9/06

The Greenwood Library of
# AMERICAN WAR REPORTING

# The Greenwood Library of
# AMERICAN WAR REPORTING

| VOLUME 7 | The Vietnam War & Post-Vietnam Conflicts |

The Vietnam War, Russell J. Cook
Post-Vietnam Conflicts, Shannon E. Martin

David A. Copeland, General Editor

Greenwood Press
Westport, Connecticut • London

**Library of Congress Cataloging-in-Publication Data**

The Greenwood library of American war reporting / David A. Copeland, general editor.
    v.  cm.
    Consists chiefly of contemporary first-person and news accounts.
    Includes bibliographical references and index.
    Contents: v. 1. The French and Indian War & the Revolutionary War—v. 2. The War of 1812 & the Mexican-American War—v. 3. The Civil War, north and south—v. 4. The Indian wars & the Spanish-American War—v. 5. World War I & World War II, the European Theater—v. 6. World War II, the Asian Theater & the Korean War—v. 7. The Vietnam War & post-Vietnam conflicts—v. 8. The Iraq wars and the War on Terror & index.
    ISBN 0–313–33435–8 (set : alk. paper)—ISBN 0–313–32885–4 (v. 1 : alk. paper)—ISBN 0–313–32931–1 (v. 2 : alk. paper)—ISBN 0–313–32941–9 (v. 3 : alk. paper)—ISBN 0–313–32990–7 (v. 4 : alk. paper)—ISBN 0–313–32888–9 (v. 5 : alk. paper)—ISBN 0–313–32942–7 (v. 6 : alk. paper)—ISBN 0–313–32930–3 (v. 7 : alk. paper)—ISBN 0–313–32933–8 (v. 8 : alk. paper)
    1. Military history, Modern—Sources.  2. United States—History, Military—Sources. 3. United States—Armed Forces—History—Sources.  I. Copeland, David A., 1951–  . II. Greenwood Press (Westport, Conn.)
    D5.G84   2005
    973—dc22      2005010122

British Library Cataloguing in Publication Data is available.

Library of Congress Catalog Card Number: 2005010122
ISBN: 0–313–33435–8 (set)
        0–313–32885–4 (vol. 1)
        0–313–32931–1 (vol. 2)
        0–313–32941–9 (vol. 3)
        0–313–32990–7 (vol. 4)
        0–313–32888–9 (vol. 5)
        0–313–32942–7 (vol. 6)
        0–313–32930–3 (vol. 7)
        0–313–32933–8 (vol. 8)

First published in 2005

Greenwood Press, 88 Post Road West, Westport, CT 06881
An imprint of Greenwood Publishing Group, Inc.
www.greenwood.com

Printed in the United States of America

The paper used in this book complies with the Permanent Paper Standard issued by the National Information Standards Organization (Z39.48–1984).

10 9 8 7 6 5 4 3 2 1

# THE GREENWOOD LIBRARY OF AMERICAN WAR REPORTING

**Volume 1**

The French and Indian War & The Revolutionary War
David A. Copeland and Carol Sue Humphrey

**Volume 2**

The War of 1812 & The Mexican-American War
David A. Copeland, Carol Sue Humphrey, and Ralph Frasca

**Volume 3**

The Civil War, North and South
Amy Reynolds and Debra Reddin van Tuyll

**Volume 4**

The Indian Wars & The Spanish-American War
John M. Coward and W. Joseph Campbell

**Volume 5**

World War I & World War II, The European Theater
Ross F. Collins and Patrick S. Washburn

**Volume 6**

World War II, The Asian Theater & The Korean War
Bradley Hamm, Donald L. Shaw, and Douglass K. Daniel

**Volume 7**

The Vietnam War & Post-Vietnam Conflicts
Russell J. Cook and Shannon E. Martin

**Volume 8**

The Iraq Wars and the War on Terror & Index
Brooke Barnett

# CONTENTS

**28 Clan Wars in Somalia, 1992–1993**                                                                  379

*Set Index can be found in Volume 8.*

# SET FOREWORD

Few events that involve humankind affect people more than war. Ask anyone who remembers World War II, Vietnam, or the events of 11 September 2001. Ask anyone who has a direct connection with conflict in Korea, Bosnia, or Iraq if these experiences have changed their lives. Because of the far-reaching effects of war, we want to know as much about it as possible. For that information, we turn to media. "This is the first line of history," veteran CBS anchor Walter Cronkite said of the relationship between media and war.

*The Greenwood Library of American War Reporting* provides the "first line of history" as its 8 volumes use primary sources to reconstruct the events of America's major military conflicts and present them to readers. Each volume gives readers the information that contemporaries of the conflicts experienced. The words, the images, and the emotions of the time are captured in these volumes from the front lines to the home front. The set begins with the French and Indian War and ends with the conflicts that have encompassed the nation since 9/11. In between, one finds some of the most important events in the history of the United States— events that in many cases continue to shape the nation. Besides the books containing the French and Indian War (combined in Volume 1 with the Revolutionary War) and post-9/11 America (Volume 8), the set includes volumes on the War of 1812 and the Mexican-American War (Volume 2), the Civil War (Volume 3, which includes sections on both the North and the South), the Spanish-American War (Volume 4), World War I, World War II (Volumes 4 and 5, with sections on the European and Asian theaters), the Korean War (Volume 5), and the war in Vietnam (Volume 7). Other parts of this set tackle less obvious conflicts that, nonetheless, affected the nation. Volume 4 also covers the Indian wars of the nineteenth century. Volume 7 takes readers inside the "little wars" that have plagued the nation from the end of the Vietnam War to the tragic events of 11 September 2001. In addition to the primary documentation and images, each volume provides readers with a comprehensive overview of its respective wars and/or conflicts and a bibliography of sources.

The ability of media to deliver the impact of war is always powerful. It only changes with the advancement and development of technology. For Americans in 1755, the words that described the massacre of General William Braddock's forces in the Pennsylvania backcountry were just as powerful to the people of that era as the television images that riveted Americans during four days of nonstop television coverage after the attacks on the World Trade Center and the Pentagon in 2001. Media have the power to bring war to us. As a reviewer in the *New-York Times* of 20 October 1862 said of Matthew Brady's photographs of the horrific Battle of Antietam: "Mr. Brady has done something to bring home to us the terrible reality and earnestness of war. If he has not brought bodies and laid them on our dooryard and along our streets, he has done something very like it."

*The Greenwood Library of American War Reporting* offers readers a chance to experience war as those who lived through those conflicts did. Some of the wars are removed from us by centuries, and the language and images from them will, at times, seem odd to us. For the people of that time, the language conveyed powerful images. Other wars and conflicts will be chillingly familiar to readers because they still remember them. The imagery and language of those wars will evoke emotions and thoughts that may be similar, yet each will be unique. These volumes also demonstrate to us the power of media in our lives and the lives of those Americans who lived before us. Truly, as Walter Cronkite said, media reports are the first line of our history, and, as the *Times* correspondent said nearly a century and a half ago, they bring the events of war to our doorsteps and into our living rooms.

# READER'S GUIDE TO THE DOCUMENTS

## BATTLES AND CAMPAIGNS

## CONTROVERSIES, ATROCITIES, AND CIVILIAN CASUALTIES

## DAILY LIFE/HOME FRONT

**Chapter 18**

8 May 1964, Edwin Shank: Criticizing the War from the Grave—American Pilot's Last Letters from Vietnam

July 1966, Don Duncan: Interview with Sergeant Smith—A "Surviving" Casualty of Vietnam

28 July 1968, John Fetterman: "Pfc. Gibson Comes Home"

27 June 1969, *Life*: Faces of American Dead in Vietnam—One Week's Toll

**Chapter 25**

25 October 1983, United Press International: "Family Has Marine Son in Beirut, Another in Grenada"

**Chapter 30**

21 May 1992, Kim Christensen: In Orange County, Bosnians Despair for Relatives, Friends in Homeland

22 November 1992, Joel Brand: "Siege Pins Americans Far from Home"

3 March 1993, Manley J. Anderson: New York Resource Center Making Bags for U.S. Airdrop

## FOREIGN LEADERS AND GOVERNMENTS

**Chapter 1**

12 October 1963, Bernard B. Fall: Interview with Pham Van Dong and Ho Chi Minh

15 September 1969, *Newsweek*: Profile of Ho Chi Minh upon His Death

**Chapter 2**

17 December 1955, Peggy Durdin: Account of Hanoi after Vietminh Victory over French

20 October 1969, Marc Riboud: Account of Hanoi after Death of Ho Chi Minh

**Chapter 3**

6 January 1962, Don Schanche: Report on Ineffectiveness of Diem Regime against Vietcong

**Chapter 6**

6 November 1963, David Halberstam: Detailed Account of Coup That Overthrew South Vietnamese President Diem

7 July 1969, *Newsweek*: Political Intrigues of President Thieu

**Chapter 26**

2 April 1986, Bob Woodward: Reagan's Efforts to Overthrow Libya's Qaddafi

6 April 1986, United Press International: Libyan Opposition to Qaddafi

## MEDIA AND THE MILITARY

30 August 1969, Hugh Van Es: Report Says All of Alpha Company Refused to Fight

## Chapter 23

15 June 1970, *Newsweek*: Editorial Questions Journalists' Decision to Go to Cambodia

19 February 1971, Ralph Graves: Editor's Note—Profile of Late Photographer Larry Burrows

19 February 1971, John Saar: A Great Photographer's Last News Story

## Chapter 24

19 September 1969, Larry Burrows: A Photographer's Growing Doubts about the War

## Chapter 25

25 October 1983, Fred Rothenberg: "Networks Denied Ability to Cover Grenada"

26 October 1983, Tom Jory: "News Coverage of Grenada Invasion Restricted by Distance, Order"

26 October 1983, Michael Kernan: "Grenada: The Reaction to the Action; On TV, Picturing the Invasion"

26 October 1983, Ira R. Allen: White House Press Restrictions in Grenada

28 October 1983, Ira R. Allen: "Larry Speakes vs. The Press"—Bitter Clashes at White House Press Briefings

28 October 1983, Felicity Barringer: "FCC Defends Ruling on Ham Radio Use"

29 October 1983, Elmer W. Lammi: "Senate Votes for End of Grenada Press Restrictions"

29 October 1983, Phil McCombs: "The Bad News Is No News"—Media Frustration with Press Restrictions

## Chapter 28

24 December 1993, Paul Quinn-Judge: Pentagon Restricts Access to Somalia Battle Tape

## NORTH VIETNAM AND VIETCONG

## Chapter 1

12 October 1963, Bernard B. Fall: Interview with Pham Van Dong and Ho Chi Minh

15 September 1969, *Newsweek*: Profile of Ho Chi Minh upon His Death

## Chapter 2

17 December 1955, Peggy Durdin: Account of Hanoi after Vietminh Victory over French

20 October 1969, Marc Riboud: Account of Hanoi after Death of Ho Chi Minh

## SOUTH VIETNAM: CIVILIANS

## SOUTH VIETNAM: GOVERNMENT AND ARMY

## TERRORISM

13 April 1986, Kevin Costelloe: Libya Reportedly Sends Foreigners to Bases, Oil Fields, and Other Possible U.S. Targets

## U.S. MILITARY AND POLICE ACTIONS: AFRICA

## U.S. MILITARY AND POLICE ACTIONS: CARIBBEAN AND LATIN AMERICA

### Chapter 25

## Chapter 27

22 December 1989, Eloy O. Aguilar: "U.S. Planes Bomb Resistance Pocket in Panama City"

22 December 1989, John M. Broder and Robin Wright: How the United States Is Hunting Noriega

22 December 1989, Marjorie Miller: Chaos, Lawlessness, and Panic in Panama's Streets; Roving Gangs Terrorize Countrymen and Foreigners; U.S. Troops Fire at Irregulars

22 December 1989, George Skelton: Americans Strongly Back Bush on Panama Invasion

28 December 1989, Walter V. Robinson and Philip Bennett: "Harrowing Tales of an Untidy Invasion"

28 December 1989, Diego Ribadeneira: Endara Tries to Establish His Credibility as New Panamanian President

28 December 1989, Joseph B. Frazier: United States Declares February Troop Pullout from Panama Unlikely

28 December 1989, Tom Raum: "White House Says Noriega Fate up to Vatican, Sees No Hostage Problem

28 December 1989, Douglas Grant Mine: "Panama Strives to Resume Normal Life; Noriega Standoff Continues"

28 December 1989, Douglas Jehl: U.S. Troops Move from Battle to Police Beat

7 January 1990, David Brinkley: The United States and Panama

7 January 1990, Maria Victoria Gonzales: "New U.S. Ambassador Calls for Enduring Friendship with Panama"

10 January 1990, Susana Hayward: "Blowtorches, Chainsaws, Hammers Pick Apart Noriega Headquarters"

10 January 1990, Susanne M. Schafer: More Than 200 Civilian Dead in Panama

10 January 1990, Kenneth Freed: "Invasion Aftermath"—Report on Civilian Casualties in Panama

## Chapter 29

3 June 1994, Peter Copeland: "U.S. Weighs Sending Troops to Seal Off Haitian Border"

4 June 1994, Kenneth Freed: Restoration of Aristide Sparks Fear in Haiti

4 June 1994, Bob Deans: "Invasion of Grenada Offers Model for Action in Haiti"

5 June 1994, Susan Rook and Bob Cain: "Repression in Haiti"

7 June 1994, Tom Squitieri: "In Haiti, Some Hope for Invasion/Army Chief Compared to Noriega"

8 June 1994, Doyle McManus: U.S. Rules Out Immediate Military Action in Haiti; Will Rely Instead on Stepped-up Sanctions

8 June 1994, Steven Greenhouse: "Governments Are Joining Haiti Force"

8 June 1994, John M. Goshko: "U.S. Asks Allies to Pledge Troops for Haiti"

23 June 1994, Ed McCullough: Americans Staying Behind in Haiti Express Doubts but No Regrets

## U.S. MILITARY AND POLICE ACTIONS: EUROPE

### Chapter 28

### Chapter 30

## U.S. PRESIDENTS AND ADMINISTRATIONS

# I

# THE VIETNAM WAR

Russell J. Cook

# TIMELINE

**1945**

2 September — Nationalist Ho Chi Minh declares independence of Vietnam after Japan's surrender to the Allies.

**1946**

December — Beginning of the Indochina War as Vietminh nationalist guerrilla forces attack French garrisons, then withdraw from Hanoi to rural bases.

**1949**

8 March — French president Vincent Auriol and former Vietamese emperor Bao Dai sign the Elysée Agreement, giving France control of Vietnam's defense and finances.

1 October — Chinese Communists under Mao Tse-tung proclaim the People's Republic of China after driving out Chiang Kai-shek's nationalist forces.

**1950**

14 January — Ho Chi Minh defies French colonial rule and declares the Democratic Republic of Vietnam.

7 February — United States and Great Britain recognize Bao Dai as the rightful ruler of Vietnam.

26 June — North Korea invades South Korea. President Truman commits U.S. troops to the conflict without congressional authorization.

**1952**

January — In the Red River valley of Vietnam, French forces under General

Jean de Lattre de Tassigny turn back Vietminh offensive under General Vo Nguyen Giap.

**1953**

27 July — Armistice agreement ends Korean conflict in stalemate, with a large U.S. garrison remaining.

9 November — Prince Norodom Sihanouk declares Cambodia's independence from France after taking command of the Cambodian army.

December — Vietminh forces penetrate Laos.

**1954**

13 March — Battle of Dienbienphu begins, a showdown between the French and the Vietminh. Britain and the United States decline to intervene.

7 May — The Vietminh defeat the French at Dienbienphu.

July — Geneva Agreements end hostilities in Vietnam, Cambodia, and Laos. Vietnam is to be partitioned at the seventeenth parallel, with the Vietminh in control of the north and the French in the south.

9 October — French forces leave Hanoi. Control of the south is assumed by Ngo Dinh Diem, Bao Dai's prime minister, with U.S. backing.

**1955**

January — The United States provides $100 million in aid and military trainers to Diem's South Vietnamese army.

26 October — Diem defeats Bao Dai in a referendum, becomes chief of state, and proclaims the Republic of Vietnam in the south.

**1957**

October — Hanoi sends thirty-seven guerrilla companies to assassinate minor South Vietamese officials in the Mekong Delta.

**1960**

11 November — South Vietnamese army units fail to overthrow Diem.

20 December — Hanoi leaders form the National Liberation Front for South Vietnam.

**1961**

19 January — Retiring U.S. president Eisenhower warns his successor, John F. Kennedy, that Laos is the key to stopping global Communism. Laos is racked by civil war between Souvanna Phouma's neutralist forces in the north, backed by the Soviet Union, and General Phoumi Nosavan's rebels in the south, backed by the United States.

May — U.S. vice president Lyndon B. Johnson visits South Vietnam and pledges substantial military aid increase to Diem's government, including helicopters.

## 1962

| | |
|---|---|
| 6 February | U.S. military assistance command is formed in South Vietnam. |
| 27 February | Two renegade South Vietnamese pilots bomb Diem's palace, but Diem and his family survive. |
| March | The South Vietnamese army launches Operation Sunrise, a pilot "Strategic Hamlet" program, to isolate rural peasants from the guerrillas. However, the mismanaged program disrupts peasant life and spurs sympathy for the Vietcong. |
| May | The Vietcong organize battalion-size units in central Vietnam. |
| July | U.S. military advisors in South Vietnam increase from 700 to 12,000. |
| 23 July | Geneva accords on Laos are signed, establishing a neutral coalition government under Souvanna Phouma. |

## 1963

| | |
|---|---|
| 2 January | Vietcong guerrillas defeat South Vietnamese regulars at the Battle of Ap Bac. |
| 8 May | Government troops shoot at Buddhist demonstrators in Hué. |
| 11 June | In Saigon, Buddhist monk Quang Duc commits suicide by lighting himself afire to protest the Diem government's repression of political dissent. |
| 21 August | Security forces under Diem's brother, Ngo Dinh Nhu, attack Buddhist temples. |
| 2 September | President Kennedy criticizes Diem in a television interview by Walter Cronkite. |
| 1 November | Encouraged by U.S. ambassador Henry Cabot Lodge, South Vietnamese army generals stage a coup d'état against Diem and Nhu, who are murdered following surrender the next day. |
| 22 November | President Kennedy is assassinated in Dallas, Texas. Hours later, Lyndon Johnson is sworn in as U.S. president. |
| December | U.S. aid to South Vietnam grows to 15,000 military advisors and $500 million annually. |

## 1964

| | |
|---|---|
| 20 January | General Nguyen Khanh arrests competing generals and seizes power in Saigon. Duong Van Minh is figurehead chief of state. |
| March | U.S. secretary of defense Robert McNamara visits South Vietnam and pledges U.S. support for Khanh. |
| 2 August | In the Tonkin Gulf of North Vietnam, patrol boats attack the U.S. surveillance destroyer Maddox, causing minimal damage. |
| 4 August | The Johnson administration uses false reports of a second confrontation in the Tonkin Gulf as an excuse to demand congressional endorsement of extraordinary war powers. |
| 7 August | The U.S. Congress passes the Tonkin Gulf resolution, which |

empowers President Johnson to wage undeclared war in Southeast Asia.

| | |
|---|---|
| 21 August | Thousands of students and militant Buddhists protest in Saigon against Khanh's repressive policies. Demonstrations continue for months. |

**1965**

| | |
|---|---|
| 18 February | General Khanh loses support of other South Vietnamese generals and relinquishes power. |
| 24 February | United States begins Operation Rolling Thunder, sustained bombing of North Vietnam. |
| 8 March | The first deployment of U.S. combat troops consists of two marine battalions to defend the Danang airfield. |
| 7 April | In a speech at Johns Hopkins University, Johnson offers massive U.S. economic aid in exchange for peace, rejected the next day by North Vietnamese prime minister Pham Van Dong. |
| October | In the first large conventional battle of the war, U.S. forces defeat North Vietnamese units in La Drang valley. |
| December | Nearly 200,000 U.S. troops are stationed in Vietnam. |
| 25 December | Johnson suspends bombing of North Vietnam to induce the enemy to negotiate. |

**1966**

| | |
|---|---|
| 31 January | Johnson resumes bombing of North Vietnam. |
| 23 May | Government troops repress Buddhist demonstrations against the Saigon regime in Danang, and in Hué on 16 June. |
| December | U.S. troops in Vietnam total nearly 400,000. |

**1967**

| | |
|---|---|
| 25 August | Defense Secretary Robert McNamara tells Congress that U.S. bombing of North Vietnam is ineffective. |
| 3 September | National elections result in General Nguyen Van Thieu becoming president of South Vietnam and Air Vice Marshal Nguyen Cao Ky becoming vice president. |
| December | U.S. troops in Vietnam total nearly 500,000. |

**1968**

| | |
|---|---|
| 31 January | Tet offensive begins as North Vietnamese and Vietcong attack dozens of cities and towns in South Vietnam, including Saigon. |
| 25 February | U.S. and South Vietnamese troops recapture Hué. |
| 27 February | Just back from an inspection tour of Vietnam, CBS news anchor Walter Cronkite predicts a stalemate and reveals dwindling U.S. public support for the war. |
| 31 March | President Johnson announces that he will not run for reelection and halts bombing of North Vietnam. |

| | |
|---|---|
| 30 May | General Creighton W. Abrams assumes command of all U.S. forces in South Vietnam, replacing William Westmoreland. |
| 5 November | Richard M. Nixon is elected U.S. president after pledging "peace with honor" in Vietnam. |
| December | U.S. troops in Vietnam total about 540,000. |

**1969**

| | |
|---|---|
| 8 June | Nixon and Thieu meet on Midway and announce withdrawal of 25,000 U.S. troops from Vietnam. |
| 25 July | Nixon in Guam declares the "Nixon Doctrine," also called "Vietnamization," which calls for South Vietnamese troops gradually to assume their war effort from the Americans. |
| 3 September | Ho Chi Minh dies in Hanoi at age 79. |
| 15 October | The first of two nationwide antiwar demonstrations occurs in Washington, D.C., and other cities. |
| 3 November | Nixon's televised speech elicits support from the "silent majority." |
| 16 November | Seymour Hersh's investigation of the 16 March 1968 massacre of 501 Mylai peasants by U.S. troops is published. |
| December | U.S. troops in Vietnam are reduced to about 480,000. |

**1970**

| | |
|---|---|
| 30 April | President Nixon announces U.S. and South Vietnamese invasion of Cambodia to strike Communist bases, followed by antiwar protests at many U.S. college campuses. |
| 4 May | Panicked National Guard troops kill four onlookers and wound seven during a peace rally at Kent State University in Kent, Ohio. Seven demonstrators are killed at Jackson State University in Mississippi. |
| 12 November | Lieutenant William Calley is tried at Fort Benning, Georgia, for his part in the Mylai massacre. |
| December | U.S. troops in Vietnam are reduced to 280,000. |

**1971**

| | |
|---|---|
| January | South Vietnamese forces invade Laos to attack the Ho Chi Minh Trail. |
| 13 June | The *New York Times* begins serial publication of *The Pentagon Papers*. A federal injunction blocking further publication is overturned by the U.S. Supreme Court two weeks later. |
| December | U.S. troops in Vietnam are reduced to 140,000. |

**1972**

| | |
|---|---|
| 25 January | Nixon reveals Henry Kissinger's secret negotiations with the North Vietnamese. |
| 30 March | North Vietnam launches an offensive across the demilitarized zone. |

| | |
|---|---|
| 8 May | Nixon announces resumption of bombing of North Vietnam and mining of Haiphong harbor. |
| 8 October | In Paris, Kissinger and North Vietnam's negotiator, Le Duc Tho, strike a tentative peace agreement, to Thieu's protest. |
| 7 November | Nixon is reelected U.S. president in a landslide victory. |

**1973**

| | |
|---|---|
| 27 January | In Paris, Kissinger and Le Duc Tho sign agreements calling for a truce in place for North and South Vietnamese forces, withdrawal of U.S. forces, and return of prisoners. |
| 12 February | Release of about 600 American prisoners of war begins. |
| 29 March | The last U.S. troops leave Vietnam. |
| 14 August | U.S. bombing of Cambodia is stopped by Congress. |
| 7 November | The U.S. Congress overrides Nixon's veto of a law limiting the president's power to wage war. |

**1974**

| | |
|---|---|
| January | Thieu declares resumption of the war. |
| 9 August | Vice President Gerald R. Ford becomes U.S. president after Nixon's resignation because of the Watergate scandal. |

**1975**

| | |
|---|---|
| 30 March | North Vietnamese forces capture Danang. |
| 17 April | Phnom Penh, Cambodia, falls to Khmer Rouge Communists. |
| 23 April | President Ford declares the war over during speech in New Orleans. |
| 29 April | Ambassador Graham Martin and last U.S. personnel are evacuated from Saigon as Communist forces overrun the city. |
| 30 April | In Saigon, North Vietnamese colonel Bui Tin accepts the South's surrender from General Duong Van Minh. |

**1977**

| | |
|---|---|
| 21 January | On his inauguration day, President Jimmy Carter pardons most of the 10,000 Vietnam War draft evaders. |

**1978**

| | |
|---|---|
| 25 December | Vietnam invades Cambodia to stop genocide by the Khmer Rouge. |

**1979**

| | |
|---|---|
| February | China invades Vietnam and is rapidly repulsed. |

**1985**     Failed farming policies cause widespread famine in Vietnam.

**1986**

| | |
|---|---|
| 18 December | Vietnamese Communist Party general secretary Nguyen Van Linh announces economic reforms. |

**1991**

February         President George Bush declares that the U.S.-led allied defeat of Iraq after only 100 hours of ground combat has "kicked the Vietnam syndrome."

**1994**

3 February      President Bill Clinton lifts the U.S. trade embargo against Vietnam.

**1995**

11 July         The United States establishes full diplomatic relations with the Republic of Vietnam.

# INTRODUCTION

From 1961 to 1975, the United States fought a devastating war in Southeast Asia for control of South Vietnam. Nationalist guerrillas known as the Vietcong, aided by Communist North Vietnam, fought for reunification of their fatherland against anti-Communist regimes propped up by the United States to stem the spread of Communism. Because of political corruption and lack of popular support, and despite infusions of U.S. weapons, advisors, and air power, the South Vietnamese were unable to defeat the insurgents, so President Lyndon Johnson sent in U.S. combat troops in 1965. The Americans tried to eliminate the Communists through attrition but were frustrated by the enemy's guerrilla tactics and an uninterrupted flow of supplies and troops from North Vietnam through neighboring Laos and Cambodia. It took three years of bloody fighting for the United States to realize its mistake and another five years to withdraw from the conflict, leaving the South Vietnamese to defend themselves. The South Vietnamese government capitulated in 1975. Both Vietnam and the United States still are recovering.

This part of this volume examines U.S. news coverage of the war, which was a watershed in military-media relations. Press advocates applauded its revelations of failed government policies—revelations that eroded public support and inevitably led to withdrawal from an untenable position in Southeast Asia. Critics of the press accused it of abetting the enemy by feeding antiwar sentiment at home. Neither view of the press's impact on war policy was entirely justified. Contrary to historical revisionism, the U.S. news media lagged behind public opinion in their growing doubt about the war. Within a year of the United States taking over the war in 1965, public support for the war weakened. By 1967, the National Guard call-ups and mounting combat casualties caused a plurality of the public to disapprove of President Lyndon Johnson's handling of the war and to regard the Vietnam commitment as a "mistake." Most questioning dispatches filed by U.S. correspondents in Vietnam were toned down or repressed altogether by stateside editors, and editorial writers tended to toe the administration line. It took the news media another two years to adopt an openly critical posture toward the war.

The Vietnam War was the longest military conflict for the United States, and consequently the most divisive for its people. The enemy's tenacity was not accounted for in U.S. war plans until there was frustration in the field, skepticism in the press, and splintered support at home. Democracies cannot sustain unpopular wars. If previous U.S. wars had lasted as long as the one in Southeast Asia, the experience would have been the same. In 1864, after only three years of war, long-awaited Union battlefield victories came just in time to avert a negotiated settlement with the Confederacy. Though World War II was declared by the U.S. Congress in self-defense, President Franklin Roosevelt's policy of unconditional surrender required the home front's backing. Had Germany and Japan hung on against the Allies, American resolve would have melted under pressures for a compromise peace.

Compared with these previous conflicts, the American strategic and economic stake in Vietnam was questionable at best. Even with massive infusions of U.S. aid, the French could not beat the guerrillas and gave up. Compared with the French, the Americans were woefully ignorant of Vietnamese customs and politics. During the 1950s, nearly every Pentagon and State Department fact-finding mission to Vietnam returned with bleak assessments of the Saigon regime's prospects and stern warnings against commitment of U.S. forces there. U.S. military power was not suited to counterinsurgency. Indeed, Presidents Eisenhower, Kennedy, Johnson, and Nixon all were reluctant to accept the costs of fighting Communist guerrillas in Southeast Asia, but were altogether unwilling to pay the domestic political price of appearing to lose to them. Thus the gradual U.S. buildup in Vietnam was kept out of the public eye. Despite the enterprise of U.S. correspondents in Vietnam, despite their unfettered access to the ground war, and despite the lack of censorship by U.S. authorities, the American news media failed to bring the futility of the war to light until it was too late. The tragic story of American involvement in Vietnam began in French Indochina.

## COLONIAL VIETNAM

The Southeast Asian countries of Laos, Cambodia, and Vietnam comprised Indochina, ruled by the French after they consolidated their control of the region with capture of the southern city of Saigon in 1859. The French were proud of their colonial empire, which rivaled that of the British in scope and economic power. Unlike the British colonialists, who ruled with benign tolerance of native institutions and customs, the French were more domineering. They believed that it was their duty to help the Indochinese assimilate the superior values, customs, justice, and religion of the French—a *mission civiliasatrice*.

The French ruled the Asians with a heavy hand. The native religion, Buddhism, was repressed in favor of Catholicism. Cities were rebuilt in French style. The opium trade was cultivated for French profit. The French Foreign Legion ruthlessly hunted resistance fighters, who by the 1880s were forced into hiding in jungles and mountains. The French authorities were reluctant to delegate bureaucratic duties to locals. As a result, French colonial governments were much more elaborate and costly than British colonial governments. For example, in 1925, 5,000 French bureaucrats were needed to control 30 million Indochinese subjects, while a comparable number of British administrators governed ten times as many subjects in India.

Conquering Indochina during the 1850s had been a drain on the French budget, so the Vietnamese were made to pay for their own exploitation. Government cartels were established in alcohol, salt, and opium. During both abundance and dearth, Indochina's exports of rice, rubber, and tin flowed uninterrupted to the European motherland, and France's manufactured goods flowed back to its protected market. Putting the colonial budget in the black lowered French tax burdens while undercutting anti-imperialist sentiment in France.

The French overlords brutally exploited Vietnamese laborers, who suffered disease and malnutrition in French plantations and mines. The death rate at one Michelin Rubber Company plantation was one in four. Traders sold coerced workers to French businessmen in a manner reminiscent of the African slave trade 200 years earlier. Landowners were dispossessed and converted into tenant farmers. By 1940, Indochina was the world's third-largest rice exporter, without regard for domestic needs. The repression created sympathy for nationalist rebel groups, but infighting and French counterinsurgency tactics kept the rebels in check.

In an effort to pacify Vietnam, the French occupiers promoted regional identities that frustrated nationalism. In fact, regional factionalism had prevented a coordinated resistance to French occupation, much as lack of political cohesion had handicapped Vietnam in resisting its centuries-old enemy, China, the populous power on Vietnam's northern border. Life was much easier in the lush rice fields of the south, which were remote from Chinese invasions. Consequently, the northerners harbored jealousies and mistrust that persist to the present.

To bolster legitimacy for colonial rule, the French occupiers co-opted the ancient Vietnamese monarchy. The compliant Vietnamese emperor, Khai Dinh, sent his son, Bao Dai, to be educated in France, so the son was more French than Vietnamese when he ascended to the throne in 1932. Bao Dai cooperated with the French occupation, lived lavishly in European-style opulence, and overlooked his people's severe deprivations. Though he was a figurehead ruler only and powerless to resist French dictates, Bao Dai nevertheless harbored the centuries-old Vietnamese dream of self-rule. The French platitudes of republican virtue he had studied in Paris rang false in Saigon.

## WORLD WAR SIDESHOW: VIETNAM

Reeling from the French army's sudden collapse before invading Germans in 1940, French Indochina was too weak to resist concurrent Japanese invasion. Just as Germany had installed a puppet regime in Vichy, France, the invading Japanese army let the French continue to rule Indochina in exchange for access to Indochinese airfields, military bases, transportation networks, and raw materials, including rice, rubber, and coal. The agreement freed the Japanese war machine to leapfrog Indochina and to pursue other conquests in southern Asia. By appeasing Japanese aggression, the French maintained control in Indochina and avoided military action during most of World War II. Daily life in Vietnam was little changed from prewar days, except that the indigenous peoples were greatly impressed by the new Asian power that had so handily defeated the European imperialists.

The Vietnamese nationalist leader Nguyen That Thanh, later known as Ho Chi Minh, was encouraged by U.S. president Franklin D. Roosevelt's early anticolonialist pronouncements and by guarantees of self-government following the war for invaded territories in the Allies' Atlantic Charter. Born in 1890 in a small village in central Vietnam, Nguyen That Thanh spent thirty years in self-imposed exile in France, China, and the Soviet Union. There he worked for the Vietnamese nationalist cause and learned political organizing. In Paris, he edited an anticolonial newspaper called *Le Paria* under the nom de plume Nguyen Ai Quoc. His pamphlets preaching revolution made their way to Vietnam and gave hope to insurgents who were waiting for their chance to strike at the French. Quoc's political allegiances always were opportunistic. He embraced Communism as the most potent enemy of European colonialism in Asia and founded the Indochinese Communist Party in 1930, yet he later aligned himself with the capitalist Allies against the Japanese invaders. Just as Roosevelt had promised, he expected the Allies to defeat the Japanese, reject the French collaborators, and grant independence to his country.

In 1941, Quoc crossed unnoticed into Vietnam from China. There he made contact with Pham Van Dong and Vo Nguyen Giap, respected patriots who had been imprisoned briefly by the French. Having read Quoc's anticolonial treatises, they looked to him as their spiritual leader and called him "Uncle." He told them that the time was right to resist the Japanese and French collaborators in order to win national independence. Together they founded the Viet Nam Doc Lap Dong Minh independence league, shortened to Vietminh. Quoc chose a new official pseudonym, Ho Chi Minh, which means "Bringer of Light" (see Chapter 1).

Ho and Giap organized Vietminh guerrilla bands in the north to harass the Japanese and the French. They urged the peasants to resist the foreigners. The Japanese hoarded Vietnamese rice stocks for their troops and for export to Japan, a policy that continued unabated despite a severe famine in early 1945 during which a fifth of the population in the north—2 million Vietnamese—died of starvation. Vietminh guerrillas captured Japanese rice granaries and gave the rice back to the peasants, thereby winning their loyalty.

Ho Chi Minh had good reasons to think that the United States, now drawn into the war, would back Vietnamese nationalism after the war. Not only was President Roosevelt a well-known anticolonialist, but also the Vietminh had helped the U.S. Office of Strategic Services track Japanese troop movements and locate downed U.S. pilots. In return for their help, U.S. agents trained the Vietminh guerrillas in weapons use. They respected the fighting qualities of the Vietminh and recognized Ho as a nationalist leader who could be useful in the final Allied drive against the Japanese. To impress the Americans and to gain more followers, Ho ordered attacks on French outposts. On Christmas Eve 1944, Giap orchestrated coordinated Vietminh raids that overran two small French garrisons in the north. This Vietminh victory later was commemorated as the birth of the Vietnamese army. By early 1945, the Vietminh throughout Vietnam swelled to 5,000 members.

Japan's surrender to the Allies in August 1945 created a power vacuum in Vietnam. The Vietminh grappled with remnants of Japanese forces, as well as rival nationalist groups, to gain control of the country. The Vietminh had the support of the peasants in the north. On 16 August in Tran Tao, a village north of Hanoi, Ho Chi Minh declared a provisional government of the Democratic Republic of Vietnam and called for the peasants to rise up against the invaders. "The oppressed the world over are wresting back their independence," he said. "We should not lag behind. Forward! Forward! Under the Vietminh banner, let us valiantly march forward!"[1] To bolster legitimacy for the new regime, the Vietminh met with Emperor Bao Dai in Hué on 25 August and coerced him to abdicate and to acknowledge Ho's presidency. Bao Dai went to Hanoi to meet with Ho and was impressed with the Vietminh leader's nationalist zeal. He warned the French that the Vietminh would be formidable adversaries of any foreign power in Vietnam (see Chapter 2 for the U.S. press's perspective on Ho's Hanoi).

On 2 September 1945, Ho formally declared Vietnam's independence by quoting the U.S. Declaration of Independence:

> All men are created equal; their Creator with certain unalienable Rights endows them [*sic*]; among these are Life, Liberty, and the pursuit of Happiness.
>
> This immortal statement was made in the Declaration of Independence of the United States of America in 1776. In a broader sense, this means: All the peoples on the earth are equal from birth; all the peoples have a right to live, to be happy and free.[2]

In July 1945, the Allies met in Potsdam, Germany, and agreed that Chinese Nationalists would take charge of Vietnam above the sixteenth parallel and the British would take charge in the south. As the Vietminh struggled with various other Vietnamese factions for control of the cities and provinces, the British commander, General Douglas Gracey, declared martial law in the south and employed French army troops that had been interned by the Japanese to enforce peace. The Vietminh protested. Humiliated by their war losses and eager to reclaim power, the French soldiers overreacted and went on a rampage through Saigon. Vietnamese civilians were brutalized, and shops and homes were ransacked. Gracey was not able to stop the rioting. It was now clear to Vietminh leaders that the Allies did not intend to grant Vietnamese independence.

The Vietminh mobilized a general strike in Saigon on 24 September 1945—the first day of the Indochina War. Within a month, the British military pulled out altogether and let the French take over, with military equipment from the United States. Fresh from victory in Europe, General Jacques Philippe Leclerc led an army of 35,000 men on a campaign to suppress the Vietminh in Saigon, the Mekong Delta, and the central highlands. As the Vietminh retreated, they burned villages and destroyed infrastructure. As soon as the French left a sector, the Vietminh guerrillas returned.

## VIETNAMESE COLD WAR POLITICS

When Japan surrendered in August 1945, few Americans knew of Vietnam. It had been a minor theater of the world war, yet Vietnam was to become a pawn in the U.S. cold war struggle against global Communism. U.S. president Harry S. Truman adopted the domino theory, the gospel of postwar Communist aggression put forward by U.S. secretary of state Dean Acheson: The Communist menace must be stopped in Vietnam, or, like a chain reaction of tumbling dominos, the other countries of Southeast Asia would fall into Communist hands. With tragic irrevocability, the U.S. stake in defending Vietnam gradually escalated until victory became more costly than defeat. The escalation was gradual because U.S. leaders feared direct intervention by Red China or the Soviet Union. Because the war could not be pursued decisively, it lasted long enough for America to lose its way. U.S. credibility became the fallen domino.

For the Vietnamese nationalists, the struggle against the Americans and their puppet South Vietnamese regime was but a new phase of their centuries-long resistance of foreign aggression. The Americans had replaced the French, the Japanese, and the Chinese before them as usurpers of Vietnamese autonomy. Facing the threat of Soviet expansion, the United States wanted France's cooperation in Europe, for which it backed restoration of French Indochina in 1946. The Vietminh pledged to fight until independence was won and retreated to the mountains. Mao Tse-tung's new Communist government in China recognized Ho's Democratic Republic of Vietnam in 1950 and began to funnel aid to the Vietminh. The Soviet Union followed suit soon after. Thus the small Asian nation was drawn into global conflict between emerging superpowers, the United States and the Soviet Union.

Despite massive financial and military aid from the United States, the overconfident French were unwilling to adjust their tactics to neutralize the Communist guerrillas and gradually lost control of the countryside. After amassing Vietminh guerrillas in the north, Giap shifted to a conventional strategy and dealt the French a humiliating defeat at Dienbienphu in May 1954. Later that year, the Geneva accords stopped the fighting, partitioned Vietnam at the seventeenth parallel, with the Communists in control of the north and the French in the south, and scheduled national elections in 1955 for reunification of the country. However, the south's chief of state, Premier Ngo Dinh Diem, refused to sign the accords and appealed to the United States for aid to fight the Communists. In a matter of months, the French withdrew completely from Vietnam, ending nearly a century of colonial rule there and leaving the United States as Diem's only support. Over the next five years, Diem consolidated his hold on power.

## CIVIL WAR AND COUNTERINSURGENCY

The start of the Vietnamese civil war can be dated to late 1960, when Vietminh veterans in the South formed the nucleus of the National Liberation Front (NLF) against the Saigon government. The NLF's guerrilla force was labeled the Vietcong, a derisive slang for "Vietnamese Communist" that stuck. Having campaigned as a tough anti-Communist, new U.S. president John F. Kennedy needed to resuscitate his image after his Central Intelligence Agency botched an invasion in March 1961 against Fidel Castro's regime in Cuba, a humiliation he publicly acknowledged. Kennedy chose South Vietnam to take his stand. He increased U.S. presence there sixteenfold and sent World War II hero General Paul D. Harkins for a new winning impetus, along with the latest U.S. weaponry. The 16,300 Americans in South Vietnam officially were limited to advisor roles, though, in fact, U.S. aviators saw action.

With justification, the U.S. advisors complained that the South Vietnamese army, or Army of the Republic of Vietnam (ARVN), avoided confronting the Vietcong. The U.S. aid paradoxically weakened the ARVN by encouraging conventional tactics ineffective in a guerrilla war. Instead of taking risks with the infantry, Diem demanded that his commanders avoid casualties by letting air strikes and artillery barrages carry the combat load in order to preserve the troops to protect him in Saigon. He barely had survived coup attempts on 11 November 1960 and 27 February 1962, and political opposition was growing (see Chapter 3).

On 2 January 1963, the ARVN Seventh Division attacked a much smaller enemy battalion in the Mekong Delta. The Vietcong were tipped off and dug in for the attack. Eighty-seven South Vietnamese soldiers were killed. The Vietcong shot down five U.S. helicopters and killed three U.S. advisors. Only seventeen Vietcong were killed, and the rest escaped allied encirclement. It was the biggest ARVN setback of the war to date and showed that the Vietcong were capable of adjusting their tactics to neutralize superior allied firepower. The U.S. Army advisor in the battle, Lieutenant Colonel John Paul Vann, was disgusted with the ARVN leadership and leaked his criticism to American press correspondents. General Harkins, supreme leader of the U.S. Military Assistance Command, Vietnam (MACV), was furious and wanted to fire Vann but feared press retaliation.

Not only were the Vietcong's tactics improving but also their weapons. While Hanoi was busy equipping its regular army in the North, its leaders expected the Vietcong in the South to procure their own weapons. During the buildup period, weapons were more precious to the guerrillas than men, and the United States unwittingly supplied both sides of the conflict. Formerly reliant on old French bolt-action rifles and homemade shotguns, the guerrillas amassed enormous quantities of U.S.-made semiautomatic and automatic combat rifles, machine guns, and ammunition captured from ARVN troops or bartered from corrupt South Vietnamese government officials. The guerrillas learned to concentrate fire with the new weapons to stop helicopters and armored personnel carriers (see Chapter 4).

During the early phase of the war, U.S. field correspondents in Saigon included Peter Kalischer and Bernard Kalb of CBS News, James Robinson of NBC News, Stanley Karnow of the *Saturday Evening Post*, Robert "Pepper" Martin of *U.S. News & World Report*, François Sully of *Newsweek* magazine, Homer Bigart and David Halberstam of the *New York Times*, Neil Sheehan of United Press International, Malcolm Browne and Peter Arnett of the Associated Press, and Charles Mohr and Merton Perry of *Time* magazine. They had free access to the U.S. military and developed their own sources, but they often ran afoul of Diem's press restrictions. Generally supportive of the U.S. mission and troops, they nevertheless candidly reported South Vietnamese military defeats, government corruption, peasant sympathy for the Vietcong, and Saigon's exaggeration of enemy casualties. They especially admired Vann for his unguarded criticism of the Saigon regime. Diem expelled some American journalists, including François Sully and James Robinson, for writing negative articles. A credibility gap widened between the official government line and battlefield realities. The White House and the Pentagon explained away the contradictions as symptomatic of the young reporters' inexperience and lack of perspective (see Chapter 5).

A zealous Roman Catholic, Diem suspected all Buddhists of collaborating with the Communists to overthrow his government. Diem got his brother, Ngo Dinh Nhu, to engineer brutal reprisals by Nhu's Mat Vu secret police against Buddhists in the ancient Vietnamese capital city of Hué. Pagodas were ransacked, and monks were jailed. The repression sparked student demonstrations in several cities, including Saigon, and the unrest threatened to destabilize the government. The Communists took advantage by stepping up their attacks in the provinces. Ambassador Frederick Nolting threatened to withdraw U.S. support if Diem did not stop his repression of the Buddhists. Diem's defiant sister-in-law, Madame Ngo Dinh Nhu, answered by accusing the Americans of manipulating the Buddhists to blackmail Diem.

The Buddhist cause attracted worldwide attention in Saigon on 11 June 1963, when Buddhist monk Quang Duc ceremonially set fire to himself to protest Diem's regime. Malcolm Browne's AP wire photo of the self-immolation electrified newspaper readers around the world. When Diem renewed his charge that the Vietcong were behind the Buddhist protests, more Buddhist monks went up in flames.

The Buddhist uprisings in Saigon and Hué led to the overthrow of the Diem regime by a military junta on 1 November 1963, with the complicity of newly appointed U.S. ambassador Henry Cabot Lodge. Diem and his brother Nhu were assassinated, and a power struggle among South Vietnamese generals followed (see Chapter 6).

As the Saigon generals jockeyed for control (three coups d'état in six months), the Vietcong strengthened its hold on the provinces and began staging raids in the cities. Vietcong battalions were bolstered by the North Vietnamese Army (NVA) and heavy ordnance. As a result, the ARVN no longer enjoyed numerical superiority and suffered heavy losses. The Saigon government appeared on the verge of collapse, and this forced the United States eventually to take over the fight (see Chapter 7).

U.S. authorities intended to be cooperative with the press. On 7 July 1963, the State Department announced a unified, transparent press policy named "Maximum Candor." Barry Zorthian, MACV's chief public affairs officer, convinced the Pentagon to accommodate the press as the best way to curry its favor. General William C. Westmoreland, who replaced Harkins as MACV commander, invited reporters on trips to remote bases to promote positive coverage.[3] MACV held daily news briefings in Saigon and weekly backgrounders on the reporters' choice of topics. Eventually, however, candor was undercut by U.S. president Lyndon B. Johnson's desire to manage the public image of the war effort. Zorthian's pleas for openness went unheeded. As a result, the daily MACV briefings, delivered in the auditorium of the Rex Hotel in Saigon, became public relations exercises that by 1966 acquired the derisive nickname "five o'clock follies." This growing divergence between ever-optimistic official statements and the deteriorating political and military situation converted even the most gung-ho members of the press corps into skeptics (see Chapter 8).

## U.S. INTERVENTION

Lyndon Johnson was wary of being mired in an Asian land war but equally wary of appearing to give in to the Communists. His reelection opponent, conservative Arizona senator Barry Goldwater, accused the Kennedy-Johnson administration of being "soft" on Communism. Johnson also was goaded into tough action by the disgruntled right wing of his own Democratic Party in the U.S. Senate, led by John Stennis of Mississippi. On 7 August 1964, Johnson manipulated a minor naval incident in North Vietnamese territorial waters in the Gulf of Tonkin to win congressional authorization to wage war in Southeast Asia, along with $700 million in war appropriations.

Despite congressional authorization, Johnson was ambivalent about escalating the war. Pressured by his advisors, and despite substantial evidence that strategic bombing was ineffective against nonindustrialized economies, Johnson approved selected punitive air strikes against military targets in North Vietnam and Laos. On 24 February 1965, sustained U.S. bombing of North Vietnam (Operation Rolling Thunder) was launched to extort a negotiated settlement. The bombing continued for more than three years. Two marine battalions landed on 8 March 1965 to protect an airfield for the bombers in the northern coastal city of Danang—the first U.S. combat troops in Vietnam.

In an address on 7 April 1965, Johnson offered a U.S.-financed rural electrification program for the Mekong River Valley in return for Vietcong withdrawal from the South: "This generation of the world must choose: destroy or build, kill or aid, hate or understand."[4] Rural electrification of Texas had been Johnson's shining achievement as a U.S. congressman, and he was sure that "Old Ho" would not turn down a repeat performance in Vietnam. However, North Vietnamese prime minister Pham Van Dong rejected Johnson's offer, insisting on a halt of U.S. bombing of North Vietnam and creation of a neutral Saigon regime with Vietcong participation. Now convinced that force was necessary to impose his will, Johnson approved incremental escalation of the U.S. war role. On 28 July 1965, the president told a national television audience, "We cannot be defeated by force of arms. We will stand in Vietnam."[5] By December 1965, Westmoreland's force grew to 184,300 troops and eventually peaked at 543,054 on 20 February 1969.[6]

To defeat the Vietcong guerrillas, Westmoreland stuck with Harkins's attrition strategy. Disregarding Ho Chi Minh's oft-repeated pledge to resist foreign intervention regardless of casualties and underestimating the enemy's ability to replace losses, Westmoreland believed that superior U.S. technology and firepower would win a contest of body counts. His "search-and-destroy" missions would seek out and eliminate the Communist guerrillas until the North's will was broken.

The "dirty little war" in Southeast Asia had been the news beat of a handful of young correspondents representing U.S. wire services and elite newspapers, but the dramatic U.S. buildup now brought a flood of international print and broadcast media. Tensions rose between reporters and MACV. Reporters accused the military of subterfuge. The military accused reporters of intentionally crippling the war effort. MACV public relations officers were caught in the middle. An example of the confrontational atmosphere involved a seemingly minor incident that media attention magnified out of proportion to its importance on the ground. On 20 March 1965, Associated Press reporter Peter Arnett and photographer Horst Faas observed ARVN troops going into combat with gas canisters, which turned out to be nonlethal tear gas used in civilian crowd control. They broke the story two days later. U.S. editorial writers and international humanitarian organizations erupted with protests over the use of "poison gas," which violated the Geneva Conventions governing the conduct of war. Had MACV disclosed the use of tear gas in advance, the uproar could have been averted (see Chapter 9).

On 3 August 1965, a television news report by CBS correspondent Morley Safer questioned the morality of the U.S. mission in Vietnam. Safer filed film showing marines nonchalantly torching the village of Cam Ne. Safer's so-called Zippo lighter report shocked millions of viewers back home. U.S. soldiers, not the Vietcong, looked like the aggressors (see Chapter 10).

Field commander Westmoreland complained that televised war violence under-mined public support, reason enough to begin censoring the news media. However, the Pentagon feared a backlash and continued its policy of voluntary guidelines for journalists, combined with surreptitious manipulation of access for reporters and photographers who made the military look good. Correspondents identified with the soldiers they covered and understood the need to suppress information that might be helpful to the enemy. On the whole, the news media cooperated with the voluntary guidelines. By the end of the war, only a handful of the hundreds of journalists covering it had been stripped of their credentials for violations. Contradicting West-moreland's claims about the first "television war," research later showed that the networks sanitized their film reports of the Vietnam War to remove scenes of actual combat that might offend viewers' sensibilities.[7]

Wholesale destruction of civilian areas became common practice among U.S. in-fantrymen and aviators, who could not tell friend from foe (the Dink complex). Any fleeing peasant was assumed to be a guerrilla and was fired upon. MACV identified known guerrilla havens as "free-fire" zones subject to indiscriminate attack. Pam-phlets were dropped in the zones to warn civilians to evacuate their homes or risk annihilation. All dwellings in the zones were destroyed. The net effect of this prac-tice was to convert some peasants into guerrillas and others into refugees who took flight to the cities (see Chapter 11).

MACV deflected attention away from Cam Ne and other reports of civilian casu-alties by decrying Vietcong brutality. In the early years of the war, the Vietcong tar-geted government officials in the hamlets for assassination. The guerrillas generally avoided harming the peasants, on whom they relied for food and intelligence. How-ever, as both sides escalated the war, the civilians increasingly were caught in the crossfire (see Chapter 12).

Beginning in January 1966, the U.S. Senate Foreign Relations Committee de-bated the war before television cameras. The hearings questioned Westmoreland's attrition strategy and the war's costs. The committee's chairman was Democratic senator J. William Fulbright of Arkansas, who had sponsored the president's Tonkin Gulf Resolution in the Senate two years earlier. Fulbright seemed haunted by his complicity in escalating the war. Sharing party affiliation with the president lent cre-dence to his public doubts about the administration's war policy. However, commit-tee testimony did little to change attitudes and presaged the polarization of public opinion to follow. Congress waited another three years to limit appropriations for the war.

Much of the early debate centered on the president's massive bombing of North Vietnam's war industries and supply routes, which seemed to have little effect on the war in the South. The U.S. military's awesome firepower barely slowed the infiltra-tion of NVA regulars and supplies into the South via the Ho Chi Minh Trail through Laos and Cambodia. The Communists conserved their forces and neutral-ized their technological disadvantages by waging hit-and-run raids at night against U.S. bases and by confronting weaker ARVN units whenever possible.

Late in 1966, the assistant managing editor of the *New York Times*, Harrison Salis-bury, began filing stories from North Vietnam's capital of Hanoi. Salisbury's detailed dispatches and photographs showed bombed civilian districts and unscathed defense works, which contradicted Defense Secretary Robert McNamara's claims about "surgical" strikes. The administration launched a public relations counterattack that accused Salisbury and the *Times* of complicity with the enemy.[8] Eventually a board of publishers forced retraction of Salisbury's Pulitzer Prize for his Hanoi reporting. The condemnation of Salisbury showed that the news media, as well as the Congress, lagged behind American public opinion, which, despite the president's flag-waving, was turning against the war (see Chapter 13).

Secretary of Defense Robert McNamara had been an architect of strategic bombing of North Vietnam, but he eventually acknowledged its failure to a Senate subcommittee on 25 August 1967, to the consternation of hard-line senators. Soon after, Johnson replaced McNamara at Defense with the hawkish Clark Clifford.

## TET OFFENSIVE, 1968

The North Vietnamese were eager to award their elderly and ailing president Ho Chi Minh with a victory. By the Tet holiday of 1968, the rebels were strong enough to attack openly and in daylight. On 31 January, they launched a coordinated attack against twenty-four cities and hundreds of military strongholds all over the South. To dramatize U.S. vulnerability, a Vietcong suicide squad overran the U.S. Embassy in Saigon and held it briefly. On 1 February, Associated Press photographer Eddie Adams and National Broadcasting Company cameraman Vo Suu captured enduring images of the war when they photographed General Nguyen Ngoe Loan, chief of South Vietnam's national police, executing a Vietcong officer in a Saigon street. Adams's photograph dominated newspapers the next day and persists as an icon of the war (see Chapter 14).

Vietcong and North Vietnamese regulars held the city of Hué for twenty-five days. The most savage fighting of the entire war eventually decimated the city's ancient fortress known as the Citadel. About 150 U.S. marines, 400 South Vietnamese troops, and 5,000 Communist soldiers perished in the battle. Afterward, the mass graves of nearly 3,000 Hué citizens brutally murdered by the Vietcong during its occupation were revealed.

Westmoreland was convinced that the attacks on cities were a diversion from the enemy's real target, the remote base of Khesanh near the demilitarized zone. He compared Khesanh to the 1954 French fortress of Dienbienphu. He reinforced the garrison and readied replacements for emergency insertion. When the North Vietnamese attacked in strength, the U.S. command unleashed its Boeing B-52 heavy bombers, which dropped 103,500 tons of heavy explosives on a five-square-mile perimeter around Khesanh during the nine-week siege—the most intensive strategic bombing campaign to that date in the history of warfare. The Communists lost more than 10,000 lives, mostly to the bombing, at a cost of fewer than 500 U.S. marine deaths. When the marines abandoned the base in June, long after the enemy had withdrawn, critics charged that Westmoreland had wasted the lives of U.S. servicemen on a meaningless outpost (see Chapter 15).

The Vietcong's audacious Tet attacks demoralized the Saigon regime and Americans back home. MACV admitted that it had been caught off guard. Although the Communists' heavy casualties—some 50,000 Communist dead compared with 2,000 U.S. and 4,000 ARVN casualties—amounted to a U.S. tactical victory, the biggest casualty during Tet was the false optimism of Westmoreland, who was replaced after a respectful interval by General Creighton W. Abrams. Clearly the U.S. president and the Pentagon had misjudged the stamina and determination of the Communist insurgents. Public skepticism about the attrition strategy and a feeling of helplessness had been growing along with U.S. casualties and tax increases. For a brief period after Tet, Americans patriotically rallied around their flag, but disillusionment about Vietnam soon reclaimed their mood.

CBS television news anchor Walter Cronkite had been one of the country's unquestioning opinion leaders, but Tet changed his mind. He insisted on inspecting the action for himself and returned from South Vietnam convinced of the struggle's futility. On 27 February 1968, in a rare departure from journalistic objectivity, Cronkite broadcast a personal editorial that Washington should start thinking about getting out of the war: "To say that we are mired in stalemate seems the only realistic, yet unsatisfactory, conclusion."[9] Cronkite's declaration of stalemate shocked President Johnson into realizing that he had lost the people's support. On 31 March 1968, he addressed the nation: "With American sons in the fields far away . . . I do not believe that I should devote an hour or a day of my time to any personal partisan causes. . . . Accordingly, I shall not seek, and I will not accept, the nomination of my party for another term as your President."[10] He offered a bombing halt and renewed desire to negotiate a settlement, but the Communists did not reciprocate. On 5 November 1968, Richard M. Nixon won the presidency by promising an honorable end of the war for the United States.

While Americans back home were waiting for Nixon's extrication strategy, the most controversial battle of the war was fought in the Ashau Valley west of the northern city of Hué near the Laotian border. After a withering bombardment on 10 May 1969, a combined U.S./ARVN force attacked an entrenched North Vietnamese position on a mountaintop called Dong Ap Bia. The bombs had no effect on the enemy's reinforced bunkers. From their lofty position, the Communists turned back one assault after another with deadly automatic weapons fire and mortars. More bombing did little except strip away foliage. Rains converted the mountainsides into a sea of mud. The mountaintop finally was taken after twelve allied assaults in nine days. Reporters on the scene picked up the marines' cynical nickname for the battle, "Hamburger Hill."

Hamburger Hill became a public relations nightmare for the government on 20 May when Senator Edward Kennedy of Massachusetts, speaking on the Senate floor, decried the battle's senseless slaughter. The senator received letters of support from some of the battle's veterans. The attrition strategy was roundly criticized. The battle was pushed off newspaper front pages by Nixon and Thieu's conference on Midway on 8 June 1969, where they announced the first withdrawal of 25,000 American troops. Additional withdrawals halved U.S. forces in Vietnam by 1970 (see Chapter 16).

Reeling from the Khesanh and Hamburger Hill debacles, the American public was further disillusioned about U.S. war policy by a relatively minor incident that captured headlines for months. On 20 June 1969, Colonel Robert B. Rheault and seven of his Green Berets in the Fifth Special Forces Group assassinated a suspected North Vietnamese spy named Thai Khac Chuyen at the request of a station chief of the Central Intelligence Agency. The eight marines were arrested for murder and incarcerated in the U.S. military prison at Long Binh, South Vietnam. Because Colonel Rheault had covered up the affair in his report to MACV, General Abrams intended a vigorous prosecution and braced for the controversy that surely would follow. The *New York Times* broke the story in August. MACV refused to provide background information on grounds of protecting rights of the accused. Recognizing that publicity would help their clients, civilian defense attorneys made innuendos that Abrams was pursuing a personal vendetta against Rheault and his company. Families of the accused sent letters of protest to members of Congress. Debate over the Green Berets case soon ballooned into a referendum on the war in general and captured headlines for months. After intervention by President Nixon, the marines were released for lack of evidence because the CIA refused to reveal its secret operations (see Chapter 17).

One magazine issue brought home to the American public the human cost of the war more than any other media event. By 1967, Time Inc.'s publisher Hedley Donovan had decided that the war was unwinnable and directed *Time* and *Life* to cultivate critical coverage of the war. In 1969, *Life* editor Loudon Wainwright thought of a way to visualize the weekly body counts and took his idea to chief editor Ralph Graves. Graves immediately approved the idea and harnessed the magazine's full resources to publish what was remembered as the zenith of *Life*'s journalism: The 27 June issue featuring photographs of most of the 242 U.S. troops killed during a previous week of fighting.[11] Many of the pictures came from high-school yearbooks, which underscored the death of innocence. No editorial copy was needed. The pictures alone had resounding impact. The faces of the dead were disproportionately working class because college students were deferred from the military draft (see Chapter 18).

## VIETNAMIZATION AND WITHDRAWAL

Richard Nixon waited until the summer of 1969 to reveal his plan to extricate U.S. forces by building up the South Vietnamese army. A French plan of Vietnamization in the early 1950s had failed to reduce French casualties, but Nixon was sure that superior U.S. firepower would make it work this time. According to the plan, ARVN ground forces would take over offensive maneuvers, while U.S. troops assumed garrison duties. Even the South Vietnamese doubted their chances against the NVA (see Chapter 19).

Morale and discipline among U.S. troops had been deteriorating since Tet. The change of mission did not help. In the early years of the war, the United States fielded its best career soldiers and ardent volunteers, most of them true believers in President Kennedy's call to turn back Communism. Their replacements following the Tet offensive were mostly conscripts whose service was coerced in discouraging circumstances. With announcement of troop withdrawals, the U.S. infantryman's personal mission was reduced to surviving his yearlong tour of duty. Because narcotics were plentiful and cheap (the Saigon government profited from the drug trade), drug abuse became common and hurt combat readiness (see Chapter 20).

The United States fought the Vietnam War against a domestic backdrop of racial tensions. In the early 1950s, the military was the nation's only desegregated public institution. The African American leadership launched a campaign of nonviolent protest against racial segregation and social injustice in the Deep South, which goaded the federal government into passing civil rights legislation in 1964 and 1965.

However, the nonviolent protest movement foundered in the North in 1965, and riots broke out in urban ghettos across the nation. Beginning in 1968, reports of racial strife in U.S. Army and Marine units in Vietnam shattered the myth that the military was immune from racial strife. Echoing the words of civil rights leader Martin Luther King Jr., leading black newspapers such as the *Chicago Defender* and *Pittsburgh Courier* questioned whether black soldiers should support the white man's war in Southeast Asia while the struggle for equality was contested back home.

Reports of insubordination began to emerge. In August 1969, the AP's Peter Arnett and Horst Faas reported that an exhausted unit of the Twenty-third Infantry Division temporarily refused orders after five continuous days of fighting in Song Chang Valley 50 miles south of Danang. Military spokesmen disputed that the mutiny was widespread. Nine days later a second unit refused its orders. Low morale was blamed in both incidents. Several editorialists dismissed the reports as aberrations and condemned the correspondents for contributing to the morale problem (see Chapter 21).

The image of the American soldier as a liberator of Vietnamese peasants was dashed when Seymour Hersh broke a story about Vietnamese civilians massacred by U.S. soldiers on 10 March 1968 in Mylai, a hamlet about 6 miles northeast of Quangngai in the northern part of South Vietnam. Hersh learned about the massacre through Capitol Hill sources and confirmed the story by interviewing the court-martialed officer, First Lieutenant William Calley. The Mylai story was overlooked for months until it was released through the little-known antiwar Dispatch News Service on 16 November 1969. A flood of follow-up news stories revealed photographs of the dead and questioned whether there had been a cover-up. Calley's case became a plebiscite on the war. After Calley was convicted and sentenced to life imprisonment, President Nixon removed Calley from prison on grounds of prejudicial publicity. After a series of appeals, Calley was paroled in 1975. Hersh won the 1970 Pulitzer Prize for international reporting (see Chapter 22).

The first part of Nixon's two-pronged strategy to end the war was Vietnamization. The second prong, Nixon's so-called Madman theory, was kept secret. Nixon tried to capitalize on his 1950s reputation as a staunch anti-Communist to scare Hanoi into believing that he would authorize use of nuclear weapons. In secret talks with the North Vietnamese, National Security Advisor Henry Kissinger intimated Nixon's volatility to trick them into peace negotiations. When the ruse did not work, Nixon renewed daily bombing of the North, which Johnson had stopped in March 1968. The Pentagon launched regular B-52 raids on neutral neighbor Cambodia to close the Ho Chi Minh Trail. In 1971, the bombing spread to neighboring Laos. Congressional probes uncovered the secret bombing campaign in 1973.

In October 1969, President Nixon's handling of the war enjoyed an approval rating of 71 percent, but various antiwar factions were growing impatient with Nixon's lack of progress toward his election campaign promise to end the war. The factions cooperated to stage a series of war protest moratoriums on 15 October in numerous cities across the country. Nearly a quarter of a million people marched in Washington, D.C. Other cities also saw huge protests. Though still a minority, the antiwar movement had grown in size and respectability.

To buy time for his two-pronged strategy to work, Nixon gave a televised speech on 3 November. He asked for the public's patience to implement his plan to Vietnamize the war and gradually to withdraw U.S. forces as the South Vietnamese assumed increasing responsibility for their own defense: "So tonight, to you, the great silent majority of my fellow Americans, I ask for your support. . . . Because let us understand—North Vietnam cannot defeat or humiliate the United States. Only Americans can do that."[12]

As before, the renewed bombing barely slowed enemy supply and infiltration from the North. On 30 April 1970, Nixon announced an allied ground invasion of the so-called Fish Hook region of Cambodia to wipe out NVA strongholds. Previous incursions into Laos and Cambodia had been kept secret. This announced escalation of the war stunned the U.S. public and outraged antiwar groups, especially college students who had trusted Nixon's promise to end the war. Protests erupted across the nation on college and university campuses, causing many to shut down and to send their students home. On 4 May 1970, a violent clash at Kent State University in Ohio captured the nation's headlines. National Guard troops felt threatened by stone-throwing protesters and opened fire; four onlookers were killed and seven wounded. A Jackson State University riot in Mississippi had more fatalities. The nation seemed unhinged.

In Cambodia, the North Vietnamese fled before the invasion force of 20,000 allied troops with air support. The incursion temporarily disrupted Communist logistics and captured some outdated weapons and rice stocks, but the North Vietnamese restored their bases shortly after the U.S. and South Vietnamese troops withdrew from their two-month campaign. The operation's lasting effects were to erode support for Nixon's war policy and to destabilize Prince Norodom Sihanouk's neutralist regime in Cambodia.

The Nixon administration anticipated an enemy offensive in 1972 to disrupt Nixon's bid for reelection to the presidency. Nixon and Kissinger came up with the idea of a South Vietnamese thrust into Laos and Cambodia as a way to show that their Vietnamization policy was working. The U.S. Congress was about to vote to cut off funds for operations in Cambodia and Laos, but the new law had a loophole that permitted continued U.S. air operations in those countries to protect Americans who remained in South Vietnam. General Abrams came up with a plan targeting an enemy concentration suggested by South Vietnamese president Thieu: the Laotian town of Tchepone 50 kilometers northwest of the old U.S. base at Khesanh. Despite CIA warnings of the enemy's formidable antiaircraft defenses in the area, Operation Dewey Canyon II (MACV used the South Vietnamese code name "Lam Son 719" to emphasize the ARVN's role) was launched on 29 January 1971 in what turned out to be the last offensive operation for American troops in Indochina. Hoping for surprise, Abrams embargoed all news of the operation; reporters were not even permitted to report that there was an embargo. The reporters protested, arguing that the caravan of mechanized units and logistical support heading toward Laos was too big for the enemy not to find out. The reporters were right. The North Vietnamese braced for the attack and inflicted heavy losses, especially of U.S. helicopters.

The embargo was leaked in a way that could not be traced, and eventually Nixon ordered Abrams to loosen his restrictions. The South Vietnamese commander followed suit and authorized helicopter pilots to transport journalists into Laos. On 10 February, a helicopter carrying the first load of newsmen lost its way and fell to enemy machine-gun fire. All on board were killed, including photographers Larry

Burrows of *Life* magazine, Henri Huet of the Associated Press, Ken Potter of United Press International, and Sergeant Vu Tu of the South Vietnamese army. Casualties among war correspondents during the Vietnam War—especially the photographers, who tended to take greater risks than the writers—outpaced press losses during any other American war (see Chapter 23).

By the time the ARVN halted halfway to its objective of Tchepone on 13 February, it had taken so many casualties that Thieu feared loss of his best troops for protection of his regime. U.S. air strikes held the line for a time, but the enemy's counterattack on 19 February spelled the operation's doom. B-52s blasted Tchepone while the main force turned back. Administration attempts to salvage the situation by claiming to the press that Tchepone had not been the goal after all made the fiasco worse. Not only had the defeat discredited the ARVN and Nixon's Vietnamization policy, but also the government's uncoordinated handling of the press had alienated what was left of editorial support for Nixon's war policy. In a postmortem to Kissinger, Nixon said his administration's worst enemy seemed to be the press.

Nixon blamed demonstrators and their dupes—the news media—for steeling the enemy's will. Many journalists were put on a secret White House enemies list of political opponents, which became a perverse badge of honor for independent-minded journalists. Nixon harnessed Vice President Spiro T. Agnew to launch verbal attacks on the news media, especially the television networks. Agnew virtually accused them of seditious abandonment of U.S. troops in the field. His attacks were the public companion to a clandestine White House domestic surveillance campaign that featured illegal wiretaps, burglaries, and political sabotage to discredit detractors and stop war intelligence leaks.

In June 1971, the White House's worst fears were realized in the *New York Times*'s publication of the first installment of a forty-seven-volume classified report on conduct of the Vietnam War known as *The Pentagon Papers*. The government got a federal injunction to stop publication on grounds of national security and theft of government property by former Defense Department official Daniel Ellsberg. To evade the injunction, the *Times* turned over the documents for publication to a rival paper, the *Washington Post*. By a unanimous vote involving nine separate opinions forged in only two weeks, the U.S. Supreme Court ruled that the documents did not warrant prior restraint, though the disclosed facts embarrassed the government.

Nixon won a landslide reelection victory in 1972, thanks to his diplomatic breakthroughs with Red China and the Soviet Union and Kissinger's preliminary peace agreement with North Vietnamese negotiators in Paris. On 23 January 1973, Nixon and Kissinger proclaimed "peace with honor" in formal agreements to be signed on 27 January in Paris by all warring parties. The United States would retire from the conflict and leave the defense of South Vietnam to its own army. Nixon guaranteed Thieu continued air and logistical support. In February, Hanoi began releasing U.S. prisoners of war. The search for U.S. soldiers missing in action lasted two decades (see Chapter 24).

After the press uncovered illegal White House activities in the so-called Watergate scandal, Nixon was forced to resign the U.S. presidency in disgrace on 9 August 1974. Vice President Gerald R. Ford was sworn in as the new chief executive. Ford immediately reassured Thieu, but the U.S. Congress already was cutting back war appropriations.

After an interval, the NVA resumed its drive to Saigon. The ARVN crumbled before a major NVA assault with Soviet tanks in January 1975. Saigon surrendered on 30 April 1975, although the U.S. Embassy had evacuated its personnel and some South Vietnamese by helicopter from rooftops on 29 April. The fifteen-year civil war was over. Violence continued for some years in neighboring Cambodia and Laos, which had tried but failed to keep out of the Vietnam conflict and which were themselves consumed by bloody civil wars. More than 58,000 U.S. troops died in combat, and several hundreds of thousands were wounded. Vietnamese, Cambodian, and Laotian dead were in the millions.

## LESSONS OF THE VIETNAM WAR

The Pentagon's well-learned lesson from the Vietnam War was that controlling press access was the key to shaping public opinion during wartime. Thus by 1977 all branches of the U.S. military dropped their news management programs and sought ways to control access to the theater of operations, thereby forcing the press to depend on official sources.

Taking its cue from the British news blackout during the Falklands War between the United Kingdom and Argentina in 1982, President Ronald Reagan's administration opted for a total press ban during the U.S. military incursion into the Caribbean island of Grenada in October 1983. Though the ban infuriated the media, it proved highly effective and, crucially, had the full support of the U.S. public, which seemed to have tired of crusading reporters unearthing government malfeasance.

Sensing a favorable public climate to study wartime press controls, the Joint Chiefs of Staff convened a blue-ribbon panel in 1984. The panel included several distinguished retired journalists and journalism educators. The panel's chair was General Winant Sidle, who had replaced Zorthian at MACV. The Sidle Report concluded, first and foremost, that news coverage of military conflicts should respect mission security and safety of U.S. forces—a priority that, with rare exceptions, the Vietnam War correspondents voluntarily had observed. The report gave eight guidelines for maintaining security. Among them were media pools in combat areas, voluntary compliance with security rules, and expulsion of violators.

The first real test of the Sidle Panel recommendations came in August 1990 when President George H. W. Bush rushed troops to Saudi Arabia to blunt an Iraqi invasion. News media were not allowed in the initial deployment, but eventually the Defense Department set up reporter and photographer pools, press minders, and security review of all reporting. By the launch of the allied ground invasion of Kuwait and Iraq on 24 February 1991, more than 1,400 media personnel were dependent on pool reports from only 192 journalists grouped in twenty-four pools. The journalists resented the restrictions. Headquarters news briefings were suspended altogether during the 100-hour ground war. It became apparent immediately after cessation of hostilities that the military had used the news media to misdirect the Iraqis. In his "Mother of All Press Briefings" on 24 February 1991 in Riyadh, Saudi Arabia, allied commander General Norman Schwarzkopf gloated about allowing television crews to cover a phony amphibious landing in order to deflect Iraqi attention from the main allied attack.

Public opinion polls after the Gulf War showed strong support for controlling press access to the war zone. Restrictions had been for the media's own safety. The journalists themselves were far less satisfied, particularly newspaper reporters, who were scooped routinely by live television coverage. Accusations of unconstitutional prior restraint went unheeded. Swept up in the patriotic fervor following capitulation of Saddam Hussein's Republican Guard, President Bush declared, "By God, we've kicked the Vietnam syndrome," an epitaph for meddling independent media in wartime.

## A NOTE ON THIS VOLUME

The *Greenwood Library of American War Reporting* represents a significant effort to preserve pieces of history, such as newspaper, magazine and broadcast reports, which might otherwise be lost to posterity. I feel privileged to help stem this loss in my own small way. As it was compiled, this volume was conceived as part of a larger effort to preserve Vietnam War source material. That effort includes Nathanial Lande's compendium of U.S. war correspondence, *Dispatches from the Front: A History of the American War Correspondent* (1996), and the fine two-volume collection published by the Library of America, *Reporting Vietnam* (1998). Although there is some overlap in choice of news items, most of the articles in this volume, including all but one of the five broadcast transcripts and all of the photographs, do not appear in the other books.

There is no denying that reading about the Vietnam War is depressing. So much death and destruction. So many mistakes. So little understanding and compassion. Celebrating the U.S. news media's opposition to the war is a false solace; certainly individual journalists came out against the war, but the aggregate of news organizations went along with the war until it was blatantly obvious their readers and viewers no longer did. The news media did not lead; they followed. Like the protagonist in a classical Greek tragedy, America struggled for thirty years in Vietnam against its scripted antagonist, Communism, and, unable to alter its own destiny, finally succumbed. In the words of the querulous president of South Vietnam, Ngo Dinh Diem, the American news media were so many "fleas on the elephant."

Our presidents have told us that we can put Vietnam behind us and feel good about ourselves again. We've kicked the "Vietnam syndrome." I object. We should remember the Vietnam War, not as a war that America lost, but a war in which Americans lost track of their values and principles. Let us not forget.

## NOTES

1. Stanley Karnow, *Vietnam: A History*, 2nd rev. ed. (New York: Penguin Books, 1997), 161–162.

2. Bernard B. Fall, ed., *Ho-Chi-Minh on Revolution: Selected Writings, 1920–66* (New York: Praeger, 1967), 143.

3. In 2003, the Pentagon perfected this strategy of inviting journalists to "join the team" by "embedding" correspondents into combat units during the Iraq War.

4. Lyndon B. Johnson, "United States Vietnam Policy: Destroy or Build" [delivered at Johns Hopkins University, 7 April 1965], *Vital Speeches of the Day*, 15 April 1965, 386–388.

5. Lyndon B. Johnson, quoted in Karnow, *Vietnam*, 441.

6. Wendell S. Merick, "Behind Optimism about Vietnam," *U.S. News & World Report*, 1 December 1969, 41.

7. Daniel C. Hallin, *The "Uncensored War": The Media and Vietnam* (New York: Oxford University Press, 1986), 129–130.

8. The same charge was levied against Associated Press/Cable News Network correspondent Peter Arnett when he transmitted the only news from Baghdad, Iraq, to the West during the first four days of the Persian Gulf War in 1991.

9. Walter Cronkite, "Walter Cronkite's Report from Vietnam (Who, What, When, Where, Why)," *CBS News*, Columbia Broadcasting System, 27 February 1968.

10. Lyndon B. Johnson, "The Vietnam War: The President's Plans" [delivered over nationwide television, 30 March 1968], *Vital Speeches of the Day*, 15 April 1968, 389.

11. "The Faces of the American Dead in Vietnam: One Week's Toll," *Life*, 27 June 1969, 21–30, cover.

12. Richard M. Nixon, "A Vietnam Plan: The Silent Majority" [delivered over national television, 3 November 1969], *Vital Speeches of the Day*, 15 November 1969, 66–70.

## FURTHER READINGS

Cumings, Bruce. *War and Television*. New York: Verso, 1992.

Fall, Bernard B. *The Two Viet-Nams: A Political and Military Analysis*. 2nd rev. ed. New York: Praeger, 1967; London: Pall Mall, 1967.

Karnow, Stanley. *Vietnam: A History*. 2nd rev. ed. New York: Penguin Books, 1997.

Sheehan, Neil, Hendrick Smith, E. W. Kenworth, and Fox Butterfield. *The Pentagon Papers*. New York: Bantam Books, 1971.

Tucker, Spencer C., ed. *Encyclopedia of the Vietnam War: A Political, Social, and Military History*. New York: Oxford University Press, 2000.

# 1

## HO CHI MINH

Ho Chi Minh was Vietnam's George Washington and Thomas Jefferson combined—a patriotic symbol of Vietnamese independence fused with eloquent idealism. Ho aspired to the American Revolution in his propaganda and quoted Jefferson in his declaration of independence for the Vietnamese state on 2 September 1945. It was sad irony that the United States of America, the spiritual model for his independence movement, was drawn into the Vietnamese civil war and became his archenemy. Much as portraits of fallen President John F. Kennedy graced American homes throughout the war, shrines to Ho Chi Minh in nearly every North Vietnamese home gave hope for victory and peace.

Ho Chi Minh was an enigmatic figure for the Americans. Because of his use of aliases while in self-imposed exile from Vietnam for three decades, little was known about him when Kennedy decided to intervene in the Vietnamese civil war in 1961. General Maxwell Taylor, a principal architect of Kennedy's decision to fight the Communist rebels, later admitted to journalist Stanley Karnow the folly of fighting an unknown enemy:

> First, we didn't know ourselves. We thought that we were going into another Korean War, but this was a different country. Secondly, we didn't know our South Vietnamese allies. We never understood them, and that was another surprise. And we knew even less about North Vietnam. Who was Ho Chi Minh? Nobody really knew.[1]

Ho was not a military leader but a political organizer. His biggest contribution to the war effort was to train other men, such as Vo Nguyen Giap (later defense minister of North Vietnam) and Pham Van Dong (later prime minister of North Vietnam), in the necessity of merging political and military instruction so that the guerrillas always knew why they were fighting. The Vietminh, and later Vietcong, cadres were mostly Communist Party members steeped in Ho's nationalist doctrine. Unlike the privileged class of French and South Vietnamese army officers, the cadres shared the hardships of ordinary soldiers. They ate with their men, slept with them, and joined them in battle. They welcomed political and military discussions. The guerrillas looked to the cadres as "big brothers."

Ho Chi Minh's health was ruined by years of imprisonment and hiding in jungles. He was a frail old man of 71 years by the time the Americans came. At the time of his death on 3 September 1969, victory over the South Vietnamese regime was not yet in hand but seemed inevitable, thanks to the Americans' demoralization following the Communist Tet offensive in the spring of 1968. Shortly before his death, Ho Chi Minh wrote a letter in reply to U.S. president Richard M. Nixon's secret invitation to negotiate a war settlement. The letter shows that to the end, Ho maintained the rightness of his nationalist cause and his people's resolve to see it through: "Our Vietnamese people are deeply devoted to peace, a real peace with independence and real freedom. They are determined to fight to the end, without fearing the sacrifices and difficulties in order to defend their country and their sacred national rights."[2]

## BERNARD B. FALL: INTERVIEW WITH PHAM VAN DONG AND HO CHI MINH

*The following interview of Pham Van Dong and Ho Chi Minh in 1962 by Bernard B. Fall, a Franco-American scholar of Vietnam, was the first personal information about Ho published in the U.S. news media. Because the interview was considered controversial, publication was delayed until 1963. Fall was given access to Ho because he had authored several Vietnam histories critical of the French and Americans. Fall corresponded occasionally during the Vietnam War for the* New Republic *and the* Nation. *While covering a marines' operation in 1967, he was killed by a booby-trap explosion. Fall's legacy included five important books about Vietnam and an edition of Ho Chi Minh's writings.*

New Republic, 12 October 1963

As the Second Indochina War now grinds on into its fourth year, a large-scale reappraisal is under way both among Americans in Saigon and in Washington as to the ultimate objectives and outcome of that war. For the time being, no solution envisaged considers seriously the possibility of talks with the real "enemy-by-proxy," North Vietnam. In fact, it is not without significance that the *only* open reference made to such negotiations came from no one else but South Vietnam's secret police chief, Ngo Dinh Nhu, in his recent interview with an American columnist. Nhu, beyond a doubt seeks to use at least the threat—if not the reality—of such South-North contacts as a counter-blackmail against the United States which has thus far (and with conspicuous unsuccess) sought his and his wife's removal from Vietnamese politics.

Thus, negotiating with North Vietnam—or, for that matter, any kind of contact with that country—has become another bogey that, in the months to come, may supplant Cuba and even Red China in the public eye. Of course, as even a brief stay in North Vietnam shows, that attitude cuts both ways: in Hanoi, the only kind of demonstration that is allowed is directed against the United States, the Ngo family, or, on occasion, against the Indian and Canadian (not the Polish, of

course) members of the lame-duck International Control Commission which still "supervises" the implementation of the civil liberties and disarmament provisions of the 1954 Indochina ceasefire. The Commission's lack of effectiveness makes it a permanent monument to the impossibility of settling a dispute when it directly involves the prestige or interests of both of the major power blocs.

French non-Communist writers have been able, over the years, to visit North Vietnam, just as Canadian, Australian and British writers have been able to visit Red China. In my own case, the fact that I had written a solidly-documented (and, hence, unflattering) book in France about North Vietnam perhaps incited the North Vietnamese leaders to be franker than usual. What follows is based on notes taken in the course of a conversation which took place in July 1962, supplemented by a tape recording made during that conversation and by notes made immediately afterwards, while my memory was fresh. It is a verbatim translation from the original French, and leaves out only some of the usual banter.

A brief note on the North Vietnamese leaders involved: *Prime Minister Pham Van Dong*, born in 1906 in Central Vietnam, is of senior mandarin origin; in fact, say some, he outranks President Ngo Dinh Diem. While Diem's father was chief of cabinet to emperor Thanh-Thai, Dong's father held the same post under emperor Duy-Tan. A graduate of Chiang Kai-shek's own Whampoa Military Academy (class of 1925), Dong has been Ho's prime minister and probably closest associate since 1955.

*Ho Chi Minh*, born in 1890 in Central Vietnam, was a revolutionary since his age of 14, went to Europe in 1911, [and] became a co-founder of the French Communist Party in 1920 and a French delegate to the Komintern in 1923. He founded the Indochinese Communist Party in 1930 and became President of the Democratic Republic of Vietnam (DRVN) on September 2, 1945. He unquestionably is the most important Asian Communist leader after Mao Tse-tung, and the last of the Old Bolsheviks in power anywhere in the Communist world.

All remarks made by Dong are preceded by "P"; those made by Ho by "H," and those made by myself by "F." My own explanations are placed in brackets.

[Pham Van Dong meets me in the corridor of the presidential residence; wears a khaki Mao Tse-tung suit; invites me to a sitting room overlooking the formal gardens.]

P: Please make yourself at home, Monsieur le Professeur, take off your jacket [takes off his own jacket].

I know how it is here during the rainy season.

I hope you are enjoying your trip throughout North Vietnam, and that you find us cooperative.

F: Thank you, Monsieur le Prime Minister, your subordinates indeed have generally been cooperative.

P: I remember, however, that you said in your book *Le Viet-Minh* that we are not a democratic country. Do you still feel the same way about this?

F: Well, Monsieur le Prime Minister, all my color films were impounded upon my arrival at Hanoi Airport, I don't think you would call this in accordance with democratic procedures . . .

P: [laughing] Oh, those are general rules which apply to everybody. [While theoretically true, the rule obviously applies to Westerners only. In addition, black-and-white film has to be exposed prior to departure and the developed film submitted to the Foreign Ministry for censorship. Even so, the airport police again inspected my films prior to departure.]

F: Monsieur le Prime Minister, North Vietnam has had some serious economic difficulties. Do you believe that they have been mastered?

P: As you know, the recent 7th plenary session of the [Vietnamese] Communist Party's Central Committee has decided to give priority to basic heavy industries, although attention will be paid to a proper balance with agriculture and consumer goods production.

We base ourselves upon the Marxist economic viewpoint: heavy industrial development is essential to Socialist construction, but we also understand the importance of the "full belly." In any case, we do not seek to bluff and will not put emphasis on "showpiece" industries but on sound and useful economic development.

Yes, we have made economic mistakes, due mainly to our backwardness and ignorance in the field of economic planning. Not all of those errors have yet been corrected and some of their effects are still felt, but we try to overcome them rapidly thanks to help from friendly countries.

F: Monsieur le Prime Minister, President Ho Chi Minh made a declaration to the *Daily Express* [London] in March 1962, referring to the conditions under which North Vietnam would negotiate a settlement with the South. Has anything happened in the meantime which would change those conditions?

P: Our position has remained largely unchanged since President Ho Chi Minh's declaration. What has changed, however, is the extent of American intervention in South Vietnam, which has continued to increase and to take over increased responsibilities and control over the [Ngo Dinh] Diem regime.

The real enemy is American intervention. It is of little importance as to who the American agent in Vietnam might be.

F: Monsieur le Prime Minister, the International Control Commission [composed of Indian, Polish and Canadian members] has recently accused the North Vietnamese Republic of aiding and abetting the South Vietnamese rebellion. What do you think of that accusation?

P: [deprecating gesture] We understand, Monsieur le Professeur, under which outside pressures the [Indian and Canadian] members of the ICC labor. After all, India does depend for development upon large-scale American aid.

F: But would it not at least be conceivable that some of the almost 100,000 South Vietnamese who went north [of the 17th Parallel] in 1954 and whose relatives are now fighting against South Vietnamese forces, would attempt to slip across your border back into South Vietnam in order to help their relatives—even without the permission of the North Vietnamese government? Wouldn't that be at least conceivable?

P: Monsieur, in our country one does not cross borders without permission.

F: Would not a spreading of the guerrilla war entail a real risk of American reaction against North Vietnamese territory? You have been to North Korea last year, Monsieur le Prime Minister; you saw what American bombers can do. . . .

P: [very seriously] We fully realize that the American imperialists wish to provoke a situation in the course of which they could use the heroic struggle of the South Vietnamese people as a pretext for the destruction of our economic and cultural achievements.

We shall offer them no pretext which could give rise to an American military intervention against North Vietnam.

[Ho Chi Minh suddenly enters, unannounced. Mao Tse-tung suit in suntan cotton. Spry and tanned looking, springy step, arms swinging, firm handshake.]

F: I thought you were in Moscow on vacation!

H: You see, people say a lot of things that aren't true. [Looks at my jacket, tape recorder, book, next to me on sofa.] My, you have got a lot of things with you.

F: I am sorry, Monsieur le Président [Push things together. Ho sits down next to me, humorous gleam on face, slaps me on thigh.]

H: So, you are the young man who is so much interested in all the small details about my life. [In my book *Le Viet Minh* and the forthcoming *Two Viet-Nams*, I have attempted to include as complete a biographical sketch of Ho Chi Minh as possible. During my stay in Hanoi, I also interviewed many of Ho's old friends on Ho's life, and he apparently had been informed of this.]

F: Monsieur le Président, you are after all a public figure, and it certainly would not be a violation of a military secret to know whether you had a family, or were in Russia at a given date.

H: Ah, but you know, I'm an old man, a very old man [he's 73]. An old man likes to have a little air of mystery about himself. I like to hold on to my little mysteries. I'm sure you will understand that.

F: But. . . .

H: Wait until I'm dead. [In spite of this, I received just before I left Hanoi a letter containing six manuscript pages of details about Ho's life, filling in most of the gaps—no doubt on his own orders.]

P: Monsieur Fall brought you a book on the Indochina War which contains a drawing of you by his wife.

H: [with an old man's impatience] Where? Where? Let me see it. Providing she's got my goatee right. Providing the goatee looks alright. [Unwraps and looks.] Mmm—yes, that is very good. That looks very much like me. [Looks around, grabs a small flower bouquet from the table, hands it to me.] Tell her from me that the drawing is very good and give her the bouquet and kiss her on both cheeks for me.

P: Monsieur Fall is interested in the present situation in South Vietnam. . . .

F: Yes, Monsieur le Président, how do you evaluate the situation in South Vietnam?

H: Monsieur Ngo Dinh Diem is in a very difficult position right now and it is not likely to improve in the future. He has no popular support.

F: But would you negotiate with South Vietnam?

P: The situation is not yet ripe for a real negotiation. They [South Vietnamese] don't really want to negotiate.

H: That is absolutely true. They are showing no intention to negotiate.

F: But are you not afraid that the situation might degenerate into a protracted war?

H: [earnestly, turning full face] Monsieur le Professeur, you have studied us for 10 years, you have written about the Indochina War. It took us eight years of bitter fighting to defeat you French in Indochina. Now the Diem regime is well armed and helped by many Americans. The Americans are stronger than the French. It might perhaps take 10 years, but our heroic compatriots in the South will defeat them in the end. We shall marshal world public opinion about this unjust war against the South Vietnamese people.

P: Yes, the heroic South Vietnamese people will have to continue the struggle by its own means but we watch its efforts with the greatest sympathy.

H: I think the Americans greatly underestimate the determination of the Vietnamese people. The Vietnamese people [have] always shown great determination when [they are] faced with an invader.

F: But are you still willing to come to a negotiated settlement if the occasion presented itself?

H: Yes, but only with people who are willing to sit down with us at one and the same table and "talk." [French word: "causer" which means: "negotiate in good faith."]

F: You mean you would negotiate with any South Vietnamese government?

H: Yes, with any.

F: But what kind of relations would you envisage?

H: Of whatever type they [South Vietnamese] wish. After all, the East and West Germans have flourishing trade relations in spite of the Berlin Wall, haven't they? [After some further amenities, Ho leaves.]

F: Monsieur le Prime Minister, what do you think of Mr. Ngo Dinh Diem's personal position as of right now?

P: It is quite difficult. He is unpopular, and the more unpopular he is, the more American aid he will need to remain in power. And the more American aid he gets, the more as an American puppet he'll look and the less likely is he to regain popularity.

F: That sounds pretty much like a vicious circle, doesn't it?

P: [humorous gleam] No, Monsieur le Professeur. It is a descending spiral.

F: But you must understand, Monsieur le Prime Minister, that South Vietnam is in a different situation than the non-Communist parts of Germany and Korea. In the latter two cases, the non-Communist part is by far the more populated, whereas in the case of Vietnam, the non-Communist part has 13.8 million people against your 17 million. You can clearly see that they have good reasons to fear North Vietnam which also has the larger army, and one with a fearsome reputation, as we French well know.

P: Certainly, we realize that we are in the stronger position. Thus, we are also willing to give all the guarantees necessary for the South to be able to come out fairly [*pour que le Sud trouve son compte*] in such a negotiation.

You will recall President Ho's declaration with regard to maintaining the South's separate government and economic system. The Fatherland Front embodies those points in its program, and the South Vietnamese Liberation Front likewise.

We do not envisage an immediate reunification and are willing to accept the verdict of the South Vietnamese people with regard to the institutions and policies of its part of the country.

F: What, then, would be the minimal conditions under which the Democratic Republic of Vietnam [North Vietnam] would accept a settlement of the conflict which at present exists in South Vietnam?

P: [Makes a statement as below.]

F: Would you object to my making a tape recording of that answer? It is a reply that I would like to have verbatim, if possible.

P: [Thinks it over, makes notes, agrees.]

P: This is a very timely question: The DRVN [North Vietnam] government has made some sufficiently explicit declarations on the subject [but] let me underline what follows: The underlying origin and immediate cause of the extremely dangerous situation in the South of our country is the armed intervention of the USA and the fascist dictatorship of Monsieur Ngo Dinh Diem, the creation and instrument of that [American] intervention.

It is obvious, then, that in order to normalize the situation in our whole country, those factors of dissension must disappear. We support with determination the patriotic struggle of our Southern compatriots and the objectives of their struggle—I mean the program of the Southern Liberation Front.

We are certain that the massive help of all classes of South [Vietnam's] society and the active support of the peoples of the world, shall determine the happy outcome of the situation full of dangers which exist in the South of our country.

The people of Vietnam and the DRVN government remain faithful to the Geneva accords [of July 1954] which establish our basic national rights. We shall continue to cooperate with the International Control Commission on the basis of those accords, and hope that this cooperation shall be fruitful—providing that all members of the Commission respect the accords.

F: Thank you, Monsieur le Prime Minister, for that statement.

P: I would like to say something about a remark you made in your book on our Republic about our alleged "isolationism" from neutral and pro-Western countries, and from international organizations. No, no and no, we are not isolationists! On the contrary, we seek "open windows" towards any country or organization that will deal with us on a matter-of-fact basis. We are willing to trade with them and make purchases from them.

F: What would be the position of the foreign community in South Vietnam, if the war worsens? There are still 15,000 French citizens living there.

P: As you know, the Southern Liberation Front has repeatedly shown that it does not wish to hurt the legitimate interests of the Europeans who live in South Vietnam. We make a distinction between France's position and that of American imperialists.

F: What is the attitude of the DRVN towards Laos and Cambodia?

P: We shall respect the Laos accords [This was stated briefly after the signature of the 1962 Geneva accords on Laos. It has become obvious since then that North Vietnamese troops still operate in Laos to some extent, or travel through to South Vietnam.], and shall at all costs maintain good relations with Cambodia.

*Credit*: Reprinted with permission.

---

## AN ANONYMOUS REPORT: PROFILE OF HO CHI MINH UPON HIS DEATH

*As exemplified by the following* Newsweek *article, the U.S. news media honored Ho Chi Minh upon his death with reverence for an enemy leader not seen in previous American wars. Americans who did not appreciate Ho's revolutionary doctrine of total commitment to Vietnamese reunification hoped that Ho's death would dishearten the Communists and thereby improve prospects for a negotiated settlement of the conflict. Ho's passing had the reverse effect: Nationwide memorial observances distracted the North Vietnamese from the conference table and renewed the people's zeal to repel the foreigners from the South.*

*Though revering Ho Chi Minh the nationalist, the* Newsweek *writers still viewed Ho Chi Minh the Communist through the lens of cold war geopolitics as little more than a surrogate for the Soviet Union and Red China in the international Communist conspiracy. Nixon's policy of detente toward the Communists, only three years off, was unimaginable in 1969.*

*The North Vietnamese disregarded Ho's wish to be cremated and to have his ashes scattered in the hills of his beloved Vietnam. They said that "Uncle Ho" belonged to the people and interred his remains in Hanoi in a giant granite mausoleum designed by Soviet architects to emulate Lenin's tomb.*

*A note of interest: This* Newsweek *profile quotes Ho Chi Minh's 1962 interview by Bernard Fall, which is reproduced in this chapter.*

Newsweek, 15 September 1969

Alone and sick in a vermin-infested Chinese jail, an obscure, middle-aged Vietnamese picked up a bamboo brush and, with sure strokes, found poetic solace in the value of personal endurance.

The rice grain suffers under the blows of the pestle;
But admire its whiteness once the ordeal is over!
Thus it is with men in the world we live in;
To be a man, one must suffer the blows of misfortune.

The frail little man who composed those lines nearly three decades ago survived more blows than most. But last week his epic ordeal was finally over. When word of his passing came, Hanoi, the war-devastated capital of his divided country, was drenched in a monsoonal downpour. Small groups of North Vietnamese paused on their way to work and, ignoring the driving rain, listened wordlessly as loudspeakers blared out the mournful bulletin: "Comrade Ho Chi Minh, Chairman of the Central Committee of the Workers Party and President of the Democratic Republic of Vietnam, died at 0947 hours, Sept. 3, 1969, after a grave and sudden heart attack."

Somberly, with hardly any display of public emotion, his countrymen prepared to heap honor on the man whom they considered the greatest Vietnamese of this—or perhaps any other—century. For seven straight days, all of North Vietnam's newspapers ran black-bordered portraits of the 79-year-old leader. Tens of thousands of peasants, soldiers and government officials donned black-and-red armbands and badges and filed slowly into Ba Dinh Congress Hall to view Ho's body as it lay in state. And almost at once, the mighty of the Marxist world began to descend on Hanoi by jet to pay their last respects to their departed colleague. The first to arrive, barely six hours after the official announcement of Ho's death, was Chou En-lai, the Premier of Communist China. Only half a day after his arrival, Chou departed once again—presumably to avoid an embarrassing face-to-face meeting with Soviet Premier Aleksei Kosygin, who was the next major Communist leader to make his appearance. But even without Chou's presence, Ho's interment this week seemed likely to prove the most impressive convocation of statesmen since the funeral of John Fitzgerald Kennedy.

## VOICES

Nor did the non-Communist world treat the occasion as a death in the Red family. Though Mr. Nixon, understandably, refused to comment on the death of a man with whom the U.S. has for five years been locked in combat, a number of non-Communist leaders in Asia and Western Europe lent their voices to the chorus of condolences. But perhaps the most eloquent testimony to Ho's stature came from those who seemed to have the least reason to revere him—his bitter antagonists in South Vietnam. With grudging admiration, a Saigon journalist observed: "The only problem of South Vietnam is that we don't have a national hero. Now that Ho

Chi Minh is dead, we are, both north and south, on the same basis." And the Vietnamese *Guardian*, an English-language daily in Saigon, editorialized: "With his passing, for better and for worse, Vietnam loses its unique politician of truly international status. With President Ho's death, a legendary, almost mythological figure disappears from the international political scene."

That Ho had cut an impressive global swath was undeniable. A survivor of Marxism's heroic era (he personally met Lenin in 1922), Ho was waging a successful war of national liberation well before Mao Tse-tung and Lin Piao articulated the theoretical basis for such struggles. During his battle for a unified, independent Vietnam—a battle that was to inspire liberation movements from Algeria to Mozambique—he wrestled France to her knees and fought the U.S., the world's mightiest power, to a military stalemate. Ultimately, Ho's single-minded dedication changed the course of history—plunging the U.S. into a rancorous national debate, prompting the political abdication of Lyndon Baines Johnson and radicalizing great segments of American youth. Throughout the world today, anti-Establishment barricades are manned by youngsters who chant: "Ho, Ho, Ho Chi Minh."

But if youth canonized Ho as a symbol of what a seemingly powerless individual could accomplish against the arrayed power of the world's mightiest industrial and military machine, older and more sophisticated observers were often equally impressed. French journalist Jean Lacouture described Ho, whom he interviewed in 1946, as a luminous, almost saintly figure. "I didn't see him enter," Lacouture wrote years later. "I didn't even hear him. His sandals, like a mendicant monk's, seemed to glide over the shiny floor. The voice was thin, with the suggestion of a lisp. The first thing that struck me was the extraordinary glow in the eyes beneath his bushy brows, huge forehead and tuft of hair; this last stood on end to such a degree that he would have looked like a circus funny man had it not been for the dignity of his features and bearing."

## SECRECY

Such an appealing image in the Western press is, of course, hard to come by for a Communist. And Ho, more conscious of the value of public relations than any other Communist leader, did his best to keep that image intact. Quite deliberately, he cloaked his personal history in a shroud of secrecy. When pressed by the late historian Bernard Fall for some information on his past, Ho replied: "Ah, but you know, I'm an old man, a very old man. And an old man likes to have a little air of mystery about himself." Even his original name (Ho Chi Minh was a *nom de guerre* which means "He Who Enlightens") was a matter of endless scholarly speculation until Fall solved the puzzle in 1967—more than two years after the U.S. committed ground troops in a war against Ho's jungle legions. Fall's discovery: Ho was born in Central Vietnam on May 19, 1890, as Nguyen That Thanh.

Between the worlds of Nguyen That Thanh and Ho Chi Minh, biographers have uncovered an intricate cobweb of aliases and disguises that covers one of the most colorful political careers of the twentieth century. By the time he was 23, Ho had sailed across the South China Sea and Indian Ocean to Africa, Europe, and reportedly to North America. Before the end of World War I, he had worked as a seaman, a pastry cook for the famous French chef Auguste Escoffier and as a free-lance photo retoucher. With his gift for languages, he was fluent in French, English, Russian, three Chinese dialects—and could get along as well in German. With his theatrical flair, he changed his identity when it suited his purposes—or when the police were on his trail—now appearing as a Chinese businessman in Canton, now as a shaven-headed Buddhist monk in Thailand.

*... to understand Ho it was necessary to go beyond psychology to politics ...*

## HIERARCHY

Almost incredibly, this ephemeral man, when he eventually emerged from the jungles after Japan's defeat in World War II, was already a ranking leader in the global Communist hierarchy. But he was a Communist such as the world had never witnessed before. Compared with Lenin, Ho was clearly an intellectual lightweight with no special genius for Marxist dialectics. Unlike Stalin, he evinced no monomaniacal drive to establish a cult of personality; to this day, not a single street or building in North Vietnam bears Ho's name. And in contrast to Mao, Ho did not set out to prove that his brand of Communism was better than all others.

None of which is to say that Ho was a "good" Communist or that he was a man easily understood. In many ways, his politics and personality were as complex as any leader's of his time. Who was to judge, for example, whether Ho was as monkishly ascetic as he seemed to casual acquaintances? His dress— an old cotton suntan jacket frayed at the collar, a pair of sandals cut from rubber tires—made it appear so. Yet Ho, the onetime apprentice to Escoffier, had a gourmet's palate. Nor were his comrades unaware that their leader had an eye for a good figure in an *ao dai*. While fighting the Japanese in the mountains of North Vietnam, Ho made sure that his force was supplied with lissome girl "entertainers" from Hanoi. In his later years, he was an inveterate chain-smoker (like South Vietnam's Vice President Nguyen Cao Ky, he preferred Salems) and he once whiled away a sociable evening in Rangoon smoking opium with Gen. Raoul Salan, the commander of French forces in northern Indochina.

## CONTRADICTION

An even more puzzling problem for those who tried to fathom Ho was the apparent contradiction between his personal reputation for soft-spoken gentleness, on the one hand,

and his regime's ruthless treatment of opponents—both domestic and foreign—on the other. Curiously, Ho confronted his enemy, as Bernard Fall pointed out, with a "hate gap." Neither the French, whom he humiliated at Dienbienphu in 1954, nor the Americans, who have suffered nearly 300,000 casualties in Vietnam, were ever able to muster the venomous hatred against "Uncle Ho" that is traditionally reserved for the leader of an enemy nation in time of war.

Yet, at the same time, it is documented that North Vietnam, under the tutelage of the benign Uncle Ho, witnessed numerous purges—including the executions of an estimated 50,000 people during a land-reform campaign in the late 1950s. Both during the Indochina war and the present struggle in Vietnam, Ho's guerrillas made systematic use of murder—often by disembowelment—to terrorize Vietnam's peasant population. And, only last week two U.S. Navy men recently released by Hanoi told a Washington news conference that a number of their fellow prisoners had been tortured by Ho's followers; according to the released men, Lt. Comdr. Richard Stratton, one of the most frequently photographed of the U.S. prisoners, at one point had his fingernails pulled out.

Which, then, was the real Ho Chi Minh—the ascetic, the sensualist, the gentle father figure or the ruthless practitioner of terror? It seems clear that Ho's personality embraced all these traits—and that, when all was said and done, he was more than the sum of his parts. For, ultimately, to understand Ho it was necessary to go beyond psychology to politics and to place him in the context of a twentieth-century phenomenon—the politics of national Communism.

## PARTITION

Ho's Communist credentials were as impeccable as they come. He was, in his various political incarnations, a charter member of the French Communist Party, a Russian Comintern agent in Asia, a political commissar with Mao Tsetung's Eighth Route Army and, finally, the founder of the Indochinese Communist Party. Throughout his career, he faithfully toed the Moscow line—a policy that cost him dearly when, in 1954, the Russians persuaded him to settle for a partitioned Vietnam at the Geneva conference rather than to try to ram a humiliating settlement down the throats of the defeated French. To the day he died, in fact, Ho remained, in some ways, more catholic than the popes in Moscow; among the books he recommended to friends were the works of Joseph Stalin.

Yet Ho, for all his dedication to Communism, did not seek to convert all mankind to his faith; if he was a true believer, it was because he saw in Communism the weapon with which he could achieve an independent Vietnam. His patriotic fervor, a legacy from his father who never reconciled himself to

French rule of Indochina, shone through Ho's every act—from his abortive petition to the Versailles Peace Conference in 1919 to his demand, 50 years later, that all U.S. troops leave Vietnamese soil. In his single-minded pursuit of national independence, Ho was acting in the tradition of the great Vietnamese heroes such as Le Loi and the Trung Sisters who, over a period of nearly 2,000 years, fought against Chinese domination. Urged by some of his colleagues in 1946 to turn to China for help in ridding Vietnam of the French, Ho declared: "I prefer to smell French *merde* for five years rather than Chinese dung for the rest of my life."

Inevitably, Ho's death immediately raised a host of questions about the future course of the Vietnamese war. In Paris last week, a scheduled session of the peace talks was suspended so that the North Vietnamese delegates could fly home to attend Ho's funeral. And in South Vietnam, the National Liberation Front announced that it would observe a 72-hour cease-fire in Ho's honor—a proposal that caused some consternation among U.S. officials. Said one American: "We can hardly agree to a cease-fire honoring a man who has been our No. 1 enemy since this war started." Yet if the South Vietnamese Government chose to agree to the cease-fire—as it well might—the U.S. could scarcely refuse to go along.

Of more lasting importance to the U.S. was the question of how Ho's death would affect the complexion of the North Vietnamese leadership. There could, of course, be no real successor to Ho. Among those considered the most likely to succeed . . . none possessed anything approaching Ho's enormous prestige in the eyes of ordinary North Vietnamese. Only one member of the Politburo, Vice President Ton Duc Thang, 81, is accorded the honor of being addressed as "Uncle." But Thang is too old to be a serious contender for supreme power (though it was possible that he might be temporarily elevated to the post of figurehead President).

## CRUCIAL JOB

Predictably, in the days following Ho's death, his colleagues proclaimed their intention of ruling by "collective leadership." But most students of North Vietnamese affairs believed that, eventually, one man would emerge in the crucial job of Chairman of the party's Central Committee—and that the odds were that the man who so emerged would be either Party Secretary Le Duan or Truong Chinh, Hanoi's chief Marxist theoretician.

If, in fact, the succession race turns into a struggle between Le Duan and Truong Chinh, its final outcome could be of immense importance to the U.S. For these two men take a radically different approach to the conduct of the war in South Vietnam. In a recent book, Douglas Pike, one of the most knowledgeable American students of Vietnam, points out that Le Duan favors a "regular-force strategy"—the doctrine that preaches the war must be won as quickly as possible by regular North Vietnamese units. In contrast, says Pike, Truong Chinh is the leading advocate of "neo-revolutionary guerrilla war"—i.e., the use of small-scale units to wage a protracted conflict.

Because of these and other differences, some observers speculated that a bitter power struggle is bound, sooner or later, to break out among the leaders in Hanoi. And this prospect has led Zbigniew Brzezinski, an expert on Communism and a former member of the U.S. State Department's Policy Planning Council, to recommend that Washington take advantage of the opening provided by Ho's passing. "The death of a dominant political leader in a Communist country creates an external façade of unity behind which there is intense political conflict," Brzezinski said last week. "This creates the opportunity to focus the attention of Communist leaders on initiatives from abroad. A proposal now to begin negotiations on a cease-fire would possibly compel some very serious discussions in Hanoi on how to respond."

## DISAGREEMENTS

Most officials in Washington, however, do not agree with Brzezinski's analysis. For one thing, these officials point out that Ho had, over the past few years, relinquished much of his power to his subordinates and that, as a result, the members of the North Vietnamese Politburo have already had a great deal of time to work out their differences in day-to-day policymaking. For another, unless President Nixon is willing to settle the Vietnamese war on terms far more unfavorable to the U.S. than he has so far indicated, there seemed little of substance he could offer as bait to Ho's successors. "I can give you a dozen reasons why we should move politically," remarked one official. "Even if we only created the appearance of motion, it might give the leadership in Hanoi an occasion for response. But I can give you just as many reasons for a waiting period. For if there are important disagreements in Hanoi, we could provoke a power struggle that, in the end, might work against us. Or we could, by seeming to capitalize upon Ho's death, drive the North Vietnamese leaders together. It isn't simple."

Thus, it seemed that in death, as well as in life, Ho had confronted the U.S. with a dilemma fraught with unpredictable consequences. Should President Nixon make a compromise gesture—such as offering to negotiate a cease-fire—and risk a possible backlash from Hanoi? Or should he wait and see how the pieces fall into place in North Vietnam—and risk missing what might prove a unique opportunity to nudge the war closer to a conclusion? Ultimately, only Richard Nixon's personal intuition could supply the answer to these questions—and decide how the U.S. would write its epitaph for Ho Chi Minh.

## HO'S COMRADES IN ARMS: WILL ONE BECOME LEADER?

For more than a generation, Ho Chi Minh worked especially closely with four men, one of whom is likely in the end to emerge as his successor. The four:

## PHAM VAN DONG

As Prime Minister of North Vietnam, 61-year-old Pham Van Dong has for years played [French Cardinal and Royal Advisor] Mazarin to Ho Chi Minh's Louis XIV. Cautious, diligent and pragmatic, Dong has loyally applied himself to the workaday tasks of running the government and the country. "He's my other self," Ho once said of his Premier. And amongst ordinary Vietnamese, to whom Ho was universally known as "Uncle," Pham Van Dong has long been regarded as "the best nephew."

The son of a central Vietnamese mandarin—his father was private secretary to the Emperor of Vietnam—Pham Van Dong early turned to revolution as a way of life. It was as an exile in China in 1925 that he first met Ho Chi Minh, and Ho soon sent him back to Vietnam as director of "agit-prop" in the Hanoi region. This "suicide mission" led, almost inevitably, to a seven-year term in a French colonial prison, but it proved Dong's reliability. When Ho proclaimed the first Viet Minh government in 1945, Dong was named Minister of Finance. And ten years later, after an impressively tough performance as head of the Viet Minh delegation at the 1954 Geneva conference, Dong was made Prime Minister of North Vietnam.

Although he is Hanoi's chief public spokesman, Dong is by nature a secretive man; he is thought to be a widower, but his private life is so totally private that Western experts are not even sure whether he has any children. Dong is also something of a fence-sitter: he is said to favor Russia in its dispute with China, but has carefully refrained from any public commitment. Because he has stayed aloof from political squabbles, Pham Van Dong might be acceptable to all of Hanoi's factions. But for the same reason, he also lacks a personal following.

## TRUONG CHINH

As outspoken as Pham Van Dong is restrained, burly Truong Chinh is the most vocal advocate of Chinese-style Communism among Hanoi's top leaders. Even Chinh's adopted name—he was born Dang Xuan Khu—is a measure of his dedication to the way of Mao Tse-tung; in Vietnamese, "Truong Chinh" means "The Long March."

Now 61, Chinh worked his way up through exile in China and early membership in the Viet Minh to become Secretary General of the Lao Dong (Workers) Party. In 1954, he took charge of "agrarian reform," and in trying to install Chinese-style collectivization ordered vast eviction of peasants and mass executions of "landlords." In the end, the scheme had to be radically modified. And, by that time, Truong Chinh was the most hated man in North Vietnam.

In 1956, as a result, Chinh was dismissed from his party post and forced to confess to "serious mistakes" and "leftist deviationism." But undaunted and unrepentant, he soon clawed his way back to the top as chairman of the National Assembly's Standing Committee, ostensibly the No. 3 position in the government (behind Ho and the 81-year-old Vice President, Ton Duc Thang). Known as Hanoi's most devout guardian of Communist orthodoxy, Chinh is also said to be the hardest of hardliners on the war.

## VO NGUYEN GIAP

As a schoolteacher in Hanoi, Vo Nguyen Giap, 57, liked to diagram Napoleon's battles on the blackboard. When asked once whether he wasn't playing Napoleon, Giap supposedly replied, "I'm going to *be* Napoleon."

Insofar as Giap has realized that ambition, he has done so, paradoxically, primarily at the expense of France. An ardent Vietnamese nationalist from youth, he acquired personal reasons for hating France when his wife died in a French prison in 1943. Tougher in this respect even than Ho himself, Giap was instrumental in mounting the Viet Minh attack on Hanoi that signaled the start of the Indochina war.

Contrary to a widely held belief in the West, however, Giap's military record has not been consistently Napoleonic. He suffered several grave defeats in his early battles against the French, and both the 1968 Tet offensive and the siege of Khe Sanh—which he is generally credited with masterminding—were not unqualified successes. Nonetheless, his epic victory at Dienbienphu in 1954 finally drove France from Indochina and made him a towering figure at home and abroad. And despite occasional political reverses, he is now Deputy Premier, Defense Minister, commander of the armed forces—and a national institution.

Fairly enough, Giap is widely admired for his intelligence, dedication and organizational brilliance. Less often noted is a more blood-chilling quality, revealed by one of his favorite slogans. "Every minute," he likes to say, "100,000 men die all over the world. The life and death of human beings means nothing."

## LE DUAN

The current First Secretary of the Lao Dong Party, Le Duan, 61, is less well-known—both in North Vietnam and overseas—than any of his three colleagues. Truong Chinh's successor as party chieftain, Le Duan has the credentials customary among members of the Hanoi establishment: two stints in colonial jails, guerrilla service against the French and a string of secret party assignments. The only jarring note is his ancestry: he is said to be of part-Chinese extraction.

Le Duan is considered to be the man who actually founded the Viet Cong in South Vietnam. Other than that, little is known of his accomplishments—or of his intentions. But he is regarded as Hanoi's leading pragmatist—partly because he tolerates such capitalist deviations as private farm plots for increased production.

Some observers claim that, even before Ho's death, Le Duan was the *de facto* ruler of North Vietnam—or at least "first among equals." And as head of the party, he would have key support if he chose to make a bid for complete authority. Even outside Hanoi there are people who would support his candidacy. At a reception in Saigon last week, South Vietnamese President Nguyen Van Thieu suggested that if Le Duan becomes top dog in Hanoi, "the war may end soon." But that view appears to be overly hopeful. For the one common thread that seems to bind the members of Ho Chi Minh's inner circle most strongly is an unrelenting determination to reunify Vietnam under their own rule.[3]

## NOTES

1. Maxwell Taylor, quoted in Stanley Karnow, *Vietnam: A History*, 2nd rev. ed. (New York: Penguin Books, 1977), 23.

2. Letter contained in Richard M. Nixon, "A Vietnam Plan: The Silent Majority" [delivered over national television, 3 November 1969], *Vital Speeches of the Day*, 15 November 1969, 70.

3. Le Duan succeeded Ho Chi Minh as supreme ruler of North Vietnam.

## FURTHER READINGS

Buttinger, Joseph. *Vietnam: A Dragon Embattled*. Vol. 1, *From Colonialism to the Vietminh*. Vol. 2, *Vietnam at War*. New York: Praeger, 1967.

Fall, Bernard B., ed. *Ho Chi Minh on Revolution: Selected Writings, 1920–66*. New York: Praeger, 1967.

Green, Felix. *Vietnam! Vietnam!* Palo Alto, Calif.: Fulton, 1966.

Warbey, William. *Ho Chi Minh and the Struggle for an Independent Vietnam*. London: Merlin Press, 1972.

# 2

## HANOI

Hanoi was the imperial capital of Tonkin, the northernmost state of ancient Vietnam. French colonialists adopted the city as their seat of government and remade its boulevards, parks, and public buildings in the Parisian style. When Vietnam was partitioned in 1954, Hanoi, by far the largest city in the northern part, with a population of roughly 300,000 people, became the capital of North Vietnam, with an overall national population of 17 million.

After reunification, the southern capital of Saigon was renamed Ho Chi Minh City in honor of Vietnam's leading patriot, but Hanoi was truly Ho's city. Hanoi was where Ho delivered his declaration of independence from the French on 2 September 1945, Hanoi was the core of his sphere of influence during the Indochina War against the French, and Hanoi was Ho Chi Minh's capital after partition.

During the Vietnam War, Americans hotly debated whether the 1965–1968 bombing campaign against North Vietnam had targeted civilian areas in Hanoi (see Chapter 13). In December 1966–January 1967, *New York Times* assistant managing editor Harrison Salisbury reported from Hanoi facts and pictures supplied by the North Vietnamese that showed civilian deaths, maimed children, and bombed homes. The U.S. government insisted that its precision air strikes were limited to military targets and accused Salisbury of collaborating with the enemy. Rightly or wrongly, Salisbury's reports created the impression of widespread violence against Hanoi citizens. After the war, westerners were surprised to find very little bomb damage in Hanoi. The Pentagon had been right after all.

## PEGGY DURDIN: ACCOUNT OF HANOI AFTER VIETMINH VICTORY OVER FRENCH

*Despite gender discrimination and other hardships, dozens of female journalists went to Vietnam to cover the war—among them, Tad Bartimus, Elizabeth Becker, Dicky Chapelle, Judith Coburn, Beverly Deepe, Gloria Emerson, Denby Fawcett, Oriana Fallaci, Frances Fitzgerald, Martha Gellhorn, Marguerite Higgins, Jurate Kizackas, Edith Lederer, Cathy Leroy, Ann Bryan Mariano, Anne Morrissy Merick, Laura Palmer, Marlene Sanders, Liz Trotta, Kate Webb, and Tracy Wood. They had to be tough and resourceful and every bit as good as their male counterparts, usually for less pay and recognition. Sometimes women could gain admittance where male journalists were denied. This essay for the New Yorker magazine by freelance writer Peggy Durdin, written not long after the Vietminh consolidated control of North Vietnam, provided a rare glimpse into the North Vietnamese capital. Though Durdin made no effort in her writing to disguise her disapproval of the new regime in Hanoi, her insights of the place as it was enrich us today.*

*New Yorker*, 17 December 1955

Until recently, Hanoi, the largest city in northern Indo-China, was a throbbing, thriving outpost of French colonialism. It was hardly more than a year and a half ago that, during a brief stopover at its airport, I found myself surrounded by planes that were being briskly loaded with jaunty Foreign Legionnaires and smart Senegalese troops, along with their weapons, ammunition, cheese, and wine, bound for nearby French garrisons, including Dienbienphu. Soon after that, in July, 1954, Messrs. Eden, Mendès-France, Molotov, and Chou En-lai got together in Geneva and ended seven years of war between the French and South Vietnam forces and the North Vietnam, or Vietminh, forces by drawing up the armistice under which the two halves of the country now edgily coexist. In October of that year, in accordance with the terms of the armistice, the Vietminh moved into Hanoi, and since then the city, now the capital of the People's Democratic Republic of Vietnam, Southeast Asia's first Communist state, has been pretty much off-limits to Westerners, aside from a scattering of Frenchmen who, for one reason or another, have remained, and a scattering of diplomats, most of them connected with a three-nation commission—Canada, India, and Poland—that was appointed in Geneva to take on the ticklish and thankless job of seeing to it that the armistice terms are faithfully observed.

Having been acquainted with Hanoi, off and on, for fifteen years, I was curious to see what had happened to it under its new rulers, and not long ago, through the good offices of the armistice commission, I contrived to spend a week in the city, or what is left of it. I don't mean to suggest that Hanoi has been visibly scarred by its ideological transformation. On the contrary, I have never seen it looking tidier; it has fewer beggars, fewer prostitutes, fewer opium dens, and a generally hygienic air that anyone familiar with the sanitary conditions prevalent in urban Asia cannot help but find startling. For all the spit and polish, though, the place seemed depressingly lifeless. In the old days, Hanoi was a delightful mixture of homegrown raffishness and imported elegance. For the better

part of a century, the French had been molding the city to their intellectual and cultural tastes, and, by the end of their sojourn, it was far more European in looks and spirit than Saigon, the capital of South Vietnam. Strolling down one of Hanoi's broad, tree-lined *allées*, flanked by Western-style houses, one would encounter a steady flow of Europeans, and the downtown streets were buzzing with Renaults and jeeps. Five thousand French civilians lived in Hanoi, out of a population of about three hundred thousand, and the foreign colony also included a large complement of French servicemen. Many of the Vietnamese in Hanoi had been converted to Western dress and manners. The young native blades, in their tight-fitting European-style suits, were known as the "sharkskin brigade," and the town abounded with restaurants serving escargots, bouillabaisse, and crêpes Suzette. French bread was piled high in the *boulangeries*, and along the shore of a pretty little lake right in the heart of the city, where the French maintained a yacht club, one could browse at a line of bookstalls reminiscent of those on the banks of the Seine.

The character of the new Hanoi becomes evident as soon as one alights at its airport, a half hour's drive from the center of town. On arriving from Saigon, I found the terminal, which had invariably been bustling and deafening, utterly deserted, except for one small room, where an immigration man and three customs inspectors, one of them a woman, stonily awaited us new arrivals. Customs officials all over the world are inclined to be testy, of course, but those in Hanoi openly scowled at me and ostentatiously donned white gloves before condescending to touch my non-Communist luggage.

An old—and, under the circumstances, intrepid—Vietnamese friend came to meet me at the airport and drove me to Hanoi proper. On the way, we passed only one automobile; the streets were all but monopolized by rickshaws. What motorized traffic there is in Hanoi these days, I soon discovered, consists almost entirely of a few dazzling white cars belonging to the international commission and some limousines in which high government officials and members of the foreign diplomatic corps get about; now and then one sees a truck or two. A number of ordinary civilians in Hanoi still own cars, but they rarely drive any more, no doubt because a gallon of gasoline costs the equivalent of fifteen American dollars. Some time ago, the government of Hungary sent North Vietnam a welcome-to-the-family gift of seventeen shiny red buses, but during my stay these were confined to a garage, where people came to gawk at them. There isn't a sharkskin suit in sight, and the diminutive Vietminh soldiers of General Vo Nguyen Giap, many of them with Dienbienphu victory buttons in their lapels, have replaced the French troops. Outside the shops where animated French civilians once stood and argued about Dior and Sartre, phlegmatic Vietnam women now squat, dribbling betel-nut juice through their blackened teeth as they fuss over baskets of fruit, dried fish, and shredded tobacco.

There are only a hundred and fifty French people in Hanoi now. Some of them are newcomers, who belong to a diplomatic mission that is supposed to work toward an unspecified kind of rapport with the Vietminh, and some are old Indo-China hands, who have been permitted to stick to their jobs. Not one French businessman is left in the city. A group of French mechanics—they had helped run the municipal streetcar system, which is now operating somewhat creakily—pulled out just before my visit. (Unlike most of the old French residents, they were strongly urged to stay, but they refused to, and then they were strongly urged to sign farewell statements saying that they were leaving because of American imperialist coercion, but they refused to do that, either; the newspapers attributed their departure to Yankee pressure anyway.) The lakeside bookstalls are gone, and only one bookshop still offers French literature. I was told that this lone holdover is a sop to a lingering local yearning for *la culture française*, but its shelves, I noticed, contained far more Vietminh propaganda—much of it printed in China—than French literature. On the floor lay a copy of a book that had been prominently displayed in all the city's bookstores before the fall of Dienbienphu. Its title was "Faut-Il Abandonner l'Indochine?"

French bread is almost as rare in Hanoi today as Philadelphia scrapple. The only remaining French restaurant is a third-rate *bistro* on the Rue des Medicaments—a street agreeably redolent of Chinese drugs, which is what most of its shops have long been selling—and the cuisine has to compete for attention with the blaring of Vietminh propaganda over a loudspeaker and with a ceiling on which a flight of Picasso doves has just been painted. (In the old days, the city was full of reproductions of Dufys, Matisses, and non-ornithological Picassos.) The faculty of the University of Hanoi, which was for many years the wellspring of Gallic culture in Indo-China, has not a single Frenchman left in its ranks, unless one counts two so-called "advisers," who don't teach classes and apparently don't do much of anything else. The Lycée Albert Sarraut, whose student body used to be fairly evenly divided between French and Vietnamese children, has not yet sacked all its French instructors, but they teach only non-controversial subjects like algebra, while such tricky, potentially loaded subjects as history and geography are taught exclusively by Vietminh stalwarts. The only French students now enrolled in the Lycée are the two children of the cultural officer of the French diplomatic mission. As might be expected of a neophyte, North Vietnam is earnestly trying to follow in the massive footsteps of its big cousin and next-door neighbor, the People's Democratic Republic of China, and the newest academy of learning in Hanoi is the Revolutionary University, patterned after the Revolutionary University in Peiping. The purpose of both is the same—to train would-be Communist functionaries. The Hanoi version of this ultramodern institution already has two thousand students. Before the civil war, Vietnamese children were taught, with all abundance of graphic detail, that China was an aggressive, rapacious country; there is hardly a national hero in Vietnamese mythology who did not get there by warding off a Chinese invasion or otherwise outsmarting the Chinese. But the fact that for generations China has been Vietnam's traditional enemy does not seem to have prevented Communist Vietnam from sedulously and respectfully parroting Communist China.

The dean of the diplomatic corps in Hanoi today is the ambassador from Peiping. His preëminence is based on protocol, but he has taken pains to buttress it with flattery. Not long after the revolutionary North Vietnam government was set up in the jungle, this enterprising Chinese scrambled out there, beating all other foreign emissaries in presenting credentials to the Vietminh chief of state, Ho Chi Minh. Getting to see Ho at all was in itself something of a distinction, for, like Mao Tse-tung, he seems to prefer a secluded way of life; as a matter of fact, Ho has made only two public appearances since the Vietminh took over Hanoi, and nobody here had any idea where he lives or what he does with his time. There are other similarities between Ho and Mao—both are considered infallible, for instance, and both are venerated as nearly divine—but there are differences, too. For one thing, nobody would ever think of calling Mao "Uncle Mao," but Ho is "Uncle Ho" to everybody, and photographs of him benignly patting children on the head are to be seen all over town. (In view of his seclusiveness, it is a mystery where and when these pictures were taken.) In every shop and home in Hanoi, it seems, there hangs a framed portrait of Ho's gentle face, which I had found attractive before this visit, when, I suppose, I saw too much of it. One's recollections of an average day in Hanoi are apt to be filtered through a montage of Ho—Ho on books and magazines and pamphlets, Ho on postage stamps, Ho on calendars, Ho reviewing troops, Ho in Peiping, Ho in Moscow, Ho with Mao, Ho with Chou, Ho with Nehru, Ho with U Nu, Ho with Bulganin, Ho (much larger than life) outside the Hôtel de Ville, and, above all, Uncle Ho beaming at plump Vietminh youngsters.

Even during times of bubbling international spirits, when the merry clink of Communist and non-Communist goblets is broadcast around the world, there is little likelihood that an American in Hanoi would be tempted to exclaim, "I like old Uncle Ho!" If China is top dog in Hanoi, the United States is pariah dog. (The laborers building the Hanoi-Haiphong railroad are told by their foremen, "Think of every rock you crush as the head of an American imperialist.") After I had been in the city for a couple of days, my old Vietnamese friend told me with a smile—it was practically the only time he smiled—that officially everything that goes wrong in North Vietnam is the fault of the United States. Among Hanoi's loneliest residents at the moment are the five young American Foreign Service career men—their average age is under thirty—who man our consulate. No Vietnamese would dare be seen talking to them, and even some Western Europeans tend to be standoffish, lest they lose favor in influential Vietminh circles. (If there are any pro-Communist Americans tucked away in Hanoi, they are doubtless happy there. One of the community's most honored citizens is Wilfred Burchett, a peripatetic Englishman who in recent times, as a correspondent for the London *Daily Worker*, has appeared, from the left side of the stage, in Panmunjom, Geneva, and Bandung. With his wife—a handsome Bulgarian woman—and their two children, he is now settled in the Vietminh capital in bourgeois comfort, writing a book, presumably on the liberation of North Vietnam from the United States and its degenerate lackeys.) For their part, the Americans at the consulate rarely make overtures to other foreigners and Vietnamese, since they want to spare them the consequences of guilt by association. Last Fourth of July, though, the isolated quintet ventured to hold open house at their headquarters. Their hospitality was accepted by a few daring British, Canadians, French, and Indians. Halfway through the festivities, the consulate's lights went out, and there was no current for an hour. The youthful diplomats admit that this may have been pure coincidence.

Local cynics used to say that the French authorities, in dealing with the Foreign Legionnaires on duty in Indo-China, were governed by this rule-of-thumb: "Keep them so busy that they have no time for thinking." The Vietminh authorities, in dealing with their subjects, appear to be governed by a somewhat different rule-of-thumb: "Keep them so busy absorbing right thoughts that they have no time for thinking independently." The citizens of Hanoi spend a great deal of their time attending indoctrination courses and holding inspirational group discussions. One day, I stopped in at a bank to exchange some outmoded Indo-Chinese *piastres* for Vietminh *dong*, and I had to wait an hour and a half while the seven employees sat around a table engaged in an earnest conversation about the merits of the Chinese People's Republic. Such conferences, often guided by a student or an alumnus of the Revolutionary University, are held almost daily in places of business all over town, and their object, one Vietnamese told me, is "to discuss various things and arrive voluntarily at the same conclusions." Attendance at them is also voluntary, in the same sense of the word. (When the government needs work crews for roads, dikes, or the rail line to China, it sends out agents who knock on doors and order people to volunteer at once.) "If you don't attend these meetings voluntarily, they come and reason courteously with you, at any hour of the day or night," my informant went on. "They did that to me eight nights running—once from one to seven in the morning. So now I attend—voluntarily." People who show better than average dispatch in arriving voluntarily at the same conclusions are rewarded with diplomas signed by Uncle Ho.

Among the topics discussed at these seminars, land reform is one of the most popular—it ranks behind the wickedness of the United States, however—and tribute is invariably paid to the many landlords in North Vietnam who have voluntarily given up their land. During my stay in Hanoi, the newspapers carried a story about an unreasonable landlord who had declined to relinquish his land and had thereupon been sentenced to death. The intellectuals, including some who used to think they could get along with the Communists, have had almost as unhappy a time of it as the landlords. A newspaper editor I know, who was once so friendly toward the Vietminh that the French put him in jail for a year, now not only is disillusioned with North Vietnam but has become a Minister in the South Vietnamese government. Vituperation and repetition to the point of saturation are the two big weapons in the Vietminh arsenal of persuasion, and neither of these appeals greatly to the intelligent people of Hanoi. Nor do they care much for the mass demonstrations that the Vietminh is forever organizing among special groups of citizens—athletes, for example, or mothers, or youths—who parade through the streets, singing, dancing, and chanting slogans as they indulge in what one Vietminh journalist has described as "disciplined joy."

The new order of things was very much in evidence at the Hôtel Metropole, where I stayed. The titular manager is a Frenchman, but when I asked him for accommodations, he said, "Let me ask the Vietminh." I quickly learned that the hotel—which was cleaner than I had ever seen it before, and had better food and better service—was being run by a committee of three Army officers. (Their jobs, like other soft berths in the city, were parceled out shortly after the armistice among deserving veterans of the jungle war.) The hotel's employees—Vietnamese accustomed to Western ways—were kept on, and the military triumvirate set about winning their confidence by bringing in an Army doctor to look after their health. When the doctor was not sympathetically treating some elderly waiter's bunions, he would play a ukulele for the employees, and sing them Communist songs. In the past, the employees had been acutely conscious of a social barrier between themselves and the French management, to say nothing of the guests. Now they were encouraged to sit around for three or four hours a day in cozy little groups, discussing on equal terms with the management the glorious victory at Dienbienphu, or the need for a reëvaluation of their views on China, or how much tomato juice should be ordered for the kitchen. After a few such conferences, an employee who was caught stealing cigarettes from a guest's room explained blandly that he could not fairly be blamed for the offense; he was the victim of bad colonial influences.

The Metropole is the local headquarters of the Canadian and Indian representatives on the international commission that polices both halves of Vietnam. The Poles stay at the city's other big hotel, the Splendide. The commission's first task was to supervise the withdrawal of troops from their battle positions to their own portions of the divided country. (It is widely believed that the Vietminh deliberately left a good many soldiers, in mufti, down south, and there is said to be a Vietminh slogan that goes "To leave for the north is glory, but to stay behind is heroism.") The commission's chief tasks at present are to see to it that no one is made to suffer by either Vietnam government for his pre-armistice political opinions, that neither side builds up an excessive stockpile of arms or ammunition, and that any resident of either side who wants to move over to the other is allowed to do so unmolested.

Since the cease-fire, five thousand Vietnamese have moved north and eight hundred thousand, many of them Catholics, have moved south. Not surprisingly, the Vietminh authorities have come to resent the imbalance between the two exoduses, and lately they have been reluctant to tolerate the freedom of movement to which the Geneva agreements committed them. Recently, when the residents

of a Catholic village in North Vietnam announced that they wanted to emigrate en masse, the village was swiftly encircled by Vietminh troops and a soldier was assigned to stand guard in each house until its occupants changed their minds. Any resident of Vietnam theoretically may lodge a protest with the international commission against this kind of thing, but a farmer in the rice fields of the Tonkin Delta has as much hope of making contact with the commission as with 10 Downing Street. And if, by chance, he should get word to the commission, the Polish representatives are almost certain to alert the Vietminh, and by the time the commission reaches the scene to investigate the circumstances, the plaintiff, his family, and his friends are likely to have disappeared.

The Polish members of the commission agree heartily with their Vietminh hosts about the merits of disciplined joy, but when they arrived in Hanoi, even its fading cosmopolitanism was sufficiently alluring to excite them to some plainly undisciplined rapture. They swarmed through the stores, buying fishing rods, Bikinis, and all sorts of other remnants of the once lavish inventories of Hanoi's shopkeepers. The Poles' acquisitiveness seems to have been appeased by now, and it is just as well, for the stores no longer have anything to offer except simple staples like soap, pencils, matches, and blue cotton cloth from China. As I looked in through the window of one Vietnamese shop on my last day in the city, I saw its proprietor, with no customers to talk to or wares to display, passing the time by tenderly washing the clay face of a blond-haired, unclothed, and, by Hanoi's new standards, terribly archaic mannequin—Peggy Durdin

*Credit*: Originally published in *The New Yorker*.

## MARC RIBOUD: ACCOUNT OF HANOI AFTER DEATH OF HO CHI MINH

*French journalist and photographer Marc Riboud was allowed to travel to Hanoi just after the death of its leader, Ho Chi Minh. Riboud found in Hanoi a strong identification of the city with the man and an unbroken resolve among the North Vietnamese to continue the fight against the Americans. Despite the suffering they experienced during the colonial years, the Vietnamese people had a curiously conciliatory attitude toward the French following the Indochina War, as a hundred years of French culture and language had left their imprint. Though hardly an ally of the North Vietnamese, the French government nevertheless tried without success to convince the United States to abandon its intervention in Vietnam and to allow the Vietnamese people to settle their own affairs. The Americans' belief in their own exceptionalism, that they could succeed where the French had failed, had tragic consequences in Southeast Asia.*

*Newsweek*, 20 October 1969

Any discussion of American options in Vietnam must inevitably come to grips with the question of North Vietnam's intentions. Yet six weeks after the death of Ho Chi Minh, the outside world remains in considerable doubt about whether the new collective leadership in Hanoi is willing—or, indeed, even able—to negotiate a peace settlement with Washington. Among the handful of Western journalists allowed to visit North Vietnam in the aftermath of Ho's death was the French photographer Marc Riboud. This was Riboud's second trip to Hanoi in twelve months; his first stay of six weeks during the autumn of 1968 coincided with President Johnson's announcement of the complete halt of U.S. bombing raids in the north. In his recent visit of more than two weeks, Riboud traveled more than 1,000 miles inside North Vietnam. In New York last week, a few days after he left Hanoi, Riboud was interviewed by *Newsweek*. Here is his report.

"The war is still the overriding fact of life in North Vietnam today," says Riboud. "Although Hanoi has not been bombed in nineteen months and the U.S. air war was halted almost a year ago, there are no signs of any official willingness to acknowledge the change. On the contrary, everywhere I traveled I saw again the same posters urging the people to remain war-conscious and warning against any relaxation while the 'enemy' still threatens. In Hanoi, the same bomb shelters still clutter almost every street. Outside the city the same anti-aircraft guns are pointed at the skies, manned by the same sort of alert-looking soldiers that I saw last year."

For Riboud, there was often a feeling of *déjà vu*. And this absence of change was the most vivid—and most important—impression of his trip. Rationing of rice and other essentials continues. The army and militia still undergo constant rigorous training—even more openly now than before. The factories, government offices, schools and universities he saw systematically dispersed in the countryside a year ago remain there today. Almost no effort has been made to reconstruct damaged or destroyed stone buildings—"The ruins are no different than they were just after the bombing halt last November," he says. In some cases—notably in Vinh, where Riboud was told that 80,000 people once lived, 140 miles north of the 17th parallel—entire cities have been left leveled and untouched.

Except for children under 12, who have now been allowed to return to their homes, all students—and their teachers—remain scattered in improvised classrooms hidden in the mountains and rice fields. In fact, Riboud notes, party leaders have let it be known that even when full peace is achieved, the now-dispersed universities will remain largely where they are today. "We have discovered many advantages in leaving the students in the countryside," one official told him with a smile.

Peace, in short, seemed as distant as ever to Riboud. "My impression," he says, weighing his words, "is that the country's leaders will not allow the slightest relaxation in the population at large—not now or in the immediate future. It is almost as if, consciously or unconsciously, they were anxious to forestall the coming of that great unknown—peace. Not that they want the war to continue indefinitely; indeed, they speak longingly of the day when they will be able to begin the work of national reconstruction. But government and party leaders seem to worry about the possible consequences of a rapid transition from war to peace—and with some justice. For a whole generation of North Vietnamese, the word 'peace' is a hollow abstraction signifying absolutely nothing. Peace for them is another world where other people live an entirely different life. They don't know how to behave in that world."

In Hanoi, Riboud talked with some top government leaders as well as with Nguyen Huu Tho, who represented the National Liberation Front of South Vietnam at Ho Chi Minh's funeral. . . . All of them, he observed, continually stressed the need for "patience," for "moving slowly" and in carefully prepared "successive stages" toward peace. "During my entire stay," he remarks, "I saw no official directive or even a hint of any desire for rapid change on the part of the Hanoi government. Its leaders know that the period of transition from war to peace, particularly if it is rapid, will pose great problems for them and for their country. And since this is a Communist government, nothing is left to chance."

But Riboud, like other recent visitors to Hanoi, did notice some significant changes in North Vietnam's urban landscape. "For one thing," be observes, "there are simply more people in the streets of Hanoi and other large cities: more pedestrians, many of them with Chinese- or Japanese-made transistor radios in hand, more bicyclists, above all more soldiers. There are many more soldiers in Hanoi on leave; some of them simply tie their portable hammocks to trees in the park and spend the night." Damaged or destroyed main roads and bridges into Hanoi, including the famous Paul Doumer bridge over the Red River, have been—or are being—repaired by the government, although many smaller side roads remain pocked with bomb craters.

Equally important, Riboud thinks, is the changed mood of the North Vietnamese people since his last visit. "They are definitely more relaxed, more at ease—much of the tension of the bombing period is gone," he says. "I was astonished, for example, at the decidedly gay atmosphere in Hanoi's Reunification Park on a Sunday afternoon. Young couples rowed leisurely around the lake or sat for hours over glasses of beer and lemonade, chatting and smiling at one another. I honestly did not have the impression they were discussing socialism or the 'American aggressors.' And in the countryside, interestingly enough, I saw quite a few patriotic posters crudely 'improved' with erotic graffiti and sketches—pictures of heroic soldiers and women on which genital symbols had been scratched with stones."

Nevertheless, continuity and stability are what the country's leaders are seeking in the first months of the post–Ho Chi Minh era in North Vietnam. And in large measure, Riboud believes, they are succeeding—because they are skillfully using Ho's death and his last testament as an effective means of unifying the population under its new collective leadership. Curiously, for a Communist state, this involves return to age-old religious and family traditions.

"I was struck," Riboud says, "by the apparent religiosity surrounding Ho's death, his funeral and the extended mourning period—as long as nine weeks in the pagodas. It seemed to me that the authorities were encouraging this return to traditional practices, and there was no sign of that a year ago. In homes, factories, public buildings, farms, Christian churches and pagodas, there still stand today shrines containing a photo of Ho with the official funeral slogan ('Our sorrow is infinite and for the rest of our lives we will remember the glorious President Ho Chi Minh') and the traditional elements of Confucian ancestral mourning—an offering of fruit, flowers, candles, burning incense and handwritten personal messages from the mourners."

Riboud's feeling was that there was no personality cult, or deification, of Ho Chi Minh implied in the official encouragement of traditional mourning rites for him. Riboud recalls the explanation of a Communist Party intellectual who told him: "The mourning for Ho is not so much religious, in the Western sense of the word, as it is traditional Vietnamese. Our tradition is the cult of the ancestor as taught by Confucianism—to which the Vietnamese people are greatly attached. Confucianism and Marxism are not that far apart—that's why Marxism is easily implanted in Vietnam." And Riboud points out that, significantly, many of the government's leaders now sprinkle their conversation with such religious-sounding phrases as "pious duty," "true faith" and, perhaps most important, "holy war."

Whether by means of a return to "religion" or to "tradition," Riboud thinks, Hanoi's leaders are seeking to establish a spirit of sacrifice and battle around the paternal image and final testament of Ho. "The newspapers and radio continually exhort the people to transform their personal sorrow over the death of Ho—everybody's uncle or second father—into a spirit of revolutionary battle (for them, a battle against 'U.S. imperialism') and into a spirit of economic production. At four or five public meetings I attended in factories and public buildings, when Ho's testament was read aloud the men present visibly restrained their tears while many women broke down and wept aloud."

Apparently quite by accident, Riboud was brought face-to-face with yet another larger-than-life image-in-the-making of Ho Chi Minh. Knowing that Riboud's wife is a sculptor, the government invited him to visit the studio of Minh Chau, Hanoi's most important official artist. There the artist—a South Vietnamese by birth who spent much of his adult life

as a guerrilla—proudly displayed his latest work: an enormous bust of Ho, done in conventional socialist-realism style, destined for a prominent spot in Hanoi upon completion. "I began this bust," Minh Chau proudly informed Riboud, "seventeen minutes after the death of Ho Chi Minh."

It was through the medium of Ho's testament, too, Riboud points out, that the North Vietnamese people were first publicly instructed how to deal with one of the most important factors in their future—the Sino-Soviet quarrel. But Ho's exhortation to his party comrades to do their best to "reestablish unity between the fraternal [Communist] parties" clearly came as no shock to North Vietnam, where the fierce competition for influence between Russia and China has made the country a microcosm of the larger struggle between the two giants. As Ho indicated, Hanoi fervently hopes the Sino-Soviet dispute will be resolved, or at least not worsened. Meanwhile, Riboud believes, the new leadership's strategy remains the same as Ho's—walking a narrow and dangerous tightrope of strict neutrality.

"Every country makes its own revolution in its own way," officials insisted to Riboud. But there is no doubt in his mind that Hanoi's leaders are worried about the Sino-Soviet conflict. Their future course—particularly of the war and the peace talks—will, after all, be partly determined by its outcome.

For this reason as well, Riboud feels that Hanoi's overall strategy in the coming months will probably be cautious and conservative. He is also pessimistic about North Vietnam's willingness—or rather ability—to carry on negotiations involving major concessions at the present time. "The nature of the current collective leadership," Riboud contends, "makes it unlikely that Hanoi will be able to respond to offers that involve real compromises in the near future."

"I do not believe," he concludes, "that any one man in the leadership today has inherited enough of Ho's authority to risk pressing for a course of action that deviates from the present strategy—the strategy laid down under Ho himself. That, at any rate, seems to be the view of many diplomats, from both Communist and non-Communist countries, resident in Hanoi today. Everyone there is settling in for a long haul."

## A TALK WITH THE NLF LEADER

On his last day in Hanoi, Marc Riboud was accorded a formal interview with Nguyen Huu Tho, the nominal head of South Vietnam's National Liberation Front. It is the first such talk that Tho has had with a Western journalist in several years. He received Riboud at the NLF's permanent office, in the North Vietnamese capital, where the Front's flag flies alongside and—pointedly—at the same height as North Vietnam's flag. Highlights of Tho's remarks:

On the U.S.: "Why can't we come to an agreement on the basis of the [NLF's] ten points? We won't budge from that. We have said this many times: we will fight until all the American soldiers have left South Vietnam. The whole world knows it. But we do not want the Americans to lose their honor in leaving. There is no reason for that, and we are not trying to do it. We believe the Americans can leave and still preserve their honor."

On the NLF: "You know why we will win the war in the South? One major reason is because, under our system, every unit, every regiment, every region has a large measure of military autonomy. Each unit develops its own plans, its own local initiative. But the 'puppet troops' [Tho's term for the South Vietnamese Army] only move and act when they are told to do so from a higher authority. They can only follow orders. As a result, none of them really knows what he is doing, and what he is fighting for."

On Saigon: "The 'puppet government' has allowed the country to be taken over by foreigners. In some Saigon schools English is now even the language of instruction. They are trying to cut us off from our own traditions, from our own national roots. I must admit, however, that the Front's Communist ideology scares many intellectuals and students in Saigon."

On B-52 raids in the South: "For some time now, we have been unable to receive visitors in the 'liberated regions' [areas under NLF control] because we cannot guarantee their security. The U.S. possesses colossal power and these B-52 raids are terrible! But of course we have means of surviving and living even against such bombardment."

On reunifying Vietnam: "We are in no hurry for reunification. It will take a long time, and we are very patient. But we would like to begin, in the first place, by establishing economic and cultural relations with the North on an equal basis. There should be no pressure from one side on the other."

## FURTHER READINGS

Burchett, Wilfred. *My Visit to the Liberated Zones of South Vietnam*. Hanoi: Foreign Languages Publishing House, 1964.

Cameron, James. *Here Is Your Enemy*. New York: Holt, Rinehart & Winston, 1966.

Fall, Bernard. *Hell in a Very Small Place: The Siege of Dien Bien Phu*. Philadelphia: J. B. Lippincott, 1967.

McCarthy, Mary. *Hanoi*. New York: Harcourt Brace, 1968.

Sontag, Susan. *Trip to Hanoi: Journey to a City at War*. London: Panther Books, 1968.

# 3

# U.S. COMMITMENT IN VIETNAM

The cold war between Western democracies and the Communist bloc was John F. Kennedy's top concern when he took office as the thirty-fifth U.S. president in January 1961. In his inaugural address, he pledged that the United States would "pay any price, bear any burden, meet any hardship, support any friend, oppose any foe to assure the survival and success of liberty." His foreign policy focus was containment of Communism in Europe and Latin America; initially, Southeast Asia was a minor part of the strategic picture. However, a commitment to the Vietnamese civil war became one of the Kennedy administration's chief legacies.

Kennedy's inaugural address reflected American "can-do-ism" that inspired its civilian and military leaders to action—the belief that the United States could succeed where others, such as the French in Indochina, had failed. Kennedy said that Americans have an obligation to export their brand of democracy to other parts of the world. The United States called it nation building, but to the Vietnamese it seemed very much like a rehash of the old French *mission civilisatrice*—a mandate to bring Western civilization to unappreciative Asians. Leadership charged with self-confidence and optimism born of a sense of mission tends to regard subordinates' negative assessments as defeatism. Such was the mood that prevailed at the U.S. Embassy and Military Assistance Command in Saigon.

Colonel Edward Lansdale returned from his extended mission as military advisor in Vietnam during the 1950s and urged increasing aid to South Vietnamese premier Ngo Dinh Diem. Most of Kennedy's advisors agreed. Some, such as Secretary of Defense Robert S. McNamara, proposed sending a large contingent of U.S. combat troops to show resolve to the Communists. Kennedy wanted to win in Vietnam, but feared being mired in a ground war in Asia, so he chose a moderate approach toward Vietnam, as recommended by his favorite military advisor, General Maxwell Taylor, a World War II hero who was destined to serve under Lyndon Johnson as the U.S. ambassador to Vietnam. A measured response would show the enemy that the United States would not permit a Communist takeover. Taylor tended to interpret the Vietnamese conflict in strictly military terms, ignoring the fact that Diem was losing the political war with the Vietcong, and that the Communists would match every U.S. escalation.

At first, Diem did not want more Americans in the war because they undercut his image as a Vietnamese nationalist. Vietcong attacks on South Vietnamese outposts in Phuoc Thanh and Darlac Provinces, timed to coincide with Taylor's visit, changed Diem's mind. Eventually the cadre of U.S. military advisors in Vietnam was increased from fewer than 700 to more than 16,000 some of whom took on covert combat assignments. Helicopters were sent in to make the South Vietnamese army more mobile. U.S. pilots began flying secret combat missions. The U.S. military buildup was kept secret because it violated the Geneva accords of 1955.

The gradually deepening U.S. commitment could not be reversed. Each increase of aid for Saigon inevitably brought demands for more aid. Each deployment of U.S. resources made it harder to back out without losing international prestige in the fight against global Communism.

## DON SCHANCHE: REPORT ON INEFFECTIVENESS OF DIEM REGIME AGAINST VIETCONG

*The* Saturday Evening Post *published some of the best magazine coverage of the early phase of the Vietnam War, at a time when most Americans were not aware of their government's involvement in the obscure jungle war. This extensive picture story profiled the Diem regime's ineffective military and political tactics against the Vietcong guerrillas. A sense of desperation pervaded the report. Schanche predicted both the coup d'état against Diem two years later and U.S. intervention in 1965.*

*Saturday Evening Post*, 6 January 1962

SAIGON—Internal flare-ups may topple this strategically located country [South Vietnam], already dangerously open to Communist attack.

The pitifully exposed red-clay fortress of Khon Brai squats bare and ugly like a fresh wound against the lush green mountains which rise to form the high plateau in this central area of South Vietnam. It is a remote outpost in almost inaccessible territory, twenty miles by a mud road from the local center of military force and civilization, the provincial capital of Kontum. But it is worth examining in detail, for around Khon Brai, away from the conflicting voices and the press agentry of Saigon, one can study many of the ills of Vietnam and gain understanding of events in this unfortunate Southeast Asian country.

Khon Brai is typical of the hundreds of similar forts which guard remote areas in this harassed little country. It has the shape of a triangle, formed by 100-yard walls of log-reinforced mud which bristle with needle-sharp bamboo spears. Surrounding the fortress is a flat ring of dirt enclosed in barbed wire and liberally sewn [sic] with "Bouncing Betty" mines.

On the day I made my first visit to the fortress, soldiers were putting finishing touches on the "New" Khon Brai. A few weeks earlier the Viet Cong (Communist) guerrillas had swept over the barbed wire, through the minefield, past the needle-sharp spears and over the walls to wipe the place clean.

They came that day at four A.M. The first warning of attack was a loud KARUMPH! in the center of the Khon Brai compound. It was a mortar shell, and it landed squarely on Khon Brai's only chance of salvation, its radio. Then up from the foot of the hill came more than 500 screaming Viet Cong, surging like a human sea against hastily organized machine-gun and rifle fire from the fortress. Some of the guerrillas carried American M-1 rifles and Thompson submachine guns captured in earlier raids against Vietnamese units; some carried ancient French and British rifles, and others had no weapons at all.

All of Khon Brai's twenty-five soldiers fought well, but two were particularly brave. The lieutenant in command stood on a watchtower as the Viet Cong surged into his compound. Picking up the fortress's last hand grenade, he lobbed it into a cluster of guerrilla soldiers. Then he died in a burst of machine-gun fire. A Vietnamese sergeant, gravely wounded in the attack, picked up one of the post's .50-caliber machine guns and painfully dragged it down the slope of the fortress hill to the bank of the Dakbla River. There he shoved the precious weapon into the mud where the guerrillas would not find it. Then he rolled over and died. Eight other Vietnamese were killed in the action. Fifteen of the fortress's defenders fought their way out and straggled into Kontum. The Communists, meanwhile, seized the fort's food and ammunition, blew a small section out of the Dakbla River bridge which Khon Brai is supposed to protect, picked up their dead and wounded and vanished into the jungle.

When I visited the fortress, it had been rebuilt. The new lieutenant in command proudly showed me how he had strengthened its defenses. There were more mines, more watchtowers, thicker walls. Now, instead of twenty-five soldiers waiting at Khon Brai to be attacked by the Communists, there were fifty. By the time you read this it is quite possible that they, too, will have been wiped out.

At Khon Brai one can see in clear relief the pitiful military legacy which Vietnam's senior officers inherited from the French and to which they still cling: the unimaginative urge to tie down brave combat soldiers in valueless static positions where they can be battered again and again on the enemy's terms.

One also can see at Khon Brai the pattern of Communist conquest in Vietnam. About five miles to the east of the fortress, across spectacular mountain country, lies the famed Ho Chi Minh Trail, down which pour some of the most dedicated fighting men in the Communist world. The trail is not a roadway nor even a path, but a series of valleys, elephant trails and passable forests beginning in Communist North Vietnam, running down through Laos along its border with South Vietnam, and cutting in to the besieged republic along the northern border of Kontum Province. From there the Communists trickle down through Vietnam like rain through a leaky roof.

It was to protect a large body of these infiltrating Communist troops that the Viet Cong guerrillas hit Khon Brai. Their diversionary assault apparently was designed to prevent Vietnamese army patrols from intercepting the men on the trail. They could have saved themselves the trouble; patrols from Khon Brai, seldom venturing more than two miles from their post, would not have intercepted the Communist infiltrators in any case.

The infiltrators are mostly South Vietnamese who went north with the Communist Vietminh armies when the Geneva Accord of 1954 formally separated North Vietnam from South Vietnam, dividing the country into two parts, each about the size of the state of Georgia and each with a population of about 13,000,000. Their mission is to return to the provinces from whence they came, recruit men for the Viet Cong, terrorize the peasantry, harass Vietnamese Army units and wait for the big push. It may not be long in coming.

Already elements of four Communist regiments have been identified in the four-province tactical zone of which Khon Brai is a part. Remaining elements of at least two Communist divisions have been spotted, by aerial reconnaissance and intelligence agents, waiting in camouflaged, jungle-covered bases in Laos. Obviously they are not gathering in such force to continue a long war of harassment. They appear ready to take a big bite. Unless the South Vietnamese army can keep this Communist force off balance during the coming months, it seems likely that the Reds will push into the area around Kontum and stage a "little Dienbienphu," hoping to topple the uncertain government of Ngo Dinh Diem in South Vietnam.

South Vietnam must buy time in which to recast its military force with new booster shots of U.S. aid, and to recast its generally unpopular authoritarian government as well. With what currency can Vietnam buy the two years most observers agree it will take to beef up the government and armed forces so that they can maintain security in the guerrilla-infested countryside? Seeking the answer, let's go back to the area of Khon Brai, where the currency is woefully short.

The little hilltop fortress with its fifty defenders is a part of the 22nd Division of the Army of the Republic of Vietnam. Its commander is a boyish thirty-four-year-old lieutenant colonel named Nguyen Bao Tri. Colonel Tri is a graduate of the U.S. Army Command and General Staff College at Fort Leavenworth. He is intelligent and has many of the qualities of a good division commander. More important in Vietnam, he is considered politically reliable by the Diem government which, having weathered one army coup d'état in 1960, is extremely touchy about the political attitudes of its troop commanders.

The young lieutenant colonel's responsibilities are staggering. With his understrength division of about 8000 men, Tri must cover four huge provinces, all heavily infested with Viet Cong guerrillas. His area encompasses 17,000 square miles, including 150 miles of seacoast and 125 miles of unmanageable border with Cambodia and Laos. Virtually all of the territory is mountainous and overgrown with dense jungle.

"It's like assigning two cops to direct all of the Yankee Stadium traffic during a World Series," says one of the nine American Military Assistance Advisory Group officers assigned to Tri's division.

Arrayed against Colonel Tri's 22nd Division are an estimated 7000 Viet Cong, 2000 of whom are hardened, dedicated soldiers sent down the Ho Chi Minh Trail from the north. Operating in small, scattered groups, they live on food given by sympathetic mountain tribesmen or plundered from antagonistic villagers. They have intelligence sources in every village, either covert agents or misguidedly sympathetic peasants, and they even penetrate the South Vietnamese army itself. The Communist troops rely quite heavily for weapons and ammunition on whatever they can capture in raids against the army, the Civil Guard (roughly the equivalent of the U.S. National Guard), and the village Self-Defense Corps, a weak grouping of untrained part-time village guards.

The local Viet Cong leader is a shadowy figure who calls himself "Truong Son" after a mountain range in central Vietnam. When he orders a major attack, the scattered bands gather to form a single strong force. This massing for attack takes days. It is then that the Viet Cong are the most vulnerable.

Colonel Tri realizes that he can never really defeat the Viet Cong in his zone. The best he can hope to do is keep them off balance by chopping at the concentrations of enemy troops which might signal the prelude to a "little Dienbienphu." If he can accomplish this, Tri and other division commanders like him in Vietnam might buy enough time to allow the present infusion of American men and equipment to bring the ill-trained, ill-led Vietnamese army up to snuff. But under the present circumstances it is doubtful that Tri can even achieve a stalemate with the enemy in his area. More than half of his thinned-out division is tied down in static outposts such as Khon Brai. Tri is lucky when he has a battalion free for mobile operations against the Viet Cong.

It is difficult to see how Vietnam can buy the time it must have. Although the United States is bolstering this overdrawn military bank account with a massive dose of modern equipment and noncombatant manpower, many of the 1600 U.S. military men here fear that this shot in the arm has come too late. In the end, Colonel Tri's division may be better equipped; it may get more and better tactical advice from the additional American advisers assigned to its units; it may find that American helicopters give it the mobility to double its kill rate against the Viet Cong; but the division will still be no more than 8000 men covering a hopelessly vast 17,000-square-mile battlefield. Even with more American help, under present Vietnamese army leadership, half of Tri's men will remain tied down in outposts like Khon Brai.

In short, the Communists are calling the tune. If they want to bring the issue to a head in Colonel Tri's area, they have sufficient strength already in the zone or within a few days' march across the Laotian borders to do it. When they are ready to move, other Viet Cong units will strike elsewhere in Vietnam to tie down the remainder of the army. In such a case, Vietnam's only salvation will be the quick dispatch of American combat troops, bolstered perhaps by at least token units from other Southeast Asia Treaty Organization powers. From there one can picture another Korea, or the start of World War III.

In Saigon some hope derives from the fact that the North Vietnamese Communists receive their direction from Moscow rather than Peking. The Chinese are more belligerent and less sensitive to American intentions to draw the line. North Vietnam's Communist leader Ho Chi Minh, who harbors an understandable fear of becoming a Chinese puppet, recently wrote an article for a Russian publication to exult in the progress of world Communism; he didn't even mention his neighbor China. Khrushchev has his Albania; Mao Tse-tung, his North Vietnam.

This guerrilla war, which has gradually increased in tempo for seven years, could go on indefinitely. It began in 1954, almost as soon as Vietnam was partitioned at Geneva. The regular Communist Vietminh forces, compelled by the Geneva agreement to withdraw northward, left behind organizers who formed village and hamlet cells which could be expanded into guerrilla units.

During this period of relative quiet, South Vietnam's new Premier Ngo Dinh Diem had his hands full consolidating his own strength in a country which had been brought to its knees in nine years of war. Two powerful religious sects, the Cao Dai and Hoa Hao, maintained their own private armies and wanted to continue riding high as they had under the French. There was a well-organized gang of ex–river pirates called the Binh Xuyen, which had paid Emperor Bao Dai $1,000,000 for the privilege of controlling the city's vice and actually running the Saigon police force. The Binh Xuyen served notice it would fight before surrendering its prerogatives. After a perilous struggle to gain control of his own army, Diem moved with strong U.S. support to eliminate all three insurgent armies. At the same time he resettled almost a million refugees who had fled south after the partition. Then he maneuvered for popular support, which in October of 1955 ousted Bao Dai and established Diem as first president of the Republic of Vietnam.

With heavy doses of U.S. aid, which to date totals about $2,000,000,000, Diem equipped his 150,000-man army, accomplished a creditable program of land reform, introduced new crops, established Vietnam's first national educational system and developed light industry. It was a remarkable achievement. For nine years before independence, Vietnam had been embroiled in a war between the French and Communist-backed Nationalists. For eighty-two years before that the country had been under French domination. Few Vietnamese had been trained to take over when the French overlords left. Yet in a few years Diem built a modern country which showed signs of becoming a prosperous independent nation.

But Diem failed abysmally to generate popular enthusiasm for what looked like a rosy future in Free Vietnam. For this he has himself to blame. The bachelor president ruthlessly suppressed well-meaning critics who objected to his autocratic ways. In time he became suspicious of even his mildest opponents and withdrew to his trusted family circle— a few close confidants, including his brothers Ngo Dinh Nhu and Ngo Dinh Can—for counsel in running the government. Diem's opponents, who include most of the intellectuals of Saigon, found themselves with no voice in government. Lacking a free press and deprived of reliable information on steps being taken inside the fence surrounding Diem's huge "Independence Palace," the intellectual community of Saigon began feeding itself on rumors, many of which were planted by the Communists. (One heard, and still does, patently ridiculous stories of sex orgies and massive schemes for milking the country from the palace.)

In the countryside many of Diem's officials came to view their government jobs as open licenses for larceny. They often extorted money from the peasants, demanded protection money from merchants and manipulated the prices farmers got for their crops. Thus the Viet Cong guerrillas could gain popular approval by occasionally murdering a corrupt official. Soon they had thousands of peasants eager to supply them with rice and information.

Under Diem's totally centralized administration it was virtually impossible for any department or bureau of the government to act without the president's personal approval. The same was true of the army. Not even a battalion could move without first consulting the president.

Repeatedly Diem was urged by U.S. advisers to decentralize the government, surrender personal control of the army and make some democratic gestures that would regain the public support he had wasted. Until recently Diem stubbornly refused to change. But when it became clear in 1961 that his poorly organized, ill-trained, ill-led army was incapable of suppressing the Viet Cong, Diem ostensibly agreed to make some changes. He partially decentralized his one-man grip on the government by creating four super-secretaries to supervise the government departments. The army was reorganized to put command in the hands of generals instead of the president. Unfortunately, the reforms were mostly on paper.

In fairness to Diem, it can be said that he has done an extraordinary job of building a nation out of chaos, even though he has lost in the process the support necessary to keep it going. Nor are all of Vietnam's problems his fault. Some of the blame rests with the United States. In 1955 and again in 1957 the United States rejected pleas by Diem to support increases in the size of the Vietnamese army. At a time when Diem saw a definite need for a militarily trained Civil Guard to use against the guerrillas—if only to man static outposts and thus release combat soldiers to fight—we insisted that the Guard be trained as a rural police force. As late as last spring and summer, Washington promised a huge increase in military assistance, then dillydallied for six months and sent Gen. Maxwell Taylor out for another look before producing. In the meantime the Communists made spectacular gains.

With an interpreter I traveled to some of the most remote areas of Vietnam: south to Camau Point, where salt-water swamps make living perilous even without the guerrilla threat, although livestock thrives and sea life in the Gulf of Siam is the richest in the world; to Communist-infested An Giang Province in the west, where the Mekong River and its tributaries have created some of the richest riceland in Asia, only to pour out a flood which recently wiped out the fall crops and left thousands of people homeless; to the east coast around the beautiful resort city of Nhatrang, where the rolling foothills of the high plateau descend gently to the sea, offering hundreds of thousands of acres of untilled land, livestock pastureland and virgin forests; and to the rugged mountainous plateau itself, where some 60,000 primitive,

semi-nomadic tribesmen called the *Montagnard* carry crossbows and point-tipped arrows across uninhabited land which geologists suspect may be loaded with coal, iron and other mineral resources.

I talked for two hours to President Diem about the problems of his country. I also spoke to hundreds of other Vietnamese: plain soldiers, junior officers and senior commanders; province chiefs and peasants; rumor-fed intellectuals and mountain tribesmen. With the exception of the president and his government supporters, all were depressed and demoralized.

Confronted with this defeatism, Diem is fighting a slow uphill battle. But it is important to realize that despite his faults and his stubborn refusal to ease his suppression of well-meaning opposition, Diem is fighting.

To answer the soldiers' grumbling, he has pushed through a program of war relief for widows and for wounded men invalided out of the army. Previously a wounded man who was discharged was likely to wind up begging on the streets in order to stay alive. A vigorous effort to deliver their ten-dollar-a-month pay on time has begun to quiet soldiers' beefing.

To give the people in the countryside more security, Diem is regrouping many of the hamlets into larger villages where the Viet Cong will not be able to move freely about, demanding food and taxes to support the Communist cause. It is likely that when the villagers realize they are gaining in security what they lose in independence, they will be more agreeable to the change.

In Kontum Province, for example, even the primitive Montagnard are beginning to tire of the constant demands for rice and young men which the Communists make. During a single week in one mountain village, fifty-two youngsters were kidnapped, some to be used as Viet Cong soldiers, the rest as supply bearers. More than 3000 mountain tribesmen have come out of the hills around Kontum to resettle in more secure villages. Another 30,000 in the same area will be moved by February, thus drastically reducing the guerrillas' sources of manpower and food.

With American help, the retraining of the Vietnamese army is progressing. Some eighty companies of jungle-trained Rangers have been trained, and more are getting ready. Unfortunately they have not been used well to date. Too often they are assigned to regular Army units for routine duties.

The 68,000-man Civil Guard, which previously got its meager training and supplies from the dregs of the Vietnamese army, is now being trained by better men with American advisers at their elbows.

The village Self-Defense Corps, an outfit which consists of little more than farmers with guns who stand guard over outlying hamlets, also is being trained and outfitted with American equipment.

All of these changes would help in time, but there remains the question of whether South Vietnam can buy enough time to accomplish them. For in this time equation, the paramount factor is in the hands of the Communists. Through the Communist Pathet Lao they control eastern Laos and can continue sending fresh troops down the Ho Chi Minh Trail either to continue the guerrilla war or to mass for a decisive assault.

In November of 1960, hot-blooded but staunchly anti-Communist young officers led three battalions of paratroopers into Saigon and surrounded the president's palace. Instead of taking over, they tried to force Diem, by telephone, to reform the government and give the people more freedom. While they negotiated, Diem gathered strength from loyal army units and overwhelmed the insurgents.

At this writing, rumors are circulating of another *coup d'état*—not by the Communists but by Vietnamese who are fed up with poor military leadership and with waiting for the president to soften. If it happens, it is doubtful that the new band of insurgents would waste time negotiating. But it is equally doubtful whether any insurgent band could take over without first quelling resistance from loyal army units and government workers. The Communists, alerted by last year's coup, unquestionably are ready to take advantage of another. During a period of civil strife they would move in.

Together, Diem and the United States have it in their power to forestall both the possibility of a successful Communist military campaign and the possibility of a *coup d'état*. Initially, two moves would go a long way toward bolstering Vietnam against these threats:

First President Diem should acknowledge that much of the grumbling and dissension in Vietnam is of his own making. A single dramatic gesture, such as the recognition of a loyal opposition with the rights of free speech and a free press, would enhance his damaged popularity and take some of the sting from such disagreeable but necessary programs as resettlement.

Second, Diem must recognize that the quality and experience of his army leaders is simply not high enough even to fight for time against the Communist guerrillas. Some observers have suggested to him that he should establish a joint military staff in which skilled American officers actually direct Vietnamese military operations. Given this transfusion of professional skill in the Army leadership, units such as Colonel Tri's 22nd Division could be used more effectively to keep the Communists off balance. Moreover, it is doubtful that a *coup d'état* would materialize in a better-led army under a president who showed a capacity for democratic reform.

When I talked to Diem, he refused even to consider the first step, but he showed some inclination to give Americans a more powerful role in the operation of his military forces. This move alone is not much, but there is a slim chance that it will gain Vietnam enough time to win without calling on American combat soldiers to fight on such hellish battlefields as the jungle-covered mountains around Khon Brai.

---

## HOMER BIGART: ANALYSIS OF U.S. INVOLVEMENT IN VIETNAM—A "VERY REAL WAR" AND A DEEP U.S. COMMITMENT

*Known by his colleagues as the "Reporters' Reporter," Homer Bigart was the senior U.S. correspondent in Vietnam during the early days of U.S. intervention in the Vietnam War. He won two Pulitzer Prizes for reporting on World War II and the Korean War for the* New York Herald Tribune *before a six-month tour in Vietnam for the* New York Times. *David Halberstam, Bigart's* Times *replacement in Saigon, credited the elder Bigart for inspiring his own Pulitzer Prize–winning reportage. The following dispatch by Bigart shows why he was revered by the young, green Saigon press corps. His prescient analysis of the United States "inextricably committed to a long, inconclusive war" was borne out by more than thirteen years of devastating conflict in Southeast Asia.*

### New York Times, 25 February 1962

SAIGON, Feb. 24—The United States is involved in a war in Vietnam. American troops will stay until victory.

That is what Attorney General Robert Kennedy said here last week. He called it "war in a very real sense of the word." He said that President Kennedy had pledged that the United States would stand by South Vietnam's President Ngo Dinh Diem "until we win."

At the moment the war isn't going badly for "our" side. There is a lull in Vietcong activities, and the South Vietnamese forces are both expanding and shaping up better as a fighting force. But all that is needed to precipitate a major war is for the Chinese Communists and Communist North Vietnam to react to a build-up of American forces.

American support to Vietnam has always been based on

the fear that Communist control of this country would jeopardize all Southeast Asia. And it continues despite the fact that Diem's American critics—especially liberals repelled by the dictatorial aspects of his regime—have been predicting his imminent downfall.

Diem remains firmly in charge and Washington's support for his regime today seems more passionate and inflexible than ever.

## U.S. INVOLVEMENT

Actually, the United States has been deeply involved in the fate of Vietnam since 1949 when the decision was made to subsidize the continuation of French rule against the Communist Vietminh rebellion [see *Times* 05/09/50]. The first United States Military Assistance Advisory Group (M.A.A.G.) arrived in 1951 to supervise the distribution of supplies. Thereafter the United States played an increasingly important role. To use a favorite Washington term, aid was "escalated" until today $2 billion has been sunk into Vietnam with no end to the outlay in sight.

This may sound more reckless than the best brinkmanship of John Foster Dulles' days, and perhaps it is. But the United States is on this particular faraway brink because the Kennedy Administration seems convinced that the Communists won't rise to the challenge of the American presence and assistance.

### Forces and Strategy

The battle in Vietnam currently involves some 300,000 armed South Vietnamese and 3,000 American servicemen on one side, against 18,000 to 25,000 Vietcong Communist regulars operating as guerrillas.

The battle that is being fought is complex—in the nature of the fighting, in the internal political background and in its international implications.

The United States does not have any combat infantry troops in Vietnam as of now, but we are getting ready for that possibility. Marine Corps officers have completed ground reconnaissance in the central Vietnam highlands, a potential theater of large-scale action between American troops and Communist forces coming down from the north.

American combat troops are not likely to be thrown into Vietnam unless Communist North Vietnam moves across the seventeenth parallel or pushes large forces down through Laos into South Vietnam.

In that case the United States would have to move in fast. Forty miles below the frontier with North Vietnam and parallel to it is Highway 9. This road has high strategic importance. Not only is it one of the few adequate roads open across the mountains to the Laotian border but it extends across Laos to Savannakhet on the Mekong River frontier with Thailand. If Highway 9 could be held from the Mekong to the sea by American, Vietnamese, Laotian and Thai forces, South Vietnam might be saved.

The situation right now is far more stable than it was last September, when the Communists were attacking in battalion strength and were even able to seize and hold a provincial capital, Phuoc Vinh, for a few hours [see *Times* 09/19/61]. The September action seemed a prelude to an all-out Communist drive to overturn the Diem Government. It precipitated the present flood of American military advisors and service troops.

Today American warships are helping the embryonic Vietnamese Navy to guard the sea frontier against infiltration from North Vietnam and U.S. Navy servicemen presently will arrive to help clean out guerrillas from the maze of tidal waterways in the Mekong River Delta. The U.S. Army helicopter crews have come under fire taking Vietnamese combat troops into guerrilla zones or carrying pigs and other livestock to hungry outposts surrounded by hostile country. U.S. Air Force pilots have flown with Vietnamese pilots on bombing missions against reported enemy concentrations and against two frontier forts recently evacuated by the Vietnamese Army.

So far our contribution in blood has been small. One American sergeant has been killed by enemy action and another is missing and presumed captured. Inevitably our casualties will grow.

It has not been easy to change from conventional warfare, in which the Vietnamese were trained so many years by M.A.A.G., to unconventional counter-guerrilla warfare. Under French influence, the Vietnamese had developed two tendencies difficult to erase: first, the habit of staying inside forts designed for the troops' protection rather than for the security of the populace; second, the habit of good living—a leisurely lunch followed by a siesta.

### Hard Living

But counter-guerrilla warfare demands hard living. Troops must live in the jungle just as the guerrillas do and eschew the comforts of barracks life.

There are some minor difficulties: most Vietnamese recruits are from the densely populated lowlands—rice paddy boys who have a fear of the jungles, not merely fear of snakes and tigers but fear of getting lost. They move fearfully, with the instinct of a herd, tending to bunch up and thus present fat targets for a Vietcong ambush.

The Vietcong guerrillas also were former rice paddy boys, but they became inured to hardship by on-the-job training in the jungle. Further, the Vietnamese are somewhat smaller than Americans, so they get weary toting eleven-pound M1 rifles and pine for the lighter French weapons they were formerly equipped with.

At a higher level, United States advisors, besides trying to eliminate political manipulation of troops, are attempting to dissuade the Vietnamese from launching large-scale operations based on sketchy intelligence. They see no justification for such operations until a more adequate intelligence system is developed and greater tactical mobility achieved.

Intelligence will improve only when the Government is able to break the grip of fear with which the Vietcong muzzles the rural population. Greater mobility is being provided by American helicopter companies, but this is a costly and dangerous way to move troops.

## PRESIDENT DIEM

The man who is at the center of the Vietnamese effort and who is also a center of controversy—President Diem—is something of an enigma. He is a mandarin (an aristocrat) and a devout Catholic. So there are two strikes against him at the start, for mandarins were regarded by the masses as greedy and corrupt, and Catholics as an unpopular minority.

Diem, however, has proved incorruptible. Rumors of personal enrichment of members of his family have never been proved. And Diem has been careful not to arouse Buddhist hostility. He is a man of great personal courage, but he is suspicious and mistrustful. The creation of a central intelligence agency here was delayed for months until Diem found a director he could trust.

Diem, a 66-year-old bachelor, often has been accused of withdrawing inside his narrow family clique and divorcing himself from reality. Critics say he distrusts everyone except the family and takes advice only from his brothers, particularly Ngo Dinh Nhu, his political advisor. His brother Nhu and his attractive, influential wife are leaders, according to critics, of a palace camarilla which tries to isolate the President from the people.

As commander-in-chief of the armed forces, Diem keeps close tabs on military operations. His personal representative on the General Staff is Brig. Gen. Nguyen Khanh who has appalled Americans by taking general reserve troops on quick one-shot operations without coordinating with the area commander. Khanh is young, vigorous and driving but, according to his critics, lacking balance and experience.

Lieut. Gen. Le Ven Ty is Chief of the General Staff, but he is in his 60's and lacks vigor. Consequently, much of the military direction comes from the President through Khanh.

It is well to remember that Diem has been right and the United States wrong on some crucial issues. In 1955, for example, Diem wanted to crush the powerful Binh Xuyen gangster sect that controlled both the police and the gambling dens and brothels and made a mockery of government authority. President Eisenhower's special ambassador, Gen. Lawton Collins, opposed Diem's plan, fearing civil war. Diem coolly proceeded to assert his power and used loyal troops to crush the Binh Xuyen in sharp fighting in Saigon's streets [see *Times* 04/29/55].

## DENIED REQUEST

More recently the United States resisted Diem's urgent requests for aid in the creation of the civil guard and self-defense corps. The United States insisted that a 19,000-man regular army was all Diem needed for national defense. Diem went ahead and organized the two forces, arming them with antiquated French rifles. Finally, after alarm bells were ringing to the widespread revival of Communist guerrilla activity and vast sections of the countryside were lost to the Vietcong, the Americans conceded Diem's point. Last year the United States started training and equipping the civil guard.

It is now generally agreed that the civil guard and the self-defense corps are absolutely vital. For until these reserve forces are ready to take over the defense of villages, railroads, harbors, airports, provincial capitals and so on, the army will be so tied down to static defense duties that it will not have the manpower to chase guerrillas.

Last week, in another apparent concession to Diem's wisdom, the United States agreed that any relaxation of tight political controls would be dangerous now. In a speech cleared with the State Department, Ambassador Frederick E. Nolting Jr. urged Diem's critics to cease carping and try to improve the government from within.

Just how serious is the criticism is not clear and there seems to be no agreement among observers whether the President's popularity is rising or falling. One former Diem adviser said he was shocked by the loss of support among the people in the past two years. He blamed this on the fact that the Government seemed to grope from crisis to crisis without a clear policy: "It's just anti-Communist and not pro anything."

But another qualified observer, perhaps less biased, cautioned against underrating Diem. Increased guerrilla activity had not been matched, he said, by a corresponding rise in popular discontent and this failure to respond must have depressed the Communists.

Most villages, he added, were like a leaf in the wind: "When the Vietcong enters, the population turns pro-Communist; when the Government troops arrive, sentiment shifts to the Government." But generally the village people would settle for the Government side, he said, not because they admired the Government but because they wanted peace.

Consequently the Government has a great advantage. He estimated that of the 30 percent tending to the Vietcong, only a third were hard-core, another third would adhere to the Communists under adversity, while the remaining third would break off under pressure.

Freedom from dictatorship and freedom from foreign domination are major propaganda lines for the Vietcong. Americans in uniform have now been seen by the peasants in virtually all sections of the country. This has given the Communists a chance to raise the bogey of foreign military domination.

## PROBLEMS AND PROSPECTS

The lack of trained troops to keep the Vietcong under relentless pressure probably will continue to handicap the military command throughout 1962, because at least a year must elapse before the self-defense units will be really capable of defending their villages.

Whether because the Army is beginning to take the initiative and is penetrating secret areas of Vietcong concentrations or because the Vietcong has abated its activities in order to recruit and train, the fact remains that security seems better in most parts of Vietnam.

In peaceful, booming Saigon there is much speculation on how the Vietcong will react to an American build-up. Senior American officers have been studying an enemy guidebook to guerrilla warfare searching avidly for clues, as though this modest work were the Vietcong's "Mein Kampf."

There will never be enough troops to seal off the frontiers. There aren't even enough troops to ring Vietcong enclaves near Saigon. Not before summer, when the civil guard and self-defense units are slated to take over the burden of defending their villages, will enough troops be freed for a counter guerrilla offensive. Then, instead of a conventional setpiece offensive of limited duration, a counter-guerrilla drive will seek to keep Vietcong units on the run at all times, tire them out by constant pressure and force them into less hospitable country where food supplies are scarce.

The offensive cannot succeed unless the Government is able to mobilize positive popular support. This will be difficult, for the Government is just beginning to develop grass roots political cadres.

## NEED MODIFICATION

Meanwhile something more than narrowly anti-Communist goals must be offered Saigon intellectuals, who are now scorned by both Diem and the Americans. This group may be permanently alienated unless there is promise of democratic reforms. Without pressure from Washington, there is not likely to be any relaxation of Diem's personal dictatorship. The struggle will go on at least 10 years, in the opinion of some observers, and severely test American patience.

The United States seems inextricably committed to a long, inconclusive war. The Communists can prolong it for years. Even without large-scale intervention from the north, which would lead to "another Korea," what may be achieved at best is only restoration of a tolerable security similar to that achieved in Malaya after years of fighting. But it is too late to disengage; our prestige has been committed. Washington says we will stay until the finish.

*Credit*: © 1962 by The New York Times Co. Reprinted with permission.

---

# WALTER CRONKITE: KENNEDY INTERVIEW ON VIETNAM

---

*President John F. Kennedy gave two nationally televised interviews about Vietnam in September 1963. The first one appeared on the Columbia Broadcasting System's CBS Evening News with Walter Cronkite on 2 September. CBS used the long interview with Kennedy to launch its new thirty-minute newscast format. Kennedy's ambivalence about the Vietnamese conflict is evident in the interview. In the same exchange, he charged South Vietnam with responsibility for its own defense and reaffirmed the U.S. conviction to stop Communism in Southeast Asia. Most viewers did not know that he already had escalated U.S. commitment to supporting South Vietnam's fight against Communist rebels.*

*Kennedy also was questioned about French president Charles de Gaulle's criticism of U.S. involvement in Vietnam. Kennedy's dismissive response was typical of the American attitude toward the French.*

*The newscast also had a report on Henry Cabot Lodge, the new U.S. ambassador to Saigon. Lodge was sent to enforce Kennedy's new get-tough policy toward South Vietnamese president Ngo Dinh Diem. Despite U.S. warnings to seek an accommodation with Buddhist political dissenters, Diem had persisted in their repression. Lodge manipulated events to encourage a clique of South Vietnamese army generals to overthrow Diem. The generals struck on 1 November 1963. Diem and his brother, Ngo Dinh Nhu, were executed the next day. Lodge's complicity in the coup increased U.S. obligations there. Kennedy's own assassination twenty days later in Dallas, Texas, left many unanswered questions about Kennedy's intentions for Vietnam.*

### CBS Evening News with Walter Cronkite, 2 September 1963

ANNOUNCER: Direct from our Newsroom in New York, this is the "CBS Evening News with Walter Cronkite," and Nelson Benton in Tuskegee, Alabama, Dan Rather in Plaquemines, Louisiana, Bernard Kalb in Saigon, Peter Kalischer in Tokyo and Eric Sevareid in Washington.

CRONKITE: Good evening from our CBS Newsroom in New York on this, the first broadcast of network television's first daily half-hour news program.

In Alabama today, Governor Wallace ringed a public school with State Troops to delay integration ordered by a

Federal Court. And in turn the local Alabama School Board threatened defiance of the Governor.

At his summer White House in Hyannis Port on Massachusetts' Cape Cod, President Kennedy today talked with this reporter of many things. . . .

CRONKITE: Mr. President, the only hot war we've got running at the moment is of course the one in Vietnam, and we've got our difficulties there quite obviously.

KENNEDY: I don't think that—unless a greater effort is made by the Government to win popular support—the war can be won out there. In the final analysis, it is their war; they're the ones who have to win it or lose it. We can help them, we can give them equipment, we can send our men out there as advisers, but they have to win it—the people of Vietnam—against the Communists. We're prepared to continue to assist them, but I don't think that the war can be won unless the people support the effort. In my opinion, in the last two months the Government has gotten out of touch with the people. The repressions against the Buddhists, we felt, were very unwise. Now all we can do is to make it very clear that we don't think this is the way to win. It's my hope that this will become increasingly obvious to the Government, that they will take steps to try to bring back popular support for this very essential struggle.

CRONKITE: Do you think this Government has time to regain the support of the people?

KENNEDY: I do. With changes in policy and perhaps with personnel, I think it can. If it doesn't make those changes, I would think that the chances of winning it would not be very good.

CRONKITE: Well, hasn't every indication from Saigon been that President Diem has no intention of changing his pattern?

KENNEDY: If he does not change it, of course, that's his decision. He has been there ten years, and, as I say, he has carried this burden when he's been counted out on a number of occasions. Our best judgment is that he can't be successful on this basis. We hope that he comes to see it, but, in the final analysis, it's the people and the Government themselves who have to win or lose this struggle. All we can do is help, and we're making it very clear. But I don't agree with those who say we should withdraw. That would be a great mistake. I know people don't like Americans to be engaged in this kind of an effort. Forty-seven Americans have been killed in combat with the enemy, but this is a very important struggle even though it's far away.

We took all this—made this effort to defend Europe. Now Europe is quite secure. We also have to participate—we may not like it—in the defense of Asia.

CRONKITE: Mr. President, have you made an assessment as to what President de Gaulle was up to in his statement on Vietnam last week?

KENNEDY: No, I guess it was an expression of his general view. But he doesn't have any forces there or any program of economic assistance. So that while these expressions are welcomed but the burden is carried, as it usually is, by the United States and the people there. But I think anything General de Gaulle says should be listened to—and we listen.

CRONKITE: You don't think that this is another prod to get together with you—to try to call off President de Gaulle from his kind of sniping at us?

KENNEDY: What, of course, makes Americans somewhat impatient is that, after carrying this load for eighteen years, we've got to get counsel. But we would like a little more assistance, real assistance. But we're going to meet our responsibility anyway. It doesn't do us any good to say, "Well, why don't we all just go home and leave the world to those who are our enemies." General de Gaulle is not our enemy. He's our friend and candid friend; and they're sometimes difficult. But he's not the object of our hostility.

CRONKITE: Mr. President, the sending of Henry Cabot Lodge, who, after all, has been a political enemy of yours over the years, at one point or another in your career and his, sending him out to Saigon might raise some speculation that perhaps you're trying to keep this from being a political issue in 1964.

KENNEDY: Ambassador Lodge wanted to go out to Saigon. If he were as careful as some politicians are, of course he wouldn't have wanted to go there. He would have maybe liked some safe job. But he's energetic and he has strong feelings about the United States; and surprising as it seemed, he put this ahead of his political career. Sometimes politicians do those things.

CRONKITE: Thank you very much, Mr. President.

KENNEDY: And we're fortunate to have him.

CRONKITE: Thank you, sir.

Ambassador Lodge is no stranger to Saigon. In 1929, as a *New York Herald Tribune* reporter, he wrote: "There is law and order in Indo-China; there is prosperity, health and education. Your life and property are as safe as in the United States." But that was thirty-four years ago. This weekend Mr. Lodge took another look. Bernard Kalb reports.

KALB: Ambassador Henry Cabot Lodge is now taking his first walking tour of Saigon with his wife, and everybody seems to be having a good time, the Ambassador, Mrs. Lodge and Saigon. And the Ambassador has been keeping everything extremely informal. To begin with, he has not worn his jacket nor his tie. The weather has helped out by raining off and on, typical weather in Saigon for this time of year.

The Ambassador was here for the first time in 1929. He was then working as a journalist for a New York newspaper, and now he's back, re-acquainting himself with this town that was once his beat.

CRONKITE: Tonight Mr. Lodge's embassy dismissed as "nonsense" a Saigon newspaper charge that the CIA is spending millions to overthrow the Diem Government. . . .

CRONKITE: And that's the way it is Monday, September 2nd, 1963.

This is Walter Cronkite. Good night.

ANNOUNCER: Direct from our Newsroom in New York, this has been the "CBS Evening News with Walter Cronkite."

*Credit*: Reprinted with permission of the CBS News Archives.

## FURTHER READINGS

Browne, Malcolm W. *The New Face of War*. Indianapolis: Bobbs-Merrill, 1965.

Halberstam, David. *The Making of a Quagmire*. New York: Random House, 1965.

Rust, William J. *Kennedy in Vietnam: American Vietnam Policy, 1960–63*. New York: Da Capo Press, 1985.

# 4

# BATTLE OF AP BAC, 2–3 JANUARY 1963

The Battle of Ap Bac on 2–3 January 1963 exposed the weaknesses of the South Vietnamese army (ARVN). The battle was named for the nearby village of Bac ("Ap," meaning "hamlet," was included in news dispatches) in the Mekong Delta province of Dinh Tuong. Guided by Lieutenant Colonel John Paul Vann, U.S. military advisor to the ARVN Seventh Division, the plan was to surprise a Vietcong company operating near the village. However, the enemy unit turned out to be the much larger 514th Vietcong Battalion of about 350 guerrillas, which learned of the impending attack, dug in behind a tree line, and ambushed the ARVN force as it unloaded from helicopters in an adjacent rice paddy.

Vann witnessed the slaughter from his small, unarmed spotter plane flying overhead. He insisted that the ARVN division commander, Lieutenant Colonel Bui Dinh Dam, send in his ten M-113 armored personnel carriers to rescue the downed pilots and charge the enemy line. The M-113 crews panicked under massed fire from the Vietcong and turned back. Vann repeatedly badgered the ARVN corps commander, Lieutenant General Huynh Van Cao, to deploy reserve paratroopers to cut off the Vietcong escape route. Cao finally consented, but the troops were mistakenly dropped into a Vietcong killing zone and suffered many casualties. In the ensuing confusion of twilight, the South Vietnamese fired on each other, and the Vietcong slipped into the darkness. The Vietcong suffered eighteen killed and thirty-nine wounded, while inflicting roughly eighty killed and more than 100 wounded on its ARVN foe four times its size. The Vietcong also killed three Americans, wounded eight more, and downed five helicopters.

Vann's public criticism of the ARVN's leadership failures in the Ap Bac debacle ruined his standing with the Pentagon and led to his resignation from the U.S. Army within a few months after the battle. Nonetheless, Vann believed in the U.S. mission in South Vietnam. In 1965, he returned to Vietnam as a pacification worker with the U.S. Agency for International Development. On 15 May 1971, U.S. commander

Creighton Abrams put Vann in charge of the Second Regional Assistance Group in the central highlands. Vann's civilian appointment was equal to that of a two-star general in the military. Vann led the ARVN to defeat North Vietnamese regulars at Kontum on 7 June 1972 and died two days later in a helicopter crash.

Press coverage of the humiliation at Ap Bac antagonized South Vietnamese premier Ngo Dinh Diem and the U.S. mission in Saigon and forever soured their relations with the press. General Paul D. Harkins, U.S. commander in Saigon, openly criticized the correspondents for damaging the war effort; the journalists responded in kind. *New York Times* correspondent David Halberstam is reputed to have shouted at the general, "I'll get you, Paul Harkins." As the political and military situation deteriorated, Military Assistance Command, Vietnam (MACV), adopted policies to manage the news. Thus the resentment and suspicion that marked military-media relations during the Vietnam War were spawned on the rice fields of Ap Bac.

---

## AN ANONYMOUS REPORT: REPORT OF VIETCONG VICTORY OVER SOUTH VIETNAMESE TROOPS AT AP BAC

---

*On 4 January 1963, the* Chicago Daily News *published three news-wire bulletins on the Battle of Ap Bac datelined Saigon, Washington, and Tan Hiep, respectively. The first bulletin established—with inaccurate estimates of casualties and the size of the enemy force—the basic facts of the battle from the perspective of allied command in Saigon. The U.S. military advisor to the ARVN Seventh Division, Lieutenant Colonel John Paul Vann, blamed the defeat on lack of aggressiveness by the South Vietnamese division and corps commanders. Vann's criticism was attributed anonymously in the following bulletin, but its source was obvious to MACV. General Harkins was enraged at Vann for talking to reporters and wanted to fire his subordinate, but Harkins feared the press's retribution and decided to allow Vann to serve out the two months remaining in his tour of duty in Vietnam.*

*Chicago Daily News, 4 January 1963*

Daily News Wire Services, Saigon, South Vietnam—Communist guerrillas took the heaviest toll in more than a year in the furious two-day battle of Ap Bac, a government spokesman said Friday.

He said 65 government soldiers were killed and 100 wounded, the heaviest loss since about 200 were killed in a Viet Cong ambush in November 1961.

The government defeat was all the more humiliating because a 200-man Communist Viet Cong battalion managed to escape into the jungles after holding the hamlet in day-long fighting against a government force 10 times as big and supported by planes, artillery and armor.

Informed witnesses said it appeared the U.S. military mission and the South Vietnamese government would have to revise military strategy in the light of lessons learned in the costly battle.

Three Americans were killed and four were wounded in the fighting, most of them when the Viet Cong shot down five American-manned helicopters and damaged six others.

One of the slain Americans was identified as Capt. Kenneth Good, whose father lives in San Marino, Calif.

The government spokesman put Viet Cong dead at 101, but American military advisers at the scene regarded the figure as too high.

Some advisers found only three guerrilla bodies in a visit to Ap Bac, just 20 miles from Saigon, shortly after the Viet Cong fled, taking their wounded and most of their dead with them.

The humiliating performance by the government force was capped by an accidental shelling of its own troops. Three Vietnamese soldiers were killed and 12 were injured by the error.

The Communist stand at Ap Bac apparently caught government forces by surprise.

Government troops moved in to engage the guerrillas, but met stiff resistance. They threw artillery barrages, air attacks and machinegun fire at the entrenched Reds, but the guerrillas managed to hold out and eventually slip through an uncovered flank into the bush.

Many American advisers were disappointed and angered that the South Vietnamese should fail one of their biggest tests after more than a year of training.

The Americans criticized what they called the lack of aggressiveness on the part of the Vietnamese commanders.

## AN ANONYMOUS REPORT: ASSESSMENT OF BATTLE OF AP BAC BY U.S. MILITARY COMMAND IN VIETNAM

*The following Associated Press bulletin, datelined Washington, revealed General Paul Harkins's tendency to report to the Pentagon the most optimistic view of events in Vietnam. The real cause for the allied defeat at Ap Bac was flawed leadership by South Vietnamese commanders, but Harkins refused to acknowledge his ally's weaknesses and instead blamed security leaks and outmoded equipment for the setback—much more manageable problems for the United States than intransigence from its ally. Harkins went so far as to characterize Ap Bac as a tactical victory, in that the Vietcong withdrew from the hamlet after the battle.*

*Chicago Daily News*, 4 January 1963

Washington (AP)—U.S. military authorities said Friday the ambush by Communist guerrillas of a helicopter-borne force of South Vietnamese troops indicates intelligence security—one of the basic problems of that war—still is unsolved.

As many as 600 Communist Viet Cong guerrillas were reported to have lain in wait for the South Vietnamese, who came in on the battlefield southwest of Saigon two days ago in U.S. Army helicopters.

The Viet Cong opened fire on the fourth wave of helicopters, according to reports received here, and inflicted heavy casualties on the South Vietnamese while shooting down five of the 15 choppers. Three Americans have been listed as killed in the action and six wounded.

The Army is preparing for the White House a report on helicopter losses in Viet Nam, including the ambush of two days ago.

Army officers said the objective of the mission obviously was tipped off to the Communists.

These officers said both sides in the bitter South Vietnamese war tried to penetrate each other's ranks with intelligence agents.

The key to success in the helicopter strikes against the elusive Viet Cong is surprise, and this obviously was lacking in the big fight near the Mekong River.

Some officials said one lesson this action may teach is the need for newer transport helicopters equipped with effective weapons.

The 10 "flying banana" troop carriers used in the attack are not built for armament, although some craft of this type have been fitted with machineguns that fire out the side doors in what experts say is an unsatisfactory manner.

The 10 aging transport helicopters were escorted by five of the Army's most modern turbine-powered, rocket- and machinegun-armed helicopters, one of which was shot down and destroyed.

*Credit*: Reprinted with permission of The Associated Press.

## AN ANONYMOUS REPORT: U.S. PATROL TRAPS VIETCONG GUERRILLA UNIT AFTER BATTLE OF AP BAC

*The day after the Ap Bac defeat, U.S. Lieutenant Colonel John Paul Vann attempted to recoup the situation by personally taking charge of a ragtag collection of American advisory personnel to round up Vietcong stragglers. Vann's claim that his squad was acting only to protect a U.S. major was a cover story to preserve the official fiction that Americans did not take part in combat in Vietnam.*

*Chicago Daily News*, 4 January 1963

Tan Hiep, South Vietnam (AP)—A U.S. Army colonel from Texas scraped together 60 American soldiers, including cooks, and turned them into a battle patrol that trapped a unit of Communist guerrillas fleeing into the Mekong River Delta jungles Friday.

The American military advisers to South Viet Nam's government forces captured 17 Communist prisoners. Col. John Paul Vann of El Paso said his men didn't fire a shot.

Vann said he put the unit together to protect an American major with Vietnamese troops.

The Vietnamese were trying to cut off fleeing Communist Viet Cong who attacked in force from nearby Ap Bac Wednesday, killing three Americans and wounding 10. Sixty-five government troops were killed in the Communist trap.

"I'm not trying to fight these people's war for them," Vann said. "Our sole reason was to protect that major."

The Americans carried automatic weapons, but were under orders from Vann not to fire unless the Communists opened up. He said the Americans did not need to use their weapons.

Vann sent the American patrol out in jeeps and on foot at 10 a.m. By early afternoon they had completed their operation and returned to their advisory roles and field cooking stoves.

*Credit*: Reprinted with permission of The Associated Press.

---

## THOMAS P. RONAN: INTERVIEW WITH COLONEL JOHN PAUL VANN, U.S. MILITARY ADVISOR AT AP BAC

---

*Following the Battle of Ap Bac, U.S. Army colonel John Paul Vann returned to the United States from his tour of duty as a military advisor in Vietnam. He was full for ideas for how to turn around the war. He discovered that his frank criticism of the South Vietnamese army's performance in the battle, as reported to the UPI's Neil Sheehan and others, had irked Pentagon brass and ruined his chances for advancement. He gave the following interview to Thomas Ronan of the* New York Times *shortly after deciding to retire from the military. Eventually, Vann returned to Vietnam. Sheehan chronicled Vann's career in* A Bright Shining Lie: John Paul Vann and America in Vietnam, *which won the Pulitzer Prize in 1989.*

### New York Times, 31 August 1963

A United States Army officer who retired recently after more than a year's service in South Vietnam said yesterday that he doubted whether the South Vietnamese Government was really interested in defeating the Vietcong Communist guerrillas.

Lieut. Col. John Paul Vann, who was the senior American officer in the key Mekong Delta area before he returned here in April, declared his doubt was shared by other American officers "on the lower level" in South Vietnam.

He said he and they thought the Government might be interested in "containing" the Communists rather than defeating them.

The belief of many American officers, he added, is that the organized military forces of the Vietcong could be crushed in six months to a year if there were a proper effort by the South Vietnamese Army.

Colonel Vann, who now lives in Denver and who was interviewed by telephone, said the Saigon Government would still have a long way to go, possibly 10 years, before it could pacify the entire countryside. This would mean the establishment of communications and the building of roads and schools in all areas, he said.

He gave two reasons why he believed the Government might be reluctant to crush the Communists.

The first was that President Ngo Dinh Diem "or whoever is running the country" feared that the people would revolt against the Government after the defeat of the Communists.

The second was that the Government believed there would be a substantial reduction in United States aid when the danger from the Communists ended.

The 39-year-old former officer was awarded the Distinguished Flying Cross and the Purple Heart and was recommended for the Legion of Merit while in South Vietnam. He also was given the highest efficiency rating by his superior.

Despite this, his outspoken criticism of the course of the war and [of] the conduct of Vietnamese authorities got him into difficulties. It was reported that Gen. Paul D. Harkins, commander of United States forces in South Vietnam, had threatened to relieve him of his command but had been dissuaded from doing so by other high officers.

### REASONS FOR RETIREMENT

Colonel Vann, father of five children, returned to the United States in April to attend the Armed Forces Industrial College but decided to retire. He said he had been influenced by the realization that his criticism might have affected his Army prospects but that he also had been moved by financial considerations.

He declared in the interview that the South Vietnamese Government not only did not encourage its commanders to fight but that it even reprimanded those who lost soldiers in offensive actions.

He said he knew a general who had been severely reprimanded when he lost some of his men in one of these actions despite the fact that the enemy had suffered equivalent losses.

The Vietnamese, he continued, prefer to do their fighting

with planes and artillery and this means that a lot of innocent people are killed. In guerrilla fighting, he noted, it is hard enough to identify the enemy when he is close.

Every time an innocent person is killed, he said, the Government makes new enemies.

Colonel Vann stressed that there was no doubt that the Government and the commanders were strongly anti-Communist. He also said that he had never seen a coward among the soldiers but that the commanders often let the enemy escape rather than sustain casualties.

Colonel Vann was critical of American policy as "too mild" toward the government. His impression, he said, is that the United States does not demand enough.

"It was incomprehensible to me that the United States should put so much in there and get so little out and demand so little," he said.

"As an American taxpayer and an American officer, I was greatly distressed at the lack of any effort to go out and win the war."

He praised General Harkins as "a very able officer" and said he believed all those "on the American side" were "breaking their backs to win the war."

But he added that officers in the field felt that those in the top echelon were sending back to Washington reports that were much too optimistic about the course of the war.

"Unfortunately America is a success-oriented country," Colonel Vann said. "If a general there gave pessimistic reports, he might be replaced."

Colonel Vann spent two and a half months at the Pentagon upon his return in April. He said he had briefed everyone he could reach, "a considerable number," about what was really happening in South Vietnam and had been told by a high-ranking general that he had performed a real service.

He joined the Army when he was 18 years old but by attending army and night schools has obtained Bachelor of Arts and Master's degrees. He also has completed his studies for a doctorate in public administration but has not yet turned in his thesis.

*Credit*: © 1963 by The New York Times Co. Reprinted with permission.

## FURTHER READINGS

Nolting, Frederick. *From Trust to Tragedy: The Political Memoirs of Frederick Nolting, Kennedy's Ambassador to Diem's Vietnam*. New York: Praeger, 1988.

Prochnau, William. *Once upon a Distant War: David Halberstam, Neil Sheehan, Peter Arnett—Young War Correspondents and Their Early Vietnam Battles*. New York: Vintage Books, 1996.

Sheehan, Neil. *A Bright Shining Lie: John Paul Vann and America in Vietnam*. New York: Vintage Books, 1989.

# 5

## JOURNALISTIC BIAS IN VIETNAM

Vietnam War reporters individually and collectively fell victim to accusations of bias. Such accusations of failed professional integrity usually were levied by indisputably biased critics—military men, government officials, and stateside editors invested in the establishment view. Famous for his close ties with the Kennedy and Johnson presidential administrations, *New York Times* columnist James Reston summed up the collective damnation of the Vietnam press corps on 20 April 1975, the day that North Vietnamese armored columns overran Saigon: "The reporters and cameras forced the withdrawal of American power from Vietnam."[1]

The many public opinion polls during the Vietnam War showed that Reston gave the press too much credit for fueling the antiwar movement. As U.S. casualties accumulated, the public anticipated the mainstream press in questioning the war and maintained its own commonsense attitudes throughout, while on the whole supporting official government policy. It was fear of public disenchantment that restrained Presidents Kennedy, Johnson, and Nixon from more rapidly escalating the war and from censoring the news media.

The saga of *Time* magazine reporter Charles Mohr dramatizes the clash of distinctly different perspectives of the Saigon press corps and stateside editors. A rising star among *Time* reporters in May 1962, Mohr was sent to Saigon to cover the U.S. buildup. There he met *Time* part-time reporter Merton Perry, who described the growing U.S. commitment and widespread disrespect for the regime of South Vietnamese premier Ngo Dinh Diem. Reporters in Saigon noted divergences between the rosy picture painted by U.S. officials and actual events in the countryside. Mohr's own contacts and excursions with combat units convinced him that the South Vietnamese government was more concerned with political infighting than with defeating the Vietcong and "winning the hearts and minds of the people."[2]

Mohr's dispatches regularly criticized the Diem regime for its indifference and even cruelty to its own people. Such criticisms were not welcomed by *Time* editors in New

York. The magazine's pages reflected with almost messianic zeal an optimistic image of the American destiny in Asia as propounded by *Time*'s founder and publisher, Henry R. Luce. The conflict between Mohr and his editors came to a head in August 1963 when Mohr's lengthy dispatch critical of Madame Ngo Dinh Nhu, the premier's outspoken sister-in-law, was altered by the editors to say, not that the Diem government was hopeless, but that it was the best that could be hoped for. Mohr exploded with cumulative frustration and wrote to *Time*'s managing editor Otto Fuerbringer that the magazine was seriously wrong to back the Diem regime. Fuerbringer was irked that his authority had been questioned, especially because he felt that the Saigon press corps was to blame for the regime's problems. He ordered an editorial for the magazine's press section (reproduced in this chapter) that accused the Saigon press corps of journalistic failings; the editorial's real target was Mohr. Mohr protested directly to Henry Luce, but to no avail, and resigned in protest. Mohr later was hired by the *New York Times* to continue covering the war. Merton Perry also resigned and was hired by *Newsweek*. Years later, doubt about the U.S. government's war policy eventually found room on the pages of *Time* magazine, but not before it was the accepted view of mainstream America.

The troubling question of journalistic bias did not end with the Vietnam War. If anything, the debate has become more heated and earnest since, as the public has grown more aware of the news media's influence on public policy. The Vietnam War is remembered, with some justification, as the watershed event that permanently embittered military-media relations. However, for the serious journalists who covered Vietnam, nothing of permanence was resolved about the journalistic calling itself except its preeminence in a free society.

## JOHN KOFFEND: "VIEW FROM SAIGON": *TIME* EDITORIAL CRITICIZES AMERICAN REPORTING OF WAR

*Time* magazine's managing editor Otto Fuerbringer ordered John Koffend, a writer of the New York staff, to pen a scathing condemnation of journalists covering the Vietnam War from Saigon; that editorial, "Foreign Correspondents: The View from Saigon," appears here. The column's specific target was *Time* reporter Charles Mohr, who had angered Fuerbringer with his open contempt for the magazine's hawkish editorial stance toward the war. One can anticipate Mohr's reaction when he read the following words, branding him an irresponsible reprobate—he quit.

*Time*, 20 September 1963

For all the light it shed, the news that U.S. newspaper readers got from Saigon might just as well have been printed in Vietnamese. Was the war being won or lost? Was the Buddhist uprising religiously inspired or Communist-inspired? Would the government fall? Only last month, *The New York Times* threw up its hands helplessly and, beneath an editorial apology, printed two widely divergent accounts of events; one presented the picture as viewed from Washington, the other as viewed from Saigon.

Uncertainty out of Washington is not exactly news, but one of the more curious aspects of the South Viet Nam story is that the press corps on the scene is helping to compound the very confusion that it should be untangling for its readers at home.

Much of its failure can be traced to its solidarity. Foreign correspondents, wherever they are stationed, are tempted to band together into an official club; they are their own closest connection with home. When they have finished covering a story, when they have examined it from every angle, they find it pleasant to relax in each other's company. In Saigon, however, more than mere sociability brings the U.S. correspondents together.

### ALOOF & HOSTILE

The country is completely alien to their experience. It lies in the middle of nowhere: 8,000 miles from the U.S., part of a uvular peninsula jutting into the South China Sea. Everywhere they turn, the U.S. correspondents find obstacles standing in the way of dispassionate reporting. None of them speak the language with any fluency—and their Vietnamese contacts seldom speak English. When possible, they resort to the country's second language—French.

In all the land, there are only two stories to report: an extraordinary kind of war, and an extraordinary kind of government, in which the figure of the President is shadowed by his brother, who wields strong police power, and by his tiny sister-in-law—who holds no office at all. At the battlefront, both U.S. military observers and the Vietnamese brass blandly tell the newsmen stories that blatantly contradict evidence obvious to the journalists' eyes. In Saigon, the ruling family is reserved, aloof, openly hostile; it does not trust the Western correspondents—and does not trouble to hide its feelings.

## CARAVELLE CAMARADERIE

Such uncommon pressures unite the newsmen to an uncommon degree. They work hard and go their separate ways on separate assignments. But when they meet and unwind—in the field, in their homes or in the camaraderie of the Hotel Caravelle's eighth-floor bar—they pool their convictions, information, misinformation and grievances. But the balm of such companionship has not been conducive to independent thought. The reporters have tended to reach unanimous agreement on almost everything they have seen. But such agreement is suspect because it is so obviously inbred. The newsmen have themselves become a part of South Viet Nam's confusion: they have covered a complex situation from only one angle, as if their own conclusions offered all the necessary illumination.

Such reporting is prone to distortions. The complicated greys of a complicated country fade into oversimplified blacks and whites. To Saigon's Western press corps, President Ngo Dinh Diem is stubborn and stupid, dominated by his brother and sister-in-law. As a result, the correspondents have taken sides against all three; they seldom miss a chance to overemphasize the ruling family's Roman Catholicism. The press corps' attitude automatically assigns justice and sympathy to the side of the Buddhists, who are well aware of their favored position. Before the first *bonze* set fire to himself, the leaders of the Buddhist uprising tipped off a Western reporter in advance. When a young Buddhist girl tried to chop off her hand in protest against government repressions, there were reports that the Buddhists delayed her trip to a hospital for 40 minutes until the last photographer had his pictures.

The Saigon-based press corps is so confident of its own convictions that any other version of the Viet Nam story is quickly dismissed as the fancy of a bemused observer. Many of the correspondents seem reluctant to give splash treatment to anything that smacks of military victory in the ugly war against the Communists, since this would take the sheen off the theory that the infection of the Buddhist troubles in Saigon is demoralizing the government troops and weakens the argument that defeat is inevitable so long as Diem is in power. When there is a defeat, the color is rich and flowing; trend stories are quickly cranked up. Last week, after one battle, A.P. gave credit to government troops for "The most significant victory over the Reds in months" then went on to say: "But the success was tempered by renewed civilian opposition to the regime of President Ngo Dinh Diem," proceeding for nine paragraphs to talk about student demonstrations in Saigon.

A few weeks ago, a correspondent flew out from the U.S. to Saigon for a firsthand look and, ignoring the assessments of resident newsmen, reached independent conclusions. Club members were furious. The Buddhist rebellion, said the newcomer, was directed by monks who were also consummate politicians, who were less interested in redressing religious injustices than in overthrowing the Diem regime. This interpretation was greeted in the Caravelle bar by still-simmering indignation. It was the analysis of an outsider and therefore patently wrong.

*Credit:* © 1963 TIME Inc. Reprinted by permission.

---

## JOHN PAUL VANN: LETTER TO EDITOR CRITICIZES *TIME*'S "VIEW FROM SAIGON" EDITORIAL

---

*U.S. Army lieutenant colonel John Paul Vann was the advisor to the South Vietnamese army who complained about South Vietnamese leadership failures in the allied defeat at the Battle of Ap Bac in 1963 (see Chapter 4) to* New York Times *correspondent David Halberstam and United Press International correspondent Neil Sheehan. After Halberstam published Vann's criticisms and attributed them to an unnamed U.S. advisor in the Mekong Delta, Vann lost favor with the Pentagon and decided to resign his military commission. The "View from Saigon" editorial in* Time *magazine (see the preceding document) irked Vann. He fired back a letter to the editor.* Time *would not publish his letter, but* Newsweek *did.*

*Newsweek,* 21 October 1963

Regarding [the editorial critical of the press in Vietnam], as senior adviser to the Vietnamese Seventh Division commander (May '62 to April '63) I had occasion to meet and know the members of the Saigon permanent press corps, including *Newsweek's* Beverly Deepe and François Sully. Dave Halberstam I knew best of all due to his frequent paddy-field walks while accompanying troops of the Seventh Division on operations.

With respect to the situation in the Mekong Delta, it is my opinion that the reading American public was in the unique position of being better informed as to the true situation than were this country's military leaders and policymakers through official channels. This was the result of firsthand observations and analyses made by the Saigon press corps over a long period of time, not just on a fly-by-night trip to sample the frosting and ignore the cake.

No matter how astute the observer, whether it be Mr. McNamara or Mr. Alsop, it is practically impossible to evaluate the situation in South Vietnam in a week or two.

I sincerely believe that the American press corps in Saigon has rendered a greater service to this country and to the 14 million deserving Vietnamese citizens than any official American group a hundred times their number.

*John Paul Vann*
*Lt. Col., U.S. Army (Ret.)*
*Littleton, Colo.*

---

# AN ANONYMOUS REPORT: LIFE AND TIMES OF THE VIETNAM PRESS CORPS—DIFFICULTY REPORTING THE TRUTH

---

Ramparts *magazine was the best-known antiwar publication of the Vietnam War era and, not coincidentally, folded the same year that the war ended. The anonymous author of the following* Ramparts *essay, a member of the Saigon press corps, describes with bitter humor his colleagues' sense of futility at reporting a war in which truth was treated as the enemy. Note the reference in this piece to retired army colonel and Vietnam veteran John Paul Vann, who had returned to Vietnam in 1965 with the U.S. Agency for International Development. The author rode with Vann on aid missions in the Mekong River delta area of South Vietnam.*

*Ramparts*, February 1967

On a muggy, listless Saigon afternoon last August, an official spokesman for the government announced a reply, of sorts, to the charge that American bombs had been responsible for the deaths of a number of Cambodians.

The announcement was made to reporters in the JUSPAO building (the awkward acronym means Joint United States Public Affairs Office), on the corner of Nguyen Hue and Le Loi streets, in the same briefing room in which any reporters who happen to be in town gather every afternoon at five. There, the newsmen are fed the cabalistic facts and figures of the day's war: operations launched, the body count, KIAs [killed in action], WIAs [wounded in action], MIAs [missing in action], raids North and South, planes lost, number of refugees in the bank and the itinerary of the latest visiting fireman.

On this particular August afternoon, as on most afternoons, the stage held five large map boards; each of four represented one of the four military divisions, or corps areas, of South Vietnam, and the fifth depicted North Vietnam. Habitual early arrivals took their seats while the military briefing personnel were still busily cluttering the maps with celluloid numbers, red and blue arrows, and little blue bombs: the numbers are keys to items in the daily printed handout, the arrows refer to military operations or incidents (red for the enemy, blue for the U.S.), and the little blue bombs stand for bombing missions in the North or B-52 raids in the South.

The proceedings are always opened by the press representative from the civilian side of the mission. Currently that representative is a short, stocky man named John Stuart; a bureaucratic "old pro," he has cropped gray hair, small eyes, a belly obscuring his belt, and a mouth that puckers when it moves. In a relatively short time in Saigon, Stuart has already become famous for a dull wit, a sodden sense of humor, epic pomposity and a total indifference to the pronunciation of foreign words—particularly Vietnamese place names.

Ordinarily (and, many feel, blissfully) the civilian briefer has little or nothing to say. On this occasion, however, he had been assigned to read the official report of an American investigation of American planes dropping American bombs on the village of Thlok Trach. The report followed the attack by ten days. Cambodia had protested the attack, understandably enough, since the Cambodians believe (and apparently we have come to agree) that Thlok Trach is in Cambodia. In the course of protesting the attack, Cambodia also noted that a group of neutral observers, including members of the International Control Commission, had witnessed the event.

The report which Stuart read to the reporters on August

12 said simply that attacks did occur on "targets in the vicinity of Thlok Trach village on 31 July and 2 August." They were launched, it said, in response to fire which U.S. helicopters had received from the area. The U.S. was sorry that the observers were endangered; however, according to the maps studied in the course of the investigation, the targets were on the Vietnamese side of the border. Reporters don't like to work any more than anybody else, especially on sultry afternoons, but sometimes they have to ask questions, and on this occasion those questions led to a quick, dizzy spiral into the looking-glass world of officialese. It went something like this:

Q. You said the targets were in Vietnam. The Cambodians say we bombed a Cambodian village. Can we take this as a denial of the Cambodian charge that we hit one of their villages?

A. It is not my purpose to answer Cambodian charges. This is a report of our investigation of the incident.

Q. Did we hit a Cambodian village?

A. We hit targets which our maps show to be in Vietnam.

Q. Did we hit the village?

A. Apparently some bombs fell in one corner of Thlok Trach.

Q. Well, if we hit the village, and the village is on the Vietnamese side of the border, how is it that the group from Phnom Penh was endangered?

That one called for a quickly drawn map. The delegation, the spokesman said, had been brought to the hamlet of An Long Chuey ("which is here"), definitely within Cambodian territory. They had walked from there to Thlok Trach, further east. Also shown on the quick sketch were the unquestionably Vietnamese village of An Long Trach, still further east, and the Vietnamese-Cambodian border—drawn by Stuart as a vertical line between An Long Chuey and Thlok Trach.

Q. Then the observers crossed into Vietnamese territory, right?

A. No, I'm not saying that.

Q. (a touch of hysteria intruding) But, goddamn it, you've drawn it on the blackboard! You've said the group walked from an area you've shown as Cambodian territory, across a line you say represents the Cambodian-Vietnamese border, and into an area you say is in Vietnam, and where you've placed Thlok Trach. What do you mean, you're not saying that?

A. That's your interpretation. I'm not saying that.

I hate to see grown men cry.

Further questions by those who could get their heads out of their hands squeezed out the admission that it was not certain who administered the village, but it was thought to be the Viet Cong. The information was also elicited that the inhabitants of the village are *ethnically* Cambodians (his emphasis, my italics).

As an anti-climax, the United States spokesman, asked whether any on the observer team had been injured, replied in the negative, adding graciously, "Though I understand some

of them dirtied their pants—in the dirt, I mean." Stuart also "understood" that "most of 'em were halfway to Phnom Penh before the last bomb fell. Har!"

Some days later, it was decided in Washington that Thlok Trach—obviously damaged goods and stolen by the NLF anyway—should be awarded to Cambodia.

Only two days before, discussion at the briefing had centered around another village bombing, this one a few miles south of the delta city of Cantho. Twenty-four or more civilians were killed and 82, or 182, wounded (briefing officials had one total, doctors at the hospital to which the wounded were taken had another). The casualties, according to the briefing, were the fault of the Viet Cong, who had forced the inhabitants to remain in the village when the attacking planes arrived.

That line came up again the following day, and was angrily challenged from the floor by Charles Mohr of *The New York Times*, who had taken the trouble to go to Cantho and to interview a number of the wounded in the hospital. They all told him that there had been no Viet Cong in the village.

Not every day in the JUSPAO briefing room is so contentious, but there have been enough such days to warrant nicknaming the daily sessions "the Five O'clock Follies." They are a running battle in that other war in Vietnam, the one between reporters and officials, known as The Information War.

Since the American build-up, the total number of foreign newsmen in South Vietnam (i.e., representatives of non-Vietnamese media) has ranged between 300 and 400, including photographers and TV cameramen and soundmen. In June of 1966 there were approximately 360 accredited foreign newsmen.

But between January 1 and June 30, 1966, the Special Projects Office of Military Assistance Command Vietnam (MACV to the press) had accredited more than 1100 persons. That represents a turnover of better than 300 per cent in six months.

Most of the turnover is due to what the press corps calls the "tourist trade"—reporters, columnists, editors, TV personalities and others, who arrive on short junkets of a month's duration or less. The standard tour for regular correspondents is about one year; there is a handful who have been working the Vietnamese story for several years. By and large, the press corps of 1965 was a different group of people from the press corps of 1964, and that of 1966 different from that of 1965.

Though the personalities may have changed, The Other War continues unabated; the attitudes of officials toward the press are among the few constants in the ever-changing Vietnamese scene. Never has there been a press corps so frequently and harshly attacked by government officials, by headline-hunting politicians, by indentured columnists, and even, at times, by wise men in the home office. And the attacks rarely vary.

American reporters in Saigon, their attackers insist, are young and immature, inexperienced and irresponsible. They are infatuated with their own importance and with the importance of their personal opinions. They are lazy, cowardly and clannish. They seldom, if ever, get out of Saigon, and they spend their time in hotel bars lapping up gin-and-tonics and interviewing each other. Their criticisms are carping, their judgment uninformed and unsound, their attitudes a product of fashionable cynicism and unconcerned ignorance. They are supercilious, arrogant, rude and thoughtless. They don't bathe often enough. And last but far from least, it is the newsmen—not the briefing personnel or the policymakers or, heaven help us, the President—who are responsible for all the confusion in the American public mind about the war and about American policy in Vietnam. No one yet has seriously attacked the entire American press corps as a mass of agents for the National Liberation Front, but it is virtually the only accusation left for the day when somebody really gets mad.

Arthur Sylvester, ex–assistant secretary of Defense for public affairs and Great White Father of all the PIOs [public information officers]—for whom the news (and, obviously, the newsman) is "part of the weaponry"—spelled it out during a meeting with a group of correspondents in Saigon. Morley Safer of CBS, who was there, wrote about it for a publication of the Overseas Press Club:

> Then he went on to the effect that American correspondents had a patriotic duty to disseminate only information that made the United States look good. . . . [Sylvester told the correspondents], "Look, if you think any American official is going to tell the truth, then you're stupid. Did you hear that? Stupid. . . . I know how to deal with you through your editors and publishers back in the States."

For the press corps as a group, there are other tactics, such as rumors of imminent censorship that are periodically floated always to be officially denied, of course. Then there is the counterattack proper, launched whenever some aspect of truth begins to reach too many people.

Let too many stories go out saying that anti-Americanism is the rule among Vietnamese, for instance; or that a pet fiasco like Revolutionary Development is in fact a fiasco; or describing the terrible slaughter being inflicted by American arms on the civilian population; or showing the vaunted progress in the delta to be a delusion if not a lie; or pointing out that the military junta in Saigon has little more support around the country than its guns (and ours) can command—let these stories begin to reach home, and the counterattack begins.

The ski troops of established policy—regulars like Sylvester and his minions, volunteer guerrillas like Joe Alsop, Henry Taylor and a dozen or so others—begin to lock and load. Frequently these friendlies will journey to Vietnam itself to stock up on fresh ammunition—a chore that rarely takes more than a week or possibly two; when they arrive, they're force-fed a VIP treatment that would aston-

ish a general. They get individual briefings, special tidbits, exclusive interviews, individual transportation—even, in at least one case, a special plane to fly the patriot in and out of the country. Back at home, they describe the progress, praise the policy, parrot the reigning opinions of the Saigon brass—and screech at their negative and immature young colleagues left behind to do the dirty work of reporting a dirty war.

One of the more dishonest, and irritating, aspects of the standard attack on the press in Vietnam (there must be State and Defense Department manuals on it by now) is that it's directed at the wrong people for the wrong reasons. Take for example the old standby about reporters who sit contentedly in Saigon and don't get out where the action is.

Those who confine themselves to the relatively safe, comfortable limits of the capital rely for their information on MACV handouts and their oral counterparts. These are the reporters who faithfully echo the official version not only because they tend to be personally inclined in that direction, but also because they aren't often troubled by confrontation with contradictory fact.

But it's the reporters who have been around the longest and who get around the most who are unpopular with local officials (and who are most respected by their colleagues). The reporters who make the establishment unhappy are the reporters who do just the opposite of what the establishment says they do.

The Saigon press corps is no aggregate of Jack Armstrongs. If your job in Saigon were to paint a nasty picture of the group, you wouldn't need to invent anything outright. There's the stumbling, incoherent 24-hour lush; the lazy reporter who does, indeed, spend all of his time in Saigon, writing about the rest of the country by picking the brains of others who have been there; the incredibly obtuse reporter who couldn't spot a snow job if he were buried in a drift; the ignoramus who (like a lot of American pilots) thinks black pajamas mean Viet Cong. There are the inventors who meet their deadlines out of their imaginations. There are the reporters who aren't reporters at all, but petty crooks who have managed to get and use press credentials to further whatever con game they're involved in at the moment. And there are the mentally unzipped, hiding and somehow making it in a vast asylum where only the abnormally sane stand out as kooks.

But all of them together are too few in number and too professionally unimportant to "explain" what's "wrong" with the press in Vietnam. The press corps' faults and failures are far more profound.

Of the 300-odd newsmen accredited on July 1, 80 belonged to the three American television networks; fewer than 20 of those 80 were correspondents. The rest were technicians. Another 40 of the accredited newsmen were Vietnamese nationals, employed by foreign news agencies as technicians or interpreters—rarely as reporters. Thus 100 of the 360 were not reporters at all in any sense.

Of the 60 dailies listed, 21 are American, including such esoteric entries as *Hometown Features* and the *Pocket Testament League*. Most of the dailies were represented by a single correspondent. Nine magazines were accredited, including the three newsweeklies, *Life*, *National Geographic*, *Flying* and *Adventist Mission*. Among them they have 20 registered employees. Another 23 accreditations were accounted for by photo and newsreel services.

Out of the total of 360, not more than 115 were actually American correspondents—and that includes the "tourists" on the list and the possibly ten or twelve correspondents temporarily out of the country on special assignment or vacation. There is still a fairly sizable press corps left, of course—but it's something less than the thundering legions of American reporters which are sometimes pictured over the tiny handful of soldiers and government officials in Vietnam.

The principal assignment of most American reporters now in Vietnam is to cover Americans at war. The heavy emphasis is on the American effort—especially the military effort—often to the virtual exclusion of Vietnamese affairs. Many reporters have neither contacts with, nor interest in, the Vietnamese, and spend their tours enclosed in a kind of American envelope.

A number of reporters I know—diligent, hard-working men who frequently risk (and sometimes lose) their lives covering military activities around the country—nonetheless spend most, if not all, their time in that envelope and have little interest in doing otherwise. It is here that the "old hands," the leftovers and returnees from the pre-buildup days, stand out from the newer arrivals. They have developed an interest in, and some knowledge of, the country. A few have even picked up a word or two of the language.

*Newsweek's* Mert Perry, a great, round mountain of man with prematurely white hair cropped close to his skull, took a 300-mile drive through the [Mekong] delta last summer with John Vann, a former U.S. advisor in Vietnam who is now back as a civilian employee of USAID [U.S. Agency for International Development].

The drive was an incredible feat; you can get ambushed on any three-mile stretch of road in the country. But Vann makes such trips regularly. He knows the country, has studied the incident reports for each sector, and knows his enemy—whom he regards with a kind of exasperated affection—from long experience. He knows what section of road is safe at what time of day (or night).

The Viet Cong, Vann claims, are, like all other Vietnamese, creatures of habit to a remarkable degree, and if you study their habits closely, you can do a lot of things you couldn't get away with otherwise. Besides, he says (quite correctly), you can't learn to know the delta by flying over it.

Perry, too, had valuable experience to profit by. When he returned to Saigon he filed a story whose basis was a comparison of notes he had taken on this trip with notes taken on the same trip the previous year. Perry's story (which *Newsweek* gutted) concluded that the much-heralded progress in the delta was arrant nonsense; that things had, rather, gone from bad to worse in almost every category.

It is unfortunate that other reporters don't have Perry's background; but it is also unavoidable. It is scarcely possible for a foreign correspondent to take a six-month cram course every time he gets a new assignment. But it is far more unfortunate that few reporters consider the lack to be important. For many, the war part of the story is quite enough.

With some, this tendency lessens as their time in Vietnam lengthens, as the country begins to get to them. They begin to see Vietnam as a nation—albeit a benighted one—and not just as a proving ground for opposing battalions of armed men and their weapons. For others, however, personal inclination and the heavy pressure to join, or stay with, the team keeps them pretty snugly wrapped in the envelope for their entire tours.

In a sense, the strongest pressure in that direction comes not from any agency or individual, but from the most elementary aspect of the reporter's personal situation: he is still an American in Vietnam, all political arguments and attitudes notwithstanding. It matters little that he may have arrived thinking U.S. policy wrong; he may even feel that the Viet Cong are probably as right as anyone else around. He soon learns that his ideas don't stand out in neon on his forehead, and that any given Vietnamese who might pass him on the street or observe him through a gun sight will recognize him only by the lightness of his skin, the roundness of his eyes and (in most cases) his inordinate size.

An experienced and usually competent correspondent in Da Nang, who had been with the Vietnamese Marines a number of times and liked them ("First-rate little bastards"), looked forward gleefully during the Buddhist crisis to the prospect of watching the Marines tear the Buddhists apart. Aside from that, he was simply disgusted that the goddamned Buddhists had gummed up the war machine—and that seemed to be the sum total of his thinking. If he had any interest at all in political ramifications, he kept it superbly to himself.

Still, most reporters decline to climb completely onto the brass bandwagon, and there are a few—in my opinion usually the best—who refuse even to trail along in its wake. These are the "negativists" whose frequently berated negativism really comes from having seen too much, learned too much, [and] talked to too many people.

These reporters get their stories from the people who do the work of American policy in Vietnam, as opposed to those who order it done: from the province rep who is too busy trying to get the fingers of the province chief out of his building funds to write rosy handouts—and who is too bitter and frustrated and despairing of the hopelessness of his job to have it in him anyway; or from the officers and men, from the DMZ to Saigon, who have grown bitter and cynical over the weeks and months of fighting for people who want, more than anything else, peace—and that at almost any price.

They get their "negativism," in short, from talking to people who have to cope with the reality of the thing, and who tend to use it occasionally in their speech. They also get it from things like past predictions of imminent victory made in the midst of imminent collapse. But one of the greatest sources is in the spectacle of responsible public officials blaming all their failures on the reporters.

Nothing the press can do, no concessions it can make short of professional suicide, will please the bureaucrats of power who clearly want the entire tradition of a free press dismantled and the concept repealed. Charles Mohr of *The New York Times* described last September's elections as the first fair and honest elections the Vietnamese people have ever had—certainly a piece of positive thinking at best—and for part of his reward read on his paper's editorial page a letter from Frederick E. Nolting Jr., former U.S. ambassador to (Diem's) South Vietnam.

Nolting castigated Mohr for implying that Diem's elections were not fair and honest—and then went on to charge the *Times* and its Saigon correspondents with collective responsibility for the overthrow of Diem, the subsequent dispatch of more than 300,000 American troops to Vietnam, and the casualties (100 or more deaths a week) which followed!

One spring day in Da Nang, as bullets slapped the air and ricocheted off pavement and houses, two American correspondents made their way toward the Tinh Hoi pagoda, command center for the Buddhist struggle forces. The Buddhists, whose press treatment the day before had not been favorable in their eyes, had already turned away several reporters. At the outer defense perimeter, one reporter asked the officer in charge whether he and his companion could proceed to the pagoda.

Without a flicker of expression, the officer said, "Yes. But if you do, I will shoot you."

There is in that scene the quintessence of Vietnam today and of the situation in which the reporter finds himself. Whatever else may be said of him, no one can call his job a simple one. And whatever else may be said about the press in Vietnam, the fact that The Other War still continues—after years of pressure, propaganda and intimidation from on high—leaves small but badly needed hope for the survival of a free press as we approach 1984.

*The author, who wishes to remain anonymous, spent 18 months in Vietnam as an accredited reporter.*

---

## PETER ARNETT: CORRESPONDENT REFLECTS ON VIETNAM, THE PRESS, AND AMERICA

*Veteran foreign correspondent Peter Arnett talked to a group of journalists in 1972 about his reporting in Vietnam. In the following transcription of his address published in* Nieman Reports, *Arnett candidly mused on journalistic bias and other fundamental issues of his craft. He also paid tribute to his mentor, the Associated Press Saigon bureau chief Malcolm Browne.*

*Perhaps the severest test of Arnett's journalistic judgment came on 5 October 1963 at noon in the Saigon central market. He witnessed the sixth public suicide by a Buddhist monk to protest the central government's political repression. Should he have tried to prevent the suicide? Arnett reflected on his fateful decision.*

*Nieman Reports,* March 1972

Mr. Arnett is an Associated Press correspondent. Following are excerpts from his address at the Pennsylvania Press Conference in Harrisburg.

God knows we are not perfect as professionals. To be honest, after eight years of covering the Vietnam war, after grinding out those thousands of words and seeing many of them build into big, black, bloody headlines; after agonizing over what to write and when to write it; after talking it all over with publishers and editors and senators and congressional investigators through the years—I am still not sure in my own mind whether what we did as reporters in Vietnam was enough or too much, whether we were neophytes or prophets, whether we performed the classic American press role of censuring Government policy or whether we botched the whole job and aided and abetted the enemy. And it might be argued that we never really satisfactorily figured out who the enemy was.

But if I am to be judged, better in the broad context of the American press tradition than the narrow interests of venal politicians or partisan colleagues.

Saigon, 1962. Vietnam then was just a problem in counterinsurgency. You could sit at a sidewalk cafe with an aperitif, ogle the graceful girls strolling down the Rue Catinat, and talk politics into the warm evening hours. No signs that Vietnam would become a word synonymous with ugliness, horror and butchery.

I was 27, a gadfly in the journalistic backwaters of Southeast Asia, expelled from three countries in an area where you have not really made the grade with Old China hands until you have been expelled from at least six.

And here was the cubbyhole the AP called its Saigon bureau, cluttered, smelly. Malcolm Browne was the sole AP reporter in Vietnam then. He was beating a two-finger tattoo on his old Remington the day I arrived, trying to complete the daily 700 words of copy we used to send them to Tokyo by morsecast—a far cry from the batteries of teleprinters tied in directly to New York that would eventually grace a much expanded AP Bureau.

Mal didn't look up when I walked in. I surveyed the cluttered room. A withered hand hung on a wall, brought back I learned later by our Vietnamese photographer who had been to an ambush scene. Browne had hitched it to the wall to remind visitors that there was a war beyond the casually luxurious life of the foreign community in the Saigon of the early sixties. Hanging below the hand was a bloodied water container picked up at another ambush. I wanted to leave.

Mal looked up and grinned at my queasiness. He introduced himself and tossed across a mimeographed booklet entitled "A Short Guide to News Coverage in Vietnam." He had authored it for the neophytes like me who came into Vietnam from time to time to assist him in his reporting task. What Mal wrote in 1962 applied up to the day I left late last year. Reading about the press problems in covering the Laos incursion, I guess it still applies.

"Coverage in Vietnam requires aggressiveness, resourcefulness and, at times, methods uncomfortably close to those used by professional intelligence units. You can expect very little help from most official sources, and news comes the hard way. Correspondents in Vietnam are regarded by the Saigon Government as 'scabby sheep' and treated accordingly. At the same time the Vietnamese people are friendly and agreeable, and private sources can be cultivated." That from the introduction.

Here are some Tips to Stringers: "Avoid the crowd. Newsmen and newswomen come to Vietnam by the hundreds, and there is a tendency to gather in bunches—in bars, in offices, on operations and so forth. One of the best stringers we ever had never went to the Caravelle Bar, never went out on a story with another person. Blaze new trails, and do it alone. The fresh story, the new angle, the hitherto unreported—these are the things we want . . . "

Here is Browne's advice on first aid. "Battle casualties often die from loss of blood. Belts, ropes and field straps make good tourniquets, and the experts recommend thinking of tourniquets first if you are bleeding heavily. Whenever flying in a helicopter try to borrow a flak jacket from the crew—two, if possible. The second one is to sit on. You won't be considered chicken. All crew members must wear them . . . "

Here is his advice when encountering the Enemy: "Carrying pistols is not condoned officially either by Vietnamese or American authorities, but American officers privately approve of the practice. Under no circumstances try to shoot it out with the Vietcong if you are alone. They also outnumber you, and generally pack Tommyguns. If you are stopped by the Vietcong tell them truthfully who you are and what you are doing. Don't try to throw away your identification papers—identity-less suspects are regarded with great suspicion and are subject to very bad treatment. If you are American and happen to speak fluent, accentless French you might get off with just a brief lecture . . ."

In those early days the war was just an aspect of the story. Like foreign correspondents in other capitals we were obliged to make the rounds of the diplomats, and here is what Browne said about that:

"A resident correspondent in Saigon is invited to three to five cocktail parties a week, sometimes more. It is wise to attend as many as possible because while the faces and the subjects don't change much the most influential people in town often go. People you can't get to interview any other way you often can nail down at receptions. Here are some subjective judgments of news value of the various embassies in Saigon:

"U.S.—Variable, the higher the official the more vague he is likely to be. British—Generally close-mouthed but extremely well informed. Excellent sources. French—Except for the ambassador (who won't talk at all) rather poorly informed. Deeply suspicious of the press, particularly American correspondents.

"German—Very good company, excellent press dinners, good on cultural developments but worthless for any other kind of news. Ambassador useful if German is kidnapped or killed, however. Japanese—Generally well informed and anxious to swap information with correspondents. Indonesian—Fairly well informed, extremely talkative, apt to be inaccurate. Korean—Friendly to press and well informed. Chinese (Nationalist)—Well informed but difficult to tap because of delicacy of its relations with Vietnam.

"Philippines—Poorly informed, mainly concerned with boosting relations with the Vietnamese Government. Cambodian and Laos—Cooperative, but not kept well informed. Indian—Generally well informed, good on news from Hanoi. Polish—Good parties, little information."

You could detect in that pamphlet the "probing, questioning, disputatious" attitude towards Vietnamese authorities and the war.

Were these guidelines adequate?

Working in Vietnam over all those years, I could never understand the drumfires of antagonism that reverberated about our reporting. I won't go into the gory details here, because in retrospect they were not important: You stuck by us; you published our material. And that was all that mattered.

The press did not send American troops into Vietnam and is not bringing them out. The official cries of anguish about our reporting was the classic syndrome of blaming the bringers of bad news rather than the news itself. The most famous example in history being Peter the Great, the Czar of Russia, who strangled the man who brought him the news of the defeat of Russian troops at Narva by the Swedes under Charles XII. We were never strangled, and thanks again.

Before making a few remarks about the War as I see it, and where it may be heading, I would like to mention the "new journalism." This is sometimes called the activist approach which is essentially determining which side is right and then becoming the advocate of that side. A journalism student corralled me last week in Urbana and brought up Neil Sheehan's article in *The New York Times* Book Review that American commanders might be guilty of war crimes in Vietnam. I was asked, "why didn't Sheehan write about war crimes when he was in Vietnam: why now, four years later?"

I bring this up because the intensity for the "new journalism" disturbed me. I am all for involved journalism, but not for the AP: we deal in facts. So I mentioned that I accompanied Neil Sheehan on some of those military operations he wrote about; I watched hooches burning down; I saw the civilian dead. I didn't write about war crimes either.

We took pictures of those burning buildings, we told of the civilian dead and how they died, but we didn't make judgments because we were witnesses, and like witnesses to robbery, accident or murder surely it was not for us to be judge and jury. I said my attitude might be broadly classed as objective, but I would prefer to consider it more experience, an intelligent approach to our craft. I said that the way I saw it, if we are to believe in popular decision-making, we have to believe in a responsible press that will provide the information upon which those decisions will be based.

Then how do you remain objective, or better, intelligent, about your copy? That is the test of your professionalism, to be able to observe with as much professional detachment as possible to report a scene with accuracy and clarity. I said it might be called a sense of mission and in the AP it must take precedence over national patriotism in war, regional propaganda or municipal boostering back home. If you fail in this professional detachment you become an advocate, a worthy enough mission but not journalism.

One example of my attempted detachment:

I stood one hot noon outside the Saigon market and watched a Buddhist monk in brown robes climb from a taxi and squat on the pavement. He squirted gasoline over himself from a rubber bottle and flicked a cigarette lighter. Here was a political immolation a few feet in front of me. I felt horror and disgust as his body blackened and puffed out like burned pastry.

I could have prevented that immolation by rushing at him and kicking the gasoline away. As a human being I wanted to. As a reporter I couldn't. This monk was one of many who committed suicide to dramatize the iniquities of the Diem Regime in Saigon. If I had stopped him, the Secret Police who were watching from a distance would have immediately arrested him and carried him off to God knows where. If I had attempted to prevent them doing this I would have propelled myself directly into Vietnamese politics. My role as a reporter would have been destroyed along with my credibility.

What did I do? I photographed him burning on the sidewalk. I beat off half a dozen Secret Police trying to grab my camera. I raced to the AP office, wrote the story and sent a radiophoto. It was on America's front pages the next morning. Three months later, mainly because of the monk immolations, the Vietnamese public unrest and the worsening war, the American Government gave the signal for the Army to overthrow Diem.

What will happen when the Americans leave? The South Vietnamese are doing most of the fighting now. If they kept it up they could hang on indefinitely. But this situation must be looked at in its entirety: compared to North Vietnam, the South is a fragile entity. It is vulnerable to political change; it is economically imperiled. The population is war weary. On the other hand North Vietnam is politically stable and has successfully mobilized the population for [fighting] us. The occasional rumbles of war discontent from the North are insignificant to the cries of anguish in the South.

So what will happen? The American withdrawal from the war will not end it. What it will end is effective American participation in a political settlement. The Communists have made it quite clear they will fight until a compromise is reached, and that will mean putting neutralists or Communists in the Saigon Government. I think the Communists will fight until that objective is reached, that they mean what they say.

I can see the South Vietnamese army after American withdrawal fighting with decreasing enthusiasm, losing control of one remote district after another, until the Saigon Government will have to make a deal or go under totally. Only then will the war end, and it could come in three years or come in ten. And I don't think it can be looked at as a victory for the Communists or the neutralists, or a defeat of America or the free world.

If there is any victory, it will be the victory of Good Sense.

## NOTES

1. James Reston, "The End of the Tunnel," *New York Times*, 30 April 1975, 38.
2. Charles Mohr, "South Vietnam: 'To Liberate from Oppression,'" *Time*, 11 May 1962, 24–28.

## FURTHER READINGS

Fawcett, Denby, Ann Bryan Mariano, Kate Webb, Anne Morrissy Merick, Jurate Kazickas, Edith Lederer, Tad Bartimus, Tracy Wood, and Laura Palmer. *War Torn: Stories of War from the Women Reporters Who Covered Vietnam*. New York: Random House, 2002.

Halberstam, David. *The Powers That Be*. New York: Dell Publishing, 1979.

Mecklin, John. *Mission in Torment: An Intimate Account of the U.S. Role in Vietnam*. Garden City, N.Y.: Doubleday, 1965.

# 6

## POLITICAL INTRIGUE

There would have been no Vietnam War without Ngo Dinh Diem, for he was the only South Vietnamese leader with strong enough nationalist and anti-Communist credentials to win backing from the United States. But Diem would not have secured power without the help of Colonel Edward G. Lansdale of the U.S. Central Intelligence Agency.

Lansdale was an agent for the Office of Strategic Services during World War II, with a specialty in "psychological warfare." After the war, he established a reputation as a counterinsurgency expert by helping Filipino leader Ramón Magsaysay put down the Communist-led Hukbalahap rebels. The Eisenhower administration hoped that he could repeat his magic against the Communists in Vietnam. The shadowy figure of Lansdale, pulling strings to support an anti-Communist dictatorship that he thought was a democracy, was immortalized in works of fiction. William J. Lederer and Eugene Burdick recast Lansdale as Colonel Edwin Hillendale in their 1958 novel *The Ugly American*. In Graham Greene's novel *The Quiet American* Lansdale was the model for the title character, Alden Pyle, a naïve U.S. agent.

Lansdale landed in Vietnam in June 1954. He built a constituency in the South for Diem, a fervent Roman Catholic, by procuring U.S. and French ships and transport planes to launch "Operation Exodus," the relocation of nearly a million Catholics from North Vietnam to the South. When a rival faction, the Binh Xuyen, challenged Diem's government in April 1955, Lansdale procured U.S. aid to enable Diem's army to rout the Binh Xuyen in house-to-house fighting in Saigon. To legitimate the regime (the Americans liked the trappings of democracy), Lansdale and other Americans rigged a South Vietnamese referendum for Diem in October 1955. Diem's henchmen intimidated voters and destroyed ballots for rival candidate Bao Dai, the exiled Vietnamese emperor who had appointed Diem as his prime minister. Diem claimed a 98 percent election victory and declared himself president of the Republic of Vietnam on 26 October 1955. His first official act was to renounce nationwide reunification elections mandated by the Geneva accords.

Familiar with American culture from his exile years in the United States, Diem was able to fool Lansdale, making the colonel believe that as leader of South Vietnam he wanted democracy and social justice, when what he really wanted was to reestablish a family dynasty in South Vietnam (the Ngos had ruled Vietnam in the tenth century). Diem's brothers, Ngo Dinh Nhu and Ngo Dinh Can, ruled the central provinces as virtual warlords and competed for rice exports and U.S. aid contracts. Another brother, Ngo Dinh Thuc, as archbishop, plundered the coffers of the Catholic Church.

Diem next turned his attention to persecuting Vietminh remnants that had remained in the South after partition. Anyone with a personal enemy or covetous neighbor could be accused of being a Vietminh suspect and turned over to the secret police. Torture was common. Corrupt province chiefs flourished by extorting bribes from innocent peasants. Non-Catholics were particularly vulnerable. In May 1957, Diem visited the United States, where President Dwight D. Eisenhower feted him as the "miracle man of Southeast Asia" who had smashed the Communist rebels. Lansdale's cache soared. However, when the Vietminh resurfaced in 1960 as the Vietcong and challenged the Diem regime, Lansdale fell into disrepute and was recalled by Washington, never to regain his former influence on events.

Lansdale's maneuvering in the background both instigated Diem's rise to power and unwittingly sowed the seeds of its destruction. The Buddhist majority viewed Vietnamese converts to Catholicism with suspicion because they had helped the French pacify the colony in the 1800s. The Catholics eagerly embraced the Americans as their new protectors. By singling out the Catholic minority for assistance, Lansdale and Diem signaled to the peasants that the Americans were in Vietnam to replace the French aggressors. Thus, by embracing his religious identity, Diem stamped himself as the puppet of foreign aggressors. The more U.S. aid and advisors he accepted, and the more he persecuted the Buddhists, the less Diem looked like a nationalist, and the more the Vietcong grew. The more the U.S. ambassador pushed Diem to temper his handling of the Buddhists, the more he resented the Americans' interfering ways (for he did consider himself a nationalist) and the more he lashed out at the Buddhists to demonstrate his independence.

The situation spiraled out of control for Diem and the Americans in the summer of 1963. Convinced that he had no option, President John F. Kennedy gave General Duong Van Minh the go-ahead for a coup d'état by Diem's generals, and a revolving door on the seat of power in Saigon began to spin out of control.

On 1 November 1963, the conspirators routed Diem and his brother Nhu from the presidential palace in Saigon, caught up with them the next day in the Saigon Chinese quarter of Cholon, and executed them. Minh led a triumvirate of generals that assumed power. On 20 January 1964, Major General Nguyen Khanh overthrew Minh and arrested four generals, but retained Minh as figurehead chief of state. Political chaos ensued with each regime change, because province chiefs had to be replaced with loyalists to the new leader. Each change weakened Saigon's hold over the peasants. On 7 August 1964, Khanh declared a state of emergency in South Vietnam, annulled the state constitution, and declared himself president. Shortly after, a coup against Khanh was narrowly averted. A civilian premier, Tran Van Huong, was appointed. Khanh, Air Vice Marshal Nguyen Cao Ky, and Brigadier General

Nguyen Van Thieu dismissed Huong and South Vietnam's legislative body, the High Council, on 19 December 1964. Under U.S. pressure, the generals reinstated Huong and promised national elections. On 18 February 1965, Khanh retired from the government. Dr. Phan Huy Quat became premier. A military junta took control in Saigon on 11 June 1965. Ky became premier and Thieu chief of state. For a time, it appeared that the two generals were able to turn around the war against the Communists. They promised nationwide elections. On 3 September 1967, Thieu was elected president and Ky vice president amid claims of voting irregularities.

Just as corrupt and self-serving as Diem, Nguyen Van Thieu, unlike Diem, was a South Vietnamese leader the Americans could manipulate. Thieu was totally dependent on the United States to protect his regime and was therefore ambivalent about his powerful ally, which eventually abandoned him.

---

## DAVID HALBERSTAM: DETAILED ACCOUNT OF COUP THAT OVERTHREW SOUTH VIETNAMESE PRESIDENT DIEM

*David Halberstam was widely regarded as the most talented and aggressive member of the Saigon press corps in 1963. Halberstam learned his craft by reporting on the civil rights movement in the South, first at the* Daily Times Leader *in West Point, Mississippi, and later at the Nashville Tennessean. The* New York Times *hired Halberstam in 1960 and assigned him to its Saigon bureau in 1962. Halberstam's questioning of official optimism about the war so rankled the government that on 22 October 1963, President Kennedy asked the publisher of the* Times, *Arthur Ochs Sulzberger, to transfer Halberstam to another bureau. "Don't you think he's too close to the story?" Kennedy asked.[1] Sulzberger refused and delayed Halberstam's vacation to avoid appearing to cave in to pressure. In 1964, at age 30, Halberstam earned a Pulitzer Prize for his reporting from Vietnam. His best-selling books* The Making of a Quagmire *(1965) and* The Best and the Brightest *(1972) chronicle the development of U.S. war policy in Vietnam.*

*New York Times*, 6 November 1963

Special to *The New York Times*—SAIGON, South Vietnam, Nov. 5—Plot and counterplot in a complex pattern of intrigue culminated in the military *coup d'état* in South Vietnam Friday.

The vanity of an ambitious young general, Ton That Dinh, appears to have been a key factor in the train of events that led to the overthrow of the Ngo family regime and the deaths of President Ngo Dinh Diem and his brother Ngo Dinh Nhu.

Buddhist dissatisfaction with the Ngos, which had long been simmering, erupted into demonstrations and violence during the summer and the climate was ripe for a coup. Generals who had been considering a coup at various times began to plan seriously.

One of the first allies they needed was Ton That Dinh.

Ton That Dinh, at 38 years of age, had risen meteorically to the rank of brigadier general. He owed much of his success to the fact that the Ngo family trusted him as it trusted only one other general, Huynh Van Cao.

The family gave Ton That Dinh a command to the north of Saigon so that it could block any attempt to overthrow the Government from that direction. Defense to the south of Saigon was in the hands of Huynh Van Cao in the Mekong Delta area.

Thus, when other generals who were disaffected with the Ngo family persuaded Ton That Dinh to join the plot, the Ngo family's carefully planned system of self-protection was left with a big hole. The Ngos did not know the hole was there, so great was their faith in Ton That Dinh.

Ton That Dinh shows the marks of vanity and driving ambition. He likes to wear a tightly tailored paratrooper's uniform, a red beret at a jaunty angle and dark glasses. Behind him there usually is a tall, silent Cambodian bodyguard. Newspaper photographers who take pictures of Ton That Dinh have always been warmly treated.

The dissident generals played upon his vanity to bring about his defection.

What follows is a recapitulation, as complete as can be obtained today, of what actually went on at the secret meetings of the plotters and the secret meetings of Government officials from the beginning of the critical period.

The Buddhists' discontent with the Ngo family, which is

Roman Catholic, became overt in the spring when the Government forbade the Buddhists to fly their religious banners along with the national flag. The Buddhists drew up a list of demands to remedy what they considered the Government's repressions. The Government promised action, but there was none.

The Buddhists began to demonstrate for what they considered their rights, and nine Buddhists were killed in one protest, at Hué. This city, the capital of the central region, is a strong Buddhist center as well as the see of Archbishop Ngo Dinh Thuc, another brother of the President.

The Buddhist centers of worship, the pagodas, then became centers of political as well as religious unrest.

Three generals began to plot in June, when the Buddhist crisis began to grow from a religious dispute into a full-scale political crisis.

One of the three was Duong Van Minh, known as Big Minh, who had a distinguished record as a combat leader, but who had been shunted aside because of Ngo Dinh Nhu's jealousies.

The second was Tran Van Don, a suave, aristocratic graduate of St. Cyr, the French West Point.

The third was Le Van Kim, virtually an unemployed general who was called by one military man the shrewdest of generals.

## GENERALS FORESAW CRISIS ON BUDDHIST ISSUE

These men felt that the Government was provoking a major crisis and that its refusal to meet some of the Buddhist demands was arrogant and self-defeating.

They brought in other key officers step by step. In all this early planning, Duong Van Minh's prestige gave the plot respectability.

The officers moved slowly and gained the consent of Gen. Nguyen Kanh of the II Corps, and Gen. Do Cao Tri of the I Corps.

They had no set plan and too few troops. Their main problem would be to get troops into Saigon.

The Ngos, however, had prepared a military structure to guard against such threats. Great emphasis was placed on loyalty among the high officers, particularly those in and directly north and south of Saigon.

There were two reasons for this:

First, a disloyal commander could turn his troops around and head up the highway and storm the Presidential Palace. Second, if other troops rebelled, then Ngo Dinh Diem and Ngo Dinh Nhu could call in their loyal commanders. This had happened in the past.

In 1960, when paratroopers had all but scored a *coup d'état*, they began negotiating with Ngo Dinh Diem only to find that the President had moved in tanks and loyal units from the Seventh Division.

The palace also depended on two élite units. These were the Special Forces and the Presidential Guard, with about 24 tanks. Their main job, if there was a rebellion, was to hold off rebel units until a loyal force could arrive.

Such loyal forces were the troops under the command of Ton That Dinh to the north and Huynh Van Cao to the south of Saigon. The latter, perhaps the most vigorous prosecutor of the war against the Communist guerrillas, the Vietcong, was known as the most political of the generals. He also had advanced quickly in the military because of his personal loyalty to Ngo Dinh Diem.

## THE DISSIDENT GENERALS HATCH A PLOT

In August the secretly dissident generals hatched a plot to circumvent the careful protection set up by the regime. They suggested to Ngo Dinh Diem and Ngo Dinh Nhu that martial law be declared and that troops be moved into the town from the distant areas where the three had supporters.

The three generals planned to stage the coup the moment the troops were in the city.

Ngo Dinh Nhu, however, had been planning to raid the pagodas with his Special Forces and the police. When he heard the generals' suggestions, he decided to work it into his plan.

He went ahead with the raid, but he declared martial law to make it look as if the army had forced him to take action and to make it appear that the anti-Buddhist move had enjoyed wide popular support.

Ngo Dinh Nhu brought his trusted general, Ton That Dinh, to Saigon and let him plan the raid on the pagodas. They were carried out Aug. 21, with international repercussions.

The raids were violent and they scarred Saigon's relations with the United States—the chief support of South Vietnam in the war against the Communists. The military, which had been growing progressively uneasy about the progress of the war, was angered further by the fact that the army had been used as a front for violent attacks on civilians.

After the pagoda raids, however, Ton That Dinh felt that he was the hero of the republic. In private he told other officers that he had "defeated" the United States Ambassador, Henry Cabot Lodge, who had arrived to take up his post just as the raids occurred.

"He came here to hold a coup," Ton That Dinh said, "but I, Dinh, have conquered him and saved the country."

Soon afterward, Ton That Dinh held a news conference. That conference, in effect, sealed the doom of the Ngo regime by opening the way for the dissident generals to woo Ton That Dinh. The generals played upon his vanity.

At the news conference, Ton That Dinh spoke of plots by "foreign adventurers," indirectly called the United States Central Intelligence Agency "crypto-Communist," and assailed the Buddhists as Communists.

Ton That Dinh was questioned sharply. He is a man with a quick temper and he became angry. On several occasions, newsmen—including Vietnamese reporters for Government controlled newspapers—broke into laughter at some of the general's accusations. This added to the general's fury.

When Ton That Dinh left the news conference he was in a

Ton That Dinh also had 20 tanks brought to his headquarters at Camp Le Van Duyet. Fifteen were used during the coup. All told, the plotters had more than 40 tanks and armored personnel carriers and they were a decisive factor in the showdown around the palace.

When these movements began, the security police called Ngo Dinh Diem and Ngo Dinh Nhu. They were reassured by Ngo Dinh Nhu that the movements were legal and part of a palace plan.

The coup came shortly before noon on Friday when the navy commander, Capt. Ho Tan Quyen, was assassinated while he was driving along the Bien Hoa Highway.

At 1:30 marines began occupying the central police headquarters, the radio station and the post office. Shortly afterward, the central police called Ngo Dinh Diem and told him the marines were there and they were not friendly.

Ngo Dinh Diem immediately ordered his military aide to call Ton That Dinh's headquarters. An aide to Ton That Dinh answered and the President took the phone at his end.

The President said that the marines were at the police station and told the aide to tell Ton That Dinh to send troops there immediately. The aide said Ton That Dinh was not in.

In the meantime, a group of high-ranking military men were having luncheon at the officers club of the general staff. The luncheon had been called nominally for a discussion of changes in corps boundaries.

At 1:30, Gen. Tran Van Don announced that a coup was on and arrested all of those at the lunch.

At about this time, there was some fighting between some of the Special Forces and troops from General Headquarters. The plotters forced Col. Le Quang Tung to get on the phone and tell his troops to surrender.

## PRESIDENT WAS DECEIVED ON LEADER'S LOYALTY

Half an hour after his first call, the President's aide again called Ton That Dinh's headquarters, and was again told that Ton That Dinh was not there.

In the background, according to the report, President Ngo Dinh Diem could be heard saying that Gen. Ton That Dinh must have been arrested by the other generals.

Fighting was developing between some of the Presidential Guard units and marines near the post office. Insurgent troops were also moving up on the Presidential Guard's barracks and firing.

At this point, the President and his brother began broadcasting on a palace transmitter. The first broadcast called on all division commanders and province chiefs to send troops to protect the President.

The message asked for acknowledgment and there was none.

As time passed, the palace receiver got messages from division commanders pledging loyalty to the military leaders.

The Presidential Palace became lonelier and lonelier. Ngo Dinh Nhu began calling the provincial chiefs to send irregular units to protect the President. The last of these messages, at 4 o'clock the next morning, called on the Republican Youth and paramilitary women's groups to move into Saigon to save the Government.

One of the insurgents' vital goals was to keep the Seventh Division from attempting to save Ngo Dinh Diem as it had before.

This division was to be transferred on Friday to the III Corps under Ton That Dinh's command.

Ngo Dinh Diem had ordered Col. Lam Van Phat to take command of this division Thursday, but according to tradition, he could not assume command until he had paid a courtesy call on Ton That Dinh, his new corps commander. Ton That Dinh refused to see him and told him to come back at 2 P.M. Friday.

In the meantime Ton That Dinh got Gen. Tran Van Don to sign orders transferring the command of the Seventh Division to Nguyen Huu Co, his deputy.

Nguyen Huu Co went to My Tho by helicopter, locked the staff officers in a room and took command.

Then Nguyen Huu Co called Huyhn Van Cao,[2] who, like Lam Van Phat, is a southerner. Nguyen Huu Co is from the central region and he was afraid Huyhn Van Cao would detect the difference in accent, but he did not.

Word of what was happening in Saigon reached Huyhn Van Cao in mid-afternoon, but he told the Seventh Division officers that Ngo Dinh Nhu had assured him this was a false coup and that the idea was to turn against the dissident element before they could act. Huyhn Van Cao, however, ordered one regiment and some armor to prepare to move if necessary.

By early Saturday, Huyhn Van Cao realized it was a real coup. When he radioed My Tho, Nguyen Huu Co identified himself and taunted him, "Didn't you recognize my accent?" Nguyen Huu Co then told Huyhn Van Cao that he had pulled all the ferryboats to the Saigon side of the Mekong River and that Huyhn Van Cao should not attempt to cross the river unless he wanted to die.

This left no one left to help the President and his brother.

By this time the coup was going by clockwork; the radio station, the telephone office and police headquarters were sealed off.

After Col. Le Quang Tung was captured, most of his Special Forces were through. Then the insurgents moved to seal off the Presidential Guard's barracks.

The fighting there was heavy and there was stiff resistance. The barracks were heavily mortared for several hours and then surrounded by tanks. At midnight the barracks fell.

Then Ton That Dinh began to plan the attack on the palace itself. During the entire evening, the generals kept asking the President and his brother to surrender to save Vietnamese lives. If they surrendered, the generals pledged, the two brothers would be protected and sent out of the country, but if they did not, they would be killed.

The President asked the commanders to send a delegation to the Palace to talk. The rebels feared this was a repetition of 1960 and did not agree.

It was reported that at 4 A.M. Ngo Dinh Diem called Ambassador Lodge. Mr. Lodge was reported to have told the President that he was concerned for the President's safety and would do all he could to insure that he and his family were honorably treated.

The coup, in the view of one observer, went slowly because the rebels made every effort to talk troops into surrendering to avoid killing Vietnamese.

The attack on the palace was scheduled to start at 3:15 A.M. with a heavy artillery barrage.

In the early morning, civilians watching the struggle from roofs noted the flashes of double flares that can be used in gauging artillery fire. At 4 A.M. the President's military aide called Ton That Dinh for the last time and asked for troops to save the palace. This time, according to the story, Ton That Dinh came on the phone "and cursed, using insulting phrases to describe the family." According to one source, he told the brothers, "You are finished. It is all over."

"I saved them on Aug. 21, but they are finished now," he said after the conversation.

Most of the real fighting was done around the palace by opposing armored units. One observer described the maneuvering as "two boxers fighting in a closet."

Atop the United States Embassy a cluster of staff members watched. Early in the morning one decided to go downstairs and tell Thich Tri Quang, the Buddhist protest leader who had taken refuge there.

"Reverend," the American said, "there is a *coup d'état* taking place."

The priest replied: "Do you think I am deaf?"

When the rebels brought in flamethrowers, the issue was decided. For the rest of the early morning, the tanks blasted at the palace. At 6 A.M., the firing ceased and then marines stormed and took the palace.

But Ngo Dinh Diem and Ngo Dinh Nhu were gone.

## THEY WAIT AT CHURCH BUT ARE ARRESTED

There are said to be three main tunnels leading from the palace but the rebels knew and guarded the exit of only one.

According to one report, Ngo Dinh Diem and Ngo Dinh Nhu escaped through a tunnel leading to a park north of the palace where they were picked up by a vehicle.

The vehicle, reported to have been a Landrover, took the brothers to a church in suburban Cholon where they apparently hoped to wait for rescue.

Armored vehicles were sent to the church where the brothers were arrested. It was reported that they had a large sum of money with them. They were placed in an armored personnel carrier.

When the news was telephoned that they were dead, Ton That Dinh grabbed the phone and made the officer repeat what he had said.

Then Ton That Dinh slowly let his arms fall.

At this point the others contended that the Ngos had committed suicide. One of Ton That Dinh's aides demanded how they could have committed suicide. The officer answered that they had grabbed a rifle from an enlisted man. Then Ton That Dinh's aide asked why only one officer was guarding them.

"Someone was careless," was the answer.

Then all was over. Duong Van Minh became chairman of the committee. Tran Van Don became Minister of Defense and Ton That Dinh became, as he had wanted, a major general and the Interior Minister.

The Government had fallen, the Ngos were dead and the military leaders had won all they had sought.

The war with the Vietcong, the questions of subversion, loyalty, poverty and religious conflict at this point became theirs to deal with.

# AN ANONYMOUS REPORT: POLITICAL INTRIGUES OF PRESIDENT THIEU

*The following* Newsweek *article showcases the talents for political intrigue of Nguyen Van Thieu, president of South Vietnam from 1967 until its fall to the Communists in 1975. Colonel Thieu commanded the attack on the Presidential Palace in Saigon during the 1963 coup d'état to remove Ngo Dinh Diem. Thieu himself came to power in 1965 in another coup on the coattails of the audacious Nguyen Cao Ky and, over the next four years, quietly outmaneuvered Ky to wrest supreme power for himself. During this interval, the United States confidently took over prosecution of the war, fought the Communists to a stalemate, and began its Vietnamization process of handing the war back to Thieu's Army of the Republic of Vietnam.*

*Newsweek,* 7 July 1969

Byzantine is hardly a strong enough word to describe the politics of South Vietnam—or of that nation's pre-eminent practitioner, Nguyen Van Thieu. Two weeks ago, to take the latest case in point, the South Vietnamese President carefully leaked to newsmen in Saigon the information that he was on the verge of making an announcement that would significantly enhance the prospects for peace. Among other things, Thieu let it be known that he intended to invite his Communist adversaries to join him in organizing nationwide elections next year and that, in the meantime, he would set up a broadly based "advisory council" headed by Duong Van (Big) Minh, a highly popular retired general. Yet last week, when the time came for Thieu's much-heralded pronouncement, he suddenly changed his tune and, instead, savagely lashed out at the foreign press for printing "groundless" reports.

Outside South Vietnam, Thieu's abrupt reversal was explained away as a matter of personal pique. The South Vietnamese President, so the conventional wisdom went, was furious at Mr. Nixon for having disclosed at a press conference that Saigon would soon come forth with important political concessions and so had clammed up rather than place himself in a position where he would appear to be doing Washington's bidding. In Saigon, however, things did not seem quite that simple. Rather, some experienced observers believed that Thieu, looking for a way to stall for time, had purposely leaked the details of his "conciliatory" offer in the hope that both the Communists and Big Minh would be forced to turn him down before he made an announcement. And that, as it turned out, was precisely what happened.

If, in fact, Thieu had acted out of Machiavellian motives, this would not come as a surprise to anyone who has observed his remarkable talent for political intrigue. When he became President nearly two years ago, the mild-mannered Thieu cast a far smaller shadow than did his flamboyant Vice President, Nguyen Cao Ky. Acting in his characteristically cautious way, Thieu gradually placed South Vietnam's most important (and coup-prone) army units under the command of officers whom he trusted. One by one, Ky's hawkish, northern-born supporters were nudged out of crucial government ministries and replaced by Thieu's own friends—men such as Tran Thien Khiem, the current Interior Minister, and Gen. Dang Van Quang, the chief of intelligence. Perhaps most important of all, while Ky went off on one of his frequent holidays to the seashore, Thieu announced the appointment of a new Prime Minister—an aging southern civilian named Tran Van Huong.

## RUMORS

As a result of all this, Thieu has succeeded in transforming the once-powerful Ky into a political supernumerary. Yet few people in Saigon believe that the South Vietnamese President will be content to rest on his laurels. "Thieu is like a man who makes his own orange juice," says one South Vietnamese politician. "He squeezes people until he's got all the juice out of them and then he throws them away." Currently, Saigon is full of rumors that the next head to roll will be that of Prime Minister Huong—one of the few men remaining at the top who is not a Thieu crony. According to the kind of logic favored by Vietnamese insiders, Thieu may find it convenient to have the Prime Minister shepherd several unpopular tax bills through the National Assembly—and then deliver Huong's resignation as a sop to the restless lawmakers.

But even if Thieu decides to scuttle Huong, he will still be a long way from controlling all the levers of power in South Vietnam. For in matters concerning war and peace, he must still consult with his colleagues in the South Vietnamese Army—and with U.S. Ambassador Ellsworth Bunker. Indeed, a large part of Thieu's apparent deviousness is explained by the fact that he is walking a tightrope between the hawkish generals in Saigon and the peace-minded Nixon Administration in Washington.

## NEW PARTY

So far, Thieu has managed to keep his balance. And recently, he has felt secure enough to move into the political arena and try to organize a new party which could compete with the Communists for mass support. Unfortunately, Thieu's efforts met with only meager success; late in May, he announced the formation of the National Social Democratic Front—an amalgam of six right-wing parties which together claim the active support of less than 5 per cent of South Vietnam's population. To make matters worse, it appeared that many of the South Vietnamese politicians who joined this new grouping had done so with little real enthusiasm. "If you don't side with the government," explained one of the politicians who signed up, "you are treated as an enemy—maybe even worse than the Communists. So we joined the President's Front. You know, it's better not to fight on two fronts at once."

For all its obvious weaknesses, however, some U.S. experts believe that Thieu's newly recruited Front may provide him with the opportunity to fulfill a pledge he made to President Nixon during their Midway summit—that is, to broaden the appeal of his government by bringing more civilian politicians into the Saigon Cabinet. But should Thieu deliver on that promise, it now seems clear, the result would be a government composed of staunch conservatives who—civilian or not—would be just as unwilling as the present crop of leaders to strike a bargain with the Communists.

## NOTES

1. John F. Kennedy, quoted in Neil Sheehan, *A Bright Shining Lie: John Paul Vann and America in Vietnam* (New York: Vintage Books, 1989), 366.

2. Name misspelled in original article—should be Huynh Van Cao.

## FURTHER READINGS

Currey, Cecil B. *Edward Lansdale: The Unquiet American.* Boston: Houghton Mifflin, 1989.

Greene, Graham. *The Quiet American.* London: W. Heinemann, 1955.

Lansdale, Edward Geary. *In the Midst of Wars: An American's Mission to Southeast Asia.* New York: Harper & Row, 1972.

Lederer, William J., and Eugene Burdick. *The Ugly American.* New York: W. W. Norton, 1958.

Lodge, Henry Cabot. *As It Was: An Inside View of Politics and Power in the 50s and 60s.* New York: W. W. Norton, 1976.

# 7

## NATIONAL LIBERATION FRONT

As revealed in the war dispatches presented in this chapter, most Americans went to South Vietnam expecting easy victory but soon gained grudging respect for the bravery, cunning, and dedication of their tough little foes in black pajamas, the Vietcong—the military component of the National Liberation Front (NLF). The Vietcong were remnants of Vietminh guerrillas who had fought the French in the Indochina War and remained in the South after Vietnam was partitioned by the Geneva Agreements in 1954. Forced into hiding by the South Vietnamese army (ARVN), the Vietcong rebels employed political indoctrination and terrorism to win support from the peasants while slowly building a viable guerrilla force armed mainly with captured U.S. weapons. In 1960, the NLF announced its "war of liberation" against the Saigon government. The Vietcong nearly had beaten the ARVN by the time the United States sent combat troops in 1965.

### STANLEY KARNOW: "THIS IS OUR ENEMY"—THE VIETCONG

*Stanley Karnow's expertise in Vietnam's history and culture was unique among U.S. war correspondents. Karnow served in the U.S. Army in the Asian theater during World War II before studies at Harvard, the Sorbonne, and the Ecole des Sciences Politiques in Paris. He began reporting for* Time *magazine in Paris in 1950. In 1959, he went to Asia for* Time *and* Life *and later reported from there for the* Saturday Evening Post *and the* Washington Post. *In 1983, he served as chief correspondent for the award-winning documentary series* Vietnam: A Television History *and wrote the series's companion volume,* Vietnam: A History. *Karnow won the 1990 Pulitzer Prize in history for his book* In Our Image: America's Empire in the Philippines.*

*Karnow wrote the following article shortly after the Tonkin Gulf incident, a minor skirmish between U.S. destroyers and North Vietnamese patrol boats. President Lyndon Johnson used the incident to cajole Congress into granting limited war powers to expand the war in Southeast Asia.*

*Saturday Evening Post,* 22 August 1964

Of all the difficult and dangerous crises facing President Johnson and the American people in the months ahead, none is more difficult or more dangerous than the endless struggle for Vietnam. The danger this month was as darkly clear as the headlines that shrieked of Communist PT boats attacking two U.S. destroyers, and of U.S. warplanes retaliating against North Vietnam. Extension of the fighting immediately raised the specter of massive intervention—and a repetition of the Korean War. To some this risk seems a necessary price for "victory" in Vietnam; to others the only hope seems to lie in withdrawal and "neutralization" of the ravaged peninsula. Yet the war goes on, as it has for nearly 20 years, in a no-man's land where there is no victory and no neutrality.

Monsoon heat drugged the early morning air. Two South Vietnamese Ranger companies fanned out across the flat grassland and scrub jungle 25 miles north of Saigon. On a routine mission to relieve an outpost attacked by Communist Vietcong guerrillas, the 200 men moved cautiously. They paused in a grove of rubber trees, then emerged into a field and headed toward a cluster of huts 400 yards away.

Suddenly, from all sides, the fierce rattle and clatter of enemy gunfire erupted. Men crumpled before they heard the noise. Others scattered. Lt. William Richter, their wiry American adviser, dived to the soggy ground. Looking up, he saw Vietcong regulars in green fatigues advancing for the kill. Richter leaped to his feet and ran for cover. But other Vietcong riflemen, crouched at the firing of the field, caught him in murderous crossfire. Bullets slammed into his thigh. He fell, crawled into the sheltering underbrush, and somehow kept going. For six hours, helped by survivors, he dragged himself back to Binh My, his home base. He was lucky; on the field beyond the rubber trees, 51 Rangers lay dead.

"They just lured us through a trapdoor, closed it on our behinds and let us have it," Richter later explained. "We were caught flatfooted and cut to pieces."

"The same damned story," a senior U.S. officer in Saigon grumbled. Different only in detail or degree, similar stories unfold week after week in South Vietnam. Posts are raided, officials assassinated, hamlets burned, towns assaulted. And they all add up to one gloomy conclusion: Despite inferior firepower and strength, the Communists are beating a South Vietnamese force of more than 400,000 soldiers backed up by nearly 17,000 American advisers and almost two million dollars a day in U.S. aid.

Everywhere the Communist offensive is growing hotter—and deadlier. Deep in the southern Mekong River delta, where half the population lives, Vietcong battalions are fighting fixed, daylight battles, ambushing large government units, and openly assaulting towns. In central Vietnam they threaten to push through to the sea and cut the country in two.

Around Saigon, where the military regime of Premier Nguyen Khanh has appeared unable to mobilize an effective anti-Communist war effort, the Communists dominate all but the principal towns and roads, and these are unsafe at night. In suburban Long An province, Vietcong units operate with impunity right under the noses of Vietnamese army battalions. A couple of weeks ago, for example, Vietcong raiders kidnapped 12 youths from a hamlet only 800 yards from the province chief's headquarters. "Conditions are miserable and getting more miserable," says a veteran United States official who works in the area. "We're getting our pants whipped and everyone knows it."

Even the sky is insecure. Vietcong bullets have torn holes in two jet airliners coming into Saigon airport, and more than half the U.S. helicopters that leave the ground are damaged by Communist fire. Barely three minutes after a chopper swung into the air out of Saigon one recent morning, the freckle-faced American sergeant next to me swung his 30-caliber machine gun out the door and released its safety. "Mister," he shouted over the rotors' din, "that's *North* Vietnam down there."

Carrying the war into Saigon itself, Vietcong terrorists are striking directly at Americans. Their lethal explosives have rocked a softball park and a movie theater, killing six Americans and injuring 70 others. Their frogmen blew a gash in the steel hull of the 9,800-ton *U.S.N.S. Card,* a helicopter transport berthed at a Saigon wharf. When Defense Secretary Robert McNamara came to visit Saigon, his schedule was kept secret, and he drove surreptitiously through the city, his car lined with bulletproof flak jackets.

Statistics reflect the war's mounting pace. Government casualties, the highest ever, now average some 200 killed and 500 wounded per week, and government troops are losing three to four times the weapons they take from the Vietcong. Last month U.S. casualties reached a record of 15 killed and 83 wounded. So far this year more than 100 American advisers have died in combat—as many as lost their lives in all of 1963.

By now the bland optimism of U.S. officialdom has evaporated—replaced by a sharp sense of urgency and the realistic recognition that the United States is in a dangerous predicament. Defense Secretary McNamara not long ago predicted American troops would be home before 1966. Now he says, "It's going to be a long war, and we shouldn't delude ourselves into thinking it's not."

So serious is the situation that when Ambassador Henry Cabot Lodge resigned last June, the job went to no less a figure than Gen. Maxwell Taylor, Chairman of the Joint Chiefs of Staff. As his deputy, Taylor brought out Deputy Undersecretary of State U. Alexis Johnson, the fourth-ranking official in the State Department. Since his arrival last month, Taylor has begun a vast reorganization of the American mission in Vietnam. He has put the formerly freewheeling U.S. military under his direct control, and has filled the establishment with experts studying everything from Vietnamese commerce to Vietcong motivation.

Rumors to the contrary, Taylor and his team are introducing nothing radically new to the problem. They are cool to talk of massive strategic bombing of North Vietnam. They're against shipping in U.S. combat troops, and they shy away from suggestions that U.S. officers take command of the Vietnamese army. "I know it doesn't sound very aggressive," explained a top U.S. diplomat in Saigon, "but our policy is 'more of the same.'"

More of the same means more money, materiel and men. Some 5,000 additional American advisers may be sent into the war. South Vietnam's army will be expanded by 50,000 men, and its economic and social programs strengthened by fresh supplies of fertilizer, medicine, schoolbooks and the like. President Johnson has extracted an extra $125 million from Congress for this "stepped-up activity." As McNamara vowed, Washington will provide "whatever is required for however long it is required."

But several experienced Americans in Vietnam are uncertain whether increased doses of material assistance are the answer. "You simply don't get greater output by injecting more input," says a U.S. official who has worked in Vietnam for the past decade. "The problem is qualitative rather than quantitative. We have to think about how we can help the Vietnamese to shape new attitudes, to give them something to fight for." Explains another American specialist: "We have everything U.S. industry can offer, but our Vietnamese are functioning in an ideological vacuum. There's nothing for people to pin their hopes to. We can't invent an ideology for the Vietnamese. Their own leaders must develop that themselves, and unless they do, no amount of money is going to solve this problem."

In Vietnam the United States is involved in a curious sort of civil war. Prompted by Communist China, the North Vietnamese unquestionably direct the Vietcong. Some heavy weapons are infiltrated down through neighboring Cambodia, and more than 10,000 Vietcong officers and agents, trained in North Vietnam, have been sent south. But nearly all Vietcong troops are southerners by origin. They usually serve in their home districts, using captured U.S. arms. Are they aggressors? To Saigon and Washington, yes. To many peasants around them, however, they are native sons and relatives returned, as they claim, to "liberate the fatherland from the American imperialists and their treacherous lackeys."

They are impossible to isolate. Modern U.S. technology counts for very little when the battlefield is everywhere, when the Vietcong blends into the peasantry and innocent peasants are too often considered Vietcong. In a letter to *Newsweek* recently, Vietnamese army Lt. Col. Doan Chi Khoan wrote: "The man who happens to come and tell us how to distinguish a Vietnamese Communist from a peasant will be our greatest benefactor."

In Saigon, all that was needed was a discreet hint to a Vietnamese friend, and I met Huynh, as he introduced himself, at a Chinese restaurant one recent evening. A handsome man in his early 40s, he was neatly dressed in an open-necked white shirt, tan slacks and sandals. We got acquainted over cold beer and the amiable, aimless talk that flows so easily in French. Did John Steinbeck still write, he inquired, and what ever became of Clark Gable? But soon we steered into Vietnam, and the distance between us, narrowed by trivia, quickly widened. As if abruptly hypnotized, Huynh slipped into oratory, and the casual conversationalist became a Vietcong preacher. "We want only peace," he declared. "The American troops must leave, and we will form a neutral coalition government to settle our own affairs."

Wouldn't that inevitably lead to a Communist take-over in Saigon? Huynh pondered a moment, then admitted that "yes, we'd probably have a socialist regime." Earnestly, almost apologetically, he added, "You know, we're not against Americans—just Americanism."

How about the terrorist attacks on American women and children here in Saigon? "Why not?" he countered calmly. "American airplanes bomb our villages. We are not so strong as you. Terrorism is a weapon of the weak."

So the war intensifies, and more and more people are killed? Huynh smiled faintly. "That's up to you Americans," he said. "We want peace, but we can go on fighting indefinitely. We fought the French for eight years and won. If we do not triumph in our lifetime, our children will carry on. We represent the people, and they cannot be defeated."

Invented by the Saigon government as a contemptuous term meaning "Communist Vietnamese," the nickname Vietcong has stuck, and now even the Communists themselves use it. Officially, it is the National Liberation Front, which claims to be a shadow government for South Vietnam, and maintains "ambassadors" in Cairo, Havana and the Communist capitals of Eastern Europe. On the ground inside South Vietnam its military commander is a veteran guerrilla fighter known as Gen. Bay Quang—his real name is believed to be Tran Nam Trung—who is based in the jungles of Tayninh province, about 50 miles northwest of Saigon. Its nominal political head is Nguyen Huu Tho, a colorless leftist lawyer, who spends most of his time in the security of nearby Cambodia, at a French rubber plantation where his cousin works. On visits to Vietcong headquarters within Vietnam, Tho drives to the border in a battered Cadillac, then walks the rest of the way.

But the Vietcong's "revolutionary base," as the Communists themselves admit, is in North Vietnam. Its real guiding prophet is North Vietnam's frail President Ho Chi Minh, the father of Vietnamese Communism. And its strategic master-mind is the brilliant, energetic General Vo Nguyen Giap, 52, Defense Minister of North Vietnam.

Although the Vietcong has suffered an estimated 10,000 casualties in the past six months, U.S. intelligence indicates that the movement keeps growing. On the ground inside South Vietnam, the Vietcong's gains are some 10,000 agitators, propagandists, officials and *canbos*, senior Communist cadres who keep a firm hand on all activities. Its backbone—about 25,000 regulars organized in seven regiments and 23 autonomous battalions—is concentrated in the southern Mekong delta and around Saigon, and stretches into the central provinces. The rest of the Vietcong is made up of regional troops, part-time guerrillas, tax collectors, medics, spies, couriers and even entertainers. (A U.S. officer recently captured a prisoner who turned out to be a violinist with a Vietcong "USO" troupe.) All in all, it has about 300,000 followers.

The government and the Vietcong are only poles. Both seek to attract enough of the country's 15 million inhabitants so that—to use Mao's well-worn analogy—their troops can move among the population like fish in water. In strength the government can penetrate and clear any region. But it lacks the manpower to hold areas, and it inspires few citizens to defend themselves in its name. Nor does the Vietcong—despite its claim to have "liberated" two thirds of the country and half the population—really occupy much real estate or arouse willing support. The guiding consideration for most Vietnamese is *Che Do Nao Cung Vay*: "All regimes are alike."

Yet the Vietcong clearly has the edge, for a mixture of complex, even intangible reasons. It has discipline, leadership, experience and dedication. It is flexible, mobile and, above all, it keeps the initiative. It can dazzle the population by its ability to strike when and where it wants. And the Vietnamese peasants, unconcerned with the finer points of democracy and Communism, will incline toward the potential victor. As a recent American-embassy analysis concluded, "whether they believe the government will actually *beat* the Vietcong is generally more important in determining their actions than whether they *hope* it will."

Vietcong initiatives surprise and confuse government troops, corroding their will to fight. Vietcong terror—"armed propaganda" in Communist jargon—is generally selective and calculated. A district chief in the Mekong delta town of Kien Long is publicly disemboweled to shock local folk into submission. At An Binh, a tiny hamlet near Saigon, the two teen-age daughters of an official are shot as a warning against helping the government. A bus bumping along a back road in Long Kanh province is stopped by a Vietcong squad. Two men are dragged off, trussed up and summarily beheaded

> The guiding consideration for most Vietnamese is *Che Do Nao Cung Vay*: "All regimes are alike."

with a broadsword. "They were police agents," the squad leader tells the trembling passengers. Nobody questions the statement. The bus chugs on. The bodies remain by the roadside, pinned with identical notes: "He betrayed the people."

Communist terror often goes to savage extremes. One night last month, a Vietcong battalion swarmed into Sung Hien, a district town some 50 miles southwest of Saigon. Its aim was to gain local favor by punishing an unpopular government Civil Guard unit garrisoned in the settlement. Instead of attacking the troops directly, the Communists went for their dependents, burning their houses and butchering their families. Among the 50 victims were the wife and five children of the post's deputy commander, and a reporter who saw the carnage afterwards described the bodies as looking like "charred stumps of wood."

Whatever their tactics, the Communists could not have progressed as they have without the help of bumbling by both the U.S. and Vietnamese governments. Sen. Mike Mansfield's Southeast Asia study mission found that, after seven years of sovereignty and over two billion dollars of U.S. aid, South Vietnam was worse off than when it began. "The pressures of the Vietcong guerrillas do not entirely explain this situation," it reported. "In retrospect, the government of Vietnam and our policies . . . must bear a substantial, a very substantial share of the responsibility."

Yet even as the Mansfield report was being written, the late President Ngo Dinh Diem and his neurotic brother Nhu were engaged in a crash program to build 11,000 fortified stockades—"strategic hamlets."

Traditionally attached to their ancestral lands, peasants were uprooted and forcibly shunted to the new settlements. An average family house costs $200 to build, but the government allocation was only $20. And surveying 1,500 families in Long An province, a U.S. Information Service team found nobody who had received more than $10 and many who got nothing. At tiny Ap Moi, with a population of 62 families, the bamboo walls were down, the hamlet council had fled, and the Vietcong passed through at will. The USIS team noted: "Evidence of overwhelming neglect."

Worst of all, the government has failed to protect people. Its legions can sweep through the countryside like beaters at a rabbit shoot. But massive, noisy maneuvers rarely provide permanent security for hamlets. Theoretically, the task of daily, static defense belongs to *Dan Ve*, the Self-Defense Corps. These recruits are poorly trained and ill-equipped, however, and the ease with which their posts are invaded suggests that many are Vietcong confederates. On salaries of $10 per month—when they get it—they are seldom eager to take risks. At Vinh Xuong, not far from Saigon, they live 500 yards from the hamlet and enter it only after alerting resident Vietcong agents.

If things were bad during Diem's days, they deteriorated after his death. General Duong Van Minh's new government fired all but 6 of the 41 province chiefs and shook up the top army commands. Gen. Nguyen Khanh again housecleaned after his January 30 [1964] *coup d'état*. These changes may have been necessary. But their haste and brutality disrupted already fragile authority in the provinces, and the Vietcong easily filled local power vacuums.

A Communist insurgency doesn't erupt overnight. It grows with the slowness of a coral reef, submerged for years. Such are the depths of the Vietcong. A group of Vietcong prisoners I saw not long ago had enrolled in the movement in the late 1940s, and literally had grown up in the Communist apparatus.

Nguyen Xuan, as he called himself, was typical. A slight, intense man of 37, he was a key propaganda agent in the southernmost Camau peninsula where he was captured last year. Xuan could recall, as a farm boy, his resentment against the French settlers who owned thousands of acres of rich paddy in his home region near the southern coast. The vague nationalism prompted him into the *khong chien*, the resistance, as his native villagers called the Communist Vietminh. "To liberate the fatherland," said one of their slogans, "start by liberating your own hamlet."

Like coral, the Vietminh chiefs were building from the bottom. Patiently they organized peasants, women, Buddhist monks and others into clubs. Xuan joined the "Youth Resistance League," and before he was 21 he headed a three-man propaganda team in the district.

Day and night, Xuan and his aides roamed the countryside, making the same promises to the peasants—land, health, prosperity. Xuan took the code name of Ba Cuong, "hardwood tree." At clandestine schools there were technical courses on organization and perplexing lectures on Marxism. But they were followed by promotions and elegant new titles, like "Sub-Sector Youth Delegate." Xuan had found his vocation. Even his marriage was appropriate: She was an official in the "Women's Liberation League."

In 1954 the French were encircled at Dienbienphu and the armistice left two Vietnams: a Communist north and Diem's south. For Xuan and his comrades, though, the crusade was unfinished. The country had yet to be reunified under Communist control. Transferred north in 1954, thousands of Vietminh veterans were training for eventual infiltration southward. Others, like Xuan, faded into the southern landscape.

All seemed calm in Saigon. Internal Communism has "disintegrated," declared Diem's government. His American military advisers concurred, and built him a heavy, road-bound army. As for counterinsurgency training, the U.S. commander in South Vietnam told a reporter, "We've translated the U.S. Army manual on guerrilla techniques into Vietnamese."

The quiescent Vietminh—or incubating Vietcong—had a superior handbook, based on its own experience fighting the French. It was General Giap's *People's War, People's Army*. In it Giap prescribed a protracted war of gradual, flexible stages: from subdued mobilization and small-scale guerrilla forays to larger, mobile operations and finally a classic offensive.

In the late 1950s, old Vietminh comrades emerged from underground.

As he had a decade before, Nguyen Xuan formed a village propaganda team. Orders came by messenger from a leader Xuan never met. His five subordinates, dispersed through the district, were unknown to one another. "We didn't take chances on security," Xuan explained to me. "If one man knew too much, he could compromise the entire setup."

Working deep in the jungles, Vietcong ordnance specialists assembled weapons. They brought out hidden Indochina War remnants such as U.S. Springfield and French MAS rifles. To these they added a primitive arsenal of ingeniously homemade equipment: Water-pipe shotguns that discharged rusty nails; crude tin-can grenades; barbed wooden spikes that could penetrate thick combat boots. For more modern material the Red guerrillas assaulted government posts and ambushed patrols. By 1961 they had collected nearly 14,000 U.S. weapons, including 600 machine guns and mortars— enough to outfit about 30 battalions.

But hardware alone doesn't make an army. The Vietcong needed leadership and training. The men for that task were the Vietminh veterans sent north in 1954. They were ready to return home. Communist drives in Laos had secured the mountainous jungle trails that lead south. Down trekked first-rate officers, non-coms and political agents—and they still come, at the rate of more than 300 per month. And over the past two years they have whipped the Vietcong into a hardened military establishment.

At its lowest level there are still the poorly armed peasant-guerrillas. District companies, better equipped, ambush convoys, attack posts, or enforce Vietcong tax gathering. The real elite, however, are the *chu-luc* battalions. "These battalions are good," says an American general in Saigon, "because their individual soldiers are good."

The emphasis on individuality is vital. Government troops think and function as units; the Vietcong fighter is a craftsman. Vietcong individuality and localism begin with recruitment. Government draftees are assigned to outfits all over the country, but Vietcong rookies, whether induced or coerced into joining, are usually kept on their native ground. The Vietcong partisan thus feels he's defending his own neighborhood. And he has known the terrain and people since childhood.

In training, too, the stress is on local affairs. Vietcong battalions recently organized south of Saigon, for instance, were marched back and forth across their province eight times to make sure they knew the topography. Since guns are more valuable than men, Vietcong arms instruction accents individual responsibility. A Vietcong machine-gunner guards his weapon with his life, and he doesn't waste ammunition. "Listen to Vietcong and government troops shooting automatic weapons, and you know who's who," explained an experienced American colonel. "With U.S. industry behind him, the government man just leans on the trigger." The Vietcong soldier's auxiliary gear also reflects thrift and inventiveness. They tailor hammocks out of U.S. parachute nylon, and make tiny oil lamps from perfume bottles. Their durable sandals are fashioned from truck tires.

From recent successes and stepped-up North Vietnamese shipments, however, Vietcong stores are growing more modern. They now have Red Chinese 81-mm. mortars and 75-mm. recoilless rifles. But the standard Vietcong weapons are still captured U.S. carbines, Garand rifles, BARs [Browning automatic rifles], and a powerful sprinkling of 57-mm. recoilless rifles and 60-mm. mortars. The reason for their preference for American equipment is obvious. Ammunition and spare parts are available at the nearest government post or around the next bend in the road. Says one U.S. adviser in the area: "I wish they were on our side."

Among other ailments, our side is crippled by anemic leadership. Government troops, as tough and resilient as their Vietcong cousins, are commanded largely by mediocrities. Fearful of a military revolt, Diem weeded out dynamic officers, and only the weakest thrived. A high-school diploma is still the prerequisite for a commission in the government army. This automatically narrows the potential officer pool to a thin layer of upper-class city boys. Their focus is on Saigon, where life is gay, and friends, relatives or political connections bring promotions. Like officers in other Asian armies, they often have civil servants' mentalities, putting a premium on survival at the expense of victory. In a way, too, their combat shyness inadvertently results from U.S. aid. Time and again—and over the pleas of his American adviser—a government officer nettled by Vietcong snipers will stop his column and call for a cannonade.

"We've thrown in helicopters, aircraft, artillery," says an American officer, "and with each new machine the ante goes up. Nobody wants to fight because some new gadget is supposed to be coming along to win the war painlessly. But war isn't painless."

## NEW RED REGIMENTS

Following the famous Giap timetable, larger Vietcong forces now are inching from guerrilla hits over the threshold into "mobile" operations. Intelligence sources have already identified seven Vietcong regimental organizations, each composed of three 500-man battalions, most of them stationed north of Saigon up to the 17th parallel [the border between North and South Vietnam]. Some military analysts believe that they may be used in large-scale strikes, such as a major assault on the central Vietnamese city of Hué—an operation which, if successful, would shatter the prestige of the Saigon regime. Other military experts doubt, however, that the Vietcong will ever phase into the stage of conventional warfare. American military muscle in the Far East, they say, precludes the probability of a classic climax, another Dienbienphu.

General Giap seems to have altered his master plan. Instead of the great conflagration that ousted the French, he is starting an array of lesser brush-fire wars from central Laos down to South Vietnam's Mekong delta. By slow means he hopes to exhaust and frustrate the war-weary Vietnamese, Washington, and U.S. public opinion. As Giap put it, the enemy "does not possess . . . the psychological and political means to fight a long, drawn-out war."

Recognizing this peril, former Ambassador Lodge said not long ago that the major American adversary in Vietnam is "impatience back home." More serious at the moment, however, is the inability of South Vietnam's own leaders to pull their own forces together.

General Khanh's government, a mixture of military men and civilian politicians, has been frayed by internal feuds. Chief of State General Duong Van Minh, who never forgave Khanh for staging a *coup d'état* last January, has offered little help to the Premier. Other generals resent the fact that Khanh, their contemporary, was able to seize power.

Preoccupied with trying to hold his fragmented government together, Khanh has had no time to lead the country. As it has before, the spreading decay in the nearby countryside worries Saigon into dark talk of plots and revolts. Assorted army officers, ambitious politicians and others assert that, as one of them told me, "we can do the job better."

Another *coup d'état* could lead to the establishment of the neutralist government the Communists want. Its likelihood is difficult to gauge, but Khanh is clearly aware of the danger. He quietly shifts from one to another of his two Saigon houses, and he frequently changes cars to avoid identification.

The shakiness of his regime has led Khanh to a new pitch. In recent weeks he began to advocate a march on North Vietnam. At a Saigon rally commemorating the tenth anniversary of the Geneva accords, Khanh told a crowd of 50,000 that "the push northward [is] an appropriate means of fulfilling our national history," and he ended his speech with a shout of "Bac Tien—to the north!" A few days later his eccentric air force commander, Commodore Nguyen Cao Ky, went further. With Khanh's approval, he declared, "We must attack the north and even Communist China."

In several tense exchanges Maxwell Taylor tried to impress upon Khanh that escalating the war is not American policy at this time. Under pressure, Khanh reluctantly softened his stand. But American officials in South Vietnam are still fearful that Khanh might try to touch off a general conflict and then beg for massive American support.

Nothing has less appeal for the average Vietnamese than the idea of expanding the conflict. Weary of war, more and more of them are saying that "we don't care who wins as long as we have peace." What both sides are really fighting for is a position of strength from which to negotiate. The Communists already have a strong position so they constantly call for an international conference. More than ever the U.S. is striving to give South Vietnam the strength that would make an honorable bargain possible. The pessimists say the situation is deteriorating dismally. The optimists claim it is not degenerating as rapidly as it was six months ago.

But whichever reading makes sense, the United States can reflect on one disheartening fact: In Vietnam it has thus far failed to cope with its first major test in counterinsurgency. This whooping guerrilla-warfare fad of two or three years ago—its invocations of flinty American Indian fighters mingled with sociological theorizing—did not meet the real challenge on the ground. There will be other tests. And before the next time the United States must prepare itself and its allies more effectively to meet the ragged, fervent, defiant youth lurking in the jungle of a continent that is no longer so far away.

*Credit*: Reprinted from The Saturday Evening Post © 1964. Renewed BFL & MS Inc. Indianapolis.

## LEE HALL: CAPTAIN GILLESPIE'S MONTAGNARD SPECIAL FORCES UNIT

*The antecedent of the U.S. Army Special Forces that fought in Vietnam was a special U.S. Army unit during World War II nicknamed "the Devil's Brigade" for its proficiency in "black ops." The first permanent special forces group was activated in 1952 at Fort Bragg, North Carolina. Five years later, U.S. Special Forces troops were sent to South Vietnam to train the first Vietnamese special forces units. On 21 September 1961, President John F. Kennedy announced his program of increased military and economic aid for South Vietnam to fight the Vietcong insurgents. Kennedy was especially intrigued by the promise of "counterinsurgency" techniques to defeat Communist "wars of liberation" and looked to the Special Forces for a new impetus to defeat the Vietcong. By his authorization, the U.S. Special Forces began wearing their distinctive headgear, the green beret.*

*Whereas the main thrust of the U.S. military aid to the South Vietnamese was main-force conventional units, the Green Berets concentrated on building irregular civilian defense groups—hamlet militias, mountain scouts, and counterinsurgency squads comprised primarily of Montagnards, a mountain tribe of the central highlands. The tribesmen were valued for their fighting qualities and wilderness savvy, but were ethnically shunned by the Vietnamese. Because of the notoriously bad relations between the Montagnards and the Vietnamese, it was common for South Vietnamese Special Forces commanders to defer during combat to their U.S. advisors. The special forces were considered most effective at neutralizing Vietcong influence among the rural peasants. However, they often were assigned incompatible duties. Because the special forces units were known as the best fighters in the army, the South Vietnamese generals tended to squander them as main-force units in large engagements with the Vietcong.*

*The friction between Montagnards and their South Vietnamese commanders exploded into a general uprising among five special forces camps on 19–20 September 1964 in the central highlands along the Laotian and Cambodian borders. The Montagnard troops kidnapped their Vietnamese overseers, killed many of them, and mounted an insurrection against the Saigon government. The rebelling Montagnards eventually returned to their camps. The only camp that did not join the insurrection was Buon Brieng because of the cool-headed leadership of its U.S. commander, Captain Vernon P. Gillespie Jr. Life magazine correspondent Lee Hall filed the following profile of Gillespie, photographed by Larry Burrows, shortly after his heroics at Buon Brieng.*

*Life*, 27 November 1964

Buon Brieng—For a moment, Special Forces Captain Vernon Gillespie Jr. stood alone, rifle crooked in his arm, quickly surveying a clearing deep in the South Vietnamese jungle. Then, as the clatter of the helicopter which had put us down died away, Gillespie raised his right arm. Small, tough troops in black-and-brown camouflage uniforms—125 in number, including their own officers and noncoms—slid swiftly through high grass into the clearing. At the clearing's edge Gillespie jerked up his arm again in the move-out sign and we all moved into the jungle.

The patrol headed west toward the high jungle, which touches the Cambodian border and is controlled by the Communist Vietcong. Perhaps 3,000 V.C.s roamed the immediate area through which the patrol passed. Gillespie's mission: to seek out and destroy any Vietcong contacted, look for refugees, destroy crops in the area.

In Saigon our high officials call Americans like Gillespie and his 12-man Special Forces team "advisers." It is possibly the most inaccurate description since the Chinese Communists were termed "agrarian reformers." The 31-year-old Gillespie, a tough, outspoken 6-footer, is in fact the leader of a battalion of highly trained *Montagnard* strike-force troops—"Yards," as he affectionately calls the fierce, dark-skinned mountain tribesmen. They in turn, officers and enlisted men alike, not only admire and respect their towheaded "dai-uy," or captain, but superstitiously treat all Americans serving with him as talismans—nothing can go far wrong so long as they are safe.

The jungle growth thickened; trails narrowed, then disappeared completely in spiky vines that shredded the point men's trousers from ankle to groin. The jungle pressed so closely that Vietcong soldiers could fire from three feet away without being seen.

Although they carried rifles, carbines, M-79 grenade launchers and Browning automatic rifles almost as tall as themselves, the *Montagnards* moved lightly. Soon we spotted the V.C.s' *punji* stakes—pieces of bamboo about as long as a Tinker Toy stick, but sharpened at both ends and covered with human excrement as a crude poison. Almost invisible in the matted jungle floor they stood slanting toward the trail. They will slice right through a boot.

Three hours later Gillespie took out his compass and consulted briefly with his two Special Forces teammates, Sgt. Lowell Stevens and Sp. 5 Ricardo Davis. "We should be close to a V.C. contact area now," he said. Cautiously the patrol moved onto a small field.

A hurried whisper passed back to the column's center and Gillespie took off running for the point of the column, the troops racing after him shouting their strange animal-like battle cry—"Ur! Ur!"—and came upon two surprised men sitting on a log eating a hot lunch of rice and peppers, their rifles hung carelessly on a tree. The two gave up at once. Items found in their clothing and packs indicated both were connected with the V.C. Squatting, Gillespie began, through an interpreter, to question the younger prisoner, a flat-faced, light-skinned man in his 20s who wore a Vietnamese copy of a U.S. Army fatigue cap.

"I can tell from your face that you are a *Montagnard*," Gillespie told him. "We do not want *Montagnards* fighting and killing *Montagnards*. You should be brothers. Show us where we can find the Vietcong and you can come back to our camp with us . . . but first we must be finished with the V.C. Where are they?"

The prisoner listened, then said slowly, "I will show you our jungle camp. You must follow the trail over there." Leaving half the company to cut down the rice in the field so it would not be harvested by the V.C., Gillespie led the patrol, almost at a trot, a mile and a half down a twisting path lined with hundreds of *punji* stakes. Then safeties clicked on rifles and the battle cry sounded again. Followed by Stevens and

Davis, Gillespie ran up front. Topping a steep slope, he came upon the jungle camp. Men were rushing out of four huts, their hands up in surrender.

In five minutes, the camp was secured. Ten men of fighting age stood in front of the largest hut. A pile of weapons lay in front of it. Not a shot had been fired and everyone breathed easier. Then, from about a mile away, came three quick carbine shots, fired to warn V.C. of the patrol's presence. "Damn, someone's bugged out," Gillespie yelled. A platoon hurried off in the direction of the shots, but returned empty-handed.

From one of the other huts, three brown-skinned girls appeared. These were "joy girls," here to give V.C. couriers pleasure as they stopped by on their way south.

Seven of the men Gillespie questioned admitted that they belonged to the Vietcong, and further search turned up a captured M-1 carbine made by a division of General Motors in World War II, a French rifle, an American Springfield, three U.S. grenades and a supply of American-made ammunition.

This was an important V.C. camp, a fact verified as Gillespie burrowed into a brown canvas knapsack left by one of the escaped V.C. First he pulled out a Vietcong uniform—saggy black cotton shirt and trousers—a 3×4–foot blue and red Vietcong flag and a bright red banner with a hammer and sickle sewn crudely in the center—the latter probably a guidon for a V.C. company in parades in the larger camps. The pack also produced a wad of documents and the final prize of the day: a ragged Vietcong songbook. It had English titles at the bottom of each page—among them *Praise God from Whom All Blessings Flow*, *When I Survey the Wondrous Cross* and *What Can Wash Away My Sin?*—but Vietcong lyrics had been substituted.

"All we need now is an organ," said Gillespie.

Gillespie paced restlessly while the troops ate dinner, fretting about a possible V.C. attack. After dinner most soldiers not on perimeter guard quickly slung their jungle hammocks and slept, rifles beside them. Gillespie sat finally beside a small fire and put his rice on to boil, flavoring it with dried monkey meat found in the camp.

"You know", he mused, with his gift for analogy . . . , "South Vietnam is like this pot. You can put a bigger lid on it, but it will still boil and eventually the pressure inside will blow the lid off. Unless we can take away the fire we're going to lose. I've got a lovely wife and two sons back on Okinawa, but this is the second tour I've served back here, trying to figure out if there isn't a way we can win."

The next morning the company turned out at first light, and penicillin syringes were poked into the rear ends of the "Yards" who had been stuck by *punjis*. After a quick breakfast, Gillespie ordered the camp set afire. As we moved out, burning bamboo hut supports popped like gunfire—"We don't want the V.C. using it again," said Gillespie. The 16 older people in the camp shouldered packs of their few belongings and joined the company. "We've got to get back to

Buon Brieng now," Gillespie explained. "We've promised these people we'll take care of them."

An hour's march from the burned camp, a helicopter sounded overhead and radioed to ask if Gillespie needed help in moving the refugees. Gillespie declined; with the V.C. controlling the area, a helicopter landing would be too dangerous. The patrol marched as fast as the refugees could go through the jungle. En route, Gillespie made radio contact with the base and arranged for trucks to meet us. "By the way," the base operator said. "Johnson won the election."

The news recalled to me another President whose words, written in rough crayon, I saw nailed to the Buon Brieng headquarters hut: "In the long history of the world, only a few generations have been granted the role of defending freedom in its hour of maximum danger. I do not shrink from this responsibility. I welcome it." Underneath John Kennedy's words is penciled a sentence which has become the motto of Gillespie's team: "God knows we tried."

When Gillespie re-entered Buon Brieng, his operation base 190 miles northwest of Saigon, he saw to the care of the refugees in the convoy and had the prisoners locked in a makeshift jail. Then he took a hot shower and shaved.

That night, men in Gillespie's team not on patrol or guard got settled down in the mess hut to the serious business of poker.

As the game heated up, Gillespie walked back to his hut. "I don't gamble, even for pennies," he said. "I can't stand losing."

Of what he has accomplished in five months at Buon Brieng, Gillespie is proudest of the 400-student schoolhouse, a tin-roofed, bamboo building that was to be dedicated while we were in camp.

Under tents made from camouflaged parachute cloth, the captain and his team partook of a traditional *Montagnard* "sacrifice"—a ritual enacted whenever an event of great significance has taken place.

A half-naked priest, bright in his ceremonial shirt, squatted between the heads of two newly killed water buffalo—their hacked-off tails placed above their eyes. Taking blood from the animals, the priest mixed it with rice wine from nine earthen jugs placed in a row. His honored American guests drank of the strong, rancid liquid through long, curving wooden straws. The priest ended the sacrifice by giving simple brass bracelets, signifying the *Montagnards'* acceptance of the Americans as brothers. Then a plain stone monument was unveiled in front of the school, in memory of George Underwood, one of Gillespie's men, killed in ambush July 23.

As the Vietnamese flag beside the monument was raised to the top of its 50-foot staff, a strong wind caught it and snapped the rope. The flag tumbled to the ground. A *Montagnard* soldier pulled off his boots and, with perfect balance, climbed the pole and replaced the flag. Just as he climbed down, another gust again broke the line. *Montagnards* and Americans stood watching below as the soldier attempted a second repair. I could not escape the feeling that no matter how many times the flag came down, there would be someone to put it up again—and that one day it would stay there.

## CAPTAIN GILLESPIE TALKS ABOUT THE WAR HE'S IN

In every war, the front-line soldier has his own outspoken viewpoint. Captain Gillespie's views below reinforce those of the U.S. top command in Vietnam. . . . They are based both on what he has gone through and on what he has seen of the troubles of other Americans.

In South Vietnam there is leadership at the national level, but it's almost nonexistent at the local level. And this is all the people see—this and the American adviser. The adviser is directed to support his Vietnamese counterpart but has no power to make needed changes. . . . Even though inspired on his arrival in Vietnam and desiring to do his bit to win the war, he is too often beaten down by his own lack of authority. In a few months he is counting the days until his return home. . . . We could always bring in more advisers, I suppose, to relieve the situation, and we could spend more money. But I don't think you could convince any U.S. businessman that the way to sell more of a product which has no demand is to spend more money and produce more of it. I think he'd want to change his product to increase the demand before he put any more money into it. It isn't that our product is bad; it's just that it needs a few improvements. . . . By meeting the V.C. on their own terms, we may be able to buy the politicians enough time to come up with the reforms they've got to have to form a stable government. But we've also got to sell democracy on a local level to win. . . . It's like I tell the "Yards"—democracy is a big loaf of bread. If you try to gulp the whole loaf at once you'll choke and die. But unless you take the first bite, you starve to death.

*Credit*: © 1964 TIME Inc. Reprinted by permission.

## FURTHER READINGS

Asprey, Robert B. *War in the Shadows: The Guerrilla in History*. 2 Vols. Garden City, N.Y.: Doubleday, 1975.

Burrows, Larry. *Larry Burrows: Vietnam*. New York: Alfred A. Knopf, 2002.

Vo Nguyen Giap. *People's War, People's Army: The Viet Cong Insurrection Manual for Underdeveloped Countries*. New York: Praeger, 1964.

# 8

# NEWS MANAGEMENT

If one agrees with *New York Times* columnist James Reston that American reporters and cameras forced the withdrawal of U.S. power from Vietnam, then the decision in 1963 of Military Assistance Command, Vietnam (MACV), not to censor the press was perhaps the most momentous decision of the war. There had been precedent for wartime censorship, which can be defined as *prior restraint* or the prevention of communication. The administration of President Franklin D. Roosevelt imposed press restrictions on 31 December 1940, almost a year before the United States entered World War II. On that date Secretary of the Navy Frank Knox prevented the media from publishing, without prior authorization, information about shipbuilding and troop movements. Such prior restraint of vital war information was legal according to the U.S. Supreme Court's interpretation of the U.S. Constitution. What was striking about the situation is that the United States was not yet at war

Congress created the Office of Censorship by passing the War Powers Act on 18 December 1941, ten days after the United States declared war against Japan. Roosevelt appointed Byron Price to direct the office. In cooperation with the news media, Price's office prepared a set of guidelines for domestic news organizations, the *Code of Wartime Practices*, which took effect on 15 January 1942 and remained in effect throughout the war. The media were asked to conform voluntarily to the code, although the government occasionally threatened legal action to get its way.

Military commanders in the European and Pacific theaters of World War II censored the press far more severely than the code called for, especially in the Pacific, where reporters were totally dependent on the U.S. Navy for information and communication channels. General Douglas MacArthur required all news copy to be reviewed and allowed only positive stories to pass the system. Reporters were treated with less disdain and more cooperation in North Africa and Europe. U.S. and British military officials worked out a joint plan that assigned accredited journalists (numbering 500 by D day) and teams of censors to combat units. The supervising censorship board was housed in the British Ministry of Information in London and moved to Paris, France, after it was secured from the Germans. The Allied high command's Operational Memorandum Number 27, dated 25 April 1944, stated the goal of the censorship operation: "The minimum amount of information will be withheld consistent with security."[1] The Allied censorship scheme worked fairly well, although there were numerous complaints about having to submit copy in duplicate, which was difficult for correspondents at the front, and about sluggish processing of stories owing to the huge volume of correspondence. Undoubtedly, some stories were censored for their political rather than military content, particularly as U.S. forces and Soviet forces converged in Germany, but by and large the censorship scheme during World War II (1941–1945) served the purposes of the news media, the military, and the U.S. audience.

Press censorship during the Korean War (1950–1953) was a different story. Military censors were unclear and inconsistent about the rules, and friction with the news media grew. Reporters resented repression particularly of their nonmilitary dispatches, such as GI profiles and stories about South Korean civilians. Following the peace treaty at Panmunjom, the Defense Department developed a joint service manual titled *Field Press Censorship* and published it in August 1954. The manual was intended for use in future wars, although the U.S. Army maintained a censorship office in peacetime. The idea that military censorship should occur only in time of war gradually was eroded.

When the Vietnam War came along, the U.S. civilian government overruled the military censorship program and chose voluntary guidelines instead. The reason given was the logistical complexities of enforcing a censorship scheme in an undeclared guerrilla war; reporters had their own means of transportation and channels of communication and did not rely on military authorities (except for coverage of the air war). The real reason censorship was not imposed was that the U.S. government did not want to call attention to what it was doing in Vietnam.

In the early years, the U.S. role in Vietnam officially was strictly advisory. It was the Saigon government's war to win or lose. The Pentagon sought to downplay the presence of U.S. military advisors, who naturally attracted the attention of American field correspondents. This attitude was reflected in the Defense Department's directive of February 1962 to MACV in Saigon, known as Cable 1006. The directive's objective was avoidance of news reports that Americans were leading combat missions, when, in fact, they were. Various deceptions were employed to hide the active participation of U.S. advisors in enemy engagements. For example, U.S. pilots were instructed always to take along a South Vietnamese passenger on strike missions so the Americans could claim that they were only "advisors." Because of the official cover-up, numerous advisors wounded or killed in action were denied combat medals. The cable directed MACV public relations specialists to encourage positive news coverage of the Saigon government's fight against the rebels. To that end, they were to give "maximum cooperation" to the press to the extent that security allowed and to repress embarrassing facts, such as the use of napalm, a form of jellied gasoline. This contradictory assignment of cooperating with the press while deceiving it put the MACV public relations officers in an impossible position with the reporters. Friction was inevitable.

Though American correspondents uncovered ARVN battlefield setbacks and growing political unrest against the Diem government in Saigon, they continued to believe in President Kennedy's mission to stop Communism in Southeast Asia, but they believed that the deteriorating military and political situation needed to be corrected. For example, the most confrontational correspondent, David Halberstam of the *New York Times*, wrote so favorably about the ARVN during his initial months in Vietnam that the U.S. State Department commended his accuracy and fairness. Later, when things began to go badly for the Saigon government, and MACV increased its dissembling, Halberstam became their pariah. "We didn't have hawks or doves when I was in Vietnam," he later observed. "The war was a given. We covered the war. The debate was about the deceptions and the lies. It was all lies and lies and lies."[2]

Thus "news management" became synonymous with lying. The following war dispatches show the reporters' preoccupation with and resentment of news management practices by the civilian and military authorities in Vietnam.

---

## DAVID HALBERSTAM: MILITARY DIRECTIVE—AMERICAN OFFICERS TO AVOID CRITICISM AND REPORT WAR EVENTS POSITIVELY

---

*By June 1963, it was evident to the Defense Department that field commanders were leaking information about ARVN defeats. Defense Secretary Robert S. McNamara instructed the army to clamp down on its officers in Vietnam. A new policy directive was implemented that confined field commanders to comment to the press only on matters under their immediate authority and not to make generalizations about war progress. The directive went on to require all military personnel to put a positive spin on events and to avoid criticisms. Perhaps in violation of the policy itself, David Halberstam obtained a copy of the directive and wrote about it for the* New York Times. *The "recent dispatch by a United States correspondent" singled out by the directive as an example of "bad reporting" was in fact Halberstam's own report, in which he anonymously cited Lieutenant Colonel John Paul Vann, U.S. military advisor to the ARVN Seventh Division in the Mekong Delta region.[3] The Pentagon suspected Vann of leaking the story and reassigned him to Washington.*

*New York Times, 24 June 1963*

Special to *The New York Times*—SAIGON, Vietnam, June 23—United States servicemen coming to South Vietnam are now being told by their officers to give a more positive picture of events here to American reporters. They have been told to avoid "gratuitous criticism."

An official Army directive on the subject says, "As songwriter Johnny Mercer put it you've got to accentuate the positive and eliminate the negative."

The written directive was prepared in the United States to be read by officers to their troops. It reflects a growing concern over both recent reporting from South Vietnam and the attitude of many of the 12,000 American servicemen estimated to be here in support and advisory roles.

### TROOPS' ATTITUDE CRITICIZED

The directive quotes a team of senior officers just back from a tour of South Vietnam as having said: "The majority of the team was impressed by the careless and frequently erroneous subjective interpretation of fact, rumor and fancy by a large number of U.S. military personnel . . . these individuals quickly and gratuitously drew gross generalizations as to what was wrong with the country, the Government and its leaders and almost any allied subject."

"The bitter truth is that critical comments by indiscreet or uninhibited advisers are producing 'bad' stories which adversely affect public understanding of American policy in Vietnam. Continuation of this trend would unjustifiably weaken public support of that policy," the directive says.

The directive was prepared this month by the headquarters of the United States Continental Army Command at Fort Monroe, Va., as a briefing to be given to all servicemen going to South Vietnam. It has been sent to commanders in charge of men going overseas by Col. B. Miller, Deputy Adjutant General.

A letter from Colonel Miller says, "Indoctrination of military personnel on the importance of suppressing irresponsible and indiscreet statements is necessary."

The orientation speech outlined in the directive emphasizes that soldiers should not discuss major matters because "it is difficult for you to see the big picture."

As to bad reporting, it cites a recent dispatch by a United States correspondent about deterioration of the military situation in the Mekong delta region, where, in the view of high American military advisers, a virtual stalemate prevails.

A check showed that Army officials had taken the references cited out of context. Qualifying phrases were omitted to make it appear that the dispatch had been written about all of South Vietnam instead of the delta region alone.

The orientation speech comments:

"These quotations were not the result of a briefing or interview with a spokesman who knew the whole picture of our activities in Vietnam." It said the information had come from military advisers "who, though they may have been very knowledgeable about their particular patch of terrain and their own particular Vietnamese unit, were necessarily limited on the knowledge of overall conditions."

The speech refers to "well-meaning but nonetheless indiscreet advisers who no doubt failed to appreciate their uninhibited views would be widely published in this critical fashion."

Actually, the report about the Mekong delta that was cited was thoroughly detailed and documented specific troubles. The sources for the information knew what the reaction would be but felt the seriousness of the situation there warranted giving the information.

The orientation speech adds: "Your approach to the questions of the press should emphasize the positive aspects of your activities and avoid gratuitous criticism. Emphasize the feeling of achievement, the hopes for the future, and the instances of outstanding individual or unit performance and optimism in general, but don't destroy your personal credibility by gilding the lily."

*Credit*: © 1963 by The New York Times Co. Reprinted with permission.

## PAUL BRINKLEY-ROGERS: CONSEQUENCES OF REFUSING TO GIVE U.S. TROOPS ACCURATE INFORMATION

*For news on the war, American military personnel in Vietnam relied almost entirely on the Pacific edition of the military newspaper,* Stars and Stripes, *and the radio and television services of American Forces Vietnam, which were widely regarded as propaganda organs.* Newsweek *correspondent Paul Brinkley-Rogers contended that refusing to trust U.S. soldiers with accurate information about the war harmed the war effort and stimulated an active underground press. The satirical title of his piece was "Where There Is No Napalm."*

### Newsweek, 20 October 1969

The announcement by South Vietnam's Vice President Nguyen Cao Ky that the U.S. planned to withdraw an additional 40,500 troops went unreported to the troops in the field. Comic references to the war in Vietnam of reruns of "Rowan and Martin's Laugh-In" were bleeped out by a Stateside colonel before shipment to the American Forces Vietnam radio-television network (AFVN) in Saigon. An improbable vocabulary guideline for military reporters has been issued: "selective ordnance" is to be used in their stories, never napalm, a mercenary is a "civilian irregular-defense-group volunteer," operations that hitherto were search and destroy are now referred to as "search and clear," and Hamburger Hill is now "Hill 937."

In these and other ways the U.S. military endeavors to shape the news and information received by the 500,000 U.S. troops in Vietnam. Last week, for example, while Stateside front pages were full of accounts of the Oct. 15 [1969] moratorium plans, the story was being downplayed in the Pacific edition of *Stars and Stripes*, well buried on inside pages where most controversial domestic election and racial news is carried.

In theory, there are many channels the troops can turn to for news. Perhaps the chief source is the Pacific edition of *Stars and Stripes* (circulation: 500,000). Though the paper relies heavily on wire services and syndicated news stories, it does have a competent staff of civilian military reporters. Daily, some 127,000 free copies are delivered to the Vietnam war zones, where GIs can read such [conservative] columnists as William Buckley, Max Lerner and Evans and Novak.

### CONTROL

American Forces Vietnam radio, its producers claim, reaches 95 percent of all U.S. troops. And AFVN television is available to GIs in base camps near most major cities. AFVN is under direct control of Military Assistance Command, Vietnam (MACV). Post exchanges are also well supplied with paperbacks and magazines ranging from *Playboy* to *The New Republic*. But the PX manager alone decides which magazines will be ordered. No one opens a GI's mail, and many GIs get free subscriptions to underground newspapers—which may be confiscated by ranking career men who object to their antiwar bias.

In practice, reports *Newsweek* Saigon correspondent Paul Brinkley-Rogers, there are other, subtler forms of censorship. Indeed, the test for military news seems to be not whether the media tell the truth but whether they hurt morale.

For example, when the Ky announcement about the U.S. troop withdrawals was made Sept. 15, Sp/5 Michael Maxwell, 22, of AFVN says he was ordered by the MACV information duty officer in Saigon not to use the material. Later, Maxwell recalls, when it was announced in Washington that 35,000 troops would in fact be withdrawn, it took five hours before MACV cleared it for broadcast. "The only thing going out of here," observes Maxwell, "is what MACV wants going out of here."

"Military commanders consider us an outlet for their opinions," says *Stars and Stripes* reporter Bob Hodierne, 24. "They think we should be handing out the party line." Hodierne, who was drafted right from a UPI [United Press International] reporting job in Vietnam into the Army, recalls the flak he received for stories filed from Ben Het in July. "Every time the word 'siege' appeared, we got a call from MACV. They said siege means completely cut off, and since they were air-dropping supplies, Ben Het could not be said to be under siege." Adds *Stars and Stripes* Saigon bureau chief Pat Luminello: "My feeling is the grunt in the field is the Army and we are writing for him. We are not a morale builder." Luminello and his staff daily get some 1,000 press releases put out by individual outfits or commanding officers. "Many IO's [information officers] are considered personal public relations men by many generals," says Luminello. "For many career officers, a favorable mention of them or their unit is the best thing that can happen to them; they know their commanding officer is going to read it."

## TREASON

For its part, the brass claims that *Stars and Stripes'* coverage is antimilitary. "Most *Stripes'* reporters are malcontents," complains one officer. "If a guy wants to read anti-establishment trash, he shouldn't get it in *Stripes*." When Col. James Campbell was named by the Defense Department as the new editor-in-chief of *Pacific Stars and Stripes*, he quickly let it be known that he was displeased with the paper's performance. A flamboyant former UPI bureau chief and editor of the European edition of *Stripes*, Campbell said a story about a U.S. unit being battered in battle, written by Hodierne, was an example of "treason," and suggested renaming the paper "The Hanoi Herald." Such reporting, he added, "is of tremendous aid and comfort to the enemy." Campbell also complained that editors ran pictures of U.S. casualties, but never any of the enemy. The flap created by his remarks forced the Pentagon to withdraw his appointment as editor and instead assign him as information officer of the U.S. Army Air Defense Command in Colorado.

Yet the battle of the brass and the grunts goes on. Army clerk Kenneth Anderberg printed three issues of an underground paper named *GI Says* before it was shuttered, supposedly for offering a $10,000 reward for "the neck" of the battalion commander responsible for the assault on Hamburger Hill—that is, Hill 937—last May. Other GIs have commandeered Army field transmitters and set up pirate radio stations. Programs include acid rock and war news heavily studded with obscenities. But Luminello thinks these are only diversionary skirmishes. "AFVN and *Stripes* are the sources of news here," he says. "If *Stripes* is censored, then GIs are at the mercy of the military for all their information and their view of the world."

## NOTES

1. Memorandum, quoted in Everette E. Dennis, David Stebenne, John Pavlik, Mark Thalhimer, Craig LaMay, Dirk Smillie, Martha FitzSimon, Shirley Gazsi, and Seth Rachlin, *The Media at War: The Press and the Persian Gulf Conflict*, eds. Craig LaMay, Martha FitzSimon, and Jeanne Sahadi (New York: Gannett Foundation Media Center, 1991), 12.

2. David Halberstam, quoted in William Prochnau, *Once upon a Distant War: David Halberstam, Neil Sheehan, Peter Arnet—Young War Correspondents and Their Early Vietnam Battles* (New York: Vintage Books, 1996), 585.

3. David Halberstam, "Saigon Reported Avoiding Clashes," *New York Times*, 1 March 1963, 1.

## FURTHER READINGS

Carruthers, Susan L. *The Media at War: Communication and Conflict in the Twentieth Century.* New York: St. Martin's Press, 2000.

Dennis, Everette E., David Stebenne, John Pavlik, Mark Thalhimer, Craig LaMay, Dirk Smillie, Martha FitzSimon, Shirley Gazsi, and Seth Rachlin. *The Media at War: The Press and the Persian Gulf Conflict.* Eds. Craig LaMay, Martha FitzSimon, and Jeanne Sahadi. New York: Gannett Foundation Media Center, 1991.

Hallin, Daniel C. *The "Uncensored War": The Media and Vietnam.* New York: Oxford University Press, 1986.

# 9

## "POISON GAS" STORY, 22 MARCH 1965

Civilians frequently were injured or killed when they refused to evacuate their dwellings during pacification missions by the South Vietnamese army (ARVN). General William C. Westmoreland, head of the Military Assistance Command, Vietnam (MACV), decided to provide crowd-control agents such as tear gas to South Vietnamese commanders as a more humane means of coaxing the peasants from their hiding places. In December 1964, public relations officers attached to the field units immediately recognized the plan's potential for misinterpretation and informed MACV in Saigon. MACV press officers recommended to Washington that the ARVN's use of tear gas be disclosed to the American press, together with its laudable purposes. Washington refused on grounds that the announcement would give a propaganda opportunity to the enemy—a shortsighted decision, as things turned out.

Associated Press reporter Peter Arnett heard rumors about use of tear gas and went to MACV for an explanation. Having been gagged by Washington, MACV declined to respond. Arnett held the story pending further developments. On 20 March 1965, an incident occurred that became the vehicle for Arnett to break the tear-gas story. Radio Hanoi had been claiming that the ARVN and Americans were using "poisonous chemicals" and that a child had suffered a swollen face in a recent attack. Arnett spotted gas canisters being carried by ARVN troops going into combat. Arnett's partner, Associated Press photographer Horst Faas, snapped the picture. Arnett's illustrated wire story clarified that the gas used was nonlethal and perhaps more humane than other crowd-control techniques, but he also quoted a U.S. advisor who pointed out the potential confusion with poison gas of the type used in World War I.

The press immediately refuted the military's claim that crowd-control gases such as tear gas are nontoxic and humane. In fact, their use could be lethal to children as well as to elderly and infirm adults (see Chapter 11 for William Pepper's detailed analysis of the effects of chemical warfare on Vietnamese children).

As the MACV public relations officers had feared, Arnett and Faas's wire service story drew a firestorm of protests from all public quarters. The outcry included the accusation that the United States was using Asians as "guinea pigs." MACV's news conferences to defend the practice went unheeded. Because Arnett had used the quote about mustard gas from World War I, Chief Information Officer Barry Zorthian concluded that Arnett had intended to sabotage the government. Arnett for his part claimed that he was only doing his job.

As a result of the hue and cry, Westmoreland temporarily discontinued the use of tear gas, as well as other combat chemicals such as sprayed herbicides, until the story subsided. Use of the chemicals later was restored. The only lasting effect of Arnett and Faas's "poison gas" story was to make Westmoreland and Washington more inclined toward outright censorship of the Saigon press in the future.

## PETER ARNETT: REPORT ON USE OF TEAR GAS ON SOUTH VIETNAMESE CIVILIANS BY SOUTH VIETNAMESE TROOPS

*Having been expelled twice from Laos and once from Indonesia, New Zealander Peter Arnett already had a reputation for tough, confrontational journalism when he arrived at the Associated Press bureau in Saigon on 26 June 1962. "In Vietnam, the Arnett legends mounted," wrote William Prochnau, another U.S. correspondent in Vietnam. "He stayed longer, took more chances, and wrote more words read by more people than any other war correspondent in any war in history."[1] Arnett won the Pulitzer Prize for international reporting in 1966 for his Vietnam coverage. Some of his colleagues thought that Arnett had rushed too quickly to file the "poison gas" story, but, as explained earlier, he actually sat on the story for three months before releasing it.*

*Associated Press photographer Horst Faas was a perfect partner for Arnett; they did some of their best work together. The German came to Vietnam from an assignment in Laos and arrived the same day as Arnett. The two were given bureau chief Malcolm Browne's unofficial guidebook on reporting in Vietnam; its basic advice was not to believe official sources. Both took the advice. Fellow Saigon correspondent David Halberstam of the* New York Times *considered Faas the best reporter among them. Faas went on more combat missions and took more chances than his colleagues, but he survived the war, won Pulitzers in 1965 and 1972 for his combat photography, and in 1998 coedited with Tim Page, another Vietnam news photographer,* Requiem, *a book memorializing news photographers who lost their lives in the Vietnam War. Following is the "poison gas" story that Arnett and Faas filed for the AP.*

Columbus (Ohio) *Evening Dispatch,* 22 March 1965

SAIGON, Viet Nam (AP)—South Viet Nam's armed forces are now using non-lethal gases in certain tactical situations against the Viet Cong, a U.S. military spokesman said Monday.

Temporary disablement is the aim, to make the enemy incapable of fighting.

The spokesman here and the Pentagon in Washington issued statements after highly reliable Saigon sources reported U.S. and Vietnamese forces were experimenting with this kind of warfare.

Various types of gases have been used in action against the Communist guerrillas in the 2nd and 3rd Corps regions, a broad belt across central Viet Nam, the sources said. Some were believed to induce tears, others nausea, vomiting and loosening of the bowels.

As officially explained, the gas is released from dispensers operated by Vietnamese personnel in helicopters to obtain the same disabling effect as gases normally used in riot control.

The Pentagon's statement said:

"In tactical situations in which the Viet Cong intermingle with or take refuge among noncombatants, rather than use artillery or aerial bombardment, Vietnamese troops have used a type of tear gas.

"It is a non-lethal type of gas which disables personnel temporarily, making the enemy incapable of fighting."

Some of these experiments have succeeded, it was reported, but others have failed. The experiments are expected to continue.

The nature of the gases is classified information, but they are believed to be mixtures that include the universal riot control weapon—tear gas. One gas reportedly causes extreme nausea and vomiting; another loosens the bowels.

Effects of the gases are reported to be temporary only.

Both helicopters and fighter-bombers have reportedly been equipped to dispense the gases over battlefields.

One objective of this gas warfare is to immobilize the enemy quickly to permit the rescue of prisoners held by the Viet Cong. Several such operations have reportedly been held since last December but without result.

Another use for gas, military sources said, is neutralization of the enemy in tunnel areas.

Associated Press Photographer Horst Faas was on one such operation Sunday. Gas was to be used if the Viet Cong pinned down the attacking government force.

There proved to be a major shortage of gas masks. One tank unit had 51 masks and 116 men. Those without gas masks were given pieces of lemon and handkerchiefs.

An infantry battalion in the operation had 170 masks for its 400 men.

The Vietnamese troopers were obviously unfamiliar with the gas masks, Faas reported, and the masks were also too big.

As it turned out, gas was not used. Vietnamese infantry officers said they were hesitant to use it because their men were not familiar with it. But all agreed it would be a valuable aid in areas where the Viet Cong was dug in.

"It is a humane way of clearing out an enemy area where women and children are being held," one Vietnamese officer said.

U.S. helicopters have been used in some experiments spraying gas in powdered form or laying down a barrage of gas grenades.

Information sources pointed out that the use of gas is still in the experimental stage.

"Even if it does work over here, there are real problems of getting it accepted," a U.S. officer said. "The difficulty is in getting the American public used to the idea.

"Even though the stuff used here is non-lethal and has no lasting effects, the idea of it all brings back memories of World War I and mustard gas."

---

# PHILIP GEYELIN: OUTCRY OVER USE OF GAS PRESAGES POLITICAL TROUBLE FOR U.S. ADMINISTRATION

---

*To Philip Geyelin of the* Wall Street Journal, *the overblown controversy resulting from the trivial misunderstanding leading to the "poison gas" story was an omen that the growing U.S. investment in Vietnam would become a political liability for President Lyndon Johnson.*

### *Wall Street Journal,* 26 March 1965

Washington—If Washington's policymakers were ever in much doubt, they now have a grim measure of just how much support or understanding they can count on, even from fast friends, if the struggle in South Vietnam gets rougher, or even if it just drags on.

The answer, all too explicit in the current uproar over the use of riot gases against Communist guerrillas, is that already the U.S., for all practical purposes, is pretty much going alone. Officials had suspected as much, of course. So, in a sense, the current hysteria over "gas warfare" only confirms their fears.

Most officials are now hopeful that the outcry over the riot gases, like the gases themselves, will do no lasting harm and eventually blow away. But the real significance of the gas "crisis" is that it should ever have stirred such an uproar at all; that friendly nations and friendly peoples should have been so quick to misconstrue and so ready to seize upon even the frailest pretext to belabor the whole U.S. effort in South Vietnam.

What this suggests, at the least, is a very large gap indeed between the public pledges of support and the true feelings of a good number of Allied nations. It also suggests that grudging public support would give way quite quickly to open opposition, should the U.S. war effort in Vietnam really give the world something more than the use of riot gas to worry about.

Perhaps most important, it suggests that the U.S. has failed dismally in its effort to get across its own concept of what the struggle in South Vietnam is all about. If that's indeed the case, the achievement of any sort of reasonable political settlement, within the framework of a big multi-nation, international accord, is going to be even more complicated than many advocates of a negotiation solution have supposed.

For the lesson many officials are reading into all the scare headlines of the past few days is that the world is a lot more nervous than might have been suspected about just what the U.S. is up to, a lot more skeptical about the U.S. side of the argument, and a lot more eager for any kind of solution, however injurious to Western interests, so long as it heads off the danger of a wider war.

## THE FACTS OF THE MATTER

What, after all, were the facts of the matter? As explained here, they were that stocks of gas canisters, containing three sorts of commercially available gases, were made available to the South Vietnamese Army last year. In addition, the South Vietnamese apparently had supplies of riot-control gases left behind by, of all people, the French, who now are doing so much of the hand-wringing about the heartlessness of employing such materials. Local commanders, the story is, were authorized to use the gases, at their own discretion, but their employment was presumed to be most useful in controlling street demonstrations in Saigon or other cities.

What apparently happened, in the first instance, was that a local military commander, confronted with the assignment of rescuing civilian hostages being held by Communist Vietcong forces in a village, was struck with the thought of trying riot gas as a technique for springing the prisoners and capturing the enemy without civilian bloodshed. "The irony is that if he had ordered an air attack on the village nothing would have been said," comments one U.S. official.

Eventually, of course, word leaked out of this and several other scattered uses of riot gas; indeed, the local authorities apparently did not feel they had anything to hide. Result: A quick and almost universal conclusion that the U.S., as part of a planned campaign to "escalate" the war against the Communist insurgency, had turned to the use of gas. That was the impression, despite the fact that the gas incidents preceded the big Vietcong raid on a U.S. encampment at Pleiku in early February, which in turn triggered the U.S. decision to bomb North Vietnam and embark on a measured tightening of pressure against Hanoi.

That was also the quick conclusion, even though the use of ostensibly more pacific measures is precisely the opposite of what "escalation" is all about; "escalation" is aimed, after all, at attempting to persuade the enemy that the U.S. is in a rough, tough, resolute frame of mind, ready to raise the level of conflict, if need be, and certainly not the sort of paper tiger that goes around using riot control devices in a war.

Part of the problem, of course, was semantical. "Gas" is an ugly word; when used in the context of "war," it conjures up dread recollections of World War I. This is apparently so even though "gas" is also packed into handy spray guns and tucked away in automobile glove-compartments or bedside tables by the nicest sort of people for emergency use against hold-up men. And even though the strange, cruel conflict in South Vietnam—with its night infiltrations, its guerrillas doubling as rice farmers by day, its terrorism, its political assassinations and its subversion—could hardly be further removed from the stand-up, toe-to-toe trench warfare of Verdun.

Clumsy public relations, of course, was a big part of the trouble, too. Or possibly the real villain is the natural gulf between the military and diplomatic mind. In any event, spokesmen on the spot could hardly have chosen more awkward definitions of what was being done. The term "non-lethal," used to describe the gases, leaves more than enough room for speculation about excruciating pain or disabling effects. Tear gas would have sounded better, but would not have embraced the one nausea-inducing material employed. Somehow the latter category seemed more hideous, as if being rendered temporarily bilious is in some way more terrible than being rendered temporarily blind.

## LEADING WITH THE CHIN

When the use of the gases was described as "experimental," the way was wide open for the inevitable propaganda barrage picturing the Vietnamese as human "guinea pigs" for the Pentagon: what was meant, of course, was simply that a new technique was being attempted to cope with a new and infinitely tricky kind of war.

What makes it all the more galling to the diplomats is the thought that if the matter had been properly handled, with some advance preparation of the public and immediate disclosure of the use of the gas, it might just conceivably have been turned into something of a plus. At least that's the implication that can be drawn from some of the commentary that blossomed in the British press, once the facts were in. A commentator in London's *Daily Mail* was downright effusive in praise of U.S. use of gas, calling it "the first halting step toward something that has eluded mankind since mankind existed—a war that does not kill." Three other London papers found riot gases infinitely preferable to most other types of weaponry.

But the fact remains that most people, on the basis of first impressions anyway, all too evidently do not agree, and some of the loudest disagreement came from what might have been considered the least likely sources.

That the Communists should seize upon all this with shrill cries of Yankee barbarism is understandable enough; the whole thing was made to order for Red propaganda mills. Nor should the French reaction come as any great surprise, even though the French Army might be able to teach us much from their long, hard struggle in Vietnam and Algeria about disagreeable ways to counter guerrilla war. Getting the Vietnam struggle over, and the U.S. out of Southeast Asia, is the obvious objective of President de Gaulle. So the Paris press, more often than not responsive to the French government's purposes, could have been counted on to put the whole matter in the worst possible light for the U.S.

## ANY EXCUSE TO CRITICIZE

Much the same can be said about reaction in other areas of the world already hostile to U.S. policy and eager for any excuse to attack it. But this does not explain the extraordinary haste with which the West Germans leapt to the darkest conclusions, or the reaction in Sweden, for another example, or in Japan and Canada. "It's just been incredible," says one U.S. official whose duties oblige him to keep close tabs on the U.S. image overseas. "In countries that are supposed to be friends, supposed to be supporting us, opinion has been almost unanimous against us."

To U.S. officials, even with all that can be said about the special emotional impact of the word "gas," and all that can be said about the awkward public relations and sensationalized press reports, this can only reflect a powerful yearning, worldwide, for an early solution to South Vietnam, and never mind the terms. Firmly, U.S. officials insist they've never kidded themselves that world sentiment was otherwise, and certainly don't intend to permit the latest reading to influence their calculations. But the gas affair has given them the most unpleasant sort of evidence of just how alone the U.S. is in Vietnam.

*Credit*: WALL STREET JOURNAL by PHILIP GEYELIN. Copyright 1965 by DOW JONES & CO INC. Reproduced with permission of DOW JONES & CO INC. via Copyright Clearance Center.

## NOTE

1. William Prochnau, *Once upon a Distant War: David Halberstam, Neil Sheehan, Peter Arnett—Young War Correspondents and Their Early Vietnam Battles* (New York: Vintage Books, 1996), 108.

## FURTHER READINGS

Arnett, Peter. *Live from the Battlefield*. New York: Simon & Schuster, 1994.

Hammond, William. *Public Affairs: The Military and the Media, 1962–1968*. Washington, D.C.: U.S. Army Center of Military History, 1988.

Menzel, Paul T., ed. *Moral Argument and the War in Vietnam*. Nashville: Aurora Publishers, 1971.

# 10

## CAM NE, 3 AUGUST 1965

The myth that the Vietnam War was the first "television war" has lasting implications. Fostered by newspaper columnists and government hacks, the myth said that by bringing the war into American living rooms, television had sabotaged the U.S. military in an otherwise winnable contest. The reality was that the Columbia Broadcasting System's Cam Ne story was the exception that proved the rule—a filmed war report with graphic destruction and violence. Very few such reports got through the network editors in New York and onto home screens. Cam Ne was different, perhaps because it was the first.

Like most cultural myths, Vietnam as the first television war defied rational counterarguments. The myth was accepted uncritically because it explained how rebels in a small, nonindustrialized Asian nation could derail the omnipotent U.S. war machine. Having partnered in propagating the myth, the Pentagon parroted it as gospel in several fact-finding commissions after the war to rationalize new rules restricting the news media during combat. The public for its part believed the myth and happily approved the restraints; after all, the new rules were for the media's own protection.

More than any other television news story from Vietnam, the Cam Ne incident gave life to the myth of Vietnam as television war by revealing the emotional power of television magnified by television's audience reach. Newspapers had reported Vietnamese civilian deaths and displacements in the past, but the printed words demanded the reader's effort to bring them to life; the distance of their meanings buffered the emotions. The Cam Ne film was different; the moving pictures had direct, undeniable import.

When CBS News president Fred Friendly read correspondent Morley Safer's initial cable on 3 August 1965, followed by news film two days later (it had to be flown from Saigon to New York), he knew that the story was dynamite. David Halberstam later described the scene:

So Friendly and Ernie Leiser, the executive producer [of *CBS Evening News with Walter Cronkite*], and Cronkite, sat in a small room in New York City and watched on their screen film of American Marines setting fire to Vietnamese thatched huts, Americans leveling a village. It was awesome, the full force of television, the ability to dramatize, now fastening on one incident, one day in the war, that was going to be shattering to an entire generation of Americans, perhaps to an entire country.[1]

They went with the story, though they realized that it bordered on advocacy journalism and surely would damage CBS's reputation for impartiality.

The network got a flood of calls and telegrams from angry viewers, including President Lyndon Johnson, lashing out at CBS and Safer for portraying "our boys" as murderers. Safer's report actually depicted no deaths (he toned it down considerably from what he witnessed), but the image of a nonchalant marine setting fire to a thatched hut with his cigarette lighter, while the dwelling's helpless former inhabitants shuddered in terror, was too much to bear for a public that had been sheltered from the inhumanity of this distant war. Despite his considerable experience as a war correspondent, the scene shocked Safer, too. That American solders would so wantonly, so haphazardly, disregard the safety of civilians was new for him—a news story that compelled airing.

## MORLEY SAFER: CABLE REPORT ON AMERICAN ACTION AT CAM NE

*In July 1965, CBS News sent 36-year-old veteran correspondent Morley Safer to Saigon to cover the U.S. buildup announced by President Johnson. In August, Safer went to Danang to report on the U.S. Marine Corps contingent stationed there. On his first combat operation out of Danang on 3 August, Safer and Vietnamese cameraman Ha Tue Can accompanied a marine unit that had orders to destroy a suspected Vietcong stronghold south of the Danang airbase. Like most Vietnamese villages, Cam Ne was a complex of small hamlets. The marines crossed wetlands in amphibious carriers, approached the village on foot, and opened fire with rockets and grenades. No enemy combatants were found. The commander claimed that Vietcong snipers wounded two U.S. marines, but Safer thought that they had been shot accidentally by fellow marines.*

*Later on 3 August, Safer cabled his initial report on the marines' Cam Ne operation to CBS. The accompanying news film was flown out of Danang soon after and arrived at CBS studios in New York two days later. Though the producers of* CBS Evening News with Walter Cronkite *did not yet have the film on 3 August, the Cam Ne story led the newscast that evening. Substitute news anchorman Harry Reasoner's matter-of-fact delivery revealed the network's cautious approach to the potentially controversial material. A transcript of the 3 August Cam Ne report follows.*

*CBS Evening News with Walter Cronkite, 3 August 1965*

REASONER: Good evening. We received today a cable from Morley Safer, our correspondent in South Vietnam. It seems to us to be worth quoting directly. "I was the only correspondent," Safer says, "at today's burning of a hamlet by U.S. Marines surrounding the village of Cam Ne. According to a Marine officer on the operation, they had orders to burn the hamlet to the ground, if they so much as received one round [of enemy fire]. After surrounding the village," Safer goes on, "and receiving one burst of automatic fire from an unidenti-

fied direction, the Marines poured in 3.5 rocket fire, M-79 grenade launchers and heavy and light machinegun fire. The Marines then moved in," still quoting Safer, "proceeding first with cigarette lighters, then with flame throwers, to burn down an estimated 150 dwellings. Old men and women," we're quoting Morley Safer, "who were pleading with the Marines to spare their houses, were ignored, and the houses were burned with the total belongings of the people. Pleas to delay the burning so that belongings could be removed were also ignored. All rice stores were burned as well." Then Safer goes on. "I personally eyewitnessed all the above, but I subsequently learned that a Marine platoon on the right flank wounded three women and killed one child in a rocket barrage. The day's operations netted about four prisoners, old men. Two Marines were wounded, both by their own fire, although this had been denied." Still quoting Safer. "During the operations, the Marines were telling the people in English to get out of their underground shelters before they burned the houses. The people therefore stay put, causing several close shaves until pleas from this reporter," Safer, "that our Vietnamese cameraman should be allowed to speak to them in the Vietnamese language, which did bring them out of their shelters." Safer goes on: "The Marines had with them no official bilingual interpreters, only three Vietnamese troopers who spoke no English, and thus could not relay instructions."

That's the end of Morley Safer's cable. Tonight a Defense Department official commented indirectly on what Safer reported, and we quote what this official said: "There is no new policy of toughness toward civilians. Our policy is still to bend over backwards, even at possible cost of U.S. lives. All our troops," he said, "are constantly reminded of the need to protect civilians and win their confidence. The U.S. Marine Corps has made a special effort in the Danang area. They have resettled some civilians," the spokesman said, "set up dispensaries for them and lost a number of Marines killed just helping the civilians."

*Credit*: Reprinted with permission of the CBS News Archives.

## MORLEY SAFER: FILM REPORT ON AMERICAN ACTION AT CAM NE

*Morley Safer's film report on the Cam Ne operation was aired on the* CBS Evening News with Walter Cronkite *on 5 August 1965. The film images showing marines torching the village unequivocally refuted official claims that most of the Cam Ne huts had been destroyed in an exchange of gunfire with the enemy. Safer followed two days later with a film report that few of the marines had remorse, and all defended their "shoot first, ask questions later" policy.*

*Claiming that Safer had manipulated the infantrymen, the marine commanders banned Safer from their operational zone, but U.S. headquarters in Saigon countermanded the ban. Instead, the Pentagon tried unsuccessfully to get CBS to recall Safer. Friendly unflinchingly defended his reporter's integrity and stood behind Safer's Cam Ne reporting. Safer later learned that the marine intelligence report placing Vietcong in Cam Ne was concocted by the local South Vietnamese province chief so that the Americans would punish the villagers for not paying their taxes.*

*Following is a transcript of Safer's 5 August film report on the Cam Ne operation, which was introduced on the* CBS Evening News *by substitute news anchorman Harry Reasoner. While describing the Cam Ne operation on camera, Safer gave impromptu instructions to his cameraman, Ha Tue Can.*

### CBS Evening News with Walter Cronkite, 5 August 1965

REASONER. Good evening. Two days ago we began this broadcast with a cabled report from CBS News Correspondent Morley Safer in Vietnam.

The cable told of a U.S. Marine operation against a village named Cam Ne. Safer reported that the Marines, ordered to retaliate in the face of any sniper fire, shot up the village, and used cigarette lighters and flame throwers to burn down about 150 homes. The Marines ordered the houses evacuated, but gave the orders in English because there were no interpreters with them. Safer and his cameraman were the only newsmen with the Marines.

SAFER: We're on the outskirts of the village of Cam Ne with elements of the First Battalion, Ninth Marines, and we were walking into this village when, you can hear what happened.

Can, let's move in with these other guys.

This is what the war in Vietnam is all about. The old and the very young. The Marines are burning this old couple's cottage because fire was coming from here. Now you walk into the village and you see no young people at all. Fire was coming from automatic—light automatic weapons' fire was coming from all of these villages. It's not really one village. It's a string of huts. And the people that are left—come this way, Can—the people that are left are like this woman here, the very old.

Seen action like this before, Marine?

MARINE: No, I haven't. Not like this, I haven't.

SAFER: Did you set fire to these houses?

MARINE: No, we were just off to the left of it [the hamlet] when it was burning.

SAFER: Were you getting fire from them?

MARINE: Somewhat—not too much. Just a little sniper fire.

SAFER: It first appeared that the Marines had been sniped at and that a few houses were made to pay. Shortly after, an officer told me he had orders to go in and level the string of hamlets that surrounds Cam Ne village. And all around the common paddy field that feeds these hamlets, a ring of fire. 150 houses were leveled in retaliation for a burst of gunfire. In Vietnam, like everywhere else in Asia, property, a home, is everything. A man lives with his family on ancestral land. His parents are buried nearby. Their spirit is part of his holding. If there were Vietcong in the hamlets they were long gone, alerted by the roar of the amphibious tractors and the heavy barrage of rocket fire laid down before the troops moved in. The women and old men who remained still never forgot that August afternoon.

The day's operation burned down 150 houses, wounded three women, killed one baby, wounded one Marine and netted these four prisoners. Four old men who could not answer questions put to them in English. Four old men who had no idea what an I.D. card was. Today's operation is the frustration of Vietnam in miniature. There is little doubt that American firepower can win a military victory here. But to a Vietnamese peasant whose home is a—means a lifetime of back-breaking labor—it will take more than presidential promises to convince him that we are on his side.

Morley Safer, CBS News, near the village of Cam Ne.

REASONER: A U.S. military spokesman in Saigon said today that the Marines do not burn down houses and villages unless they are fortified. The spokesman described Cam Ne as a Vietcong stronghold and said that 50 houses were destroyed. The U.S. spokesman said the house set afire by a cigarette lighter was a tactical installation with a concrete basement leading to tunnels rather than a peaceful dwelling. The spokesman said that as the Marines moved into Cam Ne, they came under heavy fire. The spokesman maintained that U.S. helicopters had warned the village prior to the ground attack. This was denied by Correspondent Safer in a subsequent cable to CBS News.

*Credit*: Reprinted with permission of the CBS News Archives.

## NOTE

1. David Halberstam, *The Powers That Be* (New York: Dell Publishing, 1979), 682.

## FURTHER READINGS

Safer, Morley. *Flashbacks: On Returning to Vietnam*. New York: St. Martin's Press, 1991.

Steinman, Ron. *Inside Television's First War: A Saigon Journal*. Columbia: University of Missouri Press, 2002.

Trotta, Liz. *Fighting for Air: In the Trenches with Television News*. Columbia: University of Missouri Press, 1994.

South Vietnam battle sites during the Vietnam War, 1961–1975.

Robert Capa was the greatest combat photographer of his generation, photographing the Spanish Civil War (1936–1939) and the European theater of World War II (1939–1945). He often risked death to get compelling images and his photos of the Allies' D-Day invasion of Normandy on 6 June 1944, rank among the most stunning war images ever captured on film. On 21 May 1954, while on assignment for *Life* magazine, Capa recorded this poignant moment at a military cemetery for French and Vietnamese soldiers in Namdinh, Vietnam. Moments later he stepped on a land mine and was killed, making him the first American correspondent to die in the Vietnamese conflict. (Robert Capa/Magnum Photos)

*Saturday Evening Post* photographer John Bryson took this photograph of a Vietnamese Self-Defense Corps training with wooden cutlasses for jungle combat. The defense forces of South Vietnamese president Ngo Dinh Diem tried without success to convert peasant villages into strongholds against Communist Vietcong guerrillas. The South Vietnamese villagers were expected to participate in their own defense, although with inferior weaponry, but Vietcong agents infiltrated most of the strongholds. Bryson's photograph accompanied Don Schanche's *Post* article, "Last Chance for Vietnam" (see Chapter 3), which assessed the situation in January 1962 as desperate for the U.S.-backed government of South Vietnam. Despite escalating U.S. military aid, Diem's defense forces were losing the military and political war against the Vietcong. Within two years, Diem was overthrown by his generals, and the United States took over the war against the Communists. (Reprinted with permission of The Saturday Evening Post, © 1962 [Renewed], BFL&MS, Inc., Indianapolis.)

Primitive antipersonnel weaponry proved very effective during the Vietnam War. This photograph by John Bryson for the *Saturday Evening Post* article "Last Chance for Vietnam," published in January 1962 (see Chapter 3), shows an earthen fortress bristling with wooden spikes to fend off attackers. The fortress was typical of fortified villages constructed by South Vietnamese defense forces to isolate villagers from Communist Vietcong guerrillas. Often the wooden spikes were treated with human feces as a natural poison. Despite the defenses, the fortified villages were infiltrated by Vietcong spies and eventually were abandoned. (Reprinted with permission of The Saturday Evening Post, © 1962 [Renewed], BFL&MS, Inc., Indianapolis.)

South Vietnamese president Ngo Dinh Diem distrusted the Buddhist majority in his country and accused it of sympathizing with the Vietcong rebels. For their part, the Buddhists were suspicious of Diem, despite his reputation as a nationalist, because he was a Roman Catholic who favored the customs of former French colonialists. Diem used his secret police to persecute Buddhist enclaves in Saigon and Hué. The Buddhists retaliated by staging public protests for the benefit of Western media. The protests went unnoticed until 11 June 1963, when an elderly Buddhist monk, Quang Duc, burned himself to death in a Saigon street while fellow monks and policemen looked on. Only his heart was not consumed by the fire. Associated Press Saigon bureau chief Malcolm Browne was present because of a tip from the Buddhists. Browne's photograph of the suicide shocked newspaper readers around the world. Despite U.S. pressure to moderate his stance toward the Buddhists, Diem continued his repression, and more Buddhist self-immolations followed. Within five months, a military junta overthrew Diem after the U.S. government secretly signaled its approval for a coup d'état. (AP/Wide World Photos)

U.S. president John Kennedy announced his administration's Vietnam policy in an interview on CBS *Television News* on 2 September 1963 (see Chapter 3). Kennedy and newsman Walter Cronkite faced each other in lawn chairs outside the president's summer home at Hyannisport, Massachusetts. Kennedy attempted a partial commitment to the anti-Communist regime of South Vietnamese president Ngo Dinh Diem by sending military equipment, but officially limited U.S. personnel to advisory roles. Combat missions by U.S. pilots were kept secret. Kennedy told Cronkite that success or failure in the war ultimately depended on the will of the South Vietnamese people to resist Communist aggression, a not-so-veiled message to President Diem that the United States would withdraw support if Diem continued his brutal repression of political opponents, particularly militant Buddhists. Despite the noncommittal nature of his Vietnam policy, Kennedy's escalation of the conflict was matched by the enemy and increased the U.S. stake in the region. (Library of Congress)

*Left:* Mrs. Edwin G. Shank and her two children were photographed on their way to the funeral of their husband and father, Captain Edwin "Jerry" Shank, Jr. Shank was one of 15,000 U.S. military advisors sent to South Vietnam to help stop a Communist takeover. Officially the advisors were limited to noncombat roles, but in fact, U.S. pilots such as Shank carried the load in the air war. Shank's letters home revealed the government's deception. In one letter to his wife, Shank wrote, "we fight and we die, but no one cares." After his death, Shank's widow released the letters to the press, thereby sparking debate over the Vietnam War in the U.S. Senate. This photograph accompanied *Life* magazine's 8 May 1964 publication of Shank's letters (see Chapter 18). (Getty Images)

*Right:* In 1964 *Life* magazine correspondent Lee Hall and photographer Larry Burrows accompanied a border patrol of Montagnard moutain tribesmen led by U.S. Special Forces captain Vernon Gillespie, Jr. Their report became the cover story for the magazine's 27 November issue and featured this portrait of Gillespie on a patrol in search of Vietcong. The Montagnards were known as formidable fighters who hated their ethnic Vietnamese brothers. Gillespie became a hero in September 1964 when his decisive leadership prevented the Montagnards under his command at Buon Brieng, South Vietnam, from joining a general insurrection against their Vietnamese commanders. (See Chapter 7 for Hall's report.) (Getty Images)

*Left:* Hovering U.S. Army helicopters pour machine gun fire into a tree line to cover the advance of South Vietnamese ground troops in an attack on a Vietcong camp 18 miles north of Tayninh, northwest of Saigon near the Cambodian border, in March 1965. The photographer, Horst Faas of the Associated Press, won the Pulitzer Prize in 1965 for his Vietnam War photography. (AP/Wide World Photos)

*Top left:* North Vietnam sent troops and weapons into the South over the "Ho Chi Minh Trail," a network of footpaths, roads, and waterways wending through the mountains, uplands, and river delta regions of Laos, Cambodia, and South Vietnam. This photograph was taken in 1965 by an anonymous Vietcong photographer in South Vietnam and depicts Vietcong porters carrying supplies up a "corduroy" mountain trail fashioned from jungle foliage. Most shipments were human-powered and could easily be diverted to alternate trails if threatened by government forces. U.S. aerial bombardment was ineffective in interdicting shipments along the trail, but the trail was bombed throughout the war. (Library of Congress)

*Bottom right:* This modern image of a Vietnamese military cemetery on the Ho Chi Minh Trail gives silent testimony to the supreme price paid by millions on both sides of the Vietnamese colonial war (1946–1954) and civil war (1956–1975). The Communists, led by Ho Chi Minh, saw both struggles—first against the French and later against U.S.-backed regimes in the South—as a continuation of the centuries-old Vietnamese struggle to evict foreign aggressors from their homeland. The French and Americans viewed the Communists as the aggressors in South Vietnam. The Vietnamese peasants were caught in the middle. (Corbis)

*Bottom left:* This 16 April 1965 cover of *Life* magazine features a Larry Burrows photo taken on 31 March 1965. Helicopter crew chief James C. Farley holds a jammed machine gun as he shouts to his crew, while wounded pilot Lieutenant James E. Magel lies dying beside him. Burrows risked injury or death many times to capture the graphic violence of war in Vietnam and other corners of the globe. While covering an allied incursion into Laos in 1971, Burrows died in a helicopter crash, along with three other combat photographers. (Getty Images)

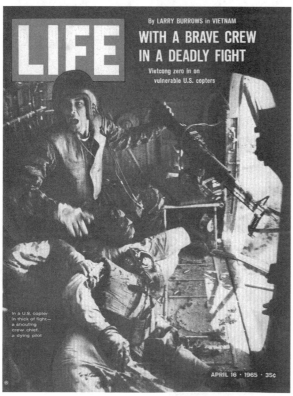

*Right:* On 3 August 1965, CBS news correspondent Morley Safer and a Vietnamese photographer accompanied a U.S. Marine unit on its search-and-destroy mission into the village of Cam Ne, south of the U.S. airbase at Danang, South Vietnam. Two days later, Safer's film report was broadcast on the *CBS Evening News with Walter Cronkite.* The report depicted Marines matter-of-factly torching peasant homes, which caused a sensation among viewers because it seemed to cast the Americans, not the Communists, as the aggressors in Southeast Asia. Safer's so-called "Zippo lighter" story gave birth to a resilient myth that the television networks had willfully undercut the U.S. war effort, when in fact Safer had been careful to tone down the more violent aspects of his report. See Chapter 10 for transcripts of Safer's Cam Ne reports. (CBS/Landov)

*Left:* Henri Huet took this photograph of U.S. G.I.s at Anthai, South Vietnam, in 1966. Huet was born in Vietnam and schooled in France. He returned to Vietnam to photograph the war, first for United Press International and later for the Associated Press. While accompanying Operation Lam Son 719, Huet died on 10 February 1971 in a helicopter crash in Laos in which three other photographers also died. (AP/Wide World Photos)

*Right:* Two South Vietnamese children gaze at an American paratrooper holding an M-79 grenade launcher as they cling to their mothers who huddle against a canal bank for protection from Vietcong sniper fire. Associated Press photographer Horst Faas took this picture on New Year's Day 1966, as the 173rd Airborne brigade made a sweep in the Baotrai area, 20 miles west of Saigon, to round up Vietcong suspects. To "pacify" this area, which was long held by the Vietcong, Vietnamese, American, and Australian battalions rounded up the farmers and their families. Faas won the Pulitzer Prize in 1965 for his Vietnam War photography. (AP/Wide World Photos)

**FEBRUARY 9 · 1968 · 35¢**

*Left:* The Communist Tet Offensive of January–February 1968 was the turning point in the Vietnam War because it proved beyond all doubt that, despite their superior military might, the Americans were not winning the war (see Chapter 14). This *Life* magazine cover photograph symbolized this bitter conclusion better than any other image of the offensive. Taken on 31 January 1968 by an anonymous Associated Press photographer, it shows two American G.I.s towering over their diminutive captive at the U.S. Embassy in Saigon. A squad of Vietcong guerrillas had raided the presumably impregnable embassy and held it for nine hours before succumbing. The message was clear: If the center of U.S. power in Vietnam was not safe from this small but determined foe, all of South Vietnam was vulnerable. (AP/Wide World Photos)

*Above:* The shadow of this picture's Vietnamese photographer, named The Dinh, looms over an artillery position after North Vietnamese forces overran several South Vietnamese government artillery bases south of the Demilitarized Zone dividing North and South Vietnam. The only identification on this uncaptioned picture was the photographer's name and the Vietnamese word *chet,* meaning "dead." (Indochina Photo Requiem Project)

U.S. bombing of North Vietnam began in March 1965 and continued unabated for three and a half years, during which Operation Rolling Thunder (see Chapter 13) dropped a million tons of bombs, rockets, and missiles on military targets, roads, railways, and ports. The bombing did not crack the morale of Communist leaders in the North Vietnamese capitol of Hanoi, nor did it stop the flow of men and materiel into South Vietnam; in fact, the bombing backfired. Scenes of Hanoi's heroic resistance, such as this photograph of a Hanoi air raid on 5 July 1967, inspired North Vietnam's allies, the Soviet Union and Communist China, to step up their military aid to make up for North Vietnam's bombing losses. The huge U.S. investment in bombing North Vietnam was out of proportion to its minimal impact on the enemy. By 1968, the United States lost more than 700 aircraft valued at $900 million, while inflicting only $300 million in damage on North Vietnam. (Corbis)

On 1 February 1968—the second day of the Tet Offensive—Associated Press photographer Eddie Adams tripped his camera's shutter at the moment that South Vietnamese National Police Chief Brigadier General Nguyen Ngoc Loan executed a Vietcong officer with a single revolver shot in the head. The victim grimaced at the impact of the fatal bullet. Carrying a pistol and wearing civilian clothes, he was captured near An Quang Pagoda, identified as an officer, and taken to the police chief. The photograph was published in newspapers around the world and won a Pulitzer Prize for Adams in 1969. (AP/Wide World Photos)

During the siege of Hué in February 1968, United Press International photographer Kyoichi Sawada took this picture of a U.S. Marine keeping his head low as he dragged a wounded buddy from the ruins of the Hué Citadel's outer wall. Despite the Americans' devastating bombardment, the Communists held the Citadel for twenty-five days before withdrawing. Hué experienced some of the most furious fighting of the Vietnam War. Sawada won a Pulitzer Prize for his combat photography in 1965. (Corbis)

In February 1968, CBS newsman Walter Cronkite went to South Vietnam to personally inspect the aftermath of the Communist Tet Offensive. This image shows Cronkite reporting in the field. The CBS broadcast entitled "Walter Cronkite's Report from Vietnam (Who What When Where Why?)" was aired on 27 February 1968. Cronkite's concluding remarks (see Chapter 14) declared that the United States was mired in a stalemate in Southeast Asia. His pessimism about the war convinced President Lyndon Johnson that the American public no longer supported his war policy. A few weeks later, Johnson announced a halt to bombing in North Vietnam, renewed his appeal for a negotiated settlement, and withdrew from the upcoming U.S. presidential election campaign. (CBS/Landov)

In late 1967, the U.S. field commander in Vietnam, General William C. Westmoreland, became convinced that the Communists intended a showdown at Khesanh, a remote U.S. Marine outpost near the Demilitarized Zone separating North and South Vietnam. Westmoreland redeployed his forces for emergency reinforcement of Khesanh, which made South Vietnamese cities more vulnerable to attack during the Communists' Tet Offensive in January–February 1968. This Richard Swanson photograph of Khesanh for *Life* magazine was captioned, "A sprawling arsenal that was delivered by air." As part of the enemy offensive, 40,000 North Vietnamese regulars and Vietcong surrounded Khesanh and bombarded it for weeks before withdrawing. Though the Americans were never in serious jeopardy, the battle showed that the Communists could fight large-scale engagements on their own terms. Westmoreland's replacement, General Creighton W. Abrams, eventually ordered abandonment of the vulnerable Khesanh outpost. (Getty Images)

*Top left:* Shortly after Associated Press photographer Oliver Noonan took this photograph in August 1969 at a U.S. firebase south of Danang, South Vietnam, he died in a helicopter crash along with the firebase's commander. The enemy fiercely resisted five recovery attempts by the U.S. Army's 23rd Infantry Division. One unit, the notorious Alpha Company, temporarily refused orders for a sixth attack. Media commentators in the United States debated the incident's significance for morale of U.S. troops in South Vietnam. See Chapter 21 to read news coverage of the Alpha Company incident.

*Top right:* The Green Berets incident, recounted in Chapter 17, ended inconclusively in October 1969, when Colonel Robert Rheault and seven other members of U.S. Army Special Forces were released from murder charges on grounds of insufficient evidence. In this photograph, Rheault is celebrating with his wife and daughter as he arrives home in Boston, Massachusetts. (AP/Wide World Photos)

*Louisville Times* reporter John Fetterman took this photograph in 1968 of U.S. Army pallbearers carrying the casket of Vietnam War casualty James Thurman "Little Duck" Gibson to his grave at Resthaven Cemetery in Perry County, Kentucky—a scene reenacted in thousands of American communities during the war. Fetterman's 28 July 1968 article, "Pfc. Gibson Comes Home," won a Pulitzer Prize in 1969 (see Chapter 18). (© The Courier-Journal)

**Philip W. Strout, 21**
Army, SP4
So. Portland, Maine

**John A. Gillen, 25**
Army, SP4
Broadview, Ill.

**Edward O'Donovan, 19**
Marines, Pfc.
Chicago, Ill.

**Michael D. Melton, 20**
Army, SP4
Little Rock, Ark.

**Melvin Green Jr., 31**
Army, S/Sgt.
Manhattan, Kan.

**Gary C. Fassel, 20**
Army, Pfc.
Buffalo, N.Y.

**John W. Kirchner, 19**
Marines, Pfc.
La Crosse, Wis.

**Keith B. Janke, 26**
Army, Sgt.
Poplar, Wis.

**Joseph L. Rhodes, 22**
Marines, L. Cpl.
Memphis, Tenn.

**William L. Anderson, 18**
Army, Sgt.
Templeton, Pa.

**David L. Mills, 22**
Army, SP4
Decatur, Ill.

**Ramon L. Vazquez Nieves, 21**
Army, Pfc.
Puerto Nuevo, P.R.

**Carl R. Martin, 26**
Army, SP5
Rapid City, S. Dak.

**Daniel L. Pucci, 22**
Marines, Cpl.
Berea, Ohio

**Howe K. Clark Jr., 22**
Army, S/Sgt.
Rockdale, Texas

**Thomas P. Jackson Jr., 23**
Army, Pfc.
Westbury, N.Y.

**Clifford Haynes Jr., 19**
Marines, Pfc.
Carnegie, Pa.

**Scott E. Saylor, 22**
Army, SP4
King of Prussia, Pa.

**Jose M. Galarza-Quinones, 21**
Army, Pfc.
Hato Rey, P.R.

**David R. Mann, 20**
Army, SP4
Earlville, Ill.

Two facing pages are shown here from "The Faces of the American Dead in Vietnam: One Week's Toll," the *Life* magazine cover story on 27 June 1969 that fueled antiwar sentiment more than any other piece of print journalism during the Vietnam War. (Time/Life)

**Henry R. Hausman Jr., 19**
Army, Pfc.
Hilliard, Ohio

**Robert J. Randall, 19**
Army, Pfc.
Miami, Fla.

**David F. Bukowski, 20**
Army, SP4
West Islip, N.Y.

**John M. Vollmerhausen Jr., 18**
Army, Pfc.
Ft. Lauderdale, Fla.

**David A. Hargens, 19**
Army, Pfc.
Nickerson, Neb.

**Matthew J. Baurle, 20**
Marines, L. Cpl.
Gloversville, N.Y.

**John L. Rosemond, 21**
Army, Pfc.
Dallas, Texas

**Richard F. DuBois, 20**
Marines, L. Cpl.
New Orleans, La.

**Duane C. Bowen, 20**
Army, SP4
Ramona, Calif.

**John N. McCarthy, 20**
Army, SP4
Glen Cove, N.Y.

**Andrew W. Rice Jr., 20**
Navy, GMG3
Bedford, Pa.

**Byrle B. Bailey, 19**
Marines, Pfc.
Omaha, Neb.

**Charles P. Smith Jr., 20**
Army, Pfc.
Richmond, Va.

**Robert H. Carter Jr., 35**
Army, Lt. Col.
Morganton, N.C.

**Stephen L. McCarvel, 19**
Army, Sgt.
Great Falls, Mont.

**Jackie D. Bass, 21**
Army, Pfc.
Cochran, Ga.

**William A. Evans, 20**
Army, Sgt.
Milwaukee, Wis.

**Richard L. Patterson, 25**
Army, 2nd Lt.
Harriman, Tenn.

**Robert W. Getz, 19**
Army, Pfc.
Decatur, Ill.

**James Boston Jr., 20**
Army, Pfc.
Gainesville, Fla.

Legendary *Life* magazine photojournalist Larry Burrows's compassion for the Vietnamese people was famous among newsmen covering the Vietnam War. Burrows took this photograph after Communist forces abandoned Hué in spring 1968. The image illustrated a Burrows essay, "Vietnam: A Degree of Disillusion," published in the 19 September 1969 issue of *Life* magazine (see Chapter 24). Its caption read, "A woman wails over the bundled remains of her husband, discovered in a mass grave near Hué." Burrows was notorious for risking death to get just the right picture. His luck ran out on 10 February 1971, when he and three other combat photographers died in a helicopter crash while covering South Vietnamese Operation Lam Son 719, an incursion into Laos to interdict enemy supply routes. (Getty Images)

For nineteen months, the U.S. Army managed to repress news of the atrocities committed by its forces at Mylai hamlet of the village of Songmy in South Vietnam, until Seymour Hersh's breaking news story in November 1969 put an officer accused of Mylai killings on the cover of nearly every news publication in America. Lieutenant William L. Calley, Jr., became the poster boy for U.S. war crimes in Southeast Asia. Calley was convicted of personally executing 109 villagers and sentenced to life in prison. Hersh won the Pulitzer Prize in 1970. (Newsweek)

U.S. Army public information officer Sergeant Ronald L. Haeberle was present at Mylai, South Vietnam, on 16 March 1968, when U.S. Army soldiers on a "search and destroy" mission killed hundreds of civilians. Haeberle photographed what happened, kept the pictures, and retired from the Army. "It was done very businesslike," Haeberle said, "They were getting ready to shoot these people and I said hold it—I wanted to take a picture. They were pleading for their lives. The looks on their faces, the mothers were crying; they were trembling. I turned my back because I couldn't look. They opened up with two M 16s." Moments later, the peasants lay dead. After a breaking newspaper story about the massacre by Seymour Hersh in November 1969 (see Chapter 22), reporter Joseph Eszterhas obtained Haeberle's photographs, including the image shown above, for publication in the Cleveland, Ohio, *Plain Dealer*. Later the photographs were used in Calley's prosecution by the army. Calley was convicted of murder and paroled in 1975. (Getty Images)

Associated Press photographer Huynh Cong Ut, known to his colleagues as "Nick," was in Trangbang, South Vietnam, on 8 June 1972, when a South Vietnamese Skyraider accidentally dropped napalm on its own forces, as well as on some villagers. After Nick Ut took this photograph of the aftermath, he helped the girl in the middle of the picture, Phan Thi Kim Phuc, get to a hospital. Both survived the war. The picture won the Pulitizer Prize in 1973 and became an icon of the war. Nick Ut and Kim Phuc were reunited twenty-eight years later at an observance of the event in London, England. (AP/Wide World Photos)

This widely published photograph was taken on 29 April 1975 by Hubert Van Es of United Press International. It shows evacuation of Vietnamese refugees from an apartment complex at 22 Gia Long Street, approximately one-half mile from the U.S. Embassy in Saigon, South Vietnam. The next day Communist forces invaded the city. The apartment complex housed offices of the CIA and the Agency for International Development. The helicopter was flown by Air America, an airline owned by the CIA. Van Es correctly captioned the location of the evacuation, but editors in the United States misread the caption and incorrectly identified the location as the U.S. Embassy building. (Corbis)

# 11

# PACIFICATION

In the war against the National Liberation Front to win the "hearts and minds" of the South Vietnamese peasants, President Ngo Dinh Diem often was his own worst enemy. To secure the peasants from Vietcong influence, Diem and his brother, Ngo Dinh Nhu, enacted a series of ill-advised policies that resulted in antagonizing the peasants and enhancing the Vietcong's prestige as "liberators."

In 1959, Diem's land reforms left powerful landlords in control of most arable acreage and required peasants to pay for land they had been granted for free by the Vietminh during the war against the French. The government further alienated peasants in the rich Mekong River delta by forcibly relocating them to fenced farm communities called *agrovilles*. Many farmers had to travel great distances each day to tend their assigned fields without pay. To them, this was forced labor. Vietcong spies identified "collaborators" and government officials in the camps for assassination. The peasants, most of whom had never traveled outside their villages, felt trapped between powerful forces that did not care about them. The *agrovilles* program was abandoned.

Despite the political damage caused by the *agrovilles*, Diem and Nhu resurrected the idea in early 1962 by corralling the peasants into armed stockades called "strategic hamlets." Nhu personally took charge of the massive building program, which was financed by the Americans. U.S. defense secretary Robert S. McNamara was glad to have concrete progress to cite when asked about the U.S. ally in South Vietnam. Nhu claimed that one-third of the population was in strategic hamlets by October 1962. As before, however, the forced relocation, intensive labor without pay to build the stockades, and violation of the traditional way of life converted peasants into Vietcong sympathizers. Later it was learned that Nhu's principal administrator for the strategic hamlet program, Colonel Pham Ngoc Thao, was a Vietcong agent who pushed the program as rapidly as possible in order to subvert government support in the countryside. The hamlets were abandoned after South Vietnamese generals conspired to overthrow the Ngo brothers in November 1963, with tacit approval of the American embassy.

While the generals struggled for control of the Saigon government, the counterinsurgency campaign foundered. With inadequate troop support, the strategic hamlets were neglected and abandoned. Thus the U.S. military establishment in Saigon faced a dismal political situation in 1964. It announced a new, comprehensive strategy to combat Vietcong influence called "pacification." Agency for International Development director James S. Killen described the program to a panel of *Life* correspondents in Saigon:

It is the responsibility of the province chief who is supposed to bring to bear on this problem all the instruments and weapons and tools at his disposal. These may represent regional forces and popular forces; they represent police; they represent civil administration; they represent the means of social and economic development judiciously used to strengthen the image of government in the eyes of the people of the province.[1]

## JOHN FLYNN: PROFILE OF CIVILIAN AID WORKER

*The U.S. mission in Vietnam harnessed Peace Corps–style civilian volunteers to distribute food and farm implements in the villages. The following 1964* Life *magazine picture story, photographed by Terrence Spencer, profiles an aid worker, accompanied by his wife, in the Mekong River delta area. The story highlights the fragility of "pacification" against a backdrop of guerrilla war.*

*Life*, 27 November 1964

Phu Vinh—Out in the Mekong Delta province of Vinh Binh, half or more of which is controlled by the enemy, I stood watching a young American who sat on the ground talking animatedly with some Vietnamese women about a range of everyday topics, including how best to dry shrimps. Their time-encrusted custom had been to spread their shrimps on the germ-laden dirt to dry under the tropical sun. Gesturing in frustration at his imperfect command of the language, he argued amiably that it would be cleaner and quicker to spread the shrimps on plastic sheets that he brought with him.

These are the terms of the war that Rob Warne is fighting. Warne calls it a "silent war," because he must move gently, persuading rather than ordering, counting his gains in inches and intangibles, always smiling.

Warne is field representative in this 1,000-square-mile province for a U.S. State Department aid mission which is known on the scene as USOM (United States Operations Mission). He is a civilian and his job is critically important, for everyone agrees that the government must win the peasants to win the war. Unlike some touchier civilians, he has no trouble working with the U.S. military, and he in turn is respected by the military both for his guts and his savvy in the eel-barrel enigma that is Vietnam. "No problem here is solely economic or solely military," Warne shrugged, tiredly wiping his eyes under his horn-rimmed glasses. "This is a political war. Political problems outrank both military and economic."

Warne uses U.S. funds and know-how to help peasants exist in areas which the Vietnamese army is trying to keep free of Vietcong. It is not easy. Vietnam's peasants are desperately weary of endless war; the lives of many have been shattered in the whipsaw pressures from both sides. The village of My Long . . . is an example. The enemy has cut the road to My Long from Phu Vinh, where Warne lives with his wife and small daughter—in a house constantly under guard. But My Long still can be reached by river, and Warne had brought 150 bags of wheat and 150 tins of soybean oil in a launch. A machine gunner aboard swept the riverbanks with slugs occasionally to discourage a Vietcong ambush. Warne has been pinned down by Vietcong fire. "I break into a slight sweat sometimes when I hear small arms," he admits. This trip he had read a book until he waded ashore at My Long.

Before the government forcibly moved in 1,000 refugees from a combat zone, this had been a quiet village. With U.S. financing, the government drilled wells for the newcomers, built schools, a clinic and 50 thatched homes, and gave each family a pig. But less than 100 of the refugees were men; gradually women began to slip away to rejoin their menfolk, who are with the Vietcong. Two-thirds of the new homes now stand empty; only 292 refugees remain in My Long.

Warne watched his supplies unloaded, then turned to talk, forcefully but very politely, with the district chief. The food was distributed and then we moved about the village, Warne sadly pausing at the empty houses. Warne checked the villagers' pigs, listened to complaints and worries, analyzed their wells, looked into the clinic. He went to the edge of town where a 40-man garrison staves off the Vietcong, whose guerrillas are so near that they speak to the villagers by loudspeaker. Not long before, we were told a child had been killed in the street by a stray bullet. No one dares go beyond the edge of town. Warne slept on his own cot that night; we left the next morning. As we went to the launch, he noticed an old woman arranging shrimps on his plastic sheet. "By gosh," he cried in real pleasure, "she's using it!"

Warne is 27, a Princeton graduate and a former Army lieutenant. This is his first post as a career foreign service officer. He feels his cause deeply; he believes democracy will win here and though the peasants discourage him sometimes, he patiently says, "They're like any other underdeveloped people worried about getting enough to eat: They have no idea of community action."

He deals in pigs and corn, medicine and books. And he spends much of his time fortifying civil government, bolstering local officials, leading by persuasion.

There are 77 U.S. field representatives in South Vietnam's 45 provinces, and Warne's work is illustrative of them all. With U.S. aid, he has put into his province 113 classrooms, 18 bridges, 124 water wells, eight dispensaries, six open-air markets, 108 culverts and a village lighting system. This is low-scale, self-help aid: to make a bridge, for example, the U.S. provides 100 bags of cement, 10 tons of steel and $1,400 in cash; the villagers supply the labor. Warne makes loans to small farmers and has a rehabilitation program for guerrillas who surrender. He travels constantly, a circuit-riding advocate of both physical and governmental improvement.

Yet the Vietcong is gaining in Vinh Binh. Last year the government counted 375 villages on its side. Now there are 274. Vietcong military forces have doubled. Every month they murder a couple of village officials. They can cut any road in the province—Warne now must use helicopters to reach more than half his territory.

One morning Warne and I entered the village of Tra On to find soldiers interrogating a hard-core Vietcong woman, who had entered town carrying a grenade in her market basket. Her plan was to throw it into a cafe where U.S. soldiers collect. Such simple terrorist tactics succeed all too frequently, as happened last week when someone tossed a plastic bomb into the snack bar of the Saigon airport, injuring 18 GIs.

Warne is frequently fired on by snipers. He tries to ignore it, but he sandbags the bottom of his jeep in the hope it will protect him from mines. Susie Warne, Rob's pretty 24-year-old wife, suffers the most from tension and fear and the general insecurity of life in Vietnam.

Susie is one of four wives of field representatives who live out in the provinces with their husbands. She is the only American woman in Phu Vinh. She boils and filters water for her family, constantly worried about the health of their 2-year-old daughter, Robin Jane. Susie has had amoebic dysentery for 14 months, but ironically Robin Jane has thrived. "It saps your energy so," Susie says, "and I get depressed. I'm getting tired of living in danger all the time and worrying about Rob. We're so cut off. I don't like to stay in the house when Rob's away for the night." He often is away.

Susie has learned to speak Vietnamese quite well—better than Rob—but she says, "Even with my best Vietnamese friends, there is only so far I can communicate." She used to bicycle around Phu Vinh, taking Robin Jane along. But she stopped when a grenade was thrown at a U.S. Army house in town. Her only other real recreation is taking the little girl to the airport to meet the USOM planes that occasionally fly the 80 miles from Saigon.

Warne's duty tour will be up in January and they will return to the States. U.S. Army advisers in the area hate to see Rob go, because he knows this province better than any [other] American. Susie is relieved that the nerve-racking days are drawing to an end.

When the Warnes returned to Phu Vinh from a recent trip to Saigon, where they take a three-day break each month, I rode beside Susie in the little plane. As we circled the muddy little landing field, she looked down at the town in which she had spent 14 months. "I hate to land," she said softly, almost to herself, "I hate to land."

*Credit:* © 1964 TIME Inc. Reprinted by permission.

## WILLIAM F. PEPPER: DEVASTATING EFFECT OF WAR ON CHILDREN OF VIETNAM

*Ramparts* magazine was the most widely read and slickly produced leftist, antiwar U.S. publication of the Vietnam War era. The magazine was launched in 1962 shortly after U.S. commitment to the war and folded during the final year of the war, 1975. The editorial staff, led by Warren Hinckle, drew spiritual *energy from opposing the war.* Ramparts *was known for clever and articulate writing on a host of counterculture topics of conscience, including Ho Chi Minh, Chairman Mao, Kennedy assassination conspiracy theories, the Black Panther Party, civil rights, hippies, the California drug culture, and, of course, the Vietnam War. The magazine targeted the far-left audience, but the mainstream audience gravitated to its politics as the antiwar movement grew. Though it operated on a shoestring,* Ramparts *fostered some first-rate long-form journalism on stories neglected by the mainstream professional press. The following heart-rending study on the war's brutality toward children (excerpted) was meticulously researched in South Vietnam by Professor William Pepper. The preface is by Dr. Benjamin Spock, also known for the care of children and for his leadership in the antiwar movement in the United States.*

*Ramparts,* January 1967

## PREFACE BY DR. BENJAMIN SPOCK

A million children have been killed or wounded or burned in the war America is carrying on in Vietnam, according to the estimate of William Pepper. Not many of them even get to hospitals, which are few and far between, but when they do, they may lie three in a bed or on newspapers on the floor. Flies are in the wounds. Even such simple equipment as cups and plates are in short supply. Materials for the adequate treatment of burns—gauze, ointments, antibiotics and plasma—are usually non-existent. This contrasts with the incredible speed and efficiency with which American troops napalmed by mistake are given elaborate first aid while being lifted out of the battlefield and then flown to a Texas hospital for treatment.

When Terre des Hommes, a Swiss humanitarian organization, asked for American government assistance in flying burned and wounded children to Europe for repair, our officials refused. With crocodile tears they explained children are unhappy when separated from their families. The fact is that a third of all Vietnamese children in institutions have already lost both parents or been abandoned.

Can America, which manufactures and delivers the efficient napalm that causes deep and deforming burns, deny all responsibility for their treatment?

Many American physicians are now volunteering to treat the children if they are brought to America. But citizens must be asked to pay the bill for transportation and hospitalization. They will also have to persuade our government to allow the children to be brought here.

William F. Pepper, executive director of the New Rochelle Commission on Human Rights, instructor in Political Science at Mercy College in Dobbs Ferry, New York, and director of that college's Children's Institute for Advanced Study and Research, spent between five and six weeks this spring [1966] in Vietnam as a freelance correspondent accredited by the Military Assistance Command in that country, and by the government of Vietnam.

During that period, in addition to traveling, he lived in Sancta Maria Orphanage in Gia Dinh Province and in the main "shelter area" in Qui Nhon, for a shorter period of time. His main interests were the effects of the war on women and children, the role of the American voluntary agencies there and the work of the military in civil action.

His visits took him to a number of orphanages—among them: An Lac, Go-Vap, Don Bosco, Hoi Duc Anh, Bac Ai—hospitals: Cho-Ray, Holy Family, Phu My, Saigon-Cholon (central hospital) and shelters in Saigon, Cholon, Qui Nhon and outer Binh Dinh.

Mr. Pepper interviewed, frequently, the following Cabinet ministers of South Vietnam: Dr. Nguyen Ba Kha, Minister of Health; Dr. Tran Ngoc Ninh, Minister of Education; Mr. Tran Ngoc Lieng, Minister of Social Welfare; Dr. Nguyen Thuc Que, High Commissioner for Refugees.

In addition, he conferred with the leaders of the Voluntary Agency Community and the USAID Coordinator for Refugee Affairs, Mr. Edward Marks, as well as the USAID child welfare specialist, Mr. Gardner Monroe, with Mademoiselle E. La Mer of UNICEF and Mr. Pierre Baesjous of UNESCO.

As Mr. Pepper makes clear, by far the majority of present refugees in South Vietnam have been rendered homeless by American military action, and by far the majority of hospital patients, especially children, are there due to injuries suffered from American military activities. The plight of these children and the huge burden they impose upon physical facilities has been almost totally ignored by the American people.

—From remarks before the Senate of the United States, August 22, 1966, by the Hon. Wayne Morse.

For countless thousands of children in Vietnam, breathing is quickened by terror and pain, and tiny bodies learn more about death every day. These solemn, rarely smiling little ones have never known what it is to live without despair.

They indeed know death, for it walks with them by day and accompanies their sleep at night. It is as omnipresent as the napalm that falls from the skies with the frequency and impartiality of the monsoon rain.

The horror of what we are doing to the children of Vietnam—"we," because napalm and white phosphorus are the weapons of America—is staggering, whether we examine the overall figures or look at a particular case like that of Doan Minh Luan.

Luan, age eight, was one of two children brought to Britain last summer through private philanthropy, for extensive treatment at the McIndoe Burn Center. He came off the plane with a muslin bag over what had been his face. His parents had been burned alive. His chin had "melted" into his throat, so that he could not close his mouth. He had no eyelids. After the injury, he had had no treatment at all—none whatever—for four months.

It will take years for Luan to be given a new face ("We are taking special care," a hospital official told a Canadian reporter, "to make him look Vietnamese"). He needs at least 12 operations, which surgeons will perform for nothing; the wife of a grocery-chain millionaire is paying the hospital bill. Luan has already been given eyelids, and he can close his mouth now. He and the nine-year-old girl who came to Britain with him, shy and sensitive Tran Thi Thong, are among the very few lucky ones.

There is no one to provide such care for most of the other horribly maimed children of Vietnam; and despite growing efforts by American and South Vietnamese authorities to conceal the fact, it's clear that there are hundreds of thousands of terribly injured children, with no hope for decent treatment on even a day-to-day basis, much less for the long months and years of restorative surgery needed to repair ten searing seconds of napalm.

When we hear about these burned children at all, they're simply called "civilians," and there's no real way to tell how many of them are killed and injured every day. By putting together some of the figures that are available, however, we can get some idea of the shocking story.

Nearly two years ago, for instance—before the major [U.S.] escalation that began in early 1965—Hugh Campbell, former Canadian member of the International Control Commission in Vietnam, said that from 1961 through 1963, 160,000 Vietnamese civilians died in the war. This figure was borne out by officials in Saigon. According to conservative estimates, another 55,000 died during 1964 and 100,000 in each of the two escalated years since, or at least 415,000 civilians have been killed since 1961. But just who are these civilians?

In 1964, according to a UNESCO population study, 47.5 percent of the people of Vietnam were under 16. Today, the figure is certainly over 50 percent. Other United Nations statistics for Southeast Asia generally bear out this figure. Since the males over 16 are away fighting—on one side or the other—it's clear that in the rural villages which bear the brunt of the napalm raids, at least 70 percent and probably more of the residents are children.

In other words, at least a quarter of a million of the children of Vietnam have been killed in the war.

If there are that many dead, using the military rule-of-thumb, there must be three times that many wounded—or at least a million child casualties since 1961. A look at just one hospital provides grim figures supporting these statistics: A medical student, who served for some time during the summer at Da Nang Surgical Hospital, reported that approximately a quarter of the 800 patients a month were burn cases (there are two burn wards at the hospital, but burned patients rarely receive surgical treatment, because more immediate surgical emergencies crowd them out). The student, David McLanahan of Temple University, also reported that between 60 and 70 percent of the patients at Da Nang were under 12 years old. . . .

Cantho, Saigon, Da Nang, Quang Ngai—it is by putting together reports such as these that the reality of extrapolated figures becomes not only clear but plainly conservative. A quarter of a million children are dead; hundreds of thousands are seriously wounded. There must be tens of thousands of Doan Minh Luans.

Manufacturer Searle Spangler, American representative for the Swiss humanitarian agency Terre des Hommes, describes what his agency has found to be the pattern when children are injured in remote villages: "If he's badly ill or injured, of course, he simply won't survive. There is no medical care available. Adults are likely to run into the forest, and he sometimes may be left to die. If they do try to get him to a hospital, the trip is agony—overland on bad roads, flies, dirt, disease, and the constant threat of interdiction by armed forces." McLanahan says that virtually every injury that reaches the hospital at Da Nang is already complicated by serious infection—and describes doctors forced to stop during emergency surgical operations to kill flies with their hands.

Torn flesh, splintered bones, screaming agony are bad enough. But perhaps most heart-rending of all are the tiny faces and bodies scorched and seared by fire.

Napalm, and its more horrible companion, white phosphorus, liquidize young flesh and carve it into grotesque forms. The little figures are afterward often scarcely human in appearance, and one cannot be confronted with the monstrous effects of the burning without being totally shaken. Perhaps it was due to a previous lack of direct contact with war, but I never left the tiny victims without losing composure. The initial urge to reach out and soothe the hurt was restrained by the fear that the ash-like skin would crumble in my fingers.

In Qui Nhon two little children—introduced to me quietly by the interpreter as being probably "children of the Viet Cong"—told of how their hamlet was scorched by the "fire bombs." Their words were soft and sadly hesitant in coming, but their badly burned and scarred bodies screamed the message. I was told later that they evinced no interest in returning to their home and to whatever might be left of their family.

I visited a number of the existing medical institutions in South Vietnam, and there is no question that the problems of overcrowding, inadequate supplies and insufficient personnel are probably insurmountable. The Da Nang Surgical Hospital is probably as well off as any Vietnamese hospital outside Saigon—but it is for surgery only; there is also a Medical Hospital not so well equipped.

Even in the Surgical Hospital, there are a number of tests that can't be done with the inadequate laboratory and X-ray equipment. Frequent power failure is a major problem (suction pumps are vital in surgery rooms; one child died in Da Nang, for instance, because during an operation he vomited and—with no suction pump to withdraw the stomach contents from his mouth—breathed them into his lungs). Though 100 burn patients every month reach Da Nang Surgical Hospital, McLanahan reported that while he was there, the hospital had only one half-pint jar of antibiotic cream—brought in privately by a surgeon—which was saved for "children who had a chance of recovery." In Sancta Maria Orphanage, I frequently became involved in trying, with a small amount of soap and a jar of Noxzema, to alleviate the festering infections that grew around every minor bite and cut.

In the nearby Medical Hospital, there are frequent shortages of antibiotics, digitalis and other equipment. While the Surgical Hospital makes use of outdated blood from military hospitals, most Vietnamese hospitals are chronically short of blood. According to another medical student, Jeffrey Mast, a hospital at Quang Ngai (60 miles south of Da Nang) occasionally "solved" a shortage of intravenous fluids by sticking a tube into a coconut—a common practice in outlying areas and, reportedly, among the Viet Cong. . . .

There is, of course, an official United States position on the use of napalm in Vietnam. The Department of the Air Force set it forth on September 1, 1966, in a letter to Senator Robert Kennedy:

> Napalm is used against selected targets, such as caves and reinforced supply areas. Casualties in attacks against targets of this type are predominantly persons involved in Communist military operations.

I am compelled to wonder what military functions were being performed by the thousands of infants and small children, many of whom I saw sharing hospital beds in Vietnam, and a few of whom appear in photographs accompanying this article.

In the brutal inventory of maimed and killed South Vietnamese children one must also include those who are the helpless victims of American defoliants and gases. The defoliants used to deprive the Viet Cong of brush and trees that might afford cover are often the common weed-killers 2,4-D and 2,4,5-T. Yet the pilots spraying from the air cannot see if women and children are hiding in the affected foliage. These chemicals "can be toxic if used in excessive amounts," says John Edsall, M.D., Professor of Biology at Harvard.

The U.S. has admitted it is using "non-toxic" gas in Vietnam. The weapon is a "humane" one, says the government, because it creates only temporary nausea and diarrhea in adult victims. Yet a *New York Times* editorial on March 24, 1965, noted that these gases "can be fatal to the very young, the very old, and those ill with heart and lung ailments. . . . No other country has employed such a weapon in recent warfare." A letter to the *Times* several days later from Dr. David Hilding of the Yale Medical School backed up this point: "The weakest, young and old, will be the ones unable to withstand the shock of this supposedly humane weapon. They will writhe in horrible cramps until their babies' [*sic*] strength is unequal to the stress and they turn blue and black and die . . ." Once again, the children of Vietnam are the losers. . . .

It is a ghastly situation. And triply compounded is the ghastliness of napalm and phosphorus. Surely, if ever a group of children in the history of man, anywhere in the world, had a moral claim for their childhood, here they are. Every sickening, frightening scar is a silent cry to Americans to begin to restore that childhood for those whom we are compelled to call our own because of what has been done in our name.

William F. Pepper is Executive Director of the Commission on Human Rights in New Rochelle, New York, a member of the faculty at Mercy College in Dobbs Ferry, New York, and Director of that college's Children's Institute for Advanced Study. On leave of absence last spring [1966], he spent six weeks in South Vietnam as an accredited journalist.

---

## PETER ARNETT: REASONS FOR DESTRUCTION OF VILLAGE OF BOKINH

*Having witnessed the destruction of the South Vietnamese town of Bentre by allied heavy guns and fighter-bombers in pursuit of the enemy, Associated Press correspondent Peter Arnett asked, "When does the infliction of civilian casualties become irrelevant as long as the enemy is destroyed?" An unnamed U.S. advisor responded, "It became necessary to destroy the town to save it."[2] In the following poignant Associated Press dispatch by Arnett, entitled "Decision in Vietnam: Death of a Hamlet," the threshold for destruction of the village of Bokinh was the death of a single American officer.*

*New York Times*, 1 June 1969

Bokinh, South Vietnam—For half a day the fate of this hamlet and its two neighbors south of Saigon hung in the balance: Would they live or die?

The scales tipped when an American colonel, who was counseling restraint, was killed. The orders were sent, and fighter-bombers and artillery came in.

The destruction of Bokinh typifies two problems that have burdened the United States ever since it committed major forces to South Vietnam. One is that reliable intelligence information, the clue that something is coming, is often lacking or faulty. The other is that pacification provides no sure answer.

And Bokinh showed again that while people are regarded as the key to victory in Vietnam, they become a secondary consideration when the choice is between saving them or securing a military objective.

That a choice had to be made at all in Bokinh was caused by the sudden appearance of 200 North Vietnamese soldiers. They had slipped across the Plain of Reeds and had entered Bokinh and part of two adjoining hamlets at night, digging bunkers and deploying their heavier weapons.

The hamlets are situated a few hundred yards from Thuthua, a district capital, an area long proud of being the most pacified in Longan Province.

## ALARM WAS NOT RAISED

Pacification is dependent on people's willingness to resist the enemy. Yet when the North Vietnamese troops appeared, no one raised the alarm. Saigon's Popular Force troops, supposedly out in night ambush positions, did not see anyone.

The North Vietnamese roused people from their beds to ferry them across a wide canal and to help build their bunkers. No one in the hamlet's self-defense forces fired his weapon or even attempted to slip a few hundred yards down the dark road to let the district chief know what was going on. Even the dogs were still.

When the North Vietnamese were ready, they announced their presence with a clatter of machine-gun fire at the main village outpost.

Then they waited the two hours until dawn for the reaction.

The exact mission of the enemy troops who slipped into Bokinh is still not clear. But they disrupted the pacification program in a way that gave them the maximum advantage— and they used allied firepower to do the job for them.

A Vietcong general explained the technique to a meeting of a Communist cadre in Quangtri Province late last year. According to a captured document, he told them that the easiest way to destroy a town or a village was to occupy it, hoist the Vietcong flag, and let the United States Air Force do the job.

"The Americans cannot resist bombing our flag, no matter from where it flies, from the public school or the church steeple," he was quoted as saying.

## TET WAS INSTRUCTIVE

This was a lesson the enemy leadership learned from the 1968 Tet offensive when many Vietnamese towns and cities were partly destroyed by allied bombing. The general instructed the cadre to utilize this American eagerness as a means of causing maximum disruption.

Bokinh was a textbook example. By sneaking undetected into Bokinh, the North Vietnamese posed a problem for allied commanders: What was the best course of action?

The enemy had surfaced and was vulnerable, particularly because fairly open terrain surrounded the neatly laid out hamlets. The temptation was to strike with as much firepower as possible, accomplishing the mission with a minimum of allied casualties.

But then, hundreds of civilians who had been patiently courted over the years and had been promised protection, were in the hamlets with the enemy. They had seemed to have been developing confidence in the central Government. Would this confidence withstand the bombing?

## "THE OTHER IMPERATIVES"

The problem was resolved in the inevitable manner. "In the cool of a room a couple of weeks later," said Maj. Donald Vogel, the United States adviser to the district, "you might think it would have been better to cordon off the hamlets with a lot of troops, and starve the North Vietnamese out. But when you are the commander on the spot, and the battle is raging, there are other imperatives."

Maj. Vogel was pinned down in a rice paddy all that day. The "other imperatives" were determined by officers from the United States Ninth Division and the Vietnamese province chief.

The decision to bomb was made at noon. Attempts to enter the hamlets that morning had been resisted with heavy fire. Rockets knocked out two American armored personnel carriers advancing across the rock-hard paddy fields.

The senior American province adviser, Col. Asa T. Gray, 50 years old, of Battle Creek, Mich., who had often visited Bokinh and knew some of the people, counseled restraint. He did not even let the American armored vehicles fire their .50-caliber machine guns.

Then a sniper killed the colonel. The bombs arrived soon after.

Parts of Bokinh and the neighboring hamlets of Anhoa and Vamthu were methodically destroyed in bombardments that continued into the evening.

Next morning, "the tears sprang to my eyes when I saw it all," said Stan Ifshin, a tall New Yorker formerly with the Peace Corps and now a civilian adviser to the district. "Nine months of my work, all gone," Mr. Ifshin thought as he walked in the smoking ruins of the hamlets.

Three hundred eighty homes were destroyed, some by fires that swept through thatch-roof houses earlier in the day.

The civilian dead totaled 19, including a family of nine. Fifty civilians were injured, many of them seriously.

"They got off easily," Mr. Ifshin said bitterly. He wasn't referring to the civilians. He meant the North Vietnamese who had slipped away in the darkness, mission accomplished. Twenty enemy bodies were found in the hamlets.

Efforts to rebuild Bokinh and its neighbors are proceeding with the same degree of energy used to destroy them. The United States Ninth Division, the province administration, Boy Scouts, religious groups and medical teams have converged upon the dazed refugees.

"The input has been superb, and we have discerned no anti-Americanism, even though the villagers seem disappointed that the enemy got that close," commented John Zeroias, the province refugee adviser. The Americans based in the district where they used to brag "nothing ever happens" wonder why they didn't get any early warning from the people of the enemy's arrival.

Major Vogel said: "We can reconstruct the hamlets. There will be very few scars to show for it all. But the mental impact on the people—how long will it take to remove those scars?

"Maybe these people just want to be left alone."

*Credit*: Reprinted with permission of The Associated Press.

---

## MAYNARD PARKER: TRUE REASON FOR HIGH CIVILIAN CASUALTIES

*The careless disregard for human life that marked "pacification" of Vietnamese peasant villages by U.S. soldiers usually was excused because "friendlies" were indistinguishable from Vietcong guerrillas. The following* Newsweek *article, entitled "GIs in Battle: The 'Dink' Complex," was compiled from dispatches by the magazine's Saigon bureau chief Maynard Parker, who raises the specter of a more fundamental and odious explanation for civilian casualties—racism.*

*Newsweek*, 1 December 1969

Although the full truth about the massacre at Song My may never be known, even the details that have emerged so far point up a distressing fact about the Vietnam war: many U.S. fighting men, under the stress of combat, display a profound contempt for the people of South Vietnam. With hearty distaste, GIs commonly refer to the South Vietnamese—allies and enemies alike—as "dinks." And in the view of many longtime observers of the war, it is not unreasonable to conclude that the strong antipathy underlying such epithets—or the "dink syndrome" as it is known in Vietnam—sometimes plays a part in the casual killing of civilian bystanders. "Psychologically and morally," says a U.S. civilian official, "it's much easier to kill a 'dink' than it is to shoot a 'Vietnamese'."

Friction between allies, of course, is not a new phenomenon. During World War II, American troops in the China-Burma-India theater often derided their native comrades as "wogs," "chinks" or "slopes." In Korea, the people of both north and south were lumped together by American GIs under the derisive term "gook." But in these earlier wars, there was at least a frontline on most occasions, and the enemy, by definition, was on the other side of it. By contrast, in Vietnam there is often no way to tell friend from foe, and the constant suspicion sometimes prods tired and frustrated soldiers into rash actions.

### CONTEMPT

Sometimes these acts are mindless impulses. Late last year, as he whizzed by a rice field in his Jeep, one soldier took a playful pot shot at a Vietnamese farmer's hat: he missed, blew the man's head off and drew a five-year prison term. In other cases, contempt for Vietnamese lives is demonstrated in a more premeditated way. One U.S. battalion commander, observed a few months ago by Saigon bureau chief Maynard Parker, dubbed his helicopter a "Gookmobile" and recorded his kills on its fuselage with a neatly painted row of conical hats. Another officer liked to stalk Vietnamese in "free-fire" zones (where anything that moves is fair game), plinking at them from his helicopter with a pistol. His shooting sprees were perfectly legal—and the victims may even have been Viet Cong.

Officially, the U.S. command takes infinite precautions to avoid civilian casualties; six or eight separate clearances are often required to fire a single round of artillery. "I'm sometimes astounded," says an American diplomat, "that they ever get a round out of the tube." But the use of such devices as free-fire zones and random "H&I" (harassment and interdiction) artillery fire inevitably create the unintended impression that Vietnamese life is cheap. Young GIs, moreover, soon learn that the main business of all army in wartime is killing, and that success is measured almost solely by body count. A brigade commander once ran a contest to rack up his unit's 10,000th kill: the prize was a week of luxury in the colonel's own quarters, and the happy winner was even shown off to a visiting journalist.

### TRAPS

The problem is compounded by the isolation of most GIs from ordinary Vietnamese citizens. The U.S. soldier lives in his own "world of the big PX"; the civilians he sees most frequently include panhandlers, black marketeers, prostitutes, taxi drivers and VC suspects—none of whom inspire much affection. And the GI soon learns from bitter experience that even apparently friendly villagers may be his mortal enemies. Fully a third of the Americal Division's casualties this year have been caused by booby traps, and many of the explosives were probably made by meek-looking farmers and grandmothers. "It gets maddening going into the same place again and again and seeing your people's legs blown off," an Army captain said last week. "You know the VC couldn't do it without support. You know even the kids are making grenades. When you're under that kind of stress, anything can happen."

The fact that "anything" does not happen more often is a credit to the American soldier. But the GI's bitter and sometimes violent distaste for the people he is supposed to defend hardly stands as a good omen. Since the first American combat soldier set foot in Vietnam, U.S. officials have repeatedly stressed the crucial importance of winning the hearts and minds of the South Vietnamese people. "Dinks," almost by definition, do not possess hearts and minds worth winning.

*Credit*: From Newsweek, 12/1/69. © 1969 Newsweek, Inc. All rights reserved. Reprinted with permission.

## NOTES

1. Lee Hall, Marshall Smith, Robert Morse, and John Flynn, "A Life Panel: The Lowdown from the Top U.S. Command in Saigon," *Life*, 27 November 1964, 46, 46A–46B, 51–52.

2. Bernard Weintraub, "Survivors Hunt Dead of Bentre, Turned to Rubble in Allied Raids," *New York Times*, 8 February 1968, 14.

## FURTHER READINGS

Just, Ward S. *To What End: Report from Vietnam*. Boston: Houghton Mifflin, 1968.

Sack, John. M. New York: New American Library, 1967.

Tanham, George K. *War without Guns: American Civilians in Rural Vietnam*. New York: Praeger, 1966.

# 12

# VIETCONG TERRORISM

In the early years of the Vietnamese civil war, the Vietcong Communist rebels had orders not to kill American military and civilian advisors so as not to provoke increased U.S. involvement. Vietcong policy changed when it became clear that the Americans would not go away, although the guerrillas tried to avoid harming civilian aid workers who helped the peasants.

The central government in Saigon condemned the Vietcong as a cruel, ruthless enemy of the people; however, the South Vietnamese soldiers, most of whom were city boys who disdained the rural population, treated the peasants with greater barbarity. They swept through the rural villages in pursuit of the enemy, raping the women, stealing food, and torturing suspected Vietcong prisoners with an alacrity that horrified their American advisors.

In the classic manner of insurgents facing an established foe, the National Liberation Front and its Vietcong fighters used terrorism as an instrument of political warfare—selective assassination of village chiefs and government collaborators, usually by shooting or beheading, but sometimes by more gruesome means, such as disemboweling. Most victims were found with a death notice pinned on their bodies; the message would explain their "crimes against the people" declared by an official-sounding group, such as "the People's Court," which everyone understood was the Vietcong. Their doctrine forbidding torture was violated selectively. Because their medical supplies were limited, the Vietcong shot seriously wounded prisoners. Torture was reserved for the walking wounded and unharmed who could not be reindoctrinated, usually officers. When feasible, American captives were treated as valuable commodities, reserved for higher-level interrogation, and sent to camps for potential prisoner exchanges.

Beginning in 1964, the terrorist objective was shifted to striking at Americans in the refugee-choked cities. The usual technique was detonation of grenades or homemade bombs in public places frequented by U.S. GIs and civilian officials. Innocent

Vietnamese pedestrians invariably also suffered, but they were considered expendable in the patriotic struggle against foreign imperialists. "Every minute," North Vietnamese general Vo Nguyen Giap observed, "thousands of men die all over the world. The life and death of human beings means nothing." The wantonly careless use of terrorism in the cities confounded the political campaign and came back to haunt the Vietcong in its Tet offensive of January–February 1968. Synchronous strikes against allied positions in every city in South Vietnam were calculated to foment a popular insurrection against the government, but the city dwellers did not rise up.

## WILLIAM TUOHY: INTRODUCTION FOR AMERICANS TO THE CONFLICT IN VIETNAM

*Vietnam was unlike any previous war for the Americans. On 28 July 1965, President Lyndon B. Johnson announced, "We will stand in Vietnam," and sent thousands of young Americans to that faraway land. This picture story for the Sunday supplement to the* New York Times *by the Saigon bureau chief for Newsweek, William Tuohy, introduced many Americans to the bewildering and unsavory conflict that their fathers, sons, and brothers soon would enter. Quoting his sources, Tuohy titled his piece, "'War Is Hell and, by God, This Is One of the Prime Examples': A Big 'Dirty Little War.'"*

New York Times, *28 November 1965*

Saigon—In the wan, yellow light of an officers' mess near Saigon's ramshackle Tan Son Nhut airport, two tired helicopter pilots sipped beer after a punishing day flying missions over Vietcong territory. The men, both U.S. Army captains in their late 20s with wives and children back home, were asked what they would do if forced down in enemy-held areas.

"I'd be thinking in the back of my mind about my family," said the tall, crew-cut captain who flies a medical evacuation chopper. "I think the four of us in the crew—with four rifles and four pistols—could hold them off long enough for rescue. But if it came to the point where we couldn't resist any longer, I don't know what I'd do."

The second pilot, who commands an armed helicopter platoon, had no doubts about what he would do. "I've made up my mind," he said. "They won't take me alive. They are not going to parade me around or make me grovel."

Drastic as it sounds, the second captain's attitude was undoubtedly shared by many other Americans in Vietnam. U.S. soldiers and civilians captured by the Vietcong have been dragged through villages like prisoners in the Roman wars, jeered at, laughed at, spit upon, kept in solitary confinement, and executed. Sometimes their bodies have been mutilated.

Recently, when two captured U.S. soldiers were killed by the V.C. in reprisal for the Saigon Government's execution of three terrorists, a State Department spokesman called it "an act of wanton murder." But most U.S. servicemen took the news more stoically: they have long accepted the fact that mercy is not to be expected from the Vietcong.

The conflict in Vietnam is often called "a dirty little war."

With U.S. combat troops and equipment pouring into the country, the war is getting much bigger. But it is no less dirty. In large part, it remains one of stealth, ambush, cut and run, treachery and bloody acts of terror inflicted on the populace by assailants they call "the men of the dark night."

To the aching frustration of U.S. commanders trained in more conventional tactics, this is a war in which countless hours are spent vainly tracking an elusive quarry through almost impenetrable jungle, muddy rice fields and blazing sand dunes. Friend is often indistinguishable from foe. Napalm and fragmentation bombs sometimes fall on defenseless peasants; artillery shells are fired at random into the paddy fields. An appalling number of victims are women, children and old men; some are participants but most are noncombatants.

"War is hell and, by God, this is one of the prime examples," says a top U.S. military commander. "There is no more ruthless s.o.b. than the Vietcong. This bastard will do anything that suits his purpose and he uses every dirty trick in the book."

To many, the dirtiest trick in the Vietcong manual is the widespread use of terror as an instrument of warfare. So far this year the Vietcong have murdered—by shooting, decapitation and disembowelment—about 400 Government officials, mostly at the hamlet and village level. Terrorists have mined and grenaded scores of buses and taxis, killing and mutilating hundreds of innocent Vietnamese.

Much of the terror is calculatedly barbaric. V.C. raiders in the Mekong delta gouged out a chunk of a village official's calf and ate it before killing him; in the mountains, pieces of skin were flayed from the thighs of women to force them to divulge their husbands' whereabouts. In northernmost Quang Tri Province, the wife of a bright young Vietnamese captain whose work had earned him a promotion to A.I.D. headquarters in Saigon returned home for a visit. She was seized by the V.C., disemboweled and her body hung on a fence post as a warning to those who become "U.S. agents." The catalogue of Vietcong atrocities is long and sickeningly repetitious.

Since there is no battlefront in Vietnam, terror is employed in the cities, too. In Saigon, the U.S. Embassy, restaurants, stadiums, police stations, and military billets have all been targets for bombs, plastique and mines. Grenades are tossed into the open windows of passing military vehicles. Sometimes, a bicycle laden with explosives prematurely detonates, leaving a gaping hole in the street.

The passenger terminal at the Saigon airport has been singled out for repeated attacks. The last time a bomb exploded there, Gen. William C. Westmoreland, U.S. commander in Vietnam, had just taken off in a helicopter and was less than 100 yards away when a puff of white smoke and debris burst through the roof of the terminal. Circling over the scene, Westmoreland calmly remarked to a passenger, "I thought they'd do that one of these days. It is typical of the Vietcong, striking a civilian terminal. They have no concern for human life." He paused, then added: "I'm always amazed they haven't been more strongly condemned by world opinion."

Nowadays, in Saigon, West German television crewmen pointedly display their national flag on their car, British citizens paint the Union Jack on their villa gates and French hotels and restaurants conspicuously fly the tricolor at every opportunity. The flag waving is not chauvinism, of course, but merely a way of saying: "We are not Americans. Don't waste your bombs on us."

But if the Vietcong cruelly employs terror, South Vietnamese troops have behaved brutally, too. Anyone who has spent much time with Government units in the field has seen the heads of prisoners held under water and bayonet blades pressed against their throats. Photographs of such incidents were common until the Government decided the publicity was not improving Saigon's public relations. In more extreme cases, victims have had bamboo slivers run under their fingernails or wires from a field telephone connected to arms, nipples, or testicles. Another rumored technique is known as "the long step." The idea is to take several prisoners up in a helicopter and toss one out in order to loosen the tongues of the others.

Some Vietcong suspects do not survive long enough for the third degree. Earlier this year, in an operation along the central coast, a Government detachment failed to flush V.C. troops suspected of lurking in the area. However, several villagers were rounded up and one man was brought before the company commander. The Vietnamese officer briefly questioned the suspect, then turned to his adviser, an Australian warrant officer, and said, "I think I shoot this man. Okay?"

"Go ahead," said the adviser.

The officer fired a carbine round point-blank, striking the villager below the chest. The man slumped and died. The patrol moved on. Later, a correspondent asked the adviser, who had seemed a decent enough fellow, why he had given his approval. The Australian cited the British experience in putting down the Malayan insurgency and said, "These people could have moved to a Government area. In this war they are either on our side or they are not. There is no in-between."

Few American military advisers would sanction such brutality or, for that matter, subscribe to the "with-us-or-against-us" theory. The most able U.S. advisers have learned to respect the subtleties and complexities of the war; General Westmoreland himself warns new arrivals of the "frustrations and perplexities" they can expect. No village is totally pro-Communist or totally pro-Government. Few peasants have the luxury to choose freely. But these lessons come slowly to newly arrived combat troops trained to assault more conventional objectives.

On some occasions the tactics of U.S. troops have been sadly inept for the situation. Thus, in a remote hamlet in the central highlands, a burly, red-faced captain entered with a patrol of paratroopers and ordered the villagers rounded up. "Ask these people where the Vietcong went," the captain told a nervous Vietnamese interpreter. An old man who might have been the village elder began speaking rapidly. "Sit down and shut up, loudmouth," bellowed the captain in English.

Then the captain ordered a soldier, "Take him 100 yards down the road. Maybe if they think we're going to blow his head off, they'll talk."

The villagers did not talk; the women and children wailed and sobbed. Embarrassed, the paratroopers began loading two dozen peasants aboard a truck to take them to the district town. The soldiers were gentle as possible and courteous, but the villagers continued to cry. For all they knew they were being packed off to exile, imprisonment or execution. A lieutenant wondered about the efficacy of such tactics, but asked plaintively, "Well, if they're not V.C. sympathizers, what are they doing way out here? Why don't they live in the city?"

The paratroopers meant well and were only trying to do their job, but the gospel as taught at Fort Benning is often inappropriate in the villages of Asia.

To many Americans, the war in Vietnam seems bewilderingly savage. Yet there seems to be no other way to wage it.

Despite the U.S. attempt to make the struggle more conventional, it is still basically a guerrilla war and, by definition, dirty. It is also a civil war, inevitably unleashing violent passions. It is a war fought by Asian standards, without even lip service to the niceties of warfare prescribed by Western convention.

Further, many Vietnamese on both sides hold primitive animistic beliefs that are sometimes responsible for macabre brutality. They believe that eating the liver of a dead foe instills the victor with strength and courage. They believe that the soul does not immediately leave the body after death, and so, if the body is mutilated the soul is condemned to wander.

There is still another reason for much of the brutality. As Gen. Maxwell Taylor said while he was Ambassador in Saigon, "This whole war is a matter of intelligence." Intelligence, or more simply, information, is a vital commodity and the attempt to get it or withhold it explains much of the terror and torture inflicted by both sides.

American advisers find it hard to dissuade the Vietnamese from using force on prisoners. Says one U.S. specialist, "The Vietnamese do their questioning out of our sight because they know we feel guilty about their methods. They say, 'You people are a bunch of softies. This is a rough war and this is the way to get information—the only way.' So the Vietnamese major says to the American adviser, 'I suggest you take a walk and don't come back for half an hour. We're going to do this anyway, so it is better if you aren't here.'"

"I myself don't believe in the effectiveness of torture, but it is very difficult to tell a Vietnamese paratrooper whose buddies have just been wiped out to go easy on a prisoner and make sure he gets back for questioning."

"There are better ways of getting information from prisoners than torture," says another American paramilitary expert. "Sure, you can start cutting off fingers and the guy will talk. But you never know whether the information is accurate. If I were being tortured, I'd whip out so much stuff it would take them six months to check it. But you can't walk away from it. You've got to watch them do it, run through five or six guys, even if it turns your insides. Then you ask, 'Why do you do it that way? Did you get any information you could act on? No? Then why not try it another way?' Most of these prisoners have been warned to expect brutality. But if you say, 'I'm your friend,' they don't know how to react. Their orders don't cover this, so being humane is much more effective."

This specialist is one of the handful of Americans in Vietnam practicing the arcane (some call it "black") art of revolutionary warfare. Their job is to train specially motivated political-military Vietnamese cadres and infuse them with skill, confidence, pride, [and] national fervor. Since the cadres are taught to fight the V.C. on their own terms the training draws heavily on Communist techniques.

"They've had 25 years' experience at this," explains one black warrior. "Why not adapt it to our aims and resources?"

The ultimate ideological task of the cadres is convincing the people that the Vietcong is trying to steal the national revolution. Through lectures and indoctrination they teach that since the overthrow of Diem, it is the Communists—not the Government—who are the oppressors, who wish to tyrannize the people, exploit their land and will not leave them in peace. A vital practical job of the cadres is to lead platoons of local militia "like a soft wind into a hamlet," to patrol at night, lay ambushes, bribe, subvert, assassinate.

Like many other peoples, the Vietnamese have been slow to borrow from the casebook of Communist insurgency techniques—even though the enemy comes from the same cultural and ethnic stock. Then, too, the Vietnamese Army is largely a product of American training, and no soldier in the world has been more loath to adopt the bloody tactics of revolutionary warfare than the average senior U.S. officer. "It's a great pity we didn't begin training these motivated platoons when we moved back here in 1954," laments a top U.S. official.

The Americans who train these cadres pass unnoticed in the streets of Saigon, dressed in casual sports shirts. In the field they wear black pajamas like the men they train. They are fluent in Vietnamese and have a high regard for their adversaries. Their guidebooks are not U.S. Army field manuals, but the works of Mao Tse-tung, Vo Nguyen Giap, Che Guevara and the ancient Chinese military philosopher, Sun Tzu. Speaking the language of revolutionary warfare, they believe the war must be won by revolutionary means.

"This is not so much a dirty war as a different war," says one of these men. "It is total war involving all the people. The American Army thinks terror is unconventional. But terror is not unconventional to the Vietcong. It is part of the human hardware. Assassination would horrify General Westmoreland. Air and artillery, that's what the military understands. But assassination is what the peasant understands."

These specialists discuss the use of terror analytically, not emotionally.

"Vietcong terror is bloodthirsty but selective," an expert explains. "It is a scalpel, not a hammer. It is aimed at the leaders. In three years they drove out 50 percent of the Vietnamese leaders from the countryside. They went after the very best and the very worst. As a result, there is a premium on mediocrity among civil servants. The purpose of most V.C. terror is to teach a lesson. They behead a village chief and kill his wife and kids. It's messy but the next chief won't bring his family to the town, and the V.C. will stress this in their propaganda.

"Usually, they have a specific reason for every act of terror. They don't kill for the sake of killing. But in the past six months, they have been making mistakes, probably by using poorly trained cadres. A green kid sits under a tree with orders to touch off a mine under a military truck. He gets impatient and blows up a bus.

"Terror is effective over the short range. But if you use too much, people begin to think: 'Eventually, it's going to be me, so I might as well help get rid of these guys.' And every time a father is beheaded, all his sons join the Army."

The experts turn the terror against the Vietcong; assassination teams are "sanitation" squads who take pride in their work. "I'm a great believer in getting the guys responsible for the war," says an American who has been trained to clean up. "Go for the head, get the commander, or the deputy political commissar for the whole battalion. The Vietcong is susceptible to this kind of attack because there is no clear chain of command to assume authority and responsibility."

"I believe in bribing guards to assassinate their officers, buying them off, working through their relatives, putting prices on their heads, sowing suspicion in every way. In warfare you try for the command post. And killing their communications and liaison people is like putting out their eyes and ears. I'd rather kill a political officer of a district than his whole company, because as long as he's alive he can recruit five companies.

"Too many people think our job is only to kill Cong," he notes, "but ultimately it is to convert them."

In Dinh Tuong, a crucial province south of Saigon, a superb black operation was carried out last summer. An informer fingered the top V.C. commissar in the province at a nighttime meeting. A sanitation squad closed in and chewed up the hut with automatic weapons fire. Killed with the V.C. chieftain were a half-dozen of his aides. The Vietcong apparatus in the province was paralyzed for weeks.

"If you can repeat this kind of thing with any regularity, you'll shorten the insurgency by years," says a U.S. specialist. "But few people know how to apply counter-terror properly. It must be selective, discriminating and teach a lesson. A little bit of terror goes a long way. One act will be understood by 95 percent of the villagers concerned. You can't allow it to be used to settle grudges. You can't allow it to turn into a monster.

"In burning the village of Cam Ne the Marines made the mistake of using mass terror instead of being selective. I've been in hamlets where kids have thrown rocks at me and I've been spat at but there is always someone who will make your visit worthwhile. The Marines should have found out the five or six homes sheltering snipers and burned them, and they should have explained why they were doing it."

Nothing infuriates these revolutionary warfare tacticians more than indiscriminate air strikes and wild artillery fire in the countryside. "It's madness," says one. "The U.S. is always looking for the easy way, the gimmick. Tactical air strikes are fine when the V.C. are attacking a position, but you don't napalm a whole village because of a couple of snipers."

The specialists also criticize some aspects of the U.S. psychological warfare program. Says one: "Writing Churchillian messages to toss out of a plane is much less dangerous than getting out to the villages personally. It is much less effective, too, since most peasants have a low literacy rate.

"Leaflets are fine to warn them of air strikes. But peasants don't follow leaflets. They follow people. You've got to have cadres on the ground to follow up. Otherwise, all you have are a bunch of activity reports but no real results."

It is a brutal war in Vietnam, but the men fighting it try not to become brutalized.

"We all want to avoid wanton ruthlessness," says a senior U.S. military commander, "and we are trying to minimize the number of noncombatants under fire. But in 20 years there has been a hell of a lot of fighting. When you receive Vietcong fire from tunnels and bunkers, the only thing to do is go in after them. If you find old people and kids, it is grievous and regrettable. But there it is.

"Yet," this officer adds, "it is curious how our point of view has changed. Twenty years ago we were dreaming up every device possible to devastate people—maximum destruction from the air—and I don't recall a great deal of concern about where the bombs landed." He went on to point out that individual acts of terror, because they are more personal, in a sense, than the mass cruelty of World War II, tend to create the impression that the struggle in Vietnam is more brutal than it really is. "What is more brutal," he asked, "killing a village chief, disemboweling his wife and cutting up his kids—or blasting Hiroshima? Burying a man alive as a warning to other villagers—or exterminating six or seven million Jews? I don't think there is a higher order of brutality here than we've had in the past."

"You can't keep a war humane," adds another American. "It's hard to argue that we're not being brutalized, but I think we can still stand for a set of ethics: respect for the dignity of life, a sense of limits to what we can and cannot do, a complete rejection of the theory that the end justifies the means. This is the cutting edge between us and Communism.

"Even in practical terms we're better off being as humane as possible because then the enemy is less reluctant to surrender."

One of the most experienced practitioners of revolutionary warfare, whose work includes counter-terror, discussed his job with candor and thoughtfulness. "Look," he said, "there's no humane way to kill a man. Terror is terror. Murder is murder. Counterterror is a word used by Americans because it sounds clean. The important thing is not the degree of cleanliness of the war but the degree of necessity.

"Let's not kid ourselves. The hero of 'Catch 22' was right—wars are basically insane. We are trying to kill each other. But I also believe in Mao's distinction between just wars and unjust wars. If you believe this is an unjust war, then you've got to get out, because you will get yourself zapped.

"The main thing is to see the relation between our aims and what the Vietnamese farmer wants—to protect his land, be left in peace, and get the V.C. out of his village. U.S. combat troops spend so much time on patrol and in bivouac that they have little contact with the people. They are more likely to become brutalized by the fighting, and this is a real danger.

"I don't think you can become really hardened if you share the involvement with the people.

"One night a Vietnamese officer and I were talking about personal things. We were sitting in a field. He showed me his wife's picture and then broke down and cried. She had left him because he wasn't at home enough. He said he still loved her. I think that when you share things like that with the people here you can't be brutalized. The important thing is to be involved."

The "dirty little war" in Vietnam is an untidy, unclear conflict, but it is the kind the United States may be fighting for many years to come—if not in Asia, then in Africa or in Latin America. It is a grim prospect, but one with a consolation of sorts. As Brig. Gen. Samuel B. Griffith, a perceptive student of insurgency, has written, "Guerrilla warfare is suffused with and reflects man's admirable qualities as well as his less pleasant ones. While it is not always humane, it is human, which is more than can be said for the strategy of extinction."

*Credit*: © 1965 by The New York Times Co. Reprinted with permission.

## DON MOSER: VIETCONG URBAN TERRORISM

*A result of months of probing the shadowy alleys of Saigon, the following extraordinary piece of investigative journalism by* Life *magazine's Don Moser, photographed by Co Rentmeester, documents urban terrorism that typified the Vietcong's revised strategy against the Americans. The Vietcong coordinated terrorist attacks in South Vietnamese cities as the preliminary phase of its ambitious Tet offensive of January–February 1968.*

### *Life*, 12 January 1968

The first *inside* report on an elite unit of secret killers known as F-100—The past few weeks in Vietnam have seen a sharp rise in Vietcong terrorist attacks. In hamlets and cities, using bombs, grenades and assassinations, well-organized V.C. units have tried to kill Americans and intimidate Vietnamese who support the government. In this remarkable report, put together after months of study, *Life* Correspondent Don Moser details the workings of the most dangerous V.C. terrorist unit now in operation.

Having synchronized watches and gone over the plan one last time, the three men struggled through the thick late-afternoon traffic toward the Ong Lanh marketplace—Sam and Tam on their motorbikes and Trong on his bicycle. The peasant woman was there waiting, sitting with her baskets of produce, just at the spot that Sam had shown her.

Sam sat astride his cycle for a moment, checking the scene. The two baskets of crude sugar were beside her. Good.

He got off and walked toward her. "How is your business today?" he asked.

"I have sold half my sugar," the woman replied.

"Did you get a good price?"

As they made casual conversation, Sam looked over the baskets. Each had a bit of wire protruding from the side. Sam opened one of the baskets and scooped some of the sugar from it; the woman did the same with the other. Sam had been meticulously trained, but this was the first operation he had run by himself, and he wanted everything to go smoothly. He plunged his hand into the remaining sugar and felt about. The day before, in the Secret Zone outside Saigon, he had carefully blocked the mine into position and now he found it still perfectly aligned with the crude but effective sighting wire. The second basket was all right too.

Without talking, he and the woman carried one of the baskets to Trong's bicycle and lashed it to the side, the wire pointing out. Trong and Tam meanwhile were tying the other basket to Tam's motorbike. To anyone in the busy marketplace who might be watching, they were just men buying sugar.

Sam then got on his own cycle and rode along to the little park by the waterfront. He sat down on a bench there—a small man, nondescript and inconspicuous. When the others arrived they did not greet him. Tam went across the park and found a bench by himself. Trong sat on the other end of Sam's bench, but the two men did not speak.

It was a long wait. Sam did not normally smoke but he smoked now. He read the newspaper. He watched the boats out on the Saigon River, the Americans enjoying themselves speeding up and down in motorboats and drifting by in little sailboats. He was worried about Trong. Tam was an old hand, a professional, but Trong was only 19 and he had handled nothing but a couple of grenadings, never a job like this.

Trong was nervous. "I am afraid it will go off early," he blurted finally. "While I am still on the bicycle."

Sam tried to settle him down. "Do not worry," he said. They had prepared the watches themselves, he explained. They had tested them carefully, and they were very good watches, the best kind. The boy should be patient now, and calm.

At precisely 7:45 Sam reached into his pocket and took out the wristwatch and the tiny battery pack. The watch had no second hand or hour hand, and he set the minute hand exactly 40 minutes back from the wire inserted through a hole drilled in the face. At 8:25 the hand would touch the wire and close the circuit.

He passed the watch to Trong, and the boy walked over to his bicycle. Pretending to fix something on the bike, Trong swiftly connected the watch to the mine in the basket and scooped sugar over it.

Then, instead of waiting for another 15 minutes as he was supposed to do, Trong climbed on his bicycle and took off down the street.

Sam stared. This could be disastrous. The whole operation could fail. Trong would park his bicycle at the target far too early—and parked bicycles bearing large, suspicious-looking burdens were not ignored by the police. Five to seven minutes was the maximum time allowed according to directives, and Trong would arrive at the target more than 15 minutes early.

Sam moved quickly to his motorbike and took after the boy. Trong was pedaling fast. Sam pulled up alongside and motioned sharply with his hand for Trong to slow down. But the boy did not even acknowledge him. He just kept pedaling, his face tight with fear.

There was nothing more Sam could do. He sped on ahead to the My Canh floating restaurant, parked his motorcycle at the appointed place and sat down on a bench to watch. Trong arrived a few minutes later, parked his bicycle near the restaurant entrance—as the plan had specified—and fled. Too early, too too early.

At 8:15, exactly on time, the experienced Tam pulled up and parked his motorcycle, positioning it carefully so that the wire on the basket was aimed directly at the restaurant where all the Americans and their Vietnamese friends were dining. Then Tam walked nonchalantly down the street, got onto Sam's motorbike and rode away. Three minutes.

Sam got up and strolled down the street. The police had noticed nothing. Perhaps the plan would work, after all. At precisely 8:20 Tam's motorbike disappeared in a blast of flame and smoke as the huge claymore mine drove its hundreds of steel pellets through the side of the restaurant. In two or three minutes policemen and firemen and soldiers would be milling about at the scene, right in front of the second mine on Trong's bicycle.

A taxi came down the street and Sam flagged it. "God, something exploded there!" Sam said as he got in.

The taxi was halfway down Flower Street when the second mine went off, and Nguyen Van Sam did not even hear the explosion.

In the two years from the day he blew up the My Canh floating restaurant in June 1965, killing 44 Americans and Vietnamese and wounding 80 more, until his capture last July 31—the very day that he intended to pull his biggest coup—Nguyen Van Sam commanded 28 other terrorist operations in the city of Saigon which were directly responsible for the deaths of 58 Vietnamese and Americans, and for injuries to 226 more. Sam was the leader of Special Action Unit 69, an element of one of the most lethal terrorist organizations in history: F-100.

F-100—known also as C-10, C-44 and by various other cover designations—is an organization of trained, professional terrorists. Its various cells and spin-off special action units have run every major terrorist operation in Saigon for the past two and a half years. Besides the My Canh restaurant, these include the bombings of the U.S. Embassy, the Metropole enlisted men's quarters, the Victoria officers' quarters and the National Police Headquarters. It was F-100 which rocketed the Vietnamese National Day celebration, attempted to mortar General Westmoreland's headquarters, and did mortar Independence Palace during [U.S.] Vice President Humphrey's recent visit. F-100 agents have also carried out assassinations, grenadings and small-scale attacks beyond count. At a conservative estimate, F-100 has killed at least 250 people and wounded 1,400 more.

While it is commonly supposed that Vietcong terrorism is haphazard, or spur of the moment, F-100's operations are planned with an almost fanatical attention to detail, painstakingly rehearsed, carried out with split-second timing, and endlessly critiqued. F-100's table of organization includes mapmakers, photographers and demolition experts. It has its own finance section, its own communications section and a specialist who converts wristwatches into mechanisms for detonating time bombs. Though some of its most active cells have lately been broken by the Vietnamese police, the parent organization itself has continued to grow in size and power. From its base deep in the Secret Zone of the jungles of Binh Duong province, and under the direction of a man known only as Brother Hoang, F-100 has the primary responsibility for terrorism not only in Saigon but in every other city and sizable town in the vicinity.

F-100 was formed early in 1965, when the three sapper platoons that had handled all Saigon terrorism were combined under a single command. Today it includes sapper units of all sizes and functions: groves, groups, cells, intercells, and special action units, of which Sam's Unit 69 was one. F-100's setup calls for a roster of 1,200 men although its actual strength is much less. Its arsenal includes every weapon from a heavy mortar on down, and the unit has even issued instructions explaining how its men can make flamethrowers from commonplace equipment easily found in Saigon—instructions which, fortunately, have not been put into practice.

F-100's men must move constantly between Saigon and headquarters in the Secret Zone of the jungle areas outside the city. There is no problem: excellent counterfeit I.D. cards are turned out on the V.C.'s jungle printing presses, and legitimate blank cards stolen from government offices are available on the black market at prices ranging from 5,000 to 20,000 piasters. Throughout the city the organization maintains a vast system of safehouses—secret meeting places—purchased with an apparently inexhaustible treasury. Some of these safehouses are private dwellings. Others are small business establishments such as bicycle repair shops or food stores, and no trouble is spared to make the cover perfect. One of the unit's more active operatives, a man known as

Chin the Barber, was trained in all tonsorial techniques before setting up a safehouse in a barbershop.

All of F-100's agents use aliases and cover names. In Vietnam people are often known by their filial rank. The second son, for example, is known is "Brother Three" (no one gets the rank of one). This custom makes a convenient basis for F-100 cover names; agents are often known just by their filial-rank numbers and initials. Nguyen Van Sam's commander, for example, is called 7-N. These numerical names are also sometimes used as sign and countersign. When two agents meet, neither being certain of the other's identity, one man will ask, "Are you Brother Four?" The other will reply, "Yes, are you Brother Six?" If the two numbers add up to 10—or whatever the correct code number for the day is—each man knows that he has made the correct contact.

To maintain security, F-100 uses a system of "compartmentalization" or "vertical organization." The unit is divided into many small units, and each man knows only his immediate commander. He may only know his comrades in the cell by aliases and see them only during operations and planning sessions.

Messages between command levels are commonly written in invisible ink made from the Chinese herbal medicine used for treating cold sores. Dispatches into the city are often carried by non-V.C. who have no idea that the paper-wrapped parcel they are delivering actually bears invisible plans for blowing up a police station. To maintain compartmentalization, agents use letter-drops—prearranged spots where messages are dropped off by one agent and picked up by another, neither man learning the identity of the other.

Recruits for F-100 are schooled in sabotage techniques in the Secret Zone, and during classes, to keep identities secret, they are separated from each other by sheets of cloth or opaque plastic. They are led about blindfolded and allowed to bathe or relieve themselves only separately or at night. After returning to Saigon, a recruit gets further on-the-job training. His squad leader gives him a grenade, drives him about on the back of a motorbike until he finds a good target, and observes how the new man performs. The scores of apparently random grenade attacks in Saigon are nearly all training exercises of this kind.

Weapons and explosives are smuggled past police checkpoints and into the city by the "ant method." Instead of a single truck carrying 200 pounds of TNT, scores of couriers using many routes of access bring in a pound or two each. F-100 is ingenious. Grenades are hidden inside pineapples, blocks of TNT are stuffed into hollow lengths of bamboo, [and] messages are secreted in loaves of bread and sewn into potatoes. Recently an American official in one U.S. office in Saigon—an admitted admirer of the female form—was attracted each morning by a curvy Vietnamese girl in his office. But when she went home at the end of the day, she no longer seemed so appealing. For a while the American thought he was simply tired from the day's work and therefore less appreciative. "But then I knew I wasn't getting that old," he said. When he ordered a body search pulled on the girl next morning, police found her brassiere packed with plastic explosives. A few more days and she would have had enough smuggled in to blow the building off the map.

> But underneath the shallow layer of water lay 300 pounds of TNT.

During 1965 and 1966, two cells of F-100—B-4 under a graduate science student and demolitions expert named Tuan, and B-5 led by a mastermind named Bay Be—ran a series of spectacularly successful operations in Saigon. Working sometimes separately, more often in concert, Tuan and Bay Be and their small groups hit the U.S. Embassy, killing 22 and wounding 179, the Metropole enlisted men's billet, killing 13 and wounding 152, [and] the Victoria officers' billet, killing eight and wounding 126. They grenaded bars and restaurants all over town, and even mounted an incredibly brazen attack on the National Police Headquarters itself. In this intricate, commando-style raid, Bay Be and his men sped up to the compound gates in two cars and laid down a screen of automatic weapons fire while another man drove a third car into the middle of the central compound and blew it up right under the noses of the cops. Then, covered by a preplanned diversionary attack on a nearby police substation, Bay Be and all of his men escaped scot-free. For the police, the attack was doubly humiliating because it is the Vietnamese police, rather than the military, who are directly responsible for fighting F-100.

Early in 1966 the national police Special Branch got its first big break with the aid of a Mata Hari–style double agent who established herself as Tuan's girl friend and confederate. The girl set up a tailor shop as a safehouse for Tuan and his men. From Tuan's point of view everything was perfect. The girl was his lover, the tailor shop was good cover, and explosives were sent in from the Secret Zone, hidden in bolts of cloth. He did not know that the tailor shop was bugged, that his conversations were recorded, and that the woman who appeared frequently to order clothes was a Special Branch agent picking up the tapes from Tuan's girl friend.

By January 1966 Tuan had worked out a formidable plan to blow up an American billet called the Alabama. He constructed an ingenious water cart. Anyone looking in the top would see that it was filled with water and if one turned the spigot, water ran out. But underneath the shallow layer of water lay 300 pounds of TNT. Just as Tuan and his men wheeled the water cart up to the Alabama, the police closed in.

Bay Be, the B-5 commander and most active terrorist of all, was also unlucky in love. He began a dalliance with the wife of another V.C. The outraged man defected and gave police the location of Bay Be's safehouse. Bay Be was arrested a few days later. A Special Branch captain thereupon saw a way to make Bay Be's capture pay further dividends. The Vietnamese Buddhists were in the midst of their 1966 demonstrations and the captain forced Bay Be to write a letter to his commander, suggesting that F-100 exploit the political crisis with a series of grenadings and minor incidents which the government would blame on the Buddhists. Many cadres should be sent in, Bay Be wrote, to work under his direction.

The letter went back up the line, the plan was approved, and F-100 started sending agents down to the city. In one week Special Branch arrested 10 key men. Ironically, the Buddhists on their own created a great deal of trouble during this period and the F-100 commander, misinterpreting who had been responsible for what, sent a message down to Bay Be, congratulating him on his effective exploitation of the situation.

Its two top cells broken with the capture of Bay Be and Tuan, F-100 subsided briefly. Then Cell B-11 and Grove A-4 went into operation with heavy weapons, shelling Tan Son Nhut airbase and the National Day celebration in the center of Saigon. In Cholon, the Chinese quarter of the city, a Chinese sapper unit also began working, although its relationship with F-100 was and is unclear. Some police believe that the organization may be a Maoist group only casually related to the Vietcong. The bombing of the Nationalist Chinese Embassy in September of 1966, however, had all the earmarks of an F-100 operation. But in the city itself, a great deal of the terrorist work was taken over by Special Action Unit 69, under the command of Nguyen Van Sam.

Nguyen Van Sam does not fit the image of a master terrorist. He is a small man with a hedgehog shock of hair and a disarming smile. He appears to be neither an ideologue nor a pathological killer, but a craftsman who has learned well a certain line of work and takes professional pride in his competence: he would approach the problem of blowing up a building in about the same frame of mind as a plumber tackling a blocked drain. He was born in 1932 in Binh Duong province, the son of a Buddhist farmer. He never attended school, but worked as a buffalo boy until he was 16, when he was recruited by his uncle into the Vietminh. During the resistance against the French he was a liaison agent, running messages from one Vietminh unit to another. When the country was partitioned in 1954, Sam went to the North where he became a truck driver and later a driving instructor. In 1963 he was recruited into Unit B, an organization for training saboteurs and terrorists to be infiltrated into the South, and attended Unit B's highly secret special school in Ha Dong province. For six months he was trained in techniques of sabotage, assassination and terrorism. He learned how to build mines and time bombs, how best to sabotage ships, offices, trains and airplanes. He received political indoctrination and

studied until his head swam. In 1964, Sam infiltrated back into the South, and headed for F-100's headquarters in the then Secret Zone in Cu Chi outside Saigon. With a fake identification card, Sam took a bus to Saigon. There, riding behind another agent on a motor scooter, Sam began learning every street and alley in the city. For the next few months he traveled back and forth between the city and the jungle. Romance can flower even among the Vietcong; in the Secret Zone, Sam fell in love with a short, rounded V.C. liaison girl and the two were married by Sam's commander.

After the success of his first independent operation at the My Canh restaurant, Sam's life fell into a weird sort of routine. When he was in Saigon, only one man—his reliable deputy Tam—knew where he lived. Sam would meet his men by prearranged appointment in a coffee shop. They would then go to one of the outdoor TV receivers scattered throughout the city and stand in back of the crowd talking softly while pretending to watch the program. Each operation was planned to the last degree. Sam and his men scouted proposed attack sites for days. They prepared meticulous maps, plans, [and] sometimes even took photographs. The plans were then carried or forwarded back to the Secret Zone for approval by Sam's commander, 7-N. When the plan was approved Sam and his men practiced the operation on a sand table until they had every movement letter perfect. Meanwhile, the necessary weapons and explosives were smuggled into the city to him.

Over the months, Sam rolled up an impressive list of accomplishments. In February of 1966 he mined the Vietnamese General Staff Headquarters gate, killing 13 and wounding 60. In May he mined an American bus station, killing five and wounding 29. Around election time in September of 1966 he ran six operations, killing one and wounding 27, and the following month he hit the Ky Son American billet, killing three and wounding 10. He bombed a warehouse in December and for the first few months of 1967 grenaded and mined several U.S. and Vietnamese military and police vehicles. On July 10 he mined the Capitol billet, killing four and wounding 27.

By this time, Sam had invested several hundred thousand V.C. piasters in a network of safehouses. He had a virtual motor pool of old cars, motorbikes and bicycles—he went through a lot of bikes and motorcycles because they were used to bear the mines and explosives and were commonly blown up in his attacks. He had a budget of 40,000 piasters a month for operating expenses, ran a training program for new recruits, and he had munitions cached all over the city.

In April of last year [1967] Sam moved his wife and their baby son into one of the safehouses in the city, obtaining the necessary identity documents for them all by the simple expedient of telling a district chief that he was a refugee from a V.C.-controlled area and therefore not on any census rolls. He established himself—or rather his wife—as a seller of soup, rice sticks and sweets.

But Sam was not happy. His superiors were demanding an impossible amount of work from him—10 to 20 operations a month. It took a long time to train "a good fighter." All too frequently his men were captured by police, it was getting harder and harder to find replacements and the bombing in the Secret Zones and the improved government control of the roads made it more difficult to get explosives into the city. Once Sam did get three big claymores and buried them along a canal in the city. But then a boat family came along, upended their sampan on his buried mines and started to repair it. For a month they camped on top of the precious mines while Sam fumed helplessly.

Moreover, Sam was growing tired of the war and tired of the killing. He was a fighter. He had always known that he had to go on fighting and that one day he would die. This had not bothered him before, but now he had a baby boy, and he hated the idea of dying without seeing his son grow up.

But work was work. In June, with his deputy Tam and the others, he began to plan his most ambitious operation yet: an attack on JUSPAO—the big Joint U.S. Public Affairs Office in the heart of Saigon. His plan called for using three huge DH-10 mines, each capable of blasting through eight inches of reinforced concrete from a distance of 100 feet. Two of the mines would be set to go off at 12 noon, as the Americans in the office were swarming out for lunch. The third would go off seven minutes later, just in time to catch the rescue workers and police. Sam was sure the blasts would kill at least 100 people.

But in an office at Saigon municipal police headquarters a barrel-shaped, flashing-eyed man was waiting for Sam to make a mistake. He was Pham Quant Tan, chief of Saigon's Special Branch. Captain Tan is a former intelligence and psychological warfare officer who devours books on criminology, chain-smokes king-sized cigarettes and functions best at 3 or 4 o'clock in the morning. During those small hours he prowls his city, meets with his agents and informers and tirelessly interrogates suspects. Captain Tan has the patience of a cat watching a mouse hole, and he is obsessed with the idea of catching terrorists. One of his diversions is the Asian chess game known in Vietnam as Co Tuong, and he is the master of a maneuver involving the two powerful "cannon" pieces. This maneuver he calls "double morte"—double death. Captain Tan is a very tough man.

While the Vietnamese police have earned something of a reputation as people not to be taken prisoner by, torture is not the captain's line. He likes to think of himself as a psychologist, and to watch him deal with a prisoner is to see a craftsman happy in his work. He interrogates prisoners for weeks, even months. "You squeeze them like a lemon, until you have every drop of juice," he says. He keeps a suspect perpetually off-balance. When a man is brought in for interrogation Captain Tan may bark a question the moment the suspect walks in the door. Next time he may ignore the man entirely for half an hour while pretending to peruse papers on his desk. During questioning his moods shift rapidly from purple-faced rage to bland reassurance. But mostly he is paternal, concerned, an agreeable relief from the surly jailers.

"Are you getting proper food?" he enquires solicitously of a prisoner. "Perhaps you would like some breakfast." Or: "Are you in good health? Your color does not look too good." His tongue clucks sympathetically and he produces vitamin pills from his desk. "You must take these, one each day, and you will feel better."

Captain Tan's interrogations form floral patterns; his questions circle, wander apparently aimlessly until the trap is set, then suddenly drive right at the guts of things.

The captain had known about Special Action Unit 69 for some time when, acting on an informer's tip, he put out an alert for the young man named Tam. When Tam was picked up at a police checkpoint he was carrying five wristwatches prepared as timebomb detonators. In spite of this solid evidence, Tam refused to talk during an entire night of questioning at a police precinct headquarters. Next morning, the captain took over the interrogation personally. When the terrorist was brought to his office Tam refused to speak or sit down. The captain stared at him. Then he told a subordinate that no one else was to question the man or even speak to him, and that he was to be placed in solitary confinement. "All right, you refused to speak," the captain said to Tam. "I will let you rest now till 9 o'clock. You can prepare all your lies in your mind. After 9 p.m. I will begin my investigation."

That night the captain had his men take Tam out of the cell, offer him food, coffee and cigarettes. Then they brought him to the captain's office. Again the V.C. refused to sit down. Captain Tan simply smiled and took out his military identification card. "I show you this to show you that I am not really a policeman," he said pleasantly. "Until recently I have always been a soldier, an infantry captain. So we are both soldiers, both fighters. So let us talk together as soldiers."

Then he began to ask, very conversationally, questions about Tam's personal life. He took no notes, and the questions were very innocent. Eventually Tam began to talk. After 20 minutes, Tam sat down for the first time. For two days the captain interviewed the V.C. until he felt that he had found the man's weakness. Finally he ordered Tam brought to his office again. "You are a sentimental guy," Captain Tan said brusquely, "I know what you want to do—you want to die. You don't want to denounce your friends; you want to die with honor as a man who would not talk. You want to be a martyr—you want your name to be among those of the heroes.

"But I am not so stupid as to let you die that way. I will tell you what I am going to do if you do not begin to talk. Late tonight I am going to take you and your motor scooter and a big truck and go to the street near your house. I am going to smash the motor scooter and then drive the truck back and forth over your head a few times. Then I am going to call the newspapers. And tomorrow the newspapers will say that you got killed by a hit-and-run driver. So none of your friends will ever know that you were a martyr who refused to talk. You will just be a man who died like a dog in the streets."

Tam began to talk. He was, he admitted, the deputy leader of Special Action Unit 69. He started leading the police to hidden weapons caches. Ultimately the police were to discover 295 charges of TNT, five claymores, six pistols, one machine gun and 108 grenades. He told the captain that his leader was the man named Sam, who lived in a house on Bay Coc Street.

Captain Tan was now ready to set what he calls "the rat trap." He stationed five of his plainclothes agents around the house on Bay Coc Street.

Sam, meanwhile, knew that something had gone wrong. He and Tam had planned to meet in front of a shop on Nguyen Hue Street to work on plans for the JUSPAO building attack. When Tam did not appear at the appointed time, Sam grew nervous. Tam was not the kind of agent to be late. His wife had had a miscarriage and was in the hospital. Everything seemed to be going wrong.

Sam waited at the rendezvous for two hours and then left, feeling deeply troubled. Tam was the only one of his men who knew where he, Sam, lived. Tam was a trusted deputy, but if he had been captured . . .

Sam slept that night at one of his safehouses. The next evening, still not having heard from Tam, he went to the house of a shopkeeper named Minh, an agent who had been keeping the mines for the attack. Minh's wife met him at the door. She did not know that her husband was a terrorist, and Sam said to her: "Is your husband here? He promised to sell me some rubber bands."

The woman was frightened. Her husband was gone, she said. Some men had come to her house, bringing the man she knew as Tam with them. Tam had led them to a place in the house where some mines were hidden. The men took the mines and her husband away with them.

Sam realized that the visitors were undoubtedly plainclothes policemen. Tam had indeed been arrested—and, furthermore, was talking. That night Sam stayed in the house of another agent named Dong, but couldn't sleep. Next morning he sent a message by courier to his commander in the Secret Zone explaining what had happened. Then he got his wife from the hospital. She must go to the Secret Zone immediately. He would follow her as soon as possible, but for now he had to stay in the city to find out how many of his men had been captured and how many of their weapons caches had been discovered. His wife, long accustomed to a life on the run, said nothing. She would simply do as he told her.

Sam returned to Dong's house. A little later there was a commotion outside. Sam looked out and saw Tam in the street with a group of plainclothesmen. Tam seemed to be pretending that he could not remember which of the houses on the street belonged to Dong. Obviously he was trying to delay the police long enough for anyone inside to escape. Sam slipped out the back door and got away with seconds to spare.

There was now clearly no safe place left in the city for Sam to hide. He took a bus out of town and stayed with his sister in Long An province for two days. To return to the city would be fatal, but Sam felt that he must make one last check on the house and weapons cache on Bay Coc Street. Perhaps Tam would not reveal that one. So on the 31st of July, the very day that he had planned to assault the JUSPAO building, Sam returned to Saigon. When he reached Bay Coc Street he looked around very carefully. Some cycle drivers, a couple of men playing elephant chess at the edge of the street, the usual gaggle of children—nothing out of the ordinary. He went on down toward the house.

At 6:45 that evening Captain Tan was enjoying the rare treat of a dinner at home with his wife when the telephone rang. It was the duty officer. The trap had sprung. When Tan reached his headquarters his men brought Sam in to him. This, the captain felt sure, was the man he had been waiting for. He ordered the blindfold removed. Sam stood there blinking in the bright light. Captain Tan watched him carefully. Suddenly Sam started screaming: "What do you bring me here for? Kill me! I want to die! I will never tell you anything!" Then he started yelling about the ultimate victory of the Liberation Front. "I want to die!" he shouted again.

Captain Tan smiled. This was the kind he liked. The silent ones, the calm ones like Tam, were difficult. But this one, this man who wanted to yell and scream his undying loyalty to the Front—this one would be easy.

*Credit*: © 1968 TIME Inc. Reprinted by permission.

## FURTHER READINGS

Sully, François. *Age of the Guerrilla: The New Warfare*. New York: Parents' Magazine Press, 1968.

Truong Nhu Tang. *A Vietcong Memoir*. New York: Harcourt Brace Jovanovich, 1985.

Tuohy, William. *Dangerous Company*. New York: Morrow, 1987.

# 13

# OPERATION ROLLING THUNDER, 24 FEBRUARY 1965—31 MARCH 1968

Operation Rolling Thunder dropped a million tons of high explosives on North Vietnam from March 1965 to November 1968—about 800 tons per day for three and a half years. It backfired. Not only were the enemy's morale and supply of the southern insurgency not broken, but also the bombing campaign renewed the enemy's resolve and stimulated increased aid from China and the Soviet Union. These facts were well known in 1966, acknowledged even by the U.S. commander, General William C. Westmoreland, and later by Defense Secretary Robert S. McNamara. Yet the U.S. government persisted because Westmoreland's attrition strategy to defeat the Communist insurgents was not working, and there was nothing else to be done.

On the advice of Wilfred Burchett, a pro-Communist journalist from Australia, Hanoi granted a travel visa to Harrison Salisbury, assistant managing editor of the *New York Times*. When he arrived just before the Christmas truce of 1966, Salisbury was taken on a tour of civilian areas that the North Vietnamese claimed had been bombed by the Americans. Salisbury posted several illustrated dispatches, at first failing to identify his sources. The U.S. military leadership at the Pentagon was aware that North Vietnamese civilians inadvertently had been bombed, but strenuously denied the errors to the news media. Legions of Pentagon researchers were put to work in an effort to refute and discredit Salisbury.

A furor erupted among government elites in Washington and media elites in New York. Reaction to Salisbury's reporting tended to track already held beliefs about the war in general. Antiwar opinion leaders condemned the bombing and applauded Salisbury's courage, while Johnson administration supporters chastised Salisbury for irresponsibly spreading enemy propaganda. The *Times* at first backed its correspondent, but later recanted when numerous respected journalists, including *Times* columnist Hanson Baldwin, openly questioned Salisbury's ethics. Eventually, a Pulitzer Prize awarded to Salisbury for his Hanoi reporting was withdrawn.

The Salisbury affair was a media event that did not significantly alter the course of the war. It did not stop the bombing, nor did it win converts to the antiwar movement. Its only lasting effects were to supplant more important news stories from the news agenda and to demonstrate to Hanoi leaders the potential propaganda advantages of permitting westerners to visit their country. Average U.S. citizens did not pay much attention to the controversy; their concerns were the war's mounting toll of lives lost, bodies broken, and treasure misspent. In hindsight, the episode's only accomplishment was to demonstrate that the government and media elites were out of touch with the American people.

## HARRISON E. SALISBURY: REPORT ON EFFECTS OF AMERICAN BOMBING ON HANOI

*Following is the first of several reports filed by Harrison Salisbury from Hanoi in December 1966 and January 1967. Suspicions of Salisbury's inaccuracies and exaggeration of U.S. bomb damage of Hanoi were confirmed after the war, but on the whole the reports accurately depicted the unbroken will of the North Vietnamese people.*

*New York Times*, 25 December 1966

**A Purposeful and Energetic Mood in Embattled Capital Found by a Times Man**

**2 Recent Attacks Cited**

**Witnesses Certain American Bombs Dropped Inside City Dec. 13 and 14**

The writer of the following dispatch is an assistant managing editor of *The New York Times*, who reached Hanoi Friday.

Special to *The New York Times*—HANOI, North Vietnam, Dec. 24—Late in the afternoon of this drizzly Christmas Eve the bicycle throngs on the roads leading into Hanoi increased.

Riding sidesaddle behind husbands were hundreds of slender young Hanoi wives returning to the city from evacuation to spend Christmas with their families. Hundreds of mothers had small children perched on the backs of bicycles—children being returned to the city for reunions during the Christmas cease-fire.

In Hanoi's Catholic churches mass was celebrated, and here and there in the small foreign quarter there were more elaborate holiday observances. Five Canadian members of the International Control Commission had a fat Christmas goose brought in specially for them from Vientiane, Laos, on the I.C.C. flight into Hanoi yesterday.

**VISITORS HAVE A PARTY**

And in Hanoi's rambling, old high-ceilinged Thongnhat (Reunification) Hotel (formerly the Metropole), there was a special Christmas party for a handful of foreign visitors who chanced to be here.

But this random evidence of Christmas spirit did not convey the mood of North Vietnam's capital, at least not as it seemed to an unexpected observer from the United States.

The mood of Hanoi seemed much more that of a wartime city going about its business briskly, energetically, purposefully. Streets are lined with cylindrical one-man air-raid shelters set in the ground at 10-foot intervals.

The shelters are formed of pre-stressed concrete with concrete lids left ajar—for quick occupancy—and they are reported to have been occupied quite a bit in recent days with the sudden burst of United States air raids. There is damage, attributed by officials here to the raids, as close as 200 yards from this hotel.

Hanoi was laid out by French architects with broad boulevards over which arch leafy trees, and with squares, public gardens and pleasant lakes. Today it seems a bit like a mixture of the Moscow and Algiers of World War II. There are khaki and uniforms everywhere and hardly a truck moves without its green boughs of camouflage. Even pretty girls camouflage their bicycles and conical straw hats.

Christmas Eve found residents in several parts of Hanoi still picking over the wreckage of homes said to have been damaged in the United States raids of Dec. 13 and 14. United States officials have contended that no attacks in built-up or residential Hanoi have been authorized or carried out. They have also suggested that Hanoi residential damage in the two raids could have been caused by defensive surface-to-air missiles that misfired or fell short.

[Although American authorities have said that they were satisfied no bombs fell inside Hanoi and that only military targets were attacked, the State Department said Thursday that "the possibility of an accident" could not be ruled out. A spokesman said that if the bombing had caused civilian injury or damage, the United States regretted it.]

This correspondent is no ballistics specialist, but inspection of several damaged sites and talks with witnesses make it clear that Hanoi residents certainly believe they were bombed by United States planes, that they certainly observed United States planes overhead and that damage certainly occurred right in the center of town.

## LARGE, SPRAWLING CITY

Hanoi is a very large, sprawling city. The city proper has a population of 600,000, and the surrounding metropolitan area brings the total to 1,100,000.

The built-up, densely populated urban area extends for a substantial distance. . . .

For instance, the Yenvien rail yard, which was listed as one of the targets in the raids Dec. 14 and 15, is in a built-up area that continues southwest to the Red River with no visible breaks in residential quarters. Much the same is true of the Vandien truck park south of the city, which was another listed target.

Oil tanks between Yenvien and Gialam, listed as another target, are in a similarly populated region. It is unlikely that any bombing attack on such targets could be carried out without civilian damage and casualties.

The location of two of the damaged areas inspected today suggests that the western approaches to the Paul Doumer Bridge may have been aimed for.

Both damaged areas lie in the Hoankiem quarter of Hanoi. Other administrative quarters of the city are Badinh, Haiba and Dongda. All have suffered some damage.

The first area inspected was Pho Nguyen Thiep Street, about a three-minute drive from the hotel and 100 yards from the central market. Thirteen houses were destroyed—one-story brick and stucco structures for the most part. The Phuc Lan Buddhist pagoda in the same street was badly damaged.

Five persons were reported killed and 11 injured, and 39 families were said to be homeless.

## SAYS BOMB EXPLODED

Tuan Ngoc Trac, a medical assistant who lived at 46 Pho Nguyen Thiep Street, said he was just going to the clinic where he works when an air alert sounded, indicating planes 25 kilometers (about 15 miles) from Hanoi. He had stepped to the street with his medical bag in his hand when he heard a plane and flung himself to the ground.

He said that the next instant a bomb exploded just over a row of houses, collapsing nine on the other side of the street. Tuan Ngoc Trac displayed an American leaflet, which he said he had found in the street, warning Hanoi residents not to remain in the vicinity of military objectives.

The North Vietnamese say that almost simultaneously—also about 3 P.M. Dec. 13—about 300 thatch and brick homes and huts along the Red River embankment, possibly a quarter of a mile from Pho Nguyen Thiep Street and equally distant from the Thongnhat Hotel, were hit. The principal damage was again done by a burst just above the houses, but there were also three ground craters caused either by rocket bursts or small bombs.

This area, 200 by 70 yards, was leveled by blast and fire. Four persons were reported killed and 10 injured, most of the residents having been at work or in a large well-constructed shelter.

Another damage site inspected was in the Badinh quarter, which is Hanoi's diplomatic section. There, on Khuc Hao Street, lies the rear of the very large Chinese Embassy compound, backing on the Rumanian Embassy. Minor damage was done to the roofs of the Chinese and Rumanian Embassies by what was said to have looked like rocket fire. Both embassies produced fragments, which they said had come from United States rocket bursts.

## HOUSE IS INSPECTED

Also examined was a house on Hué Lane in the Haiba quarter. It was reported hit Dec. 2, with the death of one person and the wounding of seven others, including two children.

Contrary to the impression given by United States communiqués, on-the-spot inspection indicates that American bombing has been inflicting considerable civilian casualties in Hanoi and its environs for some time past.

The North Vietnamese cite as an instance the village of Phuxa, a market gardening suburb possibly four miles from the city center. The village of 24 houses was reported attacked at 12:17 P.M. Aug. 13 by a United States pilot trying to bomb a Red River dike. The village was destroyed and 24 people were killed and 23 wounded. The pilot was shot down.

A crater 25 feet deep was reported blasted in the dike, but it was said to have been filled within three hours. The village has now been completely rebuilt, and has a small museum of mementos of the attack. In the museum is the casing of a United States fragmentation bomb, which bears the legend, "Loaded 7/66." A month after that date it was said to have fallen on Phuxa village, releasing 300 iron spheres, each about the size of a baseball and each loaded with 300 steel pellets about the size and shape of bicycle bearings. Those missiles are reported to have caused most of the Phuxa casualties.

It is the reality of such casualties and such apparent byproducts of the United States bombing policy that lend an atmosphere of grimness and foreboding to Hanoi's Christmas cease-fire. It is fair to say that, based on evidence of their own eyes, Hanoi residents do not find much credibility in United States bombing communiqués.

## HOWARD K. SMITH: EDITORIAL CRITICIZING SALISBURY'S REPORT ON HANOI BOMBING

*American Broadcasting Company television news anchor Howard K. Smith wrote the following guest editorial for the conservative magazine* National Review. *His purist view that Salisbury had broken the journalists' code outlawing unnamed sources denied the reality that most reporters of the era disguised their unofficial sources for fear of retribution.*

*National Review*, 24 January 1967

In the shifting sands of a difficult era this reporter's one-time employer, *The New York Times*, has always been a rock to cling to. In its pages truth was to be found as nearly as mortal reporters working under pressure of deadlines could approach it.

It is a matter of concern now to find that on the issue of Vietnam—which should call forth *The Times*' qualities of hard digging for facts and full, careful reporting of them—the old lady has begun cutting corners and abandoning pretenses of balanced reporting.

This dismay is crystallized, though not originated, by the reporting of Harrison Salisbury from Hanoi. Mr. Salisbury is one of the dozen best reporters using this language. He knows that Hanoi let him in not in the interests of scientific truth but for a special purpose: North Vietnam's lone hope is to erode the morale of Americans at home and cause them to give up. It was therefore incumbent on Mr. S. to exercise with double care all the usual requirements of good journalism.

When we both worked for the United Press, Salisbury and I had it drummed into us that the very first fact in any dispatch had to be the name of the source of the ensuing information. Yet he reported from Hanoi the other day detailed figures of civilian casualties in our bombings and gave no source at all. The impression was that he had satisfied himself that the figures were right.

Two days later, after the impact had gone too far in papers all over the nation to be caught up with, he casually revealed that the source was the Communist information apparatus whose respect for truth has not been famous. A week later, we find that Hanoi published the figures in a propaganda pamphlet a month before.

Asked about this purveying of Communist propaganda information without qualification, *The Times*' Managing Editor, Mr. Clifton Daniel, asked innocently where else would Salisbury get information? Well, Mr. Daniel should know that American correspondents in totalitarian countries go to great lengths to acquire a list of alternate sources of information.

In Nazi Germany one of *The Times*' own alternate sources was an excellent German journalist named Ernst Lemmer who after the war became Adenauer's minister for All-German Affairs. In Hanoi, Salisbury himself reported the existence of a Western colony, whose members might have useful information. In any case, we on *The Times*' staff in Berlin would never have been permitted by our managing editor to propagate Nazi information without clearly labeling it.

There is a good deal more in Mr. Salisbury's dispatches that falls below the belt. He reported extensive damages by us in the town of Namdinh and said we have never in any communiqué "asserted that Namdinh contains some facility that the U.S. regards as a military objective." He is wrong, which is forgivable; but he does not try to be right, which is not: There have been at least three U.S. communiqués reporting attacks on military objectives in Namdinh.

This set of reports is not isolated. *The Times* reported early last year that American soldiers had turned Saigon into one big brothel. The report was one of the sort Winston Churchill used to call "terminological inexactitudes" in order to avoid use of the ugly little blunt monosyllable. However, Senator Fulbright picked it up and used it to dirtify a generation of U.S. soldiers.

*The Times*' editorials have been using questionable language for some time. The other day one said, "Hanoi has made it clear to all questioners that it will not negotiate while North Vietnam is being bombed." Now if there is any purpose to stating the situation that way, it is to imply that North Vietnam would negotiate if bombing stopped. Well, there is not an iota of substantiation for that. The ways of diplomacy are infinite, and if that is what Hanoi thinks, it could convey it without loss of face, and the bombing would stop. The present Administration is anxious to the point of incaution to quit fighting if given a crumb of hope.

Every reporter makes mistakes. Heaven knows this reporter has made his share. Deadlines dominate journalism and they do not wait till a reporter has all the information that will be available to historians ten or twenty years hence. However, *The Times*' carelessness about the simple basic precautions of fair and accurate reporting has become suspicious. If one were given to phrase-mongering one might say it has dug its own credibility gap.

# AN ANONYMOUS REPORT: EDITORIAL ASKS "WHO'S IN CHARGE?"—PRESIDENT JOHNSON OR THE GENERALS

*Eight months after the Salisbury controversy, the Senate Preparedness Investigating Subcommittee on the war against North Vietnam took testimony from Pentagon officials. The admirals and generals unanimously supported Operation Rolling Thunder. On 25 August 1967, Defense Secretary Robert S. McNamara shocked the assembly by testifying that the bombing had been a total failure and should be discontinued. The senators rejected McNamara's assessment and recommended that President Johnson should listen to the generals: "What is needed now is the hard decision to do whatever is necessary, take the risks that have to be taken and apply the force that is required to see the job through."[1] In the following editorial, entitled "Generals out of Control," the New York Times asked who was in charge, the Pentagon or the president?—a question that at least partially vindicated Salisbury's earlier Hanoi dispatches.*

*New York Times, 1 September 1967*

Serious issues of civilian vs. military control of defense and diplomatic policy are raised by the public campaign of some of the nation's top generals for an extension of the bombing of North Vietnam—a campaign that has now brought them an initial Senate victory.

The spectacle of General Greene, the Marine Corps Commandant, taking to an American Legion podium to tell the country that the war in Vietnam is more important than the plight of America's riot-torn cities is the latest and most grotesque distortion of the traditional role of the military in American life.

Two days earlier, the Marine member of the Joint Chiefs of Staff emerged from a closed hearing of the Senate Preparedness Investigating Subcommittee to urge the bombing of four additional MIG airfields in North Vietnam. In the hearing itself, General Greene reportedly criticized past Administration slowness in approving enlarged target lists as an aid to Hanoi.

The Army Chief of Staff, General Johnson, joined the insurrection by calling for bombing the port of Haiphong and other off-limits targets in North Vietnam. He differed with his civilian superior, Secretary McNamara, who told the subcommittee such attacks would not hamper Hanoi's war operations in the South but would be costly in American casualties and involve great risk of conflict with Russia and China.

Earlier a third member of the Joint Chiefs, Air Force General McConnell, told the subcommittee that an extra 800,000 American troops would have been needed in South Vietnam without the bombing. The imaginary nature of this "statistic" is clearly revealed in the official intelligence estimates released by Mr. McNamara last week. They showed that the volume of war-supporting supplies entering North Vietnam and moved to the South is "significantly [less than] 100 tons per day, a quantity that could be transported by only a few trucks."

Nevertheless, President Johnson, his antennae more attuned to the 1968 elections than to any battlefront developments, evidently was so concerned about the subcommittee hearings that he surrendered to the military before the sessions began. The very first witness—Admiral Sharp, the Pacific Commander, who had already aired his desire for more bombing—brought word from the President that another group of targets had been taken off the prohibited list. The President's capitulation did not prevent the subcommittee from insisting yesterday on a further step-up of bombing to close the port of Haiphong and to hit other targets, even if it does mean war with China.

This has not been the first Administration surrender to military pressure. The public campaign conducted by General Westmoreland last spring for more ground troops led to his trip to the United States, his controversial attack on dissenters and the open negotiation with the President that ended in last month's announcement that 45,000 more troops would be sent to Vietnam.

After two and a half years of escalation in Vietnam, a buildup to 500,000 troops and a level of bombing exceeding that in Europe in World War II, the military situation in South Vietnam is no better today than when American entrance into direct combat began. American escalation has been matched by the Communists and the stalemate has merely been moved to a higher level of combat, casualties and destruction.

Responsibility for this tragic miscalculation undoubtedly belongs to the President more than to any other man. Yet, the military leaders who advised him—and have failed dismally to produce any military improvement for this huge investment—are now the chief opponents of another bombing pause, an indispensable precedent to opening negotiations with Hanoi for a political solution.

The sputtering of the Congressional debate over the Tonkin Gulf resolution has underscored the erosion in the constitutional requirement for legislative control over the war-making power. Now a similar erosion is taking place in the constitutional balance that supposedly puts the military under civilian direction. Senator Mansfield's protestations that it is really Secretary McNamara who speaks for the Administration are poorly supported by the record. Only Mr. Johnson can exercise his Presidential prerogatives under the Constitution and restore civilian control of national policy.

*Credit*: © 1967 by The New York Times Co. Reprinted with permission.

## NOTE

1. "Text of Senate Subcommittee's Report on the Bombing Policy in North Vietnam," *New York Times*, 1 September 1967, 10.

## FURTHER READINGS

Salisbury, Harrison E. *Behind the Lines: Hanoi, December 23–January 7*. New York: Harper & Row, 1967.

———, ed. *Vietnam Reconsidered: Lessons from a War*. New York: Harper & Row, 1984.

Turner, Kathleen J. *Lyndon Johnson's Dual War: Vietnam and the Press*. Chicago: University of Chicago Press, 1995.

# 14

# TET OFFENSIVE, 31 JANUARY—25 FEBRUARY 1968

On the night of 31 January 1968, about 70,000 Communists, mostly Vietcong sapper commandos, broke their own truce for the Vietnamese lunar new year called Tet and launched a combined offensive throughout South Vietnam of shocking breadth and ferocity. Most attackers were quickly repelled by U.S. forces; some tenaciously clung to their targets, such as Hué and Khesanh. All eventually yielded to the Americans, at an extraordinary cost in lives, even for the Communists—the Vietcong lost an estimated 50,000 seasoned troops and required several years to recover. Despite their fleeting gains, the attackers proved beyond a shadow of a doubt that the United States was mired in a stalemate in South Vietnam. Within weeks, the Americans began their slow process of withdrawal.

The list of Vietcong targets in the offensive included nearly every allied installation, provincial capital, and district seat in the South: coastal cities An, Danang, Hoi, Nhatrang, Quinhon, and the huge U.S. complex at Camranh Bay; northern mountain cities and outposts at Ashau, Khanduc, Khesanh, Lanvei, and the ancient Vietnamese capital of Hué; central highland towns of Banmethuot, Dakto, Kontum, Pleiku, and Dalat, a previously unmolested enclave; Mekong Delta provincial capitals Bentre, Bienhoa, Camau, Cantho, Chaudoc, Mytho, Vinhlong, and nine others; and dozens of district pacification headquarters.

The Vietcong's most audacious assault struck at the heart of the Saigon government. Saigon defenses were understaffed because the U.S. field commander, General William C. Westmoreland, was convinced that the enemy's real target was the U.S. military base at Khesanh. Four thousand guerrillas in small groups set off mines, lobbed mortars, occupied communications centers and utilities, surrounded the airport, and stormed U.S. and central government facilities throughout the capital city. Nineteen commandos broke through the outer defensive wall of the recently constructed U.S. Embassy compound, security for which had been neglected by Saigon police. The Vietcong would have taken the embassy but for the heroics of a handful of U.S. military guards and embassy diplomats. The attackers lay dead after a six-and-a-half-hour gunfight.

Tet was the biggest media story since the assassination of President Kennedy in 1963. Vivid color television images conveyed the carnage and confusion of Saigon street fighting to 50 million Americans. Westmoreland went on the air to denounce the Communists for deceitfully violating their own truce and declared the enemy decisively beaten. The television footage and newspaper headlines said otherwise.

On the second day of the offensive, Westmoreland's confident assurances were overshadowed by a single memorable image of the war: the execution of a Vietcong officer by the chief of the South Vietnamese national police, General Nguyen Ngoc Loan. Loan was infamous for his merciless dispatch of Buddhist protesters in Hué in 1966. Loan's handgun firing point-blank into his victim's head was captured on film by Associated Press photographer Eddie Adams and National Broadcasting Company cameraman Vo Suu. The next day NBC aired an edited version of its exclusive film to spare its viewers. Adams's picture, featured on newspaper front pages across the United States, spared nothing. Like the prisoner's frozen grimace as he slumped to the ground, the losing cause in Vietnam stared America in the face.

Tet was a bewildering morass of contradictions. Militarily, it was a demonstrable defeat for the Communists and played directly into Westmoreland's attrition strategy, yet the offensive was perceived as an allied setback. Strategically, the offensive was the worst U.S. intelligence failure since Pearl Harbor, yet Westmoreland had been informed of enemy preparations and had chosen to disregard them. Politically, the Communists failed in their primary objective of fomenting a popular insurrection against the Saigon government, yet the offensive so thoroughly disheartened the American public that its president stopped the bombing of North Vietnam, declined reelection, replaced his military commander, and began the war's long denouement. That Tet was the turning point of the Vietnam War was beyond dispute.

Westmoreland never forgave the news media, particularly television, for painting what he considered a distorted picture of the Tet offensive. Sixteen years later, in 1984, Westmoreland sued CBS News for libeling him in a documentary based on claims by former Central Intelligence Agency analyst Sam Adams, who said that Westmoreland had scaled down estimates of enemy strength prior to the Tet offensive in order to justify his optimism about the war. After recriminations in the journalistic community, CBS settled with Westmoreland out of court. However, a pall on his reputation lingered.

## AN ANONYMOUS REPORT: REPORT ON GENERAL GIAP'S TET OFFENSIVE

*For years the lively, colorful, and opinionated* Time *magazine was the most influential news publication in America. The* New York Times *commanded the small audience of elite intellectuals, but* Time *was Middle America's source for news, and its pages unabashedly promoted the hawkish views of its founder, Henry Luce. After Luce's retirement in 1965, a new guard at Time, Inc., gradually softened the magazine's stance on the war.* Time's *old naïve American "can-do-ism" is missing from the following comprehensive report on Communist general Vo Nguyen Giap's Tet "gamble." Though drawn almost entirely from U.S. officialdom, the article hints at the fallibility of its sources.*

*Time*, 9 February 1968

Though ominous harbingers of trouble had been in the air for days, most of South Viet Nam lazed in uneasy truce, savoring the happiest and holiest holiday of the Vietnamese year. All but a few Americans retired to their compounds to leave the feast of *Tet* to the Vietnamese celebrators filling the streets. Vietnamese soldiers made a special effort to rejoin their families. Relative visited relative, threading through thousands of firecrackers popping and fizzing in the moonless night. The Year of the Monkey had begun, and every Vietnamese knew that it was wise to make merry while there was yet time; in the twelve-year Buddhist lunar cycle, 1968 is a grimly inauspicious year.

Through the streets of Saigon, and in the dark approaches to dozens of towns and military installations throughout South Viet Nam, other Vietnamese made their furtive way, intent on celebrating only death—and on launching the Year of the Monkey on its malign way before it was many hours old. After the merrymakers had retired and the last firecrackers had sputtered out on the ground, they struck with a fierceness and bloody destructiveness that Viet Nam has not seen even in three decades of nearly continuous warfare. Up and down the narrow length of South Viet Nam, more than 36,000 North Vietnamese and Viet Cong soldiers joined in a widespread general offensive against airfields and military bases, government buildings, population centers and just plain civilians.

The Communists hit in a hundred places, from Quang Tri near the DMZ in the north all the way to Duong Dong on the tiny island of Phu Quoc off the Delta coast some 500 miles to the south. No target was too big or too impossible, including Saigon itself and General William Westmoreland's MACV headquarters. In peasant pajamas or openly insigniaed uniforms, by stealth or attacks marshaled by bullhorn, the raiders struck at nearly 40 major cities and towns.

They attacked 28 of South Viet Nam's 44 provincial capitals and occupied some, destroyed or damaged beyond repair more than 100 allied planes and helicopters. South Viet Nam's capital, which even in the worst days of the Indo-China war had never been hit so hard, was turned into a city besieged and sundered by house-to-house fighting. In Hué, the ancient imperial city of Viet Nam and the architectural and spiritual repository of Vietnamese history, the Communists seized large parts of the city—and only grudgingly yielded them block by block under heavy allied counterattacks at week's end.

## A VICTORY OF SORTS

Allied intelligence had predicted that there would be some attempted city attacks during *Tet*, but the size, the scale and, above all, the careful planning and coordination of the actual assaults took the U.S. and South Vietnamese military by surprise. In that sense, and because they continued after five days of fighting to hang on to some of their targets, the Communists undeniably won a victory of sorts. "This is real fighting on a battlefield," admitted Brigadier General John Chaisson, Westmoreland's combat operations coordinator for South Viet Nam. The Communist attack was, he said, "a very successful offensive. It was surprisingly well coordinated, surprisingly intensive and launched with a surprising amount of audacity." Westmoreland himself called the enemy campaign "a bold one," though marked "by treachery and deceitfulness."

Some psychological success could hardly be denied the attackers. In the raid on the poorly defended U.S. embassy in Saigon, they embarrassed and discomfited the U.S., still coping with the stinging humiliation of the *Pueblo* incident [a U.S. destroyer recently seized by North Korea]. They succeeded in demonstrating that, despite nearly three years of steady allied progress in the war, Communist commandos can still strike at will virtually anywhere in the country. Though the smoke must clear before any realistic assessment can be made, the slow process of pacification has probably suffered a major setback on two fronts. The promise of security in a hamlet may not seem so credible to a peasant who has learned that even Saigon and the U.S. embassy are not enemy-proof. And, amid the furor in the cities, no one yet knows how many pacification workers and members of revolutionary development teams have been assassinated out in the countryside. Fourteen American civilians working in the pacification program near Hué alone were killed last week.

## ANOTHER PRICE

In the end, however, the Communist victory may be classed as Pyrrhic. The allied command reported nearly 15,000 of the attackers killed. Even if the total is only half that—and some observers think that that may be the case when all the combat reports filed in the swirl of battle are crosschecked—it would still represent a huge bloodletting of the enemy's forces in South Viet Nam. Even the lower estimates leave no doubt about who won the actual battles: U.S. dead numbered 367 and South Vietnamese military dead about 700.

Many of the attacking units, like the one that hit the U.S. embassy, were avowedly suicidal; few of them, even when they did seize towns or installations, managed to hold them for long. Some were promised reinforcements within 48 hours—and never got them—or were given food and ammunition for only five days of foray. Such recklessness of life deprived the Communists of some of their best men, since in many cases the attackers were highly trained demolition experts or battlewise guerrillas.

The Communists also paid another kind of price. By choosing for their attack the time of *Tet*, the sacred family time of the year for the Vietnamese, they undoubtedly alienated major portions of the population. They also brought bullets and bombs into the very midst of heavily populated areas, causing indiscriminate slaughter of civilians caught in the crossfire and making homeless twice over the refugees who had fled to the cities for safety. Moreover, they totally misjudged the mood of the South Vietnamese. Believing their own propaganda, the Communists called for and expected a popular uprising to welcome the raiders as liberators. Nothing approaching that myth occurred anywhere in Viet Nam, with the possible, and as yet unverified, exception of some residents of Hué.

In its timing and total effect, the Communist offensive changed the rules of the war in a way that will make it more difficult for the enemy in the future. In making a mockery of the Tet truce, proposed in the first instance by the Viet Cong and reluctantly agreed to by the allies, the Communists, as U.S. Ambassador Ellsworth Bunker indicated, made it highly unlikely that there would ever be a holiday truce again. By demonstrating their resources of manpower, the resiliency of their communications and command networks and the quantity and quality of their weapons in the widespread attacks, the Communists also made it highly unlikely, as President Johnson all but said, that there would be any bombing pause over North Viet Nam.

## AN IMPRESSION OF STALEMATE

There was no doubt about who was the strategist behind the Communists' desperate thrust: North Vietnam's Defense Minister, General Vo Nguyen Giap, the charismatic victor over the French at Dienbienphu in 1954 and creator of the North Vietnamese army. In its surprise, its boldness, the sweep of its planning, and its split-second orchestration, the general offensive bore all the unmistakable marks of Giap's genius. All the evidence indicated, in fact, that probably for the first time since the war against the French, Giap was personally directing the entire campaign in South Viet Nam.

Giap's precise intention in launching the general offensive remains to be learned. As always in Communist military doctrine, Giap doubtless considered the political effect at least as important as outcome on the battlefield. "Guerrilla activities and large-scale combat coordinate with each other, help each other and encourage each other to develop," Giap said in a speech last September. "At the same time, they closely coordinate with the political struggle to score great victories in both military and political fields, thus leading the resistance toward final victory."

Some of Giap's political aims were evident: to embarrass the U.S. and undercut the authority of the South Vietnamese government, to frighten urban South Vietnamese and undermine pacification in the countryside, to give the impression to the U.S. public that the war is in a stalemate. Some U.S. officials also see the offensive as a prelude to North Viet Nam's coming to the conference table, aimed at enhancing Hanoi's hand in negotiations.

But both General Westmoreland and President Johnson interpreted Giap's attacks primarily in hard military terms: as a specific effort to draw U.S. troops away from the U.S. Marine base of Khe Sanh, where Giap has assembled some 40,000 men for what could be the largest single battle of the entire war. Not all of Westmoreland's and Johnson's subordinates agree. The dissenters suspect Giap of intending just the opposite—of having created the threat to Khe Sanh as a diversion designed to draw U.S. forces away from cities and towns and thus give him a foothold in the populated areas that has consistently been denied him.

Whatever Giap's immediate aims, it has been clear to Hanoi for some time that something drastic had to be done in South Viet Nam. Captured cadre notes spoke of a "counteroffensive." Depressed by constant defeats on the battlefield and consigned to stay in South Viet Nam until the war was over, the infiltrated North Vietnamese regulars were growing weary and restive. They badly needed a victory to bolster their morale, or at least a major initiative that they could call their own.

The allies had not only dominated the battlefield but had also seized the political initiative with the successful series of elections last year that culminated in the installation of Nguyen Van Thieu as civilian President under a new constitution. Increasingly, the bulk of the war was being fought on South Viet Nam's peripheries, leaving a virtual vacuum in the countryside that allied pacification efforts were moving to fill. A dramatic demonstration of Communist power and prowess was required. To Giap, the countryside general offensive seemed tailor-made for the task.

## TOUR DE FORCE

It was undoubtedly an extraordinary tour de force, unprecedented in modern military annals: the spectacle of an enemy force dispersed and unseen, everywhere hunted unremittingly, suddenly materializing to strike simultaneously in a hundred places throughout a country. Nowhere was the feat more impressive, or its art more instructively displayed, than in the assault on Saigon, the capital city of 2,000,000 people and the core of the allied commands.

Into Saigon in the days just before *Tet* slipped more than 3,000 Communist soldiers armed with weapons ranging up to machine-gun and bazooka size. Some came openly into the open city, weapons concealed in luggage or tinder baskets of food, riding buses, taxis and motor scooters, or walking. Others came furtively: some of the Viet Cong who attacked the U.S. embassy had ridden into town concealed in a truckload of flowers. Once in town, they hid their weapons. Only after the attack did Vietnamese intelligence realize that the unusual number of funerals the previous week was no accident: the Viet Cong had buried their weapons in the funeral coffins. They even test-fired their guns during the peak of the *Tet* celebrations, the sound of the shots mingling with that of the firecrackers going off.

## GUERRILLA GUIDES

In the An Quang Buddhist pagoda, the Communists set up a fully equipped command post for the attack. Shortly after midnight, the raiders assembled in units ranging from small suicide squads to well-armed company-size teams, and were led to their targets by local Communist guides. Some were dressed in neat, white button-down shirts and khakis, others in parts of ARVN uniforms or ragtag sports clothes. Dark clouds hung over the city, and only an occasional Jeep moved quickly through the eerie silence. Warned to expect something through captured enemy documents, military police had donned flak jackets and guard duty had been doubled. Saigon was a city waiting for trouble.

*"This is the Liberation Force come to liberate the city! Please be compatriots! Help us liberate the city!"*

It began when a guard in his cement-lined outpost at the side entrance of the Independence Palace saw a distant blur of moving men. There was a shout: "Open the palace gates! We are the Liberation Army!" Then, rockets blazing, the Viet Cong commandos charged. From that moment on, fighting broke out all over the city, to the crack and boom of rockets, mortars and bazookas, the chop of machine-gun fire and the whine of ricocheting bullets. For the would-be liberators of the Independence Palace, the reply was a hail of fire. Retreating across the streets, the Communists took up positions in a half-completed hotel, killed the first two Jeep loads of U.S. MPs who raced to the scene and commandeered their M-60 machine gun. In a pattern of stubborn pocket resistance to be repeated throughout Viet Nam, it took two days to shoot the Viet Cong out of the hotel.

An enemy force of at least 700 men tackled the city's most vital military target: Tan Son Nhut airstrip and its adjoining MACV compound housing Westmoreland's headquarters and the 7th Air Force Command Center, the nerve centers of U.S. command in the war. The Communists breached the immediate base perimeter, slipping past some 150 outposts without a shot being fired, and got within 1,000 feet of the runways before they were halted in eight hours of bloody hand-to-hand combat. All told, the Communists attacked from 18 different points around Tan Son Nhut, getting close enough to MACV to put bullets through Westy's windows. Westmoreland's staff officers were issued weapons and sent out to help sandbag the compound, and Westmoreland moved into his windowless command room in the center of MACV's first floor. Other Communist units raced through the city shooting at U.S. officers and enlisted men's billets (BOQs and BEQs), Ambassador Ellsworth Bunker's home, Westmoreland's home, the radio and TV stations. Wearing ARVN clothes, raiders seized part of the Vietnamese Joint General Staff Headquarters, turned the defenders' machine guns against helicopters diving in to dislodge them.

## SUMMARY VERDICT

Other Viet Cong had less militant assignments. Near the Free World Force Headquarters, a score of Viet Cong paraded through the streets singing songs and waving flags and shouting: "This is the Liberation Force come to liberate the city! Please be compatriots! Help us liberate the city!" Two- and three-man teams with the same message went from door to door, like census takers, asking for the names of local police and government officials, the addresses of ARVN and government families. Those they got—or found—they killed on the spot.

In nearby Bien Hoa, Viet Cong took over the town and set up their own roadblocks. When two American GIs were stopped, the Viet Cong hauled them from their car, delivered a "verdict" on them and summarily shot them for the benefit of the gathered townspeople. Some of Saigon's worst fighting took place in Cholon, the Chinese sector and a traditional stronghold of anti-government feeling. As elsewhere in the city, where resistance was heavy in house-to-house fighting, the ARVN warned the civilians out of the area, [and] then called in helicopters to strafe and Skyraiders to dive-bomb.

At week's end, Saigon was still a city shuddering with the roar of bombs and the splat of bullets. After five days of fighting, the stubborn attackers at Tan Son Nhut airstrip were still entrenched near the field as F-100 jets, Skyraiders and helicopters blasted at their positions. Fighting flared in one part of the city and, when troops moved in with air support to damp it down, broke out in another area. Though the allies claimed 2,000 enemy dead in the city, the U.S. command was worried by the presence of a reserve unit of some 1,000 Viet Cong still lurking in Saigon and not yet committed to battle. Allied troops ringed the city to cut off their retreat.

The violence in Saigon was only a small portion of the fighting that raged through the rest of the country. The first attack fell on Danang, site of the giant Marine base, where 300 Viet Cong infiltrated to the boundary of the Danang airfield and the walls of the South Vietnamese I Corps headquarters before being driven back. Then, in a domino pattern, the attacks moved southward through the coastal cities of Qui Nhon, Tuy Hoa and Nha Trang, leapfrogged over into the highland cities of Kontum and Pleiku and continued southward into the Delta—where some of the first attacks came only at week's end. The timing was as sequential as a mammoth string of *Tet* firecrackers going off one after the other, obviously aimed at tying down allied forces the progressive length of the country.

In Dalat, pleasure spot for South Vietnamese generals and site of the nation's fledgling military academy, the cadets got an early introduction to combat. The Viet Cong seized the highland town, [and] still held it at week's end. On the Bong Son plain, where the 1st Cavalry (Airmobile) has so often punished the enemy, the Communists hit an Air Cav base, destroyed two helicopters and penetrated the perimeter before being repulsed. At the Dong Ba Thien airfield just north of Cam Ranh Bay, attackers using satchel charges destroyed nine helicopters. In the Mekong Delta, long a Viet Cong haven, the situation seemed even more serious. The Communists held half the important city of My Tho and parts of several provincial capitals.

## CIVILIAN SHIELDS

In the fighting throughout the country, the Communists, as Westmoreland pointed out, showed "a callous disregard for human life," attacking hospitals as well as military compounds, using churches and schools as defense posts and captured civilians as shields. In the highland town of Ban Me Thuot, the Viet Cong killed six American missionaries in a sweep through a leprosarium operated by the Christian and Missionary Alliance, leaving their bodies wired with booby traps.

Such tactics no doubt contributed to the failure of the Vietnamese to heed the call to a "general uprising." No sooner had the general offensive got under way than both the Viet Cong radio and Radio Hanoi began calling for the South Vietnamese to greet the attackers as liberators, for ARVN soldiers to throw in their arms with the Communists and help overthrow the Thieu government. In Hué and Saigon, the Communists announced the formation of revolutionary Committees of the Alliance of National and Peace Forces. But throughout South Viet Nam there were few takers. In Danang, when a Viet Cong rose at a Buddhist *Tet* service with a pistol in one hand and a bullhorn in the other, bidding the crowd to support the "uprising," the Buddhists seized him and his two comrades and turned them over to the South Vietnamese police.

It was in Hué, sitting on the lush banks of the Perfume River, that the Communists, recognizing both its symbolic importance and the greater likelihood of some support from the population, made a maximum effort. There, for the time being, they enjoyed their most signal success. The seat of South Viet Nam's militant Buddhists and the home of many disaffected university students, Hué has long been South Viet Nam's capital of discontent. Into Hué last week Giap sent elements of five of his North Vietnamese regulars, supported by Viet Cong local soldiers—an estimated 2,000 men in all. They seized the Citadel of the ancient royal palace, dug in and raised the Viet Cong flag atop its crumbling battlements. Then they released from jail some 2,500 prisoners, including 400 Viet Cong.

South Vietnamese infantry units closed in on the city from all sides, and three companies of U.S. Marines, spearheaded by a platoon of army tanks, moved in to rescue a besieged U.S. military advisory unit trapped in its command. That mission accomplished, they turned to aid the South Vietnamese in rooting out the NVA, who reportedly were being guided and led by Hué students. In the twisting alleyways of the old city, digging out the Communists turned out to be a tough task. After two days of combat, President Thieu phoned ARVN I Corps Lieut. General Hoang Xuan Lam and demanded that he get Hué back in allied hands—and "get it back fast."

Lam and U.S. Marine Lieut. General Robert E. Cushman, Jr., knew how to get it back fast, but only at the cost of reducing it to ruins, and turning much of Viet Nam's heritage to crumbled stone. So the Skyraiders, wheeling and diving over Hué in support of the allied counterattack, at first used only guns and rockets no larger than 2.5 in. in order to protect the city's buildings and royal tombs and monuments. When after four days the Communists still held more than half the city, heritage was reluctantly sacrificed to necessity and the bombs loosed on the Citadel. The U.S., however, insisted that the South Vietnamese do the bombing themselves.

Hué, with Route 1 running through it, lies directly astride the main allied supply line from the Marine bases at Danang and Phu Bai to the encircled outpost of Khe Sanh. There are alternate means of supplying Khe Sanh, but Route 1, which connects with Khe Sanh via Route 9, is the best, and will thus not be left gladly in enemy hands. One of Giap's aims in his general offensive is to stretch U.S. lines—and U.S. troop deployments—as thin and as wide as he can, forcing General Westmoreland to make difficult choices of priority.

## CIRCULAR REASONING

Westmoreland sees the assault on Khe Sanh as the capstone of a three-phase campaign devised by Giap last September to win the war. Some captured documents show that Communist cadres in South Viet Nam have been told that the first three months of this year are the crucial period. During this period they are urged to win a decisive victory, which in turn will be followed by a coalition government, dictated by the Viet Cong.

The first phase, which produced the battles of Loc Ninh and Dak To along the Cambodian border, was designed to draw American forces away from population centers and rural pacification areas and "force us," as Westmoreland said, "to dissipate our military strength." The second phase erupted in the past week's widespread attacks on population centers and military installations, aimed at rendering impotent for a time the U.S. ability to react quickly to the third-phase "main attack" against the Marines in northern Viet Nam.

The captured enemy documents of recent months are even more explicit in revealing the Communist strategy, and give some remarkable insights into the tunnel vision with which Hanoi views the U.S. and the course of the conflict in South Viet Nam. One says that "the time is ripe for implementation of a general uprising to take over powers in South Nam. The masses are ready for action." The reasons: "Deteriorating morale in the U.S., the conflict between American and 'puppet' authorities, the unpopularity of G-xon (Viet-Congese for Johnson) and friction between 'doves' and 'hawks.'"

A Communist circular dated Oct. 3 specified that the general offensive should emphasize "attacks on enemy key units, cities and towns, [and] lines of communication." Another, noting that the U.S. "has proved weak and passive during recent battles at Dak To and Loc Ninh," goes so far overboard in its confidence that it says the Viet Cong revolution will succeed by mid-1968 and that civilians should be advised to expect their Viet Cong and North Vietnamese family members at war to be home around Aug. 5, 1968.

## VIOLATING HIS OWN PRECEPTS

Such explicit counsel would seem to run counter to Giap's oft-expressed public warning that North Viet Nam is ready to fight for 5, 10, 15 or 20 years to defeat the U.S. in Viet Nam. And there is also much in Giap's new strategy that flies in the face of his own guerrilla doctrine of warfare. One of his maxims is to fight only when the odds are overwhelmingly in his favor and success is certain, a precept that his troops violated nearly everywhere they struck in the course of his general offensive last week. What lies behind Giap's turnabout, which in its sanction of attacks on cities and towns constitutes the most important change of tactics by either side in the war?

In the argument within the Hanoi hierarchy on how to meet the allies' growing momentum, Giap, true to his own maxims and proven experience against the French, argued for an abandonment of large-scale or big-unit fighting and a return to guerrilla warfare in the south that might last for 10 or 20 years. His chief opponent and longtime rival, General Nguyen Chi Thanh, wanted to stick with big-unit warfare. Thanh had the advantage of being closest to the action as head of all Communist operations in South Viet Nam from his headquarters northwest of Saigon along the Cambodian border, and he prevailed in the Politburo.

Then Thanh died last summer, and no successor appeared in South Viet Nam. Instead, Giap disappeared from Hanoi, even missing the 23rd anniversary party on Dec. 22 of the founding of his own army. The best evidence is that he has set up a headquarters just north of the DMZ, determined, even if it is against his own instincts, to make big-unit war work against the U.S. He has said, in effect, to the Politburo: If this is what you want to do, I'll show you how to do it.

The first phase of his campaign was pure Giap: trying to draw U.S. forces to the periphery of South Viet Nam, into isolated areas where they had little to gain and lives to lose. He did much the same thing to the French in 1952 and 1953. Last week's series of urban attacks was a radical departure, but it has some logic and some advantages. A major element in U.S. strength is mobility in the air; if enough damage could be done to airfields and aircraft, that element would be sharply reduced. Fighting inside cities also nullified much of the U.S. firepower; neither artillery nor heavy bombing could be employed to any widespread populated areas.

For the first time since the U.S. committed itself to combat in Viet Nam, the Communist foot soldier was thus able to fight during the week with little fear of shells and bombs, rifleman to rifleman. Giap knew that he would take huge losses, but he hoped that the cost in allied lives would also be great; he has

long since proved that he considers one American life worth five of his own in the campaign to weary the U.S. of the war. That, too, characterized his war against the French, where at Dienbienphu he even budgeted 100% casualties—and took 8,000 dead to wipe out 2,000 of the camp's defenders.

## TEAK & MAHOGANY

Those U.S. analysts who believe that Khe Sanh will be attacked are convinced that Giap envisages it as a second Dienbienphu. He is out after a victory that would completely smash the will of the U.S. to continue a hard and dirty war of rising casualties and fitful overall progress in bringing South Viet Nam to where it can defend itself. Around Khe Sanh he has ringed 40,000 troops. Northward is grouped his 325C Division, to the South lies the 304. To the east lies the 324B and another division, and to the southeast there are elements of a fifth division. Across the Laotian border and north of the 17th parallel are Giap's Russian-made 152-mm. howitzers.

Well over 5,000 U.S. Marines oppose Giap in the base camp of Khe Sanh, elbow-to-elbow in their bunkers and trenches inside a perimeter only half a mile wide. But U.S. units numbering 40,000 men support the Marines within reinforcing range, with all the massed artillery and air power that Westmoreland and the Joint Chiefs of Staff believe are needed to defend the Marines. In the past ten days alone, B-52s have averaged four strikes daily on the Red-held hills around Khe Sanh.

It is an imposing setting for a large battle. Around the plateau occupied by the Marine base lie tier after tier of higher ground, mountains ranging from 4,000 to 8,000 feet. Separating the enemy looking down on Khe Sanh lie deep ravines and draws, layered with a triple canopy of foliage on teak and mahogany trees as high as 200 feet. In topography, Khe Sanh looks like a smaller version of Dienbienphu, but the terrain and underbrush are far worse for an attacker. The Communists must go downhill through terrible maneuvering grounds, cross the ravines, [and] then climb the plateau on which Khe Sanh sits—all in the face of intensive artillery fire and air attack that the French at Dienbienphu did not have.

## SYMBOLICALLY VITAL

Khe Sanh is eminently worth holding—and defending. It is a major point on the DMZ defense line, the barrier that U.S. forces have sought to string from the sea below the DMZ to the Laotian border. It now blocks off the easiest supply line that Giap has into South Viet Nam. By taking Khe Sanh, the Communists would outflank all the allied forces in Quang Tri province and part of Thua Thien province as well, probably forcing a fallback to a new defense line—perhaps as far back as Hué. As Giap well knows, Khe Sanh has become almost as vital symbolically as it is militarily; a Communist victory there would have immense propaganda and psychological value to Hanoi.

The U.S. is convinced that Khe Sanh cannot only be held, but that Giap will suffer crushing losses in manpower if he tries to take it. Giap's alternatives to a direct attack are either to pull back and miss his chance or to sit in the hills with his mortars and artillery and try to bleed Khe Sanh to death in daily barrages. At week's end Khe Sanh took minor shelling while the two sides waited and carefully watched each other. The U.S., slightly apprehensive, was ready for an attack—and even hopeful that Giap would strike. As for Giap, he no doubt was calculating the gains and losses of his big week in South Viet Nam, deciding whether he could afford another bold venture.

## THE BATTLE OF BUNKER'S BUNKER

The most daring attack of the week, and certainly one of the most embarrassing, occurred when 19 Viet Cong commandos of the C10 Sapper Battalion made the U.S. embassy their target. When Ambassador Ellsworth Bunker opened the white reinforced-concrete complex last September, few American missions ever settled into more seemingly impregnable quarters. Looming behind a 10 ft. high wall, the six-story symbol of U.S. power and prestige is encased in a massive concrete sunscreen that overlaps shatterproof Plexiglas windows. The $2.6 million building contains such an array of fortress-like features that Saigon wags soon dubbed it "Bunker's Bunker." Yet the Viet Cong attackers gained access to the embassy compound and rampaged through it for 6-1/2 hours before all were killed and the embassy was once again secure.

At 1:30 a.m., supporting V.C. troops positioned around the embassy began lobbing mortar fire onto the grounds. Then the 19 commandos appeared wearing civilian clothes (with identifying red armbands) carrying automatic weapons, rockets and enough high explosives to demolish the building. Attacking simultaneously, some of the guerrillas blasted a hole in the wall with an antitank gun and swarmed through it; others quickly scaled a rear fence. Though allied intelligence had predicted the attack, the embassy's defense consisted of only five U.S. military guards, just one more than normal. They fought back so fiercely that only their courage denied the enemy complete success. Sergeant Ronald W. Harper, 20, a Marine guard, managed to heave shut the embassy's massive teakwood front doors just seconds before the guerrillas battered at them with rockets and machine guns, thus denying the V.C. entry to the main building.

Unable to penetrate the main chancery, the V.C. commandos ran aimlessly through the compound, firing on everything they saw. Meanwhile, small groups of Marines and MPs began arriving outside the walls of the embattled embassy. The Viet Cong burst into the embassy's consulate building and various other buildings in the compound, but the Americans on the scene threw such heavy fire at them that the guerrillas were kept too busy to set off their explosives.

Finally, just before 8 a.m., Pfc. Paul Healy, 20, led a counterattack through the front gate, personally killing five V.C. with grenades and his M-16 rifle. Minutes later, two paratroop platoons from the 101st Airborne Division at nearby Bien Hoa landed on the embassy's rooftop helipad. Working their way down, they met no resistance. Though V.C. prisoners are usually turned over to the Saigon government, this time the troopers had orders to kill every V.C. in sight, lest any had seen secret codes or plans in the embassy.

As the troopers advanced, a wounded guerrilla staggered into Mission Coordinator George Jacobson's white villa behind the embassy. When U.S. troops tried to flush him with tear gas, he started upstairs, spotted the retired 56-year-old Army colonel there, and fired three shots. The guerrilla missed and Jacobson finished him off with a .45 that had quickly been tossed up to his second-floor window by troops below. That fearsome finale ended the 6-1/2 hour battle. Five Americans lay dead, as did two Vietnamese chauffeurs for the embassy who were apparently caught in the crossfire.

## THE MAN WHO PLANNED THE OFFENSIVE

It is one of those little ironies of fate that General Vo Nguyen Giap's name contains the Vietnamese words for force (Vo) and armor (Giap). The commander of North Viet Nam's armed forces and the overlord of the Viet Cong, he is a dangerous and wily foe who has become something of a legend in both Viet Nams for his stunning defeat of the French at Dienbienphu. He is one of the principal developers, along with Mao Tse-tung and Cuba's late Che Guevara, of the art of guerrilla warfare, a tactician of such talents that U.S. military experts have compared him with German Field Marshal Erwin Rommel. "You know when he's in charge," said a top Pentagon official last week. "You can feel him there." Yet, Giap had no formal training as a soldier. "The only military academy I have been to," he boasted after Dienbienphu, "is that of the bush."

Giap, 56, was not born to the bush. The son of a poor but educated landholder in what is now North Viet Nam, he was sent to an exclusive college in the old imperial capital of Hué, got a law degree from the French-run University of Hanoi and finally emerged as a history teacher at Hanoi's Thang Long School. His idol, even then, was Napoleon. "He could step to the blackboard," one of his former students recalls, "and draw in the most minute detail every battle plan of Napoleon." But his admiration for the French stopped there. A fervent Vietnamese patriot, he had joined an anti-French clandestine organization when he was only 14, [and] later became a member of Viet Nam's fledgling Communist Party.

In 1939, the French banned the party, and Giap, together with scores of other Communists, fled to China. There he met Ho Chi Minh and became a charter member of a group that the French will long remember, the Viet Minh. His assignment, based largely on his blackboard battlegrounds, was to organize Ho's ragtag guerrillas into a fighting army. That was in 1941, and Giap has been in charge of the army ever since.

Giap is an ascetic man who neither smokes nor drinks, wears baggy, high-collared uniforms, and frequently goes about shod in sandals made from rubber tires. Yet there are streaks of vanity in him. Because of his short stature (5 ft.), he likes to stand on boxes to deliver his speeches. On visits to his troops, he is liable to shuck his uniform, four-starred helmet and all, and show up dressed conspicuously in civilian clothes. He is a ruthless taskmaster, utterly contemptuous of the value of human life—even that of his own troops. "In every minute, thousands of men die all over the world," he tells his officers. "The life and death of human beings means nothing."

Giap's life has not been easy. He married in 1938 and fathered a girl, but his wife was arrested by the French and died in prison while he was in China; he has since remarried. An emotional man whose temper often got the better of his cool and earned him the nickname of "The Volcano and the Snow," he has, at times, been put down by Ho. An outburst against a French general in 1945 cost him a place on the negotiating team that tried to win independence from France at the end of World War II. A running feud with two powerful Politburo members, whose pro-Peking sentiments were resented by the strongly nationalistic Giap, kept him well down in Hanoi's Communist pecking order. Although he is North Viet Nam's Defense Minister, military commander and Vice Premier, and a popular hero second only to Ho Chi Minh, Giap has still not risen above sixth place in his party's official hierarchy.

According to the evidence available, in fact, his total command of the current Communist offensive in South Viet Nam was accorded him quite by accident. One of his Politburo archfoes, Nguyen Chi Thanh, who had shared control of operations in the South, died last summer of what Hanoi describes as a heart attack, but U.S. officers refer to as "B-52-itis" caught in the South. Thanh's death left Giap unchallenged, and he has spent a large part of the past six months planning the New Year's offensive that began last week.

*Credit: © 1968 TIME Inc. Reprinted by permission.*

## LEE LESCAZE: REPORT ON TET OFFENSIVE IN HUÉ

*Before French colonization, Hué was the imperial capital of Vietnam and home of its holiest Buddhist shrines, including the Citadel. Consequently, Hué was the most nationalistic population center and a natural hotbed of resistance to French and U.S. control. Buddhist riots against the central government started in Hué in 1963 and flared up again in 1966. Among all cities in South Vietnam, the North Vietnamese planners of the Tet offensive of 1968 viewed Hué as the best bet for a popular insurrection against the Saigon regime.*

*North Vietnamese regulars and Vietcong captured large portions of the city and presented themselves as liberators to the residents. The Vietcong visited deadly retribution on approximately 3,000 civilian "collaborators," religious missionaries, and government functionaries. Their shallow graves were discovered after the Communists left. Secret government death squads then entered the city and unleashed another wave of terror on citizens suspected of having cooperated with the Communists.*

*The Communist troops garrisoned the Citadel and prepared for the allied counterattack. From their fortified heights, they poured withering fire onto their attackers. For some days, the U.S. command restrained its fighter-bombers and artillery in order to spare the holy sites, but the intractable enemy required a change of priorities. By the twenty-fifth day of bombardment and shelling, the most savage fighting of the war ceased, the last Tet outbreak to be silenced except for Khesanh. About 5,000 North Vietnamese and Vietcong lay dead, most felled by the heavy ordnance, which slew many civilians as well. Allied deaths included 150 U.S. marines and 400 South Vietnamese infantry.*

*The following battlefield report by* Washington Post *correspondent Lee Lescaze, "Hué Marines: Bitter as They Are Brave," captured the marines' feelings of pointless sacrifice after the Tet offensive had changed everything for the Americans.*

### Washington Post, 20 February 1968

As the American Marines sweep through the southeastern part of Hué's Citadel, Vietnamese are coming back to their homes to recover and evacuate their belongings.

"They've got great intelligence," a Marine said. "Every house we set up in, the gooks are back here the next morning to clean up."

Bravo Company, 1st Battalion, 5th Marines, was set up in a rich man's house this morning. The liquor cabinet was full of Johnny Walker, Seagrams and beer.

A Buddhist altar took up one wall and the other walls had pictures of Vietnamese rural scenes mixed with centerfolds from *Playboy* magazine.

"He's the Hugh Hefner of Vietnam," a Marine said, settling into one of the absent host's armchairs.

One Marine was worried. "There's a baby's crib in there. What's a married man doing with all those *Playboy* pictures on his walls?"

The night had been rough for Bravo Company. At dusk firing broke out on three sides of the command post in the house and the Marines waited for an attack that never came.

At 7:00 A.M., as the Marines were opening C Rations and shaking off the cold of the 45-degree night, the rich man's servants came to collect what they could.

They brought a note in English which ended:

"Let us take back my things and come back to the safe region. Thank you very much. We wish you a happy new year and a complete victory."

The note said that rice and salt and "other precious things" were to be salvaged. Bravo Company watched as the servants carried out the television set first, then the refrigerator, then several lamps, plates and small decorations, then the radio phonograph and finally a 100-pound bag of rice. It took four of them three trips before they were finished. They took the Johnny Walker, but the Seagrams bottle had been broken and the Marines had taken care of the beer.

The Marines in Hué are angry. This month, Bravo Company has taken 137 casualties and the other companies of the 1st Battalion have been hit equally hard.

From heavy fighting in Phuloc, a district town south of Hué, they were brought into the former imperial capital on Feb. 12.

At first there were restrictions on the air and artillery support they could have because the Vietnamese government hoped to retake Hué with minimal damage to the city, which houses much of the country's political, religious and cultural tradition. The restrictions have since been lifted but bad weather has held down the number of air strikes.

The street fighting in Hué is terrifying. There is cover everywhere and nowhere. Walk into a street and a sniper may kill you. Stick your head out of a window and you may draw fire. Run into a building and you may find an enemy soldier there, waiting.

"The Vietnamese have better intelligence following our advance than they ever gave us about where the enemy was," one Marine said.

Every Marine casualty who is evacuated, wounded or killed, is driven through the secure blocks of Hué into the headquarters compound of the Vietnamese 1st infantry to wait for a helicopter. Vietnamese civilians stand along the road watching the dreadful cargo pass by.

In the compound, Vietnamese soldiers look on as the Marines angrily wrap their dead in ponchos and leave them on stretchers by the landing pad until the next helicopter comes in.

Individually, the Marines have shown enormous restraint. Groups of civilians who suddenly appear in front of them looking to recover their possessions from their homes do not draw fire. But the young Vietnamese civilians and the soldiers of the Vietnamese detachment that has been left at headquarters make the Americans angry. Their comrades are dying and being wounded a few blocks away in one of the hardest battles of the war.

For the Marines in the southeast part of the Citadel, it is an American battle against a very good enemy. They don't know anything about what the Vietnamese Marines are doing on the Citadel's west wall.

It has never been clearer that the Marines are fighting for their own pride, from their own fear and for their buddies who have already died. No American in Hué is fighting for Vietnam, for the Vietnamese or against Communism.

They are as bitter as they are brave. "You tell Lyndon Johnson I said 'Hi'," a wounded Marine said to a cameraman as he was carried down the street. The Marine waved his hand at the camera. "Here I am, Mr. Johnson," he said.

One seriously understrength Marine battalion has been given an enormous job here. Their inability to get the job done quickly has angered them and amazed several Vietnamese civilians who don't understand the tactical situation in Hué.

What the civilians see are American troops taking many casualties and making little progress against Vietcong and North Vietnamese soldiers—soldiers who are going to be driven out by air, artillery and U.S. Marines, but soldiers who have put up a frighteningly successful fight.

## WALTER CRONKITE: REPORT FROM VIETNAM (WHO, WHAT, WHEN, WHERE, WHY)

*Walter Cronkite was known in his youth as an accomplished war correspondent who covered the European theater of World War II for United Press International, but during the Tet offensive he hesitated to leave his CBS anchor desk to return to the field. On the* CBS Evening News, *Cronkite had assiduously cultivated a reputation for impartiality—a neutral referee of world events. He had his enthusiasms on the air—the space program, environmentalism—but those stories had no downside. Getting personally mixed up in so partisan a story as the Vietnam War risked his standing with the audience, but the cataclysmic battles of Tet compelled him to go to Vietnam to see for himself. He felt that he (and CBS) owed the audience his best insights during that perilous and confusing time. With encouragement from CBS News president Richard Salant, Cronkite flew to Vietnam in mid-February 1968.*

*Cronkite and his producer, Ernie Leiser, had trouble getting to Saigon because all airports were closed by the fighting. When they arrived, Westmoreland briefed them about the enemy's huge losses amounting to a decisive allied victory. Cronkite and Leiser wanted to go to the besieged base at Khesanh, but it was simply too dangerous for a media celebrity. They went to Hué instead. U.S. marines there were locked in a desperate battle with North Vietnamese regulars holed up in fortified positions in the Citadel. It was obvious to them that Westmoreland's optimistic estimate of the situation was either poorly informed or delusional.*

*On the way back to Saigon, Cronkite visited an old World War II buddy, Creighton W. Abrams, Westmoreland's second in command. Behind closed doors, the general admitted that they had been caught off guard by the enemy's surprise offensive, an astonishing admission by the deputy commander. In Saigon, the print reporters who had been covering the war for years complained to Cronkite about their frustrations at getting their stateside editors to believe their pessimistic but realistic dispatches that contradicted the official rosy picture. Cronkite realized that he had been part of the system that had kept the truth from the American public and determined to do something about it.*

*Cronkite's half-hour Vietnam War special aired on the Columbia Broadcasting System on the evening of 27 February 1968. Filmed reports from Hué and Saigon concluded with his studio editorial, reproduced here. He said that the evidence was undeniable that the United States was mired in a stalemate in Vietnam and should find a way out.*

*Within a month of Cronkite's broadcast, Lyndon Johnson announced a bombing halt, appealed to Hanoi for negotiations, and withdrew from the coming presidential election campaign. In November the public voted his party out of the White House and elected a peace candidate. Pundits later hyperbolically observed that Cronkite's revelations to his audience had single-handedly changed U.S. foreign policy in Southeast Asia. This judgment followed from the well-known story told by presidential aide Bill Moyers that Johnson had been stunned by the editorial and said, "Cronkite was it"—if he had lost Cronkite, he had lost the American public. This interpretation of events overstates the media's influence on the audience. Actually, public opinion had been turning against the war for some time. The Tet offensive forced the Washington establishment to catch up with the rest of the country. It was Johnson, not the public, who was moved to action by Cronkite's broadcast.*

## CBS News, 27 February 1968

Tonight, back in more familiar surroundings in New York, we'd like to sum up our findings in Vietnam, an analysis that must be speculative, personal, subjective. Who won and who lost in the great Tet offensive against the cities? I'm not sure. The Vietcong did not win by a knockout, but neither did we. The referees of history may make it a draw. Another standoff may be coming in the big battles expected south of the Demilitarized Zone. Khesanh could well fall, with a terrible loss in American lives, prestige and morale, and this is a tragedy of our stubbornness there; but the bastion no longer is a key to the rest of the northern regions, and it is doubtful that the American forces can be defeated across the breadth of the DMZ with any substantial loss of ground. Another standoff. On the political front, past performance gives no confidence that the Vietnamese government can cope with its problems, now compounded by the attack on the cities. It may not fall, it may hold on, but it probably won't show the dynamic qualities demanded of this young nation. Another standoff.

We have been too often disappointed by the optimism of the American leaders, both in Vietnam and Washington, to have faith any longer in the silver linings they find in the darkest clouds. They may be right, that Hanoi's winter-spring offensive has been forced by the Communist realization that they could not win the longer war of attrition, and that the Communists hope that any success in the offensive will improve their position for eventual negotiations. It would improve their position, and it would also require our realization, that we should have had all along, that any negotiations must be that—negotiations, not the dictation of peace terms. For it seems now more certain than ever that the bloody experience of Vietnam is to end in a stalemate. This summer's almost certain standoff will either end in real give-and-take negotiations or terrible escalation; and for every means we have to escalate, the enemy can match us, and that applies to invasion of the North, the use of nuclear weapons, or the mere commitment of one hundred, or two hundred, or three hundred thousand more American troops to the battle. And with each escalation, the world comes closer to the brink of cosmic disaster.

To say that we are closer to victory today is to believe, in the face of the evidence, the optimists who have been wrong in the past. To suggest we are on the edge of defeat is to yield to unreasonable pessimism. To say that we are mired in stalemate seems the only realistic, yet unsatisfactory, conclusion. On the off chance that military and political analysts are right, in the next few months we must test the enemy's intentions, in case this is indeed his last big gasp before negotiations. But it is increasingly clear to this reporter that the only rational way out then will be to negotiate, not as victors, but as an honorable people who lived up to their pledge to defend democracy, and did the best they could.

This is Walter Cronkite. Good night.

*Credit*: Reprinted with permission of the CBS News Archives.

---

## MICHAEL HERR: CORRESPONDENT'S RECOLLECTIONS OF TET OFFENSIVE AND BATTLE OF HUÉ

*Michael Herr went to Vietnam in 1967 as a freelance correspondent for* Esquire *magazine. His gritty, empathetic anecdotes and razor-sharp insights about the harrowing life of the "grunts," the nickname adopted by American infantrymen, became legend for Herr's flashing imagery and drug-induced hallucinations. In 1978, Herr published a collection of his war stories,* Dispatches, *to universal acclaim. The following essay became a chapter in the book. Herr's recollections of the Tet offensive and the Battle of Hué in this piece titled "Illumination Rounds" illuminate the war's contradictions and pathos. Herr also coauthored screenplays for two Vietnam War feature films,* Apocalypse Now *(1979) and* Full Metal Jacket *(1987). The title "Illumination Rounds" is word play referring to tracer munitions that trail to the target to help the enemy shoot down aircraft, as well as to Herr's terror-filled "rounds" riding helicopters and accompanying combat missions in the bush—interspersed with indulgences back in Saigon.*

*New American Review*, August 1969

We were all strapped into the seats of the Chinook, fifty of us, and something, someone, was hitting it from the outside with an enormous hammer. *How do they do that*, I thought, *we're a thousand feet in the air!* But it had to be that, over and over, shaking the helicopter, making it dip and turn in a horrible out-of-control motion that took me in the stomach. I had to laugh, it was so exciting, it was the thing I had wanted, almost what I had wanted except for that wrenching, resonant metal-echo; I could hear it even above the noise of the rotor blades. And they were going to fix that, I knew they would make it stop. They had to, it was going to make me sick.

They were all replacements going in to mop up after the big battles on Hills 875 and 876, the battles that had already taken on the name of one great battle, the Battle of Dakto. And I was new, brand-new, three days in-country, embarrassed about my boots because they were so new. And across from me, ten feet away, a boy tried to jump out of the straps and then jerked forward and hung there, his rifle barrel caught in the red plastic webbing of the seatback. As the chopper rose again and turned, his weight went back hard against the webbing and a dark spot the size of a baby's hand showed in the center of his fatigue jacket. And it grew—I knew what it was, but not, really—it got up to his armpits and then started down his sleeves and up over his shoulders at the same time. It went all across his waist and down his legs, covering the canvas on his boots until they were dark like everything else he wore, and it was running in slow, heavy drops off of his finger-

tips. I thought I could hear the drops hitting the metal strip on the chopper floor. Hey! . . . oh, but this isn't anything at all, it's not real, it's just some thing they're going through that isn't real. One of the door gunners was heaped up on the floor like a cloth dummy. His hand had the bloody raw look of a pound of liver fresh from the butcher paper. We touched down on the same LZ [landing zone] we had left just a few minutes before, but I didn't know it until one of the guys shook my shoulder, and then I couldn't stand up. All I could feel of my legs was their shaking, and the guy thought I'd been hit and helped me up. The chopper had taken eight hits, there was shattered plastic all over the floor, a dying pilot up front, and the boy was hanging forward in the straps again; he was dead, but not (I knew) really dead.

It took me a month to lose that feeling of being a spectator to something that was part game, part show. That first afternoon, before I'd boarded the Chinook, a black sergeant had tried to keep me from going. He told me I was too new to go near the kind of shit they were throwing around up in those hills. ("You a reporter?" he'd asked, and I'd said, "No, a writer," dumbass and pompous, and he'd laughed and said, "Careful. You can't use no eraser up where you wanna go.") He'd pointed to the bodies of all the dead Americans lined in two long rows near the chopper pad, so many that they could not even cover all of them decently. But they were not real then, and taught me nothing. The Chinook had come in, blowing my helmet off, and I grabbed it up and joined the replacements waiting to board. "Okay, man," the sergeant said. "You gotta go, you gotta go. All's I can say is, I hope you get a clean wound."

The Battle for Hill 875 was over, and some survivors were being brought in by a Chinook to the landing strip at Dakto. The 173rd Airborne had taken over 400 casualties, nearly 200 killed, most of them on the previous afternoon and in the fighting that had gone on all through the night. It was very cold and wet up there, and some Red Cross girls had been sent up from Pleiku to comfort the survivors. As the troops filed out of the helicopters, the girls waved and smiled at them from behind their serving tables. "Hi soldier! What's your name?" "Where you from, soldier?" "I'll bet some hot coffee would hit the spot about now."

And the men from the 173rd just kept walking without answering, staring straight ahead, their eyes rimmed with red from fatigue, their faces pinched and aged with all that had happened during the night. One of them dropped out of line and said something to a loud, fat girl who wore a Peanuts sweatshirt under her fatigue blouse, and she started to cry. The rest just walked past the girls and the large, olive-drab coffee urns. They had no idea of where they were.

At one time they would have lighted your cigarette for you on the terrace of the Continental Hotel. But those days are almost twenty years gone, and anyway, who really misses them? Now there is a crazy American who looks like George Orwell, and he is always sleeping off his drinks in one of the wicker chairs there, slumped against a table, starting, up with violence, shouting and then going back to sleep. He makes everyone nervous, especially the waiters: the old ones who had served the French and the Japanese and the first American journalists and O.S.S. types ("Those noisy bastards at the Continental," Graham Greene called them) and the really young ones who bussed the tables and pimped in a modest way. The little elevator boy still greets the guests each morning with a quiet "Ça va?", but he is seldom answered, and the old baggage man (he also brings us grass) will sit in the lobby and say, "How are you tomorrow?"

"The Ballad of Billy Joe" plays from speakers mounted on the terrace's corner columns, but the air seems too heavy to carry the sound right, and it hangs in the corners. There is an exhausted, drunk master sergeant from the First Infantry Division who has bought a flute from the old man in khaki shorts and pith helmet who sells instruments along Tu Do Street. The old man will lean over the butt-strewn flower boxes that line the terrace and play "Frère Jacques" on a wooden stringed instrument. The sergeant has bought the flute, and he is playing it quietly, pensively, badly.

The tables are crowded with American civilian construction engineers, men getting $30,000 a year from their jobs on government contracts and matching that easily on the black market. Their faces have the look of aerial photos of silicone pits, all hung with loose flesh and standing veins. Their mistresses

were among the prettiest, saddest girls in Vietnam. I always wondered what they had looked like before they'd made their arrangements with the engineers. You'd see them at the tables there, smiling their hard, empty smiles into those rangy, brutal, scared faces. No wonder those men all looked alike to the Vietnamese; after awhile, they all looked alike to me. Out on the Bien Hoa Highway, north of Saigon, there is a monument to the Vietnamese war dead, and it is one of the few graceful things left in the country. It is a modest pagoda set above the road and approached by long flights of gently rising steps. One Sunday, I saw a bunch of these engineers gunning their Harleys up those steps, laughing and shouting in the afternoon sun. The Vietnamese had a special name for them to distinguish them from all other Americans; it translated out to something like "The Terrible Ones," although I'm told that this doesn't even approximate the odium carried in the original.

There was a young sergeant in the Special Forces, stationed at the C Detachment in Can Tho that served as the SF headquarters for IV Corps. In all, he had spent thirty-six months in Vietnam. This was his third extended tour, and he planned to come back again as soon as he possibly could after this current hitch was finished. During his last tour he had lost a finger and part of a thumb in a firefight, and he had been generally shot up enough times for the three Purple Hearts which mean that you don't have to fight in Vietnam anymore. After all that, I guess they thought of him as a combat liability, but he was such a hard-charger that they gave him the EM Club to manage. He ran it well and seemed happy, except that he had gained a lot of weight in the duty, and it set him apart from the rest of the men. He loved to horse around with the Vietnamese in the compound, leaping on them from behind, leaning heavily on them, shoving them around and pulling their ears, sometimes punching them a little hard in the stomach, smiling a stiff small smile that was meant to tell them all that he was just being playful. The Vietnamese would smile too, until he turned to walk away. He loved the Vietnamese, he said, he really knew them after three years. As far as he was concerned, there was no place in the world as fine as Vietnam. And back home in North Carolina, he had a large, glass-covered display case in which he kept his medals and decorations and citations, the photographs taken during three tours and countless battles, letters from past commanders, a few souvenirs. The case stood in the center of the living room, he said, and every night his wife and three kids would move the kitchen table out in front of it and eat their dinner there.

At eight hundred feet we knew we were being shot at. Something hit the underside of the chopper but did not penetrate it. They weren't firing tracers, but we saw the brilliant flickering blips of light below, and the pilot circled and came down very fast, working the button that released fire from the flex guns mounted on either side of the Huey. Every fifth round was a tracer, and they sailed out and down, incomparably graceful, closer and closer, until they met the tiny point of light coming from the jungle. The ground fire stopped, and we went on to land at Vinh Long, where the pilot yawned and said, "I think I'll go to bed early tonight and see if I can wake up with any enthusiasm for this war."

A twenty-four-year-old Special Forces captain was telling me about it. "I went out and killed one VC and liberated a prisoner. Next day the major called me in and told me that I'd killed fourteen VC and liberated six prisoners. You want to see the medal?"

There was a little air-conditioned restaurant on the corner of Le-Loi and Tu Do, across from the Continental Hotel and the old opera house which now served as the Vietnamese Lower House. Some of us called it the Graham Greene Milk Bar (a scene in "The Quiet American" had taken place there), but its name was Givral. Every morning, they baked their own *baguettes* and *croissants*, and the coffee wasn't too bad. Sometimes I'd meet there with a friend of mine for breakfast.

He was a Belgian, a tall, slow-moving man of thirty who'd been born in the Congo. He professed to know and love war, and he affected the mercenary sensibility. He'd been photographing the Vietnam thing for seven or eight years now, and once in a while he'd go over to Laos and run around the jungles there with the government searching for the dreaded Pathet Lao, which he pronounced "Paddy Lao." Other people's stories of Laos always made it sound like a lotus-land where no one wanted to hurt anyone, but he said that whenever he went on ops there he always kept a grenade taped to his belly because he was a Catholic and knew what the Paddy Lao would do to him if he were captured. But he was a little crazy that way, and tended to dramatize his war stories.

He always wore dark glasses, probably even during operations. His pictures sold to the wire services, and I saw a few of them in the American news magazines. He was very kind in a gruff, off-handed sort of way; kindness embarrassed him, and he was so graceless among people, so eager to shock, that he couldn't understand why so many of us liked him. Irony was the effect he worked for in conversation, that and a sense of how exquisite the war could be when all of its machinery was running right. He was explaining the finish of an operation he'd just been on in War Zone C, above Cu Chi.

"There were a lot of dead VC," he said. "Dozens and dozens of them were from that same village that has been giving you so much trouble lately. VC from top to bottom—Michael, in that village the fucking *ducks* are VC. So the American commander had twenty or thirty of the dead flown up in a sling-load and dropped into the village. I should say it was a drop of at least two hundred feet, all those dead Vietcongs, right in the middle of the village."

He smiled (I couldn't see his eyes).

"Ah, Psywar!" he said, kissing off the tips of his fingers.

Bob Stokes of *Newsweek* told me this: In the big Marine hospital in Danang, they have what is called the "White Lie Ward," where they bring some of the worst cases, the ones that can be saved but who will never be the same again. A young Marine was carried in, still unconscious and full of morphine, and his legs were gone. As he was being carried into the ward, he came to briefly and saw a Catholic chaplain standing over him.

"Father," he said, "am I all right?"

The chaplain didn't know what to say. "You'll have to talk about that with the doctors, son."

"Father, are my legs okay?"

"Yes," the chaplain said. "Sure."

By the next afternoon the shock had worn off, and the boy knew all about it. He was lying on his cot when the chaplain came by.

"Father," the Marine said, "I'd like to ask you for something."

"What, son?"

"I'd like to have that cross." And he pointed to the tiny silver insignia on the chaplain's lapel.

"Of course," the chaplain said. "But why?"

"Well, it was the first thing I saw when I came to yesterday, and I'd like to have it."

The chaplain removed the cross and handed it to him. The Marine held it tightly in his fist and looked at the chaplain.

"You lied to me, Father," he said. "You cocksucker. You lied to me."

His name was Davies, and he was a gunner with a helicopter group based at Tan Son Nhut airport. On paper, by the regulations, he was billeted in one of the big "hotel" BEQs [enlisted men's billets] in Cholon, but he only kept his things there. He actually lived in a small two-story Vietnamese house deeper inside of Cholon, as far from the papers and the regulations as he could get. Every morning he took an Army bus with wire-grill windows out to the base and flew missions, mostly around War Zone C, along the Cambodian border, and most nights he returned to the house in Cholon where he lived with his "wife" (he'd found her in one of the bars) and some other Vietnamese who were said to be the girl's family. Her mamma-san and her brother were always there, living on the first floor, and there were others who came and went. He seldom saw the brother, but every few days he would find a pile of labels and brand names torn from cardboard cartons, American products that the brother wanted from the PX.

The first time I saw him he was sitting alone at a table on the Continental terrace, drinking a beer. He had a full, drooping moustache and sharp, sad eyes, and he was wearing a denim work shirt and wheat jeans. He also carried a Leica and a copy of *Ramparts Magazine*, and I just assumed at first that he was a correspondent. I didn't know then that you could buy *Ramparts* at the PX, and after I'd borrowed and returned it, we began to talk. It was the issue that featured left-wing Catholics like Jesus Christ and Fulton Sheen on the cover. *"Catholique?"* one of the bar girls said later that night. *"Moi aussi,"* and she kept the magazine. That was when we were walking around Cholon in the rain trying to find Hoa, his wife. Mamma-san had told us that she'd gone to the movies with some girl friends, but Davies knew what she was doing.

"I hate that shit," he said. "It's so uncool."

"Well, don't put up with it."

"Yeah."

Davies' house was down a long narrow alley that became nothing more than a warren at the end, smelling of camphor-smoke and fish, crowded but clean. He would not speak to Mamma-san, and we walked straight up to the second floor. It was one long room that had a sleeping area screened off in an arrangement of filmy curtains. At the top of the stairs there was a large poster of Lenny Bruce, and beneath it, in a shrine effect, was a low table with a Buddha and lighted incense on it.

"Lenny," Davies said.

Most of one wall was covered with a collage that Davies had done with the help of some friends. It included photos of burning monks, stacked Vietcong dead, wounded Marines screaming and weeping, Cardinal Spellman waving from a chopper, Ronald Reagan, his face halved and separated by a stalk of cannabis; pictures of John Lennon peering through wire-rimmed glasses, Mick Jagger, Jimi Hendrix, Dylan, Eldridge Cleaver, Rap Brown; coffins draped with American flags whose stars were replaced by swastikas and dollar signs; odd parts clipped from *Playboy* pictures, newspaper headlines (Farmers Butcher Hogs to Protest Pork Price Dip), photo captions (President Jokes with Newsmen), beautiful girls holding flowers, showers of peace symbols; Ky standing at attention and saluting, a small mushroom cloud forming where his genitalia should have been; a map of the Western United States with the shape of Vietnam reversed, and fitted over California and one large, long figure that began at the bottom with shiny leather boots and rouged knees and ascended in a microskirt, bare breasts, graceful shoulders, and a long neck, topped by the burned, blackened face of a dead Vietnamese woman.

By the time Davies' friends showed up, we were already stoned. We could hear them below, laughing and rapping with Mamma, and then they came up the stairs, three blacks and two white guys.

"It sure do smell *peculiar* up here," one of them said. "Hi, you freaky li'l fuckers."

"This grass is Number Ten," Davies said. "Every time I smoke this grass over here it gives me a bad trip."

"Ain' nuthin' th' matter with that grass," someone said. "It ain' the grass."

"Where's Hoa?"

"Yeah, Davies, where's your ole lady at?"

> One of them handed off a joint and stretched out. "Hairy day today," he said.

"She's out hustling Saigon tea, and I'm fucking sick of it." He tried to look really angry, but he only looked unhappy.

One of them handed off a joint and stretched out. "Hairy day today," he said.

"Where'd you fly?"

"Bu Dop."

"Bu Dop!" one of the spades said, and he started to move toward the joint, jiving and working his shoulders, bopping his head. "Bu Dop, budop, bu dop dop *dop!*"

"Funky funky Bu Dop."

"Hey, man, can you O.D. on grass?"

"I dunno, baby. Maybe we could get jobs at the Aberdeen Proving Grounds smokin' dope for Uncle Sugar."

"Wow, I'm stoned. Hey, Davies, you stoned?"

"Yeah," Davies said.

It started to rain again, so hard that you couldn't hear drops, only the full force of the water pouring down on the metal roof. We smoked a little more, and then the others started to leave. Davies looked like he was sleeping with his eyes open.

"That goddam pig," he said. "Fuckin' whore. Man, I'm paying out all this bread for the house, and those people downstairs. I don't even know who they are, for Christ's sake. I'm really . . . I'm getting sick of it."

"You're pretty short now,"[1] someone said. "Why don't you cut out?"

"You mean just split?"

"Why not?"

Davies was quiet for a long time.

"Yeah," he finally said. "This is bad. This is really bad. I think I'm going to get out of here."

A bird colonel, commanding a brigade of the 4th Infantry Division: "I'll bet you always wondered why we call 'em Dinks up in this part of the country. I thought of it myself. I'll tell you, I never *did* like hearing them called Charlie. See, I had an uncle named Charlie, and I liked him, too. No, Charlie was just too damn good for the little bastards. So I just thought, What are they *really* like? and I came up with rinky-dink. Suits 'em just perfect, Rinky-Dink, 'cause that's what they are. 'Cept that was too long, so we cut it down some. And that's why we call 'em Dinks."

One morning before dawn, Ed Fouhy, a former Saigon bureau chief for CBS, went out to the 8th Aerial Port at Tan Son Nhut to catch the early military flight to Danang. They boarded as the sun came up, and Fouhy strapped in next to a kid in rumpled fatigues, one of those soldiers you see whose weariness has gone far beyond physical exhaustion, into that state where no amount of sleep will give them the kind of rest they need. Every torpid movement they make tells you that they are tired, that they'll stay tired until their tours are up and the big bird flies them back to the World. Their eyes are dim with it, their faces almost puffy, and when they smile, you have to accept it as a token.

There was a standard question you could use to open a conversation with troops, and Fouhy tried it. "How long you been in-country?" he asked.

The kid half-lifted his head; that question could not be serious. The weight was really on him, and the words came slowly:

"All . . . fuckin' . . . day," he said.

["]You guys ought do a story on me suntahm," the kid said. He was a helicopter gunner, six-three with an enormous head that sat in bad proportion to the rest of his body and a line of picket teeth that were always on show in a wet, uneven smile. Every few seconds he would have to wipe his mouth with the back of his hand, and when he talked to you his face was always an inch from yours, so that I had to take my glasses off to keep them dry. He was from Kilgore, Texas, and he was on his seventeenth consecutive month in-country.

"Why should we do a story about you?"

"'Cause I'm so fuckin' good," he said, "'n' that ain' no shit, neither. Got me one hunnert 'n' fifty-se'en gooks kilt. 'N' fifty caribou." He grinned and stanched the saliva for a second. "Them're all certified," he added.

The chopper touched down at Ba Xoi and we got off, not unhappy about leaving him. "Lis'n," he said, laughing, "you git up onna ridgeline, see y' keep yer head down. Y'heah?"

["]Say; how'd you get to be a co-respondent an' come ovah to this raggedy-ass motherfucker?"

He was a really big spade, rough-looking even when he smiled, and he wore a gold nose-bead fastened through his left nostril. I told him that the nose-bead blew my mind, and he said that was all right, it blew everybody's mind. We were sitting by the chopper pad of an LZ above Kontum. He was trying to get to Dakto, I was heading for Pleiku, and we both wanted to get out of there before nightfall. We took turns running out to the pad to check the choppers that kept coming in and taking off, neither of us were having any luck, and after we'd talked for an hour he laid a joint on me and we smoked.

"I been heah mo'n eight months now," he said. "I bet I been in mo'n twenny firefights. An' I ain' hardly fired back once."

"How come?"

"Shee-it, I go firin' back, I might kill one a th' Brothers, you dig it?"

I nodded, no Viet Cong ever called me honky, and he told me that in his company alone there were more than a dozen Black Panthers and that he was one of them. I didn't say anything, and then he said that he wasn't just a Panther; he was an agent for the Panthers, sent over here to recruit. I asked him what kind of luck he'd been having, and he said fine,

real fine. There was a fierce wind blowing across the LZ, and the joint didn't last very long.

"Hey, baby," he said, "that was just some shit I tol' you. Shit, I ain' no Panther. I was just fuckin' with you, see what you'd say."

"But the Panthers have guys over here. I've met some."

"Tha' could be," he said, and he laughed.

A Huey came in, and he jogged out to see where it was headed. It was going to Dakto, and he came back to get his gear. "Later, baby," he said. "An' luck." He jumped into the chopper, and as it rose from the strip he leaned out and laughed, bringing his arm up and bending it back toward him, palm out and the fist clenched tightly in the Sign.

One day I went out with the ARVN on an operation in the rice paddies above Vinh Long, forty terrified Vietnamese troops and five Americans, all packed into three Hueys that dropped us up to our hips in paddy muck. I had never been in a rice paddy before. We spread out and moved toward the marshy swale that led to the jungle. We were still twenty feet from the first cover, a low paddy wall, when we took fire from the treeline. It was probably the working half of a crossfire that had somehow gone wrong. It caught one of the ARVN in the head, and he dropped back into the water and disappeared. We made it to the wall with two casualties. There was no way of stopping their fire, no room to send in a flanking party, so gunships were called and we crouched behind the wall and waited. There was a lot of fire coming from the trees, but we were all right as long as we kept down. And I was thinking, Oh man, so this is a rice paddy, yes, wow! when I suddenly heard an electric guitar shooting right up in my ear and a mean, rapturous black voice singing, coaxing, "Now c'mon baby, stop actin' so crazy," and when I got it all together I turned to see a grinning black corporal hunched over a cassette recorder. "Might's well," he said. "We ain' goin' nowhere till them gunships come."

That's the story of the first time I ever heard Jimi Hendrix, but in a war where a lot of people talked about Aretha's "Satisfaction" the way other people speak of Brahms' Fourth, it was more than a story; it was Credentials. "Say, that Jimi Hendrix is my main man," someone would say. "He has definitely got his shit together!" Hendrix had once been in the 101st Airborne, and the Airborne in Vietnam was full of wiggy-brilliant spades like him, really mean and really good, guys who always took care of you when things got bad. That music meant a lot to them. I never once heard it played over the Armed Forces Radio Network.

The sergeant had lain out near the clearing for almost two hours with a wounded medic. He had called over and over for a medevac, but none had come. Finally, a chopper from another outfit, a LOH [light observation helicopter], appeared, and he was able to reach it by radio. The pilot told him that he'd have to wait for one of his own ships, they weren't coming down, and the sergeant told the pilot that if he did not land for them he was going to open fire from the ground and fucking well bring him down. So they were picked up that way, but there were repercussions.

The commander's code name was Mal Hombre, and he reached the sergeant later that afternoon from a place with the call signal Violent Meals.

"God *damn* it, Sergeant," he said through the static, "I thought you were a professional soldier."

"I waited as long as I could, sir. Any longer, I was gonna lose my man."

"This outfit is perfectly capable of taking care of its own dirty laundry. Is that clear, Sergeant?"

"Colonel, since when is a wounded trooper 'dirty laundry'?"

"At ease, Sergeant," Mal Hombre said, and radio contact was broken.

There was a spec 4 in the Special Forces at Can Tho, a shy Indian boy from Chinle, Arizona, with large, wet eyes the color of ripe olives and a quiet way of speaking, a really nice way of putting things, kind to everyone without ever being stupid or soft about it. On the night that the compound and the airstrip were hit, he came and asked me if there was a chaplain anywhere around. He wasn't very religious, he said, but he was worried about tonight. He'd just volunteered for a "suicide squad," two jeeps that were going to drive across the airstrip with mortars and a recoilless rifle. It looked bad, I had to admit it; there were so few of us in the compound that they'd had to put me on the reaction force. It might be bad. He just had a feeling about it, he'd seen what always happened to guys whenever they got that feeling, at least he thought it was that feeling, a bad one, the worst he'd ever had.

I told him that the only chaplains I could think of would be in the town, and we both knew that the town was cut off.

"Oh," he said. "Look, then. If I get it tonight . . ."

"It'll be okay."

"Listen, though. If it happens . . . I think it's going to . . . Will you make sure the colonel tells my folks I was looking for a chaplain anyway?"

I promised, and the jeeps loaded and drove off. I heard later that there had been a brief firefight, but that no one had been hurt. They didn't have to use the recoilless. They all drove back into the compound two hours later. The next morning at breakfast he sat at another table, saying a lot of loud, brutal things about the gooks, and he wouldn't look at me. But at noon he came over and squeezed my arm and smiled, his eyes fixed somewhere just to the right of my own.

For two days now, ever since the Tet Offensive had begun, they had been coming by the hundreds to the province hospital at Can Tho. They were usually either very young or very old or women, and their wounds were often horrible. The more lightly wounded were being treated quickly in the hospital yard, and the more serious cases were simply placed in one of the corridors to die. There were just too many of them to treat,

the doctors had worked without a break, and now, on the second afternoon, the Viet Cong began shelling the hospital.

One of the Vietnamese nurses handed me a cold can of beer and asked me to take it down the hall where one of the Army surgeons was operating. The door of the room was ajar, and I walked right in. I probably should have looked first. A little girl was lying on the table, looking with wide dry eyes at the wall. Her left leg was gone, and a sharp piece of bone about six inches long extended from the exposed stump. The leg itself was on the floor, half wrapped in a piece of paper. The doctor was a major, and he'd been working alone. He could not have looked worse if he'd lain all night in a trough of blood. His hands were so slippery that I had to hold the can to his mouth for him and tip it up as his head went back. I couldn't look at the girl.

"Is it all right?" he said quietly.

"It's okay now. I expect I'll be sick as hell later on."

He placed his hand on the girl's forehead and said, "Hello, little darling." He thanked me for bringing the beer. He probably thought that he was smiling, but nothing changed anywhere in his face. He'd been working this way for nearly twenty hours.

The courtyard of the American compound in Hué was filled with puddles from the rain, and the canvas tops of the jeeps and trucks sagged with the weight of the water. It was the fifth day of the fighting, and everyone was still amazed that the NVA or the Cong had not hit the compound on the first night. An enormous white goose had come into the compound that night, and now his wings were heavy with the oil that had formed on the surface of the puddles. Every time a vehicle entered the yard he would beat his wings in a fury and scream, but he never left the compound and, as far as I knew, no one ever ate him.

Nearly two hundred of us were sleeping in the two small rooms that had been the compound's dining quarters. The Army was not happy about having to billet all of the Marines that were coming through, and they were absolutely furious about all of the correspondents who were hanging around, waiting until the fighting moved north across the river, into the Citadel. You were lucky to find space enough on the floor to lie down on, luckier if you found an empty stretcher to sleep on, and luckiest of all if the stretcher was new. All night long the few unbroken windows would rattle from the air strikes across the river, and a mortar pit just outside fired incessantly. At two or three in the morning, Marines would come in from their patrols. They'd cross the room, not much caring whether they stepped on anyone or not. They'd turn their radios on and shout across the room to one another. "Really, can't you fellows show a bit more consideration?" a British correspondent said, and their laughter woke anyone who was not already up.

One morning there was a fire in the prison camp across the road from the compound. We saw the black smoke rising over the barbed wire that topped the camp wall and heard automatic weapons' fire. The prison was full of captured NVA and Vietcong or Vietcong suspects; the guards said that the fire had been started to cover an escape. The ARVN and a few Americans were shooting blindly into the flames, and the bodies were burning where they fell. Civilian dead lay out on the sidewalks only a block from the compound, and the park that ran along the Perfume River was littered with dead. It was cold during those days, the sun never came out once, but the rain did things to the corpses that were worse in their way than anything the sun could have done. It was on one of those days that I realized that the only corpse I could not bear to look at would be the one I would never have to see.

Between the smoke and the mist and the flying dust inside the Citadel, it was hard to call that hour between light and darkness a true dusk, but it was the time when a lot of us would open our C-rations. We were only meters away from the worst of the fighting, not more than a Vietnamese city block in distance, and yet civilians kept appearing, smiling, shrugging, trying to get back to their homes. The Marines would try to menace them away at rifle-point, shouting, "Di, di, *di* you sorryass motherfuckers, go on, get the hell away from here!", and the refugees would smile, half-bowing, and flit up one of the shattered streets. A little boy of about ten came up to a bunch of Marines from Charlie Company. He was laughing and moving his head from side to side in a funny way. The fierceness in his eyes should have told everyone what it was, but it had never occurred to most of the Grunts that a Vietnamese child could be driven mad, too, and by the time they understood it the boy had begun to go for their eyes and tear at their fatigues, spooking everyone, putting everyone really up-tight, until one of the spades grabbed him from behind and held his arms. "C'mon, poor l'il baby, 'fore one a these Grunt mothers shoots you," he said, and carried the boy to where the corpsmen were.

On the worst days, no one expected to get through it alive. A despair set in among the members of the battalion that the older ones, the veterans of two other wars, had never seen before. Once or twice, when the men from graves registration took the personal effects from the packs and pockets of dead Marines, they would find letters from home that had been delivered days before and were still unopened.

We were running some wounded onto the back of a half-ton truck, and one young Marine kept crying from his stretcher. His sergeant held both of his hands, and the Marine kept saying, "Shit, sarge, I ain' gone make it. Oh damn, I'm gone die, ain' I?" "No, you ain't gonna die, for Christ's sake," the sergeant said. "Oh yeah, sarge, yeah, I am." "Crowley," the sergeant said, "you ain't hurt that bad. I want you to just shut the fuck-up. You ain't done a thing 'cept bitch ever since we got to this fuckin' Hué City." But the sergeant didn't really know. The kid had been hit in the throat, and you couldn't tell about those. Throat wounds were bad. Everyone was afraid of throat wounds.

We lucked out on our connections. At the battalion aid-station in Hué we got a chopper that carried us and a dozen dead Marines to the base at Phubai, and three minutes after we arrived there we caught a C-130 to Danang. Hitching in from the airfield, we found a Psyops official who felt sorry for us and drove us all the way to the Press Center. As we came through the gate we could see that the net was up and that the daily volleyball game between the Marines assigned to the Press Center was in progress.

"Where the hell have *you* guys been?" one of them said. We looked pretty wretched.

The inside of the dining room was freezing with air conditioning. I sat at a table and ordered a hamburger and a Remy Martin from one of the peasant girls who worked the tables. I sat there for a couple of hours, and ordered four more hamburgers and at least a dozen brandies. (I had no idea of it until the check came.) It was not possible, it was just not possible to have been where we'd been before and to be where we were now, all in the same afternoon. One of the correspondents who had come back with me sat at another table, also by himself, and we just looked at each other, shook our heads, and laughed. I went to my room and took my boots and fatigues off, putting them under the bed where I wouldn't have to look at them. I went into the bathroom and turned on the shower. The water was hot, incredibly hot, for a moment I thought I'd gone insane from it, and I sat down on the concrete floor for a long time, shaving there, soaping myself over and over. I was using up all the hot water, I knew that, but I couldn't get interested in it. I dressed and went back to the dining room. The net was down now, and one of the Marines said hello and asked me what the movie was going to be that night. I ordered a steak and another string of brandies. Then I went to bed and smoked a joint. I was going back in the morning, I knew that, it was understood. But why was it understood? All of my stuff was in order, ready for the five o'clock wakeup. I finished the joint and shuddered off into sleep.

Major Trong bounced around in the seat of his jeep as it drove us over the debris scattered across the streets of Hué. His face seemed completely expressionless as we passed the crowds of Vietnamese stumbling over the fallen beams and powdered brick of their homes, but his eyes were covered by dark glasses, and it was impossible to know what he was feeling. He did not look like a victor; he was so small and limp in his seat, I was sure he was going to fly out of the jeep. His driver was a sergeant named Dang, one of the biggest Vietnamese I'd ever seen, and his English was better than the major's. The jeep would stall on rubble heaps from time to time, and Dang would turn to us and smile an apology. We were on our way to the Imperial Palace.

A month earlier, the palace grounds had been covered with dozens of NVA dead and the burned-over leavings of three weeks' siege and defense. There had been some reluctance about bombing the palace, but a lot of the bombing nearby had done heavy damage, and there had been some shelling, too. The large bronze urns were dented beyond restoring, and the rains poured through a hole in the roof of the throne room, soaking the two small thrones where the old Annamese royalty had sat. In the great hall (great when you scaled it down to the Vietnamese) the red lacquerwork on the upper walls was badly chipped, and a heavy dust covered everything. The crown of the main gate had collapsed, and in the garden the broken branches of the old cay-dai trees lay like the forms of giant insects seared in a fire, wispy, delicate, dead. It was rumored during those days that the palace was being held by a unit of student volunteers who had taken the invasion of Hué as a sign and had rushed to join the North Vietnamese. The final assault had been a privilege reserved for a battalion of elite South Vietnamese Rangers called the Hoc Bao, the Black Panthers, but once the walls had been taken and the grounds entered, there was no one left inside except for the dead. They bobbed in the moat and littered all the approaches. The Marines moved in then, and empty ration cans and muddied sheets from the *Stars and Stripes* were added to the litter. A fat Marine had his picture taken pissing into the locked-open mouth of a decomposing North Vietnamese soldier.

"No good," Major Trong said. "No good. Fight here very hard, very bad."

I'd been talking to Sergeant Dang about the palace and about the line of emperors. He seemed to know a lot about it. We stalled one last time at the foot of a moat bridge, and I asked him the name of the last of the emperors to have occupied the throne. He smiled and shrugged, not so much as though he didn't know, but as though the answer didn't much matter.

"Major Trong is Emperor now," he said, and gunned the jeep into the palace grounds.

The Intel report lay closed on the green field table, and someone had scrawled "What does it all mean?" across the cover sheet. There wasn't much doubt about who had done that; the S-2 [intelligence officer] was a known ironist. There were so many like him, really young captains and majors who had the wit to cut back their despair, a wedge to set against the bitterness. What got to them sooner or later was an inability to reconcile their love of service with their contempt for the war, and a lot of them finally had to resign their commissions, leave the profession.

## NOTE

1. Being short is GI slang for nearing rotation home.

We were sitting in the tent waiting for the rain to stop, the major, five grunts and myself. The rains were constant now, ending what had been a dry monsoon season, and you could look through the tent flap and think about the Marines up there patrolling the hills. Someone came in to report that one of the patrols had discovered a small arms cache.

"An arms cache!" the major said. "What happened was, one of the grunts was out there running around, and he tripped and fell down. That's about the only way we ever find any of this shit."

He was twenty-nine, young in rank, and this was his second tour. The time before, he had been a captain commanding a regular Marine company. He knew all about grunts and patrols, arms caches and the value of most Intelligence.

It was cold, even in the tent, and the enlisted Marines seemed uncomfortable about lying around with a stranger, a correspondent there. The major was a cool head, they knew that; there wasn't going to be any kind of hassle until the rain stopped. They talked quietly among themselves at the far end of the tent, away from the light of the lantern. Reports kept coming in: reports from the Vietnamese, from recon, from Division, situation reports, casualty reports, three casualty reports in twenty minutes. The major looked them all over.

"Did you know that a dead Marine costs eighteen thousand dollars?" he said. The grunts all turned around and looked at us. They knew how the major had meant that because they knew the major. They were just seeing about me.

The rain stopped, and they left. Outside, the air was still cool, but heavy, too, as though a terrible heat was coming on. The major and I stood by the tent and watched while an F-4 flew nose-down, released its load against the base of a hill, leveled and flew upward again.

"I've been having this dream," the major said. "I've had it two times now. I'm in a big examination room back at Quantico. They're handing out questionnaires for an aptitude test. I take one and look at it, and the first question says, 'How many kinds of animals can you kill with your hands?'"

We could see rain falling in a sheet about a kilometer away. Judging by the wind, the major gave it three minutes before it reached us.

"After the first tour, I'd have the goddamndest nightmares. You know, the works. Bloody stuff, bad fights, guys dying, me dying . . . I thought they were the worst," he said, "But I sort of miss them now."

## FURTHER READINGS

Braestrup, Peter. *Big Story: How the American Press and Television Reported and Interpreted the Crisis of Tet 1968*. Boulder, Colo.: Westview Press, 1977.

Herr, Michael. *Dispatches*. New York: Alfred A. Knopf, 1977.

Nolan, Keith William. *Battle for Hué: Tet, 1968*. Novato, Calif.: Presidio Press, 1983.

Oberdorfer, Don. *Tet!* Garden City, N.Y.: Doubleday, 1971.

# 15

# SIEGE OF KHESANH, 21 JANUARY—7 APRIL 1968

The Battle of Khesanh was perhaps the most controversial and misinterpreted battle of the Vietnam War. The two supreme military commanders, Generals William C. Westmoreland and Vo Nguyen Giap, dueled each other for seventy-seven days, from 21 January to 7 April 1968. Though the U.S. base at Khesanh stood, and awesome U.S. firepower inflicted terrible losses on the North Vietnamese Army (NVA) before it withdrew, the battle was viewed as a military and political mistake for the United States and led to Westmoreland's nadir in Vietnam.

As early as 1964, reconnaissance missions staged from the U.S. base at Khesanh detected main-force NVA units crossing the demilitarized zone (DMZ) into the northernmost Quantri Province of South Vietnam and funneling down the Ho Chi Minh Trail in Laos to points further south. Because Westmoreland viewed Khesanh as the key to controlling enemy movements, he assumed that General Giap placed the same strategic importance on its capture. To that end, a major airstrip was built and supplies were stockpiled.

To deploy his forces properly for the Communist offensive scheduled for January 1968, General Giap needed to know whether the Americans would counterattack into Laos or North Vietnam. During March to August 1967, he launched a series of spoiling attacks on Khesanh and other outposts along the DMZ. Westmoreland did not pursue. Giap therefore reassigned defensive NVA battalions for the coming offensive.

Giap tested U.S. belligerency one more time by unleashing the Route 9 Front, equal in size to a U.S. Army corps of approximately 40,000 soldiers, on Khesanh on 21 January 1968, just ten days before the full countrywide offensive. This attack was not a diversion, nor an attempt to capture the U.S. base, but rather, a test of U.S. intentions to counterattack. Westmoreland believed that this attack on Khesanh was Giap's main thrust and ordered reinforcements, which drew strength away from defense of South Vietnam's major population centers.

In the grip of his own interpretation of enemy movements, Westmoreland publicly called the Khesanh action a vain attempt by the North Vietnamese to restage Dienbienphu, the five-month encirclement of a French outpost in 1954 by General Giap's Vietminh army that ended in French surrender and withdrawal from Vietnam. Echoing the general, U.S. news commentators and government officials predicted a showdown at Khesanh. President Johnson became obsessed with the specter of entrapment. Giap tried to capitalize on the American obsession with Khesanh by planting a false report with Wilfred Burchett, an Australian Communist journalist, that the general was personally in command at Khesanh, as he had been at Dienbienphu.[1]

U.S. airpower guaranteed that Khesanh would be no Dienbienphu. The Americans had more than 2,000 bombers and 3,000 helicopters on call and flew an average of 320 combat mission flights delivering 1,282 tons of bombs per day. The bombing devastated the NVA attackers, but they were unrelenting. Westmoreland was so fearful that he pondered use of nuclear weapons in the last resort to defend Khesanh. A public flap in Washington over his idea had to be quelled by the president. Westmoreland was quietly instructed to repress contingency plans involving nuclear weapons.

Early on 7 February, NVA tanks overran the Langvei Special Forces camp 8 kilometers from the Khesanh base and used it to launch artillery and rocket barrages at the main base. Other outposts fell. Several C-123 and C-130 transport planes and marine helicopters crashed. The deteriorating situation at Khesanh dominated the U.S. news agenda in March. Disturbing reports also surfaced about feuding between army and marine commanders and a Pentagon request for 205,000 more troops. The negative news coverage hurt President Johnson's approval rating just when he was being challenged by Minnesota senator Eugene McCarthy in primary elections for the Democratic presidential nomination. On 12 March, McCarthy came within a few hundred votes of winning the New Hampshire primary. By the end of the month, Johnson viewed his domestic political situation as hopeless and announced his decision not to run for reelection.

On 28 March, President Johnson announced that four-star general Creighton W. Abrams, known as "the fightin'est man" in the army, would become the new commander of Military Assistance Command, Vietnam, effective 30 May. Johnson ordered Abrams to keep a low profile for his command while he tried to coax the Communists into negotiations. To that end, Abrams decided to dismantle the Khesanh base, which invited renewed attacks by the North Vietnamese, who were seeking to disrupt domestic U.S. politics. To avoid unfavorable interpretations of his decision, Abrams gagged the press, but *Baltimore Sun* correspondent John S. Carroll published the base closure story, which asked whether Khesanh had been a U.S. defeat. Carroll's defiance of the gag order led to his expulsion from Vietnam.

## DON SIDER: REPORT ON AMERICAN SOLDIERS AT KHESANH—READY TO FIGHT

*This dispatch by* Time *magazine's Don Sider is in the fine tradition of U.S. war correspondents—in the manner of Scripps Howard's Ernie Pyle—who braved war's front lines to capture compelling portrayals of combat soldiers.*

### *Time*, 16 February 1968

*Time* Correspondent Don Sider spent several days at Khe Sanh last week ducking incoming shells, and observing the unique quality of life in the besieged Marine base. His report:

A chill, grey mist hangs over the jungled hills around Khe Sanh and drifts down onto the base's metal runway. The morning mist often lasts into the afternoon, the bright sun of recent weeks is lost in monsoonal overcast, and the air is raw and wet with winter. The camp seems to have settled into a dull, lethargic pace to match the dull, damp weather that envelops it. In a mood of resignation, Marines go about their life-or-death work, digging into the red clay, filling sandbags, bolstering the bunkers they know are their one protection against the real rain: the whining rockets and the mortars that come with no warning—just the awful cracking sound as they explode.

The dash for cover is part of every man's routine. "It's a modus vivendi," says Protestant Chaplain Ray Stubbe, 29. "The men run for shelter, but they don't cringe when they get there." Except for an occasional case of what the corpsmen call "acute environmental reaction" (shell shock), the Marines at Khe Sanh are taking their ordeal with considerable composure. Only their unwelcome bunkermates—the rats—become frantic under fire. When the "incoming" starts, the rats race for the bunkers and wildly run up to the ceilings made of runway matting and logs. One sergeant has killed 34 rats, establishing a base record.

Khe Sanh grows steadily shabbier. More and more "hardbacks" (metal roofed shacks) are tumbled by the incoming: day-by-day the protective sandbags and runway matting rise higher on bunkers. Even so, the bunkers cannot withstand direct hits. A rocket or mortar round will collapse a bunker and likely kill its occupants. The Sea-bees are finishing strong underground bunkers for the control-tower crew of Khe Sanh's airstrip and the evacuation hospital, rushing to complete the work before the threatened battle erupts. Meanwhile, the doctors must make do in cramped quarters: the operating room is an empty metal box used to ship military goods and measuring 6 ft. by 6 ft.

The top Marine at Khe Sanh is Colonel David E. Lownds, 47, the mustachioed commander of the 26th Marine Regiment, who oversees the defense of the base from an underground bunker left over by its original French occupants. Sitting in a faded lawn chair, he seldom rests, night or day. He keeps constant watch over the nerve center, a labyrinth of whitewashed rooms lit by bare bulbs and bustling with staff officers and enlisted aides. Is he worried about the huge enemy concentration surrounding him? "Hell, no," says Lownds. "I've got Marines. My confidence isn't shaken a bit." He fully recognizes his stand-and-fight mission: "My job is to stay here. My job is to hold. I don't plan on reinforcements."

Several large U.S. combat units are ready at nearby bases for just such a necessity, but the fact is that there is neither space nor cover for them at Khe Sanh. Its buildup completed, Khe Sanh is waiting to fight. Last week, to cover their attack on nearby Lang Vei, North Vietnamese hit Khe Sanh with a massive barrage of up to 1,500 rounds of 60-mm. and 82-mm. mortars and 122-mm. rockets—50% more than Con Thien ever received in a single day at the peak of its shelling last year. Fortunately, the Reds' aim was bad: they scored no direct hits and caused no serious wounds or deaths

Not all the metal was incoming. Even under that pounding, Khe Sanh's artillerymen fired back 3,000 rounds. Fighter-bombers rake the surrounding hills on a seemingly nonstop basis, while B-52 strikes lay a carpet of bombs on suspected enemy positions four to six times a day. This outpouring of U.S airpower may have delayed the Communist attack on Khe Sanh, though some officers wonder about the effectiveness of bombing against dug-in artillery and troops and trucks moving under triple-canopy jungle.

Nonetheless, airpower is what keeps the entire effort at Khe Sanh afloat. Because there is no really passable road in the area and the North Vietnamese control the ground, the mammoth supply needs must be flown in by helicopters and C-123 and C-130 transport planes. Because of the danger of incoming fire, supply planes now unload in as little as three minutes. Cargoes are shoved down their rear loading ramps while the transports taxi slowly toward takeoff. Airdrop systems are planned in case heavy fighting or poor weather prevents any landings at all.

Most Marines at Khe Sanh feel more than ready for the battle they know they are there for, but they are becoming impatient. The waiting is wearying and frustrating, as day by day they undergo incoming, see friends wounded and killed (total casualties equal 10% of the base's men), and remain unable to fight back. "I wish they'd come and get it over with," said Pfc. Larry Jenkins, 18. Despite their perilous position, Jenkins and his comrades at Khe Sanh are spoiling for a fight.

## JOHN S. CARROLL: CORRESPONDENT CRITICIZES HIS PUNISHMENT FOR REPORTING AMERICAN ABANDONMENT OF KHESANH

*Baltimore Sun reporter John S. Carroll embarrassed the U.S. mission in Vietnam by breaking the news story that the U.S. base at Khesanh would be abandoned. On 27 June 1968, Brigadier General Winant Sidle, chief U.S. information officer in Saigon, announced that he was disaccrediting Carroll—forcing him to leave Vietnam—for an indefinite period because he had violated U.S. commander Creighton Abrams's news embargo. After a firestorm of protest by editorialists back home, Carroll's suspension was reduced to sixty days. In the following report for* Atlantic Monthly, *Carroll made his case that his punishment was politically motivated.*

### *Atlantic Monthly*, October 1968

Some months and many disasters ago, when both Vietnam and the United States were more peaceful than they are now, the first American troops arrived on the green plateau that was to become the Khesanh Marine combat base. In those days there was little doing in the northwest corner of South Vietnam, so these Special Forces troops spent their spare hours fishing the cascading mountain streams, or hunting tigers and boars.

All this changed, of course. First, the Special Forces were displaced by the Marines. Then, last year, there was a series of vicious battles on the jungle-clad slopes near the base. Finally came this year's big victory—or defeat, depending on whom you ask—at the base itself.

As a correspondent for the Baltimore *Sun*, I visited Khesanh several times between the first of this year and June 24. On that day I wrote that the base was being abandoned, and subsequently I had my military press accreditation suspended for breaking the embargo on the story. One could say I asked for it; in fact, that is exactly what the military command did say. I will save a defense for another occasion. What is important is the nature of the battle of Khesanh—how we got into it and how, once we were there, we found ourselves entangled in a double web of military and public relations considerations.

Military-press relations were different in World War II, when the press was very much part of the team. The reporting of that war focused on how the combat was going and what the individual soldier was enduring.

In the Vietnam War the press has addressed itself to issues like the feasibility of our aims. Vietnam has no Ernie Pyle, and none seems likely to emerge. The military has come to realize that while fighting well against the Viet Cong is important, looking good to the press, and through the press, to the world, is equally critical.

By the time the shells were pouring down on Khesanh, the military had learned its lesson. This time the psychological war, waged through the press, would not be neglected. Khesanh would be a victory—on the battlefield as well as on the front pages and television screens of the world.

Coming as it did in concert with the climactic Tet offensive against South Vietnam's previously unmolested—and largely unguarded—cities, the battle of Khesanh marked the end of the American military's delight at finding the enemy willing to stand and fight in the remotest corners of the country. While the cities were ravaged, the resources tied up in the Khesanh venture were considerable: a six-thousand-man garrison, supported by thousands more—plus aerial bombardment heavier than the United States' total bombing effort in Europe during 1942 and 1943. And throughout the 77 days of repeated ground probes and heavy shelling at the base, there was always the fear that the North Vietnamese in the hills, estimated variously from ten thousand to forty thousand, would mass and swarm over Khesanh, inflicting a military blow and perhaps a crippling psychological defeat on the United States.

My first visit to Khesanh was on January 23, the fourth day of what came to be called the "siege." I was as green a war correspondent as had ever wandered into Vietnam, and my imagination was working double time as the four-engine C-130 transport whined along the runway at Danang and lumbered into the gray monsoon clouds. There were several other correspondents along, all of whom had been under fire before, and I resolved to do as they did. If they ducked, I would duck. If they ran for a bunker, I would run for a bunker. If they flattened themselves in a ditch, I would flatten myself in a ditch.

As it turned out, there was no cause for panic. January 23 was a relatively quiet day at Khesanh. We came tumbling out of the plane onto the metal tarmac with flak vests zipped up tight and helmets low over our eyes, but it was immediately apparent that the shelling was in a lull.

### SORE

The Khesanh of January 1968 was no longer a place for fishing or tiger hunting. The green plateau had become a red-brown sore on the face of the earth, and everything—the sandbagged bunkers, the jeeps, the stubble-bearded

Marines—was tinted the reddish color of the dirt. Around us were the lush, sinister hills. Above were the oppressive layers of dark clouds that gradually lifted late each morning and then, in the evening, settled down inexorably around the plateau like a giant candlesnuffer.

We walked along the dirt road that was Khesanh's main street, skirting the craters. As we approached the command post, everything that was not sheltered by sandbags seemed to be slanting back toward the tarmac. The forest of antennas, the makeshift utility poles, and the battered wooden "hootches" (shacks) all leaned in the same direction. This, we were to learn, was because an enemy round had detonated the main ammunition dump a few days before.

In the dim yellow light inside the sandbagged command-post bunker, a plainspoken man told us about the situation at Khesanh. In contrast to the Marines outside, this man managed to keep unstained by the dirt and the billowing clouds of dust, and his neatness all came to focus in his marvelous mustache, impeccably waxed to two sharp points. He was Colonel David Lownds, the Khesanh commander. "Our reconnaissance team and patrols have made contact in every direction," Lownds said. "I have no doubt that we will be attacked." A twenty-three-year-old corporal took a break from sandbagging to tell me: "The hills are full of gooks. They'll probably start a barrage of artillery and then run right through the base."

It was in January that public concern about Khesanh began to build. The military command knew it had problems. Some high-ranking officers had opposed holding Khesanh at all. Militarily, the base was simply not worth it, they believed. But there were problems in pulling out. One was the fact that many of the guns would have to be destroyed if the Marines fought their way out on the ground. The guns had been flown in, and the prime movers—the machines that tow the guns and carry the ammunition and crews—had been left behind.

Another problem, the decisive one, was that a withdrawal under pressure would have all the earmarks of a defeat. By the last ten days of January the world was watching Khesanh, and the first grim parallels with Dienbienphu had been drawn. So to withdraw at this time would be to take a terrific drubbing before a huge audience.

## "WESTERN ANCHOR"

What was needed, then, was a good, solid, militarily sound explanation of why we were holding Khesanh. The American public could be counted upon to take a dim view of it all if the military were to announce frankly: "Your sons are at Khesanh to win a psychological victory, or at least to prevent a psychological defeat."

The military explanation that finally emerged was twofold. It goes as follows: Khesanh is critical to American military interests in Vietnam because it sits "astride" major infiltration routes from North Vietnam and Laos. Moreover, it is the "western anchor" of the defensive line of bases along the demilitarized zone.

In reality, Khesanh sat astride nothing but Khesanh. To the North Vietnamese Army, which can do without valleys or roads in making its way into the south, Khesanh was merely a speck of flotsam—an irritating speck, to be sure—in a sea of infiltration routes.

The "western anchor" concept was equally fallacious, based as it was on a simplistic Maginot scheme for keeping the North Vietnamese out of South Vietnam.[2] One might think that if our western anchor were lost, the enemy would be able to turn our flank. Of course the flank was being turned every day, Khesanh or no, by means of the Ho Chi Minh Trail in the mountains of nearby Laos.

It has been put forth in defense of the decision to hold Khesanh that, as it turned out, the cost was not inordinately high, as battles go: fewer than a hundred Marines killed on the base, with roughly another hundred deaths in the surrounding hills, and 1600 Marines wounded, in addition to South Vietnamese and Special Forces casualties. The cost of a withdrawal under fire might have been as great. But to figure the real cost of Khesanh, one must take into account the forces held in reserve, ready to move into the base. Add to this the cost of mounting the most intensive aerial bombardment in the history of warfare (commanders in some parts of the country practically wrote off their chances of getting any air support during the Khesanh bombing). The logistic effort, too, was costly in terms of man-hours, casualties, and aircraft lost.

## THIN SPREAD

While all these resources were being poured into a remote outpost in the farthest corner of South Vietnam, the enemy turned up at the gate of the Presidential Palace, in the front yard of the United States Embassy, and in Vietnam's old imperial throne room in Hué.

One had only to go to Hué during the Tet offensive to see how thinly spread our resources were at that time. I flew into this most graceful of Vietnamese cities (it still is, despite devastation) aboard a Marine Medevac helicopter on February 6, landing in the front yard of a battered Hué University. The Marines on the south bank of the Perfume River had problems, far worse problems than anyone realized at the time. On February 6 the Marines had an enclave of perhaps a half-dozen city blocks along the riverfront, and progress was agonizingly slow. At the heart of the enclave was the bullet-scarred building that served as the American military advisers' compound. Hué was so noisy that night that hardly anyone who slept at the compound noticed when the North Vietnamese, only a few blocks away, detonated a huge charge that dropped the two center spans of the highway bridge into the murky green river.

The battle for Hué lasted weeks, longer than anyone expected. Every day in Saigon the correspondents would file into the air-conditioned auditorium for the afternoon briefing—the "five o'clock follies," as it is known—expecting to hear of the North Vietnamese collapse in Hué.

It was a long wait. Never during the fight did the Marines have the forces they felt they needed to move effectively. And never was the combined American–South Vietnamese force that fought at Hué adequate to prevent the North Vietnamese from feeding troops and supplies into the city. Just short of a month after taking Hué, the North Vietnamese withdrew, having impressed all observers with their strength and tenacity, and leaving behind a shattered city with most of its progovernment leadership captured or resting in mass graves.

The withdrawal from Hué signaled the end of the Tet offensive, but there was still Khesanh. By this time it was evident that the bombing was taking a high toll. This massive bombardment is where we won our victory, according to those who consider Khesanh a victory. Our success was in terms of enemy forces tied down and enemy soldiers killed. General Westmoreland stated later: "With only one percent of my forces, I tied down two enemy divisions and seriously defeated them. It was a major victory."

Certainly we were successful in keeping the North Vietnamese from massing and overrunning the base, as, it appears, was their intention. But tied down? This claim ignores the obvious fact that only one party to the Khesanh battle retained his options: General Vo Nguyen Giap, the North Vietnamese commander. His forces could leave any time they felt their losses were outweighing their gains. We, on the other hand, were committed for the duration.

In terms of enemy forces destroyed, no doubt terrible losses were inflicted on the North Vietnamese at Khesanh. By American standards, such losses would simply be unacceptable; the North Vietnamese are far more willing to sacrifice men, and there has been no strong sign that they are having trouble replacing the thousands who fall in battle.

Giap's withdrawal finally came late in March, when the monsoon clouds were growing thin and the Army's First Air Cavalry was about to mount Operation Pegasus to relieve the base. Reporters on the scene started picking up signs of the withdrawal a week or two before Pegasus started, as did one or two Pentagon reporters with sources outside the official briefing circle. The briefers, for their part, denied any knowledge of the enemy's withdrawal. For this reason some members of the Saigon press corps strongly suspected the image-conscious command of attempting to conceal the withdrawal so that it would appear that Operation Pegasus rather than any decision by Giap had cleared the Khesanh area of North Vietnamese forces.

### "YOU MUST NEARLY DIE"

To those expecting a big battle, Pegasus was an anticlimax. The Air Cavalry sliced through to Khesanh like a knife through butter. At the end of the operation, George Wilson, the *Washington Post's* military writer, and I wandered through the rolling country near the base, inspecting the battered North Vietnamese bunkers and the shallow trenches that snaked their way toward Khesanh's perimeter.

The force of the bombing defied comprehension: where the 2000-pounders had hit soft dirt the craters were big enough to contain a small house. The ground was littered with torn North Vietnamese and shattered supplies. On one hillside we found what we believed to be the remains of the last Marine patrol to go any distance outside the perimeter wire. Marines are fond of writing slogans on their helmets, and on one scorched and battered helmet was an ironic touch of Marine bravado: "To really live you must nearly die."

That afternoon we hopped a lift to Danang to interview Lieutenant General Robert E. Cushman, Jr., the commander of the Marines in Vietnam. We asked him whether Khesanh was going to be abandoned in the near future, and he replied that it would be kept for the time being. But he added that the base might be closed later—if enemy activity dropped off in the area.

### "MOBILE POSTURE"

Two months later the withdrawal started, but not for the reason General Cushman proposed. An official statement cited an increase in the enemy's forces in I Corps, which consists of the five northernmost provinces of South Vietnam, from six divisions to eight since January. "This," the statement noted, "gives him the capability of mounting several sizable attacks concurrently." Such attacks, of course, were precisely what had happened at the end of January in the Tet offensive. At any rate, the statement went on to say that the United States forces were adopting a "mobile posture," which would mean continued operations around Khesanh without a need for a large fixed base.

Before this statement came out, I made my visit into Khesanh aboard a slow, throbbing, deafeningly noisy Marine helicopter. (The Marines seem to revel in old equipment; "We do with men what the Army claims it does with all its gadgets," a Marine sergeant boasted at the Danang press center bar.) The word had been out in Saigon, and again in Danang, Phubai, and Dongha, that Khesanh was being abandoned, but I had no idea how far along the withdrawal had gotten until we approached the base itself.

Portions of the base that had been crowded with sandbagged bunkers and antennae were now broad fields of raw, red earth. Marines were tearing down bunkers, and bulldozers were filling the remaining holes with rubble and dirt. Big tandem-rotor helicopters were shuttling in and out, carrying slings full of cargo east to Landing Zone Stud and returning empty. The unloading tarmac of the metal runway was being peeled up and stacked in strips, ready to be hauled out.

In talking to the Marines on the ground, I learned that the North Vietnamese Army had seen everything I had. Patrols had encountered enemy troops on the hills overlooking the base, and there had been sniper fire within only a few hundred yards of the perimeter. It was clear that the news of the withdrawal was being held up for political, not military, reasons. The North Vietnamese Army knew about the withdrawal; the American public did not.

## BREAKING THE EMBARGO

Writing the story would mean trouble from the command, for stories about troop movements and future plans are embargoed until released by the Saigon headquarters. For the command, releasing the story at this time would have meant headache after headache. Correspondents would flock to the base to file eyewitness accounts of the last days of Khesanh. Instead of disposing of the issue in a single day after the completion of the move, the command would have to answer questions every day for nearly two weeks. Television watchers and newspaper readers would want answers. What would happen when our forces no longer sat *astride* those infiltration routes? What would become of the defensive line of bases along the demilitarized zone if the western anchor was hauled in? Above all, why was Khesanh worth all that effort a few months ago and not now?

As things worked out, the command ultimately faced the questioners with its lame answers, and I lost my press card. At first the suspension was indefinite, then it was set at six months. At that point the whole issue was hashed over publicly, and after some protests, the command agreed to reduce the suspension to sixty days, leaving neither of us entirely satisfied. My own hassle was one of the less significant unresolved questions about the military's role in political and propaganda aspects of the war which remain as the Khesanh episode passes into history, and the trenches and crumbled bunkers become overgrown with the lush foliage of Southeast Asia.—*John S. Carroll*

*Credit*: Reprinted with permission from John S. Carroll.

## NOTES

1. James I. Marino, "Vietnam: Strategic Crossroads at Khesanh," *Vietnam*, December 1999, http://historynet.com/vn/blkhc_sanh/index2.html.

2. Maginot was a line of fortifications in France that were effective against entrenched forces during World War I but were made obsolete by the mobile armies of World War II.

## FURTHER READINGS

Hammel, Eric, ed. *Khe Sanh: Siege in the Clouds: An Oral History*. New York: Crown Publishers, 1986.

Nalty, Bernard C. *Air Power and the Fight for Khe Sanh*. Washington, D.C.: Office of Air Force History, USAF, 1973.

Pisor, Robert. *End of the Line: The Siege of Khe Sanh*. New York: Ballantine Books, 1982.

Prados, John, and Ray W. Stubbe. *Valley of Decision: The Siege of Khe Sanh*. Boston: Houghton Mifflin, 1991.

Spencer, Ernest. *Welcome to Vietnam, Macho Man: Reflections of a Khe Sanh Vet*. New York: Bantam Books, 1989.

# 16

# BATTLE OF DONG AP BIA ("HAMBURGER HILL"), 10–18 MAY 1969

Following the inauguration of Richard M. Nixon as the thirty-seventh U.S. president on 20 January 1969, the American public waited to hear about the new president's plan to withdraw U.S. forces from the Vietnam conflict—a plan he did not have. He needed a way to increase pressure on the North Vietnamese to negotiate while reducing U.S. casualties. To buy time, Secretary of Defense Melvin R. Laird ordered the U.S. commander in South Vietnam, General Creighton W. Abrams, to shift a greater combat burden to the South Vietnamese and to avoid unnecessary major engagements with U.S. forces. For his part, Abrams did not believe that his allies were up to the task. His Communist foes took advantage of the Americans' dilemma by shifting tactics to focus attacks on U.S. units.

In the spring of 1969, the United States had approximately 540,000 combat troops in South Vietnam, supplemented by a larger South Vietnamese force (ARVN). They were opposed by only 80,000 North Vietnamese regular troops (NVA) and half that number of Vietcong fighters, yet the allies were, in fact, losing the war. Abrams clung to the attrition strategy and search-and-destroy tactics he had inherited from his predecessor, General William C. Westmoreland, yet enemy strength did not wane. On the contrary, NVA reinforcements flowed unabated along the Ho Chi Minh Trail through neighboring Laos and Cambodia, and assaults on allied positions more than doubled the previous year's rate. Before the end of Nixon's first year in office, nearly 10,000 more Americans would be killed, for a total of 40,000 U.S. casualties to date.

On 17 April 1969, the chairman of the Joint Chiefs of Staff, General Earle G. Wheeler, stunned Abrams with notification that the withdrawal of U.S. combat units would begin in July. Abrams's commanders in the field were emphatic that the ARVN was not ready to take control in their sectors. Time was running short for the Military Assistance Command, Vietnam (MACV). Abrams hoped to regain initiative and stem the enemy influx by pressing a massive search-and-destroy mission in the northern mountains of South Vietnam near the Laotian border. U.S. intelligence detected fortified enemy positions in the Ashau Valley west of the northern city of Hué. Forward units of the U.S. 101st Airborne Division reported that a North Vietnamese regiment occupied Dong Ap Bia (Hill 937), a small mountain about 2 kilometers from the Laotian border. Under the code name Operation Apache Snow, the 101st attacked on 10 May, resulting in one of the fiercest and most controversial battles of the entire war.

The Americans pounded the mountain with 1,750 tons of bombs, rockets, artillery, and napalm that denuded the jungle, but the enemy was well dug in. Rains made footing treacherous for the attackers. Enemy machine guns fired down on the exposed attackers and pushed back one futile infantry assault after another. After twelve assaults, the enemy position was overtaken on 18 May. Official tallies of the dead were 56 Americans, 5 South Vietnamese, and 630 of the enemy. When reporters arrived on the scene, they saw a cardboard C-ration box nailed to a charred tree trunk. Its handwritten scrawl read, "Hamburger Hill. Was it worth it?"

On 20 May, U.S. senator Edward M. Kennedy of Massachusetts denounced the Dong Ap Bia mission as "senseless and irresponsible" because it risked U.S. lives for no reason other than military pride. Newspapers across the country editorialized about the battle, some supporting Kennedy's view, others criticizing the senator for not supporting the troops. The debate kept the battle in the news for several weeks. On 11 June, a survivor who had since left the military told Columbia Broadcasting System reporter David Culhane that the battle had been a "turkey shoot, and we were the turkeys." It became a public relations nightmare for the government, which launched a series of media counterattacks to try to stem the controversy. On 8 June, the headline story of Hamburger Hill gave way to coverage of president Nixon's meeting with South Vietnamese president Nguyen Van Thieu on the Pacific island of Midway, where they together announced a withdrawal of 25,000 U.S. combat troops from Vietnam.

---

## DAVID CULHANE: HAMBURGER HILL INTERVIEW

---

*Following is David Culhane's "turkey shoot" interview of a candid Hamburger Hill veteran for the* CBS Evening News with Walter Cronkite. *The news segment was not titled.*

### CBS Evening News with Walter Cronkite, 11 June 1969

CRONKITE: The bloody battle of Hamburger Hill in Vietnam is now over, but the controversy continues. Today a squad leader wounded in those assaults, Sergeant Ken Tepper, talked about the fight. Tepper, who's now out of the Army, was questioned at his Grand Rapids [Michigan] home by CBS News Correspondent David Culhane.

CULHANE: How did you feel about this whole attack, this hill assault?

TEPPER: I wasn't for it, myself, and many of the guys weren't, because it seemed so useless, because they just, they just kept sending us up there, and it wasn't, we weren't getting anywhere. They were just, you know, slaughtering us, sort of, like a turkey shoot, and we were the turkeys, because there wasn't anything to hide behind. They were picking us off. No matter where you were, if you were near the bottom or you were near the top, they were just, everything was coming right straight across from the side, and really, really doing a job on us.

CULHANE: What do you do, what could you do in a circumstance like that, just flatten out on the ground?

TEPPER: Right. Crawl a lot, and we did a lot of that. My best friend was right behind me with his machine gun; he got killed right there, got a bullet through his head, and it was pretty awful. One of my friends asked me what it felt like to, when while you were there, to have somebody, one of your best buddies, get killed. And I told him you really don't think about it that much, because you're too busy and you're trying to do everything you can to save yourself and to do what you're supposed to be doing. And then you don't think about it till after it's all over and you're back down off the hill, and you've got your wounded evac-ed and everything is hunky-dory, and you get on the perimeter, and you've got all night to sit there and think about it. And I cried that night, and many guys did. One of the guys that had his, his best friend [killed] was just, just really bad off up on the hill; he was holding him in his arms, right in the middle of it all, just sitting there holding him in his arms, crying.

CULHANE: Did other people who were with you, other soldiers, have the same misgivings that you did about the attack?

TEPPER: Yes, they did.

CULHANE: How do you yourself feel about the war? Do you think the United States should be there in Vietnam or not?

TEPPER: Yes, I do. I'm, I'm not a protester of the war. It was just that certain little spot in the war that I disagreed with. But as a whole, I think the war is a thing that is necessary.

*Credit*: Reprinted with permission of the CBS News Archives.

---

## NEIL SHEEHAN: LETTERS FROM HAMBURGER HILL VETERANS TO SENATOR TED KENNEDY

*Neil Sheehan had a distinguished journalistic career covering the Vietnam War. In 1963, as United Press International correspondent, Sheehan was a member of the fledgling Saigon press corps that was destined for honor. Sheehan later reported in Vietnam for the* New York Times. *In June 1971, from the* Times' *Washington bureau, he broke the Pentagon Papers story, which exposed Vietnam War miscalculations of President Lyndon Johnson's administration. In 1989, Sheehan won a Pulitzer Prize for his biography,* A Bright Shining Lie: John Paul Vann and America in Vietnam. *(For more information about Neil Sheehan and John Paul Vann, see Chapter 4.)*

*Neil Sheehan collected letters sent by Hamburger Hill vets to Senator Edward Kennedy for the following* Harper's Magazine *article. The letters poignantly portray the soldiers' frustrating uncertainties about the war that colored the entire U.S. mission during the period of U.S. withdrawals. What was the point of risking death in an unwinnable war?*

### *Harper's Magazine,* November 1969

Mr. Sheehan spent three years in Vietnam reporting, first for UPI and then for *The New York Times*. He is now *The Times* Washington Bureau's investigative reporter.

On our way home from Vietnam in the fall of 1966, my wife and I stopped off in London and visited the crypt in Saint Paul's Cathedral. There, engraved on marble tablets commemorating the dead of the Empire's wars, were the names of those who had perished in the two conflicts with Afghanistan in the nineteenth century. Both had been ill-starred wars, in which imperial Britain overreached her limits and sought to subjugate a spirited and hardy people who would not yield. Finally, after much dying, the British armies marched back into India and the men who governed then in London acknowledged that the wars had been unwise. I wondered, reading the names and the places where they had fallen—Kandahar, Kabul, Jalalabad, strange-sounding places like the battlegrounds of Van Tuong, Plei Me, and Ia Drang still so vivid in my memory—whether any of the dead had questioned the meaning of their end. I wondered if they had understood they were to die in vain and if they had rebelled—if only in their minds and in their fear—against such a death. Perhaps there is no difference, but it ought to be one thing to perish on the beaches of Normandy or Iwo Jima in a great cause and another to fall in a rejected and unsung war.

At Van Tuong and Plei Me and Ia Drang there had been no doubts. There was fear and anguish for the loss of a buddy, and the riflemen complained about the heat and the dust, yet they seemed to accept their lot as a bitter and necessary duty for their country. They believed the generals and the diplomats and the President who told them that if they did not win here they would have to fight the yellow-skinned Communists, the eternal Gooks, at Waikiki or San Francisco. So it was better to shoot and bomb in another man's country. As the war went on and the dissent grew at home, there still seemed to be no doubts among the infantrymen.

At Khe Sanh in April and May of 1967, the Marines cheered as they clambered to the tops of three high hills north of the camp. The cheers were that much louder for their 138 comrades who had been killed on the slopes. At Hill 875 near Dak To that November, the officers shouted, "Airborne," and the paratroopers yelled back, "All the way," and rushed up again and again into the grenades and the bullets until the vocal cords of 158 were permanently silenced and the North Vietnamese were driven from the summit.

But there comes a time in some wars when the killing, or just the manner of dying, appears so senseless that even the obedient soldier who is "not to reason why" begins to question the meaning of his sacrifice. Perhaps that time has come in Vietnam. This August 24, [1969,] in the first such instance reported during the Vietnam war, a company of the 196th Light Infantry Brigade refused an order to attack [see Chapter 21]. The company had lost more than half of its 109 men killed or wounded during the previous five days assaulting a complex of enemy-held bunkers and trenches in the Nui Lon Valley near the Central Vietnam coast. The 46 men left unscathed said they would not go down into the valley again. They eventually went, shamed into going by the gibes of a veteran sergeant sent down by the battalion commander to lead them. Afterwards, there were many explanations for their refusal, all of which argued it had nothing to do with the futility of the war. The men were tired, it was said, they had had little sleep and little food and no mail. Most of their squad and platoon leaders were casualties. Perhaps these explanations were true and perhaps they were not. What could not be explained away was that men had suffered equally before and had not balked when ordered to endure more.

If the time of doubt, of pause, has come for the ordinary American soldier in Vietnam, its advent may one day be traced back to an earlier battle last May in the desolate A Shau Valley for a ridge called Ap Bia by the Vietnamese and Hill 937 on the U.S. Army maps. The soldiers, or some imaginative reporter, named it Hamburger Hill for the 55 paratroopers who did not survive the eleven consecutive assaults to seize the ridge from the North Vietnamese.

On May 20, the day the summit was taken, Senator Edward M. Kennedy stood in the Senate and protested the orders that had ordained these deaths as "senseless and irresponsible." Why were American youths still being killed for such godforsaken ridgelines, he asked, when the diplomats (having settled on their seating arrangements) were supposedly negotiating a peace in Paris? A week after the paratroopers gained its summit, Ap Bia was abandoned, just as Hill 875, the three hills north of Khe Sanh, and countless others had been before. The North Vietnamese have since reoccupied it.

"The hill itself had no tactical significance," said Maj. Gen. Melvin Zais, the commander of the 101st Airborne Division that fought the battle, but Ap Bia was "a gallant victory" just the same because the enemy losses had been much greater. Fifty-five dead paratroopers, in short, had been well traded for 629 North Vietnamese corpses. Attrition has been the Bible of the generals in this war. Seek out the enemy wherever he is and fight him wherever he decides to stand.

Kill enough, they have read out in each sermon, and some day he will quit. "We found the enemy on Hill 937 and that is where we fought him," General Zais said. Whenever the American dead have embarrassingly filled too many aluminum coffins, enemy bodies at a dozen to one have been conjured up in justification until even the computers may have wondered at the macabre statistics.

Ap Bia, however, was different from previous meat-grinder battles. How different is apparent in the letters Senator Kennedy received after his denunciation of Hamburger Hill, from the obedient soldiers who were there. For among them now is a type of infantryman who was virtually nonexistent in Vietnam in earlier years—a college-educated soldier who reflects the antiwar movement so prevalent on the campuses at home. He goes into combat with the disenchantment and developed sensitivity of his generation. He thinks about what is happening to him and what his country is doing to that tattered Asian land about the size of the state of Washington. He has seen the fallibility of the generals projected starkly on the screen of defeat. His letters are a passionate and eloquent protest against both the battle and the war itself. The appearance of this soldier in the combat ranks is, ironically, the apparent fruit of President Johnson's abolition of graduate school deferments in February of 1968. In the fiscal year ending this June, approximately 45,000 college graduates, more than double the 20,000 of two years ago, were drafted into the Army or enlisted because they faced a choice of conscription or jail.

The letters also reveal something else that was different and important about Ap Bia. Now, for the first time, some, at least, of those simple soldiers who had once cheered and shouted, "All the way," no longer believe. Through their letters, innocent of grammar but wise in the ways of war, flows a bitterness, uncomplicated, apolitical, and abiding.

Here are just a few of the letters. The names and other identifying details have been withheld to protect the men. The first is from a 1968 graduate of an Eastern university who had hoped to enter Harvard Law School last fall. . . .

Dear Sir:

At the present time I am with about a platoon of men about 10 miles upstream from Hué guarding a small Navy depot. This is very easy duty and to pass the time we sleep, drink, sleep, play cards, clean our weapons, watch movies, swim in the river, talk to the little children who speak incredibly good English. . . . In addition, we think about last week at "Hamburger Hill."

I don't suppose any war has ever been pleasant, nor has anyone suggested it to be. So while watching my partner under the "buddy system" get shot six times in both legs going up the hill, or seeing one guy in my foxhole get shot in the mouth, when we finally reached the top I was simply more depressed than angered. For if we are indeed going to fight a war, all the horrors are certainly going to be there too. No, the test must be whether the war, with all of its attendant insanity, is worth the price. That this war has not ever been, is not now, and can never be, worth the colossal price we have paid, in a thousand different ways (first the 35,000 dead, the hundred of thousands wounded, the wasted years of our youth, the $ $ $ down the drain, the neglect the war has forced on our cities, the atmosphere of violence it has encouraged in our streets) is glaringly obvious. It is simply a fact that this war was a mistake.

Perhaps the greatest lesson to be learned from all of this is that our military machine is simply not equipped to fight this sort of political war. We have all the best techniques and equipment, but our generals are apparently baffled when the bombing of the North stops or when we can't pursue the NVA [North Vietnamese Army] into Cambodia or Laos. This mentality was particularly apparent at "Hamburger Hill"—the enemy was on the hill, ergo we had to take it and we talk about the VC "human wave" attacks! There was some CS [tear] gas used and never will I forget the grisly, surreal sight of hundreds of bemasked, helmeted GIs with fiberglass and steel M-16s, scrabbling up a jungle ridge denuded of a trace of green. The artillery and air strikes had transformed the lush vegetation into plowed earth and blackened stumps. A more unearthly sight I never shall see. Indeed, what sort of victory do we seek?

There seems to be a vigorous national belief among us Americans that any great event must have equally great origins and causes. We have seen it in the tragic assassinations of this decade wherein many found it almost psychologically unacceptable that such momentous events were triggered by such insignificant people. Hence there must have been "conspiracies." In the same way most Americans must feel that a war so tragic and costly as the one in Vietnam must have some great purpose. That this purpose has remained elusive is apparent in our national debate, wherein we are often reminded that if South Vietnam and Laos fall so eventually will and must Wyoming and Ohio.

The answer to all this lies not in a gradual fade out of Vietnam fraught with face-saving devices, but in an immediate cessation of all offensive activities such as "Hamburger Hill." It is fine to secure the cities and hamlets. It is maniacal to seek out every enemy in the country. Five years of fighting have proven its virtual impossibility, and to claim "Hamburger Hill" as a victory because we killed five times as many as we lost seems absurd. Once again I must advocate the enclave method until we can extricate ourselves from this mess. For we all know that the day this war ends not one thing significant, not a goddamn thing, is going to be different from this May morning or any May morning a year ago except that many of us alive now will be dead then.

Sincerely,

[      ]

Dear Senator Kennedy,

I am a combat medic serving with an infantry company of the [   ] Battalion, 501st Infantry, 101st Airborne Division. My battalion is presently located on top of Hamburger Hill. It is raining now and we're thankful because the odor of decaying bodies is not as strong as it is when the sun is shining. Most of those bodies are North Vietnamese but my battalion has found at least two GI bodies left behind on the fingers leading to this hilltop.

Near the helicopter landing zone there is a cardboard sign with the scrawled words, "Hamburger Hill. Was it worth it?" That is a question everyone on this hill is asking. Apparently the brass at division headquarters plan to give an affirmative answer. They may change their minds but at present, they plan to establish a permanent firebase on Hamburger to secure the area and an airstrip in the A Shau Valley below. Thus they will save their faces. They can claim those 39 men died in order to open up this whole area of the A Shau.

I want to thank you for standing up for us in Vietnam. Men like you are on our side. Perhaps if more of your colleagues join with you, I will make it home to my wife.

Sincerely yours,

[      ]

Hello Senate—

I just want to say a few things about Hamburger Hill (937 Hill) 1st of all I realize war is hell and leaders will get blamed for things they do or fail to do. I am a career soldier 19 years active. Leaders like Gen. Zais Commander of the 101 Div. are glory happy. They feel that to get my next star, next promotion in BN [battalion] commanders, regiment commanders, infantry leaders, we must get our unit in a firefight we must make it big no matter what the cost. . . . So when this war is over and there is no chance to show yourself, only the officers with so-called Good Combat Records will be promoted. Now this is the way I saw it and I heard other officers as high as regiment commanders say and think the same. Phase one air strikes dumped more than two million pounds of bombs [and] more than 100 tons of napalm on the hill; about 7,000 artillery shells were fired into the Red stronghold. More of the same could have been done, but this the point—still no glory for the General! Save some for me. Phase 3. Human assault World War II tactics—not that those tactics are not good tactics, but all three phases do not have to be used. A captured NVA [North Vietnamese Army soldier] told interrogators that the first bombs kill 80–100 members of his company. Experts, both air and artillery, said that roughly 80% of the NVA on the hill was casualties. More of the same could have be done—meaning bombardment or seal all exits and wait. Captured NVA said there wasn't long before the bad need of medical aid would have forced them to walk out hands up. But, there still would not have been glory for the general and staff. At that point U.S. KIA [killed in action] or WIA [wounded in action] was [nothing] to talk about.

But who cares about that when I have my next star in sight So the outcome, as you put it, senseless and I am going to use a different word than irresponsible (Glory Hunting) because 50 young American and 50 mothers, girl friends, or wives, the soldiers to loose their lives and the other to loose their love ones. Not to say about the 300 or more to loose legs, arms, hearing, eyes [, you] name it. Because the mighty Screaming Eagles [nickname of the 101st] had to scream up Hill 937, that will give my sons [and] others' sons some thing to brag about. "My father charged up Hamburger Hill." But the real story will never be told.

Now last but not least on Hill 937 there [were] hundreds of defeated enemies trying to decide whether to give up or not. And look up and see thousands of fighting men coming to kill what's left. Surely they had to fight, causing death to us as well as them. Now the main point is this: the NVA that got away can tell the story. Something like this. Fight until the last man is dead because the American will kill you anyway. My motto is "fight and kill" as long as there is an enemy but when an enemy becomes defeated he then needs help.

From a piece of Hamburger
on Hamburger Hill[1]

Fellow American,

The papers and radio all seemed to give false facts on our wounded and killed on hill 937. Our Battalion had 33 KIA and well over the 300 mark for WIA. We of [   ] Company tried nine times to take that hill loosing more than half our company, which should have been declared incapable for the field. Headquarters don't do no fighting; they were in the rear and didn't know of our true situation. I believe the hill should never been taken in this way. Our Company only had 1 day rest between operations, was not supplied [well] at all on the operation. Was out of water for three days, and really outnumbered. Also we cannot get a 3-day pass or 7-day leave in our Battalion. The EM [enlisted man] stays on the line five days prior to his DEROS [rotation home], while officers spend only a 6-month tour on line. The men do not get proper rest and spend too long on a tour on line. They should serve the last several months on some sort of rear job. I believe this Battalion should be investigated, and go along with you, and your statements.

Do you know who will get all the big medals? The lifers— not the man who was up front with the rifle doing the job. It's a damn shame that the men that should get it, wouldn't. Thank you much for your time. The men will give you all the information you want, if you so desire. Please let us know what is going to be done here about the situation. Men no longer feel they are fighting for there country but just for there own lives. If I had to do over again I'd refuse to go to Viet Nam.

I am short now and only have three months left. I am going

---

## If I had to do over again I'd refuse to go to Viet Nam.

---

to try and put up with what's happening here. But please do something for the other men and the men to come.

A fellow American,
[         ]

Dear Sen. Kennedy:

At the moment we are on "Hamburger Hill" about 2000 meters from the Laotian border, which has become, according to our information, so criminally infamous. As veterans of the assault on this remote mountain we would like to add our support to your timely criticism of the appalling slaughter which took place here. Sen. Kennedy, air strikes from B-52s would have saved a great many of the lives lost here! We ask you to continue your investigation of this and other military operations which are destroying American lives needlessly and reducing an already low morale to nil. There is a great deal of bitterness here, not only from incidents such as this hill but poor supplies, lack of support and general disillusionment with America and its people. We hope by writing this letter that we can add some timely support to your efforts to end the holocaust in Viet Nam. It is our considered opinion that America has nothing to gain and has lost enough already by her involvement in this War.

We freely and gladly sign our names to this letter but respectfully request you not reveal our identity as repercussions will reflect upon us. The men on this hill thank you deeply for your support and peace endeavors.

Sincerely,
[         ][2]

Dear Senator Kennedy,

I write to inform you of a situation in the 101st Airborne Division, regarding a certain "Hamburger Hill" which lies within the A Shau Valley. This hill lies in the 3rd Brigade Area of Operation and our Battalion of the 2nd Brigade was in to lend a helping hand.

The 187th was ordered to take a meaningless hunk of dirt in the middle of nowhere and of no logistic importance at the rumored cost of 58 killed, 290 plus wounded and 3 missing in action.

I say rumored, because this information seems to be quite confidential.

We are a member of the [   ] Battalion, 2nd Brigade, of the 501st Infantry (101st Abn. Div.). Since we recently acquired a new Battalion Commander, we were lent out to the 3rd Brigade until we were assigned our own area of operation.

We came up this hill to lend support after it was taken. After the other battalions were pulled out, we too had orders to leave. Our courageous Lt. Colonel refused to leave when asked by Gateway 3 (3rd Brigade Commander) because the 187th of the 3rd Brigade left some of their *dead unrecovered*, a trail of thousands of rounds of both M-60 machine gun and M-16 rifle ammunition, M-16 rifles, numerous grenades, gas masks, a 90-mm. recoilless gun with an estimated 30 rounds, over 100 helmets, flack jackets, 3 starlights scopes, many claymore mines, rucksacks, canteens, M-72 laws [rocket launchers], etc. (enough to practically supply an entire Battalion).

Sir, this is not exaggeration, the hill was not thoroughly searched—even for the dead. If it wasn't for our Battalion [    ] Bn., 501st Inf. (101st Abn.) and our commander, 3 dead GIs would not have been recovered, along with all the equipment which the NVA could have used against our own men.

I know our Colonel [        ] is under considerable pressure from higher. All his men are behind him as well as his company commanders. We definitely do not need any further association with the 3rd Brigade, a sorry outfit.

Thank you for your attention.

Cordially,<br>[Signed by 41 men]

P.S. if 400 NVA were killed upon this hill, 80% or more of their bodies must have evaporated.

Mr. Ted Kennedy,

Right now I am drunk. Maybe this won't mean anything to you. If not so what.

My name is [        ]. My people call me Sgt. [      ]. I have been for a long time a platoon Sgt. in [    ] Co. [    ] BN, 506th, 101st ABN. I am what "they" call an "instant NCO!" This means I am a U.S. (draftee) who involuntarily became an NCO at Ft. Benning to be sent to RVN [Republic of Vietnam] as an NCO. So the normal slot for an E-5, NCO, is team leader—but the only thing is that rank is so scarce in RVN that I have either been a platoon Sgt. or Plt. Ldr. [platoon leader] since I have been here.

Well you are probably asking why I am writing you. . . . I am drunk by choice (I leave V. Nam in eleven days) and disgusted because I have seen how the glory hungry so-called professional officers (major and above) think only of their record and not of the well being of their troops.

Maybe if the troops were all volunteer[s] they would function better (although an all-volunteer army is "nonsense"). But as it is, the draftees are continuously asked to give their lives or limbs in order that battalion and certain brigade commanders can make their stars or bird [eagle insignia of a full colonel].

I am not saying that your critique of "Hamburger Hill" is justified. Everybody that participated will think differently (at least because of pride). What I say is why have you waited so long to expose these rank-seeking, impersonal, self-satisfying battalion commanders to the truth—producing showdown or public exposure?

I may be a fool (which is more than likely) but I believe in myself to say that "something" with the 101st ABN is very, very wrong; why should draftees be slaughtered to prove or to support the promotion of some "professional officer"???

I am twenty-four years old. I have four years of college (without degree but drafted anyway). Maybe I am stupid like all the older NCOs say (I am an "instant"). But my opinion of Vietnam is that many, too many, decisions are made with the sole criterion, "Will this contribute to my chances to make Bird or my first Star?"

War is hell, and I have many days of war behind, "war is hell." But God, at least a man should feel that his death will not be shallow, not lacking in patriotism (which you would be surprised how many men base their actions on such—when you come to the "nitty gritty").

Like the white wash that is taking place right now. Col. [    ] is "mentally ill." The Col. of the 3rd, 187th is hurting also. He didn't even use proper military procedure—but still lost almost three-quarters of his people killed or wounded. (The talk among professionals is that this insures his first star—let alone the bird.) . . .

I was not with my platoon [    ] Plt., [    ] Co., [    ] Bn. 506th, 101st ABN, when they took the hill (Hamburger). But, all I can say is that quite a few people are suffering because of how fucked this war (of senior officers) has become.

Sgt. [        ]

## NOTES

1. Footnote from original article: "The return address on the letter was a convalescent hospital."

2. Footnote from original article: "The letter was signed by two paratroopers."

## FURTHER READINGS

Pelfrey, William. *Hamburger Hill*. New York: Avon Books, 1987.

Smith, Charles R. *U.S. Marines in Vietnam: High Mobility and Standdown, 1969*. Washington, D.C.: History and Museums Division, Headquarters, U.S. Marine Corps, 1988.

Zaffiri, Samuel. *Hamburger Hill, May 11–20, 1969*. Novato, Calif.: Presidio Press, 1988.

# 17

## GREEN BERETS CASE, 20 JUNE 1969

It is the nature of daily journalism to present news with imperfect understanding, for the full meaning and context of events rarely are attainable quickly, and fully understood events no longer are news. Combine these inherent process limitations with the news media's white-hot glare, and sensationalism results. The case of the Green Berets was one of many examples of sensationalized news during the Vietnam War—imperfectly understood, taken out of context, and emphasized out of proportion to its significance in human events. The Green Berets case occurred just at a moment during America's war in Vietnam when small events were likely to have big consequences.

The summer of 1969 saw a lull in the fighting. In June, U.S. president Richard M. Nixon announced the first of a series of U.S. troop withdrawals, followed in July by his plan to "Vietnamize" the war by giving the fighting back to the South Vietnamese. He started back-channel communications with Hanoi through his national security advisor, Henry A. Kissinger. The Communists appeared to take a wait-and-see attitude. U.S. field officers reported "all quiet" in their sectors. Having exhausted the Hamburger Hill and Vietnamization stories, the news media reported the lull with a sense of urgency. Everyone was waiting for something to happen. The Green Berets affair filled this vacuum.

In July, the commander of the Fifth Special Forces Group in South Vietnam, known as the "Green Berets" (see Chapter 7), Colonel Robert B. Rheault, and seven of his subordinates were implicated in the murder of a suspected enemy spy. Their prosecution was being pushed by none other than the commander of U.S. forces in Vietnam (MACV), General Creighton W. Abrams. Abrams confined the group at the U.S. military prison at Long Binh after discovering that Rheault had lied to him about the incident.

The impending trial was fraught with hazards for the U.S. government for several reasons. Rheault was a popular officer with a stellar record in the Special Forces. Its highly classified intelligence operations might be compromised in a public trial. In addition, there was evidence that a station chief of the Central Intelligence Agency had requested the assassination. If an officer and his men were tried for following orders, every combat soldier would start to question the rightness of orders he received. Finally, notwithstanding the articles of war, the idea of decorated soldiers being tried for murder amid the mayhem and slaughter of war in Vietnam bordered on the ridiculous.

Because the CIA refused to reveal its secrets, Rheault and his men were released for lack of evidence and allowed to retire from the army if they chose, but not before their case had been debated in Congress, the Pentagon, the White House, and nearly every parlor in America. When MACV declined to provide information to reporters, the soldiers' civilian attorneys obliged with stories of unfair incarceration and vendetta theories. Most major print media and television networks prepared investigative reports. When the U.S. government announced it had agreed to pay restitution to the widow of the Vietnamese agent assassinated by the Green Berets, the *Washington Post* observed that America's reputation also was a casualty in the affair.[1]

After the Green Berets came home, the nation's attention shifted to other events. As the United States continued to reduce its involvement in the war, other bigger scandals—combat mutinies, the Mylai massacre, racial strife in the military, GI drug use in Vietnam, and the Watergate scandal—claimed their own moments in the media spotlight and further impaired the Nixon administration's ability to negotiate an end to the war on its own terms.

---

## AN ANONYMOUS REPORT: "THE CASE OF THE GREEN BERETS"

---

*The following* Newsweek *column typified the sensationalized national news coverage of the Green Berets affair.*

### Newsweek, 18 August 1969

To his fellow Green Berets, Col. Robert B. Rheault, 43, was known as a "straight arrow"—tough, smart and incorruptible. It was also common knowledge that he was a friend of Army Chief of Staff Gen. William C. Westmoreland and highly regarded in the Pentagon. And so last July 20, when Colonel Rheault (pronounced "roe") was suddenly relieved as chief of the 2,500-man Special Forces group in South Vietnam, less than two months after he had taken command of it, the scuttlebutt was that he had been quietly moved to a hush-hush assignment—perhaps one that would carry a general's star. How wrong that scuttlebutt was became apparent only last week when it was announced that Colonel Rheault and seven other Green Berets [the other men under arrest: Maj. Thomas C. Middleton, Jr.; Maj. David E. Crew; Capt. Leland J. Brumley; Capt. Budge E. Williams; Capt. Robert F. Marasco; Chief Warrant Officer Edward M. Boyle and Sgt. Alvin L. Smith, Jr.] were under arrest at the Long Binh military complex outside Saigon. The reason: suspected murder of a Vietnamese national.

The terse announcement stunned Green Berets stationed at Rheault's former headquarters at Nha Trang and in villages and outposts scattered all across South Vietnam. It also provoked more mystification than any other incident in the recent history of the U.S. Army. Not that most people found anything inherently improbable in the notion that an errant Vietnamese might have been summarily disposed of by the Green Berets. Among old Vietnam hands, there has long been gossip to the effect that the Berets—who work with mercenaries and with the Vietnamese Special Forces on countless clandestine missions—sometimes treat prisoners or suspected double agents with what can best be described as rude frontier justice. Though never solidly documented, stories of torture, drumhead trials and clandestine executions by Special Forces personnel abound. But that

Robert Rheault—a topflight career officer with Exeter, West Point and the Boston Social Register in his background—could be involved in such practices was inconceivable to those who knew him.

## MYSTERY

For reasons that are still unclear, moreover, the army did nothing to clear up the mystery. After the initial announcement, U.S. military authorities from Nha Trang to the Pentagon clamped a tight lid on information. Officially, the allegations against Rheault and his subordinates were said to be under investigation—a situation comparable to having a civilian case under the consideration of a grand jury. Whether the Green Beret case would actually be brought to the stage of a formal charge and a court-martial would take perhaps two weeks to determine. And until then, an Army spokesman said, information would be withheld from the public.

The Army, the spokesman declared, did not want to prejudice the case against the eight. But inevitably, the unexplained circumstances surrounding the case and the arrest of so senior an officer touched off waves of speculation. One rumor had it that a Vietnamese working for the Special Forces had led a unit into a North Vietnamese trap while on a mission across the Cambodian border. Evidence of this betrayal, the story went on, was brought to Colonel Rheault, and he gave his permission to "get rid" of the man, possibly not realizing how broadly that phrase might be construed. The Vietnamese, so it was said, was then shot at Nha Trang on June 20, his body wrapped in a weighted sack and dropped from a helicopter into the South China Sea.

## LOGIC

This story, however, left many unanswered questions. Why would such an affair—a relatively routine matter in the cold logic of secret war—be carried all the way up to the commander of all the Green Berets in South Vietnam? One possible answer was that the Vietnamese who had disappeared was no ordinary agent. Perhaps, some observers suggested, he was a man with friends or relatives in high places in Saigon. And that was easily the most straightforward speculation making the rounds. "Maybe," said one U.S. official cryptically, "Rheault and the others killed someone they thought was a bad guy and he was someone else's good guy. Maybe they killed someone who was a trusted agent for some other berets—say, the Vietnamese Special Forces." More fancifully yet, it was suggested in some quarters that the victim—if victim there was—might have been a high official, a member of the South Vietnamese General Staff, perhaps, who had been serving as a contact in secret negotiations between Saigon and the North Vietnamese.

All this was at best simply unsupported conjecture. But conjecture was all that was possible in the absence of a forthright statement by the Army. Bitterly, attorney George Gregory of Cheraw, S.C., who had undertaken to defend Major Middleton, complained that the Pentagon was withholding information from him. "The only information I've been getting is from the newspapers," he told *Newsweek* before he flew off to Saigon last week in an attempt to see his client. "But they're not going to try my man in a vacuum. There's going to be some bloodletting."

The families of the eight Green Berets shared Gregory's bitterness over the lack of information. The case against her husband, snapped Mrs. Rheault, was "preposterous." And that, in the absence of further information, seemed to be the almost universal feeling of Rheault's fellow officers. "He was a very highly respected officer—the epitome of the Green Beret soldier," said one. "And he still is."

---

## AN ANONYMOUS REPORT: "THE GREEN BERETS COME HOME"

---

*A lack of resolution in the Green Berets affair dissatisfied* Newsweek *editors and eroded already sagging public confidence in the Nixon administration's Vietnam policy. Two days after publication of this article, thousands of war protesters took to the streets in Washington, D.C., and other large cities across the United States.*

*Newsweek*, 13 October 1969

On a sultry afternoon last June, a CIA agent strode into Fifth Special Forces headquarters in the coastal city of Nha Trang and delivered an "eyes only" message to Maj. David E. Crew, the camp's commander. Signed by a senior U.S. intelligence officer in South Vietnam, the message read: "Return agent to duty. If unable to do so, must inform [Gen. Creighton] Abrams and [Ambassador Ellsworth] Bunker. Has highest moral and flap potential." Unfortunately, the message came too late, for the agent in question was a Vietnamese named Thai Khac Chuyen—and Chuyen had "disappeared" the day before. "We're expert in a great many things," commented a top-ranking Special Forces officer after learning about the order, "but not the art of resurrection."

And so began one of the most bizarre episodes in the Vietnam war—the case of the eight Green Berets arrested last July 20 and charged by the U.S. Army with premeditated murder. For many Americans, the case came to symbolize the war itself. Beginning with an obscure and seemingly inconsequential incident, it unfolded through a series of mistakes until the glare of publicity and the clamor of public disapproval could no longer be ignored. Finally last week, Secretary of the Army Stanley R. Resor announced that all charges against the Green Berets were being dismissed because the Central Intelligence Agency—which was involved in the case—would not permit its agents to testify at a trial. "While it is not possible to proceed with the trials," Resor said in a statement that seemed close to a tacit admission of the Berets' guilt, "I want to make it clear that the acts which were charged, but not proven, represent a violation of Army regulations, orders and principles."

Within 24 hours, seven of the eight Green Berets had held a jubilant early-morning beer party in the Long Binh barracks where they had been confined, packed their bags and boarded a plane for the long trip home. Landing at Travis Air Force Base in California, they were met by a jostling throng of reporters and cameramen. In the ensuing news conference, Col. Robert B. Rheault, the former commander of the 3,000 U.S. Special Forces troops in South Vietnam, denied that a murder had occurred. Then he delivered a curious qualification. "War is a nasty business," Rheault said, "in which you assign a number of high-sounding objectives such as 'freedom' and 'defense against the evil aggressor' to justify killing people."

With that, the seven Green Berets flew off to rejoin their families and to make the agonizing decision of whether to stay in the military service after their 30-day leaves were up. Capt. Robert F. Marasco, the Beret charged by the Army as the officer who actually shot Thai Khac Chuyen, had already made up his mind. "I've had it with the Army," Marasco said. "I'm hurt and disappointed over the treatment we got." Marasco's lawyer, a flamboyant New Yorker named Henry Rothblatt, was even less reserved in expressing his feelings about the way the Army had handled the case. "I'm going to make Resor eat those words," he growled. "We don't play that way in a democracy. The whole dirty business stinks from the beginning."

### FILM

Few would disagree. According to most accounts, the affair began in May when members of the Special Forces' B-57 detachment, a unit specializing in clandestine across-the-border forays from South Vietnam, overran a Viet Cong camp in Cambodia and found a roll of undeveloped film. Upon processing, the film showed a man the Berets identified as Thai Khac Chuyen in the company of North Vietnamese officers.

Since Chuyen worked for the Berets as an interpreter and low-level operative, he was in a position to provide extremely damaging information to the enemy. Thus, in mid-June he was picked up in Saigon and transferred to the Nha Trang headquarters of the B-57 detachment for interrogation. Using truth serum and lie-detector tests (and possibly more violent methods) the Berets soon determined to their satisfaction that Chuyen was a double—or "penetration"—agent.

Over the next few days, the Berets contacted the CIA and asked for advice in dealing with Chuyen. According to the Berets' story, the CIA mission chief in Saigon refused to take a hand in the matter and the CIA strongly implied that Chuyen would have to be murdered—"terminated with extreme prejudice" was the alleged phrase. Thus on June 20, according to the U.S. Army specifications against the Berets, the suspected double agent was bundled into a 30-foot-long boat, drugged with morphine, shot in the head and dumped in a weighted sack into a shark-infested area of the South China Sea. The CIA steadfastly denies that any of its agents knew of the Berets' intention to commit the murder and claims that it had advised the Berets not to kill Chuyen. In either case, the CIA learned that the actual assassination had been carried out when one of the Berets, Sgt. Alvin L. Smith, reported the incident—presumably because he had disagreed with the decision to kill Chuyen and feared that the other Berets might kill him to prevent his talking.

### MASQUERADE

The CIA then informed General Abrams of the matter, and he ordered Rheault to come up with an explanation. Rheault insisted that Chuyen was still alive—that, in fact, he had been sent on a mission into Cambodia. (To sustain this cover story, Rheault had a Japanese-American member of the Berets masquerade as Chuyen and leave the country in the presence of witnesses.) But Abrams knew the truth and, according to a widely accepted version of the story, he seized the opportunity to corner Rheault—a starchy paratroop officer to whom Abrams had taken a dislike. Not only did Abrams order the arrest of the Berets, but he may have violated the Uniform Code of Military Justice by confining the men to 5- by 7-foot cells and also Army regulations by failing to list Rheault as an officer in the imprisonment records.

When pressure from Washington began to build up, Abrams transferred the Berets to more comfortable quarters—but reportedly threatened to resign from his post if the Army failed to prosecute the case. In the meantime, for their pretrial hearing the Berets had lined up an impressive array of civilian defense attorneys—Rothblatt, Edward Bennett Williams and F. Lee Bailey. Arriving in Saigon, Rothblatt gave the Army a taste of what was in store. "I've never seen a weaker case in all my life," he declared, and thereupon unleashed a barrage of motions for a mistrial.

**TOES**

Realizing that a public airing of the case could well jeopardize U.S. intelligence-gathering activities in Vietnam, CIA director Richard Helms insisted that the trial be called off. Soon President Nixon found himself involved in a classical squeeze, for no matter which way he moved, sensitive toes were sure to be stepped on. The result was that the Administration equivocated. Army Secretary Resor announced that the charges against the Berets were being dropped only ten days after he had publicly affirmed that they would be pressed. And to make matters worse, the White House, through Presidential press secretary Ronald Ziegler, first claimed that the matter was entirely in Army hands, [and] then later admitted what everyone always assumed—that the President had indeed been "involved" from the first.

The President's decision to squash the case was perhaps inevitable. "It is simply unimaginable," said a CIA official in Washington, "that we could allow our chief of mission in Saigon to be grilled about his methodology by F. Lee Bailey." That may be true. But it was nonetheless deplorable that a case that had been so grossly mismanaged by the CIA and the U.S. Army would be permitted to pass into history without the scrutiny of an impartial public.

*Credit*: From Newsweek, 10/13/69. © 1969 Newsweek, Inc. All rights reserved. Reprinted with permission.

## NOTE

1. Michael Neal, "Widow Paid $6,473 by U.S. in Beret Case; 'In the Missing Category;' 'A Few Lousy Bucks,'" *Washington Post*, 10 October 1969, A10.

## FURTHER READINGS

Kelly, Frances J. *Vietnam Studies: U.S. Army Special Forces, 1961–1971*. Washington, D.C.: U.S. Army Center of Military History, 1989.

Moore, Robin, and Henry Rothblatt. *Court Martial*. Garden City, N.Y.: Doubleday, 1971.

Simpson, Charles M., III. *Inside the Green Berets—The First Thirty Years: A History of the U.S. Army Special Forces*. New York: Berkeley Books, 1984.

# 18

## AMERICAN CASUALTIES

In many ways, the Vietnam War was different from other U.S. wars, but when the flag-draped coffins came home, it was the same. Words were not enough to pay tribute to the American dead. More was required of the survivors: perhaps a call to a reexamined life and a pledge, "Never again."

The Vietnam War Memorial in Washington, D.C., bespeaks this silent pledge. The names of the dead etched onto its two rising black marble walls meeting 10 feet above ground level at a vertex of 125 degrees. The names are listed chronologically by date of death. The memorial's mirror surfaces mingle the names with the reader's reflection.

A myth was perpetuated by the American press that the walls of the Vietnam Memorial are populated primarily by the poor and disadvantaged, and that a disproportion of blacks and Hispanics served and died in Vietnam, while rich whites stayed home. Referring to the famous "Faces of the Dead" issue of *Life* magazine reproduced in this chapter, the distinguished Vietnam War correspondent David Halberstam embraced this myth when he wrote: "Vietnam had been a truly unfair war in which the upper class went to college and the rural and the black and the blue-collar went to Vietnam."[1]

Of 217 faces of the dead in the *Life* article, the African American and Hispanic faces are in proportion to the overall population at the time: twenty-three black faces, or 11 percent of the total, and only three Hispanic faces. Of the African American dead, six were officers. Contrary to the myth that the racial minorities and poor predominantly fought the war, it was non-college-bound young men, mostly from middle-class and working-class families, who served and died. In the 1960s, many middle-class youth did not attend college; a college education was not the least common denominator that it would become for them in later decades. The poor had an only slightly higher chance of dying in Vietnam than the rich (31 Vietnam deaths per 100,000 population compared to 26).[2]

Certainly class distinctions contributed to inequities, as in most aspects of society, but income and race had less to do with dying in Vietnam than did going to college.

# EDWIN SHANK: CRITICIZING THE WAR FROM THE GRAVE—AMERICAN PILOT'S LAST LETTERS FROM VIETNAM

*On 28 March 1964, the* Indianapolis News *published a collection of poignant letters home from Captain Edwin "Jerry" Shank, a U.S. Air Force "advisor" killed in Vietnam. The flyer's voice from the grave spoke of the deception, hypocrisy, and contradictions of U.S. policy in Vietnam. By May, nearly every influential newspaper and newsmagazine in the United States had reprinted the letters. Senator Margaret Chase Smith of Maine submitted the letters for the* Congressional Record *and appealed for an honest accounting of the war. The following reprint of the letters in* Life *magazine got the attention of millions of American citizens and prompted the government to develop a coordinated public relations strategy for the war.*

## *Life*, 8 May 1964

Along with reports out of South Vietnam last week of attack, counterattack and general foreboding, news was also being made by letters from a U.S. flyer who was killed there. The author was Air Force Captain Edwin G. Shank, Jr., 27, one of a tiny band of Americans flying obsolescent T-28 trainers in support of ground attacks. The letters were addressed to his wife Connie, who was at home in Winamac, Ind., caring for their three children—and expecting a fourth.

Captain Shank's letters were critical of the way the war was being conducted—the inferior equipment and unqualified personnel—and his criticisms were discussed in Congress and the press. But Captain Shank was also a lonely father trying to keep up the bonds with his family. Above all, he was a dedicated soldier who believed that his frustrating war had to be fought—and that the American people did not know enough or care enough about it. On these pages, *Life* presents a full selection from Captain Shank's letters about his lonely war.

### Thursday, 14 Nov. 63
Dear Connie and Kids,

Up to 12 missions now. All checked out for nite work and I'm second up for alert tonite. Had another 3 hr. flt. this morning. We escorted choppers back and forth to a landing zone where they put troops in the field. Then we went over and struck some suspicious areas.

We're using equipment and bombs from WW II and it's not too reliable. There are only about 6 maintenance men, 6 armament men and 11 pilots down here. We 23 run the whole T-28 war in the Mekong Delta. This will give you some idea of Uncle Sam's part in the war. I goofed on my third mission out of here. I told you we had a real short runway. One approach is over trees and bushes and a couple of barbed wire fences. There is only one barbed wire fence now. I brought about 20 ft. of fence home with me.

### 23 Nov. 63

Been real busy with the armament job. Got all kinds of problems—can't get parts or books or charts describing the different bombs and systems. The Air Force hasn't used any of this equipment since Korea, and everybody seems to have lost the books. Main problem is personnel—no good officers or NCOs over here that really know their business. Most of them are out of SAC [Strategic Air Command] and have dealt only with nuclear weapons. This doesn't apply over here. What we need is some from WW II. Some days it's like beating your head against a brick wall.

### 27 Nov. 63

Happy Thanksgiving—no different here than any other day. You know damn well where I'd like to be today.

First of all woke up Saturday to the news of Kennedy's assassination. Such a terrible thing—the world is full of animals. Sunday all hell broke loose with the Vietcong. We had a big airborne operation against them—both choppers and parachutes. I'm up to 20 missions now and am real confident in myself. I feel like a veteran. I think I am older.

Although this is called a dirty little war and is far from the shores of the old USA, it's a big mean war. We are getting beat. We are undermanned and undergunned. The US may say they are in this, but they don't know. If the US would really put combat people in here, we could win and win fast.

### Wednesday Nite, 4 Dec. 63

It's about 9:30—I guess, broke my watch. But I'll get it fixed next time into Saigon. Got my toe rot healed up and also my spider bite. I'm fully operational now.

I have debated for a week and a half now over telling you about Black Sunday—Nov. 24, 1963. I'm going to tell you, and if you don't want to hear about these things again, well say so. You do have a right to know. Anyway, here is what I saw.

At 4:30 Frank Gerski and I took off after a fort under attack. Our airborne interpreter was very poor. The first target he said to hit was in an area about the size of your dad's farm. Well, this is much too large a target, but it's all we had. After the first 2 bombs, we spotted the bad guys shooting at us. So Frank directed me in and I burned them with napalm. Then I spotted another bunch shooting great big bullets at me, so I told Frank to follow me in and shoot where I shot. Well, just as I had them in my gun sights my damn guns jammed. By now, dawn had broken. We were out of goodies and gas, so we came home, landing at around 0700.

We then got word that a big airlift of troops was taking place. Four of our T-28 birds went out—2 to escort the choppers and 2 to soften up the landing zone. They came home about 2 hrs later—said it was pretty hot. 2 more birds took off to do the same thing for the second wave of choppers. 1-½ hrs later they came home screaming "battle damage." Just after the hurt birds landed 2 others took off—almost. I watched the first go, then waited for the second. But he didn't make it. His engine quit just at takeoff. Since the runway was short he didn't have time to stop. Hit a hidden hole and tore a gear off. So now we're down to 2 airplanes out of 6 and it's my turn. We bombed like no one has ever bombed before—we literally obliterated about 600 acres of Vietcong woods and then came home.

The Vietcong hurt us bad. What they had done was pull into the little village and commit their usual atrocities. Headquarters thought they would teach this little group of Vietcong a lesson. But the crafty little bastards withdrew from the town into foxholes and bunkers they had been secretly building all week. So when the first wave of troops went in—thinking it was just a routine chase of Vietcong—they soon ran against the Vietcong wall.

We were lucky. No T-28 pilot received so much as a hangnail. We've got a tremendous *esprit* and we're all skilled—so you can be proud of us. I am. There are no heroes over here, but there are a lot of fine men. America better not let us down. We've either got to get in all the way or get out. If we get out, the Vietcong will be in Saigon the next day.

I wouldn't read this to the kids. They might not understand. You can understand now why I have a duty over here, why it's a serious duty and no one could possibly shirk it. I believe in our cause—it's just. We must win.

Saturday Nite, 21 Dec. 63

Talked to a guy today—his wife had a baby at 7:30 Saigon time on the 19th and he heard about it today about 0900—approx. 48 hrs. later. I still haven't found out how you'll get hold of me. I don't even know where I'll be. I'll bet you are miserable by now. God, how I wish I could help you. I worry about the delivery—just know that I'm with you, only I can't hold your hand. Have strength, Hon.

We got a briefing today on the total result of that operation on 24 November [Black Sunday]. The airpower got credit for 150–200 kills. No one can be sure, for the Viet-

cong carry off their dead and wounded. Anyway, there were still a lot of pieces left, and this is how we got the estimate.

No Army (Vietnamese or U.S.) troops engaged the enemy at all. It was strictly Air Force against ground. The Army was there with 1,500 troops, but the leaders kinda didn't want to fight. After we had hurt them so bad, the army let them get away.

Anyway there were approx. 700 Vietcong dug in with three 50 cal. antiaircraft guns and three 30 cal. antiaircraft guns, plus many hundred with machine guns. They were waiting for us. But we hurt them even though we lost. We lost because we had them trapped and they got away.

Pretty quiet here tonite. Christmas is near, and nobody wants it to come, really.

Sunday Nite, 22 Dec. 63

Opened Christmas presents tonite. Can't put them in my suitcase, so I opened them. They meant a lot. It's something for you instead of against you—love instead of hate and killing. Flew another mission today. I'm credited with destroying a 50 cal. antiaircraft gun. I guess I'm a true killer. I have no sympathy, and I'm good. No sense being a gentleman about it, because it's not appreciated. I'm not proud of killing. But I am proud of my skills. I'm telling you facts so you'll know what I do. *You* have to know.

I talked to Major Lengfield tonite. I said, "I'm going to put in leave papers for February to see my wife and our new-born baby. Will you approve it?" He said, "Yes, *but* it will not be approved by headquarters; I can guarantee that." I'm going to put it in anyway. All they can do is say no.

Oh, how I miss you. This life is too hard. I need softness and love.

Have faith in my love, and strengthen yourself with it for the baby. Don't give up. I still may be there.

Monday Nite, 30 Dec. 63

Missed mass yesterday—many things happened. I'm up to 38 missions now—I've been pretty busy.

Well, here goes. I got shot down yesterday. We were escorting a C-123 and I picked up 3 slugs in my airplane. I made it to a field called Con Tho and landed safely. Me and the airplane are both OK—not a scratch except the 3 bullet holes. No sweat.

Thought I should tell you.

Friday Nite, 3 Jan. 64

Missed supper. Conn Deken and I were loading some napoleon [napalm] tonite for an evaluation tomorrow. I'll try and explain the experiment. One of the airmen came up with the idea of putting chunks of charcoal into our napoleon tank. Napalm is gasoline which is jelled into a mass about the consistency of honey. When you drop it, it ignites and spreads fire about 200–300 ft. With charcoal in it, the charcoal is thrown another 200 ft., like a burning baseball, and does further damage to Vietcong houses.

Tomorrow 3 birds are going out with half their load straight napalm and the other half with charcoal in it (Madame Nhu cocktail). If higher headquarters thinks it's alright, then they'll buy us the charcoal. So far we've been buying it ourselves, or else "borrowing" it from the kitchen.

I'm going to hit the sack. It's 1130 pm here now and 1030 am for you—about time for your favorite soap opera, "As The World Turns." Wasn't that it? How are things for those people? Same as last May or are they worse?

Tuesday Nite, 7 Jan. 64

Got another letter today. You can't possibly know what a letter does for morale.

Lost 2 guys today. One was a pretty good friend of mine. The only guess is—the airplane just came apart. B-26. 3rd or 4th that have done that now.

One more bit of good news. The guy who got emergency leave for their first baby. Just as he was getting on the airplane, they took him off because the commander changed his mind. Finally the guy went to the second in command over here and got ordinary leave—not emergency leave.

With ordinary leave it will take him forever to get across the Pacific. He'll have to wait for available space. Then, if he can't get back in time he's AWOL. I don't know what the US is doing. They tell you people that we're just in training situations. But we're at war. We are doing the flying and fighting. We are losing.

Let me write again—I'll write happy. But honey, I'm so frustrated.

Thursday Nite, 9 Jan. 64

Had a good target today finally. Felt like I really dealt a blow to the Vietcong. On my second round I got a secondary explosion. This means that after my bomb exploded there was another explosion. It was either an ammo dump or a fuel storage area. It made a huge burning fireball. You really can't tell when you roll in on a pass what is in the huts and trees you're aiming at. Just lucky today, but I paid them back for shooting me down.

Wednesday, 15 Jan. 64

Another B-26 went in yesterday. Nobody made it out. A couple guys I knew pretty well bought the farm. I had met one guy's wife—real nice and they had 2 kids.

We can no longer save face over here, for we have no face to save. We are more than ever fighting this war. The South Vietnamese T-28s used to come down here and fly missions with us. But lately, since we've getting shot at so much, they moved up north. I kid you not. I can't help wondering if you're in the hospital tonite—or when you get this letter. If so, you know my prayers are with you as are my thoughts. I worry very much. I hope and pray you have a good delivery and you are strong. Please don't think I've forgotten you during all those pains. God knows I'm with you as much as humanly possible.

Monday, 20 Jan. 64

I'm back at Bien Hoa. Back for 2 weeks. Two long weeks, but they add up towards the 52 I've got to spend over here. It's really not 52 weeks. It's closer to eternity. I'm over here to do the best job possible for my country—yet my country will do nothing for me or any of my buddies or even for itself. I'm sure nothing will be done over here until after the elections. Why? Because votes are more important than my life or of my buddies' lives. What gets me most is that they won't tell you people what we do over here. I'll bet you that anyone you talk to does not know that American pilots fight this war. We—me and my buddies—do everything. The Vietnamese "STUDENTS" we have on board are Airmen basics. They don't even know their own serial numbers. The only reason they are on board is: in case we crash there is one American "advisor" and one Vietnamese "student." They are sacrificial lambs. They're a menace to have on board.

I got three letters from you today. Actually, 2 from you and 2 from kids. Hope Bart's party went alright. [Bart is Captain Shank's five-year-old son.] Wish I could have been there. A birthday party is for kids and kids only. It gives them a chance to be big. It's not for grownups. Hurrah for you for sticking by your guns.

Sunday Afternoon, 26 Jan. 64

It's a very lazy Sunday. At 1700 is church, and maybe tonite I'll get out some more letters. I'm very behind. Sorry I wrote some bad letters, but you're the only one I can express myself to. You need someone just absorb it and take it off your mind. Can't say things like that to my buddies, for they're experiencing the same emotions, I'm sure, and it just doesn't help to bitch to each other. Anyway, I'm ready and willing to go up again now.

Bart's right. Billy's got a brother, so I think we should have one.

Friday, 31 Jan. 64

Greetings from the Soc Trang duty officer. I should get relieved around 500 to either fly or get a haircut—whichever comes first.

Not much word about the coup. From what we've got, this new general [Premier Nguyen Khanh] is pro-American.

President Johnson says we're going to stay & win. I hope he's right. We can't keep up like we've been 'cause we're losing. Everyone over here seems unqualified for his job. Take me. I'm a multi-engine pilot, but I'm flying TAC fighters. We have no fighter pilot in our outfit.

Thursday, 6 Feb. 64

I thought for sure today was the day. It was all I could think of last nite, so I've been expecting some kind of notification all day. It's got to be soon now. What do you think at nite? Are you nervous?

Had another big chopper assault today, but we flew

mostly escort. Pretty quiet assault—very few shots fired. I think they're planned that way so that no Vietnamese soldiers get hurt. I'm serious. I'm pretty well convinced that these people only go into areas that are free of Vietcong. But the Vietnamese can still put up a good front to the U.S. so they can get more aid. It's a known fact over here that the ARVN (South Vietnamese army units) don't receive many casualties. You know how a cornered rat fights. Well, that's the Vietcong. So the ARVN always leaves them a way free. This is fact, not rumor.

### Nite, 6 Feb. 64

This is my second letter today, so before you read this read the other one. After the last letter—at about 6:30—we scrambled after a fort under attack. We hit & hit good, but it got dark, so we headed up here for Bien Hoa. Pretty hot target and both of us got hit.

Coming in here to Bien Hoa, they warned us that the Vietcong were shooting at airplanes on the final approach.

Well, we made a tight, fast approach and held our lights—it was pitch black until almost over the end of the runway.

I forgot my gear and went skidding along in a shower of sparks down the runway. Airplane's not hurt too bad. I'm not even scratched. My pride is terribly wounded.

I imagine everything will turn out alright. I still had enough wits to prevent the aircraft from burning or turning over.

Well, I wanted you to know. Don't worry any more now. Now it's someone else's turn. I'm still coming home, so don't get any wild ideas. You're still married to the "World's Greatest."

All my love and prayers.

### Saturday Nite, 9 Feb. 64

This will be a one-page letter. Because this is the last sheet of stationery I have.

I'm not in trouble. Got up yesterday and flew another airplane. The only reprimand I got was taking me off lead status. That's pretty good. My squadron CO picked me up after the crash and said, "When they put retractable gear on airplanes they knew that someday someone would forget." That's all he said. Everyone stuck behind me real good. Flew one mission yesterday and one today. Didn't forget my gear, though. Boy, that was some ride—100 mph on concrete in a lead sled.

### Monday Evening, 17 Feb. 64

I'm on alert now. We don't usually pull nite alert here, but all B-26s are grounded, so we are the only strike force left. A B-26 crashed last week—another case of the wings just coming off.

I'm so anxious to see my new pretty little daughter. She's probably home now. How does she like our home? I wished she missed me, too, but hell—she doesn't even know I exist.

Have you got her in the crib, or is she in a bassinette? Is she sleeping with you, or by herself in the back room?

### Friday Nite, 21 Feb. 64

Haven't felt much like writing. Tuesday evening Maj. Lengfield got shot down. He bellied his airplane in next to a special forces camp and got out without a scratch. The airplane burned completely up, though. Bernie Lukasik, one of his wingmen, kept the Vietcong away from the plane by using his prop. He was out of ammo, so all he could do was dust off the Vietcong with his prop. Took a lot of guts. We got pretty stoned that nite in celebration of no one's getting hurt. Next morning, Bernie Lukasik and Denny Sides took off for Sol Trang and had a strike on the way. Bernie was going in on his 7th strafing pass and never came out of it. That was 2 airplanes in 2 days. Kinda shook us up. Not only that, but the B-26s have been grounded since Monday. So the whole USAF fighter force is down to six airplanes. This should set an example of how much Uncle Sam cares. 6 airplanes might as well be none.

I imagine there has been something in the papers, and I thought I should explain. Needless to say, flying is down to nothing. They're saving the T-28s for emergency action only. We're changing our tactics now to decrease any chance of getting hit.

I miss you more than ever, and I will try to come home for a good long look at Patty. I hate to spread this mood to you. Have patience. Happy letters will come soon.

### 24 Feb. 64

I make captain this Friday. I'll be at Soc Trang, so I'll be throwing my party down there. I'd like to pay for it by check 'cause it would take too much of my green. Is this OK—can we afford it?

We're down to 5 airplanes now. Five airplanes to fight the war—that's just ridiculous. Tell this to my dad—let him know, too, how much the country is letting EVERYONE down. We over here are doing the best we possibly can; we fight and we die, but no one cares. They lie to my country about us—we really don't officially exist. They've just got to help us and soon, or we are going to have another Dien Bien Phu [surrender]. God help us.

You and the kids are my only motivating factor. I would love to be with you now, but I would not like to be back in combat after leaving you.

### 29 Feb. 64, Sat. Morn.

I'm a captain now—put the new bars on yesterday. Had the big party early this morning. Then a flight of four hangovers. We had a reporter in no. 4 ship, and he got to watch an actual strike. We want somebody to tell our story over here.

Got a lot of pictures from the baptism. She sure is a cute little girl. I'd love to get my hands on her. Don't feed her too much, so she'll still be tiny when I get home. Might just as well spoil her real good, too, so she'll still need a lot of picking up when I get there.

We've got a new general in command now and he really

sounds good. He has ordered B-57 (bombers, jet) to replace them [the B-26s] and he asked for immediate delivery. He's also demanded that they replace our T-28 with the AD-6. This is a much more powerful single-engine dive-bomber. It was designed for this type of work & has armor plating. We're pretty excited. These were 3 of my main gripes. Morale has just gone up 100%. I think we're going in the right direction. I sure hope so.

I've got 74 missions now. One more and I earn another Air Medal. I may go to Hong Kong Saturday. Don't have to take leave that way and can save it for you and me. All the pictures dad sent are stuck together. They threw me in the shower last night and I got everything wet. Give all the kids a big love for me—their daddy is very lonely.

Friday Nite, 13 Mar. 64

This is the second installment of a letter, so if you've opened this one first, put it away and open the other.

Kinda found out by grapevine that Luke Lukasik, the T-28 jock who got killed, was not shot down. He flew into the ground. This is terrible—but good. It means of the 3 T-28s which have been killed, only one was shot down—and even this is debatable. So I put more trust in the airplane. If it can take the beating, it increases our odds.

I figure after my next 3 trips to Soc Trang I may get home for that visit.

Rumors are fast and furious. Nothing yet on B-57s. That thing you saw on TV is not true—B-26 should NEVER fly

again. Even if rejuvenated. Also rumor that B-26 pilots will get instructions in another kind of single-engine dive-bomber. All is still in the air—all rumors.

Well, I've really filled the pages tonite. I hope this makes up for my not writing for so long. Got to Hong Kong and just lived as if every day was my last. It's an unexplainable mood, but I'm alright now. I can fight again for 3 or 4 months without a break—at least I think I can.

I wish I could have told you all these things in front of a roaring fire. It's hard to be a man sometimes. I sure need your shoulder.

May God be with you and help you until I can come home.

Sunday Morning, 22 Mar. 64
My Dear Connie,

Forgot to tell you they put me back on lead status again. Been flying pretty heavy. We'll soon be back up to 13 airplanes again. Hope these last for a while.

I miss you all very much, but time is passing and we're almost halfway. I love you all,

*JERRY AND DADDY*

Two days after he wrote this last letter home, Captain Shank was helping to bomb a Vietcong force some 10 miles from his own airbase when his T-28 came under heavy groundfire. The wing fell off his plane, and the T-28 crashed. Both Captain Shank and Tit Le Trung, the Vietnamese student pilot who was with him, were killed instantly.

*Credit:* © 1964 TIME Inc. Reprinted by permission.

---

## DON DUNCAN: INTERVIEW WITH SERGEANT SMITH—A "SURVIVING" CASUALTY OF VIETNAM

*Don Duncan was a Vietnam War correspondent for a prominent antiwar magazine,* Ramparts, *which was known for tackling politically controversial material that the mainstream press would not touch. He returned to the United States and wrote the following tender, nonjudgmental essay about a surviving American "casualty" of the Vietnam War.*

*Ramparts,* July 1966

Past the sign advertising the racetrack, Highway 30 dips downhill onto the main street of Chester, West Virginia. Quiet and unknown by day except for those interested in steel mills, this panhandle town is well known by those seeking action at the "wheel" by night. Left along the main street, past the small cafes, the American Legion and the Post Office, is the house. It is a two-story frame and sits well back from the street. What should be a large front yard is a car lot for the Ford agency next door. Inside, the living room has a collection of deep, stuffed furniture, a large new Admiral AM/FM console that hasn't found its place yet, and a tape recorder sitting on a table.

With me, sitting on the couch, is a young man in a blue shirt and slacks. He is tall, lean and tanned. Through the tan,

dark shadows are apparent under his eyes. He sits forward on the couch, the fingers of one hand alternately holding and releasing the fingers of the other. If not suspicious, he is at least wary. Conversation is awkward—he volunteers nothing and responds only to a direct question and then in most cases, indirectly.

The young man is George E. Smith, until his recent discharge a staff sergeant in the "Green Berets." Captured by the Viet Cong at Hiep Hoa in November 1963, he was released along with Staff Sergeant Claude D. McClure in November 1965. At the time of their release in Cambodia several statements were attributed to the sergeants: that they wanted to quit the Army to conduct a campaign to get the United States out of Vietnam; that the U.S. had nothing to gain from the war;

that the Viet Cong are the people; that they were treated well, unlike prisoners of Saigon's troops; that there was no brainwashing; that they never saw any regular North Vietnamese soldiers; that the U.S. could never defeat the Viet Cong.

However, being released from the Viet Cong was not the end of detention for the sergeants. They were sent to Thailand under U.S. military supervision and immediately isolated from the news media. Then, after a brief examination, the men left Thailand for debriefing and to return to their own families for Christmas. They never made it. Instead the two men were flown to Okinawa and were charged on December 21 with violating Article 104 of the Uniform Code of Military Justice—aiding the enemy. Specifically, the men were charged with "preparing, furnishing and delivering to the Viet Cong certain documents, statements and writings inimical to the interest of the United States."

These charges of "aiding the enemy" came as a complete surprise. They came during the debriefing from information given voluntarily. The debriefing continued at the request of the two soldiers. During this period the Army claimed that the men were able to move around freely, which included going to town. But what the Army neglected to mention was that this freedom had its limitation, lack of privacy—counter-intelligence was always in tow. Fellow soldiers with whom they came in contact displayed no special animosity. While in Okinawa, Smith was assigned to a garrison head quarters company, not exactly the "normal duty" for a Special Forces soldier, as the military has claimed.

As he talked about Okinawa, Smith spoke slowly, giving the impression that he was selecting his words with great care. He said there had been no psychological pressure put upon him other than the charge itself and the restricted frame of reference in being on a U.S. military island. As part of pre-trial procedures he was interviewed by a psychiatrist, but said nothing and the interview was very brief. Of his lawyer, Captain Anthony Nelson, he said he was young and perhaps too cautious, but he had no complaints. Smith had no knowledge of his mail being censored but counter-intelligence often stood by while he read and asked permission to look at certain letters. He specifically mentioned a letter from the May 2nd Movement.

In short, he had been in military custody on a military island, charged by the military with a military crime, investigated by the military, represented by a military attorney, and facing a military trial if the military so decided. He smiled and called it "a real closed shop."

When asked how he felt about the way the military handled his case, George Smith replied that he thought the Army had hurt themselves in the eyes of the public. He has no intention of attacking the Army, obviously harboring the feeling that he could add little to their self-defeating attitude. He felt that the investigation consisted mainly of communications between the Pentagon and Naha testing public opinion to determine what effect a trial would have.

Attempts by *Ramparts* and other news media to contact the men as far back as January proved fruitless. The Army charged the men with a crime punishable by death and then assigned them a military lawyer who advised them not to talk with the press. Until the month of April, the only thing the military would reveal was that the charges were still being investigated and "debriefing" was continuing. Without warning, on April 17, it was announced that both men were in this country and had been discharged to return to their respective homes.

When asked why he won't discuss the period during which he was a prisoner, Mr. Smith informed me that counter-intelligence had classified the circumstances of his detention and had warned him that discussing the matter would be a violation of the Espionage Act. The only way these men can clear themselves is in a public trial or by disclosing the circumstances of their internment. The former has been denied, and they are told they cannot do the latter or they will be guilty of disclosing classified information. Classified from whom? The Viet Cong? Surely they know what happened during the two years the men were their prisoners. The only ones who may never find out are the American people. Most emphatically George Smith does not consider himself a "turncoat," but a loyal American. However, when the men were released the Army wouldn't say the men were cleared, but only that charges had been dropped. And the Army gave the two ex-prisoners general discharges under Army regulation 635-209, rather than standard "honorable discharges." All of this maintains an aura of suspicion, and also renders them ineligible to re-enlist in the armed forces.

He says that someday he may discuss his imprisonment, but he asked for understanding for now. For two years as a prisoner, his frame of reference was narrow. After imprisonment he was transferred to another narrow frame of reference—Okinawa. He understands this is the reason why he was sent there rather than to a stateside Army post. He now wants to get properly oriented and broaden his perspective. Perhaps then, and only then, he will discuss the matter. I think he shows good sense; considering the ordeal of the last two and a half years, his position is quite understandable.

Mr. Smith told me that Hiep Hoa (the camp where he was captured) was probably the worst example of security in Viet Nam. He has heard that the commanding officer has since been relieved and expressed little sorrow over that fact. And he seemed amazed when I told him I had worked with effective members of the Vietnamese Special Forces. After commenting on the general worthlessness of that organization he said at Hiep Hoa they had found that the Vietnamese commander had 50 non-existent people on the payroll. Talk of what is called "discriminate bombing" brought forth a cynical snort. He added that he thought U.S. reports of Viet Cong losses were ridiculous. Smith was fully cognizant of the pressures put on the U.S. government to release him, by various peace groups and other concerned citizens, and is appreciative of their concern, but he doesn't know if they expedited or hindered his release. In any event, he knows little or nothing about these groups and most definitely doesn't want to be adopted by any organization.

During our conversation George's stepfather appeared intermittently, and a friend, a Korean War vet, was in the room. George's mother, with whom I had talked many times, made a brief appearance prior to going to work. A friendly woman with a broad regional accent, she expressed her happiness in having George home, but as on the telephone, she gave the impression of being bewildered by all that had occurred. I was invited to share a good meal of beans and franks with homemade bread and fresh butter prepared by George's stepfather. "All West Virginia men must learn to cook if they want

to eat." A younger brother came in briefly before starting out on his paper route in a newly acquired '59 Olds.

I asked him, "Once you get your breath, what are you planning to do, George?"

"Well, there is a new GM plant opening near here. I'll put in an application and maybe get accepted. I'd like to travel a little and see some of the country; see what's happening, what people are saying and thinking. Maybe even come to California."

"Is there anything we discussed today that you don't want published?"

He hesitated, then said, "No, I don't think so." Then with the first obvious intensity he had shown during the three-hour meeting, he added, "If you do write anything, please clear up that business about the documents. There were no documents."

## JOHN FETTERMAN: "PFC. GIBSON COMES HOME"

*The family and friends of one dead American GI spoke for themselves, but also for communities across the United States, in John Fetterman's simple tribute, "Pfc. Gibson Comes Home," which won the Pulitzer Prize for local general spot news reporting in 1969.*

### Louisville Times, 28 July 1968

It was late on a Wednesday night and most of the people were asleep in Hindman, the county seat of Knott County, when the body of Private First Class James Thurman (Little Duck) Gibson came home from Vietnam.

It was hot. But as the gray hearse arrived bearing the gray Army coffin, a summer rain began to fall. The fat raindrops glistened on the polished hearse and steamed on the street. Hindman was dark and silent. In the distance down the town's main street the red sign on the Square Deal Motor Co. flashed on and off.

Private Gibson's body had been flown from Oakland, California, to Cincinnati and was accompanied by Army Staff Sgt. Raymond A. Ritter, assigned to escort it home. The body was picked up in Cincinnati by John Everage, a partner in the local funeral home, and from that point on it was in the care of people who had known the 24-year-old soldier all his life.

At Hindman, the coffin was lifted out while Sgt. Ritter, who wore a black mourning band on his arm, snapped a salute. One funeral home employee whispered to another: "It's Little Duck. They brought him back."

Most of his life he had been called Little Duck—for so long that many people who knew him well had to pause and reflect to recall his full name.

By Thursday morning there were few people who did not know that Little Duck was home—or almost home. During the morning the family came; his older brother, Herschel, whom they call Big Duck; his sister Betty Jo; and his wife Carolyn.

They stood over the glass-shielded body and let their tears fall upon the glass, and people spoke softly in the filling station next door and on the street outside.

The soldier's parents, Mr. and Mrs. Norman Gibson, waited at home, a neat white house up the hollow which shelters Flax Patch Creek, several miles away. Mrs. Gibson had been ill for months, and the family did not let her take the trip to Hindman. Later in the morning, they took Little Duck home.

Sweltering heat choked the hills and valleys as Little Duck was placed back in the hearse and taken home. The cortege had been joined by Maj. Lyle Haldeman, a survival assistance officer, sent, like Sgt. Ritter, to assist the family. It was a long, slow trip—over a high ridge to the south, along Irishman Creek and past the small community of Amburgey.

At Amburgey, the people stood in the sun, women wept and men removed their hats as the hearse went past. Mrs. Nora Amburgey, the postmistress, lowered the flag of the tiny fourth-class post office to half-mast and said, "We all thought a lot of Little Duck."

At the point where Flax Patch Creek empties into Irishman Creek, the hearse turned, crossed a small wooden bridge and drove the final mile up Flax Patch Creek to the Gibson home. The parents and other relatives waited in a darkened, silent home.

As the coffin was lifted upon the front porch and through the door into the front living room, the silence was broken by cries of grief. The sounds of anguish swelled and rolled along the hollow. Little Duck was home.

All afternoon and all night they came, some walking, some driving up the dusty road in cars and trucks. They brought flowers and food until the living room was filled with floral tributes and the kitchen was crammed with food. The people filled the house and yard. They talked in small groups, and members of the family clasped to each other in grief.

They went, time and time again, to look down into the coffin and weep.

The mother, a sweet-faced mountain woman, her gray hair brushed back and fastened behind her head, forced back the pangs of her illness and moved, as in a trance, among the crowd as she said:

"His will will be done no matter what we say or do."

The father, a tall, tanned man, his eyes wide and red from weeping, said:

"He didn't want to go to the Army, but he knew it was the right thing to do; so he did his best. He gave all he had. I'm as proud of him as I can be. Now they bring him home like this."

Around midnight the rain returned and the mourners gathered in the house, on the porch and backed against the side of the house under the eaves.

The father talked softly of his son.

"I suppose you wonder why we called him Little Duck. Well, when the boys were little they would go over and play in the creek every chance they got. Somebody said they were like ducks.

"Ever since then Herschel was 'Big Duck' and James was 'Little Duck.'

"You worked hard all your life to raise your family. I worked in a 32-inch seam of coal, on my hands and knees, loading coal to give my family what I could.

"There was never a closer family. Little Duck was born here in this house and never wanted to leave."

Other mourners stepped up to volunteer tributes to Little Duck.

"He never was one to drink and run up and down the road at night."

"He took care of his family. He was a good boy."

Little Duck was a big boy. He was 6 feet 5½ inches tall and weighed 205 pounds. His size led him to the basketball team at Combs High School where he met and courted the girl he married last January.

Little Duck was home recently on furlough. Within a month after he went down Flax Patch Creek to return to the Army, he was back home to be buried. He had been married six months, a soldier for seven.

The Army said he was hit by mortar fragments near Saigon, but there were few details of his death.

The father, there in the stillness of the early morning, was remembering the day his son went back to the Army.

"He had walked around the place, looking at everything. He told me, 'Lord, it's good to be home.'

"Then he went down the road. He said, 'Daddy, take care of yourself and don't work too hard.'

"He said, 'I'll be seeing you.' But he can't see me now."

An elderly man, walking with great dignity, approached and said, "Nobody can ever say anything against Little Duck. He was as good a boy as you'll ever see."

Inside the living room, the air heavy with the scent of flowers, Little Duck's mother sat with her son and her grief.

Her hand went out gently, as to comfort a stranger, and she talked as though to herself:

"Why my boy? Why my baby?"

She looked toward the casket, draped in an American flag, and when she turned back she said:

"You'll never know what a flag means until you see one on your own boy."

Then she went back to weep over the casket.

On Friday afternoon Little Duck was taken over to the Providence Regular Baptist Church and placed behind the pulpit. All that night the church lights burned and the people stayed and prayed.

The parents spent the night at the church.

"This is his last night," Little Duck's mother explained.

The funeral was at 10 o'clock Saturday morning, and the people began to arrive early. They came from the dozens of hollows and small communities in Letcher, Knot, and Perry counties. Some came back from other states. They filled the pews and then filled the aisle with folding chairs. Those who could not crowd inside gathered outside the door or listened beneath the windows.

The sermon was delivered by the Rev. Archie Everage, pastor at Montgomery Baptist Church, which is on Montgomery Creek near Hindman. On the last Sunday that he was home alive, Little Duck attended services there.

The service began with a solo, "Beneath the Sunset," sung by a young girl with a clear bell-like voice; then there were hymns from the church choir.

Mr. Everage, who had been a friend of Little Duck, had difficulty in keeping his voice from breaking as he got into his final tribute. He spoke of the honor Little Duck had brought to his family, his courage and his dedication. He spoke of Little Duck "following the colors of his country." He said Little Duck died "for a cause for which many of our forefathers fought and died."

The phrase touched off a fresh wail of sobs to fill the church. Many mountain people take great pride in their men who "follow the colors." It is a tradition that goes back to October 1780, when a lightly regarded band of mountaineers handed disciplined British troops a historic defeat at Kings Mountain in South Carolina and turned the tide of the Revolutionary War.

Shortly before Little Duck was hit in Vietnam, he had written two letters intended for his wife. Actually the soldier was writing a part of his own funeral. Mr. Everage read from one letter:

"Honey, they put me in a company right down on the Delta. From what everybody says that is a rough place, but I've been praying hard for the Lord to help me and take care of me so really I'm not too scared or worried. I think if He wants it to be my time to go that I'm prepared for it. Honey, you don't know really when you are going to face something like this, but I want you to be a good girl and try to live a good life. For if I had things to do over I would have already been prepared for something like this. I guess you are wondering why I'm telling you this, but you don't know how hard it's been on me in just a short time. But listen here, if anything happens to me, all I want is for you to live right, and then I'll get to see you again."

And from another letter:

"Honey, listen, if anything happens to me I want you to know that I love you very very much and I want you to keep seeing my family the rest of their lives and I want you to know you are a wonderful wife and that I'm very proud of you. If anything happens I want Big Duck and Betty Jo to know I loved them very much. If anything happens also tell them not to worry, that I'm prepared for it."

The service lasted two hours and ended only after scores of people, of all ages, filed past the coffin.

Then they took Little Duck to Resthaven Cemetery up on a hill in Perry County. The Army provided six pallbearers, five of whom had served in Vietnam. There was a seven-man firing squad to fire the traditional three volleys over the grave and a bugler to sound taps.

The pallbearers, crisp and polished in summer tans, folded the flag from the coffin and Sgt. Ritter handed it to the young widow, who had wept so much, but spoken so little, during the past three days.

Then the soldier's widow knelt beside the casket and said softly, "Oh, Little Duck."

Then they buried Little Duck beneath a bit of the land he died for.

*Credit:* © 1968 The Courier-Journal. Reprinted with permission.

## AN ANONYMOUS REPORT: FACES OF AMERICAN DEAD IN VIETNAM—ONE WEEK'S TOLL

*Department of Defense archives recorded 58,152 U.S. servicemen and women who died in the Vietnam War and 153,303 who were wounded seriously enough to be hospitalized, for a total of 211,455 casualties, or one in every ten Americans who served in the war. These records do not include casualties of civil aid workers and journalists or deaths and incapacitation caused by illness. The army suffered the greatest number of casualties with 134,982 killed or wounded (64 percent of all casualties), but the marines' 66,227 killed and wounded represented the highest casualty rate for a service branch, 25 percent. Of course, numbers do not tell the whole story.*

*When Defense Secretary Robert S. McNamara finished his whirlwind inspection tour of South Vietnam in 1962, United Press correspondent Neil Sheehan asked, "Mr. Secretary, how can you be so optimistic when you've been here such a short time?" "Every quantitative measure we have shows that we're winning this war," McNamara said. Like McNamara's previous job as president of Ford Motor Company, he managed U.S. war policy by the numbers. The generals confidently pursued the attrition strategy: Wield superior technology to eliminate enemy soldiers faster than they can be replaced. It appealed to the American sense of competition. Whoever tallies the highest number of casualties at the end of the day wins. The television networks liked the sports metaphor; it was precise and direct. Popular National Broadcasting Company news anchor Chet Huntley referred to the war's casualty totals as the daily "score." Quantification also had the advantage of trivializing the war's cost in human misery. The dead and wounded were reduced to digits that rendered anonymous the suffering and spent futures of U.S. servicemen and women. Numbers played better in the news media than did faces.*

*The way to bring home the cost of the war was to turn the numbers into faces. This idea of* Life *magazine writer Loudon Wainwright inspired a cover story for the magazine that had more influence on the American public than any other piece of print journalism during the course of the war. Editor in chief Ralph Graves approved Wainwright's idea. They would present photographs of American deaths from one week in the war without commentary. The faces would speak for themselves. It was the perfect way to make a statement against the war without confronting the government.*

*The* Life *editors chose the week of 28 May–3 June 1969, selected because it included Memorial Day. Of the 242 names released by the Pentagon, they got families' permissions and located pictures— service photographs, high-school yearbook poses and casual snapshots—for all but twenty-five of the deceased, who were named. The solders' faces showed youth, optimism, and naïveté. The same understated but powerful imagery adorned the magazine's cover—an enlargement of one soldier's face (William C. Gearing Jr., U.S. Army SP5, Rochester, New York) behind the headline and familiar "LIFE" logotype. Two adjoining pages from this 27 June 1969 feature are reproduced in the photo essay for this section.*

## NOTES

1. David Halberstam, *The Powers That Be* (New York: Dell Publishing, 1979), 676.

2. Arnold Barnett, Timothy Stanley, and Michael Shore, "America's Vietnam Casualities: Victims of a Class War?" *Massachusetts Institute of Technology Operation Research* 40, no. 5 (September–October 1992), 856–866.

## FURTHER READINGS

Duncan, Donald. *The New Legions.* New York: Random House, 1967.

Landers, James. *Weekly War: Newsmagazines and Vietnam.* Columbia: University of Missouri Press, 2004.

Steinman, Ron. *The Soldiers' Story: Vietnam in Their Own Words.* New York: Barnes and Noble, 2000.

# 19

# THE ARVN (ARMY OF SOUTH VIETNAM)

The United States created the Army of the Republic of Vietnam (ARVN, pronounced "Arvin" by the Americans) to thwart the Communist menace in Southeast Asia. Like Jekyll and Hyde, the ARVN and the Vietcong were two sides of the same apparition—the Vietnamese peasant of fighting age. From the American perspective, the ARVN represented the side of right and light. Equipped with the latest U.S. weapons and backed by U.S. firepower, the ARVN's battalions ruled the countryside during the daylight hours. The dark side, the Vietcong, owned the countryside at night and ruled the jungle at all times. The Vietnamese were naturally afraid of the night and of the jungle, so the Vietcong trained its soldiers to control their fears, to make the night and the jungle their allies. The Vietcong had a daunting reputation for ferocious, even desperate, determination; like a wild beast, the Vietcong fought tenaciously when trapped, so ARVN commanders rarely failed to leave their adversaries an avenue of escape. By avoiding direct confrontation with the Vietcong, the ARVN gradually came to believe in its own inferiority.

Despite the ARVN's low reputation, the U.S. military advisors liked and respected the ARVN soldiers. The Americans admired their Asian comrades' bravery under fire (when commanded effectively), their stoic handling of pain, and their physical strength and inurement to the labor of rural life. The Vietamese peasant was slight of build but wiry and enjoyed a substantial diet by Asian standards. The American weapons and uniforms were too big and heavy for their small, slender frames and hid their individual strength from the casual observer. The U.S. advisors who lived and fought with the ARVN knew that they were strong and wanted to help them win the war.

The ARVN's handicap was not its soldiers but its leadership. The central government was controlled by unpopular dictators who feared military coups d'état and maneuvered to replace skilled, energetic military officers, who might challenge them, with sycophantic lackeys. The remaining ARVN generals and colonels who might have been aggressive by nature soon learned to avoid confronting the Vietcong in firefights, losses from which might compromise their units' readiness to come to the aid of Saigon. The punishment for taking casualties was demotion in rank, retribution visited on the officer's family, or worse. Such was the ARVN, the ally that the United States created in its own image, goaded into action, and then abandoned in Southeast Asia.

## MAYNARD PARKER: AMERICAN ASSESSMENT OF THE ARVN AT WAR

*In July 1969, President Nixon announced that Americans had carried the South Vietnamese long enough. Now, after a transition, the ARVN would have to do its own fighting. Most American soldiers greeted this news with disbelief, if not derision. In light of the U.S. military's own failure to put down the Communist insurrection in South Vietnam, Americans showed considerably inappropriate condescension toward the South Vietnamese, who were cast by the following* Newsweek *article, "Baby-Sitting with ARVN," as infants in the art of war.*

*The Americans' superior attitude toward their Asian allies was ironic, given that the South Vietnamese army was in fact a creature of U.S. foreign policy. The Eisenhower administration pumped aid into a fledgling anti-Communist government in South Vietnam after the defeat and evacuation of the French in 1954. Had the Americans not supported the new southern regime of Ngo Dinh Diem, national elections scheduled for 1956 probably would have given Ho Chi Minh control in the South and reunified the partitioned country. Compounding the injustice of impending U.S. abandonment of their South Vietnamese allies was the Americans' misplaced confidence in conventional force, which proved ineffective to combat guerrillas in the jungles of Vietnam, but which nevertheless fostered a dependency on air power and technology that the ARVN could not shake.*

*Newsweek, 10 November 1969*

"President Nixon has a program to end the war in Vietnam. That program is Vietnamization." Thus once again last week did Secretary of Defense Melvin Laird underscore the Administration's hope that a re-equipped and retrained South Vietnamese Army can replace most American combat troops by the end of 1970. To date, the U.S. has turned over to the ARVN more than 700,000 M-16 rifles, 12,000 machine guns, 1,200 tanks and personnel carriers, 50,000 wheeled vehicles and 900 artillery pieces. And as part of the crash program, U.S. units have been dispatched throughout the country to help "upgrade" the ARVN's performance with its new weapons. For a firsthand look at how this plan is working, *Newsweek*'s Saigon bureau chief Maynard Parker visited the 18th ARVN Division and last week filed this report:

Headquartered in Long Khanh Province—an area known for its rubber plantations, rich forests and the Communist redoubt of War Zone D—the 18th ARVN Division sits astride one of the main infiltration routes into Saigon. But despite its strategic position, the 18th has long been regarded as one of South Vietnam's sorriest outfits, with a reputation for slackness of discipline, excessive caution in battle and a record rate of desertion. If Vietnamization is to work, it was clear to the U.S. command that sad-sack divisions like the 18th

would somehow have to be trained to do their job without the aid of American combat troops. The question of course was: how could this be done?

In the case of the 18th Division, the problem was not simply a matter of more equipment—the 18th had plenty of that as well as a full quota of U.S. military advisers. More drastic measures were needed. And so last May, Gen. Creighton Abrams, the U.S. commander, moved the U.S. 199th Light Infantry Brigade into Long Khanh Province to show the 18th by deed as well as by precept how to fight the enemy. "We are going to move the 199th in there," growled one top American general at the time, "have them crawl into bed with the 18th, and make sure they get up at reveille every damn day."

### HABITS

Getting the 18th up for reveille was, of course, only part of the task. For the 18th's units habitually stuck close to their bases and seldom sought out the enemy. In order to get the 18th out and operating, the commander of the 199th, Brig. Gen. William K. Bennett, and the 18th's newly appointed commander, Brig. Gen. Lam Quang Tho, began by carving up the area into four zones of responsibility—one for each ARVN unit. Then a U.S. battalion was "co-located" with each of them. And from these four bases, the Vietnamese and Americans began to carry out joint operations, ranging from squad-size patrols to systematic battalion-size sweeps over wide areas.

In addition, the 199th set up training platoons which gave local regional force troops instruction in such elementary subjects as ambush techniques and marksmanship. Then the Vietnamese and Americans moved out into the jungle to translate their learning into practice. The U.S. troops gave advice and made suggestions all along the line—particularly trying to reach the South Vietnamese junior officers and sergeants, whose competence as a rule has been far below that of U.S. or enemy standards. But the Americans provided more than advice. "By our being out there," says one U.S. officer, "they felt that someone cared about them and therefore their confidence was built up. And I guess they didn't want to look bad in front of us."

## POOLING

There were other ways in which the U.S. troops tried to mold the 18th into a better unit. Intelligence gathering was improved by convincing the ARVN that it should pool information with the police and regional forces instead of hoarding it. And the Americans also tried to help the commanders of the 18th solve the critical problem of desertion, which was running as high as 25 per cent. After being prodded into studying the question, the Vietnamese soon discovered that most of their deserters were young Saigon draft dodgers who had been arrested and then carted off to serve in the 18th Division. "They hardly set their feet down here before they were over the wire," commented an ARVN officer. In order to reverse this trend, the 18th mounted a major recruiting campaign to find young men in its own area who, presumably, would be more interested in defending their villages against the Communist guerrillas.

The immediate results of the U.S. tutelage have been encouraging. Since the 199th arrived in Long Khanh, the 18th's "kill ratio" has risen from five enemy soldiers for one ARVN to twelve to one. The South Vietnamese are much more confident and aggressive, and—if official spokesmen are to be believed—now control many more villages than they did before the advent of the 199th. I myself can attest that I drove from Saigon to Xuan Loc, the provincial capital of Long Khanh, and that this is something I would not have dared to do six months ago.

## CONFIDENCE

But the true test of Vietnamization—at least for the province of Long Khanh—will come when the 199th is pulled out, probably next year. For the most part, the ARVN commanders are confident that they can hold their own without U.S. troops. "There will be problems," General Tho told me, "but we can cope with them as long as we have American helicopter support." Most Americans in the area are not so confident. They are doubtful that the poor caliber of leadership in the South Vietnamese Army can be rooted out by a few months of joint operations. And almost no one I talked to believed that the 18th, even by next year, will be able effectively to take on the Viet Cong Fifth Division should it choose to reemerge from its lair in the jungles of War Zone D.

Thus, I left with the feeling that as with so many things in Vietnam, the improvement of the 18th may not be as good as it looks. True, there has been undeniable progress. But will it prove all too fragile when the crunch comes? While I was in the 18th Division headquarters, for example, the Viet Cong assassinated a hamlet chief just 2 miles away in a supposedly pacified area. And I was told that in the nearby rubber plantations, the tough Viet Cong cadres were spreading the word to their men "to lie low until the Americans leave . . . then we will see the 18th's heels." And in spite of everything, they may very well prove to be right.

---

## GLORIA EMERSON: LAMENT FOR THE ARVN AND SAIGON

---

*Gloria Emerson was a foreign correspondent for the* New York Times *from 1965 to 1972, the last two years covering the Vietnam War. Her special beat was the war's impact on civilians. Among her books written after the war are* Winners and Losers *and* War Torn.

*Emerson witnessed the ruination of Saigon by America's big war. She had been in Saigon in 1955 just as the French were leaving. When she returned in 1970, the city's lovely boulevards and Gallic promenades were overflowing with fast-food joints, black marketeers, drug peddlers, and pushy GIs. The government officials and other reporters did not like having a female journalist around, but that was their problem. She could not help feeling guilt for what her brethren had done to that city and its people. Had the Saigon press corps served any noble or even useful purpose in covering the war, or had it simply been part of the leviathan that "Americanized" the city beyond recognition? Emerson's doubt, regret, and nostalgia come through in the following doleful lament for the ARVN, which collapsed before the North Vietnamese juggernaut in the spring of 1975. Emerson's piece was titled, "A Gift from ARVN: For What We Have Received, We Can Never Be Truly Grateful."*

*Esquire*, November 1975

Gloria Emerson, who spent two years in Vietnam for *The New York Times*, is writing a book on the effects of the war on America. Photographed by Denis Cameron.

It was supposed to be a war memorial, but some Vietnamese believed it was human while others said it was a gentle ghost who could not rest. The memorial was a thirteen-foot concrete statue of a Vietnamese infantryman, resting, a rifle across his knees. He was ARVN, as the Americans called both the South Vietnamese Army and its soldiers. It was a statue of a spent and haunted man; its name was Sorrow. The figure was put up at the end of 1966, below the entrance to the Vietnamese national military cemetery close to the Saigon–Bien Hoa highway, some twelve miles north of the capital.

There were people who swore the statue came alive: they had heard it sigh and ask for water. A Vietnamese military policeman had once seen it step off the pedestal, take off its helmet and pack, and lie down on the grass. There were villagers who believed the statue had moved at night, during the 1968 Tet offensive, to warn people of the fighting. Once, they said, the statue had stopped a twenty-vehicle convoy headed for an ambush. There were even Vietnamese who said they had seen the statue cry in the spring of 1971 when the South Vietnamese were sent into Laos to cut the Ho Chi Minh Trail and could not do it.

Once, the statue was moved from its site to be sent back to the workshop of its sculptor, Nguyen Thanh Tu, so he could recast it in bronze. Women in the neighborhood thought of the statue as a shrine. They came to see it, very quietly, placing flowers and joss sticks before it, kneeling to pray below the huge boots. The taxi driver in Saigon who drove to Mr. Tu's house was startled to see the statue again.

"I thought it ran away early this year—we heard it was lost," he said.

There is no one now who will write me if the statue can still be seen from the highway; perhaps it is lost for good, like the sad and ruined army it symbolized for so long. When the total collapse of ARVN came at last in the spring of 1975, Americans were surprised, some even outraged, as if we hoped for more. "A spectacle of cowardice, cruelty and confusion," one American journalist wrote of the South Vietnamese retreat, the last act in Vietnam.

The eyewitness reports told of soldiers who seemed to have gone insane. An American named Paul Vogle, a U.P.I. reporter who speaks Vietnamese more perfectly than any foreigner I have ever heard, was on the last plane to leave Danang. Soldiers kicked, battered and fired upon civilians trying to get aboard. There was no pity in them. Two hundred seventy people made it.

"Only two women and one baby were among them," Vogle wrote. "The rest were soldiers, the toughest of the tough, meanest of the mean. They didn't talk to each other or us. They looked at the floor."

The soldiers were men of the First Division, always considered a crack infantry unit by the American military, and this group was Hoe Bao, or Black Panthers, whose courage and spirit had never been questioned.

There were hours of madness before that Easter weekend ended. South Vietnamese troops threatened, drank, wept, pillaged, murdered; some begged French nuns for civilian clothes so they could destroy their uniforms. They fought with no one but their own. Order was restored shortly after the Communist troops arrived.

The war ended with the army, trained and paid for by the United States, taking revenge on the Vietnamese it was supposed to protect, victims finding their own victims. There had been orders to retreat. But the panic of the soldiers, the fear that led to their convulsions, did not come to them on a certain day. They were always an army without a country, an army without belief, an army that was not loved.

But, there is a great gift that ARVN, the decomposed and dishonored army, gave to the United States: the final, incontestable proof that the Vietnamization could not work for them and that it will work for no other people we might hope to guide, inspire and send into battle. Their failure may save us and free us from such illusions at last. It shocked many Americans that ARVN, the rangers, the marines and the airborne fled as they did, spreading their panic, each man thinking only of his own life. But this was always the deep infection that sickened South Vietnam; any American who lived there had to know it. The Saigon government, the generals, the politicians and the men in power in the provinces were held together by American money, not by political ideals, all of them caring only for their own separate survival.

The G.I.s in Vietnam did not much care for ARVN: too lazy, too small, too poor, too shiftless, too greedy, too eager to escape a war that had no ending for them. ARVN was always wanting: C rations, our money, our dustoffs, our gunships, our B-52s. At Fire Support Base Apollo, thirty miles north of Saigon, the Americans of the First Division—the Big Red One, they called it—made a line across the base: no Vietnamese was allowed to cross over into the American area without permission. The G.I.s wanted to stop ARVN from stealing. It was not quite clear to me what there was of value to steal: some food perhaps, an apple or a piece of bread, a paper, cup or canteen. One Vietnamese tried to explain how fortunate the Americans appeared. It did not matter that they, too, lived in bunkers.

"It is, perhaps, the ice," the Vietnamese said. "Ice is a luxury and the Americans have so much of it. Then, too, the Americans have so much water for washing and drinking, or so it seems to the Vietnamese. And they eat chicken all the time and that is important."

The Vietcong and the North Vietnamese troops did not have chicken, did not have ice. They did not have dustoffs or blood plasma or helicopters to pick them up and put them down. They did not have bombs, napalm or defoliants.

For nineteen years, Americans advised the South Vietnamese military. We gave them the M-16s and the Hueys, good helmets and good boots, a brutal inflation, artillery, jeeps, tanks, jobs as servants and clerks, more inflation, and a sense of their own helplessness. Money was all that mattered; we helped to make it so. With money, a man could stay out of the army for a little while, buy a deferment or a commission, arrange for service in the rear instead of being sent to the field, and get an early discharge. There was nothing that money could not fix; even the simplest Vietnamese understood this.

ARVN were the foot soldiers, the servants, the men who mattered to no one. When no longer useful they became the "friendly" dead and the "friendly" wounded at the briefings in Saigon for the press. Even the South Vietnamese pilots, who often had an excess of courage, were considered clowns. Once, during a huge operation, the American chopper crews made their contempt for their allies very clear. A Vietnamese major, who was chief of operations, tried to defend his men. He could not push his squadron too far, the major said. He reminded me that there was no mess hall for them, no free food, which the Americans took for granted.

"They do not have proper food. They are so poorly paid," the major said. "One of my door gunners was wounded and do you know how much money he had in his wallet? Two hundred piasters, that's all." It was less than a dollar. The door gunner was paid twenty-one dollars a month. It made the major quite sad, but there was nothing he could do.

American reporters did not, in the years before the Paris peace accords, know the other army. We could not move with the National Liberation Front or with Vietnamese units from the north fighting in the south. We only saw their soldiers when they were dead, captured or had defected. The Saigon government had a Chieu Hoi—open arms—program to entice men to switch to their side. The Americans, who thought up the idea, had high hopes for the program. One defector was a twenty-nine-year-old farmer from the delta named Le Van Day who had been in a Vietcong infantry unit for four years. We met when he was a scout for the Third Squadron of the Eleventh Armored Cavalry Regiment. He remembered what he had been taught.

"Ho Chi Minh wanted us first of all to be simple, second to be honest, third to be ready for sacrifice and fourth to stop worrying about our families," Le Van Day said.

But it was too dreadful a life, he said, too dreadful. For four years he had never set foot in one town. He was given the equivalent of seventy-four cents a month to keep. He could not bear the company commander who spoke constantly of victory even when so many of his men were killed.

"When I first joined this unit with the American Army I felt myself suddenly to be the son of a very rich family," he said. There was enough of everything: sleep, food, cigarettes, money. It seemed to astonish him still. So the Vietcong had unhappy men, too: the miracle was that so many of them endured for so long.

In the years to come, American generals and colonels will look back and wonder when the beginning of the end came. They will be wrong if they try to fix a date, but some of them might think it was in January 1975, when the capital of Phuoc Long Province fell. The North Vietnamese had T-54 tanks; the ARVN tried to stop them with American-made shoulder-fired rocket launchers. It did not stop them. An officer in Saigon later described what happened.

"We took aim on one of them, waited, waited until it was well in good range and then fired," he said. "Oh, it did not explode. It did not stop. To our amazement, the turret was moving, the big gun was pointing toward our trenches. Oh, God, we sank down to the bottom of our trenches, crawled away like rats, our mouths open in amazement." Troops, their wounded, and military doctors were among the hundreds killed when the South Vietnamese Air Force, forced to fly at altitudes of ten thousand feet because of heavy machine-gun fire, bombed their own positions. American analysts of the battle felt ARVN fired their rocket launchers at too close a range; they had to be fired at thirty feet away to destroy a tank. There were indications of uncertainty and confusion at the highest command levels, poor intelligence and fictitious reporting from the colonel who commanded the town.

It was too late to stop any of it. In the fiscal years 1973–1975, the South Vietnamese forces had $4,900,000,000 in military aid from the United States. North Vietnam had $1,570,000,000 from China and the Soviet Union.

"I won't give up! Not President Thieu!" the former head of state in Saigon said in an interview with *The Washington Post* in January. Thieu wanted $300,000,000 in emergency military aid from the U.S. Congress. And if the American people abandoned the South Vietnamese, Thieu said he knew what the people would do.

"They will fight to the last cartridge on hand," he said. But Nguyen Van Thieu knew nothing and spoke for no one. It was always that way. He did not go to Cong Hoa Hospital, the largest in South Vietnam for its own wounded, where paralyzed men lay in their own filth; he did not permit the mutilated veterans of his own army to ask for help. When they demonstrated for benefits and housing and jobs, he turned the combat police on them. They were easily moved. They had no way to defend themselves.

It had all happened before; the first defeat did not come this year. It happened other times. In 1971, in order to prove how well Vietnamization was working, the Americans sent the South Vietnamese into Laos to slash the Ho Chi Minh Trail, to cut off the supplies and troop movements of the North Vietnamese. The operation, which had American air and ground support but did not use U.S. troops in Laos, was called Lam Son 719.

There was much talk in daily briefings of thrusts and sweeps and plunges, of ARVN driving deeper, punching ahead, capturing supplies. There was always this kind of talk. In March of 1971, three battalions were lifted out. It was a rout. The survivors could often be seen straggling on Highway 9, the French-built road that ran across the border. ARVN came out of Laos like dazed men walking in their sleep, unable to find their beds. A platoon sergeant named Co had escaped by clinging to the runners of a helicopter. The South Vietnamese had stampeded the aircraft; the American crew had to kick the men back or the chopper could never have risen. There had been four hundred men in his unit, Co said, one hundred were still alive. He had never seen anything like the rush toward the chopper: the shouting, the pushing, the look on men's faces.

"Each helicopter could have been the last one, so what chance was there for me?" Co said. "Only the madmen would stay and politely wait for the next helicopter."

Corporal Ti was a marine who fought on Hill 547 in Laos. "The papers and the radio in Saigon kept on saying there was a Laos victory, I have learned now, but what a joke," he said. "We ran out like wounded dogs."

Some faces will not go away. There was Private Moc, who came out of Laos with the legs of his pants ripped off but who had never dropped his rifle. After escaping a North Vietnamese attack, he had walked for two nights and a day before being picked up in an airlift. Private Moc needed to talk; he needed to be sure he was really alive.

"The whole brigade ran down the hill like ants," he said. "We jumped on each other to get out of that place. No man had time to look for his commanding officer. It was quick, quick, quick or we would die." The private and twenty other marines moved like ghosts, fearing an ambush. After the men bumped into a North Vietnamese unit that opened fire, they scattered.

"After each firing, there were fewer and fewer of us," Private Moc said. "Nobody cared for anybody else at all."

It was an army that always wanted to go home, and now at last it can. They have been forgiven by those who beat them. There are some Americans and Vietnamese who wanted to see ARVN, and the other forces, fight to the last man, use the last bullet, hold the line, send in the sixteen-year-olds. There are always men like that, willing to have the others do the dying if it keeps them safe or proves them right. There were, of course, many South Vietnamese soldiers who did what was expected. They are the half million men who are missing or who are dead.

## FURTHER READINGS

Bui Diem and David Chanoff. *In the Jaws of History*. Boston: Houghton Mifflin, 1987.

Emerson, Gloria. *Winners and Losers: Battles, Retreats, Gains, Losses, and Ruins from a Long War*. New York: Random House, 1977.

Fawcett, Denby, Ann Bryan Mariano, Kate Webb, Anne Morrissy Merick, Jurate Kazickas, Edith Lederer, Tad Bartimus, Tracy Wood, and Laura Palmer. *War Torn: Stories of War from the Women Reporters Who Covered Vietnam*. New York: Random House, 2002.

Hirschman, Charles, Samuel Preston, and Vu Manh Loi. "Vietnamese Casualties during the American War: A New Estimate." *Population and Development Review* 21 (December 1995): 783–812.

# 20

# VIETNAMIZATION

Richard Milhous Nixon won a narrow election victory for the U.S. presidency in 1968 by promising to get the United States out of the war in Vietnam, or so his "peace with honor" stump speech was interpreted by the voters. What the voters did not know was that Nixon did not have a specific plan to end the American war and that he was not about to concede anything to the Communists.

Nixon's hard-line views on the Vietnamese conflict, rooted in the old domino theory of Communist world domination, had been published in the August 1964 issue of *Reader's Digest*:

> History shows that the appeasers, the compromisers who refuse to stand up against aggression, *have* to take a stand sooner or later—and always at a less favorable time and place. . . .
>
> The crisis [in Vietnam] is one not of competence but of *confidence*. It is a test not of power but of our capacity to use our power correctly and with courage. All that is needed, in short, is the will to win—and the courage to use our power—*now*.[1]

It was clear that Nixon would not hesitate to use U.S. power to compel the enemy to meet his terms.

He read Harvard professor Henry Kissinger's ideas about negotiating with the North Vietnamese that had been published in the January 1969 issue of *Foreign Affairs*:

> However we got into Viet Nam, whatever the judgment of our actions, ending the war honorably is essential for the peace of the world. Any other solution may unloose forces that would complicate prospects of international order. A new Administration must be given the benefit of the doubt and a chance to move toward a peace which grants the people of Viet Nam what they have so long struggled to achieve: an opportunity to work out their own destiny in their own way.[2]

Kissinger alluded to Nixon's campaign verbiage for maintaining credibility in global affairs—ending the war "with honor." The flattery won Kissinger a post in Nixon's cabinet as national security advisor.

According to public opinion polls in the spring of 1969, most Americans were willing to give Nixon time to work out his plan, but Congress, controlled by the opposition Democrats, was getting impatient. Senators who had acquiesced during Lyndon Johnson's escalation of the war were now openly demanding withdrawal. Nixon knew that he would have to show some progress soon or lose his political base. To bypass Congress and appeal directly to the public, he gave a televised address on 14 May 1969 in which he asked the people to trust him. He said, "The time has come for new alternatives."[3]

His new alternative—Vietnamization—not only was not new but also had failed twice before. The French had tried unsuccessfully to deploy Vietnamese troops to fight the Vietminh insurgents in the early 1950s. A decade later the head of the U.S. Military Assistance Command, General Paul D. Harkins, predicted that U.S. air power, armor, and artillery would enable the South Vietnamese army (ARVN) to turn the tide against the Communists, thereby permitting U.S. "advisors" to withdraw completely by 1965. Instead, political chaos in Saigon and poor leadership and corruption in its army led to near collapse of the southern regime.

Nixon planned to back up Vietnamization with other ploys: He would intimidate Hanoi with renewal of strategic bombing. He also would send Kissinger as a secret envoy to threaten use of nuclear weapons. If Hanoi remained truculent, he would offer to the Soviet Union a thaw in the cold war in exchange for its pressure on Hanoi to compromise at the bargaining table.

In July 1969, Nixon announced Vietnamization as part of a comprehensive foreign affairs policy that his publicists dubbed the "Nixon Doctrine." Henceforth, countries receiving U.S. military and economic aid would be required to do their own fighting, which would liberate the United States to project its power around the globe. It sounded good, but there was widespread doubt that the South Vietnamese would be able to sustain the conflict without American combat troops on the ground. As the ARVN gradually took over the fighting and was increasingly brutalized by the Vietcong and North Vietnamese, Vietnamization became a cynical euphemism for incompetence, defeat, and abandonment of an ally.

## PETER R. KANN: IS VIETNAMIZATION WORKING? A DRIVE THROUGH THE MEKONG DELTA

*Peter Kann was a staff reporter of the* Wall Street Journal. *Kann wondered whether President Nixon's Vietnamization policy was working and braved a car trip in the Mekong Delta area south of Saigon to see for himself. In the early years of the war, such a trip would have been considered suicidal, for the delta was the hot spot for Vietcong activity, but in the fall of 1969 the delta was a backwater of the war. Kann titled his report, "Vietnam Journey: A Long, Leisurely Drive through the Mekong Delta."*

Wall Street Journal, 10 November 1969

## VIETNAMIZATION MOVES SLOWLY
### Forces from North Dig in
### but the Roads Seem Safe
### High Comedy & Grim Tragedy

SAIGON—The war drags on. President Nixon has ruled out any quick withdrawal, and enemy attacks seem to be increasing once again. No progress is reported in Paris. But if there is no progress at the peace table, is there at least progress on the battlefield?

There isn't a clear answer. "Progress" is measured here in many ways. The Air Force computes the tonnage of bomb loads dropped. The Army tots up enemy bodies. Pacification planners neatly categorize hamlets on computerized evaluation charts. Psychological warriors conduct mini–Gallup Polls among taxi drivers. Economists plot curves on the shipments of rice. Embassy officers sip tea with Saigon legislators and seek to divine their Delphic utterances.

And still, Vietnam seems to defy analysis. The Vietnam war remains a kaleidoscopic conflict over a splintered society in a fragmented nation, and the bits of Vietnam that one man sees probably are no more typical—and no less valid—than the fragments perceived by another.

### THREE MEN IN A VW

With such thoughts in mind, three Americans recently set out in a 1954 Volkswagen on a week-long drive through the Mekong Delta, that densely populated rice bowl of Vietnam where, it has often been said, the war ultimately will be won or lost. The trip covered some 400 miles by road, with side trips on motor launches, sampans and helicopters. The route ran from Saigon southwest to Can Tho, the administrative hub of the Delta; then westward through the tranquil province of An Giang and on to Chau Doc province along the Cambodian frontier; then back through onetime Vietcong base areas of Sandec province and finally northeast back to Saigon.

The trip offers some glimpses of recent progress and of perennial problems, of new threats like North Vietnamese battalions and of more esoteric dangers like a nine-nostriled water monster allegedly loose in the Mekong River. The trip provides no grand conclusions, only the observation that three unarmed Americans were able to spend a week driving through rural Vietnam without being shot at. That, perhaps, is progress.

Scenically, the Delta is both beautiful and boring, a lush green blanket of marshy rice paddies stretching to the horizon. The flat monotony sporadically is broken by small mounds of earth encasing tombs, by narrow belts of palm trees and by the small clusters of thatch houses that constitute Vietnamese hamlets. Less frequently, one passes larger villages, usually with an aluminum-roofed schoolhouse (courtesy of U.S. aid), a pastel pagoda and a bustling marketplace crammed with delicacies like river eel and skinned paddy rat. Crisscrossing this landscape at intervals of every few miles are the French-built canals, which, far more than the potholed roads, serve as the Delta's economic lifelines.

Despite the war, there is an overwhelming sense of peacefulness and prosperity about the Delta. The Delta has a way of enveloping, almost swallowing up, the war. Conflict seems to encroach upon the peaceful Delta setting only as isolated incidents—here a Vietcong raid on a mud-walled militia outpost, there a string of U.S. helicopters swooping down to strafe a tree line. Unlike the dusty plateaus and jagged hills of the northern areas, the placid green Delta seems unsuited to a war.

The Delta traditionally has been an area of "low profile" U.S. involvement, with Americans serving only to advise and support Vietnamese troops in a slow-paced struggle against locally recruited Vietcong. In mid-1968, this pattern was jarred when the U.S. Ninth Division moved into the upper Delta, chalking up staggering (some skeptics say unbelievable) Vietcong body counts. Then, this past summer, the Ninth was shipped home as the first installment on President Nixon's troop-withdrawal promise.

### ON TO CAN THO

Wherever two or more American officials gather together these days the talk is of "Vietnamization," the turning over of a greater share of the war burden to the Vietnamese. So it goes in Can Tho, the Delta administrative center, where visitors can be briefed on everything from Vietnamese adaption to the M-16 automatic rifle to Vietnamese receptivity to participatory democracy. The prevailing new theme is sounded by Maj. Gen. Roderick Wetherill, ranking American in the Delta, who says: "The Vietnamese have just about everything we can give them. Now it's up to them, and we're confident they can hack it."

But if the talk of Can Tho is Vietnamization, the visible evidence still bespeaks Americanization. The massive USO building near the center of town has just unveiled a new barbecue pit, dedicated with military honors. Down the street is the even busier Hollywood Bar where GIs can buy "Saigon tea" from miniskirted, de-Vietnamized girls. Nearby is Palm Springs, a Hawaiian-style enclave for U.S. civilian advisers on everything from hog raising to intelligence gathering. Like the American military compound across town, Palm Springs boasts a well-chlorinated swimming pool.

Driving west out of Can Tho you pass several miles of impressive testament to American logistical capabilities: An airbase, warehouses, storage depots, helicopter fleets, truck yards, a naval support base, [and] office buildings for civilian contractors. Scores of American trucks and Jeeps clog the narrow road. A giant American road grader rumbles along, its treads cracking the pavement of this road even as it heads off to build a new road somewhere else. For perhaps five miles the Vietnamese are visibly represented only by a few militiamen rooting through the American tin cans on a roadside garbage heap.

## A PAPER WAR IN AN GIANG

A few miles farther on, the rural Delta reemerges, and the view once again is of small boys draped over the backs of water buffalo, which are wallowing in the wet green paddies. A two-hour drive over relatively smooth road (potholes no deeper than six inches) brings you into An Giang province, heartland of the Hoa Hao religious sect. This sect's militant anti-Communism (the result of the sect's founding father's having been decapitated by the Viet Minh) makes An Giang the most pacified province in Vietnam.

Indeed, the senior American adviser in An Giang, an Agency for International Development official named Bill Small, sleeps alone in an unguarded house on the outskirts of the province capital. (He's considerably more confident than the several dozen U.S. military advisers working under him; they live in a well-armed, walled compound defended by a platoon of Vietnamese militiamen, a minor incongruity in light of the American priority program to get Vietnamese troops off static defense.)

Mr. Small has been seeking to reduce the U.S. advisory presence in An Giang, but with limited success. One problem: The An Giang advisory team is required to file 144 separate reports to Can Tho and Saigon every month, and many Americans are needed here just to fight this paper war. Another problem is the "adviser cult" that has developed among Government of Vietnam (GVN) officials. "To rate a U.S. adviser means status to a Vietnamese. To be Vietnamized out of your adviser is to lose much face," explains a young American.

With Mr. Small, the American visitors board an outboard motor launch for a spin through An Giang's inland waterways. There's a stop in a Cho Moi district capital where Lt. Col. Nguyen Quang Hanh, the urbane district chief who holds a French passport and has a son studying in Paris, welcomes visitors to his office, its walls gaily decorated with red, yellow and green paper flowers of the sort associated with the Eugene McCarthy campaign [for U.S. president in 1968].

## THE NINE-NOSTRILED SNAKE

Breaking out a sealed bottle of Chivas Regal shortly before 10 a.m., Lt. Col. Hanh volunteers the view that because of the death of Ho Chi Minh, the war will be over by the end of this year. "There will be a couple of months of power struggle in Hanoi and then the war will end, militarily and politically, end completely," he says with absolute assurance.

Cho Moi district has been peaceful recently—except for the appearance several months ago of the nine-nostriled water snake. The snake is said to have been raised by a Cho Moi necromancer who let it loose in the Tien Giang River. The snake rapidly grew to a length of 15 feet, and it is rumored recently to have gobbled up an old fisherwoman. Reports on the river monster have circulated as far as Saigon. To many Vietnamese, magic and monsters remain far more interesting subjects than politics and war.

Taking a shortcut down a network of narrow canals, the motorboat runs afoul of some floating weeds and the engine jams in reverse. Luckily there's a Vietnamese Popular Force (PF) militia outpost nearby, and the boat backs over for assistance.

It's a fairly typical PF outpost, thick mud walls built around a tin-roofed shack in which the 12 PF soldiers and their families all live together. Startled by this surprise mid-afternoon visit, the PF scurry off to locate their new M-16s, to strap on ammunition belts and to don their steel helmets (most of which had been put to use collecting rainwater).

The PF return and try to look vigilant. One is asked if the outpost has had any contact with the Vietcong. "Oh, yes." When was the most recent contact? "The VC fired a mortar at us two years ago." (To be a PF in An Giang province is to be a lucky PF. In less secure provinces, the PF take heavier casualties than any other allied unit.)

The outpost is hardly equipped to handle motor repairs, and so, to the delight of laughing PF lining the mud walls, the Americans begin backing their way home. Pride is forgotten soon enough, and the costly American speedboat is strapped to the side of a Vietnamese sampan with a tiny put-put engine and is towed on home.

## A DRIVE TO THE "WILD WEST"

The next morning's drive brings the Americans into Chau Doc province, which has a common border of nearly 50 miles with Cambodia. Chau Doc often is called Vietnam's "Wild West" because it was one of the last Vietnamese frontier areas to be settled and because it has a tradition of professional banditry, smuggling and general lawlessness that predated the present war and no doubt will continue long after it is over.

Cambodia and South Vietnam have no diplomatic or legalized trade relations, but there is a considerable cross-border commerce greased by bribes to Vietnamese, Cambodian and Vietcong officials. At the small village of Nui Sam, some 50 beef cattle are milling and mooing as local merchants negotiate sales with Saigon buyers. The cows have recently been smuggled into Chau Doc from Cambodia through a complex procedure involving cross-border communication by coded message and Indian-style smoke signals.

At Nui Sam's only soup kitchen–coffee house, one can watch the last coats of grease being applied to the cattle-smuggling operation. The Cambodians and Vietcong already have been paid off. The GVN district chief at the border crossing point has pocketed 200 piasters ($1.60) per head (enough money so that after three months in his lucrative job he is said to have built new homes in Chau Doc, Saigon and the seaside resort of Vung Tau).

In the soup kitchen, official papers now are being drawn up

for the approval of the local GVN police chief, tax agent, economic service chief, animal husbandry representative and village chief—all of whom are accustomed to a small gratuity for their services. The room is crowded with old women clutching sheafs of paper, young clerks with stamps and chops, buyers and sellers exchanging wads of cash. Vietnamese soldiers meander among the tables cadging cigarettes. Under the tables, dogs, chickens and pigs poke around on the earthen floor looking for scraps of food. Perhaps $150,000 of business will be transacted here today. And as a result Americans and wealthy Vietnamese will continue to be able to buy beefsteak in Saigon restaurants at $10 a plate.

## "JUST HONEST SMUGGLING"

But cattle and other commercial commodities being smuggled across the border are of little concern to U.S. officials. "Hell, it's just honest smuggling," says a military officer in Chau Doc. American concern is focused on the infiltration of enemy troops and supplies across the border, and this sort of smuggling is on the rise.

In recent months, nearly two North Vietnamese regiments—up to 3,000 men—have crossed into Chau Doc from their Cambodian sanctuary. This represents the first appearance of regular North Vietnamese Army (NVA) units in the Mekong Delta and is doubly significant, and doubly dangerous, since it has occurred hard on the heels of the withdrawal of the U.S. Ninth Division. Some of the NVA troops are ensconced in cave and tunnel complexes on several of the heavily forested "Seven Sister" mountains, which dot the otherwise flat riceland of Chau Doc; others have moved south of Chau Doc into the swamp areas of the lower Delta.

There are conflicting interpretations on practically everything in Vietnam, and the NVA influx is no exception. In Saigon, some American military officers believe the Delta Vietcong have been so badly battered in the past year or so that the NVA have been called in as a "desperation move." Some U.S. diplomats think the NVA are moving in to solidify enemy control of long-time base areas in anticipation of a future cease-fire and territorial settlement. In Can Tho, senior U.S. officers suggest the NVA may move up into the eastern Delta and attempt to overrun several district capitals—a sort of "mini-Tet" campaign—and thereby score a propaganda coup.

In Chau Doc, some officials believe the NVA may break down into small units and spread across the Delta, combining with local VC forces to attack targets far more diverse and widespread than a few district capitals. "We better get over this Tet-mini-Tet psychology because I think Charlie has," says one Chau Doc officer.

In any case, whichever tack the NVA take, it likely would serve the political and psychological purpose of demonstrating South Vietnamese military vulnerability at a time of perhaps too much, too optimistic talk about Vietnamization. It could also serve to warn President Nixon that Hanoi isn't about to make American withdrawal pains any easier.

## IGNORING THE BODIES

How the NVA are infiltrating the Delta is seen next day at a small village near the border. It's 9 a.m., and a military operation is in progress. Vietnamese Regional Force (RF) troops in helmets and flak jackets are cautiously moving up a hillside just off the road. They're searching for the remnants of a Vietcong unit that in the early morning hours overran a PF outpost on the hilltop, killing four PF along with a PF wife and four children. The PF had deployed no troops to set up night ambushes outside their outpost, a move that might have intercepted the enemy attack.

Lying at the edge of the road, caked in dust and crusted blood, are a wounded PF and a little girl, her face split open by a grenade fragment. Three-wheeled Lambretta buses, packed with passengers and sacks of brown sugar smuggled from Cambodia, rattle down the road. The war-hardened passengers barely bother to glance at the wounded or at the RF troops moving up the hillside 20 yards away.

*Hanoi isn't about to make American withdrawal pains any easier.*

The significant thing about this Vietcong attack isn't the body count. The VC attack was merely one of a dozen encounters around Chau Doc province the previous night with the aim of diverting allied forces—and particularly helicopter gunships—from border surveillance to defensive support. The local VC were attracting allied attention so the NVA regulars could slip smoothly across the border. The plan succeeded: An NVA battalion crossed from Cambodia during the night, it was later learned.

American military men have long been frustrated by the sanctuary that enemy troops have in Cambodia. A helicopter flight along the Vinh Te canal, which separates Chau Doc from Cambodia, illustrates the point. A mile or two inside Cambodia are several clusters of buildings considerably larger than thatched peasant huts. "That over there is an NVA supply depot. And that one there is a VC training center," says a young American major, casual as a tourist guide.

## ON TO TRE TON

Allied military forces, of course, aren't permitted to attack enemy troops or facilities in Cambodia. This is partly to avoid angering Cambodia and forcing it actively into the war on the side of the Communists. And, while allied strikes might yield instant tactical dividends, the longer-range result likely would be to widen the scope of the war and necessitate still more U.S. troops.

The chopper swings away from the border and lands at Tre Ton, one of five district capitals of Chau Doc province. A district is the smallest military-administrative division of Vietnam, and it is the American advisory team at this level (generally four to eight men) that has the worm's eye view of how the war is going. The senior U.S. district adviser in Tre Ton is Maj. William R. Fields, an exceptionally able two-year veteran of Vietnam.

The town of Tre Ton lies in the shadow of Nui Co To, one of the dark, forbidding Seven Sister mountains. Nui Co To is both Tre Ton's most dramatic success story and one of its most persistent problems. For nearly two decades, the Vietcong dominated the mountain. Last year the allies mounted a major campaign for Nui Co To and by April of this year succeeded in capturing the enemy's vast cave and tunnel complexes. Some 250 allied troops, many of them Cambodian mercenaries working for the U.S. Special Forces, died in the campaign.

Next, the allies tried to render the caves and tunnels uninhabitable by pounding them with B-52 air strikes, by exploding tons of TNT, by trying to fill the holes with motor oil and even snakes. The rock vaults proved indestructible. Consequently, to keep the 100 or so VC who still roam the mountainsides from moving back into their former refuges, Vietnamese troops are occupied in static defense positions in the caves, a waste of much-needed mobile manpower.

An intense pacification program in hamlets at the base of Nui Co To has made modest gains. Most of these hamlets were solidly controlled by the Vietcong seven months ago but now have at least a daytime GVN presence. Driving through these hamlets one is met by sullen stares. "These people don't know yet if the GVN is here to stay or if the VC are coming back. They haven't decided which way to lean yet, but at least they're debating it for the first time," says Maj. Fields.

## HAZARDS FOR CIVILIANS

It's dusk, and along the road a thin line of peasants, many leading cows or water buffalo, is moving away from the mountainbase hamlets and toward the town of Tre Ton. These people feel reasonably secure farming their fields by day but dare not sleep in their home hamlets for fear of VC reprisals or allied artillery fire. It's a chancy business being a Vietnamese civilian in a "contested" area. This same morning, for example, two civilians had been killed by an American helicopter as they ran across a rice paddy to try and retrieve a parachute that had been used to drop a flare the night before.

Throughout the district, the most significant progress, says Maj. Fields, has been in providing village and hamlet security through the Popular Self Defense Force (PSDF) program. Begun last year, this program provides minimal training and hand-me-down weapons to the residents of villages and hamlets and thus, for the first time since the war began, permits them to defend their homes and families.

"PSDF is the single best investment ever made in this country. Most people here wouldn't support the VC if they had a reasonable choice. PSDF gives them that choice. It lets them make and defend that choice," the major says. He recounts the case of a VC tax collector who sauntered into a long-compliant village one recent night to pick up monthly tax revenues. He was nabbed by a newly formed PSDF unit and hacked to death on the spot.

While the PSDF gets rave reviews from Americans here, Vietnamese army units seem more of a mixed bag. Regular army troops (ARVN), who operate only sporadically in the district, haven't been noticeably aggressive in seeking out enemy forces on the mountains. The district's Vietnamese Regional Force companies generally operate only by day and return to static defense positions at night.

And in the critical struggle to root out the Vietcong infrastructure, it's the U.S.-controlled Provincial Reconnaissance Units (PRU) that have proved highly effective at unorthodox night strikes, while the GVN-controlled National Police Field Force operates only in the late afternoon between the end of siesta and dinnertime.

Thus, here in Tre Ton, as elsewhere, the truth about the Vietnamese armed forces lies somewhere between the view of a Can Tho colonel who calls them "a bunch of real little tigers" and the opinion of a Chau Doc sergeant who says "the only way to get them to move is to stick a bayonet up their rear ends."

## A SPECIAL PROBLEM

The small U.S. advisory team in Tre Ton has one domestic problem all its own. As told by Sgt. James Smith: "We had the mother of all rats living in our outhouse. That damned rat must have measured three feet long, weighed maybe 40 pounds. It flipped our big old tabby cat half way 'cross the compound. Haven't seen that cat since. Dogs were scared to go near that mother rat. We had this master sergeant visiting one time, and he went out to the outhouse at night and next thing we hear is pots flying and water splashing and old sarge comes screamin' out of that outhouse. From then on that mother rat owned that outhouse after dark. Man, that rat used to eat poison like it was bread. We finally got the mother, but it took enough poison to kill a couple of cows."

If U.S. advisers at the district level get thoroughly involved in both the mundane and arcane aspects of Vietnamese life, there are other American units that could profit by a bit more contact with the Vietnamese.

For example, back in Chau Phu, capital of Chau Doc province, the U.S. Navy, which helps patrol the Delta's rivers and canals, has arranged a demonstration of military gadgetry to impress the Vietnamese province chief. The gadget is an MSD (mine sweeper drone), an unmanned, remote-controlled, armor-plated boat about 15 feet long. Directed by radio waves from a black control box, the MSD can drag a chain across waterways to cut enemy mines. ("We could also use it to ram and explode enemy sampans, but that would get pretty expensive," says a Navy officer. An MSD costs about $45,000, he adds.)

The province chief and entourage are welcomed aboard a U.S. Navy patrol boat by a natty USN lieutenant commander and his well-starched staff. The black control box is unveiled and the MSD is made to loop, circle, turn right-angle corners and zigzag back and forth across the river. The province chief, a worldly colonel who has spent the better part of three years studying in the U.S., including a term at the National War College, and who consequently speaks fluent English, is in excellent humor. At least he is until the lieutenant commander calls on a young U.S. seaman to explain the MSD controls.

## LOOK, LOOK, LOOK

"You see boat. Hard work boat. Boat go far away. No good. Boat go quick quick. Good. Stop boat push button. Box make stop go. Make boat go. Quick quick. Same same other boat no men . . ." rattles off the proud young seaman in flawless pidgin English of the sort that snows Vietnamese bargirls but not Vietnamese colonels. The innocent U.S. Navy officers smile on happily. The province chief manages a forced smile. And so ends the U.S. Navy's public relations program for this particular day.

The return trip to Saigon is remarkably uneventful, interesting only in that the road through Sandec province is now considered reasonably safe whereas ten months ago it assuredly was not. At mid-afternoon, nearing Saigon, the Americans drive past three companies of regular ARVN soldiers, accompanied by armored personnel carriers, marching down the middle of the road—hardly the place to locate and engage enemy forces. "Maybe it's a parade," murmurs an optimist.

It's nightfall, and the dusty Volkswagen rolls into downtown Saigon. At the city's busiest intersection, directly in front of the colonnaded National Assembly Building, a beefy American construction worker in a gray Chevrolet collides with two Vietnamese soldiers on a Honda who are trying to run a red light.

The American rolls up his windows and accelerates, dragging along the battered Honda that has hooked on the Chevy bumper. The two Vietnamese soldiers give chase. They run alongside the moving car, pounding on the windshield and screaming "dirty American bastard! Stinking American son of a bitch!"

Saigon's normal assemblage of dirty picture peddlers, sidewalk moneychangers, barhopping GIs, prostitutes, pickpockets and beggars go on blissfully about their business. Home again.

## GARY SHEPARD: GI INTERVIEWS: "POT-SMOKING AT FIREBASE ARES"

*During the Vietnamization phase of the war, U.S. forces in Vietnam were relegated to defense, while the ARVN took over the offense, a flip-flop of their previous roles. The boredom of garrison duties, combined with doubts about their new mission, hurt morale among the American soldiers and caused an epidemic of hallucinogenic drug use. Commanding officers disregarded the trend, but the U.S. news media raised an alarm. Government officials claimed that the news stories exaggerated the situation and that combat readiness had not been affected in the incidents reported. However, when the following filmed interview of pot-smoking GIs was shown on the CBS Evening News, the seriousness of the problem seemed irrefutable. Trying to control the damage, the Pentagon charged that reporter Gary Shepard had staged the event, but a MACV investigation revealed that the officer who had been assigned to accompany Shepard and might have gagged the soldiers had gone off to another duty. The Pentagon acknowledged that drug abuse was a problem in the military, just as it was in American society.*

*CBS Evening News with Walter Cronkite*, 13 November 1970

WALTER CRONKITE: Good evening. Congressional investigators say the problem is skyrocketing away from any solution. Army authorities acknowledge that the crisis is real, and they're going all out to cope with it. Both groups are talking about marijuana, and the extent to which American servicemen are using the drug in Vietnam, as the war fades away for them. You will see for yourselves this evening, in this graphic report from Gary Shepard.

SHEPARD: This is Fire Support Base Ares, a small clearing in the jungles of War Zone D, 50 miles northeast of Saigon. Like most American installations, Fire Base Ares isn't very busy these days. The war is at its lowest level in five years, and there just isn't much to do. The big guns, which normally would be firing around the clock if the war were raging, now remain silent most of the day and the men have a lot of time on their hands—time for such former luxuries as haircuts, and games of volleyball, and even occasional live entertainment by the First Cavalry Division Band during a leisurely noon-hour lunch break. Time also for a trip to a muddy swimming hole less than two hundred yards from the fire base perimeter. But in this case, the trip is more than a mere stroll through the jungle. Most of these soldiers are about to turn on with marijuana.

SOLDIER: Orangutan, get your hair cut.

SHEPARD: Grass is as plentiful in Vietnam as C-rations. One pipeful, which the soldiers call a bowl, can easily take care of five or six men. Marijuana cigarettes are just as easy to get, and just as potent. This man is a medic assigned to the First Cavalry Division's First Battalion, 12th Cavalry.

The stuff smells pretty strong.

MEDIC: It is. It's really nice stuff over here.

SHEPARD: How often do you come down here?

MEDIC: I make it down here maybe twice a day. Sometimes in the morning I'll come down here, sometimes in the afternoon. Then we really get it on in the evening, up there at the fire base.

SHEPARD: Aren't you worried about maybe getting attacked and not being able to react properly?

MEDIC: No, nobody usually seems to worry. That's about the last thing that [unintelligible] worried about. We're worried—more worried about lifers. I think we're—we're constantly on guard for lifers when we smoke.

SHEPARD: Who are the lifers?

MEDIC: Colonel, Major, our CO, E-6 and above.

SHEPARD: The career guys.

MEDIC: The career guys. They're usually down on it. But actually, there's not too many guys that are down on it. Even—especially on the fire base. Out in the bush it's a little different, but you get on the firebase and there's not too many guys that are really down on it.

SOLDIER: Somebody give me some illumination. Dig it. That's cool to mix.

SOLDIER: Aw, come on, man. Don't want to light, man. Try it with yours.

SOLDIER: Try it with yours.

SOLDIER: These Army issue lighters, something, man?

SOLDIER: It ain't even lit, is it?

SOLDIER: Yeah, lit; it's lit. Only TT. Needs some. There it is, man. You owe it to yourself.

SHEPARD: You were telling me about a special way you do it.

SOLDIER: Oh, Ralph? Good old Ralph. Ralph's this shotgun this guy carries. And you empty it out and you stick the bowl in the barrel, blow into the bowl, and when it comes out, you get really stoned. Then, you know, like who cares about the war?

SOLDIER: This war.

SHEPARD: Do that very often?

SOLDIER: Whenever Vito's around.

SHEPARD: Vito is a 20-year-old draftee from Philadelphia. A photographer before he entered the Army, Vito is now a squad leader, responsible for the lives of a dozen men.

What's that you got there?

SOLDIER: This is—this is what they were telling you about, Ralph. This is what—well, we use it for also, you know, killing gooks and all, plus little added pleasures, it's really—well, shotgun. It's you know, the term means . . .

SOLDIER: Wild chickens. (Indistinct)

SHEPARD: How does Ralph work?

SOLDIER: Well, to (indistinct). Works real good. What we basically use it for on the LC, and I guess even out in the field, too, if you want to know, is that we use it to shotgun, from a bowl, you know. You just put the bowl in the chamber and all. Give me a bowl.

SOLDIER: (Indistinct) you got to blow real hard and (indistinct).

SOLDIER: I don't think this one's going to work. Where's the other one? We got another one around here. Paul, let me borrow that bowl for a minute. This is—this is probably all seeds and we're getting busted, but I don't care.

SOLDIER: Shotgun.

SHEPARD: Fire Base Ares is not unique. What's happening here is also happening, to some extent, at virtually every other American installation in Vietnam. Recent surveys estimate that well over 50 percent of the soldiers in Vietnam use marijuana.

SOLDIER: That's my good buddy, Sam.

SHEPARD: Gary Shepard, CBS NEWS, in War Zone D.

*Credit:* Reprinted with permission of the CBS News Archives.

## NOTES

1. Richard M. Nixon, "Needed in Vietnam: The Will to Win," *Reader's Digest*, August 1964, 43.

2. Henry Kissinger, "The Viet Nam Negotiations," *Foreign Affairs*, January 1969, 234.

3. Richard Nixon, "Address to the Nation on Vietnam, May 14, 1969" (Yorba Linda, Calif.: Richard Nixon Library and Birthplace), http://www.nixonlibrary.org/Research_Center/1969_pdf_files/1969_0195.pdf.

## FURTHER READINGS

Fitzgerald, Frances. *Fire in the Lake: The Vietnamese and the Americans in Vietnam.* Boston: Little, Brown, 1972.

Nguyen Cao Ky. *Twenty Years and Twenty Days.* New York: Stein and Day, 1976.

Stone, Robert. *Dog Soldiers.* Boston: Houghton Mifflin, 1974.

# 21

# MUTINY OF ALPHA COMPANY, 24 AUGUST 1969

Amid the U.S. military's miscalculations and frustrations during the Vietnam War, desertion of duty was the one cardinal sin that could not be tolerated. It was not for the grunts to question their orders, or else the whole effort would collapse. Though not widespread or debilitating, several desertions marred the record of U.S. infantrymen in Vietnam. The first desertion shocked the American public. The others that followed were swallowed up in the post-Tet malaise.

On 12 August 1969, a helicopter crashed during enemy attacks on a U.S. firebase in the Song Chang Valley 50 miles south of Danang. Among the eight persons killed in the crash were the firebase's battalion commander, Lieutenant Colonel Eli P. Howard, and Associated Press photographer Oliver Noonan. The replacement battalion commander ordered an all-out effort to reach the crash site. After five days of heavy fighting, in which the 109-man company sustained thirty casualties, the GIs of the battalion's Alpha Company refused to go on the sixth day.

Associated Press photographer Horst Faas overheard Alpha Company's commander, Lieutenant Eugene Shurtz Jr., radio his superior for instructions. Faas relayed the conversation to his partner, Peter Arnett, who put it on the AP wire. Alpha Company eventually yielded to cajoling from Sergeant Okey Blankenship, a battle-wise veteran who knew how to "press the men's buttons." Arnett gave Faas lead authorship of the day's final dispatch.

In a now familiar pattern, the controversial news story immediately became grist for the mills of newspaper columnists, and their columns in turn sparked a defensive response from Military Assistance Command, Vietnam (MACV), in Saigon and follow-up coverage by the elite press and television networks. MACV made Shurtz and Blankenship available at the base to the press and spun their contention that only five soldiers had mutinied, not the whole company. The men firmly asserted that they all had gone out and that "morale was at rock bottom." Television commentators debated on air whether the entire U.S. mission in Saigon was infected with poor morale. As usual, some editorialists blamed the press for stirring up a hornet's nest. All soldiers complain, they said, up to the moment they grab their rifles and fight. In their view, that was all that Alpha Company had done. Veteran Vietnam War correspondent Neil Sheehan later pondered, "[T]here comes a time in some wars when the killing, or just the manner of dying, appears so senseless that even the obedient soldier who is 'not to reason why' begins to question the meaning of his sacrifice. Perhaps that time has come in Vietnam."[1] (Sheehan's complete article appears in Chapter 16.)

## HORST FAAS AND PETER ARNETT: OLD VET TALKS TIRED GIS OF ALPHA COMPANY BACK INTO VIETNAM WAR

*Following is Faas's and Arnett's AP wire story that sparked the controversy about the mutiny of Alpha Company.*

### Chicago Tribune, 26 August 1969

Song Chang Valley, Viet Nam, Aug. 25 (AP)—"Do they know what it means to disobey orders under fire?" the officer asked.

The men of A company knew. Still they refused to go once again down that jungled rocky slope where unseen North Vietnamese had waited in bunkers and trenches.

The ranks of A company of the 196th infantry brigade's battle-worn 3rd battalion were riddled. The men were exhausted, their uniforms ripped and caked with dirt.

#### WON'T DO IT AGAIN

They had made the push down the slope of Nui Lon mountain repeatedly for five days. Each time the enemy survived a rain of bombs and artillery shells and picked them off in a deadly crossfire at close range. Those who remained decided they would not do it again.

"I am sorry, sir, but my men refuse to go: we cannot move out," Lt. Eugene Shurtz, Jr., reported to his battalion commander over a crackling field telephone. That was when Lt. Col. Robert C. Bacon asked if they knew the penalty for disobeying orders.

The lieutenant said they did, "but some of them have simply had enough. They are broken. There are boys here who have only 90 days left in Viet Nam. The situation is psychic here. Most of our squad and platoon leaders have been killed or wounded. We've got a leadership problem."

#### KILLED IN CRASH

Bacon had taken over the battalion after Lt. Col. Eli P. Howard was killed in a helicopter crash with Oliver Noonan, Associated Press photographer, and six other men. The battalion had been trying to reach the wreckage ever since the crash last Tuesday.

The colonel said he was certain the enemy had moved on, that there was no danger. He told Shurtz to order his men out once more. Again they refused. Then Bacon sent one of his seasoned Viet Nam veterans—Sgt. Okey Blankenship of Panther, W. Va.—to "give them a pep talk and a kick in the butt."

Blankenship found them bearded and beaten, crouched in the tall, blackened elephant grass, one of them crying.

#### SICK OF FIGHTING

They said they were sick of the endless fighting and heat, firefights by day and mortar shells at night, no sleep, no mail, no hot food, none of the little things that made war bearable. The sergeant saw youngsters of 19 and 20 with fear in their eyes.

Blankenship's temper flared and he began to argue. "One of them yelled to me that his company had suffered too much," Blankenship recalled. "I said another company was down to 15 men and still on the move—lied to him. I said maybe they have got something a little more than what you have got."

"Don't call us cowards. We're not cowards," the soldier shouted and ran toward Blankenship with his fists raised.

Blankenship turned his back and walked away.

Behind him the men began to stir. Slowly they picked up their rifles.

They followed him down the cratered slope.

*Credit*: Reprinted with permission of The Associated Press.

## AN ANONYMOUS REPORT: ALPHA COMPANY COMMANDER RELIEVED OF DUTY

*The day after Faas and Arnett broke the mutiny story, the Associated Press wired the following dispatch from information supplied by MACV, apparently in an effort to lay blame for the incident at the feet of Alpha Company's inexperienced commanding officer.*

*Chicago Tribune*, 27 August 1969

Saigon, Viet Nam, Aug. 27 [Wednesday] (AP)—The company commander who had a small anti-war revolt on his hands in the battlefield Sunday has been relieved of his job and is being transferred to a new post, his battalion commander said today.

Lt. Eugene Shurtz, Jr., 26, of Davenport, Ia., commander of Alpha company, will be given a new assignment with the 196th brigade of the American division.

The battalion commander, Lt. Col. Robert C. Bacon of Falls Church, Va., said in a telephone interview from Landing Zone Center, south of Da Nang, that he went into the field Monday morning to relieve Shurtz.

Sunday, the battle-worn and understrength Alpha company at first refused to move down the jungled, rocky slope on Nui Lon mountain into a deadly labyrinth of North Vietnamese bunkers and trench lines. The company had made the same push and had been driven back five days in a row.

But after calm persuasion by Bacon, his executive officer, Maj. Richard Waiten of Reynoldsville, Pa., and Sgt. Okey Blankenship of Panther, W. Va., the company finally moved out.

Bacon said today he had made the decision to relieve Shurtz Sunday night.

"The company wasn't responsive; it was dragging its feet. It was slow getting its gear together. I didn't think the company moved when I wanted it to. I would tell them to move out at 6 A.M. They would move out at 6:30."

Bacon said he talked to Shurtz about the company personally and "explained the situation."

At the same time Bacon relieved Shurtz, he brought with him a new company commander, Capt. Bernard F. Wolpers, a native of Germany, now a United States citizen.

Shurtz had been in Viet Nam only a month and had command of Alpha company for three weeks. Bacon took over the 3rd battalion of the 21st regiment, 196th brigade, last Thursday. His predecessor, Lt. Col. Eli P. Howard, 41, of Woodbridge, Va., was killed last Tuesday when his command helicopter was shot down.

Both Bacon and the spokesman said that in their knowledge no charges are pending against anyone.

*Credit*: Reprinted with permission of The Associated Press.

## HUGH VAN ES: REPORT SAYS ALL OF ALPHA COMPANY REFUSED TO FIGHT

*AP reporter Hugh Van Es filed the following dispatch that pitted MACV's claim that only five members of Alpha Company had refused orders against the soldiers' unanimous insistence that they all had balked at what seemed like a suicide mission.*

*Chicago Tribune*, 30 August 1969

Song Chang Valley, Viet Nam, Aug. 29 (AP)—The former commander of A company said today that only five soldiers refused to obey his order Sunday to go into combat, but some of the soldiers said the whole company rebelled.

Lt. Eugene Shurtz, Jr., 26, of Davenport, Ia., relieved of his command Monday, said five men "desired to see the inspector general rather than move with the company. . . . The remainder of the company was ready to go."

**REPORT LOW MORALE**

Interviewed in the field, a group of the soldiers said the whole company was together in refusing to obey orders after

five days of hard fighting because, as one of them put it: "Morale was at rock bottom." None of the soldiers who heard this contradicted the statement.

Some men of the company, a unit of the American division's 196th brigade, agreed that Shurtz was a good soldier and had been required to take over the company in a bad situation. He had been put in command three weeks earlier.

Shurtz also had a good word for his men when talking with reporters at Landing Zone Baldy, headquarters of the 196th brigade, where he has been reassigned as assistant personnel administrative officer. It was the first time he had talked with reporters since his removal.

## PRAISES HIS TROOPS

"All my men did go into the day's action and performed their assigned missions in an extremely professional manner," he said. "I believe company A is definitely an excellent unit, and for anyone to believe otherwise would be a slap in the face to the men who gave their lives, families and friends, those who suffered wounds and the remainder of the unit who executed their mission courageously and to the best of their ability."

The battle-worn and understrength company went into action only after the commander sent an officer and a veteran sergeant to talk to the men.

Reporters went into the field to get the company soldiers' views on Shurtz's statement that only five men were involved.

"It's probably right that there were five who said they wouldn't go," said Pfc. Fred Sanders of Aiken, S.C., a medic. "But when they stood up and said they wouldn't go, others said they wouldn't go either. I reckon it was moral support because nobody . . . we didn't want to go."

## TROOPS TELL VIEWS

Pfc. Carl Morton of Elmsford, N.Y., said: "The whole company definitely was behind the refusal. None of us thought we would withstand being pinned down another day or spend another night out there.

"So we decided somebody had to see the I.G. [inspector general]. Everybody couldn't, so those five volunteered and everybody agreed that they would represent the entire company to try to get someone out there who could do something about what was going on.

"Now they're trying to say that only those five men were ones that wanted to refuse. The whole company was not ready to move out."

Sanders explained this was why the company refused to obey the order: "Everybody was afraid we'd get somebody more killed and wounded. I felt we should wait for more support. We didn't know what they [the enemy] had out there."

## FEARED SAME MISTAKE

Pointing out that the company had been repulsed repeatedly in attacks on enemy bunkers, Sanders said: "We thought we'd be making the same mistake twice. Everyone was scared. It was not a matter of discipline."

Shurtz was asked if the company's refusal to obey his order was failure of his leadership. "No, I think it just stemmed from fear," he replied.

Pfc. Morton agreed, saying: "Fear? Yes. We'd all been thru it quite a bit. It was a green company and most of us had not seen the hard-core NVA [North Vietnamese] troops in any kind of numbers. Everyone knew we didn't have the numbers to stay out in the field much longer."

## INEXPERIENCE IS CITED

One of the five mentioned by Shurtz, who declined to give his name, said inexperience was a factor.

"That is the whole problem," he said. "I wouldn't say that he [Shurtz] was an inefficient lieutenant. The best of captains would have a rough time. He just wasn't equipped to handle the situation."

Added Pfc. Sanders: "I wish he had been able to take over the company in a better situation, a more normal situation, and been able to get the company under way. He was brought in right in the middle of the operation. Most of us knew more about what was going on than he did."

Asked about A company's morale now, Capt. Bernard F. Wolpers, the new commander, replied: "It is just as good as any company in Viet Nam. As a matter of fact, it is rather high right now. I didn't find it too much down. It's something that came up on the spur of the moment and nothing that would last."

Company A's soldiers said no disciplinary action had been taken against them, and Shurtz said he had recommended none. Lt. Col. Robert C. Bacon of Falls Church, Va., the battalion commander, relieved Shurtz, saying he was not satisfied with the company's progress and Shurtz lacked experience.

*Credit*: Reprinted with permission of The Associated Press.

## NOTE

1. Neil Sheehan, "Letters from Hamburger Hill," *Harper's*, November 1969, 40.

## FURTHER READINGS

Donovan, David. *Once a Warrior King: Memories of a Vietnam Officer*. New York: McGraw-Hill, 1985.

Laurence, John. *Cat from Hué: A Vietnam War Story*. New York: Public Affairs, 2002.

McDonough, James R. *Platoon Leader*. New York: Bantam Books, 1986.

# 22

# MYLAI MASSACRE, 16 MARCH 1968

Mylai was the one news story of the Vietnam War that crystallized for a generation of Americans their country's fall from grace. As the man who broke the story said, "Americans simply did not believe such things went on in America."[1] The details of the massacre are laid out in the news stories presented in this chapter. Seymour Hersh's initial report was published by newspapers nationwide on 13 November 1969, twenty months after U.S. GIs slaughtered 501 Vietnamese peasants in a hamlet called Mylai 4, part of the Songmy collection of hamlets 6 miles northeast of the provincial capital of Quangngai. Long dominated by the Communists, the area had been nicknamed "Pinkville" by the Americans. Three platoons on a search-and-destroy mission entered Mylai on 16 March 1968. Many soldiers participated in the subsequent atrocities, but the army charged only one man with murder: Lieutenant William L. Calley Jr.

"[T]hey're trying to burn me," Calley later said as he faced trial. On 29 March 1971, a military jury found Calley guilty of premeditated murder for commanding his platoon to execute 109 peasants, whose bodies were dumped in a ditch. Upon receiving the court's sentence of life in prison at hard labor, Calley responded, "I'll do my best, sir," and raised his arm in a sharp salute that said that he still believed in the system.[2]

The jury did not buy Calley's defense that he was only following orders, but President Nixon did and declared that he would review Calley's case after the courts had finished. On 20 August 1972, the commanding general at Fort Benning reduced Calley's imprisonment from life to twenty years. A later reversal of the conviction on grounds of prejudicial publicity was overturned by a higher court on 10 September 1975. By then Calley already had been granted a parole.

Other men charged in the massacre were either acquitted or had their cases dropped for lack of evidence. Of twelve officers accused of covering up the massacre, only one, Colonel Oren Henderson, went to trial, and he was released for lack of evidence. The army appeared to have taken care of its own.

It was a measure of the news media's reluctance to challenge the government's Vietnam War policy that it participated in the cover-up. "I instinctively knew I was not the first reporter to hear about the charge against the lieutenant, whoever he was, but I also knew I was probably one of the few who would believe," Hersh said.[3] Hersh broke the story by getting a tip, snooping around the corridors of Washington, and eventually tracking down the accused under house arrest at Fort Benning, Georgia. "I remember thinking," wrote Hersh of his cordial reception by Calley, "'This is the man who shot and killed 109 people.' Hell, he was nice."[4]

## SEYMOUR M. HERSH: OFFICER CHARGED WITH MURDERING 109 IN VIETNAM

*The following article is Seymour Hersh's scoop about the Mylai massacre. After the major media refused the story, a Washington, D.C., syndicate known as the Dispatch News Service, run by David Obst, picked up Hersh's story and sent it by collect wire to fifty major U.S. newspapers. Thirty-six printed the story at a copyright fee of $100 each. Over the next five months, Hersh filed four more Mylai stories by tracking down other GIs who were in Mylai on that fateful day. His later reports clarified his reference to "Pinkville" as the site of the massacre. Hersh won the Pulitzer Prize for international reporting in 1970.*

*St. Louis Post-Dispatch*, 13 November 1969

Fort Benning, GA.—Lt. William L. Calley Jr., 26, is a mild-mannered, boyish-looking Vietnam combat veteran with the nickname of Rusty. The Army says he deliberately murdered at least 109 Vietnamese civilians during a search-and-destroy mission in March 1968, in a Viet Cong stronghold known as Pinkville.

Calley has formally been charged with six specifications of mass murder. Each specification cites a number of dead, adding up to the 109 total, and adds that Calley did "with premeditation murder . . . Oriental human beings whose names and sex are unknown by shooting them with a rifle."

The Army calls it murder; Calley, his counsel and others associated with the incident describe it as a case of "carrying out orders."

Pinkville has now become a widely known code word among the military in a case that many officers and some well-informed congressmen believe will become far more controversial than the recent murder charges against eight Green Berets. In terms of numbers of slain, Pinkville is by far the worst known U.S. atrocity case of the Vietnam war.

Army investigation teams spent nearly one year studying the incident before filing charges against Calley, a platoon leader of the 11th Brigade of the American Division at the time of the slayings.

Calley was formally charged on or about Sept. 6, 1969, with multiple homicides, just a few days before he was due to be released from active service.

Calley has since hired a prominent civilian attorney, former Judge George W. Latimer of the U.S. Court of Military Appeals, and is now awaiting a military determination of whether the evidence justifies a general court-martial. All sources agreed that the court-martial will be ordered within a week or two. It is expected to begin early next year.

Calley, meanwhile, is being detained at Fort Benning, where his movements are sharply restricted. Even his exact location on the base is a closely held secret; neither the provost marshal nor the Army's Criminal Investigation Division knows where he is being held.

The Army has steadfastly refused to comment on the case, "in order not to prejudice the continuing investigation and rights of the accused." Similarly, Calley—although submitting to an interview—refused to discuss in detail just what did happen on that day, March 16, 1968.

### THIS IS ACCEPTED AS FACT

But many other officers and civilian officials, some angered by Calley's action and others angry that charges of murder were filed in the case, talked freely during interviews at Fort Benning and Washington.

These facts are not in dispute:

The Pinkville area, about six miles northeast of Quang Ngai, had been a Viet Cong fortress since the Vietnam war began. In early February 1968, a company of the 11th Brigade, as part of Task Force Barker, stormed through the area and was severely shot up.

Calley's platoon suffered casualties. After the Communist Tet offensive in February 1968, a large assault was mounted, again with high casualties and little success. A third attack was quickly mounted and it was successful.

The Army claimed 128 Viet Cong dead. Many civilians also were killed in the operation. The area was a free-fire zone in which all non–Viet Cong residents had been urged, by leaflet, to flee. Such zones are common throughout Vietnam.

One man who took part in the mission with Calley, in recounting what happened, said that in the earlier two attacks "we were really shot up."

"Every time we got hit it was from the rear," he said. "So the third time in there the order came down to go in and make sure no one was behind.

"We were told to just clear the area. It was a typical combat assault formation. We came in hot, with a cover of artillery in front of us, came down the line and destroyed the village," he said.

"There are always some civilian casualties in a combat operation. He (Calley) isn't guilty of murder," he said.

The order to "clear the area" was relayed from the battalion commander to the company commander to Calley, the source added.

## ATTORNEY'S ANGLE ON THE CASE

Calley's attorney, Latimer, said in an interview:

"This is one case that should never have been brought. Whatever killing there was was in a firefight in connection with an operation. . . .

"You can't afford to guess whether a civilian is a Viet Cong or not. Either they shoot you or you shoot them. . . .

"This case is going to be important—to what standard do you hold a combat officer in carrying out a mission? . . .

"There are two instances where murder is acceptable to anybody: where it is excusable and where it is justified. If Calley did shoot anybody because of the tactical situation or while in a firefight, it was either excusable or justifiable."

Adding to the complexity of the case is the fact that investigators from the Army Inspector General's Office, which conducted the bulk of the investigation, considered filing charges against at least six other men involved in the action that March 16.

Included were Capt. Ernest Medina, Calley's company commander, and Sgt. Manuel Lopez, Calley's main noncommissioned officer. Both are now stationed at Fort Benning.

They, and at least four other men from Calley's unit, were flown to Benning sometime in late summer during the Army's Article 32 hearing, the military equivalent of a grand jury proceeding. The hearing was conducted by Lt. Col. Dwayne G. Cameron, a Fort Benning infantry officer.

Sources report that Calley was personally accused of all of the slayings under his and Sgt. Lopez's command. At the Article 32 hearings, the young lieutenant refused to say whether the order to fire came from Medina, his company commander.

## OTHER OFFICERS ARE INDIGNANT

Calley's friends in the officer corps at Fort Benning, many of them West Point graduates, are indignant but, knowing the high stakes of the case, express their outrage in private. "They're using this as a God-damned example," one officer complained. "He's a good soldier. He follows orders.

"There weren't any friendlies in the village," the officer added. "The orders were to shoot anything that moved."

Another officer noted, "It could happen to any of us. He's killed and seen a lot of killing. . . . Killing becomes nothing in Vietnam. He knows that there were civilians there, but he also knows that there were VC among them."

A third officer, also familiar with the case, added: "There's this question—I think anyone who goes to Nam asks it. What's a civilian? Someone who works for us at day and puts on Viet Cong pajamas at night?"

There is another side to the Calley case, one that the Army cannot reveal as yet. Interviews have brought out that the investigation into the Pinkville affair was initiated six months after the incident, only after some of the men who served under Calley complained.

The Army has photographs of what purports to be the incident, although these have not—thus far—been introduced as evidence in the case, and may not be.

"They simply shot up this village and he (Calley) was the leader of it," said one Washington source. "When one guy refused to do it, Calley took the rifle away and did the shooting himself."

Asked about this Calley refused to comment.

One Pentagon officer discussed the case in a caustic manner, reaching down to tap his knee with his hand, and saying at the same time: "Some of those kids he shot were this high. I don't think they were Viet Cong. Do you?" (None of the men interviewed about the affair denied that women and children had been shot at the Pinkville incident.)

A constant source of amazement among all those interviewed was that the story had yet to reach the press. "Pinkville has been a word among GIs for a year," one official said. "I'll never cease to be amazed that it hasn't been written about before." A high-ranking officer commented that he first heard talk of the Pinkville incident soon after it happened; the officer was on duty in Saigon at the time.

## ARMY MOTIVES DISCUSSED

Why did the Army choose to prosecute this case? On what is it basing the charge that Calley acted with premeditation? The court-martial should answer these questions, but some men already have their opinions.

"The Army knew it was going to get clobbered on this at some point," one knowledgeable military source noted. "If they don't prosecute somebody—if this stuff comes out without the Army even taking some action—it would be even worse."

Another view, mentioned by many, was that the top level of the military is concerned about possible war crime tribunals after the Vietnam war ends. "Some of those commanders are thinking of future war crimes," one source said.

As for Calley, he's now smoking four packs of cigarettes daily, and getting out of shape. He's short (5-foot-3) and slender, with expressionless gray eyes and thinning brown hair. He seems slightly bewildered and hurt by the charges against him. He wants nothing more than to be cleared and return to the Army.

"I know this sounds funny," he said in an interview, "but I like the Army . . . and I don't want to do anything to hurt it."

Friends described Calley as a "gung-ho Army man . . . Army all the way." But even his staunchest supporters admit his enthusiasm may be somewhat to blame. "Maybe he did take some order to clear out the village a little bit too literally," one friend said, "but he's a fine boy."

Calley had been shipped home early from Vietnam, after the Army refused his request to extend his tour of duty. Until the incident at Pinkville, he had received nothing but high ratings from his superior officers. He was scheduled to receive, he said, the bronze and silver stars for his combat efforts. He's heard nothing about the medals since arriving at Fort Benning. The lieutenant was born in Miami and flunked out of the Palm Beach (Fla.) Junior College before enlisting in the Army. He was commissioned second lieutenant in September 1967, shortly after going to Vietnam. The Army lists his home as Waynesville, N.C.

An information sheet put out by the public affairs officer of the Americal Division the day after the March 16 engagement contained this terse mention of the incident: "The swiftness with which the units moved into the area surprised the enemy. After the battle, the 11th Brigade moved into the village, searching each hut and tunnel."

*Credit*: Reprinted with permission of the St. Louis Post-Dispatch, copyright © 1969.

---

## JOSEPH ESZTERHAS: "CAMERAMAN SAW GIS SLAY 100 VILLAGERS"

---

*Cleveland, Ohio,* Plain Dealer *reporter Joseph Eszterhas read Hersh's breaking story on the Mylai massacre, did follow-up research, and learned that the army photographer on the scene and subsequently discharged from the service was a native of Cleveland. Eszterhas tracked down the photographer and obtained rights to publish exclusives in the* Plain Dealer *and* Life *magazine.*

*Plain Dealer* (Cleveland, Ohio), 20 November 1969

U.S. Army troops "indiscriminately and wantonly mowed down" civilian residents of a tiny South Vietnamese hamlet on March 16, 1968, a former Army photographer has told *The Plain Dealer*.

Along with his eyewitness account, the former photographer has made available to *The Plain Dealer* a set of photographs taken at the village. They are being reproduced today on two pages of *The Plain Dealer*. This is the first publication of the photos, which also are in the hands of U.S. Army authorities investigating the sensational accounts of the village deaths.

Ronald L. Haeberle, 28, of Cleveland, then a sergeant and an Army public information staff member, was attached to C Company, 1st Battalion, 20th Infantry Regiment, 11th Light Infantry Brigade when the troops entered the hamlet of My Lai No. 4.

In an exclusive *Plain Dealer* interview, Haeberle described how U.S. soldiers "recklessly, wantonly and without any provocation" carried out the mass murder of South Vietnamese civilians.

In August of this year, Haeberle provided the Army's Criminal Investigation Department (CID), an arm of the Army Security Agency, with prints of the exclusive pictures he shot in the village during the operation and gave investigators a six-page statement.

Since then, 1st Lt. William L. Calley, Jr., 26, of Miami, Fla., and Staff Sgt. David Mitchell, 29, of St. Francisville, La., have been charged in the case—Calley with murder and Mitchell with assault with intent to murder.

On Tuesday, Capt. Aubrey Daniel, a lawyer with the adjutant general's office at Ft. Benning, Ga., confirmed to *The Plain Dealer* that Haeberle was present in the hamlet as an Army photographer March 16, 1968.

The mission that Haeberle witnessed and photographed with C Company in the little "Pinkville" village was his last mission in Vietnam. He was honorably discharged at the end of that same March.

Haeberle said U.S. forces did not engage in a firefight with Viet Cong while in the village. No Viet Cong were sighted; there were no reports of Viet Cong fire, he said.

U.S. forces, he related, mechanically killed the civilians, some in their beds in huts. The murders were carried out, he said, with M-16 rifles and machine guns.

He said he saw as many as 30 American soldiers murder as many as 100 South Vietnamese civilians, many of them women and babies, many left in lifeless clumps.

The only U.S. casualty he saw was a soldier who shot himself in the foot accidentally. Afterwards, he said he heard the soldier shot himself purposely.

"He couldn't stand what was going on and wanted out of there," Haeberle said.

He told his story firmly, without emotion, recounting

scenes vividly. "I was shocked. I've never been able to forget what I saw there," he said.

He described himself as "just an average American with an upper middle-class background who was drafted." He said he is not against the war in Vietnam but was appalled by the kind of brutality he witnessed.

"I never saw U.S. GIs act like that before," he said.

He describes the soldiers who did the shooting as "intent on what they were trying to accomplish. There was no feeling, nothing human about it. It was, for the most part, grim, though later some of the men tried to be humorous about leaving the bodies for the dogs and the rats."

He emphasized he does not know whether the men were ordered to kill the civilians. "All I know is that I saw it happening and I had a camera with me." He said he made no effort, as an Army person, to photograph actual killings.

His description:

"At about 5:30 in the morning of March 16, I left where I was stationed, Duc Pho, by helicopter for Task Force Barker. That is an outlying area for the base camp. I was supposed to hook up here with C Company. I hooked up with C Company at 6 or 6:30—I'm not sure—sunrise.

"No one really explained the mission, but from what I heard from the men, it was suspected that these villagers were Viet Cong sympathizers and it was thought there were Viet Cong there.

"I came in on the second lift, which came about a half hour after the first. We landed in the rice paddies and I heard gunfire from the village itself, but we were still on the outside of the village.

"There were some South Vietnamese people, maybe 15 of them, women and children included, walking on a dirt road maybe 100 yards away. All of a sudden the GIs just opened up with M-16s. Besides the M-16 fire, they were shooting at the people with M-79 grenade launchers. I couldn't believe what I was seeing.

"Off to the right, I noticed a woman appeared from some cover and this one GI fired first at her, then they all started shooting at her, aiming at her head. The bones were flying in the air chip by chip. I'd never seen Americans shoot civilians like that.

"As they moved in, closer to the village, they just kept shooting at people. I remember this man distinctly, holding a small child in one arm and another child in the other, walking toward us. They saw us and were pleading. The little girl was saying 'No, no' in English. Then all of a sudden a burst of fire and they were cut down. They were about 20 feet away. One machine gunner did it. He opened up.

"There was no reaction on the guy doing the shooting. That's the part that really got me—this little girl pleading and they were just cut down.

"I had been on the ground maybe 45 minutes at this point. Off to the left, a group of people—women, children, and babies—[was] standing around. The machine gunner was standing in front of them with the ammo bearer and all of a sudden I heard this fire and here the machine gunner had opened up on all these people in the big circle, and they were trying to run. I don't know how many got out.

"There were two small children, a very young boy and a smaller boy, maybe 4 or 5 years old. A guy with an M-16 fired at them, at the first boy, and the older boy fell over to protect the smaller boy. The GI fired some more shots with a tracer and the tip somehow seemed to be still burning the boy's flesh. Then they fired six more shots and just let them lie.

"The GIs found a group of people—mothers, children, and their daughters. This GI grabbed one of the girls, in her teens, and started stripping her, playing around. They said they wanted to see what she was made of and stuff like that.

"I remember they were keeping the mother away from protecting her daughter—she must have been around 13—by kicking the mother in the rear and slapping her around.

"They were getting ready to shoot these people and I said hold it—I wanted to take a picture. They were pleading for their lives. The looks on their faces, the mothers were crying; they were trembling.

"I turned my back because I couldn't look. They opened up with two M-16s. On automatic fire, they went through the whole clip—35, 40 shots—and I remember actually seeing the smoke come from the rifle. The automatic weapons fire cut them down.

"I couldn't take a picture of it, it was too much. One minute you see people alive and the next minute they're dead.

"I came up to a clump of bodies and I saw this small child. Part of his foot had been shot off, and he went up to this pile of bodies and just looked at it, like he was looking for somebody. A GI knelt down beside me and shot the little kid. His body flew backwards into the pile.

"I had emotional feelings. I felt nauseated to see people treated this way. American GIs were supposed to be protecting people and rehabilitating them and I had seen that. But this was incredible. I watched it and it wouldn't sink in.

"I left the village around 11 o'clock that morning. I saw clumps of bodies, and I must have seen as many as a hundred killed. It was done very businesslike."

Haeberle said he later saw a news story of C Company's operation in the tiny hamlet listing a large number of Viet Cong killed.

"There were no Viet Cong," he said. "They were just poor, innocent illiterate peasants."

## RONALD L. HAEBERLE: PHOTOS OF MYLAI MASS SLAYINGS

*The following profile of Mylai photographer Ron Haeberle accompanied the* Plain Dealer's *exclusive publication of the Mylai photos, which the newspaper also put on display in a downtown Cleveland public lobby to collect reactions from its dismayed citizens.*

### Plain Dealer *(Cleveland, Ohio), 20 November 1969*

Exclusive—This photograph will shock Americans as it shocked the editors and the staff of *The Plain Dealer*. It was taken by a young Cleveland area man while serving as a photographer with the U.S. Army in South Vietnam.

It was taken during the attack by American soldiers on the South Vietnamese village My Lai, an attack which has made world headlines in recent days with disclosures of mass killings allegedly at the hands of American soldiers.

This photograph and others on two special pages are the first to be published anywhere of the killings.

This particular picture shows a clump of bodies of South Vietnamese civilians which includes women and children. Why they were killed raises one of the most momentous questions of the war in Vietnam.

### THE PHOTOGRAPHER

Ronald L. Haeberle, 28, works as an industrial supervisor at a downtown manufacturing company.

He is a 1960 graduate of Fairview Park High School and a 1969 graduate of Ohio University.

He was drafted April 4, 1966 after completing three years at Ohio University.

He took his basic training at Ft. Benning, Ga., and was trained as a mortarman at Ft. Ord, Calif.

He was assigned to the 11th Infantry Brigade in Hawaii and served as a clerk.

"I put in some paperwork to get into photography," he said.

He was assigned to Vietnam as a combat photographer and arrived there in December 1967. He went on numerous combat missions.

What he saw in the little village in the Pinkville Sector March 16th will forever be imprinted on his memory.

"I wanted to tell my story," he says, "because there is a greater truth here which must be told."

## HAL WINGO: "BEFORE, AMERICANS ALWAYS BROUGHT US CANDY AND MEDICINE"

*After initially declining the Mylai story,* Life *magazine made up for its reluctance by sending a phalanx of journalists to Vietnam to check facts and collect interviews.* Life's *extensive picture story included Hersh and Eszterhas's reporting, Haeberle's photographs, and new eyewitness accounts, such as the following collection of moving testimonials reported by* Life's *Hal Wingo.*

### Life, *5 December 1969*

Songmy—Crouched in the doorway as a heavy rain puddles in front of her thatch hut, the old woman looks suspiciously at those who pass by. She is wary of people she doesn't know well, and that includes even many of the Vietnamese living near her in the Songmy resettlement village of Quangngai province. Songmy is not the woman's home. It is a government corral where civilians can be protected while troops pursue the Vietcong through every other village in the area.

The old woman is Nguyen Thi Doc, like many in the refugee center a survivor of the massacre at Mylai.

The old woman recalls she was just beginning a morning meal with 13 of her family, including nine grandchildren, when she heard the Americans "come down from the sky."

"They had been in the village before," she says, "and always brought us medicine or candy for the children. If we had known what they came for this time, we could have fled."

The entire family was taken out of the hut and ordered into a field, she says, and then "the soldiers started shooting at everyone."

She was hit through the shoulder and left for dead. She saw her 8-year-old granddaughter, Tran Thi Oanh, shot through the foot and watched her fall over the bodies of her dead brothers and sisters. Nguyen Thi Doc says the Americans must have thought everyone was dead when they left the village about noon.

"I thought Oanh was dead, too," she says. "And I lay in the field until the next morning, when people came from nearby villages to help us."

They were taken to a Vietnamese hospital where they stayed four months. With the exception of Oanh's 6-year-old brother, who miraculously was not hit, everyone else in the family was killed. When she was sent to the resettlement village, other survivors from Mylai told Nguyen Thi Doc they had counted 370 dead. Her voice gets excited when she recalls the number and then trails off—there is nothing more to say.

Down the path in the settlement live two other women, both of them widows of Truong Van Vinh, a 71-year-old farmer. The younger wife had gone to the market at another village the day of the attack. But the older woman and Vinh were sitting inside his hut, cringing from the artillery barrage that had been pounding near the village for hours. When it stopped, the old woman looked out and saw many Americans walking through the village. Vinh left the hut to see what was happening.

"When he got outside the door," the old woman says, "there was a shot, and I heard him fall to the ground. The soldiers came in and saw me, and motioned for me to come outside. One of them lifted his rifle to shoot me, but another group of Americans sitting around the well shouted to him and he walked away." The woman ran back into the hut where she hid for hours.

All of the Mylai villagers who talked of the incident said they could hear the Americans shouting when they arrived, but the only words they could understand were "VC, VC." The villagers deny there were any Vietcong in the village, though American battle reports for the day indicated sniper fire and resistance had been directed against the American units for some time before they entered the village. The entire coastal strip of Quangngai province has been a battleground for most of the war. Even today the area around Mylai is frequently visited by the Vietcong.

One of the few male survivors from Mylai is Truong Quang An, a wizened peasant who looks much older than his 59 years. "When we saw the helicopters landing," he says, "I ran with my two nephews to the family shelter outside the hut." The shelter is no more than a four- or five-foot hole covered with thatch and a wooden pallet. An dropped in first and the nephews took their place on the outer edge, closest to the entrance.

"We heard the soldiers walking through the village and when they saw the shelter, they stopped. One of them could see inside, and he pointed his rifle at close range and shot both my nephews." Then the soldiers moved on to the next hut, and An could hear Mylai burning as he curled up in the darkness, sheltered beneath the bodies of the two young men.—Hal Wingo

## NOTES

1. Seymour M. Hersh, "How I Broke the Mylai 4 Story," *Saturday Review*, 11 July 1970, 46.
2. John Sack, "Afterthoughts on Lieutenant Calley," *Esquire*, June 1973, 144, 204.
3. Hersh, "How I Broke the Mylai 4 Story," 46.
4. Ibid., 49.

## FURTHER READINGS

Gershen, Martin. *Destroy or Die: The True Story of Mylai*. New Rochelle, N.Y.: Arlington House, 1971.

Hersh, Seymour M. *Cover-up: The Army's Secret Investigation of the Massacre at My Lai 4*. New York: Random House, 1972.

———. *My Lai 4: A Report on the Massacre and Its Aftermath*. New York: Random House, 1970.

Knoll, Erwin, and Judith Nies McFadden, eds. *War Crimes and the American Conscience*. New York: Holt, Rinehart and Winston, 1970.

Lane, Mark. *Conversations with Americans*. New York: Simon & Schuster, 1970.

# 23

## WAR ON JOURNALISTS

Vietnam was a dangerous news beat, especially for the journalists who were not satisfied to cover the war from the Caravelle Hotel in Saigon. By William Prochnau's count, more than fifty men and women representing U.S. media were killed in the Vietnam War, with another twenty missing and presumed dead.[1] By comparison, thirty-seven American correspondents were killed in the global war against the Germans and Japanese. The Vietnam War was more deadly for correspondents because it had no defined fronts and few zones sealed off by the military. Danger lurked behind every clump of elephant grass and under every dusty provincial road and could strike at any moment without warning. In the early years, the Vietcong avoided killing the *bao chi*, who helped discredit the "puppet" regime of Ngo Dinh Diem. When the war lost its restraint, newspeople were swept up in the indiscriminate ferocity of large battles. Over protests of their editors, some war correspondents took unwise risks to get their stories. Daredevils such as Malcolm Browne, Peter Arnett, and Horst Faas were lucky and survived the war. Larry Burrows, Dickie Chapelle, and François Sully did not.

American correspondents had more than the Communists to fear. Paranoid about even slightly critical coverage, Diem was openly hostile toward the Saigon press corps. A dictator who maintained the trappings of democracy only to please the Americans, Diem kept the Vietnamese press in line and did not understand why the American leaders did not control their own media. Did they not want to win the war? His Sûreté regularly billy-clubbed reporters and smashed cameras during street demonstrations. David Halberstam went into hiding in Saigon after hearing rumors that he had been marked for assassination by Diem's secret police. This chapter presents a sample of the war's correspondence about the war on the correspondents, whose reportage momentously influenced events during the Vietnam War and redefined the profession for all future wars.

## AN ANONYMOUS REPORT: EDITORIAL QUESTIONS JOURNALISTS' DECISION TO GO TO CAMBODIA

*For years, Cambodia's Prince Norodom Sihanouk kept his country out of the war seething in neigh-boring Vietnam by maintaining strict neutrality. Encroachments of his frontier were permitted as long as Cambodian nationals were not involved. On 18 March 1970, the Cambodian National Assembly ousted Sihanouk from power and installed his prime minister, Lon Nol, who was openly pro-American. The United States opened negotiations with Lon Nol to prepare for an invasion of Cambodia should North Vietnam threaten the capital city of Phnom Penh. Joint operations of the Cambodian and South Vietnamese armies were prepared. On 5 April, an armored South Vietnamese column, with U.S. air and artillery support, invaded Cambodia to interdict enemy supplies. To avoid charges of escalating the war, the operation was not announced to the press. Dozens of foreign correspondents stationed in Saigon heard about the invasion and went to Cambodia on their own to cover this new phase of the war. Many of them became casualties in the tense melee. The following* Newsweek *article, "Beyond the Checkpoint," questions the journalists' motives and judgment in risking perils for uncertain gains.*

*Newsweek*, 15 June 1970

CBS correspondent George Syvertsen woke up with a bad cold and fever in Phnom Penh's Hotel Royal early last week. Over the protest of his Polish-born wife, Gusta, who thought he should spend the day resting, Syvertsen prepared to drive down Route 3 toward the small town of Takeo, where the Cambodian Army reportedly was on the move. "It's my job," was his stock reply to his wife's concern about his safety. "That's what they pay me for."

Certainly, few correspondents seemed better able to handle the job. Syvertsen, 37, a graduate of Columbia College and fluent in several languages, was not only an intelligent, thoughtful newsman but had more than two years of experience as a combat reporter in Indochina. He climbed into a gray canvas-topped jeep, picked up Gerald Miller, a CBS reporter-producer who had been in Cambodia for only a month, and headed south on the two-lane road. They were followed, in a blue Mercedes, by another CBS crew including one Indian and two Japanese technicians.

At about the same time that morning, Welles Hangen, 40, NBC's Hong Kong bureau chief—a scholarly China watcher with a thorough command of Mandarin and also a veteran war correspondent—was finishing his breakfast at the Royal. "I think there's something interesting on the road to Takeo," he told an NBC colleague. "See you later." He got into NBC's Opel sedan along with a Japanese cameraman, a French soundman and Cambodian driver. Probably unaware that the CBS team was just ahead, the NBC crew drove off toward Takeo.

Cambodian soldiers halted the CBS jeep and Mercedes at a checkpoint 30 miles south of Phnom Penh, warning the newsmen that the road ahead was dangerous. But they let the two vehicles pass through. A few minutes later, the NBC Opel slowed down as it approached the checkpoint but was allowed to pass.

**GRAVE**

What happened next is based partly on the report of the NBC driver, who later escaped, and partly on conjecture. Syvertsen's jeep, which could have been mistaken for a military vehicle, apparently came under Communist fire more than a mile past the checkpoint. The jeep went off the road, crashed into a tree and burned, hit most likely by a grenade. A badly maimed body found in a freshly dug grave near the jeep was identified later by a CBS newsman as Syvertsen's. Miller and the other two occupants of the jeep were presumably also dead or taken captive. When the remainder of the CBS crew, in the Mercedes, and the NBC crew in the Opel heard the shooting farther up the road, they stopped. But all of them, too, were quickly captured by Communist soldiers.

The incident on Route 3 raised to a staggering total of 24 the number of newsmen listed as dead or missing in action during the past two months in Cambodia. (Among them: photographers Sean Flynn and Dana Stone, on assignment respectively for *Time* and CBS; Richard Dudman, chief Washington correspondent of *The St. Louis Post-Dispatch*; Elizabeth Pond of *The Christian Science Monitor* and Mike Morrow of Dispatch News Service International.) The most obvious reason for the soaring casualty rate among correspondents is that, since the entrance of U.S. and South Vietnamese troops into Cambodia, the level of combat—or at least predictable, observable combat—has increased dramatically. And, unlike South Vietnam, where correspondents can be briefed in Saigon about battle conditions and then travel in the relative safety of U.S. helicopters, the Cambodian campaign almost always thrusts newsmen out on their own.

At least one veteran television newsman seriously questions whether a trip to the front is necessary at all. "We could have just one strip of action film we put on every night with a different narration to fit the day's action," he suggests cynically.

"When you get right down to it, all of the action looks just about the same." Indeed, earlier in the war many critics chided network newsmen for focusing their lenses on minor, if exciting, skirmishes in the field while failing to cover adequately either the pacification program or the political turmoil in Saigon.

But in Cambodia these days, covering the shooting war does seem to be right to the point. At the front, newsmen can observe the performance of South Vietnamese troops and thus can begin to evaluate the effectiveness of the Administration's Vietnamization program. They can also double-check the accounting of the huge caches of enemy arms and supplies the military claims to have captured. Moreover, ever since the My Lai revelations, it has become increasingly important for newsmen to find out exactly who is being killed in the Indochina war. Against the advice of an American commander, one NBC newsman barged into the Cambodian town of Snoul just after it had been bombarded by U.S. planes and interviewed the surviving villagers. He came to a conclusion that the U.S. commander would never have suggested: Snoul wanted the American soldiers to go away and not come back.

## HEAT

Not all the journalistic bravery stems from such lofty motivations. No news executive asks his men to risk their lives to scoop a rival network, magazine, newspaper or wire service; in fact, many editors urge their men to be cautious. But the subtle pressures of competition often command otherwise, particularly among network TV reporters. Several weeks ago, the Nielsen ratings of the evening news programs, which showed NBC's "Huntley-Brinkley Report" on top, were sent to TV newsmen in the field. "No one had to say anything," says a network reporter. "The heat was on."

There is an additional competitive spur for most of the younger TV newsmen who go to Indochina. They often arrive with the rank of reporter, knowing that an outstanding performance can win them the coveted status of correspondent. Nothing will catch a TV editor's eye faster than a film sequence showing one of his newsmen crouched, microphone in hand, behind a hedgerow while bullets whiz over his head. "When we watch thousands of feet and suddenly there is shooting," admits one film editor, "that is what excites us."

No war, of course, can be covered without some danger to newsmen. And an enterprising combat reporter will often incur additional risk on his own initiative. But after the record of the past two months in Cambodia, the time has come for editors—and especially TV editors—to reward discretion as well as valor.

*Credit*: From Newsweek, 6/15/70. © 1970 Newsweek, Inc. All rights reserved. Reprinted with permission.

---

## RALPH GRAVES: EDITOR'S NOTE—PROFILE OF LATE PHOTOGRAPHER LARRY BURROWS

---

Life *magazine's preeminent Vietnam photographer, Larry Burrows, died in a helicopter crash on 10 February 1971 while covering an allied offensive into Laos. The crash claimed three other photographers. His meticulously composed images (he was known as a perfectionist who would take hundreds of exposures to get just the "right" shot) vividly illustrated the Vietnam War from 1962 until his death. He had nine* Life *cover stories to his credit. A few of Burrows's Vietnam images questioned the war, such as his 1962 cover photo of a napalm explosion in Vietnam a year before the government conceded its use; some of his images humanized the war, such as his cover story on Captain Vernon Gillespie Jr. (see Chapter 7); most of his images dramatized the war, such as his final story, "A Frantic Night on the Edge of Laos" (reproduced below in this chapter, with a salute by Burrows's editor, Ralph Graves); but all Burrows's images made the war immediate.*

Life, 19 February 1971

### LARRY BURROWS, PHOTOGRAPHER

Last week a helicopter carrying Larry Burrows once again to the battlefronts of the Indochina war was shot down over Laos. Also in the helicopter were photographers Henri Huet of AP, Kent Potter of UPI, Keisaburo Shimamoto of *Newsweek* and Vietnamese army photographer Tu Vu. There is little hope that any survived.

I do not think it is demeaning to any other photographer in the world for me to say that Larry Burrows was the single bravest and most dedicated war photographer I know of. He spent nine years covering the Vietnam war under conditions of incredible danger, not just at odd times but over and over again. We kept thinking up other, safer stories for him to do, but he would do them and go back to the war. As he said, the war was his story, and he would see it through. His dream was to stay until he could photograph a Vietnam at peace.

Larry was English, a polite man, self-effacing, warm with his friends but totally cool in combat. He had deep passions, and the deepest was to make people confront the reality of the war, not look away from it. He was more concerned with people than with issues, and he had great sympathy for those who suffered. A few years ago he did a story on a little Vietnamese girl who had lost a leg in the war, and long after the story he would return to her remote village to see if she needed anything, to see that she was all right. He realized that if she became dependent on him she could become estranged from her own village, and he took care to treat her with tender, avuncular good humor that masked his deep concern and his affection.

He had been through so much, always coming out magically unscathed, that a myth of invulnerability grew up about him. Friends came to believe he was protected by some invisible armor. But I don't think he believed that himself. Whenever he went in harm's way he knew, precisely, what the dangers were and how vulnerable he was.

John Saar, *Life*'s Far East Bureau Chief, had been with Larry on the Laos border, returning to Saigon to ship us the story. . . . He had often worked with Larry, and today he sent this cable:

"The depth of his commitment [and] concentration was frightening. He could have been a surgeon or a soldier or almost anything else, but he chose photography and was so dedicated that he saw the whole world in 35-mm exposures. Work was his life, eventually his death, and Burrows I think wouldn't have bitched.

"As a photographer he began where most others stopped—exposure, speed, focus were always reflexively correct, but he worried constantly about composition and most of all, meaning. He ran terrible risks because he was a perfectionist and he had to take the risks to get perfect pictures—the only kind he found satisfactory.

"One last point, my own lingering faith in the resilience of Burrows is such that I suggest this week we just call him missing, and hope that he's beaten the odds once again."

—Ralph Graves, Managing Editor

*Credit*: © 1971 TIME Inc. Reprinted by permission.

---

## JOHN SAAR: A GREAT PHOTOGRAPHER'S LAST NEWS STORY

---

*President Richard Nixon wanted to show his political enemies that his "Vietnamization" policy to wind down U.S. involvement in Vietnam was working. He ordered General Creighton Abrams to plan a military operation to prove that the South Vietnamese army was capable of taking over defense of its own country. The operation was codenamed "Lam Son 719" by the South Vietnamese. Launched on 29 January 1971, the secret incursion into Laos by mechanized South Vietnamese units, supported by U.S. helicopters and bombers, was intended to surprise Communist strongholds along the Ho Chi Minh Trail. The South Vietnamese advance was sluggish, failed to achieve surprise, and eventually was turned back by the Communists.*

*At first Abrams embargoed press coverage of the operation to maintain its secrecy. Within a week, the embargo was lifted, and journalists were allowed access.* Life *magazine photographer Larry Burrows and correspondent John Saar were in the first wave of journalists airlifted to the Lam Son 719 sector along the Laotian border. They came upon a South Vietnamese task force decimated by its own bombers. Their chronicle of the tragedy, "A Frantic Night on the Edge of Laos," was Burrows' last report for* Life *magazine; Burrows died in a helicopter crash the next day.*

### *Life*, 19 February 1971

Four days after he took the photographs on these pages, Larry Burrows was reported missing in Laos. He had covered the war in Indochina—and survived it—for nine years. . . . When South Vietnamese troops began moving to the Laotian border early this month, Burrows and Correspondent John Saar went with them. They were at Langvei when the terrible incident shown here took place. Saar went back to Saigon to file this report. Burrows stayed on at the border, hoping for a chance to get into Laos. Last Wednesday he got his wish: a ride in to Laos with a squadron of five South Vietnamese helicopters. Four of them lost their way in the green-swathed, jagged mountain ranges and wandered north. There they came under heavy North Vietnamese antiaircraft fire. Two of the aircraft, including the one carrying Burrows and four

other photographers, were hit. They went down and were seen to burn on impact. An aerial survey of the crash site reported no sign of life.

Late afternoon, 6 February 1971. I first hear the distant whistle of a plane as Larry Burrows and I stand chatting at the roadside headquarters of Task Force 11 just three kilometers from the Laos border. Tomorrow, or maybe the day after, this amalgam of elite South Vietnamese army units will pull its armored track carriers back on to dusty Route 9 and head into Laos. We plan to ride with them.

The U.S. advisers are relaxed and pleasant and Task Force 11's commander, Lt. Colonel Bui The Dung, returns our greeting with a warm smile. Everyone knows that across the border in Laos there will be hard battles, but today the mood is lighthearted, almost festive. Chattering and joking, the paratroops are settling in, gouging out slit trenches, stringing tents. Rice savored with onions and vegetables bubbles over dozens of fires, scalding tea in blue-and-white china bowls passes delicately from one hand to the next.

Like a horn on New York's Fifth Avenue, the rising whine of a jet fighter is simply a background noise in Vietnam. I hear it, think "jet on a strike run" and ignore it. Why not? Every so often someone will say, "Hey, look at that jet roll out," and you watch—detached, safe, vaguely sympathetic to the recipients of the ton of high explosive or tanks of napalm. To the allied armies and the press who travel with them, our air power is as innocuous and reliable as home electricity. Only this time the jet was rolling in on us.

In the fading light the diving plane is hardly visible. But two men, a Vietnamese officer and his American adviser, see it, and the three bombs tumbling toward them. They go headlong into a trench. Alabama-born Staff Sergeant Bob Logan later spoke of it as "high diving without a pool."

Burrows is talking about film shipments. Two bangs snatch my attention—close, but safe. Then explosions are on us, in us, among us. The world is one terrible *kkerrussh* of sound and blast—and the brain lurches with the impact. For a frozen microsecond I read incredulity and horror on the faces around me, then we are all down and scrabbling for cover.

A shallow cooking trench. Two big fires, two simmering pots inches away. Christ, I'm going to roast to death. But my head is saying, don't move, mortars, mortars, another salvo any moment. I carry that helmet everywhere, where is it? I look around. One man is moving—fast, decisive—toward the impact area: Larry Burrows. In a thought vacuum I follow. The sunset is still pale gold on the mountaintops. Now there is a stronger, wickeder yellow: flames are licking from the turret of a burning track. We run on and Burrows goes prone to frame the scene. We are the first ones here, and the brain can't accept the visual evidence as real. People bleeding, tattered, broken people strewn everywhere by the steel cyclone. Nightmarishly outlined in the half light, dust-gray apparitions already showing ominously dark, spreading blotches rise to an elbow and extend a pleading arm. From all sides comes the elemental moan of men beseeching help.

Pandemonium. Two officers are already on the radio, calling for Medevac helicopters, but most are momentarily shocked into inactivity. And pandemonium in my head. Again it is Burrows who gives me the lead. "Come and help me bring that chap in," he says. No stretchers. Awkwardly, we pick him up by legs and arms. God, this is not only macabre, it's difficult and tiring as well. We stumble across the broken ground. My hands are slick with the man's blood and I feel its seeping wetness in my clothes. He is hard hit to the chest and stomach; now I know he must be hit in the head as well. From the depths of him comes a groan of unspeakable pain. It wrings from Burrows an answering groan of commiseration.

We bring in two more badly wounded and lay them at the edge of a bomb crater where a dressing station is hubbubbing into action. Excited voices gabbling into radios, figures blundering into one another. A wide-eyed medic arrives running barefoot with a "panic bag" in hand. A roar of exploding ammunition from a burning armored personnel carrier adds to the confusion.

Now the wounded are coming in thick and fast, very few walking. The talk is not of NVA rockets or mortars but of something called CBU dropped accidentally by a friendly plane. These cluster bomb units leave the plane as a single bomb, then explode apart into numbers of oval grenades, which in turn explode individually to create a blizzard of steel. If one plane on one run can inflict such savage hurt, I think, what unimaginable suffering has been inflicted by thousands of planes on thousands of runs?

For perhaps 10 minutes Task Force 11 has been overwhelmed by shock. Now paralysis passes and the pressure of emergency reveals personality. Most assertive is Major Todd, Georgian, senior adviser to the paratroops, who bellows orders in a mixture of pidgin English and bastard French which reduces everything to stark essentials. When the first helicopter is coming in, we hear him yell, "Only the man. No stretchers. 'Cause so beaucoup many."

Major Bill Aiken, senior adviser to the cavalry squadron, is on his second tour, but he has seen nothing like this. He sits, head sunk, shoulders hunched, and when one of his team tells him that "So-and-so is badly shaken up," Aiken replies, "He ain't the only one." But later, when there is work to do, he is on hand.

In his command center, neat in a long greatcoat, Colonel Dung coordinates the recovery of the wounded and alerts his outer defenses. He is outwardly calm, but his emotions are suppressed, not absent, and in the morning he allows himself a single telling comment: "It is sad to lose men in this way."

One of two wounded officers is paratrooper Major Nguyen Son Ha. A chirpy man of exquisite manners and delightfully deplorable English, he declines to be Medevaced until 12 hours later. By that time his broken arm is grossly swollen and his face is blanched with pain.

After 30 minutes the wounded are still coming in. Among the last is a man with a broken leg who staggers in unaided. How many are there? Thirty, forty, Christ, at least fifty. Two medics were killed outright and even at full strength there is no way the aid teams could cope with these numbers. As I watch, it becomes plain that the two doctors have been forced to leave some of the worst casualties untended in order to save those with a better chance. Two of the men Burrows and I brought in are dying where we left them. Some of the bandaging has been too hasty. One man squelches in a pool of his own blood as he rocks to and fro with pain. Three medics come over and replace the blood-soaked field dressings. The man is still contorted with pain and rams his head into the side of a corpse alongside.

The moon glides from behind clouds and lights the small

slope. It is littered with wounded, blood stains showing starkly against the gleaming white bandages. The medics and the other unwounded figures who scurry about are impossible to distinguish as American or Vietnamese. One man, whose left leg is nothing but bone and shredded flesh, raises his head to see while the medics are scissoring away the cloth. He sees and falls back soundlessly. The thought of what he sees chills me inside. Another man lying on the ground in the crucifix position moves inch by inch to the man next to him. He gropes for the man's hand and clasps it tight. The wounded are talking to one another. I can't imagine, nor do I want to know, what they say.

The Vietnamese follow the Chinese philosophy: pain must be borne with minimum display, and to a Westerner the stoicism is awesome. Men in terrible fear and pain are murmuring for the aid of their Creator and whimpering gently. I yearn for someone to scream so that I too may cry. No one does. But there is no unobtrusive exit for men who are 20 years old and want to live. They fight for breath until you long for them to die. Chest heaving with the effort, one man emits a rasping, almost metallic rattle as he sucks air through a blood-filled throat. At last he dies, chest expanded, as though that last effort stopped his heart. The man whose blood stained my trousers is also dead. One of the two doctors working with frenzied speed is 29-year-old Dr. Phan Van Chuong, who joined the army only six weeks ago. He is appalled by the number and severity of the casualties. In the morning, close to tears, he will say, "It was impossible, impossible."

The first American Medevac helicopter circles cautiously down through the cloud cover and clacks in to land, then pulls away.

"What's the problem?"

"He can't see to land." Route 9 is ankle-deep in dust, and the blades throw up a cloud which drowns the bright landing light.

"Throw water to damp the dust."

The helicopter lands and there is another obscene drama half-seen through the dust. There are too many casualties, no place for stretchers. Little groups of half-real, half-glimpsed figures run out with the worst wounded in their arms. The blinking red lights on the chopper glow eerily on their helmets and seem to pulse HURRY, HURRY, HURRY. Forced to treat their comrades like so many carcasses, the paratroops shove wounded on top of one another until the cabin is a surreal slaughterhouse. Then the chopper sets off on its dangerous return flight.

The airlift goes on for three hours. The accidental bombing by an American aircraft, probably Navy, cost seven dead and 54 wounded. Several of the wounded were expected to die. But slowly Task Force 11 recovers its confidence, turns its face away from the grave of personnel calamity and back to the war. After two hours the first quiet laugh is heard. Clunking shovels heap fresh soil on the blood-stained ground, the dead are packaged in ponchos, tied with bandages, packs and weapons of the missing men are heaped for removal. An American voice suggests that the helicopter pilots should be called in to back-haul the bodies tonight without being told they are running risks for the dead. Fortunately, Major Todd will have none of that nonsense. The bodies stay. Before they are taken away in the morning, a Vietnamese trooper looks for, finds and removes a pair of boots which are apparently his size.

But now there are still more wounded to move. "How many to go?" a paratrooper asks.

"Three, I think." And then to me, "Is that one dead?"

I stoop over a man whose face is shrouded from the dust by a towel. My hand is on his chest and I feel a slight movement. "No, he's alive."

"Okay, make it four."

*Credit*: © 1971 TIME Inc. Reprinted by permission.

# NOTE

1. William Prochnau, *Once upon a Distant War: David Halberstam, Neil Sheehan, Peter Arnett—Young War Correspondents and Their Early Vietnam Battles* (New York: Vintage Books, 1996), 326.

# FURTHER READINGS

Faas, Horst, and Tim Page, eds. *Requiem: By the Photographers Who Died in Vietnam and Indochina.* New York: Random House, 1997. Also available at *The Digital Journalist*, http://digitaljournalist.org/issue9711/req1.htm.

Knightley, Phillip. *The First Casualty: From the Crimea to Vietnam: The War Correspondent as Hero, Propagandist, and Myth Maker.* New York: Harcourt Brace Jovanovich, 1975.

Pyle, Richard, and Horst Faas. *Lost over Laos: A True Story of Tragedy, Mystery, and Friendship.* Cambridge, Mass.: Da Capo Press, 2003.

Wyatt, Clarence R. *Paper Soldiers: The American Press and the Vietnam War.* Rev. ed. Chicago: University of Chicago Press, 1995.

# 24

## DISENGAGEMENT

"The point seems paradoxical, if not whimsical," wrote Leslie Gelb of the *New York Times* about the irony that the system worked during the Vietnam War.[1] U.S. government leaders were convinced that they had to stop Communists from overtaking Vietnam, and, despite their many mistakes, they succeeded in doing just that for twenty-five years, until the end of the Vietnamese civil war in May 1975. Gelb argues that more or better news coverage of the war would not have appreciably altered the outcome, though it might have reduced dissension and better prepared the American public for the long haul. The debate in government circles was never *whether* to contain Communism in Vietnam but *how*. Disengagement simply was the final phase of that fight, an approach of last resort when no other options remained.

When they took the reins of power in 1969, both President Richard M. Nixon and his national security advisor, Henry A. Kissinger, knew that South Vietnam probably would fall to the Communists after the United States withdrew. The goal of their foreign policy was to obtain by whatever means necessary a "decent" interval between the two events. If the Watergate scandal had not destroyed Nixon's political support, the interval might have been longer than two years.

---

### LARRY BURROWS: A PHOTOGRAPHER'S GROWING DOUBTS ABOUT THE WAR

---

*Legendary* Life *magazine photographer Larry Burrows was regarded by his fellow journalists as a "company" man, generally supportive of U.S. intervention in Vietnam—the only attitude tolerated at Time, Inc., by publisher Henry Luce. But after Luce's retirement in 1965, the new leadership slowly moved the company's editorial position on the war to the political center. Doubts about the war now were permissible on the pages of* Life. *Burrows discusses his own shift in attitude in the following appraisal of U.S. disengagement from the war. He rarely wrote copy to accompany his photographs, but in the autumn of 1969 he was moved by what he saw to give voice to his growing doubts. Another theme of the following article, "Vietnam: A Degree of Disillusion," is Burrows's well-known compassion for Vietnamese civilians rocked by war.*

### Life, 19 September 1969

*Larry Burrows went to Vietnam early in 1962 and, with occasional breaks, has been covering the war there ever since. He was with South Vietnamese troops until 1964 and developed affection and sympathy for them and for their war-shattered country. Since then he has been with American troops. This year [1969] he returned for a look at the people who seemed destined to inherit the war. This is his personal report, in words and pictures.*

All over Vietnam you see the faces—more inscrutable and more tired now than I have ever known them to be. Their eyes do not meet yours, because they are aware that the enemy is still, even today, all around them, watching. They are in the middle. The pressure on them is terrible and has existed for some 30 years.

I have been rather a hawk. As a British subject I could perhaps be more objective than Americans, but I generally accepted the aims of the U.S. and Saigon, and the official version of how things were going. This spring, impressed by government statistics showing that conditions were improving, I set out to do a story on the turn for the better. In the following three months I indeed found some cause for optimism— better training and equipment in the South Vietnamese army, more roads open and safe—but I also found a degree of disillusion and demoralization in the army and the population that surprised and shocked me. The story became an attempt to show—and explain—that feeling in the South Vietnamese, and why it is such an uphill battle to try to change it.

Two months ago the first small group of American troops was pulled out of the country. More will follow, and eventually the question will be whether or not the South Vietnamese can fight and survive on their own if there is no peace treaty. Whether they can will be partly a matter of loyalty to a government, partly a matter of national pride, partly a matter of plain endurance. On each score, the prospects seem to me doubtful. The old woman [pictured], for example, is finally getting money to help rebuild in a pacified area. She has waited for months to get it, and in the meantime someone in the government may very well have been lending it at 30% interest. Whatever gratitude she feels is laced with cynicism and sapped by weariness. Many others like her simply no longer care. Perhaps the years of fighting have left them too dazed to believe in anything except the land on which they live.

### THE ONLY LOYALTY—TO FIELD AND FAMILY

Near Sadec, about 80 miles from Saigon, I met Tran Van Duoc. He and his family farm a half-acre of vegetables, which gives them a relatively good living. They are not isolated—his wife goes daily to market. Two of their sons are in the militia.

I asked him what he felt about the peace talks. He shook his head. What did he think about the Americans helping his country? "I don't think about it," he said. What did he think about? "My fields, my crops, my family."

Tran Van Duoc is not selfish or dull. It is just that his loyalties are limited to those things that he believes count. Yet the war constantly smashes families and makes less lucky men than Tran into refugees. At a training camp, I saw families and soldiers alike crying when they parted. Who is to care for the man's wife and children? If he is killed, the government will give his widow a year's pay (perhaps $700) and that is all. I don't suppose a widow in North Vietnam gets much either.

At Pleiku I met a woman who kept a shrine in memory of her husband. She gave me an American cigarette from those carefully arranged under his picture and told me how during the 1968 Tet offensive Vietcong agents came to the house at 3 a.m. and asked to talk to her husband and his brother. They went out; she and her children shivered in terror until dawn. Then neighbors came to the door to say that both men had been bound and murdered. Now she ekes out a living for her family by working for the Americans. When they leave she will be destitute, for she can expect little help from anybody.

### MORALE AND MASS GRAVES

I arrived at Hué in late April, just after they found the first of the mass graves, some 800 people buried under four feet of sand. The killings had happened during Tet—February 1968—when the enemy occupied Hué. Hundreds were rounded up—some officials, some military, some women, some children—and under the cover of darkness were taken into the countryside. Eventually, under the pretext of being moved to a "reeducation center," they were tied with bamboo strips or communications wire, marched to open graves and shot or clubbed to death. The people of Hué knew only that they had disappeared.

When the graves were discovered and opened more than a year later, after the area had been pacified, the bodies were no more than collections of bones held together by rotting cloth. The bodies were then wrapped in plastic sheets and laid out in rows. The people of Hué came in tears to seek their missing relatives. Jewelry and clothing made identification possible in a few cases; the rest were put in wooden coffins [pictured] and buried again in a mass ceremony. When it was over the people walked back to their homes in stunned silence.

There is a limit to the resiliency of spirit of any people, no matter how strong. The Tet offensive, costly as it may have been to the enemy, demonstrated to many South Vietnamese that there is no place really safe from the V.C. True, large-scale attacks on the cities have now slacked off, in part because of much heavier U.S. and South Vietnamese troop concentrations on the perimeters. But the V.C. keep on making their point in other ways: in the first six months of this year there were 4,674 South Vietnamese civilians kidnapped, 200 more than in the last six months of 1968. Many of these were government officials, police and teachers. The recent drop in the level of ground fighting and surprise attacks has so far had little impact on the villagers. Tet may not have been repeated, but it is remembered. Of course the Vietcong, over on the other side, are known to fear the bombs of the unseen B-52s overhead. But it is also true that when darkness falls every local defense militiaman thinks about the V.C.'s seeming ability to go anywhere, and when he thinks about it enough, or is frightened enough, he may be ready to make an accommodation. I asked a friend if he knew of a dedicated and honest village chief. "They are as rare as the autumn leaves," he said. There is no autumn in Vietnam.

## THE DESPAIR OF THE SEWER-PIPE DWELLER

He owned a motorscooter shop in Hué, employed 10 people, made good money, got home every night and appeared to be able to spend as much time at his business as he chose. I found him living a hike and he told me that after three years in the army he had been transferred to the Revolutionary Development cadre near home where his responsibilities appeared minimal. Such a transfer is not easily secured, but just the same, South Vietnam is full of such arrangements for those with money.

An extraordinary cynicism pervades South Vietnam. Inequality exists in any war, just as it does in peace, but it is never easy to accept great sacrifice cheerfully when you know that your neighbors with money are not required to sacrifice at all. Of course, graft is a way of life in most Oriental countries, but in a South Vietnam at war it seems more conspicuous, and more damaging. The disparity between those who have been hurt by the war and those who prosper is easy to see. Families live in concrete sewer pipes in Saigon . . . while 50 buildings, built originally as brothels, stand empty and crumbling in Pleiku. Wives of high South Vietnamese officers own a number of the bars and brothels that cluster around military bases, and have interests in the nightclubs where a Scotch may cost as much as a sewer-pipe dweller could earn in a week (or a South Vietnamese private in a day or two). Less than a mile from the sewer pipes are parking lots filled with rows of shiny motorbikes. They are worth about $500 each, and although I recognize that they are useful and perhaps even necessary if people are to move to and from work in a modern city, I could not help being struck by the contrast they made with the terrible poverty all around them.

## A CASE OF COWARDICE UNDER FIRE

Near Dakto one morning the enemy ambushed a group of seven Americans and 25 South Vietnamese troops out clearing a road of mines. Two Americans and a South Vietnamese were killed; the Americans called for help and then saw with amazement that the South Vietnamese were running away under fire. A relief column set out immediately from Dakto and I was in the second vehicle.

Near the ambush point we saw the South Vietnamese troops huddled in a ditch. The trucks stopped. A helicopter dropped an American lieutenant colonel; before it could lift off, its copilot and observer had been hit. It lifted again and I moved onto the road, put my back against a truck and began recording the scene with my camera. An American soldier was firing savagely and a lad without a helmet moved to join him, but the South Vietnamese soldiers remained huddled, an inviting target, not firing. Then the bareheaded soldier stood up to fire a long burst before another American heaved a grenade. By this time a few of the South Vietnamese had entered the fight but most were still not firing. At last, after a third American had been killed, other troops came in to relieve us and we pulled out.

It was only one skirmish, too short and too fast to justify large generalizations about the morale and capabilities of South Vietnamese troops. But in the eyes of the American troops standing silently around the tailgate of the truck which brought the broken, bleeding bodies of their buddies back to Dakto, you could see what they felt. At that moment I was ready to agree.

*Credit:* © 1969 TIME Inc. Reprinted by permission.

---

## BURR SNIDER: "LAST DAYS OF SAIGON"

---

*In the following excerpt of an* Esquire *magazine essay, Burr Snider's thick description of Saigon in the months following U.S. disengagement paints unforgettable mental images of the approaching end— among them: the refugees' desperate, pieced-together, nonpartisan existence; at the exclusive Saigon tennis club, contrasting court tactics parodying the Vietnamese, French, and American approaches to the war; journalistic inanities of the "five o'clock follies"; the American mission's metaphorical mugging*

*in a Saigon alley by Asian street urchins too weak to overcome their victim but too quick to be captured;*
*and the ultimate Saigon status symbol, the wristwatch.*

*Esquire*, January 1973

Quiet mornings; interludes, with familiar landmarks; quiet evenings; night

It is still dark at six a.m. when curfew is lifted. If it has been a night when the whump-whumps of the outgoing artillery have originated from points sufficiently far out in the exurbs, the noisiest city in the world is luxuriating in the seventh hour of its tranquility. At first light and for a poignantly brief moment thereafter one can enjoy freshness of the tropical dawn, cool, dewy, altogether sweet. But then with precisely timed fury the quiet is murdered with a quick chop: suddenly, the vacant avenues are inundated with traffic. Honda-swarms rasp and roar and spit and hoot and corrupt the air with a low ceiling of acrid clouds, billowing blue-white effluents of crude petrol burned imperfectly in a million popping little machines. A boilerworks nightmare. The streets erupt, vehicles scraping, weaving, meshing and emerging from random knots of traffic, minor casualties left in their wakes. In the interior city, market stalls spring up, reducing the thoroughfares to lanes of narrow passage. In box-backed motor scooters called *lambros* produce comes streaming in from surrounding farmlands over perilous highways.

By seven-thirty, the beginning of office hours, the sun is high and bright and the walls are dripping with humid sweat. In Cholon, the Chinese sector, seated over bowls of Chinese soup and tea in a few select cafés, members of the various cartels fix the black-market rate for money exchange and the day's prices for rice, sugar and opium. Military convoys roar helter-skelter through the streets, sirens screaming. The city undulates and totters on its rotted, flimsy underpinnings through another morning, Saigon morning. . . .

The devastation in the countryside has brought three million people together in a space meticulously designed for a few hundred thousand, and now Saigon is among the most densely populated cities in the world. Life spills into the streets simply because there is no other place for it. An odd corner, a couple of empty oil drums draped with a patch of olive-drab poncho (the dominant color of the city) becomes instant lodging for a refugee family. If they manage to remain without interference from the police or objections from already horribly cramped neighbors, they will attempt to expand, will erect a wall or two from scraps of corrugated tin roofing stolen from some American supply depot, or from sheets made of flattened-out beer cans. They will drag in pallets and fashion a cook stove out of a discarded can or a shell casing. They will hang an icon, erect a small altar, they will attempt life. Gouged and disfigured by the loss of their homes among the ancestral villages and fields, they exist dully in irretrievable limbo. But they persist . . . scrounging, grubbing,

hustling, living off bones already picked clean, sucking the juice from discarded fruit, snatching at scraps fallen from the tables of the street restaurants. Soon, if they are able to reconcile themselves to this city, they will enter into elemental business . . . the father perhaps will arrange for his youngest son to receive a tray of black-market cigarettes to sell in the streets. The mother and a daughter will buy a can of mess-hall cooking oil on credit and will fry up bananas to be dropped into little pouches holding a sticky white sweet sauce, or doughnuts, heavy and sugary, also to be moved on the streets. Or they might sell a sort of iced limeade in little cellophane bags tied at the top by a knot through which a straw is inserted. Another daughter might take a stab at prostitution, although now with the exodus of the Americans that market is badly glutted. The father might rent a pedicab which he will pump laboriously through the streets looking for fares. The nature of the family business is apt to change abruptly, governed as it is by the whims and vagaries of the black market. One day a few cases of Pepsi-Cola might become available to them and for a while the whole family will load their shoulder poles with buckets filled with chunks of ice and the drinks. Or it could be that a couple of dozen pairs of PX underwear comes by their way and a temporary stand will be set up in one of the outdoor sky markets until the goods are sold. In this city of primitive entrepreneurs not much is required to launch a business. Dotting the street corners in every precinct are tiny concerns whose single capital asset is a stolen tube-patching kit for repairing the blown tires of the countless motorbikes. It's not so much a living that the refugee pursues in the city as an alternative to dying.

At the movies in downtown Saigon (all films Chinese except where noted):

Champion of Club
Dai La The Invincible
Trang Tu Trying To Find Out If His Wife Is Unfaithful
The Battle Of Phi Long
Vampires
Boxing Champion
Dissipated Young Girl
Ape Causing Scandal in Hong Kong
Cantonese Boxing Champion
One-Armed Hero
The Tigers Of The Sea
Good-Natured Girl
War-Provoking Letter
Squadrons Of Sea Eagles
The Bell's Sabre
Lucky Meeting Of The Predestined
Love News
The Miracles Of Battles (Indian)

The Saigonese are apolitical, neither capitalists nor Communists nor much of anything else except expert tasters of the wind. They are of course filled with apprehension but not so much over the ideological future of their city as over the question of their own survival in any event. The dry season brings the threat of the Communists' post-monsoon Fall Offensive and many fear that if it comes off it will be equal in intensity to Tet of '68, with wholesale reprisals against those connected with the present government or the Americans. Any coalition agreement is bound to be shaky and the Saigonese feel that the next few months will bring radical change to their lives. They know a little something about how power vacuums are filled. After decades of armed conflict and political upheaval, the people, given the choice, would probably opt for a continuation of present conditions rather than take the risk that any change would be for the better. After all, they've lived with this war for a long time, accommodating themselves to normality within a great armed encampment. Patrols of soldiers in the streets are part of the everyday scenery, machine gun bunkers guard major intersections and bridges. The sight of high officials being whisked through the offices and between their elaborately fortified villas in the safety of wailing motorcades is to the cynical Saigonese only a source of mild amusement. In Graham Greene's *The Quiet American* (the only good novel ever written about Vietnam), Fowler, the dispassionate, Weltschmerzy journalist, describes existence in wartime Saigon: "Ordinary life goes on. . . . Just as in an air raid it proved impossible to be frightened all the time, so under the bombardment of routine jobs, of chance encounters, of impersonal anxieties, one lost for hours together the personal fear." Today in the city one loses it for days, sometimes weeks, but then again there have been four long years since Saigon has had to endure anything like the concerted bestiality of the Tet '68 uprising. Maybe it is only that memories are short.

Anyway the apprehension always comes flooding back. There is the inescapable feeling that apocalypse is galloping near, that the crunch is at hand. American ground troops are gone—the last remaining combat unit pulled out in August—and although the planes remain, the capacity of the Communists to wage war in the South has not, under the bombing of the North, appreciably diminished. Vietnamization is the egregious flop everyone knew it would be and even though there are a few passably good units, Thieu seems intent on wasting them in bloody showcase battles like Quang Tri just to make political points. His power, putative at best, is blatantly derived from American money. Were it not for the fact that the regime grows more repressive by the minute, his rule might be providing some comic relief for the people. The N.L.F. [National Liberation Front] refuses to deal with him and there is no one around strong enough to supplant him. What chances remain for a viable coalition government to survive under these conditions? Like the song says, there's no laughs left 'cause we laughed 'em all.

"The majority are probably afraid of the Vietcong, they are probably against a Communist takeover," says a half-Vietnamese, half-French girl of her fellow citizens. "But it is not out of any love for Thieu or an American-imposed democracy, even out of a particular hatred of communism. It's just that they are afraid the VC will take away their Hondas and TVs and they went too far into debt to get them."

Of course strong pockets of VC sympathy exist in Saigon and there are elements which are ripe for radicalization. Driving out of the city on the American-built Long Binh highway you see lining the road long miles of unbelievably rank and squalid hoovervilles composed of crowded shanties squatting deep in the dirt, built from the discarded remnants of the American military presence. This is where the war veterans live, scraps of land illegally appropriated from the city or private owners. The police have tried in the past to evict the squatters and raze their shacks but the veterans refuse to budge and now the issue is so explosive that the government seeks to ignore it. The veterans—there are millions of them in the country—comprise a powerful and potentially volatile group. Thieu plays stick-and-carrot with them—alternately granting them a concession or coming down hard and fast when they threaten to get too far out of hand—but there is plenty of doubt that they can be controlled indefinitely. They have already held large and loud demonstrations demanding better medical benefits and decent housing, forcing the government to call out the riot police.

Another element of dissent is the refugees. Thousands upon thousands of them are jammed into camps just around Saigon alone; some estimates number them at a third of the total population of South Vietnam. The loss of their homes has left them alienated and in deep spiritual distress and the mean conditions in the camps provide a classic revolutionary breeding ground. The VC move among them with ease and although no effective widespread organization has been achieved it may be only a matter of time before the refugees become strong enough to provide real political worry for the government.

But mostly for the Saigonese it's business—meager as it is—as usual, every man for himself in an atmosphere of nervous waiting. Meanwhile Thieu is taking no chances. On Saturdays he appears on TV to announce new emergency measures which tighten down the clamps just that bit more. Opposition newspapers are being silenced, parliamentary dissent is stilled, civil rights forgotten. Wearily the people acquiesce to spot searches, identity checks and summary interrogations. They have been through it all before but now they brace themselves for even more. They wait for the immediate future, hoping they have not entered the season of death for their city.

Ah, those long and lazy lunches at the Cercle Sportif Saigonnais. Sitting on the deck by the pool watching the tawny Vietnamese and the lithe French ladies taking the sun in their St. Tropez–inspired bikinis. Ah, the langouste with mayonnaise, a *citron pressé*, the desultory, risqué conversation, the gossip. You can forget all here. In the background the thwock thwock thwock of the tennis courts where the Vietnamese, French and American gentry sweat out the perfection of their separate game styles in the brutal midday sun: the Vietnamese, defensive demons, no power but capable of uncanny placements with their short-stroke, pistonlike swings, playing tightly and monotonously and concentrating on position and utility at the expense of grace; the French, leisurely and stylish, playing chops to preserve strength and steps, covering the court with smooth glides; and the Americans, crew-cut power and audacious risks, always taking the offensive and trying for outrageous slams. In the parking lot beside the courts the chauffeurs busy themselves polishing the staff cars. [Nguyen Cao] Ky used to play here almost daily before his fall from grace and the club members still get a little chuckle out of the spectacle. At just around noon one of those screaming motorcades so familiar in the streets in the city would come roaring into the Cercle's driveway and a bunch of his personal goons would jump out and sweep the courts clean of players. About ten minutes later the sirens would be heard again off in the distance and soon Ky would come gunning in, his limo surrounded by a phalanx of booted motorcycle cops (white boots, that's right). He'd play for about an hour or so, jump back in his car and roar off. Only then could the members resume their games.

Jean-Claude, the French planter's son who makes his living building ski boats for members of the Club Nautique, looks up from his papaya, and his eyes are so clean and clear in his handsome, swarthy face, so free of any overt Gallic cynicism that you *have* to believe that what he says comes from the heart. "Your government must not abandon Vietnam as so many Americans would like you to do," he says fervently. "You cannot say, 'F—— Vietnam.' Yes. And that would be the end. No, you must honor your commitments. Of course I agree that democracy is not the answer for this country, it cannot work in Asia. But neither is communism. What then? I will tell you. A proper politic." Well, you certainly got it by the handle there, Jean-Claude, but what'd you have in mind specifically? "A proper politic. Like in Thailand. There they got a king and ministers, but they got a proper politic. The people are happy. You think the people are happy in the North? I have an old man working for me. He will tell you. Everybody must work for the government. Everybody must work for the war. There is no rest. That is why so many come to the South. I talked once with an N.V.A. [North Vietnamese Army] officer who was captured. You know what he say? To have the right to eat, to have the right to *sleep*, a man must volunteer to fight in the South. He *must* come to the South and fight. Sure everybody volunteers. Listen. America has made many mistakes in Vietnam but she has helped. Do you know

her biggest mistake? She sent draftees. If she too had sent all volunteers it would have worked. You know what the French do to fight the wars in Africa? They make a secret recruiting. They say quietly: You want to fight in Africa? They don't make a big deal out of it. . . ." Jean Claude's voice trails off as he pauses to watch a near-naked lovely wriggle past in the pool. It's so easy to forget it all here at the Cercle. Thwock thwock. Time for maybe one more café noir before everybody retires to an air-conditioned room to wait out the hot part of the day.

In the frenzied uproar of the last few minutes before the inexorable tolling of curfew, a fat American civilian emerges unsteadily from a cab on an inky corner barely a block from the well-lit expanse of Lam Son Square. Just as he completes his transaction with the hack he is suddenly set upon by a pack of street urchins who have been milling about the sidewalk. These case-hardened little furies with empty eyes and no expectations have been street creatures ever since they could walk; they are wild and uncontrollable. They rip into the fat American like dervishes, tiny hands clawing at anything they can grasp, expertly working at his watchband, his wallet, his pockets and even his spectacles. Under the shock of the attack his mouth drops open with disbelief and he howls with rage. Almost to the ground under their shoving, he rallies . . . flails wildly with the only weapon at hand—his rolled umbrella—and catches several of them with glancing swipes. The others back off cautiously. Regaining leverage he slashes away again and again but they are too nimble for him and easily dodge his blows. Some are able to slip in under his roundhouse swings and they continue to rifle his pockets in split-second dashes. He howls again, desperately and unsuccessfully appealing to the few indifferent bystanders, among whom is a Vietnamese policeman, for help. From behind, a tiny girl, ragged and filthy, certainly no older than six, creeps up on him holding a three-legged stool so heavy that she must struggle under its weight. She raises the stool, the effort requiring all her puny strength, and brings it crashing down on the American's unprotected head. He freezes with pain. "Goddaaaaaaaaam!" he bellows, quite unable to conceive that this is really happening to him. He turns to seek out his tormentor, spots her, still holding the stool, and charges blindly, a great, mad wounded beast. She drops the stool and from a standstill accelerates to top speed flashing down the street, the American lumbering in pursuit. At the corner she slows momentarily to make the turn, her little fists describing elaborate cornering movements as if she's playing motorcar. "A-choogo-chooga-chooga-choog," she puffs merrily, confident of her swiftness and cunning, and disappears among a jumble of parked cars, *cyclos*, and Hondas. The fat American, winded, gives up the chase. He returns to the scene of his assault and among the jeers of the scattered attackers, kneels to the street to

> I agree that democracy is not the answer for this country, it cannot work in Asia. But neither is communism.

retrieve the papers that have fallen from his briefcase, still breathing with difficulty and muttering at the outrage. While he stuffs the papers into his bag another child, equally as small as the first, picks up the fallen stool, tiptoes up behind the stooped man, and smacks him another vicious blind-side shot which knocks him sprawling to the pavement.

The Continental Palace Hotel, a sprawling and beautifully preserved vestige of the lazy and laid-back French colonial days, emanates an ambience which might be described as Somerset Maugham Tropical Gothic. Inside its *raffiné* white-washed exterior, musty, high-ceilinged halls lead into spacious and decrepitly elegant rooms strewn with heavy old furnishings. Louvered French doors open out onto the smoky streets below and the *de rigueur* revolving overhead fans whir the brooding air. Downstairs there is an interior garden heavy with the scent of myriad blooms where one can linger decadently over a late breakfast of café au lait and the best croissants east of Montparnasse while aging servants patter about in slippers and wilting uniforms of starched white cotton.

The ground-floor terrace, a sort of exaggerated veranda which looks out onto Lam Son Square, the heart of downtown Saigon, is the jangled nerve center of the city's wartime nightlife. It is known among its English-speaking habitués, for whom it serves as a nightly gathering point, as the "Continental Shelf." The hotel management, French and eminently pragmatic, long ago discovered that the presence of the cadre of Vietnamese prostitutes which had staked out the Shelf as a private preserve wasn't doing business any harm at all. A tacit arrangement of easy tolerance was worked out and the ladies were given the run of the place. Over the years the *poules* at the Continental, many of them quite lushly sensational, became a sort of Saigon tradition.

It's a true *Cabaret* scene. From late afternoon until eleven-o'clock curfew the carefree hookers lounge around the tables on cushioned rattan and wicker chairs, happily chattering and gossiping, throwing winks and sunny smiles at prospective customers, and serenely watching the beat of Saigon life flow past on Tu Do Street. In a row of tables along the back wall reserved for them by unspoken agreement usually sit several of a marvelous troupe of Vietnamese drag aristocracy chirping away. These languid, giddy creatures coexist with the hookers in a spirit of friendly competition and often offer empathetic advice to the lovelorn among them. "The Queen," their undisputed but benevolent despot, is as spectacularly lovely as any girl in Saigon.

Fowler, the cynical, opium-smoking reporter who narrates the action of *The Quiet American*, cohabited with a beautiful Vietnamese dance-hall girl in a flat on Tu Do Street a few blocks down from the Continental toward the Saigon River, only in those days, before the government removed the French names from all the streets and public places, it was called the rue Catinat and it was pretty swank.

Today, Tu Do, which means liberty, is a blend of Fifth and Seventh Avenues, plush alternated with sleaze. Chic restau-rants, expensive shops, and airline offices are sandwiched in uncomfortable contiguity between bars where girls hustle the few remaining American soldiers for "Saigon tea." Most of the bars on Tu Do which once thrived are locked and shuttered now, forced to close by the dreadful lack of business. The same is true, only more so, of Hai Ba Trung, the next parallel street over, which was once lined almost exclusively with honky-tonks, and also of Le Loi, the great latitudinal thoroughfare, and of Plantation Road out in Cholon near Tan Son Nhut Air Base, where the G.I.s went to dance and drink and smoke dope in garage-like bars that featured either hill-billy or soul music (but never both), or to relax in massage and bath parlors known to the grunts more accurately as skull palaces and steam-and-cream joints.

Dancing is prohibited now in Saigon, as are private parties—the government being engaged in an assiduous campaign to convince the people that it is time to get serious about this war—and as summer ends, the troop level is down below the thirty-thousand mark and dropping fast. The sub-culture which sprang up to service the needs of soldiers is now rather suddenly a market with no buyers.

A few joints still limp along however. Most of them have reverted back to the original Vietnamese names they had before the buildup, but some, like Mimi's, The New York Bar, and The You And Me Club, hang on in English. There are still enough support and administrative troops on the staffs of the various American military headquarters in the vicinity, plus some nominal Australian and Korean forces hanging around, to provide a little action. In addition there is always the semi-permanent American community that exists here on the periphery of the military—businessmen, lawyers, journalists and such—and for the most part these types have no immediate plans for leaving. (It shouldn't surprise anyone that the American Chamber of Commerce has a thriving Saigon chapter, that there is an American Legion Post here, and that the park benches in downtown Saigon were donated by the local Lions Club.)

To a great degree though, untold thousands of pimps, whores, drug dealers, pickpockets, black marketeers and knock-off artists are just simply out of business. This is not to say that they have all made their bundles and have gone straight. It only means that they have turned inward and now feed viciously off each other and off their uncrooked countrymen. Of course the few Americans left are increasingly prone to assaults and random violence from frustrated thugs, targets for every two-bit hustler on the street. "Buy watch?" The whiny supplication is familiar by now to every American in Saigon. Walking down virtually any street in town, you'll hear footsteps rapidly approaching from behind. "Buy watch?" the voice will whisper in your ear. No, you'll say if you're practiced at this sort of thing, and increase your pace. So will the owner of the voice. "Buy watch?" No. "Look watch. Buy watch?" You don't even look. No. Then he'll grab your arm. "Sell watch?" Maybe you're in the mood to dump your time-piece. Oh for Christ's sake. No! "M.P.C.?" M.P.C. stands for

Military Payment Certificates, the scrip with which soldiers are paid in a somewhat futile attempt to curb inflation and keep greenbacks off the black market. No. "Sell dolla?" No. You are becoming more and more emphatic but you know it is of no avail. He's got his catalog and it's like a ritual—he's got to go through it item by item. "Can sa?" (Marijuana.) No. (He might be a fink.) "Skag? Buy skag?" No, babe. "Dirty pitcher?" Oh come on. Is there any place in the world except Saigon where somebody will still try to flog you a dirty pic? That's usually the last item on the list so he'll melt back into the crowd and you're free. You turn the corner. A voice whispers: "Buy watch?"

The wristwatch, as a matter of fact, is *the* Vietnamese status symbol, Hondas notwithstanding. When you pass people in the street, they don't look at your face but at your watch. When meeting a Vietnamese you'll notice that as he is shaking your hand he will be taking surreptitious peeks at your watch. There are mobile teams of thieves cruising the streets on Hondas who are unbelievably adept at ripping watches off the wrists of foreign pedestrians and then speeding off almost before they know what hit them.

In the bloated sex market the hookers are having a hard time keeping the price of an all-nighter up around the standard three to four thousand piasters (seven to ten dollars). There are too many young semipros now who are feeding habits (heroin incidentally is easier to score than grass in Saigon today) and have no scruples about price-cutting. The Continental Hotel girls still get along all right, although nothing like in years past, but the regular streetwalkers and the Honda girls—who ride around on the backs of motorbikes driven by their pimps looking for a score—are facing real trouble. To make matters worse, hundreds of pros, maybe thousands, have drifted in from Vung Tau, the seaside resort about fifty miles to the east of Saigon which was once a major R.&R. center for allied troops. As many as 30,000 G.I.s a week once passed through Vung Tau on in-country leave and the town boomed to the point of explosion. Now the beaches, once jammed solid, are deserted (except for the nihilistic Vietnamese hippies who gather there to strum their guitars and smoke that good grass the long day through), and the bars and hotels and skull palaces are boarded up—a very eerie scene. And the battalions of seven-day girl friends who prospered beyond belief during the "good" years have come streaming into Saigon to further depress an economy already mortally shaken.

Should auld acquaintance lapse among the members of the foreign press corps they can always be renewed at the daily briefing at the National Press Center on Lam Son Square, conveniently located catty-corner from the National Assembly Building whence nothing flows, and across the street from the newshawks' hangout, The Hotel Caravelle, whence flows The Truth.

At four-fifteen sharp from time immemorial, to an audience of somnolent staffers (still yawning from the three-hour siesta) representing rags and mags the world over, an A.R.V.N. [South Vietnamese army] press officer rattles off surreal stats which paint the official picture of that day's ebb and flow. This is immediately translated into backstroke English and taken down by the press as writ—except for the few wise guys who ask a couple of snide questions to let the A.R.V.N. cat know ain't nobody putting nothing over on them. When the A.R.V.N. monotonously repeats the same answer the wise guys will shrug, their duty to journalistic integrity done, and write the answer down as writ. "At 0400 this morning, in an area NW of ———, an infantry company of the A.R.V.N. engaged an enemy force of unknown size, X enemy were killed and X weapons were captured. Friendly casualties were not available."

Then a U.S. Air Force slickie takes the rostrum, *really* takes it, grasps it by the edges like he's going to hurl it at anyone who dares question his figures. A real powerhouse, this major, making his own special salute to Forties' fly-boy urbanity with a pencil-line moustache. Knowing he's got the voice, sure of his style, or why else would they put him in Public Information?—comes on like a clarion. "X tanks destroyed yesterday, X more today in an area X miles inside the Cambodian border."

A hand is raised. "Question?" he trumpets, really bull-moosing it.

"Were B-52s bombing in that area?"

"Question is were B-52s bombing in that area. I do not have that information."

"Is it a question of not having that information or of simply not making it available?"

"Question is: is it a question of not having that information or of not making it available. Answer is: it is a question of not having that information."

The press starts to shuffle sleepily out. Then two quick questions from the back, biff-baff: Why is it that the N.V.A. reports of planes shot down are always higher than reported by official friendly spokesmen and why are casualty figures always so divergent? "The answer to both these questions is I don't know."

In the insular—if not to say incestuous—press community, one question blazes the grapevine in fruitless quest of illumination: What is Kissinger telling Thieu? Nixon's man is in town again, just blown in from Paris for one of his periodic hush-hush jawjaws with Nguyen. Every bureau chief and correspondent in town has been told in very clear terms by the home office to get the skinny on the talks. But there are no leaks this time and the hacks are getting desperate.

On a quiet Sunday morning a lawyer named Ed, who provides free legal aid for indigent G.I.s (and who is known to have good press connections), is enjoying a leisurely game of chess with a friend. Enter a dashing, safari-suited Italian who strings for *Der Spiegel* out of Singapore. He has just arrived in town.

"Hello Ed. Beautiful morning. Oh, what a *splendide* chess! Where did you get it, Ed?"

"Hello. Just downstairs in the shop," says Ed, trying to be polite but utterly engrossed in his game.

"Oh, it's *splendide*," repeats the Italian, then quickly down to business. "Ed, tell me please, what did Henri tell to Thieu? Do you know? Does anybody know?"

"Sure I know," says Ed. "I'll give it to you exclusive. Kissinger walked into the palace and said, 'Your Excellency, I have a personal message from the President of the United States.' Then he pulled a pistol out of his coat and blasted old Nugent right through the heart."

"Oh Ed," laughs the Italian. "Oh, no."

"Believe me," Ed insists. "Thieu fell to the floor mortally wounded. Then he lifted up his arm and pulled back his sleeve and said to Kissinger, 'Hey, you wan' buy watch?'"

"Ho, ho, ho," chuckles the Italian. "Oh Ed. Too much." And still chuckling and shaking his head he departs.

Ad in the Saigon *Post*:

*Our Way is Brutal*
But It's The Surest One
To Get Passport For Your Fiancé
Apply: Prof Hong 145 Do Tham Square
Phone 99860

In the corridors of drowsy confusion that are the Immigration Office, a dissolute, sun-wrinkled, old-before-his-time retired N.C.O., staff sergeant or petty officer for sure, applies for a residence permit or an extension of his visa so he can continue a blissful concubinage with his "Vietnamese darlin". A tattoo on his arm pictures a naked and laughing lady in a champagne glass and kicking up her long legs in gay abandon. The caption inscribed underneath: My ruin. . . .

Blackness descends like a layer of smudge. Harsh unshaded light bulbs from the sidewalk food stalls throw fingers of unkind illumination back into the unfathomable alleys. Deep in a shadow, an old man drowsily unbuttons his all-purpose pajamas and lays his head on a fetid burlap mat. On the slum corner tiny children squint in the murk to finish their game of marbles. A hesitant breeze stirs the higher branches of the occasional tree along the street but the air below remains as tepid as bathwater. Although traffic in the road is heavy as usual it seems lulled in the new darkness; the rasp of the Honda and the put-putting of the ancient little Renault taxicabs provide a low and leisurely background din, nothing compared to the bedlam which will erupt later as curfew approaches. Whiffs of garlic and soy and *nuoc mam*, the vilely puissant and ever-present fish sauce, drift in from the cook stoves into the dead air to join in confluent wafts with the funk of the smashed and rotting garbage piled between the stalls. Steam rises with a gush from an open pot of Chinese soup simmering on a charcoal fire at streetside. Sudden reports from the far corner elicit a watchful momentary pause from the street dwellers, but when no concussion is felt the flow of the open-air life resumes. It is only a restless band of *cao bois*, the nomadic delinquents spawned of the slums, lurching their Hondas into a unified roar as they blast off into the smoky sable on another search for the unutterable. Saigon evening.

## PETER ARNETT: DEPICTION OF BLIND PANIC OF SOUTH VIETNAMESE ARMY IN FINAL HOURS OF WAR

*Associated Press correspondent Peter Arnett had seen more death and destruction than perhaps any other journalist covering the Vietnam War, and more than most American soldiers as well. He told his comrade at CBS News, Morley Safer, "I took a hardboiled approach to the Vietnam War . . . I've always tried to look past [the carnage]." But by 1970, after eight and a half years of covering the war full-time, the steel had left him. "I just don't want to see anymore bodies."[2] Arnett left the war briefly, but could not stay away for long. He was back in time for the fall of Saigon to the North Vietnamese Army on 30 April 1975. Most Western journalists were evacuated by the U.S. consulate, but, true to his nature, Arnett was among the handful who risked the invaders to get the capitulation story.*

*New York Times, 25 May 1975*

SAIGON, South Vietnam, May 24—Survivors of the last two divisions defending Saigon in the hours before its fall last month tell of men fleeing in blind panic, of officers deserting, of complete resignation to defeat by whole units and of the few who tried to salvage some honor from the sudden stunning victory by the Communist forces.

Reports of the final hours of the war have trickled into Saigon from survivors of the two divisions—the Fifth north of the capital and the 25th to the northwest. They tell of a commanding general shooting himself after ordering his 15,000-man infantry division to surrender without a fight and of another fleeing in panic after commandeering the last jeep in his camp after heavy shelling.

It was the finale of the 50-day rout of the million-man

South Vietnamese Army that began in the Central Highlands and spread down the coast until Saigon was left defenseless and defeated.

The pattern of defeat became evident early in April when élite units around Hué and Da Nang fled as Communist forces massed in the hills.

The debacle allowed Communist forces to encircle Saigon a full week before the fall of the city, and the message was apparent—surrender or else.

In the last week, only the 25th and 5th Divisions stood between the Communists and mastery of the capital. The Communists moved first against the 25th, firing shells for three days at the Cu Chi base camp, which the United States 25th Division had carved out of the jungle 20 miles northwest of Saigon in 1966.

"Casualties were innumerable and dead and wounded were lying around on the ground unaware of each other" by the morning of April 29, the day before Saigon fell, one officer who was there said.

"All ammo depots had been hit and all soldiers sought a way out of the base," he said.

"But the barbed-wire gates were closed by the high command and the slogan was given out, 'Live or die right here.' Particularly hard on soldiers was that their families were living and dying with them."

The Communist forces launched the overwhelming last attack on the Cu Chi base at 6 A.M. on April 29.

The first target was a division training center whose soldiers broke and ran in the first minutes. An hour later Communist tanks were inside Cu Chi. The division commander, Maj. Gen. Ly Tong Ba, ordered all his troops to stay in place. But within three hours a company commander reported the tanks were through the sprawling base's second line of defense and were threatening the command bunker. The general ordered his command staff into two groups and ran out.

"At that moment I saw that all men were going their own way and not following orders," said a staff officer who was present. "All looked for a way of escape to avoid fire and shelling. I myself ran away, jumping over any kind of obstacle including barbed wire toward the main gate of the base to seek a way out. What was most dramatic were the wounded. Some had lost one leg but still tried to drag themselves on—to where nobody knew. Other wounded were ignored by fellow combatants.

"When General Ba and his staff reached the main gate at the base more than 1,000 men were trying, each in his own way, to escape, climbing over the gate, crossing fields of mines. Quite a few had been shot dead by fellow combatants for earlier having refused to obey the order to resist.

"Gen. Ba himself jumped on the only jeep left, belonging to the artillery commander. He ordered the gate opened so he could flee. After the gates opened, a fleeing crowd swelled to more than 2,000 as families joined soldiers. They looked like bees fleeing an endangered hive. Communist guns began

firing from nearby but they were firing into the air to stop the soldiers and not to kill them."

The officer was captured and held for a few days in a school building, then released to his family in Saigon.

Meanwhile, the staff of the Fifth Division at Lai Khe, about 35 miles north of Saigon, was apprehensively assessing the situation. The Lai Khe base, also created by American forces, stood across Route 13, long regarded as an obvious Communist approach to Saigon. By late in the day of April 29, the division headquarters had lost contact with the corps headquarters at Bien Hoa, and the division commander, Brig. Gen. Le Nguyen Vy, was reduced to following the war news on the Saigon radio. It told him nothing of what was happening to the 25th Division.

General Vy was a well-regarded officer, chosen by President Nguyen Van Thieu to lead the Fifth Division because it was Mr. Thieu's old outfit and had a favored place in the army. But the once-effective division was worn down from fighting earlier in the year and its morale was weak.

General Vy ordered all vehicles regrouped in preparation for the whole division to move to Saigon for a final defense of the capital. But on the morning of April 30 General Vy decided on another course.

## AN ACT OF "HONOR"

He called a staff meeting at 7 A.M., which was three hours before President Duong Van Minh announced an unconditional surrender. All were present except the deputy division commander, who fled from the country in an American plane.

General Vy told his staff that Saigon would soon fall. He turned over command to Col. Tu Van and said: "As an officer of the South Vietnamese Army, I must act for the honor of the army, but you must protect the lives of the soldiers. Good luck to you."

The general went to his house, lit a cigarette and shot himself.

The colonel found the body and ordered it buried with full military honors.

As Communist tanks made their last push on Saigon 35 miles to the south, the full Fifth Division assembled at the Lai Khe flagpole. "In a short but emotional funeral General Vy was buried and the honor of the division was saved," one officer said later. "We were all very proud of this event."

At 1 P.M., after the surrender announcement from Saigon, the whole division boarded 200 trucks and drove south to the town of Ben Cat, which the Communists had occupied.

The convoy stopped outside the town. The soldiers dismounted, dropped their weapons and took off their uniforms as about 50 Communist soldiers carrying AK-47 rifles stood by.

The men stayed under guard for two days in Ben Cat. Then all were released except officers of the rank of captain and above, who were held for "retraining." Some have since returned to Saigon.

*Credit*: Reprinted with permission of The Associated Press.

## NOTES

1. Leslie H. Gelb with Richard K. Betts, *The Irony of Vietnam: The System Worked* (Washington, D.C.: Brookings Institution, 1979), 353.

2. Morley Safer, "Peter Arnett Interview," CBS *Evening News with Walter Cronkite*, Columbia Broadcasting System, 7 July 1970.

## FURTHER READINGS

Cao Van Vien. *The Final Collapse*. Washington, D.C.: U.S. Army Center of Military History, 1984.

Nolan, Keith William. *Into Laos: The Story of Dewey Canyon II/Lam Son 719: Vietnam, 1971.* Novato, Calif.: Presidio Press, 1986.

Sheehan, Neil. *Two Cities: Hanoi and Saigon*. London: Jonathan Cape, 1992.

Snepp, Frank. *A Decent Interval: An Insider's Account of Saigon's Indecent End Told by the CIA's Chief Strategy Analyst in Vietnam*. New York: Random House, 1977.

# SELECTED BIBLIOGRAPHY

## BOOKS

Carruthers, Susan L. *The Media at War: Communication and Conflict in the Twentieth Century.* New York: St. Martin's Press, 2000.

Cook, Russell. "The Vietnam War." In *History of the Mass Media in the United States.* Ed. Margaret Blanchard. Chicago: Fitzroy Dearborn, 1998.

Cumings, Bruce. *War and Television.* New York: Verso, 1992.

Dennis, Everette E., David Stebenne, John Parlike, Mark Thalhimer, Craig LaMay, Dirk Smillie, Martha FitzSimon, Shirley Gazsi, and Seth Raehlin. *The Media at War: The Press and the Persian Gulf Conflict.* Eds. Craig LaMay, Martha FitzSimon, and Jeanne Sahadi. New York: Gannett Foundation, 1991.

Faas, Horst, and Tim Page. *Requiem: By the Photographers Who Died in Vietnam and Indochina.* New York: Random House, 1997. Also available at *The Digital Journalist,* http://digitaljournalist.org/issue9711/req1.htm.

Fall, Bernard B. *The Two Viet-Nams: A Political and Military Analysis.* 2nd rev. ed. New York: Praeger, 1967; London: Pall Mall, 1967.

———, ed. *Ho Chi Minh on Revolution: Selected Writings, 1920–66.* New York: Praeger, 1967.

Fawcett, Denby, Ann Bryan Mariano, Kate Webb, Ann Morrissy Merick, Jurate Kazickas, Edith Lederer, Tad Bartimus, Tracy Wood, and Laura Palmer. *War Torn: Stories of War from the Women Reporters Who Covered Vietnam.* New York: Random House, 2002.

Greene, Graham. *The Quiet American.* London: W. Heinemann, 1955.

Halberstam, David. *The Making of a Quagmire.* New York: Random House, 1965.

———. *The Powers That Be.* New York: Dell Publishing, 1979.

Hallin, Daniel C. *The "Uncensored War": The Media and Vietnam.* New York: Oxford University Press, 1986.

Hammond, William. *Public Affairs: The Military and the Media, 1962–1968.* Washington, D.C.: U.S. Army Center of Military History, 1988.

———. *Public Affairs: The Military and the Media, 1968–1973.* Washington, D.C.: U.S. Army Center of Military History, 1996.

———. *Reporting Vietnam: Media and Military at War*. Lawrence: University Press of Kansas, 1998.

Isaacson, Walter. *Kissinger: A Biography*. New York: Simon & Schuster, 1992.

Just, Ward S. *To What End: Report from Vietnam*. Boston: Houghton Mifflin, 1968.

Karnow, Stanley. *Vietnam: A History*. 2nd rev. ed. New York: Penguin Books, 1997.

Kennedy, William V. *The Military and the Media: Why the Press Cannot Be Trusted to Cover a War*. Westport, Conn.: Praeger, 1993.

Kissinger, Henry. *White House Years*. Boston: Little, Brown and Company, 1979.

Lande, Nathaniel. *Dispatches from the Front: A History of the American War Correspondent*. Oxford: Oxford University Press, 1996.

Lederer, William J., and Eugene Burdick. *The Ugly American*. New York: W. W. Norton, 1958.

McLaughlin, Greg. *The War Correspondent*. London: Pluto Press, 2002.

Mueller, John E. *War, Presidents, and Public Opinion*. New York: Wiley, 1973.

Prochnau, William. *Once upon a Distant War: David Halberstam, Neil Sheehan, Peter Arnett—Young War Correspondents and Their Early Vietnam Battles*. New York: Vintage Books, 1996.

*Reporting Vietnam, Part One: American Journalism, 1959–1969*. New York: Literary Classics of the United States, 1998.

*Reporting Vietnam, Part Two: American Journalism, 1969–1975*. New York: Literary Classics of the United States, 1998.

Sheehan, Neil. *A Bright Shining Lie: John Paul Vann and America in Vietnam*. New York: Vintage Books, 1989.

Steinman, Ron. *The Soldiers' Story: Vietnam in Their Own Words*. New York: Barnes and Noble, 2000.

Wyatt, Clarence R. *Paper Soldiers: The American Press and the Vietnam War*. Rev. ed. Chicago: University of Chicago Press, 1995.

## NEWS SOURCES

Associated Press
*Atlantic Monthly*
*CBS Evening News with Walter Cronkite*
*Chicago Daily News*
*Chicago Tribune*
*Columbus* (Ohio) *Evening Dispatch*
*Esquire*
*Harper's Magazine*
*Life*
*Louisville Times*
*National Review*
*New American Review*
*New Republic*
*New York Times*
*New Yorker*
*Newsweek*
*Nieman Reports*
*Plain Dealer* (Cleveland, Ohio)
*Ramparts*
*St. Louis Post-Dispatch*
*Saturday Evening Post*

*Time*
*Wall Street Journal*
*Washington Post*

## WEB SITES

The American Experience and WGBH Interactive. *Vietnam Online*. Boston: WGBH Educational Foundation, 1983. http://www.pbs.org/wgbh/amex/vietnam/.

Faas, Horst, and Marianne Fulton. "The Survivor: Phan Thi Kim Phuc and the Photographer Nick Ut." *The Digital Journalist*. http://digitaljournalist.org/issue0008/ng_intro.htm.

Halstead, Dirck. "Larry Burrows: Vietnam." *The Digital Journalist*. http://digitaljournalist.org/issue0302/lb_intro.html.

Newseum. *War Stories*. Arlington, Va.: Freedom Forum. http://www.newseum.org/warstories/index.htm.

Texas Tech University. *The Vietnam Project*. Lubbock, Tex. http://www.vietnam.ttu.edu/.

U.S. Army Center of Military History. *U.S. Army Center of Military History Website*. Fort Lesley J. McNair, D.C. http://www.army.mil/cmh-pg/.

WETA. *Reporting America at War*. Washington, D.C.: Greater Washington Educational Telecommunications. http://www.pbs.org/weta/reportingamericaatwar/.

# II

## POST-VIETNAM CONFLICTS

Shannon E. Martin

# TIMELINE

**1981**

January           Ronald Reagan becomes U.S. president.

August            Libyan planes attack a U.S. aircraft carrier on maneuvers in the
                  Gulf of Sidra, which Libya claims is national territory. The
                  Libyan planes are shot down.

**1982**

September         About 2,000 U.S. troops are deployed to Lebanon as part of an
                  international peacekeeping force.

**1983**

19 October        There is a coup in Grenada.

23 October        A truck bomb explodes and kills 241 U.S. marines in Beirut,
                  Lebanon.

25 October        Coalition forces take control of the Grenada capital city in an
                  overnight raid code-named "Urgent Fury"; reporters are excluded
                  from the operation.

26 October        President Reagan reports to the American public that operation
                  "Urgent Fury" in Grenada is a complete success.

**1984**

January           U.S. troops are largely withdrawn from Grenada, and U.S. media
                  and professional organizations issue "Statement of Principles on
                  Press Access to Military Operations" demanding that the mili-
                  tary accommodate reporters during wartime situations; Sidle
                  Military-Media Relations Panel is initiated by the Pentagon, and

the panel's report is then used as guidelines for national media pool organization and deployment.

## 1986

16 April      President Reagan orders U.S. surprise air strikes on Tripoli, Libya, in retaliation for terrorist attacks in West Berlin that killed two American servicemen; the media have no foreknowledge of the strike and are not escorted, even after the strike, to the site.

## 1987

24 July      U.S. military makes first use of media pool to report operation "Earnest Will," an at-sea operation to protect Kuwaiti ships by escorting them from the Strait of Hormuz to Kuwait so that Iranian forces will not launch an attack in the Persian Gulf.

## 1988

United Nations agrees to and delivers food relief to Somalia.

## 1989

January      George Herbert Walker Bush becomes U.S. president.

May      Elections in Panama are declared fraudulent; Noriega declares his candidate the winner.

October      There is an attempted coup of Noriega leadership in Panama.

16 December      An American is killed in Panama.

20 December      The number of U.S. troops in Panama rises from 13,000 to 24,000, while new leadership is sworn in to the presidency, and operation "Just Cause" is launched; military use of media pool is activated and is deemed a failure by both the military and the media.

24 December      Noriega requests political asylum in the Panama City papal nunciature.

## 1990

7 January      A new U.S. ambassador arrives in Panama City, proclaiming a renewed partnership of respect for human rights and rule of law.

30 March      New guidance is issued by U.S. military for public affairs officers' use of media pools during military operations.

2 August      Iraq invades Kuwait.

16 December      Jean-Bertrand Aristide is elected president of Haiti.

## 1991

15 January      Coalition forces launch U.S.-led liberation of Kuwait, codenamed "Desert Shield" and then "Desert Storm"; media pools are deployed exclusively where there are no journalists already in the conflict areas.

March      Coalition forces are said to have liberated Kuwait and stabilized the border with Iraq.

| 20 September | Jean-Bertrand Aristide is deposed by a military junta in Haiti. |
| December | United Nations suspends food shipments to Somalia. |

**1992**

| March | United Nations brokers a cease-fire so that food shipments can resume to Somalia. |
| May | Sarajevo, the capital of Bosnia and Herzegovina, is under siege and surrounded by rebels and militia loyal to Croats and Serbs; the United Nations sends peacekeeping troops with orders that they are not to fire, even if fired upon. |
| 21 May | Pentagon announces new guidelines in the use and deployment of media pools. |
| 28 May | The United States commits $9 million to aid refugees in Bosnia and Herzegovina. |
| 9 June | The United Nations votes to deploy additional troops to Bosnia and Herzegovina. |
| 3 December | U.N. Security Council votes to send U.S.-led military force to Somalia to assure food distribution. |
| 4 December | The United States announces that 28,150 troops will be deployed to Somalia; the mission is code-named "Restore Hope." |

**1993**

| January | William Jefferson Clinton becomes U.S. president. |
| 5 June | Dozens of peacekeepers are killed or wounded in Somalia, and four foreign journalists are killed by a mob the next day. |
| 8 August | Four U.S. soldiers are killed by a land-mine detonation in Somalia. |
| 31 August | The United States makes plans to deploy an additional 20,000 troops to help U.N. peacekeepers in Bosnia and Herzegovina. |
| 25 September | U.S. soldiers are killed by Somali rocket-propelled grenades. |
| 3 October | Twelve U.S. soldiers are killed in fifteen-hour battle with Somali militiamen. |

**1994**

| June | Coalition troops increase the embargo enforcement efforts in Haiti. |
| August | U.N. Security Council approves sending an international military force into Haiti to restore deposed president Jean-Bertrand Aristide, and the military junta is given a deadline to turn over power. |
| 19 September | A U.S.-led multinational force enters Haiti to facilitate power change in Haiti, and more than 20,000 U.S. troops are ordered by President Clinton to participate in the operation, code-named "Restore Democracy." |
| 15 October | Jean-Bertrand Aristide returns to office as Haiti's president. |

| 21 October | The Haitian Senate passes a bill outlawing paramilitary groups. |
| 30 November | The multinational force in Haiti reports that it has collected 14,943 weapons, and 8,670 U.S. troops remain in Haiti. |

**1995**

| March | U.N. troops withdraw from Somalia, and the United States officially transfers the security operation in Haiti to a multinational force under U.N. command. |
| November | The United States opens peace talks in Dayton, Ohio, for Bosnia and Herzegovina, and NATO commits 60,000 troops to the peacekeeping effort. |
| December | René Préval wins a comfortable majority for the presidency in Haiti. |

**1996**

| 5 January | U.S. troops begin a phased withdrawal from Haiti. |
| February | René Préval is sworn in as Haiti's president. |

**1997**

| December | 8,500 U.S. troops remain in Bosnia and Herzegovina as a peace-keeping mission. |

# INTRODUCTION

## THE U.S. MEDIA AND U.S. MILITARY CAMPAIGNS FROM LIBYA IN 1981 TO BOSNIA-HERZEGOVINA IN 1997

Democracy as a functioning form of government is based on an open exchange of information among all constituents. News media have long served as a conduit for that information exchange. But in times of war even democratic governments restrict some aspects of news coverage to help maintain social order and protect national interests.

The United States began implementing formal information controls on the news media as early as the Civil War of the 1860s. This introduction will describe the kinds of restrictions placed on the news media during more recent U.S. troop deployments in the 1980s and 1990s. Examples of the news stories from these military operations include Grenada, Libya, Panama, Somalia, Haiti, and Bosnia and Herzegovina in separate chapters, as well as Lebanon and Iraq, discussed in this introduction.

The pivotal condition that shaped the U.S. news reports during this period was whether the U.S. news organizations already had media professionals in the field before the U.S. intervention began. The likelihood of this precondition was directly correlated to, though not caused by, the specific U.S. president at the time of the troop deployment. The research conclusions discussed in this introduction will include a report of the history of media restrictions and the effect of these restrictions on the American public's perception of the military campaign.

## MILITARY INTERVENTIONS

Military action can have a variety of goals that can include vanquishing a political enemy or an intruder, territorial expansion, or restoring peace. But among the reasons for military engagement useful to a discussion of events in this part are the desire to control a particular physical place so that local changes in government can occur, or the need to administer aid to those unable to protect and provide for themselves. In most cases, both of these outcomes are part of the desired goals. Often, however, there is a stronger emphasis on one or the other when troops are initially ordered to ship out.

The first of these desires—local change in government—can be seen as a primary concern in the call for U.S. military deployment to Libya, Lebanon, Grenada, Panama, and Iraq and initially in Haiti. The military goal in each of these interventions is somewhat evident from the code names used for the interventions. The deployment to Grenada was called "Urgent Fury," and the action in Panama was called "Just Cause." The military operation in Iraq was called "Desert Storm," and Haiti was initially code-named "Support Democracy." All of these suggest a desire for direct political change.

The second of these military goals—distribution of humanitarian aid—can be inferred from the code names used in the call for military action in Somalia, later in Haiti, and in Bosnia and Herzegovina. "Provide Hope" was the name of the operation in Haiti, "Operation United Shield" in Somalia, and "Operation Joint Endeavor" in Bosnia and Herzegovina. These code names suggest protection and administration as the military goals.

These missions were not without cost in human lives, which is something the American armed forces very much want to minimize. In all of these examples, U.S. military personnel were killed while trying to achieve the military objective of the mission. The biggest challenge to any officer is to balance an achievement of all the military goals. Minimizing the loss of soldiers is high among these goals. This necessarily means that information about these military deployments must be controlled in order to provide as much protection of military personnel as possible in a hostile environment. The use of military censorship of an operation's news has been part of many campaigns.

Even in a democracy, where information about the government's actions is integral to the framework of that system, there is an expectation or an appreciation by the public of the need to limit information flow during times of war or military action. The public also expects that these information controls remain in place only during the conflict itself, or when there is imminent threat of hostilities. Even when the conflict is far from American borders, there is still an understanding that American troops—as an extension of the nation—deserve the protection that information controls can provide.

## CHRONOLOGY OF MILITARY CONTROL OF NEWS DURING WAR

Following is a summary of the periods in which military control of information about particular wars or military interventions has been put in place and administered.

1864     *Civil War*: Military leaders actively inhibit reporters' news collection by interfering with access to the front or misrepresent facts; sanctions for publication include forced suspensions for *New York Journal of Commerce*, the *New York World*, and the *Chicago Times*.

1898    *Spanish-American War*: Navy institutes censorship units in Key West, Florida, Washington, D.C., and New York through telegraph and transportation venues.

1917    *World War I*: Committee on Public Information is established; restrictions and regulations prepared by the State Department, as well as the War and Navy Departments, are accepted by news organizations and are instituted upon declaration of war; statutory sanctions include prison and fines; credentials are revoked for five of the sixty journalists covering the war from abroad.

1940    *Before World War II*: President Franklin D. Roosevelt institutes restrictions on publication of war preparation information.

1941    *World War II*: FBI provides censorship control over media and telephones until Byron Price is named director of the Office of Censorship created under the War Powers Act; guidelines are issued, and the media accept them voluntarily; news copy prepared in the field requires clearance.

1950    *Korean War*: Voluntary self-censorship prevails among media for first six months; then field reports and film have to be submitted to field military headquarters for clearance.

1954    Joint services manual is published for use during future military interventions, *Field Press Censorship*.

1962    *Cuban Missile Crisis*: Controls follow *Field Press Censorship* guidelines.

1964    *Tonkin Gulf*: Resolution is passed to expand troop commitment in Vietnam; media censorship in the field is deemed infeasible because U.S. troops do not control civilians there; about 2,000 journalists agree at one time or another during the conflict to voluntary restrictions of their reporting: six have credentials revoked because of violations of these restrictions.

1971    Defense Department changes the name of the censorship program to the Wartime Information Security Program (WISP).

1974    Congress ceases funding the WISP units, which are then all closed by 1977.

1982    United States deploys troops to Lebanon as part of a coalition effort to enforce peace.

1983    *Grenada*: Surprise invasion is launched, with a total ban on media presence in or near the field during the campaign.

1984    Sidle Report endorses media pooling in the combat zone and voluntary media restrictions—ground rules—with the only sanction being exclusion from subsequent pooling.

1986    *Strike on Libya*: Media are shut out of operation.

1987    First U.S. military use of media pool to report operation "Earnest Will" at sea is deemed a success by both military and media.

1989    *Panama*: Intervention implements pool system, which is assessed by both military and media to have unsatisfactory result.

1990    *Persian Gulf*: Troop commitment to Dhahran, Saudi Arabia, allows only seventeen-member press pool with six military officers accompanying the pool.

1991    Williams guidelines are issued that require all news media to be under pool restrictions, with twelve categories of information excluded from reports, during the conflict in the Persian Gulf. CNN reports live from Baghdad, Iraq, during "Desert Storm." Legal challenges are brought against the pool system and restrictions, all of which eventually fail.

1992    Pentagon announces new guidelines in the use and deployment of media pools, and United States announces 28,150 troops deployed to Somalia as part of a coalition peacekeeping effort; military complains about media presence.

1993    United States deploys troops to help U.N. peacekeepers in Bosnia and Herzegovina; media restrictions are difficult to impose because control of the field is not unilateral, and are voluntary at the point of publication or transmission.

1994    U.N. Security Council approves sending an international military force, with U.S. troops a significant majority, into Haiti to restore deposed President Jean-Bertrand Aristide; military junta is given deadline to turn over power; media restrictions again are hard to enforce and are voluntary at the point of publication or transmission.

It is clear from a review of the history of news controls that the military tried a variety of restrictions or guidelines to effect change in the way war information was delivered. These variations were the result of changes in the kinds of conflicts being reported and changes in political attitudes about what was acceptable to underreport. Protection of soldiers has always been a tenable reason to leave out of the news reports the kind of details that would give the enemy a military strike advantage.

The kinds of information controls that are almost always disputed are those that deprive Americans of fair knowledge about how the war is progressing and what the government is doing in support of the military deployment. But often the reason for the call to arms is just as important to the public as the actions being taken or the results of that action by their government. Therefore, some of the information controls are just as much about controlling the evidence of the reasons for the conflict as they are about controlling news about the progress or outcome of that conflict.

During the historical period reviewed in this part, there was a significant shift in the way that the executive branch, which is ultimately in charge of the armed forces, tried to control news about military action. This change was due in part to the fact that none of the military deployments described here were on American soil, and they were not the result of imminent threat to the United States. The most notable military intervention just before this historical period was the Vietnam War. During that military operation, control of information became very relaxed in comparison with World War II because the military hoped to improve public opinion of the troop commitments in Southeast Asia, and because it was harder and harder to control media in that particular field of battle.

## EVOLUTION OF MEDIA POOLS

After the Vietnam intervention, the Pentagon continued to look for ways of controlling information distribution during military campaigns. In a November 1981 memo to the Joint Chiefs of Staff, it was noted that both Congress and the Office of the Under Secretary of Defense agreed that field censorship was nearly impossible because of new communication technologies and improved transportation. The Reagan administration's solution to the problem of news media and information control was simply to eliminate the media from military operations. The 1981 Gulf of Sidra maneuvers and the 1983 Grenada surprise landing were early experiments in this exclusionary model.

There is some irony in the fact that a former actor, whose movie career depended on media exposure and who then rose to become president of the United States in part because of his media career, was the most enthusiastic about excluding the media from his military operations during most of the 1980s. That policy was softened when he was succeeded in the White House by his vice president, a slightly more moderate George H. Bush, in 1989. The 1989 Panama operation under the Bush administration was the first military use of the modern conception of media pools and was said by nearly everyone involved to be a failure. The next large-scale use of media pools was during the coalition strike against Iraq. The media pools were so effectively controlled in that operation that very few reporters could provide firsthand reports, and little information that had not been approved by military censors was ever learned by the general public. The exception was CNN's reporter in Baghdad, Peter Arnett, who had remained after all the other reporters were evacuated on the eve of the military strike there and broadcast live from behind Iraq battle lines.

Though the public generally agreed that the military operations were necessary, there was some outcry from some Americans about the lack of firsthand reports that were usually provided by the media. The media organizations, too, responded with proposals that were intended to challenge the general principle of exclusion but acknowledged the occasional military need for surprise and swift action. After nearly a decade of variations on the idea of a media pool for reporting on military operations, the Pentagon established rules and guidelines that specified what could not be part of a news report. The implementation of these rules, however, varied from Pentagon administration to administration, depending on who occupied the White House.

The *Pentagon Rules*, as they were known, included a section restricting the kind of information that could be reported, items 1 through 12, and a second section that detailed how news media pool members should handle themselves and what would be expected of them in the battlefield. Here are the January 1991 guidelines and rules:

*The following information should not be reported because its publication or broadcast could jeopardize operations and endanger lives:*

1. For U.S. or coalition units, specific numerical information on troop strength, aircraft, weapons systems, on-hand equipment, or supplies (e.g., artillery, tanks, missiles, trucks, water), including amounts of ammunition or fuel moved by or on hand in support and combat units. Unit size may be described in general terms such as "company size," "multibattalion," "multidivision," "naval task force," and "carrier battle group."

Number or amount of equipment and supplies may be described as "large," "small," or "many."

2. Any information that reveals details of future plans, operations, or strikes, including postponed or canceled operations.

3. Information, photography, and imagery that would reveal the specific location of military forces or show the level of scrutiny at military installations or encampments. Locations may be described as follows: all Navy embark stories can identify the ship upon which embarked as a dateline and will state that the report is coming from the "Persian Gulf," "Red Sea," or "North Arabian Sea." Stories written in Saudi Arabia may be datelined "Eastern Saudi Arabia," "Near the Kuwaiti Border," etc. For specific countries outside Saudi Arabia, stories will state that the report is coming from the Persian Gulf region unless that country has acknowledged its participation.

4. Rules of engagement details.

5. Information on intelligence collection activities, including targets, methods, and results.

6. During an operation, specific information on friendly force troop movements, tactical deployments, and dispositions that will jeopardize operational security or lives. This would include unit designations, names of operations, and size of friendly forces involved, until released by CENTCOM.

7. Identification of mission aircraft points of origin, other than as land- or carrier-based.

8. Information on the effectiveness or ineffectiveness of enemy camouflage, cover, deception, targeting, direct and indirect fire, intelligence collection, or security measures.

9. Specific identifying information on missing or downed aircraft or ships while search and rescue operations are underway.

10. Special operations task forces methods, unique equipment, or tactics.

11. Specific operating methods and tactics (e.g., air angles of attack or speeds, or naval tactics and evasive maneuvers). General terms such as "low" or "fast" may be used.

12. Information on operational or support vulnerabilities that could be used against U.S. forces, such as details of major battle damage or personnel losses of specific U.S. or coalition units, until that information no longer provides tactical advantages to the enemy and is, therefore, released by CENTCOM. Damage and casualties may be described as "light," "moderate," or "heavy."

*For news media personnel participating in designated CENTCOM Media Pools:*

1. Upon registering with the Joint Information Bureau (JIB), news media should contact their respective pool coordinator for an explanation of pool operations.

2. In the event of hostilities, pool products will be subject to review before release to determine if they contain sensitive information about military plans, capabilities, operations, or vulnerabilities that would jeopardize the outcome of an operation or the safety of U.S. or coalition forces. Material will be examined solely for its conformance to the attached ground rules, not for its potential to express criticism or cause embarrassment. The public affairs escort officer on the scene will review pool

reports, discuss ground rules problems with the reporter, and in the limited circumstances when no agreement can be reached with a reporter about disputed materials, immediately send the disputed materials to JIB Dhahran for review by the JIB Director and the appropriate news media representative. If no agreement can be reached, the issue will be immediately forwarded to Office of Assistant Secretary of Defense (Public Affairs) (OASD [PA]) for review with the appropriate bureau chief. The ultimate decision on publication will be made by the originating reporter's news organization.

3. Correspondents may not carry a personal weapon.

Reporters are often said to be loners by nature. What is reported, day to day, may sometimes seem like herd mentality news selection, but very few reporters are ever willing to share their reports. The very essence of media pools, however, is that the reporters must share their reports. This element alone would be enough to make most news organizations think twice about participating.

The fundamental reason the news executives agreed to pools was that there was very little likelihood that the reporters could or would get to a particular military strike site during the action unless they were escorted by military personnel. The costs of independent reporting for a particular media outlet would include hiring transportation that could withstand military assault in the field, and communication technology that could withstand military operations' jamming and blackouts. These realities of the modern military operation forced the media organizations to acquiesce in the use of pools during a military campaign.

The timeline that precedes this introduction provides a more detailed listing of the events that surround those military interventions that are more fully reported in separate chapters of this part. A careful reading of the timeline will reveal how frequently the military operation was about either local political change or humanitarian aid, rather than about territorial expansion or colonialism, and how frequently the new tool of media pools was used as a way of controlling the stories about the particular military action.

## MILITARY INTERVENTIONS AND PUBLIC OPINION

All of the interventions described in this part were undertaken because the president, as chief military officer, decided that a military goal should be achieved and undertook that action on behalf of the American people, sure that he could convince them of the deployment's necessity. Public support for all of these military interventions was expressed at some point during the operation, but the timing of that support was critical to how long the operation could exist and how successful the president would be considered. It is the pairing of these considerations that will be discussed more fully in this introduction.

The necessity in a democracy to persuade constituents to support a particular government activity is sometimes the only restraint on that government's leadership. In the case of the military operations discussed in this part, the righteousness of putting U.S. troops in mortal danger and spending millions or billions of dollars in a foreign land are very much on the minds of the constituents. The news media have traditionally carried the reports on which the public has come to rely for bat-tlefront information used for judging the particular military success or failure.

Media analysts suggest that the court of public opinion was to some degree influenced by the way the media handled the story, and this in turn was influenced by the way the White House and the Pentagon handled the media. It is important to remember that during the deployment of troops to Grenada the media were completely excluded. In the operations to Panama and Iraq, military media pools were instituted. During the Lebanon, Somalia, and Haiti engagements, media were already in the location when deployment orders were issued.

What follows here is a comparative look at public opinion for some of the military deployment discussed in this book. The first sampling of public opinion is across these engagements and is the most telling. Notice that those operations where the media were most carefully controlled or excluded were highest in the category of "right thing" to do. There are samplings of public opinion polls that follow for each of the military operations discussed more fully in separate chapters. These polls were conducted by various media outlets. The questions listed were part of the survey instrument in each of the respective surveys and are reprinted verbatim.

## DEPLOYMENTS FROM 1982 TO 1991

*Question*: Now I'll name some major events in our history. I'd like to know for each whether you think what this country did was the right thing, or the wrong thing, or somewhere in between? [*Only "right thing" and "wrong thing" noted here.*]

Sending Marines into Lebanon in 1982: 35 percent said it was the right thing, 23 percent said it was the wrong thing.

Invading Grenada in 1983: 69 percent said it was the right thing, 21 percent said it was the wrong thing.

Bombing Libya in 1986: 49 percent said it was the right thing, 15 percent said it was the wrong thing.

Sending troops into Panama to overthrow Noriega in 1989: 61 percent said it was the right thing, 15 percent said it was the wrong thing.

Going to war against Iraq: 68 percent said it was the right thing, 14 percent said it was the wrong thing.[1]

### Grenada

*Question*: Now I want to ask you a few questions about the events in the Caribbean island of Grenada. First, would you say you approve or disapprove of the invasion of Grenada by U.S. troops?

No opinion: 7 percent

Disapprove: 22 percent

Approve of the invasion of Grenada by U.S. troops: 71 percent.[2]

## Libya

*Question*: Do you approve or disapprove of the United States having launched the military air strike against Libya?

Approve of U.S. jets bombing Libya last night: 77 percent.

Approve of United States having launched the military air strike against Libya on 14 April 1986: 75 percent.[3]

## Iraq and the Persian Gulf

*Question*: Given the loss of life and the other costs of the war in the Persian Gulf, do you think the war to defeat Iraq is likely to be worth the cost (January–February)? Given the loss of life and other costs of war in the Persian Gulf, do you think the war to defeat Iraq was worth the cost, or not?

|              | *Worth it*  | *Not*       |
|--------------|-------------|-------------|
| January 1991 | 59 percent  | 29 percent  |
| February     | 72          | 17          |
| June         | 66          | 30          |
| October      | 61          | 33          |
| January 1992 | 59          | 36          |
| December     | 58          | 37          |
| January 1993 | 60          | 34[4]       |

## Somalia

Americans supported U.S. humanitarian efforts in Somalia, though they apparently did not like an open-ended commitment. As the reporting increased about the humanitarian and political situation in Somalia, the approval ratings fell. Here is a sample of the public opinion polls conducted immediately around, as well as long after, the events of September and October 1993.

### 1992

*Question*: Do you approve or disapprove of the way George Bush (is handling his job/has been handling the situation in Somalia)?

Approve of the way George Bush: 73 percent.[5]

### 1993

*Question*: Now I'd like to turn to the issue of American troops in Somalia. In general, do you approve or disapprove of the presence of U.S. troops in Somalia?

Approve of the presence of U.S. troops in Somalia: 79 percent.[6]

*Question*: Do you approve or disapprove of the way Bill Clinton is handling the situation?

Approve: 62 percent; Disapprove: 29 percent; No opinion: 10 percent (as of 28 June 1993).

Approve: 33 percent; Disapprove: 53 percent; No opinion: 14 percent (as of 5 October 1993).

*Question*: Should the United States keep troops in Somalia until there's a functioning civil government or do you think the United States should pull its troops out very soon?

Keep troops in: 28 percent; Pull out: 64 percent; No opinion: 8 percent (as of 5 October).

*Question*: If U.S. prisoners can't be freed through negotiations, do you think the United States should respond with a major military attack?

Should attack: 75 percent; Should not: 19 percent; No opinion: 5 percent (as of 5 October).

Other findings from the 5 October poll:

69 percent do not think that America's vital interests are at stake.

51 percent believe that the United States should continue trying to capture warlord Mohammed Farah Aidid.

56 percent back the president's plan to send more support to troops already there.[7]

## 1994

*Question*: [President Bill] Clinton says he's sending 5,000 more U.S. troops to Somalia now, and then will withdraw all U.S. forces from Somalia by March 31, [1994]. Do you approve or disapprove of his decision to send the additional troops?

Approve: 43 percent

Disapprove: 53 percent

No opinion: 4 percent[8]

## Bosnia

Public opinion on the conflict shifted slightly during the years of seeking a peaceful resolution, but as in other foreign conflicts, the American people did not want too much American involvement. There was little pragmatic control of information out of the region. Stories in the U.S. media included humanitarian, as well as political, coverage. Here are the polling results for 1993 during the greatest media attention to the situation, as reported by a variety of news organizations and pollsters.

*Question*: As you may know, violence has erupted in the city of Sarajevo and the surrounding area called Bosnia, one of the new republics that used to be part of Yugoslavia. Should the United States do more to stop the war in Sarajevo and Bosnia, or has the United States already done enough?

| | United States has done enough to stop the war in Sarajevo and Bosnia | Should do more |
|---|---|---|
| August 1992 | 49 percent | 37 percent |
| January 1993 | 59 percent | 30 percent[9] |

*Question:* Do you favor or oppose the United States sending troops to the former Yugoslavia to try to help stop the civil war there?

Not sure: 12 percent

Favor: 34 percent

Do not favor sending U.S. troops to help stop civil war there: 54 percent.[10]

In an August 1992 NBC News/*Wall Street Journal* survey, 33 percent favored sending troops and 54 percent opposed this measure.

*Question:* Please tell me if you support or oppose the following polic[y] in . . . Bosnia. . . .

Support sending the United Nations troops including some U.S. troops to help Bosnians defend themselves against the Serbs: 62 percent.[11]

## Haiti

Very little information control was exercised in the Haiti news coverage. The reports included both humanitarian and political news. There were a number of reporters already in place or near the capital when significant U.S. troop deployment was ordered. American public opinion of the prospects of sending troops early in June 1994 was not supportive. Less than 30 percent of Americans favored such an action, according to an NBC News/*Wall Street Journal* telephone survey of about 1,500 respondents.[12] But by the time former President Jimmy Carter had brokered a peaceful change of power in Haiti that would require American troops on the island during the political shift, Americans were overwhelmingly in favor of troop deployment. According to a CBS News/*New York Times* telephone survey of about 500 respondents in early September, 77 percent favored the initiative.[13] But by the following December, Americans were once again leery of the U.S. troop deployment. Only 40 percent thought that it had been the right thing to do, while 51 percent thought that the United States should have stayed out, according to a 13 December 1994 CBS/*New York Times* poll.

## EXTREME EXAMPLES IN LEBANON AND IRAQ

The long, slow military deployment to Lebanon and the quick, sharp military strike in Iraq provide stark examples of the news media controls that the Pentagon and the president saw as necessary. The military involvement in Lebanon spanned several decades, beginning in 1976. Deployments were usually in response to the need to evacuate some special group of people threatened by the civil war there or as part of a peacekeeping mission with unspecific objectives. This kind of military operation proved more difficult to "win" than the deployment of troops to the Persian

Gulf with the expressed purpose of immediate liberation of Kuwait after the surprise invasion by Iraq.

In a manner similar to the troop deployments to Lebanon, the news media gradually built a small installation of reporters who filed stories not only about military action, but also about the political situation and the effects of both the civil war and the international interventions. The stories varied in both their perspective and their objectivity and often did not provide the kind of supportive spin that the White House would have preferred.

The next several pages contain examples of the kinds of stories that appeared in U.S. media immediately before and after the suicide car-bomb attack of the U.S. embassy in Beirut. That explosion killed sixty-three, and another that followed in October killed 241 U.S. Marines in their barracks near the airport. Each of these story examples contains the reporter's byline, the headline for the story, and a bit of description that includes the publisher or distributor and the date of distribution. The first story was dated about one month before the attack.

## EARLEEN F. TATRO: "LEBANESE SOLDIERS IN SOUTHERN LEBANON WAIT BEHIND THE WALLS"

*This wire service story would have been available to most newspapers across the United States and would, therefore, have been widely read. It is not the kind of story available to reporters when the Pentagon Rules were in effect because it included many sources that were not part of the U.S. military installation.*

### Associated Press, 20 March 1983

SIDON, Lebanon: Confined to their barracks in this Israeli-occupied city, Lebanese army soldiers pass the time with idle chatter, housekeeping chores and practicing how to fire weapons for which they have no ammunition.

They are waiting, in the words of one veteran officer, for "the politicians to find a solution so the foreign armies will leave Lebanon and we can do the job we are supposed to do."

Whether Lebanon's untested 21,600-man army can impose security in this war-shattered nation is one of the thorniest issues in the negotiations among the United States, Israel and Lebanon for the withdrawal of the estimated 60,000 Israeli, Syrian and Palestinian troops from Lebanon.

Israel maintains the Lebanese army isn't up to the job.

Lebanon says it is, with help in the beginning from United Nations soldiers or the multinational force now deployed in Beirut, the capital. The United States, committed to bringing about the withdrawal of all foreign armies, rejects Israeli proposals to retain Israeli observation posts or a border force inside Lebanon.

While the negotiations go on, 2,000 Lebanese army soldiers stay inside the walls of their barracks at Sidon and the villages of Salhiyeh and Kfar Falous in the hills east of the city. The Israeli army, like the Palestine Liberation Organization which used to control this area, does not allow Lebanese soldiers to patrol the countryside or carry weapons on the streets of Sidon.

Lebanese soldiers stationed here are disarmed by Israelis and sometimes turned back when they try to travel to their headquarters in Beirut, 25 miles to the north, or to the United Nations zone in the south where 700 Lebanese soldiers serve with the 6,300-man U.N. Interim Force in Lebanon.

"We can't even train here. The Israeli forces prevent us from going out of the barracks for training," said a Lebanese army officer who requested that his name and rank be withheld.

The officer, a Shiite Moslem from a southern Lebanon town which was once a PLO stronghold, said his garrison has been occupied by Palestinians, Syrians and Israelis in the past eight years.

He rejected Israeli suggestions that the Lebanese army, which split along sectarian lines during the 1975–76 civil war between Moslem leftists and Christian rightists, has too many PLO sympathizers to be entrusted with the security of southern Lebanon.

"That's not right, because during the last years the only barracks that opened fire on the PLO was in the south. Many of our men died and many of our men were wounded and are still having medical treatment today," said the officer, who said he himself was wounded in a seven-hour shootout with Palestinian guerrillas June 3, 1980.

Newspaper files show that at least a half-dozen Lebanese soldiers were killed and dozens wounded in 1980 and 1981, either in ambushes or repelling attacks by the PLO.

Despite the periodic clashes, the army here, as in the rest of Lebanon, did not present a challenge to the authority of the PLO and local Lebanese militias.

Israel's invasion last June 6 put an end to the PLO domination in Sidon, the Lebanese officer conceded, but he said his garrison has been weakened because the Israelis disarmed the Lebanese units.

About a half mile up the hill from the garrison is the new Sidon headquarters of the Israeli-backed militia of Maj. Saad Haddad, a Greek Catholic who broke away from the Lebanese army during the civil war and later fought alongside Israel against the PLO.

The Israelis have proposed entrusting security duties in southern Lebanon to Haddad's men, who have been trained and supplied by Israel for at least five years. Lebanon has rejected the idea of a separate Haddad force as well as the return of Haddad to the army.

However, Lebanese and Western diplomatic sources say there is a tentative agreement to compromise by incorporating some of Haddad's men into the regular army provided Haddad himself retires.

With Haddad's militia variously estimated at 900 to 1,500 men, it could not control southern Lebanon alone.

At present the Lebanese army controls only Beirut and its immediate suburbs, with the help of the multinational force composed of U.S., French, Italian and British troops.

A recruitment drive, complete with patriotic posters and television commercials extolling the virtue of serving one's country, started recently in an attempt to triple the size of the army by 1985.

Like the Lebanese soldiers who stay behind the walls of their garrison in Israeli-occupied Sidon, the army garrisons in northern Lebanon are also surrounded by Syrian and PLO troops. On March 4, six Lebanese soldiers were killed and 12 wounded in an ambush and ensuing shootout with Iranian revolutionary guards and their Lebanese allies near the Bekaa Valley town of Baalbek.

*Credit*: Copyright 1983 Associated Press. All rights reserved. Distributed by Valeo IP.

---

# AN ANONYMOUS REPORT: "LEBANON ISSUES ULTIMATUM ON TROOP WITHDRAWAL TALKS"

---

*This uncredited wire service story reported the political situation, but from the Lebanese perspective. In this intervention, the United States was often said to be favoring Israel because so much of the Israeli weapons arsenal was American.*

United Press International, 24 March 1983

Lebanon warned it will pursue other alternatives unless Israel moves by next weekend toward withdrawing its troops from Lebanon but Israeli officials said there was no major progress made on U.S. compromises for a pullout.

Frustrated by the occupation of their country, Lebanese officials quoted by the state-run National News Agency said Wednesday their demand for progress on troop withdrawals was "final and can't bear any further discussion."

State-run Beirut Radio, broadcasting the ultimatum from a Lebanese government source, did not spell out what alternatives Lebanon might pursue to pressure Israel to move toward acceptance of U.S. compromise proposals for withdrawal.

"The source warned that if the reverse happened and Israel gave a negative response (to the U.S. proposals), Lebanon will have other alternatives within American President Reagan's initiative," Beirut Radio said.

There was no immediate reaction from Israel on the Lebanese ultimatum of action on the withdrawal by April 2.

The Beirut statement setting the deadline came as neither Lebanon nor Israel appeared willing to compromise beyond the current impasse on new U.S. proposals aimed at reviving the moribund troop withdrawal talks.

In Jerusalem, state-run Israel Radio quoted an Israeli source saying "no major progress" was made in a meeting between Israeli Foreign Minister Yitzhak Shamir, Defense Minister Moshe Arens and U.S. Middle East envoy Philip Habib.

Habib returned to Israel Wednesday after briefing Lebanese President Amin Gemayel Tuesday on Israel's reaction to the U.S. compromise plan, which Lebanon reportedly had accepted.

But the Israeli stance was considered negative by Lebanese officials, said government sources in Beirut.

U.S.-led troop withdrawal talks, begun Dec. 28, are aimed at securing the pullout of 30,000 Israeli, 40,000 Syrian and 10,000 Palestine Liberation Organization troops occupying about two-thirds of Lebanon.

The negotiations have bogged down over Israeli demands for a military presence in southern Lebanon to prevent infiltration of PLO guerrillas along its northern frontier once Israeli forces pull out from Lebanese territory.

The new U.S. proposals reportedly call for Lebanese troops and multinational peace-keeping forces to jointly patrol southern Lebanon.

Israel television said Gemayel had rejected a proposal that Israeli-backed Lebanese Maj. Saad Haddad be responsible for the security of southern Lebanon.

The April 2 deadline coincides with the approximate date set for a meeting in Jordan between King Hussein and PLO Chairman Yasser Arafat on whether Jordan should join U.S.-sponsored peace talks with Israel.

Reagan's Middle East peace plan, unveiled Sept. 1, envisions the PLO giving Hussein power of attorney to negotiate with Israel. The United States rejects direct talks with the PLO until the group recognizes Israel's right to exist.

*Credit*: Reprinted by permission of UPI.

## THOMAS L. FRIEDMAN: "AMERICA'S FAILURE IN LEBANON"

*This 8,000-word story would certainly not have made the White House or the Pentagon happy. What is contained here is just a portion of the article as it appeared about one year after the deadly U.S. Embassy explosion in Beirut.*

*New York Times*, 8 April 1984

"They sent us to Beirut
To be targets who could not shoot.
Friends will die into an early grave,
Was there any reason for what they gave?"

THAT POEM WAS SCRAWLED IN blue pen on a 4-by-4 piece of lumber serving as a door frame of an underground bunker at Echo Company. It was an innocent bit of verse that some lonely marine had etched one night during the midnight watch at the Beirut airport. It should have been forgotten in the fading memories of Beirut, but it wasn't.

Sitting below deck on the U.S.S. Guam, shortly after the marines' withdrawal from the Lebanese capital, I asked a group of men from Echo Company what they remembered most about their experience. Several of them piped up in unison: "Tell him about the poem." They all seemed to have memorized it. When one of them recited it incorrectly, he was quickly set right by the others. It was their unofficial anthem.

The marines spent a total of 533 days in Beirut, suffered 240 deaths and more than 130 wounded and accomplished virtually nothing. It wasn't a group of radical students at Berkeley who were passing that harsh verdict, nor revisionist historians come to look at the record anew. It was the marines themselves.

"We had a friend, his name was Sergeant Cox, whose wife delivered a baby daughter last December," said Lance Cpl. John McCrey, sitting with a few fellow marines in the well deck of the Guam helicopter carrier.

"He was so excited. He could have gone home if he had wanted to, but he felt he should stay. The day after his daughter was born, Sergeant Cox was killed. I've been wondering . . . I've been wondering when his daughter grows up and says, 'Mom, why did daddy die?' what his wife is gonna tell her. I was here, but I don't know why he died."

What is most frustrating and embittering for the marines who served in Beirut is the fact that they did their job exactly as it was assigned to them—protecting the perimeter around Beirut International Airport—and they did it with the dignity, professionalism and discipline for which the Marine Corps is legendary. Yet when they pulled out of Beirut on the perfectly clear morning of Feb. 26, 1984, many of them complained of feeling utterly empty, of having lost friends in combat without having been able to bring any meaning to their deaths. For soldiers, there can be nothing more confusing or hurtful.

"When we were in Grenada, I really enjoyed myself," said Lance Cpl. Gordon Brock. "You were out there with your gun, shooting, taking prisoners, doing everything marines are supposed to do. I felt like Vic Morrow in one of those movies. But you got nothing to brag about from being in Beirut. We were just here, that's all. When I get home, I don't want anyone to ask me about it. I just want to get in my car and drive and forget the whole thing."

In most military operations, the marines' success or failure rests in their own hands, but in Beirut their ultimate success was always contingent on the ability of Lebanese leaders and American policy makers to produce an internal settlement and a withdrawal of foreign forces. The marines were supposedly giving them time to do that. Ultimately, the policy makers' failure became the marines' failure.

What went wrong? Why in the end did the marine mission in Beirut become so incoherent that many of the men who served there still don't understand what they were doing?

Discussions with a wide range of marines, Lebanese officials and analysts, and Western diplomats in Beirut lead to the conclusion that the marines got caught in the middle of a series of American and Lebanese miscalculations that ended in a grand failure of policy. And with that failure, the American-backed regime of President Amin Gemayel was forced to knuckle under to Syria, the American-trained Lebanese Army splintered into fragments and the American-brokered May 17, 1983, Israel-Lebanon withdrawal accord was abrogated.

Few marines today would take exception with Lance Cpl. Nick Mottola's assessment of their whole experience in Lebanon.

"What was our mission?" asked Corporal Mottola. "I'll tell you what our mission was. A lot of people died for nothing and then we left." . . .

## THE DAMAGE

The Reagan Administration turned Lebanon into a test of strength it never had to be. It made promises it never had to make and couldn't keep. In doing so, it took a small Syrian victory—which amounted to nothing more than Damascus reasserting over Lebanon—and turned it into something that will almost certainly have regional implications. Although Washington seems anxious to walk away from the Lebanon debacle as though from a bad car crash, the effects of America's failure there will not disappear easily.

America's main role in the Middle East for the last decade has been as the key peace broker between the Arabs and Israel, a part of the Soviet Union could never play. It is a role in which America's guarantees to one party or another at a difficult stage in the negotiations, its willingness to use force to protect its allies and its ability to insure that promises made are promises kept were often the critical ingredients.

But it is precisely these unique and often intangible attributes of American diplomacy that suffered so badly as a result of United States behavior in Lebanon and the abrogation of the American-sponsored May 17 accord.

The Syrians have already begun to use their victory in Lebanon to intimidate Jordan's King Hussein from having anything to do with the Reagan peace initiative for a solution to the Palestinian problem. And they have now intensified their efforts to have Egypt scrap the Camp David accords.

"We scuttled American designs in Lebanon, and we are capable of scuttling American designs in Amman," crowed Radio Damascus, in reference to Jordan's capital, after Lebanon scrapped the May 17 agreement.

It is unfortunate that Lebanon had to become the latest testing ground for American credibility in the Middle East. As the Turks, Syrians and Israelis learned before, the best of intentions don't go very far in Lebanon: the society is too splintered for anyone to save it. In Lebanon, where people put their family, village and religious loyalties first, the abstract concept of nation and state has never taken a very deep hold.

That point was driven home clearly to the marines on the morning of Feb. 26, just before the last American soldier left the Beirut airport compound.

Lieut. Col. Ernest Van Huss was the chief of operations for the last marine contingent in Beirut, and when it came time to leave, he and Colonel Faulkner decided to hold a formal ceremony to turn the airport complex back over to the Lebanese Army and to retrieve the Marines' American flag that was hanging in the Lebanese Army liaison office at the airport.

The Marine officers planned to take the flag back home and present it to the widow of one of their friends, who was the last marine to die in Lebanon.

At 8:15 that morning, a few Lebanese Army officers who had been hanging around the airport were rounded up to attend the ceremony. The marines didn't know who half of them were or whether they were loyal to the Government or some Moslem militia. But to insure that some quasi-official officer was there, they had Col. Fahim Qortabawi, the Lebanese Army officer who was in charge of liaison with the marines, flown in by helicopter.

Colonel Faulkner delivered a few brief remarks thanking the Lebanese for their cooperation and then requested that he and his men be allowed to "strike our colors," which were hanging on a flagstick on the wall, crossed with a red, white and green Lebanese flag.

The marine officers reached up, took the Stars and Stripes off the flagstick and began to fold it with great dignity into a precise triangle according to United States military regulations.

"We did it all with the dignity the U.S. flag deserves," remembered Colonel Van Huss. "The Lebanese Army officers were watching us very carefully, and, well, I guess they were a bit overwhelmed by what we were doing."

Just as the American officers finished folding their flag, Colonel Qortabawi reached up, grabbed the Lebanese flag off the wall and handed it to Colonel Faulkner.

"Please," he said, "you might as well take our flag too."

*Credit*: © 1984 by The New York Times Co. Reprinted with permission.

These are very different kinds of reports than were prevalent during the Persian Gulf strike. During that operation the *Pentagon Rules* were fully enforced, and all news reports from the region were screened for unacceptable content. Much has been written about the media pools and the effect that the system had on usual news-reporting practices. Though many media organization members spoke out against the use of pool reports, many of the public opinion polls taken during and after Desert Storm suggest that the public was unconcerned by, and even favored the use of, a pooling system.

The difference between the news reports out of Lebanon and the reports out of the Persian Gulf illustrate how differently the news media were handled, and the information was controlled, by the Pentagon. It seemed that the *Pentagon Rules* successfully managed the story and the subsequent public opinion that supported the U.S. military interventions. The remaining chapters of this part examine the kinds of stories that the American public could read and listen to during each of the U.S. troop actions of the 1980s and 1990s and note whether military-imposed media restrictions were in place.

## THE SELECTED DEPLOYMENTS

The military interventions chosen for extensive review here were those after Vietnam where the conflict was unprovoked by direct enemy assault on U.S. land domains and where the intervention resulted in U.S. troop deaths. There were many U.S. troop deployments during the 1980s and 1990s that happily did not result in deaths. These operations included Nicaragua, the Sudan and Chad, "Blast Furnace" in Bolivia, "Sharp Edge" in Liberia, "Desert Falcon" in Saudi Arabia, "Provide Promise" in the former Yugoslavia, "Support Hope" in Rwanda, and "Safe Border" in Peru and Ecuador. The numbers of troops deployed and lives lost in the selected interventions included in the following chapters are as follows: Grenada, 8,800 troops and 19 deaths; Libya, 100 aircraft and 2 deaths; Panama, 27,351 troops and 23 deaths; Somalia, 25,800 troops and 35 deaths; Haiti, 21,000 troops and 2 deaths; and Bosnia and Herzegovina, 20,000 troops and 1 death.[14]

The stories selected for inclusion in each chapter came from a search in the Nexis "more than two years old" archive file. The decision to use database searching as a means of collecting a complete selection of articles and transcripts was made so that there would be no researcher bias, but the author recognizes that there is an inherent bias in database building that comes from the upload and self-selection process. The author reviewed many databases for an appropriate collection that would yield a cross section of news media and organizations. The Nexis "more than two years old" archive file was chosen, and the same search string protocol was used to collect each sampling:

<CountryName and (U.S. w/5 troops) and DateLimiter>

Country names were Grenada, Lebanon, Libya, Kuwait or Iraq or Persian Gulf, Panama, Libya, Bosnia or Herzegovina or Bosna or Hercegovina, and Haiti. Date limiters were one year on each side of the intervention date. Dataset yield was about 250,000 articles. Some of these were duplicates in separate country searches (i.e., two countries in the study and "U.S. w/5 troops" mentioned in the same article, pulled into two separate searches).

For those interested in media effects on the social understanding of particular events, the question to consider is whether or not there is an evident difference in the kinds of stories that are provided by the media when media pools are installed by the military. In order to learn the answer to that question, the chapters of this part will provide a detailed review of the stories available in U.S. media. The chapters that follow provide a sampling of the media's coverage of particular U.S. military interventions. The story samples should make it clear that the restrictions enforced by the activation and installation of media pools very effectively controlled the kind of conflict information that was available to most of the American public.

## NOTES

1. Surveys by the Roper Organization (Roper Reports 91-3), latest that of 9–23 February 1991.

2. Surveys by ABC News/*Washington Post*, 3–7 November 1983.

3. Surveys by CBS News/*New York Times* and ABC News/*Washington Post*, latest that of 15–19 May 1986.

4. Surveys by CBS News/*New York Times*, latest that of 12–14 January 1993. For months when more than one survey was conducted, the latest asking is shown here.

5. Survey by CBS News/*New York Times*, 7–9 December 1992.

6. Surveys by Yankelovich Partners, Inc., for *Time* and CNN, 13–14 January 1993.

7. ABC News poll based on random telephone interviews with adults nationwide of more than 500 respondents, 5 October 1993.

8. ABC News national poll of 506 respondents by telephone, 7 October 1994.

9. Surveys by Yankelovich Partners, Inc., for *Time* and CNN, 13–14 January 1993.

10. Surveys by NBC News/*Wall Street Journal*, 23–26 January 1993.

11. Survey by Louis Harris and Associates, 22–26 January 1993.

12. NBC News/*Wall Street Journal*, national adult telephone survey of 1,502 respondents, 10 June 1994; "Do you favor or oppose the United States sending troops to Haiti to try to help restore democracy?" Favor sending troops to Haiti: 29 percent; Oppose sending troops to Haiti: 65 percent; Not sure: 6 percent. Survey conducted by Hart and Teeter Research Companies.

13. CBS News/*New York Times*–sponsored national telephone survey of 504 adults: "Over the weekend, the delegation led by former President Jimmy Carter met with the Haitian military rulers and reached an agreement for U.S. troops to enter Haiti peacefully and for the Haitian military rulers to leave office by October 15 (1994). Do you favor or oppose that agreement?" Favor: 77 percent; Oppose: 15 percent; Do not know/No answer: 8 percent. Respondents in this survey were originally interviewed on 18 September 1994, and were reinterviewed on 19 September after the agreement between the United States and Haitian leaders that they would step down.

14. "U.S. Military Deployments/Engagements, 1975–2001," CDI Military Almanac 2001–2002 and Military Department Public Affairs Offices, http://www.cdi.org/issues/US Forces/deployments.html.

## FURTHER READINGS

Combelles-Siegel, Pascale. "The Troubled Path to the Pentagon's Rules on Media Access to the Battlefield: Grenada to Today." Report, 15 May 1996. Strategic Studies Institute, http://wwwcarllisle-www.army.mil/usassi/.

Denton, Robert, ed. *Perspectives on Media and the Persian Gulf War*. Westport, Conn.: Praeger, 1993.

Fialka, John J. *Hotel Warriors: Covering the Gulf War*. Washington, D.C.: Woodrow Wilson Center Press, 1992.

Gottschalk, Jack A. "Consistent with Security: A History of American Military Press Censorship." *Communications and the Law* 5 (1983): 35–52.

Hohenberg, John. *Foreign Correspondence: The Great Reporters and Their Times*. Syracuse, N.Y.: Syracuse University Press, 1995.

Knightley, Phillip. *The First Casualty: From the Crimea to Vietnam: The War Correspondent as Hero, Propagandist, and Myth Maker*. New York: Harcourt Brace Jovanovich, 1975.

LaMay, Craig, Martha FitzSimon, and Jeanne Sahadi, eds. *The Media at War: The Press and the Persian Gulf Conflict*. New York: Gannett Foundation Media Center, 1991.

MacArthur, John R. *Second Front: Censorship and Propaganda in the Gulf War*. New York: Hill and Wang, 1992.

Mott, Frank Luther. *American Journalism: A History from 1690–1940*. New York: Macmillan, 1941.

Salmon, Lucy Maynard. *The Newspaper and the Historian*. New York: Oxford University Press, 1923.

Sloan, Wm. David, ed. *The Media in America*. N.p., Ala.: Vision Press, 2002.

Twentieth Century Fund. *Battle Lines: Report of the Twentieth Century Fund Task Force on the Military and the Media*. New York: Priority Press Publications, 1985.

# 25

## GRENADA, 1983

In 1974, Grenada gained colonial independence from the British after more than 200 years of intermittent struggle against European possession and became a dominion of the British Commonwealth. Government responsibility was in the hands of a thirteen-member senate and fifteen-member house of representatives. Because of its location among the Caribbean islands, near Central America, and particularly near Cuba, its strategic value to the United States was not lost on the American government. An island nation of about 200 square miles, it is among the smallest countries in the Western Hemisphere. It supports a resident population of less than 100,000 by 2002 estimates. Exports of fruits and clothing total about $78 million, while imports of fuel, chemicals, and machinery are about $270 million.

Within a half a dozen years after Grenada declared nationhood, there was some concern among neighboring islands and the United States that the country was becoming a Marxist state. When a bloodless coup in 1979 deposed the elected premier, the U.S. government was prepared to intervene. Grenada was one of several countries that the American administration watched with concern. One day before the Grenada invasion, the *Washington Post* published a story about those governments that the Reagan administration thought were dangerous. In addition to Lebanon, the Persian Gulf, and Grenada, crisis spots on the government watch list included Nicaragua, Korea, and the Philippines.[1]

When a second coup in October 1983 brought the fledgling nation into what appeared to be anarchy, the neighboring islands met to discuss a possible joint reaction. A trade embargo was reportedly considered.[2] An appeal for help in controlling the situation came the same day to the American government. Both the *Washington Post* and the Associated Press reported that the U.S. response to the coup and the request for help was a diversion to the Caribbean of military personnel en route to Lebanon.[3] What followed was a surprise to everyone except those closest to the Pentagon and the troops who were dispatched.

The United States immediately organized and launched six days later what was dubbed a rescue mission. On 25 October, thousands of coalition forces took control of the capital, Saint George's, and rounded up those who were said to be Cuban advisors. The mission occurred so quickly that American public opinion had little opportunity to waver or vary from complete support of the president's action. In a telephone survey of adult respondents conducted for ABC News/*Washington Post* a few weeks after the invasion, 71 percent said that they approved of the mission, versus 22 percent who disapproved.[4] The international response was less supportive, and within a year the Grenadian government returned to free elections closely monitored by U.S. officials.

At the time of the Grenada invasion, it was estimated in a wire service story that about a quarter of America's 2 million soldiers were stationed outside the United States. The Pentagon reported that 121 nations housed American troops on a variety of missions. Though most of those personnel were part of diplomatic missions like embassies, many were on other kinds of peacekeeping and reconstructive assignments. For example, about 240,000 were stationed in Germany. Others were stationed in South Korea (38,800), Lebanon (1,600 marines plus 100 army and marine trainers), and the southern Sinai desert (800 troops, most of them army, as a peacekeeping force to prevent incidents between Israeli and Egyptian soldiers).[5]

This mission, too, was the first effective use of media pools by the military to limit news coverage of the operation. The Pentagon's model was gleaned from a successful media control action by the British in the Falkland Islands in 1982. The news media complained, but too little, too late, for any reprieve from the severe constraints imposed. Soon the outcome of the event was secondary in the reporting community to the fact that no firsthand reports could be filed. A forty-eight-hour blackout of on-the-scene reporting not only limited what the American people learned of the invasions but masked what could be learned even months later about the successes and failures of the action.

What follow are the kinds of reports that were given by the media as the invasion was unfolding. A great majority of the stories were by a small number of news outlets because most reporters did not have direct access to Grenada and were restricted in what they could verify. Rather than many local or hometown stories, there were instead rather bare-bones wire service versions of what little could be learned of the U.S. military intervention as the Pentagon allowed the reports to be given by those who had been "rescued" from the island.

## KERNAN TURNER: INITIAL REPORTS ON U.S. ACTION IN GRENADA

*This was among the first stories to be released about the activity in Grenada. Notice that the dateline was not Grenada but Barbados. Also notice that most of the report quoted government sources and U.S. military facts. While there was some attempt to get competing information by quoting Cuban sources, most of the story relied on secondhand reports and accounts. This long story was part of a package of stories provided by Associated Press and would have been published across the country. The shorter stories by AP on the same day that also follow here carried, in some cases, no byline or headline.*

Associated Press, 25 October 1983

BRIDGETOWN, Barbados: Nearly 2,000 U.S. Marines and Army paratroopers invaded Marxist-ruled Grenada in airborne assaults Tuesday, clashing with Grenadian troops and armed Cuban workers.

The U.S. forces, ordered to protect some 1,000 Americans on the tiny eastern Caribbean island and "restore democracy," were followed in by 300 soldiers or national police from six Caribbean nations.

President Reagan said the operation began before dawn and 1,900 Marines and Army Ranger paratroopers quickly seized the two airports on the mountainous, 21-mile-long island that has a population of 110,000.

He told a mid-morning news conference the operation was "completely successful." But an administration official said Tuesday night "there was more resistance than we thought there would be."

The official, who asked not to be identified, said units of the 82nd Airborne Division probably would be sent to control one of the two airports and free the Rangers to attack pockets of resistance. The airborne division is based at Ft. Bragg, N.C.

The U.S. Defense Department announced Tuesday night that two American troopers had been killed and 23 were wounded, while more than 200 armed Cubans were captured. It added, "Resistance has been encountered but most objectives have been taken." Cuban and Grenadian casualties were not given.

Defense Department sources said several U.S. helicopters had been lost, including some that were shot down, but they gave no details.

U.S. administration and congressional sources in Washington had reported earlier that three members of Grenada's 1,200-man armed forces were killed, and 30 Soviet advisers were captured along with the Cubans.

Jamaica was one of the six island nations contributing troops to the invasion force and Prime Minister Edward Seaga told the Parliament in Kingston he had received a report at noon saying 12 Cubans and three civilians had been killed. He also said the allied forces seized a large quantity of Soviet-made arms at the new airport being built by more than 600 Cuban workers at Point Salines.

Cuba's official news agency, Prensa Latina, issued a report in Havana indicating the resistance was crumbling.

The dispatch, monitored in Mexico City, said, "We inform the nation that at 2 P.M. (EDT), after seven hours of combat, with the ammunition of the defenders exhausted, some positions and high ground defended by the Cuban constructors and collaborators fell to the enemy."

In a later report, Prensa Latina said U.S. paratroopers had captured some Cuban defenders at the airport but others were being led by Cuban army Col. Pedro Tortolo Comas.

It said he arrived in Grenada Monday on a "work visit," and was told in a message from "the commander-in-chief" that "The Cuban people are proud of you. Do not surrender under any condition." It did not name President Fidel Castro, but he is also the commander-in-chief of the Cuban armed forces.

Medical students who make up the majority of the Americans on Grenada were reported unharmed, although pinned down by the fighting.

U.S. helicopter gunships circled the American-operated St. George's Medical College, drawing fire from Grenadian snipers, Mark Barettella of Ridgefield, N.J., reported by ham radio.

"Every time a gunship goes over, there's fire all around us," he said in a broadcast monitored by The Associated Press.

Barettella, a student at the medical college, said witnesses told him they saw three U.S. helicopters shot down by small-arms fire.

The medical school, with its offices in Bay Shore, N.Y., has two campuses, located on opposite sides of the Point Salines airport, called Grand Anse and True Blue. Grenada's only operating commercial airport is Pearls Airport located on the eastern side of the island and 10 miles from the capital of St. George's.

In his account to other ham radio operators, Barettella said, "We have a load of incoming wounded U.S. troops at True Blue. The other six (wounded) Americans were medevaced. The mortar has stopped at the present. Nothing (no mortar rounds or shellfire) has gotten into the True Blue campus. Trying to keep the morale up and the panic down." He said later the six Americans evacuated by medical helicopters were Marines.

Barettella said 196 students at the two campuses were safe as were some 205 students who lived off campus and had been contacted. He said nothing had been heard from 120 other students living in or around St. George's.

The invasion, coming just two days after a deadly bomb attack on Marines in Lebanon, stirred new unease about foreign U.S. military operations among some in Washington, particularly Democrat congressmen.

Secretary of State George P. Shultz told a midafternoon news conference in Washington the decision to invade Grenada was taken because of the "atmosphere of violent uncertainty" and the fear that Americans on the island might be "hurt or taken hostage."

He said the U.S. forces "will leave promptly; we have no intention of staying there," but gave no timetable.

Shultz said Cubans, "presumably construction workers," were "resisting and firing at our forces." He added, "There are no reports of injuries to any American civilians."

The other Caribbean countries contributing troops to the invasion force were Barbados, Dominica, St. Vincent, Antigua and St. Lucia.

In Castries, St. Lucia, the Organization of Eastern Caribbean States (OECS) issued a statement saying it had sought the "pre-emptive defensive strike" against Grenada. It said the six-member OECS asked the "friendly" governments of the United States, Jamaica and Barbados to assist them.

The OECS members and Barbados, which gained its independence from Britain in 1974, are English-speaking countries. Two of the smallest OECS countries, Montserrat and St. Kitts-Nevis, did not send troops.

The Soviet Union demanded that U.S. forces withdraw immediately from Grenada. The British government expressed reservations about the attack. And medical school officials and another American ham operator on the island insisted U.S. citizens had been in no danger from Grenada's new authorities.

In London, the domestic news agency Press Association said Britain had been asked to contribute troops to the invasion force but refused. It did not say if the request came from the United States or the Caribbean countries.

Martin Rickers, first secretary of the British High Commission in Barbados, said the British cruiser Antrim was standing off Grenada but had been ordered to stay clear of the battle operations. He said it was believed that some 250 Britons in Grenada were safe.

The Organization of American States called for a meeting of the governing body to be held Wednesday in Washington and some members were expected to claim the invasion was a violation of the OAS charter.

Nicaragua's left-wing Sandinista government asked for an urgent meeting of the U.N. Security Council and the 15-member council opened debate on the invasion in a session that opened at 11 P.M. EDT.

Grenada has been under Marxist sway since a coup in 1979. But in a new government upheaval that began two weeks ago, a military-led group identified by Washington as hard-line Marxists took command, and Prime Minister Maurice Bishop and some of his Cabinet ministers were slain.

The new Revolutionary Military Council was headed by Gen. Hudson Austin.

The U.S. administration said a Marxist government on the island, 1,500 miles southeast of Miami, posed a strategic threat to the United States because Soviet-bloc aircraft might eventually use the airport at Point Salines, whose runway was being extended to 10,000 feet by the Cuban work force.

Reagan, appearing at a White House news conference, listed three reasons for the invasion: protecting American lives, "to forestall further chaos" and to "restore order and democracy."

The U.S. chief executive asserted that the island had been under the control of "a brutal group of leftist thugs."

He said the joint operation had been mounted at the request Sunday of the Organization of Eastern Caribbean States. But a senior State Department official in Washington, who declined to be identified, said the decision to invade was made in the "middle of last week."

The prime minister of Dominica, Eugenia Charles, appeared with Reagan before reporters and said the operation was aimed at "preventing this thing (Marxism) from spreading to all the islands."

A Reagan administration official said Grenada's British-appointed governor-general, Paul Scoon, who had been under house arrest, has the power to form a provisional government that would plan elections.

Seaga told the U.S. Cable News Network that the U.S. forces would remain on Grenada only a few days, but the Caribbean nations' forces would stay up to six months.

Ham radio reports from the island, U.S. officials in Washington and Cuban reports gave this picture of the early hours of the attack:

At 4:30 A.M., students at the medical school, near the Point Salines airport, heard a plane circling overhead—the first sign of the invasion.

Witnesses here in Bridgetown, 150 miles northeast of Grenada, counted 18 U.S. Army transport planes departing for Grenada. A 12-ship U.S. Navy task force, led by the aircraft carrier Independence, stood off the Grenadian shore, just beyond the horizon.

At about 5:45 A.M. the students reported hearing gunfire near the airport. Marines from the naval force landed by helicopter at Pearls Airport, on the northeast coast, and the Rangers parachuted into southernmost Point Salines, 12 miles to the southwest.

The "powerful Yankee forces" attacked the Cuban contingent "from various directions" at 9:40 A.M. and surrounded them, Havana's official news agency reported.

The allied forces encountered fire from small arms, machine guns and mortars as they moved out from their landing zones and headed toward St. George's, five miles north of Point Salines. Firm resistance was reported at the capital's old Fort George, the Grenadian army command center.

Barettella radioed that there was heavy gunfire around the campus at about 11:25 A.M.

"We are on the ground, waiting for the firing to stop," he said. "There's obviously snipers surrounding the entire campus. There are Cobra gunships passing over at this very minute." He then asked that the State Department try to call off the gunships.

The 300 troops and national police from the six Caribbean nations were flown into Grenada by U.S. Air Force planes after the initial assault.

The invaders broadcast a statement to Grenadians telling them they had "arrived in Grenada to protect lives and restore order." They told residents to stay in their homes.

"Your cooperation will ensure that peace and democracy are restored in the near future," they said.

The Grenadian Embassy in Moscow claimed 1,200 invaders and 700 Grenadians were killed, but such figures seemed irreconcilable with the reported scale of fighting.

U.S. officials said the captured Cubans would be allowed to leave on a Cuban ship that was in a Grenadian harbor. The handling of the 30 detained Soviets was still under consideration, they said.

U.S. House Speaker Thomas P. O'Neill, who said the Marines and Rangers would be pulled out of Grenada within a week, declined to criticize Reagan's actions. But other dissident voices were quickly raised in Washington.

"It's incredible that we are involved in a fight in still another place," said Sen. Alan Cranston of California, a Democratic presidential candidate, alluding to the recent Beirut bloodshed. Other Democrats also criticized the administration's move.

In announcing the invasion, Reagan declared that "American lives are at stake"—a reference to the medical students and about 200 other Americans on the island. The St. George's school generally draws Americans unable to win entry to U.S. medical colleges.

Seaga said "the greatest fear we had" was that "some of the madmen that now run the country would have taken the opportunity to hold them (the American residents) hostage."

Some of the Americans most directly involved disagreed.

Don Atkinson, an American ham operator living on Grenada, told The Associated Press: "Quite frankly, there has been no threat to any of us Americans. In any event, they were moving along orderly to the evacuation of anybody that wished to go."

The medical school's chancellor, Dr. Charles Modica, said at his Bay Shore, N.Y., office that the Americans were "in no real danger whatsoever." He noted that some Americans had left the island Monday.

At least three Americans—the pregnant wife of a medical student, and a vacationing couple—left Monday aboard a plane chartered by the U.S. Embassy in Barbados. But the departure of other Americans desiring to leave was delayed because the island's new military leaders had barred scheduled commercial flights.

*Credit:* Reprinted with permission of The Associated Press.

---

## DORALISA PILARTE: REACTION TO GRENADA

---

*This accompanying wire service story was an effort to put a local and obviously supportive face on the surprise action.*

### Associated Press, 25 October 1983

MIAMI: Leaders of the Cuban community here said Tuesday they support the invasion of Grenada but fear Fidel Castro will use the operation to base new ideological attacks against the United States.

Grenadians in Miami's ethnic mosaic also welcomed the lightning-fast arrival of U.S. forces backed by troops of six other Caribbean nations.

"We are even happier that the Caribbean states were involved and it was not a unilateral decision by the United States," said Yolande Rapier, a Grenadian who has lived in Miami for 13 years.

The action was quickly denounced in Cuban government broadcasts by Radio Havana, as expected in Miami's large Hispanic community.

"Castro is using this as a symbol," said Huber Matos Jr. of the anti-Castro Democratic and Independent Cuba organization. "We've been monitoring radio transmissions from Cuba since 7 A.M. They're talking about how the international workers are resisting the invasion."

Radio Havana transmissions monitored here put the number of Cuban workers on the island at 400 with 200 more arriving after last week's coup which deposed Granadian Prime Minister Maurice Bishop. Bishop and other government officials were shot and killed by factions that apparently are to the left of Bishop's Marxist regime.

"This is like a drop of support to the rest of the American nations," said Ceferino Pérez, press secretary of another anti-Castro organization, the Cuban Patriotic Board. "At last some action is being taken against terrorist acts in our hemisphere."

Matos said the coup came after it seemed that Bishop was going to hold general elections and push his government toward a more moderate position in order to benefit from Reagan's Caribbean Basin Initiative. The plan was formulated to funnel economic help to Caribbean and Central American countries.

"Apparently, Cuba and the Soviet Union didn't like the man taking a more independent line," Matos said.

Pérez said his organization supports not only the U.S. action "but also the way in which it has been done."

"We hope this serves to open the eyes of the rest of the nations of the hemisphere," Pérez added.

Carl Checkley, chairman of the newly formed United Grenadians, said members of his organization feared the Castro government would seize control of the island.

"We are so happy," he said.

Similar endorsements were heard in Miami's Little Havana community.

"If the United States tightens the screws a little more, that would be fine, too," said retired chef Carlos Martínez, 51, who has lived in Miami since 1962.

"Anything against communism is fine," said Martínez. "First, we'll go in there, then I hope we'll go into Nicaragua and then I really hope we'll go into Cuba."

Brush salesman Jose M. García said the United States has to support Latin American nations facing the threat of communism.

"The U.S. had to take that measure and fully support those islands with forces and morale," said García, 49. "The Rus-

sians didn't need any permission to go into Afghanistan or Hungary. This is the most correct invasion and they should have gone in before.

"What the United States is doing is giving back to these nations their right for self-government," he added. "You have to consider the distance there is between Grenada and Venezuela, Cuba and Puerto Rico."

*Credit*: Reprinted with permission of The Associated Press.

---

## AN ANONYMOUS REPORT: CUBANS RESIST U.S. ATTACK

*Not all Cubans were happy about the invasion. Because of the dearth of news sources, the wire service was reduced to repackaging reports offered out of Cuba, the military enemy of the U.S. troops in this operation. The story that follows is an example of the kind of news available to Miami Cubans.*

### Associated Press, 25 October 1983

MIAMI: Cuban workers on Grenada "are resisting heroically the attacks of the Army and Navy of the United States" and suffered casualties in the invasion of the Caribbean island early today, Radio Havana reported.

In its second broadcast since troops from the United States and six other countries landed on the island, the radio said U.S. troops were attacking work camps and other areas occupied by Cuban personnel.

Cuban casualties have been reported, but a precise number of deaths and injuries wasn't known, according to the broadcast monitored in Miami.

In Washington, a Pentagon official who demanded anonymity said the U.S. invaders "have been engaged" in battle with some of the estimated 500–600 Cubans on the island.

Radio Havana carried a report credited to the Cuban Revolutionary Government which stated, in part:

"After being attacked from different points by powerful Yankee forces, the Cuban construction crews are resisting heroically the attacks of the Army and Navy of the United States.

"They are totally surrounded."

In an earlier broadcast, Radio Havana said the army and people of Grenada were prepared for an invasion and that the Grenadan people were ready to defend their country "with dignity and determination."

"Because of the virtual aggression by the United States, the people's militia were mobilized throughout the national territory," said the broadcast.

That earlier broadcast appeared to have been prepared before Grenada radio said an invasion was under way.

The second report, however, said fighting was under way and that there were casualties.

Havana radio said Grenada was not seeking confrontation with any country or group of countries and was willing to hold discussions to "assure good relations and mutual understanding with other states."

"The army and the people (of Grenada) are ready to defend the sovereignty and integrity of the country with dignity and determination," the initial broadcast said.

*Credit*: Reprinted with permission of The Associated Press.

---

## ELAINE GANLEY: "INTERNATIONAL COMMUNITY EXPRESSES CONCERN WITH U.S. INVASION"

*Others in the international community were less than enthusiastic about the surprise invasion. The following story is an example of the kinds of comments made by American allies and foes around the world.*

### Associated Press, 25 October 1983

The Soviet Union branded Tuesday's U.S. invasion of Grenada "an act of open international brigandage" and demanded an immediate withdrawal. Britain expressed strong

reservations about the attack on the Commonwealth nation and France expressed surprise.

The U.N. Security Council prepared to meet to consider

the action in response to a request by Nicaragua, which called the invasion "a new aggression against the people of Latin America and the Caribbean."

U.N. Secretary-General Javier Pérez de Cuellar said he was "particularly disturbed over the possibility that the escalation of tensions could further complicate an already complex situation in the region." General Assembly President Jorge Illueca of Panama said the "use of force is regrettable."

As details of the invasion by hundreds of U.S. troops became known, nations from China to Egypt to Nicaragua issued responses, mostly negative.

Canadian Prime Minister Pierre Trudeau said he was waiting for proof American lives were in danger before commenting on whether the invasion was justified.

"I knew we had permission from Grenada to evacuate our nationals and I do not know if—for some reason or other—the Americans did not have that permission from Grenada," Trudeau told Parliament.

". . . Obviously if they had the authority to do that I cannot see any reason for invading to protect your nationals."

Soviet allies denounced the U.S. action as a violation of the eastern Caribbean nation's sovereignty. Pro Cuban Gen. Hudson Austin seized power in a bloody coup in Grenada last week.

". . . Peaceloving humanity demands an immediate withdrawal from Grenada of the interventionist troops of the United States and their puppets . . ." the official Soviet news agency Tass said.

A U.S. Embassy spokesman in Moscow said without elaborating that the Soviet Union had "made a diplomatic contact" over the invasion.

Tass charged the aim of the United States was to "subordinate that country to neocolonialist rule" and said the participation of some Caribbean forces in the invasion was "a fig leaf" to cover the United States' tracks.

China's official Xinhua news agency said President Reagan used "the usual pretext of 'requested invasion'" in an attempt to justify the American action.

At the House of Commons, British Prime Minister Margaret Thatcher said her government had asked the United States to "weigh carefully" a number of issues before going ahead with its invasion plan. Opposition politicians denounced the action as an "unpardonable" humiliation of an ally and demanded the government protest.

Mrs. Thatcher said Washington had consulted Britain before launching the invasion.

"We communicated our very considerable doubts that Her Majesty's government had about initiating action and asked them to weigh carefully several points before taking any irrevocable decision to act," Mrs. Thatcher said.

When it became clear the invasion would go ahead,

Mrs. Thatcher had a telephone conversation with Reagan that was "short, sharp and to the point," British government sources said. They spoke on condition they not be identified.

In Paris, France's socialist government called the attack "surprising," while the Communist Party, which holds four seats in the government, demanded U.S. forces withdraw.

"The French government was not informed of the latest events in Grenada and therefore cannot appreciate the reasons which provoked this surprising action in relation to international law," the Foreign Ministry said.

Communist Party spokesman Pierre Juquin said: "The news is falling like bullets. . . . We demand that the United States' aggression cease immediately."

The Socialist International, an organization of socialist and labor parties, said in a statement that after the U.S. invasion "the worst must be feared for the political solution of the general crisis in Central America."

Italy's Communist Party, largest in the West, condemned the American action as "an unacceptable act of war."

In Cairo, a senior Egyptian official said his government believes the U.S. action was legitimate under the U.N. charter and noted that it was requested by other Caribbean states.

U.S. forces, bolstered by troops from six Caribbean nations, landed in Grenada early Tuesday and took over the two main airports.

Reagan said the goals of the operation were to "protect innocent lives," including up to 1,000 Americans on Grenada, "to forestall further chaos," and to work for "the restoration of law and order and democracy."

Former Prime Minister Maurice Bishop and a number of Cabinet officials were killed after Austin seized power last week.

A U.S. official said 30 Soviets and 600 Cubans were seized during the Tuesday invasion.

"We condemn this crude violation of Grenada's sovereignty," said Cuba's U.N. Ambassador Raul Roa-Kouri. "It demonstrates once more what is the policy of the imperialist government of Mr. Reagan. Its aggressive character scorns the elemental rules of the international law . . ."

Nicaragua's leftist Sandinista government, which itself has been under attack by U.S-backed rebels, said the invasion was "a violation of the inalienable right of a nation to decide its own destiny, free of foreign intervention."

"We urge the international community to demand the withdrawal of the United States invading troops from the sovereign territory of Grenada and the movement of non-aligned countries to mobilize its political and moral resources in defense of the sovereignty of a sister nation," a government communiqué said.

*Credit*: Reprinted with permission of The Associated Press.

## AN ANONYMOUS REPORT: "FAMILY HAS MARINE SON IN BEIRUT, ANOTHER IN GRENADA"

*Because of the surprise and speed of the operation, there was little time for the media to put much of a humanitarian face on it. The following wire service story is one of only a few that were available the first day of the invasion.*

### United Press International, 25 October 1983

SLICKVILLE, Pa.: With one Marine son seriously injured in Beirut and another Marine son en route to strife-torn Grenada, the Valore family is angry, hurt and wants both their boys back home.

The family waited anxiously Sunday in their home 30 miles east of Pittsburgh before hearing that the youngest son, Marine Lance Cpl. Terry Valore, 22, had survived the Beirut bombing. Valore is a member of the 24th Marine Amphibious Unit.

"My son was the luckiest boy in that building because he didn't have one broken bone. My son made it," said Orlando "Mike" Valore Sr., 52, a light equipment operator for a steel company.

Valore talked to his son Tuesday and said he had suffered second-degree burns over his body, and had lost much of his hearing and the use of a leg muscle.

The family's relief, however, was short-lived.

Another son, 2nd Lt. Orlando "Mike" Valore Jr., 24, a member of the 22nd MAU, was on a ship en route to join U.S. troops in the invasion of Grenada and did not know his brother had survived.

His parents' attempts to reach their older son have met with frustration. Although the Red Cross said it would be willing to notify him, "their hands are tied," until the Marines give them official word of Terry's condition.

"Mike knows Terry was in that blown-up building. I want my son to have a clear mind," said their mother, Janice, 43.

The Valores—who also have a daughter, Marcy, 17—question the fairness of the Marines' sending two members of the same family to two "battled areas."

"One of my boys already gave his blood. I don't want the second one to have to give his blood too. Why do we have to go through this again?

"Why do I have to go through with my older boy what I just went through with my younger boy?" asked Mrs. Valore, a corporate secretary.

"I went through this once. One son put his blood there, I don't feel we should have to go through this again. I feel I have a right to demand my other son is on safe grounds," she said.

*Credit*: Reprinted by permission of UPI.

## MICHAEL PUTZEL: "PROVISIONAL GOVERNMENT TO BE REINSTALLED IN GRENADA"

*President Reagan's plans for the aftermath of the invasion were available almost simultaneously with the announcement of the invasion.*

### Associated Press, 25 October 1983

WASHINGTON: The United States and its Caribbean allies in the invasion of Grenada plan to reinstall the British governor general and have him appoint a provisional government for the island nation, U.S. officials said Tuesday.

The governor general, appointed by Queen Elizabeth II, is Paul Scoon, a Grenadian citizen, whose role as the queen's representative in the Commonwealth country was largely undercut when Grenada's constitution was suspended after a coup d'état in 1979.

In London, a Buckingham Palace spokesman said Tuesday that Scoon would be prepared to form a provisional government for Grenada. "Those are the constitutional rights of a governor-general," the spokesman said.

U.S. officials, briefing reporters at the White House shortly after President Reagan announced the invasion, also said members of the military council which seized control of the island following the ouster and later murder of Prime Minister Maurice Bishop would be arrested. It was not immediately clear whether they would be detained to face charges in connection with the coup and assassination or what might be in store for them, said the officials, who spoke on condition they not be identified.

One of the first military objectives of the operation was to secure the two campuses of St. George's Medical School, where about 600 American students were trapped when the military council imposed its "shoot-on-sight" curfew and closed the island's airport to international flights.

Plans called for the 600 Cuban construction workers and military advisers on the island to be given safe passage to a Cuban ship already in the harbor at St. George's, Grenada's capital, and permitted to return to Cuba if they choose, officials said.

There also are about 30 Soviet advisers, who officials said would be treated with "diplomatic courtesy" and would be allowed to remain or leave if they wish.

But until order has been restored to the island, one official said, the Soviets and Cubans "obviously will be neutralized and detained."

"Following the restoration of order on Grenada, it is envisioned the governor general, who is a Grenadian living in Grenada, will form a provisional government," one official said. "That government then will go through a process of elections and restore the constitution."

Although Grenada has been plagued by political turmoil and violence since before it was given independence by Britain in 1974, the island operated with a parliamentary system of government with a British-style constitution until Bishop took power in a leftist coup in 1979.

"The process as we envision it is the flow of constitutional authority from the governor general to a provisional government, which he appoints," the American official said. Although the official claimed the governor general has the legal authority to name a provisional government, British officials familiar with the constitution said that was not clear.

The queen's representative, according to the constitution, is empowered to appoint members of the Grenadian Senate.

But the U.S. official predicted the provisional government "will hold elections for a more permanent government."

"Once a provisional government is established," the official added, "the United States expects to reopen its embassy" to be headed for the time being by Deputy Assistant Secretary of State Anthony Gillespie, now on Barbados.

Asked how long the U.S. troops would remain on the island, the official said, "Our object is to remove them as soon as possible after order is restored."

It is hoped, he added, that the forces of the eastern Caribbean allies "will be able to maintain order as this constitutional process, going from the governor general to a provisional government to elections, goes forward."

*Credit*: Reprinted with permission of The Associated Press.

---

## FRED ROTHENBERG: "NETWORKS DENIED ABILITY TO COVER GRENADA"

---

*For months after the story of Grenada broke, the story that most interested journalists was the clampdown on reporters during the invasion. This story that moved with all the preceding wire service examples was much discussed in newsrooms across the nation. The American public, however, seemed unconcerned or at least untroubled by these military impositions.*

### Associated Press, 25 October 1983

NEW YORK: CBS News showed videotape Tuesday of the airport runway at Grenada and an American aircraft carrier and several warships in the waters around the island. But the footage did not capture any fighting between U.S. forces and Grenadian soldiers.

The tape of the U.S. ships, which was shot through a thick fog, was shown on the "CBS Evening News" Tuesday night. It was believed to be the only videotape of Grenada after U.S. Marines invaded the Caribbean island Tuesday morning. The assignment desk at ABC News said it had no footage from the island. NBC News said it had no footage of Grenada.

The networks are negotiating with the White House and the Defense Department for permission to cover the fighting on Grenada. U.S. forces seized control of the island's two airports Tuesday. At the time of the invasion, there were no network personnel on Grenada, but each network had correspondents reporting from nearby Barbados.

According to Mary Lou O'Callaghan, a spokeswoman for NBC News, a pool request by the three networks for access to Grenada was turned down by the White House because it said the operation there was "covert."

Several hours after the Marines landed, CBS News chartered a plane that circled the island. A film crew and correspondent Sandy Gilmour were aboard the plane, which tried to land "but was waved away by people on the ground," according to Ramona Dunn, a spokeswoman for CBS News.

Edward Joyce, president of CBS News, wrote a letter to Secretary of Defense Caspar Weinberger protesting the Defense Department's decision not to let CBS News land its plane in Grenada.

Roone Arledge, president of ABC News, also sent a letter to Weinberger asking the Defense Department for "assistance and approval" to cover the military operation in Grenada. "Suffice it to say that the U.S. troops on Grenada deserve as much coverage as the debate in Washington over their presence there," Arledge wrote.

*Credit*: Reprinted with permission of The Associated Press.

## JAMES GERSTENZANG: "REAGAN DECLARES INVASION 'COMPLETELY SUCCESSFUL'"

*Before the day was out, President Reagan declared the operation a success, and there were no firsthand media accounts to contradict his version of events.*

Associated Press, 25 October 1983

WASHINGTON: President Reagan said Tuesday that U.S. and Caribbean troops invaded Grenada to protect 1,000 Americans from a new government run by "a brutal group of leftist thugs" and to restore order to the tiny nation. Officials said the fighting involved some Cubans on the island.

The president called the initial operation "completely successful," but acknowledged there were casualties. Secretary of State George P. Shultz said Cubans are "resisting and firing at our forces."

The Soviet Union demanded in a meeting with a U.S. official in Moscow that the U.S. troops withdraw immediately. Nicaragua asked for an urgent meeting of the U.N. Security Council.

The U.S. embassy in Moscow advised Soviet officials about the action shortly after the invasion began and "their initial reaction was to say 'it's illegal,'" said a U.S. official in Washington. He characterized the complaint as "pro forma."

Shultz said at a news conference that Grenada had been gripped in an "atmosphere of violent uncertainty," and the president decided to act before American citizens there were "hurt or taken hostage."

Reagan, who dispatched the troops with a decision made late Monday, said the United States "had no choice but to act strongly and decisively" because "American lives are at stake."

The Pentagon said 1,900 Marines, who landed by helicopter, and Army Rangers, who made an airborne assault, were part of a force that included troops or police units from seven Caribbean nations opposed to the regime of Gen. Hudson Austin. The general overthrew Prime Minister Maurice Bishop, who was killed in the Oct. 19 coup. Since then, the island has been under a nearly 24-hour curfew.

A Pentagon official said that Grenada, about 100 miles north of Venezuela, maintained an army of about 1,200, and a militia of 4,000 to 5,000 called up in recent days.

The invading troops secured the island's two air strips, Pearls Airport on the northeastern coast and Point Salines on a southwestern peninsula. Those at Point Salines, where Cuban workers were building a 10,000-foot runway, then fanned north toward St. Georges, the island's capital, a senior administration official said.

The official, speaking on the condition that he not be identified by name, said that 30 Soviet advisers and 600 Cubans, including 50 advisers, were "secured." He said the Cubans would be taken to a Cuban ship in a Grenadian harbor, and that arrangements would be made for the Soviets to leave.

The landing forces were said by U.S. officials to have encountered some resistance, from ground fire and an anti-aircraft unit that was silenced from the air.

"I know there are casualties, but I don't have any official report right now," the president said during a mid-day picture-taking session with the president of Bangladesh, Gen. H. M. Ershad.

Reagan, in a 9 A.M. EDT nationally broadcast announcement, 4½ hours after the invasion began, said he ordered the invasion to protect the Americans, 600 of whom are students at the St. Georges Medical College at the end of the Point Salines runway, "to forestall further chaos," and to help restore law and order to the island nation of 110,000.

Referring to the coup, Reagan said: "A brutal group of leftist thugs violently seized power, killing the prime minister, three Cabinet members, two labor leaders and other civilians, including children."

However, Dr. Charles Modica, chancellor of the medical school, disputed Reagan's assertion that the Americans were in danger and said, "this was an unnecessary risk for our U.S. citizens as well as from other countries in Grenada." He made his comments in an interview with NBC's Today Show, in Bayshore, N.Y., where he maintains offices.

"If any of the Americans or other citizens of any country in Grenada were hurt by this action, I think he should be held accountable," Modica said of Reagan.

Ever since taking office, Reagan has been sharply critical of Grenada, where Bishop, a leftist aligned with Moscow, took power in 1979. On a Caribbean visit in April, 1982, the president said in Barbados that Grenada "bears the Soviet and Cuban trademark, which means it will attempt to spread the virus of Marxism throughout the region."

On Tuesday, he said, "let there be no misunderstanding: this collective action has been forced on us by events that have no precedent in the eastern Caribbean and no place in any civilized society."

The president said that the U.S. troops would be withdrawn as quickly as possible. Prime Minister Eugenia Charles of Dominica, chairman of the Organization of Eastern Caribbean States, said this could be as early as the end of the week.

Mrs. Charles conferred with Reagan in the Oval Office at 7:30 A.M. Reagan briefed key congressional leaders about the invasion plan on Monday evening, and reported to an expanded congressional group after meeting with the prime minister.

Standing at Reagan's side when he made the announcement of the military action, Mrs. Charles said, "it is not a matter of an invasion. It is a matter of preventing this thing (Marxism) from spreading to all the islands."

The initial request for U.S. participation in the invasion was received from the Caribbean group last week, a senior administration official said. A State Department official said that by Friday, information on the best landing sites, location of coral reefs, and details on Grenada's armed forces and arms caches began pouring in.

The other participants in the invasion were 120 Jamaican soldiers, 50 from Barbados, and 130 from St. Lucia, St. Vincent, and Antigua, according to the administration official. He said they made up 50 to 65 percent of the nations' armed forces.

A Pentagon official also counted St. Christopher-Nevis, which does not have an army, as among the participants. He said none of the Caribbean forces took part in the initial invasion, but followed the U.S. troops.

He said that U.S. officials who had visited with the Americans on the island found "a very high anxiety level" in recent days. At mid-morning, several hours after the invasion began, he said he could not give "ironclad assurances" that they were safe.

On Capitol Hill, members of Congress stunned by the deaths of more than 200 Marines in Lebanon questioned Tuesday Reagan's action.

"One day we've got the number of Marine deaths which shocked us all and the next day we find we are invading Grenada," said Sen. Lawton Chiles, D-Fla. "Are we looking for a war we can win?"

"If Americans are in danger," said Rep. Peter Kostmayer, D-Pa., "the United States government has an obligation to do all it can. The question is were they in danger or was this used as a pretext for the invasion."

But there were shows of support from congressional leaders.

"Our hope is to have our forces out very quickly," said Sen. Charles Percy, R-Ill., chairman of the Senate Foreign Relations Committee, "just as soon as we can and as quickly as we can restore a semblance of order."

House Speaker Thomas P. O'Neill Jr. said angrily, "It's no time for the press of America or we in public life to criticize our country when our troops are being committed."

Assistant Senate Democratic leader Alan Cranston of California, a candidate for the 1984 Democratic presidential nomination, said, "it is incredible that we are involved in a fight in still another place."

Discussing plans for restoring a constitutional government on the island, a senior administration official said that Governor Gen. Paul Scoon, a Grenadan appointed by Queen Elizabeth II, was authorized under the Grenadan constitution suspended by Bishop to form a provisional government, which would be expected to set up elections leading to a permanent government.

Meanwhile, the head of the governing body of the Organization of American States—the Permanent Council—said he began urgent consultations with members of the OAS on the Grenada situation, and questioned whether the OAS charter had been violated by the invading nations.

*Credit*: Reprinted with permission of The Associated Press.

---

## ROBERT MacNEIL AND JIM LEHRER: REPORT ON GRENADA INVASION

*Despite the news media blackout on the shores of Grenada, some television news broadcasts included extensive coverage of what could be reported. Here is an example of the first-day reporting done on one show. One successful aspect of the administrative spin of this day's events is the insistence, repeated often in the news reports, that the Grenada action was taken as a retaliation for violence done to U.S. troops in Beirut the previous week.*

*MacNeil/Lehrer NewsHour* (PBS), Transcript 2107, 25 October 1983

JIM LEHRER: Good evening. There was another stunner today, again involving U.S. military forces in a foreign land. Some 1,900 U.S. Marines and Army Rangers invaded the small Caribbean island of Grenada before dawn this morning. President Reagan explained why.

Pres. RONALD REAGAN: The United States' objectives are clear—to protect our own citizens, to facilitate the evacuation of those who want to leave, and to help in the restoration of democratic institutions in Grenada.

LEHRER: But others in Congress and elsewhere are not so sure. With the Marine death toll in Sunday's Beirut tragedy up today to 215, there is a lot to report and talk about tonight. Robin?

ROBERT MacNEIL: And tonight we'll be covering the latest on the situation in Grenada with Undersecretary of State Lawrence Eagleburger and Prime Minister Eugenia Charles of Dominica, one of the six Caribbean nations joining the invasion. We'll hear from foreign and American critics who think the action was a bad idea. A group of regional newspaper editors tells us how Americans outside Washington are taking the Marine casualties and the Grenada invasion. And we have the latest from Beirut.

LEHRER: It began under the cover of early morning darkness. First came the Army Rangers by parachute, then the Marines by helicopter. It was an action President Reagan said was to protect the lives of U.S. citizens on Grenada and to restore order to the island country of 110,000 people now ruled by what he termed "leftist thugs." Tonight, U.S. officials say, the island's two airports and the situation are secure, except for remaining pockets of resistance from the Grenadian army. There have been at least two unconfirmed dead among American troops, but no further details other than the overall description of U.S. casualties as "minimal." There was armed resistance from some 600 Cuban construction workers; at least 12 of the Cubans died, according to one report. That's the overview. We go back for the details now, beginning at 9 A.M. Eastern Time in the White House briefing room. That's when President Reagan, accompanied by the prime minister of another Caribbean island, Dominica, announced the action to the public.

Pres. REAGAN: On Sunday, October 23rd, the United States received an urgent formal request from the five member nations of the Organization of Eastern Caribbean States to assist in a joint effort to restore order and democracy on the island of Grenada. We have taken this decisive action for three reasons: first, and of overriding importance, to protect innocent lives, including up to 1,000 Americans whose personal safety is, of course, my paramount concern; second, to forestall further chaos; and, third, to assist in the restoration of conditions of law and order and of governmental institutions to the island of Grenada where a brutal group of leftist thugs violently seized power, killing the prime minister, three cabinet members, two labor leaders and other civilians, including children. Let there be no misunderstanding. This collective action has been forced on us by events that have no precedent in the Eastern Caribbean and no place in any civilized society.

EUGENIA CHARLES, Prime Minister of Dominica: I think we were all very horrified at the events which took place recently in Grenada. We have to isolate the persons who have committed the acts that they did last week in killing off most of the cabinet. And we have to ensure that in fact an interim government of persons who are good administrators and who are Grenadians who can run the country for a few months with the pure purpose of putting the country back on a democratic status.

MacNEIL: Joining the Americans were forces from six Caribbean countries, four of them members of the Organization of Eastern Caribbean States—Antigua, Dominica, St. Lucia, and St. Vincent—and the others, two larger Caribbean nations, Jamaica and Barbados. The 300 soldiers and policemen represented more than half of the military forces of the six islands, which had been disturbed that their neighbor,

Grenada, had an army of more than 2,000. The invasion was mounted from Barbados, 110 miles northeast of Grenada.

[voice-over] The first sign that something was brewing was seen late yesterday when about 50 Marines in combat gear boarded helicopters at the airport in Barbados. Shortly afterwards, the helicopters took off in the direction of Grenada. Then there was silence overnight until Radio Grenada broke the news this morning: the island was being invaded and Barbados was obviously being used as a staging point. Today, big American Hercules planes capable of carrying heavy loads of troops and equipment were taking off from the airport at Barbados. The task was obviously to ferry in supplies for the American Marines and soldiers and the troops from the other Caribbean islands until a seaport could be secured in Grenada.

[on camera] So far there are no reports of any injury to the Americans living on Grenada, whose safety was one motive for the invasion. Charlayne Hunter-Gault has been finding out what news there was today of the U.S. citizens on the island. Charlayne?

CHARLAYNE HUNTER-GAULT: Since the phone lines went dead shortly after the invasion, the main source of news coming out of Grenada has been ham radio. The voice that has dominated the ham radio airwaves belongs to a man identified only as Mark, an American. He appears to be broadcasting from one of the two campuses of the St. George's University Medical School. His broadcasts were being monitored in the United States by ham operators, the news media, as well as a voice identifying itself as being from the State Department. At one point late this afternoon, Mark described the situation at the True Blue campus.

MARK, American student, Grenada: Our latest report is that True Blue is under mortar fire. True Blue is under mortar fire. The students are under tables. We don't know—that's the last report; that came in about 10 minutes ago. We're waiting an update on that. Again, no student to this point, and there is no further report that any students are being harmed in any way. Over.

HUNTER-GAULT: Late this afternoon, Mark described some of the first casualties—U.S. troops and Grenadian citizens being brought into a makeshift hospital at the True Blue campus.

MARK: Okay. First piece of info. For the States there. We have a [report] of "a load of incoming wounded U.S. troops." U.S. troops, probably at—we're at True Blue. At True Blue. They are at True Blue; they are treating U.S. troops and Grenadian civilians only. Okay, there are seven or eight wounded Grenadian civilians, possibly fatal, not yet though, but not looking good, though. Over.

HUNTER-GAULT: The State Department broke in to warn Mark not to discuss specific military targets, but throughout the day Mark was fed and attempted to answer questions from worried parents. There were no indications when normal communications would be restored on the island. Jim?

LEHRER: For most Grenadians the first concrete word on what was really happening this morning came on the radio in a most unusual message broadcast by the invading forces. Here are excerpts from that broadcast as monitored in nearby Barbados and recorded by National Public Radio's "Morning Edition" program.

RADIO BROADCAST, by invading forces, Grenada: People of Grenada, your Caribbean neighbors and the United States are concerned for your safety and welfare, as well as that of all foreign citizens residing in Grenada. Our forces are here to restore peace and order in Grenada for everyone's benefit. For your safety, please remain in your homes until further notice. Do not hinder our efforts to stabilize your nation. Foreign citizens in Grenada should remain neutral and stay in their quarters. No one has anything to fear from our forces.

LEHRER: Judy Woodruff now chronicles the story behind that broadcast. Judy?

JUDY WOODRUFF: Jim, planning for the invasion began in the middle of last week after what one U.S. official called a straw poll of the Caribbean nations in the area. At that time U.S. intelligence agencies began assessing the military forces on the island and the best landing sites for an armed incursion. Also, a Navy task force that had been heading for Lebanon from waters off Nicaragua was redirected toward Grenada. With the Navy aircraft carrier *Independence* and its force of some 70 planes cruising in nearby waters, and another naval task force, including the helicopter carrier *Guam*, located to the east of Grenada, the Americans prepared for action. At 5:30 this morning the invasion began. About 500 Marines on board helicopters landed near Pearls Airport on the island's northeastern coast. Some 700 to 1,000 Army Rangers, meanwhile, who had been based on Barbados, parachuted in near the island's other airport, Pt. Salinas International at the southwestern tip of the island about three miles from the capital city of St. George's. The U.S. forces, followed by a 300-man contingent from several neighboring Caribbean islands, quickly captured the airports. There were reports of fighting at both locations and, at a news conference, Secretary of State Shultz described the contacts American troops had with Soviets and Cubans.

GEORGE SHULTZ, Secretary of State: It's my understanding that the Soviets that are there have been identified; they are safe, and their safety is being looked to. On the other hand, in the case of the Cubans, there are many more there. I think there are some 600 Cubans there, presumably construction workers. But it is the case that some number—I don't know how many, and perhaps the military don't know at this point how many—are resisting and firing at our forces, and of course that would cause us to fire back.

WOODRUFF: Much of the fighting with the Cubans apparently took place at the Pt. Salinas airport, which Cuban nationals have been helping to expand. This airport has been a major source of concern to U.S. strategists who fear that it could become a base for Cuban and Soviet military activities in the Southern Caribbean, including a source of supplies for Nicaragua. The paratroopers at Point Salinas then moved to secure the two nearby campuses of the St. George's Medical School, where most of the estimated 1,000 Americans on Grenada are located. On the surface it appears that the Grenadan force of some 2,200 men with less than two dozen pieces of artillery, 24 mortars, about a half-dozen anti-aircraft guns, are badly outgunned by the 2,000 American troops backed up by 11 naval ships and dozens of planes. But the fighting continues. Jim?

LEHRER: For an update on where matters stand right now on the ground in Grenada and elsewhere diplomatically, first to the number-three man in the State Department, Undersecretary of State Lawrence Eagleburger. Mr. Secretary, first of all, can you confirm the two dead Americans among the American troops?

LAWRENCE EAGLEBURGER: I can't confirm them. We had a report before I left of at least one dead, but I can't confirm that there are two.

LEHRER: Marines or—was it a Marine or a Ranger?

Sec. EAGLEBURGER: I think it was a soldier, but I'm not sure.

LEHRER: What about wounded?

Sec. EAGLEBURGER: We've heard reports of maybe a dozen or so wounded, but again I don't have any specific figures, and I think you'll understand that I can't get into much detail on a military operation that's still going on, so I can't be too specific, but we have had at least the report of one dead and somewhere around a dozen wounded.

> Our forces are here to restore peace and order in Grenada for everyone's benefit.

LEHRER: The number that I used at the beginning of the number of Cubans killed, that was attributed to—that was in an interview that Jamaican Prime Minister Seaga gave. Does that jell with what you know, too?

Sec. EAGLEBURGER: The number that I had heard was two confirmed killed and a number captured, but there may be later figures on that as well.

LEHRER: Now, these were construction workers, the Cubans, right?

Sec. EAGLEBURGER: Well, that's an interesting fact that I think we're beginning to get a little more insight into. They certainly have been called construction workers, but I must say they are better armed than most construction workers I've ever heard of, and they are clearly under command of somebody, and there have been a number of them, at least, that have been fighting, and I therefore would have to at least hazard a guess that we may still call them construction workers, but I suspect they were something more than that.

LEHRER: When you say they were armed, in what way?

Sec. EAGLEBURGER: Well, they clearly had arms and were firing at our troops. I—obviously, generally rifles. I can't go beyond that because we haven't had any further reports, but they have been fighting against our troops, and they have been doing so in what I would clearly say was a military manner.

LEHRER: Now, the pockets of resistance that remained. Does that include Cubans, or does that mean the Grenadian army?

Sec. EAGLEBURGER: Well, again, my latest understanding of this is that there were some Cubans still fighting, and there may be a few Grenadians that are continuing to fight, but it's hard to say how many of each.

LEHRER: Are there any reports on deaths to civilians, to Grenadian civilians?

Sec. EAGLEBURGER: Only the sorts of reports that we heard here tonight. Some reports over radios and so forth. That's all I've seen. Luckily, the reports we have so far, at least, indicate that there have been no American deaths.

LEHRER: American civilians—American civilian deaths, of the 1,000 who were already there.

Sec. EAGLEBURGER: That's right.

LEHRER: Any word on how the U.S. forces were received by the Grenadian civilians?

Sec. EAGLEBURGER: I haven't heard anything about that at all.

LEHRER: You don't know whether they resisted or any of that?

Sec. EAGLEBURGER: No idea. We did have one report that while the Grenadians have tried to call up the militia, at least a substantial part of the militia did not show up.

LEHRER: That's in addition to the army of what Judy said a moment ago was about—what did you say, Judy? About—

WOODRUFF: Twenty-two hundred.

LEHRER: About 2,200, and in addition to that, the militia.

Sec. EAGLEBURGER: They had tried to call up the militia and a number of them apparently didn't show up.

LEHRER: Any word on how long this fighting is going to go on?

Sec. EAGLEBURGER: I couldn't give you any guess at this point.

LEHRER: What is the scenario for how long the U.S. troops will be there?

Sec. EAGLEBURGER: Well, the Secretary tried to deal with that in his press conference today, and I think the answer is, at this point there's no way that we can give you a specific time that they will be there. The Secretary said, and we intended, that the American forces will leave the island just as quickly as they can after they have met the purposes that they were there for, which is, first of all, to secure the safety of American citizens, and secondly to assist the Organization of Eastern Caribbean States in the process of stabilizing the island.

LEHRER: Earlier today there was a report that the prospect was for maybe just five to seven days. Does that make sense?

Sec. EAGLEBURGER: Well, again, I just don't want to be tied down to a specific time frame, but it will be as fast as we can get out.

LEHRER: But are we talking about a matter of days or weeks or months or—

Sec. EAGLEBURGER: You keep pushing me—

LEHRER: I know, I know, but I mean, you can give me a ballpark, can you not?

Sec. EAGLEBURGER: I'd rather just stick with, "We'll get out as quickly as we can."

LEHRER: All right. The President said that the action was justified on two grounds: the safety to the American civilians, and, as we sit here tonight, no American civilians that you know of have been injured.

Sec. EAGLEBURGER: So far as I know.

LEHRER: All right. Now, the second one is the initiation from the six other—from the six Caribbean nations. Why was it that this request could not be refused?

Sec. EAGLEBURGER: Well, you know, to argue that it couldn't be refused is, I think, the wrong way to put it.

LEHRER: Why was it so compelling?

Sec. EAGLEBURGER: Well, that it was compelling is a different point. It could obviously have been refused. We are, after all, a sovereign state. It was compelling because here were countries in the area who are culturally close to the Grenadians, who themselves are democracies, and who came to us and said that here is a situation of great instability. "It is threatening to the area as a whole, and we need the help of the United States to straighten this out." And we felt that under those circumstances, appealed to as we were by other democracies, and with the interests of the Caribbean in mind, we felt it was essential that we reply affirmatively but, again, I would suggest that the Prime Minister can give you at least as good an answer as I can on this.

LEHRER: We're going to hear from him now—from her now.

Sec. EAGLEBURGER: I hope—

LEHRER: Mr. Secretary, thank you. Robin?

MacNEIL: Mary Eugenia Charles, who made the announcement with President Reagan this morning, became the prime minister of Dominica in 1980. That's two years after the island became independent from Britain. Ms. Charles is a lawyer educated in Canada and Britain; she's the first and only woman head of state in the Caribbean, or head of government in the Caribbean. Prime Minister, who initiated this idea?

Pr. Min. CHARLES: The OECS organization.

MacNEIL: That's the Organization of Eastern Caribbean States.

Pr. Min. CHARLES: That's right.

MacNEIL: When did that happen?

Pr. Min. CHARLES: On Friday we first had talks with the ambassador, and then on Sunday we made the formal request.

MacNEIL: Well, what about this straw poll that our reporter Judy Woodruff referred to on her information by the U.S. of these nations? When did that take place?

Pr. Min. CHARLES: I know nothing about a straw poll, and you have to explain it to me, what a straw poll is.

MacNEIL: Well, it's canvassing opinion, I would gather.

Pr. Min. CHARLES: No, well, certainly my opinion wasn't canvassed, and I am chairman of the OECS.

MacNEIL: And did you gather the other six states—other five states together?

Pr. Min. CHARLES: We had a meeting concerning what was happening and we called it in Barbados, and at that meeting we decided on certain sanctions to be taken, and we also considered it was necessary to do more than this because, first of all, Grenada has a very large armed—I've always been afraid of this, this very large army and all the equipment they built up there. Also we know that there are, let us say, persons, outside of the Grenada kin who live there, who operate there, who have had reasons to have interest in some of the people we have in Dominica who spend a lot of time over there and get resources from those people, and we are quite worried that with the vacuum that existed in Grenada and this might continue on the chain of islands and affect us badly.

MacNEIL: If the decision was made only Sunday, how could the invasion be mounted so quickly? A rather complicated thing to do.

Pr. Min. CHARLES: Well, I don't know how. I'm not a military person. I don't know how it's done. But we do know that we asked America because they already had ships in the area, because they'd come close to [unintelligible]; they had to evacuate the people.

MacNEIL: I see.

Pr. Min. CHARLES: But we also asked Barbados and Jamaica to assist us.

MacNEIL: As a lawyer yourself and a head of government, what is the legal justification for this invasion?

Pr. Min. CHARLES: Generally Section—Article 8 of our treaty, which allows us to get together to prevent this sort of thing happening.

MacNEIL: To prevent what sort of thing?

Pr. Min. CHARLES: The breakup of peace and stability in our part of the world.

MacNEIL: The interior of Grenada is mountainous jungle-like terrain. What happens if the Grenadian army retreats in there? Do you not risk being pinned down in very long guerrilla warfare?

Pr. Min. CHARLES: It may be. It could be. I hope not though because I think that—I believe, quite frankly, the Grenadian people are not going to be wanting to have this done. They're wanting to have the return to normalcy, which they haven't had for some time.

MacNEIL: You expect it all to be over very rapidly?

Pr. Min. CHARLES: I think so.

MacNEIL: What is your estimate of how long it will take?

Pr. Min. CHARLES: You have to ask the military people that. I am not good at that sort of thing. I wouldn't know. But all I do know is that we have asked Americans to come in and help us and to leave as soon as possible so we can have a peacekeeping force of Caribbean people.

MacNEIL: And what kind of government are you and your fellow Caribbean nations going to set up in Grenada in the interim, if you are successful in restoring order?

Pr. Min. CHARLES: It will be an interim government of administrators who can run the country, run the affairs of the country and put into effect the method of allowing the Grenadian people to choose for themselves the government they want.

MacNEIL: How do you choose who they should be, the administrators?

Pr. Min. CHARLES: Well, really the governor general will do this, and I think he might confer with some of us on this. There are Grenadians outside of Grenada, especially in international organizations, who are non-political and who are in fact devoted to Grenada and would, I hope, be glad to come and see this country put back to normalcy.

MacNEIL: What will you do with General Austin and other leaders of the coup if you catch them?

Pr. Min. CHARLES: Well, I presume that they will be charged. I will not presume they would be detained for three years, as has been done in the past. I believe that they will be charged and brought to trial. This is the way that we think it should be done. This is the way the constitution of Grenada, which was suspended, shall we say? in '79, would require.

MacNEIL: Well, Prime Minister, thank you. Jim?

LEHRER: We turn now from exposition and explanation to analysis and criticism of what the United States and the six Caribbean nations did today, and that begins where it always begins, at the Congress. There was a mixture of reaction among the individual senators and House members. Some supported it; some deplored it. Here's a sampling.

Rep. DON BONKER, (D) Washington: It is clear that this administration has a cavalier attitude about using military force to deal with diplomatic problems.

Rep. IKE SKELTON, (D) Missouri: We cannot allow power-hungry dictators to knock off our neighbors to the south one by one.

Rep. THOMAS DOWNEY, (D) New York: Mr. President, you've got a lot of questions to answer to allay the fear that this member has that this is an administration that shoots first and asks questions later.

Rep. CARROLL CAMPBELL, (R) South Carolina: If we are to be the nation we are, and our neighbors ask for help, are we in fact to turn our back? Are we to leave our citizens there to be whatever happened to 'em in the face of this? I think not.

Rep. EDWARD MARKEY, (D) Massachusetts: Gunboat diplomacy has a new king. Move over, Teddy Roosevelt.

Sen. CHARLES PERCY, (R) Illinois: One thousand American citizens and 600 medical students at St. George's Medical School had to be secured; they have been secured.

Sen. CHRISTOPHER DODD, (D) Connecticut: We've certainly not been shy, and I think correctly so, in castigating the Soviet Union from time to time when they have engaged in such behavior. If we now perform likewise, I think the credibility of our arguments against the Soviets lose some of their validity.

Sen. JOHN TOWER, (R) Texas: I think the President acted properly. I don't think that he could have taken any other action when he was requested to do so by the Organization of Eastern Caribbean States because they felt that their security was threatened.

Sen. DANIEL P. MOYNIHAN, (D) New York: I don't know that you bring in democracy on the point of a bayonet.

LEHRER: Later in the day members of Congress's Black Caucus expressed their special concerns about the invasion of Grenada.

Rep. JULIAN DIXON, (D) California: It is particularly disturbing to us that this administration has not seen fit to consult in any manner with the black members of Congress, despite our close ties with the leaders of the Caribbean region, and sensitivity to the issues involved.

Rep. MERVYN DYMALLY, (D) California: We see the response based on the East-West conflict, an ideological one, and the request gave this administration just the excuse that it's been looking for for the last 3½ to four years.

Rep. RON DELLUMS, (D) California: This is incredibly dangerous what we are doing here, and I take the position that we ought to, in this country, oppose with as much fervor as humanly possible what this country has done in using other black Caribbean nations as a veil, a thin veil for the exploits of this militaristic administration.

MacNEIL: The Grenadian invasion brought negative reaction from predictable hostile quarters like Moscow, but also friends like Britain. The Soviet news agency Tass called the landings "banditry and terrorism" and demanded immediate withdrawal. Nicaragua demanded an emergency meeting of the United Nations Security Council; members are meeting informally tonight to consider the request. United Nations Secretary General Pérez de Cuellar issued a statement expressing grave concern. Two Caribbean nations, Guyana and the Dominican Republic, itself invaded by U.S. Marines in 1965, both condemned the invasion. And British Prime Minister Margaret Thatcher, normally President Reagan's staunchest ally, said she had refused to join the expedition.

MARGARET THATCHER, Prime Minister, Great Britain: We communicated to the United States our very considerable doubts which Her Majesty's government had about initiating action, and asked them to weigh carefully several points before taking any irrevocable decision to act.

MacNEIL: In Ottawa, Canadian Prime Minister Pierre Trudeau refused to condemn or applaud the action, but in Parliament he asked pointed questions: were there other ways of insuring the safety of the Americans there than by proceeding by invasion? In the case of Canada, he said, we had authority from Grenada to take our citizens out. Trudeau also said, what would happen if the United States had given itself the authority to invade any country where a democratic system didn't exist? Jim?

LEHRER: Another critical view of the Grenada action now from an American. He's Richard Feinberg, who was formerly a Latin America and Caribbean specialist on the State Department's policy planning staff. He's now vice president of the Overseas Development Council and is the author of a recent book, *The Intemperate Zone: The Third World Challenge to U.S. Foreign Policy.* From your perspective, what was wrong with doing this today?

RICHARD FEINBERG: Well, Jim, I think the administration managed to seize defeat from the jaws of victory in Grenada. The coup and countercoup and bloodshed in the last two weeks on the island served to discredit an unfriendly government and a government friendly to Cuba; by indirection, bolstered the cause of democracy in the region. We have now changed the debate from a discussion of the failure of a leftist regime in Grenada to a discussion of American intervention in the Caribbean and in the Third World.

LEHRER: All right. Let's go through the two basic justifications that the administration has given that Secretary Eagleburger has gone over again. First of all, the safety to the American citizens there. You don't buy that as a justification?

Mr. FEINBERG: Well, first, I don't think the administration has presented convincing evidence of that, and Larry Speakes, the press man from the White House, just about two or three days ago said that in fact there was no danger to American citizens. Even if there were, however, then it would seem to me a more limited military operation would be called for rather than an attempt to impose a new government on the island.

LEHRER: You heard—the second aspect. You heard what Prime Minister Charles says. She said that she and her fellow leaders in that area felt that their security was in jeopardy; they came to the United States and asked for help. Why shouldn't the United States have said yes?

Mr. FEINBERG: Well, first, of course, often governments come to us and ask for our assistance or military force and we turn them down, so we don't have to. Secondly, I think we should have operated within the broader OAS framework. Grenada is a member of the OAS.

LEHRER: That's the Organization of American States of all Latin America.

Mr. FEINBERG: Exactly. That's right. The hemispheric-wide organization, which is much more important historically. And we've sidestepped them because I think we realized we could not get a two-thirds majority which would be necessary to mount such an invasion.

LEHRER: All right, now that it's done, you object to it; what's the harm?

Mr. FEINBERG: I think there are a number of costs involved here. One is the image of the United States, the colossus, stepping on an ant, a country of 100,000 people. Second, the apparent justification for intervention by a great power in small countries. The Soviets, I'm sure, are quite pleased; the Afghans, the Cambodians, the Czechs, the Poles disturbed by this sort of precedent. Third, the sidelining of the OAS, weakening of the most important regional organization; and, finally, the question of getting out. Easy to get in; how easy it will be to get out remains unclear. There are two major political parties in Grenada. One, the New Drew movement [?] that we are repressing presumably will not easily participate in any sort of interim government or democratic government—

LEHRER: These are the folks that committed the coup a few days ago and that are—

Mr. FEINBERG: That's right. Who are the strongest political force on the island. The second strongest political force is that the—a fellow by the name of Gairy, who essentially was a dictator elected initially but, sort of like Marcos, gradually became undemocratic, and was also involved in supporting UFOs in Washington, in the U.N. in New York, and drug deals and this sort of thing—an unsavory character. But, so that's the choice that exists in Grenada now in terms of political forces. In other words, I think it's not going to be easy to set up any sort of stable interim government, and even harder to establish some sort of reasonable democracy.

LEHRER: So it'll all be in vain, you say?

Mr. FEINBERG: I think that we may have trouble. I think that one reason that Mr. Eagleburger and others have hesitated to give you a leaving date is that it may be very difficult, in fact, to restore some sort of stable constitutional government.

LEHRER: Thank you. Robin?

MacNEIL: The administration's statement that Americans in Grenada were in danger was disputed by the chancellor of the American-funded medical college in St. George's, the capital of Grenada, Dr. Charles Modica. Roughly half of the 1,000 Americans on the island are students at the medical school. Dr. Modica is presently in the United States. You said early today on NBC that the President's information was wrong. How do you know that?

CHARLES MODICA: Well, I was very involved with this whole crisis to begin with. When the coup took place I made it my business, because of the large American enrollment we have in St. George's, to communicate with the State Department and with the U.S. Embassy. And my only interest has been all along, and it remains today, the safety of our students and faculty. I, quite frankly, have been up for the last 48 hours, well in advance of this particular crisis, in order to maintain communications with the appropriate officials to ensure that things would go smoothly.

MacNEIL: If the American forces had not gone in, in your view, would the students and faculty have been in any danger?

Dr. MODICA: In my view there was no immediate threat to the students or faculty. And I have to assume that the President had some information that I was not privy to, and I would like to think that he did because otherwise there are many suspicions to be raised as to the motive of the U.S. forces going in today.

MacNEIL: Like what?

Dr. MODICA: Well, let me put it this way. I worked very hard on Thursday, the day after the revolution, to make it my business to communicate to the leaders who were announced that day my concern for the safety of our American students.

MacNEIL: That's General Austin and Mr. Coard?

Dr. MODICA: Well, Mr. Coard was not involved in that—

MacNEIL: But General Austin?

Dr. MODICA: Yes, General Austin and one of the majors, Major Stroud. We at the university felt that if they could guarantee the safety of Americans this would be a very good, positive first step, and if we had silence on their part we ought to think very carefully and quickly about getting students out of there.

MacNEIL: And what did you get?

Dr. MODICA: We got a very good response. They asked what our needs were because they had a curfew into effect. We replied, well, one campus was running low on water and, lo and behold, within two or three hours there were two or three fire trucks full of water.

MacNEIL: Did any of the Americans you know want to leave there, and could they have?

Dr. MODICA: Well, in fact, 30 of our students out of the 650—and I think it was on Sunday—were interested in leaving the country, and we had arranged—I had personally arranged to have U.S. Embassy officials flown into Grenada during the time of the curfew. This was a special favor that I asked of the government at that time—

MacNEIL: And it happened?

Dr. MODICA: And it happened. And I got U.S. officials into Grenada on Saturday late in the day. We had a few problems, and it almost didn't come off, but I worked very hard at it. I got U.S. officials in there, and they met with the students Saturday night and Sunday.

MacNEIL: Something else you also said this morning would lead me to ask you this question. Do you believe that the lives of the Americans have been put at greater risk by the invasion than they were in before?

Dr. MODICA: I believe that they were put in much greater risk by the invasion, and in fact I have been just speaking to some of our students that are still on the floor of a dormitory with a ham radio asking us for instructions as to what to do, because they're not sure if the area has even been secured yet.

MacNEIL: Well, thank you. Jim?

LEHRER: Back to Secretary Eagleburger now. Let's take the Chancellor's comments here. He says those folks were not in jeopardy unless the President knows something he doesn't know.

Sec. EAGLEBURGER: Well, obviously we disagree with him.

LEHRER: Does the President know something that he didn't know?

Sec. EAGLEBURGER: Well, if he's the President of the United States, I would certainly hope so. The point of the matter is that, in our view, the first thing that should be remembered, I think, is that we can't really even say that after the execution of Prime Minister Bishop, in our view, there has been any effective government. There have been some people who have said that they were nominally in charge, but in our view over the course of the last week there has been great instability, and our concern was that in fact that instability would get worse and that there was, in fact, potential for a real threat to American citizens, particularly those students. I think we share with the Doctor a great concern over the well-being of those American citizens. I think we differ on the judgment as to how serious the threat to their well-being was. And obviously we can have differences of view on this, but we felt rather strongly that it was the responsibility of the President to assure the safety of American citizens and that in this case that it was a great danger to their security.

LEHRER: Doctor, what's wrong with that?

Dr. MODICA: I feel that—first of all, I have to say that I would like to believe—I'm very proud to be an American, and I would like to believe that the President of the United States did have the interests of our students at heart. But there are some things that occurred today that bother me tremendously. I was in close touch with the embassy at the highest levels in Barbados and the State Department for the past 48 hours in a row, in addition to a few days before that, and at 4:30 A.M., when I received on our Telex machine in New York a mention from the students there operating it that planes were heard overhead, and they were getting very panicky, I immediately called the State Department. I thought perhaps something like this might be taking place, and I wanted to at least advise the students that in fact it was a friendly force coming in, to remain into their dorms and not to worry. And instead, from 4:30 until the time that President Reagan made the formal announcement, no one in the State Department would confirm nor deny that it was American military forces there. Certainly I was not about to give that information to the enemy, but only to the students that I had direct contact with.

LEHRER: Mr. Secretary, know anything about that?

Sec. EAGLEBURGER: Well, certainly. And, again, I understand what the Doctor is saying, but let's start with an understanding here now that, with an operation of this sort we are also dealing with the lives of troops involved, and therefore it is essential that in an operation like this we maintain the highest degree of secrecy that we can. I understand the Doctor's concern, but here again the point was he was asking us to tell him something that—not that he would deliberately pass on to anybody who would then go out and try to shoot the Americans as they came onshore, but he would be passing it on to others. We couldn't be sure of how that information would then proceed on

the ground in Grenada. And we had no choice, and have had no choice over the last day, as the President made his decision, but to remain as buttoned-up on this as we could.

LEHRER: Let's go to some of the points that Mr. Feinberg raised, and the policy points that, by doing this, the United States, to use his term, took defeat from the jaws of victory because this was already a negative thing for the left, and now we've turned it into a debate about the United States.

Sec. EAGLEBURGER: I don't argue at all that the execution of Prime Minister Bishop and the access to some form of power over the course of the last week or so by what the President—I think rightly—described as "thugs," was a black eye for the left. But—and if that were all that there were to it, I suppose he would have a point, but I have to come back again to the two points I started with, the first of which is, our judgment was and our judgment continues to be that the security of American citizens on that island, the safety of American citizens on that island was threatened, and that we had an obligation to try to do what we could to protect them. And, secondly, I cannot forget, nor should we forget, whether Dr. Feinberg agrees that we should have gone ahead with it or not, that a number of democratic states in the area, extremely concerned with the course of events in Grenada, had asked us to assist them in bringing about some stability in the island itself.

Mr. FEINBERG: If I might, Jim, in terms of—if we were worried about a deteriorating situation in Grenada, then presumably we could have gradually withdrawn American citizens, as we often do in other cases. I would also point out that we have, in previous occasions, for example, in the Dominican Republic in 1965, used the safety of American citizens as a pretext for a much wider operation.

LEHRER: And you think that's what happened here? You agree with the Doctor?

Mr. FEINBERG: I think unquestionably that the administration was looking for, in the broader sense, a quick, cheap victory in the Third World.

LEHRER: That's a very serious charge, Mr. Secretary.

Sec. EAGLEBURGER: You know, on occasion I get tired of being called a liar, but I'll forget that for the moment. But the fact of the matter is, and it goes back to something the Doctor said as well, yes, it is true, we finally got two embassy people from Barbados onto the island. It took a great deal of effort; they were turned back at least once. When they got on the island there was no guarantee that anybody was going to be able to get off the island. I do not agree with what Dr. Feinberg has just said, that presumably we could get them off the island. The fact of the matter was that, on the basis of our own experience, we could not get them—be sure that we could get them off the island. Indeed, the government of Grenada had announced that charter flights would be permitted onto the island on Monday; they did not permit those charter flights to land on the island on Monday. There was, in fact, no guarantee that we would be able to get them off the island.

LEHRER: What about his point, also, Mr. Secretary, that

if stability is the purpose of this excursion, that it's going to be impossible or nearly impossible to accomplish, and you're going to have to be there—the U.S. is going to have to be there a long time?

Sec. EAGLEBURGER: You know, Dr. Feinberg has his judgment on this subject, and he's an expert on it. I don't deny that. Again, what I have to say is that those other democratic states in the area, who also know that island, and we heard from the prime minister of one of them a few moments ago, believe that in fact there is an alternative, and that there can be a return to democracy on that island. With all respect to Dr. Feinberg, I have to, in this case, I think, bow to the judgment of the people who live there.

Mr. FEINBERG: Well, it is a judgment call, and I think often we have underestimated the difficulty of restoring constitutional government. How legitimate will a government be in Grenada that is put into power by external forces?

LEHRER: Well, what about the Secretary's point, though, that the better judge of that are the people from the surrounding islands rather than, he's saying, you, or anyone else?

Mr. FEINBERG: Yeah, I can understand there was great unhappiness in the region first with the Bishop government, which was not democratic, and then with the following bloodshed, and I can understand that, and it was a strong emotional reaction. I think over the last week or so a couple of things happened. One, there was an overreaction in the region. I think people with cooler heads—and I respect Prime Minister Charles, but I think that people with cooler heads—were urging caution. I also think that we need to examine carefully, historically, exactly how this decision came about. The Organization of Eastern Caribbean—the security arrangement, after all, was essentially pushed and created by the United States, and the countries in the area also know or hope that there will be a substantial reward or payoff for participating with us in this arrangement. So I think it's a little more complex.

LEHRER: Mr. Secretary, are you at all disturbed about the reaction of Great Britain?

Sec. EAGLEBURGER: Oh, I think it's clear that we would have preferred that the Prime Minister would have taken a different view, but let me make one point clear that earlier in the program was a little bit hazy. The United States at no time asked the United Kingdom to join us in this operation. We did never—we never asked that. Now, whether the Caribbean states in fact appealed to London or not is something for them to discuss. But we did not ask them to join us.

LEHRER: Gentlemen, thank you. Doctor, in New York, thank you.

*Credit*: Reprinted with permission from MacNeil-Lehrer Productions.

## TOM JORY: "NEWS COVERAGE OF GRENADA INVASION RESTRICTED BY DISTANCE, ORDER"

*For the next week there were reports that slowly leaked off the island as more Americans who had been residents in Grenada were brought home, but many news organizations reported the lack of journalists' access to the invasion zones. The next several stories all appeared the day after the invasion was announced by the government but before firsthand reports by journalists were available.*

### Associated Press, 26 October 1983

News reporters covering the invasion of the Caribbean island of Grenada were restricted—as they had been in recent months on other major world stories—by distance and government order, in their access to information.

The island of Barbados, 150 miles from Grenada, was swarming with reporters and television camera crews Wednesday, all awaiting clearance to fly to the besieged island. Much of the information on the invasion came, meanwhile, from Washington.

Reporters from Western news organizations were expelled from Grenada last week, and none was allowed to accompany the invading forces early Tuesday. There was no indication that the Defense Department was about to lift the restriction.

"We find ourselves in the same position we were in when the British government wouldn't allow us to go to the Falklands, and when the Soviets wouldn't allow any reporters in the area (near the Soviet island of Sakhalin) where the Korean Air Lines plane went down," said Wick Temple, managing editor of The Associated Press.

"We're covering it from U.S. government reports in Washington," Temple said, "and from reporters scattered all over the Caribbean." He said the AP had three correspondents on Barbados, one in Jamaica and one in Trinidad, all filing through the news agency's bureau in San Juan, Puerto Rico. Another AP reporter was allowed to report from Havana, Cuba, by the Cuban government.

Other news organizations said they were covering the story in much the same way.

"We would just like to have reporters and photographers in Grenada, and we don't," said Paul Varian, foreign editor for United Press International.

"We have a reporter trying to get to the scene . . . with the crowd in Barbados," said Myron Beckenstein, assistant foreign editor of the Baltimore Sun. He said the newspaper was unhappy with the way it was forced to report the important international story, and added: "We're upset, too, with the way the government is handling this."

In fact, several news organizations complained to the Pentagon, and to President Reagan, about the restrictions on reporters.

Keith Fuller, president and general manager of the AP, asked Reagan in a telegram sent Wednesday that "our correspondents be permitted to cover the military operations involving our forces in Grenada.

"Despite the perils, such coverage has historically been the rule," Fuller said. "There is no substitute for accurate, factual, firsthand reports. In their absence, only public confusion and misunderstanding can follow."

Said Roone Arledge, president of ABC News, in a letter to the Defense Department: "Suffice it to say that the U.S. troops on Grenada deserve as much coverage as the debate in Washington over their presence there."

Reuven Frank, president of NBC News, said in a statement, "Eyewitness reports by seasoned correspondents would serve the cause of accuracy and thereby improve understanding by the public."

Larry Speakes, Reagan's press secretary, said the ban was imposed to protect the safety of reporters. "When the Pentagon deems it safe, they will let you in," he said.

Defense Secretary Caspar Weinberger told reporters Wednesday that the decision to exclude reporters was made by the military commanders. "As soon as the commanders notify us that it is appropriate, and I hope it can be as soon as tomorrow, newsmen can go in," he said.

Richard S. Salant, president and chief executive officer of the National News Council, sent a telegram to Reagan Wednesday, saying it was "unconscionable that American troops should be involved in a shooting war while the press is totally barred from direct coverage of the combat zone."

The restrictions left the TV networks without pictures of the invasion and the fighting on Grenada.

"If you have pictures of the Marines going in," said Jeremy Lamprecht, director of foreign news for NBC, "it helps to show the story. It would be nice to see the Soviets and Cubans they say they captured."

The "CBS Evening News" ran a videotape Tuesday night showing several U.S. warships around the island, through a thick fog. It was thought to be the only film of the island shot after the invasion.

Covering the story from the outside was not without its hazards. An Associated Press reporter and three photographers were detained by Barbados police for over an hour Wednesday as they watched military transport planes being loaded with ammunition and supplies at the airport near Bridgetown, Barbados.

Police escorted the newsmen, including the AP's Richard Pienciak, from the third floor of an abandoned terminal building, forced three of them to strip to their underwear, and confiscated their film.

Pienciak said the policemen threatened the four with arrest if they returned to the terminal.

Other reporters on Barbados spoke by telephone with anyone they could reach on Grenada, and scrambled for bits of information from ham radio operators in contact with the besieged island. And they listened to the Caribbean Broadcasting Corp. station in Bridgetown, which frequently carried reports from Radio Free Grenada.

"We're all doing it the same way, I guess," said Desmond Maberly, editor and deputy manager of Reuters, the British news agency, "out of Barbados, out of Washington, and in our case, also out of Havana."

Reuters, unlike most other news organizations in the West, has had a correspondent in Cuba for some time, and Maberly said officials there "started talking pretty early.

"They came across not only with their criticism," he said, "but they came across with their first casualty figures, too. They did say yesterday they had injuries and wounded, the usual official statements, but also they seemed to be fairly candid about problems their own people were encountering in the fight."

Invading forces were known to have skirmished with armed Cuban construction workers building an airport in Grenada.

Barbara Crossett, deputy foreign news editor of the New York Times, said the newspaper had two reporters on Barbados and one in Havana, and another "constantly watching" the U.S. office in Bay Shore, N.Y., for the medical school in Grenada, where many of the Americans on the island were students.

The Times reporters in the Caribbean are in daily contact with ham-radio operators on Grenada. "It's been interesting because it's given some idea of the scale of the fighting, particularly around the campuses," she said.

AP technicians set up a ham-radio link from East Brunswick, N.J., to American medical students in Grenada, and AP stories carried considerable eyewitness information from them.

*Credit*: Reprinted with permission of The Associated Press.

# MICHAEL KERNAN: "GRENADA: THE REACTION TO THE ACTION; ON TV, PICTURING THE INVASION"

*This story provides an overview of the confusion and distress among media outlets when they discovered that they would not be allowed access to Grenada, and how ill informed they were about the operation at all. It also helps explain why there was so little television coverage of the conflict. Television needs images for broadcast, rather than just the news anchors reading reports.*

*Washington Post*, 26 October 1983

Americans who are accustomed to television taking them straight to the scene of wars and disasters were flying blind this time.

The invasion of Grenada remained largely a matter for the imagination throughout the day yesterday, as TV networks made the most of maps, shots of helicopters, and many, many talking heads: at the Pentagon, at the White House, on the Hill, at the State Department, on Barbados.

From the island itself there were only voice reports.

Edward M. Joyce, president of CBS News, sent a letter to Defense Secretary Caspar Weinberger protesting the refusal to allow news crews to land on the island, with or without military protection.

"I would also like to protest the attitude expressed by your Public Affairs office," he wrote, "as indicated in the statements . . . to our correspondent Bill Lynch that 'we learned a lesson from the British in the Falklands.' To use the censorship by the British as an example to be followed by the United States in this military operation is baffling to me and deeply disturbing because it refutes the principles of the First Amendment. . . ."

ABC also sent a letter to Weinberger. "Suffice it to say that the U.S. troops on Grenada deserve as much coverage as the debate in Washington over their presence there," ABC News president Roone Arledge wrote.

At 3:34 P.M. CBS did have an aerial shot of the Grenada landscape, taken from a chartered plane sometime after the landings at the airports. Planes have been forbidden to fly within 50 miles of the island since the invasion stepped off at 5:40 A.M. yesterday.

The size of the invading army was successively reported as 1,000, 1,500, 1,700 and 1,900, and word of a helicopter crash—passed along by a student at St. George's medical school with a ham radio—went unconfirmed for some hours before the Pentagon finally acknowledged that one had been shot down. The student later reported having seen six wounded soldiers and the fall of a second copter. Pentagon sources stuck to the word "minimal" to describe American casualties, rejecting a report of 22 casualties.

As to which network got the story first, there seemed to be several answers. Monday evening, all three networks as well as print journalists learned that 50 U.S. Marines had landed on Barbados Monday and had flown off immediately in three helicopters around 5 P.M. The American embassy there indicated

the force might help evacuate the 1,000 Americans living on Grenada.

CBS had that on the "CBS Evening News" at 6:30 P.M. Monday, with Sandy Gilmore reporting from Barbados. The White House denied that Americans were in any danger on Grenada but admitted that, as Deputy Press Secretary Larry Speakes put it, "the situation remains unstable."

In any case, this was not the invasion.

At 6 A.M. yesterday, on "World News This Morning," ABC reported from Barbados that the 50 Marines had flown into Grenada, and showed their planes leaving Barbados. At 6:07 A.M. ABC had the first confirmed report out of Barbados of Marines landing at a Grenada airport. Photos of planes leaving Barbados were featured. A more comprehensive report followed at 7, with ABC news correspondent Mark Potter on Barbados. At 6:30 A.M. NBC had word from State Department correspondent Fred Francis on "Sunrise" that the invasion was under way. And CBS' Gilmore reported the event on "Morning News" at 7:05.

"At 7 A.M. we were working on Lebanon and our minds were on that," said Steve Freedman, executive producer of NBC's "Today" show. "Then we get a phone call from Dennis Murphy on Barbados, who says they've invaded Grenada. And we say, who invaded Grenada? Then he says, I think there are Americans here. The story evolved. Then Tom Pettit, executive vice president of NBC News, calls at 8 and says, Can you do another hour? We were a little worried, but we got real lucky: The president came out, our Washington staff lined up a lot of people, correspondents at the White House, the Pentagon and the State Department, so we had all those perspectives. . . . The really extraordinary thing was that we had to do a whole new two hours for the West Coast. We were on the air from 7 A.M. to noon."

Through the morning, all the networks continued to run special reports and bulletins of varying length, about every hour, leading up to the fairly complete recap at 3 P.M. with the press conference by Secretary of State George Shultz.

Cable News Network sent a reporter and crew to Barbados on Monday, after receiving a tip on the impending invasion from a news source. Ed Turner, senior vice president of CNN, said the source was "pretty solid, and the president of the network said okay, send down Mike Boettcher and the crew. So it became the joke of the network—everyone assumed it would be a month sunbathing on the beaches of

Barbados awaiting invasion—and it just didn't happen that way."

As they awaited permission to go to Grenada, the networks mobilized their coverage. For example, CBS also sent correspondents to Jamaica, Trinidad, Cuba and Barbados, and will send a crew to Puerto Rico.

David Burke, vice president and assistant to the president of ABC News, said his people also are covering the American military bases from which the attacking force took off and have chartered planes and a boat in their attempts to reach Grenada for first-hand reporting.

"We're getting almost as much from the news as we're getting from intelligence sources," commented Sen. Patrick J. Leahy (D-Vt.) at midmorning. And that wasn't very much.

All three networks tended to use the same detailed map of Grenada, with their pointers indicating over and over the same two invasion points at the airfields and the location of the medical school, where many of the Americans are staying. At 1:42 P.M., ABC brought out a new map, a National Geographic version of the island. NBC relied mostly on quickie 30-second bulletins throughout the morning and afternoon, plus somewhat longer reports hourly.

All three networks scheduled special coverage last night of the invasion.

Gradually, the facts were sorted out. The fighting was down to "pockets of resistance" by early afternoon and presumed to be all over but the mopping up. Voice reports from Havana and Moscow were added to the mix, as well as Margaret Thatcher's negative comments from London and reaction from members of Congress. In fact, as the firing died down, the voices were all that were left.

*Credit:* © **1983, The Washington Post, reprinted with permission.**

---

## IRA R. ALLEN: WHITE HOUSE PRESS RESTRICTIONS IN GRENADA

---

*The White House continued to defend its directive to limit access to the island of Grenada. This report captures the reasons given by the White House and the stall responses provided to specific requests.*

United Press International, 26 October 1983

WASHINGTON: The policy of the White House is "to tell the truth," deputy press secretary Larry Speakes said Wednesday, while coming under fire from reporters for misleading them before the invasion of Grenada.

Speakes also said he would take note of demands by reporters to intercede with President Reagan to allow U.S. news organizations onto the island for first-hand coverage.

Speakes was questioned in detail about why on Monday he and other spokesmen carried out instructions to "knock down hard" reports that an invasion was imminent and told to call such reports "preposterous."

The deputy press secretary said he originally denied a question about a Marine landing taking place Monday based on "narrow guidance" given him by the National Security Council, then said "no" to a question about a landing possibly occurring the next morning, when it in fact took place.

"The policy of the White House is to tell the truth," Speakes said, although he conceded, "There could have been confusion."

Tuesday, he said it was possible reporters were "misled."

Reporters usually are not barred from accompanying U.S. troops, although they have been subject to wartime censorship and limited "pool" coverage by designated representatives in past actions.

Speakes cited the Pentagon's rationale for not letting reporters onto the island as "safety," although he declined later to characterize the shooting as "combat," a term that could have congressional ramifications under the War Powers Resolution.

Speakes' daily morning briefing was marked by bitter exchanges. He called reporters' behavior "venomous," and network correspondents accused Reagan of "stonewalling."

As he lectured reporters about "restoring some civility," CBS correspondent Lesley Stahl replied, "Don't censor us in here either."

When ABC correspondent Sam Donaldson started to ask vigorously why no coverage of the invasion was allowed, Speakes told him, "I realize you're carrying your management's water."

"The president certainly has the power to order the Department of Defense to allow this to be covered," said CBS correspondent Bill Plante, asking that Speakes "personally express to the president our concern that we cannot cover this war."

"Your request is noted and I will carry it—" Speakes said, his last words drowned out by the clamor of more questions.

In recounting what he knew and when he knew it, Speakes said public affairs officials were not informed until late in the planning Monday night and he was not finally notified until one hour after the invasion took place.

"I do not think they will deliberately mislead you," Speakes said of White House higher-ups. "I think they may tell you nothing, but they will not mislead you."

While explaining why Monday's questions about an imminent invasion were knocked down so hard, Speakes, referring to NSC spokesman Bob Sims, said: "Perhaps Sims assumed—I did—that that was a pretty well preposterous thought" that an invasion would occur.

*Credit*: Reprinted by permission of UPI.

---

## CHRISTOPHER SULLIVAN: "PROTESTS OVER GRENADA INVASION, JOY OVER EVACUATIONS"

---

*This report of the mixed public response provides an overview of the concerns expressed by some politicians and members of the public over the precipitous action of the White House. Largely, though, the public and politicians supported the operation, as is presented by this story two days after the invasion was announced.*

### Associated Press, 27 October 1983

More than 3,000 demonstrators marched in several cities to protest the U.S.-led invasion of Grenada, while supporters—including Reagan administration officials—defended the military strike, and evacuated Americans kissed the soil of their homeland.

Chanting, "USA, CIA, out of Grenada today," about 2,500 protesters rallied in New York near the United Nations on Wednesday night, as a dozen speakers denounced the invasion by about 2,000 U.S. troops and 300 more from Grenada's Caribbean neighbors.

Calling it "a sad day," the Rev. Herbert Daughtry, leader of a Brooklyn community group, told the rally he could not understand why the tiny island nation had "struck such fear in the heart of Ronald Reagan."

In Boston, 22 protesters were dragged away and arrested for refusing to leave the office of House Speaker Thomas P. O'Neill, a spokeswoman for the U.S. Marshal's office said.

In a telephone conversation with O'Neill, who was in Washington, members of the Ad Hoc Citizens' Group Opposing U.S. Invasion said they were "profoundly disappointed" in the speaker's refusal to speak out against the attack.

In other demonstrations Wednesday, 250 people marched in San Francisco, 250 rallied in Ann Arbor, Mich., and a half-dozen people were on hand with placards in Albany, N.Y., where presidential counselor Edwin Meese said U.S. leaders "would have been abdicating our responsibility" if they had ignored pleas for help from Grenada's neighbors.

About 20 picketers protested outside an Army recruiting station in Los Angeles, and in downtown Chicago, a group of Vietnam veterans demonstrated against the invasion, carrying a sign that said: "Get your bloody hands out of Grenada."

In contrast, 40 supporters of U.S. action gathered on the Florida State University campus in Tallahassee, one carrying a sign that read: "Reagan Hero of Freedom; Stop the Soviets Now."

About 10 opponents marched outside a federal building in Charleston, S.C., where two planes landed at an airbase Wednesday, bringing home the first 141 American evacuees from Grenada. Some kissed the ground as they left the planes. More evacuees returned today.

Banners wished them "Welcome Home" and a crowd of 60 cheered.

"I don't think there's a more beautiful sight than being back in the United States," said Jean Joel of Albany, N.Y., who, like many of the 1,000 Americans on Grenada, had been a student at St. George's University Medical School, a focal point of fighting between American-led troops and Grenadian and Cuban defenders.

Following last week's toppling and execution of former Grenadian leader Maurice Bishop, "Conditions were ripe for terrorist activity aimed against them (the students)," said House Republican leader Robert Michel, who defended Reagan's "bold step" in a statement released from his Peoria, Ill., office Wednesday.

Former President Gerald Ford agreed, terming the action "totally justified" to combat growing Soviet influence in the Caribbean.

But former CIA director Stansfield Turner, speaking in Atlantic City, N.J., said the invasion appeared to be "not worth it" and suggested a U.S. force may have to remain on the island for a long time.

Alan S. Whiting, a former U.S. intelligence analyst now teaching at the University of Arizona in Tucson, said the captured Cuban airfield on Grenada was strategically insignificant and said the invasion will only encourage anti-American attitudes.

Meanwhile, families of American residents of Grenada and invading servicemen waited anxiously for news.

"We're very upset and concerned, but there's just not much we can do," said Bernard McCormack of Charlton, Mass., whose daughter, June Diliberto, remained in Grenada.

*Credit*: Reprinted with permission of The Associated Press.

## IRA R. ALLEN: "LARRY SPEAKES VS. THE PRESS"—BITTER CLASHES AT WHITE HOUSE PRESS BRIEFINGS

*Relations between the White House and the press corps dropped to unusual levels of hostility by week's end. This report is an example of the things said during press briefings that are usually formal and very polite.*

United Press International, 28 October 1983

WASHINGTON: White House spokesman Larry Speakes clashed bitterly with reporters for the fourth straight day Friday over the administration's handling of news coverage of the U.S. invasion of Grenada.

While denying he was justifying censorship, Speakes said the first report by a journalist reaching Grenada "was wrong as heck" and a "bum story."

Speakes has been under fire from reporters since the American invasion Tuesday for having unintentionally misled them about the impending action, the government's refusal to let reporters onto the island for two days—and only then under strict military control—and on conflicting information supplied by the Pentagon.

Speakes' daily briefing for the White House press corps again broke down into bickering Friday as Speakes defended the administration's actions.

"Now, the media's there, and the first story out of there last night was just as wrong as heck," Speakes said. "It was a UPI bulletin precede that indicated there was a major firefight going on . . . and it was totally erroneous, and the guy was there and the guy saw some aircraft come in and he totally over-reported."

"Why aren't reporters allowed to cover the war?" Speakes asked, repeating an oft-asked question. He replied, "The guy who covered the war and saw it personally came out with a bum story."

"Mr. Speakes' credibility as a spokesman for the White House is fast approaching the vanishing point," said Maxwell McCrohon, editor in chief of United Press International in a statement following the briefing. "After four days of stonewalling and at least one example of misinformation, his first response today was to attack a UPI reporter's story from Grenada."

"The reporter based her story on information supplied by a senior military officer taking part in the invasion.

"Instead of engaging in recriminations with reporters on the scene and those covering the White House, Mr. Speakes should address himself to the question of providing information that would enable them to report fully a story of great national and international concern," McCrohon said.

The one-sentence United Press International bulletin cited by Speakes reported fierce combat between U.S. troops and Cubans entrenched near the Cuban-built jet airport at Point Salines. A subsequent bulletin filed to UPI subscribers within minutes focused on details of the fighting—U.S. air strikes and artillery fire.

"Mr. Speakes probably objected to use of the expression 'fierce combat' in the initial bulletin," UPI Foreign Editor Paul Varian said in New York. "Our coverage went far beyond subjective characterizations and zeroed in quickly on the details of the fighting to let readers decide for themselves."

CBS correspondent Bill Plante, replying to Speakes' comments at the White House, said, "That's what the system is all about."

"Bum stories?" asked Speakes.

"Yes, sir," Plante continued. "This system is about the right to be wrong and the right to observe it for ourselves and to be wrong. That's what this is about. We don't guarantee accuracy, but you should guarantee access."

"I have never . . ." Speakes began, then asking "The right to be wrong?"

"You're goddamn right. The right to be wrong—for ourselves," Plante said.

When a reporter told Speakes he "just gave the rationale for censorship," the deputy press secretary replied, "No I didn't."

Later, Speakes and CBS correspondent Lesley Stahl got into this exchange over Speakes' complaint that reporters shout questions at him all at once.

Speakes: I wish you wouldn't interrupt.

Stahl: Larry, don't tell us how to act.

Speakes: Let me tell you one thing, Lesley, (Speakes rises and points his finger). I've had about enough of you.

Stahl: Well, I've had enough of you . . .

Speakes: If you can't be—not interrupt me back . . .

Stahl: I want you all to report he's pointing his finger at me.

Speakes: I sure am. Now you're the greatest violator of this thing, and I am sick and tired of you. I am sick and tired of you.

Stahl: Every time somebody asks you a question in this room you try to tell us how to act.

Speakes: I try to tell you don't interrupt me.

Stahl: Well, don't interrupt someone else . . . You have just as much as we have. And none of us appreciates being told how to conduct ourselves . . . And don't make it so personal to me because I'm speaking for all of us.

Speakes: Well, it is very personal with me. If you conducted yourself in some way where we could have a logical conversation—

Stahl: Larry, it has nothing to do with that.

Speakes: You're interrupting me again.

Stahl: (Sarcastically). I'm so sorry. I'm not really sorry at all.

Speakes: You know what you can do. You can walk out again like you did last time.

Stahl: I don't feel like walking out.

Speakes: I know, but you did last time.

*Credit*: Reprinted by permission of UPI.

---

# FELICITY BARRINGER: "FCC DEFENDS RULING ON HAM RADIO USE"

---

*This story is an example of the ways in which the news media tried to go around the Pentagon restrictions on direct reporting by nonmilitary personnel.*

*Washington Post*, 28 October 1983

Federal Communications Commission officials said yesterday that they were reiterating their standing rules Wednesday when they sent an advisory to amateur or "ham" radio operators and commercial broadcasters that the amateur frequencies could not be used for active newsgathering.

The advisory was sent when administration officials were still refusing reporters permission to go to the Caribbean island of Grenada, invaded by U.S. forces early Tuesday morning. Four reporters encountered on the island by U.S. troops Wednesday were airlifted to the carrier USS Guam.

Under the circumstances, amateur radio was the only available independent source of information from the scene of the invasion.

"The commission was not shutting down some 'loose end' here that was violating a blackout," said Ray Kowalski, chief of the FCC's special services division. "The commission was using, as much as it could, amateur radio to facilitate communication within the amateur rules."

The rules involved, in effect informally for years but codified only last July, prohibit the use of amateur frequencies for "business communications on behalf of any party."

In an official notice July 20, the FCC explained: "For example . . . an amateur radio station may not be used for a medical or law enforcement communication which does not fall within the exception of immediate danger to life or property." Many other frequencies are available for this purpose, it said.

The notice made no specific mention of newsgathering. Under the FCC's interpretation, reporters legally may monitor amateur broadcasts, but interviewing, either directly by reporters or indirectly by ham operators relaying reporters' questions, represented a prohibited "business" use of the airwaves.

The notice was issued Wednesday, Kowalski said, because dozens of commercial radio and television broadcasters were requesting permission to use a normally restricted frequency that was being used by an American medical student on Grenada. The student, Mark Barettella, broadcast for about 36 hours from his dormitory at the St. George's University School of Medicine on Grenada.

Kowalski said that because of an urgent request from the State Department Tuesday night, he allowed Barettella and at least three U.S.-based hams to use a frequency normally restricted to communications in international Morse code. But he and other FCC officials repeatedly denied news organization requests to communicate with Barettella.

According to Kowalski and a CBS spokesman, CBS News made such a request Tuesday night and again Wednesday, asking permission to patch Dan Rather, anchorman of the "CBS Evening News," into the amateur frequency so he could conduct an interview with Barettella.

Asked for comment on the FCC interpretation of newsgathering as business, a CBS spokesman said, "We would agree this was not the kind of use for which the amateur frequencies were intended." Asked if the agency should have made an exception for the Rather interview, CBS responded that while the request was "not an emergency, it would have hurt no one and the American people would have been better informed."

Earlier Tuesday, the State Department had intervened on Barettella's behalf, asking the FCC to let him use a normally restricted frequency, according to Kowalski. "I gave the waiver based on what I was told by the State Department was a life-and-death emergency," Kowalski said.

*Credit*: © **1983, The Washington Post, reprinted with permission.**

# DAVID HOFFMAN AND FRED HIATT: "PRESIDENT DEFENDS INVASION, MARINES IN BEIRUT; CUBAN ARMS CACHE FOUND ON GRENADA"

*This front-page story reported the shift in rationale for the invasion of Grenada. President Reagan was responding to a variety of political pressures at home to protect Americans around the world, as well as advance the U.S. position in hostile, crisis-prone locations. The constraint on direct media coverage of the war was still a point of concern here.*

*Washington Post*, 28 October 1983

President Reagan, shifting his justification for the American invasion of Grenada, said last night that U.S. forces had discovered a "complete Cuban base with weapons and communications equipment" that made it "clear a Cuban occupation of the island had been planned."

Saying that U.S. troops found warehouses with "weapons and ammunition stacked almost to the ceiling, enough to supply thousands of terrorists," the president called Grenada "a Soviet-Cuban colony being readied as a major military bastion to export terror and undermine democracy."

While the administration presented only fragmentary evidence of what Reagan called the major Cuban buildup, the president said in his nationally televisied address, "We got there just in time."

Hours earlier a senior Pentagon official, also referring to what he called signs of a Cuban buildup on the island, said U.S. forces may have to remain there "indefinitely" to combat likely Cuban efforts to return, inspire guerrilla activity and regain control.

"I don't think the Cubans are going to give up," said the official, who declined to be identified.

He observed that it would take a large naval and ground force to keep Cuba from sending small boats with weapons to Grenada in ensuing months.

Initial response in Havana early today came from deputy foreign minister Ricardo Alarcón, who told Washington Post correspondent Alma Guillermoprieto that Reagan's description of Cuban military installations in Grenada was "a great lie . . . because we don't have any military installations or structures in Grenada."

The administration had said earlier—and still was saying officially yesterday—that the U.S. military operation on Grenada would be surgical and brief.

The Pentagon said yesterday that eight U.S. servicemen had been killed in the invasion, eight others were missing and 39 were wounded.

The theme of Cuban involvement on the island built in a crescendo yesterday, with administration officials repeatedly raising their estimates of the Cuban presence, saying they had been surprised by it and citing it as justification for the action.

There had been almost no mention of Cuba at the outset.

Officials had said then that the invasion was ordered to protect U.S. citizens on the island and to support neighboring island governments that had asked for help.

Most of the Americans on Grenada were students and faculty members at St. George's University School of Medicine, 409 of whom had been flown to the United States by yesterday, officials said.

Administration officials said U.S. forces had encountered twice as many Cubans in Grenada as expected and discovered a "combat engineer battalion" and a Cuban colonel on the island. One official said the "indications are they were building a major Cuban base."

Late in the day, Pentagon officials showed reporters videotapes that were said to have been made early yesterday morning in Grenada and that showed six warehouses of Soviet-made small arms ammunition and weapons. An unidentified U.S. colonel narrating the tape said the weapons cache, discovered five miles north of Pt. Salines airport, was "far above what any force on any island this size would need for self-defense."

The weapons shown in the videotape were small arms, assault rifles, machine guns, mortars and, in one case, an antiaircraft battery that the unseen narrator described as "extremely lethal." It was impossible to gauge the amounts of weapons discovered, however, and the tape did not reveal any larger equipment that might belong to an aggressive or invading force such as helicopters, ships, tanks, missiles or armored personnel carriers.

After a White House meeting with Reagan yesterday, Prime Minister John Compton of St. Lucia, one of the eastern Caribbean nations that participated in the invasion, said the Cuban "military buildup" was the main reason that his nation and others had sought U.S. military help.

"The United States came to our aid because we thought the military buildup was threatening the whole of the southern Caribbean," he said.

In the one clear response to the invasion on Capitol Hill yesterday, the House Foreign Affairs Committee adopted, 32 to 2, a declaration that the War Powers Act of 1973 applied to the use of American troops in Grenada. As approved, the resolution would require the removal of the troops after 60 days with the clock starting Tuesday, when the invasion began.

Also yesterday, Federal Communications Commission officials said they were reiterating standing rules when they sent an advisory Wednesday to amateur or "ham" radio operators and commercial broadcasters that amateur frequencies could not be used to transmit news stories. The advisory was sent when administration officials still were refusing reporters permission to cover the invasion.

After sharp criticism from news organizations across the nation, the administration eased a news blackout it had imposed on coverage of the first two days of the invasion. The Pentagon late yesterday gave 12 reporters an escorted glimpse of Grenada.

On the Cubans, Reagan's new national security affairs adviser, Robert C. McFarlane, told reporters yesterday, "The discoveries that have been made are extraordinary in terms of capability and infrastructure and what it portended for the future."

Reagan last night linked the Soviet Union to the Cuban presence. He said it was "no coincidence" that when a leftist military junta took over earlier this month, "there were 30 Soviet advisers and hundreds of Cuban military and paramilitary forces on the island." Administration officials had said previously that the 20 to 30 Soviets on the island were embassy officials.

A senior administration official, briefing reporters at the White House before the president's speech, said that there were about 1,100 Cubans on the island, more than twice as many as previously believed, and that several hundred remained at large.

It had been known that there were Cuban construction workers on Grenada helping to build a large airstrip that the administration had feared could be of possible military use to hostile powers. But the construction workers had not been considered a military force.

The official said the weapons stores on the island were "sufficient to equip terrorists in the thousands." He said this meant that the Cubans apparently intended to "exploit Grenada as a forward Cuban base." He added that the military preparations on Grenada were "enough to sustain a significant ground force or terrorist operations."

This official added that U.S. forces had discovered large quantities of automatic weapons, mortars, ammunition and equipment for light infantry during the invasion. He added that "extremely sophisticated" communications equipment had also been discovered.

Presidential spokesman Larry Speakes told reporters earlier yesterday, "Clearly you had a substantial Cuban organization there that was well equipped. It was following a pattern of previous Cuban behavior in Angola and Ethiopia."

The strong emphasis on Cuba's military buildup contrasted with the administration's insistence in the first two days of the invasion that the action was motivated by concerns about the safety of American citizens in Grenada and was designed only to restore order and "democratic institutions" on the island.

The eight-minute videotape which the Pentagon unveiled for reporters tonight was filmed at 5 A.M. yesterday, Pentagon officials said. It showed six moderate-sized warehouses roofed in tin or plastic sheeting, and at least two sheds covering what a narrator said were Soviet-made heavy trucks and ambulances, all surrounded by a low barbed-wire fence.

Inside the warehouses were hundreds of crates of ammunition for machine guns, Soviet made AK-47 automatic rifles, 120mm mortars and antiaircraft guns, the narrator said. Some of the crates were marked with Russian letters and others had stamped on them, "Oficina Economica Cubana."

The narrator said U.S. forces found "millions of rounds and thousands of weapons" at the complex which appeared to be surrounded by low green vegetation not far from the ocean. The film also showed several hundred men who were said to be Cuban prisoners being guarded by Barbadan and possibly other Caribbean nations' soldiers.

The prisoners were lying close together on the pavements, many of them covering themselves with large straw hats from what was apparently hot sun. Some of them appeared to be in their early 20s in khaki uniform, while others were quite bedraggled and apparently middle-aged.

Even as the administration was disclosing what it described as surprising evidence of Cuban military involvement in Grenada, officials suggested the possibility of a longer stay for U.S. forces than was originally forecast.

Administration officials repeatedly have refused to set a specific timetable for withdrawal. Last night, Reagan said, "It is our intention to get our men out as soon as possible." A senior administration official said it was expected U.S. troops might remain some weeks, but not months.

A senior Pentagon official said he believed that the United States will try to install a force from neighboring Caribbean nations, Great Britain or elsewhere that might be able to take the place of U.S. forces and still maintain order. This official, however, was pessimistic on the chances of finding a force capable and willing to do so.

"The tendency in government is to worry about what has to be done now, and then worry about the rest later," he said, suggesting that the Pentagon may not have had time to plan carefully for the occupation during the few days that the invasion was put together.

"Over the next six months, I just hope to God we can find a force that can maintain order and prevent infiltration," he said. "I would think neither Defense Secretary Caspar Weinberger nor Gen. John Vessey, chairman of the Joint Chiefs of Staff, wants to pin us down any further than we're pinned down already, but you can't leave a vacuum. . . . They could just establish a constabulary, if it weren't for the Cubans."

Administration officials originally had envisioned a police force for Grenada made up of troops from the Caribbean nations that joined the invasion. But Compton, the St. Lucia prime minister, suggested that the island nations had at their disposal a combined force of only about 500 men. He said leaders of the Organization of Eastern Caribbean Nations, joined by leaders of Jamaica and Barbados, would meet Saturday to discuss the post-invasion force.

Compton also predicted that U.S. forces would be needed in Grenada for only a matter of weeks.

Administration officials said that the island's governor-general, Sir Paul Scoon, was returned to Grenada yesterday from the USS Guam and was to give a radio speech to the populace. Scoon had been held under house arrest after the 16-member military junta seized control of the island.

Compton said yesterday that before the invasion Scoon had written a letter seeking help for the island from the other Caribbean states. But the letter, dated Monday, Oct. 24, the day before the invasion, wasn't delivered until after Scoon was removed from his house by U.S. forces in an armored personnel carrier.

Compton said word of the request had been passed to the OECS states by an unidentified western ambassador on Grenada.

He added that the Cuban buildup on the island had been under way since 1979, but while former prime minister Maurice Bishop was in control he had a "restraining hand" on the leftist forces on Grenada. Bishop was placed under house arrest two weeks ago by the island's armed forces and was killed Oct. 19.

Compton said that the Caribbean nations expect a provisional government to hold elections in about six months. The administration has provided no timetable.

In London, Commonwealth Secretary General Shridath Ramphal urged that the group create a peace-keeping force for Grenada to replace the Marines, which he said should be withdrawn from the island "very, very quickly."

One question still unresolved is how the administration intends to evacuate at least 600 Cuban prisoners on the island whom Reagan said "will be sent to their homelands."

There were lingering questions at the White House yesterday about how the administration had tried to control news coverage of the invasion. Speakes, responding to The Post's report that he had discussed resigning after senior officials misled him about the invasion, said, "the thought never crossed my mind."

Speakes told reporters that he had consented to allow the Pentagon to manage the flow of news about the military actions because "that is the way they want to do business and I have no objection to that." The Pentagon continued to restrict tightly the amount of information available about the invasion, reportedly on the orders of Gen. Vessey.

*Credit*: © **1983, The Washington Post, reprinted with permission.**

---

# PHIL McCOMBS: "THE BAD NEWS IS NO NEWS"—MEDIA FRUSTRATION WITH PRESS RESTRICTIONS

---

*This report about not getting to report is the story as told among the media professionals. The sentiments expressed here were common among the news media, but were largely not shared by members of the public, who were said to be quite happy with the restrictions as a way of protecting the surprise element of the invasion and completion of the operation.*

## *Washington Post*, 29 October 1983

BRIDGETOWN, Barbados: It's got all the elements—the bearded palm trees, the sugar cane waving in the hot sea breeze, the native taxi drivers careening down narrow streets, the expensive but sleazy hotels, the slowly rotating ceiling fans above ranks of sweating diners in dark restaurants, the bikini-clad tourists on the beach, the U.S. combat troops walking around the airport with that special saunter. You almost expect Joel McCrea, the jaunty reporter-hero from Alfred Hitchcock's "Foreign Correspondent," to come wandering through.

It's also got 325 crazed journalists.

But this is Barbados, not Grenada.

"Seven days down here and it's been a bitch," said Time magazine photographer Michael Luongo, standing outside the old shambling airport building that has become the press center. "Press liaison has been nil. We've had no briefings to speak of."

"Everybody in the press is outraged," said Newsweek correspondent Elaine Shannon in the air-conditioned restaurant at the airport, where she had sought a cheeseburger and respite from the heat. "I've never seen so much pent-up fury."

Of course, both Luongo and Shannon might be happier had they not been left out of the limited press pool that U.S. military forces flew yesterday and today from this island paradise 150 miles across an azure sea for a few hours' look at Grenada.

But of the 325 journalists from all over the world that U.S. officials said are here today, so far only about 35 have been given the limited press tour.

They are "pool reporters," which means that when they get back after their tour they are duty-bound to give all details of their reporting to their comrades in the press corps. The result is a madhouse, a frustrating mob scene.

"People were screaming 'Talk! Talk!'" Shannon said of last night's pool report. "Nobody could file because the flight was so late coming back. We were faced with a pool report that quoted paratroopers who would not give their names quoting Grenadans as jumping up and down shouting, 'We're free!'"

But the frustration is real, and what is happening here among the press, the soldiers and the U.S. government is strange and slightly unnerving. For example, a camouflaged trooper sitting at the airport here today was asked if he was a Ranger. He replied, with a curl to his lip, "I don't know, man."

"I've just never seen such a mad dog and pony show before," said a senior editor of a major media outlet who asked not to be identified. "I just think the g——damn thing is such a flagrant manipulation of the press. They keep talking about how they're concerned for our safety, which I find truly touching."

Carole Agus of Newsday said U.S. Embassy officials at the airport yesterday tried to confiscate her notes after she walked past Marine guards and interviewed officials that apparently she was not supposed to interview.

"I don't think you should release that—anything you hear here you can't write," Agus quoted an embassy official as saying. Agus said she failed to obtain complete identification of the embassy officials, and got out of the situation by laughing and saying, "Hey, come on fellows, let's be reasonable." She said she then walked away and the officials did not press the point.

Luongo, the Time photographer, had an even more hair-raising experience—this one with Barbados police officers who, he said, seemed to think he should not be taking photographs near the airport, where U.S. military aircraft are plainly visible going about their operations.

Luongo said he was detained and strip-searched. "I was personally stripped naked . . . by airport security police," he said. Three other photographers also were strip-searched at the same time in a small room where police took them, he said.

"They didn't touch us . . . they wanted our film. We gave them bogus rolls."

Facilities at the press center, several miles outside of town, are minimal. Only about a dozen telephones are installed, and when the pool reporters returned last night all phone connections out of the island were jammed for hours.

The big, linoleum-floored press room smells of stale sweat and is littered with trash. Reporters nervously fidget about, some talking on the phone to their editors, others pumping information out of one another. The U.S. military command post for airport operations here is nearby, but there seem to be only minimal and quite formal relations between the press and the military. The nearby airfield contains many C-130 and other transport aircraft for ferrying U.S. troops to the combat zone, as well as transport and fighter helicopters. The whine of aircraft engines and the thumping of rotor blades form a continual backdrop.

For example, to find out how many reporters are here, one had to submit a written request. About an hour later, a very polite Capt. Dean Chamberlain returned with the answer—325—but since he was new on the scene, and could not be substantively questioned about anything, and because he was the only available military officer at 2:30 P.M., reporter frustration was buzzing in the air.

Eventually Chamberlain emerged with a mimeographed "Grenada update," which he handed out to about 100 reporters.

"Between Oct. 25 and Oct. 27," the news release said, "all major military objectives on the island of Grenada are secured . . . Our forces have been well received by a friendly populous [sic] . . . the fighting is continuing."

About the time the news release was being handed out, there was a sudden flurry among the reporters as someone rushed into the room and shouted, "There are evacuees out front!"

There was a great scrambling and grabbing of camera and other equipment as reporters rushed outside to see what was going on. Many evacuees from Grenada were there—it was not clear exactly how they got there, but as the press interviewed them it was clear that they had been evacuated by American forces.

Most appeared to be not too happy about it. As cameras clicked and rolled and as microphones were thrust into her face, an evacuee who identified herself only as Marina said, "We're not happy because we did not feel it was necessary" for the American troops to invade Grenada.

"How do the Grenadans feel?" shouted a reporter.

"They were very scared," said Marina.

Another evacuee, Kathleen Robinson from Great Britain, was standing nearby. "Would you go back?" shouted a reporter.

"Once the Americans clear out, yes. I liked it very much," Robinson said.

Another evacuee, a German who identified himself only as E. Bock and who demanded that no photos be taken of him, said, "The opinion of most Grenadans is they want to finish it but they have such a strong anti-sympathy to the Americans that it will probably continue."

"He's an engineer," joked a cynical reporter, "and part-time terrorist."

Other reporters nearby laughed.

"There's something strange going on here," said Luongo of these evacuees. "They won't talk much. They're making some gross exaggerations."

Another photographer, Alan Oxley of Sipa Press, said, "Are they Canadians, these weirdos?"

Later, speaking of the American military, Oxley said, "All this crap. We need to be on the island!"

By 6:45 last night, the press pool due in at 5 had still not returned from Grenada. The press center was jammed with roughly 200 reporters growing more and more restless.

"What an abortion this thing is," said Tampa television correspondent Rob North. "So many high journalistic hopes dashed. I'm so sick of looking at network crews and foreign crews and everyone else, I could throw up. I just want it to be over."

That seemed to reflect the mood of many of the people here, and as the minutes and missed deadlines continued to tick by, it promised to be a long, frustrating night.

*Credit*: © 1983, The Washington Post, reprinted with permission.

## ELMER W. LAMMI: "SENATE VOTES FOR END OF GRENADA PRESS RESTRICTIONS"

*By the end of the first week of the invasion operation, Congress finally acted to end the news media's restrictions. The Pentagon responded very slowly to open up access over the weekend.*

United Press International, 29 October 1983

WASHINGTON: The Senate Saturday voted for an end to restrictions on news coverage of U.S. military operations in Grenada with Sen. Edward Kennedy, D-Mass, asking, "What does the administration have to hide?"

But the Senate will reconsider the 53–18 vote Monday in view of objections that the amendment calling for an end to the restrictions may have gone too far.

"You could have reporters from Tass," objected Sen. John Tower, R-Texas. "Is that what you want?"

Sen. Donald Riegle, D-Mich., offered the amendment to a routine bill raising the nation's debt ceiling, debated during a rare Saturday session.

Riegle joined news organizations in objecting to the fact that reporters did not accompany the U.S.-led invasion force that landed on the Caribbean island Tuesday. It was only after more than two days of fighting that a small group of reporters were allowed on the island, and then only under tightly controlled conditions.

Tower's attack on the resolution triggered an angry shouting match, with the Texas Republican and Sen. Ted Stevens, R-Alaska, on one side, and Sens. Riegle, Kennedy, and Paul Sarbanes, D-Md., on the other.

Kennedy charged that the administration was continuing "to put roadblock after roadblock" in the way of efforts "to find out what the real facts are on this issue."

"What does the administration have to hide?" he asked.

Tower said Riegle's resolution went too far in saying the press should not be prevented from "freely accessing news sources of its choice." He and Stevens said it might give Soviet KGB agents access to military secrets.

Tower said military operations had never been so "wide open" for news coverage and it could endanger the lives of U.S. troops.

But Sarbanes charged that the administration had taken "unprecedented actions" to keep the people from learning what is going on in Grenada.

Stevens called the U.S. troops landing in Grenada "a rescue mission," which he compared to the unsuccessful effort to rescue the hostages in Iran.

Riegle's amendment said, "Since a free press is an essential feature of our democratic system of government and since currently in Lebanon, and traditionally in the past, the United States has allowed the press to cover conflicts involving United States armed forces, restrictions imposed upon the press in Grenada shall cease."

Such restrictions, it said, would include "preventing the press from freely accessing news sources of its choice."

It also calls for an end to "unreasonably limiting" the numbers of reporters permitted to enter Grenada and their freedom of unsupervised movement on the island.

Before adopting the amendment, the Senate added language saying that nothing in the resolution would "require any action which jeopardizes the safety or security of U.S. or allied forces or citizens in Grenada."

*Credit*: Reprinted by permission of UPI.

## DAN SEWELL: "GRENADA AND THE MARINES"

*This report from Grenada was among the first to make its way into print despite Pentagon restrictions. It was later dismissed by White House spokesmen, who suggested that stories like these were largely inaccurate, and that was why there were such heavy restrictions on the media access to the fighting zone.*

Associated Press, 29 October 1983

ST. GEORGE'S, Grenada: Assault rifles and pistols were aimed at U.S. Marines Saturday as they surrounded the house of the former deputy prime minister whose drive for power precipitated Grenada's bloody coup.

"Come out or we'll blow the house up," warned one Marine.

The warning was ignored. The Marines then pointed a light anti-tank gun at the house and shouted that they were ready to "blow the house apart."

This time, Bernard Coard, a hard-line Marxist, walked out. With him were his wife Phyllis, their two children, former cabinet minister Selwyn Strachan and Lt. Col. Leon James, a member of the military junta that emerged after the coup.

They gave up without a struggle but Coard uttered a comment "that's not worth repeating," said Capt. David Karcher.

Coard's capture was described to the third group of reporters flown from Barbados to Grenada in as many days, after the U.S.-led invasion of the tiny Caribbean island on Tuesday.

U.S. forces encountered only scattered sniper fire Saturday. Military sources indicated they planned to "starve out" the remaining 200–300 Cuban defenders and an unknown number of Grenadian soldiers who have scattered into the mountain jungles.

Marines said an informant pointed out the house where Coard was hiding in the suburbs of St. George's, the capital.

Coard and the others were taken to Queen's Park, where hundreds of Grenadians chanted "C is for Coard, Cuba and Communism!" and "Give us Phyllis! We deal with Phyllis!" said Kenneth Kerr, owner of a snack shop.

Coard's Jamaica-born wife was a vice minister and head of the national women's organization in the former government. Foreign Minister Unison Whiteman said after Prime Minister Maurice Bishop was put under house arrest Oct. 12 that Coard and his wife were "running the show" in Grenada.

Whiteman was killed along with Bishop in the coup one week later that brought Gen. Hudson Austin's "revolutionary military council" to power and set the stage for the invasion by U.S. and Caribbean troops.

Karcher said the Marines had to protect Coard from the growing crowd.

"We want to take him apart piece by piece," said Martin Henry, a bartender.

Navy Vice Adm. Joseph Metcalf III, commander of the U.S. task force that invaded Grenada at dawn Tuesday, declined to say where Coard was being held.

"I'm not going to tell you what we're going to do with him. We're not going to give him a good-conduct medal," Metcalf said.

Coard, 39, a political scientist and economist, apparently felt Bishop wasn't radical enough.

Two days after Bishop was confined to his home, Strachan, the information and mobilization minister, announced that Coard had become prime minister. Later that day, Coard announced his resignation, saying he wanted to quell rumors that he and his wife were plotting to assassinate Bishop.

Bishop was freed by a crowd of supporters on Oct. 19, but he and three of his Cabinet ministers were killed in the resulting confrontation with the army.

Kerr, who said he was in the crowd that freed Bishop from house arrest, recalled, "He was weak, he told the crowd 'Don't push me, I'm tired.' He said he hadn't eaten because he was afraid they'd poisoned his food."

Kerr said he was in a crowd that followed Bishop to Fort Rupert, where some of his cabinet ministers were being held.

Without warning, two rocket launchers fired into the crowd, he said.

"Everybody started running. They kept shooting. None of us had guns. Most of them were schoolchildren," Kerr said.

He said George Louison, the agriculture minister, fell to the ground wounded.

"I saw them put a gun in his mouth and kill him," Kerr said.

Kerr said he believed Bishop and others who went inside Fort Rupert were executed. He estimated at least 60 people died, including some who fell over a cliff.

Kerr, a Bishop supporter, said he welcomed the U.S. invasion despite a broken arm suffered in fire from U.S. warplanes.

"We needed them to save us. I'm happy unless I lose my arm," he said.

There were reports of continued looting in St. George's Saturday, and reporters saw dozens of stores that had been boarded up after their windows had been smashed.

Garbage was strewn in the streets, but officials said electricity, water and local television service had been restored to the capital.

*Credit*: Reprinted with permission of The Associated Press.

## LOREN JENKINS: "THE INVASION OF GRENADA; U.S. TROOPS PREPARE FOR LONGER FIGHT AGAINST CUBAN HOLDOUTS"

*Finally, by Saturday reporters were allowed on the island to report what they saw in the streets of the capital and heard from U.S. military personnel.*

*Washington Post*, 29 October 1983

ST. GEORGE'S, Grenada: The U.S. military today turned over security duties in this seaside capital city to a small Caribbean force as American troops continued to fight against what they said were an estimated 500 Cubans holding out in parts of the island.

As the first contingent of the joint Caribbean Security Force arrived, both the U.S. military commander and the chief of the Caribbean nations force predicted that U.S. troops would have to remain in Grenada for some time to come.

"How long we continue operations here is a factor of how long the Cubans want to fight," said Admiral Joseph Metcalf III, commander of the U.S. joint task force that landed on Grenada four days ago. In an interview with a pool of 26 foreign journalists at the Cuban-built airport at Point Salines south of the capital, Metcalf said: "If the Cubans want to play games and go into those hills it will take quite a while [to end military operations]."

Col. Ken Barnes of Jamaica, the Caribbean Security Force commander, predicted the United States would not be able to leave Grenada "before a matter of months."

While his force would now take over security in the capital, Barnes said, his men are not trained to fight the snipers thought to be in the city and in the hills beyond it.

Barnes made his comment here minutes after U.S. Marine Corps Blackhawk helicopters landed 250 of his 300-man force in Grenada at the Queen's Park cricket grounds.

There was no official handover ceremony, and Barnes' men marched off the cricket grounds into the city immediately after landing, behind two U.S. Marine Corps amphibious armed personnel carriers.

The decision to leave the security of the capital city to a force of about 250 soldiers and police from six Caribbean nations was designed to underline the allies' participation in the military occupation of the island.

The city was calm today, despite the evidence of recent bombings, looting and a fire in at least one police station.

But there were signs that the fighting on the island was still not over after four days of U.S. military operations.

Journalists saw evidence of continued military clashes on the outskirts of the capital as well as in the densely vegetated mountainous interior of this small island.

Witnesses said that U.S. Rangers from the 82nd Airborne Division were still fighting against elusive bands of snipers in and around the holiday beach hotel strip along the Grand Anse Bay, just south of the capital.

The sounds of battle were also heard throughout the afternoon just east of the still-uncompleted air strip at Point Salines.

The air strip, which the Reagan administration claimed was being built not for the commercial traffic as the Grenadan government insisted but as an important strategic military base for Cuba and its Soviet sponsors, has been the main staging area for the U.S. military force.

Metcalf said the force had now reached about 5,000 men on the ground and another 10,000 men afloat with his battle group off the Grenadan coast.

[In Washington, the Pentagon said more than 6,000 U.S. troops are participating in the invasion, including 5,000 from the 82nd Airborne, 500 Marines, several hundred support personnel and the Rangers already stationed on the island.]

In the rolling hills just a few miles off the air strip's 5,000-foot-long runway, the odd crump of outgoing mortar fire could be heard intermittently throughout the afternoon.

Overhead, a gray C-130 Spectre gunship circled into the night, firing occasional deep-throated salvos from its awesome rapid-fire 100mm howitzers.

Journalists, escorted by Rangers to view a cache of captured Grenadan arms and ammunition in a group of corrugated tin warehouses about a mile from the airport, saw a Ranger platoon deployed in a perimeter defense position just beyond the warehouses.

The soldiers, their young faces smeared with green camouflage paint, crouched in ditches along the road, their guns pointing east into the hilly tropical brush where the sounds of gunfire could be heard. Behind them, in a truck park, a row of 80mm mortars had been mounted to provide protective covering fire if necessary.

Along the road back to the airport, less than a quarter of a mile from the runway, the body of a dead man in civilian clothes was lying on its back under a canopy of a frangipani tree. Both legs had been blown off below the knees and the torso had begun to darken and swell in the stifling heat of a tropical sun.

According to the U.S. Rangers, the man was believed to have died Thursday evening when an air strike by two U.S. Navy A-7 Corsair carrier-based fighter bombers were called in to blow up a concrete house where snipers were believed to have holed up. The house was demolished, but whether the snipers were ever found could not immediately be established.

Metcalf, a feisty and slight naval officer in gold-rimmed eyeglasses, insisted that "organized resistance" on the island had in fact already ceased.

His men, he said, were now just conducting a "bush operation of light fighting" to flush out snipers who continued to make large parts of Grenada unsafe.

"Sniping is going to be a continuing problem," Metcalf said. "It has been a problem all along. They are still shooting at us but we have been lucky because they are bad shots."

Metcalf said the United States was able to set the number of remaining Cubans at about 500 through information provided by captured combatants.

The admiral said the number of Cubans was higher than expected, one reason why the U.S. felt the need to increase the level of its own forces. Asked whether that meant that U.S. intelligence had been faulty, Metcalf snapped: "I don't know, I'm not an intelligence officer. Let's just say it wasn't adequate."

Metcalf spoke with journalists from a press pool who had been flown here from Barbados for a five-hour guided visit.

The interview was held in the still-unfinished airport terminal building before the troupe of journalists was taken by helicopter over sniper-threatened roads north to St. George's.

The admiral referred all questions about the total number of U.S. casualties during the operations to Defense Department spokesmen in Washington. These spokesmen today gave the U.S. casualty toll as 11 dead, seven missing and 67 wounded.

Metcalf said however that his men to date had killed 36 Cubans or Grenadans who had resisted the U.S. advances.

He gave the number of wounded enemy combatants as 56. Metcalf said his men had had no chance to break down this casualty figure by nationality. But he said he thought most of the resistance came from Cubans rather than Grenadans loyal to the island's now-toppled Marxist Revolutionary Military Council.

Despite the dead body of an unarmed man lying near where goats grazed and yellow butterflies flitted over purple bougainvillea flowers, Metcalf said there had been no civilians killed since his force of U.S. Marines and Rangers assaulted the island in a two-pronged helicopter attack shortly after dawn Tuesday.

The admiral said that of the now estimated 1,100 Cubans believed to have been on the island at the time of the U.S.

landings, almost 650 have now been captured and more are either giving themselves up or being captured by the hour.

[The Pentagon today said 638 Cubans and 17 Grenadans had been captured.]

How many of those captured were combatants no one in the U.S. command here seems to know for sure.

Cuba has insisted all along its men were mostly construction workers laboring on the airfield while the Reagan administration has alleged they were almost all armed members of an engineering battalion there not only to work on the airstrip but to help defend the island's pro-Cuban regime.

Just above the airport, on a hill dotted with ramshackle wooden barracks that once housed the Cuban workers, a prisoner of war center now holds more than 500 Cuban prisoners, according to a U.S. Ranger officer.

At least 200 of them were in three pens surrounded by razor-sharp rolls of concertina wire laid out on an asphalt parking lot between the barracks.

The men looked relaxed and were all dressed in civilian clothes. Most wore straw hats or had bandanas tied around their forehead. Many joked among themselves while smoking long Cuban cigars. Most were either squatting or stretched out on small cotton mattresses that had been stripped from their barracks.

The only Cuban who could be interviewed through the wire before U.S. military officials forbade any talking to the prisoners said his name was Fulgencio Gonzalez Molina.

"We are noncombatants here; we are just laborers," he said through the wire enclosure. "I was just a cook here, not a fighter."

Chief Warrant Officer Rolf Milton, the 37-year-old Ranger in charge of the prisoners, said all of them were Cubans and most had come from the airport area. "Which are active combatants we really don't know," Milton said, "not one of them has admitted to being a soldier."

A Ranger officer showed journalists through the Cubans' barracks which had been looted and rifled. Family photographs of wives and children back in Cuba, personal letters, Cuban political magazines extolling Marxist-Leninism, clothes, assorted shoes and boots, and other personal effects, were scattered over the floors.

Outside the barracks, Ranger officers pointed out half a dozen shallow rifle trenches as proof that the Cubans had planned to resist from their barracks—although there were no signs of any fighting having taken place in the immediate area.

*Credit*: © **1983, The Washington Post, reprinted with permission.**

## JAMES FERON: U.S. TROOPS PATROL AS GRENADA SLOWLY RETURNS TO NORMAL

*By the weekend, many news organizations were presenting wrap-up stories about what had happened during the previous week. This front-page story from the* New York Times *is an example of an overview report published just six days after the invasion was authorized.*

*New York Times, 31 October 1983*

ST. GEORGE'S, Grenada, Oct. 30: United States forces patrolled here today amid signs that this Caribbean island capital was approaching near normal life.

Sniping continued from the hills around the city. But less than a week after United States and Caribbean forces invaded, electricity has been fully restored and with it an adequate water supply.

Food was available although some stores have been looted and supplies remained a problem. Local telephone service was restored although international service was still out.

(In Bridgetown, Reuters, quoting the Barbados Defense Ministry, reported that American forces in Grenada had captured Gen. Hudson Austin, leader of the leftist military council that took power in the coup last week that partly instigated the United States invasion. The Defense Department in Washington said only that the general had apparently been captured.)

### APPEAL TO GRENADIANS

Sir Paul Scoon, the Governor General, has asked Grenadians to open their shops, return to work and send their children to school Monday morning.

He has also asked them to maintain an 8 P.M. to 5 A.M. curfew.

On Saturday, Sir Paul said in a radio broadcast that he planned to appoint a "representative body of Grenadians to assist as an interim measure in administering the affairs of our country."

The Defense Department today increased the number of American reporters and camera crews allowed into Grenada. It said they were free to remain overnight or for indefinite stays. Reporters were officially barred from the island until two days after the invasion began and were subsequently allowed in only in small groups with military escorts. (Page A12.)

American troops guarded checkpoints and patrolled the city but Grenadians also were out in force walking the hilly streets and crowding the seafront.

The American death toll rose to 16 today, with 77 wounded and three missing since thousands of United States troops and a seven-nation Caribbean force invaded Grenada at dawn last Tuesday and deposed the leftist military junta.

### MARINES EXPECT TO LEAVE

Capt. Dean Chamberlain of the 22d Marine Amphibious Unit said he thought his force would be completely out of Grenada soon, with the 82d Airborne serving as a replacement force. The marines had been on their way to Lebanon when they were diverted to this island for what the announcement aboard ship said was "an evacuation" operation.

At the airport at Point Salines, C-5's and C-130's continued to arrive from Bridgetown, the capital of Barbados, and beyond, shuttling supplies and soldiers to and from the island. Soldiers still guarded gun emplacements, one with a sign reading "Fire Base Gator—you yell, we shell."

A fishing boat left the harbor for the first time since the invasion. A small crowd cheered.

A man shouted to a friend near the police barracks facing the seawall, "Are you working tomorrow?" The answer came quickly, "Yeah, I am." The first man said O.K. as if he required the confirmation.

### TOWN'S ROADS ARE BUSY

A battered Soviet-made tank and an armored personnel carrier stood wrecked off a road that was also dotted with smashed cars. But vehicles were operating busily in town, some of them apparently requisitioned to carry American soldiers to and from their positions.

In the afternoon two jeeploads of United States soldiers pulled up to the telephone company building in the city and raced inside, presumably responding to a tip. They said they found uniforms, a radio and some ammunition clips, but would not provide details.

The road over the mountain linking the airport at Port Salines and St. George's was opened to allow several busloads of journalists flown in from Bridgetown to wander freely through the city.

Smaller groups had been lifted by helicopter to the city because the road was not secure. Today the buses traveled through a half-dozen checkpoints. One of the most heavily guarded was just outside St. George's at the Ross Point Hotel, selected as the site of the new American presence on Grenada, where there had been no embassy or consulate. The chargé d'affaires is Charles Gillespie, who will be attached to the United States Embassy in Bridgetown.

## FOOD SUPPLIES SENT

A staff is already assembled and cars parked outside have tags reading "U.S. Embassy." One of the first tasks will be to administer a $25,000 emergency food shipment.

Meanwhile, a few small restaurants have been opened and the St. James Hotel was offering rooms and meals to journalists and others who stayed overnight.

The city offered a relaxed Sunday atmosphere with children playing in the harbor waters and couples strolling. But a reminder of the days of fighting remained.

A United States marine at the Queens Park area just at the edge of town was approached by a small boy and three girls offering him a live grenade they had found in the woods. It had Russian markings.

Another marine, Lance Cpl. Brian Polito, said his patrol had discovered a booby-trap grenade Saturday in the wooded hills that rise sharply from St. George's.

Lance Cpl. Leonard Mota of New Bedford, Mass., one of the marines who landed at a beach three miles from St. George's on Tuesday, said: "The people have been nice to us. They've been coming out slowly since we've been here."

## ARMY TROOPS TAKE OVER

"They come around with fruit, soda, cigarettes and water nuts," a coconut that provides a cool sweet drink popular with the servicemen. "And they also turn in P.R.A.'s," he said, referring to former members of the People's Revolutionary Army.

The Defense Department said Saturday in Washington that most of the 1,200 marines who came here as part of a 6,000-member United States invasion force had been replaced by Army troops. The marines, the department said, would be sent to Lebanon in the next few days to relieve the Marine force stationed there. Today, officials in Washington said the marines were still standing by awaiting transport to their assignment in Lebanon.

Agnes Williams, a 65-year-old native of St. George's, was walking with a reporter when one of a group of young men shouted at her.

"They said 'don't tell him lies,'" she said, "but they're P.R.A.'s." So young? she was asked of the teenagers. "Yes, very young," she said.

Grenada's Government was taken over in a coup by Maurice Bishop in 1979 but he died at the hands of soldiers in the aftermath of another coup initiated two weeks ago by extremists in his own left-wing Government.

The group that took over was headed by Deputy Prime Minister Bernard Coard, who was captured here Saturday after his hiding place was disclosed by Grenadians.

## WHEREABOUTS NOT KNOWN

His present whereabouts are not known, but marines guarding Queens Park pointed to a barracks area nearby saying, "much of the questioning goes on there."

On the hilly streets of St. George's there seemed to be enthusiasm for the Americans' intervention but division over what was to come.

Don Phillip, a manager of a lumber department, said the stores would open Monday and food would be coming in "but it will take years for our economy to recover."

He was referring to tourism. "We would sometimes have two or three cruise ships a day but then it dropped to two or three a week" under the Bishop Government, he said.

"It was getting very heavy, the ideology," he said. "Soldiers would knock on your door asking youngsters to join the N.Y.O.," or National Youth Organization.

Signs of ideology, and some recent counter-ideology, are everywhere in the capital. "Long live the third anniversary of People's Power," said one slogan. Another read, "Long live the revolution," but scrawled beneath it was "No way Coard" and "No to Coard."

There seemed to be a nostalgic recollection of Mr. Bishop by Grenadians and a sense of despair over the political future.

Genty Jacobs, the owner of the Crescent Inn, said, "Most of the middle class and respectable left under Bishop." He did not know who was left to form the interim government that Sir Paul Scoon said he will seek to install as a transition to general elections.

## ROBERT MacNEIL AND JIM LEHRER: THIS WEEK IN GRENADA

*This television report also was a wrap-up report of the week's operation in Grenada. Though questions about the legitimacy of the invasion were asked, few respondents seemed to question the need for quick and decisive military intervention.*

*MacNeil/Lehrer NewsHour* (PBS), Transcript 2111, 31 October 1983

ROBERT MacNEIL: Good evening. The aftermath of the Grenada invasion still leads the news and our program tonight. As the fighting there stops, we have a report from Grenada by Charlayne Hunter-Gault and her exclusive interview with an aide to murdered Prime Minister Maurice Bishop. We also talk to a top State Department official, Kenneth Dam, about evidence revealed by captured documents. Jim?

MacNEIL: There was no fighting reported in Grenada today as the island, under U.S. military occupation, started to return to normal. Several hundred Marines were pulled out, leaving U.S. forces ashore at 5,000. The Governor General, Sir Paul Scoon, asked people to re-open their businesses, return to work and to school. The White House and the Pentagon acknowledged that a U.S. carrier-based bomber had mistakenly bombed a mental hospital. The incident, revealed by the Canadian newsmagazine *MacLean's* and the *New York Post* today, occurred on Tuesday, the first day of the invasion. The news accounts said 13 bodies had been recovered at the 183-patient hospital, and quoted a nurse as saying there will be many more. Pentagon officials today put the toll at 14 dead. White House spokesman Larry Speakes said the hospital was in an area thought to be exclusively military. The White House also said that the leader of the coup which brought on the invasion, General Hudson Austin, had been captured and was being questioned on a U.S. ship. Jim?

LEHRER: There were several Washington developments on Grenada today. House Speaker Thomas O'Neill announced he was sending a congressional leadership delegation to Grenada next weekend. Headed by Majority Whip Thomas Foley, the congressmen will seek information on how threatened American civilians there were before the invasion and whether the U.S. invasion force had adequate intelligence, among other things. The House is to vote tomorrow on whether to impose a 60-day War Powers restriction on the use of troops in Grenada; the Senate passed the measure last week, and O'Neill predicted the House will now do the same. At the White House, a senior press officer resigned over the way information was handled during the Grenada invasion. Leslie Jank, deputy press secretary for foreign affairs, said in his resignation letter to President Reagan that he had lost his personal credibility as a result, and the best thing to do was to quit. On a similar issue, the American Society of Newspaper Editors today lodged a formal protest with the Defense Department over its refusal to permit reporters to cover the first phases of the Grenada action. And the State Department said today U.S. troops found secret treaties which called for the training of Grenadian armed forces in the Soviet Union and the integration of Cubans into those forces. A spokesman said the treaties with the Soviet Union, Cuba and North Korea had been signed by the late Maurice Bishop when he was prime minister of Grenada. Robin?

MacNEIL: The Pentagon has now relaxed those restrictions on reporting from Grenada, although telephone and telex communications are still difficult. On Friday, Charlayne

Hunter-Gault was in the second group of journalists permitted on the island in tours organized by the U.S. military. She went back to Grenada over the weekend and compiled this report.

CHARLAYNE HUNTER-GAULT [*voice-over*]: We glimpsed Grenada for the first time since the invasion as we approached the island in the large C-130 provided by the Army. In the days that followed, that would be our routine. The Army would provide us with escorts and glimpses. Each day the window would open just a little more, enough to get an impression of what was going on there, but not enough to tell the whole story. But what we do know now begins here, at this 10,000-foot runway, one of the main ingredients in the U.S. case for the invasion. The United States argues that this airport was being readied to serve as a base for Cuban-Soviet operations throughout the Caribbean. It was here, in the Port Salines area, that the Army landed, encountering the first wave of resistance from fighters on the ground at the airport. Here we learned for the first time from a military official on the ground that the resistance was a lot stronger than they had anticipated. Vice Admiral Joseph Metcalf III, commander of the joint military operations, was asked why the intelligence was so poor.

Vice Adm. JOSEPH METCALF III, Commander, Joint Military Operations: How do I know? I'm not an intelligence officer. All we—well, let's put it this way. It wasn't—it wasn't what I would have desired, sir.

HUNTER-GAULT [*voice-over*]: Up to now there had been conflicting reports of the size of the American military forces so we pressed Admiral Metcalf for a precise figure.

Adm. METCALF: Oh, I'd say it's about 10,000 sailors, Marines afloat.

1st REPORTER: Ten thousand afloat?

2nd REPORTER: So 15,000 American troops in the water and on land.

Adm. METCALF: That's right.

HUNTER-GAULT [*voice-over*]: The Army conducted its press tours by dividing us into two groups. Some of us were taken to see two Russian-made tanks that had been used against the Americans in the early hours of the invasion, then on to a compound just northeast of the airport where the second wave of fighting took place. This was also the second pillar in the U.S. case for the invasion. Several warehouses containing weapons and other materiel bearing Soviet, Chinese and Cuban markings. On the ground, military spokesmen offered their evidence to support President Reagan's charge that this sophisticated arsenal made it clear that a Cuban occupation of the island was planned.

MILITARY SPOKESMAN: This island is absolutely an arsenal. Everywhere—you look around you. Everywhere around you there is stores of ammunition. There is enough arms and ammunition on this island to issue more than one weapon to every man, woman and child on the entire island. It's unbelievable.

HUNTER-GAULT [*voice-over*]: Having gotten the military point of view, many of us were anxious to find out what the Grenadian people thought. To give us a shot at that, our military tour guides took us by helicopter to the town of St. George's, but instead of civilians we ran into more military. Our arrival at the sports field coincided with a landing of the multinational force, a 300-man unit made up of military and police from several neighboring Eastern Caribbean islands. We asked the commander of those troops, Colonel Ken Barnes, how long they expected American troops to occupy the island.

KEN BARNES, Commander, multinational forces: I think it's going to be maybe months.

REPORTER: Maybe months? Maybe six months?

Comm. BARNES: No, I don't think as long as that, but. . . .

HUNTER-GAULT [*voice-over*]: But Marine Colonel Roy Smith had a different answer.

Col. ROY SMITH, USMC: I don't have any idea.

HUNTER-GAULT: Obviously this is an answer that nobody can give with any certainty. Given the commitment of men and materiel, it is clear that the original speculation that this campaign would be over quickly was probably overly optimistic. But amid all of that uncertainty, we found one area where there seemed little doubt. It was in the responses of the Grenadian people who were finally allowed to talk with us on our guided military tour.

REPORTER: Do you feel free now?

GRENADIAN WOMAN: Yeah, we feel free, but you know we still feel nervous and so.

REPORTER: Are you glad to see the Americans come in?

WOMAN: Yeah, we are very glad and really thankful to you and also to God for his mercy.

2nd GRENADIAN WOMAN: Well, we are very happy to have you all here.

REPORTER: You don't want the Cubans back?

WOMAN: No, no, no. No. Cubans. We want Americans.

HUNTER-GAULT [*voice-over*]: On subsequent day trips that we've taken, we learned that Grenadians are also helping the military in their efforts to ferret out members of the People's Revolutionary Army, the contingent that helped the Cubans resist the American invasion. As the military drove the press through St. George's, two men who had been fingered by Grenadians as members of the PRA were being arrested.

MILITARY SPOKESMAN: One is an intelligence officer in the PRA and the other appears to be possibly a company commander in the PRA. However, that's pretty common.

HUNTER-GAULT [*voice-over*]: The PRA are the military arm of the group which overthrew the Bishop government, assassinated Bishop and others, and sparked the invasion. On our tour we also learned that Grenadians had led the military to Deputy Prime Minister Bernard Coard and his wife Phyllis who reportedly masterminded the overthrow of Bishop. After four days, the official military tours ended, but not the questions. What we have now is mostly the official version of events. Now that the window to this picturesque but troubled little island will be opening wider, perhaps we will be able to find additional answers as well.

MacNEIL: After filing that report by satellite from Barbados, Charlayne has gone back to Grenada and will be sending a follow-up report in the next few days. In the meantime, she has also sent us an exclusive interview with an official of the government of Prime Minister Maurice Bishop, who was killed in the coup two weeks ago. The interview, which was taped in Barbados, is with Donald Rojas, Bishop's press secretary. Rojas said he was not killed because at the last minute Bishop asked him to go to the telephone office to tell the outside world what was happening.

HUNTER-GAULT: Part of the explanation for the invasion was that the United States feared a Soviet-backed, Cuban takeover of Grenada. What's your reaction to that?

DON ROJAS: Oh, I don't accept that at all, and I think that that is hyperbole and simply untrue and inaccurate.

HUNTER-GAULT: What was the role of Cuba in Grenada?

Mr. ROJAS: The Cuban presence in Grenada was one of cooperation with the People's Revolutionary government in developing Grenada economically and trying to lift Grenada out of a legacy of backwardness—economic, social, political backwardness.

HUNTER-GAULT: So specifically what did that translate into in terms of what they were doing?

Mr. ROJAS: They were doing things like helping to build an international airport. They were not the only ones, by the way, assisting in building this international airport. Seventeen countries have given aid, including many Western countries, including the European Economic Community, including Venezuela, including Mexico have given assistance in the construction of this airport. Cubans were there to help build the airport. Cubans were there to help construct and set up other economic enterprises, such as an asphalt plant, such as a concrete and block-making plant which would have the capacity to produce up to 500 low-income housing units per year. The Cubans had doctors and dentists there. They had teachers. They had technicians and auto mechanics. In a variety of areas of economic cooperation there were Cuban personnel in Grenada assisting in the development plans of the country. There were of course also military personnel; that is undeniable.

HUNTER-GAULT: What were they doing there?

Mr. ROJAS: They were there on the invitation of the

People's Revolutionary government to assist in training the People's Revolutionary Army. But to be trained—to train the People's Revolutionary Army in the techniques of defensive warfare, not offensive warfare.

HUNTER-GAULT: One of the other pillars in the United States' case for the invasion was this huge arms arsenal near the airport. Were these arms that were being used to train Grenadians in self-defense, or what were those arms? You knew about—those were not secret.

Mr. ROJAS: No, they were not secret to Grenadians.

HUNTER-GAULT: The Grenadian people knew about—

Mr. ROJAS: And one has to understand "huge" in relative terms. What does huge mean? I mean, they were automatic rifles; they were anti-aircraft guns. There were AK-47 rifles and so on, machine guns and so on. But—and ammunition. Nothing extraordinarily sophisticated about that kind of weaponry.

HUNTER-GAULT: Well, one of the officers, one of the military officers said that there were enough armaments there to arm the entire population of Grenada, including women and children.

Mr. ROJAS: One hundred thousand?

HUNTER-GAULT: One hundred thousand people?

Mr. ROJAS: There were one hundred thousand arms found?

HUNTER-GAULT: Well, he didn't say how many arms. He said that there was just an arsenal that was large enough to arm every man, woman and child in Grenada.

Mr. ROJAS: I don't know. I can't—I can't argue with him, but I'm telling you—

HUNTER-GAULT: Well, you're saying that there was a legitimate reason for those arms.

Mr. ROJAS: Yes, absolutely. Absolutely. Given the history of hostility and aggression encountered by the Grenadian revolution ever since March of 1979, given the history of military maneuvers—U.S. military maneuvers—and, in many cases, NATO force military maneuvers in the Caribbean region from 1981 up until the first quarter of 1983—I draw your attention to the famous Marines operation of August of 1981, when a United States task force conducted military maneuvers off of Vieques Island, off of Puerto Rico, and it was a, in fact, a rehearsal for a potential invasion of Grenada. That is as far back as August of 1981. Subsequent to that they have been—

HUNTER-GAULT: Excuse me. Are you just saying that the Grendans feared that the United States was going to invade?

Mr. ROJAS: There was a lot of justification for apprehension on the part of the majority of Grenadians that there was either the real possibility or certainly the threat of military aggression from the United States. And this is not recent, huh?

HUNTER-GAULT: This is during the Bishop regime?

Mr. ROJAS: Yes, this is during the Bishop regime. Certainly. I draw your attention, too, to President Reagan's speech in March of this year, the so-called "Star Wars" speech, in which

he—he said that Grenada was a threat to the national security interests of the United States—tiny Grenada—because of the airport which was supposed to be, in his view, being constructed as a Soviet and Cuban military base.

HUNTER-GAULT: You say that's not the case.

Mr. ROJAS: That is not the case.

HUNTER-GAULT: The Army in its argument that it's clear that this airport was being built as a base to export revolution by the Cubans cites the heavy concrete, the long lengthy—what is it?—10,000-foot airport—

Mr. ROJAS: It is 9,000 feet, by the way.

HUNTER-GAULT: —and they argue that clearly this was intended for large military-type carriers.

Mr. ROJAS: No, but Charlayne, a 9,000-foot runway is nothing abnormal in the Caribbean. In fact, that runway is the seventh—would have been, upon completion, the seventh-longest runway in the Caribbean. I draw your attention to Grantley Adam's airport—the length of the runway is over 10,000 feet. Does that in itself mean that, you know, Grantley Adam's airport is a military base? In fact, it is being, for all practical purposes, being used at the present moment as a military base. I mean, an airport is an airport.

HUNTER-GAULT: Well, why do you think that so many Grenadans that the press has been able to talk to are so enthusiastic about the presence of the Americans now?

Mr. ROJAS: The people in Grenada, and I will say the majority of the people in Grenada, were relieved that the invasion brought a solution, I suppose, of sorts, in that it rid them of the yoke of the revolutionary and military gangsters and these madmen who had arrested the country at gunpoint. They are relieved at that. But, quite frankly, they did not expect, and I am now speaking out of my knowledge of the Grenadian people, I'm not speaking on behalf of the Grenadian people—I don't have any such right—but I would think that they certainly did not expect an invasion of such magnitude—they certainly did not expect that an invasion would constitute the use of 5,000 Marines and other military personnel on land, the use of jet fighters and jet bombers, the use of medium and, in some cases, heavy artillery, the use of helicopter gunships, the destruction of much property on Grenada, and 10,000 troops on ships off the coast of Grenada ready to be deployed if necessary. In my view this is excessive. It is overkill.

HUNTER-GAULT: How do you see all this ending?

Mr. ROJAS: Well, I would hope it would end very quickly. I hope that as rapidly as possible all non-Grenadian forces be withdrawn from the country, and I would hope that the Grenadian people will be given the opportunity to exercise their right to determine and fashion the destiny of their own country, and the way in which they want to build their future. They alone can determine that and should be allowed to do that.

HUNTER-GAULT: Well, along with Mr. Bishop, many of the ministers of the government were murdered; you are now out of the country. Who should form a new government?

Mr. ROJAS: Tough question. Very tough question. I don't know, quite frankly. The Grenadian people will have to decide that themselves. They will have to throw up their own leaders, and leaders cannot be imposed on them from the outside or prescribed by any foreign country. The Grenadian people themselves will have to choose their leaders.

LEHRER: Reaction to that interview and a further update on Grenada generally now from Kenneth Dam, the deputy secretary of state, number-two man at the State Department. Mr. Secretary, what is the schedule now for establishing an interim government or, as Mr. Rojas says, to let the Grenadian people now decide what kind of government they want?

KENNETH DAM: Well, that's a question for the Governor General. I understand that he said today that he hoped to be forming an interim government in several days, but it's his constitutional duty to do that, and it's up to him.

LEHRER: And from the United States' point of view, is there a schedule now or an anticipated schedule as to when U.S. troops will start moving out in large numbers?

Sec. DAM: Well, first of all, all of the Rangers, as I understand it, have now left, and we expect the Marines to be leaving within a few days. After that it remains to be seen. After all, there's still much of the island which we have not yet fully covered. There's still sniper fire and so it depends a bit on what happens.

LEHRER: But on the ground, the reports today that, for all practical purposes, the main fighting is over. That is correct, right?

Sec. DAM: Well, I would—the way I would characterize it is to say that organized resistance is probably over, but there still is isolated fighting going on.

LEHRER: Well, what is the military mission now? To make sure that every ounce, or every square foot of land on Grenada is free of anybody with a weapon who might be used not only against American troops but against another Grenadian, and then when that happens then it will—then the U.S. will leave?

Sec. DAM: Well, I think we have to leave the island in a situation where the Caribbean defense force and the local police and so forth can maintain law and order, and there are constitutional processes in place. That is to say, an organized government is in control. So long as there is a possibility of a good deal more fighting I think we'd be derelict in our responsibilities if we were to leave.

LEHRER: But are we, as one of the men said in the earlier piece by Charlayne, are we talking about months now for the U.S. troops to remain there?

Sec. DAM: I don't—I don't think we're talking about months when we're talking about these large numbers. What we may be able to do to facilitate the re-establishment of organized process of government and so forth remains to be seen. I don't want to prejudge what the—first of all, what the actual military situation will be with regard to resistance. We don't know that much about what we remains. We don't know how many people are hiding out in the hills. We don't know what kind of armaments we have. I have seen reports that, as we go around the island, we find many more places where there are caches of weapons. And so we've got to establish the facts there before we can set a schedule.

LEHRER: Has the State Department or has the U.S. government established the facts on the mental hospital attack that apparently killed at least 14, maybe even more, people?

Sec. DAM: Well, let me tell you my understanding of it, subject to correction as we—as the Pentagon nails down the remaining facts. When we were in the position of securing the safety of the Governor-General, we were receiving fire from the fort, Fort Fredericks, and in order to neutralize that we called in air support. We did not realize at that time that right next to the fort was a mental hospital. In fact, as I understand it, we did not realize until Sunday that there had been some civilian casualties as a result of the suppression of the hostile fire from Fort Fredericks.

LEHRER: Is the death toll that was mentioned—that Robin mentioned at the top, about it? Fourteen dead.

Sec. DAM: That's my understanding of what we're talking about, but again, I don't have information that is that precise.

LEHRER: Now, let's go through some of the things Mr. Rojas told Charlayne. First of all, what do you think of his version of the Cuban connection with the Grenadan government under Maurice Bishop, for whom he worked?

Sec. DAM: Well, first of all, I thought it was interesting that, despite what he has been saying in the past and what the Bishop government said in the past, he is now conceding that there were Cuban military personnel there. These weren't just construction workers. In addition to that, there were Cuban military personnel. And he concedes, contrary to what was said before, that in those buildings—Cuban-style buildings—around the airport there were large volumes of weapons. As a matter of fact, they were very, very large indeed. Over a million rounds of ammunition had been made available by the Cubans and others to the Grenadians. So what we're now hearing is well, that it was just because they feared an invasion from the United States.

LEHRER: You don't buy that?

Sec. DAM: Well, I don't buy that because the fact of the matter is that when you look at the situation the volume of supplies is far too large for that. There also was an ideology of spreading this new view of the world. It's the same sort of pattern we've seen elsewhere where the Cubans have been involved—in Angola and other places in Africa. In Nicaragua. It seems to me it's sort of confession and avoidance: "Yeah, what you say is true, but we were pure of heart." And in any event, the government of Mr. Bishop included these various people—these very people who he's saying now are the only cause of the trouble.

LEHRER: You mean the people who turned on him?

Sec. DAM: Yes.

LEHRER: I see.

Sec. DAM: Obviously there was a struggle for power in that government and who's to say who was dealing with the Cubans to bring in all this material?

LEHRER: Well, now, you were one of—I think you and William Clark were the two American officials who talked to Bishop when he was here, what was it? four months before the coup that led to his death. What did he say then about what the Cuban connection was?

Sec. DAM: Well, he didn't—we didn't talk about it all that much because he came to see us and he had a pitch he wanted to give to us, which was he wanted better relations with the United States. And we said, well, we were prepared for better relations with Grenada. He had some ideas about how that might be—might take place. He realized that, given the history, it couldn't happen instantaneously, so we talked about that.

LEHRER: But he didn't—you didn't ask him or he didn't say what his deal was with Cuba or any of that sort of thing?

Sec. DAM: No. It was more or less taken for granted that he had this close connection with Cuba. It was implicit in the conversation, but we weren't questioning him.

LEHRER: Did he express to you the fear that Mr. Rojas expressed to Charlayne that they were arming or feared an invasion from the United States? Did he say, "Hey, Mr. Dam, please don't invade us?" or anything like that?

Sec. DAM: No. He said that we ought to have better relationships. It was silly for us to have this kind of tension between the two governments, and we said we agreed with that and—but we had some doubts about the bonafides of his position. We were seriously worried about the human rights position on the island where he'd essentially locked up his opposition and kept them there for months and years. And we said we didn't see any basis, if he really wanted better relations, for the kind of attacks that he was carrying out against the United States verbally all the time, and we suggested that he lower his rhetoric.

LEHRER: And what did he say?

Sec. DAM: He didn't say too much about that. Then there was a period when it may have been a little lower rhetoric, but it ended quickly.

LEHRER: Finally, these secret documents, and you mentioned them yesterday in your appearance on Face the Nation. I think you called it a treasure trove of documents. Are those going to be made public?

Sec. DAM: Well—excuse me. We certainly hope to do so. I think we have to recognize that these are Grenadian government documents that I was talking about, and so they're really the property of the Grenadian government. We will be consulting with them and we do hope to make them public.

LEHRER: And when they are made public they will prove what, in a nutshell?

Sec. DAM: They will prove that there—well, first of all, there are many documents, and I was only referring to certain ones. The ones I was referring to are supply contracts covering a period of years between Grenada on the one hand and the Soviet Union on the other, Cuba on the other and North Korea. They will show that we haven't even seen all of the armaments that were coming. They will also show that the Soviet Union was trying to hide its hand by shipping through Cuba.

LEHRER: I see. Mr. Secretary, thank you.

*Credit*: Reprinted with permission from MacNeil-Lehrer Productions.

---

## CHARLES J. HANLEY: MAJOR UNCERTAINTIES STILL HANG OVER GRENADA INVASION

*A week after the invasion, there were many questions about what happened. The following wire service article is an example of the kinds of questions being asked and the kinds of answers supplied by the administration.*

### Associated Press, 1 November 1983

The Grenada invasion leaves dozens of unanswered questions, uncertainties, inconsistencies bobbing in its wake.

Some confusion stems from strict U.S. military controls on the news media. Some stems from poor communications, hasty conclusions, or the failure of U.S. authorities thus far to release any documentary evidence to support contentions of a Cuban buildup on the Caribbean island.

And some confusion apparently is the result of deliberate misstatements.

The "credibility" problem has prompted one White House press officer to quit his job, and congressional leaders to organize a fact-finding visit to Grenada.

Here, in capsule form, are the major question marks that hang over the invasion:

### WHAT WAS THE MOTIVE?

Chiefly to rescue Americans? Or to achieve "geo-political" goals by ousting Cubans from Grenada?

In announcing the invasion Oct. 25, President Reagan said the "overriding" reason he ordered it was to protect 1,000 American residents of Grenada in the aftermath of a bloody coup. Two other reasons: "to forestall further chaos," and to help restore "governmental institutions."

Two nights later, in a nationally televised address, Reagan

reaffirmed his concern for the American residents, but focused more sharply on the Cuban presence on the island and what he said was a communist plan to turn Grenada into "a major military bastion to export terror." The U.S. troops "got there just in time," he said.

Prime Minister Eugenia Charles of Dominica, which contributed forces to the invasion, described the invasion as "a matter of preventing this thing (Marxism) from spreading to all the islands."

## WHEN DID THE U.S. DECIDE TO INVADE?

Reagan administration officials said the president made a tentative decision late Sunday, Oct. 23, after receiving a "surprise" request Saturday from a half-dozen eastern Caribbean states for intervention. But Caribbean security forces were already assembling in Barbados by Sunday.

A State Department official, who spoke with reporters on condition he not be identified, said the decision had been made in the middle of the previous week. And Tom Adams, the Barbados prime minister, said plans for U.S. action were in the works a week earlier than that.

Adams said he was informed Oct. 15 the United States was planning with Caribbean nations to rescue Grenadian Prime Minister Maurice Bishop from house arrest. This was four days before Bishop was killed in a bloodbath cited by U.S. officials as the ultimate reason for the invasion.

## WERE AMERICANS IN SERIOUS DANGER?

U.S. officials said the invasion was necessary because Americans, most of them medical school students, were threatened by a reign of terror on Grenada. "The nightmare of our hostages in Iran must never be repeated," Reagan declared.

But the day before the invasion, White House spokesman Larry Speakes said there was no indication of danger to the American residents. And the day before that—Sunday, Oct. 23—U.S. diplomat Kenneth Kurze returned from a visit to the Grenada students and said, "We have not recommended they leave."

The Grenadian military junta, meanwhile, repeatedly assured U.S. authorities that the Americans' safety was guaranteed.

The students themselves sounded divided. After evacuation, some said they had been nervous about Grenada's "shoot-on-sight" curfew, although that was lifted before the invasion. All were terrified during the invasion.

Student Nick Mongillo's diary may have typified the reaction.

"I hope the Beirut killing of over 100 U.S. Marines doesn't aggravate old President Reagan to do something here," he wrote on Sunday, Oct. 23.

But two days after the invasion, he wrote, "It is over! . . . The good ol' Marines did the job."

Last Friday, senior Reagan administration officials acknowledged to the Senate Intelligence Committee there had been no actual threats or overt actions taken against the American residents of Grenada.

## WAS THERE A PLAN TO TAKE AMERICAN HOSTAGES?

Defense Secretary Caspar Weinberger said last Friday there were "indications" from "intelligence reports" of plans to take Americans hostage on Grenada.

But U.S. intelligence sources later said there was no clear evidence any of the Americans were in danger of being taken hostage.

## WAS GRENADA'S AIRPORT CLOSED, STRANDING THE AMERICANS?

White House spokesman Speakes said the Grenadian military junta kept the island's small Pearls Airport closed, blocking the departure of Americans who wanted to leave.

But at least one flight, carrying three Americans, is known to have left Pearls Monday, the day before the invasion. And Dr. Charles Modica, chancellor of the St. George's University medical school on the island, says air controllers reported that four airplanes took off that day, after a week-long airport shutdown.

Modica says the military junta delayed other Americans' departure with "red tape"—insisting, for example, that no U.S. military planes be sent to Grenada, and limiting the size of planes that could land.

But the worst complication could not be blamed on the Grenadians: Other Caribbean states had decided that weekend to suspend scheduled airline flights into and out of Grenada.

## HOW MANY CUBANS WERE ON GRENADA?

As the Reagan administration focused on the alleged Cuban buildup in Grenada, the U.S. invasion commanders raised the estimated number of Cubans on the island, finally hitting 1,200.

Later, U.S. officials acknowledged the figure the Cuban government reported all along—784—was probably correct.

## WAS GRENADA BEING TURNED INTO A CUBAN "BASTION"?

Speakes said of the Cubans who were building an airport on Grenada, "In reality, it was a combat engineer battalion there." But no evidence of that has been produced thus far.

U.S. officers said warehouses of weapons found on Grenada could equip "10,000 guerrillas." Cuba said the arms were intended for Grenada's home militia of several thousand.

What Cuban buildup there was may have been precipitated, at least in part, by U.S. actions. "When it appeared U.S. intervention was likely, Cubans took over control of the island," said the U.S. Atlantic commander, Adm. Wesley McDonald.

## WAS THE CUBAN-BUILT AIRPORT A STRATEGIC THREAT?

Grenada's Marxist leaders said the new airport's 10,000-foot runway would allow jetliners to land on the island for the first time, boosting tourism. But the U.S. government expressed concern the airport might be put to military use by the Cubans or Soviets.

Some of the airport's financing came from the British government and European Common Market, and a British firm was a prime contractor. A British government source noted that the airport was not built to military specifications—it had no protected fuel dumps or hardened shelters for warplanes.

## WHAT WAS THE NON-AMERICAN CASUALTY TOLL?

Although an uncensored news film showed U.S. soldiers lining up Cuban bodies, U.S. officers said the non-American dead were not being counted.

Finally, on Friday, the operation commander, Vice Adm. Joseph Metcalf III, said there were 36 dead and 56 wounded among the defenders. A day later, although no new combat had occurred, he said he had "heard" as many as 69 Cubans were killed.

On the invasion's first day, U.S. warplanes mistakenly bombed a Grenada mental hospital, killing perhaps 20 patients. It was not until six days later, after a Canadian magazine journalist reported the bombing, that U.S. officials acknowledged it.

## WAS THE INVASION "LEGAL"?

The U.N. and Organization of American States charters forbid such a violation of a nation's territory.

Secretary of State George P. Shultz, asked about this, cited the two-year-old treaty that formed the Organization of Eastern Caribbean States as justification for the military operation.

But that treaty, to which the United States is not a party, stipulates that collective military action can be taken against "external aggression," and then only by a unanimous vote of the eight member states. Only five members voted to take action on Grenada.

*Credit*: Reprinted with permission of The Associated Press.

---

## DAVID MASON: "EUROPEAN CRITICISM OF GRENADA INVASION COOLING"

*Less than a month after the invasion of Grenada, the European community was backing away from its original condemnation. The following article is an example of the kinds of stories that chronicled that change.*

Associated Press, 5 November 1983

LONDON: As American troops withdraw from Grenada, sharp criticism of the invasion from America's Western European allies is fading, and some government officials suggest that damage to the Atlantic alliance will be minimal.

There have been some signs of second thoughts since the virtually unanimous castigation of the Oct. 25 mission, conducted with hardly a nod toward the allies, who constantly press Washington for more consultation on major international issues.

President Reagan said the reason he sent U.S. troops into Grenada was to rescue hundreds of Americans following the bloody Oct. 19 military coup on the Marxist-ruled island.

Some Western European officials, noting the quick American success on Grenada and the fact there were minimal casualties, have turned from condemnation to welcoming Grenada's new opportunity to install a democratic regime.

Prime Minister Margaret Thatcher tempered her initial criticism by saying, "Whenever people have the yoke of communism lifted I am delighted. . . . to be perfectly honest I am delighted that the people of Grenada are free."

Asked about the effect of Grenada on relations with the Untied States, a senior British official who would not be quoted by name, said:

"Grenada is receding into a proper perspective. It doesn't mark a giant watershed after which nothing will be the same."

Western European criticism initially followed three distinct themes:

The invasion of sovereign, independent Grenada was a violation of international law.

It handed the Soviet Union strong arguments to counter criticism of Moscow's occupation of Afghanistan.

Coming a few weeks before scheduled deployment of new American missiles in Western Europe, doubts were expressed over whether America could be trusted to take European interests into account in case of a nuclear showdown with the Soviets.

The most pointed reaction to the invasion of Grenada came initially from Britain which felt it should have been more closely consulted on America's plan to invade a country that is a member of the British Commonwealth of former colonies.

Mrs. Thatcher in a worldwide radio call-in repeatedly chided the United States for "walking into" Grenada. She declared herself strongly against communism and terrorism, but said if the United States continues to march into countries for those reasons "we are going to have really terrible wars in the world."

Britain is due very soon to take the first of its 160 cruise missiles as part of a NATO plan to site 572 rockets in five European countries starting in December should the U.S.-Soviet arms talks in Geneva remain deadlocked.

The issue of ultimate control of the missiles was rekindled by the Grenada invasion. The opposition British Labor Party argued there would be as little consultation on the rockets as there was over Grenada.

In West Germany, which is due to take the biggest share of the American missiles—96 cruises and all 108 Pershing 2s—the opposition Social Democrats charged the United States had done a disservice to the alliance. Foreign policy spokesman Carsten Voigt demanded a veto right over firing missiles from West German territory.

But Juergen Sudhoff, spokesman for the conservative Bonn government, watered down initial criticism of the Grenada invasion by saying "We have full trust in the United States that their action contributes to securing democratic freedoms for the people of Grenada."

In Italy, which with Britain and West Germany will take the first of the American missiles, Socialist Premier Bettino Craxi called the Grenada invasion a "dangerous precedent." But later, Italian officials generally were less critical and let the matter drop.

In the Netherlands, preparation continues for deploying 48 cruise missiles, although a final decision on accepting them is still pending. The invasion of Grenada appeared to have no immediate effect on the missile question.

In France, the invasion was initially condemned by government leaders, but by the end of the week criticism had all but died away.

France's Socialist president, François Mitterrand, remains a strong supporter of NATO's missile deployment decision, and there is broad public support for it which did not seem to be altered by the invasion.

*Credit*: Reprinted with permission of The Associated Press.

---

# ED MAGNUSON, WILLIAM McWHIRTER, AND CHRISTOPHER REDMAN: GETTING BACK TO NORMAL— AS GRENADA BEGINS TO REBUILD, SUPPORT SOLIDIFIES FOR INVASION

---

*One month after the invasion, newsmagazines were providing an overview of what happened and trying to explain why it all happened so quickly. Here is an example of such a report.*

### *Time*, 21 November 1983

Two squads of U.S. paratroopers roared down onto the soccer field in their choppers, kicking up clouds of dust. The combat-equipped men hit the dry field running, then flopped prone into defensive positions, their rifles ready. Ahead of them, youths of the small seaside town of Gouyave, on Grenada's west coast, sat watching from a bridge railing. They broke into loud applause. So, too, did local women at the sides of the field. The American troops, who had been searching for armed Cuban or Grenadian hold-outs in the little war that was over, had been given a bad tip. They stood up to return the waves of the villagers.

Three weeks after the Oct. 25 U.S. military invasion, life on the tiny island took on an Evelyn Waugh flavor. The week's only known military casualty was a paratrooper who hurt himself while body surfing. Marijuana sales resumed along Ganja Alley, a colourful corner of St. George's, and local businessmen had their first post-invasion Rotary Club luncheon. Even Gail Reed, the American-born wife of the Cuban ambassador, whose embassy had been ringed for days by U.S. troops, was able to joke before flying back to Havana: "I'm sorry I left my Jane Fonda workout videotape at home."

Still, there was serious business to be done in Grenada. The last of the 634 Cuban prisoners were returned to their homeland. Tons of American construction supplies and equipment were flown to the island, where U.S. military engineers will supervise the rebuilding of roads, water systems and telephone and power facilities. Some $3.5 million in emergency U.S. funds had been allotted to the task, but the total seemed likely to fall far short of eventual needs.

Sir Paul Scoon, the once ceremonial representative of the British Queen in the Commonwealth nation, was running the island as Governor-General. With a British lawyer at his side, he announced the appointment of the nine-man "advisory council" that will help administer affairs in Grenada until a new government is elected, presumably under a democratic constitution. No one could say when that might be. The council, composed of non-political Grenadians with administrative skills, is to be headed by Meredith Alister McIntyre, 51, now deputy secretary-general of the U.N. Conference on Trade and Development in Geneva. Scoon gave high priority to forming "an efficient and effective police service free of politics." Police duties were being performed by troops from neighboring Caribbean nations, as well as by some 3,000 U.S. paratroopers still on the island.

In Washington, before leaving for the Far East, Ronald Reagan solidified the broad popular support for his decision to invade Grenada. He basked in the virtually unanimous praise of American students from St. George's University School of Medicine, whose perceived peril on Grenada had been one of the President's rationales for what he called the "rescue mission." Addressing about 300 of the returned students, whom he had invited to the White House, along with some of the troops who had helped them get off the chaotic island, Reagan criticized those who "belittled the danger that you were in." The President added: "It is very easy for some know-it-all in a plush protected quarter to say that you were in no danger. I have wondered how many of them would have changed places with you." The students' cheers rolled across the South Lawn.

In another effort to shore up support for the invasion, the Administration placed captured Cuban weapons on display in a hangar at Andrews Air Force Base. The most formidable were two Soviet-built BTR-60 armored personnel carriers. Twelve of them had been spirited at night into Grenada 18 months ago by the Cubans, after electric power had been cut and roadblocks installed to conceal the unloading. Also on display were twelve ZU-23 antiaircraft guns, 291 submachine guns, 6,330 rifles and 5.6 million rounds of ammunition. The Pentagon termed the arms cache sufficient to equip two Cuban battalions (about 500 men each) for up to 45 days of combat.

A congressional study group concluded, after a three-day trip to Grenada, that Reagan's move had been justified. The 14 members of Congress, headed by Democrat Thomas Foley of Washington State, reported to House Speaker Tip O'Neill that most of them felt that the students had been possible targets for a Tehran-type taking of hostages. This caused O'Neill, who had denounced Reagan's decision, to reverse himself. Noting that "a potentially life-threatening situation existed on the island," the Speaker said that the invasion "was justified under these particular circumstances."

There were a few dissenters among the congressional fact finders. "Not a single American child nor single American national was in any way placed in danger or placed in a hostage situation prior to the invasion," insisted Ohio Democrat Louis Stokes. The Congressional Black Caucus denounced the intervention. Seven other Democratic Congressmen, led by Ted Weiss of New York, introduced a quixotic resolution to impeach Reagan for sending in the troops, which would, of course, go exactly nowhere. Just outside the White House on Saturday, a youngish crowd of at least 20,000 gathered to demonstrate their displeasure with the Grenada adventure and with U.S. military involvement in Central America.

But overall the Grenada operation seemed to produce a new public pride in the military. It infused Veterans Day observances last week, and was evident as Army Rangers and some of the paratroopers returned from the Caribbean, "It's great to

feel wanted," Ranger Sergeant Tracy Hickman told one reporter at Georgia's Hunter Army Airfield, contrasting the bitter homecoming from Viet Nam with last week's warm reception. A post-invasion poll taken by the Washington *Post* and ABC News showed that 63% of Americans approve the way Reagan is handling the presidency, the highest level in two years, and attributed his gain largely to the Grenada intervention.

While the Administration had gained wide public approval at home for its Grenada action, the question of how long the U.S. should maintain troops on the island was still open. The Administration had predicted quick withdraw, stressing that the U.S. had no intention of occupying or imposing political decisions on the islanders. Defense Secretary Casper [sic] Weinberger said he expected U.S. troops to be off the island by Christmas. Schoon and many Grenadians familiar with the island's factional politics warned the visiting Congressmen that U.S. forces should stay far longer to ensure stability.

An ironic problem for the Americans is that many of the Marxist-inspired social projects were welcomed by Grenadians, who now expect the U.S. to continue them with U.S. dollars. They include medical clinics, adult-education courses, scholarships for study abroad, housing assistance, an uncompleted new sports stadium and, of course, the controversial 10,000-ft. airstrip, which had been budgeted as a $71 million project. It is three-fourths completed.

One preliminary estimate of the cost of restoring Grenada's lagging economy and its basic physical facilities is $100 million. That is close to a third of the Administration's proposed spending for its entire Caribbean Basin Initiative. Concedes one U.S. Caribbean specialist: "Whatever we give here has to be matched in the neighboring island states. Otherwise they will draw the undesirable conclusion that the best way to receive U.S. aid is to turn Red and then be rescued."

While the Administration's Grenada venture had turned out a popular success, the Government's information apparatus was still in some disarray. Last week, for example, State Department Spokesman John Hughes officially confirmed a rumor that a grave holding more than 100 bodies of Grenadians slain by Marxist forces in the "bloody Wednesday" massacre of Oct. 19 had been found on the island. Next day he had to admit there was no such discovery. U.S. military authorities later located a grave believed to have held the burned bodies of former Prime Minister Maurice Bishop and three Cabinet members slain with him in the coup.

Confusion over casualty counts continued. Major General Norman Schwarzkopf, deputy commander of the invasion force, said that 160 Grenadian soldiers and 71 Cubans had been killed during the invasion. The Pentagon had given a much lower count of 59 Cuban and Grenadian combat deaths, offering no breakdown on the nationalities. There was agreement that 18 Americans had died.

The glaring lack of advance intelligence about Grenada and the haste with which the military was ordered to mount the invasion showed in the fact that the U.S. forces, as it turns out, were unaware that the medical students were located on two campuses, True Blue and Grand Anse, some four miles apart. The soldiers reached 130 True Blue students early on the invasion day. But it was not until 30 hours later, during which time a student ham-radio operator on

Grand Anse kept listeners throughout the hemisphere informed that his campus was still cut off from U.S. forces, that Army Rangers finally rescued the 224 students there. For so successful an operation, it was clear there were still post-mortems to be conducted and lessons to be learned.

*Credit:* © 1983 TIME Inc. Reprinted by permission.

## PETER O'LOUGHLIN: "COMMONWEALTH NATIONS TAKE SOFT LINE ON U.S. GRENADA INVASION"

*Despite the direct military intervention by a foreign government on a Commonwealth member, member states decided against a formal condemnation. The following story reported the decision.*

Associated Press, 30 November 1983

NEW DELHI, India: Commonwealth leaders, despite harsh comments in the past week, have decided not to denounce the U.S. invasion of Grenada or to urge that American forces withdraw from the island.

The 48-nation association of Britain and its former colonies, in a 12-page communiqué wrapping up a week-long summit, did attack the United States on one issue—but it was in regard to Namibia, not Grenada.

Namibia, formally known as South-West Africa, is administered by South Africa under an old League of Nations mandate, abrogated by the United Nations. The United States was criticized for impeding independence for the territory.

Many of the Commonwealth leaders, when they arrived here a week ago, were opposed to the Oct. 25 invasion of Grenada. But the communiqué issued Tuesday made no mention of the United States and did not call for the withdrawal of about 2,000 American troops still on the Caribbean island.

"Heads of government agreed . . . that the emphasis should be on reconstruction but not recrimination," the communiqué said.

It also said that an all-Caribbean force was ready "to assist in the maintenance of law and order in Grenada" if requested by the current interim administration of technocrats.

At a news conference after the final session, Prime Minister Indira Gandhi said she would have preferred the communiqué to call for an "unconditional withdrawal" of U.S. troops from Grenada.

"We, India, consider what has happened as a warning to all countries small and not so small and even some I could call big countries," Mrs. Gandhi said.

U.S. Marines and Army soldiers invaded Grenada in the wake of a Marxist-led military coup for the stated purpose of restoring order and protecting Americans on the island.

Australian Prime Minister Robert Hawke's attempt to have the Commonwealth call for the withdrawal of Syrian and Israeli troops from Lebanon resulted in a compromise that said "many heads of government" wanted all foreign armed

forces to quit, other than the four-nation Western peacekeeping force.

Mrs. Gandhi, objecting to any implicit criticism of Syria, tried to have the communiqué read that only "some" heads of government endorsed the call, while Hawke wanted it to read "most."

Regarding southern Africa, the Commonwealth took its hardest line to date against Washington for being the only nation supporting South Africa's contention that Cuban troops must withdraw from Angola before it will permit elections and independence in the territory.

"Hopes that (Namibian) independence might be imminent, had been frustrated when the United States and South Africa insisted on the withdrawal of Cuban troops as a precondition," the communiqué said.

The White House issued a statement in Washington responding to the Commonwealth communiqué on Namibia and stood firm on its Cuban-Namibian linkage.

It said the "implementation of a Namibian government can take place only if the fundamental concerns of all the parties are addressed, and . . . South Africa's position regarding the withdrawal of Cuban forces from Angola does remain as an issue to be resolved."

"For the past two years, we have worked hard on the search for a solution based on reciprocity, with full mutual respect for security and sovereignty about Namibia's independence," the unsigned statement said. "We will remain engaged in this effort as long as it appears there is a chance for a peaceful solution."

The Commonwealth leaders condemned white minority-ruled South Africa in strong terms for repeated violation of the territorial integrity of neighboring black states and for "economic sabotage and blackmail."

They called for the withdrawal of South African troops from Angola and stricter enforcement of a mandatory arms embargo on South Africa.

*Credit:* Reprinted with permission of The Associated Press.

## LOU CANNON, DAVID HOFFMAN, AND FRED HIATT: "SENTIMENT FOR PULLOUT INCREASING"

*This front-page story reflects the national sentiment about bringing the troops home after a mission that looked pretty successful in Grenada and hopeless in Lebanon.*

*Washington Post*, 30 November 1983

President Reagan is facing growing political and military sentiment within his administration to remove U.S. Marines from Lebanon or to redeploy them soon to safer positions, officials said yesterday.

"The involvement in Lebanon is the Achilles' heel in the administration's foreign policies," said one Reagan adviser. "If we don't solve it in the short run, it will be critical for us in the long run."

This view is reportedly shared by Pentagon officials who see the Marines, according to one source, as "sitting ducks" at the Beirut airport.

"This is a rare instance when White House chief of staff James A. Baker and Secretary of Defense Caspar W. Weinberger see the world the same way, but we still don't have a plan to remove the Marines," one official said. The Joint Chiefs of Staff also is reported to be uneasy about the continued deployment of the Marines there.

However, officials said that Secretary of State George P. Shultz and national security affairs adviser Robert C. McFarlane, both former Marines, remain firmly committed to keeping the Marines in Lebanon as part of the multinational peace-keeping force intended to support the government of President Amin Gemayel, who will meet with Reagan here on Thursday.

An administration official emphasized last night that Reagan also is committed to the "security of Lebanon and the reconciliation process there" and that the accomplishment of this "would enable the Marines to be withdrawn." Other administration officials expressed increased concern about continued deployment of the Marines at the Beirut airport, where 239 U.S. servicemen were killed in a suicide truck-bomb attack a month ago.

One official said French forces had "botched" a Nov. 17 retaliatory air strike against a training center in Lebanon for Iranians blamed by U.S. and French officials for apparently coordinated bombing attacks on U.S. and French troops in Beirut on Oct. 23. The French government had claimed that the retaliatory strike was "a surgical operation without error."

Administration officials also said the United States and France had cooperated in selecting joint targets for the retaliatory air strike and that the French acted after U.S. officials were unable to decide on what action to take.

According to the officials, aerial photographs assessing the damage caused by the French bombing confirmed that much of the target east of Beirut, which reportedly included barracks

occupied by Iranian revolutionary guards, was not destroyed.

"Let's put it this way," one official said, "the French were not satisfied with their performance."

Administration officials considered a range of retaliatory options, including air strikes and ground commando raids, according to officials. Although it is true that the Joint Chiefs of Staff had serious reservations about some of the options, as has previously been reported, it expressed support for others, according to Pentagon officials.

Officials said the United States plans no further retaliation unless a "preemptive attack" is required to forestall another strike against the Marines.

What emerged from interviews with administration officials who discussed the options in Lebanon on condition that they not be identified was a growing concern that U.S. policy in Lebanon faces military and political imperatives that cannot be ignored.

One Pentagon official said the administration "is still looking for ways to get the Marines out of the bunker mentality and into more active peace-keeping" but has no clear ideas about how to do this. Since the attack on the Marines, U.S. officials have been preoccupied with their survival and would like to find a way to transform them from targets into more active participants.

On the other hand, there reportedly is no enthusiasm for increasing the support role of the 1,800 Marines for the Lebanese army if the fighting heats up again. "Getting our people more involved isn't something that's being pushed in this building," a Pentagon official said.

A Reagan political adviser called the involvement of the Marines in Lebanon "the single most negative issue we face" in a reelection campaign. The adviser said Americans were "diverted" from the Beirut bombing by the subsequent successful invasion of Grenada, but that the Middle East had "Vietnam possibilities in political terms" if the Marines remain in Lebanon well into the 1984 general election campaign.

Within the White House, the concern is more measured but deepening. One official said yesterday that "we can live with the involvement in Lebanon for a while" but that "withdrawal is an imperative within a matter of months."

The formal imperative, as defined by the War Powers Resolution compromise with Congress that Reagan signed on Oct. 12, would require the Marines to be withdrawn from Lebanon by April, 1985, well after Election Day. The principal argument for allowing the administration this much time was that it would demonstrate U.S. resolve and discourage Syria from waiting out a U.S. withdrawal.

But the view in the White House is that Reagan will be in deep political trouble unless the Marines are withdrawn by next summer despite the breathing room given the White House by House Speaker Thomas P. (Tip) O'Neill Jr.'s (D-Mass.) support of the war powers compromise.

"It is not just the Reagan administration time clock, it is not just the Republican time clock, but it is the speaker's, too," one official said.

While this may shield Reagan for the time being from criticism by Democratic leaders, it is no protection against what White House polls show to be a rising tide of voter concern about U.S. involvement in Lebanon.

*Credit*: **© 1983, The Washington Post, reprinted with permission.**

## NOTES

1. Don Oberdorfer, "The Beirut Massacre; U.S. Resources Worldwide Face Further Strain," *Washington Post*, 24 October 1983, A12.

2. Edward Cody, "Caribbean Nations Discuss Response to Violence in Grenada," *Washington Post*, 23 October 1983, A24.

3. G. G. LaBelle, "International News," Associated Press, 22 October 1983.

4. Survey by ABC News/*Washington Post*, 3–7 November 1983: *Question*: Now I want to ask you a few questions about the events in the Caribbean island of Grenada. First, would you say you approve or disapprove of the invasion of Grenada by U.S. troops? No opinion: 7 percent; Disapprove: 22 percent; Approve: 71 percent.

5. Associated Press, "U.S. Troops Scattered around the World," 25 October 1983.

## FURTHER READINGS

Adkin, Mark. *Urgent Fury: The Battle for Grenada*. Lexington, Mass.: Lexington Books, 1989.

Beck, Robert. *The Grenada Invasion: Politics, Law, and Foreign Policy Decisionmaking*. Boulder, Colo.: Westview Press, 1993.

O'Shaughnessy, Hugh. *Grenada: An Eyewitness Account of the U.S. Invasion and the Caribbean History That Provoked It*. New York: Dodd, Mead, 1984.

U.S. Congress. *Full Committee Hearing on the Lessons Learned as a Result of the U.S. Military Operations in Grenada: Hearing before the Committee on Armed Services, House of Representatives*. 98th Cong., 2nd sess., 24 January 1984.

# 26

# LIBYA AND THE GULF OF SIDRA, 1986

Modern Libya is a patchwork of territories previously held by foreign powers for centuries. Much of the area came under Ottoman rule in the sixteenth century. The governor sent from Constantinople was frequently overruled or sidelined by the more local professional soldiers in Tripoli. The leaders of these militarily entrenched families were called deys, and the Ottomans eventually gave way to one of them who installed himself into a hereditary governorship in 1711.

The Karamanli family ruled until 1835 as dey and governor, with the help of pirated riches taken from ships and land missions along the Mediterranean. The United States fought an unsuccessful war against the pirating during the early 1800s. It was not until 1815 that some of the European countries began a more successful campaign to stop the Tripoli-sanctioned pirating. That effort led to the reinstitution of direct Ottoman Empire administration in Tripoli twenty years later and interrupted the dey powerhouse.

Though the Italians claimed to have conquered Tripoli during the Turko-Italian War of 1911, the treaty that ended that war granted Tripoli autonomy. Italy continued to occupy and overpower portions of Libya during the next twenty years. The colonists built an infrastructure for transportation, health care, and education, and Libya as a nation was made part of Italy in 1939.

When Italy entered World War II in 1940, North Africa became a battleground that eventually was under Anglo-French military control. When a peace treaty between Italy and the Allied forces that were overseeing the outcome of Libya could not be reached in 1947, the United Nations was given jurisdiction in 1949. Libya petitioned for independent statehood and was named the United Kingdom of Libya in 1951. King Idris I was named ruler, with Tripoli as the capital city, and the new nation quickly joined the Arab League. Libya was admitted, as an independent nation, to the United Nations in 1955.

The nation of about 5 million shared relatively peaceful borders with Algeria,

Chad, Egypt, Niger, Sudan, and Tunisia. Though the interior of the country is mostly barren desert, it also has about 1,000 miles of lush Mediterranean coastline. The country is about the size of Alaska. Because of a poor agricultural environment and many years under the rule of foreign powers, the new country required substantial financial support from the wealthier Western governments, such as the United States and Great Britain. In exchange for startup financing, Libya allowed the establishment of U.S. and British military bases in strategic locations across the country.

The discovery of oil in Libya just after the installation of the new government quickly made a few residents of the predominantly poor country very rich. With this newfound wealth came a desire for political power, and in 1969 a coup led by 27-year-old Colonel Muammar al-Qaddafi deposed King Idris. The constitution was redrafted, and a twelve-member Revolutionary Command Council became the government. That council named Qaddafi as prime minister until 1972, when he named himself president.

Qaddafi wanted to limit Western political views and influence in the region, so he expelled U.S. and British military installations within Libya. He also initiated a cultural revolution in 1973 that reoriented the nation toward Muslim principles and Middle East military alignments with Egypt and Syria. Qaddafi survived several coup attempts, but during the 1980s he began ordering assassinations of Libyan dissidents living outside of Libya. These actions led to hit-and-miss murders committed primarily in Europe where Libyan exiles resided.

Closer to home, Qaddafi was emphatic about his national borders. In 1981, he ordered his fighter planes to attack a U.S. ship in the Gulf of Sidra, which Libya claimed was national water. The Libyan planes were shot down by the U.S. forces, and these hostilities led to Qaddafi's declaration of subsequent terrorist activities against the United States and the U.S. ban of Libyan oil imports. The rhetoric on each side escalated with small contests of will and force displayed. In 1986, President Reagan ordered strikes against military targets near the coast, and then on Tripoli when Qaddafi was thought to be there.

The American public was concerned by the threats issued on each side, but was evidently sure that Reagan would not let Qaddafi get the better of the United States. At the end of March, after a U.S. strike from the Gulf of Sidra along the Libyan coast, *Newsweek* conducted a public opinion survey to find out if Americans were confident of the U.S. position against Qaddafi.[1] Seventy-five percent of those polled thought that the attacks were justified, though there was a nearly even split about whether the sea maneuvers were intended to provoke a fight. A 64 percent majority of Americans thought that the U.S. attacks might provoke retaliatory terrorism, but the same percentage thought that it was worth the risk to teach Qaddafi a lesson in U.S. might. Nearly two-thirds of those polled said that they would not travel abroad because of these fears, but a majority also said that they thought that Reagan made wise use of military force in foreign policy issues.

The results must have been reassuring for Reagan, though he seemed to need little confidence building on the issue of Qaddafi, a "mad dog," as the president had characterized him in a televised interview. Within a week of this poll's publication, Reagan ordered a surprise predawn air raid over Tripoli. In an effort that reportedly targeted Qaddafi himself, the United States launched a 100-craft air strike on Tripoli and Benghazi on 14 April.

The raid was pronounced a retaliatory strike in response to the suspected Libyan-sponsored terrorist attack in West Berlin that had killed two U.S. servicemen earlier in the month. Most of the international community was not pleased with the U.S. unilateral action, and many governments were vocal about their displeasure. Some of the leaders wondered aloud if this was just another indication that the Americans were taking international law into their own hands. Reagan did not seem to shy away from calling on military solutions for political problems.

The 14 April 1986 air attack was the third time Reagan ordered a strike against Libya, and the fifth time that U.S. troops had seen combat since he took office in 1981. The first call to arms under the Reagan administration occurred when U.S. naval warplanes were practicing maneuvers near Libya and were ordered to shoot down two Libyan fighter planes that were said to have attacked the U.S. jets. Through 1986, American ships continued to hold positions off the Libyan coast, and in March 1986 they were again fired upon by antiaircraft missiles from Libya. U.S. forces responded by sinking at least two Libyan patrol boats and twice attacking SA-5 radar sites. No Americans were killed in the first two engagements with Libya. Two were killed in the third strike. The other two military campaigns were in 1983. That year U.S. Marines went to Beirut on a peacekeeping mission. A few days after an explosion there killed 241 servicemen, U.S. marines and army rangers invaded Grenada. In that campaign, nineteen Americans were killed.

What follows is a selection of the news reports of that brief air strike campaign aimed very specifically at Qaddafi and the international reaction. Nearly all the reporting was about the political implications, and very little was about the human cost of the conflict. Few American journalists were allowed into Tripoli during the conflict, and so reporting from the city was limited, not by U.S. censorship, but by Qaddafi. In the United States, the Pentagon had shut out the media from the surprise strike and had limited response to those questions asked by the media before and after the air attacks. Note that the various spellings of Qaddafi's name in news reports are an indication of how little agreement there was about how to cover this intervention.

---

## BOB WOODWARD: REAGAN'S EFFORTS TO OVERTHROW LIBYA'S QADDAFI

---

*This front-page story two weeks before the surprise air raid over Libya reported the uneasiness that many people felt about the prospect of fighting there, but also about the relentlessness of President Reagan's efforts to rid the world of Qaddafi.*

### Washington Post, 2 April 1986

Eight months of secret U.S. efforts to win Egyptian approval for a U.S.-Egyptian military operation designed to overthrow Libyan leader Muammar Qaddafi appear to have foundered following public disclosure and rejection of the plan by Cairo, informed sources said yesterday.

Still, there were contradictory reports yesterday on whether the plan had been abandoned by the United States. Officials were quoted this week in Cairo as saying that the Egyptian government had rejected three U.S. overtures in recent months for a joint attack on Libya. U.S. sources, however, said that secret discussions in Cairo in February were productive and the joint planning was continuing.

One option of the plan called for U.S. military air operations in coordination with Egypt, which would attack across the 600-mile Libyan-Egyptian border. U.S. support was to include extensive bombing in what one source said would have been the most ambitious and aggressive foreign policy decision in the Reagan administration.

President Reagan authorized the planning and in the last eight months sent two high-level emissaries to Egypt for secret military planning, according to informed sources. One emissary, Vice Adm. John M. Poindexter, now Reagan's national security affairs adviser, headed a team of military planners that visited Cairo late last summer around Labor Day; a senior Pentagon general assigned to the Joint Chiefs of Staff continued the efforts this February in meetings that one source said "went very well."

Reagan never gave final approval to carry out the military plan even if Cairo had assented and sources disagreed yesterday about how close it came to realization. "It was really a plan for a surprise attack on Libya in conjunction with Egypt, nothing less," one source said.

The Defense Department last year also slowed its planning when strategists concluded that as many as six divisions, or 90,000 men, would have to be used if direct U.S. military involvement was required.

"The whole attitude of the Pentagon study was," said one source, "'Do we want a war with Libya?'" Libya's armed forces include 73,000 regular troops and 535 combat aircraft.

The joint U.S.-Egyptian military discussions were one of the most closely held undertakings in the Reagan White House, sources said. "A small group of mostly senior advisers took the war-making power unto themselves," one source critical of the planning said recently. "They had insufficient understanding of the Middle East. . . . It could have been a disaster."

Even while disagreeing over details of the plan and its current status, a number of sources agreed that it was not to be executed until there was a clear-cut military or terrorist provocation by Libya and Qaddafi, its erratic leader.

One part of the U.S. plan called for Egypt to attack Libya on the ground, occupying perhaps half the country. Then, at Egyptian request, the United States would step in to assist. Another scenario suggested that once in control of half of Libya, Egypt would have sufficient leverage to force Qaddafi out of power.

In another alternative, U.S. bombers and tactical fighters would strike major Libyan military installations before the Egyptian attack or in concert with Egypt's attack.

Despite Egyptian hostility toward Qaddafi, the sources said, some U.S. strategists believed that Arab solidarity likely would have prevailed, preventing Egypt's participation with the United States in any large-scale attack against an Arab neighbor unless Libya attacked first.

Some administration officials have described the plan as "precautionary" and a "contingency." Several sources have said that the U.S. Navy exercise last week in Libya's Gulf of Sidra—code-named "Operation Prairie Fire"—may have satisfied the administration's goal of sending a message of U.S. resolve to Qaddafi. Three U.S. aircraft carrier groups retaliated against a Libyan missile attack by sinking at least two Libyan patrol boats and bombing a missile radar site.

In December and January when The Washington Post learned of some of the secret planning with the Egyptians, certain details about ongoing military plans were omitted from articles after a request from senior administration officials. On Dec. 21, The Post reported that a high-level emissary for anti-Libyan military contingency planning had been sent to the Middle East. In a Jan. 24 article, Egypt was first identified as a key participant in the secret planning. Poindexter was not identified as one of the emissaries to Cairo until an article last Wednesday in The Post in the wake of the Gulf of Sidra action.

Poindexter's role as the planning emissary to Cairo was a closely held secret and apparently triggered a response in Egypt.

Ibrahim Nafeh, editor in chief of the semiofficial Al-Ahram and a man close to Egyptian President Hosni Mubarak, wrote on Monday that "the United States has attempted more than once to join in an action with Egypt against Libya." He cited three such attempts and said that Egypt had rejected the proposal each time.

The Washington Times yesterday said that administration sources confirmed these reported rejections.

Well-placed administration sources, however, said the Egyptian reaction was not outright rejection and that during the February meetings in Cairo a senior Defense Department planner reported positive results. The White House had no comment yesterday.

There is apparent division in the Egyptian government about the U.S. plan, and one source said that Egyptian Defense Minister Abdul-Halim Abu Ghazala, a defense attaché in Washington during the mid-1970s, was more inclined to at least listen to U.S. plans.

U.S. relations with Egypt were strained last October after the hijacking of the Italian cruise ship Achille Lauro, when U.S. jets intercepted an Egyptian airliner carrying the four hijackers. An article the next month in The Washington Post detailing a covert CIA plan to attempt to undermine the Qaddafi regime—which has been only a portion of the administration's anti-Qaddafi plans—also increased Egyptian fears that any joint undertaking against Qaddafi with the United States would become public.

Abu Ghazala was apparently upset about the CIA disclosure, according to an intelligence report, and was told by the U.S. embassy in Cairo that the story would not arouse much controversy because nearly everyone in the United States favored unseating Qaddafi.

The seriousness with which the anti-Libyan planning was undertaken by the White House is illustrated by one written analysis about probable Soviet reaction to a military strike against Libya prior to the November summit meeting. The analysis concluded that the Soviets would keep their distance, and any U.S.-Egyptian move would not hurt the summit.

As details of the plan were disclosed to Pentagon and intelligence analysts over the last eight months, serious objections began to surface. No one in the White House had fully grasped the extent to which Qaddafi, who has ruled since 1969, has a hold on the Libyan population of 3 million people, according to one informed source. Through a series of so-called revolutionary committees, Qaddafi has organized and armed the population, in some instances down to individual blocks in the Libyan capital of Tripoli. These people's committees are fiercely loyal to Qaddafi, according to some U.S. analysts.

The Pentagon, according to sources, was also concerned that the planning did not fully deal with the task of launching and coordinating such a military operation across the Atlantic.

"This wasn't Grenada," one source said, though there were frequent references to it in the discussions.

*Credit:* © **1986, The Washington Post, reprinted with permission.**

---

## AN ANONYMOUS REPORT: LIBYAN OPPOSITION TO QADDAFI

*The desire by Americans to see Qaddafi out of power was very strong. This wire service story reinforced the view that Qaddafi was thought to be a bad man even by his own people. The dateline of West Germany, site of the recent terrorist attack that the United States credited to Qaddafi, probably added more significance to the story.*

### United Press International, 6 April 1986

HAMBURG, West Germany: The Libyan army will overthrow Libyan leader Moammar Khadafy because of the war in Chad and other problems, an opposition leader said in an interview published Sunday.

"Time is running out," Abd Hamid Bakusch, who was prime minister in the government toppled by Khadafy in 1969, told the West German news magazine Der Spiegel.

He said the army is dissatisfied with Libyan involvement in the civil war in Chad, money is scarce because of falling oil prices and the supply of consumer goods is critical.

"Things are coming to a head," he said. "Khadafy will not be able to hold out much longer. Time is running out."

Bakusch, head of the Libyan Liberation Organization based in Egypt, said the army has been purged so often and so many officers and soldiers executed that it would like to topple Khadafy.

"They will do it very soon. The decisive thing is the Chad fiasco. . . . The Chad war is unpopular in Libya. Recently there was a mutiny among the Libyan troops. That is the beginning of the end."

Bakusch criticized the United States for not striking hard enough at Khadafy. He said by limiting its recent action to the Gulf of Sidra it gave Khadafy the chance to pose as a hero and embarrassed Arab countries that would like to see Khadafy overthrown.

"The Americans should have inflicted serious military losses on Khadafy to such an extent that he could not have denied it," he said. "Then the army and people would have been encouraged to put an end to the rule of horror of this bloody dictator."

Khadafy has met violence in the past. According to intelligence reports reaching the United States, in May 1984 unidentified commandos attacked Khadafy's fortress home on the outskirts of Tripoli. Most of the attackers were killed during the heavy rocket and mortar attack.

Khadafy has accused Britain, Sudan and the United States of conspiring to overthrow him. Britain severed diplomatic relations with Tripoli in April 1984 after a policewoman was shot to death by gunfire from within the Libyan mission in London.

Bakusch said all Arab states, even Syria, want to see the end of Khadafy, although they fear openly opposing him.

He called it a "scandal" that European countries put their economic interests ahead of humanitarian interests. He said European countries are financing terrorism in Europe by buying Libyan oil.

*Credit:* Reprinted by permission of UPI.

---

## EVAN THOMAS: REAGAN FLEXES U.S. MUSCLE IN LIBYA, CENTRAL AMERICA

*The U.S. government control of information about Libya was quite tight, and as a result daily news was limited. This gave the weekly newsmagazines an opportunity to develop stories that were at least as timely as daily news could produce. This story focused on the recent developments in Libya alongside another Reagan target region, Central America.*

*Time*, 7 April 1986

Navy warplanes firing missiles at Libyan patrol boats. Army helicopters ferrying troops into the jungles of Central America. American might was unleashed and on display last week, resonating with echoes of fights for right and freedom from the halls of Montezuma to the shores of Tripoli. As the images of far-flung war flickered over television screens, Americans could hardly be blamed for humming a bar or two from the *Marines' Hymn*—but not too loudly and more than a bit nervously.

To most Americans, smiting Libya's Muammar Gaddafi certainly felt good: taking up his "line of death" dare, double-daring him back, winning a public slapping match, sailing away. Yet, now what? America might seem just a bit less like a helpless giant, but could a breezy flick really be expected to chasten Gaddafi? And the sight of Army choppers kicking up dust in a foreign bush was disquieting, an eerie evocation of *Apocalypse Now*. In Ronald Reagan's two-front muscle flexing last week, the images and the reality were hard to sort out. Power, yes, and the will to use it, yes. But to what end? And with what effect? Will briefly disabling Gaddafi's radar mean less terrorism or more? Will aiding Honduras serve to keep Nicaragua at bay or drag U.S. troops into a thickening morass?

This much was certain: under President Reagan the U.S. is determined to back words with symbolic displays of force, to carry a big stick as well as speak loudly. To be sure, the battle of Sidra will be, at most, a footnote in the annals of naval engagements. Trafalgar or Midway it was not. And the helicopters whirring toward the battle zone in Honduras were not transporting American troops. Even the symbolism was curiously muted by partial pretexts—about concern for freedom of the seas and Honduran sovereignty—that served to blur the true aims of the actions. Nevertheless, in the wake of American-aided democratic triumphs in Haiti and the Philippines, the Administration last week was clearly feeling confident, seeking to show once again that the U.S. is willing to assume some carefully limited military risks.

If last week's show of force somehow seemed contrived, it was partly by political necessity. In the nuclear age, particularly after Viet Nam, the U.S. is perforce muscle-bound. It may have enough firepower to flatten the globe, yet Presidents are understandably loath to use force except under the most tightly circumscribed conditions. There is public opinion to worry about, as well as Congress and nervous allies, not to mention the Soviet Union. Even the Pentagon, still smarting from Viet Nam, is chary of waging war without unequivocal support.

Reagan's intent is unambiguous: to stop Gaddafi from fomenting terrorism and to stop Nicaraguan President Daniel Ortega Saavedra from spreading Marxist revolution. Indeed, Reagan would not mind going one step further and getting both men right off the world stage. But eliminating such nemeses is not so easy. For all his make-my-day bluster,

Reagan is no less bound than were his immediate predecessors by rules of military engagement that, while rooted in the best democratic traditions, have been carried to unreal extremes: American boys should not be seen dying on the nightly news. Wars should be over in three days or less, or before Congress invokes the War Powers Resolution. Victory must be assured in advance. And the American public must be all for it from the outset.

To satisfy the onerous requirements of public relations both at home and abroad, Reagan had to find a pretext for sailing the Sixth Fleet into harm's way. But assuring free passage in international waters had only a little more to do with the actual reasons for sending ships across Gaddafi's line of death than rescuing American medical students did with invading Grenada in 1983; as pretexts go, it was about on a par with citing arms shipments to rebels in El Salvador in order to aid the *contras* in Nicaragua. Scoffed Senator Gary Hart of Colorado: "There is always some fig leaf being used."

By the same token, although the Nicaraguan incursion last week was very real, Reagan's decision to send $20 million in emergency aid to Honduras and to permit U.S. helicopters to ferry Honduran troops was very much a part of his larger struggle to rally congressional and public support for $100 million in aid to the *contras*. Set back by the House a week earlier, the Administration needed a win in the Senate to keep the aid package alive and unencumbered by too many strings. What better way of showing that the *contras* need help than to make the most of Nicaraguan troops crossing the border to attack the rebels in their Honduran sanctuaries? Speaking at a political fund raiser in New Orleans last week, Reagan was not subtle in his message: The Nicaraguan attack, he declared, was a "slap in the face" to those in Congress who voted against *contra* aid.

Administration spokesmen tried to transform public backing for standing up to Gaddafi into support for the less popular policy of aiding the *contras*. "Americans understand what type of people we have to deal with in this world," said White House Communications Director Patrick Buchanan, speaking of Gaddafi, "and they expect that from time to time we as a great power have to assert our right. That has to carry over into the Central America issue. Sure, *contra* aid is a divisive issue in a dirty little war, but it takes courage to do what's right in that situation."

It was difficult to tell how seriously the targets of Reagan's bellicosity took it. On the night the Sixth Fleet sailed from the Gulf of Sidra, a fireworks display in Tripoli commemorating the 16th anniversary of the departure of the British military from Libya turned into a celebration of Gaddafi's latest skirmish with the U.S. In Nicaragua citizens enjoyed Holy Week by going to the beach, apparently unconcerned about the battle raging along the Honduran border. Nor did the President of Honduras, José Azcona Hoyo, seem overly concerned that his country was being invaded. He too went to the seashore for a vacation. For that matter, Reagan made no attempt to maintain a crisis atmosphere; at week's end he headed to his California ranch for Easter, stopping in New Orleans on the way.

Gaddafi's navy was no match for the Sixth Fleet. But aside from having the U.S. seem to stand tall again, it was difficult to discern any long-term strategic policy behind Reagan's show of force. In fact, long-range policies are in short supply in this Administration. Reagan swats a fly here or a gnat there while ignoring the insects' breeding areas. Says the President's former National Security Adviser Robert McFarlane of last week's action: "I don't see the kind of strategic framework that would make it a new phase. It is more a case of reacting to events."

Tweaking Gaddafi without defanging him may be like "wounding a dangerous animal," says Edward Luttwak, an analyst at Georgetown University's Center for Strategic and International Studies. Even a former foreign policy adviser to President Reagan last week questioned the wisdom of sending in the Sixth Fleet. "It's all right to give Gaddafi a bloody nose," he said. "But if you do it without a game plan, what

does it get you? If there is now more terrorism aimed at Europeans and Americans, what have you won?"

In some ways Reagan has managed to break the post–Viet Nam syndrome that has paralyzed U.S. foreign policy. Yet he is hardly free of its shadow. With the significant exception of sending the Marines to Beirut on an ill-fated mission 3 years ago, Reagan has become the master of staging small shows of force, tidy little wars carefully calibrated to win public approval without costing too many American lives.

American ambivalence about its superpower mantle is illustrated by the fact that congressional doves, many of them fearful of being labeled "soft" because of their opposition to *contra* aid, rushed last week to applaud Reagan's easy victory in the Gulf of Sidra. Yet they shy away from the tougher issue: how to apply steady and vigilant force as part of a policy for dealing with Nicaragua. Smacking Gaddafi may be cathartic and quick. But if the U.S. is truly going to face its responsibilities as a superpower, it will have to find a way to grapple with threats that are far more difficult and dirty, especially those closer to home.

*Credit:* © 1986 TIME Inc. Reprinted by permission.

---

## DAVID L. BARNETT AND JOSEPH FROMM WITH BOB HORTON, ROBERT A. MANNING, AND JOSEPH P. SHAPIRO: REAGAN ADMINISTRATION'S MILITARY PLAN

*This newsmagazine report, too, was concerned with the long-term military plan that Reagan's administration might be organizing. Readers were obviously worried about military action that would commit troops in distant trouble spots.*

### U.S. News & World Report, 7 April 1986

President's use of arms: Warning to adversaries, reassurance to friends. It also reflects a more flexible pursuit of interests, applying both aid and diplomacy. By ordering U.S. forces into action in two of the world's hot spots in late March, Ronald Reagan sent a clear message to friend and foe: No longer paralyzed by memories of Vietnam, Washington is prepared to use military power when its interests are at risk.

The message was a warning to the Soviet Union's Mikhail Gorbachev as well as to Libya's Muammar Qadhafi and Nicaragua's Daniel Ortega. It was meant as reassurance to allies who respect the use of power. All now are on notice of new meaning behind Reagan's tough language and the vast military buildup during his Presidency.

But the policy evolving in recent months is even broader. The United States, its defenses bolstered and its economy strong, is beginning to assert interests more vigorously through non-military means as well. They range from pragmatic abandonment of old friends—such as Ferdinand Marcos in the Philippines—to pressure in the name of democracy against extremists of the right as well as the left.

The sharpest immediate message, of course, was to Qadhafi and Ortega. Qadhafi, after being pummeled by a carrier armada that he challenged, must reckon on retaliation against his homeland for any future terrorist acts against Americans. Nicaragua's Ortega, with U.S. helicopters ferrying Honduran troops to counter a Sandinista invasion, must recognize Reagan's resolve to neutralize his leftist government. Chances are now high that Congress will provide military aid to the contra forces trying to overthrow the Sandinistas.

The Soviet Union's Gorbachev, watching closely, cannot avoid the judgment that Reagan's interest in superpower summitry and arms control does not mean a softer line against Soviet expansionism.

There are clear risks in the President's more assertive posture. Qadhafi has vowed to retaliate for his humiliation. Several other Arab leaders could be goaded into supporting him. In Central America, the U.S. faces a greater likelihood that its troops could be drawn into conflict. With a few exceptions, such as Margaret Thatcher of Britain, European allies are reacting nervously to U.S. actions. While Moscow's first reactions were relatively mild, the possibility also grows that Soviet-U.S. relations will turn cold again.

But for now, the administration's thrusts against Libya and Nicaragua represented clear triumph. They followed a recent pattern that included—

- The dispatch of two warships loaded with sensitive electronic equipment through the Black Sea near the Soviet coast, asserting the right of passage. Moscow's reaction was angry, but not threatening.
- Staging an underground nuclear test and treating as propaganda a Soviet offer to end all testing. The administration also hinted that it may soon end compliance with the un-ratified SALT II Treaty because of Soviet violations.
- Ordering the expulsion of a third of the Soviet personnel at the United Nations in New York on the ground that they are engaged in espionage.

Meanwhile, the administration was probing at Soviet interests elsewhere. It pursued aid for Jonas Savimbi's guerrillas fighting the Marxist government in Angola, and increased covert support of tribesmen resisting the Soviet occupation of Afghanistan.

Former Secretary of State Alexander Haig sees a form of national recovery in the activity. "I think it's very clear," he said, "that the American malaise, which seemed to paralyze American foreign policy in the latter part of the '70s, has been transformed into an attitude in which we are more rather than less willing to assume the responsibilities of international leadership. Such leadership requires risk taking."

The degree of popular support for a more assertive and complex foreign policy is yet to be seen. A USA TODAY survey showed 67 percent of Americans backing a military counterstrike against Libya and 83 percent glad "the U.S.A. is standing up for rights around the world even if it means taking some military risks." But another poll indicated 53 percent are opposed to the campaign for more military aid to the Nicaraguan contra forces.

Reagan plainly hopes to gain wider understanding by emphasizing that he opposes extremists of whatever stripe. "The American people," he said in a recent message to Congress, "believe in human rights and oppose tyranny in whatever form, whether of the left or the right. We use our influence to encourage democratic change in careful ways that respect other countries' traditions and political realities."

As evidence, administration officials cite their role in helping to replace authoritarian regimes in the Philippines, Haiti, Guatemala and El Salvador. Now, pressure is being applied for reforms in Chile, South Africa and South Korea.

In Chile, U.S. Ambassador Harry Barnes has been marching, candle in hand, in human-rights rallies against the Pinochet regime. Such behavior would have been unthinkable not long ago.

Still, directly or indirectly, Reagan's policies are oriented to the East-West competition. Military moves above all are meant as a message to Moscow. Libya's Qadhafi, after all, gets billions of dollars' worth of military hardware from the Soviet Union. But the support of democracy anywhere counters Moscow's fondness for fishing in troubled waters. In that regard, the administration believes it has the Soviets on the run.

A high-ranking Reagan aide, though contending the administration hasn't changed its policies, says that the U.S. is more assertive now because Moscow is preoccupied with internal problems. Secretary of State George Shultz borrowed a phrase from Moscow recently to remark that the "correlation of forces" in the world now favors Washington.

Given that view, the administration seems to have concluded that no major concessions are needed to encourage summitry or an arms-control pact. By this argument Gorbachev, overextended abroad and in economic trouble at home, needs both more than Reagan does.

There is nothing foolhardy in the evolving policy. Recent shows of assertiveness have been on the fringes of Soviet expansionism—not where the Soviets could easily intervene.

Norman Podhoretz, editor of Commentary magazine, finds Reagan's policy too mild. Though Congress is partly to blame, he says, the President has not supported anti-Communist insurgencies "as consistently or as vigorously as I would like."

Others reflect doubts for different reasons. Zbigniew Brzezinski, national-security adviser during the Carter administration, questions whether military assertiveness is properly focused. "I am concerned that it not be overly dissipated on sideshows," he says. "I think Libya is a sideshow."

Reagan obviously would not agree. Well into his second term, he appears resolved to achieve the foreign-policy successes that eluded him earlier. Having used his power successfully, it is all but certain that he will have to do so again—perhaps in Central America, perhaps elsewhere. How well he manages the challenge may yet be the primary measure of his Presidency.

## BOYD FRANCE AND BILL JAVETSKI: "MEASURING THE IMPACT OF REAGAN'S SHOWDOWNS ABROAD"

*This newsmagazine's report not only focused on the political implications of military maneuvers for relations with U.S. allies, but also seemed to urge the president on to some finality that came very close to justifying assassinations of those leaders Americans opposed.*

*Business Week*, 7 April 1986

The attack on Libyan ships and installations in the Gulf of Sidra is the latest example of what has become a pattern in President Reagan's foreign policy—low-risk but highly visible military ventures that are wildly popular at home. Reagan sent a carrier task force to challenge Libyan strongman Muammer Qadaffi's claim to sovereignty over the gulf, a claim unsupported by international law or custom and unrecognized by any major nation. And as in similar previous ventures, where the Administration overthrew a leftist regime in Grenada in 1983 and seized an airline carrying Arab terrorists last year, moving against the detested Qadaffi drew near-unanimous political support.

The impact in the Middle East and among U.S. allies is less certain. In moderate Arab governments, many would be privately pleased to see Qadaffi taken down a notch. But the Arab man in the street instinctively sides with Qadaffi as an Arab brother. "If anything, we have given Qadaffi a new lease on life at home and in the Arab world," says Joyce R. Starr, a Middle East expert at the Center for Strategic & International Studies at Georgetown University. "Unless we take Qadaffi out, almost anything we do is likely to strengthen him." In Europe, British Prime Minister Margaret Thatcher and the Bonn government backed Reagan's move, but Italian Prime Minister Bettino Craxi rebuked the U.S. and Qadaffi for using "military means." The Soviets, who were briefed on U.S. plans in advance, decried the action but made no move against it.

### STRAINED RELATIONS

Yet the net result of the Libyan fracas is likely to be little basic international political change. In fact, few of Reagan's foreign policy initiatives in his five years as President have produced major results. Reagan's preference seems instead to be for carefully circumscribed ventures such as the invasion of Grenada. The toppling of leftist rule on that small island by a U.S. task force enabled the President to proclaim that the U.S. was once again "standing tall." Last year, when the Administration orchestrated the capture of terrorists aboard an Egyptian airliner, the action displayed U.S. technical and management prowess, although it strained relations with Italy and Egypt.

Such an approach backfired, though, with the attempt to influence Lebanon's civil war by sending a token contingent of marines and putting U.S. military might on display by dispatching the battleship New Jersey to fire thunderous salvos from offshore. Instead of a low-risk operation, the intervention became costly when 241 marines were killed in their barracks by a suicide bomber. Rather than raising the ante by sending more forces, Reagan pulled out.

But the Reagan foreign policy venture that is most divisive at home is in Central America. As the carefully staged challenge to Qadaffi got under way, a battle flared on the Honduran-Nicaraguan border between U.S.-supported contras and Nicaraguan troops. The fighting should help Reagan get Congress to give more aid to the contras. Such aid is another low-cost attempt by Reagan to deal with a foreign problem—in this case one that he depicts as a Soviet threat to the U.S. But Reagan's foreign policy dilemma, says William B. Quandt, a Middle East expert at Washington's Brookings Institution, is that the Administration feels it must oversell its objectives to get public support. It thus creates, in Quandt's view, a "huge gap" between its declared perceptions of threats to our national security and what it is willing to do about them.

The challenge to Qadaffi, advocates argue, is an important symbolic projection of U.S. power. To build support among allies on major issues, from arms control to East-West relations, Reagan will need to show how U.S. power and commitment will be matched to broader common policy goals.

## ROBERT MacNEIL, JIM LEHRER, CHARLES REDMAN, AND RICHARD VAUGHN: "NEWS SUMMARY"—GULF OF SIDRA ATTACK, RECENT TERRORIST ATTACKS

*The television reports of action in Libya were often coupled with other reports of casualties. This story of the U.S. military's Gulf of Sidra strike against Libya was placed in counterpoint to the reports of deaths at the hands of terrorist attacks around the world and in the context of America's ongoing efforts to find peaceful settlements in areas of continued conflict.*

*MacNeil/Lehrer NewsHour* (PBS), Transcript 2747, 8 April 1986

JIM LEHRER: West German authorities today named a Libyan diplomat as the leading suspect in the weekend disco bombing that killed two people and injured 200. Authorities in Bonn said he was assigned to the Libyan Embassy, called a People's Bureau, in East Berlin. They identified him as 47-year-old El-Amin Abdullah El-Amin. They said a manhunt had been launched for him. In Washington, State Department spokesman Charles Redman also spoke today about Libya's People's Bureaus.

CHARLES REDMAN, State Department spokesman: All I'm saying is that there's a very intensive, active investigation, which is under way, that we're working closely with the German officials, that on the question of People's Bureaus in a more generic sense, that's obviously a matter of concern. Where there are indications or reasons to believe that the Libyan People's Bureaus are involved in actual or potential terrorist activities, it is certainly to the advantage of the host government as well as others to take appropriate action to deal with those who pose such terrorist threats.

LEHRER: The Libyan foreign minister said in an interview today 56 Libyans died in the Gulf of Sidra confrontation with the United States. The official was quoted in an Egyptian newspaper. He said the Libyans were killed by U.S. bombing raids on patrol boats and a missile site.

MacNEIL: Two bombings made news in widely separated places. In Bangkok, Thailand, a powerful bomb went off in the parking lot of a hotel which Defense Secretary Wein-

berger was due to visit 90 minutes later. The bomb wounded three people. Thai officials were not sure whether it was linked to Weinberger's visit.

In the Lebanese port city of Junieh, a car bomb exploded at lunch hour, killing at least 10 people and injuring more than 100. We have a report by Richard Vaughn of Worldwide Television News.

RICHARD VAUGHN, Worldwide Television News *[voiceover]*: For the militiamen of President Amin Gemayel the explosion was much too close for comfort. Offices of Gemayel's Phalange Party are located only 100 meters from the site of the blast. It happened in the Christian enclave of Junieh, the latest sign of the tension that's rising between Gemayel's Phalangists and rival Christian groups determined to dislodge the embattled Lebanese president once and for all. Some Christians and the Syrians, too, are angry with Gemayel for rejecting a Syrian-sponsored peace accord. The bloody struggle for power among the Christians is heightening fears that fullscale civil war is about to erupt.

MacNEIL: Vice President George Bush said today that the U.S. is pursuing a new initiative towards a Middle East peace settlement. Richard Murphy, the State Department's top Middle East troubleshooter, split off from Bush's tour of Arab states to go to Egypt and Israel. Murphy said, "We're looking for a way to restore the momentum in the peace process."

*Credit:* Reprinted with permission from MacNeil-Lehrer Productions.

## KEVIN COSTELLOE: LIBYA REPORTEDLY SENDS FOREIGNERS TO BASES, OIL FIELDS, AND OTHER POSSIBLE U.S. TARGETS

*This wire service report out of Tripoli would have been widely read because it was one of just a handful of American reporters' stories available to Western media from Libya's capital.*

Associated Press, 13 April 1986

TRIPOLI, Libya: Col. Moammar Khadafy's government claimed Sunday it had moved foreign workers, including U.S.

citizens, to oil fields in the desert and army bases purportedly targeted for attack by American forces.

But a Western diplomat told The Associated Press he had spoken to several representatives of his country in Libya, and "none of them reported any such incident." He spoke on condition he not be identified by name or country.

Tripoli has remained quiet for days, and there were no signs Sunday of any military preparations.

The U.S. 6th Fleet, meanwhile, was poised in the Mediterranean off Libya, awaiting President Reagan's decision on a possible strike in retaliation for Khadafy's reputed support of international terrorism.

(In a report monitored in London, the official Libyan news agency JANA carried a Foreign Ministry statement reiterating Libya's determination to strike back if attacked.

("Libya does not want aggression and does not work to cause it . . . ," the statement said. "However, if aggression is carried out against it, it will retaliate forcefully against all targets which constitute rear bases for the aggression.

(The statement did not say what was meant by rear bases, but Khadafy has threatened targets in southern Europe, mentioning Spain and Italy, in the event of a U.S. military move.)

Reagan and Chancellor Helmut Kohl of West Germany have said Libya is a prime suspect in the April 5 bombing of a West Berlin discotheque that was a gathering place for U.S. troops stationed in West Germany.

A U.S. Army sergeant and a Turkish woman died in the blast, and 230 people were injured, including 63 Americans. Reagan said he would consider a retaliatory strike if evidence proved Khadafy was behind the bombing.

(In New York, *Newsweek* magazine said it had obtained U.S. intelligence reports showing Khadafy has stepped up surveillance of American citizens, government posts and commercial interests abroad.

(The magazine said the reports also indicate Libya has targeted U.S. embassies in NATO countries and 10 African nations as well as commercial interests in Europe and the Middle East for terrorist attacks.

(The reports also reveal that Khadafy is prepared to offer $100 million for the six Americans being held hostage in Lebanon by Islamic radicals, said the magazine.)

A statement released by a Libyan Information Department official, who refused to be identified, said: "Foreign workers have been forced to live in them (oil fields), taking into account that the majority are Americans."

Diplomats and business people estimate 800 Americans still live in Libya, including executives, oil field workers and about 100 American women married to Libyans.

Reagan ordered all Americans out under risk of a 10-year prison sentence and cut all U.S. economic ties with Libya after terrorists attacked the Rome and Vienna airports Dec. 27, killing 20 people, including five Americans.

The United States blamed Palestinian terrorist Abu Nidal, whose real name is Sabry al-Banna, of carrying out the attacks and accused Khadafy of harboring him.

Other Westerners in Libya include Europeans. The British community, for example, is estimated at 5,000.

Hundreds of foreign workers already live in the desert oil fields, often on rotating shifts lasting about one month.

Oil is Libya's largest single source of income, although Western analysts say revenues plunged from $22 billion in 1984 to about $8 billion in 1985.

The Western diplomat told the AP only five major docks are used to load oil on tankers, so there would be no need for U.S. warplanes to hit the widely scattered oil fields.

"The Americans could take out the jetties' loading points, and that would stop the oil flow," the diplomat said.

The Libyan statement also said: "The military camps have been handed over to foreigners to repair them and to use them to live there. Foreign workers have been moved to army camps.

"Libya has got information that America is going to attack several army camps and oil fields and petrochemical companies," the statement said.

The statement said the moves to the oil fields and military bases took place Saturday, and the army has been moved to undisclosed locations.

---

## TIMES WIRE SERVICES: "COMMON MARKET IMPOSES CURBS ON LIBYAN DIPLOMATS; PLEADS FOR RESTRAINT ON 'ALL SIDES' "

---

*While all sides seemed to be praying for peace, the Reagan administration had already given the order for an air strike that was in progress as this story was published.*

*Los Angeles Times*, 14 April 1986

THE HAGUE: The 12 Common Market countries today imposed diplomatic sanctions against Libya, including reductions in embassy staff levels and tighter visa requirements—

but they rejected imposing economic sanctions against Tripoli and urged U.S. military restraint.

The Common Market foreign ministers, after meeting for

four hours in an emergency session, also pledged to work against all governments that support terrorism.

In Washington, U.S. officials who would comment only on the basis of anonymity gave a tepid welcome to the Common Market's moves.

"These are reasonably solid steps," one official said.

"Obviously there has been some movement and that's a good sign," said another.

But the officials said the moves would not satisfy the Reagan Administration entirely.

## "GLASS HALF-EMPTY"

"I'd say this was a glass half-empty rather than half-full," one official said.

West German Foreign Minister Hans-Dietrich Genscher was to arrive in Washington late today and present the position taken by the 12 European Community ministers to President Reagan, a West German spokesman said.

A communiqué issued after the European meeting, which was convened to deal with the U.S.-Libya crisis, called for "restrictions on the freedom of movement of diplomatic and consular personnel; reduction of the staff of diplomatic and consular missions, (and) stricter visa requirements and procedures" for Libyan nationals.

Although rejecting calls for economic sanctions against Libya, the foreign ministers reaffirmed a Jan. 27 ban on arms sales to countries supporting terrorism, specifying that such a ban applies to Libya.

In an obvious reference to the threat of a military confrontation in the Mediterranean, the nations said that "in order to enable the achievement of a political solution, avoid-

ing further escalation of military tension in the region, with all the inherent dangers, the 12 underline the need for restraint on all sides."

## U.S. FLOTILLA ON ALERT

A flotilla of U.S. air and naval forces is assembled in the Mediterranean on alert for possible action against Libya, which the United States has blamed for fostering terrorism and has labeled a prime suspect in the April 5 bombing of a West Berlin discotheque frequented by U.S. troops.

As current head of the Common Market, the Dutch called the meeting in response to appeals from Spain and Italy, which have been threatened by Libya with reprisals if U.S. forces attack.

Before the start of the Common Market meeting, sources in several delegations said the Europeans would try to steer the United States away from attacking the North African nation. The sources all spoke on condition of anonymity.

"We want to do everything we can to avoid a military escalation," an aide to Genscher said.

## NO CHANGE OF POLICY

Meanwhile, French President François Mitterrand told U.S. Special Envoy Vernon Walters today that France is ready to fight terrorism but will not change its policy toward Libya.

A statement issued after Walters' 45-minute meeting with Mitterrand at the Elysée Palace said Mitterrand "reaffirmed his determination and that of France to continue to fight without flagging against terrorism."

*Credit*: Copyright © 1986, Los Angeles Times. Reprinted with permission.

---

## AN ANONYMOUS REPORT: WASHINGTON BRIEFING ON LIBYAN SITUATION

---

*This wire service report simply told what had been provided to the press corps in Washington, D.C. It stuck to the facts as they were presented, with no outside confirmation because none was yet available.*

### United Press International, 14 April 1986

WASHINGTON: Secretary of State George Shultz said Monday night "an escalation" of terrorist violence by Libyan leader Moammar Khadafy forced President Reagan to decide "it was time to act and so he did."

"The action was proportionate to the sustained, clear, continuing and widespread use of terror against Americans and others by Khadafy's Libya," Shultz said.

The secretary of state made his comments at a nationally broadcast briefing with Defense Secretary Caspar Weinberger after President Reagan, reading his own statement from the Oval Office, confirmed that U.S. warplanes had attacked Libya, including the capital city of Tripoli, earlier Monday night in retaliation for a terrorist bombing that killed an American GI.

Weinberger said U.S. planes from the aircraft carriers America and Coral Sea struck in Libya's eastern zone and 18 F-111s dropped 500-pound and 2,000-pound laser-guided weapons and precision-guided bombs.

He said all of the F-111s except one were accounted for. Asked if he had information that that plane had been shot down, he said only that it had not been heard from.

It was the second time in less than a month that U.S. warplanes have attacked targets in Libya. On March 24, U.S. jets bombed a Soviet-built anti-aircraft missile base. Reagan ordered that attack after Libyan missiles were fired at U.S. jets flying over the disputed Gulf of Sidra, crossing Khadafy's so-called line of death.

Reagan made the decision to wage the strike on Libyan cities, including Tripoli and Benghazi, after weeks of gathering evidence linking Khadafy to the bombing of a West Berlin night club that killed one American serviceman and a Turkish woman and wounded 240 others.

"Self-defense is not only our right," Reagan said. "It is our duty."

Weinberger said the attacks went "precisely as planned." He said U.S. troops showed "very great skill—both navigational and organization of attack. All the targets were terrorist related," he said.

The defense secretary said that until the planes returned to their bases—expected about 2 a.m. EST—he would not be able to give an accurate assessment of the bombing damage to the Libyan targets, which he said included Khadafy's headquarters near Tripoli.

"The targets were the military airport near Tripoli, a training area including a maritime training unit for terrorists, and (an) air base for which suppressive air activities would be launched," Weinberger said.

"All of the Navy planes have returned without casualty. All of the F-111s are accounted for except one."

"We have no idea that we killed anybody," Weinberger said, as well as no indication that the F-111 unaccounted for went down.

Reagan said U.S. forces had "succeeded in their mission" against Libyan targets and that intelligence information leading to the U.S. attack was "exact, precise (and) irrefutable" that Libya was responsible for the bombing of the discoteque in Berlin.

"I made it clear we would retaliate if there was evidence presented that Libya was responsible. This monstrous brutality is but the latest evidence in the Khadafy regime," Reagan said.

Said Shultz: "It's not a question of settling scores, it's a question of acting against terrorism.

"That is the primary objective: To defend ourselves in the immediate and projectively.

"All of our embassies are on alert of course," Shultz said. "We have reports and indications of Libyan intention to attack up to 30 of our embassies. When I say Khadafy's planning is widespread . . . I think the evidence bears this out."

Reagan had said U.S. sources had "solid evidence about other attacks Khadafy" had planned against U.S. targets worldwide.

Shultz also said the United States didn't "have any real damage assessment as yet."

"We seek to reduce his capability of carrying on terrorist acts," Shultz said. "And I'm sure to some degree that was done. And we also have registered the point with him and with other Libyans that they will pay a price—that there is a cost—to engaging in terrorism around the world. So they know that."

Reagan said, "What is clear is that the United States will take military action as is needed."

"We have done what we had to do," the president said. "If necessary we shall do it again."

*Credit*: Reprinted by permission of UPI.

## AN ANONYMOUS REPORT: U.S. ENVOY WALTERS MEETS WITH FRENCH PRESIDENT MITTERRAND ON U.S.-LIBYAN SITUATION

*This wire service report out of Paris is an indication of just how much the U.S. administration was willing to misinform the media about what was already in progress. In response to a direct question about military action, Vernon Walters was dismissive and derisive.*

### Associated Press, 14 April 1986

PARIS: U.S. special envoy Vernon Walters today met with President François Mitterrand in another attempt to rally European support for the Reagan administration's policy toward Libya.

Walters, the U.S. ambassador to the United Nations, was asked as he left the Elysée Palace if the subject of military action against Libya was discussed. "It's a far-fetched suggestion you make," he responded.

Walters would only say he and Mitterrand discussed during the 45-minute meeting "problems which interest France and the United States. We perhaps (also) discussed other things outside the European or African geographic region."

A communiqué issued by the presidential palace said the two men "examined the current situation in the Mediterranean" and that Mitterrand reaffirmed France's intention to combat terrorism.

The U.S. 6th Fleet has been cruising the Mediterranean, awaiting President Reagan's decision on whether to launch a military strike in retaliation for Libyan leader Col. Moammar Khadafy's alleged support of international terrorism.

Reagan has branded Libya a prime suspect in the April 5 bombing of a West Berlin discotheque frequented by U.S. troops. A U.S. Army sergeant and a Turkish woman died in the blast, and 230 people were injured, including 63 Americans.

Walters met Sunday with Prime Minister Jacques Chirac after arriving from the West German capital of Bonn, where he held talks with Chancellor Helmut Kohl and Foreign Minister Hans-Dietrich Genscher.

After his meeting with Walters, Genscher was quoted as saying that there was no danger of a military clash between the United States and Libya.

Reagan has said he would consider a retaliatory strike if evidence proved Khadafy was behind the bombing.

Walters met Saturday with Prime Minister Margaret Thatcher in London. He is expected to go to Italy later for meetings with Italian officials.

A U.S. spokesman in Bonn said Walters' mission was similar to that of Deputy Secretary of State John Whitehead, who visited Bonn and other European capitals in January seeking support for U.S. economic sanctions against Libya.

Those sanctions were imposed after the Dec. 27 terrorist attacks at the Rome and Vienna airports that left 20 dead. The United States blamed the attacks on the renegade Palestinian faction led by Abu Nidal, which is believed linked to Libya.

---

## TIM AHERN: CONGRESSIONAL RESPONSE TO U.S. RAID ON LIBYA

---

*This report on the congressional attitude response after the air raid had been ordered and executed was part of a series of articles that highlighted the displeasure by some members about their exclusion from the rationale and planning of the strike.*

### Associated Press, 15 April 1986

WASHINGTON: Senate Majority Leader Bob Dole said today he thought that President Reagan had complied with the War Powers Act when he notified congressional leaders about the U.S. attack on Libya a few hours before American bombers struck.

"I think the president complied with the act," Dole, R-Kan., told reporters.

Besides, said Dole, the question of legality "isn't the important issue. I think the issue is whether we're going to deter terrorism, not whether some congressman is going to be called."

The 1973 War Powers Act, passed in the wake of the Vietnam War after congressional concerns about presidential use of American troops, requires the White House to consult with Congress within 48 hours after U.S. forces are put into a situation where they may become engaged in hostilities.

In addition, the law requires that U.S. troops be withdrawn within 60 days if Congress doesn't declare war.

Dole was one of about 10 lawmakers who attended a secret briefing at the White House late Monday afternoon by the president and top administration officials.

During the two-hour meeting, Sen. Robert Byrd, D-W.Va., said he and other legislators had raised questions about compliance with the War Powers Act.

Asked about consultation with Congress under the War Powers Act, Byrd said, "This was not consultation, it was notification. . . . We were told of a decision that already had been made.

"I'm not going to say the action violated the War Powers Act. . . . But I did urge those (administration officials) who were there that from here on out to be sure they observe the requirements of the War Powers Act."

Sen. Strom Thurmond, R-S.C., who also attended the administration briefing, said requirements of the act had been met. "Sometimes when you have to strike you just can't wait," he said.

Some legislators, including Rep. Dante Fascell, D-Fla., chairman of the House Armed Services Committee, complained last month that Reagan had not complied with the War Powers Act when U.S. Navy ships fired at Libyan naval vessels and missile sites.

While trying to comply with the War Powers Act, the Reagan administration also tried to justify its strike under international law.

Both Reagan and Secretary of State George Shultz said the United States was operating under Article 51 of the United Nations charter.

That provision outlines the use of force in international relations and provides that countries can act in self-defense. But it also requires that any force must be proportional to the offense that preceded it.

Shultz, in a Jan. 15 speech at National Defense University, said that under international law, "a nation attacked by terrorists is permitted to use force to prevent or pre-empt future attacks, to seize terrorists or to rescue its citizens, when no other means is available."

Both Reagan and Shultz said the U.S. strikes were not retaliation, which is not permitted under the U.N. charter. Instead, they said, the United States had evidence that the April 5 bombing of a West Berlin disco was part of a Libyan plot to hurt the United States by attacking American citizens.

Shultz called the U.S. attacks a "proportionate" and "measured" response.

But Prof. W. Thomas Mallison, director of the international law program at the George Washington University law school, took issue today with the administration's legal justification.

"It's not justified under article 51," he said. "First of all, it is not proportional. The article requires that the response be in relation to the original attack and this was all out of proportion to anything that Libya may have done to the United States."

---

# ROBERT H. REID: WESTERNERS IN LIBYA WARNED TO STAY INDOORS; QADDAFI TOURS HOSPITAL

*While this report probably brought no surprising news, it was one of just a few that came out of the Libyan capital after the raid.*

Associated Press, 17 April 1986

TRIPOLI, Libya: Embassies warned Westerners to stay off Tripoli's streets Thursday as Arab anger seethed over the U.S. bombing raid and explosions and anti-aircraft fire again echoed through the city.

Some nervous foreigners sought a way out of this isolated country to escape the confrontation between the United States and Libyan leader Col. Moammar Khadafy. But land borders were closed and the airport was largely inactive.

The Libyan capital appeared calm through most of the day. But several heavy, unexplained explosions rocked Tripoli Thursday afternoon, and after nightfall the racket of anti-aircraft guns could be heard—for the third straight night following Tuesday's pre-dawn U.S. air raids.

Streams of tracer rounds lit the sky as guns fired for several minutes starting about 9 p.m. (2 p.m. EST). It was not clear what they were firing at, and there was no indication of bombing raids.

Khadafy, who emerged from two days' seclusion Wednesday to denounce President Reagan in a televised speech, was shown on Libyan TV again Thursday night as he visited a Tripoli hospital, touring the wards and shaking hands with bandaged victims of the American attack.

"Thank God, you're all right," one woman said to Khadafy as she struggled to rise from her bed.

Hospital workers and patients cheered and chanted, at one point shouting, "Reagan is the killer of children!"

Khadafy's 15-month-old adopted daughter was reported killed and two small sons were reported injured in the American assault. Western diplomats estimated the attack left at least 100 people dead in Tripoli alone. The eastern city of Benghazi also was hit, but casualties there could not be learned.

The U.S. administration said it ordered the military action as both a retaliatory and pre-emptive blow against what it says is Libyan-sponsored international terrorism.

Libyans tried to return life to normal in the city Thursday. Schools and banks reopened and many shops raised their shutters for the first time since the raid.

Long lines formed at bread stores as Libyans stocked up on food and other essentials that have been in short supply since the raid.

An Italian diplomat, speaking on condition of anonymity, said no evacuation was being organized, "but it's obvious some women who have been subjected to strain and tension want to leave." Among them was the wife of an Italian consular official who suffered facial cuts during the U.S. air raids.

About 8,000 Italian citizens are in Libya, the largest foreign contingent among some 18,000 Westerners who work in the oil and construction industries here.

Embassies of several other countries, including Belgium, Spain and Canada, reported that no full-scale evacuation was in the works, but they said contingency plans had been prepared in case the situation here deteriorates.

"We advise people just to stay put and wait, not to go outside," said an official at the Belgian Embassy. "There is no evacuation, not for the time being."

The Belgian Embassy looks after the interests of the estimated 800 Americans still living in Libya despite President Reagan's previous order that they leave by last Feb. 1.

Canadian Vice Consul Michel Tessier said about one-third of the 1,000 Canadians working in Libya had expressed an interest in leaving.

A British diplomat, who said the 5,000 Britons in Libya were also being advised to stay indoors, said an evacuation would be difficult to arrange because Libya's borders with its north African neighbors Egypt and Tunisia have been closed.

Libyan officials said Tripoli Airport had reopened Thursday for both international and domestic flights. But foreign airlines canceled Thursday's flights, saying they would consider resuming service after studying the situation. The airport's military section was among the targets of the U.S. air raids.

A Boeing 727 of the Yugoslav airline JAT with 12 passengers aboard was refused landing permission in Tripoli Thursday and returned to Belgrade. Libyan authorities said the Tripoli airport had insufficient security because of war operations, the Yugoslav news agency reported.

An Air Malta flight to Tripoli was canceled Thursday while the plane was waiting to take off from the Mediterranean island of Malta. But a Libyan airliner did leave Tripoli Thursday evening for Rome.

Roadblocks were removed Thursday from around Tripoli's Azziziyah barracks, where Khadafy maintains a residence and his headquarters. Gunfire erupted around the compound Wednesday, but Libyan officials insisted troops were firing at a U.S. reconnaissance plane.

Libyan officials relaxed restrictions on movements by foreign journalists and permitted them to move about the city without official escort.

In related developments:

Terrorists retaliated for the U.S. air strike in several capitals, killing three kidnapped Britons in Lebanon, trying and failing to place a bomb aboard an Israeli El Al jetliner in London, and hurling a firebomb at the U.S. Marine embassy guard quarters in Tunis. Anti-American protesters rallied in cities around the world.

European Common Market foreign ministers, meeting in Paris, urged "utmost restraint" on both the United States and Libya and said they would launch a worldwide diplomatic effort to find solutions to terrorism.

In Moscow, the Soviet government formally reasserted its right to sea and air passage near Soviet-aligned Libya, possibly indicating it intends to move naval vessels or other military equipment into the area.

In the face of violent repercussions from the air attack, the Reagan administration reiterated its belief that it was "absolutely the right thing to do."

The Pentagon officially declared the two crewmen from an Air Force F-111 bomber lost in the raid as killed in action. Pentagon officials said it had not been determined whether the plane was hit by a Libyan missile.

---

## AN ANONYMOUS REPORT: TRIPOLI AIR STRIKE PROMPTS U.S. SECURITY PRECAUTIONS

---

*The fears of reprisal expressed by Americans before the air strike on Tripoli were evident in this report as security preparedness increased everywhere.*

### Associated Press, 17 April 1986

WASHINGTON: The Army has clamped a nighttime lid on its personnel in West Germany, imposing a midnight to 5 A.M. curfew in five large American military communities in a move aimed at improving security against terrorism.

Maj. Phil Soucy, an Army spokesman at the Pentagon, said he could provide few details of the order. But he said the curfew has been established in the Munich, Nuremberg, Frankfurt, Darmstadt and Heidelberg housing areas.

"This was a decision made at the command level, not at the Pentagon," said Soucy. "I can confirm that a curfew directive has been issued for those five areas. I don't know how long it might be in place."

The move follows the April 5 terrorist bombing of a West Berlin discotheque frequented by Americans. After this week's American air raid on Libya, U.S. installations and embassies worldwide were put on high alert.

About 250,000 U.S. troops are based in West Germany.

Stars and Stripes, the unofficial newspaper for the U.S. armed forces overseas, disclosed the curfew orders. Army officials at the Army's European headquarters in Heidelberg refused to confirm or deny the report, saying they could not discuss security matters.

Stars and Stripes said the order was contained in a letter distributed by the Munich deputy community commander.

"These security measures will cause a great deal of inconvenience; however, they are appropriate and necessary for the protection of our community," the paper quoted the letter as saying.

The Stars and Stripes said military authorities had canceled games in the finals of the Army's basketball league, which were scheduled for Wednesday night. It said the Army's Information, Tours and Travel offices had been directed to cancel tours through Sunday.

"U.S. personnel are again strongly encouraged to avoid bars, restaurants and other off-post establishments frequented by large groups of Americans," the newspaper quoted the letter as saying.

"Group activities involving large numbers of personnel that are planned to take place in uncontrolled areas should be rescheduled or canceled," the letter was quoted as saying.

Stepped-up security in the past 10 days has caused long backups of U.S. soldiers, their dependents or other civilians seeking to enter American installations in Western Europe.

Military police have taken to opening car hoods and engine compartments, rolling mirrors under vehicles in search of bombs, and elaborately examining identity cards.

# DON OBERDORFER: NEWS ANALYSIS—THREE SCENARIOS OF MILITARY CONFRONTATION IN LIBYAN DISPUTE

*This front-page story provided more analysis than news, which was what the news organizations were forced to do in the absence of on-site reporting in Libya and informative White House briefings.*

*Washington Post*, 20 April 1986

The United States and Libya, as the result of developments in the past month, are fighting an undeclared but increasingly violent war that administration officials say has three possible results.

Under the best outcome from the U.S. perspective, Libyan leader Muammar Qaddafi will be killed or ousted, with his successors in Tripoli abandoning the tactics of international terror.

A more guarded prospect envisions Qaddafi alive and in power, but his terrorism thwarted by western vigilance and economic pressures.

The third and most disturbing prospect is the reason much of the world now has a first-class case of the jitters: the spiral of violence increases, with Qaddafi-inspired terrorist attacks continuing on Americans and with President Reagan retaliating with increasingly forceful bombardments, blockades or even an invasion of Libya.

Thus far, the world's newest and perhaps most dangerous war has been conducted on one side by terrorists with 10-pound packages of plastic explosives and on the other by waves of U.S. warplanes, which last week bombarded Tripoli and Benghazi with more than 100 tons of bombs and missiles.

The disparity in military means is only one of many strange aspects of hostilities between the United States and a Third World desert country 5,000 miles away that is peripheral to any U.S. national interest except one: the security and safety of American citizens, diplomats and military personnel.

"A great power can't easily go to war with a small power," said retired general Bruce Palmer, former U.S. Army vice chief of staff and a historian of the Vietnam war. Last week's bombing of Libya, Palmer said, "is reminiscent of how we tried to punish Hanoi and make them cease and desist" guerrilla warfare and other attacks in South Vietnam through carefully calibrated U.S. bombing. "I thought we'd learned our lesson, but obviously we didn't," he said.

The war was triggered, so far as Libya was concerned, by a March 24 clash arising from U.S. naval exercises in nearby international waters, which Libya adamantly claims. In the face of a massive and calculated show of U.S. military power, Libya launched antiaircraft missiles and patrol boats. U.S. forces attacked the missile sites and sank the boats.

For the United States, the causus belli was a coded message from Tripoli March 25 authorizing Libyan diplomatic missions around the world to mount attacks on Americans. Qaddafi virtually announced his intentions that day in Tripoli when he

proclaimed, "It is a time for confrontation—for war. . . . If they [U.S. officials] want to expand the struggle, we will carry it all over the world."

The March 25 secret message was the first time, according to U.S. officials, that Qaddafi had issued a general order through Libyan diplomats to attack Americans. It drew an immediate response from the State Department, which began consulting other governments quietly and announced March 26 that Libyan agents were conducting surveillance against "American installations and interests around the world" in ways which suggested "that Americans are targeted for attacks."

When that March 25 Libyan message and follow-up instructions, which the administration says were intercepted, were translated into death and injury of U.S. service personnel in a West Berlin discotheque April 5, Reagan decided to retaliate with U.S. warplanes.

A crucial point in the April 14 U.S. bombing raid was the declaration by Reagan that "if necessary, we shall do it again." Thus last week's U.S. raid could well be not an isolated episode but the beginning of a long confrontation.

The U.S. military action last week has some elements in common with previous American experience, including U.S. raids on Libya at the time of the Barbary pirates in the early 1800s, U.S. retaliatory bombing of North Vietnam in the early phase of the Vietnam war and U.S. ground combat action based in part on the protection of American citizens in the Dominican Republic in 1965 and Grenada in 1983.

However, the current U.S. conflict is different in important respects from all earlier models, which makes them of little use to officials studying the three major near-term possibilities.

The early overthrow, assassination or death of Qaddafi and his lieutenants in U.S. military raids, leading to a reversal of his policies, would be a resounding defeat for state-sponsored terrorism. In the administration view this would have major impact, especially in the Middle East, and bring domestic and international political gains across a broad front similar to those arising from Grenada several years ago.

A clear if less dramatic success would be the frustration of Libyan-sponsored terrorism through heightened security measures, improved intelligence and increasingly tough economic and political sanctions by a united western alliance.

Administration officials said that if such a combination of measures can be achieved with currently reluctant allies, it might bring a change in operational policy, though not a change of heart by Qaddafi.

Under the third and darkest scenario, however, a continuation of dramatic Libyan-sponsored attacks on U.S. targets would lead to more extensive American bombing raids or other U.S. military actions, such as a naval blockade of Libya or use of U.S. or allied ground troops. Such a deepening struggle has the potential for enflaming radical states and splinter groups to new acts of terrorism. If Americans are harmed by such acts, the Reagan administration would find itself facing yet another series of questions about how to respond appropriately.

This "worst case" possibility for the Libya conflict could produce increasingly serious disputes within the Atlantic alliance, heightened political tension and potential military tension with the Soviet Union and increased instability and disaffection from the United States in moderate Arab states and other Third World nations. As military action and reaction continue, public support in the United States for administration policy toward Libya could erode.

Notably absent from the present conflict is diplomatic contact with Libya in search of a settlement of differences, despite or perhaps due to the fact that Secretary of State George P. Shultz has taken a dominant role in fashioning U.S. policy. The Reagan administration withdrew all U.S. diplomats from Libya, ejected Libyan diplomats from Washington and has rejected overtures for contact with Qaddafi. The U.S. ambassador to the Vatican, William A. Wilson, was reprimanded for holding unauthorized discussions with Libya in January.

In contrast to Reagan's words and deeds, President Jimmy Carter took a different approach when faced with intelligence reports in 1977 that Qaddafi had ordered the assassination of the U.S. ambassador to Egypt, Hermann F. Eilts. Carter notified the Libyan leader through diplomatic channels that the plot had been discovered and that Qaddafi would be held "personally responsible" if Eilts were harmed. Eilts, now a professor at Boston University, said last week that one "hit team" was arrested in Egypt and Qaddafi is believed to have recalled another group and to have dropped the assassination plan. At Carter's insistence, Eilts said, the episode was not made public and came to light years later.

In terms of military muscle and economic resources, there is no comparison between the United States and Libya, a backward if oil-rich nation of 3 million. As the United States learned in earlier conflicts with Third World nations, however, usable and effective power cannot be determined by gross national product or numbers of aircraft carriers.

Barry M. Blechman of Georgetown's Center for Strategic and International Studies and author of a book on the uses of U.S. military force since World War II, said a forceful response to state-supported terrorism is justified and necessary but that "the way the United States went about it was quite odd."

Blechman noted that two carrier task forces, which the Pentagon said involved 17 naval vessels, 155 warplanes and 14,700 U.S. military personnel, were required to drop bombs on a limited number of Libyan targets. To employ such forces costing billions of dollars to retaliate against terrorists wielding 10-pound plastic bombs shows "the muscle-bound nature of the U.S. military," as well as "the U.S. inability to employ limited covert operations" and other alternative means, he said.

The rules of international conduct among nations changed several years ago "when normal, civilized states began to be subject to planned nonstate and state-supported terrorism," said former undersecretary of state Lawrence S. Eagleburger. He approved last week's U.S. action because "we tried for the better part of five years to get the European allies to agree on a set of nonmilitary sanctions and they wouldn't."

Eagleburger said he is concerned, though, about divisions in the Atlantic alliance and especially about U.S. frustration and anger with European countries that refused to cooperate.

Prof. Robert E. Osgood of Johns Hopkins School of Advanced International Studies, who was a senior State Department policy planner in 1983–85, said, "Terrorism directed at Americans abroad has become the functional equivalent of the aggression of states."

Osgood expressed concern that due to the disparity between the Libyan and U.S. means of waging war, "the United States has defined a battlefield in which the other side has most of the advantages."

The circumstances that gave rise to the U.S.-Libyan dispute and the actions taken in recent weeks were foreshadowed in striking fashion by a 1977 Rand Corp. report for the U.S. Air Force, "Military Implications of a Possible World Order Crisis in the 1980s."

The report by Rand analyst Guy J. Pauker outlined the possibility in the 1980s of "a breakdown of global order as a result of sharpening confrontation between the Third World and the industrial democracies" that could bring about increasingly nationalistic responses, lawlessness, chaos and anarchy in world affairs.

The United States would be expected to use its forces to protect others and its interests and citizens as order breaks down, Pauker wrote. Such a U.S. role would raise such difficult choices as whether the United States should "be prepared to project its power into all parts of the world where Americans may wish to travel, trade, study and engage in any other normal and peaceful activity. . . . If not, where should one draw the line?"

*Credit:* © **1986, The Washington Post, reprinted with permission.**

## RICHARD COHEN: INCIDENTAL VICTIMS OF AIR STRIKES

*This column reminded people that the strikes against other cities included harm to residents who were not the intended victims of military action, but the bystanders who bore the brunt, nonetheless.*

*Washington Post,* 22 April 1986

I remember a picture—an official White House photo taken in 1975 during the Ford administration. It showed Gerald Ford, Henry Kissinger, Donald Rumsfeld and two other officials, dressed in formal wear, exulting in news they had just received about the U.S. attempt to rescue sailors from the Mayaguez, a ship captured by communist Cambodians. The rescue operation, as it turned out, was something of a botch.

Hard to tell, though, from that picture. Kissinger is leaning back in a broad smile; Rumsfeld is beside himself with laughter; Ford, holding a pipe, is gesturing and laughing; and Robert McFarlane, then a staff member of the National Security Council, obviously thinking the matter not so funny is—pictures do not lie—smiling weakly. Since then he has learned to control himself.

But not the Reagan administration. For more than a week, it has been playing out its own version of that night. In exquisite bad taste, it has shown the same capacity to celebrate the odious. White House Chief of Staff Donald Regan even had a joke to tell. He said a friend of his had suggested new lyrics for the Marine Hymn: "From the Halls of Montezuma to what's left of Tripoli." It is reported that no one laughed.

As for the Defense Department, it has almost daily released information celebratory of the Libya strike. Unmentioned in all the hurrahs for this or that technical feat is the fact that civilians were killed, that some of the F-111 planes from England did not drop their bombs and one of them did not return. Two American servicemen were killed.

Americans have been treated to war as a televised video game. On the TV screen, we zoomed in on the coast and then swung toward the barracks where Muammar Qaddafi is said to live. We passed it once, and then doubled back at something like nine miles a second and—there!—released our bombs. In the corner of the screen, you could see nine little bombs, just like in the video games, and then—Kerpow!—you were told they hit. The president says we may have to play again.

And so we may. It may be our only recourse—something we have to do because we can think of nothing else to do, nothing that will work. There is no sense of obligation in some of the statements coming from the administration—no sense that we are off into something where the end is unknown. Already, hostages have been murdered in Lebanon; a U.S. diplomat shot in Khartoum; and the U.S. maneuvered into being seen by much of the Arab world as a colonialist-Zionist caricature. In attempting to control events, we just may have lost control of them. This is the way it is sometimes.

Official Washington, though, seems to have little appreciation of this. When it is not busy celebrating a military victory over a sandbox nation ruled by a kook in a doorman's uniform, it is thinking of ways to compound the problem by showing contempt for history. House and Senate Republicans, led by Senate Majority Leader Robert J. Dole, have introduced legislation that would give the president an even freer hand to respond to terrorist attacks. In an unintended assessment of their own worth, these Republicans would no longer require the president to consult with Congress before sending U.S. troops into a hostile situation.

But if the strike against Libya proves anything, it is how much the president ought to consult with Congress. With every day, the second-guessers are looking better and wiser. If ever there was a time to ensure the maximum participation of people with wisdom, experience and a different point of view, it is now. Instead, some members of Congress can hardly wait to give the president carte blanche, and some journalists seem to equate reflection and dissent with cowardice and virtual treason. The fashions of the 1950s are back in more than just clothing.

War is ugly and the celebration of it nearly as ugly. The raid on Libya was necessary, but it is hardly a cause for celebration, a reason to ignore history, or a rationale for squelching criticism. The United States did what it thought it had to do—just as it did in 1975 when 41 U.S. servicemen died attempting to rescue 39 captured seamen who may have been already freed. That incident should serve as a reminder. The first laugh is easy. The last one is best.

*Credit:* © **1986, The Washington Post, reprinted with permission.**

## MICHAEL R. GORDON: "BARRACKS OF QADDAFI'S GUARDS SURVIVED U.S. RAID"

*The careful release of information about the strike meant that little was known about any failures. The report here appeared ten days after the strike and came out of Washington, D.C., where apparently some less-than-outstanding results of the strike were leaked.*

*New York Times*, 24 April 1986

WASHINGTON: United States Air Force planes that attacked the Azziziya compound in Tripoli on April 15 failed to strike two buildings that serve as quarters for Col. Muammar el-Qaddafi's elite guard, military experts familiar with the Pentagon reports on the raid said today.

The buildings were among five that were targeted in the compound, the experts said. The F-111 planes that carried out the attack bombed two buildings and possibly a third, they said, including one that is used as a command and control center.

The Navy A-6's that attacked Benghazi at the same time may have had more success, the experts said. They said the planes appear to have struck the quarters for the elite guard at the alternative command post there.

Administration officials have suggested that by striking at Colonel Qaddafi's elite troops the United States hoped to foster a coup or weaken his power in Libya. The attack came at 2 A.M. local time when the Libyans would have been asleep.

Pentagon officials said the mission was generally successful.

"The planes got there in secrecy and the Air Force and Navy performed their coordinated strikes with precision," one said. "They were able to attack most of their targets, given the constraints on them."

"The raid was executed well," a Congressional expert said. "It was not perfect but no military operations are."

Nine of the 18 F-111's in the raid were to attack the Azziziya compound, but five aborted the mission.

"It was not a case of the pilots missing their targets," a Pentagon official said. "They did not have the full number of aircraft assigned to the target."

Pentagon officials have said that three of the five planes that aborted the mission did so because some of their equipment was not in working order.

They said that the rules for the mission were stringent to minimize the risk of civilian casualties and that if one of four navigation and target-acquisition systems of the F-111's were not in working order the planes were not to attack.

Of the two other F-111's that did not attack, one could not find the target, officials said. The other did not arrive in time for the operation.

Pentagon officials are still evaluating the reports on the raid and information on the targets has been limited.

Members of Congress, for example, have been told the military has not yet been able to confirm that the F-111 lost in the raid was shot down over Libya and cannot exclude the possibility that it crashed before reaching Libya.

A Pentagon spokesman has urged reporters to be skeptical about Libyan claims that civilian areas were damaged in the operation. At the same time, the Pentagon has not disclosed any new information about "collateral damage" that may have been inadvertently caused in civilian areas.

The Libyans have suggested that cluster bombs were used against civilian areas. But Pentagon officials said that these bombs were used by the Navy A-6's to attack planes at the Benina airfield near Benghazi.

Officials said that attacks on an intelligence installation close to the French Embassy and the former Wheelus Air Force Base were ruled out because they were near residential areas.

Officials say it is not clear what may have caused the destruction in the civilian neighborhood near the French Embassy and the Libyan intelligence installation in Tripoli.

The French weekly magazine Le Canard Enchaine said today that, contrary to American statements, the F-111's had flown over the Pyrenees Mountains, on the French-Spanish border.

The magazine, quoting "well-informed French officers," said the planes had flown low enough to escape radar detection.

The United States has said that, since France and Spain barred the use of their airspace, the planes had to make a detour to reach Libya from bases in Britain by flying entirely over water, around the Iberian Peninsula.

## WILLIAM PFAFF: EDITORIAL—NATO FOCUSES ON WAR OPINION, NOT VICTIMS OF AIR RAIDS

*Most of the reporting on the Libya strike was about the political fallout. This opinion piece reflected how much the media had focused on what other leaders thought of the air raid, and how little attention was focused on the humanitarian concerns.*

*Los Angeles Times,* 24 April 1986

PARIS: The trouble between the United States and its European allies over the Libyan affair is considerably more serious than a difference of opinion over whether bombing Col. Moammar Kadafi is the way to end terrorism.

Europe's polls are interesting. Two-thirds to three-quarters of the public in Great Britain and West Germany condemn America's punitive expedition against Libya. Two-thirds of the French favor it. The French government, on the other hand, objected to the raid, and the British and German governments supported it.

This is not, perhaps, the paradox that it seems. The French public is expressing exactly the activist approach to foreign affairs that inspired its government to take an independent and nationalist line. If the French government did not keep its policies conspicuously independent of the American, on this as on most issues, the public would also be upset.

The West Germans and British, on the other hand, are deeply, even cripplingly, conscious of a dependence on the United States—a dependence provoking resentment. In London last weekend the best arguments that anyone could produce in favor of allowing the United States to use British bases for the raid were that U.S. help in the Falklands war had to be repaid (Margaret Thatcher's position) and that appeasement of the United States is essential to keep the Atlantic Alliance together.

This was an argument made in the right-wing Sunday Telegraph, whose editor went on to say: better a muddled raid on Kadafi, and all the dangers that flow from this in the short term, than the appalling long-term dangers that would flow from a U.S. withdrawal from Europe. This does not amount to a very ringing endorsement.

It amounts, in fact, to a deeply patronizing, if complaisant, approach to the United States, serving to justify the angry complaint made by the U.S. ambassador to the United Nations, Gen. Vernon Walters, after his trip to Europe to try to muster support for the U.S. attack on Libya. He said that Europeans have a complex that Americans are ignorant, naive and stupid. (Another British commentator, in another conservative paper, the Spectator, said that when Americans get hurt they are tremendous crybabies, canceling their holidays and generally behaving in a fashion that displays what in the RAF used to be called "lack of moral fiber.")

Walters also said that European critics of the United States have never forgiven us for the Marshall Plan. That is not true. Europeans fear that it is the Americans who have never forgiven Europeans for the Marshall Plan. They fear that Americans have forgotten what lay behind the Marshall Plan, and NATO, and the stationing of U.S. troops in Europe—concern for the strategic security of the United States as much as for that of Western Europe.

The United States is thought by Europeans, and not only by Europeans, to be in a mood today to put its strategic priority on what happens in Libya, with its date palms and 3 million inhabitants, or in Nicaragua, rather than on what happens in Western Europe, an industrial and economic community more populous, richer, with a larger military potential than either the United States or the Soviet Union.

The Libyan affair has dramatized what everyone has known for some time—that things are going badly between the European allies and the United States. Whether West Europeans think Americans stupid, incompetent or crybabies, or whether Americans think Europeans yellow-bellied appeasers—to take the more colorful things being said—is of little consequence in itself. The problem is what lies behind the epithets.

The American perception of national interest and national security increasingly diverges from that of most West Europeans. The NATO alliance is not what it was meant to become when it was conceived in 1948. Its members have certain enduring interests in common, and have divergent interests as well—or divergent perceptions of interests. The time has come to face this.

NATO was formed as an association of continuous and effective self-help and mutual aid on matters of international security. That was too grand an aim. It is responsible for the bitterness that Americans feel when they don't get the unqualified support that they expect from their allies in affairs such as the Libyan raid, and equally for the resentment that Europeans feel when the United States charges off on its own, with little concern for what Europeans think or for whether it may be the Europeans who eventually have to take the consequences for U.S. actions.

It is time to rethink the transatlantic relationship. It is time to think of replacing the NATO treaty with something more modest and more realistic that will rest on the strategic interests that continue to be held in common on the two sides of the Atlantic but that will renounce the impossible ambition of strategic cooperation on many fronts. One could put it this way: The time has come for an Atlantic Coalition to take the place of the Atlantic Alliance.

## AN ANONYMOUS REPORT: GERMAN HOSTILITY TO U.S. RAIDS ON LIBYA

*This wire service report told of anti-American sentiment in a place where many Americans would have expected to find support. Though few would challenge the air strike as a retaliatory action rather than as an instigation of hostilities, many were concerned about the safety of U.S. troops in Germany. The hostile feelings there could not be ignored because of the large number of Americans at risk for more terrorist attacks.*

### Associated Press, 26 April 1986

FRANKFURT, West Germany: Officials say leaflets have turned up in the Frankfurt area urging cab drivers to refuse customers bound for a U.S. military installation.

The 1,700-member Frankfurt Taxi Association, the city's major group of cab operators, said it was not responsible for the leaflets and had reported the matter to police.

The leaflets were signed by the "Frankfurt Taxi Drivers Initiative" and also called for a protest demonstration at the U.S. Rhein-Main Air Base in Frankfurt on June 15.

The motive for the boycott campaign was not clear, but could be linked to the April 15 U.S. air raids on Libya. Anti-U.S. demonstrations occurred in several European cities after the raids.

About 250,000 U.S. troops are stationed in West Germany.

## BARRY JAMES: "LIBYA AND THE NATO CONNECTION"

*This wire service story also told of the international reaction to American military action, but worked as an apologist's report. The straining of relations between the United States and NATO was not news in the United States, but the efforts by the British to support Reagan without confrontation elsewhere were the kind of story that would be widely read in the United States.*

### United Press International, 26 April 1986

LONDON: European foot-dragging over Libya has raised questions in Britain about the health of the North Atlantic Treaty Organization, a factor that probably was uppermost in Prime Minister Margaret Thatcher's mind when she authorized the use of British bases to launch the U.S. raid.

Judging from opinion polls and an outpouring of letters to newspapers, the decision brought Thatcher enormous unpopularity.

Liberal Party leader David Steel jibed that Thatcher had "turned the British bulldog into a Reagan poodle," and some political commentators predict the issue could cost her the next election.

Libya is an "out-of-area" problem for NATO, which was set up to oppose Soviet expansion in Europe. But political sources said Thatcher was concerned the alliance could suffer serious damage if Reagan felt he could count on no help from his allies on an issue of such domestic political resonance.

She appears to have been persuaded several days before the raid that Reagan intended to go ahead with it, with or without Britain or America's other NATO allies. Reagan later made it clear that America was prepared to act "with others, if possible, and alone if necessary."

To have stood aside, Thatcher apparently reasoned, would have increased isolationist tendencies in the United States and strengthened the voice of those who want to bring U.S. troops home, with incalculable consequences for European security.

With the European allies seemingly unable or unwilling to take firm collective action against Libya, Thatcher decided she had no option but to stand shoulder-to-shoulder with Reagan.

Immediately after the raid, she told Parliament that Reagan had every right to protect the 300,000 American servicemen posted to Europe to defend its freedoms—particularly after uncovering evidence linking Libya with the Berlin disco bombing.

Secretary of State for Defense George Younger later acknowledged that the future of the alliance was an important factor in deciding whether to lend British support, despite the inevitable domestic unpopularity of such a move.

"Do we refuse our principal ally the use of his bases when he's defending himself, while we're very happy to let him spend his money in defending us?" Younger asked.

"We are a very important ally of the United States. One of the principal objectives of our enemies is to divide us. We have very clearly shown that we are not to be divided. We will stick by each other as far as I'm concerned."

Peregrine Worsthorne, editor of the conservative Sunday Telegraph, made the point that in an alliance it is as important to know your friends as it is to know your enemies, particularly when a friend is crucial to your defense.

He said Thatcher "has . . . helped significantly to head off such a backlash of anti-European resentment in the United States as could have wrecked NATO. Such an achievement may not any longer be the stuff of which electoral victories are made. But it is the stuff, nevertheless, of statesmanship."

It would be ironic, however, if Thatcher's action opened the way for the opposition Labor party to take power in the next election, which must be held within two years.

For Labor not only can be expected to dismantle Britain's nuclear defenses but is also likely to take a close look at the agreement covering the air bases from which the Libya raid was mounted. In strictly military terms, a Labor victory could mean a weaker alliance.

Another irony is that while Britain has reaped American gratitude for its help, France has emerged as the popular villain of the affair for refusing to allow U.S. F-111 fighter-bombers to cross its territory.

It seems to have been forgotten that of all the European countries, France has done the most to confront Col. Moammar Khadafy, committing troops to oppose him in Chad and promising naval support to Tunisia when it came under Libyan threat.

And French public opinion, in contrast to Britain's, emerged largely in favor of Reagan's raid.

The French appear not to have shared Thatcher's concern about the effect on NATO of saying no to Reagan. For while Britain has come to rely more on its "special relationship" with the United States, France has pursued an independent policy within NATO since pulling out of the alliance's military command in the 1960s.

*Credit*: Reprinted by permission of UPI.

---

## HENRY TREWHITT: PLANNING THE LIBYAN RAIDS; PUBLIC REACTION TO ATTACKS

---

*This weekly magazine report on the surprise strike gave an overview of the kinds of concerns the public had about what had happened. It emphasized the planning and attention the strike had received before it was ordered.*

### *U.S. News & World Report*, 28 April 1986

After months of talk, Reagan's bold night raid on Libya takes Qadhafi by surprise but tests U.S. relations with much of the world. In time, the tactics may bring a united international front against terrorism, but for now more violence seems likely.

The U.S. air assault against a pariah Arab leader has launched America into a new high-risk war against terrorism, one that will be hard to sustain and even harder to win.

The critical step in Ronald Reagan's promised campaign against state-sponsored terrorism was long in coming. But with the April 14 strike against Libya's Muammar Qadhafi, he set a course that showed readiness to answer terrorism wherever it threatens Americans.

By striking the capital of an Arab land, the U.S. had dramatically raised the stakes. There was no suggestion of military action against Syria or Iran. Both are primary sponsors of political terrorism, but both are also far more formidable militarily than Libya. Syria has closer ties to the Soviet Union.

Yet the U.S. attack, in effect, was an assertion of leadership with obvious risk to lives and national prestige. There could be no turning back, without humiliation, from a U.S. foreign policy that in recent months has become newly assertive around the world.

Victory against terrorism appears possible only if the fragmented democracies unite. Even so, the cost in money and blood will be high in light of the certainty that for now the plague is spreading.

Reagan left no doubt about his reaction to future offenses traceable to Qadhafi. Buoyed by overwhelming support at home, he warned as his bombers returned to base that, if necessary, "we shall do it again."

The occasion might come soon. A new wave of terror flashed across Europe and the Mideast following the U.S. attack. An early measure of the cost: The murder in Beirut of Peter Kilburn, a librarian at the American University in Beirut who was kidnapped 16 months ago, along with two

Britons—deaths soon tied to Libya. The shooting of a U.S. Embassy employee in Khartoum prompted Washington to begin a rapid evacuation of Americans from Sudan. U.S. analysts said they expected Qadhafi, enraged by the death of one of his children and injury to two more, to order yet more assaults on Americans. An administration official warned of "open season" on those who travel abroad. In response, Americans hunkered down, many canceling international trips, some avoiding even domestic flights.

Initial world reaction to the U.S. attack was tumultuous—and generally hostile. The most dramatic came from Moscow, supplier of arms and political support for Qadhafi. Postponing a planning session of foreign ministers next month, Soviet leaders all but ruled out a summit meeting of Reagan and Soviet leader Mikhail Gorbachev this summer. That left summit prospects open for late this year at the earliest, with a dark shadow over arms-control decisions pending in the meantime.

The most painful fallout for Washington came from the North Atlantic Treaty Organization (NATO). Only Britain's Margaret Thatcher, among European allies, supported the U.S. action. "Reagan's poodle," opponents jeered after she approved the use of British-based U.S. F-111 bombers. Other Western European leaders mostly waffled, urging American restraint while criticizing Qadhafi's sponsorship of terrorism. Their reasons—domestic political considerations—were evident in the anti-American slogans shouted by demonstrators in dozens of cities. Canada was the only NATO member besides Britain to publicly support the United States.

Especially bitter debate swirled around France and Spain. Both denied overflight rights to the American bombers, forcing a long detour over the Atlantic—and thus extra-hazardous aerial refuelings—before the attacking planes reached Libya. For France, the refusal was a familiar expression of fierce independence in foreign policy, in this case possibly against public opinion.

In Spain, where the government recently won narrow approval for remaining in NATO, the overflight ban plainly spoke for the crowds denouncing the American action.

At the United Nations, at a meeting of nonaligned nations in New Delhi and in scores of small nations, the Third World joined in the chorus of reproach. In Japan, the government had little reaction but began beefing up already intense security preparations for a meeting May 4–6 of the leaders of major democratic industrial powers. Israeli leaders predictably praised U.S. emulation of their own policy of striking back directly against terrorism.

Other Mideast reaction was equally predictable, hostile—and deceptively uniform. The usual obligatory sense of Arab brotherhood inspired denunciation of the surprise attack. But U.S. officials carefully distinguished between the criticism from Egypt and Jordan, both dependent on Washington's aid, and that of radical Arab governments and non-Arab Iran. "Arab nations have to react negatively in public," a U.S. official said, "but in private they tell us to go for it."

Reagan administration reaction to the turmoil was mixed. Soviet postponement of the summit-planning session between Secretary of State George Shultz and Foreign Minister Eduard Shevardnadze came as a surprise. "We regret the Soviet decision and consider it a mistake," White House spokesman Larry Speakes said.

U.S. diplomats also were putting the best face possible on European attitudes. Several hinted that private allied support was greater than the public record indicated. Secretary Shultz, while lamenting France's denial of overflight rights, carefully emphasized that French police recently foiled a Libyan plan to attack visa applicants at the U.S. Embassy in Paris. One official, in fact, reported that the French privately encouraged a strike against Libya, "the harder the better."

Reagan had no such problems on the home front. Members of Congress and private citizens alike united behind him. A bill introduced in Congress would give him a free hand in dealing with terrorism, including the use of "deadly force." In effect, the legislation would nullify the War Powers Act, a product of the Vietnam War, requiring the President to consult Congress on the use of military power.

The nation methodically went about tightening security in public places. Dump trucks were being parked around the Capitol after working hours. Airports in major cities were adding guards, bomb-sniffing dogs and experts on terrorism. Military bases at home and abroad reinforced security.

Both Congress and the public appeared less tolerant than the administration of European criticism, especially France's. Snapped Senator Pete Domenici (R-N.M.): "It is inconceivable to me that our European allies should disagree with us 100 percent of the time and still expect to be treated as allies." Robert Hunter, a foreign-policy adviser during the Carter administration, remarked that "I haven't seen so much anger, bitterness and contempt toward the European allies in this town since 1967, during Vietnam."

The military strike against Libya had been building for a long while, but reached a climax when an explosion ripped through a discotheque frequented by U.S. troops in West Berlin, killing an American sergeant and a Turkish woman. President Reagan, reporting to the nation later, claimed to have "conclusive" evidence that the Berlin attack was ordered from Tripoli. Shultz reported the discovery of Libyan plans for at least 30 attacks on Americans or U.S. installations.

Once again, the U.S. fleet began maneuvering in the Mediterranean, while persistent leaks in Washington foretold another attack. It came at 2 A.M. Libyan time on April 15, coinciding with the previous evening's 7 o'clock news in Washington. This time, the administration used British-based F-111s, with their heavier bomb load, as well as planes from the Sixth Fleet, to strike at five military installations.

After 11 minutes of thunder from exploding bombs and massive antiaircraft fire, it was over. Despite the loss of one F-111 and its two crewmen and at least one misplaced bomb that damaged the French Embassy and other foreign missions, U.S. authorities described it as a near perfect mission.

The one possible error: The U.S. failed to kill Qadhafi. Officials later told the Washington Post that he had been a target and that U.S. planes had dropped four 2,000-pound bombs on his barracks. President Reagan later insisted that Qadhafi was not a target, but the White House did not challenge Secretary Shultz's assertion that it would be better if Qadhafi were replaced.

In execution, the attack was a more powerful rerun of the March 24 clash. The earlier strike was advertised as defense of free navigation. This time, Reagan cited the right of self-defense under the U.N. Charter. It was the first against a state for sponsorship of terrorism. Therein lay the central message to the rest of the world.

What the raid did not do was quell terrorism. As events left a fresh trail of blood in the Middle East, Washington policymakers tried to anticipate where the struggle may lead and if it can be won. The U.S. has armed heavily against a superpower foe like the Soviet Union, but, as with Vietnam in the 1960s, the fight against terrorism is thrusting the nation into uncharted territory.

A central question is whether Washington has a comprehensive strategy. Administration officials claim a set of coherent policies based on economic, political and military steps that will be taken when necessary. But critics see an administration that has a reactive policy and is divided between hawks and doves. Even the attack on Libya was briskly debated, with Secretary Shultz cast as a hawk and Defense Secretary Caspar Weinberger, ironically, as a dove.

Still to be determined is whether the American public will support a sustained fight against terrorism, especially if it involves the shedding of American blood in full view on prime-time television. To many planners, U.S. military action must be quick, decisive and without casualties to be popular. The two recent attacks on Libya have come close to those requirements. Nonetheless, there is concern that if violence spreads to the U.S., requiring curtailment of travel and civil liberties, public support will fragment.

Washington recognizes the role of historic Middle East issues, especially the Arab-Israeli conflict, behind terrorism. But no one appears certain how to deal with those issues. Some analysts believe the U.S. must first revive the stalled negotiations to resolve the future of Palestinians. Conservatives in the administration claim that the Palestinian cause is unrelated to Qadhafi-style terrorism. With no answers in sight, the new struggle could easily rival Vietnam as one of America's longest and most painful military involvements.

The immediate prospect is that the growing violence would fuel a bitter debate over whether, as Reagan's critics charged, the U.S. had provoked new terrorism or merely anticipated it. The answer may never be known. But the growing bloodshed threatened an early test of Reagan's declaration that there can be no "appeasement of evil . . . no sanctuary for terror."

No one pretended that Washington could easily mount punitive attacks against Syria and Iran, though there is ample evidence that their leaders sponsor more terrorism than does Qadhafi. Both political and military considerations argue caution. Syria's troops are far better trained to use sophisticated arms. An attack on Iran, more difficult because of geography, could widen the current war with Iraq into a general Persian Gulf conflict that could, in turn, expand into a confrontation between the United States and the Soviet Union.

"Qadhafi is not the full extent of the problem, for sure," said Shultz. "There may be other things we have to do." But he did not detail them, and he vowed that "we're not going to get put in a position where there is some sort of automatic" U.S. response.

Zbigniew Brzezinski, national-security adviser under President Carter, saw the Libya attack as "a message to smaller states supporting terrorism that it is unwise to do so." But he also cautioned that "no two incidents of terrorism are similar. . . . This doesn't establish any precedent to be followed rigorously."

Some of the same caution was voiced by Lawrence Eagleburger, a senior policymaker under both Democratic and Republican administrations, now retired. The U.S. attack "does mean that when terrorists are planning activities, they'll have to put something new into the equation," he remarked. "It's now less likely that there will be no response."

But the central question, he concluded, echoing the judgment of many administration officials, is whether Reagan's policy finally awakens the West to the need for collective action. "If this action achieves nothing more than beginning to create that consciousness," he said, "it will have been worth it."

*Credit*: Copyright 1986 U.S. News & World Report, L.P. Reprinted with permission.

# NOTE

1. "Fearing Trouble: A Newsweek Poll," *Newsweek*, 7 April 1986, 23. The Gallup Organization interviewed a representative national sample of 606 adults by telephone 26 and 27 March. The margin of error is plus or minus 5 percentage points. Some "Don't know" responses are omitted.

## FURTHER READINGS

Davis, Brian L. *Qaddafi, Terrorism, and the Origins of the U.S. Attack on Libya.* New York: Praeger, 1990.

Haass, Richard N., ed. *Transatlantic Tensions: The United States, Europe, and Problem Countries.* Washington, D.C.: Brookings Institution Press, 1999.

Simons, Geoffrey L. *Libya: The Struggle for Survival.* New York: St. Martin's Press, 1993.

*Top:* A Palestinian woman brandishes helmets during a 27 September 1982 memorial service in Beirut for victims of Lebanon's Sabra refugee camp massacre. She claimed the helmets were worn by those who massacred hundreds of her countrymen. (AP/Wide World Photos)

*Right:* Palestinian leader Yasser Arafat is greeted by children in Beirut, Lebanon, on 28 August 1982. (AP/Wide World Photos)

The destroyed American Embassy in Beirut, Lebanon, following a car bomb, 19 April 1983. (AP/Wide World Photos)

"ON TO CENTRAL AMERICA!"

LEBANON POLICY

©1984 HERBLOCK

*Left:* Despite the strong role of television and photographic imagery in informing and influencing American sentiment after the Vietnam War, more traditional methods—the political cartoon, for instance—still carried weight and represented the thoughts and views of the time quite well, as this "On to Central America!" cartoon, and others following, demonstrate. (From *Herblock Through the Looking Glass* [W.W. Norton, 1984]. Reprinted with permission.)

*Right:* In the shadow of an American M-60 tank, two U.S. soldiers stand guard over three Grenadian prisoners in St. George's, Grenada, in October 1983. U.S. troops invaded the island of Grenada on 25 October to overthrow the Marxist government. (AP/Wide World Photos)

A U.S. soldier, left, and a Barbados policeman stand guard over a group of Cuban prisoners of war at a compound near the airport in Port Salines, Grenada, 29 October 1983. The Cubans are among the nearly 600 taken prisoner by the multinational forces earlier in the week. (AP/Wide World Photos)

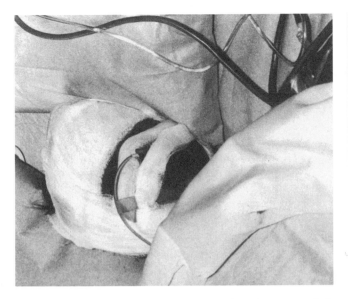

Khamis Gadhafi, three-year-old son of Libyan leader Col. Moammar Gadhafi, is shown in his hospital bed with his head and face wrapped in bandages as he is treated for injuries in Tripoli, Libya, 20 April 1986. Other members of the Gadhafi family were injured in the same U.S. bombing raid, including the colonel himself and an infant daughter, who was killed. The U.S. attack was in response to terrorism allegedly traced to Libya. (AP/Wide World Photos)

Libyan president Moammar Gadhafi poses between two of his eight children, Sadi, left, and Asha, inside his tent headquarters in Tripoli, Libya, on 11 January 1986. (AP/Wide World Photos)

LET A THOUSAND FLOWERS BLOOM.

"Let a thousand flowers bloom" (Oliphant © 1986 Universal Press Syndicate. Reprinted with permission. All rights reserved.)

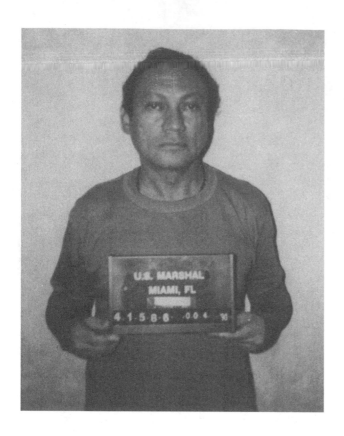

A January 1990 file photo of deposed Panamanian General Manuel Antonio Noriega, serving a forty-year sentence in Miami for drug trafficking. He was ousted by an American invasion of Panama in December 1989, tried in the United States, and convicted in 1992. On 6 November 1996, authorities confirmed that Noriega had begun collecting his Panamanian government pension of about $1,500 a month. (AP/Wide World Photos)

Doonesbury, "The heat, the bad food, the nasty mood toward Americans—what a hellhole this country is." (© 1990 G. B. Trudeau. Reprinted with permission of Universal Press Syndicate. All rights reserved.)

General Colin Powell, chairman of the Joint Chiefs of Staff, is interviewed by the news media outside the Comandancia, the former Panamanian Defense Forces headquarters in Panama City on 6 January 1990. In the background is a logo for the "Macho Mountain Brigade," one of Manuel Noriega's elite fighting units. (AP/Wide World Photos)

U.S. soldiers carry an American flag through the streets of Panama City as they celebrate with Panamanian citizens in January 1990 following Noriega's surrender. (AP/Wide World Photos)

A Somali clansman shows off his rocket launcher outside Mogadishu's main port in Somalia, 8 December 1992. The clansmen were commonly seen driving through the city with machine guns mounted on the roofs of their vehicles. U.S. intelligence officials said that a prolonged American stay in Somalia probably would expose American troops to hit-and-run guerrilla attacks from the country's heavily armed and undisciplined clans. (AP/Wide World Photos)

U.S. Marines are surrounded by members of the media after landing on the beach at Mogadishu's main airport in Somalia on 9 December 1992. U.S. armed forces arrived in Somalia as part of the U.N.'s peacekeeping effort. (AP/Wide World Photos)

Somali dock workers pile wheat bags unloaded from an aid relief ship, 29 December 1992, in Mogadishu's port warehouse. With the start of Operation Restore Hope, ships lined up to offload donated goods for famine victims, but transport to the stricken areas of Somalia was inadequate due to a shortage of trucks, and the port's warehouse soon filled to capacity. (AP/Wide World Photos)

Bearers carry one of seven flag-draped coffins into the front of a C-5 transport plane in Mogadishu in this 17 March 1994 photo, for shipment to Dover Air Force Base in Delaware. (AP/Wide World Photos)

President Bill Clinton, accompanied by Haitian president Jean-Bertrand Aristide, speaks at the White House on 14 October 1994 during a farewell ceremony for the Haitian president. On the eve of his return to Haiti, Aristide received a warm White House farewell from President Clinton who said a "new era of hope" was opening for Haiti with the restoration of democracy. (AP/Wide World Photos)

On 7 December 1995, ten days before the Haitian presidential election, Haiti presidential candidate Rene Preval waves to supporters at a rally in Hinche, Haiti. (AP/Wide World Photos)

*Right:* Sergeant 1st Class Curtis Stapleton, from Oklahoma City, Oklahoma, a member of the U.N. peacekeeping forces in Haiti, flies the U.S. flag while boarding the plane that will return him, and 143 of his fellow soldiers, to Fort Bragg, North Carolina, on 17 January 1996. (AP/Wide World Photos)

*Left:* Patients who have traveled more than 120 miles to the Grace Childrens Hospital in Port-au-Prince, Haiti, wait to see a doctor in this 20 March 1996 photo. A 1996 health and demographic survey revealed that more children under five died in Haiti than in any other country in the Western Hemisphere. (AP/Wide World Photos)

*Right:* The slogan of the French Revolution and the name of leader Jean Tatoune appear on building wall in Gonaïves, Haiti. (Photograph by Danny Lyon, courtesy of Edwynn Houck Gallery)

Muslim and Croatian prisoners sit up in what is described as a sleeping room in the detention camp in Manjaca, some 150 miles northwest of Sarajevo, Bosnia and Herzegovina, 9 August 1992. (AP/Wide World Photos)

A father's hands press against the window of a bus carrying his tearful son and wife to safety from the besieged city of Sarajevo during the Bosnian War on 10 November 1992. Roman Catholic Croat and Muslim-led government forces fought together against Bosnia's Eastern Orthodox Serbs early in the war, which started after Bosnia seceded from Serb-dominated Yugoslavia. All sides in Bosnia's war were accused of "ethnic cleansing." Thousands of Muslims and Croats were also killed in Serb-run concentration camps. A peace accord was signed on 14 December 1995, with NATO delegated to keep peace. The conflict left about 250,000 dead and 2.5 million refugees. (AP/Wide World Photos)

*Top:* U.N. peacekeepers and Sarajevo citizens take cover from gunfire on the city's infamous "Sniper Alley" during Bosnia's 1992–1995 war between the country's Muslims, Serbs, and Croats in this March 1993 photo. The end of the U.N.'s decade-long peacekeeping mission to the war-torn country came on 31 December. (AP/Wide World Photos)

*Right:* An unidentified Serbian woman holds a skull she believes belongs to a relative, during a reburial in the village of Fakovici, in eastern Bosnia, on 17 May 1993. The skeletal remains, reburied in a common grave, are believed to be of Serbs reportedly killed by Muslim forces when they briefly occupied the village in July 1992. (AP/Wide World Photos)

*Bottom:* "Thank you for not interfering" (Oliphant © 1993 Universal Press Syndicate. Reprinted with permission. All rights reserved.)

*Top:* "Here I am, a simple cat from Arkansas, thrust up close to all the big questions that face America in our time" (Oliphant © 1993 Universal Press Syndicate. Reprinted with permission. All rights reserved.)

*Left:* Pat Gray was among the many demonstrators carrying signs and chanting "Give money to the poor, not to the war, U.S. Troops out of Bosnia," on 15 December 1995 during rush hour in San Francisco. The United States planned to send 25,000 troops to Bosnia, but due to the poor weather conditions no more troops arrived at that time. (AP/Wide World Photos)

*Right:* U.S. Army soldiers walk through the snow as they patrol the perimeter of Tuzla airbase on 19 December 1995. They were in Bosnia as part of the NATO Implementation Force to enforce the Bosnia peace agreement. (AP/Wide World Photos)

# 27

# NORIEGA AND PANAMA, 1989

The U.S. government's military presence in Panama spanned almost all of the twentieth century. When Panama seceded from Colombia in 1903, this action was quickly followed by the signing of a treaty between the new Panamanian government and the United States for the construction of the Panama Canal by the U.S. Army Corps of Engineers. Construction began the next year, and U.S. troops were immediately dispatched to protect the American investments there. The United States remained in control of the canal until 1977, when transfer to the Panamanian government began. That transfer was completed at the end of 1999.

This relatively small country, about the size of South Carolina and largely coastal, is bordered on the north by Costa Rica and on the south by Colombia. The slender tropical landmass supports a population of almost 3 million, most of whom are Spanish speakers and Roman Catholics. The country is sometimes described as the land bridge that connects North and South America. Forestry and fishing support the residents, though much of the national economy depends on the attractive banking, insurance, and tourism businesses housed primarily in the capital, Panama City. Well-known exports from Panama include fruit, sugar, coffee, and shrimp.

A step-up in the number of American troops stationed in Panama occurred briefly in 1989 when Manuel Antonio Noriega was deposed as president there. His political heavy-handedness was undeniably observed during the national elections that year, though it was already well known that the U.S. government was not pleased with the kind of leadership he provided in the region. Additional U.S. troops were called into Panama during the summer, the Pentagon said, to protect American interests, but many believed that they were also there to help accomplish the coup.

The U.S. military intervention began slowly. In May 1989, Panama held presidential elections, and international observers reported that Democratic Alliance of Civic Opposition candidate Guillermo Endara had won the election by a substantial margin. The candidate supported by General Noriega, Carlos Duque, claimed victory, however, that same day, 7 May. On 8 May Panamanian troops raided the vote-counting centers while demonstrators marched in support of Endara. The Panamanian government released partial results on 9 May, two days after the election, that showed Duque winning. Former President Jimmy Carter, who had gone to Panama as a member of the international observers committee, said that he thought that there was fraud in the government version of the results.

President Bush asked Noriega to resign, and the Panamanian government announced that the elections were annulled because of international interference. When the Panamanian government troops were reported to have nearly beaten to death Endara and vice presidential candidates Ricardo Arias Calderón and Guillermo Ford, President Bush sent 2,000 additional U.S. troops to Panama on 11 May. The U.S. ambassador to Panama withdrew from the mission there on 15 May. By 17 May, just ten days after the elections had been held, the Organization of American States met in Washington, D.C., and passed a resolution condemning election abuses by Noriega. The situation in Panama continued under a cloud of disapproval, but Noriega remained in control of the government.

Early in October, several hundred rebel soldiers, reportedly led by Major Moises Giroldi Vega, seized the Panamanian Defense Forces headquarters in Panama City, captured General Noriega, and announced that they now controlled the government. But the demise of Noriega was not a fact. Troops loyal to him, within hours of the coup, recaptured the headquarters and freed Noriega.

Noriega blamed the United States for the coup attempt, but President Bush said only that the United States had been informed of the coup plans and had not supported it. If the United States had supported the toppling of Noriega's government, the White House said privately, it would have succeeded. The U.S. government did admit several days later that U.S. troops had blocked two roads near the Defense Forces headquarters at the request of the rebels. On 4 October, it was reported that Noriega had summarily ordered and carried out the execution of Giroldi and some of the rebel soldiers. By 10 October, the Panamanian government adopted a state of emergency that included the retroactive firing of government employees suspected in any activities that had opposed the government—that is, Noriega.

By mid-December, the National Assembly unanimously voted a declaration of war with the United States and named Noriega as leader. The next day, 16 December, an American was killed by Panamanian soldiers, and there were several reports of U.S. citizens being harassed and assaulted across the country. President Bush dispatched orders for U.S. troops to mobilize, and on 20 December a Panamanian judge, acting on U.S. instructions, swore in the opposition candidate of the 7 May elections, President Endara, and vice presidential candidates Calderón and Ford. That same day 11,000 additional U.S. troops were added to the 13,000 already in Panama. They took over the airfield, power stations, and Defense Forces headquarters. Though several Americans were held hostage by Noriega supporters, all were released or rescued within a few days.

The United States reported that during the first week of deployment twenty-four American soldiers and 139 Panamanian soldiers had been killed. Noriega remained at large during that week and finally requested political asylum in the home of the papal nuncio to Panama on 24 December. When this was learned, U.S. troops surrounded the residence and demanded Noriega's surrender. The Vatican said that it would not surrender Noriega on demand but did say that he was being asked to leave of his own free will by the end of the month. He was later captured and eventually brought to the United States to stand trial for drug-trafficking offenses.

Though U.S. public support of American involvement in international politics was already quite high—a reported 68 percent approval—the troop deployment was characterized by the White House as nothing more than an effort to get rid of one very bad guy, Noriega, and to support free and fair elections that would overcome a cruel and unjust dictator, Noriega. Even the Panamanians seemed to approve of the U.S. action. An early January, Spanish-language public opinion poll taken in Panama of more than 700 residents asked, "In general, do you approve . . . of the US sending troops to Panama to remove Manuel Noriega from power?"[1] The results were a resounding affirmation. Only 6 percent disapproved, while more than 60 percent strongly approved and almost 30 percent somewhat approved.

What follows are the news reports of this short war, code-named "Just Cause," that saw swift U.S. intervention and summary justice. Because of the longtime presence of the United States in the region, there were many reporters in place, whose movements were relatively unrestricted during the December 1989 events.

---

## WILLIAM BRANIGIN: "NORIEGA APPOINTED 'MAXIMUM LEADER'; PANAMA SAYS 'STATE OF WAR' EXISTS WITH U.S."

---

*This story out of Mexico City was among the early alerts that the U.S. military had been put on notice by Noriega's government, and that if an intervention was going to take place, it had better be done quickly and decisively.*

*Washington Post*, 16 December 1989

MEXICO CITY: A Panamanian legislative body formed by Gen. Manuel Antonio Noriega today named him head of government, formally granted him sweeping powers and declared the country to be "in a state of war" with the United States because of American economic sanctions.

The National Assembly of Representatives, a 510-member body appointed by the Panamanian strongman in October, passed a unanimous resolution naming Noriega as "chief of government" and "maximum leader for national liberation." The resolution said the move was prompted by U.S. "aggression," a reference to a series of economic sanctions imposed since April 1988 and recent military maneuvers by the U.S. military's Panama-based Southern Command.

The sanctions, aimed at depriving the Noriega government of income and forcing him from power, were tightened earlier this month when the Bush administration banned Panamanian-registered ships from U.S. ports effective Feb. 1, 1990.

"The Republic of Panama is declared to be in a state of war while the aggression lasts," the resolution said. "To confront this aggression, the job of chief of government of Panama is hereby created, and Manuel Antonio Noriega is designated to carry out these responsibilities as maximum leader for national liberation."

The move formalized a situation that already existed, as Noriega has held dictatorial power over the military and all branches of the government since he became commander of the Panama Defense Forces in 1983. Officially, he now also outranks civilian "provisional president" Francisco Rodríguez, a high school chum whom Noriega installed in the post after annulling presidential and legislative elections in May to prevent a landslide opposition victory. Rodríguez now becomes a ceremonial president, which he had been anyway for all practical purposes.

In an acceptance speech, Noriega asserted that he had not sought the new post, but that "you have invited me to occupy a trench, and I will not fail you."

He reminded the audience that President Ronald Reagan had invoked the economic sanctions against Panama under the U.S. war powers act, and he raised the specter of armed conflict with the United States over the Panama Canal, which he claims Washington seeks to retain beyond its scheduled transfer to Panama at the end of the century.

"We will sit by the canal and watch the bodies of our enemies float by," Noriega said. "But we will never destroy the canal."

Although Noriega's Panama Defense Forces (PDF) has periodically harassed American servicemen and is held responsible for a series of intrusions at U.S. military installations in Panama, the 16,000-member force so far has avoided any direct military confrontation with the 12,000 troops of the U.S. Southern Command.

In the latest episode in the campaign against the United States, a municipal official allied with Noriega has asked the PDF to arrest two American generals for ignoring three summonses to appear in court on charges of disturbing the peace. The case accuses Gen. Maxwell Thurman, the commander of the Southern Command, and Maj. Gen. Marc Cisneros, commander of U.S. Army South, of "constant harassment" against citizens living near U.S. bases, citing noise from movements of troops, armored vehicles, helicopters and airplanes.

The Southern Command dismisses the allegations, insisting that all its activities are within its rights under the 1977 Panama Canal treaties. The command said Tuesday that it would consider any attempt to arrest Thurman or Cisneros as an act of terrorism.

Another target of Noriega's ire lately has been Fernando Manfredo, the deputy administrator of the Panama Canal Commission. In keeping with a treaty requirement that a Panamanian take over the position in 1990, the White House named Manfredo as its temporary choice for the post until a Panamanian government recognized by the United States nominates a candidate. The United States does not recognize Noriega's government.

In another resolution today, the assembly called on the government to strip Manfredo of his citizenship if he accepts the administrator's position.

(Special correspondent Berta R. Thayer in Panama City contributed to this report.)

---

## RONALD J. OSTROW: ADMINISTRATION SEEKS LEGAL BASIS FOR ARREST OF NORIEGA

---

*This front-page story out of Washington, D.C., seemed to suggest that the White House approach to the political problems posed by Noriega was going to be to discredit him on the basis of a variety of activities illegal in the United States. It was apparently looking for grounds on which to arrest him legally when the opportunity presented itself.*

*Los Angeles Times*, 17 December 1989

WASHINGTON: U.S. military forces have the legal authority to conduct law enforcement operations outside the United States, including pursuing and apprehending international terrorists and drug traffickers, Atty. Gen. Dick Thornburgh's top legal adviser has ruled.

In a Nov. 3 memorandum that opens the door to direct participation by the military in stepped-up offensives in other nations, Assistant Atty. Gen. William P. Barr concluded that a Reconstruction Era ban on such involvement was not intended to apply outside U.S. borders.

Barr's ruling, first reported Saturday by the Washington Post and confirmed by Administration sources, was made after questions were raised about the military's authority to arrest Panamanian strongman Manuel A. Noriega if a coup attempt against him were successful.

Although the 28-page legal opinion cleared the way for such action, Administration officials emphasized that a policy decision "at the highest inter-agency levels" would be required before the military embarked on any law enforcement mission in other countries.

"Even though we may have the legal right to do some things, we may not—for political reasons—want to exercise all those rights," a senior Defense Department official said.

Asked whether the Barr opinion had led to specific military actions, such as in the escalating offensive against South American cocaine traffickers, one Administration source declined to comment, while another said: "Not to my knowledge."

The ruling could remove potential obstacles to the involvement of U.S. military forces in the escalating offensive against cocaine producers and traffickers in the South American nations of Colombia, Peru and Bolivia.

U.S. troops have been deployed to South America to work with local officials as part of an "Andean initiative" contained in President Bush's anti-drug program, but their ability to apprehend traffickers was not clearly established until Barr's opinion was issued.

However, any direct involvement by U.S. military personnel in the drug-producing nations would be certain to provoke significant nationalist opposition within those countries by citizens who view the U.S. involvement with suspicion.

The memorandum on law enforcement actions by military personnel addresses a different legal question than a controversial June 21 opinion by Barr that said the FBI had authority to seize fugitives overseas without obtaining permission of the foreign government.

And the assurances made by Administration officials that military actions would not be undertaken without prior approval at high levels illustrates their sensitivity to congressional criticism of the earlier opinion.

The Justice Department declined to make public Barr's latest ruling, just as it had the June 21 opinion, on grounds that the documents constitute "private communications" between Barr and his "client"—Thornburgh, and, through him, President Bush.

But an Administration official said Barr's latest written ruling was in line with a verbal opinion that his office of legal counsel had formulated during the Ronald Reagan Administration before Barr joined the government.

"OLC looked at the issue and wrote a rough first draft, but the issue abated," and the opinion was never completed, an Administration official said. He declined to explain the facts under consideration at that time, but he said the verbal opinion did not lead to any action by the military.

Barr's opinion reviews the history of the 1878 Posse Comitatus Act, passed in response to opposition to military oversight of Reconstruction Era elections. The ruling concludes that the act sought to bar military interference in functions of the states and was not meant to address military actions in other countries, an Administration official said.

"All the legislative history (of the act) related to interference with the states, with the military in conflict with Americans that could undermine confidence in the military," he said. "It was not Congress' intent for it to apply extraterritorially."

Until recent years, the Pentagon had avoided any involvement in the fight against drugs entering the United States by citing the ban on military involvement in civilian law enforcement. But during the Reagan Administration, the act was amended to permit the use of the military for intelligence in drug interception along U.S. borders.

Defense Secretary Dick Cheney has invited proposals for broader military involvement in anti-drug efforts, and he has been considering initiatives submitted by the 10 principal U.S. military field commanders.

Several of these proposals "pushed the envelope on what we could or could not do" in fighting drug trafficking, a senior Pentagon official said. He added that Cheney has rejected some of the proposals on grounds that they went too far.

Doubts over the military's limited powers in battling drugs were raised during the Noriega coup attempt. Gen. Maxwell Thurman, commander of U.S. forces in Panama, felt it necessary to have a federal law enforcement agent standing by in case the coup succeeded and Noriega could be arrested on federal narcotics charges he faces in Florida.

The White House then sought clarification of the limitations, which resulted in Barr's opinion, an Administration source said.

(Staff writer Melissa Healy contributed to this story.)

*Credit*: Copyright © 1989, Los Angeles Times. Reprinted with permission.

---

## ELOY O. AGUILAR: "PANAMA ACCUSES UNITED STATES OF 'CONTINUED VIOLATIONS'"

---

*This wire service story out of Panama reported both a step-up in the U.S. military action and tensions in the region. It would be only hours before "Just Cause" was in play.*

Associated Press, 19 December 1989

PANAMA CITY, Panama: Panama accused the U.S. armed forces Tuesday of violating its air space with "observation planes and helicopters" in preparation for military action.

Frequent movements of U.S. soldiers and equipment have been seen within U.S. military installations the past three days. About 12,000 American soldiers are stationed along the Panama Canal.

"It is a way to keep pressure on until the United States drops the other shoe," a U.S. source said privately.

U.S. troops were put on maximum alert and restricted to base after Panamanian soldiers killed a U.S. Marine lieutenant Saturday.

NBC News broadcast segments Tuesday evening showing what it said were C-141 Starlifter transports landing in Panama in the afternoon. It said one plane was landing every 10 minutes and that security had been tightened around the air base.

This reporter drove through Howard Air Force Base Tuesday night and said he saw at least 10 large transport planes, an unusually high number. There also were six to eight helicopters parked there, in contrast to the usual three or four.

It was not clear what kind of planes the reporter saw or whether they transported troops or cargo.

Residents of Veracruz, a town next to Howard air base, said they had heard what sounded like frequent landings over the past hour and a half.

A U.S. Southern Command spokesman said earlier Tuesday "no unusual military activity" was taking place. Later he said he knew nothing about the reported arrival of C-141 planes.

At Fort Clayton, headquarters of the U.S. Army South, tanks were pulled into a circle in an open area and troops climbed on and off them in routine cleaning and exercises Tuesday afternoon. Trucks and armored personnel carriers also were moved into public view.

Telephone lines to the Southern Command offices at Quarry Heights and to officers' homes were busy late Tuesday. Access to Quarry Heights is limited, but a public road goes through Howard.

Earlier Tuesday, C-141 transport planes were seen in the air around Fort Bragg, N.C., home of the Army's 82nd Airborne division. It was not known if they were connected to any U.S. military activity in Panama.

Lt. Pascual Gonzalez, director of civil aviation, said Panama has "a critical situation" with the United States. "We think the level of aggression and intimidation will increase," he told The Associated Press.

"There are helicopters flying during the night over our installations," he said.

At the State Department in Washington, spokeswoman Margaret Tutwiler said Gen. Manuel Antonio Noriega's declaration last week that a state of war existed with the United States, followed by "indiscriminate and unprovoked violence against Americans, clearly increases tensions in Panama."

"We find the unwarranted use of violence against Americans by the Noriega regime unacceptable," she said.

Ms. Tutwiler would not say what contingencies or options were under consideration.

The United States has tried to oust Noriega, who controls the Panamanian military and the country, since he was indicted on federal drug trafficking charges in February 1988.

U.S. sanctions have depressed the economy, but have not budged Noriega, and two coup attempts failed to unseat him.

Noriega denies the drug charges and says the United States wants to renege on treaties that require the canal to be turned over to Panama at the end of the century.

Panamanian officials say the American officer was killed when he and three others drove a car past checkpoints, then fired at Noriega's military headquarters building, wounding two civilians and a soldier.

The United States says the four were unarmed, in civilian clothes, when they got lost near the headquarters.

Lt. Robert Paz, 25, who had been in Panama since September, was killed when the group fled civilians and soldiers who tried to force them from their car at the checkpoint, Southern Command said.

On Monday, a U.S. Army officer wounded a Panamanian police corporal because he thought the man was about to draw a weapon, according to Southern Command.

Police Cpl. César Tejada, who was shot once in the left arm, told journalists permitted to interview him in a hospital Tuesday the American had initiated the incident.

"I was merely standing there, doing my job, when this car went by at high speed and the driver fired two shots at me," he said. "I never gave him a reason for it."

Journalists also were permitted to interview another patient, Alex Correa, who said he belonged to the security detail at military headquarters. Correa said he was shot in the arm Saturday by the Americans.

He said he heard shots and saw the American car pass by, apparently after going through a checkpoint. The car had a flat tire, he added, and the occupants were yelling.

Southern Command officials have said repeatedly the only shooting was by Panamanian troops.

*Credit*: Reprinted with permission of The Associated Press.

## ANDREW ROSENTHAL: PRESIDENT BUSH CALLS PANAMA SLAYING "AN ENORMOUS OUTRAGE"

*This front-page story not only reported the most current events in Panama but also provided a lengthy overview of the situation. Because of its placement and timing, the story would have been widely read not only in the United States but internationally as well.*

*New York Times*, 19 December 1989

President Bush today called the weekend slaying of an American Marine officer by Panamanian soldiers "an enormous outrage." With tensions high, a United States military officer in Panama City wounded a uniformed Panamanian a few hours after the President spoke.

Frustrated by the success of Panama's military leader, Gen. Manuel Antonio Noriega, in thwarting American vows to depose him, Mr. Bush and his senior aides said they were leaving open the possibility of military action in Panama after Panamanian soldiers shot and killed a Marine officer at a roadblock on Saturday night. The officer's identity and rank have not been made public.

### TROOPS, OR STRONG LANGUAGE?

But it is not clear whether the Administration is seriously considering specific plans or whether officials, still smarting from criticism of their handling of the failed coup attempt in Panama in October, are simply employing more muscular language to keep the heat on General Noriega while they decide how to proceed.

Mr. Bush, who was interviewed today by four reporters from news services, avoided giving a direct answer when asked how he would respond to the new violence in Panama. "All Presidents have options," he said, "but they don't discuss what they might be."

The United States Southern Command in Panama City, which has about 12,000 soldiers, has a set of contingency plans to deal with Panamanian provocations or attacks against United States military or diplomatic personnel. The troops are in the region as a rapid deployment force and to defend the Panama Canal, but in the months since General Noriega annulled free elections, they have often been on heightened alert because of tensions between the two countries.

Marlin Fitzwater, the White House spokesman, said today that the shootings were part of "a pattern of indiscriminate violence" touched off by General Noriega on Friday when he declared that a state of war existed between Panama and the United States.

## DETAILS SKETCHY ON NEW SHOOTING

Details of the shooting in Panama today were sketchy. But American military officials here and in Panama City said a United States Army lieutenant was leaving a laundry near the headquarters of the United States Southern Command when he was approached by a uniformed Panamanian. There were conflicting reports about whether the Panamanian was a police officer or a member of General Noriega's army.

At first, Pentagon officials told reporters that the Panamanian drew his own gun and the American then fired twice. But the Pentagon later gave a different version. In a written statement, the Pentagon said the American was leaving the laundry when he was approached by the Panamanian, who "signaled the serviceman to stop and then approached him."

"The U.S. serviceman felt threatened when he saw the Panamanian apparently reach for his weapon," the statement said. "The American responded defensively by pulling a weapon and fired two shots. The Panamanian went down, then got up and left the scene. The extent of his injuries is unknown at this time and the event is currently under investigation."

The Associated Press, reporting from Panama, quoted a Southern Command official, who refused to be more specifically identified, as saying that the Panamanian was an army corporal.

The shooting was the second violent episode in 48 hours involving American and Panamanian forces. On Saturday night, Administration officials said, Panamanian soldiers shot and killed one of four American officers who had taken a wrong turn in their car and wound up at a roadblock near the headquarters of General Noriega's forces.

In an interview today with the New York radio station WBAI, General Noriega said the Americans started the shooting by firing first and wounding several people, including a girl, a night watchman and an elderly man.

## "A GRAVE ESCALATION"

Panama's Foreign Minister, Leonardo Kam, said at a news conference in Panama City that two civilians and a soldier were wounded by the Americans in that confrontation. He called the episode "a grave escalation in the permanently hostile policy of provocation and intimidation that the U.S. Army has been systematically pursuing against the Panamanian people."

But Administration officials said the American officers were unarmed. They said they were in civilian clothes and lost in the Chorrillo neighborhood, near the military headquarters. At a roadblock, Panamanian soldiers tried to pull the Americans out of their car and then opened fire when they fled, killing one and wounding another in the ankle, Administration officials said.

The American military in Panama was on a Delta One alert today, restricted to bases that were patrolled by guards in combat gear. Panamanian Government troops with machine guns blocked the street in front of the Panamanian military command.

## HANDLED PERSONALLY BY BUSH

In Washington tonight, the Panamanian situation was reportedly being handled personally by Mr. Bush and his top-level advisers, including Brent Scowcroft, the national security adviser, Secretary of State James A. Baker 3d, Secretary of Defense Dick Cheney and Gen. Colin L. Powell, the Chairman of the Joint Chiefs of Staff.

If the top echelon was considering specific military action, orders had apparently not been passed down to lower-level planners and strategists in the Pentagon. The Joint Chiefs did not convene a formal session on Panama today. Senior officers said there was considerable sentiment for not allowing the shooting to pass unanswered, but there was no clear sense of what form such a response would involve.

Mr. Fitzwater also cited American reports that Panamanian soldiers had beaten and interrogated an American naval officer on Saturday night and sexually threatened his wife. Other members of the American military were detained and had their weapons and radios taken away at a Panama airport during the weekend, he said.

Last week, American officials said a Panamanian soldier pointed a gun at a United States officer near a garbage dump, but no shots were fired.

"When you put all of these together, you begin to discern a certain climate of aggression that is very disturbing," Mr. Fitzwater said.

## "IT'S PRETTY OPEN-ENDED"

Asked about the possibility of military action in Panama, a Pentagon official said: "There is always the potential that things can get elevated, but at this point we're going to see what develops. It's pretty open-ended and we haven't closed the door on the military option, but it's conditional on what happens next."

The official said the shooting today was not thought to have been linked to the killing of the American officer and the other incidents over the weekend.

Another Administration official said that the Panamanian military "tried to reassure us that the Saturday night shooting was an accident, an isolated incident that was unintended."

The official would not say whether the United States had accepted that explanation. "We don't think there's an excuse for what happened," he said.

Earlier today, reports that elements of the Army's 18th Airborne Corps were on alert prompted speculation that the United States might be planning a military response in Panama. The 18th Airborne is the Army's fast-reaction force and includes paratroopers of the 82d Airborne Division.

But the Pentagon issued a statement this afternoon saying the units were involved in previously scheduled exercises to test their readiness. The exercises "are not related to the incident in Panama," the statement added.

The Pentagon did not identify the units of the 18th Airborne Corps involved in the exercise, but some officials said that it involved the 82d Airborne.

*Credit:* Copyright © 1989 by The New York Times Co. Reprinted with permission.

---

## JOHN OTIS: "U.S. CRITICIZES PANAMA MEDIA REPORTS ON SHOOTING"

---

*This wire service story out of Panama City provided U.S. readers with the kind of inside view that supported the U.S. troop intervention soon to come.*

### United Press International, 19 December 1989

PANAMA CITY, Panama: The U.S. Southern Command Tuesday accused the pro-government Panamanian media of distorting weekend events that have increased tension between the two countries.

"I am very concerned to see the false stories in the official regime newspapers," said Mercedes Morris, a spokeswoman for the Southern Command.

Since the Saturday night slaying of a U.S. Marine lieutenant by Panamanian troops, the local pro-government media has stressed claims by the Panamanian Defense Forces that several Americans ran a checkpoint near PDF headquarters and fired on Panamanian soldiers and civilians, injuring two civilians and a PDF soldier.

The PDF has not acknowledged that an American died in the incident.

Morris denied the Panamanian version, saying the U.S. servicemen never fired into a crowd of people.

"That is a blatant lie. They (the U.S. military officers) were unarmed. They had no weapons in the car," Morris said.

The newspaper Critica Tuesday quoted Foreign Minister Leonardo Kam as calling Saturday's shooting "acts of terrorism and intimidation . . . by four U.S. soldiers." The story was headlined: "Our Country Will Not Kneel Before Anyone, Least of All Before the U.S."

Critica columns and editorials cast doubt on the U.S. version of the events.

Morris said the local press is trying to confuse Panamanians.

"They are trying to mislead public opinion," Morris said. "It was the PDF that fired."

According to the Southern Command, the four Americans felt threatened when they were stopped at a PDF checkpoint at about 9:05 P.M. Saturday. As they fled the scene in their car, PDF soldiers fired five times at the car, killing one U.S. officer, the command said.

In Washington, the Pentagon Tuesday identified the U.S. military officer killed in Panama City as Marine Lt. Robert Paz, 25, of Dallas.

The U.S. Southern Command has said Paz was one of four off-duty officers wearing civilian clothes who were stopped by about 40 Panamanian civilians and five or six Panama Defense Forces soldiers on Saturday night.

According to the Southern Command the Panamanians attempted to pull the officers out of their car. As the servicemen sped away, shots were fired and Paz was hit. He was taken to Gorgas Hospital in Panama City, where he died.

Morris said the incidents of Saturday and Monday, in which a U.S. serviceman shot and wounded a Panamanian police officer, were under investigation.

*Credit:* Reprinted by permission of UPI.

## JOHANNA NEUMAN AND JUAN J. WALTE: "U.S. ALERT FOR ATTACKS IN PANAMA"

*This front-page national newspaper story would have made everyone in the United States aware that U.S. troops would soon be in action.*

### USA Today, 19 December 1989

The Pentagon said a Panamanian was shot after appearing to reach for a weapon during a standoff at a laundry.

The incident follows Saturday's killing of a U.S. officer. President Bush, voicing "enormous frustration" that Gen. Manuel Noriega still leads Panama, refused to rule out military retaliation.

"I think a president, all presidents, have options, but they don't discuss what they might be," Bush said.

The White House—whose first response was low-key—Monday upped the ante, calling the weekend death a murder.

Noriega's declaration of war against the U.S. Friday—at first shrugged off by the White House—"may have been a license for harassment and threats and, in this case, murder," said spokesman Marlin Fitzwater.

He cited two other incidents Saturday between U.S. troops, Panamanian Defense Forces:

- U.S. military policemen were detained, interrogated and stripped of weapons and radios by the PDF.
- A U.S. Navy lieutenant was questioned for four hours, beaten, kicked in the groin; his wife was sexually threatened.

"When you put all of these things together," Fitzwater said, "you begin to discern a certain climate of aggression." Experts say they could be more significant than thought:

- Former U.S. Ambassador Ambler Moss: "This is one more indication of the last stage of the dictatorship—the 'bunker' stage, the one where things start to come apart."
- Panama opposition leader Ricardo Arias Calderón: "The danger is that this can provoke a greater confrontation."

*Credit*: From USA TODAY, a division of Gannett Co., Inc. Reprinted with Permission.

## BRYNA BRENNAN: OAS ISSUES MILD RESOLUTION CALLING FOR U.S. TROOPS TO LEAVE PANAMA

*This wire service story reported the opposition of the Organization of American States to the U.S. troops entering Panama to seek Noriega, but it was coupled with other wire service stories that reported the White House statements of necessity and success in Panama.*

### Associated Press, 22 December 1989

WASHINGTON: The Organization of American States, in a rare move, closed ranks formally against the United States on Friday for invading Panama. A State Department spokesman said: "We are outraged."

A pre-dawn OAS vote followed a marathon emergency session that began Wednesday hours after thousands of U.S. troops assaulted Panama and attempted to capture dictator Manuel Antonio Noriega.

OAS members cast aside Nicaraguan and Panamanian calls for condemnation, approving instead a resolution "to deeply regret the military intervention in Panama" and call for the withdrawal of troops used in the U.S. action. It did not specify a timetable.

The written resolution was considerably milder than the oral debates in which even staunch U.S. allies spoke out against the invasion. But it was the first time since the so-called tuna wars along South America's Pacific coast in early

1970s that the OAS issued such a strong document against an American action.

The United States, however, said it opposed any type of rebuff.

"We are outraged," State Department spokesman Richard Boucher said. "It is unacceptable."

A prepared State Department statement said: "We are disappointed that the OAS missed an historic opportunity to get beyond its traditional narrow concern over nonintervention. The resolution is unbalanced. It does not cite the root problem—Noriega. It also fails to recognize the threat to Americans in Noriega's 'state of war' declaration, our Panama Canal Treaty rights and our sovereign right to self-defense."

The State Department statement noted that the language of the resolution was to "regret" rather than condemn. The Spanish version of the resolution, however, translates closer to "deeply deplore."

"That's how they sold it to the Caribbean nations," said a State Department official who asked not to be identified.

Shastri Ali, the No. 2 at the Trinidad and Tobago Embassy, said Friday: "What we voted in favor of was to deeply regret. It seems we agreed to different things."

John Maisto, the U.S. deputy permanent representative to the OAS, earlier called the final resolution "a mixed bag. . . . We're a little disappointed. It certainly wasn't an extreme resolution, but it's a little detached from what is really happening in Panama."

The OAS approved the resolution on a 20–1 vote. Abstentions came from El Salvador, Honduras, Venezuela, Antigua and Barbuda, Costa Rica and Guatemala.

The resolution noted "the serious events (in Panama), especially the armed clashes resulting from the military intervention by the United States and the deplorable loss of lives and property."

The State Department statement said "part of the explanation" for the resolution was "that the rightful representative of the new Panamanian government was not at the meeting."

The OAS members rebuffed a request by Panama's newly installed President Guillermo Endara to seat his appointed representative. Noriega loyalist, José María Cabrera, spoke out repeatedly against the "criminal abuse" by the United States.

U.S. Ambassador Luigi Einaudi cast the only negative vote on the motion outlined by Peru, Brazil, Mexico, Colombia, Uruguay and Argentina.

He failed on an 11–4 vote with two abstentions to add to the resolution a mention that the OAS charter itself allows each nation the right of self-defense.

Einaudi said that once Noriega declared a state of war against the United States, U.S. officials "clearly have the legitimate right of self-defense."

The ambassador also said the United States has tried to work out a peaceful solution of the Panamanian situation through the OAS but "it is impossible to reason with a dictator. At the end, Noriega has got what he deserved."

A U.S. attempt to label the invasion a "military action" failed with only three votes among the 26 delegates who attended the 17-hour debate and negotiation.

*Credit*: Reprinted with permission of The Associated Press.

---

# ELOY O. AGUILAR: "U.S. PLANES BOMB RESISTANCE POCKET IN PANAMA CITY"

*This wire service story out of Panama City is an example of the necessity for U.S. troops in Panama that the White House pointed to during press conferences during this week in December.*

## Associated Press, 22 December 1989

PANAMA CITY, Panama: Two U.S. planes late Thursday bombed a strong pocket of resistance in the capital manned by troops loyal to fugitive Gen. Manuel Antonio Noriega as the second day of the American invasion ended.

Flares lighted the moonless sky. Helicopters flew low over parts of Panama City, shining bright lights.

On Thursday afternoon, hours before the bombing, U.S. troops on armored personnel carriers shouted over megaphones for residents near the Tinajitas garrison in the northeastern San Miguelito neighborhood to evacuate. Sporadic machine-gun fire could be heard.

U.S. soldiers throughout Thursday ducked occasional gunfire in mop-up operations and ringed the Nicaraguan and Cuban embassies with armored personnel carriers in case the elusive Noriega was inside.

Thousands of U.S. servicemen swept into Panama City on the second day of their huge offensive, trying to wipe out diehard resisters and hunting for Noriega, while also searching for missing Americans believed to be hostages.

President Bush pledged in Washington Thursday that U.S. forces would scour Panama "as long as it takes" to capture Noriega. He said the military operation he ordered created stability in Panama and said "it's been worth" the American lives it cost, while expressing sorrow over the deaths.

He has ordered a $1 million bounty for the capture of Noriega, who has been charged in the United States with drug-running and money-laundering.

Looters swarmed the streets of Panama City like locusts Thursday. Thousands, from children to grandparents, stripped store shelves down to bare wood on Central Avenue.

U.S. soldiers were too busy with snipers and small bands of armed Noriega loyalists to challenge the looters.

The force in San Miguelito was composed of fighters from the civilian, paramilitary "Dignity Battalions" and other Noriega loyalists.

U.S. armored personnel carriers were seen heading Thursday night toward San Miguelito, a large working-class neighborhood of 340,000 people.

Residents said people they believed were Panamanian combatants were fleeing to more secure areas and the poor were being evacuated.

Elsewhere, machine guns rattled and explosions boomed near Cerro Patacón hill behind Santa Maria University, close to U.S. Army communications installations.

Pentagon officials said U.S. troops had military control of Panama City. They said most units of Noriega's Defense

Forces had fled into the jungles, and U.S. troops may be ordered in to follow them.

They reported 21 Americans killed, 208 wounded and four missing in two days of fighting.

Figures for Panamanian casualties were hard to come by.

An official in the office of Leonardo Diaz, medical director of the Santo Tomás Hospital, said the hospital had taken in 80 dead and more than 1,000 wounded.

"We have really lost count of the wounded," she said, refusing to give her name. She said many of the wounded were civilians coming from areas of fighting near Defense Forces barracks.

"The morgue is now full. We have no place to put the dead," she said.

She added the hospital was running low on medical supplies.

Santo Tomás is the hospital nearest the bombed and burned-out Panamanian Defense Forces headquarters, flattened on the first night of the invasion.

An exhausted emergency room doctor at the hospital could give no breakdown of civilian or military casualties. The Dignity Battalions and some of Noriega's elite units, such as the Machos de Monte, wear civilian clothing.

A Spanish photographer was killed and a French and an English photographer were wounded Thursday in crossfire between U.S. troops who mistook each other for Panamanian forces in the Marriott Hotel parking lot, other journalists said.

An Associated Press photographer saw flares being fired Thursday night near Anton, 60 miles southwest of Panama City and a few miles from the Panamanian Defense Forces base of Río Hato. People were taking refuge in a local school.

Troops from the 82nd Airborne Division stopped the photographer, Matias Recart, at Anton and refused to let him continue to Panama City.

Residents said Panamanians attacked American positions at Río Hato, then apparently went into the mountains.

Dignity Battalions were seen at several points between Anton and the western city of David.

China on Friday came to Noriega's defense, saying U.S. troops invaded because the Panamanian strongman opposed U.S. attempts to gain permanent control over the Panama Canal. The official Xinhua News Agency called it a "rather novel and sensational" cliché that America sent troops to bring to trial "what it called a 'drug trafficker.'"

In Managua, the Nicaraguan capital, officials ordered troops and armored vehicles to encircle the U.S. Embassy because its embassy in Panama City was surrounded by American forces.

Defense Secretary Dick Cheney said in a TV interview that reinforcements sent to aid the troops based in Panama may be able to leave "within a few weeks." Earlier, officials said they hoped the action could take three days.

Looters who capitalized on the chaos set up stands in alleyways and sidewalks to hawk their wares to jostling hordes of Christmas buyers.

Slumdwellers peddled designer brassieres, French champagne and Gucci watches at bargain prices. Ritzy stores on Avenida España, Panama's main thoroughfare, were stripped of goods.

"Look," a young man said proudly, showing a gold watch. "I bought it for $20, the salesman didn't even realize it is a Gucci."

New President Guillermo Endara, sworn in by a Panamanian judge as U.S. forces invaded at midnight Tuesday, announced an 18-hour curfew that ends at 6 A.M. Friday. It had no immediate effect on the crowds.

Panama's newly installed leaders appeared at the legislative assembly building under heavy U.S. guard. U.S. soldiers in jeans, sweatshirts and other civilian clothes were sprinkled throughout the building.

Scattered bursts of gunfire came from San Miguelito and from a central hotel district taken over temporarily by armed Noriega supporters. They did not appear to be seeking confrontation with U.S. forces, however, but vandalized and looted hotel rooms and stole cars.

In Chitre, 100 miles southwest of Panama City, a Panamanian Defense Forces officer said the garrison of about 200 men had not been attacked.

"We are with . . . (Noriega) until the last bullet. We are ready for the gringos. We are waiting for orders," he said.

In David, 230 miles west of Panama City and 30 miles from the border with Costa Rica, residents reached by telephone said Noriega supporters controlled the streets and little looting occurred.

A U.S. military source at Southern Command said Noriega's brother-in-law, Lt. Col. Aquilino Sieiro, surrendered with some of his men in La Chorrera, 25 miles west of Panama City.

It was unclear if Noriega remained in control of the Defense Forces. In a clandestine radio broadcast late Wednesday, he called for a guerrilla war against the United States.

U.S. officials said 59 Panamanian soldiers had been killed and 66 wounded.

Officials said American troops had taken about 1,500 prisoners in the first 36 hours of armed combat.

After rumors spread that Noriega or other members of his high command were in the Nicaraguan and Cuban embassies, U.S. troops surrounded the missions.

Israel television reported from Jerusalem that Noriega had been spotted within the last 24 hours on Contadora, a resort island 40 miles south of Panama City. It said he was planning to escape to Nicaragua.

In Panama City, an armored personnel carrier driver had to ask a reporter for directions, and a soldier laying concertina wire at the Nicaraguan Embassy said, "We're just securing exits."

In Managua, Foreign Minister Miguel d'Escoto said: "We have ordered exactly that the same thing be done here, around the U.S. Embassy, as was done in Panama City."

U.S. Defense Department spokesman Pete Williams said reports surfaced of Americans held against their will. He said they included a group of 11 Smithsonian Institution scientists and John Myerson, a CBS News producer.

Later Thursday, the Smithsonian Institution said the 11 had been found and were awaiting rescue by U.S. troops. The group had been based on the San Blas Islands off Panama and included five Americans, five Panamanians and one Venezuelan.

But it was unclear if they were still captured or had been released.

Juan Antonio Rodríguez, a photographer for Spain's largest newspaper, El Pais, was killed when two groups of U.S. troops mistakenly exchanged fire, said Tomás Lozano, the Spanish ambassador. Two other journalists were wounded.

Patrick Chauvel of the Sygma photo agency was shot in the stomach and badly wounded, said French Ambassador Jacques Rummelhardt. Chauvel was on assignment for Newsweek magazine.

Malcolm Linton, an English photographer for Reuters news agency, was shot in the leg, said Tom Brown, a Reuters editor. Linton was listed in good condition.

The hotel was occupied by U.S. troops who arrived to rescue Americans trapped there.

Maruja Torres, a correspondent for El Pais, said six journalists were standing in a hotel parking lot when a U.S. armored personnel carrier approached. Apparently thinking it was a Panamanian forces vehicle, U.S. troops inside the hotel yelled at the six to get out of the way, then fired, Torres said.

The personnel carrier returned fire, said Torres.

Bush said Wednesday that the United States launched the invasion, the biggest military action since the Vietnam War, to bring Noriega to trial on the drug charges and to ensure the safety of the 35,000 Americans living in Panama.

American officials helped install Endara as president and Ricardo Arias Calderón as first vice president and Guillermo Ford as second vice president.

Outside observers said the three opposition politicians were winning elections here last May 7 when the Noriega-controlled government nullified the balloting.

The Panama Canal opened Thursday after closing Wednesday, the first time anything other than a landslide has forced the 75-year-old canal to close. The 43-mile-long waterway will be open only during daytime until at least the weekend, for fear of terrorist attack, the Panama Canal Commission said.

About 13,000 troops are regularly stationed in Panama to protect the canal. About 9,500 others were flown in for the invasion. Reinforcements were sent in Wednesday to assist exhausted troops.

American forces appealed Thursday in radio broadcasts for Noriega's forces to surrender.

"Do not fight for a small group of drug traffickers," one broadcast said in Spanish.

Officials said they believed the dictator remained in Panama, despite reports that placed him in Colombia, Mexico and the Dominican Republic.

On Wednesday night, Noriega tried to rally his supporters by making a brief radio address in which he vowed to "win or die."

The wily dictator has eluded 24,000 U.S. soldiers after managing to withstand intense U.S. political and economic pressure for two years. The invasion followed Noriega's declaration last Friday that Panama was in a "state of war" with Washington and the shooting death Saturday of a U.S. Marine lieutenant in what American officials called an unprovoked shooting.

*Credit*: Reprinted with permission of The Associated Press.

---

## JOHN M. BRODER AND ROBIN WRIGHT: HOW THE UNITED STATES IS HUNTING NORIEGA

*This story reported another aspect of the White House's more subtle efforts to capture Noriega in a community that was particularly concerned with drug trafficking.*

*Los Angeles Times*, 22 December 1989

WASHINGTON: The call came into the Pentagon at 2:20 P.M. Thursday.

"My code name is MKO. Noriega is at 78.3 degrees west latitude and 9.3 degrees north longitude in the jungle moving east with 18 men, heading toward the coast, where a 20–25 foot surface boat is prepared to take him out of the country."

Right, one military officer sighed, "and Elvis is out there waiting for him."

American officials in Washington and in Panama sorted through hundreds of such tips Thursday as they pressed a massive manhunt for deposed Panamanian dictator Manuel A. Noriega.

U.S. troops combed Panama for the crafty fugitive, using an array of high-tech electronics tracing gear, sophisticated "movement analysis" techniques and a small army of informants—as well as the promise of a $1-million bounty for Noriega's capture.

Despite the unprecedented efforts, the only thing American officials said they knew for sure late Thursday was that Noriega had not left Panama.

President Bush said the United States is "concentrating every way we possibly can to find Noriega" and said that the hunt is "open-ended" until the former dictator is located.

"His picture will be in every post office in town," Bush declared in a televised news conference. "He's a fugitive drug dealer."

Noriega was being pursued by teams of Army Delta Force and Navy SEAL commandos, other military special troops, FBI and Drug Enforcement Administration agents and perhaps, U.S. officials have speculated, hit men from the Medellín drug cartel who have put a price on Noriega's head because he cheated them in a drug deal some years ago.

Gen. Colin L. Powell, chairman of the Joint Chiefs of Staff, declined to discuss the manhunt, saying that he does not want to jeopardize an "ongoing operational mission." But he said that there is "a difference between tracking Mr. Noriega and tracking reports of Mr. Noriega."

He acknowledged that the Panama operation failed in one of its key missions—to capture Noriega at the outset. "A plan only exists up to the time of execution," Powell said. "Then you're into audibles"—a football term for improvising at the line of scrimmage.

Defense Secretary Dick Cheney said U.S. agents tried to tail Noriega closely in the days before the invasion but frequently lost him. "There were periods of time when we knew where he was with precision and sometimes when we didn't," Cheney said.

The officials said that consideration was given to mounting a limited kidnap operation before the invasion, but it was rejected because "we didn't have sufficient confidence in his location" to assure the operation's success.

U.S. officials endeavored to cast the Noriega manhunt as a law enforcement operation rather than a military exercise, in part by including the FBI and the DEA, sources said.

"If we hunt him down as a criminal by people who professionally hunt down criminals, then it looks better," an Administration source said. "We don't want to make him a fugitive *bandido* being hunted by Marines. He's not Pancho Villa, he's John Dillinger. We don't want to give him the honor of arms. He is not an honorable soldier."

A sincere effort was being made to take him alive, one official in Washington involved in the manhunt said. "I have no indication that anyone has quietly said, 'Terminate with extreme prejudice,'" the official said.

"At the same time," he conceded, "some people would not be saddened by his death. A smart person would not want to get Noriega alive. You don't want a long trial where he makes his big speeches, where the wound stays open, where people demonstrate, where he might say things people don't want to hear. He might name names, for example."

U.S. intelligence agencies know that Noriega has prepared a substantial number of "trap doors" in Panama to disappear through in case he had to run, officials said. He is thought to maintain as many as 11 safe houses in and near Panama City and may be employing a series of tunnels to move from one to another, sources said.

Noriega was expected to try to escape by air from Paitilla airport in the eastern part of Panama City, and the airfield was one of the first objectives seized by American commandos in the early hours of the invasion. Four Navy Seals were killed in that operation.

Noriega also is believed to maintain redoubts at David and Chiriqui, near the Costa Rican border and in the San Blas Islands, off the Caribbean coast.

All these known hide-outs came under American control or surveillance early in the operation, Administration officials said.

The search for Noriega has spawned scores of reports on his location; most, like the anonymous call to the Pentagon, were not very credible.

"There are so many wild rumors, from the French Riviera to Santo Domingo to Paraguay," said an Administration official involved in the manhunt.

Israeli television reported that Noriega and a renegade Israeli intelligence agent who served as his bodyguard were on the island of Contadora off Panama, plotting their escape to Nicaragua.

A U.S. intelligence source dismissed the Contadora report out of hand. "It's the most unlikely place I can think of," he said. "How would he get there? It's wide open. It's hot as hell. And it does not have its own water, so it's very expensive to survive there."

Another American law enforcement official predicted that Noriega would next appear in Havana, but he gave no concrete evidence to support the theory.

Neal Livingstone, an American terrorism consultant who formerly had extensive business dealings in Panama, said Noriega most likely is holed up in Panama City or its suburbs.

"It's much easier to hide there. He hasn't lived in the jungle in years, and he's easier to see there. And all it takes is one guy who wants to make a million bucks, and he's history," Livingstone said.

Noriega probably was being protected by a small band of loyalists trained in Cuba and East Germany, Livingstone said. These guards themselves are wanted by Panamanian and American authorities, so they have nothing to gain by turning in Noriega, he said.

Noriega has to watch his back, however, U.S. government sources said. "The biggest incentive is the reward. In Panama, a million bucks is a lot of money, an awful lot of money," one official involved in the operation said. "Noriega's operation survived off corruption and greed, so the money is the most potent weapon against him."

## THE NORIEGA INDICTMENTS

The intended capture of Gen. Manuel A. Noriega would enable U.S. authorities to bring him to trial on drug trafficking charges in Miami and Tampa, Fla. Indictments unsealed Feb. 5, 1988, marked the first time that federal charges were filed against a foreign leader who was not in the U.S. Noriega could receive up to 145 years in prison and more than $1.1 million in fines if convicted. The charges:

THE MIAMI INDICTMENT charges Noriega with conspiracy, racketeering, importing drugs and traveling to further conspiracy. It accuses him of:

- Accepting a $4.6-million bribe from Colombia's Medellín drug cartel to protect shipments of cocaine, launder money, supply drug laboratories and shield drug traffickers from the law.
- Allowing smugglers to use Panama as way station for U.S.-bound cocaine.
- Traveling to Havana so that Cuban President Fidel Castro could mediate dispute with Medellin cartel after Panaman-

ian troops seized drug laboratory that Noriega had been paid to protect.

- Using his official positions both before and after he took control of Panama, in 1983, to provide protection for international criminal narcotics traffickers.
- Arranging for shipment of cocaine processing chemicals, including those seized by Panamanian police.
- Laundering cartel's narcotics proceeds in Panamanian banks.
- Allowing cartel leaders to shift operations to Panama to escape crackdown in Colombia after assassination of that country's anti-drug minister of justice.

THE TAMPA INDICTMENT accuses Noriega of:

- Conspiring to import and distribute marijuana.
- Attempting to import more than 1.4 million pounds of marijuana.
- Accepting $1-million bribe from drug dealers for his authorization to smuggle drugs and launder cash in Panama.

*Credit*: Copyright © 1989, Los Angeles Times. Reprinted with permission.

---

## MARJORIE MILLER: CHAOS, LAWLESSNESS, AND PANIC IN PANAMA'S STREETS; ROVING GANGS TERRORIZE COUNTRYMEN AND FOREIGNERS; U.S. TROOPS FIRE AT IRREGULARS

*This story out of Panama City, paired on the front page with the preceding story, would have been confirmation that the U.S. efforts in Panama were manyfold and very necessary.*

*Los Angeles Times,* 22 December 1989

PANAMA CITY: Torn by the invasion of American troops, the capital of Panama erupted into chaos Thursday as panic, gunfire and lawlessness swept the city.

Because the Panamanian army, which doubled as domestic police, had fallen in defeat, roving gangs of thugs—many of them loyalists of strongman Manuel A. Noriega—took to the streets, terrorizing countrymen and foreigners alike.

They fired into 100 screaming guests and employees at the Marriott Hotel, gunned down an American schoolteacher returning from dinner with friends, used two other American women as shields and stole a school bus to go on a shooting and stealing spree.

The U.S. Embassy was hit by a rocket-propelled grenade and six rounds of small arms fire, Col. Ron Sconyers, a U.S. commander who toured the city after nightfall, told reporters. He said that the embassy was secure on only three sides. During his tour, he said, he saw shattered store windows by the hundreds and bonfires in the streets.

Looters carrying refrigerators, microwave ovens, tires and gasoline shouted, "Viva Bush! Viva Bush!" and chanted, "Bush! Bush! Bush!" One, the new owner of a knife sharpener, waved it at members of a Pentagon media pool that ac-

companied the U.S. troops to Panama and joked, "It is a present from Bush."

The slain schoolteacher was identified as Gertrude Kandi Helin of Dixon, Ill., who taught in Panama City. The two women held hostage were Mary Rebhan, 24, of Hollywood, Fla., and Tara King, 25, of Dallas. Both were freed unharmed.

The school bus stolen for the shooting and robbing spree ended up abandoned. It was not known whether it had held any children when it was taken, but no Panamanian youngsters were reported hurt.

As his first official act, newly installed Panamanian President Guillermo Endara closed all public and private establishments and clamped a curfew on the country.

It did little good, however. "It's bad downtown, 10 times worse than you've ever seen, worse than El Salvador was last month," Lt. Col. James L. Swank, a spokesman for the Southern Command, told reporters.

A dozen civilians were missing, Swank said. He did not say how many were Americans. But he added: "There's some indication that some are hostages."

He said 1,500 to 2,000 U.S. military police were patrolling Panama City. But a Panamanian resident told The

Times that some American troops became so disoriented they had to beg natives for directions.

One GI, who asked to remain anonymous, said mortars had shelled Howard Air Force Base.

Was this a mop-up operation? he was asked.

"Hell, no!" he replied.

The mayhem began before dawn. While looters turned the streets of Panama City into an early Christmas bazaar, U.S. troops prepared to evacuate guests and employees from the Marriott.

As they were about to be moved from the hotel cafeteria into waiting trucks, Panamanian irregulars opened fire from a passing car, wounding at least one American soldier in the chest and stomach.

Screaming in panic, guests in the cafeteria dived for the floor. Heavily armed U.S. soldiers, their faces daubed with camouflage, shouted, "They're coming in from the front! They're coming in from the back! Get a gun position! Everyone stay down!"

"We returned the fire," an American officer told Reuters news agency. "One of them was hit, and they sped off."

Calm returned. The troops shouted orders for the civilians to leave behind all their luggage and to move quickly into a pair of airport delivery trucks. These two trucks, with armed soldiers mounted on each, drove in a convoy. Two Sherman tanks and a jeep equipped with a 15-millimeter machine gun led the way. They drove to safety in the ruins of a pirate fortress.

By the time the pre-dawn darkness had turned to morning and then to afternoon—and the busy looters had set up shop on the sidewalks, hawking everything from designer brassieres and French champagne to Gucci watches—Manuel Cupas, a lawyer in an upscale part of Panama City, reported the school bus theft and shooting spree.

He gave a tense account to The Times by telephone as the action unfolded.

"There's no police at the moment," he said, looking out his window. "There is a big bus full of people. . . . About 50 to 60 persons moving out toward the Mansion Dante (boutique) right at this moment. . . .

"It's an 'Instituto Pedagogico' (school) bus. . . . They probably stole the bus. . . . Listen . . . they are breaking in. . . . They are trying to get into the boutique. That's a gun. . . . Who's shooting? All of them are getting in for the merchandise. . . . There's a car stopped with people with guns, and they've started firing at all those guys. . . . The bus is still there. Jesus Christ! Nobody is hurt. . . .

"They just shoot to move the people. They are running. . . . I don't know them. I don't recognize that car. One of the people who got the gun . . . Wait. Wait. (To his pregnant wife) Get down! Jesus, I am on the floor now! I am on the second floor, but the bullets are going. . . . (To his wife) Go over there! . . . My wife is expecting our first baby in April. . . . Are they moving away? Wait a second, I will see what I can see. They just left. Everybody left. . . .

"I hope my wife is OK. She was afraid. We have a balcony enclosed with windows facing the street. . . .

"They are robbing now at the other side of this building. It's the Taxi store. Still shooting. . . . Do you hear this? I am on the floor again. One of the stores is called Taxi. (To his wife) What do they sell there? They sell men's clothes. They are destroying it."

Cupas said the first band of robbers, those who arrived in the school bus, looked like members of the Dignity Battalion, a violent paramilitary group loyal to Noriega. The second group, he said, looked like armed civilians.

Rebhan and King, the two American women taken as human shields, told their story to members of the Pentagon media pool. They said they were taken captive at the Panama City airport Tuesday night, shortly after U.S. troops arrived.

The women said they had gone to the airport to pick up Rebhan's brother, flying in for her wedding at the end of the month.

As U.S. forces closed in on the terminal, the women said, 30 armed Noriega loyalists took the two of them captive and holed up in a sweltering customs room.

"They had us in chokeholds for most of the time," Rebhan said.

"They made us kneel down," King added. "(They) held guns to my back and to her head."

American troops began to arrive in force to take over the airport, but the Panamanians held them off with the women.

"For six hours they made us keep shouting, 'Go away. We're Americans. They're going to kill us . . . if you come,'" Rebhan said.

Just before dawn, the Americans set a deadline of 6:30 A.M. for the Panamanians to surrender and told them they were surrounded and that Noriega was already dead. In fact, Noriega's whereabouts were not known. But his loyalists fell for the bluff—and gave up.

A number of Panamanians reported attempts to organize private security teams.

Leticia Arias, 39, a lawyer who lives in a two-story home in the upper-middle-income neighborhood of La Loma near downtown Panama City, told The Times by phone that 200 families were taking turns as "watch teams" while other families slept.

Nearly all armed themselves with small-caliber weapons, including .22 pistols and hunting rifles, she said.

She said the families were terrified that members of Noriega's Dignity Battalion would raid their neighborhood Thursday night. The families prayed for the arrival of American soldiers who could restore peace.

"I don't know why the Americans have not come to take care of the neighborhoods," Arias pleaded. "Tonight (roving gangs) are going to kill all of us. We all have guns. We are armed—not heavily, with .22s and .45s or hunting rifles. They are the only things we have to defend ourselves.

"There are no police in the streets, no one to take care of

us. We are very afraid of what will happen to us tonight. We are waiting for American soldiers to come. We haven't seen one."

Arias described the day as "horrible for the businessman in downtown Panama."

"All the people went to the streets, especially low-class people . . . and destroyed businesses, drug stores, department stores, hardware stores, everything—the whole city," Arias said. "They have been stealing cars, which they load with refrigerators, furniture.

"In the cars are men armed with shotguns and heavy arms. All these people have had so many needs over the past two years, they feel now is the time to get what they need. They rob supermarkets because they are hungry. That is the mind of these people.

"The Dignity Battalion . . . calls the people from the street and tells them, 'You can get whatever you want.' The poorest people are listening to them."

In downtown Panama City, fear was just as keen.

Celia Cabrera, who lives in a second-story apartment, said by telephone that she was afraid to leave her building. At dawn, she said, she heard planes overhead and saw soldiers surrounding a government building nearby.

"Maybe," Cabrera said, "they thought he (Noriega) was hiding in there.

"There is a lot of vandalism," she added. "People are breaking windows, taking everything they can. I have gone down to the first floor, but I don't want to go outside. I see people running by, some of them shooting."

Rodrigo Vives, a lawyer living in a fourth-floor condominium near the banking center, said he had stockpiled enough food for himself, his wife and two children to live for five days without having to venture outside his building.

"We are tired of disorder," he said. "Now that night is coming down, my neighborhood is letting others know that we are going to defend ourselves. We are shooting any person coming nearby. We need more permanent protection. At least a couple of small American jeeps would help."

Staff writers Richard E. Meyer, Maria Newman, Louis Sahagun and Tracy Wilkinson in Los Angeles and researchers Edith Stanley in Atlanta and Anna Virtue in Miami contributed to this story.

---

## GEORGE SKELTON: AMERICANS STRONGLY BACK BUSH ON PANAMA INVASION

---

*This third front-page story reassured Americans that they were unified in their support, and confirmed the need for such military intervention.*

*Los Angeles Times*, 22 December 1989

Americans strongly support the massive U.S. invasion of Panama and agree with President Bush that "it's been worth it" despite the loss of American lives, The Times Poll found Thursday.

If Panamanian dictator Manuel A. Noriega manages to escape capture, however, this enthusiasm could cool some. And the public does not believe the invasion has made life any safer for the 35,000 Americans in Panama, the survey showed.

Two reasons cited by Bush for unleashing the largest U.S. invasion force since the Vietnam war were "to bring General Noriega to justice in the United States," where he is wanted on drug-trafficking charges, and "to safeguard the lives of American citizens."

But Americans think the invasion has accomplished two other goals enunciated by Bush: "To defend democracy" and to protect U.S. rights under the Panama Canal Treaties.

The Times Poll, directed by I. A. Lewis, interviewed 700 adult Americans by telephone Thursday afternoon and night. The margin of error for a survey this size is five percentage points in either direction.

"There is a tendency for Americans to rally 'round the flag whenever U.S. armed forces are first sent into battle," pollster Lewis noted. "But if the situation drags on, the public could easily become more critical.

"What we are measuring now is mostly first impressions. A number of factors will have a lot to do with the final public attitude—things like how quickly Noriega is captured, the extent of American casualties, the reaction of other Latin American governments and how soon American troops can pull out."

But on the second day of the invasion by more than 20,000 U.S. Marines, paratroopers, infantrymen, sailors and airmen, American citizens interviewed by The Times Poll were supporting the attack by a ratio of more than 5 to 1, with 77% approving and only 15% disapproving. In fact, 56% approved "strongly."

Politically for Bush, coming on the heels of a generally successful summit meeting with Soviet President Mikhail S. Gorbachev, the invasion seems to have increased his popularity. Eighty percent now approve of how the President is "handling his job," compared to 66% during a pre-summit survey by The Times Poll and just 59% last March.

In Thursday's poll, two-thirds of those interviewed agreed

with Bush's statement at a press conference a few hours earlier that the invasion had "been worth it" despite the loss of American lives. As of late Thursday, the Pentagon was reporting U.S. combat casualties of 21 dead, 208 wounded and four missing.

But nearly a third of the people surveyed said they will consider the invasion to be "less successful" if Noriega is not captured. On Thursday, Bush vowed to keep U.S. troops hunting for Noriega "as long as it takes." And in the survey, people on the average said they expect that it will be nine months before American forces can be withdrawn.

Roughly a third of the people also worried that U.S. troops could get "bogged down" in Panama as they did a generation ago in Vietnam, although nearly two-thirds thought this to be unlikely.

Underscoring their concern for the safety of possible American hostages in Panama, half of those surveyed feared that the invasion had "further jeopardized" U.S. citizens living there. Only 37% felt that American lives had been made "more secure."

But half believed that the attack had resulted in a more secure Panama Canal. Less than one-third thought it was now in further jeopardy. Only about 1 in 6 advocated scrapping the Panama Canal Treaties, which call for turning over the canal and U.S. military bases to Panamanian control on Dec. 31, 1999.

Roughly 6 in 10 people said the U.S. military operation "has brought democracy closer to realization in Panama," where a new government was sworn in as the invasion began.

Emphasizing their approval of the attack, a majority of people considered it to be "morally justified." And two-thirds asserted that the United States had "made every effort to negotiate a peaceful settlement" before invading.

*Credit*: Copyright © 1989, Los Angeles Times. Reprinted with permission.

---

## WALTER V. ROBINSON AND PHILIP BENNETT: "HARROWING TALES OF AN UNTIDY INVASION"

---

*This story published on the opposite coast mirrored those of the* Los Angeles Times *and reinforced the necessity and the success of the U.S. troops' actions.*

*Boston Globe*, 28 December 1989

At picturesque Fort Amador on the Panama Canal, years of peaceful coexistence between U.S. and Panamanian troops ended abruptly at 1:15 A.M. last Wednesday with the staccato burst of machine-gun fire and the crack of artillery rounds hitting home.

The invading U.S. military forces, leaping from assault helicopters onto a golf course in front of a row of six dormitories of the Panamanian Defense Forces, literally drove their quarry into the sea.

Thousands of bullets pierced the stone walls of the barracks. Every window was blown out. Deafening howitzer rounds rained on the red-tile roofs of the buildings. The sidewalk was littered with concrete rubble and severed palm fronds.

In the aftermath, a lone Panamanian boot pierced by a machine-gun round provided striking evidence of the firepower and the flight it provoked.

The boot, resting on a footlocker inside one of the devastated buildings, corroborated U.S. accounts of the action; most of the Panamanian troops, including the owner of the boot, were so stunned by the ferocity of the attack that they fled barefoot out the back door of the barracks and down a grass-covered slope to Panama Bay, where they swam for their lives.

"Five hundred of them were captured there, many of them pulled from the water by Navy patrol boats," said Staff Sgt. Enrique Salcido, a member of the U.S. assault force. And what of those who stayed to fight? "They died there," he said.

So began the largest hostile U.S. military operation since the end of the Vietnam War—the invasion of a sovereign nation in order to overthrow its government and capture its leader, a corrupt but shrewd military dictator despised at home and wanted on drug-trafficking charges in the United States.

During the next hours and days, two dozen Americans and hundreds of Panamanians, most of them civilians, would lose their lives and livelihoods in an extraordinary demonstration of U.S. firepower, in the desperate resistance of government supporters and in the frenzied looting of a society pushed to the brink of disintegration.

But the military success of the U.S. invasion hinged most heavily on the decisions of thousands of Panamanian soldiers, like those at Fort Amador, to avoid the fight in the face of overwhelming odds. They faced superior soldiers and weapons that included the $600 million Stealth fighter.

In many respects, this was the chronicle of an invasion foretold. It was the result of detailed U.S. planning during more than two years of political and economic pressure by two U.S. administrations that failed to force Gen. Manuel Antonio Noriega from power. Noriega predicted the invasion, the U.S. hinted at it, Panamanians awaited it and, even in its destructive aftermath, found reason to applaud it.

But like any conflict of its size and complexity, the invasion did not unfold according to either side's script. After being followed for days by U.S. intelligence agents, Noriega escaped capture. U.S. forces failed to secure a major hotel, the Marriott, and American civilians were taken captive as a result. While the Panamanian Defense Forces crumbled more quickly than analysts expected, paramilitary groups loyal to Noriega provided more resistance than anticipated.

After eight days, U.S. military might has quieted most of the shooting and driven Noriega, who once vowed never to surrender, into refuge at the Vatican Embassy. A monumental task of rebuilding confronts the new civilian government. And the United States, once again the preeminent force in Panama's affairs, faces an indefinite economic and military commitment to the country.

What is more, troubling moral questions remain for U.S. policy makers and for an American public that appears to support the military solution to the irksome Panamanian question.

The rubble of Chorrillos, the poverty-stricken neighborhood where American bombs and artillery rounds killed scores of civilians and devastated the homes and possessions of hundreds of others, illustrates the problem: U.S. policy forbids, and the American public opposes, the use of assassination—"the 45-cent solution," as one soldier put it, referring to the price of a bullet. But it condones military action of the sort that, at least for the poorest in Panamanian society, has had immeasurably higher costs.

It now seems clear that the failure of U.S. intelligence agents to locate Noriega early last Wednesday, despite having tracked him for several days, prolonged the shooting and led to additional deaths. Diplomats say there was evidence that Panama's intelligence service, which the general once headed, may have alerted Noriega to the invasion as much as 72 hours in advance.

By most accounts, Noriega moved as many as 20 times a day to avoid U.S. forces before fleeing the apartment of the mother of his mistress minutes before U.S. troops arrived there. He rushed to the Vatican Embassy, several blocks away, on Sunday.

Although U.S. military officials now say that Noriega abandoned his troops and hid from combat, Gen. Maxwell Thurman, the commanding general of the U.S. Southern Command, said three days into the operation that the general was leading organized resistance by his scattered troops.

The confusion following the invasion spawned another war, too, with its own grim costs to Panama. Evidence of its destructive path can be found in virtually every street in the city and on the faces of many Panamanians as they seek to come to grips with a relatively prosperous society that was torn asunder in a day's time.

Within hours of the start of the invasion, the disintegration of the Defense Forces contributed to anarchy on the streets. Without police, Panama became a lawless place, its commercial and retail sectors looted, its streets piled with trash and many of its residents heavily armed and at war with one an-

other. Some of its most thoughtful citizens are convinced that it may be difficult to reestablish civilized behavior.

In Betania last Saturday night, a skirmish in the street war convinced Leonardo Montenegro, an accountant who lives in that middle-class Panama City neighborhood, that it will be a long time before Panama regains its footing.

Throughout the city, and in Betania, too, neighborhood vigilante groups patrolled against marauding gangs of Noriega supporters and other hoodlums bent on taking advantage of a cowed populace with no police force to protect it. That night, three such hoodlums invaded a neighbor's home, according to Montenegro, robbing the family and, for a few frightening moments, threatening to kill their daughter.

The men fled, but alert neighborhood vigilantes apprehended two of them, according to Montenegro. The enraged father, bearing a revolver a friend had taught him to use only hours earlier, rushed up to the two suspects and, at point-blank range, shot them dead. Their bodies were left on a street corner, and the men returned to be with their families.

Americans died here, too—23 soldiers as of yesterday and two American civilians. As is so often the case in war, soldiers die from making the wrong split-second decisions. That is what happened to the first American, and the only Marine, to die here.

By 1:05 A.M. last Wednesday, the war began and ended for Marine Cpl. Garreth C. Isaak of Greenville, S.C. Isaak, just eight days shy of his 23d birthday, drew an unlucky straw that night: He was the point man for a force of 110 Marines assigned to capture a Panamanian Defense Forces outpost at Arrijan, just outside the city.

The Americans crawled through a fence toward the outpost. Once in position, according to 1st. Lt. Dan Kraus, they yelled to the soldiers inside to surrender. There was no response.

Isaak moved forward, reached the door and pushed it open. A single shot from inside pierced his neck, killing him instantly. The Marines returned fire, peppering the building's front wall with 39 bullets. One Panamanian soldier was killed; the three others inside, who had been asleep when the Americans arrived, surrendered meekly.

The 82d Airborne Division's first brigade, 2,000 men from Fort Bragg, N.C., was more fortunate. Thanks to U.S. firepower and rigorous training, the entire brigade parachuted onto a runway at Omar Torrijos International Airport and secured much of the airport without sustaining a single casualty.

The men had sat shivering, mostly from the cold but some from fear, for nine hours before stepping into the darkness over the airport—four hours on the ground at Pope Air Force Base in Fayetteville, N.C., waiting for their aircraft to be deiced for takeoff, and five more hours aloft, all the while clad in summer-weight tropical uniforms.

Before the brigade boarded the aircraft, chaplains of different denominations conducted services, and many of the men clambered aboard carrying pocket-sized editions of the New Testament handed to them along with their ammunition.

En route to Panama, recalled Maj. Baxter Ennis, "some men read the Bible. Others prayed. It was a somber, mildly apprehensive feeling. We expected a fight."

But the 82d did not get one, at least initially. Shortly before they parachuted, an AC-130 aircraft "hosed down" the airport and a Panamanian barracks there, destroying the barracks with a combination of howitzer fire and 20mm cannon fire. The defenders were either killed or fled before the 82d arrived.

Simultaneously, U.S. forces were punishing Noriega's downtown headquarters and the surrounding slum of Chorrillos with fierce air attacks and ground fire. Minutes before the area was leveled and civilian homes incinerated, U.S. troops shouted in Spanish through megaphones for residents to evacuate.

"The soldiers told us all to leave," said Carmen Herrera, the mother of three. "People were crying and praying. I thought we would all die there."

Her tenement ablaze, Herrera carried her baby daughter from the apartment followed by her two other young children. They ran through a hail of gunfire to a Catholic church, Our Lady of Fatima, where they cowered on the floor. They escaped in the morning to a refugee center in the Canal Zone.

"You see why I say that the invasion was good and bad," she said later. "Many soldiers and people died. Young soldiers who were defending Panama because they had been ordered to. They were there all over on the ground."

A short distance away, just minutes from the headquarters of U.S. Army forces, 20 young members of Noriega's feared investigative police, known as the DENI, were thrown from their beds by an assaulting company of U.S. troops. The Panamanians inside the building began to argue.

"Ten of us wanted to leave and 10 of us wanted to stay and fight," said a soldier who was in the building. "Their force was so much greater than ours. I thought that this was the end. So I took off my uniform and ran. The 10 who stayed all fell there."

By late last week, the soldier, who asked that his name not be used, had joined the new Panamanian Public Force, the security body loyal to the U.S.-installed civilian government. He mustered with former members of the Defense Forces in a parking lot outside an apartment complex for the U.S. military.

Among those in the parking lot was Maj. Juan Antonio Guizado, once an officer loyal to Noriega and now the new chief of police cooperating with U.S. forces. He had been in a restaurant with his wife when the invasion broke. He drove home, he said, and "never looked back."

"Someday, we'll all forget this unfortunate episode," he said. "We have always been such good friends, the United States and Panama."

*Credit*: BOSTON GLOBE by WALTER V. ROBINSON AND PHILIP BENNETT. Copyright 1989 by GLOBE NEWSPAPER CO (MA). Reproduced with permission of GLOBE NEWSPAPER CO (MA) via Copyright Clearance Center.

---

## DIEGO RIBADENEIRA: ENDARA TRIES TO ESTABLISH HIS CREDIBILITY AS NEW PANAMANIAN PRESIDENT

*This story out of Panama City begins to put more of the human face on the abrupt invasion of the U.S. troops. Though the United States has had a long history with Panama, the day-to-day life of the people there was initially not part of the reports when troops moved in and the political situation grabbed the headlines and most of the media attention.*

*Boston Globe*, 28 December 1989

PANAMA CITY: As businesses struggled to reestablish themselves in this war-torn city, the newly installed Panamanian leadership worked yesterday to establish credibility and move away from being seen as a proxy U.S. government.

In a well-orchestrated ceremony at the government's new headquarters, guarded by American soldiers, Panama's Electoral Commission released revised results showing that in elections in May, Guillermo Endara handily defeated the candidate chosen by the deposed leader, Gen. Manuel Antonio Noriega.

Meanwhile, tension in the capital continued to ease on the eighth day of the invasion by 26,000 American troops. For the first time since U.S. forces toppled Noriega, no American soldiers were reported shot yesterday, and scores of members of the former Panamanian Defense Forces continued to surrender.

At various sites established by American troops across Panama City, Panamanians relinquished hundreds of weapons, including AK-47s.

U.S. soldiers surrounded the Vatican Embassy in the southern sector of Panama City, where Noriega sought refuge Christmas Eve. While American officials tried to exert pressure on the Vatican to release Noriega to U.S. authorities so he can stand trial in the United States on drug charges, the Vatican gave no indication that it might turn over the deposed Panamanian strongman.

Not far from the Vatican Embassy, the new Panamanian government scrambled "to regain Panama's national sovereignty."

Endara appeared to be the winner in the May 7 elections, but Noriega nullified the results. Yesterday, Endara was presented a certificate declaring him president, and he donned a sash bearing the colors of the Panamanian flag.

"Today we begin a new era of democracy in Panama," said Endara as he sat between his two vice presidents, Guillermo Ford and Ricardo Arias Calderón, inside the heavily protected Foreign Ministry, which is serving as presidential headquarters.

But it is clear that the new Panamanian democracy is still dependent on the security supplied by the American soldiers.

The streets around the Foreign Ministry were surrounded by barbed wire. U.S. soldiers armed with machine guns behind sandbags kept a watchful eye on people around the building. Access was limited to those with government-issued passes.

While invading U.S. forces struggled to establish the new Panamanian Public Force to replace the Defense Forces, the streets of Panama City are still patrolled by U.S. military police, only some of whom are accompanied by Panamanian police officers.

"You can imagine what it is like to totally take out a police force of a large American city and then try to replace it with something completely new," said Lt. Col. Jerry Murguia, an Army operations official. "You can imagine the scope of the problem. But we are progressing at a positive pace."

As Panama City recovered from the fighting, which sparked widespread looting and destroyed thousands of homes, traffic in the center of the city gridlocked. With no police to enforce traffic regulations, drivers devised their own rules, going down sidewalks, across parks and down the wrong way on one-way streets to cut through the city.

Despite pleas from the Endara government for business owners to help restore a semblance of normalcy to commerce, the vast majority of businesses remained closed yesterday.

However, the nation's banks, vital to Panama's economy, are scheduled to reopen today.

In some of the poor sections of the city, black markets appeared, with vendors plying goods that had been looted just a few days ago. Along Central Avenue, vendors sold everything from sunglasses to portable stereos to clothes.

"Venao," shouted several sellers in Calidonia, a lower-income neighborhood. The word is a Panamanian slang for people who sell stolen contraband.

One 21-year-old man, who said his name was Pedro, wheeled a large Samsonite suitcase down the avenue. The suitcase contained several designer sweaters that he was selling for $20 each.

"Everybody has to make a living somehow," said Pedro.

The hottest topic of conversation was the fate of Noriega.

On Tuesday night, American soldiers shot out the lights around the Vatican Embassy without explanation. Yesterday afternoon, American soldiers were seen tinkering with phone lines into the Vatican Embassy.

According to a 1904 treaty between the United States and Panama, Panama can surrender Panamanians sought in the United States to American authorities.

"We believe Noriega's crimes are not political but that instead he is a common criminal of the worst type," Endara said. He added that the Vatican Embassy "should in the very near future ask that criminal to leave its premises."

Asked what would happen if Noriega is expelled, Endara said, "As of this moment, we are not thinking of anything in particular."

Trying to bolster his fledgling government, Endara also named four more government officials, including the director of social security and the deputy minister of planning and economic development.

*Credit*: BOSTON GLOBE by DIEGO RIBADENEIRA. Copyright 1989 by GLOBE NEWSPAPER CO (MA). Reproduced with permission of GLOBE NEWSPAPER CO (MA) via Copyright Clearance Center.

## JOSEPH B. FRAZIER: UNITED STATES DECLARES FEBRUARY TROOP PULLOUT FROM PANAMA UNLIKELY

*This report seems to reflect the public view that troops should come home soon, though the White House appeared less willing to withdraw until Noriega was in custody.*

Associated Press, 28 December 1989

PANAMA CITY, Panama: The United States would like the extra troops it sent here out by February but that is unlikely because Panama's security forces must be rebuilt from scratch, a senior U.S. Embassy official said Thursday.

The official told a press briefing the newly formed security forces are made up largely of officers and troops from Gen. Manuel Antonio Noriega's old Panama Defense Forces and that adjustments are being made province by province.

"We cannot get to that fully in one month," he said, speaking on condition of anonymity.

He said one change already was made in the southern city of Las Tablas in Los Santos province.

While people there were celebrating, he said, the zone military commander told them to whoop it up all they wanted but to bear in mind that the Americans were leaving—and he was staying.

The man was arrested and replaced, but this is the type of thing that needs to be sorted out, the official said.

"It is no secret that the new government does not have a lot of confidence in some of these people," he said.

He said former officers who were exiled, arrested or retired because Noriega didn't like them were called back to duty, but they make up a small minority of the officer corps.

He said no indication emerged of a guerrilla movement taking to the hills following last week's U.S. military invasion that drove Noriega from power. Should that happen, he said, the United States—not Panama—probably would deal with it.

The United States had 12,000 troops stationed in Panama and 14,000 more were brought in as reinforcements. The official said authorities had hoped to be able to withdraw all the extra troops by February.

"That's probably not meetable," he said.

He said one problem is that the strength of Noriega's paramilitary "Dignity Battalions" is not known. He said the battalions are "still there to be turned back on again."

U.S. troops are convinced of Cuban troop involvement but no evidence has surfaced, he reported.

He said about 3,300 "shooters" were in the 16,000-strong Defense Forces and about three-fourths of those have been accounted for. The rest were in support or police roles, he said.

The official said he believes the new government is looking at forming a security force at a lower level than a conventional army but stronger than a police force. Also, there may be a move to decentralize and move some functions to other agencies. Noriega had consolidated all police-related functions within the Defense Forces to keep better control.

The AP reported Tuesday that U.S. military officials want to establish a professional army but officials of President Guillermo Endara's government fear an army would become a threat to democracy. The armed forces ruled Panama the last 21 years.

The U.S. official said a list exists of people sought by Panamanian and American forces. Most were caught, but some are believed to be in the Vatican Embassy and the Cuban Embassy residence.

Noriega's wife, Felicidad, is in the residence. She is not on the wanted list, but investigators want to see if she came by all she has legally, he said.

He said former Finance Minister Orville Goodin, who holds Panamanian and American citizenship, had $3 million in cash with him when arrested.

"I think they just gave it back to the bank he took it from," the official said.

He said the United States does not want to be seen as running a puppet government in Panama.

"What we want to do is fix it right," he said. "We sure don't want to do this again."

*Credit*: Reprinted with permission of The Associated Press.

---

## TOM RAUM: "WHITE HOUSE SAYS NORIEGA FATE UP TO VATICAN, SEES NO HOSTAGE PROBLEM"

*This report, on the same day as the preceding one, evidenced the White House's frustration with the recent surprise from Noriega and political relations with the Vatican.*

Associated Press, 28 December 1989

CORPUS CHRISTI, Texas: The White House said today the fate of ousted Panamanian leader Manuel Antonio Noriega is now "in the hands of the Vatican," although President Bush's spokesman said U.S. troops surrounding the Vatican embassy are prepared to move in if hostages are taken.

Presidential press secretary Marlin Fitzwater said that the U.S. position on Noriega remains the same: "We believe that he is, as an indicted person, a criminal and not a political refugee in the normal sense of someone who seeks political asylum."

However, the spokesman suggested negotiations on Noriega remain delicate.

"We continue to make our views known, the Vatican continues to consider this matter. And we leave it to them to work this out as they see fit," he said.

"This matter is now in the hands of the Vatican," said Fitzwater, briefing reporters in Corpus Christi as Bush enjoyed a hunting vacation on an isolated ranch near the south Texas community of Beeville.

Asked about a reported letter from the papal representative in Panama City saying U.S. troops could go into the embassy if a hostage-situation arose, Fitzwater said:

"We have no indication there is trouble within the nunciatura. There are no hostages that we're aware of."

But, he added, "Certainly, would there be any danger there, we would be prepared to offer assistance to help.

"However, we do not see any at this time. We do not anticipate any," he added.

Noriega has been holed up in the Vatican embassy since Christmas Eve.

Fitzwater said that, although some Noriega loyalists that had been in the embassy with Noriega have been released to U.S. authorities, "most of his cronies are still there."

Fitzwater said that, overall, "the situation is good and

steadily improving" in Panama, with the U.S.-backed government of Guillermo Endara "continuing to expand its control."

Although Bush has voiced continued determination to have Noriega returned to the United States, administration officials said privately that little headway has been apparent in prying Noriega from the Vatican embassy to face drug trafficking charges in the United States, and they expressed some frustration at the pace of negotiations.

"I want to see this man who is under indictment brought to justice for poisoning the children of the United States of America and people around the world," Bush said at a barbecue held in Beeville Wednesday night in his honor.

The president and fellow Texan, Secretary of State James A. Baker III, are spending the next few days quail hunting here on the 10,000-acre ranch of William Farish, a wealthy Houston oilman and longtime Bush friend.

Bush, who has been coming here for a holiday season quail hunt annually for more than two decades, thanked the crowd of more than 700 people "for this homecoming."

Fitzwater said Bush was receiving briefings in writing and by phone on any developments in Panama, but otherwise intended to spend the day hunting.

"Look, I don't make any cover. I'm going to be enjoying myself and I think the American people understand that," Bush told reporters on his arrival at the Corpus Christi Naval Air Station.

The president spent several hours fishing on nearby San Jose Island, where he said he and Baker caught about a half-dozen fish.

Meanwhile, Justice Department officials are planning to ask "one or two" more European countries to freeze bank ac-counts where Noriega is thought to have hidden illegal drug profits, spokesman David Runkel said today.

Similar requests were made Wednesday to the governments of four nations—France, Luxembourg, Switzerland and the United Kingdom. Runkel said those governments are cooperating.

Authorities in France responded by freezing accounts in two banks holding $3.3 million under the names of Noriega and members of his families. Swiss officials placed a "precautionary" freeze on two accounts in banks in Zurich and Geneva.

Speaking to reporters in Corpus Christi, Bush congratulated Romania's new president, Ion Iliescu, and said he was "amazed and respectful" of the changes there.

"My concern is for tranquility and freedom in Romania," Bush said.

He declined to criticize harshly the quick executions of former dictator Nicolae Ceausescu and his wife, adding, "We did say that we were concerned that the trial of Ceausescu should have been more open, but that's their matter."

Regarding Noriega, the president said a Vatican refusal to simply turn over the former Panamanian dictator to U.S. officials does "complicate matters."

Hinting that trying Noriega in Panama remained an option, Bush said: "The main thing is he should be tried and brought to justice." He made clear, however, that bringing Noriega back to the United States remains a clear first choice.

Bush, speaking from a podium standing behind bales of hay, received a hearty ovation when he told the crowd in Beeville, "I am determined to bring him to justice."

*Credit*: Reprinted with permission of The Associated Press.

---

## DOUGLAS GRANT MINE: "PANAMA STRIVES TO RESUME NORMAL LIFE; NORIEGA STANDOFF CONTINUES"

---

*This story and the next one both emphasized the end to hostilities and the desire of the Panamanians to try to return to productive lives in a post-Noriega world.*

### Associated Press, 28 December 1989

PANAMA CITY, Panama: President Guillermo Endara's fledgling government worked to reopen banks and public offices today and to resume full Panama Canal operations for the first time since the United States invaded.

Endara on Wednesday appealed again to the Vatican Embassy to surrender deposed strongman Manuel Antonio Noriega for trial on drug trafficking charges.

The Vatican today said it had received no formal request from the Panamanian government and would not simply push Noriega out and hand him over to U.S. authorities.

"We have not received any letter," said Joaquín Navarro, the Vatican's chief spokesman. He said neither Pope John Paul II nor any other Vatican official had received a message from the government.

In Texas, President Bush said his administration was determined to bring Noriega to the United States to stand trial, but admitted that the Vatican's stand "complicated things."

The U.S. invasion began Dec. 20 and Noriega was on the run until appearing at the Vatican Embassy on Sunday.

U.S. troops, armored cars and helicopters have stood watch outside around the clock to ensure he doesn't escape or get spirited away.

Navarro said the Vatican still hoped to resolve the crisis within days but he gave no details about negotiations.

He also declined to comment about a story in today's Los Angeles Times in which the Vatican Embassy in Panama reportedly authorized U.S. forces to take necessary measures in the event that Noriega or his associates take the Vatican envoy or any other staff hostage.

The newspaper said the authorization has been interpreted by some U.S. officials as an invitation to the United States to seize the ousted Panamanian dictator from the embassy, while others have said that isn't the case.

Navarro said he couldn't comment on the report because he didn't know the source of information for the report.

He also was asked to comment on reports that several Noriega associates had been persuaded to leave the embassy.

"As far as I know, has been persuaded to leave," Navarro said.

The Rev. Marcos McGrath, archbishop of Panama, said today there were few of Noriega's associates left in the embassy, and he predicted Noriega would be the only one left by Friday. McGrath spoke on ABC-TV's "Good Morning America." Panama's new government hustled to restore order in the streets of the capital, screening members of Noriega's disbanded Defense Forces and incorporating a growing number of them into a new armed force that includes police.

Some former Defense Forces members were seen directing traffic, patrolling streets and guarding government buildings on Wednesday.

The U.S. Southern Command said all but a few hundred of the 15,000 members of the Defense Forces had surrendered or been arrested.

Alfredo Maduro, president of the Panamanian Chamber of Commerce, said insurance brokers had conservatively estimated losses caused by looting or other damage to businesses in the capital at $750 million to $1 billion.

Maduro said businessmen planned to ask the United States for "something like a Marshall Plan for Panama" to recover and resume operations.

A spokeswoman for the Panama Canal Commission said

the waterway planned to return to a full 24-hour schedule today.

The U.S. Justice Department asked France, Switzerland, Luxembourg and Britain to freeze bank accounts in which Noriega is believed to have stashed more than $10 million in "illegal drug money."

France froze accounts in two banks holding $3.3 million and Swiss officials placed a "precautionary" freeze on two accounts.

The United States and the Endara government, which was elected in May balloting that Noriega nullified, renewed their pleas to the Vatican to turn over the ousted military ruler.

U.S. troops cannot go after Noriega, who was thought to be trying to negotiate safe passage to a third country, because embassies are inviolable under international law.

"We feel that the nunciature, the papal nuncio should in the very near future ask the ex-dictator to leave," Endara said. "We believe that Gen. Noriega's crimes are not political. He is a common criminal of the worst kind."

Noriega was indicted by two federal grand juries in Florida in February 1988 on charges of trafficking in Colombian cocaine and money laundering.

Endara said Panama's constitution forbids extradition of Panamanian nationals to another country but said a loophole, which he did not immediately specify, might be provided by the 1904 treaty that allowed the United States to build the Panama Canal.

The Southern Command said Wednesday 23 Americans have been killed and 322 wounded since the United States invaded. It said 297 Panamanian troops were killed and 123 wounded.

Army Lt. Col. Jerry Murguia cited an army surgeon as saying at least 250 civilians were killed. That figure did not include others who were quickly buried in the first days of the invasion, Murguia said.

*Credit*: Reprinted with permission of The Associated Press.

---

## DOUGLAS JEHL: U.S. TROOPS MOVE FROM BATTLE TO POLICE BEAT

---

*This report gave the American reader a sense of normalcy returning to Panama and would have helped ease any concerns about U.S. intervention lasting indefinitely.*

*Los Angeles Times*, 28 December 1989

PANAMA CITY: When the trouble began Wednesday morning, Cpl. Eddie Sonnier of the Army's 7th Infantry (Light) was manning his post in front of the Gago supermarket.

Just up the traffic-choked Avenida Transimica, a jet-black jeep had revved its engine, shifted gears and now was struggling to create a new lane by pushing aside one of the overturned cars that still litter the capital's streets.

The city may have been a war zone just a few days ago, but by Wednesday, much of the U.S. Army here was in the business of law and order, and the black jeep was clearly breaking the rules.

Sonnier and Pvt. Santiago Hernandez sprang from their post and sprinted up the block, pulled the car to the curb and pointed their M-16 rifles at driver Oriel Mate.

"I didn't know it would be a problem," Mate said in desperation. "I had to get to work." He even pulled a wad of $100 bills from his pocket and offered them to the Americans before they declined the bribe and sent him on his way.

"We're combat troops," Sonnier said as he walked back to his post. "I thought we'd be in the jungle by now."

Instead, he and the rest of his unit were standing on street corners in the rain, an occupying force struggling to fill in for the vanquished Panamanian police.

All across the city Wednesday it was much the same, as U.S. soldiers who had only a week before felt the rush of adrenalin as they parachuted into Panama and fought fierce battles now found themselves getting lost in residential neighborhoods as they tried to patrol the streets and chase after rumored criminal hide-outs and caches of arms.

It was war at its most stultifying, leaving troops muttering beneath their yawns and hoping aloud that military police might soon take over the role of patrolling.

"Our job is over as far as we're concerned," said Sgt. Coit Darst, a paratrooper whose Bravo Company had only a week before raided the Marriott Hotel to free more than a dozen American hostages. "This is where the MPs ought to come in."

But in the wake of an invasion that left Panama without practical civilian authority and forced its citizens to cope for themselves against bands of looters and thieves, U.S. commanders seemed determined to hasten the return of the capital to more normal times—even if it meant making police out of newly arrived infantrymen who spoke no Spanish and were unsure until a few days ago whether Panamanians drove on the right or left side of the road.

"We're transitioning from combat to pacification," said Army Brig. Gen. Joseph Kinzer, second in command of the 82nd Airborne, whose units have been given principal responsibility for restoring order to much of Panama City.

"What we need to do next is to complete the transition back to Panamanian control," he said. "But that's going to take some time."

A reporter who accompanied Bravo Company on a four-hour urban patrol Wednesday afternoon found soldiers not only unenthusiastic but also ill-equipped for the pacification role.

A jeep with a .50-caliber machine gun mounted on its roof got lost several times on a journey from battalion headquarters near the beach at Panama Viejo to a hilltop command post less than two miles away, making necessary repeated U-turns in narrow residential streets.

The infantrymen stationed to patrol the hilly *barrios* nearby moved from site to site in a Mitsubishi Montero that a resourceful sergeant had hot-wired from the Marriott parking lot. Otherwise, the troops explained, the infantry wouldn't rate its own transportation.

And most of the afternoon was spent on what one soldier referred to as yet "another wild goose chase" as the company investigated citizen complaints about a squalid El Barrako tenement rumored to house "hoodlums and thieves."

Like a SWAT commander calling for backup units, Capt. Steve Phillips assembled dozens of troops outside the suspect building and called in a "psychological operations" unit to make a Spanish-language appeal via loudspeaker urging the inhabitants to surrender their weapons.

But the tenement proved to be filled almost entirely with women and children, and a suspected arms cache inside numbered exactly one gun.

Bored troops who waited outside griped about "police work" and wondered what was for dinner.

"We're very sorry for disturbing your streets," the psychological operations jeep announced in Spanish as the company rumbled its way back to base. "The Panamanian police will be back very soon."

*Credit*: Copyright © 1989, Los Angeles Times. Reprinted with permission.

---

# DAVID BRINKLEY: THE UNITED STATES AND PANAMA

*This very long television news report focused on all aspects of the relationship the United States had with Panama, but the guests were particularly outspoken on the need to capture and punish Noriega. This news show would have been seen by hundreds of thousands of Americans and would have contributed significantly to the public view of the situation.*

### This Week with David Brinkley (ABC), 7 January 1990

DAVID BRINKLEY: All right, Noriega's in jail in Miami, but what do we do with him now? Try him, yes, but his lawyers say U.S. courts have no jurisdiction over crimes committed in other countries. President Bush says he only wants Noriega to have a fair trial. Fine, but what if, for some reason, he is found not guilty? What do we do with him then?

Panama will not take him back. He'd be lynched if he went there and it is not clear that any other country will have him. So there are questions, many of them. We'll put them to today's guests: [voice-over] General Brent Scowcroft, National Security Assistant to President Bush and Frank Rubino, attorney for Manual [sic] Noriega. Some background from our man Jack Smith and our discussion here with George Will, Sam Donaldson and Cokie Roberts. All here on our Sunday program. [on camera] First, the news since the Sunday morning papers. The Papal Nuncio in Panama says he gave Manual Noriega refuge in the embassy because he threatened guerrilla warfare and massive killing if he was not taken in. The nuncio told an Italian newspaper, "He gave me 15 minutes to decide." He didn't have time to contact the Vatican for instructions, so he decided himself to let Noriega in.

Mr. BRINKLEY: A massive effort by the United States, the U.S. Army and the people of Panama have forced out Noriega, the military dictator, and sent him to a Miami jail where he is now. Well, there is a long way to go before all of this mess is settled. Before we explore it, here's some background information from Jack Smith. Jack?

JACK SMITH, ABC News: [voice-over] David, the photo seemed to say it all, "Mission accomplished." But the capture of Manual Noriega doesn't close the book on the former strongman and nowhere is that more evident than with his trial which could become one of the most difficult in U.S. history.

RUDOLPH GIULIANI, former U.S. Attorney, New York: People should not expect a quick and speedy result here.

SMITH: [voice-over] In fact, Giuliani, who prosecuted Ferdinand Marcos, says the trial could drag on for two years. The case appears to break new ground. Can the U.S., for instance, try a foreign leader it just toppled from power? Noriega's attorneys plan to make an issue out of that and the pre-trial publicity which they say will deny him a fair trial.

STEVE KOLLIN, Noriega's Attorney: Are there any jurors, potential jurors in the United States who do not have a predisposition to this matter?

SMITH: Most of all, though, the defense is expected to tie up the prosecution with requests for classified documents it will claim are crucial to Noriega's defense. For years Noriega was an informer for both the CIA and the U.S. Drug Enforcement Agency. [voice-over] If the government balks on the grounds of national security, some of the 12 counts against Noriega could be dropped. Recall that the two central charges against Oliver North were dropped for that reason and just two months ago, the government dropped its entire case in the Iran-Contra trial of former CIA agent Joseph Fernandez because U.S. Intelligence wouldn't part with documents that reportedly merely showed the existence of CIA offices in Central America.

ROBERT KURZ, The Brookings Institution: Noriega knows a lot more than that and he is likely to expose a lot more than could have come out in the Fernandez case.

BILL MOFFAT, Criminal Attorney: It is conceivable that the threat to reveal information will force a deal.

SMITH: [voice-over] However, President Bush denied that—

Pres. GEORGE BUSH: Our government is not seeking a deal with Noriega.

SMITH: [voice-over]—and the Attorney General foresees no problems.

RICHARD THORNBURGH, Attorney General: [January 4, 1990] There's nothing that's come to our attention that would indicate that this trial can't go forward.

SMITH: [voice-over] At the very least, though, the documents will be embarrassing: letters of praise, for instance, from U.S. officials like this one from former Attorney General William French Smith; the fact also that George Bush met with Noriega at least twice, though the president denies he ever knew about Noriega's drug dealing; nothing damaging to national security perhaps, just the credibility of the U.S. government which, for so long, turned a blind eye to what Noriega was doing. If Noriega's trial is more painful than assumed, the same may go for other tasks facing the U.S. now, like repairing its strained relations with Latin America. The president Friday said he was sending Vice President Quayle to the region.

Pres. BUSH: [January 5, 1990] And I am determined not to neglect the democracies in this hemisphere.

SMITH: [voice-over] Equally important is rebuilding Panama itself.

ALFREDO MADURO, Panama Chamber of Commerce: We have a heck of a long road ahead of us: the recuperation of the economy, the democratic system of Panama.

SMITH: [voice-over] Apart from the damage caused by the fighting, there's the less visible damage caused by two years of U.S. sanctions which brought down Panama's economy by wrecking its lucrative banking industry. Perhaps hardest of all to rebuild, though, will be Panama's political institutions, undermined by 21 years of military dictatorship and shattered when the U.S. destroyed the Panamanian Defense Forces.

Sen. SAM NUNN, (D) Georgia: They were not just military, they were, as you well know, police forces, but they also were customs, immigration. They just were pervasive in terms of their running of the government. So we're really talking about replacing the government there and that is going to take some time.

SMITH: [voice-over] But with a fast pullout of U.S. troops now predicted, some experts worry the U.S. could botch the reconstruction.

Mr. KURZ: If we don't separate the army from the police and if we don't have a civilian police trained by policemen—the FBI or the Costa Ricans, as opposed to the U.S. Army—you're not going to get a democratic result.

SMITH: [voice-over] Another area where the effects of Noriega's capture may have been overrated: the war on drugs. Even the staunchest supporters of intervention admit it won't affect the flow of cocaine into the U.S.

Sen. ALFONSE D'AMATO, (R) New York: No. Absolutely not. There's so much in the way of drugs that have been already placed in the pipeline, that are ready for distribution. Noriega was a money-laundering specialist.

SMITH: [voice-over] But even there, the drug cartel moved its money-laundering operations elsewhere some time ago. [on camera] In short, no matter how satisfying it is to see Noriega in a U.S. jail, his being there does not solve American problems in Panama. If anything, military intervention now burdens the U.S. with even greater responsibility for Panama's future and for all that may go wrong there. David?

Mr. BRINKLEY: Jack, thank you. Coming next, Frank Rubino, an attorney who will defend General Noriega in court and shortly, General Brent Scowcroft, National Security Assistant to President Bush, in a moment.

[Commercial break]

Mr. BRINKLEY: Mr. Rubino, thanks for coming in.

FRANK RUBINO, Attorney for Manuel Noriega: Good morning.

Mr. BRINKLEY: Glad to have you with us. Here in the studio are George Will and Sam Donaldson, both of ABC News. Now, Mr. Rubino, you will be Noriega's lawyer if this case comes to trial, as apparently it will.

Mr. RUBINO: Yes, sir.

Mr. BRINKLEY: Do you know of any evidence likely to come out that will be embarrassing to the U.S. government?

Mr. RUBINO: At this stage of the proceedings, we have not got into the discovery part of the case which is wherein we will petition the government to provide us certain various materials which we will then review for importance of those materials to be used in court. We've not reached that stage yet.

Mr. BRINKLEY: Well, I know there are some aspects of the case you don't want to discuss in advance and, in fact, can't. But you have spent some time with the general, discussed his background and so on. Is there anything in what he says that you think might embarrass the government if made public?

Mr. RUBINO: Well, at this stage, my conversations with the general since his arrest have been going over certain areas about which we'll be filing pre-trial motions to dismiss the case based on various grounds. None of those go into sensitive documents or areas yet.

Mr. BRINKLEY: I see.

GEORGE WILL, ABC News: David asks about sensitive documents that might embarrass the United States generally or the current administration in particular. You would, however, be after documents that would exculpate your client. How might that work? What might you find in American files that would wash away the liability here?

Mr. RUBINO: Well, this would all be speculation at this point as to what the government may have. I think we just have to wait to receive those documents—

Mr. WILL: But you must have some idea what you might find. Give us a hypothetical that would indicate.

Mr. RUBINO: The one thing I've never done in 16 years of practicing law is to guess what may happen. I think the better course is to wait—to look at the documents, see what they are and then try to competently use them.

> The government chose to bring General Noriega to trial and they shall have their trial.

Mr. WILL: There's a whole new raft of documents allegedly found by American troops when they went into Noriega's headquarters. They probably did not have a proper warrant when they were doing that, at least by American search and seizure standards. Would you try and attack the admissibility of that evidence?

Mr. RUBINO: Oh, obviously. I mean, there is no provision in law for armed soldiers to kick down your door and seize documents from your home. There is no question that they will be severely challenged.

Mr. WILL: You also, I gather then, will argue that your client, in any case, having been described as a narco-thug terrorist and other things by American officials, cannot possibly get a fair trial. Others will say Jack Ruby got a trial and he committed his crime on television. How do you then argue that there's no way you can get a fair trial or will you?

Mr. RUBINO: I definitely will argue that General Noriega cannot receive a fair trial. You have to look at the whole equation of what it takes to make up a fair trial. Two problems we do not have. One, the prosecutor in the case, Miles Malman, is a competent prosecutor who I honestly believe will do his best to insure a fair trial. Judge Hoover is probably one of the best jurists we have and I'm sure that he's going to, without a doubt, do his best. But the pre-trial publicity is just amazing, the amount. And not only the amount of publicity, but the type of publicity. People have equated this case to North.

Mr. WILL: Given that you have this sort of—you think, a large club with which to beat the prosecution with on the publicity issue, might you then want to plea bargain?

Mr. RUBINO: Absolutely not. The government chose to bring General Noriega to trial and they shall have their trial.

SAM DONALDSON, ABC News: Your initial complaint was that we have no jurisdiction, that Noriega did not fall under the jurisdiction of the United States. But have you lost that now?

Mr. RUBINO: Absolutely not. That is one of the motions that will be filed. We did previously litigate an area of head of state immunity, but that time, General Noriega was in fact the general of the army. After that, he has now been appointed the maximum leader. At the time he was seized by the government, he was the maximum leader of the country, which would give him, in our opinion, head of state immunity. There are other grounds also we'll be attacking it on.

Mr. DONALDSON: Now, there was one fellow—I've forgotten his name—from the Bahamas, not the Prime Minister of the Bahamas, but from some small portion of that who was technically a head of state or government and we convicted him of drug dealing.

Mr. RUBINO: I think you're speaking of the Turks and Caicos case.

Mr. DONALDSON: I'm sure I am.

Mr. RUBINO: Yes. That particular gentleman, because

that is actually a colony or a protectorate, but not an independent country, he was not, in fact, head of state.

Mr. DONALDSON: All right. Have you seen Noriega? Have you seen him? Where did you see him?

Mr. RUBINO: Oh, yes. I meet with him in the federal courthouse.

Mr. DONALDSON: In other words, not in his cell?

Mr. RUBINO: No. The Marshal's Service has been kind enough to bring him out to a room, giving us a lot more—you know, considerable size and space where we can meet.

Mr. DONALDSON: For various reasons, is there any plan that you know of to move Noriega around to various federal installations throughout the United States for his safety, for instance?

Mr. RUBINO: No. The government's very concerned and rightfully so about his safety and they have advised us that they will move him to a secure location, but make him readily available to us at any time.

Mr. DONALDSON: How long do you think the trial will take?

Mr. RUBINO: The trial itself—the government announced two months, but I extremely doubt that. I would honestly say the trial itself, from the time we actually begin the case, less picking a jury, could take about four to six months. The jury selection could go on forever.

Mr. DONALDSON: All right. What do you think—

Mr. WILL: It's a long time.

Mr. DONALDSON: All right, let's explore that. What are the challenges that you will make to prospective jurors when you're picking the jury?

Mr. RUBINO: The pre-trial publicity is not the problem in and of itself. It's—the question the judge will ask is, "You've heard of General Noriega, you've received this pre-trial publicity. Based upon that, are you able to put this out of your mind and give this man a fair trial or have you already decided in your mind as to his guilt or innocence?" Since he has been portrayed in every form of press, television—the president of the United States said that he was a thug and a purveyor of drugs to children—I mean, obviously how can someone strike that from their mind and be able to give this man a fair trial?

Mr. DONALDSON: Well, are you saying that no jury could be found in the United States anywhere?

Mr. RUBINO: Well, I think we may be able to find someone who hasn't heard of this, but is that person qualified to be on a jury? Obviously, you want a jury of intelligent people who can go through the evidence, which will be very complex in this case, and come upon an intelligent verdict.

Mr. WILL: But you're postulating a rule of jurisprudence here whereby the more infamous you are, the more you're immunized by your infamy.

Mr. RUBINO: Well, we didn't create the infamy. That's the problem. The government could have done this in such a way as to not publicize General Noriega in the horrible negative light they have. They have created their own monster in this case.

Mr. DONALDSON: Are you going to apply for bail? Perhaps you have and I missed it?

Mr. RUBINO: No. At this stage, we have not asked for bail, at the initial appearance.

Mr. DONALDSON: Will you?

Mr. RUBINO: It is doubtful we will.

Mr. DONALDSON: It wouldn't be granted?

Mr. RUBINO: I think it's quite obvious it wouldn't.

Mr. BRINKLEY: Mr. Rubino—

Mr. RUBINO: Yes, sir.

Mr. BRINKLEY: —if you were a private citizen and on the list for jury duty and you understand that this trial is going to run for months, wouldn't you be likely to give an answer that is unsatisfactory so you would not be on the jury?

Mr. RUBINO: That happens quite often. I've tried long, complex cases wherein you go through a tremendous amount of people 'til you can reach people that can spend that much time. A lot of people probably will attempt to exclude themselves. Then, on the other hand, you have the problem of people who will try to get on the jury on purpose because they have some type of evil motive and that's something we have to sort out, too.

Mr. BRINKLEY: Well, I have one other question before our time runs out. Did the U.S. government at any time offer Noriega the option of going to some third country?

Mr. RUBINO: You mean, during the negotiations at the Vatican?

Mr. BRINKLEY: Well, any time in recent weeks, months, as far as you know.

Mr. RUBINO: The last time we had—we, being the lawyers, had contact with the U.S. government with respect to this was in October. At that time, I personally met with representatives of the government and options were discussed at that time. But since that date, nothing.

Mr. DONALDSON: How much about are you going to be paid for representing Noriega?

Mr. RUBINO: At this point, I don't know that answer.

Mr. DONALDSON: Where will the money come from? 'Cause clearly, you're not going to do pro bono work, are you?

Mr. RUBINO: Well, obviously, this case is so complex, one basically will have to shut their office down and do nothing but this case, I interpret, for about a year and a half.

Mr. DONALDSON: Well, I mean, a lot of people say that Noriega's funds are illegally derived, they're drug money. Can you accept money that, in fact, is drug money?

Mr. RUBINO: I cannot accept money that, in fact, is drug money. But just because a lot of people say it is, doesn't make it true.

Mr. BRINKLEY: Well, we will have to watch you, as you perform in this, with great interest. And thank you very much for coming in today.

Mr. RUBINO: You're welcome.

Mr. BRINKLEY: Pleasure to have you. Coming next, General Brent Scowcroft, National Security Assistant to President Bush, in a moment.

[Commercial break]

Mr. BRINKLEY: General Scowcroft, thanks for coming. Glad to have you with us.

BRENT SCOWCROFT, National Security Assistant: Good morning, David.

Mr. BRINKLEY: You know everyone here.

Mr. SCOWCROFT: Yes, indeed.

Mr. BRINKLEY: I would like to ask you a question I put to Mr. Rubino and I didn't really quite get an answer. At any time in recent weeks, months, was Noriega offered a chance to go to some third country and stay away, stay out of sight?

Mr. SCOWCROFT: There was some discussion of that early in October, but not since then.

Mr. BRINKLEY: And what? Was the offer made to him?

Mr. SCOWCROFT: I don't think it was ever presented personally to him, but the president made some comments that if he went to a third country with which we did not have an extradition treaty, that that would be all right, but that was some time ago.

Mr. WILL: In the Iran-Contra trials, two Republican presidents have taken pretty stiff lines, saying, "Even if it costs us the ability to proceed with certain prosecutions, we're going to hold the line on not releasing potentially embarrassing," or, I guess, injurious classified documents. Would you expect that to be the same policy in the Bush Administration regarding Noriega, that you're prepared to see his prosecution fail rather than release certain documents?

Mr. SCOWCROFT: Well, I think it certainly—George, let's distinguish embarrassing from important issues. Embarrassing, no, certainly not. And I think it's also important to remember that General Noriega has been indicted on drug charges. That's a fairly narrow kind—narrow part of his whole relationship with the United States. So, I'm quite comfortable.

Mr. WILL: Well, I think that a lot of Americans say, "Well, we'd like some idea, hypothetical but specific idea of what might be an injurious document that would be released." Can you give us some idea?

Mr. SCOWCROFT: No, I really can't. At the moment, as far as I know, there aren't any and you had the Attorney General saying he didn't anticipate any problems of that character. I don't—you know, I don't know whether the files have been searched to the ultimate, but—

Mr. WILL: Now, you emphasized that this is a drug indictment—

Mr. SCOWCROFT: Yes.

Mr. WILL: —a sort of common criminal case we have here, but what's uncommon about this is the use of the American military as a posse to get a head of state to bring him back here—

Mr. SCOWCROFT: Yes, indeed.

Mr. WILL: —to be tried. Now, some Americans say there must be other leaders, if not heads of state, certainly people active in politics in Latin America equally vulnerable to this

kind of operation. Would you see other people being warned by this and perhaps us going after others?

Mr. SCOWCROFT: I would not say that this is a precedent for any other action. Panama, in a number of ways, is unique and therefore, I would say this case, incident, whatever you want to call it, is unique. I would not draw conclusions from it.

Mr. DONALDSON: Is it correct, General, that Colombia has resisted our effort to use our fleet to blockade Colombia or in any way interdict the drug supply?

Mr. SCOWCROFT: We haven't really started discussions with Colombia. There are some stories that have leaked in the press. We are looking at ways we might able to improve interdiction across the Caribbean. Before we undertake anything, we will, of course, consult with any of the countries—

Mr. DONALDSON: Well, one of the stories had it that Colombia refused to consult with us last week. Is that correct?

Mr. SCOWCROFT: There have been some difficulties resulting in some premature and, I think, probably inaccurate leaks about what we had in mind.

Mr. DONALDSON: Well, define "difficulties." Define "difficulties" for me, then.

Mr. SCOWCROFT: Well, I think, you know, when you start—the term that was in the paper, for example, was "blockade." Now, that's a warlike, negative term. What we would be doing is—if we did anything down there—would be a cooperative effort in conjunction with the countries there to help get better control of the drug traffic.

Mr. DONALDSON: Well, a cooperative effort, but it is apparent at the moment that President Barco of Colombia is resisting the idea of cooperating.

Mr. SCOWCROFT: No.

Mr. DONALDSON: He is not resisting?

Mr. SCOWCROFT: This is a reaction to premature and inaccurate leaks. I think it'll work out.

Mr. DONALDSON: General, if I may, sir, you can't blame the press, can you?

Mr. SCOWCROFT: I'm not blaming. I'm not blaming anyone.

Mr. DONALDSON: I'm asking you questions now about what the facts are, not what has been in the papers. You've just told us that President Barco is not resisting. So he's going to cooperate with us?

Mr. SCOWCROFT: So far as I know, President Barco has not been seized with the problem. We have not presented it in that sense to President Barco so far as I know.

Mr. DONALDSON: So it's not a case that the fleet is steaming even before we have consulted with President Barco?

Mr. SCOWCROFT: Not so far as I know.

Mr. WILL: A word that keeps appearing in press reports speculating on how long American forces might be in Panama in their current role, is "reconstruction." It depends on how fast the reconstruction of the Panamanian army, civil government, economy takes hold. Is that the aim of American policy right now, reconstruction of Panama?

Mr. SCOWCROFT: Well, the aim of American policy is to assist the new Panamanian government to be able to turn itself into an operating government. They have come to power on very, very short notice and to the extent that we can be helpful, we want to. But I think it's important to distinguish between the troops that are in Panama on a more or less permanent basis—about 12,000—and the augmented troops that were sent down for the operation.

Mr. DONALDSON: How many casualties were there in Panama of civilians? A former Attorney General, Ramsey Clark, is saying this morning that he believes there were over a thousand civilian casualties and we've heard figures of two or three thousand.

Mr. SCOWCROFT: I honestly don't know, but I'm pretty certain neither does Ramsey Clark.

Mr. DONALDSON: What would you think it would be, in the hundreds?

Mr. SCOWCROFT: Well, I don't want to speculate because, you know, there was a lot of chaos, a lot of confusion and I think until there is some kind of an inventory, it's very difficult to say how many. But I think numbers he suggests are probably quite high.

Mr. BRINKLEY: Did General Noriega at some time in the past have some relationship with the CIA?

Mr. SCOWCROFT: Yes.

Mr. BRINKLEY: Could you tell us what it was?

Mr. SCOWCROFT: Not in detail, I can't, no—

Mr. BRINKLEY: Well, in general, what was it?

Mr. SCOWCROFT: —but I—he did have a relationship in which he provided information to us.

Mr. WILL: Can you not tell us—

Mr. BRINKLEY: Was he—one more, George. Was he not at the same time acting as a double agent and telling whatever he learned to Castro?

Mr. SCOWCROFT: I don't know that.

Mr. BRINKLEY: You don't know. George?

Mr. WILL: That's, I guess, my question. Is it that you don't know his relationship with the CIA or it would be injurious to the national interest to say so?

Mr. SCOWCROFT: I don't know precisely what it was, but I think whatever it was, the Central Intelligence Agency would certainly have been aware that he could have been working for—

Mr. BRINKLEY: Let me interrupt here, briefly, Sam, George, General. We'll be back with more questions for General Scowcroft in a moment.

[Commercial break]

Mr. BRINKLEY: Sorry I interrupted. Okay, go ahead now, if you want.

Mr. DONALDSON: A couple of more questions on Panama. Can you clear up the confusion over whether there actually was a deadline given Noriega to leave the Papal Nuncio? Archbishop Laboa, says that in fact he gave Noriega no deadline, but U.S. officials have said otherwise.

Mr. SCOWCROFT: Well, I can't really clear it up. I wasn't there and I would take what the archbishop—the Papal Nuncio said very seriously.

Mr. DONALDSON: Two other stories. The Papal Nuncio says that he tried to contact General Thurmond, the U.S. commander down there, when Noriega called in and said, "Pick up me here" at the Dairy Freeze or wherever he was, in order to get U.S. troops over there. Is that correct?

Mr. SCOWCROFT: I don't know that.

Mr. DONALDSON: Well, I'll try—I'm batting zero at the moment, but let me try one more. Archbishop Laboa says this morning that, in fact, Noriega told him when he came on the phone that if he wasn't granted asylum that he would commence a series of massacres in Chiriqui Province. Do you know anything about that?

Mr. SCOWCROFT: I only know what I read about it.

Mr. DONALDSON: Over to you, George.

*Credit:* Reprinted with permission of ABC News, This Week with David Brinkley.

---

## MARIA VICTORIA GONZALES: "NEW U.S. AMBASSADOR CALLS FOR ENDURING FRIENDSHIP WITH PANAMA"

---

*This wire service story out of Panama about three weeks after the White House issued orders to launch a U.S. troop intervention reported that all was well again in the political relationship between the U.S. and Panamanian governments.*

### Associated Press, 7 January 1990

PANAMA CITY, Panama: Deane Hinton took over as the new U.S. ambassador to Panama Saturday and pledged American cooperation when Panamanians take full operational control of the Panama Canal.

Also Saturday, former U.S. Attorney General Ramsey Clark said the death toll from the U.S. invasion of Panama is higher than has been reported. Clark estimated at least 4,000 had died, and called the reported toll "an official conspiracy of silence."

U.S., Panamanian and hospital sources say at least 500

civilians are believed to have died in the operation to oust Gen. Manuel Antonio Noriega and bring him to the United States for trial on drug trafficking charges.

Clark, who is gathering information about human rights violations, did not say how he arrived at his figure of 4,000, nor did he give any other details.

"There is a strong motive for not counting the dead. Humanity should pay attention to this point," Clark said at a news conference. He did not elaborate.

Hinton, in an arrival statement, said: "Let us not look back to a troubled past but rather let us responsibly face the future. Together let Panamanians and Americans build our relations on a basis of mutual respect and enduring friendship."

"Let me stress that Panamanians and Americans must henceforth cooperate to prepare for the day less than 10 years away for (Panamanian) operation of the Panama Canal," Hinton said.

Treaties signed by then-President Jimmy Carter and Panamanian Gen. Omar Torrijos in 1977 gave full ownership to Panama of the waterway, which the United States built and inaugurated in 1913.

The agreement put control of its operation under a joint U.S.-Panamanian commission until the year 2000, when it reverts completely to Panama.

Noriega has claimed the United States sought his ouster in order to renege on the treaties.

But the Bush administration repeatedly insisted it did not want to retain control of the waterway, only to get Noriega to stand trial in the United States for drug trafficking and money laundering.

The Ecumenical Committee of Panama said in a statement Saturday that the U.S. government should repair the damage caused by the assault.

It asked that "the United States accept its responsibility to repair the damage from the invasion."

The appointment of Hinton, an experienced career diplomat, was seen as another effort by the Bush administration to reconstruct the extensive damage caused by the fighting between U.S. troops and soldiers loyal to Noriega and six years of harsh Noriega rule.

Hinton, 67, a former ambassador to El Salvador and Pakistan, replaces Arthur Davis.

He pledged to do all he could to help new President Guillermo Endara and his government "fulfill the aspirations of the Panamanian people for equitable social and economic development and for the benefits of participatory democracy, respect for human rights and the rule of law."

Panama, he said, "has a philosophical commitment to the free enterprise system. And it has demonstrated a firm commitment to the establishment of democratic institutions and the carrying out of democratic principles."

*Credit*: Reprinted with permission of The Associated Press.

---

## SUSANA HAYWARD: "BLOWTORCHES, CHAINSAWS, HAMMERS PICK APART NORIEGA HEADQUARTERS"

*This report would have been just the kind of confirmation Americans needed to feel confident about the White House decision to send troops.*

Associated Press, 10 January 1990

PANAMA CITY, Panama: Hundreds of Panamanians used blowtorches and chainsaws to tear down the military headquarters of Manuel Antonio Noriega, then carted off furniture and pornography belonging to the toppled dictator.

Hundreds of residents went to the bombed-out National Defense headquarters after U.S. troops left the four-story cement compound, which had been ringed by soldiers and coils of barbed wire since the invasion Dec. 20.

"Tell the world that this is not looting," said Lolita del Alvarado of the poor neighborhood of Chorrillo nearby. "This is money that belongs to the people. We had no medicine, no schools, nothing. People in this neighborhood lived terribly."

American troops were bulldozing dilapidated and bullet-riddled apartments and buildings in the area, site of some of the heaviest fighting of the invasion, and are to rebuild the neighborhood.

It was a family outing as parents went with their children,

grandparents and other relatives to the building where Noriega once commanded his 14,000-member Defense Forces.

No one stopped the looters, many of whom ransacked Noriega's office and removed track lighting and wood paneling.

One man showed a visitor a copy of European pornographic magazines hidden among pages of official memos.

Many sported ill-fitting military uniforms and shoulder patches belonging to Noriega's army, and laughed and danced in the streets.

Bright colored murals depicting Noriega's army in action, atop armored cars and communicating via walkie talkies, adorned the walls of the compound.

Panamanians stopped to stare and snickered when they came upon the words: "Every man must at one time in his life decide whether he dares go for victory, risking everything, or sit down and watch the victors walk by."

Noriega went into hiding the night of the invasion and on Christmas Eve sought refuge inside the Vatican embassy. He remained there until he surrendered to U.S. troops a week ago and was flown to Miami to face drug-trafficking charges.

Panamanians used blowtorches, chainsaws, hammers and ice picks to tear down the gates and iron fences surrounding the compound and carted off pieces of wall, window frames and corrugated tin roofs.

Outside the compound, a truck with "war material" painted on its side was picked apart and sat without wheels. Other vehicles lay on their sides, nothing but corrugated steel carcasses.

Earlier Tuesday, between 150 and 200 protesters marched against the invasion in the first demonstration of its kind. They passed out leaflets lambasting the "savage invasion which cut an open wound in our national sovereignty."

Another 8,000 people attended a Mass and celebrated Noriega's downfall, chanting "Viva Panama" and waving white handkerchiefs. Archbishop Marcos McGrath urged the crowd to "forget rancor and hatred" to build a new Panama.

Both events commemorated the Day of the Martyrs, a national holiday in memory of 23 Panamanians who died in anti-American riots in 1964.

Dozens of U.S. soldiers ringed the Peruvian ambassador's residence, where 11 of Noriega's top officers had sought refuge Monday.

The Peruvian government said it had granted asylum to Noriega's security aide, Capt. Gonzalo González, who is on the U.S. most-wanted list. The others included Noriega's secretary, Capt. Marcela Tason; his top press spokesman, Maj. Edgardo López Grimaldo; and Maj. Heraclides Sucre, a commander of the elite Battalion 2000.

Peru's Foreign Ministry spokesman, José Torres, told The Associated Press in Lima that they would be allowed to come to Peru if they wished, but that there had been no discussions on the matter.

"It is supposed that they will try to go to some friendly country, perhaps Peru," Torres said.

President Alan García has roundly criticized the U.S. invasion, and refused to recognize the government of Guillermo Endara.

Peruvian chargé d'affaires Luis Sandiga denied Panamanian claims that the residence was sheltering Lt. Col. Luis "Papo" Cordova, one of Noriega's most-wanted associates.

In Peru, Foreign Minister Guillermo Larco Cox said Cordova had sought refuge in the ambassador's residence, but Peruvian officials refused.

He said Cordova was considered a "persona non grata" and left the residence "of his own will." The foreign minister did not say whether Cordova was apprehended by U.S. troops or if he had left before the troops surrounded the residence.

*Credit*: Reprinted with permission of The Associated Press.

---

# SUSANNE M. SCHAFER: MORE THAN 200 CIVILIAN DEAD IN PANAMA

---

*This wire service story reported the less successful side of the intervention that would have been on many Americans' minds as they assessed the costs of these U.S. troop deployments.*

Associated Press, 10 January 1990

WASHINGTON: Nearly three weeks after the invasion of Panama, the Pentagon says it estimates 220 Panamanian civilians were killed during Operation Just Cause.

Pentagon spokesman Bob Hall, briefing reporters Tuesday, stressed the figure was an estimate and that U.S. military authorities and Panamanian officials were working to "refine the accuracy of that figure."

"The U.S. military in Panama is working in concert with representatives of all the hospitals, several agencies across the spectrum of the Panamanian government and various relief and humanitarian organizations" to determine the number of Panamanians killed, Hall said.

Ever since the military attempt to oust Gen. Manuel Antonio Noriega began Dec. 20, U.S. military officials have been unable to offer any sound estimate of the number of civilians killed in the fighting and social chaos that erupted.

Hall said the Institute for Legal Medicine, which acts as the government's coroner, has counted 203 civilians killed as a direct result of the military operation.

However, Hall said, that organization still has a number of cases to review and he said U.S. officials expect the number to rise.

"We're being conservative. We think there'll be a few more. We expect the figure to rise slightly," Hall said of the institute's figure.

Hall said 203 individuals were included in the 220 estimate reached by U.S. officials and that both numbers include "Panamanian Defense Forces and dignity battalions not in uniform and otherwise unidentifiable, as well as looters and bona fide and innocent civilians."

"The institute has been unable to make any determination whether the deaths were caused by U.S. military, PDF, dignity battalions, looters or other civilians," Hall said.

Officials estimate nearly 300 Panamanian soldiers were killed in the fighting. The U.S. military death toll was 23.

The spokesman said some 23,000 U.S. troops remain in Panama but that about 4,000 have returned to the United

States. About 13,000 troops were stationed in Panama before the invasion.

Hall said he could offer no timetable for the return of the remaining U.S. troops. He said about 700 were deployed in Panama in "nation-building exercises" to help re-establish civil and governmental operations.

Defense Secretary Dick Cheney plans to discuss troop withdrawal with Gen. Colin Powell, chairman of the Joint Chiefs of Staff, later this week, the spokesman said.

Hall said U.S. troops detained 4,320 Panamanians in the course of the military operation and 675 remained in detention by U.S. military authorities.

Those still in custody were being held pending background checks or until the Panamanian legal and justice systems are rebuilt, Pentagon officials said.

Hall also said U.S. troops were searching vehicles leaving the Peruvian Embassy in Panama City because "there have been some reports that people may or may not be in the embassy."

In Panama, government officials said the troops surrounded the embassy because two of Noriega's top associates had taken refuge inside.

Hall said decisions about the conduct of U.S. troops are made by the Southern Command, headed by Gen. Maxwell Thurman, and "policy considerations" were taken into account in the movement of U.S. troops in the region.

"General Thurman has the complete confidence" of Cheney, Powell and President Bush, Hall said.

At the State Department, spokeswoman Margaret Tutwiler said U.S. officials know who was in the Peruvian Embassy but she would not identify them. She declined to discuss the legal authority of U.S. troops involved in surrounding the embassy.

*Credit*: Reprinted with permission of The Associated Press.

---

## KENNETH FREED: "INVASION AFTERMATH"—REPORT ON CIVILIAN CASUALTIES IN PANAMA

*The news reports were not wholly about the victories and successes. This story is an example of the news that follows any military action. Because of the special interest that the California reader had in the U.S. war against drugs and the outcome of "Just Cause," this story about the often unreported aspects of conflict and civilian casualties would have been well read.*

### Los Angeles Times, 10 January 1990

PANAMA CITY: Every day, Rosa María Salcedo makes a pilgrimage to the burned-out shell of her home in the slum neighborhood of El Chorrillo. Along the way, she stops at the morgue, where she asks, "Have you seen my son?"

Salcedo has not seen her son, Archimedes, 18, since the evening of Dec. 20, when he went out to drink beer with friends in an open-air cafe. The place was just down the street from the Salcedos' two-room flat and not far from Panama's military headquarters, the Comandancia.

"I was asleep when I heard a loud noise and felt the walls shake," she said. "At first I thought Archimedes was drunk and slammed the door. Then the building began to burn."

What she heard and felt were the opening salvos of the American attack on the Comandancia, which was destroyed along with the Salcedo apartment building and dozens of other buildings. When she ran into the streets in the first hours of Dec. 21, "all I wanted was to find Archimedes," she said.

She did not, and she still has not.

**MANY IN MOURNING**

And Rosa María Salcedo is not alone. Amid the physical, economic and emotional wreckage left by the U.S. operation to capture strongman Manuel A. Noriega are the mourning relatives of many who were killed or are still listed as missing.

Of the 27,000 American soldiers who took part in Operation Just Cause, 23 were killed; 324 were wounded. Enemy casualties, as reported by the U.S. Southern Command, included 314 dead, 124 wounded and 5,704 detained.

Until Tuesday, in the absence of official estimates, there had been widely varying figures on the number of civilian casualties; some ran into the thousands. But on Tuesday, the Pentagon estimated that 220 Panamanian civilians had been killed in the operation.

Earlier, the Pentagon said it was virtually impossible to count civilian casualties.

"How do you count (Panama Defense Forces personnel) in civilian clothes, or the members of Dignity Battalions (paramilitary units) or looters who were shot?" U.S. Army Lt. Col. James Swank asked. "We are leaving that to the international agencies; that is the sort of thing they are good at."

But the International Red Cross, the Panamanian Red Cross and the Panamanian Human Rights Commission have no consensus. The most detailed figures have been supplied by the country's Human Rights Commission, a private organization with a reputation for fairness and objectivity. According to Raul Escoffery, the commission's executive director, 207 civilians were killed and 480 wounded as a direct result of the invasion.

The Panamanian Red Cross reports that between Dec. 20

and Jan. 5, a total of 129 civilians were killed and 517 were injured.

Sandra DeCorrea, speaking for the Panamanian Red Cross, said she has received inquiries on about 1,200 people believed to be missing and added, "So far, we have found 400." Most had simply fled the areas where heavy fighting took place and had either chosen not to return immediately or had difficulty getting home because of blockades and closed roads. The figures on the missing do not include the 5,000 detainees still being processed by U.S. forces.

Rosa María Mota, a representative of the International Red Cross, said she has received reports of 2,000 missing but that these "came in the hours immediately after the invasion and are not accurate."

Most of the dead and wounded came in the first three or four days of fighting, and the majority of them were shot, according to Dr. Juan Ramirez Harris, a staff physician at Santo Tomás Hospital, where many of the casualties were taken, particularly after the first day of fighting.

"However, starting about the 23rd (of December)," he said, "we noticed that more people had been cut, some of them severely." He said these people apparently were cut by broken glass as they broke into stores to loot them.

## "NO MORE THAN 300"

Roger Montero, head of the Forensic Registry, said he expects the civilian dead to total "no more than 300."

Some critics, among them former U.S. Atty. Gen. Ramsey Clark, say the U.S. military is hiding a civilian casualty rate as high as 4,000 dead and missing, but no one has provided any evidence to substantiate such figures.

In fact, Oswaldo Velasquez, president of the Human Rights Commission, said in an interview that "we have not received one complaint of American troops committing one atrocity or killing any unarmed people."

Whatever the final toll, it presumably includes Archimedes Salcedo. Chances are that he was incinerated when the building behind the sidewalk café was reduced to charred rubble. But his mother, a tiny woman whose hard life as a street vendor and part-time cleaning woman has added ages to her 40 years, continues to look.

"I think he ran away," she said, "and is afraid to come back because the gringos think he was in the Dignity Battalions."

If he were a "DigBat," as the Dignity Battalion people are commonly called, it could be that he was jailed and lied about his name.

Whatever his fate, every morning, after the curfew lifts at 5 o'clock, his mother leaves her sister's home in the outlying neighborhood of San Miguelito and on foot and by bus heads for El Chorrillo, hoping to find Archimedes, her only child.

En route, she stops at the city morgue because of a lingering fear that this is where she will find him. So far, she has not been able to identify Archimedes from the pictures of corpses shown to people asking about relatives and friends.

"We can't use the actual remains for identification in most cases," the Forensic Registry's Montero said. "Nearly all the dead were brought here in the first few days and are hard to identify. So we use photos taken when they came in, or we ask them to make the identification on the basis of clothing the victims were wearing."

Sometimes, this method works. Ramón Paredes, a San Miguelito tailor, was able to pick out his missing cousin, a member of the Panama Defense Forces, who evidently changed into civilian clothes when the attack started. Paredes had made the clothes his cousin was wearing.

"I knew it was my work," he said. "I didn't want it to be, but there was no doubt."

Still, in some cases the missing are not dead—not even really missing.

Sixta Luce, 33, a hotel maid, was working the night the invasion began. When men in civilian clothing, masked and brandishing rifles, rushed into the hotel and began rounding up guests, she fled out a service exit and spent the night hiding behind a trash bin.

The fighting that followed kept her on the run. She managed to hitch a ride out of the city. Finally, she was picked up by U.S. troops and taken to a refugee camp.

It was not until late last week that she was cleared and allowed to leave the camp. Because there is no telephone in her home and there was no mail service at the time, Luce was out of contact with her family until she got home Friday.

By this time she had been reported missing by three different relatives. Thus, her reappearance reduced by three the number of missing on lists kept by the Panamanian Red Cross and the Human Rights Commission.

*Credit*: Copyright © 1990, Los Angeles Times. Reprinted with permission.

# NOTE

1. "CBS Survey of Panama Opinion," Belden & Russonello, published 8 January 1990, 794 Panama adults, interviewed in Spanish by phone or in person 2 through 4 January 1990, before Noriega gave himself up to U.S. authorities, jointly undertaken by CBS and Belden & Russonello, 4 percent margin of error.

## FURTHER READINGS

Howe, James. *A People Who Would Not Kneel: Panama, the United States, and the San Blas Kuna.* Washington, D.C.: Smithsonian Institution Press, 1998.

Lindsay-Poland, John. *Emperors in the Jungle: The Hidden History of the U.S. in Panama.* Durham, N.C.: Duke University Press, 2003.

Noriega, Manuel Antonio. *America's Prisoner: The Memoirs of Manuel Noriega.* New York: Random House, 1997.

Reynolds, Nicholas E. *Just Cause: Marine Operations in Panama, 1988–1990.* Washington, D.C.: History and Museums Division, Headquarters, U.S. Marine Corps, 1996.

# 28

# CLAN WARS IN SOMALIA, 1992–1993

The northeastern region of Africa now known as Somalia was recognized as an independent republic in 1960 when two contiguous regions that shared the name Somaliland were united under the auspices of United Nations and British administration. Mogadishu, the largest city, located on the Indian Ocean coast, was named the capital. The new nation, slightly smaller than the state of Texas, is principally desert with about 1,800 miles of coast along the Gulf of Aden as well as the Indian Ocean. Large nomadic and refugee groups make it difficult to accurately report the population, but estimates are between 7 million and 9 million.

The two former Somaliland regions had been protectorates of Italy and Great Britain during colonial periods from the end of the nineteenth century to the mid-twentieth century. The largely nomadic population of the region often ignored the occupation by each of these colonial governments, and tribal rule has principally been the governmental organization.

After World War II, the United Nations made Italian Somaliland a trust territory, and Somali nationalists demanded assurances that national independence would be forthcoming. When elections were held in 1969, the newly elected president was assassinated. Armed forces seized control, parliament was dissolved, and the Supreme Revolutionary Council put Siad Barre in control of the nation. Somalia renamed itself the Somali Democratic Republic and declared itself a socialist state.

Still under Siad Barre as politburo head, a new constitution was organized, and in 1976 the Supreme Revolutionary Council was replaced by the Somali Revolutionary Socialist Party. Though elections were held in 1979 for People's Assembly, the country remained under the rule of Siad Barre.

Somalia continued a long-standing dispute with neighboring Ethiopia over Ogaden, a region that Somali nomads had occupied for centuries but that Ethiopia included within its governmental jurisdiction. Both countries supported guerrilla tactics in the disputed lands until a nonaggression pact was signed in 1988.

Recurrent famines and general discontent led to the 1991 replacement of Siad Barre with an interim government. Barre and resistance troops tried three times to take the capital of Mogadishu but were turned back. He fled to Kenya in 1992, and tribal wars broke out across the fledgling nation.

The U.N. shipments of food that had begun as early as 1988 were suspended in December 1991 because conditions were so chaotic. A U.N.-brokered cease-fire went into effect in March 1992 that allowed relief shipments of food to resume in April. Famine was widespread, and factional fighting continued. The United Nations estimated that at least one-third of the population suffered from starvation. When the cease-fire completely broke down, the international community decided that military intervention was the only solution available for famine relief.

On 3 December 1992, the U.N. Security Council voted to send a U.S.-led military force to assure food distribution, and the next day the United States announced that 28,150 troops would be deployed in a short-term mission. A U.S.-led multinational military force, organized by U.N. resolution, arrived the next week and established control of enough key areas that famine relief shipments could be distributed.

By mid-January 1993, the United States reported its first casualty, killed by Somali gunmen in an attack near Mogadishu's airport, but by May the U.S. forces were confident enough of peace in the region that command of the Somalia operation was returned to the sole authority of the United Nations unilateral command. By March 1993, U.N.-sponsored talks resulted in the establishment of the Transitional National Council, which assumed authority in Somalia with the promise of elections within two years. Then on 5 June, the peacekeepers came under attack. Twenty-four Pakistanis were killed, and fifty-four others were wounded in a series of ambushes, setting the stage for four months of nearly daily clashes between warlord supporters and the U.N. multinational force.

The United Nations began retaliatory raids against warlord militia, conducting an aerial assault on one warlord's weapons caches. Retaliatory raids continued with air and ground assaults, in which one such raid was reported to have killed about fifty Somalis. An angry mob killed four foreign journalists who arrived later to report on the raid site.

On 8 August, four U.S. soldiers were killed when their all-purpose humvee vehicle was detonated by a land mine. This loss of U.S. soldiers prompted President Clinton to order the U.S. Rangers to Somalia. In response, the U.S. Senate passed a resolution urging President Clinton to seek congressional authority for continued U.S. involvement in Somalia.

On 25 September, U.S. soldiers were killed by Somali rocket-propelled grenades that brought down a Blackhawk helicopter. On 3 October, twelve U.S. soldiers were killed, seventy-eight were wounded, and others were missing or held captive following a fifteen-hour battle with Somali militiamen in Mogadishu. The next day President Clinton called for more than 200 fresh troops and heavy tanks to Somalia. This quick sequence of events changed the American view of the U.S. commitment to help the Somalis. The reporting and public opinion provided here reflect this change of heart.

The last U.N. troops withdrew in March 1995, and factional fighting resumed. Famine continued to plague the population, and by the end of the twentieth century there was still no permanent government there. The Transitional National Government formed in August 2000 was charged with creating a new constitution and holding elections within three years; as of 2005, these elections have not yet been held.

Here is a sample of the public opinion polls conducted immediately around, as well as long after, the events of September and October 1993. The first set of survey responses was carried by the *Los Angeles Times* and contained results of an ABC News survey taken in June and October.

## 1993

*Question*: Do you approve or disapprove of the way Bill Clinton is handling the situation?

Approve: 62 percent; Disapprove: 29 percent; No opinion: 10 percent (as of 28 June 1993).

Approve: 33 percent; Disapprove: 53 percent; No opinion: 14 percent (as of 5 October 1993).

*Question*: Should the United States keep troops in Somalia until there's a functioning civil government, or do you think the United States should pull its troops out very soon?

Keep troops in: 28 percent; Pull out: 64 percent; No opinion: 8 percent (as of 5 October).

*Question*: If U.S. prisoners can't be freed through negotiations, do you think the United States should respond with a major military attack?

Should attack: 75 percent; Should not: 19 percent; No opinion: 5 percent (as of 5 October).

Other findings from the 5 October poll: 69 percent did not think that America's vital interests were at stake; 51 percent believed that the United States should continue trying to capture warlord Mohammed Fanah Aidid; 56 percent backed the president's plan to send more support to troops already there.[1]

*Question*: (Here are a few questions concerning the recent events in Somalia, in which U.S. soldiers have been killed or taken prisoner by forces controlled by a Somalian warlord.) (For the next few questions, suppose the United States withdraws its troops from Somalia in the next six months without establishing a stable government or capturing the Somali warlord responsible for the attack on U.S. soldiers.) And if that happens, do you think the United States would lose power or prestige when dealing with other countries in the future, or don't you think that would occur?

Would lose power or prestige: 33 percent; Would not occur: 61 percent; Not sure: 6 percent (as of 7 October 1993).[2]

## 1994

*Question*: (President Bill) Clinton says that he is sending 5,000 more U.S. troops to Somalia now, and then will withdraw all U.S. forces from Somalia by March 31, (1994). Do you approve or disapprove of his decision to send the additional troops?

Approve: 43 percent; Disapprove: 53 percent; No opinion: 4 percent.[3]

What follows is a sample of the kind of reporting about the Somalia intervention during the initial years of that conflict. The early reporting of the situation focused almost entirely on the humanitarian needs of a besieged population, plagued by bad weather and a few willful warlords. After American soldiers who were part of the multilateral forces there were killed, the reports shifted almost exclusively to the war. The reporting seemed to turn quite quickly from the optimism of relief efforts to the horror of slaughter and mayhem. The "Further Readings" at the end of the chapter list additional sources that discuss or describe the history of the Somalian nation.

## KEITH B. RICHBURG: "SOMALIA'S OVERSHADOWED TRAGEDY; WORLD ANXIOUS ABOUT BALKAN TURMOIL, ALOOF TO THAT IN AFRICA"

*This front-page story from Somalia emphasized the humanitarian needs to which Americans were responding by donations through the U.N. relief efforts. Throughout the news reports provided here, there was a note of comparing Somalia with the situation in the Balkans. Both the humanitarian needs and the prospect of military intervention were coupled here, but in these early days of reporting on Somalia, the relief efforts were given the most attention.*

*Washington Post*, 12 August 1992

MOGADISHU: The haunting images have become almost daily television news fare: pathetic, gaunt bodies, orphans with hollow eyes, hospitals overrun with gunshot victims, and rival groups perpetuating untold slaughter of each other. And each new image heightens the civilized world's outrage and revulsion, increasing pressure on Western governments to do something—anything—to halt this humanitarian nightmare.

That has been the international reaction to the crisis in the former Yugoslavia, a civil war in the heart of Europe that has attracted a major United Nations presence and now talk of direct Western military intervention.

But the images are much the same here in Somalia, half a continent away and even further in terms of the international consciousness. Hundreds, if not thousands, of people are dying daily from hunger and disease, and refugees are streaming by the thousands into neighboring Kenya each day. Civil administration has collapsed and what was once a functioning country has been reduced to a state of primordial anarchy.

If tragedy were measured simply in numbers of human lives destroyed, the one in Somalia would, by many accounts, be judged greater than that in Croatia and Bosnia. Here, civil war has been compounded by a famine that is starving entire villages. But unlike the Balkans, the Somali crisis has attracted little international attention or aid, and only faint, distant calls for Western military involvement.

The people grappling with the Somali crisis, and many observing it from the outside, immediately offer a few straightfor-ward explanations for what some have called an international double standard: the Balkans' proximity to Western capitals; the modern "novelty," at least in media circles, of a war in Europe that could spread; the neglect of African leaders in speaking up about a crisis on their own doorstep; and on a more basic level, racism—Yugoslavs are white Europeans, Somalis are black Africans.

"One, there's the proximity," said a Western diplomat in Nairobi, expressing frustration at the apparent double standard. "There are also probably more Yugoslavs living in the United States. There's color. And all the adoption fanatics [in the West] see a chance to adopt little blond kids."

"More people are concerned about Yugoslavia, so nobody is concerned about Africa," said Patrick Bongrain, a logistical officer working in the coastal town of Merca with the French aid group Doctors Without Borders. "Yugoslavia is something new—and it's very close for European people."

Rakiya Omaar, a Somali who is executive director of Africa Watch, the human rights group, calls it European racism fueled by African indifference. "It's ludicrous for Africans to argue that Europeans should be paying as much attention to Somalia as they pay to Yugoslavia," she said. "Why should Europeans care about Africans when Africans don't care about Africans? . . . Africa's own silence makes racism easier," she said. "If your own people won't speak up for you, why should the rest of the world care?"

Sanford J. Ungar, dean of American University's communication school and a journalist who has reported from and written a book about Africa, called the disparity of interest between Yugoslavia and Somalia "a classic example of a situation where the familiar crowds out the unfamiliar."

"It's a Eurocentric bias," he said. "It's part of the old myths and assumptions that the most important things happening in the world at any given time are the things happening in Europe." While racism is not entirely to blame, he said, "There is a subtle racism at work. . . . It has to do with frame of mind, with what's immediate, what's familiar, and who stirs the more immediate compassion."

U.N. Secretary General Boutros Boutros-Ghali, an Egyptian, touched on many of these points when he challenged the Security Council's decision to step up costly peace-keeping operations in Bosnia—a "rich man's war"—while relief operations in Somalia and the rest of black Africa go neglected and under-funded.

This view was echoed here last week by Boutros-Ghali's special envoy to Somalia, Mohamed Sahnoun, a former Algerian ambassador to Washington. In an interview, Sahnoun said Boutros-Ghali "was right in pointing out that operations we launched in the former Yugoslavia are costing a lot of money to the United Nations, but nothing was done about Somalia."

Sahnoun noted irony in that a U.N. cease-fire in Mogadishu, brokered in March, has made it safer for relief operations than embattled Bosnia-Hercegovina, where U.N. peace keepers have come under constant attack. While young Somalis fight in the streets with M16 rifles, the city is free of the artillery and mortar battles being fought in Bosnia with heavy weapons of the former Yugoslav army.

"People are really starving, and the security conditions are better than in Yugoslavia," Sahnoun said. Asked about the reasons for the discrepancy, he paused and fumbled briefly for the correct diplomatic answer. "Maybe because it's in Europe, I don't know," he said. "Maybe it's their neighbor's problem. . . . And the media." He also criticized the United Nations for pulling its staff out of Somalia after the fall of president Mohamed Siad Barre in January 1991 and failing to reestablish a presence until nearly a year later. "It was a very, very long delay and a tragic delay. And we are now paying the price," Sahnoun said.

In many ways, Somalia is an unfortunate victim of the end of the Cold War. During the 1970s, with his country fighting socialist Ethiopia over the Ogaden border region, Siad Barre embraced the West—and suddenly this desert country of nomads and camel herds emerged as a center of American geopolitical planning.

Strategic thinkers in Washington saw Somalia as an important new client in the troubled "arc of instability," a base from which to project power into the Red Sea and the Middle East. Siad Barre, although a recent convert to anticommunism, also provided a bulwark against anti-Western Ethiopia, which was being bolstered by Soviet hardware and Cuban troops. The United States built one of Africa's longest airstrips at Berbera, constructed one of the most expensive and colossal embassy compounds in the world and rewarded Siad Barre by helping him purchase sophisticated weapons.

By the time the civil war reached the capital and toppled Siad Barre, however, America had lost interest. Western embassies evacuated Mogadishu, never to look back. And as rival warlords battled to fill the power vacuum, the attitudes of some outsiders was summed up by a U.S. official in Nairobi who said in an interview last year that the entire country "should be paved over and turned into a parking lot."

If the West must take some blame for first arming Somalia and then turning its back, so, too, must Africa's own leaders be held accountable—largely for their inaction.

When the Yugoslav crisis first erupted last year, European leaders worked feverishly trying to broker some kind of agreement. Europe also has forced the issue to the top of the United Nations agenda—Boutros-Ghali was reported as saying he receives constant calls each day about Yugoslavia from prominent Europeans.

By contrast, African leaders have remained virtually silent on Somalia. As opposing warlords battled in Mogadishu for much of last year—shelling the city into oblivion and killing mostly innocent women and children—the Organization of African Unity took no role. The OAU secretary general never set foot there to try to talk to the combatants. And no African president has shown the courage of French President François Mitterrand, who traveled to war-torn Bosnia to dramatize the besieged people's plight.

"The point [of Mitterrand's trip] was to show the people of Sarajevo that Europe had not forgotten them," said Omaar of Africa Watch. "Why can't an African leader go to Mogadishu? If young boys and girls working for [aid organizations] can go, why can't an African leader go?"

During June's OAU meeting in Senegal, African heads of state in their private session roundly criticized the leaders of Somalia's neighboring East African states for not taking a more active role to end the conflict, Liberian President Amos Sawyer said in an interview. "The countries of that subregion have to take some bold decisions," Sawyer said.

"The OAU debated the problem, discussed the problem. But they don't have any means," said Sahnoun, the U.N. envoy here. He said that whoever brokered a Somali agreement in the early stages of the fighting would have needed to follow through quickly with guarantees of relief assistance, like food and medical supplies. "Who in the OAU can do that?" he asked.

Omaar also blamed the Islamic Conference and the Arab League for their relative silence on Somalia, which is a member of both groups. "Where is the Arab League?" she said. "It is awash with money. . . . The hypocrisy of it makes me sick."

If Western powers, African and Arab leaders and the United Nations must shoulder blame for allowing Somalia to fade from the world's view, so must the Western media. Foreign correspondents, mostly based in Nairobi, complain that when they wrote about Somalia's slide into anarchy last year, their stories received little attention from editors back home. Also, some journalists considered Somalia too dangerous for on-the-scene coverage.

Ungar of American University blames that neglect on what he calls the journalistic cycle that drives much of foreign news coverage, with the U.S. government setting the agenda.

Editors respond "to what's on television, and television and journalism are responding to what the administration is paying attention to." Crises in Africa are thus bound to receive less attention, he said.

*Credit*: © **1992, The Washington Post, reprinted with permission.**

---

## REID G. MILLER: "SOMALIA AIRLIFT BEGINS; KENYA LIFTS BAN ON U.S. FLIGHTS OVER AIRSPACE"

---

*This similar piece, which also appeared on the front page of its paper, gave a somewhat hopeful view of success in the relief mission.*

### Chicago Sun-Times, 21 August 1992

MOMBASA, Kenya: The United States today began an airlift of food to starving Somalis after Kenya lifted a brief ban on American flights over its airspace.

The first C-130 Hercules carrying 12½ tons of beans, wheat flour, vegetable oil and grain took off from this Indian Ocean port city's international airport in early afternoon for the northeastern Kenya town of Wajir. There, the food was to be unloaded and taken by truck to some of the 11 refugee camps on or near the Kenya-Somalia border.

The aid operation—involving about 100 U.S. troops, including Green Berets—comes as officials are warning that half of Somalia's children risk death from starvation because of drought and civil war. Hundreds are said to be dying daily.

Kenya had accused Washington of flying into Mombasa without its permission and late Thursday withdrew permission for U.S. planes to fly over its territory.

It also claimed in a Foreign Ministry statement that the United States was conducting an "uncoordinated food airlift" by bypassing aid agencies to use troops to distribute food.

U.S. Embassy spokesman T. J. Dowling denied each accusation. "We did have prior permission to land at Mombasa, the base for the U.S. airlift. This is not an uncoordinated operation," he said today.

Agreement to again permit the flights resulted from negotiations this morning between President Daniel Moi, U.S. Ambassador Smith Hempstone and Frank Libutti, the Marine Corps brigadier general commanding the U.S. aid airlift.

Relations between Nairobi and Washington have been frosty since Hempstone's arrival three years ago with a mission to link U.S. aid to Kenya's policies on human rights, democracy and corruption.

Kenya's record is poor in each area, and all except humanitarian aid has been cut. Kenya has accused Hempstone of racism and interference in Kenya's affairs.

Foreign Minister Wilson Ndolo Ayah said the earlier flight ban resulted from a misunderstanding. "This was a complex effort organized on short notice and some details were not adequately worked out in advance," he said.

A team of 16 U.S. soldiers was flown earlier today to a military airstrip outside Wajir to set up a communications station that will direct aid flights.

More than 400,000 people are housed in the 11 refugee camps, 330,000 of them Somalis.

*Credit*: Copyright 1992 Associated Press. All rights reserved. Distributed by Valeo IP.

---

## WILLIAM C. MANN: "U.S. AIRLIFT TO SOMALIA: TROOPS ENJOY 'FEEDING, NOT BOMBING'"

---

*This U.S. military intervention was reported very frequently in terms of providing humanitarian aid in a brutal and foreign environment. The following story distributed by Associated Press is an example of the kinds of reports given space in newspapers and on the air across the United States throughout the autumn of 1992.*

### Associated Press, 30 August 1992

MOMBASA, Kenya: On the graffiti wall of Joint Task Force Provide Relief, a soldier described the mission of the American food airlift to Somalia this way:

"1st operational deployment of survival."

In his soft Virginia accent, Tech. Sgt. Stuard M. Smith expressed the same idea.

"It's enjoyable to help people," said Smith, 38, who grew up in Richlands, in the Blue Ridge mountains. "It really is. It's nice to know you're helping these people who can't help themselves."

President Bush ordered the task force formed on Aug. 14 to carry food to as many as 2 million Somalis said by the United Nations to be in imminent danger of starvation.

Three days later, a fleet of four C-141s and eight smaller C-130 Hercules cargo planes began arriving in Mombasa, Kenya's principal Indian Ocean port and the base of the U.S relief operation. Relief flights began on Aug. 21.

On Sunday, four flights took 37 tons of rice, beans and vegetable oil to the Somali town of Belet Huen. There were seven flights to Wajir, Kenya, near the Somali border, with 125 tons of wheat, split peas and salt.

The shipment Sunday was enough to feed 372,500 people for a day.

A week into the American operation, morale among the 490 young soldiers, sailors, airmen and marines of the joint task force is remarkably good.

For one thing, shipments of food and mail arrived from home Saturday night. For another, they were given their very own military address: JTF–Provide Relief, CMR-70901 APOAE 09899-0901.

"Talking about morale, this is a group of winners," said the commander, Marine Brig. Gen. Frank Libutti, 47, of Huntington, N.Y.

It was Libutti who suggested the graffiti wall as a way of pulling his disparate troops together.

The unpainted side of a makeshift, wooden office inside the cement-block U.S. Navy warehouse is the heart of the operation. Among the other scrawled entries on the graffiti wall:

"Combat camera. We came. We saw. We took their picture."

David Coyle of the 438th combat Support Group wrote: "Proud father of Erin Vey Coyle and husband to Nancy Coyle. God Bless America."

Among several task force members interviewed, the only complaint was uncertainty about when the mission would be over.

"Our orders were cut for 60 days, but we don't know," said Tech. Sgt. Marv D. Lynchard, 34, of Houston.

"Anyhow, it's better than the desert," said the 17-year veteran combat photographer, who was in Saudi Arabia last year during the Gulf War.

Tech. Sgt. Charles Johnson, 35, of Charleston, S.C., a flight line safety specialist, also has 17 years in the Air Force but missed Desert Storm.

"You train for so many years to do a job, and then you miss the war," he said. "I sort of had a feeling that I'd missed something."

But Johnson added, "It's kind of pleasing to be out here doing something for somebody instead of making war. We're feeding people, not bombing them."

The U.S. airlift to Wajir began on Aug. 21, with food intended for Kenyan drought victims and Somali refugees. The first flights into Somalia began Friday. The shipments are distributed by relief agencies.

One ton of food feeds about 2,200 people for one day. It would take nearly 700 tons a day just to feed the Somalis in immediate danger of starvation; the Red Cross' relief effort is getting about 22,000 tons of food a month into the country.

Italy, France, Germany, Canada, Britain, Israel and other nations also have mounted airlifts or promised aid to Somalia.

At Provide Relief, 2nd Lt. Scott Magnan, 24, briefs flight crews on the weather. So far, he said, it's been fine for missions.

He also noted that there's plenty to do in Mombasa, like windsurfing, scuba diving and swimming. But the Syracuse, N.Y., native has had no time to enjoy the city. He's worked every day, briefing six to 10 flight crews daily.

He thinks about his wife, Tracy, back home "with two puppies, a lawn to mow and a full-time teacher's job. . . . She's busier than me."

But he had no complaints.

"I'll go home when they tell me to," Magnan said.

*Credit*: Reprinted with permission of The Associated Press.

---

# KEITH B. RICHBURG: "SOLUTIONS FOR SOMALIA COMPLICATED BY CHAOS; AUTHORITY IS ABSENT AND FOOD IS POWER"

---

*This front-page story is another example of humanitarian concerns rather than political concerns as the focus of the reports coming directly out of Somalia.*

*Washington Post*, 30 August 1992

MOMBASA, Kenya: U.S. Brig. Gen. Frank Libutti's first exposure to Somalia's misery came 12 days ago, during a brief tour of the famine-stricken town of Baidoa.

Libutti was immediately confronted by the chaotic and depressing scenes that have come to characterize the plight of Somalia, where an estimated 1.5 million people face imminent starvation and clan warfare and banditry rage unchecked because there is no government to impose order. His initial view came at Baidoa's airstrip, where the Marine general was described by one source as "shocked—it was a bunch of ragged guys with guns."

Libutti, wearing civilian clothes for the supposedly incognito visit, was whisked into the town center to see two feeding centers run by foreign relief agencies. "He was appalled by the hunger and the filth," the source said.

The international community is now discovering what Libutti apparently learned on his first visit to Baidoa: Recognizing suffering is one thing, but doing something about it—in a country with no government, where the rule of the gun prevails—is another matter.

Western capitals can allocate food and supplies, and diplomats can speak optimistically of cease-fires and peace conferences. But as long as Somalia remains in the grip of young armed hoodlums who hijack precious food for the power it confers, outside intervention, even for humanitarian purposes, will remain limited.

"The problem here is not resources or food," said Andrew Natsios, President Bush's special coordinator for the Somali relief effort, Operation Provide Relief, of which Libutti is commander. "It is security. It is the clan war. It is the anarchy."

Natsios has worked with other relief efforts in Africa and Asia involving civil wars waged by rival guerrilla armies. But he noted that the key distinction between those conflicts and the problem in Somalia "is that we have not developed a doctrine that works yet on how to deal with anarchy. This is not civil war—this is chaos."

The world woke up to Somalia's suffering three weeks ago, responding to the chiding of U.N. Secretary General Boutros Boutros-Ghali and to images of rail-thin, starving Somalis that began to compete for television air time with equally troubling pictures of victims of civil war in the former Yugoslavia. On Aug. 14, the White House announced plans for a massive airlift of 145,000 tons of food to help alleviate the Somali famine. Smaller food airlifts have been undertaken by the French and German governments.

But the West's difficulty in coming to grips with Somalia's grim situation may have been illustrated when the long-awaited U.S. airlift into Somalia finally began Friday. The first American C-130 cargo planes went not to Baidoa, which has come to epitomize the chaotic country's suffering, but farther north to Beledweyne. Libutti was later overheard telling some of his officers that Beledweyne was "a much more upbeat place than Baidoa."

Not only upbeat, but far safer and more orderly—and thus easier to supply. Yesterday, three more U.S. cargo planes made the trip from Kenya to Beledweyne, and so far, no plans have been announced to expand the American effort to other, far needier towns and villages such as Baidoa in the country's interior.

Part of the problem is that in a starving country, food becomes power—and thus the prey of both the organized armed looters and the freelance gunmen. Warlords who use young men to fight their battles must pay their troops not in cash but in food. And foreign relief agencies wishing to move food from place to place inside Somalia must first negotiate deals with the patchwork of clan leaders and militia commanders who have replaced organized government.

If the world needed any added reminder of the perils of food delivery amid anarchy, it came Friday just as the American airlift got underway. In Mogadishu, the Somali capital, gunmen raided the port, where a U.N. ship was being unloaded. Some 300 tons of food and 199 barrels of fuel were stolen.

Another reminder of the prevailing anarchy came that same day when two U.N. military observers—a Czech and an Egyptian—monitoring a fragile cease-fire in Mogadishu were shot and wounded as they approached a militia checkpoint, even though their vehicle bore the U.N. flag.

Also on Friday, the U.N. Security Council approved Boutros-Ghali's recommendation to send an additional 3,000 armed personnel to Somalia to bolster a 500-man U.N. contingent of Pakistani troops due in Mogadishu in early September. The extra peace keepers would be deployed to guard food supplies in the countryside.

But one of the country's most powerful warlords, Gen. Mohamed Farah Aideed, has been quoted as opposing the expanded U.N. presence.

A relief agency official who knows Aideed and has spoken with him said the general's intransigence may have more to do with his somewhat weakened position. After battling forces still loyal to ousted Somali dictator Mohamed Siad Barre, Aideed is said to be pinned down at his new base in Baardheere, unable to return to his headquarters in Mogadishu for fear of losing territory he only recently gained.

"He's in bad trouble now," said the relief official, who asked not to be named. "He's stuck down in Baardheere. He's mired down there . . . [and] when he gets stressed, he gets weird."

Any further expansion of the U.N. presence in Somalia appears daunting without at least the tacit approval of Aideed and the other principal warlords. Few countries would be willing to commit troops to a peace-keeping force in a country without clearly defined battle lines and where the major combatants openly oppose their presence.

Natsios called the planned U.N. troop expansion "a good idea" that the United States supports. But, he added, "The question is, which country will contribute the security guards?"

## GARY STRIEKER: "U.S. MILITARY CARGO PLANES BRING U.N. TROOPS TO SOMALIA"

*This television report focused on the progress made and the positive outcome expected. There is little explanation here about why there might be more of a problem than just bad weather and bad luck.*

*CNN News*, Transcript 122–2, 23 September 1992

HIGHLIGHT: Relief efforts to some villages in rural areas of Somalia are on hold because of heavy rains. Flights to these areas will resume soon, while flights continue in other towns. More U.N. troops are arriving.

JIM CLANCY, Anchor: Relief efforts to some villages in rural areas of Somalia are on hold tonight. Heavy rains have turned the dirt air strips into muddy runways. But officials hope to resume flights very soon. Meanwhile, the air lifts continue in other towns. Here's CNN's Gary Strieker.

GARY STRIEKER, Correspondent: More U.N. troops and equipment reach Mogadishu every day. By the end of this week, the full contingent should be here—500 armed Pakistani soldiers. More U.N. troops means more protection for food relief sent here for millions of starving Somalis. UNICEF's Goodwill Ambassador Audrey Hepburn was in Mogadishu to meet the troops.

AUDREY HEPBURN, UNICEF Goodwill Ambassador: Now that our blue helmets are here I think things are looking not so blue but rosy—better.

STRIEKER: U.S. military cargo planes are bringing the troops here from Pakistan.

W. O. HARTMAN SLATE, U.S. Marine Corps: We're the best in the business when it comes to moving large groups of personnel and large amounts of equipment from one country to another. It just stands to reason that we were asked to help out, and we're always willing to help out.

STRIEKER: Command and control of this operation comes from 25 miles offshore. A U.S. Naval amphibious readiness group with landing craft and 2,100 marines. The U.N. commander says U.S. support has been essential for this operation.

Brig. Gen. IMTIAZ SHAHEEN, Commander, UNOSOM: — So it's a great extension of help to the United Nations that this kind of support has been extended to bring in the peace keepers.

STRIEKER: The strongest military faction in Somalia, led by Mohammed Fara Adid, initially called the arrival of the U.S. navy ships "a provocation," but afterwards said they had no objection. The U.S. has downplayed its role in this operation, but amphibious assault craft and marines send a strong message to the warlords to back away from any confrontation with U.N. troops.

In a few weeks, the U.N. soldiers will take up positions in Mogadishu's port and airport to guard incoming relief supplies and escort food convoys to distribution points in the city. This is the first time the U.N. has sent armed troops to an African conflict since the Congo Crisis more than 30 years ago.

And while these soldiers now have a limited humanitarian mission, they could be the start of a much bigger military operation here. The U.N. Security Council has authorized 3,000 more troops for Somalia, but the main warlords have so far agreed to only these 500. There is growing support worldwide to declare Somalia a U.N. trusteeship, but that would need many thousands of troops and a huge financial commitment.

Meanwhile, the U.S. Navy and Marines will leave Somalia's coast after all 500 U.N. soldiers have arrived. These men will then be on their own in this city, surrounded by thousands of armed gunmen. Gary Strieker, CNN, Mogadishu, Somalia.

*Credit:* © 2005 Cable News Network LP, LLLP. Reprinted with permission.

## AN ANONYMOUS REPORT: "U.S. TROOPS SAY FOOD DELIVERED TO SOMALIA HAS KIDS PLAYING AGAIN"

*This is another of the human-interest stories that were frequently reported from Africa to American readers.*

Associated Press, 30 October 1992

MOMBASA, Kenya: When U.S. Air Force Capt. Casey Seabright started flying food to famine-stricken Somalia in early September, he never saw children. Now they're playing in villages near the airfields.

"It's pretty heartwarming—it makes you feel like you're doing something," said the 30-year-old navigator from St. Paul, Minn., who is on his second tour with the U.S. military airlift operating from the Kenyan port of Mombasa.

Marine Cpl. Thomas A. Burr, one of few American servicemen to visit Mogadishu, said he was overwhelmed by the devastation in Somalia, where drought and civil war have led to anarchy.

"I almost wanted to cry," said the 22-year-old satellite communications operator from Alexandria, La. "It took a long time for the world to answer. Now that we're here, maybe it will be over."

Since late August, the U.S. military has ferried food to famine-stricken towns in Somalia where at least 100,000 people have died and two million more are threatened with starvation.

So far, 14 C-130 Hercules aircraft have delivered more than 10,560 tons of food, sometimes confronted by gunmen on the tarmac. On Sept. 18, a plane was shot up in Belet Huen, and last week anti-tank mines on the runway halted flights for two days.

The United States has contributed about five percent of the nearly 200,000 tons of aid that has reached Somalia since January, and less than 20 percent of the 55,000 tons the United Nations estimates is needed every month.

Some relief agencies have criticized the Americans for being overly cautious and delivering less than they could.

But airlift commander Marine Brig. Gen. Frank Libutti said the food delivered by the United States adds up to over 35 million meals—enough to feed Washington, D.C. for two weeks.

"We've made a difference in terms of tackling hunger," said the 47-year-old from Huntington, New York.

Yet the airlift cannot meet all of Somalia's food needs. Ultimately, the ports that have been plagued by security problems must be reopened.

Some relief experts estimate that half the food is looted by the freelance gunmen and clan-based militias who have become the de facto rulers of the country. But agencies receiving food from the American effort report that 90 percent is getting to the needy, according to Army Lt. Col. Robert Donnelly, spokesman for the airlift.

More than 600 service personnel are part of Joint Task Force Provide Relief. The Marines and soldiers came with tents and sleeping bags, but the entire task force is being housed in luxurious beach-front hotels along the Indian Ocean.

"We still don't believe it," said Army Spec. Craig Hysell, 25, of Dallas, Texas, a military policemen and Gulf War veteran who was cultivating his tan by the pool at the Nyali Beach Hotel. "It's got sort of a dream quality to it. . . . Peacetime with no tensions is great."

*Credit*: Reprinted with permission of The Associated Press.

---

## RANDALL PINKSTON: "UNITED STATES PREPARING TO SEND TROOPS TO SOMALIA"

*As troops prepared for the prospect of military action in Somalia, the reports continued to be upbeat about the good work the United States was doing and the high likelihood of success. This television report is an example of that kind of story, seen and heard frequently since the relief efforts had begun months earlier.*

### CBS This Morning, 1 December 1992

HARRY SMITH, co-host: The heavily armed gangs who have brutalized Somalia's starving millions may soon be facing the kind of force that won the Persian Gulf War. And as usual, it looks as if the United States Marines will be first on the scene. Randall Pinkston is standing by at the White House with more on that. Good morning, Randall.

RANDALL PINKSTON reporting: Good morning, Harry. The first group of Marines are on the way, 1,800 troops steaming towards Somalia. They are expected to arrive off the shore of Somalia sometime tomorrow—this as the U.N. is preparing to accept a U.S. offer of a total of up to 20,000 troops to ensure the delivery of humanitarian aid to starving Somalis. In a list of options to the Security Council, Secretary-General Boutros-Ghali concluded there is no alternative but to decide to adopt more forceful measures to deliver relief supplies to the starving. The chairman of the Joint Chiefs of Staff is waiting for orders from the commander in chief.

General COLIN POWELL (Chairman, Joint Chiefs of Staff): As everyone knows, we are now putting together some plans to help the U.N. in Somalia in a much more forceful way if the U.N. makes such a request of us. It looks like they're moving in that direction.

PINKSTON: U.S. military forces would enable the delivery of food and supplies currently piled up in warehouses. While the mission would be a humanitarian one, some fear American soldiers could become mired in Somalia's gang warfare.

Mr. TED CARPENTER (Foreign Policy Analyst): Sending in the United States as the planetary nanny in Somalia or anywhere else is a blueprint for disaster for this country.

PINKSTON: But U.S. officials are emphasizing a short-term

role for U.S. troops in Somalia, with limited objectives. The next step is to persuade the Security Council to accept a key U.S. condition for participation, that the troops be under U.S. command. Harry.

SMITH: Randall Pinkston reporting live from the White House. Thanks.

## JOHN M. GOSHKO: "U.N. LEADER URGES FORCE TO HALT SOMALI ANARCHY"

*This Associated Press story appeared in many newspapers across the country and was among the first to hint that the situation in Somalia was not just a problem of food relief.*

### Associated Press, 1 December 1992

NEW YORK: An international military operation, probably led by the United States, must intervene forcibly in Somalia to disarm its warring factions if that East African country is to be saved from further starvation and bloodshed, UN Secretary-General Boutros Boutros-Ghali told the Security Council on Monday.

If Boutros-Ghali's proposal is accepted, it would be the first instance of the United Nations becoming involved in a country's internal affairs without the agreement of local authorities and with the possibility of offensive military force, instead of implementing passive peace-keeping measures such as monitoring cease-fires or elections.

In a letter to the Council, Boutros-Ghali said he would prefer such an operation to be under the direct command and control of the United Nations. But he noted that such an arrangement is unacceptable to many members—notably the United States, which has offered to provide up to 20,000 troops and other support for the operation—and he acknowledged that the United States would dominate and lead any force sent to Somalia.

Boutros-Ghali said traditional UN peace-keeping efforts have failed to halt the famine and anarchy devastating Somalia. He said he had concluded that only "a country-wide show of force" can guarantee deliveries of food and humanitarian aid in the face of attacks by warring militias.

The secretary-general's precedent-setting proposal drew a cautious reaction from the 15 countries on the Security Council and other UN members. Diplomats said they would require instructions from their governments about what position to take, and they said the Council would not begin discussing Boutros-Ghali's recommendations until today at the earliest.

It was unclear whether other countries might be willing to donate forces to such an operation. Also unclear was whether African countries, and their Third World allies, would support the idea of intervention for humanitarian reasons, oppose it for imposing a new form of colonialism on one of their

number or insist that any forces that go into Somalia be controlled directly by the United Nations.

With his proposals, Boutros-Ghali, who as an Egyptian deputy prime minister campaigned for the secretary-general's post as a representative of Africa, essentially associated himself with the U.S. view on the need for military action.

In a visit to the UN last week on behalf of President Bush, acting Secretary of State Lawrence S. Eagleburger offered to provide up to a division of U.S. combat troops and support elements if the United Nations approves an operation to safeguard deliveries of the aid. But while Eagleburger said the United States would act only under the authority of a UN mandate, he also stipulated that any U.S. troops sent to Somalia would have to remain under U.S. command.

The U.S. proposal prompted some UN members to call on the world body to establish interim control over Somalia and organize elections there. On Sunday, a senior Bush administration official said it might be necessary to follow the military operation with such a UN effort to end the anarchy that has engulfed Somalia since the overthrow of its dictator, Mohamed Siad Barre, last year.

White House press spokesman Marlin Fitzwater emphasized Monday that any U.S. role would be limited to the immediate problem of safeguarding food and medicine distribution.

In his letter to the Security Council, Boutros-Ghali also delineated the difference between the two problems. He said there was an urgent need for intervention by a force under the command either of the United Nations or individual members, but added: "In either case, the objectives of the operation should be precisely defined and limited in time, in order to prepare the way for a return to peace-keeping and post-conflict peace building."

## JEANNE MOOS: "U.S. PROPOSES DRAFT RESOLUTION TO U.N. ON SOMALI AID"

*This report focuses on the political leadership that was seeking to determine an international solution in Somalia. Though the United Nations had been looking for unilateral action for months, this was one of the few times that these activities developed into a significant television story. The story came out of New York City.*

*CNN News*, Transcript 227–1, 1 December 1992

HIGHLIGHT: The five members of the U.N. Security Council are meeting to discuss the options on the issue of aid to Somalia. The U.S. has proposed a resolution in which the council would ask the U.S. to name a commander.

FRANK SESNO, Anchor: And now Somalia. Here in Washington, the Pentagon says that a three-ship task force with some 1,800 Marines on board, accompanied by helicopters, is headed for Somalia, but the troops will not be deployed until a formal decision is made by the United Nations to intervene militarily in that East African nation.

And so, today, the United Nations Security Council is considering plans for just how and when it might send troops into Somalia. CNN has learned the U.S. is looking for a certain degree of control in all of that.

CNN's Jeanne Moos is at the United Nations, joins us now live. Jeanne?

JEANNE MOOS, National Correspondent: Well, Frank, the five permanent members of the U.N. Security Council are meeting as we speak now at the British mission to the U.N. The U.S. has proposed a draft resolution and CNN has learned some of the key details of that in which the security council would ask the U.S. to appoint a commander of the Somali operation. And we'll have more on that in a minute.

But what the U.S. is trying to do is get the agreement of the five permanent members before it brings this whole matter before the entire security council. There were some preliminary discussions this morning among all 15 members and those will continue more in-depth discussions in a couple of hours behind closed doors.

But there's no question now that the security council is moving towards a greater show of force in Somalia to get those food shipments through. The question is, how is it going to work and who's going to command it? Who is going to be in charge? The U.S.—this has been a sticking point. The U.S. has offered up to 20,000 troops but the U.S. would like to be in command of those troops, while the secretary general and some African countries have expressed the preference that the U.N. be in charge.

So now, the U.S. has proposed a draft resolution in which the security council would ask the U.S. to appoint a commander of the force. This would give the U.S. command and control, but it would also give a U.N. stamp to the whole thing. As I said, this is a draft resolution. It could change. This may not fly. Right now the five permanent members are discussing it at the British mission. I'm Jeanne Moos reporting live from the United Nations.

*Credit*: © 2005 Cable News Network LP, LLLP. Reprinted with permission.

## JEANNE MOOS: "U.N. AND U.S. AGREE ON SOMALIA RELIEF PROTECTION"

*This report from the United Nations followed on the same day. Clearly the military aspects of the relief effort were getting more attention now.*

*CNN News*, Transcript 243–1, 1 December 1992

HIGHLIGHT: A closed-door meeting between the U.N. and United States officials in regards to the command and control of a proposed military operation to protect relief efforts in Somalia has just ended.

SUSAN ROOK, Anchor: The United States and the United Nations moved closer today toward using troops to help save lives in Somalia. The U.N. Security Council has been working on a plan to ensure the delivery of desperately needed food aid. CNN's Jeanne Moos has the latest from the U.N.

Jeanne?

JEANNE MOOS, National Correspondent: A closed-door meeting of all 15 members of the Security Council ended about an hour ago, and it ended with progress towards a resolution that will leave the U.S. pretty much in charge of a military operation in Somalia. The proposed resolution would call on states to take all necessary means to make what it says is "secure the environment" so that food gets through to the starving people in Somalia. Here at the U.N. we call this "all necessary means" kind of talk "use-of-force authorization." It basically authorizes the use of force.

Now, one of the main sticking points here at the U.N. has been who would be in command and control of this operation? The U.S., which has offered to send as many as 20,000 troops over to Somalia—the U.N.—the U.S., rather, says that it wants command and control, but the Secretary-General and some of the African countries have said that they would prefer the U.N. had command and control.

Well, it looks like the U.S. will get its way, though not exactly in the language it would have liked to have seen. Earlier today there was language that the Security Council would ask the U.S. to appoint the commander of the operation. Well, that's been changed. It's been "jargonized," in the words of one U.N. delegate.

In any case, here's what the British ambassador to the U.N. had to say on this subject as he left the consultations.

DAVID HANNAY, British Ambassador to the U.N.: One of the options would involve an approach with a multinational force in which the country that was providing the largest contingent would be likely to provide the commander, and nobody took issue with that. It was generally seen to be a perfectly sensible way of proceeding. I'm not saying every country in the council supports that option, but most do, and I think that's the way the debate is going.

MOOS: Now, during the Desert Storm operation, some countries thought that the U.N. Security Council authorized the use of force and then was sort of left out of the picture as if the U.S.-led coalition had a little too much leeway. So, in this case it's likely that strings, or at least some slim threads, are going to be kept attached so that the U.N. keeps some control over the operation.

Amb. HANNAY: I think there will be very close links with the council. There will be reporting to the council. It will be the council that will have authorized the operation. It will be the council that will decide when the moment has come to conclude the operation and to switch to a more classical peacekeeping sort of operation.

MOOS: Apparently the U.S. can live with all those restrictions. The council is supposed to meet tomorrow afternoon around 5:00 to look at a final draft of the resolution, and then they're talking about a vote either on Thursday or possibly Friday. But at this point it looks like Thursday.

I'm Jeanne Moos reporting live from the United Nations.

---

# FORREST SAWYER AND TED KOPPEL: POLITICAL SITUATION IN SOMALIA

---

*As American troops were about to engage in significant combat duty, the news reports began to focus on the political leadership in Somalia. This ABC report is an example of that kind of story.*

*World News Sunday* (ABC), 6 December 1992

FORREST SAWYER: [CONVOY] A convoy of food for the starving finally makes it past the gunmen of Somalia. [KOPPEL & MAHDI] And Ted Koppel talks with the feuding warlords who say they're ready for the U.S. to bring peace.

ANNOUNCER: From ABC News, World News Sunday. Here's Forrest Sawyer.

FORREST SAWYER: Good evening. Even before U.S. troops arrive in Somalia, relief supplies have broken through the month-old siege of the port city of Mogadishu. [MAP] Planes loaded with food have also landed in the central city of Bardera. But the anarchy in the country continues to make it nearly impossible for relief workers to do their jobs, which means everyone is waiting for the U.S. to arrive. Ted Koppel reports tonight from Mogadishu.

TED KOPPEL: Forrest, it's a tough way to learn geography, but when U.S. troops are about to enter an uncertain environment in a strange place, our interest is suddenly seized. We're coming to you tonight from Mogadishu, the capital of Somalia. [RADAR] This port city is on the Indian Ocean. And as we flew in from Kenya this morning, our radar screen identified several large ships sitting just beyond the horizon from Mogadishu. [AERIAL OF CARRIER] One of them, the helicopter carrier USS Tripoli, with its contingent of Marines on board, was some 35 miles off the coast of Somalia. [SU (*a visual cue*)] This is a country where the four horsemen of the Apocalypse are on familiar territory. That makes the Marines, expected here any day now, a very desirable alternative.

MOHAMMED ALI MAHDI: I'm so happy if the United States has responded and sent in a force to Somalia to settle the peace and deliver the food to the needy people.

TED KOPPEL: His rivals call Ali Mahdi Mohammed a warlord. He calls himself "president." [MAHDI] If the Marines come and say, "Mr. President, we would like your men to give up their weapons," will you tell them to do it?

MOHAMMED ALI MAHDI: I will be very happy to hear that. We've waited for a year and my people are ready to put down their weapons because they need the peace.

TED KOPPEL: [GUNMEN] Although his gunmen control a significant piece of the country, Ali Mahdi has a precarious grip on the capital because of this man, Farah Aidid, another warlord who prefers the title "chairman." [AIDID] He, too, says he welcomes the Marines. But with a difference.

General FARAH AIDID: Only Americans, I believe, can give this possibility. It's a great country.

TED KOPPEL: What about your security forces?

General FARAH AIDID: Well, my security forces will be under my order, under my instructions.

TED KOPPEL: If they are asked to give up their weapons, will they do so?

General FARAH AIDID: I think we have to talk with American officials. And I think it is not necessary to force my forces to . . . in disarming them. This is not necessary because they are obeying my instructions.

TED KOPPEL: Aidid says he would like the U.S. government to send a delegation to meet with him before the Marines land to avoid misunderstandings. But with the Marines coming one way or another, Aidid made some concessions today, as Bill Redeker now reports.

AID WORKER: Can we lead the second convoy immediately, over.

BILL REDEKER: [RELIEF TRUCKS] More than 100 trucks loaded with 1,000 tons of wheat left the port today, leaving Aidid's turf, heading toward Ali Mahdi's. [WAREHOUSE WORKERS] The convoys made only a dent in the mountains of donated grain that have piled up in warehouses here because the feuding factions would not allow relief agencies to move it. Today, CARE agreed to pay off the faction that controls the port with 20 tons of grain so the trucks could roll—aid by extortion.

RHODRI WYNN-POPE/CARE: Donors are very realistic and very pragmatic about it all, thank goodness, because they appreciate that working here is not the easiest thing in the world.

BILL REDEKER: [SU] Although relief workers are pleased that some of this grain is finally leaving the port here in Mogadishu, it will not go directly to feeding centers. Instead, it will first head to another warehouse controlled by another warlord. [FIGHTERS] As the heavily armed convoys approached the borders between the two factions, there was tension and the fear that someone in this no-man's land might start shooting. But all of the trucks made it through safely. Ibrahim Sherill Omyer says he'll put down his gun for good once the U.S. Marines arrive, but many here are skeptical. The hired guns of Somalia's warlords earn their living fighting one another.

RHODRI WYNN-POPE: It's no good just coming in and disarming people unless there is something for those people who have been disarmed to do.

BILL REDEKER: While that may be a very real concern, the first priority is food. Tomorrow, another convoy of aid is scheduled to leave the port if the deal holds. Bill Redeker, ABC News, Mogadishu.

TED KOPPEL: Operating beneath the warlords and their gunmen, a whole commercial culture of black marketeers has grown up. It is not easy, as Jim Laurie now reports, to be a merchant in this city.

JIM LAURIE: [STREET SCENE] It is a city like no other—of gunmen, looters, black marketeers. [DEBRIS] A city mostly of rubble, of two years of civil war; a place where there is still an electric shop, but there is no electricity; a place where the devastating Somali famine can be forgotten in a black market brimming with food. [MARKET] There are back street warehouses like this one run by Adra Kahman, stocked high with international food aid: rice, flour and sorghum. [WAREHOUSE] The owner tells us, no, the food is not stolen. He says he's storing it for Red Cross feeding stations. The Red Cross says the shop is a typical example of looting on a grand scale.

HORST HOMBURG/ICRC: Looters installed some small warehouses in hidden places and they distribute now via the black market.

JIM LAURIE: [GROCERIES] As much as 50 percent of food relief winds up on the black market. The only good news about looting in Mogadishu is that the price of rice today is one-tenth of three months ago—now only six cents a pound. With those prices and the introduction of U.S. troops this week, the day of the looter may be nearing an end. Jim Laurie, ABC News, Mogadishu.

TED KOPPEL: We'll be bringing you Nightline from Somalia all this week. And when U.S. forces land, ABC News will be here to report on their arrival and the consequences. Now back to Forrest Sawyer in Washington. Forrest?

FORREST SAWYER: Thank you, Ted. Not everyone in the Bush Administration supports the rescue mission. For instance the American ambassador to Kenya, who says he, quote, "does not think Somalia is amenable to a quick fix so beloved by Americans." In a cable to the State Department obtained by U.S. News and World Report, Smith Hempstone says he believes the mission will simply, quote, "keep tens of thousands of Somali kids from starving to death in 1993, who, in all probability, will starve to death in 1994." "If you like Beirut," he goes on to say, "you will love Mogadishu." Coming up, while the military fights hunger overseas, celebrities are fighting hunger here at home; and later in the broadcast, a look at Bill Clinton's style of governing from those who've watched him work; and Charles Barkley of the Phoenix Suns, whose career is soaring on and off the court.

*Credit*: Reprinted with permission of ABC News, World News Sunday.

## SUSANNE M. SCHAFER: DEFENSE SECRETARY CHENEY SAYS OPTIONS OPEN ON DEALING WITH WARLORDS

*This wire service report out of Washington, D.C., also began to focus on the leadership concerns in Somalia and contained the preemptive statement from Defense Secretary Cheney, just before President Bush was to leave office, that U.S. troops would not "get bogged down in a guerrilla war." That phrase became a mantra for all of the U.S. military interventions after Vietnam.*

Associated Press, 6 December 1992

WASHINGTON: U.S. troops may round up and disarm the warring Somali gunmen who block the delivery of aid to the starving, Defense Secretary Dick Cheney said Sunday, but he insisted Americans will not get bogged down in a guerrilla war.

Cheney, in an appearance on NBC's "Meet the Press," said the first order of business for 30,000 troops being sent to Somalia will be to "restore some semblance of order" and that means dealing with the guns, mortars, artillery and other weaponry amassed by the nation's warlords.

"We may well want to go in and round up troops or weapons. We might want to offer a bounty" so people turn in their guns, Cheney said.

"We will be concerned about any potential military threat to our own forces, to the relief workers, and we will, in fact, have to deal with some of those elements in order to achieve our objective," Cheney said.

Marine Commandant Carl Mundy echoed Cheney's comments, saying he hoped U.S. troops encounter "a peaceful disarmament," but will be ready to meet any challenge if they don't.

"We are prepared to take whatever measures we have to to achieve disarmament," the four-star general said in an appearance on ABC's "This Week With David Brinkley."

The Marine general said he believed U.S. forces in the region will begin moving into Somalia "in about two days."

The troops will be allowed to return fire if fired upon, and also will be allowed to shoot first should someone even appear to be making threatening moves, Mundy said.

They may "need to fire because . . . someone's pointing a weapon at you, a machine gun or a tank (is) coming towards you or something, and they'll be able to engage," the general said.

Neither Cheney nor Mundy said they viewed the U.S. role as "rounding up every AK-47 in Somalia," nor remaining until peace returns to the devastated nation.

"If you're looking for the United States to stay until all Somalia's problems are solved—it's not going to happen," Cheney said.

He said U.S. officials hoped to begin turning some areas of Somalia over to U.N. peacekeepers by the end of next month.

Cheney estimated the humanitarian mission will cost the Pentagon "perhaps $300 million or $400 million."

Queried about the possibility that U.S. forces might end up in a lengthy guerrilla conflict, Cheney responded, "I think that's dead wrong."

He refused to specify any date for a U.S. departure, but said, "the idea of leaving a large U.S. combat force for a long time in Somalia is not a valid one."

National security adviser Brent Scowcroft, interviewed on CBS-TV's "Face The Nation," said the U.S. role in the operation "is strictly limited" and hopefully will prepare a groundwork of peace so Somalia can rebuild a government structure.

Scowcroft said, however, that at least "a few thousand" U.S. military personnel may be called upon to remain in Somalia after the U.S. ground troops depart.

They would be logistics specialists who would help provide support for any U.N. follow-on forces, Scowcroft said, because of the dire conditions in Somalia and the lack of such basics as fuel and water.

Meanwhile, the Navy announced that it had ordered the Baltimore-based hospital ship USNS Comfort to begin preparations to deploy to Somalia.

Lt. Cmdr. Steve Pietropaoli said it wasn't immediately clear how many medical specialists will be needed to get the 1,000-bed hospital ship under way, but he was certain the full complement wouldn't be called.

The ship is expected to get under way from Baltimore, Md., in three to four days. It will sail to Norfolk, Va., to pick up supplies before heading to Africa and it may take about two weeks for the ship to reach its destination, Pietropaoli said.

## TINA SUSMAN: "FOOD CONVOY MOVES OUT OF SOMALIA"

*This story from the wire service, in conjunction with the preceding one, reported what was actually happening in Somalia and was datelined from Mogadishu.*

### Associated Press, 6 December 1992

MOGADISHU, Somalia: A convoy of trucks carrying relief supplies to Somalia's starving moved out of Mogadishu's port Sunday for the first time in more than a month.

Elsewhere, relief planes reached the isolated city of Bardera just as food was running out.

Meanwhile, 1,800 U.S. Marines prepared to come ashore from three warships off the Indian Ocean coast to set up an operation to feed Somalia's starving.

They will be the first of about 28,150 American troops and smaller contingents from other nations that comprise a U.N.-mandated mission of mercy.

The first detachment of more than 2,000 French troops will be ready to leave the African nation of Djibouti on Monday, Defense Minister Pierre Joxe said in Paris. Egypt and Turkey also announced they will send troops.

President Bush ordered the U.S. military to organize the relief operation on Friday to secure Somalia's major ports and airports, and help deliver aid.

Mogadishu's port was closed on Nov. 11 amid clan disputes and rampant looting, and about 12,000 metric tons of wheat, rice and sorghum have yet to be distributed. The last attempt to open the port, on Nov. 25, failed when a U.N.-chartered ship was shelled as it entered the harbor.

Aid agencies estimate at least half the food donated to Somalia so far has been stolen.

Somalia descended into chaos in January 1991 after rebels drove dictator Mohamed Siad Barre from power. Since then, the government has collapsed, and drought and warfare have ravaged the nation.

About 300,000 Somalis have died this year from starvation, disease and warfare; another 250,000 could die by the end of the year without help. Some 2 million people, or one-third of the population, are at risk of starvation.

The United Nations failed in an attempt to move a food convoy out of the capital on Saturday. But the trucks rolled on Sunday.

The U.S.-led force is expected to oversee food distribution and make sure that Somalia's warring militias stay out of the way.

On Saturday, the relief group CARE canceled a convoy of 40 trucks of rice, beans and wheat it had planned to send from Mogadishu's port to the northern part of the city.

Clansmen from the north and south said they had agreed to let the trucks pass through, but by late afternoon the northern side said it could not guarantee their safety.

They later radioed CARE workers saying they had found a sufficient number of armed guards, but relief officials said the danger of being on the street near dark made it too dangerous to attempt the trip.

*Credit*: Reprinted with permission of The Associated Press.

## HOWARD GOLDBERG: "AMERICANS SPLIT OVER COMMITTING U.S. TROOPS TO U.N."

*This wire service story, which appeared the same day as the two preceding ones, focused on the confusion Americans were beginning to express over the U.S. efforts in Somalia and all the seemingly similar military efforts abroad.*

### Associated Press, 6 December 1992

NEW YORK: Most Americans think the United Nations could be relied on to fight at least some aggression worldwide, but they are divided over whether to commit American troops to such a U.N. force, an Associated Press poll found.

American public opinion is also split on the question of military intervention to alleviate suffering caused by internal conflicts in such places as Somalia and the former Yugoslavia.

Forty-five percent said the United Nations should inter-

vene if it takes military force to restore normal life, but 38 percent opposed intervention. The rest were not sure.

The telephone survey of 1,004 adults was taken Nov. 13–17 by ICR Survey Research Group of Media, Pa., part of AUS Consultants. Results have a margin of sampling error of 3 percentage points, plus or minus.

The U.N. secretary-general, Boutros Boutros-Ghali, has proposed a major upgrade in the U.N. military structure, so that the world body could roll back aggression and restore broken cease-fires.

Only 7 percent of Americans in the poll said the United States could almost always rely on the United Nations to deal with foreign aggression. Twenty-five percent rated the world body as reliable most of the time, and 55 percent said it could be relied on some of the time.

But only two in five favor assigning U.S. troops to a permanent anti-aggression force of the United Nations.

The reluctance to commit troops was strongest among women, those under age 35 and those in the lowest income category.

It also was strong among the seven in 10 Americans who believe the world is becoming a less safe place and among the four in seven who say the United States should concentrate on problems at home and worry less about the world.

Only 28 percent agreed with a less isolationist world view: that the United States has to maintain full support of its international agreements and alliances. A majority of those people favored a U.S. troop commitment to U.N. forces and intervention to restore normal life in places such as Somalia.

*Credit*: Reprinted with permission of The Associated Press.

---

## RANDAL ASHLEY: OPERATION RESTORE HOPE: EASING GRIEF AND WANT, POPE HINTS THAT HE APPROVES OF U.S. MISSION IN SOMALIA

---

*This Georgia newspaper story focused on international approval of the U.S. effort, as well as reporting on the realities of the U.S. commitment during the days in which President Bush was preparing to leave office and hand the situation to President-elect Clinton.*

### Atlanta Journal and Constitution, 6 December 1992

Pope John Paul II on Saturday issued an implicit endorsement of the imminent U.S. intervention in Somalia, saying that "internal conflicts should not condemn defenseless millions to die" and that nations have a duty to prevent such catastrophes.

The pope's words contrasted sharply with the pontiff's refusal two years ago to support Operation Desert Storm against the Iraqi invasion of Kuwait.

The pontiff skirted the military nature of the U.S. intervention in Somalia and focused instead on its stated aim: to reopen relief supply routes closed by warring militias and allow food to be delivered to millions of starving Somalis.

"The conscience of humanity demands that humanitarian intervention be made compulsory in situations which seriously endanger the survival of entire peoples and groups," Pope John Paul said.

### RELIEF WORKERS TRY TO HANG ON UNTIL GIS ARRIVE

In the tension-filled days before the arrival of U.S. troops, relief workers are facing not only their usual frustrations but also an increasingly volatile situation in Mogadishu and nearby towns.

Fearing that gunmen may rush to loot supplies or even resort to kidnappings before the Americans step ashore early this week, hundreds of aid workers have chosen to hunker down, stocking extra food and water and tightening their security precautions.

As always, their safety depends largely on the protection of hired Somali guards who follow them in heavily armed vehicles.

### MOST U.S. FORCES LIKELY TO STAY FOR MONTHS

American troops heading for Somalia as "peacemakers" may begin handing control to U.N. teams in early January, but most of the 28,000-strong U.S. force will be there until March or beyond, senior military officers told The Associated Press.

Thousands of U.S.-based Marines and Army troops were packing their gear Sunday and getting ready for a holiday season deployment, which officials said would not start before Monday. Supply ships were loading at U.S. ports this weekend.

Some 1,800 Marines, meanwhile, remained aboard ships offshore from the East African nation.

### WEDDINGS THE ORDER OF THE DAY

When Army Spec. Bernard Barber learned last week that he will soon be heading to Somalia, he hastily rescheduled his Dec. 26 wedding for Saturday.

And he wasn't alone.

There were 12 weddings scheduled for Saturday among soldiers of the Army's 10th Mountain Division, based at Fort Drum, N.Y.

"They want to make sure their sweethearts get benefits in

case anything happens," said Justice of the Peace Howard George. "When a soldier lines up and fills out their next-of-kin form, it gets to them."

Michelle Grigsby, Spec. Barber's fiancée, flew to Fort Drum from California on Friday, two days after the soldier called to tell her he was leaving for Somalia. "I cried," she said. "I broke down."

## U.S. TO GIVE $32 MILLION IN FOOD TO AFRICANS

The United States will provide $32 million in corn to starving Somalis and other victims of food shortages in sub-Saharan Africa, according to Agriculture Secretary Edward Madigan.

The aid is being donated from USDA stocks and will provide approximately 93,000 metric tons of corn for use in Somalia, Kenya and other African countries where civil strife, drought and the needs of refugees have strained local food supplies.

The donation totals 3.66 million bushels. U.S. farmers this year are expected to harvest a bumper crop of 9.33 billion bushels.

*Credit*: ATLANTA JOURNAL AND CONSTITUTION by RANDAL ASHLEY. Copyright 1992 by ATLANTA JOUR-CONSTITUTION. Reproduced with permission of ATLANTA JOUR-CONSTITUTION via Copyright Clearance Center.

---

## CARYLE MURPHY: SAUDI ARABIA SENDING TROOPS TO AID SOMALIA; MOVE SEEN AS LINKED TO CONCERNS FOR BOSNIA

---

*This story is an example of the way a connection between Bosnia and Somalia was presented. The example linked the use of the military in both conflicts as protection rather than humanitarian aid.*

*Washington Post*, 10 December 1992

CAIRO: Departing from its traditional reluctance to use its military beyond its borders, and with an eye on the Bosnian conflict, Saudi Arabia has decided to send about 1,000 troops to join U.S. forces in Somalia, a well-informed source said.

King Fahd's decision to send "no less than a battalion" of soldiers—mainly medical, engineering and administrative units—and some helicopters to the starving African nation follows earlier announcements by two other Islamic countries—Egypt and Turkey—that they will also contribute troops to the U.N.-authorized rescue operation in Somalia, which is predominantly Muslim. A 500-man unit of U.N. troops from Pakistan, another Islamic nation, has been in Somalia for several weeks.

Fahd's decision, which was communicated to Washington in the last 24 hours, was taken with a view to encourage the United States to push for U.N. military intervention in Bosnia in order to stop the killing of Muslims there, the source said.

The Saudis want to help "make the U.N. collective security effort more active and effective," the source said, adding that "you have more credibility to push on Bosnia if you are involved somewhere else."

Both Egypt and Saudi Arabia have previously told the Bush administration they are ready to contribute forces to a U.N.-sanctioned military operation in the former Yugoslavia. Both countries, along with Turkey, are deeply concerned about growing public anger throughout the Muslim world at the U.N.'s failure to halt Serbian atrocities against Muslims in Bosnia.

Islamic activists and opposition groups, complaining of a Western double standard, are demanding that their governments help Bosnia defend itself, even without U.N. authorization. And Islamic radicals are portraying the conflict as a religious war, with the West acting as an accomplice to the killing of Bosnian Muslims by Christian Serbs.

The involvement of Islamic troops in Somalia may deflect criticism from Iran, Iraq, and Egypt's main Islamic opposition group, the Muslim Brotherhood, of the arrival of U.S. forces in Mogadishu today.

"Where are the Arab and Islamic governments? Why have they not hurried to save their brothers in religion, language and history?" said a Brotherhood statement which also criticized "this suspicious American intervention."

Iran's state-run radio charged that the United States wants "to control main energy supply routes to the West" and warned of the creation of a "puppet government with U.S. backing in Somalia."

Iraqi National Assembly speaker Saadi Mehdi Saleh said, "The problem of Somalia might have been fabricated in order to [create] the pretext for military intervention."

*Credit*: © **1992, The Washington Post, reprinted with permission.**

## JEFFREY ULBRICH: "BLOODSHED IN SOMALIA AS FRENCH OPEN FIRE AT ROADBLOCK"

*As it began to become clear that the troops might see real combat, the reports grew more ominous and less upbeat. Here is an example of such a story. Because it was a wire service story, it would have been used across the country.*

Associated Press, 11 December 1992

MOGADISHU, Somalia: Marines and French soldiers fired on a truckload of Somalis who barreled through a French checkpoint on Thursday, killing two and injuring seven in the first bloodshed of the U.S.-led military mission.

The shooting came nearly two days after U.S. and French soldiers took control of Somalia's capital to protect food shipments. Several hours later, heavy fighting broke out between Somali gunmen in a tough area of Mogadishu about a half mile from the nearest foreign post.

The incidents attested to the continued volatility of Somalia, where even with Marines and French Legionnaires seizing weapons and flexing muscles, plenty of heavy weaponry remains in the capital.

The developments foreshadowed the unpredictable situation U.S. troops may face as they deploy in Somalia's interior, an operation expected to begin over the weekend.

Somalia's two main warlords, whose looting clansmen have blocked relief convoys, agreed Thursday to their first meeting since they locked horns two years ago. The fighting that broke out at midnight Thursday occurred near the dividing line between their fiefdoms and involved automatic weapons and rocket-propelled grenades, residents said.

In a statement read to reporters Friday, a Marine warrant officer said both Marines and French troopers opened fire on a truck loaded with Somalis that sped through their positions Thursday night.

According to the statement, the truck approached a French barricade "at a high rate of speed and despite efforts to get the vehicle to stop proceeded through the barricade. . . ."

The officer, Mike Hedlund, said the French opened fire and the vehicle kept going and entered an adjacent U.S. Marine position.

"The Marines opened fire. The vehicle crashed," he said, adding that two Somalis were killed and seven injured.

At the Pentagon, Lt. Gen. Martin Brandtner said the truck had been a "technical" mounted with a gun. But news photographers who arrived on the scene minutes after the incident did not see any weapons.

Two of the Somalis suffered bullet wounds and five were hurt when the vehicle slammed into a cement wall after it was shot, Brandtner said.

Both the bodies and the injured were flown to the USS Tripoli off the coast, where the injured were reported in stable condition.

On Saturday, Marines are to escort the first land convoy in a month to the strife-torn city of Baidoa, 125 miles to the northwest.

CARE International said Thursday night that its staff in Baidoa—an American, two Britons and two Australians—had barricaded themselves inside their compound in anticipation of an armed attack by clansmen.

CARE's manager in Mogadishu, Rhodri Wynn-Pope, asked American troops to provide air cover for the town Thursday night.

Army troops from Fort Drum, N.Y., were scheduled to begin arriving over the weekend in Baidoa, then split off and seize three other centers of the starvation zone—Belet Wen, Oddur and Gailassi.

About 350 fresh Marines, mostly support personnel, arrived in Mogadishu on Friday in a chartered Boeing 747.

On Nov. 11, a 34-truck relief convoy to Baidoa was ambushed with heavy casualties. Only one truck—with supplies promised for the warlords themselves—made it through. Since then, truck convoys have not ventured out of Mogadishu.

Fifty to 60 deaths are reported each day in Baidoa. Regular airlifts have done little for the hundreds of thousands of people encamped around the town because the battling clans and looters have prevented agencies from distributing food and medicine.

Even worse is Bardera, about 50 miles south of Baidoa. Unlike Baidoa, which at least has refugee camps, Bardera has neither camps nor sanitation. Heavy seasonal rains have limited food flights into Bardera's muddy airstrip.

Relief officials reported Thursday that a large convoy of Somali "technicals"—jeeps and pickup trucks mounted with guns and cannons—was spotted headed west from the Baidoa area toward the Ethiopian border.

Alarmed by sporadic gunfire near the U.S. Embassy compound in Mogadishu, Marines on Thursday raided several buildings in pursuit of snipers.

With Cobra attack helicopters hovering, Marines burst into a villa a half mile from the embassy and seized two anti-aircraft guns, two surface-to-air missiles and 10,000 rounds of rifle ammunition, according to an NBC reporter.

In a hopeful development for the violence-wracked land, warlord Mohamed Farrah Aidid announced he would meet Friday with his chief rival, Ali Mahdi Mohamed, said special U.S. envoy Robert Oakley. Oakley was also to attend.

The emergency food airlift into Mogadishu resumed Wednesday just hours after 1,700 Marines came ashore and seized the airport and seaport, the first steps in an unprecedented, U.N.-sponsored campaign to deliver aid through armed force.

A stream of C-5 and C-141 cargo aircraft landed at the airport from Germany, bringing equipment to supply the terminal with electricity, communications and water, said Col. Fred Peck, the Marines' spokesman.

There is little starvation in Mogadishu, where the Marines have been thronged by crowds of astonished, often admiring children and adults.

But relief shipments to the interior have been routinely looted by armed bands of youths set loose by clan conflict following the overthrow of President Mohamed Siad Barre in January 1991.

About 300,000 people have died of starvation, disease or warfare, U.N. officials estimate, and hundreds of thousands more are at risk of starvation.

The U.S. operation's field commander, Marine Lt. Gen. Robert Johnston, arrived Thursday to set up headquarters at the U.S. Embassy compound. The U.S. force eventually will include more than 28,000 troops.

About 150 Foreign Legionnaires in Mogadishu are the vanguard of an expected 2,000 French soldiers. Other troops have been promised by a dozen nations, including Saudi Arabia, Canada, Italy, Egypt and Turkey.

*Credit*: Reprinted with permission of The Associated Press.

---

## JAMIE McINTYRE: "EASY GOING SO FAR FOR TROOPS IN SOMALIA"

*This television report, however, continued to put a positive spin on the progress in Somalia despite casualties and wounded overnight.*

*CNN News*, Transcript 151–5, 11 December 1992

HIGHLIGHT: U.S. troops have not encountered any substantial resistance in Somalia, and that has officials smiling. Military analysts say much of the fighting outside Mogadishu is over who will welcome the U.S. troops.

BRIAN CHRISTIE, Anchor: Two rival Somali clan leaders, whose fighting necessitated Operation Restore Hope, are meeting at this hour in Mogadishu. Mohammad Farah Aidid and Ali Mahdi Mohammed will participate in talks at the U.S. Embassy. On Thursday, two Somalis were killed and seven others hurt when they were fired on by French and U.S. troops after their vehicle ran through a checkpoint. The casualties were the first since Western forces landed. U.S. troop strength in Somalia increased a few hours ago when another wave of Marines arrived in Mogadishu from California.

As the third day of Operation Restore Hope gets underway, U.S. troops have yet to encounter any major resistance. CNN's Jamie McIntyre reports U.S. military officials are monitoring the situation to make sure things stay that way.

JAMIE McINTYRE, Correspondent: U.S. troops have yet to encounter any substantial or organized resistance, and that has Pentagon officials smiling.

Lt. Gen. MARTIN BRANDTNER, U.S. Marine Corps: I am delighted to say that the casualty slide, which I will show you here, is all zeros. We hope that it stays that way.

McINTYRE: To hear U.S. military analysts tell it, much of the inter-clan fighting outside of Mogadishu is over who will, in effect, be in position to give the U.S. forces the key to the city.

Rear Adm. MICHAEL CRAMER, U.S. Navy: There is no indication, though, when U.S. and French and coalition and other forces arrive, that any of these organizations are, in an organized way, going to oppose. Just the opposite is the case.

McINTYRE: Here's the Pentagon assessment of the situation. In Bale Dogle, where U.S. planes have already landed, locals have been disarmed, the airport runway is sound, and security is good. Further west, at Baidoa, U.S. intelligence says heavy fighting between rival clans is threatening the safety of relief workers, and the overall situation is described as tense.

South in Kismayu, heavy fighting and looting forced the evacuation of 13 relief workers. The coastal road has been flooded by heavy rains, and clan warfare is further dividing the factions. The Marines plan next to quickly secure the airstrip at Bale Dogle, then be joined the next day by Army troops scheduled to arrive Saturday.

But, for relief workers in Baidoa and Kismayu, anxious for the Americans to arrive, it will be at least several more days.

Lt. Gen. BRANDTNER: As the facilities improve, and our ability to put forces and equipment through faster, the pace will obviously move, and I would submit to you, this is going to happen very quickly.

McINTYRE: Pentagon officials say it's up to commanders in Somalia to decide if the timetable can be accelerated. No one here is willing to predict how soon enough security will be in place to start accomplishing the mission's number-one goal, feeding the famished. Jamie McIntyre, CNN, the Pentagon.

*Credit*: © 2005 Cable News Network LP, LLLP. Reprinted with permission.

## BILL LAGATTUTA: SOMALI TOWN OF BAIDOA BEGINS RECOVERY

*This television news broadcast on New Year's Eve is an example of the upbeat reports that occasionally still found an ear and eye among the American public, despite the stepped-up military commitment and the reports of resistance among the Somalis.*

### CBS Evening News, 31 December 1992

PAULA ZAHN, anchor: Tomorrow the president is scheduled to fly into the heart of Somalia's famine district. He's going to a town ravaged by starvation, disease and war, where US troops have turned desperation into hope. Bill Lagattuta reports from Baidoa.

Unidentified Child: America! America!

LAGATTUTA: The children of Baidoa all know America, it's the country that rode to their rescue. When President Bush rides through Baidoa, if he peers out from the troop carrier he'll be sitting in, he'll see a miracle—a town terrorized and starving to death is coming to life again.

Unidentified Man: People are coming out, businesses are starting to open.

LAGATTUTA: And most importantly, the children are eating. This feeding center was a death camp two weeks ago. Now even the skinniest are smiling, because the Marines protect the food convoys. And if he looks over here, the commander in chief will see one of his men driving the bulldozer that's helping relief workers build the first new school.

Mr. MARK MULLEN (Concern): No Americans is no hope, as far as we're concerned.

LAGATTUTA: What President Bush will see here in Baidoa is wherever the Americans have invaded, life has become a little more sane. What he should hear is the question all of Somalia is asking: What happens when the troops go home?

How will the food keep getting where it's supposed to in this country where the only traffic cops work for free, and even then needs help? The president should know, if he doesn't already, that Somalia is a country that's been stripped bare. This is the biggest power station; this, the country's parliament; this is the cleanest hospital in Mogadishu, with an exhausted American volunteer running the emergency room.

Dr. BRODERICK FRANKLIN (Surgeon): Not enough scissors, not enough clean water. I mean, clean—clean, sterile water is a big item in a place like this.

LAGATTUTA: In a place like this, where the clans have been the only real government, Mr. Bush may be trying to figure out which warlord is the least of many evils, and should the American government give its blessing to one of them? And when he gets a look at some of the confiscated battle wagons, someone should tell the president there are countless others secreted away, waiting for the day the soldiers leave. Tomorrow, though, Mr. Bush may run into this: grateful Somalis bearing shovels, not guns, off to build that school in Baidoa.

Mr. MULLEN: The outlook for Somalia is positive at this time. We can deal with today; tomorrow is an uncertainty.

LAGATTUTA: How long would you like these troops to stay?

Mr. MULLEN: Ten to 15 years perhaps.

LAGATTUTA: If he's listening tomorrow, Mr. Bush will hear a lot of wishful thinking. Hope has been restored. The hard part is living up to the expectations.

Bill Lagattuta, CBS News, Baidoa.

*Credit:* Reprinted with permission of the CBS News Archives.

## RUTH SINAI: "BUSH SEES SOMALIA'S SUFFERING, PRAISES AMERICAN TROOPS"

*Even as the new year arrived, outgoing President Bush insisted that things were going well in Somalia. Soon this problem would be President Clinton's, and Bush was aware that his presidency would be judged in part by the success he fostered there. The following stories were provided as a package from the wire service. They would have appeared in newspapers across the United States on the traditionally slow news day of 1 January.*

### Associated Press, 1 January 1993

BAIDOA, Somalia: President Bush, stepping into the heart of Somalia's devastated interior, greeted hundreds of cheering youngsters and foreign relief workers at an orphanage in this ravaged relief center on Friday.

Accepting a red garland of local flowers that he wore over his military camouflaged shirt, Bush walked smilingly among the children, who chanted and clapped nonstop.

It was the president's second and final day in Somalia, a visit punctuated by overnight shelling in which rival clans fired on one another in the western suburbs of the capital. It was not known whether Bush heard the fire from his berth on the USS Tripoli.

After his stop at the orphanage, Bush was headed to Beli Dogle, an airstrip where some of the 18,000 troops participating in Operation Restore Hope were deployed.

From Somalia, Bush was headed on Saturday to Moscow, where he and Russian President Boris Yeltsin will sign off an ambitious treaty to cut long-range nuclear weapons by two-thirds.

The president smiled, waved and held out his hand to some of the children who were lined up in the orphanage courtyard to greet him.

The orphanage's crushing burden mirrors the burden of Baidoa itself, the place to which all roads lead in a region laid low by war, drought and famine, a place where 100 people a day were dying of starvation and disease.

It was the president's second visit to a facility serving the victims of famine and disease that has wracked this East African nation where 350,000 have died in the past three years as a result of civil war.

On Thursday he wended his way among Somalis too weak to move and children about to die, and said it was "just too emotional" to witness the suffering of this ravaged African country.

The president, in a New Year's Eve visit to the east African nation, praised the 18,000 American troops deployed throughout Somalia, saying they were performing their task of alleviating its misery in "A-1 style."

Bush was given a graphic display of the dangers of their mission when rival clans shelled each other with mortars in the western suburbs of Mogadishu Thursday night.

Flashes from the shelling lit up the sky as Bush spent the night on a U.S. Navy ship offshore. Col. Fred Peck, the Marines' spokesman, said the battle, apparently over an arms cache, was "not the first firefight but it's definitely the largest" since U.S. forces arrived Dec. 9 to aid relief operations.

Peck said he was unaware of any changes in Bush's plans to return to shore Friday for further inspections of efforts to save the starving.

Soon after arriving from Washington, via a brief stop in Saudi Arabia, Bush was taken to a private hospital, school and food center about 18 miles outside Mogadishu.

The clatter of his helicopter was almost drowned out by the chant of children and their parents shouting repeatedly, "Welcome Mr. Bush, Welcome Mr. Bush."

A group of children dressed in colorful rags handed him a purple bougainvilla branch, and he was then led through a maze of thatched huts covered with plastic sheets and tattered cloth to the hospital's school.

The center, whose name translates as "Place of Bones," was founded by a Somali doctor as a clinic in 1985, but since the civil war began more than two years ago, it has become a safe haven for thousands of refugees. Almost 30,000 people have been treated there for illness, starvation and gunshot wounds.

Bush entered a school, made of corrugated tin, to be greeted by dozens of tiny children sitting quietly on the sand floor. Outside a sign read "We need peace and education." Another sign said, "We Somalis never forget George Bush."

There were no desks or chairs, only several tattered school books.

The president, wearing fatigues and looking flushed from the heavy heat, also toured the center's hospital, walking along a hallway in which dozens of Somalis lay on the floor too weak or ill to move. In one room were malnourished children, two of whom were not expected to live, Bush was told.

"It's just too emotional for me to see this," he told reporters outside.

"I thought I had the most respect possible before now, and now it's even greater," Bush said of the U.S. troops. "It's the best of America."

Security for Bush's 44-hour visit was a daunting operation. Marines seized weapons caches, took over one building from which snipers could target the former U.S. embassy and pocked its 55-acre compound with gun pits and machine gun posts. Bush was transported from site to site in a helicopter guarded by helicopter gunships.

Sharpshooters were deployed on rooftops and Bush was tightly cocooned among Marines and Secret Service agents when he moved around on the ground.

Bush leaves Saturday for Moscow, where he and Russian President Boris Yeltsin will sign a historic nuclear arms reduction treaty.

Bush began his visit with a greeting to some 1,000 Marines and Air Force troops who turned out to see him on the grounds of the former U.S. embassy, once the largest and most modern in sub-Sahara Africa.

The embassy was completed in 1989 at a cost of $50 million and ransacked and ruined two years later in the war that ousted former dictator Mohammed Siad Barre. It is now the base of American Marines.

"We're very proud of this humanitarian effort," Bush told the troops. "This is a significantly new role" for the military and one that touches all Americans, he added.

"Ninety Six, Mr. Bush," shouted one enthusiastic soldier, referring to the next presidential election year.

Soldiers said they were pleased Bush had come to see them and boost morale on New Year's Eve.

"His visit lends a lot of credibility to this international effort and to what we're doing," said Maj. Ron Watkins of Cohasset, Mass.

"This mission you all are involved in is historic," Bush later told hundreds of cheering sailors and Marines aboard the amphibious assault ship USS Tripoli, anchored several miles off shore. Bush is spending two nights aboard the vessel.

"It's right and it's God's work and you're doing it well," Bush said before proceeding to dinner with the officers with whom he will ring in the New Year.

# MARK FRITZ: "SOMALIA'S NEW YEAR LIKE THE OLD AS FIGHTING RESUMES"

*This report was much less optimistic than the preceding accompanying story from the wire service.*

Associated Press, 1 January 1993

MOGADISHU, Somalia: Clan fighting erupted anew on Mogadishu's outskirts Friday and the thunder of tanks, artillery and mortars conveyed a disheartening New Year's message: Even as the starving are being fed, an appetite for power remains.

The new fighting, the heaviest since U.S. troops arrived on Dec. 9, came as President Bush visited Somali orphans and American Marines in Baidoa, the bleak heart of this bloodied, starving nation.

The fighting began Thursday and resumed Friday morning. It broke out when a minor clan faction unsuccessfully tried to seize a compound full of tanks and artillery from one of the main warlords, Gen. Mohamed Farrah Aidid.

Aidid's side suffered 17 dead and at least 25 wounded, said Marine Col. Michael W. Hagee, a spokesman for the multinational military force. He did not have casualties for the other side.

In many cases, the fighters were teen-agers in tennis shoes clambering over positions and firing weapons.

Hagee said the military was concerned about the fighting, even if it was not directed at troops.

"Anyone who uses (weapons) puts themselves at great risk," he said.

But he deflected repeated questions by reporters about whether the potent U.S.-led military force would try to take out the tanks, artillery and mortars if they are used again.

"We'll cross that bridge when we come to it," he said.

Several children and elderly people were among the wounded in the clashes in Mogadishu's northwest suburbs, said doctors at the capital's three main hospitals.

Two men and a child lay bleeding on operating tables in a tiny room at one hospital. Two nurses held down a man with a gaping head wound as a doctor tried to give him a shot.

The fighting gave Bush a glimpse of the rivalries and bloodshed that have plunged Somalia into the world's worst humanitarian crisis, a quagmire of clan warfare, anarchy, looting and famine.

Somalia plunged into factional anarchy and widespread looting and starvation after dictatorial President Mohammed Siad Barre was toppled in January 1991. At least 350,000 have died of disease and starvation in the past year, and 2 million more lives are endangered.

The U.S.-led mission now is restricted to providing safe passage for food delivery. But U.N. officials want U.S. troops to remain until a stable government is formed.

U.S. officials traveling with Bush said Washington so far has failed to get the United Nations to put together a cohesive plan for replacing U.S. forces with a more balanced multinational force.

The New Year's Eve firefight broke out when the small Murursade clan, led by Mohamed Kanyare, tried to drive Aidid's people from a compound containing Soviet-built tanks and artillery, which Aidid had agreed to remove from the center of the city.

The Murursade rained mortar shells on the compound, and Aidid's people responded with artillery, tank fire, mortars, rocket-fired grenades and machine guns.

Somali journalist Mohamed Aden Guled said Aidid ordered in reinforcements, and the Murursade were driven back by midday Friday.

Arden Mohamed Ali, an analyst at the U.N. Children's Fund, said the Murursade were seeking to become players in the U.N.-sponsored clan reconciliation talks set for Monday and Tuesday in Addis Ababa, Ethiopia.

"They are fighting for recognition of their faction," he said.

The peace talks remain tenuous. The U.N. spokesman for Somalia, Farouk Mawlawi, said Aidid still had not committed to them.

# KEITH B. RICHBURG: CHANGEOVER IN SOMALIA TAKING SHAPE; CONCERNS ABOUT U.N.'S FIGHTING ABILITY GROW

*Three months into the new year and the new presidency, the reports were less rosy. This story is an example of the kinds of reports that were now more frequent from the Somali capital.*

*Washington Post*, 10 March 1993

MOGADISHU, Somalia: The huge American amphibious landing vehicle that for weeks sat like a sentry at the city's strategic Kilometer Four traffic circle is gone now. In its place is a small, white tank with "U.N." painted in black on the sides.

Compared to the hulking U.S. craft, the little white tank resembles a child's toy, or perhaps a carnival bumper car. It can barely fit two people, compared to the several Marines and their gear the American vehicle can accommodate. While the massive American machine seemed to inspire awe among Somali passersby who would press against the surrounding barbed wire for a look, Somalis seem oblivious to the U.N. tank and the Nigerian soldiers standing watch outside it.

Nevertheless, the switch of vehicles is a reminder of a crucial event in this country's attempt to overcome its chaotic civil war and mass starvation. Ninety days after the first American Marines landed at Mogadishu's port and its seaside international airport under the glare of television lights, a transition from a U.S.-led intervention force to a United Nations operation appears to be finally taking shape.

A new U.N. military commander, Turkish Lt. Gen. Cevik Bir, is en route. A Security Council resolution authorizing the operation is expected to be passed soon, possibly this week. A retired American admiral, Jonathan T. Howe, took over as the new envoy to Somalia yesterday, replacing Iraqi-born Ismat Kittani, who was considered ineffective. There is even a proposed changeover date—May 1.

In replacing the U.S. troops, the United Nations is embarking on one of the largest, costliest and most difficult operations in its history, comparable only to the peace-keeping operation in Cambodia. About 28,000 soldiers and 2,800 civilian administrators will serve under the U.N. flag in Somalia.

As the inevitability of the turnover becomes apparent here, Somalis and relief workers are raising serious questions, expressing nagging concerns and a growing sense of anxiety. How aggressive will the U.N. force be in continuing the tough job of disarming the country's militias? How effective will they prove when challenged militarily—as diplomats and aid workers say they inevitably will be—by resurgent warlords and their teenaged gunmen? Will the U.N. force do a better job than the Americans in putting

down ongoing clan violence in places such as Kismaayo or farther north around Gaalkacyo?

Finally, there is concern about the ability of the U.N. force to meet its mandate to help Somalis rebuild their institutions and establish some semblance of government.

"As with the United States, there is still no real effort to sit down and figure out exactly what it is they [the U.N. force] want to do," said Rakiya Omaar, a Somali human rights activist in London who heads the new group African Rights. "You can't impose a political settlement, either on Bosnia, Cambodia or Somalia."

This week, for the first time, the number of allied coalition troops on the ground surpassed the number of American forces. On Sunday, 13,985 American troops remained in Somalia compared to 14,017 troops from 24 nations. American troops remain only in Baardheere, Merca, Kismaayo and Mogadishu. Troops from other nations are deployed in all the other Somali towns across the famine belt.

Diplomats and relief workers here expect the United Nations force to encounter obstacles that the U.S.-led forces did not—or were able to avoid.

For one, the U.S. intervention forces operate only in the southern third of Somalia, the "famine zone" that ends north at the town of Beledweyne, where Canadian troops are based. The U.N. force, by contrast, will have responsibility for the entire country, including the breakaway "Somaliland Republic," and its capital, Hargeysa, and the area around war-wracked Gaalkacyo. With fewer troops responsible for a far larger chunk of territory, the U.N. force will be stretched thin. "Yes, the land mass you're going to be covering is going up," a U.S. official conceded.

In the days before the American Marines first landed, U.S. diplomats in Mogadishu warned Somalia's main warlord, Gen. Mohamed Farah Aideed, to move his heavy equipment, men and "technical" vehicles north of the U.S. operating zone. Aideed complied, and his men and machines roam freely in a kind of no-man's land around Gaalkacyo. It will be up to the U.N. force to try to garrison them.

Marine Col. Fred Peck, the U.S. military spokesman, said at a recent briefing that U.S. forces "have a minimal sense of what's going on" in the area north of the American zone. "We don't have a good picture," he said. "There are clan militia forces up there."

Still, he said, the U.N. troop numbers should be "quite

adequate." They will be supplemented by a newly formed Somali police force of 3,000 men, and the Americans will have already contained much of the violence in the southern regions.

Ongoing violence in Kismaayo between supporters of rival warlords demonstrates how much remains to be done in terms of establishing security. Grenade attacks and running gun battles there have killed more than 20 people and injured 200 in the past two weeks. Relief workers in the southern port city spend much of their time barricaded in their compounds.

One national contingent of the U.N. force, at least, has already demonstrated that it won't back down from a fight. Last month, when snipers opened fire on a hotel, the Nigerians responded with an hour-long bullet and grenade barrage that essentially destroyed the snipers' suspected hideaway. American military officials complained about the Nigerians' lack of "fire discipline," and relief workers said stray bullets hit their compounds.

[A Nigerian accidentally fired five rounds into a Mogadishu hotel dining room while trying to clear his rifle Tuesday, the Associated Press reported. One of the bullets wounded Voice of America reporter Alex Belida of Rockville in the thigh.]

While the United States maintains that its mission was strictly limited to opening supply routes and delivering food aid, the U.N. force will be faced with the formidable task of trying to rebuild Somali society. As departing U.S. envoy Robert Oakley put it in his valedictory remarks, "Our mission never included the political restructuring of Somalia."

Sticking to the original mandate—delivering food to the starving—has made it easier for the United States to declare victory and go home, leaving behind only a residual force of about 5,000 logistics experts and a "rapid response team" to intervene if the U.N. force gets bogged down. But critics of a precipitous U.S. withdrawal say that by emphasizing only the food-delivery aspects of Operation Restore Hope, the U.S. forces are handing the job over to the United Nations while the real mission is still incomplete.

"We've only scratched the surface in disarming these people," Kittani warned in his last news conference as the U.N. envoy here.

"The Americans have stuck to what they said they would do—which is why the whole thing is irrelevant to solving the problem of Somalia," Omaar, the human rights activist, said. "They are leaving an ill-prepared U.N. to deal with the disappointment, and the prospect of a violent aftermath."

*Credit:* © **1993, The Washington Post, reprinted with permission.**

---

## PAUL ALEXANDER: "U.S. TROOPS RETURN TO KISMAYU; AIDID RETURNS TO TALKS"

---

*This story is an example of the kind of report that was appearing more frequently, coupling the political situation directly to the use of peacekeeping troops. Though the country now seemed to have settled down in some areas, there were still many hot spots of fighting.*

### Associated Press, 19 March 1993

KISMAYU, Somalia: A key Somali faction leader returned to peace talks today, apparently mollified by the deployment of a battalion of American troops to this violent city.

The 500 members of a U.S. quick reaction force moved into Kismayu Thursday, ordered back after fighters of Mohamed Said Hirsi, known as Gen. Morgan, drove supporters of Col. Omar Jess out of the town.

Tuesday's clash prompted Mohamed Farrah Aidid, one of Somalia's chief warlords and a supporter of Jess, to pull out of peace talks in Addis Ababa, Ethiopia. Aidid had said he would not return until the situation in Kismayu was "reversed."

But Farouk Mawlawi, the U.N. spokesman in the Ethiopian capital, said today that Aidid had rejoined talks. The warlord met with other faction leaders and U.N. officials this morning.

Despite U.N. efforts to expand representation by including community leaders and intellectuals, Aidid's temporary walk-

out demonstrated how much of a grip the warlords have on the peace process.

The talks were suspended after he left Wednesday, and committees met only informally on Thursday.

With Aidid back on board today, conference committees resumed discussion of issues including setting up transitional authorities that could ensure security for relief and development work.

Mawlawi had said Thursday that there was still hope an agreement would be reached by the end of the conference. But he conceded the talks were not likely to end as scheduled on Saturday. He would not say how long they would last.

Aidid had no immediate comment, and the reasons for his decision were not clear. But a U.N. fact-finding mission left for Kismayu today, as he had demanded, and the U.S. troops were charged with trying to end feuding here.

Two weeks ago, the Americans had handed over peacekeeping operations in this dusty port to an 800-man Belgian force.

The United States had more than 1,000 troops here until the handover to Belgian forces. About 150 American soldiers had remained to guard aid agencies.

Kismayu was quiet Thursday, as a team of investigators—including the U.S. military's top legal adviser in Somalia and a U.S. diplomat from Nairobi, Kenya—began trying to sort out the dispute.

"It's very complex because it involves clans and sub-clans, years of hatred," said Brig. Gen. Greg Lile, who is in charge of the American troops in Kismayu.

Lile said the troops will enforce a ban on weapons, bandits, roadblocks and "technicals"—vehicles mounted with weapons—in Kismayu and will intercede to halt unrest.

Meanwhile, at U.N. headquarters in New York today, the Security Council opens debate on taking over the Somalia relief mission from the U.S.-led task force. The council plans to send a 28,000-strong U.N. peacekeeping force to Somalia. A May 1 date has been set to begin the transition.

Some 12,000 U.S. troops remain in Somalia, along with about 14,000 troops from 22 other countries.

Somalia has been wracked by famine that was worsened by a civil war that toppled dictator Mohammed Siad Barre in January 1991. More than 350,000 people died last year before the U.S.-led coalition arrived in December to safeguard aid deliveries.

*Credit*: Reprinted with permission of The Associated Press.

---

## KATIE DAVIS: "ROBERT OAKLEY SPEAKS OUT ABOUT GAINS IN SOMALIA"

---

*Despite the recurrence of violence in Somalia, some politicians continued to insist that the U.S.-led effort had been a success. This radio broadcast interview is an example of the former President Bush administration reassuring the public that its decision to send troops and food was the best solution for clan fighting in Somalia.*

### All Things Considered (NPR), 28 March 1993

DAVIS: This is Katie Davis. Coming up on All Things Considered, the architect of the U.S.-Somalia Relief Plan talks about progress in the country. . . . Some major developments on Somalia this past week. On Friday, the United Nations Security Council voted to set up a multi-national, U.N. peacekeeping force for the country. The force, which is expected to have at least 28,000 troops, will replace the U.S. contingent there in May. And yesterday, leaders of Somalia's opposing factions reached a peace accord. Under the agreement, an interim government will be set up until elections can be held in two years time. These developments mark a turning point for Somalia, which became the focus of world attention last December when former President George Bush sent U.S. troops there to help protect relief operations. Robert Oakley was the Bush administration's special envoy in Somalia. He returned to Washington a few weeks ago.

ROBERT OAKLEY, Former Special Envoy in Somalia: The Somali people are much, much better off. The killing has stopped from clan warfare. The death from famine has stopped. The death from disease has slowed way, way down to something approaching normal, which is not very good but at least it's normal. So the problem with the Somali people, the physical problems, if you will, have been largely resolved. But because the militias are no longer able to wage war, they're no longer able to loot. They have no means of providing for their members. So individual members of these militias have taken their weapons and gone off to become bandits or robbers, if you will, using guns and they'll threaten whoever seems to have something to rob. And this is where the relief workers and other foreigners, including media people, feel much more in danger than they did before because there's more armed banditry.

DAVIS: But that certainly could create perhaps as severe a situation if the armed bandits are attacking relief agencies, looting food. The delivery of food and the stability of the country could be disrupted.

Mr. OAKLEY: No, because what's happening is that the clan warfare, which was so destructive of the stability of the country and which was the primary cause, both, as I say, the deaths from warfare but also preventing food and medical supplies from getting through to the people. That problem has been virtually stopped.

DAVIS: When you left on March 2nd, when you left the country, and now when you look back at what's going on there, do you have a feeling that, yes, I think this country is going to be okay, that it won't slide back into the chaos that existed?

Mr. OAKLEY: Yeah, the answer to that, my answer is a resounding, "Yes, it will not slide back into the same sort of chaos, anarchy and orgy of self-destruction." The mood has changed. Even the warlords don't want to see that happen. The more intelligent ones have virtually disarmed themselves and have chosen the political path. Others, including General Aidid, still have reservations and they still seem to feel that they can get their way by trying to use intimidation but not the sort of warfare that you had before. That was really an aberration in any society.

DAVIS: If you were given an opportunity to tackle this

problem all over again, is there anything you would do differently?

Mr. OAKLEY: Well, one of the things which we didn't count upon because the U.S. mandate, as I said, was fairly narrow and I think it was a correct mandate because I don't believe that the United States has any long-term responsibility for Somalia. When I was there before ten years ago, we and the Russians both deluded ourselves into thinking we had strategic interests in the Horn and what we did there and the amount of money we put in for military and other things, into Somalia and Ethiopia, and don't forget they changed sides and changed the lines and it didn't help that part of the world a bit and it didn't help us any. But in places like El Sal-vador and Nicaragua and Mozambique and Angola, from the very beginning, the United Nations envisaged plans to demobilize, disarm guerrilla groups. That was not done for Somalia. The United Nations' operation went into suspense when the U.S. came in. It wasn't part of the U.S. operation. We should have thought about that, we and the United Nations together. In that way, we could have gotten on top of the problem, of sort of individual armed violence and banditry, much earlier on.

DAVIS: Robert Oakley is the former presidential envoy to Somalia.

## PAUL ALEXANDER: "U.S. TROOPS PULL OUT OF LAST SECTOR"

*This report from Somalia a month after the preceding interview was much less upbeat.*

Associated Press, 29 April 1993

MERCA, Somalia: U.S. Army troops handed over Merca, the last area of Operation Restore Hope under American control. So why aren't they celebrating?

First, they are leaving a great beach with coral reefs little more than a stone's throw away. Then there's the loss of security: American soldiers have made Merca one of the safest spots in violence-wracked Somalia.

Finally, after transferring control to Pakistan on Wednesday, these soldiers aren't going home to Fort Drum, N.Y.

They're just moving to Mogadishu, where they'll be part of the 1,300-soldier quick-reaction force the Americans are leaving behind after the United Nations takes over full control of the coalition forces from the United States next week.

"It's like night and day," said Spec. David Hofner of Los Gatos, Calif., a Humvee driver who regularly makes trips between Mogadishu and this city of 20,000 people.

"By comparison, this is a paradise. It reminds me a lot of home. Troops here go to the beach and it's like you're not in Somalia."

Danger isn't far away. On the washboard-rough road to Mogadishu, a two-hour drive up the coast, convoys remain advisable because of the threat of bandits.

Security in the capital has improved markedly since a multinational force arrived Dec. 9 to safeguard food shipments in a country where an estimated 350,000 people died last year from famine and disease in a country wracked by civil war.

But Mogadishu's streets, with their rock-throwing youths and pistol-packing adults, remain hazardous.

Merca still bears the scars of war, with battered, roofless buildings.

But the market seems to be doing well, recent rains have turned everything green, and healthy-looking livestock abound. People wave and smile as Americans pass.

On the other side of the reddish-gold dunes lies the former communist propaganda school, a complex of seven buildings encircling a tent camp where many of the 625 soldiers have been sleeping. The surf crashes in the distance, on the other side of the double strands of barbed wire.

The Americans pumped out military songs like "Rifle Regiment" through loud, tinny speakers mounted on a Humvee for the transfer ceremony. After a Pakistani bagpipe-and-drum band performed, Lt. Col. William Martinez spoke while a Pakistani interpreter translated into Urdu.

"You can be proud in knowing you have truly restored hope in Merca," Martinez told his troops.

Martinez later spoke of the difference in the city and the surrounding area since the troops arrived in December.

"Initially, there were a lot of bandits, a lot of technicals," Martinez said. "Now it's one of the safest sectors in Somalia."

Hofner, the Army driver, said he'd think about returning someday if things keep improving.

"It's so sad that people are killing each other over food, over which clan they're from," he said. "If this place gets its act together, I'd come back.

"This could be such a beautiful country. I'd put a hotel on the beach and make millions."

# TINA SUSMAN: CHAOS RETURNS TO SOMALIA; AT LEAST 28 PEOPLE SLAIN, INCLUDING U.N. TROOPS

*In June, a serious setback occurred when Pakistani U.N. troops were killed, and dozens of civilians were wounded. This report from Somalia is an example of early reports of this new uprising.*

Associated Press, 5 June 1993

MOGADISHU, Somalia: Chaos returned to Mogadishu on Saturday as combat erupted between a warlord's fighters and U.N. peacekeepers. At least 28 people, including Pakistani U.N. troopers, were reported killed, and 130 were wounded.

Machine-gun fire and grenade blasts echoed through the capital all day as U.N. troops, Americans among them, battled Somalis loyal to warlord Mohamed Farrah Aidid.

The fighting, the worst in Mogadishu since anti-American riots erupted in February, showed the tenuous security situation in Mogadishu even after six months of foreign military presence.

The Somalis were apparently enraged by rumors that the U.N. troops—who took over command of an international military coalition from the United States a month ago—planned to occupy Aidid's radio station.

As military helicopters swooped over the city, Somalis rushed their wounded to hospitals on carts pulled by donkeys. Barricades of burning tires, boulders and wire blocked several main streets.

The city's two main hospitals reported 23 Somalis had been killed and more than 100 wounded.

U.N. sources said three Pakistani members of the U.N. force were killed, but Italian Gen. Bruno Loy said his men recovered the bodies of five Pakistani soldiers.

In an interview with Italian state TV, Loy said Italian troops, backed by a dozen tanks and armored personnel carriers and two helicopters, rescued 80 Pakistanis who were surrounded by snipers in two areas in the city. The Italian defense ministry said 10 American soldiers were also rescued.

The Italians ferried about 30 wounded Pakistani peacekeepers by helicopter to an Italian military hospital, Loy said. No Italians were injured during the rescue, which was achieved by the show of force without firing a shot, he said.

There were unconfirmed reports an American soldier was also wounded.

The Italian foreign ministry late Saturday said it was joining Pakistan's call for a meeting of the U.N. Security Council as soon as possible to discuss the situation. Italy's special representative here has been instructed to give Somalis a strong warning about the day's bloodshed.

Some of the fiercest fighting occurred near a traffic circle in the city center, a hotspot since foreign troops arrived in

Somalia in December to safeguard relief supplies for victims of war and famine.

U.N. officials warned foreign aid workers to stay indoors, and they did, huddling inside their compounds.

Bullets smacked into a hotel overlooking the circle where most foreign journalists and some U.N. workers are staying, as Pakistani troops on the roof traded gunfire with snipers.

One bullet punched through a wall of a room next to the office of The Associated Press. Journalists lay on their bellies to avoid being hit.

Fresh bullet holes pocked a low wall around the perimeter of the hotel's roof, where journalists transmit stories and pictures by satellite telephones.

Hundreds of Somalis gathered outside a United Nations building up the road, and witnesses said some tried to storm the building.

The fighting broke out about 10 A.M. as U.N. troops conducted inspections of weapons storage sites. The weapons had been taken from Somalis in accordance with U.N. demands.

U.N. spokesman Farouk Mawlawi said Aidid was informed of the planned inspections on Friday and indicated no objection. One of the sites of weapons to be inspected was near Aidid's radio station, which sparked rumors of a planned takeover of the station.

Stockwell and Mawlawi denied any plans to seize the station, which broadcast anti-U.N. chants and songs Saturday afternoon.

Among the U.N. troops facing combat Saturday was a U.S. quick reaction force, a 1,100-member team mostly composed of soldiers from the 10th Mountain Division based in Fort Drum, N.Y.

The U.S.-led multinational force arrived in Mogadishu in December to protect relief supplies intended for victims of Somalia's civil war and famine, which killed an estimated 350,000 people last year.

The United States handed over control of the operation to the United Nations last month and has withdrawn the bulk of its troops.

There are still some 4,000 American soldiers here among the 18,000 foreign troops.

*Credit*: Reprinted with permission of The Associated Press.

## KEITH B. RICHBURG: SCORES KILLED OR HURT IN SOMALI CAPITAL; U.S. TROOPS INVOLVED

*The State Department later confirmed that the attack on U.N. troops on 5 June left twenty-three Pakistani peacekeepers dead and fifty-nine wounded. Three American soldiers also were wounded. The following newspaper report is an example of the kind of follow-up story that appeared the day after the attack.*

*Washington Post*, 6 June 1993

MOGADISHU, Somalia: In the bloodiest day here in three months, U.N. forces backed by helicopter gunships fought running battles across Mogadishu today with Somali gunmen who attacked U.N. offices and foreign troops and set up barricades of debris and burning tires.

The clashes shattered the illusion of normalcy that had settled over this battle-scarred capital in recent weeks and posed the first major challenge to the U.N.-commanded peace keepers since they took over one month ago from the American-led military force sent here to restore order and deliver food to Somalia's famine-stricken people.

More than 20 Pakistani troops were believed killed and up to 60 wounded in today's fighting, according to a Reuters report, quoting U.N. sources. Two American soldiers were also said to have been wounded.

U.S. Army Maj. David Stockwell, spokesman for U.N. forces in Somalia, declined to confirm casualty figures but said there were "several dead and wounded" among the U.N. troops. He said fighting in at least one location was continuing into the night.

Pakistan called for an urgent meeting of the U.N. Security Council, and Council members scheduled a closed-door meeting in New York for 11 A.M. Sunday.

Scores of Somalis were also killed or wounded in the gun battles, which began around 10 A.M. and continued sporadically throughout the day. By late afternoon, the capital's Digfer Hospital had recorded 34 gunshot victims, including three who died. Nearby Banadir Hospital received as many as 100 casualties, including 10 dead, according to the hospital administrator. It was unclear whether the Somali victims were shot by U.N. troops or by Somali bandits who apparently took advantage of the violence to engage in widespread looting and vandalism.

Elements of the U.S. "quick reaction force"—the 1,200-man Army unit left behind to quell such outbreaks—were called into action early Friday. Stockwell said U.S. helicopters patrolling the skies may have been engaged in the fighting, but precise details were unavailable.

Most of today's fighting appears to have been conducted by Pakistani troops, who in late April replaced U.S. Marines as the main force in charge of securing Mogadishu's dangerous streets.

[In Rome, state television broadcast an interview with Italian Gen. Bruno Loy, who said Italian troops, backed by tanks, armored personnel carriers and helicopters, rescued 80 Pakistanis who were surrounded by snipers in two areas in the city, the Associated Press reported. The Italian Defense Ministry said 10 American soldiers also were rescued. No Italians were injured during the rescue, achieved by a show of force without firing a shot, Loy said.]

The violence was apparently sparked by rumors that U.N. forces had attempted to take over a radio station run by Mohamed Farah Aideed, one of Somalia's principal warlords. Aideed has been broadcasting vehement anti-foreign propaganda and accusing the United Nations of attempting to colonize Somalia. In the chaotic factional warfare that followed the fall of President Mohammed Siad Barre in January 1991, Aideed emerged as perhaps the most powerful man in Somalia. But his power was diminished by the arrival of foreign troops last December, and he has often used the radio station to try to rally his clan faction against what he calls U.N. interference in Somalia's internal affairs.

U.N. diplomatic and military officials said it was too early to determine whether the clash was an attempt by Aideed to undermine U.N. authority here.

U.N. officials said no attempt was made to enter or occupy Aideed's radio station compound. U.N. spokesman Farouk Mawlawi said the troops told Aideed on Friday that they would conduct inventories at five of the sites that had been designated for the warlord to store his weapons when U.S. troops arrived, and "one of the sites happens to be close to Radio Mogadishu."

After U.N. troops went to inspect the site, anti-U.N. demonstrations apparently began around the radio station compound. The radio station reported, apparently erroneously, that the foreign troops killed two young Somalis as they attempted to enter and occupy the station.

The administrator at Banadir Hospital said most of the gunshot victims there had been wounded in fighting around the radio station or one of the radio transmitters. He said many of the victims were women and children.

Anti-U.N. demonstrations quickly turned into violent attacks by Somalis—some armed with automatic weapons and grenades—on U.N. installations scattered around the south side of the city, a sector considered a stronghold of Aideed and his supporters. There also were reported attacks on Pakistani patrols and on Pakistani positions around a key traffic circle.

This was the second major anti-foreigner uprising in Mogadishu; two days of riots in late February left an untold number of Somalis dead or injured.

Today's fighting shattered a seductive calm that had set-tled over the capital since U.S. forces handed over command of peace-keeping operations to the United Nations a month ago.

## REID G. MILLER: "U.S., U.N. FORCES LAUNCH RETALIATORY ATTACK"

*This story a week later is an example of the reporting shift to an entirely different focus on the conflict and military action. There was attention now on anything but the combat strike.*

Associated Press, 12 June 1993

MOGADISHU, Somalia: U.N. forces attacking from the air and ground went after Somali warlord Mohamed Farrah Aidid today in retaliation for ambushes that killed 23 peacekeepers and crippled relief operations.

The pre-dawn strike on Aidid's bases of power in Mogadishu was seen as a test of the United Nations' will to continue its efforts to deliver food and restore order in lawless Somalia.

"The operation seems at this point a success. At this point it's very much on track," said Secretary of State Warren Christopher in Istanbul, Turkey. He said the city's radio tower, water reservoir and cigarette factory were destroyed.

An Aidid aide was captured by Italian troops, but Aidid had evaded arrest as of late today, said the Italian Defense Ministry in Rome. The ministry did not have details on the arrest or the name of the aide.

Flares, rockets and tracer bullets lit the night sky over several parts of the seaside city as aircraft flying without lights buzzed across rooftops for attacks on Aidid's command quarters, radio station and arms caches.

Helicopters blasted away at tanks and other vehicles that tried to make their way into the city from the countryside. But by morning, the streets were quiet, if tense, and knots of people had gathered to discuss the attack.

Pakistani troops opened fire on a crowd of rock-throwing protesters making its way toward U.N. headquarters at mid-morning, killing one man as he fled and wounding two other people.

One aim of the strike was the arrest of Aidid, who has denied responsibility for the ambush but is believed to have authorized it in an attempt to regain some of his waning power.

It was not immediately known whether he had been seized or how many casualties were suffered in the raids. The air strikes were followed by house-to-house searches by U.N. troops for Aidid and four of his chief aides.

A Pentagon official, speaking on condition of anonymity, said ground units were also ordered to secure certain areas of the city and search for additional weapons caches.

Taking part in the raids were four heavily armed American AC-130 aerial gunships and a U.S. army quick reaction force of 1,200 men based in Mogadishu.

"This response is essential if the U.N. is to be able to continue its long-term humanitarian relief and reconstruction efforts in Somalia," a statement from Defense Secretary Les Aspin said.

The assault began at 4 A.M. (9 P.M. EDT Friday) with the clatter of darkened helicopters and the whine of barely visible planes. Minutes later, the flash of rockets could be seen in at least three parts of the city.

Explosions rocked the sleeping city and buildings were briefly illuminated by flashes of brilliant light.

An hour after the assault began, explosions still rumbled across the city. But tracer fire from the ground had ceased as Aidid's militiamen stopped returning fire.

About 100 members of the Quick Reaction Force, representing the 10th Mountain Division based at Fort Drum, N.Y., were dropped outside a radio repeater station. Aidid's radio station was destroyed, but the United Nations began broadcasting on its frequency, appealing to people to remain calm.

Four hours after the raid began, the Americans were pulling out of the radio station, where they detained 38 Somalis. They were replaced by French troops who had served as a backup.

The U.N. raid had been expected for days. Last Sunday, the Security Council authorized its more than 18,000 peacekeepers in Somalia to take all necessary steps to bring to justice those responsible for the ambush that killed 23 Pakistanis and wounded 59 others.

On Friday, the United States dispatched a 4,200-man Navy and Marine assault force that had been taking part in maneuvers in Kuwait to the lower Persian Gulf for possible intervention in Somalia.

Pakistan's ambassador to the United Nations said in New York that Aidid "had to be taught in concrete terms that he could not get away with such actions.

"I expect the U.N. to act quicker and more forcibly if there are future attacks on U.N. peacekeeping forces," Ambassador Jamsheed Marker said.

Two simultaneous attacks on Pakistani troops in Mogadishu last Saturday threatened anew the international effort to restore health and order to a country wracked by famine and anarchy.

The most immediate effect of the ambushes Saturday was the closure of 35 food distribution sites in Mogadishu, which had been open six days a week and handed out enough food each day to feed about 600,000 people. Nearly 80 percent of Mogadishu's residents still depend on donated food.

Truck convoys moving 2,750 tons of food a week to far-flung areas such as Baidoa and Kismayu also stopped because nearly all the drivers were evacuated.

Hundreds of U.N. staff and relief workers were evacuated to Nairobi, Kenya, with the few remaining U.N. staffers relocated to the former U.S. embassy.

Troops this week dug foxholes, razed trees and strung barbed wire around the compound in preparation for an attack on Aidid.

The heavily fortified embassy compound became U.N. headquarters in early May when the United States turned over to the world body the humanitarian task it began last Dec. 9 with the landing of Marines on Mogadishu's beaches.

More than 350,000 Somalis died last year from famine, warfare and disease, but the U.S.-led intervention ordered by former President Bush shortly before he left office largely put an end to the problem of hunger.

Strife continued, however, as Aidid, his allies and enemies strove for land, wealth and power in the vacuum left by the overthrow of former dictator Mohammed Siad Barre in January, 1991.

*Credit*: Reprinted with permission of The Associated Press.

## BOB SIMON: "UN MILITARY WAGES ALL-OUT ATTACK ON SOMALI WARLORD GENERAL AIDID"

*This television report minced no words about how poorly the military effort was going.*

*CBS Evening News*, 17 June 1993

CONNIE CHUNG, co-anchor: There is blood in the streets and alleys of Mogadishu tonight. UN forces, including US troops, are in a fight to the finish with a defiant Somali warlord. They're trying to destroy his power base and arrest him for the ambush murders of 23 UN peacekeepers two weeks ago. Five more UN soldiers were killed today and 44 wounded, including one American. Scores of Somalis died. Correspondent Bob Simon is in the Somali capital of Mogadishu.

BOB SIMON reporting: It was a new and different kind of peacekeeping operation. It looked like war. Helicopters hovered over Mogadishu like birds of prey, firing off TOW missiles, rockets, 20-millimeter cannons. They swept low and fast over the rooftops of this sad city. They devoured their targets. The firing wasn't only from the air. Pakistani troops were the first to approach General Aidid's compound, tentatively, afraid of what might be on the other side, but no one was home. The house was not destroyed, but the general had a new skylight in his living room and a new door.

The UN command insisted that only a handful of Americans were involved on the ground, maintaining contact with the birds in the sky, but it was American troops who conducted the closet-to-closet search here, Americans who removed Aidid's household weapons—bazookas, rocket-propelled grenades—American voices who urged Aidid's followers to surrender.

UNIDENTIFIED SOLDIER: Attention, attention. US armed forces are working the area. Please evacuate the area now.

SIMON: Most of the firepower was directed towards this one area. The house of Aidid's chief lieutenant was completely gutted. But there were some mistakes. Two missiles blew holes in the compound of this French relief agency, killing a Somali woman.

As dusk fell, there was still no word as to the whereabouts of General Aidid, and there were two stories floating around. Some UN officials claimed they never intended to capture him; others said they were still looking. Then the UN's top man here announced in a telephone briefing that he had ordered Aidid's arrest.

Mr. JONATHAN HOWE (UN Special Envoy): It's my feeling that General Aidid, at this point, is a threat to the safety of Somalis and to the international community, and therefore he must be detained.

SIMON: This means that while this operation is nearing its end, a state of war between the UN and an entire faction is bound to continue. Those children who the Marines came here to feed six months ago will now be suspects in a combat zone called Somalia. Bob Simon, CBS News, Mogadishu.

*Credit*: Reprinted with permission of the CBS News Archives.

## TINA SUSMAN: AMERICAN LEGAL TEAM INVESTIGATES SOMALI CLAIMS

*Though this report is somewhat tongue in cheek, it was, no doubt, read with little humor by Americans who already were tired of overseas missions and the casualties in both human lives and millions of dollars.*

Associated Press, 29 June 1993

MOGADISHU, Somalia: The elderly man was clearly distressed as he told how a noisy American military patrol caused his camel to stop giving milk and eventually flee into the bush, where she was devoured by a lion.

Were it not for the lion—there aren't any to speak of in Somalia—his claim might have been believed by the sympathetic soldier listening to him.

Instead, it joined the claims dismissed by U.S. troops negotiating with Somalis seeking compensation for everything from lost lives to lost goats.

Each Tuesday and Saturday, about two dozen Somalis gather outside U.S. military headquarters to face an Army legal team that investigates the claims and works out settlements.

The procedure is not new. By U.S. law, American troops overseas must compensate civilians injured in non-combat incidents involving soldiers.

What is new is the challenge of verifying claims in a chaotic country stripped of official records and filled with hungry, jobless people whose desperation is sometimes made evident by brutality.

Capt. Jody Mhehr, a lawyer who heads the legal team, recalled a family seeking $5,000 for the death of a daughter hit by an American Humvee. The case was rejected when Somali witnesses backed up the driver's claim that the mother pushed the girl in front of the armored vehicle.

About 80 percent of claims are rejected, compared to about 20 percent in Germany and other places where U.S. troops are stationed.

"If it's a property claim, they have to prove they own the property, which is very hard to do here," said Mhehr, of Clinton, Iowa. "Most of what they have is copies of copies of copies."

The problem forces investigators to use methods that might be unacceptable elsewhere but work well in Somalia, where word-of-mouth is the best source of information.

In one case, a man claimed his home was damaged by an American armored vehicle. With no papers to prove ownership, Army investigators went to the property and quickly attracted a crowd of curious neighbors.

"We asked them if the person making the claim owned the house. They said 'no,'" Mhehr said. Case closed.

Claims apply only in non-combat situations, meaning damages from this month's U.N. attacks against warlord Mohamed Farrah Aidid could not be claimed.

Capt. Roger Cartwright, of West Point, N.Y., heard the nervous camel claim. He also recalled two self-proclaimed drug-dealers high on the local weed who intentionally rammed their car into an American tank and demanded compensation.

But there was also the man whose only relative, a son, was killed in March when a soldier's weapon accidentally fired at a checkpoint. The man depended on his son for support and asked for 100 camels in compensation, Cartwright said.

The military, not wanting to get involved in livestock trading, spoke to Somali farmers and decided to offer $100 per camel. The devastated father preferred camels but was forced to take the $10,000, Cartwright said.

The maximum payout is $12,500, a letdown for claimants demanding anywhere from $15,000 to $30,000 for vehicles damaged or destroyed by U.S. forces. Most cars in Somalia are dented, rusted hulks looted several times over or not worth stealing, but that doesn't stop people from trying.

Muhuyndiim Tahow Mahamoud was on line Tuesday to demand $10,000 for a pickup truck allegedly damaged by American tanks. He said he did not bring any ownership documents because of the rain; he did not want them to get soggy.

Even when people win cases, they're not always satisfied. One woman rejected her $5,000 damage payment because it was not in crisp, new $100 bills.

*Credit*: Reprinted with permission of The Associated Press.

## JAMIE McINTYRE: "MORE U.S. TROOPS DIE IN CLASHES IN SOMALIA"

*This is an initial report of the most serious military loss for the U.S. troops since they had landed in Somalia. The story would eventually cause Americans to change drastically and inalterably their attitude about continued involvement in the region.*

*CNN News*, Transcript 543–1, 3 October 1993

HIGHLIGHT: Five U.S. servicemen were killed today in clashes with Aidid factions in Mogadishu, Somalia. Nearly two dozen U.S. troops were wounded and two helicopters were downed by ground fire.

JEANNE MESERVE, Anchor: A military operation involving U.S. troops is reportedly ongoing in Mogadishu, Somalia, at this hour. CNN Military Affairs Correspondent Jamie McIntyre joins us now from the Pentagon with the latest. Jamie?

JAMIE McINTYRE, Military Affairs Correspondent: Jeanne, it's been a bloody day and night for U.S. peacekeepers in Somalia, in an operation that is still going on. U.S. forces have suffered five deaths and as many as two dozen wounded. Two U.S. Blackhawk helicopters were shot down during the operation. In one case, it's not known if anyone was able to walk away from the crash site. Sources say other casualties came when a U.S. truck convoy was ambushed and came under heavy fire. The Pentagon says elite U.S. Army Rangers were part of the military operation, which was based on information that supporters of Aidid wanted by the U.N. were in a certain location in Mogadishu.

The Pentagon has never officially acknowledged the Rangers were sent to capture Aidid, and Pentagon officials tonight refuse to confirm Aidid was the target of the raid. The Pentagon did say that 20 Somalis, who were supporters of Aidid, were taken into custody, including one high-ranking member of Aidid's leadership. President Clinton, in California tonight, issued the following statement within the last hour. Said the president, "I offer my deepest sympathies for the families and friends of the American soldiers who were killed in Somalia today. These brave Americans were engaged in a vital humanitarian mission to prevent the recurrence of mass death that resulted from the anarchy and famine in Somalia."

Earlier today, three U.S. Marines were injured when their vehicle, including a Somali interpreter, drove over a bomb that was detonated by remote control. These deaths today, coupled with the failure to capture General Aidid, is certain to increase already substantial pressure from Congress and some of the military to declare victory and pull out of Somalia. Jeanne?

MESERVE: Jamie, do we have any idea what brought down those two U.S. helicopters? There were reports earlier that shoulder-fired missiles might have been used.

McINTYRE: Well, U.S. intelligence sources have said for a number of weeks now that they've been concerned about the threat from shoulder-fired missiles. These are missiles that are designed to take out aircraft, as opposed to the rocket-propelled grenades that we've seen used against some of the helicopters in the past. Initially, there were some reports that perhaps a shoulder-fired missile had been used to bring down one of the Blackhawks. The early reports we're hearing now from Mogadishu indicate that they were perhaps brought down just by regular ground fire, or some of those rocket-propelled grenades. Not the more lethal shoulder-fired missiles, but these are initial reports, and the conventional wisdom at the Pentagon is that initial reports are never to be relied upon. But, at this point, it looks like if Aidid has those deadly missiles, he hasn't used them yet.

MESERVE: Jamie McIntyre, at the Pentagon, thank you very much.

*Credit*: © 2005 Cable News Network LP, LLLP. Reprinted with permission.

---

# J.F.O. McALLISTER, JAMES L. GRAFF, ANDREW PURVIS, AND BRUCE VAN VOORST: DOES THE UNITED STATES HAVE THE WILL FOR GLOBAL PEACEKEEPING?

---

*This weekly newsmagazine story auspiciously appeared as the worst tragedy for U.S. troops was unfolding. The overview of the political situation in Somalia was important for Americans to read as the military was reassessing its operation there.*

*Time*, 4 October 1993

On a hot moonless night two weeks ago, elite U.S. Army Rangers aboard helicopters slithered down ropes onto a roof in northern Mogadishu to arrest 39 Somalis. Under intense questioning, one man in custody confessed he was General Mohammed Farrah Aidid, the warlord whose fighters have been attacking peacekeeping troops since June. But the big catch quickly turned into an embarrassing fumble. Though he bore a slight resemblance, the arrested man was not Aidid. He turned out to be a former police chief who assumed the fake identity out of fear that the soldiers would shoot him.

Like the 1982 U.S. intervention in Beirut to keep a peace that did not exist, the Somalia deployment is beginning to founder on messy local politics, which foreign commanders do not really understand and cannot put right. As the death toll of peacekeepers and civilians mounts and Mogadishu remains resolutely unpacified, American support for the mission in Somalia has plummeted. According to a TIME/CNN poll last week, only 43 percent of respondents approve of keeping U.S. troops there, while 46 percent disapprove. Eight months ago, 79 percent of those polled supported the deployment. The death of three more U.S. soldiers when their helicopter was shot down Saturday near Mogadishu will do nothing to improve those numbers. Washington politicians are increasingly nervous, fearing that the Clinton Administration does not have a strategy for getting out.

The growing opposition raises sharp questions about whether the U.S. military is equipped, and the U.S. public has the will, to take on the nasty work of peacekeeping. An answer is needed fast: Clinton is contemplating sending 25,000 troops to enforce an awkward Bosnian peace accord sputtering toward completion.

Murky wars like Somalia and Bosnia—complicated local fights with a potential for international spillover—are a growth industry now that the cold war no longer imposes a rough order on world politics. The Clinton Administration is faced with redefining when the U.S. should intervene abroad and whether it should be done alone, through the U.N. or through permanent or ad hoc alliances. Secretary of State Warren Christopher, National Security Adviser Anthony Lake and U.N. Ambassador Madeleine Albright all gave speeches last week that sketched parts of the doctrine they are constructing for how America should manage its global obligations. Clinton is to follow them this week with an address at the U.N. expected to lay out, among other things, the criteria that will govern his decisions on sending U.S. forces abroad.

His advisers reject complaints that the President has no strong views on foreign affairs and is too prone to turn over world leadership, including the command of American troops, to a flabby and uncertain U.N. They insist he is determined to lead, alone if need be, to protect American interests. But they doubt there should be any general commitment to come to the rescue of humanitarian tragedies like Somalia's or complex ethnic implosions like Yugoslavia's. Lake says the U.S. should instead adopt a strategy of "enlargement," promoting global stability by increasing the numbers, strength and cohesiveness of free-market democracies.

Albright set a high threshold for U.S. military involvement abroad. She said the U.S. should not step in unless there was a "clear mission, competent commanders, sensible rules of engagement and the means required to get the job done." If the U.N. ran the show, Washington would also demand that a cease-fire be in place and an end to the deployment identified.

These doctrines show that the Administration is anything but trigger-happy. Why, then, is Clinton marching resolutely toward the deployment of U.S. soldiers to help NATO police Bosnia? The President promised the forces once the warring parties all agree on a settlement. The one now about to be signed will dismember the country into Serb, Croat and Muslim zones and allow the Serb and Croat regions to secede in two years. Senior U.S. officials say enforcement should not be too bloody because all three sides will gain from peace. But reluctant units must be disarmed, thousands of refugees relocated and safe passage corridors patrolled in a land where bitter hatred and the thirst for revenge still prevail.

So far Clinton has avoided investing American revenue and lives in Bosnia, while maintaining that he personally would like to do more to help its government resist aggression. The Administration says it still must see the fine print of the accord before it actually mobilizes troops. And Clinton has pledged to seek congressional approval for a Bosnia deployment—a potential escape hatch if the mission looks too burdensome.

Late last week top aides went to Capitol Hill to begin explaining the difficult options the U.S. may soon face. General John Shalikashvili, the next Chairman of the Joint Chiefs of Staff, acknowledged that the Bosnian operation could cost the U.N. $4 billion its first year. Lawmakers, led by influential Senator Sam Nunn, expressed deep anxiety that the Administration had no exit strategy. "My big question will be not how do we go about it," Nunn told the New York Times, "but how do we get out if the parties begin fighting again?"

It is hard to see how Clinton, with his heavy domestic agenda, could gain politically from putting more American troops in harm's way. Unfortunately, Washington has promised to guarantee a Bosnia settlement so long and loudly that a reversal, even if Congress provides welcome cover, will make Clinton look feckless. Says a senior Pentagon official: "If the U.S. can't take part in this operation, it will be a major blow to the structure of NATO,"—as well as a final abandonment of Bosnian civilians to bloodthirsty aggressors.

Somalia was supposed to prove that intervention could be simple. A year ago, as many as 1,000 Somalis a day were dying of starvation while feuding warlords stole relief supplies. Operation Restore Hope quickly restored the flow of foodstuffs and choked off most banditry. Starvation has all but ended. Refugees are returning. In most of the country, order now prevails. Washington has reduced its contingent from 28,000 to 4,800 soldiers. Says retired U.S. Admiral Jonathan Howe, the U.N.'s special representative in Somalia: "A lot more work needs to be done. But the story of Somalia is a good story."

In south Mogadishu, where Aidid is still defiant, the story is anything but good. Constantly on the move, always surrounded by women and children, Aidid has managed to elude arrest and assassination despite the arrival last August of 400 U.S. Rangers ordered to find him. His gunmen are marauding through the city, and U.N. forces, led by the U.S., have responded with a heavy hand. Earlier this month, more than 100 Somalis were killed and wounded when U.S. helicopters fired into a crowd that had ambushed a passing U.N.

convoy. Last week the Rangers had a small success when they captured Aidid's major banker, but the man was not in hiding.

Fifty-two foreign soldiers have died since Aidid started targeting them in June. U.S. officials admit his forces have the capacity to conduct hit-and-run attacks indefinitely. U.N. positions take mortar fire most nights as Aidid tries to wear down the staying power of the 30 countries contributing troops. His subordinates vow to fight on even if he is captured.

Some in Congress want the U.S. to pull out all its remaining troops immediately, leaving the work of nation building to other U.N. members. The TIME/CNN poll shows that only 22 percent of the public think the U.S. should engage in disarming the warlords. But Clinton advisers fear the whole U.N. mission would collapse if the U.S. military backbone were withdrawn, returning Somalia to anarchy and famine.

"Our sense is to keep picking away one lieutenant here, one bunch of militiamen there," says a Clinton official. "If we keep up the pressure, we'll eventually get there."

The Administration hopes its blizzard of foreign-policy speeches will help direct public attention away from the bloodshed in Somalia and Bosnia toward its accomplishments in other regions—propping up Boris Yeltsin, for example. Top officials worry, as Lake says, that "we have come into the new era with relatively few ways to convince a skeptical public that engagement abroad is a worthwhile investment." But there is no sidestepping the hard cases. If Washington is to remain a superpower, the public will have to bear not only comparatively light burdens like democratic "enlargement" but onerous ones like Somalia and Bosnia as well.

*Credit*: © 1993 TIME Inc. Reprinted by permission.

---

## MARTHA RADDATZ: "FIVE AMERICANS KILLED IN MOGADISHU FIGHTING YESTERDAY"

---

*This radio report left no doubt that military operations in Somalia were not going well for U.S. troops. The story here would balloon in later reports that follow this one.*

### *Morning Edition* (NPR), 4 October 1993

BOB EDWARDS: United Nations officials still are trying to assess the casualties from a 16-hour battle in Somalia's capital, Mogadishu. At least five Americans were killed in the fighting, some of the heaviest since U.S. troops went into Somalia nearly a year ago. Around 500 Somalis reportedly were wounded. There are also reports out of Mogadishu that a U.S. serviceman may have been taken hostage. NPR's Martha Raddatz reports.

MARTHA RADDATZ, Reporter: The report of a U.S. military hostage comes from Somali scouts working for foreign journalists in Mogadishu. A U.N. spokesman there, Major David Stockwell [sp (*spelling query*)], says officials can't confirm the report, nor can they rule out the possibility. Western reporters saw the body of one American soldier strapped to a wheelbarrow and being rolled through the streets of the Somali capital by a cheering crowd of some 200 Somalis. The Pentagon will not say how the five servicemen were killed, but has confirmed that at least two U.S. Black Hawk helicopters were shot down in Mogadishu during the fighting. Those helicopters each have a minimum of three people on board. Dozens of U.S. soldiers are also reported injured. The fighting was part of a U.N. assault on the forces of Somali warlord Mohamed Farah Aidid. The U.N. troops included large numbers of Pakistanis and Malaysians. There were casualties among those troops, but no figures are yet available. The U.S. troops were part of the elite Army Ranger unit. The figure of

500 Somalis wounded comes from the Red Cross in Mogadishu. There is no official death toll, but journalists report seeing truckloads of corpses driven from the battle scene. A Pentagon spokesman, Colonel Dave Garner [sp], also says a number of Aidid's supporters have been taken into custody.

Col. DAVE GARNER, Pentagon Spokesman: Approximately 20 individuals associated with the Somali National Alliance, including at least one high-ranking member of Aidid's leadership, have been detained as a result of an ongoing UNISOM II operation in Somalia.

RADDATZ: Aidid's forces are blamed for the deaths of over 50 peacekeepers since June. Yesterday, just before this most recent fighting broke out, three U.S. Marines were wounded and a Somali U.N. employee was killed when a mine exploded under the military vehicle in which the four were riding. The Marines are hospitalized in stable condition with shrapnel wounds and burns. U.N. spokesman Stockwell says the mine was detonated by remote control and was specifically targeting the Humvee utility vehicle. Somali gunmen ambushed the vehicle immediately after the blast. A Black Hawk helicopter was shot at when it arrived at the scene but managed to rescue the survivors. Stockwell said it was just another in a series of unprovoked attacks on U.N. troops in general, and on U.S. troops in particular. Aidid himself continues to elude U.N. forces, adding to the growing frustration of many U.S. lawmakers who are calling for a withdrawal from Somalia. Defense Secretary Les Aspin rejects suggestions that the United States leave Somalia immediately, saying such a move would lead to a return of the famine in the African nation. Aspin said the U.S. is looking for a date to

withdraw, but it must be done in a way so that security remains in the country. I'm Martha Raddatz in Washington.

## KEITH B. RICHBURG: "SOMALIA BATTLE KILLED 12 AMERICANS, WOUNDED 78"

*This front-page newspaper report the day after the American deaths provided more details about the breaking story, but none of it was good news.*

*Washington Post*, 5 October 1993

NAIROBI, Kenya: Twelve American soldiers were killed, 78 wounded and an undetermined number missing and believed captured in the ferocious 15-hour battle in Mogadishu, the Somali capital, late Sunday and early this morning with guerrillas of fugitive militia leader Mohamed Farah Aideed.

The Clinton administration reacted to the heavy casualties in the most intense fighting that American troops have faced in their 10-month intervention in Somalia by ordering more troops and armor to Mogadishu and threatening to "respond forcefully if any harm comes to those who are being detained," as Secretary of Defense Les Aspin said at the Pentagon. He demanded the "proper treatment and prompt return of any detainees."

In Mogadishu, a videotape apparently made by Somalis holding an American prisoner was broadcast showing a man with a cut face and wearing a T-shirt and dogtags. In response to questions asked in halting English, the man identified himself as Mike Durant and "a Black Hawk pilot."

During the course of the battle, Somali gunmen shot down two U.S. Black Hawk helicopters with heavy machine guns or rocket-propelled grenades, and a detachment of 70 to 90 U.S. Rangers was then pinned down trying to secure a perimeter around one of the copters, U.S. officials said. The U.N. command sent a multinational relief force, which encountered heavy resistance. Three other U.S. helicopters were hit and one crashed in the port area while the other two aircraft were able to land safely, officials said.

The heavy toll of American dead and wounded—far exceeding initial Pentagon reports Sunday of five GIs killed—and the specter of U.S. soldiers being held by a ruthless warlord, appear to significantly raise the stakes in what previously had been considered a confrontation with a small but determined band of militiamen. The latest violence deepened public and congressional anxiety over the U.S. role in the conflict, and aggravated a foreign policy dilemma for the Clinton administration.

"In the face of these kinds of attacks, it's a time for Americans to be very steady in our response and not talk about

getting out," Secretary of State Warren Christopher said Sunday night in an interview with the Cable News Network. Asked how long U.S. forces could expect to remain in Somalia, he said they would stay until their mission of establishing "a secure environment" has been fulfilled.

News reports from Mogadishu, quoting Toronto Star photographer Paul Watson, said the bodies of dead American soldiers littered the scene of the fighting, with the bloodied corpse of one U.S. serviceman being dragged through the streets by ropes tied to his feet, and another dead serviceman stripped naked and surrounded by a gleeful Somali mob chanting "Victory!" and telling reporters, "Come look at the white man."

In another case, the corpse of an American soldier was said to have been tied up and trundled through the streets on a wheelbarrow by about 200 cheering Somalis, Reuters news agency reported, quoting Western journalists in the capital.

As many as six American soldiers were said to be unaccounted for, but it was unclear whether some of them were believed to be dead, and their bodies not recovered, or being held as prisoners. American and U.N. officials declined to discuss specific figures on the missing, for fear of giving information to Aideed's followers in case some of the Americans are in the hands of friendly Somalis not aligned with his clan. An American spokesman in Mogadishu would confirm only that "there are some U.S. soldiers missing" and said they might be in Aideed's hands.

U.S. Army Maj. David Stockwell, the chief U.N. military spokesman in Somalia, said he was "shocked" by the reports of American soldiers' bodies being abused and put on public display, saying, "We don't treat Somali casualties that way." He appealed to Aideed's followers to treat any American captives "with the same humanitarian views in mind" that the United Nations treats detained Aideed followers. He said the Americans being held captive should be given "adequate medical treatment, food and water, and visits by the International Committee of the Red Cross."

However, U.S. and U.N. officials, who assert that Aideed is a criminal and not a lawful combatant, pointedly declined to assert the rights of the prisoners under the Geneva Convention.

A spokesman for Aideed's Somali National Congress militia said the guerrillas had captured an American officer—Aspin called the captive a warrant officer—who had a broken leg. The videotape that was broadcast showed the alleged captive's legs covered by a blanket, and he appeared to be seated on some type of mat. He also looked very frightened. When his interrogator asked him his opinion of the operation, he replied, "I'm a soldier. I have to do what I'm told." In answer to another question, the man said killing innocent people "is not good."

The Pentagon identified the American captive as Chief Warrant Officer Michael J. Durant, 32, of Fort Campbell, Ky. It also identified four of the 12 soldiers killed: Pfc. James H. Martin Jr., 23, of Fort Drum, N.Y.; Pfc. Richard W. Kowalewski Jr. and Sgt. James C. Joyce, 24, both of Fort Benning, Ga., and Chief Warrant Officer Clifton P. Wolcott, 36, of Fort Campbell.

Aspin said an Army mechanized infantry company would be dispatched to Mogadishu to bolster 4,700 U.S. forces there. The unit of 220 infantry troops contains a platoon of four M-1A1 tanks—specially fitted with plows to blow up mines—and 14 armored Bradley Fighting Vehicles. He said two additional AC-130 air gunships, replacement helicopters and 200 other troops also would be ordered to Somalia.

President Clinton said the "modest increase" in troops "does not signify some new commitment or offensive commitment" in Somalia. "I am just not satisfied that the American soldiers who are there have the protection they need under present circumstances," he said.

The president, speaking in San Francisco, expressed his regret for the loss of American lives, saying the soldiers "were acting in the best spirit of America . . . working to assure that anarchy and starvation do not return to a nation in which more than 300,000 people had lost their lives, many of them children, before the United States" intervened last December to halt starvation and anarchy.

In a statement in New York, U.N. Secretary General Boutros Boutros-Ghali expressed "deepest sympathies to the families of the brave soldiers who gave their lives in the cause of peace, reconciliation and reconstruction in Somalia" but that the incident would not "deter the United Nations from" its mission in Somalia.

The United Nations assumed command of the U.S.-led multinational humanitarian mission in May, but since mid-June has devoted considerable effort to trying to track down and arrest warlord Aideed, whom U.N. officials blame for the deaths of dozens of peace keepers in attacks by his militiamen in southern Mogadishu. Twenty-three Americans have now died in combat in Somalia—all but four since the United Nations took control of the operation.

Besides the American casualties Sunday, a Malaysian U.N. soldier was killed and six Malays and two Pakistanis were wounded, according to U.N. military officials. The Malay defense ministry in Kuala Lumpur had earlier said nine of its troops were wounded in the fighting and four Malay armored personnel carriers were burned out and destroyed. Malaysian Defense Minister Najib Razak was quoted as saying the Malay soldier killed was the driver of an armored personnel carrier that was hit by a rocket-propelled grenade.

Casualties on the Somali side were said to be heavy but American military officials, in keeping with their usual policy, declined to estimate the number of Somalis killed and wounded. The Red Cross conducted a count of Mogadishu hospitals and reported about 500 wounded Somalis from the battle, according to an agency spokesman in Nairobi. A spokesman for Aideed's Somali National Alliance militia told reporters that 30 Somalis had died in the fighting, including many women and children caught in the cross-fire.

Stockwell told reporters that U.S. troops fought back fiercely against their attackers and he acknowledged Somali casualties were likely high. "We had taken off the gloves," he said. "That is not to suggest that anyone was irresponsible. . . . We did the right thing."

He said the U.S. and U.N. troops received "hundreds" of rocket-propelled grenades and fire from small arms and heavy weapons, and that the American-led troops fired back with M-16 rifles, 40mm grenade launchers and .50-caliber machine guns. American helicopters providing aerial backup also opened fire with 20mm cannons and 2.75-inch rockets.

The Malaysians and Pakistanis were part of an American-led "task force" of several hundred foreign troops, including a company of armored American Humvee vehicles, a platoon of elite U.S. Army Rangers, and two U.S. Army infantry units that moved out of their staging area at Mogadishu's airport to rescue the Rangers pinned down at the site of the downed helicopter. The trapped rangers were in the Bakara market section of the city, an area known as a stronghold of Aideed and one of the few areas of the capital where the warlord moves relatively freely—despite the U.N. order for his arrest and a $25,000 reward offer for anyone who turns him in.

The violence began at dusk on Sunday, when American Rangers led a "search and seizure" operation about a mile east of Bakara market, in an effort to round up and arrest some of Aideed's top lieutenants. Stockwell denied today that the mission's initial goal was to arrest Aideed himself, saying in a telephone interview: "It was not aimed at Aideed, and we did not get Aideed." But late Sunday, Pentagon officials in Washington were openly telling reporters that Aideed might be captured and that Clinton might be able to announce the arrest when he arrived on the West Coast later that day.

In the end, the American troops managed to detain two dozen Somalis meeting at the Olympic Hotel, including two whom Stockwell described as "key" Aideed lieutenants, responsible for many of the recent ambush attacks against U.N. troops. Of the 24 detainees, Stockwell said three were killed in cross-fire as the troops arresting them came under attack, and a fourth was wounded and is being treated.

U.N. officials declined to provide the names of those detained, but Pentagon officials identified them as political adviser Osman Salah and Mohamed Hassan Awale, a former Washington taxicab driver who has functioned as Aideed's foreign policy adviser. Awale has long been considered a member of the warlord's inner circle.

The chief U.N. envoy in Somalia, retired U.S. Navy Adm. Jonathan T. Howe, said in a prepared statement that the 21 Somalis detained were "suspected of complicity" in the ongoing attacks against American and U.N. troops in the capital, and he said he hoped the arrests "will effectively contribute to stemming the violence in south Mogadishu."

*Credit:* © **1993, The Washington Post, reprinted with permission.**

---

## LEE MAY: THE FUROR OVER SOMALIA—AMERICANS REACT TO BRUTAL IMAGES

---

*This report from Georgia is an example of the public backlash to the reports of the previous day. Clearly public opinion had changed about the U.S. commitment to a troop presence in Somalia.*

### Atlanta Journal and Constitution, 6 October 1993

Donnie Slaton was unequivocal. "I don't think we should be there," the Georgia State University freshman said Tuesday, referring to Somalia.

His reasoning was equally simple and direct. "When we first went in, I thought it was the right thing to do; I'm all for helping someone in need.

"But when people you're trying to help start rejoicing over the helpers getting killed—well, that's too strange to me."

Emily Feistritzer, president of the National Center for Education Information in Washington, D.C., agrees, saying, "I think we ought to get out of there yesterday."

Slaton and Feistritzer are adding their voices to a growing chorus of Americans who say the humanitarian mission of feeding hungry Somalis is a colossal, humiliating, dangerous failure, that while Americans and other U.N. troops are trying to make the country safe, they're getting slaughtered.

Such resentment, anger, confusion and disenchantment were heavily fueled by developments over the past several days, including the deaths of at least 12 GIs, the wounding and disappearances of dozens of others, and photographs of dead and captured Americans.

Perhaps the chilling photographs and television footage did as much as anything to heat up U.S. feelings, setting the stage for an irony: To a large extent, pictures of starving Somalis got Americans into Somalia, and now they could take Americans out.

While President Clinton resists that conclusion, he certainly is getting heavy pressure to change his mind. Or to at least define the Somalia mission in a way that persuades.

In Washington, phone calls to congressional offices Tuesday were running heavily against U.S. involvement in Somalia. Meanwhile, about 500 Georgia troops headed for that East African nation to join the 4,700 Americans who already are part of the 28,000-member U.N. force.

"I'm sick to my stomach," one man told the office of Rep. Sanford Bishop (D-Ga.) after watching CNN's coverage.

Rep. John Lewis (D-Ga.), also deeply affected by the pictures, said, "It's Vietnam all over again. To see the body of a soldier dragged around—the American people can't take that. Even in war, that goes against all international rules and agreements and common decency."

His office phones rang 20 times as soon as the doors opened Tuesday morning, Lewis said, adding that every caller urged pulling out the troops.

Like many Americans, Lewis strongly supported U.S. troop involvement in Somalia when President George Bush deployed them last year.

Sen. Paul Coverdell (R-Ga.) said his office's phone lines were jammed with callers, most of whom urged a U.S. pullout.

"Most people have some living memory of a military quagmire," Coverdell said, "and they can spot another one pretty quickly."

The senator has introduced legislation that would limit deployment of U.S. troops under U.N. command unless authorized by Congress.

Nevertheless, some people say American troops belong in Somalia.

"We should be there," declared Michael German, director of grants development for Atlanta. "We never go places where people of color are involved in conflict unless we refer to it as 'in the national interest,' which means money or resources. We should be there to restore the democracy."

But on Tuesday at least, with the images of dead or captured Americans embedded in the national psyche, German's view was clearly in the minority.

Commenting a day earlier at a Carter Center conference, Rosalynn Carter said, "We went in for a good cause, and now we are practically at war."

The former first lady called it "devastating" that the United States could allow Gen. Mohammed Farrah Aidid, the fugitive factional leader, to "dictate what is happening in Somalia."

The question of whether Aidid speaks, or acts for a nation gets to the salient point. If he does, Clinton and other U.S. officials have an impossible task in trying to persuade the American public and the Congress to back a policy of keeping U.S. troops in Somalia.

In Donnie Slaton's view, there is no doubt that Aidid's anti-Americanism is the predominant view. He has seen the pictures.

"I think it's the majority that doesn't want us there," said the young college student. "On TV, it doesn't seem like a few that are rejoicing. It seems a few that are sad."

## PAUL QUINN-JUDGE: "SOMALIA FORCES CAN PLAGUE NEW U.S. MILITARY MIGHT"

*The news media now seemed willing to examine the vulnerability of U.S. troops after pictures earlier in the week of Somalis parading the body of a dead American soldier captured public attention across the country. This story is an example of those stories that took another look at the rosy outlook and supreme capabilities touted by both the Bush and Clinton administrations up to this point.*

*Boston Globe*, 6 October 1993

WASHINGTON: Gunmen loyal to the Somali clan leader Mohamed Farah Aidid have deployed heavy artillery and large-caliber antiaircraft weapons that could cause problems even for the new military equipment the US has dispatched to deal with him, military sources said yesterday.

US intelligence reports from Somalia described Aidid as having moved at least one 105-millimeter howitzer and a ZSU 23-millimeter antiaircraft gun into the area of last weekend's US raid in south Mogadishu.

Such weaponry could be used against the AC-130 gunships, M1A1 battle tanks and Bradley Fighting Vehicles that President Clinton ordered sent to the East African nation on Monday.

Besides gunships and tanks, forces en route include a fleet of seven Special Operations MH-60 and AH-6 helicopters designed for night raids and evacuations from hostile areas. US Army Rangers were pinned down during a 10-hour firefight on Sunday because rescue helicopters were vulnerable to ground fire and UN forces did not have the heavy armor necessary to push through to them by land.

The Pentagon confirmed yesterday that 650 troops had begun moving to Somalia by air. Previous reports had put the number of fresh US troops bound for Somalia at 200.

A spokeswoman for Westover Air Force base in Chicopee said two C-5As from the base are involved in airlifting troops and supplies from Fort Stewart, Ga., to Somalia. At the same time, a spokeswoman for Fort Devens said the base's 46th Combat Support Hospital, on duty in Somalia, treated 60 wounded soldiers in a 36-hour period this week.

Twelve US soldiers died in the raid, which took place on Sunday at the former Olympia Hotel, northwest of the Mogadishu port. Some 75 were wounded, five soldiers are missing and one, Chief Warrant Officer Michael Durant, Berlin, N.H. native, was confirmed captured.

A Somali journalist was quoted yesterday as saying that Aidid is holding US prisoners "close to him" to deter possible counterattacks.

The US military believes that the Olympia is a major command center for Aidid's forces. Besides the artillery and antiaircraft weapons, Aidid has moved an undetermined number of 106-millimeter recoilless rifles and rocket-propelled grenades into the area of the Olympia, intelligence reports said.

Deployment of the weaponry seems to be an act of defiance in the face of US warnings of swift retaliation if any captured US servicemen are harmed—a message underlined by the dispatch of the new US weaponry.

The tanks are intended to give US forces in the city greater mobility; Aidid's guerrillas have effectively closed many of Mogadishu's main roads to UN forces in recent weeks. The AC-130 gunships, meanwhile, are intended to restore control of the skies that Aidid's forces have denied to US helicopters.

But military sources say the weapons Aidid has placed around the Olympia can definitely cause problems for the new US equipment. The ZSU antiaircraft gun, which the former Soviet Union handed out liberally in the Third World, is capable of shooting down AC-130s, sources say, or could at the very least force the planes to fly higher during attacks, thus diminishing their accuracy. The 105mm howitzer could probably immobilize an M1A1 by destroying one of its tracks, military sources say.

Intelligence accounts of the fighting provide a sobering picture of unpredictable but murderously effective tactics used by Aidid's fighters, as well as the limitations under which UN troops are operating in south Mogadishu.

The Rangers and Delta force commandos who raided the Olympia Hotel on Sunday quickly found themselves seriously outnumbered. Special forces prefer to operate at night, when their superior training and equipment gives them the advantage over larger forces.

No more than 100 US troops were involved in the original raid, according to official estimates. But they found themselves facing attack from up to 200 gunmen, while another 150 Aidid militiamen secured the perimeter around the hotel.

The Special Forces were on the ground for over 10 hours as they attempted first to withdraw with their captives, then went to the rescue of comrades in two helicopters that were shot down by Aidid forces. The US Quick Reaction Force, backed by Malaysian and Pakistani troops, was ambushed several times and took about seven hours to come to the Special Forces' support.

The intelligence reports conclude that Aidid has a "crude but effective" defensive strategy. This includes a warning system, perimeter and air defenses and a reserve force, ready to deploy in an emergency.

Reports yesterday that Aidid was planning to use US prisoners as human shields injected a new element into the conflict. Noting their difficulty in finding Aidid, US officials expressed pessimism about their chances of locating five or six prisoners.

*Credit*: BOSTON GLOBE by PAUL QUINN-JUDGE. Copyright 1993 by GLOBE NEWSPAPER CO (MA). Reproduced with permission of GLOBE NEWSPAPER CO (MA) via Copyright Clearance Center.

---

## DAVID MARTIN: PENTAGON PREPARES TO DOUBLE NUMBER OF TROOPS IN SOMALIA

---

*The Pentagon, despite public outcry to leave Somalia, was preparing, instead, to redouble the efforts there. This report focused only on the administration's concerns.*

### CBS Evening News, 6 October 1993

CONNIE CHUNG, co-anchor: From the Pentagon now, national security correspondent David Martin has the latest on the growing US troop commitment.

DAVID MARTIN reporting: As reinforcements continue to load up for Somalia, the Pentagon has prepared orders to up the ante again by sending 1,500 to 2,000 more troops into the hellhole of Mogadishu. That would double the number of American combat troops in Somalia. Their mission? Prevent a repeat of Sunday's disaster in which a company of Army Rangers was nearly wiped out. Some of the wounded from Sunday's firefight, now hospitalized in Germany, told what it was like to be members of a unit that suffered 70 percent casualty.

Private First Class JEFFERY YOUNG (US Army): Sixteen hours being pinned down is definitely a downer. We had to wait for our reinforcements to come on the ground to pull us out. They hit a lot of roadblocks and a lot of obstacles so it made it difficult for us. We just had to wait and bide our time till they could get to us.

MARTIN: Without tanks to break through the roadblocks,

the reinforcements took too long to get there. Sergeant Robert Jackson rode to the rescue in an armored personnel carrier.

Sergeant ROBERT JACKSON (U.S. Army): If you've seen that movie Clint Eastwood was in when he's in a bus and—and all the policemen are firing at him, it was just like that. I mean, I was thinking, "Oh, God, I'm going to die," and you know . . .

MARTIN: The U.S. military, which could do no wrong in Iraq, suddenly seems as if it can do no right in Somalia. It's the same military but a different battleground.

Mr. DON SNIDER (Military Analyst): They're trying to establish the security in a clan stronghold in an urban area and it's not clear that that can be done with military force under the rules that we have them operating under right now.

MARTIN: No one is suggesting that putting in more troops will increase the chances of capturing Mohammed Aidid. In fact, there are those in the Pentagon who warn that more troops only mean more targets for Aidid to shoot at. Connie.

CHUNG: Thank you. David Martin at the Pentagon.

*Credit*: Reprinted with permission of the CBS News Archives.

---

## MICHAEL M. PHILLIPS: "U.S. SOLDIERS HEAD HOME, SICK OF SOMALIA, READY FOR CHRISTMAS"

---

*By the end of the year, the news reports focused almost entirely on the poor outlook for any success. These reports were in sharp contrast to those of a year earlier when outgoing President Bush had visited Somalia amid sunny predictions of a quick, decisive improvement for the Somalis. This story is an example of the kind of reports that were published across the country.*

Associated Press, 23 December 1993

MOGADISHU, Somalia: Proud of their performance but sick of Somalia, hundreds of U.S. soldiers took a welcome last look at Mogadishu Thursday with one thing in mind: Getting home for Christmas.

The last American forces to leave Somalia before the holiday, the 580 soldiers shouldered their weapons, dusted off their desert fatigues and boarded chartered jets for the United States.

"I guess at Christmas time you want to be with family and friends," said Army Spec. Esther Poulsen, 23, of Castro Valley, Calif. "But here with all those Somalis who don't like us—it was hard enough being here at Thanksgiving."

President Clinton promised to withdraw all U.S. combat troops by March 31, following a vicious street battle with militiamen loyal to Gen. Mohamed Farrah Aidid that left 18 Americans dead and 75 wounded in October.

The U.N. military operation in Somalia will be left in the hands of whichever countries are willing to try to keep the northeastern African country from sinking back into clan-based civil war following the U.S. departure.

Volunteers have been few. India and Pakistan are expected to fill in the biggest gaps left by the departing Americans, Belgians, Germans, French, Italians and other nationalities.

That's just fine with members of Poulsen's 561st Support Battalion from Fort Campbell, Ky., one of five U.S. logistical units pulled out Thursday.

"Morale was low—oh, morale was low," said chaplain's assistant Pfc. Doriveliz Ruiz, of Luquillo, Puerto Rico, whose job was to help keep the battalion's spirits up. "It was a waste of time and American money."

With their withdrawal so close, U.S. military commanders are taking pains to avoid American casualties. U.S. forces are gradually pulling back from their three main bases in Mogadishu and concentrating near the docks and airport.

While Pakistanis and Indians man the major checkpoints and patrol the streets, the Americans have been largely out of sight and their duties limited to air support and tasks associated with getting the troops and equipment out of the country.

"At least somebody gets to go home for the holidays," sighed Sgt. Wesley Arnold, 24, an MP from San Diego, Calif., who arrived a week ago to help with the withdrawal of the remaining 10,200 troops. "We're not all stuck over here."

The last to leave will probably be the 3,800 sailors and Marines stationed on ships visible from Mogadishu's beaches, ready to provide cover for the withdrawal if necessary.

As they departed Thursday, the soldiers said they were proud of what they were able to accomplish in a country where between 100,000 and 350,000 people are estimated to have died from hunger, disease and fighting before the bulk of the U.N. force arrived a year ago.

The U.S. troops planned aid convoys and set up transportation systems, among other tasks.

"If you go to the schools, the orphanages, and the feeding centers, you'll find a lot of people who are very grateful to these young soldiers," said Col. Jim Willie, commander of the 507th Logistical Task Force out of Fort Bragg, N.C.

*Credit*: Reprinted with permission of The Associated Press.

# PAUL QUINN-JUDGE: PENTAGON RESTRICTS ACCESS TO SOMALIA BATTLE TAPE

*When the stories about Somalia could not be much worse, this story broke on Christmas Eve. The report escalated the public outcry against continued U.S. troop presence in Somalia so that the government was soon forced to diminish the commitment over the next two years, until there was a complete withdrawal and no permanent peace.*

*Boston Globe*, 24 December 1993

WASHINGTON: The Pentagon is fighting a bitter rearguard action to prevent the release of a US military video of the Oct. 3 gun battle in Mogadishu, the firefight that changed US policy in Somalia and probably contributed to the resignation of Defense Secretary Les Aspin.

Citing national security considerations, the department has rejected requests by ABC News and the National Security News Agency to obtain the tapes under the provisions of the Freedom of Information Act.

Military spokesmen said that the technology used to make the film is too sensitive to reveal. But sources in the communications industry said the technology is widely known and easily available. Some military men who have seen the film want it to be released.

The Somalia issue echoes a similar one from the 1991 Gulf War. Although the Pentagon selectively released video showing air strikes by cruise missiles and smart bombs, military footage of the 100-hour ground war against Iraq has never been made public. In previous wars, the Department of Defense generally cooperated with requests by the press and historians and turned over official, unclassified footage.

Military specialists who have viewed the Somalia film said it shows scenes of outstanding bravery and professionalism and maintained that it would demonstrate that the operation, in which 18 US troops and hundreds of Somalis were killed, was not a bloody mess but a well-planned, successfully executed operation carried out under extremely difficult conditions.

Meanwhile, continued classification of the video leaves perhaps the most intriguing and sensitive question unanswered: Was a group of senior US military officers watching the battle live on television screens in Mogadishu, Washington or elsewhere? And if so, why did it take so long for a relief column to reach the embattled Army Rangers?

Informed military sources held out the possibility that senior officers watched the firefight in real time. Civilian communications specialists said that this was highly likely. The officers could have been watching at the National Military Command Center in the Pentagon or in Central Command Headquarters in Florida, which had overall charge of the US military operation in Somalia. The same sources said there is a high possibility that the images were also monitored at military headquarters in Mogadishu.

A spokesman for the Special Operations Command in Florida, which has responsibility for the Rangers and Delta Force units involved in the battle, said the command had not received images of the battle while the fighting was taking place. But the spokesman refused to rule out the possibility that some other command might have.

A Pentagon spokesman said he was "unaware" of anyone in the building seeing the images during the battle.

To transmit the video, the US military is believed to have used helicopters capable of relaying images via a microwave downlink to a ground station at the US military headquarters in the city. The images would have been sent virtually instantaneously via a satellite belonging to the Defense Satellite Communication System back to the United States.

The gun battle lasted for more than 12 hours. A relief column took many hours to arrive.

The video is said to be very dramatic. Two Ranger helicopters go down. Two members of a Delta sniper team are shown dropped from a helicopter to protect survivors of one of the crashed craft until they in turn run out of ammunition

and are killed. Another small helicopter makes a daring landing in the middle of a street to take off wounded. A third helicopter fights for control in the air after being hit by a rocket-propelled grenade as a Special Forces search and rescue team fast-ropes down to the ground.

Sources in the communications industry said they do not understand why the Defense Department is being so secretive about the tape. A spokesman for the Special Operations Command said that the main reason is the sophistication of the technology used in filming and transmitting the raid.

"It's not just a video hanging out of a camera," said George Grimes, a command spokesman.

Because of its sensitivity, Grimes said, "the film cannot be edited at all. It cannot be sanitized."

The tape also shows Ranger and Delta tactics that the military is not willing to make available to a broad audience, Grimes said.

The technology by which the video would be shot and transmitted long distances at high speed is, however, well known and readily available. Television networks and local stations have long used similar systems for covering events like the Los Angeles riots, California brush fires or the New York City Marathon.

A representative for Wescam of Hamilton, Ontario, which makes helicopter-mounted video cameras for commercial and secret military uses, says that its equipment can beam images from the helicopters to ground stations as far as 60 miles away. Relay stations then send the images out.

John Pike of the Federation of American Scientists noted that the present generation of defense communications satellites has been in operation for more than 10 years.

Pike and other specialists added, however, that the film could reveal developments in one area that the military still guards jealously: its capability to see at night or in very dusty, hazy conditions. The operation started in the afternoon and stretched into the early hours of the next morning. Combat could have stirred up a lot of dust. If the film was dramatically clearer than might have been expected, this would be a sign that infrared imaging had taken a leap forward—an advance the military would not yet wish to discuss.

*Credit*: BOSTON GLOBE by PAUL QUINN-JUDGE. Copyright 1993 by GLOBE NEWSPAPER CO (MA). Reproduced with permission of GLOBE NEWSPAPER CO (MA) via Copyright Clearance Center.

# NOTES

1. ABC News poll based on random telephone interviews with adults nationwide. The 5 October survey involved 509 responses.

2. Yankelovich Partners, Inc., sponsored by *Time* and Cable News Network, telephone survey of 500 adult respondents, 7 October 1993.

3. ABC News national poll of 506 respondents by telephone, 7 October 1994.

## FURTHER READINGS

Burton, Richard. *First Footsteps in East Africa*. Ed. Gordon Waterfield. New York: Praeger, 1966.

Cassanelli, Lee V. *The Shaping of Somali Society: Reconstructing the History of a Pastoral People, 1600–1900*. Philadelphia: University of Pennsylvania Press, 1982.

CountryReports.org. *Somalia*. http://www.countryreports.org/history/somohist.htm.

Drysdale, John G. *The Somali Dispute*. New York: Praeger, 1964.

———. *Somaliland: The Anatomy of Secession*. Hove, Sussex: Global-Stats, 1991.

Gersony, Robert. *Why Somalis Flee: A Synthesis of Accounts of Conflict Experience in Northern Somalia by Somali Refugees, Displaced Persons, and Others*. Washington, D.C.: Department of State, 1989.

Henze, Paul B. *The Horn of Africa: From War to Peace*. New York: St. Martin's Press, 1991.

Lewis, I. M. *A Modern History of Somalia: Nation and State in the Horn of Africa*. Boulder, Colo.: Westview Press, 1988.

———. *Somali Culture, History, and Social Institutions: An Introductory Guide to the Somali Democratic Republic*. London: London School of Economics and Political Science, 1981.

Library of Congress. *A Country Study: Somalia*. http://memory.loc.gov/frd/cs/sotoc.html.

Ruiz, Hiram A. *Beyond the Headlines: Refugees in the Horn of Africa*. Washington, D.C.: American Council for Nationalities Service, 1988.

Samatar, Said S., ed. *In the Shadow of Conquest: Islam in Colonial Northeast Africa*. Trenton, N.J.: Red Sea Press, 1992.

# 29

## HAITI AND DEMOCRACY, 1994–1996

Haiti, the western third of the island named Hispaniola, was ceded to France in 1697, about 200 years after Christopher Columbus first sighted it. The nation of the Dominican Republic occupies the remaining portion of the island. The terrain is mostly mountainous and tropical, with a land area slightly smaller than the state of Maryland to support a population of about 7 million.

Columbus claimed the island for Spain in 1492, and the settlers nearly wiped out the native inhabitants within a few years. During the next several hundred years, African slaves were imported to work the sugar plantations, and their labor made it one of the richest islands in the Caribbean. Poor land use and forestry management soon stripped the island of many of its natural resources.

A slave rebellion in 1791 led to the local abolition of slavery by 1793. The Spanish and French forces were driven out by the liberated slaves, and the country declared independence in 1804—the first black republic in the world. A series of monarchies ruled until 1859. Coups and poverty marked the nation's history for dozens of years. Because of unsuccessful leadership at the turn of the century, the United States occupied the country from 1915 to 1934 as a strategic base. Coups and dictatorships ended with the death of dictator François "Papa Doc" Duvalier in 1971 and the ousting of his son "Baby Doc" Jean-Claude Duvalier in February 1986 from the capital, Port-au-Prince.

A democracy was reestablished, and Father Jean-Bertrand Aristide became Haiti's first democratically elected president on 7 February 1991. When he was forced from the country following a military coup in September 1991, the United States, France, and Canada suspended aid to Haiti and refused to recognize the military junta government. When a trade embargo failed to force the junta out of power, a negotiated peace was agreed to in 1994, and multinational troops from the United States and other Caribbean nations occupied the country on 15 September to facilitate a peaceful transition. Aristide was returned to the presidency on 21 October, and the Haitian Senate passed a bill outlawing paramilitary groups.

The Haitian government began the work of setting up all the components of a working democracy, including the appointment of a new supreme court and the separation and reorganization of police and army units. In December 1994, the Provisional Electoral Council was established to begin the election process for legislative, municipal, and local elections. On 17 January 1995, Aristide and members of the U.S. Defense Department determined that the country was stable enough for a complete turnover from the multinational forces to a United Nations Mission in Haiti. This transfer was accomplished by the end of March. U.S. forces remained in Haiti for another year. On 17 December 1995, René Préval was elected to succeed President Aristide. His inauguration on 7 February 1996 was the first peaceful transfer of power between civilian leaders in Haiti's history as an independent nation.

Media coverage of the situation in Haiti had been provided sporadically for many years. There were reporters on the island who filed stories about both the Dominican Republic and Haiti because of its strategic location near Cuba. U.S. troops were stationed on the island, and there was always a political skirmish of some sort that generated a story. There had also been a long period of emigration from the island to the United States, and so the wire services were often able to file localizing reports about family members in the United States for regional U.S. newspapers. When the White House announced that it was strengthening enforcement of the trade embargo against Haiti, the story was not unknown to the American public.

Much of the early coverage of this particular sequence of actions came out of both Washington and Haiti's capital, Port-au-Prince, or the Dominican Republic. Reporters already on the island could report on the junta's activities, as well as the local population's reactions to both the junta and American initiatives. American public opinion of the prospects of sending troops, early in June, was not supportive. Less than 30 percent of Americans favored such an action, according to a NBC News/*Wall Street Journal* telephone survey of about 1,500 respondents.[1] But by the time former President Jimmy Carter had brokered a peaceful change of power in Haiti that required American troops on the island during the political shift, Americans were overwhelmingly in favor of troop deployment. According to a CBS News/*New York Times* telephone survey of about 500 respondents in early September, 77 percent favored the initiative.[2]

What follows are examples of the media coverage of the U.S. progress toward troop deployment in Haiti. At the end of the chapter, "Further Readings" lists other resources that are useful in more fully understanding the events of this military intervention.

## PETER COPELAND: "U.S. WEIGHS SENDING TROOPS TO SEAL OFF HAITIAN BORDER"

*This story is the kind of informative update about the Haitian situation that reflected the concerns that many Americans were discussing across the nation.*

*Rocky Mountain News* (Denver), 3 June 1994

WASHINGTON: The United States may send a small number of troops to the Dominican Republic to help cut off gasoline and other supplies being smuggled into Haiti, Pentagon officials said Thursday.

Until now, direct U.S. involvement in Haiti has been limited to ships offshore enforcing a U.N. embargo on Haiti's military government.

While 57 commercial ships have been boarded near Haiti since the embargo began on May 21, the border with the Dominican Republic has remained open for the most part, and goods have been streaming into Haiti.

Haiti and the Dominican Republic share a small island,

and the Dominican Republic's army of 15,000 has been unable to stop the flow of goods to Haiti, in part because of corruption that has allowed some officers to profit from the contraband, U.S. officials said.

Pentagon officials are adamant that there are no plans to invade Haiti and that any troops sent to the Dominican Republic will be used only to enforce sanctions.

Enforcement of the embargo at sea continued Thursday, and Navy commandos seized a 40-foot Bahamian sailboat after it tried to sneak gasoline past U.S. patrol ships, a Pentagon spokesman said.

*Credit:* Reprinted with permission.

---

## KENNETH FREED: RESTORATION OF ARISTIDE SPARKS FEAR IN HAITI

---

*This story out of Haiti not only told the American perspective but also included some doubt about the prospects of success. Though the story was not a negative one, it allowed for a change of heart among the leadership at home.*

*Los Angeles Times,* 4 June 1994

PORT-AU-PRINCE, Haiti: The generals still give the orders, and their gunmen still rule the streets. But as diplomats and Haitians look to scenarios for the future, the vision isn't pretty—especially, they say, if the United States succeeds in restoring President Jean-Bertrand Aristide.

Almost every Haitian expert and most foreign sources interviewed over a week's time agreed that, as one leading businessman put it, "there is no other option to the (U.S.) military option" to put Aristide back in office more than 32 months after he was driven into exile by the Haitian army.

This conviction has been strengthened by Aristide's statements this week giving qualified approval to a limited U.S. military strike to remove Haiti's ruling army officers.

With the prospect that the deposed leader might somehow be back, sources—all of whom opposed the September, 1991, coup and have worked to end military rule—are showing signs of great caution, if not outright fear, of an Aristide government.

This concern is based on what they say have been shortsighted U.S. policies and the uncompromising opposition by the ousted president to broadening his government to include differing political and economic views from his populist and partisan approach.

"It's the same old thing," said a Haitian diplomatic expert who said he voted for Aristide and wants him restored "as a matter of democratic principle."

"Aristide and his advisers in Washington (where the ousted president lives) think they can rule alone, that anyone who opposes a policy is an enemy," he said.

His view, shared by many of those interviewed, is rooted in what is seen as duplicitous Aristide actions over the last

year, particularly in insisting that he has accepted the need for a broader government.

He did this, a political analyst said, "only under American pressure and to keep American support. Now that it seems certain that he will come back, he's the same old Aristide."

The expert's main example is Aristide's failure to nominate a new prime minister to replace Robert Malval, the moderate who resigned over Aristide's refusal to accept a broadened government.

"If Aristide had learned anything or was sincere in seeking reconciliation, he would certainly have named a prime minister acceptable to more people," he said. "I know his advisers are telling him there's no need now, that he will come back and do whatever he wants."

This source, contacted after word of Aristide's acceptance of possible U.S. military action here, said even the limited endorsement was a sign of Aristide's ambiguous attitude.

"You note he called for a surgical strike, for the American forces to come in and get out and only to remove the military," the analyst said. Aristide "said nothing about the structural changes we need and can only be accomplished if there is stability imposed from the outside."

"You know what is going to happen?" he asked. "Right after he gets back and Cédras, Biamby and François are forced out, Aristide is going to condemn 'American intervention' and demand the U.S. forces leave."

The source was referring to Lt. Gen. Raoul Cédras, the military coup leader; army chief of staff Gen. Philippe Biamby; and police commander Michel-Joseph François. The three are seen as architects of the coup and the brutal policies that have followed.

Other concerns, which appear to reflect class and economic distinctions as well as differing political views, are based on a belief that in the seven months of Aristide's government, he was violently anti-business and instigated the nation's poor—the overwhelming majority here—against Haiti's middle and upper classes.

In reality, said a onetime Aristide associate who now has doubts, "that is an erroneous judgment of the past. There are plenty of reasons to worry about Haiti under Aristide when he comes back, but not because he was advocating violence or class warfare.

"There was less human rights abuse (under Aristide) than at any time in Haitian history," the source said. "Economic measures were improving. The problem was his lack of a political vision, his lack of understanding of the political process and his inability to realize he was a politician and needed more than a vision from God to govern."

Now, the source said, "Aristide believes that his only problem—the (Haitian) military—will be removed. He doesn't understand that Haiti's problems are far deeper than a corrupt and abusive army."

Others said that misunderstanding goes beyond Aristide to include the Clinton Administration, which, one source said, "is now driven entirely by domestic political concerns and seems based on the idea that if the military is driven out, the United States can forget Haiti."

Of possible U.S. military action, a political expert, once favored to be a senior Aristide Cabinet official, observed: "It is all well and good. But the Americans are totally crazy if they don't look at the day after" the U.S. troops arrive.

A businessman, who once led an effort to reconcile Aristide with Haiti's wealthy private sector, said, "As things stand, I don't think his new government will be any different from his first one."

If that assessment is correct, or even if only the anti-military sectors believe it, one diplomat said, "then Haiti is in real trouble and the Americans will only have cut off the top of the problem and not ripped out the roots."

Under the best of circumstances, Aristide's return will present huge challenges not only to him but to long-range U.S. interests here—the creation of a stable economic and political climate to finally remove the threat of massive Haitian migration to the United States.

While Aristide is still judged to hold the support of most of the 70% who made him Haiti's first democratically elected president, his enemies will remain powerful and determined to protect their economic and social advantages.

He has no political party, and what little support he had in the Parliament is dissipated, one diplomat said.

Another source, who seemed to voice the prevailing mood, said that "if nothing is done beyond disbanding the military and there are no serious efforts to dismantle the old institutions, then Haiti will remain the same. In 10 years we'll still be the mess we are."

*Credit*: Copyright © 1994, Los Angeles Times. Reprinted with permission.

## BOB DEANS: "INVASION OF GRENADA OFFERS MODEL FOR ACTION IN HAITI"

*This Cox News wire service story ran from Texas to Ohio and provided something of a community memory of U.S. military intervention recently successful.*

Cox News Service, 4 June 1994

WASHINGTON: Rejecting democratic elections, a hostile junta takes control of a poor Caribbean nation and violence erupts.

Alarmed at the mayhem in its back yard, the United States invades, citing the need to restore order and democracy.

Congressional opponents, a host of analysts and a handful of key allies leap to assail the White House action as perilous, irresponsible and perhaps illegal.

Two weeks later, though, the invasion largely is hailed as a success. International peacekeepers help the islanders restore services and build new political institutions, and most U.S. troops soon are headed home.

Haiti in 1994? No, Grenada in 1983.

Code-named "Urgent Fury," the Grenada operation—in which more than 2,000 Marines and Army Rangers, backed by 26 U.S. warships and dozens of combat aircraft, overwhelmed about 700 Grenadian troops and a few hundred Cubans—is for many military analysts the model for a prospective U.S. invasion of Haiti.

"It would be an island campaign, and it would be against a military of limited capability," a Pentagon spokeswoman said.

However, Grenada also showed that invading even a tiny place with a ragtag army is dangerous.

"This was no cakewalk," Gen. Norman Schwarzkopf, the Desert Storm leader who was deputy commander of the Grenada invasion, wrote in It Doesn't Take a Hero, his autobiography. "People were getting killed."

Six days after hard-line Marxists overthrew the leftist government of Prime Minister Maurice Bishop in October 1983, Marines and Army troops staged a dawn raid, seizing

Grenada's two airports. Over the next 48 hours, resistance by the tiny Grenadian army was quelled.

But the invasion was far from painless. At least 100 Grenadians and Cubans were killed, and at least 19 Americans died. More than 100 other U.S. soldiers were wounded.

Three U.S. helicopters were shot down. And in a horrific accident, two other helicopters collided on a crowded beach, severing limbs of and otherwise hurting 24 U.S. troops.

The official toll doesn't include the deaths of at least four special operations soldiers whose roles the Pentagon doesn't acknowledge publicly. And there were civilian casualties, including 17 patients killed when U.S. planes inadvertently bombed a mental hospital.

"The operation came within a hair's breadth of being a military disaster," wrote retired British infantry officer Mark Adkin in his book Urgent Fury, a comprehensive review of the invasion.

And the army of Haiti, where a military dictatorship headed by Lt. Gen. Raoul Cédras has ousted the elected government of exiled President Jean-Bertrand Aristide, is considerably more powerful than Grenada's. Cédras commands a force of about 7,500 soldiers—10 times what U.S. troops faced in Grenada. Thousands of other Haitians belong to army-backed paramilitary groups.

If the White House calls for an invasion, though, it can tap a broad range of powerful U.S. military resources.

"Any of the forces in the continental United States could be mobilized on short notice to move," said the Pentagon spokeswoman, who spoke on condition of anonymity. "You could come from Texas, you could come from Washington state, you could come from North Carolina, and it would just be a matter of hours, not days."

The Haitian forces, by contrast, are shabbily equipped and poorly trained. But so were the Somalian street fighters who killed 18 U.S. Rangers and wounded more than 75 others last fall in Mogadishu.

Columnist Robert Novak wrote this week that the Clinton administration "is looking at an invasion a month from now" if the sanctions fall short of their goal. Novak quoted one official as saying that a "quick-in, quick-out" operation is planned and that Latin American countries would be asked to provide troops for the occupation.

State Department deputy spokeswoman Christine Shelly said Friday that President Clinton has not ruled out military action, but, for the time being, he is focusing on economic sanctions.

*Credit*: Reprinted with permission of Cox News Service.

---

## SUSAN ROOK AND BOB CAIN: "REPRESSION IN HAITI"

---

*This was the kind of television coverage that not only reported the political situation and U.S. activities, but also stressed the humanitarian needs.*

*CNN News*, Transcript 112–3, 5 June 1994

HIGHLIGHT: U.S. ships have been only partly successful in enforcing the embargo. Some insist the embargo is hurting only Haiti's poor. U.S. policymakers are discussing potential military options.

DICK WILSON, CNN News: [voice-over] The week began with another grim reminder of military repression in Haiti. Three victims of the Haitian military were buried amid wailing, crying, and collapsing mourners. All three were supporters of the exiled Haitian president, Jean-Bertrand Aristide. Emotions ran so high, the priest saying Mass had to leave the church. More than 3,000 victims have been killed in political violence in Haiti, and that's just in the year since army strongman Raoul Cédras overthrew Father Aristide, the elected president of Haiti. Aristide waits in exile in Washington hoping to return to power.

This week, more U.S. ships were added to the naval blockade around Haiti, 12 ships to patrol 1,000 miles of the Haitian coastline. They operate under a central command post on board the U.S.S. Wasp, now anchored not far from Haiti at Guantanamo Bay, Cuba. To catch the smaller smugglers'

boats, the Navy relies on 30-foot inflatable fast-moving boats.

Capt. JEFF ZAKEM, United States Navy: So you can go right up alongside, and you don't have to bring a larger ship up, endangering the U.S. ship as well as the ship you're trying to board.

WILSON: [voice-over] But many Haitians say the embargo ends up hurting the poor, while the rich simply get richer.

RENAUD CHARLES, Aristide Opponent: Most likely, it's not going to work, and it's only the poor people of Haiti which the embargo has been killing anyway over the past two and a half years, is going to kill even more.

WILSON: [voice-over] As the week neared an end, there were signs the economic embargo will be tightened even further. This factory has already closed. International air flights to and from the island may be cut off, and there could be new restrictions on financial transactions. The embargo and blockade are hardly leak-proof. Defense Secretary William Perry tells CNN the naval operation is not totally effective. And the wide-open border with the Dominican Republic has been only partly sealed against smugglers. The prized commodity for most Haitians, gasoline.

Meantime, President Clinton says he's keeping the military option open if the embargo fails and Haiti's military rulers refuse to leave. And administration officials reportedly are working out the details of a possible invasion by the U.S. along the lines of past operations in Grenada and Panama.

[on camera] Pentagon planners say a U.S. invasion of Haiti, if it ever happens, would be easy. The hard part, they warn, could be getting U.S. forces out.

[voice-over] U.S. forces are expected to face little resistance during any future invasion, but restoring order after an invasion is expected to be a much more difficult job. In Congress, critics of an invasion say U.S. troops could wind up staying in Haiti from three to five years.

Meantime, Aristide's supporters inside Haiti are being killed, and others are ready to die for him. This man is one of them.

GERARD-JEAN JUSTE, Aristide Supporter: I'm walking with death, so at the moment that I'm caught, that's the end. The only consolation we have, myself I have, is I am—in Haiti now, I'm 48 years old, and most Haitians live between 45 to 65. So I'm in the stage of—I am ready to die now.

WILSON: [voice-over] And many other Haitians remain willing to risk death in small boats. They continue to pour out of Haiti, more than 1,400 in the past month. Most are intercepted by the U.S. Coast Guard and sent back home. Soon, the refugees will be allowed to make their cases in shipboard interviews at a Jamaican port and at two nearby islands.

The marching band plays a farewell dirge for the latest victims in Haiti, and in the country at large, the killing, the smuggling, and the military repression are expected to continue into another week.

*Credit*: © 2005 Cable News Network LP, LLLP. Reprinted with permission.

---

## TOM SQUITIERI: "IN HAITI, SOME HOPE FOR INVASION/ARMY CHIEF COMPARED TO NORIEGA"

*Comparisons to the situation in Panama and its successful outcome in the eyes of America were often made in the media. This is an example of the suggestion that the White House had an opportunity not only to provide humanitarian relief but also to make things politically right in Haiti.*

### USA Today, 7 June 1994

PORT-AU-PRINCE, Haiti: Ignored by Haiti's military regime and a virtual prisoner in his home, acting Prime Minister Robert Malval says an invasion of his violence-torn Caribbean nation would be seen by Haitians as a "salvation force."

Malval, the last remaining link to exiled president Jean-Bertrand Aristide, ousted in a 1991 coup, predicts departure of the military chiefs and easing of sanctions—or military action—by Sept. 1.

If not, he warns, "thousands of people will be taking to the seas . . ." to flee to the USA.

In an interview, Malval, shunned by the military but recognized by the United States and others as Haiti's acting prime minister, compares the possible fate of army chief Gen. Raoul Cédras to that of Panamanian leader Manuel Noriega.

Now in a U.S. prison serving time on drug charges, Noriega was arrested by U.S. troops in the wake of the December 1989 invasion of Panama. Over the weekend, Cédras met with Miami lawyer Frank Rubino, who was Noriega's lawyer.

"(Cédras) would be inspired to listen to his lawyer," Malval says, referring perhaps to allegations, voiced among others by President Clinton, that the Haitian military has links to the drug trade.

But in Washington, federal authorities say that while they've taken an initial look into drug connections, no charges are in the works.

Malval says Cédras still has time to resign and get amnesty—"if he comes to his senses."

"But he (Cédras) thinks he can outsmart the world. I got news for him. He will be forced to resign without amnesty and he must bear in mind he will have the fate of Noriega."

Regarding a possible invasion to restore the exiled Aristide to power, Malval says that "when the people who are maintaining order are promoting disorders, there is no other choice . . . there is nothing left."

As for military resistance to an invasion, "there won't be any," Malval says. "This will be viewed as a salvation force."

Under Haiti's constitution Malval remains the caretaker prime minister until someone else legally assumes the post. He also remains a symbol of democracy to many Haitians.

Meanwhile:

- Aristide says he wants "swift and determined action" to remove the military leaders who ousted him.
- The New York Times reports the Clinton administration expects to process 2,000 Haitians a week when it begins reviewing applicants for refugee status this month on a ship off Jamaica's coast.

*Credit*: From USA TODAY, a division of Gannett Co., Inc. Reprinted with Permission.

# DOYLE McMANUS: U.S. RULES OUT IMMEDIATE MILITARY ACTION IN HAITI; WILL RELY INSTEAD ON STEPPED-UP SANCTIONS

*This article is an example of the way the White House explained the president's desire to avoid military intervention if a political solution could be brokered instead.*

*Los Angeles Times*, 8 June 1994

WASHINGTON: The Clinton Administration has decided against immediate military action in Haiti, hoping instead that stepped-up economic and political sanctions can drive the military regime from power there, senior officials said Tuesday.

After weeks of debate between White House aides seeking a quick solution to the Haiti impasse and a Pentagon wary of using force, the Administration has settled on a series of diplomatic actions in hopes that the sanctions can be made effective, they said.

President Clinton may reopen the internal debate over military intervention if the sanctions fail, but he has set no deadline for that decision, the officials said.

Meanwhile, they said, the Administration is trying to make the sanctions work—and seeking commitments for a multinational peacekeeping force of 2,000 to 4,000 troops to pacify Haiti if the regime falls. "We really do want to find a peaceful multilateral solution in Haiti," Deputy Secretary of State Strobe Talbott said after returning from a trip to Latin America that focused on efforts to tighten the sanctions.

Talbott, the Administration's diplomatic point man on the issue, argued that new U.N.-sponsored sanctions can succeed in driving the Haitian military regime from power, despite the doubts of the policy's critics.

He said the Administration has made progress in winning support from Latin American countries for the new sanctions. And, he said, several countries have agreed to contribute to a new, more muscular U.N. peacekeeping force that would police the island once the military regime is toppled.

"That . . . sends a tough signal to them that the international community is serious about this," he said. "It also sends a signal to the many Haitians that are staying in their country that there is hope for the future."

Talbott and other officials refused to say which countries have agreed to participate. But Canada, France, Venezuela and Argentina have all been involved in discussions about the peacekeeping force.

The new force is being designed as an "expanded" version of the U.N.-sponsored military training force, which was scheduled to land in Haiti in October but turned back when armed Haitian thugs gathered at the dock.

Some countries said, however, that they would participate only after a peaceful transfer of power in Haiti and warned that they might not join if the United States invades the island, one official said.

The Organization of American States, meeting in Brazil, passed a resolution Tuesday endorsing the expanded force and urging all its members to join the stepped-up economic embargo. The OAS resolution was something of a diplomatic victory for the Administration. Some Latin American countries initially sought a resolution formally ruling out any use of military force in Haiti, but Talbott and other U.S. officials lobbied to avoid such a prohibition.

U.S. officials explained that even though Clinton has not decided on military action, he does not want to face an OAS prohibition—and, more immediately, he does not want to relax pressure on the Haitian military by taking the option off the table.

Some foreign policy aides, frustrated by the failure of previous sanctions to budge the military regime, had urged that military intervention be actively considered. Although Defense Secretary William J. Perry dismissed the idea, Pentagon officials later acknowledged that they had been forced to consider the step because of the depth of Clinton's commitment to solving the Haiti issue.

The main new sanctions against Haiti include a complete trade embargo, including efforts to stop smuggling across the nation's border with the Dominican Republic; a ban on commercial air flights; a halt to financial transactions; a freeze on overseas financial assets of Lt. Gen. Raoul Cédras, Haiti's military ruler, and others in the regime, and cancellation of the entry visas of the rulers and their relatives.

In additional moves to enforce the sanctions, the Pentagon said it may send a small number of U.S. troops to the Dominican Republic to maintain helicopters and other equipment for the trade embargo.

Officials said they have decided to move ahead with plans for a U.S.-funded ship-borne radio station to allow exiled Haitian President Jean-Bertrand Aristide to broadcast to his people.

"What is important now is that we are seeing more cooperation from other countries in implementing the sanctions as well," one official said.

But the United States has also been slow. Aristide's chief U.S. adviser, former Rep. Michael D. Barnes, said the State Department canceled Cédras' wife's U.S. visa—which she had used for shopping trips to Miami—only last week.

## STEVEN GREENHOUSE: "GOVERNMENTS ARE JOINING HAITI FORCE"

*Articles like this one suggested that the White House was, in fact, having some success through the political route, rather than relying on military might.*

*New York Times*, 8 June 1994

WASHINGTON: Administration officials say they have enlisted about a dozen countries to take part in a United Nations task force of more than 3,000 soldiers and civilians who would maintain order and strengthen democratic institutions after the Haitian military leaders cede power, whether voluntarily or through military intervention.

In recent days, Deputy Secretary of State Strobe Talbott and William H. Gray 3d, the special adviser on Haiti, have asked countries throughout the Western Hemisphere to join the force, which is aimed at insuring the safe return of Haiti's exiled President, the Rev. Jean-Bertrand Aristide.

The Administration's effort to line up broad participation is part of its stepped-up campaign to heighten political, economic and psychological pressure on Haiti's military leaders, who seized power in September 1991 and so far have been reluctant to give it up.

### QUICKER U.S. EXIT

For the Clinton Administration, one obvious benefit of a large United Nations mission is that if the United States invades Haiti to oust its military leaders, sending in the mission afterward would allow Washington to withdraw many of its troops quickly.

American officials declined to name the countries that have agreed to take part in the task force—officially called the United Nations Mission on Haiti—but officials in other countries said Canada, Venezuela and Argentina had agreed to contribute personnel.

"What if the coup leaders step down next week as a result of the economic sanctions?" Mr. Gray said in a telephone interview. "Who maintains order? Who protects the international relief organizations and embassies there? Who's there to protect the return of President Aristide and to insure his safety? You will need the U.N. mission right away."

Many nations in the Hemisphere oppose military intervention, and American officials recognize that the Administration could point to a broad-based United Nations mission as an international imprimatur for such intervention.

### SOME OPPOSE INVASION

According to one official, several countries have said they would not participate in the United Nations mission if Haiti's military is forced out through military intervention.

Administration officials said the task force would be vital for maintaining safety and order to allow Father Aristide to return to Haiti should Haiti's military leaders step down because of pressures from the trade embargo.

"If the military leaves in a week or two, you would probably want the U.N. mission there before Aristide returns," Mr. Gray said. "It would assure law and order. It would make sure there was no retribution and could prevent another coup. If you have a power vacuum anything could happen. You could potentially have another level of military rise up and say, 'We're taking over.'"

Some Administration officials predict that it will take months for the embargo to work, while others say that only military intervention will succeed in forcing out the Haitian military. American officials say they are not asking other countries to contribute troops to an invasion.

### U.S. FEARS ANARCHY

American officials fear an embarrassing wave of anarchy and retribution between the time the military leaders leave and the time Father Aristide returns, either from international pressure or an invasion. With Haiti's military and police force expected to be in wholesale disarray, American officials see the United Nations mission serving as the beat cops until a government is running smoothly.

One senior American official said the United Nations mission would leave Haiti in early 1996, at the earliest, after presidential elections scheduled for December 1995.

In feverish diplomacy over the last week, the United States has persuaded other countries to back a task force that would be far larger and have far greater responsibilities than one set up last July as part of the Governor's Island agreement. In that accord, the Haitian military agreed to turn over power to Father Aristide, but it later refused to honor that commitment.

The United Nations mission established under that agreement was to include about 800 soldiers and civilians and to concentrate on retraining Haiti's military and police force, who have a long history of repression and opposition to democracy.

### A PROTECTION MISSION

Mr. Gray said that the expanded, reconfigured task force not only would do such training, but that it would also be responsible for law enforcement and for protecting embassies, elected officials, human rights monitors and international relief organizations.

At a meeting today in Belem, Brazil, of the foreign ministers of the Organization of American States, the ministers called for enlarging the United Nations mission. They also backed an American-led call to ban all commercial flights to and from Haiti and to cut off financial transactions with Haiti.

Administration officials said today that President Clinton would announce unilateral action within a few days to ban flights and financial transactions between Haiti and the United States.

"It will take six months for Haiti's upper classes to be bitten" by the tougher United Nations sanctions approved last month, said a senior Administration official. "What you have to do is ratchet it up real quick so they feel the bite, so they can't keep their money in foreign banks or enjoy flying around in American planes."

Buoyed by the Dominican Republic's new efforts to clamp down on smuggling to Haiti, Administration officials have voiced increased confidence in recent days that the embargo might force Haiti's military from power.

Some Haiti specialists say the Administration adopted a more upbeat posture on the embargo after officials concluded that their privately stated pessimism about the sanctions was reinforcing the military's commitment to stay in power.

Dennis Boxx, a Defense Department spokesman, said today that a small number of American troops might soon go to the Dominican Republic to help provide "technical support" to fight smuggling to Haiti.

## JOHN M. GOSHKO: "U.S. ASKS ALLIES TO PLEDGE TROOPS FOR HAITI"

*Stories like this one, however, detailed that the White House was not excluding the possible need for military intervention should a peaceful negotiation of political change be unsuccessful.*

*Washington Post*, 8 June 1994

The Clinton administration is urging allies to pledge troops for a proposed 3,000-member peacekeeping force that would move into Haiti and keep order if democracy is restored to the troubled Caribbean nation, U.S. officials and diplomatic sources said yesterday.

The force tentatively would have a considerably broader mission than under past agreements, which foresaw a small contingent confined to training the Haitian armed forces after deposed civilian President Jean-Bertrand Aristide is returned to office.

As now envisioned by U.S. planners, the force's mission would include taking over some police duties while a corruption-free Haitian police force is being created. It would protect Aristide, the members of his government, human rights monitors and representatives of humanitarian aid organizations. It also would guard foreign embassies and important infrastructure such as roads and water systems from attack or sabotage by disgruntled supporters of the armed forces.

The force would consist of units from the United States and countries in the Western Hemisphere and Europe. Its purpose would be to prevent anarchy or civil war if the international community succeeds in forcing Haiti's military rulers from power.

That would put U.S. troops into a position reminiscent of the one encountered in Somalia, where attacks by hostile forces caused American deaths and led to congressional and public demands for U.S. withdrawal. Lawmakers have warned against getting into a similar position in Haiti.

The United States and France said they would contribute troops. The sources did not identify other countries willing to do so, but said U.S. officials feel they have made progress in obtaining tentative pledges from several nations.

In particular, the sources said, intense U.S. lobbying at the annual meeting of Organization of American States foreign ministers, which ended yesterday in Belem, Brazil, won expressions of support from several Western Hemisphere governments.

The sources noted, however, that hemispheric countries all have stressed willingness to take part in a peacekeeping operation only if Haiti's military rulers give up power peaceably. President Clinton has refused for the past month to rule out the possibility of a military intervention in Haiti, but the United States has found virtually no support within the OAS for deposing the military by force.

For the moment, at least, U.S. officials say they are counting on the near-total trade embargo imposed by the United Nations against Haiti May 21 to force out the military. Earlier, more limited sanctions proved ineffective against the Haitian armed forces, which deposed Aristide in a September 1991 coup. The sources said it is not clear what the United States will do if the latest sanctions fail.

At U.S. urging, the OAS ministers adopted a resolution calling on member states to reinforce the embargo by suspending commercial aviation traffic with Haiti and freezing assets of the military commanders, their family members and supporters.

The United States already is planning to put these additional sanctions into effect on its own within the next few days. Officials traveling with Clinton in Europe said the United States intends to give the sanctions a careful trial before considering other options such as an invasion.

"Speculation on the use of force to expel the military junta is running faster than serious consideration within the government of such a move," a senior U.S. official said in Europe.

The sources here described the planned force as "an enhanced and greatly expanded version" of the joint U.S.-Canadian military training mission that was supposed to go to Haiti last October under terms of an agreement for the armed forces commander, Lt. Gen. Raoul Cédras, to step aside and permit Aristide's return.

When U.S. and Canadian troops aboard the USS Harlan County tried to disembark in Port-au-Prince last October, they were met by armed thugs. Rather than challenge the mob, Clinton ordered the ship to leave.

Staff writer Ann Devroy contributed to this report from Paris.

*Credit:* © **1994, The Washington Post, reprinted with permission.**

---

## ED McCULLOUGH: AMERICANS STAYING BEHIND IN HAITI EXPRESS DOUBTS BUT NO REGRETS

---

*This wire service story out of Haiti was the kind of local reporting that was possible because reporters had been in the region for many years, and it was this kind of story that made the situation in Haiti seem less remote and more personal to the American reader, even if the reader did not agree with the story subjects' individual assessments of the situation in Haiti.*

Associated Press, 23 June 1994

PORT AU PRINCE, Haiti: Many Americans in this troubled Caribbean nation seem to be ignoring Washington's recommendation to leave by Friday, when a U.S. travel ban takes effect.

"I have Haiti under my skin," said Eleanor Snare, director of the Haitian-American Institute, which teaches English to about 2,000 adults.

Before arriving in 1969, "I didn't even know where Haiti was," said Ms. Snare. Now, as an international economic embargo tightens, she feels, "In the middle of a hurricane, you huddle with the people you're close to."

The U.S. ban, effective after Friday's flights, will cut off the main air connection to Haiti. However, at least one commercial airliner is maintaining service for now, and special humanitarian charters are being planned.

The Rev. Wallace Turnbull was born in Haiti to American missionary parents 45 years ago. His grandfather started and his father expanded the Baptist mission on a breezy mountainside high above the crowded, sweltering and filthy capital of Port au Prince.

Today, the mission is part of a system of 300 rural parishes that teach 47,500 students in the impoverished nation, where public education is of the lowest quality.

"We are here on a mission to serve God and the people of Haiti," said Turnbull, whose independent mission is linked to a Baptist church in Grand Rapids, Mich.

"Bill Clinton didn't send me," he added. "Therefore, unless an act of war is declared and we are ordered to leave," he, his wife and their young daughter will stay.

The U.N.-sanctioned and U.S.-led economic embargo aims to pressure the ruling junta, led by Lt. Gen. Raoul Cé-dras, to step aside in favor of elected President Jean-Bertrand Aristide, who was toppled by a 1991 coup.

It has crippled a farm- and import-based economy that already was the poorest in the hemisphere. However, Cédras has not budged, and President Clinton has raised the prospect of using U.S. troops to restore Aristide.

There were about 8,000 U.S. citizens in Haiti when the State Department recently ordered non-essential U.S. Embassy staffers and family members to leave, and recommended other Americans do likewise.

About 2,000 have left in the past two weeks, the embassy calculates. Many of the rest—mostly Haitian-Americans, U.S. missionaries and volunteer aid workers—apparently plan to stay.

"I'm cautious, but I don't feel unsafe," Dan O'Neil, a 30-year-old aid worker from Sandy Hook, Conn., said Wednesday. He arrived six months ago and plans to extend his two-year contract.

O'Neil had to postpone his wedding, set for Saturday, because guests from the States could not attend due to the travel ban. But he remains upbeat: "The diversity is incredible. Villages not far from here seem like Africa. . . . I'd like to stay."

The Rev. Ron Voss, 53, of Anderson, Ind., came to Haiti for the first time in 1980, and has been a resident for most of the past four years. He runs the Haiti Parish Twinning Program, which links Haitian and U.S. churches.

"I'd like to stay until the president (Aristide) is back, and long after that," Voss said. "I'm in love with these people and their country. I feel what I do here is worthwhile."

The capital was its usual hustle-and-bustle Wednesday,

with less traffic because gasoline, officially under embargo but smuggled in and available at about $6 a gallon, is too expensive for many to buy.

There was little sense of impending crisis. Several merchants said they hadn't even heard of a pro-army group's call for a general strike Friday, and would comply only if forced to.

"I'm a poor man. This is what I have to do," said a cigarette seller, standing on a street corner with a new product line: contraband gasoline in plastic containers.

Lines at the airport for American Airlines flights to New York and Miami were long, but orderly. Air France continued to sell tickets for Caribbean destinations on dates after the midnight Friday U.S. air embargo.

A decree took effect Wednesday barring reporters from traveling outside the capital without written permission from the Information Ministry. Nevertheless, reporters were not apprehended for working in the so-called strategic dock area or airport.

*Credit*: Reprinted with permission of The Associated Press.

---

# GISELLE FERNANDEZ: "HUNDREDS OF HAITIANS AND AMERICANS JAM PORT-AU-PRINCE AIRPORT; CATCH LAST FLIGHTS OUT BEFORE SANCTIONS TAKE EFFECT"

---

*This television report not only presented the prospective effect of the sanctions, but also the effectiveness of the political, rather than military, solutions in motivating those in Haiti to change the regime from within.*

## CBS Evening News Transcripts, 24 June 1994

DEBORAH NORVILLE, anchor: The military rulers of Haiti are under new pressure tonight with the country cut off from its most important link with the outside world. President Clinton has banned all US commercial airline flights to Haiti as of midnight. Correspondent Giselle Fernandez is in Port-au-Prince.

GISELLE FERNANDEZ reporting: In a rush to leave the island, hundreds of Haitians and Americans today jammed the airport to catch the last flights out to America. Many arrived hours before the flight and stood in long lines, carrying out as many belongings as they could. Joe Danek, a volunteer with the Catholic Church, had to beat the deadline to get two Haitian American orphans to the United States. While sad to go, he said, he can do more for Haiti at home.

Mr. JOE DANEK (Haiti Parish Twinning Program): That's where the work is now. Here you can't do anything because of the fear of being shot at, murdered.

FERNANDEZ: The closing of two American banks also had Haitians lining up outside the gates. Guards armed with automatic weapons told those holding checks and needing cash their accounts were frozen. In the financial district, Haitian businessmen called the new sanctions aimed at them "racist." They say they have no influence over military coup leaders.

Mr. STANLEY SCHRAGER (US Embassy Spokesperson): They still have influence on the military, and they have more motivation right now than they've ever had in the past three years to try to use that influence.

FERNANDEZ: While the US clamps down, Haiti's military is stepping up the propaganda war by trying to play up the threat of a US invasion. Throughout the capital, the army is setting up road blocks like this one around key government buildings trying to create a siege mentality. The government is already cracking down on journalists. Today police arrested CBS and CNN camera crews videotaping the last planes taking off. Authorities released the crews after consulting with the regime's highest officials. At the port, more signs of just how hard it is to escape the crisis. Another heartbreaking homecoming for refugees who were denied political asylum. Their dream of getting to America was shattered as the last planes to the US flew north. Giselle Fernandez, CBS News, Port-au-Prince.

NORVILLE: President Clinton has raised the threat of US military intervention in Haiti, but a new CBS News poll shows most Americans do not favor an invasion. Asked if the United States should send in ground troops to remove the military and restore democracy, two-thirds said no. Only 27 percent said they approve of President Clinton's handling of the situation in Haiti.

*Credit*: Reprinted with permission of the CBS News Archives.

## BERNARD SHAW: SECRETARY OF STATE CHRISTOPHER SAYS "SEVERE" SANCTIONS BEING PLACED ON HAITI

*This television interview gave special attention to the kind of political-solution initiatives the White House was promoting, in contrast to the use of U.S. military interventions where there had been coups and nationalistic infighting.*

*CNN News*, Transcript 805–6, 24 June 1994

BERNARD SHAW, Anchor: The United States is keeping a very watchful eye on day to day developments in all of these world hot spots we have just touched upon—Haiti, Rwanda, and also Bosnia-Hercegovina. To bring us up to date on Washington's stance on these subjects and some others, we are joined by United States Secretary of State Warren Christopher. Mr. Secretary, thanks for joining us—

WARREN CHRISTOPHER, U.S. Secretary of State: — Good evening, Bernie, thank you—

SHAW: —and I hope we can get through this without an interruption, but if we have to break away, I'm sure you'll understand.

Secy. CHRISTOPHER: I'll understand.

SHAW: Mr. Secretary, after midnight, as Susan just reported, no more flights from Haiti to the United States, you've got the sanctions. Do you really think these are going to dislodge those generals?

Secy. CHRISTOPHER: I think the generals will end up leaving, one way or the other. We're now imposing sanctions, we're now increasing the pressure, and we'll just have to see if it works. These are very severe sanctions—no more commercial flights after the end of the day today, freezing the bank accounts of those who are involved in this illegal government, and those who support them. That's real pressure, Bernie, and we'll just have to see if it works. I hope it will.

SHAW: Do you have any personal, private worries for the more than 5,000 Americans still on the island?

Secy. CHRISTOPHER: Well, they all had an opportunity to leave, and a number of them did leave. I think the departure was very orderly. The Americans who are there have not been harmed up to this point. Of course, we'll be watching it very carefully. The sanctions are severe sanctions, but, you know, there are very strong interests here in trying to restore democracy in Haiti. It's important for the stability of this entire region. This is one of the few democratic governments that've been overthrown in this region, and I think we've got a strong responsibility to restore democracy in Haiti. It'll affect the whole hemisphere if we let those illegal people get away with taking over the government and really undoing the trend toward democracy in Haiti, which has been really— swept the entire hemisphere. If it's reversed in Haiti it will be a very bad thing.

SHAW: Let's go to Rwanda. If the French can send in troops in a mercy mission, why can't the Clinton administration?

Secy. CHRISTOPHER: Well, you know, we've done a great many things with respect to Rwanda. We've supplied about $100 million in relief to Rwanda and Burundi, the neighboring nation, in the last two months. At the request of the French, we've been moving in a number of their pieces of equipment. We're also supplying a 50-armored-personnel carrier to the United Nations there—

SHAW: —but I mean troops—bodies on the ground.

Secy. CHRISTOPHER: Well, the United States troops, I think, ought to go into situations where we have a very strong national interest. In this situation, I think it's best left to either the neighboring countries in Africa or those nations which have had a long-standing interest in this part of—in this part of Africa. We're doing our part in various parts of the world. We certainly did in Somalia, but you know, the answer to every problem is not to send in U.S. troops, as there needs to be burden sharing and I think that's going to be a good part of our policy, Bernie.

## JULIA McEVOY: "TRAIN EXILED HAITIANS AS POLICE OFFICERS?"

*This radio report, like the television interviews, emphasized the compassionate side of Clinton's efforts to find a lasting solution in Haiti.*

*All Things Considered* (NPR), Transcript 1524–5, 25 June 1994

JACKIE LYDEN, Host: As President Clinton continues to search for a foreign policy success in Haiti, one key to unlocking the solution may come from Haitians themselves, Haitians living in Canada and the U.S., that is. The two countries have agreed that Canada should begin training Haitian exiles to act as the nucleus of a new civilian police force in Haiti once the military leaders have gone. It's an idea that deposed Haitian President Jean Bertrand Aristide endorses. But as Julia McEvoy reports, the idea is splitting ranks within Miami's Haitian community.

JULIA McEVOY, Reporter: U.S. Haiti policy continues to be the subject of intense debate in Miami's Haitian immigrant community and by and large the attitude is one of cynicism.

JACQUES DESPINOS, Haitian Democratic Organization: The U.S. has always said in case they go to Haiti, their problem is not to go in but to come out. I don't buy that. It's like they make you believe they're fighting an army. Which army? Or maybe it's like they're playing game with people.

McEVOY: Jacques Despinos [sp], head of Miami's Haitian Democratic Organization typifies the distrust felt by Haitian exiles towards the U.S.'s position on Haiti.

Mr. DESPINOS: I just can't believe it and just can't understand. United States is super power, let this small country playing game for years. That's why people say they believe U.S. has been behind the coup, and behind everything.

McEVOY: There is general agreement among Miami Haitians that the idea of a new police force for Haiti made up of Haitian exiles originated in Brooklyn last year. Since then the idea has generated a lot of discussion within Haitian exile communities of Canada and the U.S. The thinking seems to go along these lines. Haitians for military invasion are also in favor of a U.S.-Canadian trained police for Haiti. Those who fear military intervention see a U.S. or Canadian-trained force as a sinister presence in their country.

[sounds of trumpets]

McEVOY: Marcus García hosts "La Radio a l'Haitienne," a radio program popular with Miami Haitians. According to Garcia the majority of Haitians in his community are very much in favor of an invasion and would be willing volunteers for a new civilian police force.

MARCUS GARCIA: The idea is civilian national police force. For most of the people it is more than that. It is not a civilian police, it's like an invasion force—Haitians going to Haiti to liberate their country. That's the way it is. But inside all that, there is a lot of controversy.

McEVOY: The controversy finds its roots in the 1915 U.S. invasion of Haiti. U.S. troops did not leave the country until 1934. This past has many Haitians in the U.S. suspicious of any U.S. involvement in the future of their country.

PATRICK BOSSANT: What is being proposed here is a replica of what occurred in 1915.

McEVOY: Patrick Bossant [sp] is a member of Comité de Resistance, a community-based organization in Miami that supports democracy in Haiti.

Mr. BOSSANT: Because, basically, you know the U.S. came in, in July 1915, and the first thing they did was specifically that, they created the Haitian gendarmerie and they trained them and they controlled them, and like the big father, and it was the same relationship.

[sound of church choir]

McEVOY: The Notre Dame church is central to Miami's Haitian immigrant community. On this afternoon, one hundred children are receiving first communion, an event that has filled the church to capacity, forcing many to congregate outside. Very few of these churchgoers are willing to discuss politics of any kind. Those that do are very opinionated on whether the U.S. should train Haitian exiles to act as a new police force in Haiti.

1st MAN: That is a good idea, because this guy, the police, we have now in Haiti, we have to get rid of them because they don't like their own self because they kill all their own people, you know.

2nd MAN: If the U.S invade Haiti and they train the police force here in this community, in United States, he will be the same kind of force they got in Haiti. And in 1915 when they invade Haiti, they train that police force in Haiti to kill their own people instead of protect the Haitian.

McEVOY: According to radio host Marcus García, many of the most enthusiastic supporters of an exile-based police force are Haitians who are in the U.S. military like Ralph Suplice [sp], a marine reserve. Suplice says sending a Haitian exile force is the best way to mitigate the distrust many Haitians have towards the U.S.

RALPH SUPLICE: Short of Haitians doing the invasion themselves, the idea of Haitians going after the invasion takes place would be the next best thing. It would be to get something done, to go back and leave Haiti to us to take care of.

McEVOY: The reform of the Haitian military and the creation of a civilian police force separate from that army is central to the Haitian crisis. But it may also prove to be a factor in President Clinton's political future. An unstable Haiti means more Haitians trying to emigrate to the U.S. at a time when there is a strong anti-immigration mood among many Americans. This, according to many Haitian exiles, is why the Haiti issue is heating up and why they believe the U.S. may turn to them to help solve the problem. For National Public Radio, I'm Julia McEvoy reporting.

## ELAINE SCIOLINO: "REVISED U.S. PLAN FOR HAITI CALLS FOR LARGE PEACE FORCE"

*This story is an example of the reporting done to give readers as much explanatory information from multiple perspectives as possible in a very complicated environment. This kind of story did not come from a single press briefing but from many sources and gave the reader more than just a spot of news.*

*New York Times*, 25 June 1994

WASHINGTON: The Clinton Administration is preparing a plan for Haiti, if and when its military leaders leave power, to create an international peacekeeping force that would involve several thousand American troops, police and civilian contractors, senior Administration officials said today.

The size of the United Nations–mandated force is expected to be 12,000 to 14,000 troops, about half of them Americans, although the officials said the final number could change. (CORRECTION: Because of an editing error, an article on Saturday about the Clinton Administration's plan to create an international peacekeeping force for Haiti referred incorrectly at one point to the force's proposed makeup. The 12,000 to 14,000 members would include police officers and civilian contractors as well as troops.)

The size of the force, which would be authorized by the United Nations if the ousted President, the Rev. Jean-Bertrand Aristide, is returned to office, is much larger than earlier anticipated. Less than two weeks ago, some senior Administration officials suggested that a force of 3,000 to 4,000 would be sufficient.

Following a number of interagency meetings in recent days, the Administration concluded that a much larger force was necessary.

### PRESSING THE U.N.

Administration officials said that the United States would press the United Nations to create the larger force because Washington wants to insure that it would be able to deal with any eventuality in Haiti, particularly in light of the polarization of Haitian society and the absence of civil institutions.

It is unclear how many of the thousands of Americans participating in the force would be armed troops. But in a recent classified memo to Washington, Madeleine K. Albright, the United States representative to the United Nations, said that Washington wanted to reduce its troop contribution to 3,000 very soon after the force goes into Haiti, said one Administration official familiar with the memo.

Some senior Pentagon officials remain strongly opposed to the formation of such a large force because it would involve a large number of American soldiers and because there is no clear idea of what the force's mandate would be, Administration officials said.

Even though all relevant agencies of government have signed off on a plan for the international force, the plan could be modified or even shelved if opposition in some parts of the Pentagon is strong enough.

One indication of the opposition came after State Department officials said early in the day that the Administration intended to present the new plan to Father Aristide and to begin consultations with key lawmakers next week.

There already have been some consultations with the United Nations and with foreign governments, and President Clinton discussed the new force with Argentina's President Carlos Menem at the White House today.

But later in the day, a White House official said that President Clinton had not yet signed off on the plan and that there would be no consultations with Congress next week.

The plan, at least in its current form, has four goals for the peacekeepers: the protection of democratic leaders and institutions, the professionalization of the military and the retraining of the police, the protection of the international humanitarian and human rights workers and the maintenance of essential civil order.

Those goals were set out earlier this month at a meeting in Brazil of foreign ministers of the Organization of American States, and were endorsed by Father Aristide.

But the fourth task—maintaining civil order—is ambiguous and makes some officials uneasy.

Some senior officials said that about a dozen countries have expressed a willingness to take part in the force in small numbers, particularly in sending police officers and trainers, leaving the United States to provide the bulk of the military and logistical support.

Canada, for example, could probably be expected to contribute Royal Canadian Mounted Police officers and engineers and helicopters to the force. It has also announced that it will train about 500 Haitian exiles as police and police trainers in Canada.

### REQUEST FOR BATTALION DENIED

But the Canadians have already refused an American request to contribute a combat battalion of about 800 soldiers, the Administration officials said.

At a press briefing at the White House today, Mr. Menem said that it would be up to the Argentine Parliament to decide whether his country would participate in an invasion force to restore Father Aristide to power. He said that he, as President, could decide on his own whether to send in peacekeeping troops after democracy was restored, but did not say whether he was prepared to do so.

There are currently 870 Americans serving in peacekeeping missions around the world. But the situation in Haiti and Bosnia could change that in the coming months.

If the Bosnian Government and the Serbs move closer to a peace agreement, there is the possibility that the United States would have to deploy peacekeeping troops in Bosnia as part of a force of perhaps 50,000 troops to implement the settlement.

The United States could find itself in the position of having to contribute thousands of troops to both Haiti and Bosnia.

*Credit*: Copyright © 1994 by The New York Times Co. Reprinted with permission.

---

## BARRY SCHWEID: CLINTON ADMINISTRATION CONTENDS SANCTIONS MAY YET WORK IN HAITI

---

*This story reported the ways in which the U.S. administration was trying to deal with a humanitarian need and struggling with the effort. It was the kind of story that began to turn the tide of American opinion toward support for military intervention.*

### Associated Press, 30 June 1994

WASHINGTON: Despite heightened repression and an upsurge in Haitian boat people, the Clinton administration contends more time is needed to allow economic sanctions to bring Haiti's military leaders to heel.

Secretary of State Warren Christopher faced questioning on the Haiti policy at a Senate Foreign Relations Committee hearing Thursday.

On Wednesday, Defense Secretary William Perry played down talk of a U.S. invasion to restore democracy in Haiti, which has been under military control since elected President Jean-Bertrand Aristide was ousted by a coup in September 1991.

"I think the pressure on the Haitian military leaders is increasing very substantially as a result of the increased sanctions that we've taken," Perry said at a news conference.

"I think we should continue to believe that we should give some time to see that process work itself out and I think we may see some very substantial results from that," he said. "The conventional wisdom is that sanctions cannot be effective, that they cannot force governments to change their actions. This may be a counter-example."

The administration tightened the international sanctions Wednesday by revoking the visas of most Haitians hoping to travel to the United States. The move was largely symbolic, however, because President Clinton banned commercial air traffic between the United States and Haiti late last week.

In the meantime, the administration is struggling against a tide of Haitians desperate for U.S. asylum, and Clinton is housing them at the U.S. naval base at Guantanamo Bay, Cuba.

Hundreds of Haitian boat people were diverted Wednesday to a new tent city at Guantanamo, and hundreds more fled the troubled Caribbean nation.

Over the past six days, Coast Guard cutters and Navy warships have intercepted more than 3,300 Haitians fleeing economic collapse and political repression in their army-run country.

The upsurge in boat people was touched off by Clinton's decision to give fleeing Haitians a chance to apply for political asylum for the first time since President Bush halted the practice in May 1992.

William Gray, U.S. special envoy on Haiti, said at a White House briefing Wednesday that about 20 percent to 30 percent of applicants are being granted refugee status, up from less than 10 percent in earlier months. He attributed the increase in successful applications to "a continuing deterioration of the human rights situation."

Gray also blamed human rights problems for the increase in refugees. He said it was unclear whether the recent surge in refugees was simply a temporary spike or would continue.

In either event, he said, "we are prepared to deal with whatever develops with regard to the refugee situation."

Administration officials said they were using Guantanamo only to ease the burden until refugee processing centers were opened in the nearby Turks and Caicos Islands and possibly other countries.

Clinton criticized Bush during the 1992 presidential campaign for his policy on Haiti, saying it was immoral to send migrants home without first giving them a chance to present evidence of political persecution.

Once elected, however, Clinton continued the forced repatriations because of concern that thousands of Haitians would stream to U.S. shores in hopes of a more liberal asylum policy.

Gray said the administration's focus remained on the "source of the problem . . . the coup leaders who continue to oppress their leaders and continue to hold power against the will of their people."

The Senate, after a five-hour debate Wednesday, rejected a

proposal to require Clinton to obtain advance authorization from Congress before taking any military action in Haiti. The Senate instead approved a non-binding resolution that said the president should consult with and seek the approval of Congress before committing U.S. troops in Haiti.

Clinton has said only that he has not ruled out a military option.

*Credit*: Reprinted with permission of The Associated Press.

---

# BARRY SCHWEID: "PENTAGON SAYS U.S. TROOPS WILL GO TO HAITI"

---

*Two months later the White House was ready to put troops in the field because there seemed to be fading hopes everywhere that diplomatic efforts were going to solve the crisis.*

Associated Press, 31 August 1994

WASHINGTON: Deputy Defense Secretary John M. Deutch said Wednesday that American troops will be dispatched to Haiti—either to expel the country's military junta or to help restore order if the generals bow to international pressure and depart.

"The multinational force is going to Haiti," he said, referring to the predominantly American fighting coalition about to be trained in Puerto Rico.

Deutch told reporters some 10,000 U.S. troops would be in a coalition force supplemented by several hundred from other hemisphere countries to be trained in Puerto Rico. He said the point of such a large force was to minimize American and Haitian casualties. He offered no timetable for moving against Lt. Gen. Raoul Cédras.

Clinton administration officials have warned Raoul Cédras and his cohorts for months they risk an invasion if they do not quit and permit restoration of elected President Jean-Bertrand Aristide, who was ousted three years ago. Deutch's statement was the toughest so far.

Denying reports the Pentagon was reluctant to act, Deutch said there was no policy disagreement with the State Department, usually depicted in the media as more prone to use the force authorized by the U.N. Security Council in July.

Even so, Deputy Secretary of State Strobe Talbott said the use of force would be "a last resort." In a joint news conference, he said, "we want to make sure we use other avenues."

Deutch and Talbott headed a U.S. delegation that went to Kingston, Jamaica, on Tuesday and won unanimous support of the 13-nation Caribbean Community and Common Market for the U.N. resolution. They then went to the Dominican Republic to check on infiltration of supplies to Haiti in defiance of a U.N. embargo.

Talbott said they detected during a helicopter ride a large, makeshift pipeline, apparently to carry oil, as well as several large barrels of oil being carried across the border to Haiti. Talbott said the Dominican government had promised to enforce the embargo with troops.

Administration officials are hopeful three nations, the Bahamas, Antigua and Guyana, which did not commit troops on Tuesday, will do so eventually. They would supplement the troops Jamaica, Trinidad and Tobago, Barbados and Belize agreed in Kingston to provide.

Deutch dismissed any suggestion the Caribbean countries were making only a symbolic contribution. He said they would be part of the military coalition and also help in stabilizing the country.

However, other officials said that if there is an invasion, only Americans would be in the initial wave. Deutch emphasized they would be under the command of American officers.

"The multinational force is going to Haiti," he said. "The issue is the circumstances under which that force enters Haiti. It could be under a permissive circumstance, at the request of Haiti's legitimate government, with the authority of the United Nations, or it can be under contested circumstances if the de facto, the illegal government does not come to its senses and realize the world is determined to see a change in the government . . ."

Some 30 U.S. Army specialists will train the Caribbean soldiers, a senior Pentagon official said. The troops will be broken down into six light infantry platoons and an 80-man headquarters unit that will participate in about two to three weeks of training at the U.S. military base Roosevelt Roads in Puerto Rico.

It is expected to take up to two weeks to get the Caribbean unit organized before the training can begin, the official said.

The infantry units' training will focus on such skills as crowd control, first aid, manning road blocks, communications, weapons use and logistical issues, said the official, who spoke on condition of anonymity.

The Caribbean soldiers will supply their own small arms, but the United States will supply uniforms, helmets, flak jackets and small vehicles, the official said.

The U.S. soldiers conducting the training will be drawn from those based in the region and will be familiar with the area and its languages, the official said.

An administration official confirmed, meanwhile, that the U.S. Coast Guard had provided information to Haiti's military rulers on refugees preparing to board boats for the United States.

The official, speaking on condition of anonymity, said the information was provided on only one occasion, several months ago, and that there were no further exchanges. "We do not cooperate with the Haitian military," he said.

The administration has been urging Haitians seeking refuge in the United States to apply within the country instead of taking to sea in unsafe craft. The Coast Guard regularly patrols Haiti's shores.

*Credit*: Reprinted with permission of The Associated Press.

## CARL ROCHELLE: U.S. HAITI INVASION FORCES RECEIVE VISIT FROM DEFENSE SECRETARY PERRY

*This live report from the Pentagon is an example of how open the reporting was about the situation in Haiti.*

*CNN News*, Transcript 863–3, 18 September 1994

RALPH WENGE, Anchor: Now, the Pentagon is saying the troops are poised and ready for action if the talks in Haiti do not bring about a peaceful resolution. CNN's Carl Rochelle is at the Pentagon at this hour. He joins us now with the latest. Carl, good morning.

CARL ROCHELLE, Correspondent: Good morning, Ralph. One indication of how far things are moved along—Defense Secretary William Perry, who went out with a visit for the troops yesterday shortly after he and the Joint Chiefs of Staff finished briefing President Clinton here at the Pentagon—he took an aircraft—he and Carl Mundy, the commandant of the Marine Corps, General Carl Mundy—flew to Guantanamo Bay, Cuba, we are told, and took a helicopter out to the U.S.S. Wasp, where they visited with a number of commanders and a number of the Marines who were on board the ship. It is similar to a visit that Secretary Perry made last week to Norfolk, Virginia, where he met with some of the troops aboard the Eisenhower, Army troops and sailors and the troops on the Mount Whitney to, I guess, give them an atta boy. We were told that this is very much personal with him—that he wanted to go out, he wanted to visit with these men, he wanted to see these men who perhaps in a few days could be put in harm's way. Ralph—

WENGE: All right. Carl, what is the status of the forces right now? Do we have any idea yet when they're likely to go ashore?

ROCHELLE: What we are told—that everything is ready, everyone is ready—that all of the ships are in place, the Mount Whitney is now in place, the U.S.S. America, the U.S.S. Eisenhower. Interesting thing about the Eisenhower and the America. Both of them are carrying Army troops and helicopters. These are the long deck carriers that we've become familiar with over the years launching F-14's and F-18's and A-6's into combat in all kinds of situations. But, in this case, these carriers are being used as helicopter carriers. They've got Army helicopters on board—never heard of before—in such an operation like this, and it's part of what we can expect of a massive wave of helicopters going in when the assault takes place.

Now, when? Well, one thing I think we can probably count on is that as long as the delegation of Former President Carter and Former Chairman of the Joint Chiefs of Staff, General Colin Powell, and Senator Sam Nunn, the chairman of the Senate Armed Services Committee, are in the country, we can expect that there won't be any invasion or any installation of U.S. troops. But, I would think within hours after they come out—now, perhaps they'll come out with General Cédras with them, perhaps they'll come out with an agreement, perhaps they'll come out with no agreement—but, I would think within hours after that happens, you could see the first U.S. troops going ashore. It could be a peaceful operation; it could be a not peaceful operation, but it won't be long after that happens. Ralph—

WENGE: Obviously, this could be a very critical Sunday. Carl, thank you very much. We'll talk with you later.

*Credit*: © 2005 Cable News Network LP, LLLP. Reprinted with permission.

## BERNARD KALB: "THE MEDIA AND THE SITUATION IN HAITI"

*This show is an example of the ways in which the media had the time to talk about how their access during this crisis was different from recent past experience under different White House administrations. This kind of reflective thinking in the face of military intervention was not unusual. What was unusual was the kind of access available to the reporters this time, and the attitude of the White House about its relationship with the media during times of crisis.*

Reliable Sources (CNN), Transcript 134, 18 September 1994

BERNARD KALB: Welcome to Reliable Sources, where we turn a critical lens on the media. I'm Bernard Kalb. The lineup for this edition—Somalia, Rwanda, Bosnia and now Haiti—are the cameras driving the policy? And what's it like in Haiti for reporters on the scene?

The military is preparing for an invasion of Haiti and American news organizations are gearing up as well.

[voice-over] An invasion of Haiti could look something like this. That morning, in December, '92, when U.S. marines waded onto the beaches of Somalia, blinded by the light of American television cameras that had gotten there first. That's because hundreds of TV and print journalists have descended on the Caribbean nation and are gearing up to cover an invasion. It's unclear how the media, with its power of instant communication, will affect the battlefield. Unclear, too, what role, if any, have the media played in bringing the crisis to a boiling point. Have U.S. policymakers been nudged into action by the video images of desperate refugees and will U.S. policymakers feel pressured to leave Haiti if the images turn to this or this, as they did in Somalia?

[on camera] Joining us from Port-au-Prince, Haiti is Douglas Farah, correspondent for the Washington Post. In Miami, Spencer Reiss, the Miami bureau chief of Newsweek magazine, who has covered Haiti extensively and is on his way back, and here in Windows, Peter Arnett, the veteran CNN correspondent, who has covered wars around the world, who recently returned from Haiti.

Doug, in Port-au-Prince, do you feel as though you are at the end of a saber being rattled by the White House?

DOUGLAS FARAH, "Washington Post": [Port-au-Prince, Haiti] Well I think there's no question that as American policy has moved forward here, they've become much more interested, and we have become—at least what we're saying is being paid much more attention to up there. I think our reporting down here hasn't changed much on the human rights situation and on the effects of the embargo. It's just that people up there are now using them in Washington, the reports, to gain political support, which they were not doing before.

BERNARD KALB: Spencer, do you feel, how shall I put it, manipulated, exploited, used by the administration in Washington?

SPENCER REISS, "Newsweek": Sure, I mean all of us know, in this business, that as the ability to do the kinds of things we can now do, and this show is evidence of that, we can, we are, you know, we're manipulated by anybody that has access to a camera or a reporter's notebook, whether it's General Cédras, Bill Clinton or anybody else. It's just part of life.

BERNARD KALB: Peter, as a professional journalistic skeptic, and you've spent a lot of time in Haiti, how do you resist that manipulation?

PETER ARNETT, CNN International Correspondent: Well going beyond that a minute, I, uniquely, in my career, I was told by the American embassy on several occasions that if I or any other journalist was assassinated in the course of events there, it would have automatically triggered an American invasion, and as one who's been often criticized by U.S. administrations I thought that the fact that we were in danger and the fact that others' human rights violations were apparent, were aiding and abetting American policy at the time.

BERNARD KALB: Peter Arnett could trigger an invasion?

PETER ARNETT: Amazing as it may seem, that's what they were saying. Peter Arnett and any other journalist there.

BERNARD KALB: All right. Doug, tell us something about whatever dangers you may face down there covering this story.

DOUGLAS FARAH: Well I think, so far, to be completely honest, there hasn't been a great deal of danger. I think the danger will probably increase as an American invasion draws nearer and the anti-American sentiment comes to the forefront. I think we've all had a few minor incidents of people shoving, pushing, being extremely hostile. At this point, and I covered Salvador and Central America for eight years in the drug war, and this is, by far, the most peaceful I've felt in covering any of those major events.

BERNARD KALB: We're being told that there's something of an alert of vulnerability about the Matana Hotel, where much of the press hangs out.

DOUGLAS FARAH: Well I think, clearly, as people begin to feel that the end really is near, they may want to take a swipe at some of us, or all of us, and we are fairly vulnerable. Because of the economic situation of the country and the infrastructure, we're more or less kept in two or three hotels. That's the only place we can really operate out of. So I think if they decided to get us, they could, but at this point I haven't seen any serious indication of that.

BERNARD KALB: Spencer, what sort of restrictions have been, in effect, put there by the Haitian government when you've been covering the story down there?

SPENCER REISS: There have been a number of theoretical restrictions placed over, particularly in the last three or four months, in terms of not being supposedly allowed on beaches, around the airport, etc., but those have generally not been enforced, like most laws in Haiti, and as—for all practical purposes, people have been able to do pretty much anything they want.

BERNARD KALB: Peter, you covered the Persian Gulf, obviously, we all know that, and you've covered the Haitian story. When you do a comparison, have you encountered more restrictions imposed by American officials than you do by, say, Iraqis or Haitians?

PETER ARNETT: Yeah, I would have to say that, first of all, there was no censorship when I was in Port-au-Prince, and, with the exception of what Spence says, some limited areas we couldn't visit, basically we could pretty much see and visit wherever we wanted to go to. I must say that I was impressed with the sophisticated nature of the military leaders' supporters, the wealthy elite, the MREs, the morally repugnant elite, as they were named earlier this year. Often at the hotel, they'd be at restaurants we were at, lobbying, making their point, arguing, getting on the air, on CNN, getting quoted in the New York Times, making a very effective effort, I thought, to present the case of the military leadership. It wasn't easy, really, I found, in Haiti, to document the Clinton Administration's case that there were continuing human rights abuses, because very few of those involved in abuses, victims, wanted to go on camera and show their faces, and, of course, the bodies that lay around Port-au-Prince were anonymous. We never could figure out whoever murdered them.

DOUGLAS FARAH: I think, Bernie—

BERNARD KALB: Please, go ahead.

DOUGLAS FARAH: I was going to say, I think part of it is that the people that ran the coup here largely consider themselves to be very pro-American and believed all along that they could make a coherent case to the American public, that the American public would understand what they had done and why they had done it. I don't think they were right, but I think that's part of the reason why they tolerated us this long.

BERNARD KALB: Doug, what sort of plans are being made by the media to cover an invasion?

DOUGLAS FARAH: Well I think everyone has their own different plans. I think everybody's sort of beefed-up considerably. We're going to have two or three reporters in before, we hope, and then a couple coming in afterwards and I think, in the chaos of things, it'll more or less be every person for themselves. I don't think any of our plans will really matter, in the end. I think we'll just go to chaos.

BERNARD KALB: Just go to chaos at the end. You've had some of the heavies from television, Dan Rather already parachuting onto the scene, and I suspect the others will arrive as well. Is that story being accurately portrayed or is there a jumping at the gun, so to speak?

SPENCER REISS: I think if I could—[crosstalk] Go ahead, Doug. Go ahead.

DOUGLAS FARAH: I was going to say, I think, by and large, the people that have been here for a long time are reporting exactly the same things in exactly the same way we have before. I think things get a little distorted when people parachute in in large numbers. I think that the people who have been covering this place consistently over time, we're doing exactly the same thing and exactly the same stories.

SPENCER REISS: Yeah, I'd add, from here, that, also, people should remember that Washington has played a very big role, and Washington reporting, in a number of the false alarms or drum beating exercises that we've seen in this story, particularly since May, when the full trade embargo went on. We have been, you know, gone through a whole series of scares, and a lot of that is coming, not from here, but from Washington.

BERNARD KALB: Washington?

SPENCER REISS: Yeah.

BERNARD KALB: Peter, you're right here in Washington right at the moment. Do you feel inundated, do you feel swamped by stories projecting the administration point of view on how you write a story?

PETER ARNETT: Well, certainly, in the last few days in Washington, there's been an enormous amount written about the administration's plans. What strikes me about all the coverage of this particular coming or this crisis, is the detail the Pentagon has leaked. This is a war by fax, Bernie. We know more about this war, this upcoming operation, than any previous that I've ever known, even in Vietnam, when there was no censorship.

BERNARD KALB: Whatever happened to the phrase "loose lips sink ships"?

PETER ARNETT: Exactly. It does not apply in this particular conflict, and it indicates two things to me. One, the total confidence of the Pentagon, when they eventually launch the operation, of its success, and the other, of course, is to try and scare the military leadership into the sea.

BERNARD KALB: And, Doug, scaring the military leadership into the sea is the exploitation of the media, and you fellows are being at the end of the saber.

DOUGLAS FARAH: Well I think that that—to a degree, that's true, yes. I think one of the big differences—if I can go back to the Washington question just a second, is that when I was writing, and not just me, you have lots of other people writing the impact of the embargo stories earlier, the administration was calling up me and my paper and saying we were wildly exaggerating the situation and the human rights situation, and now that it's politically convenient for them, they're pulling out all the old clips and going back over them, as if this had been their position all along. So I think, clearly, there's a manipulation by Washington of what we've been reporting all along.

BERNARD KALB: Spence, what are you going to be reporting as soon as you arrive there?

SPENCER REISS: Well it depends. I mean, by the time we get on the air, there is some possibility that things may have changed dramatically. Assuming it doesn't, we're going to be doing the same kind of sitting around watching and waiting that everybody's been doing now for, really, it's almost three months since people moved in in force down there and it's a very difficult situation, because there's so much rumor, there's so much, as we've been saying again and again, manipulation, things are being done for effect. Everybody in Washington's aware of the fact that the Haitian general staff have all got TV sets in their offices, on which they're watching this show, if they're up on Sunday morning. And—

BERNARD KALB: But Spence will the—sorry, go ahead. Finish up.

SPENCER REISS: No, I'm just—everybody knows that, and they're, you know, so it's a game, and it's still not over.

BERNARD KALB: Well, good luck in swimming through the manipulation and nailing the facts. To you, Doug, and you, Spencer, my thanks. The same here to you, Peter. When we come back, we'll take up this subject—are the TV cameras driving U.S. policy? And, of course, we'll have our regular panelists here—Howard Kurtz, Martin Schram and Ellen Hume. Also, for a finale—the good, the bad and the ugly—this week in American journalism.

[Commercial break]

BERNARD KALB: Welcome back. Marty, a question for you. True or false—do the cameras shape foreign policy?

MARTIN SCHRAM, Scripps Howard Syndicate: Sometimes true, sometimes false.

BERNARD KALB: Then, the question is, look how effectively the media, television media, produced a positive response for intervention in Bosnia. That is not the case, clearly, in Haiti.

MARTIN SCHRAM: And think why.

BERNARD KALB: And think why?

MARTIN SCHRAM: Yeah, because there are no pictures out of Haiti, of the atrocities. We saw them in Somalia—the starving children, your heart went out, Rwanda, we've seen it, Bosnia we've seen the buildings getting shattered by the attacks of the mortars, and, in Haiti, we have not seen the pictures of the atrocities that Bill Clinton talked about in his speech. Therefore, they have to find some other way to gin up public sentiment to invade.

BERNARD KALB: Kurtz, you've lost your 20/20 vision watching television. Is he right on that? Is there not comparable horror being shown?

HOWARD KURTZ, "Washington Post" Media Reporter: Oh, not at all, Bernie.

BERNARD KALB: Not at all.

HOWARD KURTZ: This has not been that—

BERNARD KALB: And that means?

HOWARD KURTZ: That means it's been an uphill struggle, for lots of reasons, for this administration to try to make the case. This is not a situation where the administration is following television. This is a situation where they're trying to convince the public, through television, that there is a strong rationale here.

BERNARD KALB: Why hasn't that horror been on the screen?

HOWARD KURTZ: I'm not entirely sure, I guess, because—in part, because there haven't been pictures. [unintelligible]

MARTIN SCHRAM: Well, there have not been mass scenes of hundreds or thousands of people starving, shot, wounded, whatever it was, as we could see in Somalia or Bosnia.

HOWARD KURTZ: And maybe also, Marty, we've become inured to it. There have been so many years of stories about suffering and poverty and brutality in Haiti.

ELLEN HUME, Washington Annenberg Program, Media Analyst: Exactly. I mean, that's what I would talk about. I'd say that the news media are almost overloaded with one crisis and then another, and how many starving orphans are you going to have? The captions of the picture are going to be almost interchangeable, and I think, first of all, I have to do a little disclaimer here.

BERNARD KALB: Disclaimer?

ELLEN HUME: I have to explain that my husband is part of the administration's human rights team and he helped write Clinton's speech, but I'm not here to reflect his views. Let me make that clear. I've been in the business 25 years, the news business, and I'm here to talk about that. But I do think that Howie's point is correct, that, in fact, you can't expect the public to absorb every bit of pain that's out there in the world.

HOWARD KURTZ: Compassion fatigue.

ELLEN HUME: Yeah, and I wonder if the news organizations were not publishing these stories and pictures, or if, in fact, it was the fact that there were none.

HOWARD KURTZ: We were doing Cuba last month.

ELLEN HUME: Yeah.

HOWARD KURTZ: We were sort of ricocheting to [crosstalk].

BERNARD KALB: That suggests a kind of a censorship. You don't mean that, do you?

ELLEN HUME: I mean that's—no, no, not a censorship.

BERNARD KALB: Well how about the Washington Post?

ELLEN HUME: But news judgment. Was it the judgment of the editors and the producers of television that Haiti was not as gory or as awful a story as someplace else?

BERNARD KALB: Haiti is Somalia, different geography. We've had enough of that.

HOWARD KURTZ: The focus, in a lot of the coverage, has been on the refugee problem, because that's something that touches our shores, and all the Haitians that have been taken to Guantanamo. That dominated a lot of the headlines.

BERNARD KALB: Well this comes back to this headline, Marty. Rwanda, Bosnia, Sarajevo, Haiti. Does the media cover death the same way?

MARTIN SCHRAM: You know, the fact is we really do try to cover it the same way. It's sometimes harder to get the pictures than other times. If you think back, it was a long time before we really got the pictures out of Somalia. I mean there

> Rwanda, Bosnia, Sarajevo, Haiti. Does the media cover death the same way?

was death for an awful long time before the first television cameras brought it back to the United States, and everyone said, oh my goodness, there's starvation there. You can't get the pictures in Haiti if you aren't there with your cameras when the atrocities are happening, and there were not scenes, bloody scenes, streets filled with bodies. It just wasn't there.

HOWARD KURTZ: Marty, that's going to change if this invasion comes, because this administration—I've been on the phone in recent days with the State Department and the Pentagon—is assiduously courting the press, a marked contrast to the testy relations during the Persian Gulf War.

BERNARD KALB: [unintelligible]?

HOWARD KURTZ: Well they've been doing everything but offering limousines and catering to reporters who want to go cover this thing, and it's not because they're nice guys. It's because they know there isn't a lot of public support in the country for this, and they want to have the press tell the story of U.S. troops invading and they don't want a lot of stories about censorship.

BERNARD KALB: But then the question is, the question is, in the Persian Gulf, the Pentagon defeated both Iraq and the media.

HOWARD KURTZ: Absolutely.

BERNARD KALB: No question about that.

HOWARD KURTZ: Clearly.

BERNARD KALB: What sort of restrictions are there shaping up now in connection with the coverage of any sort of invasion?

ELLEN HUME: It's very different, because Haiti is an open country for media. They've been in place there for a long time. It's an open country for coverage. They have not restricted the press. Saudi Arabia, which was the launching pad for the Persian Gulf effort, was closed to the free press, and, in fact, they wouldn't let reporters in. There was no freedom of movement. Grenada, no press were alerted. There was no coverage of the invasion of either the Persian Gulf conflict or Grenada.

BERNARD KALB: Ellen, it was the—yeah, but the Pentagon was the impresario of the coverage, regardless of what was in Saudi Arabia.

MARTIN SCHRAM: Let me tell you a story about what I think is going on now. I turned on the TV a few days ago and saw, on CNN, Jamie McIntyre, one of the most extraordinary pieces I had seen, a detailed map with where each aircraft carrier is going to be, where the invasion is going to come in, arrows and all that, names, numbers of troops and everything.

ELLEN HUME: Yeah.

MARTIN SCHRAM: I called him up and I said, "my goodness, are they leaking it that bad? Do they want it all out?" And he said, "you know," he said, "all hell's broken loose here," he said. "I pieced it together from a dozen sources, and now everyone thinks I got it from one source. The Pentagon spokesman told me it was painfully accurate."

BERNARD KALB: Yeah, but, you know, Marty, what they want—the Pentagon's putting this stuff out in oceanic tidal wave, because they are trying to bomb Haiti with the media, with threats and so forth. I'm going to take us to polls in our remaining time. This constant stethoscoping of the country, instant polls. The president has 32, the president has 41. Yes for invasion, no for invasion. What about the polls? Do they reflect accuracy, or are they a discardable snapshot of the moment?

HOWARD KURTZ: I think the numbers are so overwhelming, in terms of public skepticism toward military action in Haiti, that it's a perfectly fair thing to make that a major issue, as we would in any situation like this.

ELLEN HUME: But the telephone polls, the minute after any event, whether it's a speech or an invasion, are extremely spurious. I mean no serious pollster thinks that these are correct.

BERNARD KALB: Spurious. Fancy word for false.

ELLEN HUME: False, and not reliable.

BERNARD KALB: Misleading, distorting, not reliable.

ELLEN HUME: Not a reliable source, Bernie.

BERNARD KALB: Not a reliable source. A poll is not a reliable source?

ELLEN HUME: Not an instant poll. A thoughtful poll, a scientific poll, yes. But these phone-in polls are skewed by the fact that the only people you telephone are really [unintelligible].

MARTIN SCHRAM: But even in the more detailed polls, the Gallup/CNN/USA Today poll, 370 people, after Clinton's speech—

ELLEN HUME: Oh I'm not disputing that. I'm saying every—

MARTIN SCHRAM: And it's scientific, but it's still only 370 people right after—

ELLEN HUME: And if the invasion occurs, you know darn well it's likely to change. If the invasion goes badly, it'll be worse for the president. If it goes well, it'll be better for the president.

MARTIN SCHRAM: Exactly.

BERNARD KALB: But we'll probably poll you two, without any question. When we return, this distinguished panel issues its weekly nominations for the good, the bad and the ugly, the best and worst of American journalism this week. You will not want to miss this.

[Commercial break]

BERNARD KALB: Welcome back to the careful assessments by our panel of the best and the worst in American journalism this past week. Ellen?

ELLEN HUME: I'm afraid my dart is to mother ship CNN this week, arguing in a Miami court that they were shocked, shocked to find out that they were defying a judge's order in 1990 when they broadcast Noriega tapes that were the U.S. government's property and so forth. Well, it turns out that they—a tape also exists of our anchor, Bernie Shaw, from CNN, saying at the time, right before, just a little bit later, the very tapes CNN has been ordered not to broadcast. So you see, caught in the act.

BERNARD KALB: Bad, ugly?

ELLEN HUME: Improper.

BERNARD KALB: Improper.

HOWARD KURTZ: Bernie, not too many Washington reporters enjoy the unglamorous job of actually reporting on the workings of the federal government. It's much more fun to cover politics, as you know. Well this week, the New York Times ran a terrific series on the incompetence, the corruption and the occasional stupidity of the Immigration and Naturalization Service, everything from how easy it is to buy a green card to how easy it is to sneak across the border and get in again. Journalism needs more of this kind of old-fashioned digging.

BERNARD KALB: Sensational, brilliant, good?

HOWARD KURTZ: Very very good.

MARTIN SCHRAM: Bernie, here's a plus for an editorial cartoonist from a writer. Jim Morin, of the Miami Herald, did a clever flip flop. He drew up a Kansas newspaper with a headline "Topeka Besieged By Haitian Exiles. City Police, Hospitals, Schools, Overwhelmed. Unemployment Crimes Skyrocket." And in the center, "Bob Dole Calls for U.S. Invasion, Says National Security Is Now At Stake." There's a cartoonist who said it all.

BERNARD KALB: Good?

MARTIN SCHRAM: Good.

BERNARD KALB: Excellent?

MARTIN SCHRAM: Just the way Washington works.

BERNARD KALB: I'm going to be a little ahead of my time. I'm going to be somewhere between good and spineless. Good that the media fights the Pentagon, should there be restrictions on any invasion of Haiti. Spineless, if they cave in the way they did in the Persian Gulf. Any questions?

HOWARD KURTZ: I think, inevitably, Bernie, there will be conflicts, for all the promises of cooperation we're hearing right now.

BERNARD KALB: Thank you for your last word. My thanks to our panel and to our guests, to our viewers. We'll be back again same time next week. I'm Bernard Kalb.

*Credit:* © 2005 Cable News Network LP, LLLP. Reprinted with permission.

---

# JUDY KEEN: CLINTON AND NATION WAIT FOR BREAKTHROUGH IN HAITI

---

*This front-page story in a national newspaper was a report on what everyone across the country would have wanted to know. What happened, and how did it all turn out? Had military intervention been avoided? Were the Americans still the good guys? This story gave answers to all those questions.*

### USA Today, 19 September 1994

President Clinton spent Sunday doing what many other people across the nation were doing: waiting for signs of a breakthrough in Haiti.

By the time the dramatic, last-minute agreement finally was reached, Clinton already had given the order for the military to begin its assault on the Caribbean nation—and 61 planes launched from Pope Air Force Base, N.C., suddenly were ordered back.

This was an invasion Clinton never really wanted. He was gambling that Haiti's military junta would back down in the face of overwhelming U.S. military might.

But before he could call off the invasion, he endured an exhausting day, often able to do little but tune in TV footage that focused for hours on the second floor of the army headquarters in Port-au-Prince.

Inside, former president Jimmy Carter, former Joint Chiefs of Staff chairman Colin Powell and Senate Armed Services Committee chairman Sam Nunn huddled with Haitian Lt. Gen. Raoul Cédras late into Sunday—finally leaving eight hours after their scheduled noon departure.

People in Haiti's capital waited breathlessly, too, gripped between the uncertainties of probable war and possible peace.

The negotiators' plane, engines running, sat all afternoon at the Port-au-Prince airport.

Hanging in the balance: the actions of an invasion force of 20,000 U.S. troops poised offshore and the fates of Cédras, Haiti's other military dictators and deposed Haitian president Jean-Bertrand Aristide.

Also at stake: Clinton's own foreign-policy credibility. Aides described Clinton as unwavering Sunday in his resolve to restore democracy to Haiti, but he was forced to watch from afar as emissaries who are not members of his administration searched for a way to avoid war.

"It was almost like a scene out of Dr. Strangelove," said Rep. Porter Goss, R-Fla., an observer of Haiti's 1990 elections and a former CIA agent in the Caribbean. "This was not exactly a confidence-building exercise."

At church Sunday morning, Clinton bowed his head as a prayer was said for the troops and the commander in chief who might have to send them into harm's way.

When his prayers were answered late Sunday, Clinton once again found himself indebted to Carter, who had rescued him from a possible confrontation with North Korea in June.

As Carter boarded the plane, which left Haiti at 8:37 P.M. ET, his relaxed expression told the story: He had succeeded.

Carter and his delegation will be heroes of the averted almost-war, but Clinton, too, will be credited for avoiding a conflict that polls showed most of the public did not want.

"Credit should be given in the sense that the situation never really did warrant a military intervention," said Walter Kansteiner, a National Security Council official in the Bush administration. "It should have always been a diplomatic initiative. It's 11th hour, but better late than never."

A week ago, Clinton made up his mind that he would invade Haiti this week if the military dictators had not left. Thursday night, he emphatically told the nation from the Oval Office there was no turning back.

The extraordinary detail of public disclosure of troop mobilizations and movements was designed to telegraph to Cédras that this was no bluff.

But, White House advisers say, Carter was eager to try his hand at another diplomatic rescue, and Cédras had sent word that he was eager to talk.

The White House had turned down Carter only days earlier, but late Thursday Clinton and his top aides decided they had to take one last shot at a peaceful solution to the crisis.

When Clinton agreed reluctantly to dispatch Carter, he decided to make him part of a high-powered triumvirate:

- Powell was tapped for the mission because of his military résumé. Even out of uniform, he would remind Cédras of the awesome might the U.S. military had amassed offshore and its ability to destroy the Haitian army.
- Nunn was chosen to embody Congress' support for the military operation, if not for Clinton's Haiti policies.

Late Sunday, after praising their success, Secretary of State Warren Christopher called the trio "the perfect combination."

The administration flanked Carter with Nunn and Powell, says retired Adm. Eugene Carroll, deputy director of the Center for Defense Information, "to convey to Cédras that there's no accommodation and no compromise."

Carter's instructions were adamant: discuss with Cédras only the timetable for their departure from Haiti, what kind of plane they wanted to travel on and where they wanted to go.

The former president, who during his diplomatic foray to North Korea demonstrated a penchant for discussing progress with CNN, also was asked to keep quiet about his talks in Haiti.

Carter and the delegation had a formal, mostly unproductive three-hour meeting early Saturday, then made an unscheduled late-night visit to army headquarters for a meeting that lasted until 2 A.M. Sunday.

Carter was tight-lipped about the meetings, saying only, "We're doing the best we can."

Cédras held out for Aristide's immediate resignation and took a hard line, saying he'd step down but wouldn't leave.

Clinton spoke twice with Carter on Saturday, each time reinforcing the narrow scope the former president was allowed to discuss with Cédras. At 7:30 A.M. Sunday, Clinton met in the Oval Office with top aides, then waited for the phone to ring.

Powell called at midday with a pessimistic update, and after that the hours stretched on and on.

Clinton and the rest of his aides monitored news updates on TV, and Carter and Powell called directly into the Oval Office several times, seeking Clinton's direction as they hammered out the deal. In late afternoon, Clinton authorized the delegation to tell Cédras that the invasion was about to begin.

That's when things began to change.

In mid-evening, the call came that Cédras had agreed to leave. Clinton grinned broadly, aides say. Relief was palpable.

Critics still worry about the implications of sending U.S. troops into Haiti to ensure a peaceful change of government.

"Once we get entangled, we get entangled," Rep. Goss said. "The president appears absolutely committed to throwing us into this briar patch. The only issue is whether we go in with our weapons holstered or cocked."

Contributing: Lee Michael Katz, Juan Walte.

What dictators agreed to do:

U.S.-led troops will be in Haiti to oversee the government transition. Under the agreement reached Sunday:

- Haiti's military coup leaders will leave power as soon as parliament passes an amnesty law to protect them and their supporters—but no later than Oct. 15.
- Exiled President Jean-Bertrand Aristide returns "when the dictators depart."
- Legislative elections will go forward on schedule in December.
- The economic embargo will be lifted.

Says Aristide spokesman Jean Claude Martineau: "Let's hope what we expect will happen, will happen."

Of the three-man junta:

- Haitian army chief Philippe Biamby must give up his authority.
- Biamby and Lt. Gen. Raoul Cédras are not required to leave Haiti, but are expected to do so.
- Police chief Michel François, who boycotted the negotiations, loses his post.

Cédras has reneged on other agreements to depart, most recently Oct. 30, 1993.

## AN ANONYMOUS REPORT: "TROOPS BEGIN LANDING IN HAITI"

*This uncredited wire service story from Haiti, which was part of a series of stories dispatched that day, would have been widely published and contributed to the American public knowing some firsthand details as the day's events unfolded.*

United Press International, 19 September 1994

PORT-AU-PRINCE: American troops began landing in Port-au-Prince Monday as part of a multinational peacekeeping force that will ensure Haiti's military leaders keep their word to step down from power.

The first soldiers stepped from 10 helicopters that landed on an airfield in the Haitian capital at around 9:30 A.M. EDT/1:30 P.M. GMT to begin the process to restore exiled Haitian President Jean-Bertrand Aristide to power.

U.S. Maj. Gen. David Meade, one of the first of U.S. troops to land in Haiti, said the troops had not experienced trouble. "We haven't seen any resistance and we haven't experienced any," Meade told CNN after the first wave of helicopters flew to the airfield from a command ship in the Haitian port.

The helicopters were greeted by a number of journalists. U.S. mission commander Gen. Henry Shelton arrived a short time later and was mobbed by reporters. He planned to meet with Haitian military leader Lt. Gen. Raoul Cédras.

U.S. officials said the U.N.-sanctioned military operation was expected to prepare the way for international police teams following the announcement that Haiti's military leaders would abdicate their offices by Oct. 15 and cooperate with the 15,000 coalition troops that began landing Monday.

Haiti's military leaders agreed Sunday night to give up power by Oct. 15 under an 11th-hour arrangement brokered by former President Jimmy Carter and his team of retired Gen. Colin Powell and Sen. Sam Nunn, D-Ga., after 61 American planes carrying troops already were en route to Haiti.

President Clinton announced the agreement. "The dictators have recognized that it is in their best interest . . . to relinquish power peacefully rather than to face imminent action by the forces of the multinational forces we are leading."

Clinton said in a nationally broadcast statement, "This is a good agreement for the United States and for Haiti." Under terms of the agreement, Cédras and Brig. Gen. Philippe Biamby, the Haitian army's chief of staff, agreed to step down. The third member of the ruling military troika, police chief Lt. Col. Michel François, refused to sign the accord and reportedly went into hiding.

But U.S. Secretary of State Warren Christopher told reporters in Washington that François' position "is sufficiently eroded in Haiti" that he did not pose a threat. When the 11th-hour agreement was reached, 61 U.S. warplanes were already in the air and headed for Haiti.

Urging his countrymen to "maintain calm," acting President Emile Jonassaint went on Haitian television early Monday to announce that the military regime had agreed to step down. Jonassaint painted himself and Cédras, leader of the coup that ousted Aristide in September 1991, as martyrs who were taking a heroic step to save Haiti.

Jonassaint said the leaders would leave by Oct. 15, after the Haitian Congress passes a general amnesty. Although the military leaders' resignation would clear the way for the return of Aristide, Jonassaint did not mention the exiled president in his speech.

However, he said the accord would lead to the immediate lifting of the U.N. economic embargo that has crippled the already impoverished Caribbean nation, the poorest country in the Western Hemisphere. Human rights workers said there was great confusion among ordinary citizens in Port-au-Prince, where different versions of the accord were being circulated.

Under terms of the agreement, Cédras and Brig. Gen. Philippe Biamby, the Haitian army's chief of staff, agreed to step down. The third member of the ruling military troika, police chief Lt. Col. Michel François, refused to sign the accord and reportedly went into hiding. But U.S. Secretary of State Warren Christopher told reporters in Washington that François' position was "sufficiently eroded" so that he did not pose a threat.

Acting President Emile Jonassaint, urging his countrymen to "maintain calm," announced the agreement on Haitian television early Monday and said the military regime had agreed to step down to save the Caribbean nation from "annihilation."

Although the military leaders' resignation would clear the way for the return of Aristide, Jonassaint did not mention the exiled president in his speech. However, he said the accord would lead to the immediate lifting of the U.N. economic embargo that has crippled impoverished Haiti, the poorest country in the Western Hemisphere.

Human rights workers said there was great confusion among ordinary citizens in Port-au-Prince, where different versions of the accord were being circulated. Nevertheless, the streets of the capital were calm Monday and citizens went about their everyday tasks as U.S troops began arriving.

Markets opened as usual and students lined up in downtown streets to take high school entrance exams, although many Port-au-Prince residents flocked to the airport to watch the Americans arrive.

"Many people are very satisfied to see the arrival of these troops," said businessman Pierre Fernandez. "The Haitian people believe they are here to give the country peace."

Not everyone was happy to see the U.S. troops arrive, and some Haitians expressed fear over the impending return of Aristide. "I never knew why they (the United Nations) im-posed the embargo," said Marie Rose Bousquet, one of the spectators who gathered at the airport. "I won't be happy to see Aristide come back, I think he's going to burn houses." (with additional reporting by Bryan Sierra at the Pentagon)

*Credit*: Reprinted by permission of UPI.

## ARMANDO TRULL AND PHILLIP GORTON SMUCKER: HAITIANS WATCH AS U.S. MISSION BEGINS

*This second story would have also been widely published. It reported the humanitarian aspects of the mission in Haiti.*

United Press International, 19 September 1994

PORT-AU-PRINCE: Crowds of Haitians too young to re-member the U.S. departure and the earlier promise of democ-racy six decades ago gathered in great numbers at the island's airports and seaports to watch as operation "Uphold Democracy" got under way Monday.

Some 5,000 men, women and children stood in the debris-filled air stirred by the turbulence of the arriving aircraft and watched the arrival of the U.S. peacekeepers and their sup-plies. Fascinated by the huge helicopters, uniforms and equipment, the crowd climbed trees and walls and sat on the rooftops of nearby buildings to catch a glimpse of "les Amer-icans" in an impromptu carnival that included vendors hawking sugar cane, drinks and cigarettes.

Shortly after the first squad of the U.S. 10th Mountain Di-vision landed at the airport and deployed, Emile Renoire ap-proached a heavily armed serviceman and asked, "Are you here to help the Haitian people?" U.S. Army Pvt. Jimmy Cherry answered, "Yes I am." Renoir continued, "Do you love the Haitian people?" To which the soldier replied, "I love all peoples."

When asked for his opinion, Eves Pierre said, "I am happy and also proud to find that the Americans are here to help the political situation."

Unemployed mechanic Claude Marie Lucas added, "I been robbed and beaten by my enemies, so I am very pleased to see the Americans come. We hope this will mean the end of violence."

Elsewhere the crowd was more reserved as it stood oppo-site fences that surrounded machine gun nests where U.S. soldiers perched. The GIs and Haitians often communicated through a mixture of gestures and laughter.

But the generally light mood didn't completely assuage the fears of some Haitians. "We will feel much safer once the peacekeepers are actually on the streets of the city," said a man who asked not to be identified.

The day didn't end with tired participants gradually, qui-etly going home. Instead it ended abruptly.

A contingent of the crowd that had watched and waved at Americans all day began to chant pro-Aristide slogans in Creole. But 10 policemen and several uniformed parami-litary troops decided they had had enough.

Within sight of the U.S. troops, the men began to threaten and then hit the people with the butts of their rifles until they had chased away a substantial number of the chanters.

Someone cried out to the U.S. forces no more than 40 feet away, "Why aren't they doing anything?" But there was no response.

*Credit*: Reprinted by permission of UPI.

## SID BALMAN JR.: "WASHINGTON NEWS"—HUMANITARIAN INTERVENTION IN HAITI

*This third wire service story is an example of the media reports that drove home the humanitarian point of the intervention.*

United Press International, 19 September 1994

WASHINGTON: The Rev. Jean Marie Vincent won't have a chance to comment on the deal President Clinton struck with Haiti's military dictators that provides for their "honor-able" departure from power next month. He's dead.

Haitian security forces silenced Vincent, 49, a Roman Catholic priest—who once shielded President Jean-Bertrand Aristide from assassins with his own body—with a hail of gunfire in Port-au-Prince Aug. 28.

There are at least 3,000 Haitians who the ruling junta's security forces have put to death for a variety of reasons: for supporting Aristide, for appearing to support Aristide or for merely being in the wrong place at the wrong time.

President Clinton spoke to the nation Sept. 15 of those unfortunate souls—and uncounted thousands raped or mutilated by the regime's forces during their three-year reign of terror—as one justification for a U.S. invasion.

The State Department reinforced that message the same day by releasing an eight-page report on escalating human rights abuse in Haiti. U.S. officials said providing the American public with a graphic description of the abuses would be a key factor in convincing them military action was necessary.

Clinton also said the United States must shore up its international credibility, protect its borders and promote democracy in the Western Hemisphere by restoring Aristide to power.

Clinton said achieving those objectives depended on attacking the cancer that Haiti's government had become and removing Lt. Gen. Raoul Cédras, military Chief of Staff Brig. Gen. Phillipe Biamby and security chief Lt. Col. Michel François.

"Gen. Cédras and his accomplices alone are responsible for this suffering and terrible human tragedy," Clinton said. "Cédras and his armed thugs have conducted a reign of terror, executing children, raping women, and killing priests.

"The terror, the desperation and the instability will not end until they leave. The message of the United States to the Haitian dictators is clear: Your time is up."

Numerous U.S. officials, including Deputy Secretary of State Strobe Talbott and Deputy Defense Secretary John Deutch, said Cédras and his aides would be apprehended then turned over to Aristide for punishment if they did not flee by the time U.S.-led forces arrived.

But all that changed once Clinton sent former President Jimmy Carter, Senate Armed Services Committee Chairman Sam Nunn, D-Ga., and former Chairman of the Joint Chiefs of Staff Gen. Colin Powell to Port-au-Prince for a last-ditch diplomatic effort.

As planeloads of crack paratroops were winging their way to Haiti, Carter's team managed to convince the de-facto leaders to leave power. U.S. officials said they were told they could remain in Haiti.

It was a diplomatic tour de force for the Clinton administration, officials said. Powell even pulled Cédras's wife aside at one particularly sensitive point in the talks and convinced her that relinquishing power and upholding past agreements was the only "honorable course" for her husband, they said.

It is a disturbing image. The U.S. general who brought down Iraqi President Saddam Hussein during the Persian Gulf war on bended knee, so to speak, before the first lady of terror in Haiti, appealing to her sense of honor and duty.

"The role I may have played with some effect is to appeal to their sense of honor and to appeal to their sense of what is right and what is wrong," Powell said at a White House news conference Monday.

Powell, Carter and Nunn also persuaded Clinton, who had ruled out any further negotiations unless they dealt with the details of the rulers' departure, to reverse major elements of his approach.

Clinton agreed that Cédras, Biamby and François could stay in power one more month and remain in the country afterwards without fear of arrest. Most importantly, the president said U.S. forces would work together with the repressive regime in managing the transition to power.

U.S. officials said Clinton was convinced to accept the compromise since it allowed him to have 15,000 troops land in Haiti without a fight. Once those soldiers were on the ground, they said, Clinton would be able to call the shots.

"One reason we are now modulating what we say is the big stick is there and we can talk a little softly," a senior U.S. official involved in all aspects of the Haiti strategy told reporters under conditions of anonymity.

Carter even told CNN Monday that the Clinton administration would look to Haitian troops, believed to have carried out a large share of the abuses, to quell unrest should it arise. He said a strategy of keeping blood off the hands of U.S. troops would keep them in the good graces of Haitian citizens.

Clinton justified his new alliance with the de-facto leaders—who he earlier described as the personification of evil—saying the agreement achieved the overall objectives in a way that minimized the loss of American life.

And in a subtle but significant change, Clinton indicated Cédras and his aides may not have been entirely responsible for much of the human rights abuse. "I don't take back anything I say about what has happened there in the last three years and the absence of any effort by the authorities to stop it, and sometimes some direct responsibility for it," Clinton said during the White House appearance with Powell, Carter and Nunn.

The president said amnesty for Cédras, Biamby and François was part of a pact signed last year in which they agreed to cede power. U.S. officials could not explain why the Governor's Island accord suddenly came back into force after State Department spokesman Michael McCurry said only last week that the agreement was now "moot" since the ruling junta had refused to honor it.

*Credit*: Reprinted by permission of UPI.

# KEVIN FEDARKO, REPORTED BY SAM ALLIS AND BERNARD DIEDERICH/PORT-AU-PRINCE AND MICHAEL DUFFY, J.F.O. McALLISTER, AND MARK THOMPSON/WASHINGTON: CLINTON PREPARES NATION FOR WAR IN HAITI

*Though this national newsmagazine story was published before the invasion of U.S. troops into Haiti, it focused on the dynamics of the political situation that seemed to be melting into a military situation as the nation watched each day. This inevitability was found in many of the analysis reports in all media formats during the weeks preceding the intervention.*

*Time*, 19 September 1994

Normally, senior aides to Bill Clinton do not speak with frankness about the roles, missions and vital interests at stake in Haiti. But last week they were all eagerly making themselves available to deliver one message: that, as an official put it, "there comes a point where it has to be clear that the U.S. means what it says."

The word has not yet got through to Port-au-Prince. Haiti's military junta called its supporters into the streets for what has become a familiar ritual of taunting the U.S. While onlookers sipped rum, 3,000 demonstrators screamed slogans into the microphones of foreign television crews and painted voodoo hexes on the crosswalk to hobble U.S. invaders when they arrive. As an expression of the diplomacy-of-defiance that constitutes Haiti's foreign policy, it provided a crude but telling glimpse of what Lieut. General Raoul Cédras thinks of Clinton's threats to topple him and his henchmen.

For weeks it has seemed that Cédras' contempt for the U.S. was matched only by the Clinton Administration's ambivalence over whether the Haitian leader could be shoved from power by force of argument or force of arms. Last week senior Administration officials staked out policy positions far in front of a President who has not yet made up his mind. "One way or another, the de facto government is going to be leaving," declared Secretary of State Warren Christopher. "Their days are definitely numbered."

From the corridors of the White House to the State Department to the Pentagon, officials insisted the debate was no longer about whether the U.S. would "forcibly enter" Haiti, but how and when. The flurry of highly public military preparations, said a White House official, "means we're going into an operational stage." When pressed, all these officials admitted Clinton had not set a date for invasion—although Sept. 20, according to sources in the Pentagon, is looming as a likely deadline. "If the President doesn't invade," said another official, "he's going to be hurting. There's a sense of inevitability that it's going to happen."

To make that message convincing, the White House team moved on a broader, bolder front than ever before. Just after Clinton returned from his 12-day vacation on Martha's Vineyard, he sat down to discuss Haiti with his senior foreign-policy advisers. While the President gave no final go-ahead, the issues on the table boiled down to tactics: how to handle Congress; whether to set a public deadline for invasion; and who—if anyone—should be sent to deliver to the Haitian government a "drop-dead date" by which it must step down or be kicked out.

In part, the highly visible and carefully choreographed mobilization is designed to make the threat of invasion so real that the real invasion will not be necessary. Its assertive rhetoric notwithstanding, the White House still fervently hopes the junta will believe the warnings and voluntarily call it quits. Late last week some Administration officials suggested that Cédras and his cronies may finally be realizing the seriousness of their predicament. Asked to describe evidence for this, a White House aide refused to elaborate but hinted that recent intelligence reports indicated a shift in tone among the Haitian leaders based on "how they are talking among themselves." In Port-au-Prince, a Haitian political analyst scoffed at the idea. "There has been too much bluffing, too many mixed signals in the history of this crisis," he said, "to believe the Clinton Administration is really serious about ending this."

While the beating of war drums is intended to intimidate Haiti's leaders, it is also meant to prepare the two groups Clinton must enlist before sending U.S. troops into battle: Congress and the American people. To convince the country that returning Aristide to power is worth spilling American blood, advisers told Clinton he needs to spell out the U.S. vital interests at stake, preferably in a TV speech this week.

A top official laid out four basic points Clinton would make. First, he would stress—without a trace of irony—that the U.S. must follow through on its repeated public threats of invasion to preserve "American credibility." Second, Clinton would lay out human-rights abuses in Haiti. "Bodies are found every day in gullies," said the official. The President will make it clear that "there is a different standard for savagery next door than brutality on the other side of town."

Then Clinton would explain that he has exhausted all peaceful means of resolving the conflict. The U.S. has tried—and failed—to dislodge the junta through negotiations and through economic sanctions whose effect on the Haitian poor now borders "on cruelty." Finally, the official said, the President would argue that the U.S. can no longer accept a situation in Haiti that contributes to the disastrous explosion of refugees from the Caribbean.

While Clinton realizes he needs to court public support, he does not intend to seek explicit congressional approval. Lawmakers do not seem sufficiently united to block an invasion, but Republicans can be counted on to criticize the President. They are already charging that an invasion is just a political stunt timed to boost the Democrats' sagging electoral fortunes. In fact, what most Congressmen really want, says a Capitol Hill staff member, "is to be consulted, but let Clinton take the heat." Beginning Monday, the Administration's national-security officials will launch a sortie on Capitol Hill to brief key lawmakers.

The Defense Department scrambled all week to position the military for action. In Puerto Rico, troops began warm-up maneuvers. Deputy Defense Secretary John Deutch ordered seven huge cargo ships out of mothballs; a day later, he activated five more supply vessels. They are expected to set sail this week to transport weapons and materiel for the Army's 10th Mountain Division, which will play a key part in the postinvasion peacekeeping force. On Friday, Pentagon officials said that the aircraft carrier Dwight D. Eisenhower will pull into its berth in Norfolk, Virginia, this week and begin replacing its planes with 70 helicopters, which can more easily land troops in Haiti. By late this week, the Ike and the U.S.S. Mount Whitney, which will serve as the invasion's command vessel, will leave for the Caribbean. Both ships should be in place by early next week.

Although the Pentagon has long insisted its troops would meet little resistance from the 7,000-man Haitian army, spokesmen indicated the total invasion force will probably consist of 20,000 U.S. troops, an overwhelming force intended to minimize casualties. Nearly half would be slated for peacekeeping, once returning President Jean-Bertrand Aristide settles in. Only about 13,000 are expected to actually invade Haiti, led by 1,800 Marines, who will storm Port-au-Prince to secure the airport and the U.S. embassy and then await reinforcements. The entire operation will be commanded by Admiral Paul D. Miller, a hard-charging, innovative officer. While Miller says he is "ready for whatever mission we're given," he concedes that it will not be "a one-day problem."

For that reason, Administration officials are at pains to lay out their plans for the days after the initial attack. As tensions heightened, William Gray III, Clinton's special envoy on Haiti, brought General John Shalikashvili, Chairman of the Joint Chiefs of Staff, together with Aristide for a 90-minute meeting on Tuesday, when details of the invasion were discussed. The U.S. also began enlisting Haitian refugees from Guantanamo to participate in an interim police force that would step in to replace the Haitian army and restore order. A token force of about 300 troops from eight Caribbean nations would then join a larger international peacekeeping force that would quickly replace U.S. units and train a permanent new Haitian security force. "The military mission is to restore democratic processes," says a senior U.S. official. "But we're not going in there to do nation building. This is not a 20-year exercise."

In the end, it may no longer matter whether Clinton succeeds this week in persuading Americans to support him in his venture. For better or worse, the President has drawn a line from which he can no longer retreat, and which points inexorably toward war. There is now only one person who can change that: Raoul Cédras.

---

## JOSEPH MALLIA: FOR SLAIN VICTIM'S HAITIAN KIN, TEARS AND LOSS OF HOPE

*As the worst of America's fears seemed to be melting away with glimmers of success in Haiti, stories like the following one were found, localizing the story for American readers.*

*Boston Herald*, 28 September 1994

PORT-AU-PRINCE, Haiti—Sitting on the front porch of her family's tiny but neatly kept home near Port-au-Prince Bay, Nadine Maignant wept for her father, who was slain Monday in Boston.

"I feel like it was me who died. I had no one but my father to help me. It was him who paid for school, the rent, the food—everything," said the daughter, who was dressed in a pair of black denim jeans her father had sent her.

She had hoped that one day her father would bring her to the United States, where she wants to study to become a doctor.

Jacques Maignant—who used the alias of Jacques Fritz Bruno while in the United States—was shot dead when he surprised three armed men who were robbing $15,000 in cash from his roommates. Maignant, 49, and his roommates made a living running a small-time gambling operation in their apartment.

Maignant had left his wife and four children behind seven years ago in Haiti, leaving to look for work in the United States so he could provide them food and shelter. His oldest son, Roody, later joined him in Massachusetts.

Nadine, 22, said she was stunned when Roody called with the news that her father had been shot in the heart. She said she never expected that he might be in greater danger in the United States than in Haiti, where thousands of American troops were forcing an end to a military dictatorship.

Yesterday morning, Nadine showed a visitor clothing, shoes and a portable cassette player her father had sent her.

And Maignant's wife, Marie Marthe Baine, said he sent $200 to $300 a month whenever he could to support Nadine, along with his daughter Rosaline, 15, and his son, Kisinger, 17.

"He was always good to us. He always took responsibility for his children," said Baine, who wore a tattered denim dress and scuffed sandals.

"He wanted to help us, but he couldn't find work here so he was obliged to go to New York," she said.

After a short time in New York, Maignant went to Boston, Baine said.

Maignant paid the $230 annual rent on their three-room house, along with the $5-a-month electricity bills, and $6-a-month water bills.

His remittances lifted the family out of poverty. If not for him, they would have been consigned to the slums where most of the Haitian poor live—an entire family in a one-room shack with no running water and open sewers running along the alleys.

Now the family fears they'll lose their house, with its thick concrete walls that keep out much of the noise from passing traffic, and shabby blue and red curtains that stop some of the dust.

Nadine said she had not slept since her brother in Massachusetts called her brother in Haiti Monday with the horrible news.

"I didn't have the courage to sleep. I'm afraid of nightmares," she said.

Nadine said her father was to be buried today in Boston. Because the commercial embargo against Haiti hasn't yet been lifted, none of the family in Haiti will be allowed to attend the funeral because they cannot get a commercial airflight.

"That makes me so sad, because I'll never see my father again," she said.

Jacques Maignant's mother is dead, but his father, Luc Maignant, is a Haitian army soldier. And he has a sister and brother, Gladys and Ricot Laguerre, living in Massachusetts, Nadine said.

The daughter was supposed to begin her final year of college preparatory school in October, but now she knows she won't be able to attend.

"Now I have no hope at all."

*Credit:* Reprinted with permission of the Boston Herald.

---

## ANNE-MARIE O'CONNOR: U.S. SOLDIERS' SHIFTING ROLES IN HAITI

*This wire service story was published across the nation, from the* Dayton *(Ohio)* Daily News *to the* Austin *(Texas)* Statesman-American. *It was the kind of update story that was becoming a theme among American readers who wanted to know when the mission would be over, and when the troops were coming home as Thanksgiving loomed and Christmas was soon to follow.*

### Cox News Service, 28 September 1994

PORT-AU-PRINCE, HAITI: The American soldiers gingerly cradled the Haitian teen-ager in their arms as they carried him into the hospital in the central port town of Gonaïves. They tried not to exacerbate the searing pain emanating from the wounds in his groin inflicted by pro-army militants with razor blades.

A U.S. patrol rushed to the town's cemetery after the recent attack looking for the boy's assailants, who were reported hiding among the pastel mausoleums.

Out in the hot, dusty streets of Gonaïves, meanwhile, U.S. Special Forces were conducting joint patrols with Haitian security forces and holding back crowds of civilians, emboldened enough by the American presence to vent their anger at past human-rights abuses by the military regime and its supporters.

It was a day that has become increasingly typical for the U.S. forces in Haiti—a bewildering mix of humanitarian, police and military work in which the line between friend and foe shifts from hour to hour.

As they spread throughout Haiti, U.S. soldiers find themselves freeing political prisoners, buying back guns, guarding prominent politicians, securing government buildings and trying to maintain order. They are doing it even if, as in last weekend's deadly shootout in Cap Haitien that left 10 Haitians dead, they decide that merits deadly force.

Their role is clouded by ambiguities. They are expected to prevent violence yet initially they were barred from assuming full peacekeeping duties. They are to work together with Haitian military forces yet prevent them from hurting unarmed civilians.

"We're cooperating with the people we were supposed to be fighting against. It's pretty weird," said Pfc. Robert Luiz, 22, of the 10th Mountain Division at Fort Drum, N.Y. "We're working with the army, but we're supposed to stop them if they beat up civilians. It's a real fine line. It's got to come to a head sooner or later."

As the U.S. occupation of Haiti, now numbering more

than 15,600 troops, moves through its second week, there is some satisfaction at how smoothly the mission has proceeded.

The outpouring of support for the Americans among the Haitian people has been overwhelming. The only U.S. casualty has been a soldier who died Tuesday of a gunshot wound that officials believe was self-inflicted.

Yet, U.S. officials are expressing concern over "mission creep"—that they find their role slowly expanding beyond the original goal of restoring the democratically elected government.

In parts of northern Haiti, many authorities have simply withdrawn and left the Americans in control. In Port-au-Prince, American soldiers increasingly find themselves doing even routine police work.

"We're dazed and confused," said Sgt. Ed Collins, 28, from Canton, Ohio. "We don't really know what is going on."

Pfc. Luiz, a Boston native and a veteran of Somalia, a country still mired in violence long after the withdrawal of U.S. peacekeeping forces, said he feared American forces might not achieve lasting peace in Haiti, either.

*Credit*: Reprinted with permission of Cox News Service.

## TOM SQUITIERI AND JACK KELLEY: "HAITIAN LAWMAKERS FACE TOUCHY AMNESTY ISSUE"

*This is an example of the kind of story that ran in newspapers across the country reporting the kinds of problems that the negotiated peace seemed to be causing. All had not gone perfectly, and much of the American public wondered if the Haitians were ready for democracy.*

### USA Today, 28 September 1994

PORT-AU-PRINCE, Haiti: With exiled members flown in from the USA and U.S. soldiers guarding the door, Haiti's parliament convenes today to consider amnesty for Lt. Gen. Raoul Cédras and his top aides.

The issue before the lawmakers is how broad to make the amnesty, a pre-condition to the return of exiled President Jean-Bertrand Aristide.

Many of Aristide's supporters are willing to vote for amnesty for those taking part in the 1991 coup that deposed him, shielding coup plotters from prosecution.

But these lawmakers oppose amnesty for so-called "blood crimes," murders, mutilation and rapes that characterized Haiti's post-coup reign.

Instead, many hope that Cédras, who will be in attendance, will be forced to step down without amnesty by Oct. 15, leaving him open to court prosecution and making more likely his exodus from Haiti.

Officials face another unexpected and potentially explosive political dilemma. If Aristide is returned to office, his legal successor in event of death will be the man who currently, and illegally, is president of Haiti.

Emil Jonassaint, installed as president by the Cédras military government last May, is still legally chief justice of Haiti's Supreme Court. He is in line to become president of Haiti, should Aristide resign or die while in office.

"It could be a dilemma," U.S. Embassy spokesman Stan Schrager said Tuesday. He said this was not expected by U.S. planners.

U.S. officials were also surprised when a highly publicized U.S. effort to get guns off the street got off to a slow start.

Only seven weapons, most of them old and nearly inopera-

ble, were turned over to the U.S. Army in the first day of a U.S.-sponsored "cash for guns" sale.

Soldiers hoped to reduce the threat of violence before Aristide's return. Haitian officials estimate there are 200,000 handguns in Port-au-Prince alone.

But only four handguns, two World War II vintage rifles, and a 9mm pistol were handed over. U.S. forces pay $50 for handguns, $300 for heavy weapons.

"U.S. schools taught me the basics of supply and demand," said construction company owner Christoph Deplagani, 48, who decided to keep his two handguns. "Maybe they can teach the army the same thing. They're fools to think we're going to give up our guns."

Meanwhile:

- Pentagon and State Department officials told House members the U.S. mission in Haiti will cost $1 billion.

With Congress threatening to set a date for withdrawal of U.S. troops, the House Foreign Affairs Committee today considers a bill calling for a March 1 withdrawal. The Clinton administration has urged Congress not to tie the military's hands.

But Rep. Robert Torricelli, D-N.J., speaking for many lawmakers, criticized the White House for not seeking congressional approval in the first place: "The lives of our forces have been used as a shield to defend against the shrinking of the constitutional process."

- An unidentified U.S. soldier apparently committed suicide with a gunshot to the head, the first U.S. casualty of the eight-day-old intervention.

- About 2,000 people rioted at a feeding center in central Port-au-Prince. U.S. military police drove up and the rioters fled. The soldiers remained a few minutes, then pulled away and the looting resumed.

Contributing: Jessica Lee

*Credit*: From USA TODAY, a division of Gannett Co., Inc. Reprinted with Permission.

## MICHAEL NORTON: "U.S. TROOPS BEGIN WITHDRAWAL FROM HAITI"

*Reestablishing the government in Haiti took longer than most Americans had expected. It was more than a year after the troops had landed before they began to return home. This wire service report is an example of the kind of story that reminded U.S. readers how long it had all taken.*

### Associated Press, 6 January 1996

PORT-AU-PRINCE, Haiti: Fifteen months after leading a multinational force into Haiti to restore democracy, the United States has begun withdrawing the last of its troops from the still-troubled country.

Thanking them for a job well done, U.S. Gen. Joseph Kinzer, commander of the U.N. military mission, said goodbye at the Port-au-Prince airport Friday to 66 soldiers of the 5th Special Operations Group of Fort Campbell, Ky.

"God bless you," Kinzer said, before shaking hands with each soldier.

The soldiers were the first to leave under the phased final pullout. About 2,200 U.S. troops remain in Haiti, part of a 5,800-member U.N. peacekeeping force that is scheduled to leave by Feb. 29.

The next contingent of U.S. soldiers to leave will be several hundred troops with the 46th Engineering Battalion at Fort Polk, La. They depart Wednesday.

President Clinton's pledge to pull U.S. troops out of Bosnia after a year has dampened speculation that American soldiers will extend their stay in Haiti to help its new police force maintain law and order.

"This represents the beginning of the American redeployment to the United States. And they will not be returning," said an army spokesman, Lt. Col. Dave Walker.

Walker said some U.S. logistics soldiers would remain until April to supervise the return of equipment.

On Sept. 19, 1994, a multinational force invaded Haiti and dismantled its army, which had ousted Aristide in a September 1991 coup. As many as 4,000 civilians were killed during military rule.

At its peak, the U.S.-led force had 20,000 troops.

Democratically elected President Jean-Bertrand Aristide returned from exile on Oct. 15, 1994. On March 31, the U.S. led force handed over peacekeeping duty to the U.N. mission.

A new Haitian police force being trained by U.S. and Canadian advisers will take over when the peacekeepers leave. But the police have been accused of using excessive force on several occasions, including shooting unarmed civilians.

In December, Rep. Benjamin Gilman, R-N.Y., chairman of the House Foreign Affairs Committee, froze $5 million in aid for the police training program, saying there was evidence criminals were infiltrating the force. Haitian officials deny the claim.

Robert Gelbard, the State Department's top law enforcement affairs official, told the committee Thursday the program will have to be suspended in mid-January unless the funds are released.

Concerned that he might not be able to prevent unrest, President-elect René Préval has said he might consider asking the United Nations to extend its mandate, which expires at the end of February. Préval takes office Feb. 7.

*Credit*: Reprinted with permission of The Associated Press.

## ANDERSON COOPER: SUMMARY OF U.S. MISSION IN HAITI

*This television report also reminded the viewers how long the effort in Haiti had taken, but further emphasized that it was a job well done and surely worth the effort. This sort of report reflected much of the American view of the last-resort military intervention in Haiti.*

### World News Sunday (ABC), Transcript 609, 3 March 1996

CAROLE SIMPSON: Haiti's new president, René Préval, is scheduled to visit the White House this month. He's coming to show support for President Clinton and his decision to deploy American troops to the Caribbean island to restore democracy. Eighteen months after the troops arrived, they're getting ready to come home. Canadian troops will now be in charge of keeping the peace.

As ABC's Anderson Cooper found out, American troops will come back maybe a little bit wiser, but also a little bit sadder.

ANDERSON COOPER, ABC News: [voice-over] You don't see American soldiers in Port-au-Prince anymore. They're packing up, shipping out. Everyone here knows it. To find them, you drive through streets choked with traffic, crowded with people—Port-au-Prince at night. You arrive at a dusty base by the airport, a sprawl of tents, all greens and black, where Haitian children beg for something, anything, and where Private Jennifer Gibbons [sp?] counts the days until she can leave.

Pvt. JENNIFER GIBBONS: It's sad to see the kids having to grow up like that, but I mean, what can we do to help them?

ANDERSON COOPER: [voice-over] Private Gibbons grew up in Ohio, and had never been outside the United States before coming to Haiti five months ago. She was overwhelmed by the poverty, changed by the things she saw.

Pvt. JENNIFER GIBBONS: There's certain things that I'll never forget that I've seen down here, like the dead man I seen laying in the street one day. He was laying out in the road like this, with his feet tied together, and he was all dusty, and his head was all banged up, and he had machete cuts all on his arms and his sides, and on his legs.

I'm not shocked by it anymore, I'm not surprised by it anymore, but you know, I notice it, and it—it still—umh, that's what it does to me, umh, my God.

ANDERSON COOPER: [voice-over] For months, the 3rd Platoon has patrolled this city, stars and stripes and blue berets and white Humvees, gun-toting peacekeepers moving through shadows. Reporting, observing, that was their mission, but riding with them, you knew they were the law here. A Haitian woman is kidnapped, and it's the U.S. Army MP's who search for her, though they think she's probably already dead.

U.S. SOLDIER: Somebody'll probably find her in a week or so.

ANDERSON COOPER: What do you mean?

U.S. SOLDIER: Oh, somebody'll come out one day and find her laying on a trashpile or in a ravine.

ANDERSON COOPER: [voice-over] The U.S. has spent over $20 million building a new Haitian national police force, the HNP. The 3rd Platoon has helped train them, and nightly checks the jails, looking for human rights abuses. The hope is that with experience, the HNP will become self-sufficient, gain the respect of the Haitian people. Then the U.N. peacekeepers can go. But few in the 3rd are optimistic about what will happen when they leave.

2nd U.S. SOLDIER: It's probably gonna' go to hell. I mean, the only reason half the people restrain right now from doing anything to the other half is just 'cause we're down here. Just our presence alone stops most of the stuff.

ANDERSON COOPER: [voice-over] In their off-time, the American soldiers sit by a makeshift pool they call the Santa Monica pier, drinking non-alcoholic beer and talking about home. Specialist Scott Pena married his high-school sweetheart. Now, when he calls home, she says she hears a change in his voice.

Spec. SCOTT PENA: I have never seen—I've never seen poverty like this before in my life. This is—it—my first couple of months down here, I kind of had a hard time trying to take it all in. I mean, I'm a father, I have two children and it changed me as a person, changed the way I thought about people and human life.

ANDERSON COOPER: [voice-over] So the 3rd Platoon is ready to go. Sergeant Christopher Schwartz [sp?] is leaving, proud of his role in restoring democracy in Haiti.

Sgt. CHRISTOPHER SCHWARTZ: We came in here to set these people up to be in charge of their own future. I think it's time for us to go. I think it's time for us to go, let them stand on their own two feet. You know, it's—it's what they need. It's what their country needs.

ANDERSON COOPER: [voice-over] If you've never been to Port-au-Prince before, you may not notice what's changed. Garbage still stretches for blocks, people still struggle to survive, but the American military has accomplished its mission in Haiti, maybe even more than the 3rd Platoon realizes. There's a new president, a new parliament. The 3rd Platoon leaves knowing the rest is up to the Haitian people. They leave wondering if they'll ever have to come back.

*Credit*: Reprinted with permission of ABC News, World News Sunday.

## NOTES

1. NBC News/*Wall Street Journal*, national adult telephone survey of 1,502 respondents, 10 June 1994: "Do you favor or oppose the United States sending troops to Haiti to try to help restore democracy?" Favor sending troops to Haiti: 29 percent: Oppose sending troops to Haiti: 65 percent; Not sure: 6 percent. Survey conducted by Hart and Teeter Research Companies.

2. CBS News/*New York Times*–sponsored national telephone survey of 504 adults: "Over the weekend, the delegation led by former President Jimmy Carter met with the Haitian

military rulers and reached an agreement for U.S. troops to enter Haiti peacefully and for the Haitian military rulers to leave office by October 15, (1994). Do you favor or oppose that agreement?" Favor: 77 percent; Oppose: 15 percent: Do not know/No answer: 8 percent. Respondents in this survey were originally interviewed on 18 September 1994, and were reinterviewed on 19 September after the agreement between the United States and Haitian leaders that they would step down.

## FURTHER READINGS

DiPrizio, Robert C. *Armed Humanitarians: U.S. Interventions from Northern Iraq to Kosovo.* Baltimore: Johns Hopkins University Press, 2002.

Fatton, Robert. *Haiti's Predatory Republic: The Unending Transition to Democracy.* Boulder, Colo.: Lynne Rienner, 2002.

Hendrickson, Ryan C. *The Clinton Wars: The Constitution, Congress, and War Powers.* Nashville: Vanderbilt University Press, 2002.

Rotberg, Robert I. *Haiti's Turmoil: Politics and Policy under Aristide and Clinton.* Cambridge, Mass.: World Peace Foundation, 2003.

Sheller, Mimi. *Democracy after Slavery: Black Publics and Peasant Radicalism in Haiti and Jamaica.* Gainesville: University Press of Florida, 2000.

Soderlund, Walter C. *Mass Media and Foreign Policy: Post–Cold War Crises in the Caribbean.* Westport, Conn.: Praeger, 2003.

Weiss, Thomas G. *Military-Civilian Interactions: Intervening in Humanitarian Crises.* Lanham, Md.: Rowman & Littlefield, 1999.

# 30

## WAR IN BOSNIA-HERZEGOVINA, 1992–1997

On 28 February 1992, Bosnia-Herzegovina declared independence from the former Yugoslav nation-states, which were their neighbors on all sides. Croatia and Slovenia, also former Yugoslav states, had declared their independence in 1991. Although Bosnia-Herzegovina was not the first of the breakaway states in the Balkans, its declaration significantly escalated the hostilities among those who wanted Yugoslavia to remain as closely intact as possible after the disintegration of the Soviet Union. The states that remained as part of the Yugoslav nation were Serbia, Kosovo, and Montenegro. Bosnia-Herzegovina's declaration also antagonized Croats and Serbs who wanted Bosnian lands for their own states.

The region's largest city is Sarajevo, with a population of about 400,000. Sarajevo was designated the capital of the new nation, and the government began organizing itself on a democratic model. The residents of the new nation, and especially those in the new capital, resigned themselves to the prospect of some residual hostilities, but the initial reports from the capital city were encouraging and positive.

Bosnia-Herzegovina, in southeastern Europe on the Balkan Peninsula, was quickly recognized by the United Nations and began to prepare an application to the European Union. It is bordered to the north and west by Croatia, and to the south and east by Serbia and Montenegro. It has a 20-kilometer coastline, between two sections of Croatia, on the Adriatic Sea. Most of the country is mountainous, with wood and coal as primary natural resources. Fish farms dot the nation's many streams and rivers, and there are small herds of livestock among the mountains. About 4 million residents are sprinkled among hundreds of rural villages in 51,129 square kilometers, a land area about the size of West Virginia.

Sarajevo, home to the 1984 Winter Olympics, represented for the Western nations a near-perfect hope of ethnic balance and community harmony when other emerging nations seemed to be struggling with conflict and brutality among dominant and minority groups. The new government soon held elections, but the outcome was seen among other democratic nations as less than optimal. The new officials reflected greater divisions and intractable allegiances of the religious and ethnic groups in dozens of small regions within the new nation's boundaries.

By May of that year, hostile troops surrounded Sarajevo, which is built along a river valley and surrounded by steep hills. All along the border regions there were reports of rebels and hostile troops destroying entire villages. Sarajevo suffered periodic shelling from the hills above it. The airport was shut down, and transportation of goods in and out of the city ceased. Snipers picked off those who tried to move about within the city. Within weeks, portions of the city, like the surrounding country villages, were captured and held by either Serb, Croat, or rebel troops. Both Croats and Serbs took credit and laid blame for the destruction. Eventually the United Nations entered the city in a peacekeeping role. The troops under the U.N. flag were instructed not to fire, even when fired upon.

The next three years were a period of constant struggle for the fledgling democracy, under siege and without reserves or strong central leadership. A series of peace agreements forged in Paris, London, Rome, Bonn, Madrid, Cologne, and Dayton, Ohio, as well as Sarajevo, from 1995 to 2002 eventually were successful in quelling the violence and reestablishing the government there. These documents spelled out a power-sharing arrangement among national Bosnians, Croats, and Serbs. But the international community no longer saw the region as a shining example of post-Communist countries moving decisively into a democratic, capitalist model.

By the end of the twentieth century, much was written about the 1990s war in Bosnia-Herzegovina, but the history of the region begins as early as the Bronze Age. The tribes prospered as shepherds and seamen, metal workers, and textile artisans. The region became an important nexus of trade routes between the East and the West and was conquered by the Romans, who remained in control of the area from the first to the fifth centuries.

After the slow decline of the Romans, there was a long period of self-rule until the Turkish Empire dominated the region from the fifteenth century until the end of the nineteenth century. In 1878, the Austrians gained control of the Balkans. Sarajevo was the site of the 1914 assassination of the Austro-Hungarian archduke Franz Ferdinand that was said to have instigated World War I. During World War II, the region was the site of much bloody and cruel fighting between the Italians, Germans, and local factions.

Among those who prepared analyses of the most recent war in Bosnia-Herzegovina, there was some suggestion that the United States and other Western powers missed an opportunity to help the start-up democracy before the fracturing of the region could take hold:

> The lack of Western effort to support democratic parties in Bosnia and the other former Yugoslav republics represents a missed opportunity for preventive engagement. . . . The opportunity to establish power sharing was lost when the non-nationalists who could have played the role of balancer and mediator were excluded from power. . . . Once the nationalists came to power, Bosnia entered a downward spiral of ethnic conflict that outside actors could have stopped only through intervention.[1]

Most of the news coverage initially focused on the political leaders and diplomacy. The stories were about what each leader said should happen or would happen. Most of the news came from official reports. Few of the stories were about individuals or civilians on the ground in Bosnia-Herzegovina, sometimes spelled with a c rather than a z, during the first year of the conflict.

After the 1992 election of William Jefferson Clinton, the news coverage began to shift. It was clear from campaign speeches during the summer and autumn that the war in Bosnia-Herzegovina was a more important issue to Clinton than to Bush. Clinton said that he intended to commit troops to support a stronger peacekeeping mission in Bosnia-Herzegovina. This signaled to the U.S. press that the war effort was going to receive more attention from the U.S. government after Clinton took office, and so the U.S. media coverage in Bosnia-Herzegovina began to expand soon after a winner in the election was declared in November.

Public opinion on the conflict shifted slightly during the years of seeking a peaceful resolution, but as in other foreign conflicts, the American people did not want too much American involvement. The following are reports of public opinion surveys compiled by Roper Public Opinion Research. Clearly the kind of reporting about the situation had some effect on the public's view of what was happening and what should be happening in Bosnia-Herzegovina under U.S. leadership. Here are the polling results for 1993, 1994, and 1995 during the greatest media attention on the situation, as reported by a variety of news organizations and pollsters.

## 1993

*Question:* As you may know, violence has erupted in the city of Sarajevo and the surrounding area called Bosnia, one of the new republics that used to be part of Yugoslavia. Should the United States do more to stop the war in Sarajevo and Bosnia, or has the United States already done enough?

|  | *United States has done enough to stop the war in Sarajevo and Bosnia* | *Should do more* |
| --- | --- | --- |
| August 1992 | 49 percent | 37 percent |
| January 1993 | 59 percent | 30 percent[2] |

*Question:* Do you favor or oppose the United States sending troops to the former Yugoslavia to try to help stop the civil war there?

| | |
| --- | --- |
| Not sure | 12 percent |
| Favor | 34 percent |
| Do not favor sending U.S. troops to help stop civil war there | 54 percent[3] |

In an August 1992 NBC News/*Wall Street Journal* survey, 33 percent favored sending troops and 54 percent opposed this measure.

*Question:* Please tell me if you support or oppose the following polic[y] in . . . Bosnia. . . .

Support sending the United Nations troops including some U.S. troops to help Bosnians defend themselves against the Serbs: 62 percent.[4]

## 1994

| Sending U.S. Troops to Haiti Was . . . | All | GOP | Dem | Ind | 11/94 |
|---|---|---|---|---|---|
| The right thing | 40% | 35% | 47% | 39% | 41% |
| Should have stayed out | 51% | 57% | 43% | 53% | 52% |
| | | | | | |
| War in Bosnia | All | GOP | Dem | Ind | 11/94 |
| U.S. has responsibility | 28% | 22% | 34% | 28% | 30% |
| U.S. doesn't have responsibility | 65% | 71% | 59% | 66% | 62%[5] |

## 1995

*Those who favor and those who oppose sending U.S. forces as part of an international contingent:* 47 percent to 49 percent.

*Those who believe that Clinton had not adequately explained the rationale for a U.S. military presence in the Balkans:* 58 percent.

*The president should get Congress's approval before dispatching troops:* 79 percent.

*Those who support deployment if assured of no casualties:* 67 percent.

At 25 hypothetical battlefield deaths, only 31 percent would support the Bosnia deployment; at 400 fatalities, support would drop to 21 percent.[6]

What follows are examples of the kind of coverage the war received among the U.S. media. Though the stories tell much of the war's history, other resources listed at the end of the chapter include larger overviews of the region and more recent Web materials that might be useful in understanding the many voices evident in the conflict there. As late as 2005, the internationally imposed government, the Office of the High Representative, set up by a multitude of agreements, was still in place. The selection of a national anthem and flag was still unresolved, and the Office of High Representative was still settling many domestic disputes one at a time.

---

## SYLVIA POGGIOLI: "PEACEKEEPING FORCES LAND IN YUGOSLAVIA"

---

*Sylvia Poggioli is a regular international reporter for National Public Radio. This story, which she reported from Sarajevo, aired on* All Things Considered *very early in the struggle for control of the area. Croatia is the northern neighbor of Bosnia-Herzegovina.*

### All Things Considered (NPR), 16 March 1992

LINDA WERTHEIMER: Today Croatian radio accused the Yugoslav federal army of shelling several villages overnight. Charges of new cease-fire violations come as an advance team of United Nations peacekeeping troops begins scouting areas of Croatia where U.N. forces will be deployed. Several hundred personnel are now on the ground. The total forces will be 14,000 strong, making it one of the largest U.N. operations ever. It will also be one of the most difficult.

NPR's Sylvia Poggioli is in Sarajevo, the capital of the neighboring republic of Bosnia, and has this report.

POGGIOLI: Everyone entering the Holiday Inn in Sarajevo must go through a metal detector. The hotel is temporary headquarters of the first U.N. peacekeeping mission in Europe. The force commander is an Indian, General Satish Nambiar. He says the mission's aim is to ensure peace so a negotiated settlement can be reached.

General SATISH NAMBIAR (U.N. Force Commander): Our main concern is that the two sides facing each other with weapons—we must try and keep them away from each other so that no violence takes place, there is no confrontation between them.

POGGIOLI: Disarming the warring sides will be the troops' toughest task. There are no accurate estimates on the number of Serb and Croatian armed fighters, regulars or irregulars. Before the cease-fire went into effect in January, the number of armed groups proliferated. Political parties and even factions and wealthy businessmen had their own militias in the field.

Despite an international embargo, weapons float in throughout the six-month ethnic war in Croatia. And here in Sarajevo, the black market offers a wide selection of guns and automatic weapons. And grenades are selling for only $20. But General Nambiar has deflected reporters' questions about how the troops will respond if they are attacked. The U.N. mission will be very complex. The forces comprise not only military personnel but also a large contingent of police and civilian administrators who will have to restore order in areas that have plunged into anarchy. U.N. officials say many important details still have to be worked out. It is still not clear what currency, flags and laws will be applied in areas with conflicting national allegiances. Another major concern is the U.N. mission's cost. Fred Eckhard is the U.N. troop spokesman.

FRED ECKHARD (U.N. Troop Spokesman): The problem is that when the price tag was presented to the Security Council, they balked at $634 million, and they said, "OK, start moving in the direction of deployment, but please take a second look on the ground and see if you can come back with better numbers."

POGGIOLI: The high cost of the operation had prompted the U.N. Security Council to stagger the deployment of the contingent, which is expected to be fully deployed by the middle of next month. A total of 24 countries are sending troops, none of them from Yugoslavia's neighboring countries or the United States. But for the first time since 1948, the force will include Russian troops with a battalion 900 strong. The arrival of the advance contingents has been welcomed by the local population. But here in Bosnia, whose population is a mix of Serbs, Croatians and Slavic Muslims, tension has escalated in the last few days. Militias of all three ethnic groups are on guard in their neighborhoods at night. Barricades have been set up in the southern city of Mostar, and the sound of gunfire could be heard in Sarajevo over the weekend.

The U.N. task forces are restricted to Croatia and do not cover Bosnia, but the choice of Sarajevo as command headquarters is not seen as merely symbolic. General Nambiar has told reporters he hopes the troops' presence here will help defuse the situation. This is Sylvia Poggioli in Sarajevo.

---

## AN ANONYMOUS REPORT: "2 BRIDGES BLASTED, TRAPPING BOSNIANS"

---

*This story was probably a wire service story, since there is no byline, and could have been published by any of the news organizations that subscribed to the service. The dateline of Sarajevo suggests that it was contributed by a reporter who was in Bosnia-Herzegovina sometime before 1 May.*

### *St. Louis Post-Dispatch*, 1 May 1992

SARAJEVO, Bosnia-Herzegovina—Masked commandos blew up the last two bridges linking Bosnia-Herzegovina with Croatia, and reports Thursday said at least 10 people had been killed in the explosions.

The bridges, near Brcko, were the only links left to relatively safe haven for thousands of refugees fleeing embattled northeastern Bosnia for Croatia. Meanwhile, fighting eased in Sarajevo between Serb militias seeking to carve off part of the city and Muslim defenders of the Bosnian capital.

Shooting ebbed by daylight, and no new major incidents were reported, leaving Sarajevo more peaceful than it had been for days. Clashes continued elsewhere between Serb forces opposed to Bosnian independence and Slavic Muslims and Croats supporting it.

Three people were killed and seven wounded in Mostar, where federal forces shelled the southwestern city, the Belgrade-based news agency Tanjug reported. About 300 people have been killed and more than 2,000 wounded since Muslims and Croats in Bosnia voted for independence Feb. 29.

Fighting intensified after the state won recognition from the United States and much of Europe on April 7. Commanders of the Serb-dominated federal army refuse to withdraw from Bosnia, where about 100,000 federal troops are helping ethnic Serbs do battle.

The United States and western Europe have threatened sanctions against Serbia if the army and Serbian forces do not quit the ethnically mixed republic.

Greek Premier Constantine Mitsotakis arrived Thursday in Belgrade, Serbia's capital. He was expected to warn Serbian President Slobodan Milosevic of possible EC sanctions.

The Conference on Security and Cooperation in Europe

admitted Bosnia Thursday as its 52nd member. All member nations approved, including a reconstituted Yugoslavia now made up only of Serbia and the tiny republic of Montenegro. All four other former Yugoslav republics, including Slovenia, opted for independence.

On Thursday, three days after its creation, the new Yugo-slavia established border posts with neighboring Croatia, Bosnia and Macedonia. Passports will be needed to cross the borders, Tanjug said.

*Credit*: Reprinted with permission of the St. Louis Post-Dispatch, copyright 1992.

## KIM CHRISTENSEN: IN ORANGE COUNTY, BOSNIANS DESPAIR FOR RELATIVES, FRIENDS IN HOMELAND

*An exception was a story like the following one in the* Orange County Register. *This story was localized for California readers and so was about the U.S. community of Bosnians.*

### Orange County Register, 21 May 1992

His mother is nearly 90 and huddled in a three-bedroom apartment with 20 other people as violence rages around them in Sarajevo, capital of the former Yugoslav republic of Bosnia-Herzegovina. Eric Dvinovic, a Lake Forest jeweler, waits by the phone and wonders whether he will ever see her again.

"It is very bad," Dvinovic said Wednesday. "The snipers are shooting anybody who moves. They are shooting kids, 4 and 5 years old. Nobody is safe there right now. They can't even get the dead people out of the street. Some of them are laying there for two weeks."

Dvinovic, 46, is among a small contingent of Bosnian immigrants living in or near Orange County. They keep in close touch with each other, and with relatives in Europe, hoping for a break in the fighting that has killed more than 2,500 people since the majority of Bosnians voted for independence Feb. 29.

Ethnic Serbs, who comprise about one-third of the population of 4.3 million, favored remaining aligned with neighboring Serbia.

They have been assisted in their violent opposition to independence by the Serb-led Yugoslav federal army.

While thousands of Bosnian refugees have fled to neighboring Croatia, others are trapped in their homes.

"My wife and baby, mother, two sisters and brothers are there," said Muhamed Kavazovic, 42, of Yorba Linda.

He came to the United States five years ago to work in his brother's machine shop in Los Angeles. He has visited his homeland during that time, but was unable to get his wife, Aida, 31, and their daughter, Amra, 4½, out of Bosnia before violence erupted.

Kavazovic said he speaks often with his wife and daughter by telephone, but the conversations do little to ease his concern for their safety.

"I worry all day and all night," he said. "I cannot sleep." Food and medicine are in short supply, and relief convoys have come under fire by the Serbs, according to the International Red Cross and Bosnian officials.

Dvinovic said he and other Bosnian-Americans have been trying to raise money to buy vital non-military supplies. The relief effort is being coordinated by the Red Cross, with help locally from St. Anthony's Catholic Church in Los Angeles, whose members are mostly Croatians.

"My brother said that people don't have anything to eat," Dvinovic said. "They are eating grass. They are going to starve."

In protest of the Yugoslav army's aggression, the United States on Wednesday suspended landing rights for JAT, the national airline. But Dvinovic and other Bosnian-Americans have called for more drastic measures, including sending US troops.

"We need America to stand up for freedom; they have donesobefore," he said. "America says it is for democracy, but it is always backing up the wrong sides."

Croatian-Americans also accused the United States of indifference when their homeland was engulfed in civil war after declaring its independence last year.

Relative peace has since come to Croatia, but Dvinovic and other immigrants said Wednesday they are not optimistic about the short-term prospects for Bosnia.

"I called the White House and someone there said, 'We'll see what we can do,'" said Ann Selimovic, of Anaheim Hills. "But I don't know. The way I see it, the whole world is sitting and watching what is happening to innocent people, and nobody is doing anything."

*Credit*: Reprinted by permission of the Orange County Register, copyright 1992.

## ROLAND PRINZ: "REFUGEES SPEAK OF ATROCITIES; HARD EVIDENCE OFTEN LACKING"

*The American public rarely got firsthand reports of the situation outside of Sarajevo. This Associated Press story is typical of those carried by many newspapers during 1992, the first year of conflict.*

### Associated Press, 23 May 1992

BIJELJINA, Bosnia-Herzegovina: Vidoje Vasilic, a Serb villager in his 60s, says he fled his home when Croatian attackers slaughtered his neighbors.

Pero Jovicic, another Serb fleeing Bosnia's killing fields, recalls seeing the body of a 75-year-old man with multiple cuts on the torso, and that of another man whose head had been smashed.

Just as in the bloody conflict in Croatia, tales abound in Bosnia of cruelty, indiscriminate attacks on civilians and wanton violence. There is little doubt that atrocities are being committed on all sides.

But just like the conflict in Croatia, a potent mixture of fear, willingness to believe rumor, and propaganda makes it maddeningly difficult to determine the facts.

More than 2,000 people have been killed this spring in Bosnia, and 650,000 people have fled their homes because of fighting between Serb irregulars and the Serb-dominated army on one side against the republic's majority Slavic Muslims and Croats. Serb-led forces now control more than two-thirds of Bosnian territory.

U.N. peacekeeping forces moving into neighboring Croatia, where fighting has killed more than 10,000 people, have documented cases in which Serb forces have forced civilians to leave their homes in an apparent effort to create ethnically pure areas.

*Credit:* Reprinted with permission of The Associated Press.

## JUDY WOODRUFF AND JIM LEHRER: BOSNIA TRUCE BROKEN

*The following three stories from national television and newspapers offers an example of the narrow range of coverage.*

### MacNeil/Lehrer NewsHour (PBS), Transcript 4343, 27 May 1992

Ms. WOODRUFF: Good evening. I'm Judy Woodruff in New York.

Mr. LEHRER: And I'm Jim Lehrer in Washington.

The truce in the Bosnian capital of Sarajevo was shattered today. At least 16 people were killed and more than 100 wounded when mortar shells struck a crowded street. The attack was blamed on Serbian forces. Hours later, the European Community decided to impose a trade embargo on Serbia. We have more in this report narrated by Louise Bates of Worldwide Television News. The report contains graphic pictures some viewers may find disturbing.

Ms. BATES: The bodies lay all over the street. The wounded begged for help after the reign of terror fell on the queue for bread. Families who'd ventured out into the sunshine after weeks of bombardment to get food for their loved ones—the bombs destroyed these people's lives and wrecked the cease-fire brokered only hours earlier. The attack was a massive setback for Serbia, which has been accused of staging the massacre. It was trying to stave off U.N. sanctions with the promise to cooperate with peacekeeping, but Serb irregulars, still determined to partition the mainly Muslim capital, have taken the republic closer to international condemnation. Rescuers not knowing who to help first struggled in vain to cope with the carnage. The wounded were taken to local hospitals, whose medical supplies are already stretched to the limit. As more victims arrived, staff fought to cope with the emergency. The hospitals are suffering from shortages of food and medicine because of the blockaded airport. The siege should have been lifted when the cease-fire was agreed. In Belgrade, the chairman of the self-proclaimed Serbian republic in Bosnia denied any responsibility, saying that Serbian forces had not fired any single grenade on Sarajevo. Outraged Bosnian officials in Sarajevo called the massacre "a blow against the peace," and said foreign intervention was now vital. In Brussels, U.S. Defense Sec. Dick Cheney gave no sign of that.

*Credit:* Reprinted with permission from MacNeil-Lehrer Productions.

## BARRY SCHWEID: "ADMINISTRATION OFFERS AID TO REFUGEES IN YUGOSLAVIA"

*A further example of the narrow coverage offered by the national media.*

Associated Press, 28 May 1992

WASHINGTON: The United States on Thursday offered $9 million in aid to the victims of the fighting in Yugoslavia, and against the backdrop of the bloodshed endorsed the principle of NATO peacekeepers in European hot spots under the auspices of a 52-nation security group.

Most of the aid announced by the White House is designated for refugees in Bosnia-Herzegovina, the tiny former republic where Serbian forces are at war with Muslim civilians, causing more than 480,000 of them to flee.

Administration officials acknowledged that delivering the assistance in the midst of what Secretary of State James A. Baker III has called "a humanitarian nightmare" would require either an armed escort or a ceasefire.

The fighting has not ceased, however, and U.S. officials did not approve the use of troops to cut through Serbian lines and deliver the aid.

Deaths by starvation are reported in Bosnia-Herzegovina and the country is running out of bread, vegetables and other food, although there are supplies of wheat in Sarajevo, the embattled capital, the State Department said.

Spokesman Richard Boucher declined to say whether the United States would approve using armed convoys to deliver the relief. "I don't have anything new on the general area of military force for you," he said.

*Credit*: Reprinted with permission of The Associated Press.

## JOHANNA NEUMAN: U.S. FREEZES YUGOSLAVIA ASSETS

*This is an example of the depersonalized reporting of the war, which was not worth more than a news brief.*

*USA Today*, 1 June 1992

International pressure grew Sunday to stop the bloodshed in Bosnia—Herzegovina that has left 2,200 dead and 1.3 million homeless in the worst fighting in Europe since World War II.

One day after the U.N. Security Council slapped broad economic sanctions on Serbian-led Yugoslavia, blamed for fomenting civil war since Bosnia and three other republics declared independence:

- President Bush froze $214 million in Yugoslav assets.

Bush, in a letter to Congress, expressed "outrage at the actions of the Serbian and Montenegrin governments," actions which "constitute an unusual and extraordinary threat to the national security, foreign policy and economy of the United States."

- European countries cut off air travel to Yugoslavia, leaving many passengers stranded at Belgrade's airport.

(In sports, officials banned the Yugoslav soccer team from the European championships. They meet today to banish Yugoslavia from World Cup qualifying games this summer.)

- Warring factions in Bosnia agreed to a cease-fire in Sarajevo due to start today. With residents on the brink of starvation, relief officials hope to re-open Sarajevo Airport.

In Belgrade, 50,000 people marched to mourn the dead in more than two months of bloodshed in Bosnia. Serbian forces have captured about 70 percent of independent Bosnia.

A defiant Serbian President Slobodan Milosevic, who Saturday criticized the United States and Russia for the Security Council's 13–0 vote to impose economic sanctions, told reporters on Sunday that he expects the move, which includes an oil embargo, to be lifted. Milosevic, a Serbian nationalist, hopes to legitimize his rule by winning Sunday's elections to represent Serbia and Montenegro—the two remaining republics in Yugoslavia.

*Credit*: From USA TODAY, a division of Gannett Co., Inc. Reprinted with Permission.

## WOLF BLITZER: WHITE HOUSE RELUCTANT TO EXPAND U.S. EFFORT IN YUGOSLAVIA

*This report on CNN was broadcast around the world. Though it is short, it is indicative of the kind of stories that were available on the situation in Bosnia-Herzegovina.*

*CNN News*, Transcript 84–1, 8 June 1992

HIGHLIGHT: The Bush administration says it will offer only limited logistical support to new U.N. efforts to provide humanitarian assistance in war-ravaged Sarajevo.

CATHERINE CRIER, Anchor: Thanks for joining us. We begin tonight with the escalating violence in the former Yugoslavian republic of Bosnia-Hercegovina. U.N. Secretary General Boutrous-Boutrous Ghali today recommended the Security Council send 1100 peacekeepers to Sarajevo. Their role—to secure the airport there so relief flights can land. And the U.S. backs the idea, but committing U.S. troops— well, that's another matter. CNN's Wolf Blitzer reports.

WOLF BLITZER, Military Affairs Correspondent: With the fighting in and around Bosnia's capital of Sarajevo getting worse, the Bush administration is ready to support an expanded United Nations effort to bring food and medicine to the devastated area. The White House says people there are starving, and the State Department has expressed alarm over reports that rebel Serbs have started expelling large numbers of non-Serbs.

MARGARET TUTWILER, State Department Spokeswoman: We reiterate that ethnic cleansing is totally abhorrent and savage.

*Credit:* © 2005 Cable News Network LP, LLLP. Reprinted with permission.

## JOHN M. GOSHKO, TREVOR ROWE, *WASHINGTON POST* STAFF WRITERS: "U.N. VOTES TO DEPLOY EXTRA TROOPS IN BOSNIA; DEPLOYMENT CONDITIONAL ON CEASE-FIRE"

*This was a front-page story, which was unusual this early in the U.S. news coverage of the war. Notice that the report was from U.S. official reports and described the actions of the United Nations.*

*Washington Post*, 9 June 1992

The U.N. Security Council, spurred by fears of mass starvation in Bosnia-Hercegovina's besieged capital, Sarajevo, voted unanimously last night to try to send an additional 1,100 U.N. troops to Yugoslavia to reopen Sarajevo's airport and permit delivery of supplies to the city's beleaguered residents.

The resolution, adopted by the 15-nation council without any dissent, would not dispatch the troops until a viable cease-fire is put in effect among the warring factions in Bosnia.

It authorizes U.N. Secretary General Boutros Boutros-Ghali to send an initial force of 60 military observers and related personnel to Sarajevo to oversee implementation of a cease-fire, including the removal of Serbian antiaircraft batteries and gun emplacements. The main elements of the peace-keeping force would not be dispatched until Boutros-Ghali has advised the council that the required truce is in effect.

Left unclear last night was what the United Nations would do if a cease-fire cannot be arranged. In that case, the council reluctantly would be forced to consider possible military action to relieve Sarajevo. However, last night's resolution at least gives the council a breathing space.

*Credit:* © **1992, The Washington Post, reprinted with permission.**

## JULIAN M. ISHERWOOD: "EUROPEAN MILITARY GROUPS MEET TO ACT ON YUGOSLAV CRISIS"

*This news wire service story would have been published in many newspapers that subscribed to United Press International. Notice that the reporter was actually reporting from Helsinki, Finland, on a story in Bosnia-Herzegovina.*

United Press International, 9 July 1992

HELSINKI, Finland: As Euro-Atlantic leaders heard appeals for an end to civil wars in Eastern Europe, European defense organizations moved Thursday to act independently to isolate Serbia and ensure that humanitarian aid reaches the victims of the war in Bosnia-Hercegovina.

France said it was sending 700 troops equipped with helicopter gunships next Wednesday to protect United Nations troops ferrying humanitarian aid to Sarajevo, the besieged capital of war-ravaged Bosnia-Hercegovina.

Simultaneously, the Western European Union, a defense organization of nine European powers, said it is preparing a plan for a naval blockade of Serbia to underscore U.N. sanctions against the Belgrade government, which is widely believed to be sponsoring the ethnic Serb guerrillas in Bosnia-Hercegovina.

Both WEU and North Atlantic Treaty Organization caucuses were to convene Friday in Helsinki, where senior ministers are attending the two-day summit of the 52-member Conference on Security and Cooperation in Europe.

But it remained clear that any military action would be under the authority of the U.N. and that there was no imminent likelihood of military intervention in the Bosnian civil war itself, despite a plea by the republic's president, Alija Izetbegovic.

During a meeting with President Bush, Izetbegovic urged Western leaders to intervene militarily to end the fighting. "We still do not have sufficient help from the international community," he complained.

Although Bush agreed that Serb aggression in Bosnia "must be stopped," he gave no indication how this would be done and has previously said he had no plans to commit U.S. troops on the ground in Bosnia.

Still, in an address to the CSCE meeting of heads of state and government, Bush said the CSCE should not only see to it that supplies get through to Bosnia, "no matter what it takes," but that the fighting should be stopped.

Serbia and its federation partner Montenegro were not present at the two-day summit. The two, who claim the Yugoslav CSCE seat, have been suspended from the forum for 100 days because of continued fighting in Bosnia-Hercegovina.

"We should do all we can to prevent this conflict from spreading," Bush said, again calling for a cease-fire by all sides. "Let's call with one voice for the guns to fall silent."

The CSCE leaders also worked to achieve peace elsewhere in Europe, and they complained bitterly at mushrooming violence in the region.

*Credit*: Reprinted by permission of UPI.

---

## AN ANONYMOUS REPORT: "SERBS PROMISE TO LET WOMEN AND CHILDREN LEAVE BOSNIA CAPITAL; U.N. WARNS OF NEW MUSLIM EXPULSION"

---

*By the end of the summer, many of the reports about Bosnia-Herzegovina came from reporters stationed there. This report from the* Houston Chronicle *ran inside, but in the front section of the newspaper.*

*Houston Chronicle, 12 August 1992*

SARAJEVO, Bosnia-Herzegovina—Seeking to head off international military intervention in Bosnia, Serb fighters on Tuesday promised to allow women and children to leave Sarajevo and a self-proclaimed Serb parliament pledged cooperation with the United Nations.

As they did so, United Nations officials warned Tuesday that Serbian forces are also attempting to expel about 28,000 Bosnians, mostly Muslims, from their homes around the Bihac area in northeastern Bosnia-Herzegovina.

Calling it one of the largest single acts of "ethnic cleansing" since the war in Bosnia began in May, the Office of the U.N. High Commissioner for Refugees was hoping to forestall the expulsion and to avoid becoming a pawn in the Serbian plan to remove Muslims from the area.

Lars Nielsen, field coordinator for the High Commissioner's

office, said that he, officials of the U.N. peacekeeping force and local Serb and Muslim leaders planned to meet in the Bihac area today to discuss the potential exodus.

In Washington, Bush administration officials told Congress it would take a field army of 400,000 troops to impose peace on the former Yugoslavia, and such a force would become mired in a long-term occupation of the country.

Despite the warning, the Senate approved, 74–22, a resolution calling on President Bush to seek from the United Nations "all necessary means, including the use of multilateral military force" to ensure delivery of humanitarian relief and access for inspectors to alleged concentration camps. The House later Tuesday passed a similar resolution.

"If we try to impose a solution, it will require a very large force that would have to use violence to stop violence, and that inevitably means the death of innocent civilians" as well as U.S. troops, said Stephen J. Hadley, assistant secretary of defense for international security policy.

Lt. Gen. Barry R. McCaffrey, an assistant to Gen. Colin Powell, the chairman of the Joint Chiefs of Staff, described the devastated 20,000-square-mile region as "slightly larger than South Vietnam, or four times the size of Northern Ireland" and said 400,000 troops would be needed to impose an uneasy peace.

---

## JOEL BRAND: "SIEGE PINS AMERICANS FAR FROM HOME"

---

*As the U.S. national elections approached, the coverage of the war in Bosnia was told almost entirely in terms of candidate responses to the situation. Candidate William Jefferson "Bill" Clinton announced that he would pursue military action to intervene in the conflict. President George Bush said that he was not in favor of military intervention. After the election, which Clinton won, there was more local coverage of the war, and the United States did begin organizing a military response to reported atrocities. The following several stories represent the subtle shift in the kind of coverage U.S. readers and listeners experienced. This story appeared on the front page of the Sunday edition and so would have been widely read in the nation's capital.*

*Washington Times*, 22 November 1992

SARAJEVO, Bosnia-Herzegovina—Safeta Basic and her American-born daughter, Aida, have been waiting five months for the call that never came: word that U.S. authorities have arrived to evacuate American citizens from this besieged capital.

American Air National Guard and Air Force cargo planes arriving on relief flights to Sarajevo several times a day have been authorized to evacuate the Basics and 27 other American citizens on a list provided by the U.S. Embassy in neighboring Croatia.

But no one in authority told that to the Basics or 14 others on the list who, since applying to be evacuated in June, remain cut off in a city where telephones rarely work and street travel is conducted under threat of sniper and artillery fire.

Any attempt to flee overland from the city of 400,000 has been extremely hazardous, leading past numerous sniper points and into territory held by ill-disciplined Serbian militias.

The first organized land evacuation was attempted last Sunday, when the Red Cross, taking advantage of a precarious cease-fire, managed to bus some 1,500 residents out of the city to nearby Serbian-held suburbs. But many families were split up in the evacuation and hundreds of others were left behind.

Mrs. Basic and 14-year-old Aida learned they were eligible for the airlift—unlike almost everyone else in this city—only when tracked down at their house in Sarajevo's northern hills by an American reporter last week.

"How come I didn't know about it?" Mrs. Basic, 36, asked suspiciously.

Her tall, brown-haired daughter, who was born in St. Louis, said she wanted to leave as soon as she could. "I just want to leave the war, beyond that I don't know," she said in her living room.

Mrs. Basic, who returned to Sarajevo from St. Louis after her marriage to an American broke up, said that in June she placed her and Aida's names on a list at the Bosnian Foreign Ministry of foreign nationals who wanted to be evacuated.

"I kept calling [the Bosnian presidency] every day because my daughter, she kept asking me, 'When are we going to go?' I never thought we'd really go. If it really happens, I'm going to die [of happiness]," said Mrs. Basic, who works at a hospital as an anesthesiologist.

"If something happened to her and I could have gotten her out sooner, I couldn't live with myself," said Mrs. Basic, who wants to take her daughter back to St. Louis.

Bosnian authorities said they passed the list of foreign nationals along to the United Nations but are unsure what happened to the list after that.

However, on Sept. 25, the U.S. Embassy in Zagreb, Croatia, provided a list of 28 Americans to the U.N. High Commissioner for Refugees (UNHCR) in Sarajevo and asked the United Nations to arrange their evacuation.

As of last week, UNHCR—which is understaffed and hard-pressed to carry out its primary mission of providing for up to 1.8 million people this winter—managed to contact only 13 of those on the list.

Telephones are frequently out of order and most phone numbers changed after the main exchange was hit by artillery in May. The only way to reach the others is to track them down by going to their last known address—something UNHCR has not had the resources to do.

There are no working long-distance lines from Sarajevo, making it impossible for the stranded Americans to contact the embassy in Zagreb.

In Washington, a State Department official said the United States aired television and radio advertisements in Sarajevo, advising U.S. citizens to contact UNHCR.

"We've been doing what we can to get through to people," said the official, who acknowledged that television in Sarajevo may not be working.

"We're incredibly limited in what we can do for people inside a war zone," said the official, who said the nearest embassies are in Zagreb and Belgrade, the Serbian capital.

A spokeswoman at the Zagreb embassy, which was upgraded from a consulate after Croatia was recognized as an independent country in April, pointed out that Americans were advised to leave Bosnia-Herzegovina before the war started there and that some heeded the advice.

But many stayed behind, almost all of whom had ethnic or family ties in the country. Some said they could not have anticipated what happened since Bosnian Serbs laid siege to Sarajevo.

U.N. officials said that eight of the 13 Americans reached by UNHCR were evacuated so far, seven of them in the past week.

Of the remaining 15 Americans, the Basics and another American—the 18-year-old U.S.-born son of a college professor—learned they were eligible to be removed only through inquiries for this article.

One other American citizen gave up on waiting for an airlift and undertook a hazardous overland escape from the city through the Serbian-controlled countryside, according to his neighbors. His fate could not be determined.

The whereabouts of another dozen U.S. citizens who were trapped in Sarajevo remains unknown.

Even among those who were contacted by UNHCR, there are some who feel trapped and abandoned by the U.S. government.

One of these is a contractor from Seattle who lived in the United States for 20 years but returned with his wife for a visit to Sarajevo just before the war started. He asked that their names not be used.

The contractor, who recalls watching on television as U.S. troops rescued endangered Americans from Grenada in October 1983, is angry at being left on his own to make the dangerous trip through the city to the U.N. headquarters for evacuation.

"I don't know what the life of an American is worth to the American government," he said.

Staff writer Warren Strobel contributed to this report in Washington.

---

# ROY GUTMAN: U.N. NEUTRALITY IN BOSNIA

---

*This story is an example of the more frequently read locally reported stories from Bosnia-Herzegovina about the war there.*

*Newsday* (New York), 22 November 1992

TRAVNIK, Bosnia-Herzegovina: As Serb artillery shells crashed past the minarets into the center of this historic city recently, British U.N. troops nearby winced as they described their orders, which are to do nothing beyond guarding convoys of humanitarian aid.

With their vastly superior force, the Bosnian Serbs are well placed to capture and destroy this architectural jewel of a city, the gateway to central Bosnia and home to 40,000 residents and expellees. British intelligence reports suggest that the Serbs, who stepped up the attack on Travnik last week, are "going for broke" in Bosnia before President-elect Bill Clinton takes office and considers a policy shift.

The 880-man British battalion group has just completed its deployment in Vitez, just 10 miles to the south of here. But its mission, laid out by the U.N. Security Council, is to protect trucks, not people. Should the Serbs seize Travnik and move on to capture Vitez and head toward Sarajevo, taking control of the main supply route from the Adriatic coast

to the Bosnian interior, the battlefront would pass right over them.

"We are utterly neutral," said Capt. Lee Smart, a British spokesman at the new U.N. protection force base in Vitez. "Should the fighting come past us, under the orders we have been given so far, we can't fight anyone." The exception is self-defense. "Should we be attacked, we can defend ourselves," Smart said.

For foreign relief agencies the deployment of the British and other forces under U.N. control is another case of inadequate humanitarian "band-aids" that have no impact on the war, itself. They say Bosnia could well freeze and starve despite the logistical support provided by western troops.

"Probably we are too late," said Yves Mauron, the international Red Cross representative in nearby Zenica. "I think everybody is too late. This is the characteristic of this war."

A mood of fatalism pervades Travnik, located in a narrow valley and indefensible from attack by the Serbs who have taken the high ground. Turkish viziers ruled Bosnia from this town from 1699 to 1851, and Nobel Prize–winning author Ivo Andrić was born here. But its days as a predominantly Muslim city may be numbered.

Because of a split between the ill-armed Muslim forces, who are fighting to preserve a unified Bosnian state, and the better equipped Roman Catholic Croats, who favor partition, the powerful army of the Christian Orthodox Serbs advanced last week to the edge of Turbe, a suburb four miles to the north.

In an interview earlier this month at his frontline headquarters in Turbe, the local Muslim commander expressed only forlorn hope. "The Serbs have tanks and artillery. We are fighting with hunting rifles. All we have is our hands and our hearts," said Reko Sulejman. For months, he said, the Croat forces had refused to deliver military supplies, and the only way for the Muslims to obtain any weapons was through private purchase. For weeks, according to a British intelligence assessment, the Croats took no part in the fighting.

In recent days, the Croats shifted their stance, sending reinforcements to Turbe and setting up a roadblock at the southern end of the narrow valley to prevent fighters from fleeing. But foreign observers say tension between Muslims and Croats is just below the surface and could erupt again.

In the last month, Bosnian Croats attacked Muslims in nearby Novi Travnik in a battle in which 20 died and the entire commercial district and several apartment buildings were destroyed. In Prozor, a predominantly Croat town to the west, the Croat forces sent in tanks and destroyed the Muslim business district. Extreme Croat nationalists have renamed the military police headquarters there as the "House of the Ustasha," referring to the World War II force allied with the Nazis. As fighting raged between the Croats and Muslims, the Serbs capitalized on it by seizing the stronghold of Jajce, northwest of Travnik, forcing 45,000 people to flee.

Foreign relief officials say they believe the Croats may have decided to reinforce their position in Travnik, whose population is 45 percent Muslim and 37 percent Croat, with the aim, if the Serbs allow, of later taking control and expelling the Muslim population.

Ivan Sarci, a spokesman for the Bosnian Croat army, disputed any such intent. "Muslims and Croats are defending Travnik together," he said. "There has been no conflict here. We will defend the city as best we know how."

In Travnik the tension is palpable. "This is a city where the Croat officials are reporting to Boban, and the Muslims are reporting to Sarajevo," said Davor Schopf, a local Croat journalist. He referred to Mate Boban, the head of the self-declared autonomous Bosnian Croat state. "The only way it continues to function is because the officials know each other from childhood and try to arrange practical solutions."

Travnik is not only a key northern outpost of the besieged Bosnian government and a gateway to Sarajevo, 55 miles southeast, but also the first safe haven for Muslims and Croats fleeing the terror tactics of Serb "ethnic cleansing" aimed at driving the other groups from northern Bosnia.

About 18,000 refugees who survived assaults and robbery by Serb irregulars as they walked down the treacherous Vlasic Mountain fill the schools, sport halls, kindergartens, army barracks and private homes of Travnik. But now Travnik, whose own population is about the same size, is also destitute.

"We have used up all our stocks, our money, our gasoline, our food, our communal reserves," said Mustafa Hockic, a Muslim member of the city government. "Now our own citizens have been reduced to the state of refugees. Our doctors, our teachers have to go to the public kitchens for food. We now have to organize aid for our own inhabitants."

If Serbs capture Turbe, even the treacherous path down Vlasic Mountain could be closed. And in the Banja Luka region, where the "ethnic cleansing" is proceeding full speed ahead, foreign relief officials said they had no way of guessing how people could escape. Neighboring Croatia and most of Europe have closed their borders to Bosnian refugees.

During daytime lulls in the fighting children play war in a cemetery overlooking the city. At night horse-drawn carts go back and forth to nearby villages as peasants gather their belongings and flee before the expected Serb advance.

Travnik has no heat. The official reason is that Serb artillery damaged the central heating plant and there is no coal. But in fact, sources said, the city has not started up its central heating plant to avoid offering another target for the Serbs. If the heating plant is destroyed, the city will become virtually uninhabitable in the coming winter.

But the British detachment has its hands tied. "Our mandate is to protect the U.N. food convoys and to go wherever they want us. Beyond that we're not in a position to get involved," Smart said.

About the only hope for saving the city appears to be quick action by the U.N. Security Council on an Austrian proposal to use military force to establish safe zones in Travnik and four other Bosnian cities—Sarajevo, Gorazde, Tuzla and Bihac. Austria's plan, modeled on the safe havens created by the United States and Britain for Iraqi Kurds after the Gulf war, is intended to stem the flood of refugees expected this winter if the Serbs continue their conquest of Bosnia.

It would require a far greater military force than the 20,000 U.N. troops now deployed in Bosnia, and, an Austrian official acknowledged, would amount to an "intervention through the back door."

"We are convinced that if limited military action had been taken one year ago, this war would never have occurred," said the official, who spoke on condition of anonymity. "We are also convinced that we will all be dragged in later, with far higher casualties, far higher human costs, and far more destruction."

The official said that the United States, which has no troops in Bosnia, seems in favor of its plan and that France, with 4,000 troops in Bosnia, has given tentative support, but that Britain has expressed strong reservations because it might put its 2,600 troops at risk.

A senior official at the U.N. High Commission on Refugees said the idea of a safe zone was "very appealing" but that to implement it would require a major military commitment that he doubted world leaders would make. The official, who asked not to be named, said such an approach would also be "another humanitarian solution for something which is not humanitarian. It is another case of dealing with consequences, not causes. Don't look for humanitarian solutions. Look for real solutions," he said.

## LINDA WERTHEIMER: BRITISH TROOPS IN BOSNIA FIGHT

*This radio broadcast report portrayed the sense of hopelessness and senselessness of the situation that many close to the war felt.*

### All Things Considered (NPR), 26 November 1992

Relief flights to Sarajevo resumed today, and a UN relief convoy that struck a land mine on the way finally reached the embattled eastern Bosnian city of Gorazde, where civilians have been cut off for several months. NPR's Tom Gjelten has just returned from several days with British troops assigned to escort aid convoys in central Bosnia. He joins us now from the Croatian city of Split.

Tom, tell us about the—the British troops there in Bosnia.

TOM GJELTEN (NPR Reporter): Well, Linda, this is an infantry—the heart of the British contingent is an infantry battalion of the Cheshire regiment. They are, in fact, to escort humanitarian aid convoys. Actually, it's a somewhat unusual arrangement. They are under assignment to the UN High Commissioner for Refugees, which is the coordinating body for all humanitarian aid in Bosnia, and the UNHCR officials actually can direct the British troops wherever they want them. They can call up the commander of the British troops and say, "We need—we need an escort for this convoy going on this day to such-and-such a city," and the British troops are obligated to provide it, so they're really there to help the UNHCR in any way they can.

WERTHEIMER: These battle-hardened British troops, though, Tom, they are—they're not really there to fight, are they? Can they ac—they—they can't really fight.

GJELTEN: Linda, they have a virtually impossible task. If the Serb forces, who control the hills around the routes that those convoys take, decide—if the Serb commanders decide they want to stop a convoy, they can stop a convoy by shelling it. There is virtually nothing that these guys can do. They do have very impressive fighting vehicles equipped with 30mm cannons, but they can't sh—they can't go after the Serbs who are—are shooting them.

Moreover, they are now running into problems with the people that they're supposed to be protecting. Because they have all this great firepower, the people up there who have been praying for outside military intervention for months think now that it has arrived, and when they see what all these guys are doing is essentially delivering Meals on Wheels, they get very frustrated and they start throwing rocks at the vehicles and so forth, so these guys are really in an impossible situation.

WERTHEIMER: And this—this is the group that you went into Bosnia with.

GJELTEN: Right.

WERTHEIMER: Sounds like sitting ducks, Tom.

GJELTEN: Well, they are sitting ducks, but they're very good at turning around quickly and hightailing it out of there.

WERTHEIMER: You went in with—with these British troops into central Bosnia to Travnik, which has become a center for refugees fleeing the fighting throughout Bosnia. It's surrounded now by Serb forces. We hear every day that it may fall, it may not fall. What is daily life like for civilians in—in a place like that?

GJELTEN: For the population of Travnik this is a terrifying moment because refugees have been streaming into Travnik for months, and they're arriving at a rate of 1,000 a day coming to—into Travnik. Every group that comes in has horrible stories of what they went through when Serb forces overran their cities.

Now unlike the refugees who have been coming through before, if Travnik falls, these people will have nowhere to go, because the escape routes out of Travnik go precisely through the territory that would be under Serb control if the city were to fall. The ci—I think the thing that impressed me most is that no one is making any arrangements to leave. This is completely unlike the behavior of people in other besieged cities who—who are sort of gathering their things together and making contact with relatives in distant cities and so forth. These people really do feel they have nowhere to go and they're not even bothering to prepare for it.

I was, just yesterday, visiting this family that I met a couple of months ago. This Bosnian-Muslim woman who hosted me had coffee that she had put aside and she had made some sweet cakes for me. She had her grandson over visiting, and she told me that she hates it when he comes to visit because she knows that he has to walk five blocks to get over there to her. And she keeps telling him not to come because she's so terrified that a shell is going to land in the street while he's walking over to see her. But he gets very bored where he is and frightened and he likes to come over and—and visit her and he shows up there every day.

WERTHEIMER: NPR's Tom Gjelten speaking with us from the Croatian port city of Split.

---

## AN ANONYMOUS REPORT: "KENTUCKY GUARD ASKED TO ASSIST IN POSSIBLE AIRLIFTS"

---

*This wire service story would have been available to any of the member news organizations. Since it is datelined Louisville, Kentucky, it would have been read primarily by midwesterners.*

### Associated Press, 28 November 1992

LOUISVILLE, Ky.: The Kentucky Air National Guard's 123rd Airlift Wing has been told to be prepared in case the government orders large airlifts of food and supplies to Somalia and Bosnia-Herzegovina, an official said.

The Defense Department singled out the Standiford Field–based 123rd Airlift Wing because its fleet of C-130 Hercules cargo planes has computer defense systems and can make quick takeoffs and landings, said Lt. Col. Ed Tonini.

"They contacted us about four weeks ago," Tonini said Friday. "They asked if we could ready ourselves for a tactical airlift on six days' notice, and we told them that we could."

Some members of the 123rd already have volunteered for relief missions and have had a firsthand look at devastation caused by Somalia's civil unrest.

Tonini said he didn't know whether the airlift would be affected by President Bush's offer to the United Nations to provide up to 30,000 U.S. troops to help a multinational force safeguard food supplies for starving Somalis.

Washington on Wednesday offered to send 30,000 American troops under a U.S. commander or as part of a larger U.N. force.

In Kennebunkport, Maine, National Security Adviser Brent Scowcroft said Saturday the proposal was still being discussed with the U.N. and U.S. allies.

---

## ROBERT MacNEIL AND JAMES LEHRER; KEMAL KURSPAHIC, BOSNIAN JOURNALIST; GORDANA KNEZEVIC, BOSNIAN JOURNALIST: NEWS OF BOSNIA

---

*This report featured the resourcefulness of those working and living in what seemed to the outside world like a hopeless situation.*

### *MacNeil/Lehrer NewsHour* (PBS), Transcript 4509, 30 November 1992

Mr. MACNEIL: One newspaper's effort to keep publishing amid the shelling and killing in Sarajevo, Bosnia. In eight months of civil war in the former Yugoslav republic at least 17,000 people have died. Some of the worst fighting has taken place around the offices of the newspaper Oslobodjenje, or Liberation. Its modernist building has been gutted. Its journalists have been attacked by missile fire. Six staffers have died. Serbian snipers keep rifles trained on the newspaper's entrance. Like Bosnia, itself, the newspaper staff is composed of Muslims, Serbs, and Croats. They now work in a basement shelter, producing the paper by candlelight. The newspaper's two editors are in the United States this week and tomorrow will receive the 1992 Courage in Journalism Award from the International Women's Media Foundation, and they join us now. Kemal Kurspahic is the Muslim, is the editor in chief, and was able to leave Bosnia for medical treatment. Gordana Knezevic, a Bosnian Serb, has been acting editor in chief while her colleague recovers. She was allowed to leave Sarajevo on a United Nations flight to accept her award. Congratulations on the award you will receive tomorrow. Can you just tell us as fellow journalists a little bit of how you put this newspaper out. You don't have electricity very often. How do you see, apart from candlelight? How do you run the presses if you don't have electricity?

Mr. KURSPAHIC: We have some power generators, but you know we have to save it because we don't have enough oil to operate, so it works for four or six hours a day in order to print the paper, to allow our printers to do their job. All the rest of the day we work under candlelight because the offices are in shelter underground and there is no natural light.

Mr. MacNEIL: They're in, I read, a nuclear shelter, a shelter that was designed for nuclear war, is that correct?

Ms. KNEZEVIC: That's right. That's right. And—

Mr. MacNEIL: And are you all living there too?

Ms. KNEZEVIC: We are working on shift system so few people are sleeping and working there for seven days, and we are changing this shift, but another clue for our survival is our tough editor in chief. You know, he at the beginning of the war, he told us that he doesn't know how many of us would survive, but that we have to have an issue every day, and that's how we operated for eight months.

Mr. MacNEIL: Apart from it's your profession, why is it so vital to you to keep the newspaper going for Sarajevo?

Mr. KURSPAHIC: There is first responsibility to our readers, and I would say to the idea of free press, you know, you can't allow some people just come there to push you out and to stop publishing the paper which has 50 years tradition, and the other thing is that keeping "Oslobodjenje," which means liberation, alive gives also some psychological support to people in Sarajevo. "Oslobodjenje" is now the only thing left you can buy each morning in Sarajevo. There is no bread anymore. So that's the last remaining of pre-war normal life there, and people live with us and they keep it as their, as being newly born each morning when they see the paper coming out of flame, out of ashes of our building.

Mr. MacNEIL: You get 10,000 editions—10,000 copies out a day?

Ms. KNEZEVIC: That's right.

Mr. MacNEIL: And how do you get them to people in a city that's so often under shell fire and bombardment?

Ms. KNEZEVIC: We have a special system. There is no driver in Sarajevo who would drive to our building to pick up the copies, but the journalists, themselves, are driving a few cars early in the morning, and then some other people are waiting for them at certain spots of the town and they are doing big distribution, and those 10,000 copies are sold in half an hour. And we could sell double than that but we have to spare the paper, so someone might say what is our situation in the paper.

Mr. MacNEIL: How are you getting paper?

Mr. KURSPAHIC: We didn't get any since the beginning of the war, which is the beginning of April, and in order to prolong our life we had to use number of pages and to reduce circulation, because our pre-war circulation was about 60,000 a day, so we had to reduce this to ⅕ in order to live longer, and—

Mr. MacNEIL: How much have you got left?

Mr. KURSPAHIC: I almost shouldn't say so because, you know, we are trying to smuggle some paper in the city, and I think we'll live till the end of the war.

Mr. MacNEIL: It is—all the stories I've seen about you suggest that the Serbian attackers are really aiming at the paper. I mean, hundreds of shells and missiles have hit the building. They continue to keep the entrance to the building under fire. Why did they want to so clearly stop you from publishing?

Ms. KNEZEVIC: What we think is the main course of these severe attacks is just the structure, ethnical structure of "Oslobodjenje." We are real proof that it's not possible to only live together but to work together, just because we are some Serbs, Croats and Muslims trying desperately to keep a company alive, and that makes them very nervous.

Mr. MacNEIL: Because that was the reality in Bosnia, and particularly in the city of Sarajevo before the, the Serbian attacks began.

Ms. KNEZEVIC: That's right, and in that sense, "Oslobodjenje" is somehow a symbol of this Sarajevo before the war, a symbol in a sense of common culture, of multicultural, multi-religious, multi-ethnical place.

Mr. KURSPAHIC: And you know I think that our staff reflects that picture, I mean, ethnic picture of Bosnia almost ideally. There is almost ideal percentage of Serbs, Muslims and Croats living together, and on the other hand, the basic idea of aggression is to destroy that possibility of different nations living together.

Mr. MacNEIL: And ethnically cleanse.

Mr. KURSPAHIC: Yes.

Mr. MacNEIL: Ethnically distinct groups.

Mr. KURSPAHIC: I think they, they want to destroy "Oslobodjenje" just to prove that there is nothing left of that culture of living together in Sarajevo.

Mr. MacNEIL: Do you feel being right there in Sarajevo that there is going—that this is going to stop because of a negotiated settlement? Can the U.N. get these—ultimately get the cease-fire to work? I mean, there was another one negotiated for the weekend and it was broken again today.

Mr. KURSPAHIC: Unfortunately, I don't expect a lot from those negotiations. You know, our experiences don't give us very much hope on that. I think we deal with the project and with the people who understand only the language of force, so, in my opinion, if international community, if it still exists because from our experience we doubt it, if international community wants to do something, then I think it's time either to intervene to some measure or to allow us to arm ourselves to defend the country because it's hypocrisy to tell that there is already too many arms there. There is but they're all in one hands, in hands of aggressor. I think that advantage is at least one hundred to one in all measures in arms sense. So I think that—

Mr. MacNEIL: What is your reaction then when—you know this has been debated a long time here and the Bush administration has said, we couldn't go in there effectively without getting bogged down. They want to go into the risk of getting bogged down as they did in Vietnam—what is your reaction when you hear that reason given for the U.S. not—

Ms. KNEZEVIC: People in Sarajevo I can tell you generally start to forget about the outside world, and they feel very lonely, and they feel very helpless, and there is a lot of bitterness inside Sarajevo at the moment. Just because they thought that their cause is obvious and just because people of Sarajevo are not a side in a conflict, there was not any armed forces inside the city once the city was attacked, you know, and maybe they even didn't give a lot of arguments to the rest of the world, just because they thought that the cause of Bosnian people was so justified, and why should they produce an argument to prove that, so this general mood is very much shown in the reaction over U.N. presence in Sarajevo. People sympathize with them, don't expect much of them, and they just feel that there is a long, long winter coming and nobody sees the end.

Mr. MACNEIL: What is your reaction to the reasons the Bush administration has given for not intervening militarily?

Mr. KURSPAHIC: I think there are ways to intervene without taking so much risks. There are specific military targets. There are artillery positions which each child in Sarajevo knows. We are exposed to that. They shell apartment buildings. They shell hospitals. They kill civilians there, and everyone in Sarajevo knows where the fire comes from, so I think even limited air strikes against strictly military targets, artillery positions, air fields from which they operate, and some similar things might be done in 48 hours because those people understand the unusual force and that will be a strong message to them. I think it's high time if it's not, of course, for many of us it's too late, but I think that's the only way to send them a message they will understand.

Mr. MACNEIL: The—there's going to be elections in Serbia on December the 20th. There is talk that Milan Panic, the prime minister who used to live in the United States, is going to run against Milosevic, the Serbian leader. Do you—would that make any difference to the war if, if he ran and Milosevic were defeated? Would that make any difference?

Ms. KNEZEVIC: I must admit I am not hopeful. It looks like Panic is just another good player on the Serbian stage and at least we in Sarajevo, we don't think that there is a real gap between Milosevic and Panic in the sense that Panic is to talk about peace and Milosevic is to proceed with the war, so we—we don't think that they have different national program.

Mr. MACNEIL: They're both in favor of a greater Serbia, in other words—

Ms. KNEZEVIC: That's right.

Mr. MACNEIL: —you believe?

Ms. KNEZEVIC: That's right. So in that sense we are not hopeful in any political change in Belgrade.

Mr. MACNEIL: Well, I must thank you both and end it there, and wish you both good luck. Thank you.

*Credit:* Reprinted with permission from MacNeil-Lehrer Productions.

---

## MANLEY J. ANDERSON: NEW YORK RESOURCE CENTER MAKING BAGS FOR U.S. AIRDROP

*This local story would not have had wide circulation but is typical of the kinds of localizing that the Bosnian situation received in the media. The story is not about the war, but about the U.S. efforts in that war.*

*Post-Journal* (Jamestown, N.Y.), 3 March 1993

The Resource Center in Jamestown is playing a small but important role in airdrops by U.S. cargo planes of vital food and medical supplies into war-torn Bosnia.

The aerial cargo bags, with a capacity of 2,200 pounds, used to parachute the goods to the besieged civilians are made by 18 center employees assigned to the project.

"We're in the middle of a contract for 5,600 pieces," said Gregory D. Bender, the center's director of business operations. "Then we have a backlog of 2,600 more. We are the preferred supplier, so as long as the government uses this bag they have to buy from us."

Bender described the bags as measuring 14-1/2 feet tip to tip. They have four points, like a star almost, he said, and weigh about 48 pounds empty. "They have very large pieces of hardware to attach to parachutes," he explained.

"We've been doing government projects for about 17 years now," Bender said. "This is one of seven products."

He said the others involve two different tent pins, insect bars, a ground rod assembly and another cargo bag. "We also did helmet covers for Operation Desert Storm," Bender noted.

He said the cargo bags are made of nylon duck and nylon webbing. "The weaving pattern is a manual pattern you weave with hot glue," he said, "and then it's sewn in place with heavy duty industrial sewing machines. We do about 21 a day."

Bender said the bags made locally are recognizable by the distinctive thread used in their construction. "Our thread is a natural white thread," he said, "and one of the bags (dropped in Bosnia) had a white thread so it was recognized."

The center spokesman said several Kurds were killed in previous air drops of supplies when they tried to catch the falling cargo bags. "They hold 2,200 pounds," he said, "so you're not going to catch them."

Bender said to eliminate the possibility of aid recipients trying to catch the airdrops, the parachutes now used in the operation have slits cut in them so they drop faster.

As to complaints that many of the cargo bags dropped into the Bosnian war zone fell far from their intended destination, Bender said, "There's not much you can do about dropping them from 12,000 feet."

He said The Resource Center is a set-aside supplier through National Industries for the Severely Handicapped and soon will be the only supply source of the bags for the St. Louis–based U.S. Army Aviation and Troop Command.

Bender said the cargo bags must meet very rigid government specifications. He noted that the number of employees assigned to the project may increase by two to a total of 20.

---

## JILL DOUGHERTY: "U.S. PRESCRIBES LIST OF ACTIONS AGAINST SERBIA"

*Most of the news continued to emanate from locations other than Bosnia-Herzegovina. The following transcript is an example of the continuing coverage of what the leadership said. It came from a variety of national capitals.*

*CNN News*, Transcript 327–2, 7 March 1993

HIGHLIGHT: The United States has presented the United Nations with a list of recommended actions to be taken against Serbia to bring peace to Bosnia. Advisers say tougher economic pressure against the Serbs is needed.

DAVID FRENCH, Anchor: Ministers of the European Community meet tomorrow to discuss U.S. and German calls for tighter sanctions against Serbia. U.N. Secretary-General Boutros Boutros-Ghali says peace talks must continue. But he says member nations eventually may have to commit ground troops if the talks fail.

And from Bosnia-Hercegovina the U.N. warned the evacuation of more than 2,000 sick and wounded Muslims in the Cerska region may be weeks away. The town of Srebrenica reports continued heavy shelling by Serb forces. Rough terrain and winter weather pose additional obstacles.

President Clinton will hear from two U.S. diplomatic teams who are set to return from overseas meetings with European officials. Their goal reportedly is to develop strategies to halt the flow of money and goods into Serbia. The White House says a number of options remain open to halt the Serbian aggression.

CNN's Jill Dougherty reports.

JILL DOUGHERTY, Correspondent: President Clinton is seeking, the White House says, to inflict real pain on the Serbians for sponsoring continued aggression in Bosnia—has promised the U.S. will push to crank up the international sanctions. Two possible options—tighten the embargo against Serbia by stopping shipments of oil and other supplies in and out of the country and crackdown on international transfers of Serbian money. The objective, isolate and weaken Serbia enough that it will stop supporting attacks and back acceptance of a U.N.-sponsored peace plan.

In New York Bosnian Serbs are balking at agreement on a map dividing Bosnia into 10 semi-autonomous provinces but with new indications Bosnian Muslims may join the Croats in agreeing as early as this week, the U.S. is hoping to isolate Serbia diplomatically as well.

SANDY BERGER, Deputy National Security Adviser: And the only party that will not have signed that agreement. At that point I think the spotlight of world attention and world pressure will focus on the Serbs to stop the brutal fighting and to reach an agreement.

DOUGHERTY: With Bosnian Serbs continuing to capture Muslim territory, though, the U.N. secretary-general again warned force, not negotiation, may be the only answer if the Serbs refuse to stop or withdraw.

BOUTROS BOUTROS-GHALI, Secretary-General of the U.N.: I believe that if after what ought to be done we find that we are not able to obtain the withdrawal then there is only one solution which is enforcement. And, again, the members that must be ready to send troops on the ground.

DOUGHERTY: Defense Secretary Les Aspin responded by repeating administration policy that without a peace agreement the U.S. is not yet ready to send troops. But then appeared to open the door to that possibility.

LES ASPIN, Defense Secretary: I think we'd see what happens after this. But the current policy is to use heavy diplomatic pressure.

DOUGHERTY: The White House is couching its statements on Bosnia in very careful terms. Asked whether the president has ruled out military intervention before a peace agreement is reached, a White House spokesman has said Mr. Clinton is not discussing it right now. That using ground forces is not something he wants to do.

Jill Dougherty, CNN, the White House.

*Credit*: © 2005 Cable News Network LP, LLLP. Reprinted with permission.

## SHEILAH KAST AND BARRIE DUNSMORE: CLINTON ADMINISTRATION STRATEGY IN BOSNIA

*This television report is like the earlier stories that focused on what the diplomats said. This story, however, is about the much more aggressive strategy of intervention that the recently inaugurated President Clinton had adopted over the previous wait-and-see program administered by President Bush.*

*World News Saturday* (ABC), 1 May 1993

TOM JARRIEL: Good evening. President Clinton is taking the U.S. and its allies a big step closer to military involvement in Bosnia's civil war, even as the warring parties are preparing for 11th-hour peace negotiations in Athens, Greece. Few details emerged after the President held a long strategy session with his top advisers today, but Mr. Clinton has dispatched Secretary of State Warren Christopher to Europe to secure allied support for military steps to halt Serb aggression. We have two reports, beginning with Sheilah Kast at the White House.

SHEILAH KAST: President Clinton's top diplomatic and military advisers streamed into the White House for what would be nearly four hours of discussion about U.S. options to quell the violence in Bosnia. Participants said the President decided on what they called a direction that includes military steps, although not involving U.S. ground troops. The tone was tough.

Secretary of State WARREN CHRISTOPHER: It will take deeds, immediate concrete action by the Serbs, actions on the ground, to convince the international community of their seriousness and good faith. What we're tired of is simply their words and actions and manipulation.

SHEILAH KAST: The President has acknowledged the need to foster public support for any U.S. action in Bosnia, but Christopher focused less on the moral outrage of ethnic cleansing than on what he termed U.S. strategic interests.

Secretary WARREN CHRISTOPHER: The United States does not want this conflict to spread in a way that would involve our allies, Greece and Turkey. It does not want it to spread to Kosovo or Macedonia.

SHEILAH KAST: European allies may be more excited about that motive than U.S. voters. The Secretary of State leaves tonight to consult with leaders in Britain, France, Russia, Germany and NATO.

Secretary WARREN CHRISTOPHER: I'll come back and report to the President, and he'll be reporting to the American people on this subject, but the clock is ticking.

SHEILAH KAST: While the European leaders will be told the first details of Mr. Clinton's plan, Christopher insisted they will not have a veto power. The U.S. is proceeding on its own track, he said, and will not be diverted. Sheilah Kast, ABC News, the White House.

BARRIE DUNSMORE: This is Barrie Dunsmore. While Secretary of State Christopher refused to go into detail on what military steps the U.S. is now prepared to take, he did

drop some hints. First, it is likely that before any military action is taken the Serbs will be given an ultimatum.

Secretary WARREN CHRISTOPHER: They must honor the cease-fire that was called for in the London accords. They must stop bombing the cities in Bosnia. They must permit humanitarian aid to go forward.

BARRIE DUNSMORE: Christopher's stress on the cease-fire implies the U.S., first of all, wants to protect Muslim civilians from further massacres. That suggests that Muslim cities will be declared safe havens. And if the Serbs ignore the ultimatum, NATO air forces will at some point attack Serbian military targets. U.S. and other NATO members are already patrolling the skies over Bosnia, enforcing the no-fly zone. Some combination of these planes could be used to enforce the ultimatum. Another clue to the new U.S. direction was in Christopher's confidence in European reaction.

Secretary WARREN CHRISTOPHER: I have no reason to think that my consultations there won't be well-received, and I have some confidence that we can reach a situation of unity and cohesion.

BARRIE DUNSMORE: The British and French seem ready to use air strikes to protect Muslim enclaves. In fact, Britain has already issued its own ultimatum to protect Canadian U.N. forces in Srebrenica, but Britain and France have been strongly opposed to lifting the arms embargo on the Bosnian Muslims because they say it would endanger their troops, now conducting the U.N. relief effort. So perhaps the U.S. is prepared to hold off on lifting the embargo. But on one point you don't have to read the tea leaves. [SU (a video cue)] Serbia will not be allowed to use this weekend's Yugoslav conference in Athens as a way of delaying U.S. action. Christopher made it clear that no matter what happens in Athens, the U.S. plans to proceed with its new get-tough policy until there is a genuine cease-fire. Barrie Dunsmore, ABC News, the State Department.

TOM JARRIEL: As peace mediators prepared for a final showdown at the bargaining table, there was a sharp increase in the fighting. Shelling killed eight people and wounded 60 others in a sudden attack on Sarajevo today. Throughout Bosnia, more than 40 people have died and more than 200 have been wounded in the past 24 hours. The talks in Greece are being described as a last-ditch effort to end the fighting and to ward off Western military intervention. More on that now from ABC's Jerry King.

JERRY KING: It's not the first time the leaders of the warring sides have attended a weekend conference said to be a last chance for peace. This time the mediators believe they have real grounds for optimism.

CYRUS VANCE/U.N. Negotiator: I look forward to this with hope.

LORD DAVID OWEN/EC Negotiator: Peace, which has so long eluded the former Yugoslavia, is now, I think, within our grasp, if only everyone has the courage to seize it.

JERRY KING: What has changed? The U.N. is finally enforcing its tough economic sanctions against Serbia and that has caused Serbia's President to reconsider his role as godfather to the rebel Serbs in Bosnia. "We are here", says Slobodan Milosevic, "to take a decisive step forward". Everyone hopes the Serbs will step on Serbia's allies in Bosnia, the ones winning the ground war. [SU] What happens at the conference here tomorrow, whether there's a small step toward peace or a giant leap away from it, depends in very large measure on the Bosnian Serbs. They are the only ones who have so far refused to go along with the Vance-Owen peace plan. And they're the ones the U.S. and some Europeans are threatening to bomb, which may be why the Bosnian Serb leader now says the peace plan may not be so bad after all.

RADOVAN KARADZIC/Bosnian Serb Leader: The Serbian side is ready for the peace, an immediate and unconditional peace.

JERRY KING: The problem is, the world has heard that one before. As one diplomat puts it, echoing Warren Christopher, "We need deeds, not words". Jerry King, ABC News, Athens.

*Credit*: Reprinted with permission of ABC News, World News Saturday.

---

## NANCY BENAC: CLINTON DISPATCHES SECRETARY OF STATE CHRISTOPHER WITH PLAN FOR "MILITARY STEPS" IN BOSNIA

---

*Even by midyear President Clinton's team was still struggling to grasp the complexity of the Bosnian situation. The following report by the Associated Press would have run in many newspapers. It suggested that a solution in Bosnia-Herzegovina was not imminent.*

### Associated Press, 1 May 1993

WASHINGTON: President Clinton today dispatched Secretary of State Warren Christopher to Europe to discuss stronger action against Serb aggression in Bosnia, including unspecified "military steps."

Christopher, briefing reporters after more than five hours of consultations between Clinton and his top advisers, said the president "decided on the direction that he believes the United States and the international community should now take in this situation."

"This direction involves a number of specific recommendations, including military steps," Christopher said. He did not provide specifics, saying the United States wanted to consult first with its allies.

"The clock is ticking," Christopher said.

"I think the Serbs know what they have to do and they know that they need to do it promptly," he said. "Our course of decision is well set here."

Christopher ticked off a series of measures that the United States and the world community had taken to curb ethnic violence in Bosnia, including tough economic sanctions and enforcing a "no-fly" zone to prevent the use of air power.

And yet, he said, "The outrages continue in the former Yugoslavia."

Christopher said he would leave Saturday night and consult with leaders in Britain, France, Russia, Germany and NATO and European Community officials in Brussels.

"I'm quite hopeful we can find a consensus," he said.

"I'm certainly going to try to persuade the Europeans of the directions the president has laid down."

The main options that had been under consideration by the Clinton administration were lifting an arms embargo against outgunned Bosnian Muslims and air strikes against Bosnian Serb positions.

But Christopher specifically ruled out using large numbers of American ground troops in the absence of a peace plan, which has long been Clinton's position.

Christopher emphasized that the United States is running out of patience with the Serbs.

"We're tired of their words and manipulation," he said.

He also emphasized that beyond the world-wide humanitarian concern over "ethnic cleansing," the United States believes it has important strategic interests in the Balkans as well.

However, the United States does not want to see a larger Balkan war, one that could spread into other regions of the former Yugoslavia and perhaps involve two NATO allies, Greece and Turkey, he said.

With pressure for stronger action mounting, a bipartisan group of 16 senators Friday sent a letter to Clinton expressing support both for multinational air strikes against Serbian artillery sites and lifting of the arms embargo.

But support for such action is far from unanimous in

Congress, and U.S. allies in Europe have particular concerns about the impact of such a strategy.

Clinton has been wrestling with the Bosnian issue ever since he took office, calling it by far the most difficult foreign policy question he faces. His goals are to bring a swift end to the ethnic violence there and at the same time foster prospects for long-term peace.

State Department spokesman Richard Boucher on Friday called the Serbs "clearly the main impediments to peace" and accused them of waiting until they could cause more suffering before agreeing to participate in a new round of peace talks this weekend in Athens, Greece.

The two other warring factions in Bosnia, ethnic Croats and Muslims, have approved the peace plan advanced by the United Nations and the European Community.

Administration officials have said the new Serb willingness to discuss the proposal would have no effect on Clinton's decision. But the president, during an appearance Friday in New Orleans, said he hoped talk about possibly using military force has had an impact.

"I think it may well have, and I certainly hope so," he said.

Clinton also directed U.S. envoy Reginald Bartholomew to go to Athens for the peace talks called by U.N. mediator Cyrus Vance and EC mediator David Owen.

"He will make clear to the parties, particularly to the Bosnian Serbs, that words alone will not deter the United States and the international community from pursuing further options," Boucher said.

Clinton has said repeatedly that the only option he has ruled out is sending U.S. ground troops into Bosnia and that he wants to move forward only in concert with allies.

But U.S. allies are wary of military intervention in the former Yugoslavia, with particular concern about the potential impact on British, French and Canadian forces engaged in humanitarian operations there.

Also important would be Russian support for whatever measures Clinton advocates. While President Boris Yeltsin has gone along generally with the gradual escalation of sanctions, Russia has traditional ties to the Serbs and evidently more influence with them than does the United States.

*Credit*: Reprinted with permission of The Associated Press.

---

# CRAGG HINES: THE BOSNIA QUANDARY—CRISIS COULD DO SERIOUS POLITICAL DAMAGE TO CLINTON

*The war was becoming something of a political quagmire for the president, as is evident from this* Houston Chronicle *front-page story. It is important to remember, however, that this story was published in a large newspaper housed in the heart of former President Bush's home state.*

*Houston Chronicle, 9 May 1993*

WASHINGTON—The conflict in Bosnia poses a severe test for President Clinton's past, present and future.

The new Democratic chief executive's current interventionist bent contrasts with his outspoken opposition to U.S. involvement in Vietnam 25 years ago and prompts questions about whether he is attempting to establish a strong image as a commander in chief after once going to extraordinary lengths to avoid military service.

His ongoing deliberations on sending U.S. forces into a battle from which Europeans next door are shying has further distracted Clinton from his goal of focusing on the nation's economy, as well as complicating his negotiations with Congress on other high-priority issues, including health care and campaign finance reform.

And the possibility of failure, through ensnaring U.S. forces in a deadly, prolonged Balkans engagement, raises the prospect of irreversible political damage for Clinton, who is already less popular than any recent president so early in his term.

As Secretary of State Warren Christopher has argued, Bosnia is "the problem from hell."

Americans are repulsed by the daily scenes of atrocities in the war-torn slice of the Balkans, where ancient ethnic and religious rivalries were rekindled by the breakup of Yugoslavia.

But they are far from certain that the United States should intervene militarily—and neither are many Pentagon top brass.

"This whole thing is being driven by political pressure, not strategic reasoning," argued Douglas Seay, a national security analyst with the conservative Heritage Foundation and an opponent of U.S. involvement in Bosnia.

Clinton has described the conflict as "heart-breaking, infuriating."

And even as hard as he has pushed to step up the military response to Serbian aggression—specifically with air strikes against Serb positions—Clinton concedes there must be some clearly defined purpose.

"If I decide to ask the American people and the United States Congress to support an approach that would include the use of air power, I would have a very specific, clearly defined strategy to pursue and very clear tactical objectives . . . which would have a beginning, a middle and an end," Clinton said Friday.

But many participants in the debate are unwilling to back the president until he offers convincing military aims or national security goals.

"We still don't have clear-cut military objectives," Sen. John McCain, R-Ariz., said last week in an interview on CBS' "This Morning." ["]The question is not whether we should do something. The question is what we can do and beneficially affect the situation."

One reason is the lack of support from top military leaders for intervening in the Balkans.

"I have not yet met a military expert who says that air strikes alone will beneficially affect the situation, and it's fraught with danger," McCain said.

There is widespread belief that the air strikes which Clinton has proposed will not alone be enough to stop the Serb push. And, perhaps recalling the death that came with the escalation of U.S. involvement in Vietnam, Clinton has all but ruled out the use of U.S. ground forces in the Balkans.

Gen. John Sheehan, director of operations for the Joint Chiefs of Staff, recently told the Senate Foreign Relations Committee: "I cannot in my own mind think of a military operation short of total intervention that will cause a cessation of the rape, pillaging and murder."

That is not the singular view.

Gen. Merrill McPeak, chief of the Air Force, told a Senate committee that Serbian guns raining terror on Bosnian Muslims could be silenced by air strikes.

That struck other old military hands as odd.

"I don't know what Gen. McPeak might be smoking, but it's not Marlboros and he might be inhaling," David Hackworth, a retired colonel with Vietnam experience told Reuters news agency.

And the Pentagon is not the only locus of power that's in a quandary.

"There really is very great confusion, I think, within the Congress as to what the American national interests are and what we ought to do," said Rep. Lee Hamilton, the Indiana Democrat who chairs the House Foreign Affairs Committee.

In none of the recent national public opinion polls has Clinton's proposal for air strikes—much less the use of ground troops, which some believe would eventually be needed—had majority support.

A USA Today–CNN-Gallup poll released Friday showed that 55 percent of those interviewed oppose U.S. air strikes, but 68 percent support contributing U.S. troops to a peacekeeping force.

"I'm very concerned about the will of the American people and that if we embark on a military enterprise that fails, then we are worse off than we were before we entered . . ." McCain said.

While the Republican leadership has generally supported Clinton on foreign policy, others in the party have readily compared Bosnia to Vietnam, not least because it invokes memories of Clinton's attempt to avoid serving in the divisive Asian conflict.

"It reminds me of Vietnam," said McCain, who spent five years as a prisoner of war in North Vietnam. But lest his commentary appear too partisan, McCain said the prospect of U.S. forces in Bosnia "also reminds me of Beirut, when we decided to insert peacekeeping forces in that unhappy civil war and obviously we lost 241 young Americans" during the Reagan administration.

The link, at least currently, between Bosnia and the Asian conflict two decades ago is "the belief that through air strikes, bombing bridges and supply lines, we could deter the North Vietnamese."

Another event in the historical spectrum that is being reviewed in light of Bosnia is the Holocaust, brought vividly to the mind of many opinion makers in Washington by the recent opening of a museum commemorating the slaughter of 6 million Jews by Nazi Germany.

At the dedication ceremony, Holocaust survivor Elie Wiesel told Clinton of Bosnia: "Something, anything, must be done."

Clinton's machinations have prompted several writers to remark on the irony of the Balkan mess confronting a White House filled with anti-interventionists.

"Flapping about the young president as he plots this course are a flock of squawking 'dawks'—deeply committed doves on every recent foreign intervention from Grenada to the Persian Gulf who suddenly have assumed the plumage and cry of Balkan hawks," international affairs analyst Karen Elliott House wrote in the Wall Street Journal last week.

Clinton argues that he is playing the hand that was dealt him in the Balkans, suggesting he was left a mess by the Bush administration, where the clear view was that while the bloodshed was regrettable it was not a fight that should involve the United States.

The president was fully aware of the problem and called in last year's campaign for stepped-up U.S. military action, including the air strikes against Serbian positions.

In more recent days, the Clinton administration has argued that if the Bosnian conflict is not stemmed, it could spread as far as Turkey and Greece, two U.S. allies who need little to make them go after one another.

McCain is unconvinced.

"I'm a little bit reminded of the domino theory when we were talking about Vietnam," the senator said.

Clinton, while avoiding the Vietnam analogy, has never minimized the crisis in Bosnia—and by extension the effect it could have on his presidency.

"This is clearly the most difficult foreign policy problem we face and that all our allies face," Clinton said in a news conference two weeks ago. "And if it were easy, I suppose it would have been solved before."

## ART PINE: "PENTAGON GATHERING BOSNIA INTELLIGENCE FOR TARGETS, TACTICS"

*Though news occasionally came directly from Bosnia during this year of coverage, many stories were still out of Washington, D.C., and reported how U.S. leaders were managing the crisis. The following story told more about U.S. concerns than about the Bosnian nationals' situation. The Clinton team was learning, apparently, to slow down substantially its efforts and expectations for a quick solution.*

*Los Angeles Times*, 10 May 1993

WASHINGTON: As the United States and its allies weigh possible military action against the Bosnian Serbs, the Pentagon has begun intensifying its efforts to marshal allied intelligence data to help plot possible targets and tactics, analysts here say.

Led by the Defense Intelligence Agency, the military is gathering a wide array of information, ranging from photographs taken by U.S. spy satellites to firsthand reports from allied troops on duty in Bosnia-Herzegovina and from recent refugees.

What has emerged is a picture of a combat zone in which weather and terrain would pose serious challenges to the allies. But it also appears that the potential enemy's firepower is limited to relatively unsophisticated weapons and that its supply lines could be disrupted with little difficulty.

Still unclear is the likely effectiveness of the Bosnian Serbs' fighting force—whether the 40,000-man army would prove troublesome for the United States or is undisciplined and apt to run quickly, as some experts contend.

George Kenney, an expert on Eastern Europe at the Carnegie Endowment for International Peace, says the paradox posed by Bosnian Serb troops may prove one of the thorniest—and most frustrating—challenges for any allied intervention forces.

"For the most part, the Serb forces aren't a credible fighting force and wouldn't fight very well," Kenney contends. "These are criminal gangs much more than military units. It's mainly the officers who are even trained. In any real crunch, most of them would flee."

At the same time, Kenney cautions, the absence of any real discipline means that die-hard Serbian guerrillas would likely continue to be a threat far longer than conventional forces might be. "Once you're there, you (would) have to stay there for a long time," he says.

Defense analysts say a stepped-up pace of intelligence gathering on Bosnia began early in March, when the United Nations first raised the possibility that it might need troops to enforce a U.N.-brokered peace accord and that the North Atlantic Treaty Organization might get the job.

Over the past few months, both U.S. and NATO intelligence-gathering agencies have been sharpening their focus, steadily increasing the number of passes by spy satellites over Bosnia. British, French and Canadians on U.N. humanitarian missions have also been interviewing refugees.

But weather—and the mountainous terrain—has been hampering some efforts. Adding to the difficulties, the Bosnian Serbs' arsenal is stashed in mountain caves—first used during the regime of Yugoslav dictator Josip Broz Tito—and is thus out of range of aerial photography equipment.

Jeffrey Richelson, an analyst with the National Security Archives, said that if a military confrontation came, the allies would be able to use satellites—and some ground stations in the region—to monitor the Serbian forces' radio transmissions.

Unfortunately, however, there is a shortage of skilled linguists capable of translating such transmissions. For that reason, intelligence agencies have begun advertising for former Cold War interpreters, hoping some might want to return to work.

Defense analysts say the Serbian forces' arsenal is respectable but mostly old and unsophisticated. They are thought to have no real ballistic missiles, such as the Iraqi Scuds that posed a threat to ground troops during the Persian Gulf War.

Their antiaircraft weapons also are limited—a few aging, radar-guided SA-2, SA-3 and SA-6 Soviet-made surface-to-air missiles and some SA-14 shoulder-fired surface-to-air missiles that can home in on heat emanating from aircraft.

Defense analysts say both are relatively easy to knock out or thwart through decoys or evasion tactics and that the Serbs have no network of sophisticated command centers and antiaircraft radar installations, such as the Iraqis had built up before the Gulf War.

The Serbs have one major long-range-radar tracking station at the southern tip of Bosnia, 20 miles south of Sarajevo. Experts say that undoubtedly would be one of the first targets of any allied air strike.

Military analysts say the Serbs' most worrisome weapons are its 600 artillery pieces, hundreds of mortars and 500 T-54 and T-55 tanks—the latter hidden in mountain caves. They also have antiaircraft artillery that could discourage the allies from flying at low altitudes, at least initially.

The artillery would be relatively easy to eliminate if the United States sent in ground troops. Such troops could serve as spotters and could operate TPQ-36 counter-battery radar that can help knock out enemy artillery pieces or mortars within seconds after they have been fired.

If the U.S. action is confined to air strikes, however, analysts say it would be more difficult to destroy artillery pieces—particularly without spotters. Military experts have speculated that Washington might send in a few spotters and ground artillery units despite a no-ground-troops pledge.

Bosnia's mountainous, tree-covered terrain and frequently cloudy skies also would add to the problems, although experts say that U.S. pilots are trained to cope with both factors and that the aircraft they would use are capable of conducting all-weather operations.

It is not yet clear yet whether allied air attacks would be extended into Serbia to knock out supply lines from Belgrade. Analysts said that decision probably would depend upon how well Serbian President Slobodan Milosevic keeps his word on cutting off supplies to the Bosnian Serbs.

*Credit*: Copyright © 1993, Los Angeles Times. Reprinted with permission.

---

## RALPH BEGLEITER: MILITARY ACTION IN BOSNIA ON HOLD

---

*This transcript mirrors the preceding* Los Angeles Times *story.*

*CNN News*, Transcript 408–1, 10 May 1993

HIGHLIGHT: President Clinton has turned his attention toward U.S. matters as Secretary of State Christopher explains that our European allies have chosen to await the outcome of the Serbian referendum.

FRANK SESNO, Anchor: One of the reasons the president is talking about the economy is because he wants to refocus on that amid turbulence overseas. To Bosnia now—European allies want to delay any final decision on using force in Bosnia until after a Bosnian Serb referendum, set for next week, takes place. But the White House decision to take a wait-and-see attitude may take some heat off of Bosnia's Serbs. CNN World Affairs Correspondent Ralph Begleiter reports.

RALPH BEGLEITER, International Affairs Correspondent: It may not be intentional, but the world community is giving Bosnia's Serbs a green light to continue their war against the Muslims for another week. President Clinton turned his attention to domestic matters, as polls show U.S. voters have little interest in intervening in Bosnia.

A White House spokesman told reporters the move to use force to stop the Serbs is in a holding pattern, at least until next week, after a self-proclaimed Bosnian Serb referendum takes place. Mr. Clinton's Secretary of State tried to put a better light on the delay.

WARREN CHRISTOPHER, Secretary of State: I would not say that our efforts to try to achieve a peaceful settlement in Bosnia are by any means on the back burner.

BEGLEITER: The U.S. blames European allies unwilling to decide what to do next.

RICHARD BOUCHER, State Department Spokesman: As a practical matter, we're—it appears that they will want to await the—the results of the referendum before we can agree on final steps.

BEGLEITER: But the 12 nations of the European Community are challenging the U.S. to send ground troops to Bosnia to join the allies protecting safe zones.

Lord DAVID OWEN, European Community Envoy: If there is a difference of perception, I think it stems from the fact that we have been involved on the ground, and the United States has not yet.

BEGLEITER: U.N. troops on the ground have had little effect on the campaign of ethnic cleansing, and the U.N. team reports Serb attacks on Zepa last week destroyed the Muslim town while Europe and the U.S. debated what to do. Christopher warns the Serbs against seeing a green light in the hesitation of the allies.

Secy. of State CHRISTOPHER: If they are perceiving those signals, that would not be a wise choice on their part because I think the international community is still anxious to take stronger action.

BEGLEITER: Europe and the U.S. are pinning their hopes now on Belgrade's announcement to choke off military supplies to the Bosnian Serbs. But allied officials say the blockade so far is incomplete. Meantime, threats of allied military action have again been shunted to the side.

Ralph Begleiter, CNN, at the State Department.

*Credit*: © 2005 Cable News Network LP, LLLP. Reprinted with permission.

---

## ART PINE: "PEACE PACT MAY BRING 20,000 GIS TO BOSNIA"

---

*Clinton continued to look for international coalitions in solving the political war problems in Bosnia-Herzegovina, but he seemed to be learning very slowly just how complicated the situation was. The following story illustrates the number of political players Clinton's team needed to consult before a peaceful settlement could even be accepted, let alone deployed.*

*Chicago Sun-Times*, 31 August 1993

The Clinton administration is making preliminary plans to deploy as many as 20,000 U.S. ground troops to help with United Nations peacekeeping efforts in Bosnia if talks in Geneva produce a peace agreement, U.S. officials said Monday.

But President Clinton said no final decision will be made on the precise number of troops and how they will be deployed until he is certain that any peace agreement is "fair, fully embraced by the Bosnian government, and is enforceable."

"The United States is prepared to participate in a multinational effort to keep the peace in Bosnia, but I want to see what the details are," Clinton said at a news conference. "I also want to know whose responsibility it is to stay for how long."

Clinton promised in February to provide U.S. troops to help enforce what then was expected to be the Vance-Owen peace accord in Bosnia, but that pact fell through. Officials said the promise would hold for a new peace accord.

With the three warring factions in Bosnia—the Bosnian Serbs, Croats and Muslims—edging closer to a peace agreement, U.N. mediator Thorvald Stoltenberg has asked for assurances that U.S. troops will help enforce it. The administration's statements Monday were aimed at reiterating its intention to carry out its pledge.

With Washington's approval, military planners at NATO also have begun drafting plans for about 40,000 NATO troops to take on the enforcement operations. U.S. authorities estimate that if that number holds firm, the United States will provide about 20,000 of these troops.

NATO officials say the preliminary planning now under way amounts mainly to updating and refocusing plans made in anticipation of the Vance-Owen accord.

## JACK R. PAYTON: "CLINTON'S FOREIGN POLICY OVERHAUL: TOO LITTLE, TOO LATE?"

*By the end of Clinton's first year, there had been a striking increase in the number of stories about Bosnia-Herzegovina and then a sharp drop-off as the President's foreign policy initiatives were dismissed both at home and abroad. The following is an example of the assessment that many newspapers and television broadcasters carried. The attention here is not on Bosnia-Herzegovina but on the political fallout in the United States.*

*St. Petersburg* (Fla.) *Times*, 30 December 1993

Few, other than his most devoted supporters, will argue that President Clinton's first year in office has been a success when it comes to foreign and defense policy.

Starting with Bosnia and continuing on through Somalia and Haiti, the administration wasted little time earning itself a reputation for amateurish bungling in handling the complicated affairs of the world.

And justified or not, this perception of well-meaning incompetence all but overshadowed the Clinton team's few modest successes over the past 11 months, chief among them its unwavering support for the right side in Russia.

So now, as his first year in office comes to an end, the overhaul of Clinton's national security apparatus is striking many in this unforgiving town as too little and possibly too late. A new secretary of defense and a new No. 2 man at the State Department, it's argued, aren't likely to revitalize Clinton's crisis management, much less his basic approach to world affairs.

Republicans and others already are sharpening their knives to use foreign and defense policy as a weapon against Clinton in 1996.

Nobody is arguing that Clinton's advisers lack smarts. With Warren Christopher as secretary of state, Anthony Lake as national security adviser and Les Aspin as secretary of defense, the president put together one of the most experienced and savvy national security teams ever assembled.

The problem, most experts now acknowledge, was that the team never focused its energies and many brilliant theories into coherent, well-thought-out guidelines for action in the real world.

Lake, for instance, came up with a so-called "lift and strike" proposal for dealing with Bosnia. The arms embargo would be lifted so Bosnian Muslims could buy weapons for self-defense and U.S. planes would strike Bosnian Serb targets if the Serbians violated an eventual cease-fire.

The trouble was that nobody bothered to discuss the proposal beforehand with the British and French, whose troops made up the bulk of the U.N. peacekeeping contingent on the ground in Bosnia. When Clinton went public with the Lake plan, the two allies promptly shot it down as a threat to their soldiers.

It wasn't long before Christopher declared Bosnia and its problems non-essential to U.S. national security. Direct U.S. involvement was no longer an option and the issue seemed to slip from America's radar screen.

Almost as a substitute for action in Bosnia—to show that we really cared about injustice in the world—Clinton decided to extend and deepen our involvement in Somalia. Reversing the Bush administration idea of pulling U.S. troops out of the east African nation last spring, Clinton ordered them to stay on under command of the United Nations.

Problems cropped up almost immediately.

The various national contingents in the U.N. force failed to coordinate their operations. U.N. Secretary General Boutros Boutros-Ghali decided to take sides in the civil war by opposing warlord Mohamed Farrah Aidid and his guerrillas. The Clinton administration, preoccupied with its budget battle in Congress, went along without serious question.

What started out as a humanitarian mission to deliver food to the starving quickly turned into a series of bloody skirmishes. When 18 of America's elite Army Rangers got killed in a firefight with Aidid's soldiers in early October, Clinton and his advisers came to the belated conclusion that Somalia was indeed a dangerous place.

U.S. troops would be withdrawn as soon as possible without giving the impression of a humiliating retreat. Like the hapless Bosnians, the U.N. mission and Somalia's defenseless civilians would be left to their own devices.

Right or wrong, America's failure in Somalia was eventually blamed on Aspin, who had earlier vetoed sending in tanks and armored personnel carriers that might have helped the Army Rangers escape the ambush by Aidid's men.

Within days of the Somalia debacle, disaster struck again when a shipload of American troops turned back from an attempt to dock in Haiti after a gang of thugs rioted on the docks at Port-au-Prince. The administration's tough talk about direct intervention to re-install ousted Haitian President Jean-Bertrand Aristide got put on indefinite hold.

While the world watched, the United States—the world's only remaining superpower—had once again been humiliated by a handful of ruffians. State Department officials began referring to their troubles as "Black October."

The administration's foreign and defense policy was collapsing and something had to be done.

In early November, Christopher delivered what was billed as a major policy address, saying that "regional problems" such as Bosnia, Somalia and Haiti were never really America's prime concern. Washington's first foreign policy priority, he said, was helping Boris Yeltsin to remain president and promote free markets and democracy in Russia.

While undoubtedly true, no one was persuaded that stating the obvious would get America back on track to play its special role in the world. Something more had to be done. A head or two had to roll.

The most prominent head to get chopped belonged to Aspin, whose cardinal sin was a disorganized management style, not his decisions on Somalia. His replacement, former admiral and CIA operations chief Bobby Ray Inman, is expected to bring discipline and a crisp decision-making style to the job.

The other new face near the top of the foreign policy team is that of Strobe Talbott, a former Time magazine columnist and Russia expert appointed this week to replace Clifton Wharton as Christopher's deputy at the State Department.

The big question, of course, is whether Inman at the Pentagon and Talbott backing up Christopher at the State Department will be able to sort out the administration's foreign policy mess.

Few expect they will, at least not by themselves. The best hope is that Inman's well-known persuasive powers and Talbott's friendship with Clinton will finally get the president's serious attention.

And serious attention will be essential in the coming year if Clinton wants to avoid more, and much more dangerous, foreign policy debacles.

Topping the list of potential disasters is North Korea and its attempts to build a nuclear arsenal. The CIA says North Korea probably has already built one or two bombs. The State Department says that's a worst-case scenario and there's no reason to panic, at least not yet.

Another tricky issue he'll be facing in 1994 is what to do about China. Should Washington again grant Beijing "most favored nation" trading status despite its shortcomings in human rights and arms proliferation?

The new year promises to be an interesting one, and the hope in Washington is that Clinton's revamped national security team will be up for it.

*Credit*: Copyright St. Petersburg Times, 1993. Used with permission.

## JOHN DIAMOND: CLINTON TELLS SERBS UNITED STATES READY TO INTERVENE MILITARILY

*The next several stories reported the progress, or lack of it, in moving the warring parties toward compliance with various peace agreements. Always the stories reported the threat of U.S. troop commitments in the region. The life and daily experiences of the residents in Bosnia-Herzegovina were rarely part of these reports.*

Associated Press, 23 April 1994

WASHINGTON: With 200 warplanes prepared to strike, President Clinton is cautioning Bosnian Serb forces around the Muslim enclave of Gorazde against discounting NATO's resolve.

With Serb shelling of Gorazde continuing today despite a NATO ultimatum, Clinton was taking a wait-and-see attitude, saying, "We had a good day yesterday. They're going to be up and down. We'll see."

At a White House news conference on Friday, he told reporters: "Working through NATO and working along with Russia and others, we are determined to save innocent lives, to raise the price for aggression, and to help bring the parties back to a negotiated settlement."

The administration joined several other Western governments in ordering embassy dependents and nonessential staff out of Belgrade, Yugoslavia, concerned that possible NATO attacks in Bosnia would bring retaliation.

"It seemed to be the prudent thing to do under all the circumstances," said Secretary of State Warren Christopher.

Meanwhile, Pentagon officials were cautioning that intensified air strikes against Serb forces around the besieged Bosnian city could lead to casualties among U.S. and other NATO forces.

"It's not going to be without its dangers," said one senior defense official who spoke on condition of anonymity. Pilots would be called upon to find and destroy Serb weapons tucked into the wooded hillsides around the Drina River while avoiding damage to innocent civilians.

There are at least 60 Serb artillery emplacements around Gorazde, as well as command and communications posts, supply depots and tanks that would be subject to air strikes.

Clinton spoke about developments in Bosnia after NATO's North Atlantic Council in Brussels approved his challenge to the Serbs that they lift their siege of Gorazde or face air strikes.

"The Bosnian Serbs should not doubt NATO's willingness to act," Clinton said. At the same time, he noted that "we are not in this business to enter this war on one side against another."

U.S. troops would not be sent to war in Bosnia-Herzegovina, Clinton said. The goal of the NATO ultimatum is to compel the Serbs to keep their pledge to stop shooting and start talking about a settlement to the 2-year-old war in the former Yugoslav republic.

Sharing the podium in a televised appearance with Prime Minister Andreas Papandreou of Greece, Clinton was clearly pleased with NATO's decision. It reaffirmed the leadership role the United States asserts as the world's only superpower. And it endorsed Clinton's own judgment in how to deal with his most difficult foreign policy problem.

Still, Clinton and his military subordinates remained ever-cautious about the limits of power.

The president stressed that his own goals in the Balkans were limited to stopping "the slaughter of the innocents," adding: "It is important not to be too arrogant about our abilities to dictate events beyond our shores."

Last year, only Germany and the Netherlands, of the 15 U.S. allies in Europe, supported his proposal to bomb some Serb artillery positions and to permit arms to get to the Bosnian government despite a U.N. embargo against all belligerents. Clinton had to retreat.

Without disclosing the options he might consider if the Serbs persist, Clinton dismissed a suggestion by Sen. Sam Nunn, D-Ga., chairman of the Senate Armed Services Committee, that NATO consider the option of bombing targets in Serbia itself if intermediate steps fail.

Clinton said the allies were trying to confine the war, and that bombing Serbia was not appropriate.

Nunn later issued a statement saying that any assertion that he wants immediate raids on Serbia is "an absurd distortion of my position."

Two other senators warned against widening air strikes.

Sen. John McCain, R-Ariz., a former fighter pilot and Vietnam prisoner of war, said "incremental escalation" could mean the United States will soon "face a choice between deploying American ground troops or withdrawing in abject defeat."

Sen. John W. Warner, R-Va., a former secretary of the Navy, said the battle could not be turned through the air.

"Sometimes leadership is more difficult to exercise by way of restraint than just using the forces of military as they are designed and trained to do," Warner said.

*Credit*: Reprinted with permission of The Associated Press.

## DONALD M. ROTHBERG: DEFENSE SECRETARY PERRY SAYS ANY U.S. FORCE IN BOSNIA WOULD BE OVERWHELMING

*This report suggests that the United States was looking for improvement in the situation, but did not expect it after many months with no progress.*

### Associated Press, 9 December 1994

WASHINGTON: Planning moved ahead Friday for a massive evacuation of U.N. forces from Bosnia, a pullout U.S. officials still hope doesn't take place.

"That's a decision that's going to be made by the U.N. and going to be largely influenced by the countries that have the troops on the ground there," said Defense Secretary William Perry.

But he said that if U.S. troops take part in an evacuation they will go in prepared to respond to any attacks with "overwhelming force."

At the State Department, spokeswoman Christine Shelly said the Clinton administration believes the U.N. forces in Bosnia are "performing a valuable mission."

"There hasn't been a decision to withdraw," she said. "This is only contingency planning at this point."

In Brussels, NATO ministers gave the go-ahead to complete planning for the rescue of U.N. peacekeepers in Bosnia. NATO ambassadors expressed pleasure with the U.S. offer of up to 25,000 American soldiers to help evacuate peacekeepers if the war in Bosnia worsens.

Perry said he spoke to the British defense minister, who said he favored continuing the U.N. mission in Bosnia unless the situation deteriorates.

Bosnian Serbs hold more than 200 United Nations personnel hostage for insurance against possible NATO air strikes.

The main mission of the U.N. force has been to attempt to deliver food and medicine to civilians. Perry said that if the U.N. withdraws, NATO would try to perform that task with air drops of supplies.

"It is entirely possible that it would be much more difficult to get those relief supplies to the cities," he said. He rejected a Serb threat to block an airlift unless NATO agrees to stop enforcing a no-fly zone over Bosnia.

Perry said that if the peacekeepers are evacuated the next step should be "a reinvigorated diplomatic approach designed to achieve a cease-fire, designed to reach a negotiated settlement."

But the defense secretary also pointed out that removal of the U.N. troops would provide "more flexibility in the future for applying military leverage than there is today."

France, Britain and other countries with troops in the U.N. force have been reluctant to endorse U.S. calls for air strikes. The United States has no ground troops in Bosnia.

Perry said that any evacuation would be handled by NATO.

"I see this as a NATO operation where NATO takes over command and control of the entire operation, both the troops that are brought in and the troops that are already there," he said.

There is continuing friction between NATO and the U.N. over questions of how much force should be used against the Serbs.

"If NATO goes in on this operation, we're not going in with a token force; we'll want to go in with a strong enough force that will command respect, because it's my judgment that is the best way of avoiding problems, is having a strong enough force that nobody sees it as an inviting target," said Perry.

*Credit*: Repritned with permission of The Associated Press.

## LEE MICHAEL KATZ: FRANCE "COMMITTED" TO TROOPS IN BOSNIA

*This report contrasts with the one above, as some members of the European community disagreed with the U.S. slow-down action.*

### USA Today, 13 December 1994

French Defense Minister François Leotard says France will strengthen rather than withdraw U.N. peacekeepers in Bosnia-Herzegovina, easing concern over deploying U.S. troops to rescue them.

"We will stay and we remain committed in the field in Bosnia," Leotard said Monday.

With Defense Secretary William Perry at his side, Leotard made his remarks after a tense week of diplomacy between the United States and France over the civil war in Bosnia.

Last week, French Foreign Minister Alain Juppe, in a reference to the U.S. refusal to put ground forces in Bosnia as peacekeepers, assailed "governments that want to give us lessons when they have not lifted a little finger to put even one man on the ground."

Monday, Leotard sought to soften the impact of Juppe's remarks. "We refuse to grant the Serbs the reward that they are apparently seeking: the withdrawal of U.N. forces from Bosnia," he said.

Leotard said allies were working to strengthen the "powerless" peacekeepers, hundreds of whom have been held hostage by Serb forces.

Perry left Washington on Monday to consult with NATO allies in Brussels on the future of peacekeeping efforts.

Perry suggested "new rules of engagement" for the thinly stretched U.N. peacekeepers, so they can regroup into "more defensible positions."

Bosnian Serbs have captured 70 percent of Bosnia since fighting began in 1991 against ethnic Muslims and Croats, who declared independence from Serb-dominated Yugoslavia.

On Monday, Serbs let humanitarian aid convoys pass through their checkpoints for the first time in several weeks.

Leotard said there are several proposals to overcome the problems of Bosnian Serbs thwarting U.N. aid convoys:

- Use military muscle to establish "a heavily protected humanitarian corridor."
- Fully control Sarajevo airport, now often shut down under threats from Serb anti-aircraft batteries.
- Increase airdrops to Bosnian Muslims and others trapped in remote areas.

Withdrawing troops would be "a nightmare scenario" Leotard said. This could lead not only to wider fighting, but a huge flow of refugees and even the "Islamization" of the war as Muslim countries send troops to aid their Bosnian kin.

And Leotard said French troops, who provide much of the 23,000 U.N. peacekeeping force, would withdraw "tomorrow" if Washington unilaterally allows arms to be shipped to Bosnian government forces.

*Credit*: From USA TODAY, a division of Gannett Co., Inc. Reprinted with Permission.

---

## MICHAEL DOBBS: "BOSNIA TALKS OPEN"

---

*This report of the Dayton peace initiative would have been read by many of the Washington political community and was carried in many newspapers across the country. At this point, American support for more military presence in the region was very low. There were negotiations but no news, during the nearly eleven months between this article and the preceding one.*

*Washington Post*, 2 November 1995

DAYTON, Ohio: Secretary of State Warren Christopher opened talks here today designed to end the four-year war in Bosnia and other parts of the former Yugoslavia, warning the politicians who plunged the region into ethnic turmoil that future generations would never forgive them if they failed to achieve peace.

Shortly after the opening of the talks, Christopher supported a key demand of the Bosnian Muslims by calling for the removal from power of two Bosnian Serb leaders who have been indicted for war crimes by an international tribunal in The Hague. In an interview with ABC News, Christopher said the United States would not feel "comfortable" sending troops to Bosnia as peacekeepers as long as Radovan Karadzic and Gen. Ratko Mladic remained "in a strong command position" in Bosnia.

The talks at Wright-Patterson Air Force Base, just outside Dayton, mark the first serious attempt by the United States to negotiate a peace settlement in Bosnia. If successful, they will prepare the way for deployment of up to 60,000 NATO troops, including as many as 25,000 Americans, to police a 700-mile demarcation line between the warring factions.

In a gesture that U.S. officials said had been carefully planned, Christopher maneuvered Serbian President Slobo-

dan Milosevic into shaking hands with his bitter enemies, Bosnian President Alija Izetbegovic, a Muslim, and Croatian President Franjo Tudjman, at the start of this afternoon's opening plenary session. It was the first time that the three leaders have met together since May 1993, when they attended a peace conference in Athens, one of several earlier unsuccessful attempts to end the war.

U.S. negotiators planned to hand the three leaders detailed proposals for ending the war in Bosnia, which has cost the lives of tens of thousands of people and driven nearly 2 million refugees from their homes. The American proposals include ideas for a new constitution that would preserve the principle of a united Bosnian state, as sought by the Muslims, while dividing the territory roughly equally between a Muslim-Croat federation and the separatist Serbs.

Addressing the plenary session of leaders from the former Yugoslavia, as well as representatives of the five-nation Contact Group of mediators, Christopher said that failure to achieve a peace settlement could plunge Europe into a wider war.

"If we fail, the war will resume and future generations will surely hold us accountable for the consequences that would follow. The lights so recently lit in Sarajevo would once again be extinguished, death and starvation would once again spread across the Balkans . . . threatening the region and perhaps Europe itself," he said.

All sides regard the Dayton talks as the best chance yet of bringing peace to the former Yugoslavia. They come at a time when the warring factions have fought themselves to a rough balance of power on the ground, with the Serbs and the Muslim-Croat federation each controlling roughly half of Bosnian territory.

Never before has the United States invested so much of its diplomatic and military prestige in negotiating and enforcing a peace settlement in Bosnia.

All sides also agree, however, that the negotiations are likely to prove both very difficult and protracted. U.S. officials say they are significantly more complex than the 1978 Camp David talks, on which they have been modeled. At Camp David, President Jimmy Carter played host only to the leaders of Egypt and Israel. Today, by contrast, representatives of three warring parties and six teams of international negotiators were participating.

The Dayton talks have been elaborately choreographed by U.S. officials to put political and psychological pressure on the participants to reach an agreement. No date has been set for the conclusion of the talks, which will include shuttling among the parties by the international negotiating teams as well as face-to-face meetings of all three delegations.

The three Balkan leaders and their delegations are staying in housing usually reserved for visiting Air Force officers, around a quadrangle a few hundred yards from the base's Hope Hotel (named for actor Bob Hope), where today's plenary session took place. Over the past week, the suites being used by the three heads of state have been repainted in identical colors, and refurbished with identical furniture, down to lampshades and bed covers.

"It is a little like Motel 6," quipped Muhamed Sacirbey, Bosnia's foreign minister, who lived several years in Ohio while growing up and who attended the University of Toledo. He said he and other delegates assumed that the premises were bugged with electronic listening devices planted by U.S. intelligence agencies.

Both Milosevic and Izetbegovic have agreed to remain in Dayton for the duration of the talks. Tudjman plans to return to Croatia Thursday, leaving day-to-day negotiations in the hands of his foreign minister, Mate Granic. All three delegations have agreed not to issue public statements until the end of the talks.

The Serb delegation headed by Milosevic includes three representatives of the Bosnian Serbs, including deputy leader Nikola Koljevic. Karadzic, the Bosnian Serb civilian leader, and Mladic, the military commander, have been barred from traveling to Western countries because of their indictments for war crimes.

According to U.S. officials, Milosevic has privately signaled that he would like to see Karadzic and Mladic ousted from their positions, even though both men once were considered his proteges. Milosevic now views Karadzic as a potential political rival; war crimes accusations against Mladic, including for the massacre of thousands of Muslims in and around Srebrenica in July, make him a political embarrassment.

U.S. officials said that the continued presence of Karadzic and Mladic in top positions would create serious political problems for U.S. and other NATO peacekeepers sent to Bosnia to enforce any agreement reached here. A controversy has raged within the administration over the past few weeks about whether U.S. troops would be obliged to arrest the two men, with Christopher insisting that they would be detained and Defense Secretary William J. Perry saying they would not.

State Department spokesman Nicholas Burns said that Christopher had individual meetings with leaders of the three Balkan delegations today, and later met with Milosevic and Tudjman together. The latter discussions centered on the territorial dispute between Croatia and Serbia over eastern Slavonia, Croatia's easternmost region, which was captured by the Yugoslav army in late 1993.

Burns later read a joint statement from Milosevic and Tudjman, in which the two presidents promised to work for the "full normalization" of relations between their countries and a settlement of the territorial dispute.

After the opening plenary meeting, the delegates went into closed session. U.S. officials said all three heads of government promised to work for the success of the talks. Milosevic, who helped to unleash the war in Bosnia in April 1992 by encouraging the Yugoslav army to arm the Bosnian Serbs and attack Bosnian towns, shook the hands of Bosnian leaders and had a brief conversation with Izetbegovic.

In Washington, meanwhile, President Clinton received a warning at a meeting with top congressional leaders of both parties that he is far from having majority support for sending U.S. troops to Bosnia to enforce a peace settlement. In fact, the legislators said, there is less support for the idea now than there was a month ago.

"The initial briefings have not been effective" in winning support, House Speaker Newt Gingrich (R-Ga.) said he told Clinton. House Minority Leader Richard A. Gephardt (D-Mo.) said his goal is simply to keep Democrats from committing against the idea.

White House press secretary Michael McCurry said Clinton does not dispute that there is likely more anxiety about U.S. participation in a NATO peacekeeping force than a month ago. But he said that is simply because the administration has been talking about the prospect more openly.

Staff writer John F. Harris in Washington contributed to this report.

*Credit:* © **1995, The Washington Post, reprinted with permission.**

# MIMI HALL: REPUBLICANS SPLIT ON PLAN TO SEND TROOPS TO BOSNIA

*Though the Dayton peace agreements seemed like a final effort by the Clinton administration, there was still much debate in the United States about American commitment to a resolution, as is evident in this news story.*

*USA Today*, 29 November 1995

A rift among Republicans, in many cases along generational lines, is complicating President Clinton's effort to win support for the U.S. peacekeeping mission in Bosnia-Herzegovina.

On one side are younger, constituent-minded House members, who—mindful of polls showing the public is skeptical of U.S. involvement abroad—oppose sending troops to the war-torn Balkans.

On the other side: older, establishment Republicans—among them, prominent former Defense and national security advisers and Senate Majority Leader Bob Dole, R-Kan., a veteran—who say the nation has a responsibility to act and risks its reputation if it abandons its commitments.

As a practical matter, Clinton doesn't need any approval for his plan to send 20,000 troops to Bosnia to help NATO forces police the peace pact forged last week.

Politically, however, in an election year, Clinton could use the cover of congressional backing in case the mission ends in disaster.

He may have trouble getting it in the House.

"I am extremely skeptical of this whole operation," House Majority Leader Dick Armey, R-Texas, said after a Tuesday afternoon meeting at the White House between Clinton and congressional leaders.

Hearings in the House begin Thursday, when members of the International Relations Committee are expected to grill Secretary of State Warren Christopher and Defense Secretary William Perry.

Armey said he hadn't yet spoken to many of his colleagues, but "as I told the president, if they're getting the kind of phone calls from their district that I'm getting . . . it's not going to be, I think, in any respect an easy proposition" for Clinton to win House support.

But in the Senate, Dole and other members, while cautious, seem more inclined to go along with the plan, even in the face of public opposition.

In a year's time, Dole, the GOP front-runner who has played up his World War II service as part of his campaign, hopes he'll be preparing to take Clinton's job as the next commander in chief.

So despite criticism from other GOP presidential contenders, including conservative commentator Patrick Buchanan, Dole said he is reluctant to vote to erode the power of the president to commit U.S. military forces overseas.

"I want to support the president if I can," said Dole. "I'm certain that some of my opponents on the Republican side will have a field day. But there comes a time when you have to be responsible, too."

Also Tuesday, hearings opened in the Senate Armed Services Committee, where former Republican presidential advisers encouraged members of Congress to back the president's plan—even if it might result in casualties.

Clinton may have made a bad decision to get the U.S. involved in the war in Bosnia in the first place, but now that he has, Congress should back him up, said Brent Scowcroft, national security adviser to President Bush.

"Risky as I think the situation is for U.S. troops, the alternative is a clear disaster," Scowcroft said. "To turn our backs now would be a catastrophe for U.S. reliability, which I think is our most precious issue of national security."

He and former Defense secretary James Schlesinger, who worked for presidents Nixon and Ford, told the panel a series of questions remain:

- How long will troops stay?
- How will they react if they come under fire?
- Will troops help train Bosnian forces to protect themselves if the war resumes?
- How will troops return refugees to their homes?

"We now have no practical alternative but to go in," Schlesinger said. "We have our prestige, our credibility at stake."

In the only comment that drew a laugh during the three-hour-long Senate hearing, Sen. Robert Byrd, D-W.Va., seemed to sum up the sentiments of his colleagues when he said the dilemma reminded him of what Socrates said when asked about marriage:

"You'll be sorry if you don't, and you'll regret it if you do."

Contributing: Susan Page.

## JOHN POMFRET: "BOSNIAN SERBS DEMAND NEW DEAL FOR SARAJEVO"

*This report from Bosnia was carried on the front page of the* Washington Post *and would have been seen by many Washington politicians. Though the readership may not have been as large as that of a wire service story, it was certainly read by those who made the decisions about NATO policy.*

*Washington Post,* 27 December 1995

PALE, Bosnia: Bosnian Serb leaders sought today to delay the reunification of Sarajevo under Muslim rule by more than six months and suggested that their initial compliance with the Bosnian peace plan could sour if the demand is refused.

U.S. Navy Adm. Leighton W. Smith, commander of the NATO peace force in Bosnia, said he was noncommittal after hearing the Bosnian Serbs' proposal during a meeting here in Pale, the Bosnian Serb headquarters 10 miles east of Sarajevo. But he specified that he has authority to modify deadlines set down in the Dayton peace accords, which cover a variety of steps ranging from troop pullbacks to elections.

A NATO source said, meanwhile, that Bosnian Serb military commander and alleged war criminal Ratko Mladic sent Smith a letter last week. The letter, while not solicited by the American admiral, put Smith in a difficult position because under the Dayton agreement Smith must not communicate with those charged with war crimes by the International War Crimes Tribunal in The Hague.

The source said Smith accepted the letter but had no plans to reply.

Before the 20,000 U.S. troops assigned to the NATO force began deploying to Bosnia, Secretary of State Warren Christopher said the United States would not feel "comfortable" sending peacekeepers as long as Mladic and the Bosnian Serbs' civilian leader, Radovan Karadzic, remain "in a strong command position." State Department spokesman Nicholas Burns on Nov. 15 ruled out as "inconceivable" that Karadzic and Mladic would be in positions of authority when a peace deal was reached.

The developments underscored two of the main difficulties facing the American-led operation to end the 3½-year war in Bosnia: how to deal with alleged war criminals whose cooperation is key to making peace in Bosnia and what to do about Serb-held parts of Bosnia's capital, slated to be returned to the Muslim-dominated government in less than three months.

How Smith and the rest of his NATO-led operation cope with these two problems will have a great impact on the outcome of the mission, Western officials have said. The main point they stress is that the NATO force, made up of troops from 32 nations, must work to deny the Serbs—or Muslims and Croats—the opportunity to exploit international differences in any attempt to scuttle the plan. This tactic was employed with much success, especially by Serbs and Muslims, during the failed U.N. mission in the former Yugoslavia.

Already, strains have appeared. Last Thursday, the deputy commander of Russian peacekeepers in Bosnia, Maj. Gen. Nikolai Staskov, appeared to violate the spirit of the accord by meeting Mladic in his headquarters in the east Bosnian garrison town of Han Pijesak.

NATO officials said Staskov did not break the terms of the treaty because Russia will not actually join the peace implementation force until January.

In addition, French government and military officials have made receptive noises about renegotiating the peace deal's provisions for Sarajevo, extending some of the peace plan's deadlines around Sarajevo or helping the Serbs to build a new Serb city nearby.

The Serb demands for a new deal for Sarajevo came during Smith's first trip to Pale. The request to delay and modify implementation of the deal around Sarajevo recalled other attempts to alter agreements and accords after they have been signed.

In February 1994, the Bosnian Serbs postponed compliance with a NATO ultimatum to remove heavy weapons from around Sarajevo, establishing a pattern that led to collapse of a NATO plan to stop the shelling of civilians in Sarajevo.

Under the Dayton peace agreement, the Bosnian Serbs are to withdraw from five suburbs around Sarajevo where, for almost four years, they besieged the city, plastering it with hundreds of thousands of mortar rounds and killing an estimated 10,000 people. Dozens of Bosnian Serbs interviewed in the suburbs over the last two weeks have said they are petrified of living under a Muslim government.

During the Pale talks, held in a small, ramshackle house near the aptly named Panorama Hotel, nestled in a pine forest overlooking a massive limestone bluff, Smith met with Momcilo Krajisnik, the head of the self-styled Bosnian Serb parliament; Aleksa Buha, serving as "foreign minister" of the Bosnian Serbs; and other Serb leaders.

At a news conference that followed, Buha said the Serbs asked Smith to extend until the end of September deadlines stipulated by the Dayton deal. Buha added that the Serbs would like Smith to respond to their demands by Jan. 6, Orthodox Christmas.

Under the Dayton deal, the Bosnian Serb army must vacate the suburbs by early February and the Bosnian government can take control of them by March 19—90 days after the peace plan came into effect Dec. 19. Krajisnik said he wanted the 90-day period prolonged. He added, "Things could become very serious when cooperation gets out of our hands."

Krajisnik appeared to be purposely unclear about what the Serbs want. While he said his delegation had only asked Smith to extend the deadline, he also stressed that the deal itself was unacceptable.

"Serbs will never accept Muslim authority," he said. "These proposed solutions are not sufficient for the time being; maybe they'll be sufficient in nine months or a year."

"I did not commit," Smith said, "but we will continue to watch the situation closely."

Smith went to Pale on the condition that neither Mladic nor Karadzic, who also has been indicted on charges of war crimes, be present at the meeting.

*Credit:* © **1995, The Washington Post, reprinted with permission.**

## BOB TUTT: REFUGEES IN U.S. VOICE HOPE FOR BOSNIAN PEACE EFFORT

*This is an example of the kind of localizing story that appeared occasionally in U.S. newspapers, but even these human-interest reports were few and far between as the situation dragged on and on in the minds of the American public.*

*Houston Chronicle*, 31 December 1995

Jasmina Pasic had wished to stay in Sarajevo despite dangers posed by Bosnian Serbs who besieged and regularly blasted the city.

Finally her rheumatism became so painful she reluctantly decided to leave for treatment.

She received a terrifying sendoff. As she prepared to depart from her apartment, a barrage of Serbian shells slammed nearby.

Pasic, a Bosnian Muslim who has found refuge in Houston, fervently hopes that the peace agreement negotiated to stop the war will hold.

So does Liliana Malenica, a Bosnia Serb who lives here, as, no doubt, do hundreds of others of Yugoslavian Slavic descent who live in this area as permanent residents or war refugees.

Malenica is concerned about the safety of her widowed, 70-year-old mother still living in a Serbian area of Sarajevo because under the peace plan all of the city, including Serbian neighborhoods, will fall under Muslim control.

Her mother fears someone will oust her from her home, Malenica said, and she has no other place to go.

Malenica moved here when a Canadian chemical company transferred her husband, Rajko Malenica, to Houston. She grew up in Sarajevo and remembers how various ethnic groups in that historic city lived in remarkable harmony.

Marshal Tito, a communist dictator reigning over Yugoslavia after World War II, forcefully damped ethnic conflicts that stud that region's history.

After Tito's death in 1980, old ethnic aspirations and animosities began to emerge. The war that has raged for the past four years has dismembered Yugoslavia.

Ethnic conflicts have persisted although the people share the same Slavic ancestry and language. Perhaps the most crucial difference is in religious faith. Serbs are predominantly Eastern Orthodox, Croatians predominantly Roman Catholic, most Bosnians Muslims.

Malenica recalled that when she visited her parents in Sarajevo in 1990, before the war erupted, she could sense trouble brewing.

"I asked them what they feared," she said, "and so vividly, I remember my mother leaning across the table and telling me, 'Darling, you do not remember what it means to be a Serb under Croatian occupation, but Dad and I do all too well.'" Her mother referred to the World War II period when Croats sided with the Nazi German forces that conquered Yugoslavia.

The Croats then reportedly killed about 1 million Serbs.

In Yugoslavia, Malenica said, "A volcano has erupted. There probably was a just cause for the eruption. It is very difficult to explain hundreds of years of history."

It seems inevitable that in wartime participants on all sides may commit cruel, criminal acts, but during the current Yugoslavian war, the Serbs have come across as the chief offenders. They are accused of committing mass rapes, murderous "ethnic cleansing," having their snipers pick off any exposed civilian, male or female, in Sarajevo.

Malenica maintains that the full story of atrocities committed by Bosnian Muslims has not been reported. "I know of a Serbian man, a non-combatant, seized on the streets of Sarajevo by Muslims and compelled to work as a forced laborer on a daily basis," she said. "I have heard of Serbs being verbally abused and spat upon."

Croats, it should be noted, also have been accused of racial cleansing and other atrocities during the war.

Ralph Subotich, a native of Croatia, immigrated to this country with his mother after World War II. Croatia sided with the Nazis, he said, because that was the only way the nation could gain independence from Yugoslavia.

His father, Mato Subotich, and four uncles became "Croatian freedom fighters," he said, "but they all disappeared without a trace after the war," having obviously been killed by the Serbs.

He could never learn their exact fates, he said, because the Serbs, unlike the Nazis, didn't keep detailed records of their actions.

Subotich and his mother escaped to Germany and spent six years in a displaced persons camp there before managing to immigrate in 1951.

"With the Cold War on," he said, "no one was going to force us to go back to a communist country."

He said he, like many others in the "Croatian diaspora," has made financial contributions to support Croatia's move to independence.

Who is primarily responsible for the bloodshed in what used to be Yugoslavia?

Undoubtedly the Serbs, Subotich said.

There is a collective responsibility, no one group can be singled out, said Pasic.

"It would be extremely unfair to pinpoint one person or one group," Malenica said.

What are the chances that peace will prevail?

"I think it's going to work out pretty well," Subotich said.

"Nobody wants to fight anymore, and when the NATO troops went in, this was a way for everyone to lay down their arms and try to have a peace."

"True peace is possible," Pasic said, "but what we have now is only on paper. It will take a long, long time for true peace to come."

"I am sure that anything is possible as long as it is done in a civil and honest manner," Malenica said. "I ache for that beautiful city Sarajevo, hurting for anyone who is there, but I am afraid of anything (to bring peace) that is forceful." She noted a television news report on a recent evening showing U.S. troops sent as peacekeepers battling the elements to construct a bridge over the Sava River between Croatia and Bosnia.

"One soldier said they had prepared for absolutely the worst scenario," Malenica said. "In this case the worst came from the gods in the form of bad weather. Unfortunately you can blame no side in the war for that."

---

## BOB DEANS: CLINTON SAYS U.S. TROOPS TO REMAIN IN BOSNIA INDEFINITELY

*After five years of conflict and national attention, the situation remained contentious, but U.S coverage still focused on the political fallout at home. This Cox News Service story ran in many papers across the nation and would have been read by millions.*

Cox News Service, 19 December 1997

WASHINGTON: Saying the two-year Balkans peace is too fragile to stand on its own, President Clinton announced Thursday that he would extend the U.S. troop presence in Bosnia for a second time, opening the door to American involvement in the troubled region into the next century.

Clinton has twice set deadlines for completing the U.S. mission in Bosnia—saying first it would end by 1997 and then, after missing that marker, pledging to wrap it up by June 1998—a strategy he admitted was an "error."

Conceding that he had vastly underestimated the difficulties of stitching the war-shattered Balkans back together again, Clinton declined to set a date certain for bringing the troops home this time, a dramatic departure from precedent dating to the Gulf War.

"I honestly believed in 18 months we could get this done," Clinton said, referring to his decision a year ago to extend the U.S. troop presence through next June. "I wasn't right, which is why I don't want to make that error again."

Instead, Clinton—who leaves Sunday for a one-day trip to Bosnia to rally the troops before Christmas—cited what he called "benchmarks" that must be met before the mission to Bosnia is complete. Among those, he said, are the establish-

ment of a strong civilian police force, and respect for political and legal institutions meant to meld the war-torn republic into a single nation of two entities—Serb and non-Serb.

In a remarkable flash of candor, Clinton said it was "more honest" to tell the American people what conditions must exist before the troops can come home than to hold out yet another deadline that might once again have to be missed.

"We tried it in this SFOR period, and it turned out we were wrong," Clinton said, referring to the mission of the NATO Security Force, called SFOR, he last year pledged would end next June. "I am not suggesting a permanent presence in Bosnia. I am suggesting that it's a more honest thing to do to say what our objectives are," than to offer up a specific deadline.

Clinton's Republican critics, however, blasted the decision, accusing him of leading U.S. troops into an ill-defined mission that threatens to sprawl still further with time.

"The president has now exceeded two self-imposed deadlines for American withdrawal from Bosnia, and we are embarked on an open-ended commitment that will lead us from mission creep to mission leap," Sen. Kay Bailey Hutchison, R-Texas, said in a written statement. "This is nation-building, which has been discredited in Somalia and in Haiti."

The Pentagon estimates that it has spent, to date, $5 billion on the Bosnia operation. It has budgeted an additional $1.5 billion for the operation through June.

Europe's bloodiest conflict since World War II, 3½ years of ethnic war in Bosnia ended two years ago, following U.S.-led NATO air strikes and U.S.-brokered peace talks outside of Dayton, Ohio, among warring Bosnians, Croats and Serbs.

Continued peace, however, requires continued peace-keeping, Clinton said.

"We don't believe the peace is self-sustaining," Clinton said at a White House news conference. "If we pull out before the job is done, Bosnia almost certainly will fall back into violence, chaos, and, ultimately, a war every bit as bloody as the one that was stopped."

Asked whether he could guarantee that U.S. troops would be out of Bosnia at least by the time he leaves office in January 2001, Clinton declined to give such an assurance.

"I don't think it's necessary for us to stay until, until everybody wants to go have tea together at 4:00 in the afternoon, in a civil environment," Clinton said. "But I do think we should stay there until we get the job done."

Clinton said he and his counterparts in the North Atlantic Treaty Alliance [sic] (NATO) would finalize plans in the coming weeks for a scaled-back peacekeeping force in Bosnia.

There are 8,500 U.S. troops there now—one-fourth of the total Security Force, or SFOR—and the Pentagon is weighing a continued force expected to range between 5,000 and 7,000 American troops.

NATO commander Gen. Wesley Clark—who wrote the military terms for the Dayton peace accords—has argued against a sharp reduction in U.S. troop levels, insisting that the force remain large enough to protect itself.

Clinton administration officials have signaled for weeks that the president was leaning toward extending the U.S. presence in Bosnia.

Still, Thursday's announcement came as a relief to aid workers and others struggling to help the war-torn country recover its footing.

"It's a welcomed decision, that's for sure," said Patrice Dufour, senior advisor for operations and information at the World Bank mission in Sarajevo.

The Washington-based development bank has led efforts to pump more than $2 billion—with another $1.4 billion pledged by the United States and other donor countries—into post-war restoration projects in Bosnia, work that could not be accomplished without the security backdrop the NATO forces provide.

"Reconstruction is moving ahead very well. The real challenge is reconciliation," Dufour said in a telephone interview. "The international presence is certainly needed to make sure the violence doesn't come up again."

The notion of setting a date certain for U.S. military deployments to end became popular during the lead-up to the 1990–91 Gulf War as a way to give politicians protection from public fears of being drawn into a Vietnam-style quagmire with no clear end-point.

While the date certain approach was generally supported by the Pentagon, it was widely criticized by military analysts as a precursor to failure, because it signalled to American foes the limits of U.S. commitment on any given issue.

Balkan watchers, for example, dismissed Clinton's earlier deadlines as cynical and misleading, saying there was never any serious expectation that the wounds of 3½ years of fighting in Bosnia would mend in 12 months, or even another 18 months beyond that.

War broke out in Bosnia in April 1992, when Bosnian Serbs, backed by neighboring Serbia, rejected Bosnia's decision to become an independent republic as the result of the break-up of the former Yugoslavia.

In seeking to justify a continuing U.S. presence in Bosnia, Clinton evoked the grim atrocities that stalked the region and haunted the conscience of the world for nearly four years.

"We will never be able to forget the mass graves, the women and young girls victimized by systematic campaigns of rape, skeletal prisoners locked behind barbed-wire fences, endless lines of refugees marching toward a future of despair," Clinton said. "The war in Bosnia was abhorrent to our values. It also threatened our national interests."

*Credit*: Reprinted with permission of Cox News Service.

## NOTES

1. Steven L. Burg and Paul S. Shoup, *The War in Bosnia-Herzegovina: Ethnic Conflict and International Intervention* (Armonk, N.Y.: M. E. Sharpe, 1999), 390–392.

2. Surveys by Yankelovich Partners, Inc., for *Time* and CNN, 13–14 January 1993 and 19 August 1992.

3. Surveys by NBC News/*Wall Street Journal*, 23–26 January 1993.

4. Survey by Louis Harris and Associates, 22–26 January 1993.

5. CBS/*New York Times* Survey, 13 December 1994.

6. *Los Angeles Times*/Gallup Poll, 28 November 1995.

## FURTHER READINGS

Burg, Steven L., and Paul S. Shoup. *The War in Bosnia-Herzegovina: Ethnic Conflict and International Intervention.* Armonk, N.Y.: M. E. Sharpe, 1999.

Kaplan, Robert D. *Balkan Ghosts: A Journey through History.* New York: Vintage Books, 1996.

# SELECTED BIBLIOGRAPHY

## ARTICLES

Gottschalk, Jack A. "Consistent with Security: A History of American Military Press Censorship." *Communications and the Law* 5 (1983): 35–52.

Sidle, Winant. "A Battle behind the Scenes: The Gulf War Reheats Military-Media Controversy." *Military Review* 71 (September 1991): 52–63.

## BOOKS

Adkin, Mark. *Urgent Fury: The Battle for Grenada*. Lexington, Mass.: Lexington Books, 1989.

Andrić, Ivo. *The Bosnian Chronicle*. New York: Arcade Publishing, 1945.

———. *The Bridge on the Drina*. New York: Arcade Publishing, 1945.

Beck, Robert. *The Grenada Invasion: Politics, Law, and Foreign Policy Decisionmaking*. Boulder, Colo.: Westview Press, 1993.

Burg, Steven L., and Paul S. Shoup. *The War in Bosnia-Herzegovina: Ethnic Conflict and International Intervention*. Armonte, N.Y.: M. E. Sharpe, 1999.

Burton, Richard. *First Footsteps in East Africa*. Ed. Gordon Waterfield. New York: Praeger, 1966.

Davis, Brian L. *Qaddafi, Terrorism, and the Origins of the U.S. attack on Libya*. New York: Praeger, 1990.

Denton, Robert, ed. *Perspectives on Media and the Persian Gulf War*. New York: Praeger, 1993.

DiPrizio, Robert C. *Armed Humanitarians: U.S. Interventions from Northern Iraq to Kosovo*. Baltimore: Johns Hopkins University Press, 2002.

Drysdale, John G. *The Somali Dispute*. New York: Praeger, 1964.

———. *Somaliland: The Anatomy of Secession*. Hove, Sussex: Global-Stats, 1991.

Fatton, Robert. *Haiti's Predatory Republic: The Unending Transition to Democracy*. Boulder, Colo.: Lynne Rienner, 2002.

Fialka, John J. *Hotel Warriors: Covering the Gulf War*. Washington, D.C.: Woodrow Wilson Center Press, 1992.

Gersony, Robert. *Why Somalis Flee: A Synthesis of Accounts of Conflict Experience in Northern Somalia by Somali Refugees, Displaced Persons, and Others.* Washington, D.C.: Department of State, 1989.

Haass, Richard N., ed. *Transatlantic Tensions: The United States, Europe, and Problem Countries.* Washington, D.C.: Brookings Institution Press, 1999.

Hammond, William M. *Public Affairs: The Military and the Media, 1962–1968.* Washington, D.C.: U.S. Army Center of Military History, 1988.

———. *Public Affairs: The Military and the Media, 1968–1973.* Washington, D.C.: U.S. Army Center of Military History, 1996.

Hendrickson, Ryan C. *The Clinton Wars: The Constitution, Congress, and War Powers.* Nashville: Vanderbilt University Press, 2002.

Henze, Paul B. *The Horn of Africa: From War to Peace.* New York: St. Martin's Press, 1991.

Hoffman, Fred S. *Review of the Panama Pool Deployment, December 1989.* Memorandum for correspondents. Washington, D.C.: Pentagon, March 1990.

Howe, James. *A People Who Would Not Kneel: Panama, the United States, and the San Blas Kuna.* Washington, D.C.: Smithsonian Institution Press, 1998.

Kaplan, Robert D. *Balkan Ghosts: A Journey through History.* New York: Vintage Books, 1996.

Knightley, Phillip. *The First Casualty: From the Crimea to Vietnam: The War Correspondent as Hero, Propagandist, and Myth Maker.* New York: Harcourt Brace Jovanovich, 1975.

LaMay, Craig, Martha FitzSimon, and Jeanne Sahadi, eds. *The Media at War: The Press and the Persian Gulf Conflict.* New York: Gannett Foundation Media Center, 1991.

Lewis, I. M. *A Modern History of Somalia: Nation and State in the Horn of Africa.* Boulder, Colo.: Westview Press, 1988.

Lindsay-Poland, John. *Emperors in the Jungle: The Hidden History of the U.S. in Panama.* Durham: Duke University Press, 2003.

MacArthur, John R. *Second Front: Censorship and Propaganda in the Gulf War.* New York: Hill and Wang, 1992.

Mott, Frank Luther. *American Journalism: A History from 1690–1940.* New York: Macmillan, 1941.

Noriega, Manuel Antonio. *America's Prisoner: The Memoirs of Manuel Noriega.* New York: Random House, 1997.

O'Shaughnessy, Hugh. *Grenada: An Eyewitness Account of the U.S. Invasion and the Caribbean History That Provoked It.* New York: Dodd, Mead, 1984.

Reynolds, Nicholas E. *Just Cause: Marine Operations in Panama, 1988–1990.* Washington, D.C.: History and Museums Division, Headquarters, U.S. Marine Corps, 1996.

Rotberg, Robert I. *Haiti's Turmoil: Politics and Policy under Aristide and Clinton.* Cambridge, Mass.: World Peace Foundation, 2003.

Ruiz, Hiram A. *Beyond the Headlines: Refugees in the Horn of Africa.* Washington, D.C.: American Council for Nationalities Service, 1988.

Salmon, Lucy Maynard. *The Newspaper and the Historian.* New York: Oxford University Press, 1923.

Samatar, Said S., ed. *In the Shadow of Conquest: Islam in Colonial Northeast Africa.* Trenton, N.J.: Red Sea Press, 1992.

Sheller, Mimi. *Democracy after Slavery: Black Publics and Peasant Radicalism in Haiti and Jamaica.* Gainesville: University Press of Florida, 2000.

Sidle, Winant. *Report by the Chairman of the Joint Chiefs of Staff Military-Media Relations Panel.* Washington, D.C.: Chairman of the Joint Chiefs of Staff, 1984.

Simons, Geoffrey L. *Libya: The Struggle for Survival.* New York: St. Martin's Press, 1993.

Soderlund, Walter C. *Mass Media and Foreign Policy: Post–Cold War Crises in the Caribbean.* Westport, Conn.: Praeger, 2003.

Twentieth Century Fund. *Battle Lines: Report of the Twentieth Century Fund Task Force on the Military and the Media.* New York: Priority Press Publications, 1985.

U.S. Congress. *Full Committee Hearing on the Lessons Learned as a Result of the U.S. Military Operations in Grenada: Hearing before the Committee on Armed Services, House of Representatives.* 98th Cong., 2nd sess., 24 January 1984.

Weiss, Thomas G. *Military-Civilian interactions: Intervening in Humanitarian Crises.* Lanham, Md.: Rowman & Littlefield, 1999.

## NEWS SOURCES

*All Things Considered* (NPR)
Associated Press
*Atlanta Journal and Constitution*
*Boston Globe*
*Boston Herald*
*Business Week*
*CBS Evening News*
*CBS This Morning*
*Chicago Sun-Times*
*CNN News*
Cox News Service
*Houston Chronicle*
*Los Angeles Times*
*MacNeil/Lehrer NewsHour* (PBS)
*Morning Edition* (NPR)
*New York Times*
*Newsday* (New York)
*Orange County Register*
*Post-Journal* (Jamestown, N.Y.)
*Reliable Sources* (CNN)
*Rocky Mountain News* (Denver)
*St. Louis Post-Dispatch*
*St. Petersburg* (Fla.) *Times*
*This Week with David Brinkley* (ABC)
*Time*
United Press International
*U.S. News & World Report*
*USA Today*
*Washington Post*
*Washington Times*
*World News Saturday* (ABC)
*World News Sunday* (ABC)

## WEB SITE

Combelles-Siegel, Pascale. "The Troubled Path to the Pentagon's Rules on Media Access to the Battlefield: Grenada to Today." Report, 15 May 1996. Strategic Studies Institute, http://wwwcarllisle-www.army.mil/usassi/.